LET'S GO:

The Budget Guide to

SPAIN, PORTUGAL, & MOROCCO

1989

Andrew I. Solomon
Editor

David L. Rettig
Assistant Editor

Written by Harvard Student Agencies, Inc.

ST. MARTIN'S PRESS
NEW YORK

Helping Let's Go

If you have suggestions or corrections, or just want to share your discoveries, drop us a line. We read every piece of correspondence, whether a 10-page letter, a postcard, or, as in one case, a collage. All suggestions are passed along to our researcher/writers. Please note that mail received after June 1, 1989 will probably be too late for the 1990 book, but will be retained for the following edition. Address mail to: Let's Go: Spain, Portugal & Morocco, Harvard Student Agencies, Inc.; Thayer Hall-B; Harvard University; Cambridge, MA 02138; USA.

In addition to the invaluable travel advice our readers share with us, many are kind enough to offer their services as researchers. Unfortunately, the charter of Harvard Student Agencies, Inc. enables us to employ only currently enrolled Harvard students both as researchers and editorial staff.

Maps by David Lindroth, copyright © 1989, 1986 by St. Martin's Press, Inc.

Distributed outside the U.S. and Canada by Pan Books Ltd.

ISBN: 0-312-02239-5

First Edition
10 9 8 7 6 5 4 3 2 1

Let's Go: Spain, Portugal, & Morocco is written by Harvard Student Agencies, Inc., Harvard University, Thayer Hall-B, Cambridge, Mass. 02138.

Let's Go ® is a registered trademark of Harvard Student Agencies, Inc.

ACKNOWLEDGMENTS

It has been a summer of extremes—and I'm not referring to the weather. This book long ago took on a life (and a bizarre sense of humor) all its own. To the extent that its very existence reflects a human endeavor, however, those who shaped its formation—both style and substance—must be recognized.

This bad boy's other parent deserves primary mention. Dave Rettig's good-humored style, unique phone voice, and almost womb-like attraction to Au Bon Pain brightened many a gloomy day at the office. His thoughtful writing and clever wit singed their mark on this baby-turned-Sasquatch. I only hope that Dave will recover someday from this experience—and go on to live a normal, unfrazzled life.

Five researcher/writers overhauled the body of this book, the text itself. The reordering of Spain was largely the work of Charles Ehrlich, whose bushwhacking through unexplored territory in Almeria added three new cities to the guide. Charles was really forced to rough it, covering many of Spain's beaches, the Balearic Islands, and the book's most romantic bar. George Jagoe could easily have written an entire book of his own on the Pyrenees, the Picos, and especially Barcelona. His copy batches, more like packages, managed to take even the post office by surprise. Scott Mayer authored some of the summer's most entertaining correspondence as Moroccan police chased him around the countryside, once even injecting bronchitis into his system. Nicole de Necochea proved that careful researching and having fun needn't be mutually exclusive; vastly expanded bar and disco sections in Madrid and Sevilla verify this point. Jen Wang, from our California desk, almost didn't get to Europe at all. Missed connections and the dreaded curse of the rain cloud not withstanding, Jen visited all the book's namesake countries. Our expanded Madeira and revamped Portugal sections were his loving creations.

If the work of researchers constitutes the book's blood and guts, three doctors carefully guided its maturation. Alice Ma was truly a gem of a Managing Editor. Her meticulous attention to detail—and junk food—never ceased to amaze me. Production/Communications Coordinator Joe Hayashi exceeded his job description to the point of lunacy, but thankfully so. He and IBM must have some kind of mystical alliance: He stays up all night once a month and the computer vows never to cross him. Mark Selwyn, Publishing Manager extraordinaire, must be missing several million neurons. His shocking ability to remain calm in the face of foolishly nerve-wrecking stresses at times seemed non-human. Ice cream-loving bosses are a rare commodity in today's health-conscious society.

Back in our hell hole of a basement, fellow officemates helped maintain my sanity and ensure the completion of this onus. Kay, alias Spagol magol, Jim Mazur, a.k.a friend, put up with my lunacy (or even exacerbated it) from the initial nightmare of terror sheets to the agony of choosing a place for lunch; from end of summer exhaustion to early morning phone ramblings. Pip can have a piece of a piece anytime. She's definately no lamo, so whoa! Steve and Jamey helped close down the place many a night at the end of the summer. Steve's telephone answering service and *hummus* wholesale shop, due to open after graduation, will do well I'm sure. Jamey, sanity now regained, is planning to open a used clothing shop, with an Elsieburger stand in back. Carol and Benj ensured musical diversity in the office. Jay perfected the arts of obscure movie references, Minnesotaisms, and office impersonation routines. Julianne, accent master, despite her defense of Science A, is OK in my book. Sharon and Debbie offered moral support, while Glenn singlehandedly kept the Twizzlers Corporation (and it is a corporation) in business. Alex perfected the warped ability to live on zero sleep as Lynley honed her fro yo eating talents, perpetually garbed in white. Scott's Japanese medical project took him away from the office for a spell, but his recovery was nutritionally nurtured with balanced meals of yogurt and Ovaltine. Emily and Susan were all smiles, except when Emily decided to help with this book in its hellish final days. Allen made the same mistaken life choice.

Mother-office support came in the form of Viv "wanna dance, stranger?" Hunt, whose lip syncing career may some day impinge upon her class schedules.

Above ground, Chef Wart tested new recipes on my willing stomach and advanced vocabulary on my awestruck ears. Many friends somehow were able to bear with me. Thanks Jen and Sue (lunch buddies), Love Child and Sarah et co. (dinner and party buddies), Euner-Euner (life story buddy), Andrea (reality check point), Deb (bank buddy), Michael (roommate buddy), Lizzie and Jane et co. (hanging out buddies).

My family has been a constant source of support—and food. They made this book (and everything) possible. I thank them, and I love them.

—Andy

"Everything is for the best in the physical and moral world and . . . things could not have been otherwise," Candide said after he was driven from his castle, enslaved, flogged, and broiled on a spit. But what are a couple of inconveniences if you've got a few friends and peanuts butter shakes to keep you going? At times, this summer was a rapturous delight; at others, it was something to be survived. Only because of the new-found and re-found friends also interned in Canaday were either possible. Back at the ranch, Jo Jo, Chris, and Liam, my summer and life mates, I'd be lost without you. May we always live in times of BBQs, bachelor parties, and Inquisition chairs. Polly, the orgo loving loser of bikes, you can protect me any Thursday night. Julio, may we suck octopus and make danceable pop music back in L-House. Finally, Mom, Dad, Jeff, and Susanne, though we're apart, I love you more each day.

—Dave

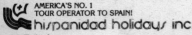

CONTENTS

vii

viii   **Contents**

LET'S GO: SPAIN, PORTUGAL, & MOROCCO

General Introduction

Don Quixote was right. Armored jousters still rampage across the Iberian peninsula and Morocco, their spirit alive in the mirages, snake charmers, flamenco dancers, hooded Berbers, and religous figures that you will find to be omnipresent. They are all part of the act: Welcome to the stage.

Giants and vast armies confronted Don Quixote as he traveled through Spain, the faithful but bewildered Sancho Panza at his side. More earthy and less imaginative than the ingenious gentleman, Sancho saw only windmills and sheep at first, but soon came to believe in his master's fantasies. The Spain of today is filled with *paella* and *gazpacho,* olive trees and orange blossoms, and, on a more serious note, insular groups struggling for autonomy, their political passions fired by vivid memories of the not long-disposed fascist, Generalissimo Franco. Eventually, Spain will find you, whether during a mystical moment in Cordoba's mosque, a political discussion in a Salamanca bar, or a face-to-face encounter with an angry bull on a Pamplona street. Traveling in Spain "in quest of Adventures," Cervantes wrote, may be "the oddest Fancy that ever enter'd into a Madman's brain," but the Spanish ambiente has never ceased to arouse potential knights-errant into new sallies and quests.

Determined to preserve its age-old culture, in a rapidly industrializing society, Spain's western neighbor faces different challenges. Five centuries ago, Portuguese explorers gambled that beyond the western horizon lay not an abyss but a new land. Setting out across the Atlantic and around the tip of Africa, they boldly forged an empire that circled the globe. No longer wealthy or powerful today, Portugal struggles not to conquer new lands but to overcome economic and political difficulties at home. The Portuguese cling to tradition in their religious beliefs, annual festivals, dress, and cuisine. Unlike the Spanish, the Portuguese share a single common language; from their fervent participation in Semana Santa to their meticulous care for ancient architectural treasures, the Portuguese preserve a common national culture as well.

It was only forty years ago that the machinations at Rick's snared Humphrey Bogart in an intricate game of cat-and-mouse. The Morocco of today hasn't changed much: You play Bogart, the hustlers will play themselves. Tourism is the number one industry, and Morocco's denizens take full advantage of it. Don't be perplexed if you are harassed at every turn by those who would guide you for money, only to be invited, steps later, to share a meal with those who seek only your friendship. Your senses will often be inundated by the droning prayers and the desert sun, only to be soothed, moments later, by the shade of an emerald fountain near an ancient mosque. You will find yourself fascinated and dismayed by the hoods and veils, the smells and songs, the poverty in the streets and the abandoned wealth of colonialism. The unparalleled natural beauty of the Moroccan countryside will also beguile you, from the snowcapped High Atlas Mountains to the endless expanse of the Sahara, which has made more than one weary traveler feel like Don Quixote.

1

Let's Go will show you the secrets of these enchanting lands, many hidden beyond the concession stands and well-traveled bus routes. We list the hot spots, cheap shops, and sleazy flops (we'll warn you about these). Like you, our researcher/writers travel on a shoestring budget in their eternal quest for tastier meals, cleaner and more spacious rooms, and decent museums.

Planning Your Trip

A Note on Prices and Currency
The information in this book was researched in the summer of 1988. Since then, inflation in all three countries will have raised prices by as much as 20%. The exchange rates listed are those of August 15, 1988. Since rates fluctuate considerably, confirm them before you go by checking a national newspaper.

For a successful trip, plan ahead. A deluge of information is yours for the asking, so let your fingers do the walking—or writing. A couple of hours spent contacting the right offices is a small investment in return for the wealth of information you will receive. You should also consider mapping out an itinerary. Even if discarded upon arrival, it will force you to think about your priorities. Are you traveling to see museum exhibits or to meet people? To sun worship or to immerse yourself in the culture? Remember, as well, that blitzing Madrid in two days or touring Fes's medina in an hour will only leave you with a postcard impression. Spend some time exploring the city streets, soaking up sounds and smells, and talking to locals. For every city, there are miles of countryside; for every museum, hundreds of cafes.

When should you travel? Fall and winter mean sparser crowds, livelier city life, greater hospitality, and lower accommodation and transportation prices. The mild Mediterranean winters will allow you to join the locals for a swim, while ski season on the surrounding slopes may prove equally alluring. Off-season airfares will allow you to travel more cheaply, while the relative lack of touring masses will free you from hours spent searching for an inexpensive bed. You'll inevitably get a better feel for the country.

However, some small towns may be virtually boarded-up in the off-season. Many restaurants close, while museums and tourist offices typically maintain shorter hours. Seaside resorts are nearly lifeless, and overcast skies and cold temperatures in certain regions may dampen spirits considerably.

In Spain, Portugal, and Morocco, there are two high seasons: the summer season in the coastal and interior regions and the winter season in the mountainous ski regions. To further complicate things, parts of Spain oberve a "mid-season" in between the high and low periods, charging prices between the two extremes. In some places, Semana Santa and other festival times will be considered part of high season as well. Wherever appropriate, we provide information and rates for varying seasons.

Useful Organizations and Publications

The organizations and publications listed below can help as you're planning your trip. Although they are in the business of luring you abroad, national tourist offices are still valuable sources of information. Remember, the more specific your queries, the more helpful these agencies will be.

Tourist Offices

National Tourist Office of Spain: U.S., 665 Fifth Ave., New York, NY 10022 (tel. (212) 759-8822); 845 N. Michigan Ave., #915E, Chicago, IL 60611 (tel. (312) 642-1992); San Vicente Plaza Bldg., 8383 Wilshire Blvd., #960, Beverly Hills, CA 90211 (tel. (213) 658-7188). **Canada,** 60 Bloor St. W., #201, Toronto, Ont. M4W 3B8 (tel. (416) 961-3131). **U.K.,** 57-58 St. James St., London SW1A IL2 (tel. (01) 499 49 93). **Australia and New Zealand,** write to the Daini Toranomon Denki Bldg., 4F, 1-10 Toranomon 3-Chome, Minato-qu, Tokyo 105.

Portuguese National Tourist Office: U.S., 590 Fifth Ave., New York, NY 10036-5089 (tel. (212) 354-4403). **Canada,** 2180 Yonge St. (Concourse Level), Toronto. Ont. M4S 2B9 (tel. (416) 487-3300) or 500 Sherbrook St. W., #930, 94 Montreal, Que. PQH3A 3C6 (tel. (514) 843-4623). **U.K.,** Newbond Street House, 1-5 Newbond St., London W1Y ONP (tel. (01) 493 38 73). **Australia and New Zealand,** refer to the New York or London office.

Moroccan National Tourist Office: U.S., 20 E. 46th St., #1203, New York, NY 10017 (tel. (212) 557-2520); 420 N. Rodeo Dr., Beverly Hills, CA 90210 (tel. (213) 271-8939). **Canada,** 2001, rue University, #1460, Montreal, Quebec PQ H3A 2A6 (tel. (514) 842-8111). **U.K.,** 174 Regent St., London W1R GHV (tel. (01) 437 00 73). **Australia and New Zealand,** refer to the office in New York or London office.

Embassies and Consulates

Embassy of Spain: U.S., 2700 15th St. NW, Washington, DC 20009 (tel. (202) 265-0190 or 265-0191). **Canada,** 350 Sparks St., #802, Ottawa, Ont. K1R 7S8 (tel. (613) 935-5235 or 935-2828). **U.K.,** 24 Belgrave Sq., London SW1X 8QA (tel. (01) 235 55 55). **Australia,** 15 Arkana St., Yarralumla A.C.T. 2600, or P.O. Box 256 Canberra, Woden A.C.T. 2606 (tel. 73 35 55 or 73 38 45). **New Zealand,** see Australia.

Embassy of Portugal: U.S., 2125 Kalorama Rd. NW, Washington, DC 20008 (tel. (202) 328-8610). **Canada,** 645 Highland Park Dr., Ottawa, Ont. K1Y OB8 (tel. (613) 729-0883). **U.K.,** 11 Belgrave Sq., London SW1 X-8PP (tel. (01) 235 53 31). **Australia,** 6 Champion St., 1st floor, Deakin, A.C.T. 2600 Canberra (tel. 85 20 84). **New Zealand,** see Australia.

Embassy of Morocco: U.S., 1601 21st St. NW, Washington, DC 20009 (tel. (202) 462-7979). **Canada,** 38 Range Rd., Ottawa, Ont. K1N 8J4 (tel. (613) 236-7391). **U.K.,** 49 Queens Gate Garden, London SW7 5NE (tel. 581 50 01).

Consulate General of Spain: U.S., 150 E. 58th St., New York, NY 10155 (tel. (212) 355 40 90). Information on study abroad and on student accommodations. **U.K.,** 20 Draycott Pl., London SW3 2R2 (tel. (01) 581 59 21). **Australia,** 50 Park St., 7th floor, Sydney, N.S.W. 2000, or P.O. Box E441, St. James, N.S.W. 2000 (tel. 262 24 33 or 262 24 43). **New Zealand,** see Australia.

Consulate General of Portugal: U.S., 630 Fifth Ave., #655, New York, NY 10020 (tel. (212) 246-4580). Other offices in Boston, Providence, and San Francisco. **Canada,** in Montreal (tel. (514) 876-1604); in Toronto (tel. (416) 360-8260). **U.K.,** Silver City House, 62 Brompton Road, London SW1E 5BH (tel. (01) 581 87 22). **Australia,** 6 Champion St., 1st floor, Canberra, A.C.T. 2600 (tel. 85 20 84). **New Zealand,** 4749 Fort St., Oakland.

Consulate General of Morocco: U.S., 437 Fifth Ave., 10th floor, New York, NY (tel. (212) 758-2625).

Travel Information and Publications

Canadian Universities Travel Service (Travel CUTS), 187 College St., Toronto, Ont. M5T 1P7 (tel. (416) 979-2406). Discount transatlantic flights from Canadian cities. Student ID cards and travel passes. Their excellent newspaper, *The Canadian Student Traveler,* is free on campuses across Canada and at branch offices in Edmonton, Halifax, Montreal, Ottawa, Saskatoon, Toronto, Vancouver, Victoria, Winnipeg, and London, England.

Council on International Educational Exchange (CIEE), 205 E. 42nd St., New York, NY 10017 (tel. (212) 661-1414; for charter flights: (800) 223-7402, in NY (212) 661-1450). Probably the most comprehensive student travel service. Information for students interested in studying, working, or traveling abroad; low-cost travel; and insurance. All the usual discount travel cards and the ISIC are available. They will send you the annual *Student Travel Catalog* (postage US$1) and *Work, Study, Travel Abroad: The Whole World Handbook* (US$8.95 plus postage). They operate branch offices in Amherst, Atlanta, Austin, Berkeley, Boston, Cambridge, Chicago, Dallas, Encino, Long Beach, Los Angeles, Minneapolis, Portland, Providence, San Diego, La Jolla, San Francisco, and Seattle.

Educational Travel Centre (ETC), 438 N. Frances St., Madison, WI 53703 (tel. (608) 256-5551). Flight information, IYHF (AYH) membership cards, Eurail, and Britrail passes. Their free pamphlet *Taking Off* gives tour and flight information.

Ford's Travel Guides, 19448 Londelius St., Northridge, CA 91325. Distributes *Ford's Freighter Travel Guide & Waterways of the World* (US$8.95), which lists freighter companies that take passengers for trans-Atlantic sea crossings.

Foundation of International Youth Travel Organizations (FIYTO), 81 Islands Brygge, DK-2300 Copenhagen, Denmark (tel. (01) 54 45 35). The FIYTO (YIEE) card is available to anyone (not just students) under 26 and gets you discounts on intra-European transportation, accommodations, cultural activities, and tours. Free annual catalog lists over 4000 discounts available to cardholders.

Forsyth Travel Library, 9154 W. 57th St., P.O. Box 2975, Shawnee Mission, KS 66201 (tel. (800) FOR-SYTH, that's (800) 367-7984, or (913) 384-3440). Well-stocked mail-order service that carries wide range of European city, area, and country maps. Sole American distributor of the *Thomas Cook European Timetable* (US$19.95 postage included), a compendium of schedules for every train in Europe. Write for their free newsletter and catalog.

International Youth Hostel Federation (IYHF), 9 Guessens Rd., Welwyn, Garden City, Hertfordshire AL8 6QW, England (tel. (0707) 32 41 70). National hostel associations include:

American Youth Hostels (AYH), P.O. Box 37613 NW, Washington, DC 20013-7613 (tel. (202) 783-6161). IYHF cards, hostel handbooks, information on budget travel, and the World Adventure Trip Program. Distributes the *International Youth Hostel Handbook, Vol. 1: Europe and Mediterranean* (US$7.50).
Australian Youth Hostel Association, 60 Mary St., Surry Hills, Sydney, New South Wales 2010 (tel. (02) 212 11 51).
British Youth Hostel Association (YHA), Treveyan House, 8 St. Stephen's Hill, St. Albans, Herts AL1 2DY (tel. St. Albs. 55 215).
Canadian Hosteling Association (CHA), 333 River Rd., Vanier, Ont. K1L 8H9 (tel. (613) 748-5638).
Youth Hostel Association of New Zealand, 28 Worchester St., P.O. Box 436, 28, Christchurch, 1 (tel. 79 99 70).

Islamic Center of New York, 1 Riverside Dr., New York, NY 10023 (tel. (212) 362-6800). Gregorian to Islamic conversion calendar and information on Islam.

Let's Go Travel Services, Harvard Student Agencies, Inc., Thayer Hall-B, Harvard University, Cambridge, MA 02138 (tel. (617) 495-9649). ISIC cards, American Youth Hostel memberships (valid at all IYHF hostels), FIYTO cards for non-students, Eurail, Britrail, and France Vacances passes, travel guides (including the entire *Let's Go* series), and travel gear. ISIC, AYH, FIYTO cards available by mail. Use the order form in *Let's Go,* or call or write for their "Bag of Tricks" discount and information packet.

John Muir Publications, P.O. Box 613, Santa Fe, NM 87504 (tel. (505) 982-4078). Distributes three very helpful books by Rick Steve: *Europe 101: History, Art and Culture for the Traveler* (US$11.95), *Europe Through the Back Door* (US$12.95), and *Europe in 22 Days* (US$6.95).

Portuguese Student Travel Office, TURICOOP, Rua Pascoal de Melo, 15-1 DTO, Lisbon (tel. (01) 531 804 or 539 247).

SSA/STA, 220 Faraday St., Carlton, Melbourne, Victoria 3053, Australia (tel. (03) 347 69 11). Standard travel services.

STA Travel, 74 Old Brompton Rd., London SW7 3LQ (tel. (01) 581 82 33) Bargain flights, accommodations, travel services.

Student Travel, 10 High St., Auckland, New Zealand. (tel. (09) 399 723) Standard travel services.

Superintendent of Documents, U.S. Government Printing Office, Washington, DC 20402. Publishes many useful travel-related booklets, including *Your Trip Abroad* (US$1) and *Health Information for International Travel* (US$4.75).

Tagus Turismo Juvenil, Praça de Londres, 9B, 1000 Lisbon (tel. (01) 884 957), and Rua Guedes de Azevedo, 34 Loja C, 4000 Porto (tel. (02) 382 763). In Coimbra, Rua Padre António Vieira (tel. (039) 349 16). Information on workcamps and *au pair* positions, low cost transportation, youth hostel cards, students halls, camping, and study visits.

TIVE/Instituto de la Juventud, José Ortega y Gasset, 71, 28006 Madrid (tel. 401 90 11, 401 90 98, or 401 90 49). Language courses, ISIC and FIYTO cards, student tours, group and individual charter flights, train tickets (BIJ), and discounts on buses and Iberia flights. Listings of cheap accommodations.

Wide World Books and Maps, 401 NE 45th St., Seattle, WA 98105 (tel. (206) 634-3453). Distributes a free catalog listing the most recent guidebooks to all parts of the world.

Documents and Formalities

Early applicants for travel documents get the worm: A backlog at any agency could spoil the best-laid plans.

Passports

For U.S. and Canadian citizens, a valid passport is the only document necessary for entering Spain, Portugal, or Morocco, and for reentering the U.S. or Canada. Australians and New Zealanders who wish to enter Spain or Portugal must obtain a visa in advance or risk being turned away at the border. Though Moroccan border officials sometimes don't check carefully, it's highly advisable to apply for a new passport if your current one bears an Israeli stamp: It is Arab League policy not to admit holders of passports with Israeli stamps, and Israeli and South African citizens. You will also not be able to send mail from Morocco to Israel. In all three countries, you must carry your passport with you at all times, since the police have the right to stop you and demand to see it.

U.S. citizens may apply for a passport, valid for 10 years (5 years if you are under 18), at any office of the U.S. Passport Agency (in Boston, Chicago, Honolulu, Houston, Los Angeles, Miami, New Orleans, New York City, Philadelphia, San Francisco, Seattle, Stamford, or Washington, DC) or at one of the several thousand federal or state courts or post offices authorized to accept passport applications. If you have been issued a passport before and your current passport is not more than 12 years old and was issued after your 16th birthday, you may renew your current passport either by mail or in person; otherwise, you must apply in person. Parents may apply on behalf of children under 13. Before you apply, gather the following: (1) a completed application; (2) proof of U.S. citizenship (a certified copy of your birth certificate or your naturalization papers, or a previous passport not more than 12 years old); (3) one piece of identification bearing your signature and either your photo or your description (e.g., a driver's license); and (4) two identical passport photographs. If you are renewing by mail, your old passport will serve as both (2) and (3). By mail, the fees are US$42, US$27 if you're under 18. If you apply in person, the fees are US$35 and US$20. Processing usually takes about two weeks if you apply in person or at a Passport Agency, three or four weeks at a court or post office; file your application as early as possible. You may pay for express-mail return of your passport. In emergencies—providing you have proof of departure within five working days (e.g., an airline ticket)—the Passport Agency will issue a passport while you wait (and wait, and wait). It's wise to arrive in the office by 1pm. For more information, contact the Bureau of Consular Affairs, Public Affairs Staff, CA/PA Department of State, #5807, Washington, DC 20520 (tel. (202) 523-1355).

Canadian citizens may apply for a five-year, renewable passport by mail from the Passport Office, Department of External Affairs, Ottawa, Ont. K1A 0G3, or in person at one of 20 regional offices. Applicants must submit (1) a completed application, available at passport offices, post offices, and travel agencies; (2) documentary evidence of Canadian citizenship; and (3) two identical photographs. Your identity must be certified on your application by a "guarantor," someone who has known you for at least two years and falls into one of a number of specified categories (e.g., minister, medical doctor, police officer, or notary public). The current fee is CDN$25. The process takes three to five days if you apply at a regional office, or two weeks by mail. More information can be found in the brochure *Canada Passport* and in the booklet *Bon Voyage, But*—both free from the Passport Office and at airports.

British citizens must apply at passport offices located throughout Britain. Subjects 16 and over may obtain a 10-year passport; those under 16 may obtain a five-year passport. The fee for either is £15. A birth certificate, marriage certificate (if applicable), and two identical recent photographs are required. All documents must be originals; copies will not be accepted. Documentation is usually waived if the applicant produces a previous unrestricted British passport.

Australian citizens must apply in person at a local post office. Citizens 18 and over may obtain a passport valid for 10 years (AUS$66); those under 18 may apply for a five-year passport (AUS$27). For more information, consult any Australian post office.

New Zealanders must contact the Department of Internal Affairs, Passports Head Office, Private Bag, Wellington, New Zealand (tel. 738 699), or their local district office for an application. The fee for a 10-year passport (5 years if you are under age 10) is NZ$49.50 if you apply in New Zealand, NZ$50 if you apply at a New Zealand consulate; the office will provide speedy processing in emergencies.

Before you leave, you should photocopy your passport number, and the date and place of its issuance; keep this apart from your passport in case the document disappears. In addition, consulates recommend that you carry an expired passport or a copy of your birth certificate in a separate part of your baggage. If you lose your passport while traveling, notify the local police and the nearest consulate of your home government immediately. Your consulate will be able to issue you a new passport or temporary traveling papers in such an emergency.

Visas

Citizens of Australia and New Zealand must obtain a visa before entering Spain, Portugal, or Morocco. U.S., Canadian, and British citizens need only a passport to remain in Spain for six months, Portugal for 60 days, and Morocco for 90 days. These periods may be extended with visas—permission from a foreign government (in the form of a stamp in your passport) that entitles you to stay in the country for a specified period of time. If you'll be staying in any of these countries longer than permitted with a passport, apply for a visa at the country's embassy or one of its consulates in your own country well before your departure. Extending your stay once you're there is more difficult, unless you're a student. You must contact the country's immigration officials or local police well before your time is up, though in Portugal you may apply to the Foreigners Registration Service seven days prior to your original date of expiration. As a rule, you'll need sound proof of financial resources.

Although a visa is not required to visit Morocco, acquiring one before arrival can decrease your chances of encountering difficulty at the border. The U.S. Department of State provides two free pamphlets, *Visa Requirements of Foreign Governments* and *Tips for Travelers.* Write to the Superintendent of Documents (see Useful Organizations and Publications above). If you'd rather have someone else deal with this bureaucracy, call **Visa Service, Inc.,** 507 Fifth Ave., #904, New York, NY 10017 (tel. (212) 986-0924). The service charge varies with the requirements of your passport; the average cost for a U.S. citizen is US$10 per visa that they obtain for you.

Customs

Your luggage may be examined when you enter and leave Spain, Portugal, or Morocco. Most personal belongings can be imported. Up to 200 cigarettes are permitted by all three countries. Two cameras are permitted by Spain and Portugal, and one for Morocco. One bottle of wine and one of hard liquor are permitted by Spain and Morocco; you may bring two liters of wine and one of liquor into Portugal. It is illegal to import or export Moroccan dirhams. On leaving Morocco, you may convert 50% of the dirhams in your possession (100% if you have been in the country less than 48 hours) by presenting exchange slips (to prove they were purchased at the official rate) to an authorized bank at your point of departure. Save your receipts as proof each time you change money, and try not to end up with too many extra dirhams.

Upon reentering your own country, you must declare all articles acquired abroad. Note that items bought at duty-free shops are not exempt from duty when you return home. "Duty-free" means only that you did not pay taxes in the country of purchase.

U.S. citizens can bring back US$400 worth of goods duty-free and pay 10% on the next US$1000 worth. The duty-free goods must be for personal or household use and cannot include more than 100 cigars, 200 cigarettes (1 carton), or one liter of wine or liquor (you must be 21 or older to bring liquor into the U.S.). All items included must accompany you; you cannot ship them separately.

U.S. customs officials screen out contraband, including non-prescription drugs and narcotics, obscene publications, lottery tickets, liquor-filled candies, and most plants. To avoid problems when carrying prescription drugs, make sure the bottles are clearly marked, and have the prescription ready to show the customs officer.

While in Europe, U.S. citizens can mail home unsolicited gifts duty-free if they are worth less than US$50. However, you may not mail liquor, tobacco, or perfume into the U.S. If you mail home personal goods of U.S. origin, mark the package "American goods returned." Spot checks are occasionally made on parcels, so make sure you mark the accurate price and nature of the gift on the package. If you send back parcels worth more than US$50, the Postal Service will collect the duty plus a handling charge when it is delivered.

Beyond your US$400 allowance, certain items purchased in Morocco may be excluded from duty under the Generalized System of Preferences (GSP), a program designed to build the economies of developing nations through export trade. For more information, write for the brochure *GSP and the Traveler* from the U.S. Customs Service, P.O. Box 7407, Washington, DC 20044 (tel. (202) 566-8195). Their publication *Know Before You Go* provides general customs information.

Canadian citizens may return any number of items per year with a maximum of CDN$100 worth of goods after 48 hours abroad or, once a year, CDN$300 after at least one week away. Your allowance may include 200 cigarettes, 50 cigars, .91kg tobacco, and 1.1 liters of wine or liquor. (You must be at least 16 to bring in tobacco, and you must meet the age requirement of the province of your port of return to bring in alcohol.) You will be assessed at a 20% tax rate on goods valued up to CDN$300 over and above your CDN$100 or CDN$300 exemption. The allowance may not include alcohol or tobacco products. You may send back gifts valued up to CDN$40 duty-free, but you cannot send alcohol or tobacco. For more information, write for the pamphlets *I Declare/ Je Déclare* and *Canada: Travel Information*, available from the Revenue Canada Customs and Excise Department, Communications Branch, Mackenzie Ave., Ottawa, Ont. KIA OL5 (tel. (613) 957-0275).

Australian citizens must purchase a AUS$20 Departure Tax stamp at a post office or international airport before you leave. Children under 12 are exempt. Citizens may return with as much as AUS$400 in goods (AUS$200 if you are under 18), including one liter of alcohol and 250 cigarettes. You may mail back personal property; mark it "Australian goods returned" to avoid duty. You may not mail unsolicited gifts duty-free. For more information, write for the brochure *Australian Customs Information* from the Australian Customs Service, Customs House, 5-11 Constitution Ave., Canberra, A.C.T. 2600.

New Zealand citizens face extensive, strictly enforced customs regulations. Upon return, for example, your plane will be sprayed with an insecticide to deal with any unwelcome visitors. Citizens are allowed to import up to NZ$500 in goods, including 200 cigarettes, 250 grams of tobacco or 50 cigars, and one of the following—4.5 liters of beer, 4.5 liters of wine, or 1125ml of spirits. For more information, pick up the pamphlet *Customs Guide for Travellers* at a customs office.

Student Identification

The **International Student Identity Card (ISIC)** is the most widely accepted form of student identification. The US$10 card can get you discounts at archeological sights, theaters, museums, accommodations and on train, ferry, and airplane travel. Among the student travel offices that issue the ISIC are CIEE or Let's Go Travel in the U.S., Travel CUTS in Canada, London Student Travel in the U.K., SSA in Australia, and Student Travel in New Zealand. (See Useful Organizations and Publications above.) The card is also available at many other university travel offices. When applying, the following must be supplied in person or by mail: current, dated proof of your student status (photocopy of your school ID showing this year's date, a letter on school stationery signed and sealed by the registrar, or a photocopied grade report); a 1½"×2" photo with your name printed on the back; and proof of your birthdate and nationality. The ISIC also provides medical/accident insurance of up to US$2000 plus US$100 per day up to 60 days of in-hospital illness coverage. The card is valid until the end of the calendar year in which it is purchased or the end of the following year if purchased after September 1. If you are taking a year off from school, you cannot purchase a new card in January unless you were a student during the fall semester. When you apply for the card, pick up a copy of the *ID Discount Guide*, listing by country some of the discounts available. You can also write to CIEE for a copy.

With the increase in phony student IDs, many airlines and other agencies now require double proof of student status; it's a good idea to carry a signed letter from the registrar with your school seal or your school photo ID.

In Spain, students with identification are entitled to free admission to state museums and monuments, at least 15% off domestic train fares, and up to 40% off international train tickets. In Portugal, cardholders will receive comparable discounts. In Morocco, the ISIC gets you substantial discounts on Royal Air Maroc flights, and it's the most convincing piece of evidence to get you across the Algerian border without having to change the required US$200 into dinars.

Travelers under 26 who are ineligible for the ISIC can take advantage of the youth card issued by the **Federation of International Youth Travel Organizations (FIYTO).** Also known as the **Youth International Educational Exchange Card (YIEE),** the FITYO card entitles you to many of the benefits accorded ISIC holders. CIEE, Travel CUTS, and budget travel agencies worldwide issue the FITYO card. (See Useful Organizations and Publications above.) You must bring your passport number, a photograph, and the US$4 fee. For further information, write to FIYTO, 81 Islands Brygge, DK-2300 Copenhagen S, Denmark.

International Driver's Permit

You can drive in Spain, Portugal, or Morocco with a valid American or Canadian license. You might want to get an **International Driving Permit** before you leave. Although not required, the IDP can help smooth out difficulties with foreign police officers and can act as an additional piece of identification. Permits are available at offices of the **American Automobile Association (AAA)** and the **Canadian Automobile Association (CAA).** In the U.S., contact Travel Agency Services Department, AAA, 8111 Gatehouse Rd., Falls Church, VA 22047 (tel. (703) 222-6334). In Canada, contact CAA, Toronto Head Office, 2 Carlton St., Toronto, Ont. M5B 1K4 (tel. (416) 964-3170). You will need a completed application, two passport-sized photographs, your valid driver's license, and the US$5 fee. Applicants must be at least age 18.

If you drive, buy, or borrow a car that is not insured, you will need a "green card" or International Insurance Certificate. Most rental agencies include this coverage in their prices; if you buy or lease a car, obtain a green card through the dealer, from an office of the AAA, the CAA, or from some travel agents. Check to see that your auto insurance applies abroad. If not, take out a short-term policy (contact AAA Travel Services about their liability insurance program).

Money

Currency and Exchange

Shop around when exchanging money. Although an exchange office may advertise an extremely attractive rate, it may milk you on the commission charge, or vice versa. Banks often offer the best rates but generally charge a commission. To minimize your losses, exchange fairly large sums at one time, though never more than is safe to carry around, especially in Morocco. More importantly, don't purchase more of a currency than you'll need; every time you convert, you incur a loss, particularly with weakening currencies. Before leaving home, buy about $50 in the currency of the first country you will visit to save you some time and money at the airport. Avoid exchanging money at the unfavorable rates offered by train stations, luxury hotels, and restaurants.

If you're willing to match wits with international financiers, or if you are adept at reading tao cards or animal entrails, you can play the currencies market for a better exchange rate. If the dollar is rising against your destination's currency, hold on to your dollars until you reach Europe. If the dollar is falling exchange in the U.S.

In Spain, banking hours are Monday through Friday from 9am to 2pm and Saturday from 9am to 1pm. In Portugal, banks are open Monday through Friday from 8:30 to 11:45am and from 1 to 2:45pm, although some regions keep longer hours. Morocco's banks are open Monday through Friday from 8:30 to 11:30am and from 3 to 5:30pm. Banks will often be closed for seemingly spontaneous public holidays. Make sure you're not caught cashless. The Spanish department stores Corte Inglés and Galerías Preciados also offer fairly good exchange rates.

Traveler's Checks

Nothing is likely to cause you more headaches than money—even when you have it. Carrying large amounts of cash, even in a money belt, is unwise. Traveler's checks are the safest way to carry money, and unlike your pesatas, escudos, or dirhams, they can be replaced.

Traveler's checks are sold by several agencies and banks, usually for face value plus a 1-2% commission. In Spain and Portugal, you should have no trouble using any of the major brands of checks. In Morocco, most banks will recognize any major check, but it's advisable to stick with American Express, since smaller hotels may refuse other checks.

American Express: Call (800) 221-7282 in the U.S.; call collect (801) 968-8300 from elsewhere. American Express offices overseas will hold mail for checkholders free of charge.

Bank of America: Call (800) 227-3460 in the U.S.; call collect (415) 624-5400 from elsewhere.

Citicorp: Call (800) 645-6556 in the U.S. and Canada; call collect (813) 623-1709 from elsewhere.

MasterCard International: Call (800) 223-9920 in the U.S. and Canada; call collect (212) 974-9496 from elsewhere.

Visa: Call (800) 227-6811 in the U.S. and Canada.

Some companies, notably American Express, offer additional services to traveler's check or credit cardholders; they may cash personal checks, send emergency cables, and cancel airline, hotel, or car rental reservations. Always ask for details about services available to checkholders.

If your checks are lost or stolen, expect red tape and delay even in the best of circumstances. As a precaution, separate your check receipts and keep them in a safe place. Record check numbers as you cash them to help you identify which checks are missing if some disappear. And leave a list of check numbers with someone at home. It is also smart to obtain a list of refund centers when you buy your checks. Most importantly, keep a separate supply of cash or traveler's checks for emergencies.It's best to use a money belt or a flat bag around your neck worn inside your clothing, and split up your money among your pockets and bags.

Credit Cards

While many low-cost establishments simply don't honor credit cards, they can be invaluable in an emergency. With major credit cards, you can get an instant cash advance as large as your remaining credit line from banks that issue the card (although these will be few in Morocco). In Spain, you can get up to 25,000ptas with a Visa card without going through the long process of obtaining approval from the U.S. Such a quick transfusion of cash may be your only source of money, since many

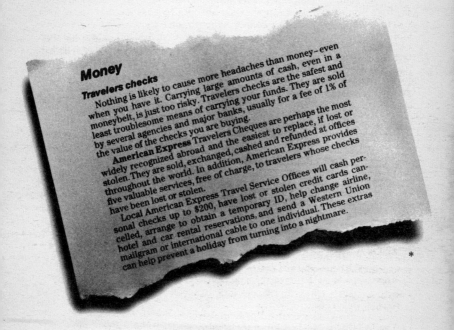

Money

Travelers checks

Nothing is likely to cause more headaches than money—even when you have it. Carrying large amounts of cash, even in a moneybelt, is just too risky. Travelers checks are the safest and least troublesome means of carrying your funds. They are sold by several agencies and major banks, usually for a fee of 1% of the value of the checks you are buying.

American Express Travelers Cheques are perhaps the most widely recognized abroad and the easiest to replace, if lost or stolen. They are sold, exchanged, cashed and refunded at offices throughout the world. In addition, American Express provides five valuable services, free of charge, to travelers whose checks have been lost or stolen.

Local American Express Travel Service Offices will cash personal checks up to $200, have lost or stolen credit cards cancelled, arrange to obtain a temporary ID, help change airline, hotel and car rental reservations, and send a Western Union mailgram or international cable to one individual. These extras can help prevent a holiday from turning into a nightmare.

*

Thanks a lot "Let's Go."
We couldn't have said it better ourselves.

traveler's check vendors will not cash a personal check, and a transatlantic cable for money takes at least 24 hours.

American Express Travel Service (tel. (800) 528-4800) provides valuable services to cardholders, cashing personal checks, holding mail at their overseas offices for cardholders, and providing access to their Global Assist network, which offers information and assistance in emergencies. Be advised, however, that in Morocco you may have difficulty convincing even airport personnel that these little squares of plastic have any value.

If you can't get a credit card on your own, a card-carrying family member can get a card issued in your name; it will be billed to the original account but still entitle you to all the benefits.

Sending Money

Sending money is complicated, expensive, and often extremely frustrating. Do your best to avoid it. Carry a credit card or a separate stash of traveler's checks.

The quickest and cheapest way to have money sent is to have someone cable money through the U.S. office of a large foreign bank whose home country you are visiting. Operating branch offices throughout their country, these banks can often reach you in remote corners, and there is less chance of delay or mix-up since the transaction is entirely in-house.

You can also have money sent through a large commercial bank. The sender must have an account with the bank or take cash to one of its branches (some won't cable money for noncustomers). These banks may charge you an additional fee to pick it up. Cabled money can arrive the same day, the next day, or a week later: It depends on when the sender tries to send the money, what time zones it must cross, and the sophistication of the receiving bank. All information the sender gives, such as your passport number and the recipient bank name and address, must be exact; expect significant delays otherwise. Using a local bank to send money will be slower and more expensive, since these banks usually go through larger banks.

Sending money through **American Express** is comparable in cost. Normally, the sender must have an American Express card to use the company's services, but some offices will waive this requirement for a commission. The money is guaranteed to arrive within 72 hours at the designated overseas office, where it will be held for 14 days before being returned to the sender. This service operates only between American Express offices proper, not their representative offices.

Western Union offers convenient but expensive service. A sender in the U.S. with a MasterCard or Visa card can call Western Union (tel. (800) 325-6000 or 325-4176) and cable up to the credit limit of the card. A sender without a card must go in person to a Western Union office with cash or a cashier's check (no money orders accepted). The money will arrive at the central telegram office of the city designated, and can be picked up upon presentation of suitable identification. Money will generally arrive within two days. Unfortunately, Western Union's service is not comprehensive; in Morocco, it services only Rabat. Rates are US$20 to send US$100-$200 and US$40 to send US$500-$750.

The **State Department's Citizens Emergency Center,** Department of State, #4811, 2201 C St. NW, Washington, DC 20520 (tel. (202) 647-5225), will send you money if you are an American citizen in a life or death emergency. For a fee of US$15, they will send the money within hours, or sometimes overnight, to the nearest consular office. The Department prefers to send sums no greater than US$500. The quickest way to have the money sent is to cable the money to the State Department though Western Union, or to drop off cash, a certified check, bank draft, or money order at the State Department itself.

Value Added Tax

A form of sales tax levied in the European Economic Community, VAT is generally part of the price paid on goods and services. The amount of tax (6-36%) varies from country to country and also from item to item. Overseas visitors not from the EEC can participate in a complex export scheme that exempts them from VAT on goods, but not services. Only certain large stores participate, and the trouble is worthwhile only if you are buying an item over US$100. Ask for a certificate of exportation when you make your purchase (they will ask to see your passport) and present the certificate with the goods to the customs officer for validation when you leave the country. You must take the goods out of the country within three months of their purchase. Once you leave the country, you can claim a refund from the store by mail. If possible, obtain it in your own currency. Making your purchases with a credit card will often speed up your refund check. Morocco does not participate in the VAT refund system. Prices quoted in *Let's Go* include VAT unless otherwise specified.

Packing

Pack light. Set out everything you think you'll need, eliminate half of it, and take more money. Extra luggage will not only get heavier each mile you have to carry it, but will also mark you as a tourist. Test your luggage by walking around the block a with it a few times before you leave.

Decide first what type of luggage suits you best. If you're planning to cover a lot of ground by foot, a sturdy, internal-frame **backpack** with several external compartments is your best bet. In comparison, external-frame packs offer added support and distribute weight better, but are more obtrusive. Knowledgeable salespeople in reputable camping stores are your best sources of assistance.

Consider a light **suitcase** or a large **shoulder bag** if you plan to stay mainly in cities or you wish to travel unobtrusively. A small **day pack** is indispensible for carrying your lunch, camera, water bottle, and *Let's Go*.

In Spain, Portugal, and Morocco, **dress** for the heat. Natural fibers or cotton blends will prove most comfortable. Forego clothes that will brand you as an out-of-towner (see Safety and Security below). Western dress may go unnoticed in larger cities, but will only draw unwarranted attention in the countryside. While no non-Muslim is permitted to enter a mosque without invitation, conservative attire will gain you entrance into Spanish and Portuguese houses of worship.

Here's a list of miscellaneous items you should consider taking: a bath towel, flashlight (especially useful for exploring the unlit caves of Spain and Morocco), canteen, clock, sunglasses, a pocket knife, needle and thread, paper and pencil, earplugs (for noisy hostels), and matches. Most toiletries will be available in cities and towns along the way, but certain items, such as tampons, toilet paper, contact-lens fluids, and contraceptives, may not be easy to find. Finally, bring a padlock to lock your pack to your bedframe at hostels—don't assume that your possessions are safe while you sleep.

If you can't live without your favorite electrical appliance, you'll need a **converter.** Its voltage will depend on where you are—current runs at both 110 and 220AC. Some machines have a switch-operated converter built in (but since European outlets are designed to receive round prongs, you'll also need an **adapter** to change the shape of the plug). To order a converter by mail, write Franzus Company, 53 W. 23rd St., New York, NY 10010 (tel. (212) 463-9393).

Camera equipment is valuable, fragile, and heavy. The more you leave behind, the less you'll worry and the better your back will feel. In many small towns and at tourist attractions, film availability is limited and prices inflated. Consider buying film before you leave home. Despite the disclaimers to the contrary, airport X-ray equipment often fogs film. Higher speed film is more likely to be damaged. Consider purchasing a lead-lined pouch from a camera store and stash your rolls there. Although developing is cheap and fast in Spain, use of non-standard chemicals and even the altitude of the developing office can affect quality, so you may prefer to develop your pictures once you return home.

Accommodations

Visit local tourist offices to find the places that *Let's Go* doesn't have room to list. Many distribute extensive listings free of charge, and many will also make room reservations for a small fee. If *Let's Go* lists one price for an establishment, it's the high-season price and you can usually book the same room for a lower price in the off-season. We list off-season prices where we can. Accommodations are listed in order of value.

Hostels remain the opiate of the budget-concerned masses. Prices are extraordinarily low—at US$3-10 for shared rooms, only camping is cheaper. They also provide opportunities to meet other travelers, exchange stories, and swap information on restaurants and sights. Most hostels, however, share certain disadvantages. An early curfew is common; no problem if you're going camel riding in the pre-dawn hours the next day, but a draconian cramp on you're style if your club-hopping in Madrid. There is little privacy, rooms are usually segregated by sex, and you may run into hordes of pre-teens. Most hostels enforce a lockout from morning to early afternoon. During the summer, be sure to arrive at hostels as early as possible to secure a bed.

Make sure to purchase an International Youth Hostel Federation (IYHF) card (US$20), available from various budget travel agencies and national hostel associations (see Useful Organizations and Publications above). Membership is valid for the calendar year. It's also wise to obtain a sleeping sack, which many hostels require. (See Accommodations under specific country introductions for more information.)

Camping

Camping gives you low prices without the rules and regulations of hostels or the drabness of cheap hotels. Stick to official sites—thieving is rife, and policemen can be unsympathetic to travelers camping illegally on beaches and other sites. Official campgrounds are abundant, however, and information is available from tourist offices. Be sure to arrive early—urban and coastal parks may require reservations.

If you need to purchase **camping gear,** it's better to spend money on high quality equipment than to try working with broken equipment in the field. In the summer, get a synthetic-filled **sleeping bag.** They're cheaper and more durable than down-filled bags. Most are water-resistant. Mummy bags are lighter and more compact than regular bags. Sleeping bags usually have ratings for specific minimum temperatures, so buy your bag accordingly. In Spain, Portugal, and Morocco be prepared for temperatures that can dip to the freezing point at night, especially in the desert and at high altitudes. Synthetic bags usually cost US$20-50, while down bags for sub-freezing temperatures start at US$150. Simple **Ensolite pads** run US$6-10, but the best air mattress or a sophisticated hybrid such as the **Thermarest** may cost upto US$50.

Modern **tents** have their own frames and suspension systems, can be set up quickly, and usually do not require staking. Make certain that your tent has a rain fly and bug netting. The material is also important: Synthetic canvas is less expensive, lighter, and more water-resistant than cotton canvas, but it is also less able to breath. Make sure that the edges of the tent floor extend several inches off the ground to prevent water seepage from the outside. Backpackers and cyclists may wish to pay a bit more for a sophisticated lightweight tent that is easily packed—some two-person tents weigh just over two pounds. Car travelers should strongly consider buying a tent larger than needed; you will appreciate the extra room, especially in the sweltering heat. Expect to pay US$65 for a simple two-person tent and around US$160 for a serviceable four-person model. Some camping equipment stores:

Campmor, 810 Rte. 17 N., P.O. Box 997, Paramus, NJ 07653 (tel. (800) 526-5784).

L.L. Bean, Freeport, ME 04033 (tel. (800) 341-4341). Write for their free catalog of goods ranging from backpacks and sleeping bags to walking shoes and sweaters.

Mountain Equipment, Inc. (MEI), 4776 E. Jensen Ave., Fresno, CA 93725 (tel. (209) 486-8211). Good-quality, reasonably priced backpacks and travel packs. Send for their catalog and the names of retailers who sell MEI products.

Recreational Equipment, Inc. (REI), P.O. Box C-88126, Seattle, WA 98138 (tel. (206) 395-3780). Customers (non-members) get a 10% discount at the time of purchase.

Non-Commercial Accommodations

For a change from the routine, consider the wide range of alternative housing options at your disposal, including student dormitories, religious institutions, and host networks.

Servas is an organization devoted to promoting understanding among people of different cultures. Traveler members may stay free in host members' homes in 80 countries. Participants are expected to contact their hosts in advance and to be willing to fit into the household routine. Prospective traveler members are interviewed and asked to contribute US$45. Approved members are given an orientation and then sent a directory (US$15) listing host members in countries they have specified. To apply, write: U.S. Servas Committee, 11 John St., #706, New York, NY 10038 (tel. (212) 267-0252).

Traveler's Directory, 6224 Boynton St., Philadelphia, PA 19144, or 1501 Wylie Dr., Modesto, CA 95355, prints a semiannual registry of its members, listing specific offers of hospitality to other members. Members must be willing to host other members in their homes. Annual membership for those living in North America is US$20, outside North America US$25. You must be in the directory for two editions before you receive a copy (or pay an additional US$10). The directory's newsletter, *Vagabond Shoes,* is available to nonmembers for US$10 per year and provides helpful advice on budget travel in Europe (see Useful Organizations and Publications above).

Pax Christi, The International Catholic Movement for Peace, has established meeting centers in Europe at places where both long spiritual traditions and important tourist industries exist. International groups of young people offer food and lodging to travelers of both sexes for a maximum of five days in summer. A "Friends of Pax Christi" card, which can be purchased on arrival at the center, is required.

Spanish and Portuguese monasteries offer peaceful lodgings in a rural setting. Note that these are functioning religious institutions and not converted dormitories. Most offer hotel-like rooms and charge 700-1500ptas per night. Others accept single men or single women at 250-500ptas per person; ask individual monasteries for details. Contact local tourist offices or churches, especially in Galicia, central Castilla, and Madrid, for locations and directions. Reservations must usually be made well in advance.

Health

For **medical emergencies,** dial 091 in Spain, 115 in Portugal, and 19 in Morocco.

The three-digit temperatures and exotic foods of the Iberian peninsula and North Africa can often bring even the healthiest of travelers to their knees. Give your body time to adjust; you may not want to try squid cooked in its own ink at your first Portuguese meal. Although cutting out nutritious food by eating at street vendors or dirty restaurants may save you money, you may pay dearly for it. Avoid unpeeled fruits and vegetables, and drink plenty of fluids. Drinking water from the village pump may prove unwise; although it may be safe for locals, your uninitiated stomach may protest vehemently. You may want to rely on bottled water in these areas. Insist on breaking the plastic seal on the bottle yourself before paying, or you may end up slurping expensive tap water. And if you can't drink the water, you can't use the ice.

In many areas of Spain, Portugal, and especially Morocco, the sun will fry you faster than a two-minute egg. The desert is a dangerous place to work on your tan. If you suffer a bout of prickly heat, you can relieve the itchy rash by taking frequent showers, dusting with talcum powder, and keeping yourself as cool as possible.

If you succumb to diarrhea, the best cure is plenty of fluids and rest. If you must eat, yogurt's your best bet, or nibble on boiled vegetables or rice; abstain from fruits, fruit juices, and roughage until you've recovered. Several antibiotics are available over-the-counter in Morocco. Pepto-bismol is a reliable stand-by. In Spain and Portugal, you can also check with a pharmacy, which gives on-the-spot advice.

If you'll need medication while traveling, obtain a full supply before you leave, since matching your prescription with a foreign equivalent is not always possible. Always carry up-to-date prescriptions and a statement from your doctor, especially if you will be carrying insulin, syringes, or any narcotic drug.

Travelers with a medical condition that cannot easily be recognized (diabetes, allergies to antibiotics, epilepsy, heart conditions) should consider obtaining a **Medic Alert identification tag.** This internationally recognized tag identifies the condition in emergencies and provides the number of Medic Alert's 24-hour hotline, through which medical personnel can obtain information about the member's medical history. Lifetime membership is US$20; contact Medic Alert Foundation International, P.O. Box 1009, Turlock, CA 95381 (tel. (800) IDA-LERT, that's 432-5378).

In areas of Spain and Portugal you may have difficulty finding emergency medical care. The **International Association for Medical Assistance to Travelers (IAMAT),** 417 Center St., Lewiston, NY 14092 (tel. (716) 754-4883), provides a worldwide directory of English-speaking doctors and country-by-country breakdowns of sanitary conditions (membership is free, donations requested). Embassies, consulates, and American Express offices should also be of help. Also try resort areas where English-speaking doctors are most likely to be available, or, in Spain and Portugal, major hospitals in cities near the resorts.

The Moroccan Red Crescent is not wholly reliable. Avoid the public hospitals. If you fall seriously ill in Morocco, see a private doctor (ask the U.S. consulate or a local, modern pharmacy for recommendations), and consider heading home. The heat and poor sanitary conditions are not conducive to speedy recovery.

Before traveling to Morocco, get a shot of gamma globulin to protect against hepatitis. If you plan to explore beyond the big cities, you should get cholera and typhoid shots, as well as malaria pills. Watch any open sores, scratches, cuts, or mosquito bites: The heat and less sanitary conditions increase the likelihood of infections, which may lead to more serious illness.

For more information, *The Pocket Medical Encyclopedia and First-Aid Guide* (US$4.95) is available from Simon & Schuster, 200 Old Tappan Rd., Old Tappan, NJ 07675 (tel. (800) 223 2336). Richard Dawood's *How to Stay Healthy Abroad* (US$11.95, postage included) is available from Viking-Penguin Inc., 299 Murray Hill Parkway, East Rutherford, NJ 07073 (tel. (201) 933-1460).

You might also want to bring along a compact **first-aid kit,** which should include mild antiseptic soap, a thermometer, aspirin, antiseptic ointment such as Bacitracin, antibiotics, medication for motion sickness and diarrhea, bandages, mosquito repellant, a Swiss Army knife with tweezers, and an antihistamine (even if you've never experienced an allergic reaction at home). No matter what the time of year, be sure to include a good sunscreen and lip balm. If you wear glasses or contact lenses, take an extra pair along. Bring contraceptives with you if you think you will need them, since they may not be readily available or reliable.

Safety and Security

To avoid falling prey to thieves and hustlers, don't act like a tourist. Conspicuous clothing, for instance, will only invite unfriendly interest. Dress codes are extremely important, and shorts (especially cut-offs), tank and tube tops, and T-shirts are signs of ignorance for men and women; they are especially offensive in religious regions.

Bare shoulders, bare knees, and shorts are inappropriate, especially in the country-side. Pants, medium-length skirts, and short sleeves are acceptable. It is best to fol-low the behavior of locals as much as possible. In Morocco, a shawl and *djellaba* (a long garment with sleeves and a hood) may help women blend in, as will long pants for men.

Always look as if you know exactly where you're going. Stay away from bus and train stations and public parks after dark. Crowded youth hostels and overnight trains are favorite hangouts for petty criminals. Keep money and valuables with you at all times, especially while you're sleeping, perhaps in a **money belt. Necklace pouches** worn under the shirt are most theft-resistant. Even during the day, never leave your valuables unattended; a trip to the shower or the telephone could cost you your camera. If you're carrying a zipper-close backpack, consider buying a small lock.

While traveling, steer clear of empty train compartments, particularly at night. Don't check your luggage on trains, especially if you are switching trains en route; it is unnecessary and luggage is often lost. If you plan to sleep outside, or simply don't want to carry everything with you, try to store your gear at a train or bus station.

In Morocco, those traveling alone will often be singled out for harassment. Hook-ing up with a companion (this is especially true for women) will make your stay much safer. Firmly saying *imshi* (go away) will sometimes take care of any harrass-ment. You can also try asking the hustler for the nearest policeman, mentioning that all of your money has just been stolen.

In Morocco's Islamic culture, where **women** may be veiled and secluded in their own homes, a female tourist walking the streets of a strange city by herself should beware. Strolling arm in arm with another woman, a common European practice, may be helpful, as may be a gold band on your left hand. More subtle forms of discrimination, such as being refused a room in a hotel that is not full (proprietors would rather not be responsible for your well-being) are also to be expected, particu-larly in larger, inland cities. Your best response to most harrassment is no response at all. If a situation becomes threatening, however, a loud and stern answer, espe-cially in the presence of onlookers, may prove effective. *Let's Go* lists emergency, police, and consulate phone numbers. Often we also list women's centers, rape crisis numbers, and special accommodations for women.

In major cities, watch out for pickpockets who are fast and professional. Remem-ber that pickpockets can come in all shapes and sizes, and will do anything to divert your attention. The following scams are currently popular in major European cities: someone blocks your view with a piece of cardboard or a map (pretending to ask directions); groups of youths, even children, pretend to scuffle and fight; pairs of people attempt to solicit money or sell posters to support political causes; someone throws mustard or yogurt on your purse and offers to clean up the mess—taking your purse in the meantime; and people tell you they have just been robbed and need to "borrow" money.

It's always a good idea to make photocopies of all important documents, includ-ing your passport, identification, credit cards, and the numbers of your traveler's checks. Keep one set in your luggage, and leave another set with friends at home. Although copies may not substitute for the original documents, you might be able to facilitate reissuances and cancellations.

Insurance

When buying insurance, beware of unnecessary coverage. Check whether your homeowner's insurance (or your family's coverage) provides against theft during travel. University term-time plans often cover summer travel as well. ISIC holders are also provided with medical/accident insurance of up to US$2000 plus US$100 per day up to 60 days of in-hospital illness coverage. Be aware that insurance compa-nies generally require a copy of the police report filed at the time of the theft before they will honor your claim. For medical expenses, you must submit evidence that you did indeed pay the charges for which you are requesting reimbursement. Always keep all receipts. Check the time limit on filing to make sure that you will be returning home in time to secure reimbursement. The following firms offer a variety of insurance programs. You can buy a policy from them or, in some cases, from a travel agent.

Access America, Inc., 600 Third Ave., Box 807, New York, NY 10163 (tel. (800) 851-2800). Offers trip cancellation/interruption insurance, stolen passport coverage, bail money, medical payments, and more. Policyholders are given a toll-free, 24-hour international number providing access to a network of multi-lingual coordinators.

Europ Assistance Worldwide, 1133 15th St. NW, #400, Washington, DC 20005 (tel. (800) 821-2828). Round-the-world services include medical coverage, medical evacuation, interpretation assistance, help in locating lost passports and visas, medical and legal referrals, and transmission of urgent messages.

Travel Guard International, Travel Guard Gold, P.O. Box 1200, Stevens Point, WI 54481 (tel. (800) 782-5151). Their comprehensive package covers medical treatment, cash advances, and lost luggage. Airplane ticket cancellation covers only 50% up to US$200 but the cancellation may be made for "any reason whatsoever."

The Travelers Insurance Co., 1 Tower Sq., Hartford, CT 06183 (tel. (800) 243-3144). Insurance for baggage, accident, sickness, trip cancellation, and emergency medical evacuation. Available through most travel agencies.

CIEE also offers an inexpensive Trip Safe plan with options to cover medical treatment and hospitalization, accidents, and even charter flights missed due to illness. (See Useful Organizations and Publications above.)

Drugs

The horror stories about drug busts in Europe and North Africa are grounded in solid fact. Every year, hundreds of young travelers are arrested in foreign countries for illegal possession, use, or trafficking in drugs. Some countries—Morocco, in particular—are especially severe in their treatment of those arrested on drug-related charges.

Don't buy drugs. Although plenty of locals may be using hashish, the openness is an illusion. In Morocco, possession is legal for citizens, but will land a foreigner in jail. Furthermore, dealers often work hand-in-hand with the police. In one racket, a drug dealer sells to a foreign visitor, heads straight for the police, describes the patron in detail, collects a fee for information, and gets the goods back when the buyer is arrested. Never carry drugs across borders. International express trains are not as safe as they might seem; you may be searched entering a country that you'll be leaving a half-hour later.

Don't expect your government to extricate you; they are powerless in the judicial system of a foreign country. Consular officers can only visit a prisoner, provide a list of attorneys, and inform family and friends. A U.S. State Department bulletin notes, "You're virtually 'on your own' if you become involved, however innocently, in illegal drug trafficking." The legal codes in some countries, including Morocco, provide for guilt by association; *you* may be charged if your companions are found in possession of illegal drugs. For more information, send for the brochure *Travel Warning on Drugs Abroad,* available from the Bureau of Consular Affairs, CA/PA #5807, U.S. Department of State, Washington, DC 20520 (tel. (202) 647-1488).

Work

The employment situation in Spain, Portugal, and Morocco is grim for natives and worse for foreigners. Unemployment is high, and all jobs, including unskilled and part-time positions, are coveted. Getting a work visa is extremely difficult. Consult the *Directory of Overseas Summer Jobs* (US$9.95), available from Writer's Digest Books, 1507 Dana Ave, Cincinnati, OH 45207 (tel. (800) 543-4644), for more information.

Teaching English is perhaps the best source of official and unofficial employment in Spain and Portugal, and probably your only source of income in Morocco. Inquire at language schools and private schools. Some English schools will arrange a work permit for you, although they tend to pay less. In Morocco, you may wish to consult the **American Language Center,** 4 rue de Tanger (tel. (07) 612 69) and 19 pl. de la Fraternité (tel. 752 70), Rabat; 2 rue Emsallah, Tangier (tel. 336 40); 2 rue du Consul Gaillard, Fes (tel. 248 50); Villa 3, Impasse du Moulin de Gueliz, Marrakech 9 (tel. 323 73). Also try the **Tangier American School,** rue Christophe Colomb, 149 (tel. 215 27).

You can also lead a tour group abroad. Positions as group leaders are available from **American Youth Hostels, Inc.,** P.O. Box 37613, Washington, DC 20013 (tel. (202) 783-6161) and from the **Experiment in International Living,** Kipling Rd., Brattleboro, VT 05301 (tel. (802) 257-7751). Jobs in restaurants and bars may be sources of under-the-table income. **International work camps** allow volunteers to work on community development projects. Spartan room and board is generally provided.

For more information on available work options:

Interexchange Program, William Sloane House, 356 W. 34th St., 2nd floor, New York, NY 10001 (tel. (212) 947-9533). Offers catalogs listing work abroad options in Europe.

Vacation Work Publications, 9 Park End St., Oxford OX1 1HJ, England (tel. (0865) 24 19 78). Publishes the *1989 Directory of Summer Jobs Abroad* (£4.95).

Volunteers for Peace: Tiffany Rd., Belmont, VT 05730 (tel. (802) 259-2759). Placement service for workcamps in 30 countries, primarily in Europe. Free newsletter.

Study

Foreign students can study in **Spain** through U.S. university programs or through courses for foreign students organized by Spanish universities or centers. If your language skills are good enough, you also have the option of enrolling directly in a Spanish university. If possible, talk to counselors at your college and use their libraries. Another resource is the **Education Office of Spain,** 150 Fifth Ave., #600, New York, NY 10011 (tel. (212) 741-5144).

U.S. citizens who are considering enrolling as regular students in a Spanish university should write for "General Information About Higher Education in Spain" and "Study in Spain," two information packets available from the U.S. Consulate in Spain. (See Consulates below). Further information is best obtained from individual universities. The universities of Madrid, Sevilla, Alicante, Granada, and Salamanca all offer some combination of language classes, supplementary cultural instruction, daytrips, and related extra-curricular activities. Address inquiries to the city (for example, Universidad Complutense, Granada, Spain). Note that in letters to University of Madrid, you must also specify Faculdad de Filosofia y Letras.

All universities in **Portugal** are open to foreign students. It's best to contact the individual institutions for specifics. Universities offering language studies to foreigners include the University of Lisbon, Faculdades de Letras, Cidade Universitária (tel. 73 11 89), and the University of Coimbra, Faculdade de Letras, Largo da Porta Ferrea (tel. 260 88). The Ricardo Espíritu Santo Foundation in Lisbon, at Largo das Portas do Sol, 2 (tel. 86 21 84), offers courses for foreigners in local arts.

For study in **Morocco,** contact one of the state-controlled universities listed here, or look into your own university's exchange program. The Université Mohammed V, BP 554, 3 rue Michlifen, Agdal, Rabat (tel. 713 18), conducts classes in Arabic and French on subjects that range from the humanities to dentistry. The Université Quaraouyne, BP 60, Fes, was founded in 859. Four faculties teach philosophy and languages, law (*sharia*), Arabic studies, and theology. Courses are offered in Arabic, French, English, and Spanish at the Universié Sidi Mohammed, BP 42, Dhar El Mahraz, Fes, where the faculties teach arts and sciences, law, economics, and social sciences.

For more information on study abroad, contact the following organizations:

Keeping in Touch

Mail

The communications systems in Spain, Portugal, and Morocco range from decent to dubious. In all three countries, the most reliable way to send a message is by wire; the least is by surface mail.

Air mail letters (*por avion*) and aerograms from **Spain** should arrive in the U.S. in a week to 10 days, while surface mail (*por barco*) is considerably less expensive but takes a month or longer. International postcards (*tarjetas postales*) cost 45ptas; they run 18ptas domestically. Postcards are considerably slower than letters. An airmail letter (*via aerea*) from **Portugal** takes a little over a week to reach the U.S. or Canada, while surface mail (*superficie*) can take up to two months. The most reliable way to send a letter or parcel home from Portugal is by registered (*registado*) or express (*certificado*) mail, either of which should take about five days. Letters and parcels that are sent registered or express rarely get lost. Postcards run 75$. Mail sent from **Morocco** is similar in speed and reliability. For almost complete certainty, send your mail express (*expres*) or registered (*recommandé*). Postcards cost 2dh to the U.S. and around 1.60dh to Europe. Stamps are available in all three countries from tobacconists, shops that post a sign outside, and hotels, as well as post offices.

Mail from home can be sent to you in care of **General Delivery.** Letters addressed "Poste Restante" in Portugal and Morocco or "Lista de Correos" in Spain will be held for pick-up at the post office handling general delivery in any city or town. Letters should be sent two weeks in advance. The sender should indicate your last name clearly by capitalizing or underlining it. In Portugal, you must pay 20$ per item picked-up; in Morocco .60dh. Mail can also be sent to you in care of American Express offices. A list of offices is available from any branch office or from American Express, 65 Broadway, New York, NY 10006. To be sure that you receive mail, ask correspondents to send photocopies of their letters to several different places you'll be visiting. You might also consider contacting **Eur-Aide,** P.O. Box 2375, Naperville, IL 60565 (tel. (800) 247-4755), which offers an answering service for travelers in Europe for a weekly or monthly fee. Anyone who wants to get in touch with you calls a "home base" in Europe and leaves a short message; you get the message by calling the "home base" as often as you like. Calls to a "home base" are much cheaper than an overseas call.

Telephone

Almost all telephones in **Spain** are coin-operated; the old token-operated models are now rare. A local call costs 5ptas. To reach the local operator, dial 009 (no coins required). For calls within Spain, insert at least 50ptas. City telephone codes are necessary for long-distance dialing within the country. *Let's Go* lists these codes in the Practical Information section of each city.

Direct-dialing **international calls** is easy and much cheaper than using central telephone offices. Just stock up on plenty of change (you can call the operator beforehand to get an idea of how much your call will be), and then follow the multilingual instructions posted in the telephone booth. International calls can also be made from central telephone offices, open 24 hours in some cities. Specify *cobra revertido* for collect, and *persona a persona* for person-to-person calls. You can now use Visa credit cards to make international calls from Spanish phone offices. If you have trouble placing calls at these offices, try placing them from a luxury hotel instead.

Public telephones in **Portugal** are available at telephone company offices, certain post offices, and street booths. The credifone system uses magnetic cards that can be purchased at locations posted on the phone booths. Long-distance calls within Portugal require a telephone code prefix. Consult the Practical Information section of each city.

Direct-dial *international calls* can be placed from post offices or from telephone offices using the prefix (0971) to the U.S. or (00) to Europe. You can not direct dial Canada. To reach the international operator, dial 098 and specify *pago no destino* for collect calls or *chamada pessoa à pessoa* for person-to-person calls. A call from Portugal to the U.S. costs 375$ per minute, or 330$ per minute from midnight to 8am and all day Sundays and holidays. Unfortunately, you may encounter difficulty getting through to the U.S. from anywhere outside Lisbon.

Telephones in **Morocco** are anything but predictable. Telephone offices exist in the major cities, but the most convenient—and expensive—way to call long distance (especially from rural areas) is to go to a luxury hotel and ask them to place the call for you. They typically levy a 30% commission, but you can wait in comfort.

Most phones are coin-operated, and each city has its own telephone code. Allow plenty of time for overseas calls. An *appel* or direct call, where you pay the cashier afterwards, can take an hour or two, while collect calls (ask for "P.C.V.") may take twice as long. Try to place your call very early or very late to avoid the long lines that stretch farther than that elusive Moroccan camel caravan.

From Rabat and Casablanca, you can dial direct at designated booths. Just lift the receiver and wait for the dial tone—a simple procedure that can take minutes or hours. Then dial "00" and wait for a musical tune, but do not wait until it has ended or you will be disconnected—dial the country code, area code, and number.

Calls to the U.S. and to Canada cost 25dh per minute, to Great Britain 6.75dh per minute.

Telegrams

If you can navigate the phone system, a three-minute call is as cheap as sending a **telegram** from Spain, Portugal, or Morocco. If you must send a telegram, you will find the offices attached to or inside of post offices. In Portugal, telegrams can be sent either through the post office or through "Marconi" offices. Telegrams to the U.S. cost 660$ plus 46$ per word. Spanish rates run about 750ptas. In Morocco, telegrams to the U.S. cost 2.03dh per word, to Canada 1.89dh per word, and to Europe roughly 1dh per word.

Additional Concerns

Senior Travelers

In Spain, senior citizens receive a 50% discount on train fares (a passport will usually do for ID; if not, purchase a RENFE "golden card" at any station for a minimal fee). Portugal offers similar transportation discounts. In many cases, student discounts are available to senior citizens as well. The IYHF card is US$10 for those over 59. The following organizations and publications provide information on discounts and services available to seniors.

American Association of Retired Persons, Special Services Department, 1909 K St. NW, Washington, DC 20049 (tel. (800) 227-7737). Those 50 years and older receive benefits from AARP Travel Services and get discounts on hotels, motels, and car rental and sightseeing companies. Annual membership $5.

Bureau of Consular Affairs, Superintendent of Documents, U.S. Government Printing Office, Washington, DC 20402. Publishes the pamphlet, *Travel Tips for Senior Citizens* (US$1), which provides information on passports, visas, health, and currency.

Elderhostel, 80 Boylston St., #400, Boston, MA 02116 (tel. (617) 426-7788). Offers short-term, residential, academic programs throughout Europe for those 60 and over and their spouses. Some programs include homestays with local families.

Mature Outlook, P.O. Box 1205, Glenview, IL 60025. Provides those 50 years and older with vacation packages, discounted travel insurance, and other discounts. Annual membership US$7.50 per couple.

Pilot Books, 103 Cooper St., Babylon, NY 11702 (tel. (516) 422-2225). Publishes the *1988 Senior Citizen's Guide to Budget Travel* (US$4.95 postage included).

Disabled Travelers

The accessibility of European countries varies greatly. When making arrangements with an airline or hotel, specify exactly what accommodations you require. Rail is usually the most convenient form of travel.

Check with the country you are visiting about the customary six-month quarantine on all animals, including guide dogs. Owners must usually obtain an import license; have current certification of the animal's rabies, distemper, and contagious hepatitis inoculations; and have a veterinarian's letter attesting to the dog's health. The following organizations can provide information and assistance:

American Foundation for the Blind, 15 W. 16th St., New York, NY 10011 (tel. (800) 232-5463). Offers information, travel books, and ID cards to the legally blind.

Disability Press, Ltd., Applemarket House, 17 Union St., Kingston-upon-Thames, Surrey KT1 1RP, England. Publishes the *Disabled Traveller's International Phrasebook* (£1.5 in the U.K, £2.35 elsewhere), a compilation of useful phrases in most European languages, including Spanish, French, and Portuguese.

Mobility International, U.S.A., P.O. Box 3551, Eugene, OR 97403 (tel. (503) 343-1284, voice and TDD). Information on travel programs, accommodations, access guides, and organized tours. MUISA distributes many useful pamphlets including the *Guide to International Educational Exchange, Community Service and Travel for Persons with Disabilities.*

Society for the Advancement of Travel for the Handicapped, 26 Court St., Brooklyn, NY 11242 (tel. (718) 858-5483). Offers advice and assistance in trip planning, including information on tour operators. Annual membership US$40; students and seniors US$25.

Travel Information Service, Moss Rehabilitation Hospital, 12th St. and Tabor Rd., Philadelphia, PA 19141 (tel. (215) 329-5715). Provides access information on specific cities throughout Europe. Send US$5 for brochures.

In recent years a number of publications have come out focusing specifically on overseas travel for the disabled. Check the travel section of any large bookstore. *Access to the World: A Travel Guide for the Handicapped,* by Louise Weiss provides useful information on transportation for the disabled and is available from Facts on File, Inc., 460 Park Ave. S., New York, NY 10016 (US$16.95 plus sales tax for NY and CA residents).

Gay and Lesbian Travelers

In Spain and Portugal, the legal minimum age for consensual sexual intercourse is 18. In general, there is a relaxed attitude towards homosexuality. Some consider the gay scene in Spain the best in Europe, while Portugal is slightly less liberal. Gay and lesbian bars and discos are prevalent in large cities, but gay people should always exercise discretion, especially in less urban areas. Conversely, Morocco, is culturally intolerant of homosexuality. Both civil and Islamic law prohibit the practice of homosexuality, and the rise of fundamentalism further complicates the situation.

For more information, check out the following publications:

Gaia's Guide: Excellent "international guide for traveling women" that lists local lesbian, feminist, and gay information numbers, bookstores, restaurants, hotels, and meeting places. However, it is rather weak on Spain and Portugal and has no listings for Morocco. The book, revised annually, is available at many local bookstores or by mail (US$12.50, postage included) from 9-11 Kensington High St., London W8, England.

Spartacus Guide for Gay Men: This book lists bars, restaurants, hotels, bookstores, and hotlines worldwide (US$24.95). Check your local bookstore or write c/o Bruno Gmunder, Lutzowstrasse 105, P.O. Box 30 13 45, D-1000, Berlin 30, West Germany.

Party: A gay monthly sold at newsstands in Spain.

Travelers with Children

Lest you find yourself touring with *l'enfant terrible,* you should plan ahead when traveling with children. Avoid hassles by booking rooms in advance, especially in summer.

Children are no different from adults: They just want to have a good time. But a child's idea of fun might be quite unique. Simply try to gear some of your plans towards the interests of the kids. This may prove surprisingly enjoyable for you as well.

Many books are written specifically to prepare young children for travel. Others can help teach your child about such topics as the wildlife or the history of the area you will be touring. Try *Baby Travel* (US$11.95), published by Hippocrene Books Inc., 171 Madison Ave., New York, NY 10016 (tel. (212) 685-4371). *Sharing Nature with Children* (US$8.95) is available from Wilderness Press, 2440 Bancroft Way, Berkeley, CA 94704. Your children may enjoy *Emma's Vacation, First Flight,* and *The Train,* by David McPhail, or *Vacation Surprises,* by Patricia Montgomery.

Vegetarians

Spain, Portugal, and Morocco can be a vegetarian's delight. While there are a number of staple meat dishes, fresh produce is cheap and omnipresent. **The Vegetarian Society of the U.K.,** Parkdale, Durham Rd., Altrincham, Cheshire, England (tel. (061) 928 07 03), publishes *The International Vegetarian Handbook* (£2.50), which lists vegetarian and health-conscious restaurants, guesthouses, societies, and health-food stores in Europe. The guide is also available through the **North Ameri-**

can Vegetarian Society, P.O. Box 72, Dolgeville, NY 13329 (tel. (518) 458-7970; US$8.95).

Nude Sunbathers

Nude sunbathing is not at all uncommon in Spain and Portugal, and almost any beach that you come upon will have at least one section dedicated to nude sunbathers. To be on the safe side, look for the signs that say *playa natural* or *playa de nudistas.* Nude sunbathing on unauthorized beaches could result in an embarrassing arrest. Any nude sunbathing in Morocco should be done discreetly, if at all. For more information, you may want to write to Harmony Books, Crown Publishers, Inc., 34 Englehard Ave., Arenel, NJ 07001 (tel. (201) 382-7600) for *The World Guide to Nude Beaches and Recreation* (US$14.95).

Getting There

From North America

Air fare to Europe will cost you anywhere between US$300 to US$1200, depending on the season, the airline, your destination, your point of departure, the amount of luggage you take, and, above all, the whims of airline executives. Start looking early and be flexible.

If possible, consider traveling in the off-season; most major airlines maintain a steep, multi-tiered fare structure. In general, fares start increasing in May and decreasing in late September. When planning your trip, try to keep your schedule and itinerary as flexible as possible; an indirect flight to London, Frankfurt, Brussels, or Luxembourg could cost considerably less than a direct flight to Madrid or Lisbon. Traveling to Europe on a one-way ticket may also save you money.

Find a travel agent committed to saving you money, and don't hesitate to shop around. Commissions are smaller on cheaper flights, so some agents may be less than eager to help you find the best deal. In addition, check the travel section of the Sunday *New York Times* or other major newspapers for bargain fares, and consult CIEE or other student travel organizations. Frequently, such organizations offer special deals to students that regular travel agents may not know about.

Charter flights are the most consistently economical option. You can book some charters up to the last minute, but most flights fill up months in advance, especially at the beginning of the summer. Later in the season, companies start having trouble filling their planes and either cancel some flights or offer special prices; watch for both. Charters also allow you to mix and match arrival and departure points in Europe. Once you have made your plans, however, the flexibility ends. You must choose your departure and return dates when you book, and you will lose some or all of your money if you cancel. Travel insurance usually doesn't help.

Although charter flights are less expensive, they are also frequently more crowded and often delayed. In addition, most charter companies reserve the right to cancel flights up to 48 hours before departure; they will do their best to find you another flight, but don't bet your backpack on it. If they do default on your flight, however, you will get your money back—eventually.

Council Charters, 205 E. 42nd St, New York, NY 10017 (tel. (800) 223 7402). A subsidiary of the Council on International Educational Exchange, Council Charters was among the first on the charter scene and offers service to cities worldwide. Their flights are extremely popular, so reserve early.

DER Tours, 11933 Wilshire Blvd., Los Angeles, CA 90025 (tel. (800) 421-4343; in CA (800) 252-0606).

Travac, 989 Sixth Ave., New York, NY 10018 (tel. (800) TRAV-800, that's 872-8800).

Travel CUTS, 187 College St., Toronto, Ont. M5T 1P7, Canada (tel. (416) 979-2406).

UniTravel, P.O. Box 16220, St. Louis, MO (tel. (800) 325-2222).

Wardair, Tel. (800) 237-0314.

The major airlines offer two options for the budget traveler: standby flights and APEX fares. The advantage of **standby** flights, which are sold only in the summer, is flexibility; you can come and go as you please. The disadvantage is that during peak season, flying standby can turn into a game of roulette. The number of available seats is established only moments before departure. Call individual carriers for the availability and price of standby fares. Tickets are usually sold at the airport on the day of departure. Most travel agents can also issue standby tickets, but may be reluctant to do so. Major international carriers restrict the cities to which one can fly standby. Madrid is an extremely rare standby destination, but London is popular, and cheap ground transportation options may make this an attractive possibility.

More expensive than the stand-by fare, **Advanced Purchase Excursion Fare (APEX)** provides you with confirmed reservations and allows you to arrive and depart from different cities. Reservations must be made 21 days in advance with 7- to 14-day minimum and 60- to 90-day maximum stay limitations. To change an APEX reservation, you must pay a US$50-100 penalty; to change your return, you must pay a US$100 penalty or upgrade your ticket, which will cost well over US$100. For summer travel, book APEX fares early.

You may wish to try the following national airlines:

Air Canada, Tel. (800) 422-6232.

Iberia, Tel. (800) 221-9741. You can also visit their offices in major cities throughout the U.S. and Canada. Spain's national airline flies directly to Spain from a number of U.S. cities. Iberia's APEX tickets must be purchased 21 days in advance.

Royal Air Maroc, Tel. (800) 223-5858. Morocco's national airline. Offices in Chicago and Montreal. Discounts for ISIC holders.

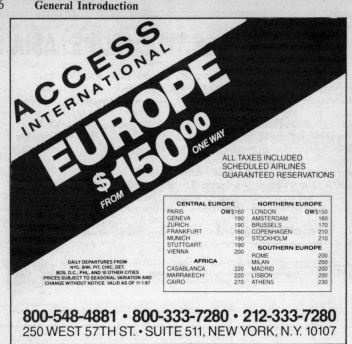
Tap Air Portugal, Tel. (800) 221-7370. Portugal's national airline flies directly to Lisbon from New York. Offices also in Boston, Toronto, and Montreal.

Virgin Atlantic (tel. (800) 862-8621) offers regularly scheduled flights to London from the eastern seaboard for about US$290 each way. A still cheaper option is their Late Saver fare, available for US$259. To qualify, you must book one week or less in advance. **Icelandair** (tel. (800) 223-5500), offers a "get up and go" fare to those booking three days or fewer in advance. Round-trip rates start at US$398.

Discount clearing houses offer savings on charter flights, commercial flights, tour packages, and cruises. These clubs make available unsold tickets three weeks to a few days before departure. Annual dues run US$30-50, but the fares offered can be extremely cheap, often less than US$200 each way. Several places to check out:

Access International, 250 W. 57th St., New York, NY 10107 (tel. (212) 333-7280).

Air Hitch, 2901 Broadway, #100, New York, NY 10025 (tel. (212) 864-2000).

Discount Travel International, Ives Bldg., #205, Narberth, PA 19072 (tel. (800) 824-4000).

Last Minute Travel Club, 132 Brookline Ave., Boston, MA 02215 (tel. (800) 527-8646).

Stand-Buys Ltd., 311 W. Superior, 4th floor, Chicago, IL 60610 (tel. (312) 943-5737).

Worldwide Discount Travel Club, 1674 Meridian Ave., Miami Beach, FL 33139 (tel. (305) 534-2082).

Enterprising travelers who can travel light might consider flying to Europe as **couriers.** Couriers accompany packages across the Atlantic on regular commercial airlines. Your fare is inexpensive, but you are allowed only carry-on bags (the company uses your luggage space).**NOW Voyager,** 74 Varick St., #307, New York, NY 10013 (tel. (212) 431-1616), is the major courier service, arranging flights all over the world for a US$45 fee. A quick warning: NOW Voyager books flights out of New York only, and they require that you visit their office in person to make sure that you "look responsible." You may also wish to check your local yellow pages under "Air Courier Service."

Once There

Transportation in Europe

By Air

For information on intra-European flights, look into **STA Travel,** 74 Old Brompton Rd., London SW7 3LQ (tel. 581 10 22), **Air Travel Advisory Board,** Morley House, Regent St., London, England (tel. 636 50 00), or **CIEE,** 51, rue Dauphine, 6ème, Paris 75006, France. Magic Bus also offers cheap charter flights within Europe (see By Bus below). Iberia, TAP Air, and Royal Air Maroc offer fast and inexpensive air service between Madrid, Lisbon, and Casablanca as well as other major cities.

By Train

European trains retain the romance and convenience that American trains have long since lost. Second-class travel is pleasant, and compartments facilitate meeting people. During the summer, you will find that most of Europe is traveling with you.

Avoid riding an overnight train in a regular coach seat: You'll be awake the whole night. A better option is a sleeping berth in a *couchette* car. Always be wary of thieves who prey on sleeping train riders. If you're sleeping on a train, keep your doors locked and your possessions on your person. For more information, contact **Ariel Publications,** 14417 SE 19th Place, Bellevue, WA 98007 (tel. (206) 641-0518), which publishes *Camp Europe by Train* (US$15.95, postage included), a thorough guide covering nearly all aspects of train travel.

If you're under 26, you will be able to utilize **BIJ** tickets (also known as **Transalpino, Eurotrain,** and **Twen-tours** tickets); they can cut up to 50% off regular second-class rail fares on international runs, but restrict users to certain trains and hours of travel. Tickets are valid for two months, six months in Morocco. Free stopovers are allowed. For example, you can travel from London to Venice for US$75, stopping off in half a dozen countries along the way and taking up to two months. The program's primary disadvantage is that you can stop only at those locations along your route. For more information, contact **Campus Holidays,** 242 Bellevue Ave., Upper Montclair, NJ 07043 (tel. (201) 744-8724).

If you're planning much travel outside Spain, Portugal, or Morocco, consider buying a railpass. Before you invest in one, make sure it will save you money. Visit a travel agent and consult the current *Eurailtariff Manual.* Add up the second-class fares for the major routes you plan to cover and remember to deduct a 30-50% discount if you're under 26 and eligible for BIJ discounts; you will probably find it difficult to make your railpass pay for itself in Spain, Portugal, or Morocco, where train fares are reasonable and distances short. If your total travel cost approaches the price of the pass, the convenience of avoiding ticket lines may make the pass worthwhile. But also watch out for supplements: On many trains other than the slowest, the railpass requires you to pay one-third the normal fare. On any trips between major cities or for distances over 250-300km, reservations are required.

The various Eurailpasses are valid in 16 European countries (not including Great Britain or Morocco) and entitle you to passage on certain ferries and reduced fares on others. If you're under 26 you can buy the **Eurail Youthpass,** good for one or two months of second-class travel (US$320 and US$420, respectively). If you're 26 or older, you must purchase a first-class **Eurailpass,** costing US$298 for 15 days, US$470 for one month, US$650 for two months, or US$798 for three months. The **Eurail Saverpass** is available to groups of three or more traveling together. It is valid for 15 days and costs US$210 per person. From October 1 to March 31, only two people need travel together to qualify for the Saverpass. Finally, the **Eurail Flexipass** is designed for use on any nine days within a 21-day period. At US$310, the pass is only US$60 cheaper than the regular 21-day Eurailpass and therefore not a bargain.

Officially, Eurailpasses must be purchased outside of Europe. They are available through CIEE, Let's Go Travel, Travel CUTS, or a travel agent (see Useful Organizations and Publications above). While not refundable, they can be replaced with some hassle. When you get the pass, sign it and detach the validation slip. This slip, and a receipt from the agent of sale, will permit reissuance for US$5.

The **InterRail** pass entitles travelers under 26 to one month's unlimited travel in even more countries. It covers the 16 Eurail countries plus Great Britain, Morocco, Yugoslavia, Romania, and Hungary. Holders receive only a 50% reduction on travel within the country where the pass is purchased. InterRail is much less expensive than Eurail (one month with ferry £169; one month without ferry £139), but can only be purchased in a country where you have resided for six months. An old airport arrival stamp on your passport can set the beginning date of your residency, as long as there is no evidence that you have left Europe since. This pass is especially useful to foreign students who wish to travel after their term of study. Since Spanish train fares are relatively cheap, Spain is a particularly choice location to purchase the pass since half-price fares will prove quite inexpensive. (See the Getting Around sections of each country for more information.)

By Bus

In Morocco, as well as in rural areas of Spain and Portugal, bus networks are more extensive and efficient than train service. You will also find that they are also slower and less comfortable. The **Miracle Bus Co.,** 408 The Strand, London WC2 (tel. (01) 379 60 55), connects London to Spain and Portugal. **Magic Bus,** 20 Filellinon, Syntagma, Athens, Greece (tel. 323 74 71), offers cheap, direct service between major cities in Europe. Ask for their student discounts. **Grey-Green Coaches,** 52 Stamford Hill, London N16 5DT, England (tel. (01) 800 80 10), also runs bus lines throughout the continent. (See the Getting Around section of each country for more information.)

By Car

Travel by **car** can be an especially cheap option for groups of three or more. For periods longer than 21 days, leasing may be more economical than renting. European car travel does have its drawbacks: Gas is extremely expensive, almost US$2 per gallon; highway tolls can be pricy; and a VAT tax of 14-23.5% is imposed on all rentals. Be sure the tax is included in the rental agreement, and check minimum age requirements with each company.

If you rent a car, be sure that you know exactly what to do in an accident or breakdown. Car insurance in the form of the standard **International Insurance Certificate,** or "green card" is required. You can usually obtain a green card through the rental dealer or a travel agent. As for license requirements, the **International Driver's Permit,** available from the **American Automobile Association** (AAA) or the **Canadian Automobile Association** (CAA), will suffice anywhere; you will need a completed application, a valid driver's license, two recent passport-size photos, and US$5. You must be at least 18. This license is valid for one year, and you must carry your regular driver's license with you as well. If there's no AAA office near you, write to the main office at 8111 Gatehouse Rd., Falls Church, VA 22047 (tel. (703) 222-6713). Although a U.S. license will be honored in Spain, preclude any hassle by obtaining the International Driver's Permit anyway.

Some agencies to contact for information on reservations:

Auto Europe, P.O. Box 1097, Camden, ME 04843 (tel. (800) 223-5555; in Canada (800) 458-9503). Car rentals and leases throughout Europe. Will match any rental rate.

Avis, Tel. (800) 331-2112. You must reserve in advance in the U.S. Rates average US$150 per week. No leasing plan.

Europe by Car, Inc.,Rockefeller Plaza, New York, NY 10020 (tel. (800) 223-1516). Economy cars for US$99-129, with 5% student and faculty discount. Tax-free leasing. Car purchasing.

Hertz Rent A Car, Tel. (800) 654-3131. Their "Affordable Europe" plan offers rates of US$100-250 per week with unlimited mileage. You must book at least 2 days in advance outside of Europe and keep the car a minimum of 5 days.

Kemwel Group, 106 Calvert St., Harrison, NY 10528 (tel. (800) 678-0678). Rentals start at US$79 per week; plan on spending US$120-150. Camper rentals also.

Nemet Auto International, 153-03 Hillside Ave., Jamaica, NY 11432 (tel. (800) 221-0177). One of the leading firms in European car purchasing plans.

Many companies require that you sign your rental agreement before you go overseas; it is generally cheaper that way. For more information about specific laws and road conditions in Spain, Portugal, and Morocco, consult the Getting Around section in the regional introductions for each country. *Let's Go* also lists rental agencies in various major cities where available.

By Moped and Bicycle

Touring by **motorized bike** is a breezy, enjoyable way to see the country, especially in the coastal areas, where you'll be stopping for the view. Mopeds cruise at an easy 40mph and don't use much gas. Unless you want to test the hospital facilities, however, play it extremely safe on a moped. The vehicles can be dangerous in the rain and on rough roads or gravel. Never ride with a backpack on; always wear a helmet. You should be able to find rental agencies in most cities (US$15-20 per day).

In coastal areas and on the flatlands of Spain's interior, **bicycling** is an enjoyable mode of travel if you're in good shape and are undeterred by the baggage limitations. Remember that touring Europe by bicycle is different from a Sunday afternoon ride. Even experienced cyclists should consider Iberia's Mediterranean climate, which can quickly drench the joy of summer pedaling. In Spain, cyclists will be sharing the pavement with motorists and mules alike. Bicycles are not permitted on toll highways, so you'll have to ride the backroads from city to city. Cycling is not an option in much of Morocco because of distances and poor road conditions.

The first thing to buy is a suitable bike helmet. The best models sell for US$30-55. You will also need a tough bike lock; the best are made by Citadel or Kryptonite and run US$30. These companies insure their locks against theft of your bike for up to two years. If you need to outfit yourself with additional equipment, don't spend a cent until you have scanned the pages of *Bicycling* magazine for the lowest prices. **Bike Nashbar,** 4111 Simon Rd., Youngstown, OH 44512 (tel. (800) 345-2453; in OH (800) 654-2453), almost always has the lowest prices; if they don't, they'll subtract 5¢ from the best price you can find.

Most airline companies count a bicycle as your second free piece of luggage. As an additional piece, it will cost US$60-80 each way. Policies vary, so check individual airline's regulations.

To Morocco by Sea

The cheapest way to get to Morocco is a ferry from Algeciras. Several boat lines run between Spain and Tangier or Ceuta (see the Algeciras and Ceuta sections), and a new French line between Nador (near Melilla) and Port Vendres (southern France). Frequent ferries connect Málaga and Tangier as well as the Canaries and Tangier.

Embassies, Consulates, and Tourist Offices

If you're ill or in trouble, your embassy will provide a list of doctors or pertinent legal advice and can contact relatives back home. In extreme cases, they can offer emergency financial assistance.

Spain

U.S. Embassy and Consulate: Serrano, 75, Madrid, 28006 (tel. 276 36 00); Consulate: Barcelona, Via Laietana, 33 (tel. 319 95 50).
Canadian Embassy: Núñez de Balboa, 35, 30, Madrid 28001 (tel. 431 43 00).
British Embassy: Caller de Fernando el Canto, 16, Madrid 4 (tel. 419 02 00).
Australian Embassy: Paseo de la Castellano, 143, 28046 Madrid (tel. 279 85 04).
New Zealand Embassy: No resident representative. Refer to Embassy in Rome: via Zara, 28, Rome 00198 (tel. (06) 85 12 25).

Portugal

U.S. Embassy and Consulate: Avda. das Forças Armadas, Lisbon (tel. 725 600); Consulate: Rua Julio Dinis, 826, 3rd floor, Oporto (tel. 630 94).
Canadian Embassy: Rua Rosa Araujo, 2, 6th floor, Lisbon (tel. 56 38 21).
British Embassy: Rua de São Domingos A Lapa, 37, Lisbon (tel. 66 11 91).
Australian Embassy: Avda. da Liberdade, 244, 4th floor, Lisbon (tel. 53 91 08).
New Zealand: Same as in Spain.

Morocco

U.S. Embassy: 2 ave. de Marrakech, Rabat (tel. 262 65); Consulates: 8 blvd. Moulay Youssef, Casablanca (tel. 224 149); Chemin de Amoureaux, Tangier (tel. 309 05).
Canadian Embassy: 13bis rue Jaafar, As Sadik, BP 709, Rabat—AGDAL (tel. 713 75).
British Embassy: 17 blvd. de la Tour, Hassan, BP 45, Rabat (tel. 209 05 or 209 06).
Australian Embassy: No resident representative. Refer to Ambassador in Paris.
New Zealand Embassy: No resident representative. Refer to Ambassador in Britain.

Tourist offices are located throughout Spain, Portugal, and Morocco. Although they are seldom used by tourists, they can provide a wealth of information. In **Spain,** many towns have an **Oficina de Turismo** that dispenses information on local lodgings, sights, and transportation discounts. Student tourist offices, **Viajes TIVE,** are located throughout Spain. Their central office is in Madrid at Fernando el Católico, 88.

The national tourist board in **Portugal,** is the **Direcção General do Turismo (DGT).** They have offices in almost every city, look for the "Turismo" sign posted on the building. Finding an English speaker at any of these offices should be no problem. The principal organizations that handle student travel in Portugal are **TURICOOP,** Rua Pascoal de Melo, 15-1, Lisbon (tel. 53 18 04 or 53 92 47) and

TAGUS Youth Travel, Praça de Londres 9B, Lisbon (tel. 88 49 57), and Rua Guedes de Azevedo, 34, 36 C, Oporto (tel. 38 27 63).

In **Morocco,** there are about a dozen **Offices Nationales Marocaine de Tourisme (ONMT),** all in the larger cities. Many towns also have a **syndicat d'initiative.** Both bureaus offer information on local monuments and markets, may help you locate accommodations, and will change money when banks are closed. These offices also arrange official tours for a fixed fee of 20-40dh per day. Official guides will take you to places you'd never find on your own—and maybe would never want to find. They tend to be safer but a bit more expensive than their unofficial counterparts. Official guides can be engaged only through the tourist offices and have numbered bronze badges; don't be fooled by hustlers flashing authentic-looking documents.

Weights and Measures

1 meter (m) = 1.09 yards
1 kilometer (km) = about 5/8 mile
1 kilogram (kg) = 2.2 pounds
1 liter = 1.76 pints

The dates in this book are given using B.C.E. (Before Common Era) and C.E. (Common Era), instead of B.C. (Before Christ) and A.D. (Anno Domini).

SPAIN

US $1 = 124.55 pesetas (ptas)	100ptas = US $0.80
CDN $1 = 103.25ptas	100ptas = CDN $0.97
UK £1 = 210.43ptas	100ptas = UK £0.48
AUS $1 = 99.83ptas	100ptas = AUS $1.00
NZ $1 = 82.43ptas	100ptas = NZ $1.21

Once There

Getting Around

It is no longer necessary to perambulate the wilds of Spain since twentieth-century technology shows its face from the isle of Ibiza to metropolitan Madrid. Given the substantial distances between Spanish cities, you should consider **flying** between major cities, especially if you've already been overland once and don't want to spend precious days in transit.

Iberia, Spain's major national airline, flies between Madrid and all principal Spanish cities as well as between Barcelona and a number of other cities. Aviaco offers the same domestic routes and is more likely to have room. Iberia's fares between major cities run US$70; Aviaco and charter company rates are often cheaper. Flying to and from the Balearic or Canary Islands is also an option. Both Iberia and Aviaco run flights from the mainland, and Iberia has service among the islands as well.

Tarifas-minis are special Iberia and Aviaco fares that run about 60% of normal round-trip and tourist-class prices; travelers under 22 can sometimes get an additional 15% discount. You must buy your ticket at least three days in advance and travel round-trip (though you can take a circuitous route). There are no refunds or exchanges, and *tarifs-minis* are available only on certain days of the week.

Despite their bad reputation, Spanish **trains** are surprisingly clean, efficient, and inexpensive. You'll encounter problems with RENFE, the national railroad system, mainly at border stops, where you must change trains because of different track widths. Expect trains between Madrid and Paris or Madrid and Barcelona to be overcrowded and in need of cleaning, especially in summer and on weekends. The best train is the *talgo*, which zips between cities in high style. Next in RENFE's pecking order are the *electro* and *ter*—both comfortable, but heavier on the number of stops. *Expreso* and *rápido* are plain trains which vary greatly in speed. Finally, the somnolent *tranvía, semidirecto, correo*, or *ferrobús* trains stop at every donkey crossing and are strictly for rural-train-stop architecture fanatics.

Whatever their speed (or lack thereof) Spanish trains are inexpensive. The base fare is about 350ptas per 100km for second-class tickets; 525ptas per 100km for first-class seats. There is, however, a supplementary charge for the faster or more comfortable trains. An overnight couchette costs about 800ptas, 1000ptas for one in an air-conditioned apartment.

You can buy tickets within 60 days of departure at RENFE travel offices, RENFE train stations, and authorized travel agencies; you can cancel your tickets up to 15 minutes before the train leaves and still receive a 75-90% refund. RENFE also offers a number of discounts. On frequent "blue days" (a calendar of "blue days" is displayed at RENFE offices and stations), there are discounts of up to 50%, depending on your age, family status, and the distance you're traveling. If you're under 26, look into the Tarjeta Joven (technically available only to Spanish citizens). Available at RENFE offices and some travel agencies, they are good for half off on many trips. Also inquire at travel agencies about BIJ tickets for international routes. RENFE offers a Cheque-trem pass, good for a 15% discount on tickets with a total value of 20,000-30,000ptas. All train travelers will find the 200-page *Guía*

RENFE a useful investment. Pick up this detailed schedule of the major national and international rail routes for 150ptas at any train station. For Eurail and Inter-Rail information, see Getting There: By Train in the General Introduction. Youth railcards and other student budget travel information can be obtained from **Viajes TIVE,** C. Fernando el Católico, 88, Madrid (tel. 401 90 11 or 243 02 08), or any of its branch offices throughout Spain.

Buses in Spain service all train destinations and other points as well. Although they may cost up to 25% more than trains, they're usually the only public transportation to hamlets in the Pyrenees or isolated fishing villages along the coast. Spain has no national busline, just a multitude of small companies that comb local routes. Be sure to shop around.

A **car** can be useful, since public transportation can be unreliable in some areas. The experience of driving in Spanish cities, especially Madrid or Barcelona, has been known to change the political views of many a foreign driver. On mountain roads, beep your horn when rounding blind curves. In general, superhighways are your best bet, and most of them are scenic as well. Be careful not to get caught low on gas, since service stations aren't common. It's a good idea to get an **international driver's license,** available from the American Automobile Association for a fee on presentation of your valid U.S. license and two 2" × 2" photos. Although U.S. licenses are honored if translated, Spanish police are likely to be much more understanding if you can produce the international ID.

Renting a car in Spain is considerably less expensive than doing so in many other European countries, though gas prices might make you wince (about US$2.40 per gallon). One-day (9am-8pm) rentals start at about 3020ptas plus 24ptas per kilometer for a Ford Fiesta. Spain's largest national car rental company is **Atesa,** with a U.S. representative at Marsans International, 500 Fifth Ave., New York, NY 10110, and branch offices in Los Angeles and Miami. The cheapest deal will run you about US$106 per week with unlimited mileage plus extra for gas, complete insurance, tax, and deposit. For more information, see Getting Around in the General Introduction, or check the Practical Information section of specific cities.

Adedo, C. Estudios, 9, Madrid (tel. 265 65 65), will hook you up with drivers going to your destination; you share expenses. Membership costs 1500ptas for drivers, 3500ptas for passengers. Membership for one trip costs only 500ptas, international trips 1000ptas. Insurance is included in the fee. Call at least 2 days in advance. Sample destinations and fares (from Madrid): Alicante 980ptas, Barcelona 1440ptas, Cádiz 1540ptas, Lisbon 2000ptas, Amsterdam 5400ptas, Geneva 4200ptas, Paris 4000ptas, and Rome 6200ptas.

If you've ever wanted to read the voluminous *Don Quixote,* try **hitchhiking;** you'll have plenty of time to pore over the pages as you breathe exhaust from passing cars. Only on small mountain roads, where public transport never followed the path of electricity, is tilting your thumb anything more than a finger exercise. Though the inhabitants of such infrequently traveled regions are friendly and curious, they may be going only to the next village a few kilometers away. Hitchhiking generally gets worse the farther south you venture. Castilla and Andalucía offer little more than a long, hot wait; hitchhiking out of Madrid—in any direction—is virtually impossible. Only the Mediterranean coast and the islands, with their millions of sun-seeking Europeans, brighten the picture. Women can depend on frequent rides but are likely to face harassment; the best combination is one man and one woman.

Though flying is cheaper and smoother, taking a **ferry** to Spain's Mediterranean and Atlantic islands is more scenic, more romantic, and a better way to get a tan. Transmediterranea is the major line plying the seas to and from the Balearic and Canary Islands, though smaller, younger companies (notably ISNASA) should also be investigated. Don't forget to inquire about special youth fares if you qualify. In high season, make reservations and expect overcrowding. Get a couchette for overnight trips; they're available for a small charge on a space-available basis. Buy your ticket at least an hour prior to departure to avoid paying a surcharge on board. A *silla,* the least expensive option, is your basic deck chair. A *butaca,* good for sleeping and sunning alike, is more like an airplane seat.

Accommodations

If *Let's Go* lists only one set of prices for an establishment, it's the high-season price and off-season prices are 200-300ptas less. In July and August, it's a good idea to reserve well in advance.

The **Red Española de Albergues Juveniles (REAJ)**, the Spanish IYHF affiliate, runs almost 50 youth **hostels** year-round and over 100 in summer. Reserve beds for July and August. Hostel prices can't be beat; a room runs around 425ptas per night; lunch is often available for 400ptas and a light breakfast for 150ptas. Rates run a tad higher for guests over 26. IYHF cards are almost always required, although some hostels will issue the card on the spot. Sleep sacks cost 100ptas per night. (Don't confuse youth hostels with the ritzy *albergues nacionales*, classy government-run establishments in out-of-the-way places for motorists.) Hostel addresses and reservation procedures can be obtained from **REAJ**, José Ortega y Gasset, 71, Apartado, 208, Madrid 6.

Inexpensive and centrally located, Spanish **accommodations options** are among the few great travel bargains left. In popular destinations, arrive early if you want to get beyond the registration desk. **Fondas** are the cheapest option and usually serve cheap food as well. **Casas de huéspedes** (guest houses) and **hospedajes** offer medium-priced rooms. **Pensiones** are the most expensive and may offer full board only (*pension completo*), which should cost no more than 1500-2000ptas. The government rates **hostales**, which usually offer a full board option, on a three-star system; **residencias**, which are in the same price range, are also on the three-star system. The highest-priced accommodations, **hotels** are rated on a five-star system. All legally registered establishments must display a blue plaque identifying their category (F, CH, P, HsR, or H).

Ask to be shown a room before you hand over your passport. You will get better accommodations and be certain of the price, since proprietors are required by law to post it prominently in every room, as well as by the main entrance. Minimum and maximum prices are fixed according to the facilities, but don't expect these to correspond exactly to low and high season. Prices can be undercut, though not legally exceeded. Breakfast is obligatory in some places, and you must pay for it even if you don't eat it. Hot showers (*duchas calientes*) usually cost 100-200ptas, while cold showers may be included in the room price or cost an extra 100ptas. Haggling for prices in small inns is still accepted. Ask for a *habitación sencilla* if you want a single, a *habitación doble* for a double, and a *cama de matrimonio* for a double bed (though you no longer need to be in the state of matrimony to request one).

If you run into trouble when it comes time to pay the bill, ask for the complaint book, *libro de reclamaciones*, which the government requires to be produced on demand. The argument will usually end immediately, since all complaints must be forwarded to the authorities within 48 hours, and hotelkeepers are penalized if caught overcharging. Day hotels, which provide such services as showers, barbershops, and shoeshines, are found in airports and major train stations; they're a good place to clean up your act when you don't have a room.

Rooms in **casas particulares** (private residences) are an excellent alternative to hotels or hostels. Pick up a list of residences at a Turismo office, or ask restaurant proprietors for names and directions. Tourist offices can provide information on **rural cottages** and **farmhouses** that offer rooms to travelers. For information on **refugios** (alpine huts), write to the Federación Nacional de Montañismo, Alberto Aguiler, 3, Madrid 15 (tel. 445 13 82 or 445 14 38).

Many castles, convents, palaces, and historic buildings have been converted into inns known as **paradores nacionales.** These are rated on a four-star system; one-and possibly two-star accommodations offer reasonable rates, especially in off-season (doubles about US$25). You can get a list of *paradores* from the national tourist office. Reservations in high season are a must.

Colegios mayores (student dormitories) are open to travelers in summer; a list is available from the Consulate General of Spain. (See Useful Organizations and

Publications in the General Introduction.) **Residencias** are private university dorms that are rented out. Universities and local tourist offices will have more information.

Camping is cheapest. Though there are no private beaches in Spain, and unofficial camping is tempting, you should stick to official sites, since thieving is rife, and soldiers and police can be unsympathetic to campers found on illegal sites. Official camping sites abound, and information is available from most tourist offices. Be sure to arrive early. In summer, the more popular campgrounds are usually packed; urban and coastal parks may even require reservations.

Spanish campgrounds are regulated by the government, and like the hotel industry, are rated by the quality of amenities and priced accordingly. Fees must be posted within view of the entrance. Prices run about 175-275ptas per person, plus 150-250ptas per tent; some sites offer reduced rates in low season. Wash basins, showers, and toilets are required by the government. You may also find a playground, a post office, and, for a little extra, use of a car wash or hairdresser. Write for *Guía de Campings,* a complete guide to all official campgrounds in Spain, available from the national tourist office (about 500ptas; see Useful Organizations and Publications in the General Introduction), or pick one up in any tourist office. Many tourist offices also have a *Mapa de Campings* in the back of their province's hotel guide.

Life and Times

History and Politics

In the minds of American schoolchildren, 1492 is notable as the year Christopher Columbus informed King Fernando and Queen Isabel of the earth's spherical dimensions. Only more advanced history students will be aware, however, that Columbus was an Italian and that Yale University is eternally blacklisted in the Spanish consciousness for its 1965 announcement that Columbus was not, by a long shot, the first explorer to come upon the Americas. Nonetheless, 1492 remains a year to be reckoned with in the annals of Spanish history. It was the year that the Jew were expelled from Spain during the Spainish Inquisition, and the keys to the city of Granada, the last Moorish stronghold were finally recovered. The country also plunged into its most prosperous century to date.

But the centuries leading up to this great and terrible year lie at the root of the modern Spanish character. Prior to 1492, the one date etched in the hearts of Spanish schoolchildren is 711, when the Moors invaded and conquered the land. Although Celts, Phoenicians, Greeks, Carthaginians, Visigoths, and Romans all occupied the Iberian peninsula, their marks—with the exception of a few Roman bridges and aqueducts—were largely erased by the Moorish conquest of 711. The succeeding eight centuries of Arab rule ushered in considerable economic prosperity and a magnificent flourishing of the arts, which remains evident in modern Spain. When the caliphate of Córdoba, which was early established as the capital of Moorish rule, divided and fell in 1031, Christian strongholds sprung up across the land. During the next four and a half centuries, Christians and Muslims lived side by side, an occasional civil war notwithstanding. An intermingling of cultures was fostered as communities of *Mozarabs* (faithful Christians going about their business under the rule of Moorish kings) and *Mudéjars* (dutiful Muslims living under Christian rulers) joined those living under monarchs of their own faiths.

The saga of the Reconquista (the era of Christian reconquest) began almost as soon as the Moors had invaded, though at first it consisted only of a group of Christian lords in the north who maintained their independence. The Christians ultimately gained the upper hand when, in 1469, the marriage of Fernando, King of Aragon, and Isabel of Castilla wed their respective kingdoms and united Spain against the Moors. Their grandson, Carlos I, became Holy Roman Emperor Carlos V in 1519, established the Habsburg dynasty on the peninsula, and ushered in a period of Spanish imperialism that would embroil the country in 400 years of intermittent warfare. Territorial expansion, both on and beyond the Continent, Spain's central position in the Counter Reformation, and the Golden Age of Spanish art and literature all conferred upon Spain the status of a principal European power. The *conquistadores* brought Mexico, Peru, and Chile under Spanish rule and the jewels of the Aztecs and Incas into the royal chest. While the small European aristocracy lived lavishly in lands where the great majority of Native Americans suffered in extreme poverty, the sixteenth century was epitomized back home by El Escorial, King Felipe II's opulent summer palace near Madrid.

Felipe's reign began Spain's long decline despite the glory of victory over the Turks at Lepanto in 1571. The defeat of the "Invincible Armada" in the English Channel in 1588 dealt a serious blow to Spanish sea power and bravado. Portugal's reclamation of independence in 1640 tarnished Spain's grand European image even further. Economic decline ensued as the country squandered its troves of gold and ceded parcel after parcel of land in a series of bloody and often pointless battles, primarily against France, Britain, and the Netherlands. With 1713's Treaty of Utrecht, ending the War of the Spanish Succession, Spain was forced to surrender Flanders, and the last vestiges of its imperial power in northern Europe vanished. War casualties and a wave of emigration to the New World had severely decreased Spain's population. While the late eighteenth century brought a measure of economic recovery and population growth, the nineteenth again saw civil and international strife. Absolute monarchies succumbed to revolution and were supplanted by representative governments, in turn replaced by reactionary rulers; wars of emancipation drained away Spanish possessions in America.

As the century drew to a close, Spain saw the rise of a working class and regionalist movements in Catalunya, Euskadi, and Galicia, as well as the loss of more colonies in the Spanish-American War of 1898. While Spain remained neutral in both World Wars, its own civil war in the intervening years caused global concern. In 1931, following the social unrest in General Primo de Rivera's military dictatorship, the Second Republic was formed and a constitution of progressive social policies adopted, including the right of a region to seek autonomous status. Catalunya won its independence in 1932, and the Basque regions petitioned for autonomy in the same year. During the next five years, however, the rightist Falange party grew stronger, bolstered by a series of government crises and deteriorating economic conditions. Then, in 1936, war broke out. General Francisco Franco's nationalist army, supported by Hitler and Mussolini, battled the Republicans, whose forces were augmented by the International Brigade—volunteer soldiers from the entire world, among them Americans, Britons, and French. Most of the regionalists threw their support behind the Republican cause, but Catholicism complicated matters, dividing the loyalties of both industrial and agricultural laborers. In 1939, Franco had already been declared head of state and Madrid fell to the Fascists. The Civil War claimed one million lives, leveled cities, and obliterated entire villages.

In the post-war era, the isolationist policies imposed by the dictatorial regime led to growing upheaval in various sectors of the population: Worker dissatisfaction, regional discontent, and student uprisings all plagued Spain in the 1950s. In the latter years of his rule, Franco sought to provide the nation with the stability it had so long desired by mordernizing the economy, encouraging tourism, and joining NATO. Nonetheless, separatist terrorism increased. When Juan Carlos I, Franco's chosen successor, came to the throne in 1975, he facilitated the nation's return to democracy by allowing for autonomous regions with their own governments, which exercised varying degrees of independence. In 1978, a referendum in favor of a democratic constitution was put to the people and ignited political passions. The streets of Spain were plastered with posters proclaiming "¡*Vota Sí*," "*Vota No*," and "¡*Arriba España!*" With the adoption of the new constitution, several welcome reforms (such as the limitation of excessive military and clerical powers) were instituted.

The failure of an attempted coup shortly after the resignation of Prime Minister Adolfo Suarez in 1981 served largely to strengthen the country's faith in democracy. Despite harsh anti-terrorist laws, the major problem of the '80s has been the violence wrought by regional autonomist movements. In the fall of 1982, the Spanish

Socialists were elected with Felipe González at the head of the party. González has been widely commended for his social reforms and the flexibility of his political ideology (not to mention his winning smile), but separatism, disagreement about Spain's NATO and EEC membership, and economic recession have not made his tenure altogether conflict-free. Spain officially joined the European Economic Community in 1986—a move that has triggered significant social change. NATO membership, which González's party sponsored, was approved in a referendum, and in June, 1986, he was re-elected for four more years with a clear majority. To keep abreast of the political situation, read the Madrid daily, *El País,* which also features columns by premier Latin American authors.

Language

The official language of the country, *castellano,* is extremely phonetic. *C* before *e* and *i,* and *z* are pronounced like *th* in *thousand; d* is pronounced like *th* in *this; g,* before *e* and *i,* and *j* are pronounced like the German *ch* in *Bach; h* is silent; ñ is pronounced *ny;* and *v* is pronounced like a soft *b.* If you speak French or Italian, you'll have a good head start. A pocket Spanish-English dictionary is indispensable. While knowing how to ask for a a single (*sencilla*) or double (*doble*) for the night may not help when someone rattles off prices or directions in rapid succession, it can't hurt to learn the numbers and the difference between right and left (*la derecha* and *la izquierda,* respectively), as well as how to ask for breakfast, lunch, and dinner (*desayuno, almuerzo,* and *cena*).

Spanish dialects abound. In the south, *ándaluz* often confuses pronunciation and reverses numerous letters; this dialect gave rise to Latin American forms of Spanish. *Catalán* is an entirely distinct language, and its various dialects, spoken in Catalunya, Valencia, and the Balearic Islands, are cherished sources of regional pride. Its dropping of final vowels and dipthongation of interior syllables make it sound from afar like Spanish with English intonation. In Basque Country and Navarre, the population speaks *euskera* (Basque), which linguists have not been able to relate to any other existing language.

Architecture

From Moorish citadels to Gothic cathedrals, the Spanish landscape tells a story of conquest, Catholicism, and commerce. Spain's architecture reflects the many cultures that invaded the Iberian peninsula, as well as the rise of a unique Spanish tradition.

Five centuries of Roman colonization are evident only in scattered ruins. Today the remains of the temples, theaters, and aqueducts that once dotted the Mediterranean coast lie in Mérida, Segovia, and Tarragona. The enormous aqueduct in Segovia, with 167 granite arches, is an example of Roman engineering at its finest.

Little remains of the period of great migrations. Not until the Moorish invasion of 711 did architecture flourish in Spain. The Moors imported Islamic culture and constructed mosques and palaces throughout southern Spain. Red and white horseshoe arches, lavish decoration, ornate tiles, blind doorways, and stylized geometric designs (the Koran forbids human and animal representation) characterize their structures. While many Moorish buildings had bland exteriors, the insides often contained inviting courtyards with pools and fountains as well as row upon row of colorful arches. The fourteenth-century Alhambra in Granada, later altered for Christian purposes, epitomizes the Moorish style.

The blending of Islam and Christianity in Spain produced two architectural styles: Mozarabic, developed by Christians under Muslim rule, and Mudéjar, developed by Muslims under Christian rule. The more pronounced and innovative Mudéjar style, a combination of Gothic and Islamic elements, peaked in the fourteenth century with churches such as Nuestra Dama del Transito in Toledo and *alcázares* in Sevilla and Segovia.

While Islam flourished in the south, Christianity struggled to survive in the north. As Christians gained a stronger foothold in Spain, so did Romanesque architecture. Linked to Italy by trade and to France by the famous pilgrimage route from southern France to Santiago de Compostela, northern Spain borrowed freely from both areas to create its own Spanish Romanesque style. Constructed of heavy hewn stone and decorated with spindly, flat figures, Romanesque churches and monasteries proliferated in the eleventh and twelfth centuries. Not too large or especially imposing, the buildings of this period, such as the old cathedral in Salamanca, conceal intricately carved stone and wood interiors.

The conquest of Moorish lands in the south and the country's growing wealth helped to establish the Gothic style. Designing churches rich in decoration and stained glass, Gothic architects experimented with airier spaces and played with lighting. Toward the end of the fifteenth century, Gothic architecture grew more ornate and flamboyant as the New World brought wealth and a sense of pride and confidence to Spain. This new style, called plateresque, featured stone so intricately carved as to resemble silverwork. Despite the carving, the Gothic builders did not strive for the delicacy of their Romanesque predecessors, but rather for size and overall impression. In Sevilla, for example, they sought to create a cathedral so large that the rest of the world would think them mad—the original tower rose so high it collapsed.

The Renaissance had a sobering impact on the plateresque style. In the province of Jaén, **Andrés de Vandeluira** began to downplay added frills in the mid-sixteenth century, concentrating instead on larger shapes, symmetry, and the treatment of each building as a whole rather than a series of separate parts. Gradually, severe lines and Italian concepts of proportion replaced the less disciplined forms of the fifteenth century. El Escorial near Madrid is an example of the unadorned style that marked Spanish architecture of this time. In the late seventeenth century, ornamentation returned stronger than ever in the Spanish baroque style known as Churrigueresque. Twisted columns and sculptural detail characterize the works of this period, including the altar of the cathedral of Toledo and the sacristy of the Cartuja in Granada.

Although the next centuries brought a hodgepodge of styles, Spanish architecture lost its vitality and originality, with one noteworthy exception: the work of **Antonio Gaudí.** Gaudí, whose works from the turn of the twentieth century are found mainly in Barcelona, combined curves and colors in a unique style exemplified in the Church of the Sagrada Familia.

Art

Spanish painters over the centuries have expressed their philosophical and often their political views on canvas. During the Renaissance **El Greco,** who was born in Crete and settled in Toledo, painted elongated figures and mystical visions that suggested the sharp division in his mind between the celestial and terrestrial spheres. Spain's Golden Age produced the realist canvases and portraits of **Diego Velázquez** and the *bodégons* (landscapes) of **Murillo.** In the early nineteenth century, **Goya** brought his social conscience to his art with his highly unflattering portraits of royalty and his macabre figures depicting war and illness.

A number of twentieth century artists from Spanish shores were leaders in modern art movements. In 1900, 19-year-old **Pablo Picasso** visited Paris. Three years later, he went back to France to live and work. Founder of cubism, he painted a universe of fragmented and overlapping planes with highly unconventional perspectives. His 1937 mural *Guernica* depicts the bombing of that Cantabrian city during the Spanish Civil War. The enormous gray, black, and white painting, completed in only six weeks, is both a political statement and a historical document. *Guernica* hung in the Museum of Modern Art in New York by order of the artist until, upon restoration of democracy in 1978, it was brought to the Prado in Madrid. **Juan Gris,** a fellow cubist, inhabited the same Paris tenement as his elder, Picasso. Gris worked to make familiar objects out of polychromatic abstract shapes with touches of bright red and yellow in honor of his native flag.

Surrealist **Joan Miró,** who died in 1983, moved from rural Catalunya to Paris at the age of 25, just after the World War I. He became known primarily for his painting of droll, rounded, biomorpic outlines in black, white, and red, based largely upon the irrational unconscious or non-analytic part of the mind. Miró, who returned to Spain after World War II, was said to have defined the term "surreal" literally, as "more real than real." He was not considered a particularly political artist, but his representation of chaos and instability emerged with the Civil War, and he painted at least one anti-Franco commentary. **Salvador Dalí,** whose name is nearly synonymous with the word "surrealism," lived the life of an iconoclast, insulting, offending, and outraging high society at every turn. Another Catalan who lived and worked in Paris, he too based the odd images of his paintings on dream consciousness. Perhaps his best known work is *The Persistence of Memory* (1931), with its bent and draped wristwatches (apparently inspired by a wedge of soft Camembert cheese) against a warm yellow sunset on a barren landscape. Though his politics were largely unknown (at one point he even announced himself an admirer of Franco—perhaps only for shock value), he painted the truly haunting *Premonition of the Civil War* (1936), subtitled *Soft Construction with Boiled Beans,* a monstrous vision of war with a distorted body conveys the putrefaction of flesh.

Literature

Vivar, near the city of Burgos in Old Castilla, is still considered the land of **El Cid,** the setting of the anonymous twelfth-century epic poem *El Canto de Mío Cid.* This tale casts Rodrigo Diaz de Vivar as the hero of the Reconquista. In reality, he was a mercenary soldier just as willing to kill fellow Christians as Islamic foes. Nonetheless, the masterful poem is the commencement of Spanish literature in *castellano.* Its subdued and realistic concern with everyday matters is closer to modern sensibility than its French and German counterparts. If it's everyday matters you wish to get away from, you can retrace the steps of deluded idealist **Don Quixote** through La Mancha as he searched for The Impossible Dream.

Though not linked to a particular region of Spain, **Fernando de Rojas's** *La Celestina* (1499) tells a universal tale of the absurdity of human existence through two aristocratic lovers and their go-between Celestina. Rojas's anguished outlook typifies the pain of the Jewish outcast in anti-Semitic Spain. Also products of Spain's Golden Age of literature (1499-1700) are **St. Teresa of Avila** and her pupil **San Juan de la Cruz,** both of whom wrote about their interior quests during the religious and political tumult of the Spanish Counter-Reformation during the sixteenth century. The most vivid depictions of backpacker-style life during this period can be found in picaresque novels: *Lazarillo de Tormes* recounts the anti-hero's dubious rise in a corrupt society, and the lengthy *Guzmán de Alfarache* reads like a rogue's travelogue.

Set in Oviedo (renamed in the novel, though still recognizable) is Leopoldo Alas's (**Clarín**) nineteenth-century novel *La Regenta,* the story of a young woman whose longing for a more poetic life is thwarted by a weak husband, a hypocritical priest, and a selfish lover. The nineteenth-century novelist and essayist **Emilia Pardo Bazán** authored a daring novella of female sexual awakening—a Spanish *Fear of Flying* called *Insolación* (Sunstroke).

Modern Spanish literature begins with the "**Generación del '98,**" a group of writers concerned with the national gloom following the country's defeat in the Spanish-American war. *El sentimiento trágico de la vida* (*The Tragic Sense of Life*) by the leader of the movement, **Miguel de Unamuno,** treats the uncertainty of human existence and the importance of constant questioning. Among the best-known of the early twentieth-century Spanish writers is **José Ortega y Gasset,** whose essay *La Rebelión de las masas* (*The Revolt of the Masses,* 1930) addresses the implications of modern democracy. In *España invertebrada* (*Spineless Spain*), Ortega y Gasset discusses the nation's body politic and its fragmenting regionalism in curiously appropriate corporeal terms. Andalusian lyric poet and playwright **Federico García Lorca,** killed by Francoists in 1936, is noted especially for his tragic dramas of strong women caught in traditional Spanish settings. Particularly moving are *Bodas de sangre* (Blood Wedding), *Yerma* (Wasteland), and *Romance de la luna.* His *Poeta en Nueva York* is a surrealist vision of America's largest city in the late '20s. The landscape of Castilla is evoked by **Antonio Machado** in the poem *Campos de Castilla (Fields of Castilla).*

Ever since **Washington Irving** took up residence in Granada and wrote *Tales of the Alhambra,* American and British authors have been inspired by Spanish landscape, and their works make wonderful traveling companions. **James Michener's** *Iberia,* subtitled **Spanish Travels and Reflections** (1968), though rather bland, enlightens the newcomer to Spain with descriptions of history, culture, and geography. For a considerably slimmer volume, read *Spain* (1979) by **Jan Morris,** a book about post-Franco Spain filled with history and personal anecdotes as well as philosophizing and flip generalizations. **Ernest Hemingway's** novels of Americans in Spain reveal much about the nation's culture as they amuse. *The Sun Also Rises* (1926), his first novel, is a portrait of the frenzied 1920s life of castrated Jake Barnes and his love, Lady Brett Ashley, including their antics at the Pamplona Fiesta of San Fermín. *For Whom the Bell Tolls* packs off disillusioned American Robert Jordan to fight with the Spanish Loyalists. For a glorification of bullfighting, pick up the essay *Death in the Afternoon* (1932), extolled by Spanish critics. For a British perspective, read **George Orwell's** *Homage to Catalonia* (1938), a brilliant account of the author's front-line participation in the Spanish Civil War. For a tale of foreign affairs, both political and emotional, pick up the highly acclaimed *Short Flights* by journalist **Barbara Probst Solomon** (no relation). This autobiographical novel, along with her earlier *Arriving Where We Started,* is a wonderful history lesson of Spain since the '40s.

Film

Spanish film boasts a growing number of acclaimed directors. **Luis Buñuel,** who died in 1983, was one of the great filmmakers of all time. A polemical figure during the Franco regime, Buñuel worked in France, the U.S., and Mexico as well as in his native land. Ever since his stormy collaboration with Salvador Dalí in *Un Chien andalou (An Andalusian Dog,* 1929) and *L'âge d'or (The Golden Age,* 1930), he has been considered a master of cinematic surrealism. His satiric documentary *Las Hurdes* (1932) was banned by the Republican government. Buñuel's major themes—the hypocrisy of social convention and the despotic power of the upper classes—rear their heads in various ways throughout his works, which include *Le Charme discret de la bourgeoisie* (1973) and *Cet obscur objet du désir* (1977), as well as the lesser-known *Viridiana* (1961) and *El Angel exterminador* (1962). His recently published autobiography, *Mi ultimo suspiro (My Last Sigh),* provides a more personal glimpse into the director's life.

Carlos Saura has also achieved a large international following with his dark and beautiful films on the self-destructive tendencies of the bourgeoisie, including *La Caza (The Hunt,* 1975), *Ana y los lobos (Anne and the Wolves,* 1972), and *Cría cuervos (Crow Babies,* 1975). One of Saura's greatest films, *La prima Angélica* (1973), deals with one man's coming of age in fascist Spain. Saura's *Bodas de sangre (Blood Wedding)* and *Carmen* are fascinating combinations of film and flamenco based on Lorca's play and Bizet's opera, respectively. Saura's most recent work, *El Amor brujo (Savage Love),* based on the ballet by de Falla, caused quite a splash.

Antoni Ribas's Catalan film *La ciutat cremada (The Burned City,* 1976) is the story of an upper-class family in Barcelona on the eve of the twentieth century. *Opera prima* (1980), an extremely popular first film by **Fernando Trueba,** is a young man's humorous love story in a liberalized yet socially demanding Madrid. An exiled writer's return to Spain is the theme of the sentimental *Volver a empezar (To Begin Again),* which received the 1982 Academy Award for best foreign film. *El Sur (The South,* 1983), by **Victor Erice,** is the beautiful story of a girl's obsession with her father's native Andalucía, which she has never seen. Vicente Molina-Fox's book *New Cinema in Spain* describes the recent renaissance in Spanish filmmaking.

Music

Foreigners who have heard no more of Spain's musical tradition than a flashy flamenco performance at a big-city tourist trap are in for a surprise. Spain boasts a diverse folk tradition and its own operetta style, as well as a number of fine composers and successful contemporary groups.

Music in medieval Spain was heavily influenced by the large Moorish population. Alfonso the Wise's *Cantigas de Santa María*, sung in praise of the Virgin Mary, are a combination of music and poetry written in Galician. Tomás Luis de Victoria, Spain's most important Renaissance composer, lived in Rome for most of his life and wrote numerous Masses. The country's most important composers, however, lived in the nineteenth century: Felipe Pedrell, with his innovative use of folk themes and melodies; Isaac Albeniz, composer of *Iberia,* a piano suite dedicated to several Spanish provinces, and *Catalunya,* a rhapsody for orchestra; **Enrique Granados,** who used stylized rhythms in his 12 *Danzas españolas* and in whose *Goyescas,* the choir of common people is virtually the protagonist (premiered at New York's Metropolitan Opera House in 1916). But Spain's towering composer is undisputedly **Manuel de Falla,** born in Cadiz. An admirer of Debussy and Ravel, he is known for his beautiful *Nights in the Gardens of Spain, Seven Spanish Folk Songs,* the opera *La Vida breve* (*The Brief Life*), and the ballet *El Amor brujo* (*Love the Magician*).

Zarzuela is Spain's sprightly answer to operetta and musical comedy. The genre was born in the seventeenth century as a form of entertainment for the royal court vacationing at the Palacio de la Zarzuela near Madrid; since then it has drawn widely on popular melodies and themes. Performances have cheerful, romantic plots full of color.

Folk music and regional dances hail from every corner of the Spanish peninsula. Andalusian flamenco, although rooted in Arab musical forms, has a strong gypsy quality. Several years ago young Spaniards looked down on flamenco as an anachronism, but recently the style has seen a resurgence in the form of very danceable *sevillanas.* You may hear these in popular discos and in aerobics classes. Galicia's *muñeira* and *redondela* bear the imprint of this region's Celtic origins. Catalans of all ages join hands spontaneously to dance their stately *sardana,* while in nearby Aragon, the *jota* has been likened to a waltz, albeit freer and more lively.

The works of contemporary singers Joan Manuel Serrat, Lluís Llach, and María del Mar Bonet are loosely referred to as *nova cançó catalana* (New Catalan song), whose political and philosophical lyrics are taken from both Catalan and *castellano* poetry or adapted from old folk songs. Modern rock, by American, British, and Spanish groups is very popular in Spain today. **Mecano,** a Madrid trio; **Ana Belen;** and **Miguel Bosé** (solo pop artists) are among the better-known Spanish groups. This modern music provides more than just rhythms—incisive political lyrics offer insight into Spanish politics .

Food

Spain's adventures in the New World may have done the invaluable service of introducing tomatoes, potatoes, peppers, corn, and chocolate to Europe, but Spanish and Latin American cuisines are not in the least interchangeable; in Spain, you'll find the spicy foods of Mexico only in Mexican restaurants. Absorbing New World and Moorish influences, Spain developed its own culinary tradition or, more accurately, traditions, for its many distinct regional cultures have produced a seemingly endless repertoire of dishes based on indigenous produce, meats, and fish. *Aceite* (olive oil) and *ajo* (garlic) may be the only truly national staples, while *paella,* gazpacho, and flan have caught on outside their regions of origin in a number of geographically unique varieties. Spanish fare is hearty, healthful, and inexpensive. For the tourist, perhaps the most difficult element of Spanish cuisine to stomach is the eating schedule—hours vary geographically.

The coastal areas prepare their catches distinctively and deliciously. In Euskadi, *calamar* (squid) is served in its own ink, and *angulas a la bilbaína* (baby eels in garlic), king crabs, and *sopa de pescado* (fish soup) are outstanding. Galicia's shell-fish, veal, meat, and fish pies retain a hint of the region's Celtic heritage: *santiaguinos* and *gambas* are spider crabs and large shrimp; *veirias* and *mejillones* are sweet scal-lops and sweet mussels. Ordering your shellfish *a la Gallega* will bring you a lightly spiced red-orange sauce made of crushed red pepper. Though *zarzuela* can be found elsewhere, Catalunya is the home of this seafood and tomato dish. The region also offers its own variety of *langosta* (lobster), as does Ibiza. Fish stews abound in the Balearics. Down south in Andalucía, the fish is fried to perfection. Also try the Mal-lorcan specialty, the *ensaininda,* a light pastry smothered with powdered sugar.

To complement the seafood and to cool the palate in hot weather, Andalucía of-fers gazpacho, a cold, tomato-based vegetable soup. It makes a great *plato primero* (1st course) and the myriad ways to prepare it guarantees that you'll never grow tired of it. On Mallorca, work up the courage to try *lenguas de cerdo con salsa de granada* (pig tongues in a pomegranate sauce), or fill up on the uniquely shaped pastries. Galicia's *queso tertilla* (a local cheese) and *millo cos xoubos* (a corn-flour pudding) accompany the meat and seafood mainstays. *Oca con peras* (baby goose with pears) is a regional favorite in Catalunya.

Inland in Asturias, up north, *fabada* (bean stew) and *queso cabrales* (a blue cheese) are specialties. Castilla is known for *cocido* (a concoction of meats, sausages, and chickpeas), *chorizo* (sausage spiced with paprika and garlic), and its pork dishes, including *cochinillo asado al horno* (roast suckling pig). Meat and poultry stews fla-vor barren Extremadura, while Aragon and Navarre spice their menus with indige-nous red peppers. In Navarre, you might undertake the gastronomic adventure called *perdiz con chocolate* (partridge in chocolate). Rice dominates Valencia, the birthplace of *paella,* the saffron-spiced dish made variously with meat, fish, poultry, vegetables, or snails (but always with lots of **saffron**).

One of the biggest pleasures of Spanish dining is the price tag. You can usually enjoy a meal for around 550ptas, and 1000ptas buys a spread fit for *el Rey.* Although the service charge is theoretically figured in, it's customary to tip 5%, 10% for good service. Although a restaurant may be open from 8am to 1 or 2am, most serve meals only from 1 or 2pm to 4 or 5pm, and in the evening from 7 or 8pm to 11pm or midnight.

Each city's tourist office rates its restaurants with a row of forks: five forks indi-cate luxury and so on down the line. Cafeterias are rated by a row of up to three cups. All cafeterias and one- and two-fork establishments will be accessible to the budget traveler's wallet. You'll notice that cafeterias serve lighter fare with less oil and garlic—and occasionally cross the line into rather Americanized comestibles. All cafeterias and the restaurants of fewer forks are required to offer a *menú de la casa* (menu of the house) or *menú del día,* also known as a *menú turístico* (MT). By law, it consists of soup or appetizer, one or two main courses, bread, dessert, and ¼-liter of wine or mineral water, and can cost no more than 80% of the sum of the separate course or beverage prices. The price ranges from about 400ptas in the cheapest bar/restaurants to well in excess of 850ptas in a four-forker. In addi-tion, many restaurants offer cheap, fixed-price *cubiertos* (set meals) or *platos com-binados* (combination plates—main course and side dishes on a single plate, plus bread and sometimes beverage).

Spaniards start their day with a continental breakfast of coffee and *bollos* (rolls). Spanish coffee is rich and aromatic. Ask for *café solo* if you take it black; order *café con leche* for something closer to the French café au lait. As in the rest of Eu-rope, dinner is served at midday, which this far south means between 2 and 3pm. (In the downtown area of big cities, the lunch hour may be shorter, but as a rule, if you want to eat a sandwich at noon, you'll have to do it alone.) The midday meal in Spain consists of several courses: an appetizer (*entremés*) of soup or an egg dish, a main course of meat or fish with vegetable or salad, and a fruit or occasionally a sweet for dessert. After such a feast you'll understand why everything in Spain shuts down during meal times; by the time you've finished all the courses and mustered the motivation to get moving, two hours will have elapsed. While pastries in Spain tend toward the gooey, the fruit is wonderful. You'll find *naranjas* (oranges), *uvas* (grapes), *dátiles* (dates), *higos* (figs), and *melones* (melons). For a sweet dessert, you can always order flan, a lightly burnt egg custard with *dulce de leche* (like a caramel) on the side. Supper, like everything else in Spain, is late—usually at 10 or 10:30pm. The offerings here will be somewhat lighter than at lunch, though three courses is still usual.

During off hours, you can fill up on *tapas* and *bocadillos,* snacks served at bars everywhere. After work Spaniards make for the local bars and *mesones* or *tascas* to meet friends and to munch on these delightful tidbits. The variety is amazing, dishes range from salads such as *ensaladilla rusa* (cold potato salad with peas) to fried seafood and mini-sandwiches. Many regions have their own distinctive *tapas,* so be sure to ask about them wherever you go. Larger portions are available as *raciones* (rations), which make an excellent and cheap light meal.

Tapas, as well as dinner and supper, are almost always washed down with a glass of wine (*vino blanco* is white, *vino tinto* red, and *vino rosada* blush) or draft beer; request *cerveza del país* for Spanish beer. Perhaps most famous of the Spanish wines is the sherry that hails (and takes its name) from Jerez in Andalucía. From dry to sweet, they are *fino* and *amontillado* (served as aperitifs), *oloroso* and *dulce* (both dessert wines). Montilla and Morilas are good dry wines from the region around Córdoba. The leading table wines in Spain are La Rioja and Valdepeñas from Castilla, but the lesser-known ones are just as good. Try Tenerife from the Canary Islands, Cariñema from Zaragoza, and Panandés from Catalunya. Also keep in mind Ribeiro in Galicia, cider in the Asturias, and muscatel in Málaga. Ordering the *vino de casa* (house wine) is usually a good choice. Sangria, a red-wine punch, is also a favorite and in Spain usually comes with citrus slices, seltzer, and sugar mixed in. Also try *tinto de verano,* a cold summer drink of red wine and gaseous mineral water. Spain offers a few non-alcoholic specialties, too, most notably *horchata de chufa,* a milky, nut-flavored syrup, and the crushed-ice *granizadas.* Memories of blazing hot afternoons and ice-cold *blanco y negro* (ice cream and coffee float) will someday bring tears to your eyes. Another good cool drink is *limón,* a sort of carbonated lemonade made by Schweppes. Most people tip a few *duros* (5ptas coins) after having a drink at a cafe or bar.

Climate

Spain's climate is as varied as its geography. Hot summers and long, fairly cold winters characterize the large and arid interior *meseta* (plateau). The Mediterranean coast, protected by mountain ranges, enjoys balmy weather year-round, while the verdant northern provinces bordering the Bay of Biscay and the Atlantic offer mild and humid weather with a mixture of sun, mist, and fine rain. The contrast between day and night can also be great; blistering heat may be followed by surprisingly cool temperatures when the sun drops. Summer will be hot all over, though less so in northern Euskadi and Galicia. Although winter tourist crowds descend on the Costa del Sol, the islands, and the mountain resort areas, the weather elsewhere shouldn't be prohibitively cold. Temperatures stay in the mid-50s during the day (except at higher altitudes), dropping about 15° at night. Autumn and spring, with their long sunny days, are wonderful times (especially in Castilla, Andalucía, the Mediterranean Coast, and the islands).

Spain recently reverted from daylight savings time to standard time. In the Canaries it is always one hour earlier than in the rest of Spain.

Festivals and Holidays

From olive harvests and medieval dancing to Easter egg painting and passion plays, big cities and rural villages alike claim their own particular festivals in Spain.

Even if you don't time your visit to coincide with a festival, you'll probably walk unexpectedly into at least one or two. **The Running of the Bulls** through the streets of Pamplona on the morning of July 7 (the fights come in the afternoon) may be the most notorious, but the **Semana Santa** (Holy Week) celebrations (March 26-April 2 in 1989) bring some of the greatest shows in Spain: From Palm Sunday to Easter, especially in Andalucía, cities and towns strive to outdo one another. Cavalcades, floral floats, and parades of life-size models of biblical characters augment the processions of shrouded mourners and traditionally costumed marchers.

Lest this evoke a mood that is too somber, Sevilla's **April Fair** follows on the heels of Holy Week. The flamenco, bullfights, and general merrymaking should sufficiently restore spirits (provided you've booked a room months in advance or plan to stay outside the city and commute). Spaniards and tourists alike flock to this world-famous fiesta.

Valencia's **Las Fallas** (literally the bonfires), held in the middle of March, bring a week-long party of fireworks, floral parades, and dancing in the streets. On the last night, great wooden *ninots* (effigies) are set ablaze in a custom dating from the Middle Ages, when the town's carpenters burned their collective timber scraps.

Among the lesser-known but no less festive *ferias* are the **winter carnivals** of Cádiz and the Canary Islands (Feb. 16-24). Forbidden during Franco's 40 years, these are now celebrated with special fervor. The succession of grape harvests, cattle fairs, gastronomic competitions, and patron saints' days (notably St. Isidro in Madrid May 8-15 and the Festival of Our Lady of Mercy in Barcelona Sept. 20-24) offers the traveler endless opportunities to join the locals on their own terms. For a complete listing of the country's annual events, write to the Spanish National Tourist Office. (See Useful Organizations and Publications in the General Introduction.)

Banks, shops, and offices shut down on legal and religious holidays. Holidays occur on the following dates: January 1 (New Year's Day); January 6 (The Epiphany); March 19 (St. Joseph's Day); March 23 (Holy Thursday), March 24 (Good Friday), and March 26 (Easter Sunday); May 1 (May Day); Corpus Christi (the Thurs. following the 8th Sun. after Easter); July 25 (Feast of Santiago); August 15 (Feast of the Assumption); October 12 (Independence Day); November 1 (All Saints' Day); December 8 (Feast of the Immaculate Conception); and December 25 (Christmas). Although some of these holidays are no longer official, business does slow down if it doesn't stop altogether.

Madrid

Castilla's dry air nearly ignites in the heat of the sun-scorched summer. But in recent years, an impressive artistic renaissance has kept the quiet flame of culture burning year-round, illuminating the richness and creativity of this cosmopolitan capital. Spanish artists and intellectuals once again flock to Madrid in search of the approval they once sought abroad. The parks, museums, and monuments of Madrid stand as tributes to Spain's many artistic and cultural achievements. Buildings here combine Madrid's grand old architectural styles with those of other world capitals. Avenues swell with pedestrians and are often choked with traffic. Newsstands display a host of dailies from all over the world, and cosmopolitan residents flaunt the latest fashions. "Post Modern" Madrid, as some here call it, has become the living symbol of Spain's search for its European identity, assertive and yet engagingly apprehensive.

Madrid superseded Toledo as capital in 1561 under Felipe II, and ever since has been an arena for conflict between central and regional power. In 1766, Madrid saw the riots against Carlos III's unpopular Neapolitan minister Marquis de Esquilache, who sought to legislate, among other things, the style of hats and the length of capes. In 1808, Madrid's center became the scene of a massive uprising against

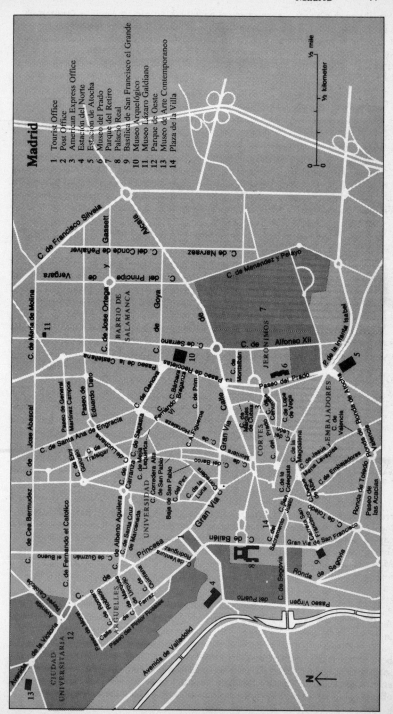

Madrid

1 Tourist Office
2 Post Office
3 American Express Office
4 Estación del Norte
5 Estación de Atocha
6 Museo del Prado
7 Parque del Retiro
8 Palacio Real
9 Basílica de San Francisco el Grande
10 Museo Arqueológico
11 Museo Lázaro Galdiano
12 Parque de Oeste
13 Museo de Arte Contemporaneo
14 Plaza de la Villa

the Napoleonic occupation, which led to bloody reprisals against the inhabitants. From 1936 to 1939, during the Spanish Civil War, the city held out as the capital of the Republic, fiercely resisting the *franquistas*. Recently, the capital has witnessed several terrorist attacks by Basque separatists, aimed mainly at police and military personnel.

The political, economic, and social renovation that followed the death of Franco has modernized and liberalized Spanish society, and nowhere is this more evident than in Madrid. A Socialist mayor, Juan Barranco, runs the city, successfully continuing the ambitious task set out by his late predecessor, the beloved mayor-philosopher Enrique Tierno Galván. A Socialist president re-elected to a second term, Felipe Gonzalez runs the country, although he is officially second in command to King Juan Carlos and Queen Sofia. Spanish conservatives, soundly defeated in the 1986 elections, utter warnings about the rise in crime and terrorism, and mutter darkly about youthful debauchery, but few dare deny that the city has experienced an unprecedented cultural flowering, aptly nicknamed "*la movida*" (the movement).

Orientation and Practical Information

Madrid's center bustles between two parks: **Casa del Campo** to the west and **Parque del Retiro** to the east. The epicenter of this area is the **Puerta del Sol,** a large square that is the geographic heart of Spain—notice the "Km O" marker on the sidewalk in front of the police station. "Km" signs appearing around the city and surrounding areas indicate distance from this center point. Many major streets intersect at the square, although the **Gran Vía,** Madrid's main commercial thoroughfare, runs parallel to and to the north of it. The free map, available at the tourist office and at all El Corte Ingleés stores, should be a sufficient path-finder. Better maps are available at local newsstands. Scattered throughout the town center are **Columnas Informativas,** which look like telephone booths and contain indexed maps of the city.

Madrid, like all cities, has its *zonas peligrosas* (dangerous areas). Walking alone after 1am in any of the following areas would be a mistake: Plaza 2 de Mayo (substance abusers and violent crime), Puerta del Sol (muggers), Calle de Preciados (more pickpocket reportings here than anywhere else in the city), and Calle de la Montera. The charming area around Plaza Santa Ana has also been targeted recently because of its appeal to tourists. If you are carrying a purse or knapsack, put the strap around your neck and torso, holding on tightly to the zipper or snaps with your hand as you walk. Bags carelessly dangling from browsing tourists' shoulders are favorite targets for thieves. The nearest police station to Pl. 2 de Mayo is at C. La Luna, 29 (tel. 521 04 11). There's a police station on the south side of Puerta del Sol, at #7 (tel. 221 65 16), the point where Spanish citizens met Napoleon's troops. If you're not near either station, call 091 and be prepared to describe your location.

The several lines of the **metro** emanate mainly from the Puerta del Sol and cover most of the city. The metro operates daily from 6am to 1:30am (60ptas per trip, 10-trip ticket 410ptas). Check the map at each entrance; they are few and far between once inside. Better yet, pick up a free map at one of the ticket booths inside the station. For metro information, call Oficina de Información de Metro, C. Retiro and C. Atocho (tel. 435 22 66), or branch offices (tel. 552 76 43 or 521 95 11).

Buses are usually faster but slightly more expensive. **Red buses** run from 5:30am to 11pm or 2am, depending on the line; the perimetral line (*Circular*) runs 24 hours. (55ptas per trip, 80ptas including transfer, 10-ride card excluding transfers 500ptas.) More comfortable, air-conditioned **yellow microbuses** (look for the prefix M) serve other routes (65ptas per trip, 20-trip book 1300ptas). Multiple-ride cards and route guides for both buses are available at the Empressa Municipal de Transportes (EMT; tel. 401 99 00) kiosk at Pl. de las Cibeles. (Open daily 8am-8:30pm.) On Sundays and holidays, special bus routes run to the parks, museums, and zoo. Check at Turismo. **Taxis** cost 90ptas plus 40ptas per additional kilometer. The airport fee adds 200ptas plus 100ptas per piece of luggage.

Tourist Offices: These offices offer maps and leaflets, but getting any other information from them may feel like pulling teeth. **Nacional,** C. Princesa, 1 (tel. 241 23 25), at Pl. de España and Torre de Madrid. Metro: Pl. de España. Friendly staff. Open Mon.-Fri. 9am-7pm, Sat. 9:30am-1:30pm. Also a branch at Barajas airport (tel. 205 86 56), in the international flight arrival area. Open Mon.-Fri. 8am-8pm, Sat. 8am-1pm. **Provincial,** Duque de Medinaceli, 2 (tel. 429 49 51). Open Mon.-Fri. 9am-7pm, Sat. 9am-1pm. **Municipal,** Pl. Mayor, 3 (tel. 266 54 77). Cramped, crowded office. Open Mon.-Fri. 10am-2pm and 4-7pm, Sat. 10am-1:30pm. For accurate information about museums, call the **Oficina de Museos,** Palacio Real (tel. 248 74 04). Open Mon.-Sat. 9:30am-12:45pm and 4-6:45pm, Sun. 9:30am-1:45pm.

Accommodation Service: Brújula, Torre de Madrid, 6th floor (tel. 248 97 05), at Pl. de España. Open Mon.-Fri. 9:30am-1:30pm and 4-7pm, Sat. 9:30am-1:30pm. Also at Chamartín (tel. 315 78 94) and Atocha (tel. 228 26 84) train stations, and at the Terminal de Autobuses Madrid (tel. 275 96 80) at the airport. These locations open daily 8am-9pm. They'll make reservations for all of Spain free of charge except for long-distance calls. You provide the location and price range; they'll search. Fast service. You must go in person.

Student Travel: Viajes TIVE, C. Fernando el Católico, 88 (tel. 401 90 11 or 243 02 08). Metro: Quevedo. Branch office at José Ortega y Gasset, 71 (tel. 401 95 01 or 401 90 11). Metro: Lista. Both open Mon.-Fri. 9am-2pm, Sat. 9am-noon. Information on student budget transportation. Some English spoken. **Tarjetas jóvenes** (youth cards) 2500ptas, allowing those ages 12-26 to travel by train at half-price distances of at least 100km (one way) or 200km (round-trip) May-Dec. (See Getting Around under the Spain Introduction for more information.) For an extra fee, you can also travel at half-price in France, Portugal, Italy, and Germany from June-Sept. InterRail passes 24,650ptas. (Only Spaniards may purchase the passes here. Foreigners should try the RENFE Office.) Also BritRail passes and not-so-great flight discounts. To London (one way 18,375ptas, round-trip 23,835ptas), Los Angeles (one way 92,600ptas, round-trip 111,150ptas), New York (one way 44,600ptas, round-trip 64,385ptas), and other international destinations.

Embassies: U.S., C. Serrano, 75 (tel. 276 34 00 or 276 36 00). Open Mon.-Fri. 9am-6pm. Call Mon.-Fri. 3-5pm for information on passports and visas, which can be arranged Mon.-Fri. 9am-12:30pm at Paseo de la Castellana, 52, 5th floor. **Canada,** Núñez de Balboa, 35 (tel. 431 43 00). Open mid-June to mid-Sept. Mon.-Fri. 9am-1pm, phones Mon.-Fri. 8:30am-5:30pm; in off-season Mon.-Fri. 9:30am-1pm, phones Mon.-Fri. 8:30am-2:30pm. Answering machine on weekends; staffmember on duty will pick up if call is urgent. **U.K.,** Fernando el Santo, 16 (tel. 419 02 00 or 419 02 08). Open July 20-Sept. 2 Mon.-Fri. 9am-1pm, visas until noon; Sept. 3-July 19 Mon.-Fri. 3-5pm, visa inquiries by phone. **Australia,** Edificio Cuzco 1, Paseo de la Castellana, 143 (tel. 279 85 01 or 279 85 04). Open Mon.-Fri. 10:30am-1:30pm. **New Zealand,** O.L.P. C. Pío XII, 20 (tel. 200 00 78 or 457 32 58).

Currency Exchange: Barajas Airport. Open 24 hours. Chamartín and Atocha train stations. Open daily 8am-10pm. Oficinas de Viaje RENFE, C. Alcalá, 44 (tel. 522 05 18 or 429 05 28). Open Mon.-Fri. 9am-3pm and 4-7:30pm, Sat. 9am-1:30pm. Banks open Mon.-Fri. 9am-2pm, Sat. 9am-1pm. 4- and 5-star hotels (e.g., Ritz of Madrid, next to the Prado, and Palace Real, on C. Duque de Medinaceli ½ block from provincial tourist office) will often exchange currency. In off hours, every El Corte Inglés department store has a currency exchange office charging a 1% commisssion on currency, a 2% commission on traveler's checks. This is very reasonable compared with the up-to-10% charged at the airport and at some local banks. If you make a purchase at the store, you may pay in foreign currency and receive change in pesetas, at no commission. Stores are located throughout the city. All stores open Mon.-Sat. 10am-9:30pm.

American Express: Pl. de las Cortes, 2, Madrid 28014 (tel. 429 57 75), at Carrera de San Jerónimo. Open Mon.-Fri. 9am-5:30pm, Sat. 9am-noon. In addition to currency exchange services (dollars to pesetas only; 1% cash and 2% traveler's check commission), they'll hold mail for American Express cardholders and check users.

Main Post and Telegraph Office: Palacio de Comunicaciones, Pl. de la Cibeles (tel. 521 81 95 or 521 91 37). Open for stamps Mon.-Fri. 8am-10pm, Sat. 8am-8pm, Sun. 10am-1pm; for certified mail Mon.-Fri. 8am-10pm, Sat. 9am-2pm, Sun. 10am-1pm; for Lista de Correos Mon.-Fri. 9am-8pm, Sat. 9am-2pm. Open for **telegrams** 24 hours; assistance available Mon.-Fri. 8am-9pm. Door H remains open for telegrams, telex, and other services. Call 522 20 00 to send telegrams by phone. **Information** open Mon.-Fri. 8am-9pm. **Postal Code:** 28070.

Telephones: Telefonica, Gran Vía, 28, at C. Fuencarral. A high-rise building with a clock at the top. Open 24 hours. Direct-dial lines to the U.S. are available. Also a branch at C.

Peligros, 10. Open daily 9am-10pm. The Palacio de Comunicaciones at Pl. de la Cibeles has a small, comfortable office for long-distance calls. Enter Puerto H, next to the gold mailboxes along Paseo del Prado. Calls in excess of 500ptas can be charged to a credit card. Open Mon.-Fri. 8am-midnight, Sat.-Sun. and holidays 8am-10pm. Long-distance calls may also be placed at Paseo Recoletos, 43, off Pl. de Colón. Open Mon.-Fri. 9am-10pm, Sat.-Sun. and holidays 10am-9pm. **Telephone code:** 91.

Airport: Barajas Airport, 15km out of the city on N-11 (tel. 411 25 45 for flight information 24 hours; 205 43 72 for arrivals). **Iberia,** Pl. de Canovas, 4 (tel. 585 85 85). Metro: Atocha. Open Mon.-Fri. 9am-7pm, Sat. 9am-2pm. Branch office at C. Princesa, 2 (tel. 585 81 58). Metro: Pl. España. Other branches are located throughout the city; they are generally open Mon.-Fri. 9am-7pm, Sat. 9am-1pm. Telephone reservations can be made daily 8am-10pm by calling 411 10 11 for domestic flights or 411 20 11 for international flights. **Spantax,** Paseo de la Castellana, 181 (tel. 279 69 00). Open Mon.-Fri. 9am-noon and 4-7pm. See Yellow Pages for other airlines. Yellow buses run between Pl. de Colón (from the underground parking lot) and the airport (every 15 min., in early morning or late evening every 20-30 min.; 190ptas). Prices of flights to major cities in Spain run 8600-12,000ptas one way. *Nocturno* rates are 25% cheaper and available on flights to some cities. Youth fares (for ages 26 and under), sometimes available, can net you up to a 70% discount.

Inter-City/International Train Stations: For information, reservations, and ticket purchases, visit **RENFE,** C. Alcalá, 44 (tel. 733 30 00 or 733 22 00). Metro: Banco de España. Open Mon.-Fri. 9am-3pm and 4-7:30pm, Sat. 9am-1:30pm. Arrive early to avoid long lines and harried staff. Eurailpass holders should be advised that reservations and supplementary fees are required to board most Spanish trains. **Main Train Stations: Chamartín,** the largest station, is located far to the north. Metro: Chamartín or the train from Atocha (see next listing); bus #27 or the M-6 to Pl. de Castilla, then bus #110 to the station. To Burgos, Euskadi (Basque Country), Cantabria/Asturias, Catalunya (including Barcelona), Bilbao, Santander, and France. **Atocha,** a few blocks south of the Prado. Metro: Atocha or bus #6, 14, 19, 27, or 45. To Andalucía, Toledo, and Extremadura. Both Chamartín and Atocha stations service Avila, El Escorial, Alicante, Guadalajara, Segovia, Valencia, and Portugal. **Norté,** also called Príncipe Pío. Metro: Norté or bus *Circular,* #1, or 46. To Barcelona, Sevilla, Granada, Galicia (including Santiago and Coruña), and Salamanca. For reservations, call 429 82 28, go the RENFE office, or visit any of the 3 major train stations. Chamartín and Atocha ticket offices open daily 9am-9pm. Norté ticket office open daily 9am-7pm. **Sample Times and Fares:** 2nd-class *expreso* to Sevilla (5 per day, 10 hr., 3395ptas), Pamplona (1 per day, 9 hr., 2675ptas), Barcelona (2 per day, 11 hr., 4060ptas), Santander (1 per day, 6 hr., 2375ptas), Algeciras (1 per day, 13 hr., 4080ptas), La Coruña (1 per day, 14 hr., 4390ptas), Lisbon (1 per day, 11½ hr., 3730), and Paris (17-19 hr., 10,805ptas). Since fares and schedules are subject to change, always check before you plan your trip. For further information, call 552 05 18, 429 05 28, or 276 30 44.

Commuter Trains (Trenes de Cercanías): Apeadero de Atocha, next to Atocha Station (tel. 227 31 60). All trains leaving from Apeadero de Atocha stop at the centrally located **Recoletos** (under Pl. Colón) and **Nuevos Ministerios** (on Paseo de la Castellana) stations before stopping at Chamartín. You need a ticket (80ptas) to travel between Atocha, the Apeadero, Recoletos, Nuevos Ministerios, and Chamartín, if you don't already have one for a destination outside Madrid. To Avila (2 hr., 540ptas; also from Estación Norté), El Escorial, Segovia (10 per day, 2hr., 460ptas), and Sierra de Guadarrama. The *Horario de trenes: Cercarvias de Madrid,* 150ptas at station newsstands, may prove helpful.

Inter-City Bus Information: Estación Sur de Autobuses, Canarias, 17 (tel. 468 42 00 or call Turismo). Metro: Palos de Moguer. Among the largest of Madrid's 8 bus stations. Almost all stations house numerous companies with various destinations. **Sample Times and Fares:** To El Escorial (1 hr., 152ptas), Segovia (1¾ hr., 297ptas), Avila (2 hr., 360ptas), and Cuenca (2¾ hr., 516ptas). Often more than one company will journey to the same destination; compare times and fares.

Car Rental (Alquiler de Coches): Atesta, Barajas Airport (tel. 205 86 60 or 205 86 63). Open daily 7am-midnight. Paseo de la Castellana, 243 (tel. 315 13 49 or 733 93 72). Metro: Pl. Castilla. Open Mon.-Fri. 9am-8pm, Sat.-Sun. 9am-1pm. Pandas, Ford Escorts, Volkswagens, Fiestas, Corsas, and Minibuses. **Autos Bravo,** C. Toledo, 136 (tel. 474 80 75 or 474 64 44). Metro: Puerta de Toledo. A wide variety of cars, including Land Rovers, Renaults, Fiestas, and Porsches. **Avis,** C. Gran Vía and Barajas Airport (tel. 457 97 06 or 457 97 07). C. Gran Vía location open Mon.-Fri. 8am-7pm, Sat. 8am-2pm, Sun. 9am-1pm. Barajas Airport branch open daily 7am-midnight. For all 3 agencies, you must be over 21 and have a valid driver's license.

Moped/Motorcycle Rental: Motocicletas Antonio Castro, C. Conde Duque, 13 (tel. 242 06 57), at Santa Cruz de Marcenado. Metro: San Bernardo. 49-cc Vespinos 1650ptas plus 2%

VAT per day (9am-8pm); 250-cc Yamahas 4200ptas plus 2% VAT per day. Deposit 6000ptas. Mileage and insurance included. You must have a valid driver's license, a passport, and be at least age 18. Clients pay for gas. Open Mon.-Fri. 9am-noon and 5-8pm, Sat. 9am-1:30pm.

Hitchhiking: Tel. 441 72 22 for route information. Legal but not safe. Use the following national routes, which emanate from Madrid: N-I (north) for Burgos and Irún; N-II (northeast) for Barcelona and Zaragoza; N-III (east) for Cuenca and Valencia; N-IV (south) for Aranjuez, Andalucía, and Alicante; N-V (west) for Badajoz; N-VI (northwest) for Avila, Sierra de Guadarrama, Segovia, Salamanca, and Galicia; E-4 (west) for Extremadura and Portugal; 401 (southeast) for Toledo and connecting country road to Consuegra.

Baggage Check: At Chamartín and Atocha train stations. Lockers fitting large backpacks 150ptas per day. **Estacíon Sur de Autobuses,** C. Canarias, 17. Also at the air terminal beneath Pl. de Colón.

English Bookstores: Turner English Bookshop, C. Génova, 3 (tel. 410 43 59), on Pl. de Santa Bárbara. Metro: Alonso Martínez. Impressive collection of English, French, and Spanish books, including the *Let's Go* series. Open Mon.-Fri. 9:30am-2pm and 5-8pm, Sat. 10am-2pm. All **El Corté Inglés** stores have a *librería* with some English-language books on Spain and Europe and often some *Let's Go* guides.

Cultural Centers: Washington Irving Center, Marqués de Villa Magna, 8 (tel. 435 69 22). Large selection of U.S. magazines. Occasional photography exhibits. Library open Mon.-Fri. noon-7pm. **British Cultural Center,** Almagro, 5 (tel. 419 12 50). Library open in summer Mon.-Fri. 9am-1pm and 3-6pm; in off-season Mon.-Thurs. 9am-7pm, Fri. 9am-3pm.

Laundromats: Lavendería Donoso Cortés, C. Donoso Cortés, 17 (tel. 446 96 90). Metro: Quevedo. Self-service. Wash and dry 300ptas per 5kg. Soap 60ptas. Open Mon.-Fri. 8:30am-7:30pm, Sat. 8:30am-1pm. **Lavandería Marcenado,** C. Marcenado, 15 (tel. 416 68 71). Metro: Prosperidad. Full service. Wash and dry 600ptas per 5 kg. Open Mon.-Fri. 9:30am-1:30pm and 4:30-8pm, Sat. 9:30am-1:30pm. **Lavandería Maryland,** Meléndez Valdés, 52 (tel. 243 30 41). Metro: Argüelles. Self-service and full service. Self-service wash and dry 500ptas per 5kg, full service 700ptas.

Swimming Pools (Piscinas Municipales): Casa de Campo, Avenida del Angel (tel. 463 00 50). Metro: El Lago. Outdoor. Open in summer daily 10am-8pm. Admission 200ptas, ages 4-13 85ptas. **Municipal de la Latina,** Pl. de la Cebada, 2 (tel. 265 80 31 or 265 10 55). Metro: Latina. Indoor. Open Sept.-July Mon.-Fri. 8am-6pm, Sat. 8am-8pm, Sun. 8am-2:30pm. Admission 200ptas. **San Juan Batista,** C. Treviana (tel. 416 42 59). Metro: La Paz or bus #11 and M-7. Open daily 10am-8pm. Admission 200ptas, children 85ptas. **Municipal de la Elipa,** Avda. de la Paz (tel. 439 30 44). Bus #28 and P-13. Adults 200ptas, children 85ptas.

Lost Property (Objetos Perdidos): For objects lost in **buses,** C. Alcantará, 26 (tel. 401 31 00). Metro: Goya. For objects lost in **taxis,** Pl. de Legazpi, 6 (tel. 228 48 06). Metro: Legapi. Open Mon.-Fri. 9am-2pm, Sat. 9am-1pm. Also at Pl. de Chamberi, 4 (tel. 448 79 26). Metro: Ruben Danó. For objects lost on the **metro,** Cuatro Caminos station (tel. 233 20 00). For objects lost **elsewhere,** Pl. de los Cibeles/Palacio de Comunicaciones. Metro: Banco de España (upstairs from the information office). Also at Almacen de Objetos Perdidos, C. Santa Engracia, 120 (tel. 441 02 11). Metro: Ríos Rosas. The latter holds lost items for 2 years.

Women's Center: Libreria de Mujeres, C. San Cristobal, 17 (tel. 221 70 43), near Pl. Mayor. Concerts, readings, lectures, political activities, and international bookstore. Some English spoken. **Women's Groups,** C. Barqillo, 44, 1st floor (tel. 419 36 89). For information, call after 8pm. **Women's Medical Issues Hotline:** Tel. 730 49 01 or 419 94 41. Unfortunately, the English here is poor. Open Mon.-Fri. 3:30-6:30pm.

24-Hour Pharmacies: Tel. 098 or check the listings in daily newspapers under Services to find pharmacies open after 8pm. Late-night duty rotates among the pharmacies. Contraceptive products are sold over the counter in most Spanish pharmacies.

British-American Medical Unit: Conde de Aranda, 1, 1st floor, (tel. 435 18 23), to the left. Metro: Serrano. Doctors, dentists, optometrists. Regular personnel on duty 9am-8pm, but assistance is available at all hours. This is *not* an emergency clinic.

Medical Emergency: For an ambulance, call 252 32 64 or 252 27 92.

Police: Puerta del Sol, 7 (tel. 221 65 16). **Emergency:** Tel. 091 or 092.

Accommodations

There are more than enough rooms in Madrid to go around. Demand rises dramatically in summer, but the persistent should have no problem. From mid-June through August, arriving in the city before noon or making a reservation will save you time. Tourist offices will not arrange accommodations.

Youth Hostels

There are two IYHF youth hostels in Madrid. Fees are more than reasonable and meals are available for a modest charge. The only things you're likely to miss are privacy and security: There are usually eight people per room, and unlocked cubby holes are used to store your belongings. Rooms fill quickly, so be sure to call or write in advance. An IYHF card is required at both hostels; you may purchase one at the hostels. Both hostels permit a maximum stay of only three nights; if a large group unexpectedly arrives, your bed may be given away even sooner. Alternative reservations are always wise.

Youth Hostel Santa Cruz de Marcenado (IYHF), C. Santa Cruz de Marcenado, 28 (tel. 247 45 32), off C. de Serrano Jover between Princesa and Alberto Aguilera. Metro: Argüelles. Modern, recently renovated facilities in a pleasant location near the student district. Glass-enclosed roof terrace. 75 beds in airy rooms. Firm mattresses. There have been reports of thefts here in years past, so hold on tight to your belongings. Hot showers. Strict curfew 1:30am. 450ptas, ages over 26 550ptas. Breakfast included. Individual meals 350-470ptas. Full pension 1100ptas, ages over 26 1200ptas. Reservations must be received at least 15 days in advance. 25% deposit required for groups.

Youth Hostel Richard Schirrman (IYHF), Casa de Campo (tel. 463 56 99). Immediately turn left as you exit metro station El Lago, then turn left again, and walk 1km on the unpaved rocky footpath along the metro tracks. Cross over the small concrete footbridge, and turn left at the Albergue Juvenil sign. Located on the outskirts of the city, in a park close to a lake and municipal swimming pool. Some travelers may feel uneasy about walking through the unlit, densely wooded park at night. 130 bunk beds. Each 8-person room has a bath. Hot showers. No curfew. 450ptas, ages over 26 530ptas. Breakfast included. Full pension 1100ptas, ages over 26 1200ptas. Same reservation requirements as above.

Hotels, Hostales, Pensiones

Between Puerta del Sol and Palacio Real

Here you will sleep close to the heart of Madrid: dusty balconies, flashy department stores, and the major sights—the Gran Vía, Palacio Real, and Plaza Mayor. Accommodations are cheap, but you get what you pay for.

Hostal Residencia Cruz-Sol, Pl. de Santa Cruz, 6, 4th floor (tel. 542 71 97), a stone's throw from the east side of Pl. Mayor. Metro: Sol. Tasteful, spacious, wooden-floored rooms, most with wrought-iron balconies overlooking the chiming Church of Sta. Cruz. Sun-lit reading room offers a pleasant view of Spanish-tiled rooftops. Your belongings couldn't be safer: Guests are not issued a key to the double-locked front door. You must ring the doorbell to be let in by the owner, an upstanding Galician *caballero* who will open the door with a smile in the wee-est hours. Highly recommended. Doubles for single use 1200ptas. Doubles 1600ptas. Hot showers 150ptas (100ptas during stays over 1 night). On the 2nd floor is **Hostal Santa Cruz** (tel. 522 24 41), with higher ceilings and prices. Owner speaks only *un peu de* French, Italian, and English. Doubles only. With shower 2600ptas, with bath 3000ptas. Reservations with 1 night's deposit.

Hostal Montalvo, Zaragoza, 6, 3rd floor (tel. 265 59 10), near Pl. Mayor. Metro: Sol. You can't get any closer to the Pl. Mayor than this. Romantic little rooms with beige wallpaper and brown bedspreads. However, the place reeks of cigarette smoke. Singles 1500ptas, with bath 2500ptas. Doubles 3000ptas, with bath 3200ptas. Warm showers 150ptas.

Hostal Residencia Miño, C. Arenal, 16, 2nd floor (tel. 531 50 79 or 531 97 89). Metro: Opera or Sol. Caring owners proud of the deer's head, marble statue, and velvet chairs in the lobby. Stucco-walled rooms with plant-lined balconies. Singles with shower 1500ptas. Doubles with shower 220ptas, with bath 2700ptas. Triples with bath 3300ptas. **Hostal Alicante,** on the same floor (tel. 531 51 78), is less plush and offers similar prices. Singles with shower 1400ptas.

Doubles with shower 2300ptas, with bath 2600ptas. Triples with shower 3300ptas, with bath 3600ptas. There is one large triple that can easily fit four people.

Hostal Residencia Malagueña, C. Preciados, 35, 4th floor (tel. 248 52 23), between Puerta del Sol and Pl. del Callao. Metro: Callao. Friendly manager. Big, clean, well-lit rooms, some with fireplace. Singles 1000ptas. Doubles 1700ptas, with shower 2000ptas. Triples 2300ptas. On the 3rd floor is **Hostal Residencia Callao** (tel. 542 00 67). Slightly more expensive, but firm mattresses. Fireplaces in some rooms. Singles 1300ptas. Doubles 1900ptas, with shower 2200ptas.

Hostal Residencia María del Mar, C. Marques Viudo de Pontejo, 7, 2nd and 3rd floors (tel. 531 90 64), 2 blocks from Pl. Mayor. Metro: Sol. Well kept, with bedside lamps. Doubles all face the street and sport balconies. Singles 900ptas. Doubles 1600ptas. Showers 200ptas. One floor up is **Hostal Residencia Encarnita** (tel. 531 90 55). The rooms are a notch down. Singles 800ptas. Doubles 1100ptas, with shower 1600ptas.

Hostal Residencia Roben, Arenal 26, 5th floor (tel. 241 91 75). Metro: Opera. Rooms are carpeted and spotless. Singles 2000ptas, with bath 2500ptas. Doubles with bath 3000ptas. Triples 4200ptas.

Hostal Maàiru, C. Espejo, 2 (tel. 247 30 88), south of Teatro Real. Metro: Opera. Well-kept rooms at some of the best prices around. Singles 850ptas. Doubles 1600ptas, with shower 1800ptas, with bath 2000ptas. Showers 200ptas.

Hostal Residencia Pinariega, C. Santiago, 1, 1st floor (tel. 248 08 19), smack dab in between Pl. Mayor and the Opera House. Metro: Sol. Friendly management eager to help. Springy beds. Rooms not facing street are a bit gloomy. For a hot shower at no extra charge, ask the *amo* (owner), Paco, to turn on the *agua caliente*. Singles 1300ptas. Doubles with bath 2000ptas. Triples with bath 3700ptas.

Casa de Huéspedes Jaén, Costanilla de los Angeles, 8 (tel. 542 34 63), off Pl. de Santo Domingo, 1 block from C. Arenal. Metro: Santo Domingo or Callao. Quite difficult to locate. Cramped, noisy rooms, but the price is right. Singles 800 ptas. Doubles 1300ptas. Showers 200ptas.

Pensión Rico, C. San Bernardo, 55, 5th floor (tel. 521 69 96). Metro: Noviciado. Rooms are small, but tidy and rarely available. Singles 800ptas. Doubles 2100ptas. Hot showers 150ptas. On the 4th floor is **Hostal Residencia "El Hostal"** (tel. 532 16 49). Gregarious owner. Most rooms face the street, allowing for ventilation and people-watching. Singles 1000ptas. Doubles 2000ptas. Triples 2700ptas. Renovations underway at press time.

Hostal Residencia Paz, C. Flora, 4, 1st floor (tel. 247 30 47), off C. del Arenal by Pl. Isabel II. Metro: Opera. Well-maintained, with owners who speak some English. Rooms are quiet since they are off the street. Singles 1100ptas. Doubles 1800ptas, with shower 2000ptas. Triples with shower 3000ptas.

Between Puerta del Sol and Atocha Stations

This central location offers some of the cheapest dives in town. Though conveniently located, the area isn't the safest. Women should be especially careful. Although streets are busy and well-lit, muggings are not uncommon. The closer you get to the Atocha station, the worse the neighborhood. The area south of C. Atocha is worse than that to the north. On streets such as **Calle Colegiata de la Magdalena,** you will find many pensions at rock-bottom prices (with loiterers out front and a long wait while the proprietor looks you over through the peephole). For safer, more comfortable rooms, walk down **Carrera de San Jerónimo** and hit any of the side streets: **Espoz y Mina, Victoria de la Cruz, de Echegaray,** and others. **Plaza Santa Ana,** with its lovely trees and benches is an ideal location to look for bargain lodgings.

Hostal Residencia Mondragón, Carrera San Jerónimo, 32, 4th floor (tel. 429 68 16). Metro: Sol. Large and clean. Brightly colored wallpaper and bedspreads create a cheery atmosphere. Private balconies or doors opening onto a red-tiled terrace with potted geraniums. Singles with showers 1200ptas. Doubles with showers 1900ptas. On the 5th floor is **Hostal Madrid Centro** (tel. 429 68 13), offering sizable rooms, some with a fireplace and sitting area. Doubles with shower 2300ptas. Up to 4 may stay in a double for 1100ptas per person. **Hostal Aguilar** (tel. 429 59 26), on the 2nd floor, is likely to have a vacancy if you arrive in Madrid at night; there are 50 rooms. TV lounge. Singles with bath 1600ptas. Doubles with bath 2700ptas.

Hotel Sud-Americana, Paseo del Prado, 12, 6th floor (tel. 429 25 64). Metro: Atocha or Antón Martín. Conveniently located across from the Prado and a block from Madrid's finest luxury hotels. High ceilings, chandeliers, and antique wood furniture provide an air of old-time elegance. Some rooms offer spectacular views. Pleasant and helpful owners. Singles 1400ptas. Doubles 2400ptas. Showers 200ptas. Reservations with 1 night's deposit. **Hostal Coruña,** on the 3rd floor (tel. 429 25 43). Young management with cute toddler daughter prancing around. The rooms are in good shape, though the view isn't as spectacular as Sud-Americana's. Singles 1400ptas. Doubles 2400ptas. Triples 3300ptas. Showers 200ptas.

Hostal Residencia María Molina, Carrera San Jerónimo, 11, 3rd floor (tel. 429 66 38). Metro: Sol. Elegant marble entrance hall and staircase. Tidy rooms. Singles 1300ptas, with bath 1800ptas. Doubles with bath 2700ptas. Triples with bath 3300ptas.

Hostal Residencia Esmeralda, C. de la Victoria, 1-2 (tel. 521 07 58). Metro: Sol. Bars on this street are hangouts for bullfighting aficionados. Spacious, freshly painted, blue rooms with carpet, high ceilings, and oak furniture. Singles 1500ptas. Doubles 2300ptas. Triples 3000ptas.

Hostal Guerra, Carrera San Jerónimo, 3, 3rd floor (tel. 522 55 77), near Puerta del Sol. Metro: Sol. Wide-smiling owner. If there's a *guerra* (war) in this hostel, it's one against dirt. Rooms with hardwood floors are well scrubbed. Singles 1200ptas, with bath 1800ptas. Doubles 2200-2500ptas, with bath 2800-3000ptas. Triples with bath 3200ptas. Warm showers 200ptas, 150ptas during stays of more than 1 night.

Hostal Residencia Regional, C. del Principe, 18 (tel. 522 33 73), off Pl. de Santa Ana. Metro: Sol. Wonderful glass and wood elevator rides a wrought-iron shaft next to a marble staircase. Rooms with hardwood floors, elaborate molding, and nice views of the street. Singles 1300ptas, with bath 1800ptas. Doubles 2000ptas, with bath 2500ptas. Downstairs, **Hostal Carreras** (tel. 522 00 36) rents big, clean rooms, some recently renovated, with natural furniture and lots of light. Singles 1200ptas, with bath 2000ptas. Doubles 2300ptas, with bath 2500ptas. Triples 3000ptas, with bath 3500ptas.

Pensión Comendador, Doctor Mata, 1 (tel. 239 07 78). Metro: Atocha. Rooms are small, but the owner keeps them comfortable and clean. Currently undergoing a noisy and messy renovation. Singles 1000ptas. Doubles 1800ptas. Triples 2400ptas. On the 3rd and 4th floors, **Hostal Residencia Aránzazu** (tel. 239 48 46). Very clean, but slightly more expensive. Singles 1300ptas, with bath 2000ptas. Doubles 2000ptas, with bath 2500ptas. Triples 3000ptas, with bath 4000ptas.

Hostal Residencia La Vera, C. Colegiata de la Magdalena, 21, 2nd floor (tel. 468 73 64). Metro: Antón Martín. A run-down street and dark entryway, but the rooms are quite clean. Singles 1000ptas. Doubles 1500ptas. Triples 1700ptas. Showers 150ptas.

Hostal Leonés, Núñez de Arce, 14 (tel. 531 08 89 or 522 71 35), off Pl. de Santa Ana. A dirty stairwell leads to clean and spacious rooms. Singles 1000ptas. Doubles 1800ptas. Triples 2700ptas. Showers 150ptas.

Along Gran Vía

Madrid's main east-west artery is lined with slightly decaying, grand old buildings that house plenty of comfortable, though more expensive, *hostales* and hotels. Rooms in this area tend to be noisy.

Alcázar Regis, Gran Vía, 5th floor (tel. 247 93 17). Metro: Pl. de España. The beautiful woodwork, stained glass, crystal chandeliers, and antique furniture will make you feel like a 1st-class traveler. Rooms are spacious and well kept, though simpler than the elaborate reception rooms. Singles 1200ptas. Doubles 2100ptas. Triples 3300ptas. Showers 100ptas. Breakfast 150ptas. **La Costa Verde,** on the 9th floor (tel. 241 91 41 or 542 26 44). Bleaker decor, but many rooms have splendid views. Singles 1100ptas. Doubles 2000ptas, with shower 2500ptas. Triples 2800ptas, with shower 3200ptas.

Hostal Margarita, Gran Vía, 50, 5th floor (tel. 247 35 49). Metro: Callao. A stairwell with stained-glass windows leads to a homey, comfortable place run by a sweet woman from Cuba. Singles 1800ptas. Doubles with shower 2800ptas, with bath 3000ptas. Triples with shower 3300ptas. Only 7 rooms. Reservations with 2500ptas deposit. **Hostal Lauria** (tel. 241 91 82), on the 4th floor, offers large, well-lit rooms with desks and baths. Airy, elegant TV lounge. Singles with bath 2100ptas. Doubles with bath 3200ptas. Triples with bath 4230ptas.

Hostal Residencia La Plata, Gran Vía, 15, 4th floor (tel. 531 97 37 or 521 17 25). In an extremely well-maintained building, with a doorman who will walk you to your door at night. Exceptional comfort. Rooms are clean and well-furnished. Friendly management. Laundry service available. Singles with shower 22000ptas, with bath 2000ptas. Doubles with bath 3200ptas. Triples with bath 4500ptas.

Hostal Residencia Lamalonga, Gran Vía, 56, 2nd floor (tel. 247 26 31 or 247 68 94). Metro: Callao or Santo Domingo. A clean, well-kept place with comfortable rooms and an efficient and caring owner. Lots o' amenities: large bathroom with rugs and tiles, TV lounge, telephones, and room service. Singles with shower 2300ptas. Doubles with shower 2800ptas, with bath 3100ptas. Triples with shower 3700ptas.

Hostal El Pinar, C. Isabel la Católica, 19 (tel. 247 32 82), just off Gran Vía. Metro: Pl. de España. Simple but clean rooms; all face the street. Wildly colorful bathrooms. Singles 1300ptas. Doubles 2300ptas. Triples 3000ptas. Showers 150ptas.

Hostal Delfina, Gran Vía, 12, 4th floor (tel. 522 64 23 or 522 64 22). Metro: Gran Vía or Sevilla. A bit of old-fashioned charm, especially the funky steel bed frames, but the owner is also proud of his Danish showers. Run-down bathrooms. Singles with bath 1700ptas. Doubles with bath 2500-2700ptas. Triples with bath 3000ptas. Reservations accepted 1-2 days in advance with a 1000-2000ptas deposit. **Hostal Los Zamoranos** (tel. 532 90 25), on the 6th floor.Nice, big, real good, decent rooms, although somewhat humid in summer. Beware of the grimy bathrooms. Family lives on separate floor, so it's quiet. Singles 1300ptas, with shower 2000ptas. Doubles 2200ptas, with shower 2600ptas. Triples 3300ptas, with shower 3900ptas. **Hostal Amaya** (tel. 522 21 51), on the 1st floor. Quaint rooms. Singles with bath 1500ptas. Doubles with bath 2000ptas. Triples with bath 3000ptas.

Along Calle Fuencarral

Along Calle Fuencarral (which radiates off Gran Vía), the rooms are somewhat cheaper, almost as convenient, and usually quieter.

Hostal Medieval, C. Fuencarral, 46 (tel. 222 25 49), at C. Augusto Figueroa. Metro: Tribunal. The manager is friendly, bird chirps in the background, and flowers fill the balconies. Singles with shower 1700ptas. Doubles with shower 2800ptas, with bath 3500ptas. Triples with shower 3700ptas.

Hostal Residencia Kryse, C. Fuencarral, 25 (tel. 522 81 53 or 231 15 12). Metro: Gran Vía. Run by a friendly family, this place boasts a reading room and a large TV lounge with a fireplace. Rooms are clean, and beds have firm mattresses. Singles 1300ptas. Doubles 2000ptas, with shower 2400ptas. Triples with shower 3000ptas. On the 2nd and 3rd floors is **Hostal Palacios Ribadavia** (tel. 531 48 47). Clean, airy rooms with high ceilings and colorful bedspreads. Pleasant sitting room with the most comfortable couch you've ever sat on. Caring manager. Singles 1100ptas, with shower 1600ptas. Doubles with shower 2200ptas. Triples with shower 3300ptas.

Hostal Residencia Ginebra, C. Fuencarral, 17 (tel. 532 10 35 or 522 37 53). Metro: Gran Vía. A little dark, but the rooms are carpeted and well cared for. Newly varnished wooden staircase. Singles with shower 1800ptas, with bath 2000ptas. Doubles with bath 3000ptas. Triples with bath 4200ptas.

Hostal Residencia Dominguez, C. de Santa Brigida, 1 (tel. 232 15 47), just off C. Fuencarral. Metro: Tribunal. Small, clean rooms with cheerful bedspreads. Singles 1100ptas, with shower 1300ptas. Doubles with shower 2200ptas, with bath 2400ptas.

Elsewhere

Hostal Senegal, Pl. de Santa Bárbara, 8 (tel. 419 07 71 or 419 10 32), sandwiched between Pizza Hut and Cervecería Santa Bárbara. Enter at C. de Orellana. Metro: Alonso Martínez. Modest but clean rooms with attractive wood paneling and furniture. Balconies face the plaza. Singles with shower 2300ptas, with bath 2600ptas. Doubles 3000ptas, with bath 3200ptas.

Hostal Residencia Asunción, Pl. de Santa Bárbara, 8, 2nd floor (tel. 410 25 28). Metro: Alonso Martínez. Well-lit rooms with high ceilings and hardwood floors; most have balconies and open to the plaza. Comfortable guest lounge. Singles with bath 2600ptas. Doubles with bath 3400ptas. Triples with bath 4500ptas.

Hostal Don Diego, C. Velázquez, 45 (tel. 435 07 60 or 435 08 29). Metro: Velázquez. A high-quality establishment in Salamanca, Madrid's most prestigious *barrio*. Excellent value for the location and the elegance. Modern rooms with lovely leather and wood furniture, spacious closets, and telephones. Comfortable TV lounge has sofas; bar serves sandwiches and breakfast. Singles with bath 3900ptas. Doubles with bath 5200ptas. Triples with bath 7020ptas. Reserve at least 1 week in advance.

Hostal Santa Bárbara, Pl. de Santa Bárbara, 4, 3rd floor (tel. 446 93 08 or 445 73 34). Metro: Alonso Martínez. Friendly, English-speaking Italian owner. Plush hotel atmosphere. Large, clean rooms with cloth wallpaper, private baths, and telephones, most face the plaza. Modern TV lounge with marble tables. Room service. Singles with bath 2915ptas. Doubles with bath 4080ptas.

Hostal Residencia Princesa, C. Princesa, 84 (tel. 243 94 54), near the Ciudad Universitaria. Metro: Argüelles. Nice rooms, but they overlook a noisy street. Singles 1500ptas. Doubles 2200ptas. Showers 250ptas. On the same floor, **Hostal Residencia La Princesita** (tel. 243 31 53) offers equally pleasant lodgings. Doubles 2100ptas. Triples 3000ptas. Showers 250ptas.

Camping

There are about 13 campsites within 50km of Madrid; the tourist offices provide information on all of them. **Camping Madrid** (tel. 202 28 35) is on Carretera N-11, Madrid-Burgos (7km). Take the metro to Pl. de Castilla, then bus #129 to the Iglesia de los Dominicos. (275ptas per person and 250ptas per tent.) **Camping Osuna** (tel. 741 05 10) is located on the Ajalvir-Vicálvaro road (15.5km). Take the metro to Canillejas, then bus #105 to Avda. de Logroño. (300ptas per person and 250ptas per tent.) Both campgrounds offer complete facilities: telephones, hot showers, washers and dryers, a playground, bar, and restaurant. Safes, currency exchange, and medical care are also available. Camping Madrid offers a swimming pool, while buses run from Camping Osuna to El Escorial, Aranjuez, and Sierra de Madrid. For further camping information, contact the Consejería de Educación de Juventud, Caballeno de Gracia, 32 (tel. 522 29 41 or 521 44 27).

Food

It requires extraordinary ingenuity to be hungry in Madrid. Although restaurants rarely open before mid-afternoon and subsequently close until evening, countless bars, *mesones* (restaurants where people stand at the bar to eat and talk), and cafes always serve lighter fare such as *tapas* and baroque pastries. In addition to local dishes, you will find regional specialties from Galicia, Valencia, Catalunya, and Andalucía. Some of the capital's delicacies are *caldereta de cordero* (lamb stewed with tomatoes and peppers), *callos a la madrileña* (tripe cooked with wine, sausage, and ham), *mojete* (mixed vegetables), and *pisto manchego* (cooked vegetables mixed with egg). While the house wine in most restaurants is from La Mancha (usually *Valdepeñas*), the best local wine is considered to be *Arganda-Colmenar de Oreja,* a slightly expensive dry wine once produced at the site of the Barajas airport.

The immense variety of *tapas* can be a bit intimidating (Madrid is Spain's *tapa* capital, with tidbits from all over), and their names are almost never translated. Your toothpick will probably find its way into the following: *atún* or *bonito* (tuna), *boquerones* (sardines), *calamares fritos* (fried squid), *cerdo* (pork), *chorizo* (spicy sausage), *champiñones al ajillo* (mushrooms in garlic sauce), *gambas* (shrimp), *jamón serrano* (ham that has been laid out on ice in the sun so that it gets smoked but doesn't spoil), *judías verdes* (green beans), *lenguado* (sole), *merluza* (hake), and *ternera* (veal). A *bocadillo* of a *tapa* is served as a sandwich on thick bread. A *ración* is a large portion and can serve as a complete meal with some *pan* (bread) and a glass of Aguila or Mahou *cerveza*.

Some of the best bargains line the streets of old Madrid, in the bars and *mesones* around the **Plaza Mayor** and the **Puerta del Sol;** Calle Ventura de la Vega, off Carrera de San Jerónimo, is lined with low- to medium-priced restaurants; you should also try Calles de la Victoria, Espoz y Mina, Echegaray, and Pelayo. For inexpensive food, the area around Ciudad Universitaria can't be beat. No trip to Madrid is complete without a visit to one of the old cafeterias, where you can experience the traditional *tertulias,* or informal literary and intellectual circles.

True peseta-pinchers can stock up on everything from yogurt and fresh fruit to meat and wine at the **Mercado de San Miguel,** an odd-looking building with metal pillars and a red-tiled, ornamented roof just off the northwest corner of the Pl.

Mayor. (Open Mon.-Sat. 9am-3pm and 5:30-7:30pm.) Also try the open-air market **El Rastro,** a flea market selling food and other goods on C. Ribera de Curtidores, off the Pl. Mayor. (Metro: La Latina. Open Sun. 10am-2pm.) **El Rastrillo de Tetuán,** Marques de Viana, offers similar fare. (Metro: Tetuán. Open Sun. and holidays in the morning.) Every **El Corte Inglés** ("English Court") department store has a food market, usually on the ground floor. Prices are lower only at an open market. (All stores open Mon.- Sat. 10am- 9pm.)

Bullfight aficionados may wish to explore **Calle de la Victoria,** off Carrera San Jerónimo, just southeast of Puerta del Sol. Although restaurants here are neither remarkable nor clean, they are thematically consistent. Try the original *patatas bravas* (potatoes in hot sauce) at **Las Bravas,** Alvarez Gato, 3 (tel. 232 26 20). This bar concocted the recipe later copied by the rest of the neighborhood.

The orange **VIPS** (pronounced "veeps") signs that pop up all over Madrid belong to a chain of modern restaurants that serve everything from sandwiches to full dinners. Though not exactly budget establishments, VIPS are extremely convenient and their *platos combinadoas* aren't bad. (Open Sun.-Thurs. 9am-3am, Fri-Sat. 9am-3:30am.) They also carry English books and magazines, as well as records, chocolate, and canned food. American fast-food joints can also be found in the commercial districts.

Around Puerta del Sol

This area is full of restaurants, but choose carefully to avoid tourist traps. Several good restaurants along **Calle Ventura de la Vega** attract a loyal local clientele.

Museo del Jamón, Carrera San Jerónimo, 6 (tel. 521 03 46), off Puerta del Sol. You can really ham it up here. Lightly smoked Iberian ham sandwiches 80ptas (3 make a meal). Baked half-chicken with salad and fried potatoes 450ptas. Open Mon.-Sat. 9am-12:30am, Sun. 10am-12:30am. Restaurant upstairs, with same prices but a longer menu, opens daily at 1pm. 5 other locations in the city.

Restaurante El Cuchi, C. Cuchilleros, 3 (tel. 266 31 08), off the southwest corner of the Pl. Mayor. Sign over the entrance proudly announces "Hemingway never ate here." *Loco* atmosphere. Roaming *mariachis* offer everyone tequila shots. Entertaining waiters. Try the delicately cooked pregnant trout (800ptas) or make your own *paella* (950ptas). Open daily 1-4pm and 8pm-midnight.

Restaurante Sobrinos del Botín, C. Cuchilleros, 17 (tel. 266 42 17), a hop, skip, and jump from El Cuchi. Metro: Sol or Opera. An expensive treat. The oldest restaurant in Spain (1725); Hemingway called it one of the best in the world. House *menú* of gazpacho, roast suckling pig, ice cream, and wine 2500ptas. Two sittings for dinner: 8 and 10:30pm. Open daily 1-4pm and 8pm-midnight. Make reservations.

Lhardy, Carrera de San Jerónimo, 8 (tel. 521 33 85 or 522 22 07), at C. de la Victoria. Metro: Sol. One of Madrid's oldest restaurants, it doubles as a museum—the upstairs dining rooms still feature the original 1839 decor. Varnished wallpaper and lavish meals are well worth the investment: full meals 4200ptas. *Cocido,* a stew of vegetables, chicken, beef, sausage, and ham, is the house specialty (2300ptas). Proper attire required. Open Sept.-July Mon.-Sat. 1-3:30pm and 9-11:30pm, Sun. 1-3:30pm. Aficionados on a budget congregate downstairs for cognac, sherry, *caldo,* and the best hors d'oeuvres in town. Bar open Sept.-July Mon.-Sat. 9:30pm-12:30am.

Cafetería-Restaurante Marfil, Pl. Jesús, 7 (tel. 429 18 91), near C. Lope de Vega. Metro: Antón Martin. Convenient place after a day at the Prado. Local clientele. Basque-style hake with shrimp and asparagus 700ptas. *Menú* 700ptas. Open Mon.-Sat. 7am-11:30pm.

Restaurante Toscana, C. Manuel Fernández y González, 10-17 (tel. 429 60 31 or 429 60 33). Metro: Sevilla or Sol. Woodwork, tiles, and Spanish plates on the wall. A hopping night spot Fri.-Sat. after 10pm. The house specialty is *morcillo* (tender veal) with fries (800ptas). Open Wed.-Mon. 1-4pm and 8pm-midnight, Tues. 8pm-midnight.

Edelweiss, Jovellanos, 7 (tel. 521 03 26), behind Congreso de los Diputados. Metro: Sevilla or Banco de España. Members of the Cortes are said to be frequent patrons. Espensive, but the *menú* is only 600ptas. Specializes in German and central European dishes. Try the *sauerbraten* with dumplings (900ptas) or the house specialty, *codillo de cerdo con chu crut,* a pork and vegetable dish that feeds 2 (1100ptas). Open Mon.-Sat. 12:45-4pm and 7pm-midnight.

Riazor Restaurante, C. De Toledo, 19 (tel. 266 54 67 or 266 54 66), 100 ft. southwest of the Pl. Mayor. *Fritura* (fried seafood platter) with clams, mussels, shrimp, and sole 850ptas. *Menú* 600ptas. Open daily 1pm-1am.

Near Ciudad Universitaria

One of the the cheapest yet loveliest areas in Madrid, the student quarter is crowded from September to June, when the university is in session. You will find some of the most attractive bargains in town here, set amid wide, tree-lined streets. The area starts at the intersection of Calle de la Princesa, Alberto Aguilera, and Marqués de Urquijo and can be reached by metro (Argüelles or Moncloa) and bus #1, 12, 61, or *Circular.* During the school year, students crowd the bars; try Calle Princesa between noon and 2:30pm and between 8 and 11pm.

Restaurante El Parque, Fernando el Católico, 78 (tel. 243 31 27), down the street from the student travel office. Metro: Moncloa. One of the largest menus you've ever seen. Choose between a number of beef, pork, lamb, rabbit, fish, and vegetable dishes. Entrees about 500ptas, *menú* 475ptas. Open Mon.-Sat. 1-4:30pm and 8:30pm-midnight, Sun. 1-4:30pm.

Parador de Moncloa, C. de Hilarión Eslava, 16 (tel. 244 10 72). Students abound here even during vacations. A lively bar-restaurant guaranteed to be "happening." Sandwiches 100ptas, full meals from 450ptas. Open Mon.-Sat. 11:30am-3:30pm and 5:30pm-midnight, Sun. 5:30pm-midnight.

Restaurante Ku'damm, C. del Conde Duque, 30 (tel. 542 21 57), off C. de Alberto Aguilera. Metro: Ventura Rodríguez or San Bernardo. A *pizzería* and *cervecería* serving Spanish, German, and Italian dishes. Funky black and white photographs line the wall. The individual pizzas, served hot on wooden butcherblocks, are especially good. *Pizza mixta* (salami, olives, onions, tomatoes, and cheese) 600ptas. Open daily noon-midnight.

Restaurante Rias Baixas, D. de Amuniel, 38 (tel. 248 50 84), off C. de Alberto Aguilera. Metro: Ventura Rodríguez or San Bernardo. A Galician restaurant: Seashells, fishing nets, and other nautical paraphernalia accent the walls. Concentrate on the *gallego* specialties (275-1350ptas), such as *pulpo* (octopus) and the tangy white wine *Ribeira.* Open Mon.-Fri. 1-4pm and 9pm-1am, Sat. 1-4pm and 8pm-midnight.

Restaurante del Estal, C. de Rodríguez San Pedro, 64 (tel. 243 30 69 or 243 70 74), off C. Princesa. Metro: Argüelles. The tasty *menú* costs 550ptas, but the *churrasco,* served on wooden platters, is the house specialty (700ptas). Open Mon.-Sat. 12:30-4pm and 8:30pm-midnight.

Between San Bernardo, Colón, and Gran Vía

The many budget restaurants here feature everything from crepes to tacos to *hamburguesas.* Cleanliness and quality vary greatly.

La Chocolatería, C. Barbieri, 15 (tel. 521 00 23), 4 blocks from Gran Vía. Metro: Chueca. Quaint Spanish decor, wooden tables, and tiled walls. The old-fashioned camera in the corner will not take your picture, and the antique cash register never breaks 900ptas, which is true of most entrees here. Unusual and delicious dishes. *Pastel de cebolla* (onion quiche) 440ptas. Save room for desserts like lemon sherbet in champagne (370ptas). Open Mon.-Sat. 1:30-3:45pm and 9pm-1:45am, Sun. 9pm-1:45am. Bar open daily 6:30pm-1:45am. Closed during Semana Santa and Aug.

La Gata Flora, C. del Dos de Mayo, 1 (tel. 521 20 20), at C. San Vicente Ferrer. Metro: Noviciado or Tribunal. Unsafe area at night. Good Italian restaurant run by friendly Argentines. A yellow and brown bohemian interior, with drawings of *gatas* (cats). Try the *cappelletti al pesto* for dumplings in a delicious sauce (550ptas) or the *escalope nona* (690ptas). Open in summer Sun.-Thurs. 1-4pm and 9pm-12:30am, Fri.-Sat. 8:30pm-1am; in off-season Sun.-Thurs. 2-4pm and 9:30pm-12:30am.

Cervecería Santa Bárbara, at Pl. de Santa Bárbara, 8, at C. de Orellana. Metro: Alonso Martínez. The *gambas* (shrimp) are packed almost as tightly as the people, and they're just as fresh. 600ptas per 100 grams. Freshly brewed beer in a tall glass 130ptas. Open daily 11am-midnight.

Restaurante Las Maravillas, Pl. Dos de Mayo, 9 (no phone), near La Gata Flora but on the plaza, and just as dangerous at night. One of the cheapest of the bohemian restaurants. Come here for an afternoon meal and sit at the outside tables facing the plaza. Individual pizzas 500ptas, hot croissant sandwiches 250ptas. Open Tues.-Sun. 8pm-2am.

Casa Gades, C. Conde de Xiquena, 4 (tel. 532 30 51 or 232 48 61). Metro: Chueca. There are 2 of these Italian restaurants, adjacent to each other. One is homey, the other chic. Don't expect friendly service, but the meals are a good deal. Pizza and most other dishes 500ptas. Open daily 1:30-4pm and 9pm-2:15am.

Valencia, Gran Vía, 44 (tel. 522 01 50 or 532 11 94). Metro: Callao. The place to try *paella especial,* a flavorful rice dish with vegetables, chicken, and various seafoods (475ptas). *Menú* of 3 courses, bread, and wine 1000ptas. Open Tues.-Sat. 12:30-4pm and 7:30-11pm, Sun. 12:30-4pm.

Elsewhere

Casa Mingo, Paseo de la Florida, 2 (tel. 247 79 18). Metro: Norté. This wild restaurant is built into the end of the train station. The walls are stacked with enormous barrels, and the tables crowded with enthusiastic clientele who come here to eat roast chicken (550ptas) and drink Asturian cider made by the Mingo family (by the *caña* or 200ptas per bottle). Don't order the *sidra natural;* it's the *sidera extrafina* that's homemade. *Madrileños* and *asturianos* pour the cider by holding the bottle high above their shoulders and pouring the cider into a glass on the floor or held low in the other hand. Open daily 11am-midnight.

Foster's Hollywood, C. Velázquez, 80 (tel. 435 61 28). Metro: Núñez de Balboa. If more Spaniards tried a meal here, they wouldn't berate American cuisine so much. The ½-lb. burgers are, *sin duda* (without a doubt), the best in Madrid. Served with baked potato or fries, and salad (555ptas). Other specialties include root beer (130ptas) and homemade apple pie (320ptas). 6 other locations in the city. Open Sun.-Thurs. 1pm-1:15am, Fri.-Sat. 1pm-2:15am.

Restaurante-Cafeteria Sabatini, C. Bailén, 15 (tel. 247 92 40), opposite the Sabatini Gardens adjacent to the Palacio Real. Large portions of *paella* with chicken, clams, and small crabs (675ptas) or garlic chicken (600ptas). Friendly, high-speed waiters. Sidewalk tables face 2 of Madrid's most famous sites. Open daily 9am-1am. Dinner served 8pm-midnight.

Choletera El Jardín, C. López de Hoyos, 219 (tel. 415 50 37). Metro: Avda. de la Paz, then cross the bridge over the highway. A tropical garden oasis in the midst of unattractive urban wasteland. The entrance is covered with ivy, and the outdoor tables hidden among trees and bushes. Delicious beef and mutton dinners about 1500ptas. Open daily 1:30pm-1:30am.

Major Sights

The many monuments, museums, and churches of Madrid lend the city an almost stern elegance. The world-famous Prado Museum impresses all with the genius of its art, the stately Palacio Real haughtily commands attention on the edge of sprawling gardens, and the cobblestoned Plaza Mayor exudes immensity. But the Spanish capital also offers a wealth of smaller museums, churches, and parks where you can escape the summer crowds. Don't overlook Madrid's quaint, narrow streets; airy squares; grand, leafy boulevards; and sublime baroque and neoclassical architecture.

Spanish-speakers can take advantage of the Ayuntamiento's *Tardes de verano* tours, designed to acquaint Spaniards with Madrid. The routes include visits to Old Madrid, Parque del Retiro, the old cafes, and surrounding parks. The tour entitled *Madrid castizo* will take you where no tourist has ever gone before. Tours on foot cost 200ptas, students 150ptas. Tours on bus cost 400ptas, students 300ptas. A package deal of six tours (3 on bus, 3 on foot), cost 1500ptas, students 1000ptas. For information, contact Conozcamos Madrid, c/o Señores de Luzón, 10 (Pl. de Santiago), 28013 Madrid (tel. 242 55 12 or 248 74 26).

The imposing **Puerta de Alcalá,** at Pl. de la Independencia, on the northern entrance to Parque del Retiro, was built in 1778 in honor of Carlos III and was financed by an unpopular wine tax. The architect who created this neoclassical granite and limestone structure also designed most of the Palacio Real. On the eastern face of the *puerta,* you can still see the marks left by bullets fired during the battle for Madrid in the Civil War.

Walking west toward Puerta del Sol on Alcalá, you will run into the triumphant, lion-drawn carriage of the goddess Cibeles on the **Fuente de la Cibeles,** located in front of the post office, the Bank of Spain, and the Ministry of Defense, and between tree-lined Paseos del Prado and Recoletos. Completed in 1799, the fountain was designed by Ventura Rodríguez, with sculptures by Roberto Michel and Francisco Gutiérrez. The scepter and key that the goddess carries symbolize her power over the seasons and the fertility of the land. During the Nationalist bomb raids over the capital, citizens successfully protected this emblem of Madrid by covering it completely with a pyramid made with sacks of sand. Paseo del Prado is graced with two other masterpieces by Ventura Rodríguez. The **Fuente de Apolo,** 1 block south of Pl. de Cibeles, features Apollo surrounded by the Seasons. Farther south, on Pl. Cánovas del Castillo, in front of El Prado, he placed the **Fuente de Neptuno,** with the proud figure of Neptune standing atop his tortoise-shell-shaped conveyance, trident in hand, pulled by two gargantuan sea chargers, and surrounded by dolphins spouting torrents of water.

Southeast of the Fuente de Neptuno, on the east side of Paseo del Prado, is the **Museo del Prado** (tel. 468 09 05). The museum contains over 5000 canvases from the Iberian peninsula and the rest of the continent, many collected by Spanish monarchs between the fifteenth and eighteenth centuries. On display here is the spiritual luminosity of El Greco; the technical sophistication of Velázquez; and the contorted imaginings of Goya; as well as Bosch's bizarre landscapes of life, death, sin, suffering, and sex; Breughel the Elder's morbidity; and Botticelli's visions.

The second floor (the first floor in Spanish usage) houses the greatest Spanish works from the sixteenth and seventeenth centuries. Several towering religious works by El Greco (1541-1614) will amaze you with their passion for transcendence. *La Trinidad* demonstrates that even in early works he had mastered much of the style that was to make him famous; the painting is a study in the deliberate use of line, the surety of emotional expression, and the intensity of color. These qualities come to the fore in his later *La Adoración de los pastores,* painted for his own tomb.

The artistic genius of Diego de la Velázquez (1599-1660) is represented by his masterpiece *Las Meninas* (*The Maids of Honor*), a fascinating portrayal of court life in the seventeenth century and the daring epitome of the painter's ideas on the unity of theme, composition, and light. The canvas's recent restoration has revealed the fullness of Velázquez's palette, doing away with previous interpretations of this work. The Prado deserves praise for the way the painting is displayed. The mirrors on both side walls underscore the play of reflected angles. The side lighting emulates the window light in the painting, bringing forth Velázquez's subtle handling of volumes. In the painting's background, you can see the reflections of King Felipe IV and his wife Mariana, who, therefore, share the spectator's point of view as they pose for the portrait the artist is painting within the canvas itself. If you look into the room directly opposite the point where *Las Meninas* is hung, you will see Velázquez's actual portraits of Felipe IV and his wife. Another recently cleaned and restored painting, *Las Hilanderas* (*The Spinners*) is so delicately rendered as to give the viewer the sensation of being inside the painting. *La Rendición de Breda* or *Las Lanzas* (*The Surrender of Breda*) depicts a surrender gracefully accepted. Nassau hands the keys to the city over to his conqueror, Spínola, whose face simultaneously expresses sympathy and triumph. Velázques's small *La Villa de Medici en Roma* demonstrates the use of impressionist devices, while his equestrian portrait of Prince Baltasar Carlos renders the unique quality of light in the Sierra de Guadarrama so well that even those familiar with it are awed.

Other Spanish painters of the same era are also well represented on the Prado's first floor. Murillo's (1618-1682) religious work sharply contrasts his genre paintings, although he combines both impulses in such works as *Familia con pájaro pequeño* (*Family with Small Bird*). The austere mysticism of Zurbarán (1598-1664) is evident in his *La Visión de San Pedro Nolasco,* which shows the saint experiencing a vision of a holy city. José de Ribera (1591-1652) also devotes himself to the pain of religion. *El Martirio de San Bartholomeo* (*The Martyrdom of Saint Bartholomew*) is an agonizing portrayal of the saint being hoisted aloft in preparation for flaying; the powerful muscles of the executioners convey the brutality of the act.

The Prado's collection of **Italian works** delights with its careful representation of Renaissance themes. Fra Angelico's (1387-1455) *The Annunciation* depicts both the story of Adam and Eve and that of Mary, and is notable for its Giottoesque, proplike representation of nature. Raphael's (1483-1520) *The Cardinal* sums up all the ambition and power of the medieval clergy. Tintoretto's (1518-1594) *The Washing of the Feet* uses great open spaces to convey a Renaissance scene, and Botticelli's (1444-1510) series *The Story of Nastagio degli Honesti* reveals much about social life in the Renaissance.

Sex, religion, and death make their unsubtle presences known in the Prado's collection of **Flemish paintings,** which has long been popular in Spain due to the commercial ties between the Low Countries and Castilla. Hieronymus Bosch (1450-1516), known to the Spanish as "El Bosco," is the most enigmatic of the Flemish painters. He is considered a futurist because his works transcend realism and delve into the "subconscious" imagination three centuries before Goya—and nearly half a millenium before Dalí and the surrealists—would do likewise. Bosch is a bitter mystic in the sanguine years of the Renaissance. While most European artists were beginning to downplay human limitations, he remained skeptical and portrayed man's vilest potentials. Nowhere is this misanthropy more evident than in Bosch's stunning *triptych The Garden of Earthly Delights,* a sharp indictment of those who seek fulfillment in the transience of worldly pleasure. The right panel, which shows seemingly innocent humans being tortured by animalistic creatures, grimly eclipses any vestige of the painter's belief in the resurrection that appears in the center and left panels. Bosch's legacy is clear in the macabre works of Peter Breughel the Elder (1525-1569). In his *Triumph of Death,* legions of skeletons wreak havoc upon the pitiable remnants of humanity. Albrecht Dürer (1471-1528) provides Germanic relief from these two glum views in his double painting *Adam and Eve.* Dürer's works are normally marked by their sobriety, as in his sensitive *Self-Portrait.* But in *Adam and Eve,* he seems to toy with viewers. Was Eve ever innocent (as one is led to believe by the unbitten apple), or had she no naïveté to shed (as the devilishness in her eyes suggests)?

The ground floor contains more treasures of Spanish art, both early and late. The collection of canvases by **Francisco de Goya** (1746-1828) chronicles his gradual transition from gaiety to despair. The painter's early period is wonderfully captured in a series of his cartoons intended for tapestries in El Escorial. Lazy afternoons, bucolic scenes, and merry drinking games are paralleled by his graceful *La Vendimia* (*The Vintage*) and *La Nevada* (*The Snowfall*), a careful and rare (for Spanish painters) depiction of a winter scene. Numerous portraits of Spain's royal family are also on display, including an unpleasantly realistic *La Familia de Carlos IV.* As Prado tour guides will repeat over and over, Goya never sacrificed realism for the sake of sentimentality. He painted what he saw: a group of listless, puffy, round-eyed royalty. Doña María Josefa, with the ugly birthmark on her right temple, looks like the *loca* (crazy) she was.

Being court painter wasn't without its advantages. When the Duke of Alba commissioned Goya to paint a portrait of his wife, the Duchess of Alba, the artist had an illicit affair with her. He gave the Duke *La Maja vestida* (*Clothed Maja*), but kept *La Maja desnuda* (*Nude Maja*) for his own viewing pleasure. You can see from her proportions that Goya's feminine ideal lay somewhere between the classical one and Mae West.

Two events following the 1780s poisoned Goya's peace of mind and dramatically altered the once-sedate mood of his paintings. When Napoleon's army invaded, Spaniards were forced to use guerilla warfare to defend themselves. *Los Fusilamientos del tercero de mayo* (The Execution of the Rioters: May 3, 1808) depicts Goya's compatriots at the moment of their slaughter by French troops. The latter are intentionally painted with little detail in order to emphasize their automation-like coldness. The *chiaroscuro,* or contrast of light and dark, between the central figure's white shirt (connoting martyrdom) and the tenebrous background, is striking.

Rumor has it that the blood on the bottom left side of the canvas is not all pigment—Goya shed some blood as he worked as a memoriam to those who died for Spain. The second event effecting a change in Goya's style was his complete loss of hearing in 1819. He retreated to a small country house outside Madrid, since nicknamed "La quinta del sordo" (deaf man's house), and decorated its inner walls with the haunting **black paintings.** The most famous one is *Saturno devorando a su hijo* (*Saturn Devouring His Son*). It is rumored that this painting, which reveals a father-son relationship reduced to the barest essentials, hung over the dining table in the deaf man's house. *Duelo a garrotazos* (*Fight with Cudgels*), which shows two men with sand up to their knees beating each other mercilessly, seems an expression of war's futility.

Primitive and Renaissance Spanish painting are well represented in such works as Bartolomé Bermejo's *Santo Domingo de Silos,* which overflows with a golden background reminiscent of Byzantine art. Two small chapels off the rotunda by the Puerta de Goya reveal fascinating eleventh- and twelfth-century paintings from the Mozarabic Church of San Baudelio de Berlanga and the hermitage of Cruz de Maderuelo. A pair of smooth New York art speculators had made off with several of these unique paintings for a pittance, but Spain eventually got them back in exchange for a monastery. Finally, the Prado also contains some fine classical Roman and Greek statues. (Open Tues.-Sat. 9am-7pm, Sun. 9am-2pm. Admission 400ptas, students free. Metro: Banco de España.) The Prado runs a cafeteria with reasonable prices.

Your ticket to the Prado is also valid for the nearby **Casón del Buen Retiro.** Once a famous porcelain factory, the *casón* was destroyed in 1808 during the war against Napoleon. The restored version now houses the *Sección de Arte Español del Siglo XIX,* a small collection of outstanding works by the nineteenth-century Spanish masters Joaquín Sorolla, Santiago Russinyol, Fortuny, Eduardo Rosales, and others. (Open Tues.-Sat. 9am-6:45pm, Sun. 9am-1:45pm. Entrance on Felipe IV.) The other side of the *casón,* facing the Parque del Retiro, houses the **Legado Picasso,** featuring the great *Guernica.* During the Spanish Civil War, numerous civilians were killed when Gernika (Guernica), a small town in the Basque Country, was mercilessly bombed by German airplanes at the nationalists' request. Picasso painted this huge work of jumbled and distorted figures to denounce the outrage. Unlike most cubist creations, *Guernica* is fraught with symbolism. The pointed tongue and spear-pierced stomach of the horse signifies the wounding of the Spanish people. According to Picasso, "the bull represents brutality and darkness;" it looks beyond the confines of the canvas to show that such genocide can recur. The lightbulb symbolizes the destructive potential of technological innovation. But Picasso was not entirely pessimistic: At the bottom center, a flower grows from martyrs' blood. Supposedly, when asked by nationalist officials whether he had painted the picture, Picasso answered, "No, you did." He gave the canvas to New York's Museum of Modern Art with the request that it be returned to Spain only when democracy was restored; *Guernica* belatedly arrived in Madrid in the fall of 1981. As a symbol of support for the present system of government, the painting remains so controversial that visitors must walk through a metal detector before entering the building, and a glass case protects the work. (Open Tues.-Sat. 9am-6:45pm, Sun. 9am-1:45pm. Admission same as to the Prado, and the same ticket lets you in.)

When the intensity of the art at the Prado proves too tiring, head to the 353 acres of green peace known as **Parque del Retiro** (about 2 blocks behind the Prado, by C. de Alfonso XII), where you will find everything necessary to put your soul at rest. Tourists paddle quietly on the central lake, while carefully arranged gardens soothe exhausted urban spirits.

Parque del Retiro spreads around the lake known as the **Estanque Grande.** A huge statue of Alfonso XII on horseback dominates the rectangular lake and is backed by a long, columned archway and fronted by statues of lions with steps leading down to the water. You can rent a rowboat here (9am-10:30pm, about 250ptas per hr.). The water looks tranquil on the surface, but drop in a piece of bread and a slew of ravenous carp will splash up to fight over it.

South of the lake are exhibit halls, ponds, and several more attractive gardens. The **Palace of Exhibitions** usually hosts an art show, as does the **Crystal Palace,** an airy building that resembles a greenhouse and faces a pond with a shooting jet of water at its center. (Both open Tues.-Sat. 10am-2pm and 5-7pm, Sun. 10am-2pm. Admission 75ptas, students free.) At the southernmost tip of the park lies **La Rosaleda,** a wondrous garden of sandy paths; small, geometrically arranged hedges; and thousands of roses of every hue—purples, reds, yellows, whites—that burst out of the ground or hang from frames. Just to the northeast of these gardens stretch the formal **Jardines de Cecilio Rodríguez,** laid out in classical style with orange flower beds, conical clipped hedges, columned walkways wrapped in ivy, and pheasants wandering the grounds.

If you leave the park through the southwest Puerta de Murillo, you can walk across Avda. Alfonso XII onto Espalter, which will lead you to the entrance of the **Jardín Botánico,** moved to its present location by Carlos III in 1755. The living collection includes species from all over the world, from California maples to Greek chestnuts. Madrid's first zoo was installed here in 1858 and then moved to El Retiro. An old law that may still be in effect allowed *madrileños* to come and gather medicinal herbs. While the lower part of the garden is organized along the rational lines typical of the Enlightenment, the upper section is undeniably Romantic, with sinuous paths and arbitrarily placed little fountains. (Garden open daily 9am-9pm. Admission 50ptas.)

From Pl. de Murillo at the northwest corner of the Jardín Botánico, follow C. de las Huertas west to C. Carretas and turn right (north) to the symbolic heart of Madrid, the **Puerta del Sol.** This plaza's streets now attract pedestrians and cars in great numbers, but the bustle belies a bloody past. On May 2 to 3, 1808, *madrileños* fought Napoleon's army here after learning that he planned to remove the Royal Infantas. Two of Goya's paintings in the Prado, *El segundo de mayo* (*May 2, 1808*) and *Los Fusilamientos del tercero de mayo* (*The Execution of the Rioters: May 3, 1808*), are gruesome portrayals of this episode.

Just southwest of Puerta del Sol, south of C. Mayor, is the **Plaza Mayor.** Since no city street passes through it, this expansive square comes as an abrupt surprise to the visitor who enters it by one of the many alley-like entrances. Facades are marked by orderly rows of modest balconies, and outdoor cafes rim the edges, but the plaza's center is unsettlingly empty except for the seventeenth-century statue of Felipe III by sculptors Juan de Bolonia and Pietro Tacca. (Their work was not placed in the plaza until 1847.) Philatelists and numismatists still congregate here every Sunday morning; Christmas decorations are sold here in December; and in autumn there is a book fair. The plaza's appearance has not changed much since 1620, when Gómez de Mora completed the project ordered by Felipe III. The royal proclamations, bullfights, and *auto da fés* of former times have given way to less momentous, though still quintessentially *madrileño,* activities: socializing in the cafes and soaking up the afternoon sun. (Metro: Sol. Buses #3, 53, M-1. From Puerta del Sol, walk to C. Mayor—by McDonald's—and proceed 1 or 2 blocks up before turning left.)

Across C. Mayor, on the western tip of central Madrid is the **Palacio Real.** Although no monarchs have dwelled in the royal palace since the war-torn 1930s, this elegant granite edifice continues to fulfill an important symbolic and diplomatic function. King Juan Carlos and Queen Sofia live in the Palacio de la Zarzuela, but they visit the building on frequent official occasions. Built by King Felipe V to replace the medieval Alcázar (which burned down on Christmas Eve, 1734), the palace initially marked the monumental inauguration of the Bourbon dynasty. More than 250 years later, this work of the Italian architects Sacchetti and Sabatini inaugurated yet another era in Spanish history: On June 12, 1985, the Royal Palace hosted 150 diplomats and heads of state for dinner and the signing of the treaty that joined Spain to the European Common Market. (Metro: Opera. Buses #4, 15, 25, 33, 39.)

The only way to see the Palacio is on a guided tour (in Spanish or amusing English; 2 hr.) that covers the endless collection of porcelain, tapestries, furniture, chandeliers, armor, and paintings. The palace is a virtual museum of decorative art, ranging from the baroque to the Victorian. The **Salón de Gasparini** is the embodiment of rococo taste, with porcelain objects featuring pseudo-Chinese motifs. In the eastern wing, the rooms decorated for Queen María Cristina are mostly from the nineteenth century, although the **Salón de Espejos** (Hall of Mirrors) incorporate quintessential neoclassicism. One of the most impressive rooms is the **Salón del Trono** (Throne Room); everything here is exactly as it was in the eighteenth century, with the exception of King Juan Carlos's and Queen Sofía's thrones, which are new. Notice Tiepolo's fresco on the ceiling, *Grandeza de la monarquía española con sus provincias y estados* (*Greatness of the Spanish Monarchy, with its Provinces and States*). Clock lovers will appreciate the hundreds of ornate timepieces arranged throughout the palace, most of them collected by Carlos IV. Other attractions include a massive sangria bowl, perhaps the largest in the world.

The **Biblioteca Real,** on the ground floor, contains an outstanding group of *incunabula,* a copy of the first edition of *Don Quixote,* and Don Juan Carlos's collection of coins and commemorative medals, as well as a music room that boasts several Stradivarius violins. The **Real Armería** (Armory) displays strangely exquisite instruments of medieval warfare and torture, including the swords of El Cid and the armor of Carlos V and Felipe II. The **Real Oficina de Farmacia** (Royal Pharmacy) features quaint crystal and china receptacles used to prepare royal medicinal concoctions. (Palace open, except during royal visits, Mon.-Sat. 9:30am-12:45pm and 4-5:45pm, Sun. 9:30am-12:45pm. Comprehensive ticket, which you can break down several ways, 300ptas, students 225ptas. To see everything in a ½-day, get here within the 1st hr. of opening; otherwise you will not be sold a ticket to both the Palacio and its satellite collections.)

Beautiful gardens and parks surround the Palacio Real. In front, across C. de Bailén, lies **Plaza de Oriente,** a small square dominated by the figure of Felipe IV rearing up on his stallion and clutching a royal proclamation in one hand. On either side of the encircling geometric hedges stand two small, wooded plazas. These are partially lined with statues of Spanish monarchs originally designed for the palace facade. Some say their current placement is due to their weight, but others claim that neoclassicists felt baroque statues would ruin the well-proportioned facade. In any case, the monarchs look rather disgruntled at having been relegated to the curb along with the parked tour buses. Notice the strange names of some of the Visigoth kings, e.g., Vilfredo el Belloso (Wilfred the Hairy One).

To the north stretch the serene **Jardines de Sabatini,** designed in the twentieth century to complement the palace's orderly eighteenth-century exterior. Behind the *palacio* is the lush and spotless **Campo del Moro,** opened to the public by Juan Carlos only 12 years ago. The view of the palace rising majestically on a dark green slope is thoroughly enchanting. (Open daily 10am-8pm. Enter on Paseo de la Virgen del Puerto.) An old greenhouse here houses the **Museo de Carruajes Reales,** a magical collection of eighteenth- and nineteenth-century horse-drawn carriages that belonged to the royal family. (Open Mon.-Sat. 10am-12:45pm and 4-5:45pm, Sun. 10am-12:45pm. Admission 75ptas.)

Nearby, on C. Pintor Rosales, **Parque del Oeste** (West Park) boasts the only Egyptian temple in Spain. The fourth-century B.C.E. **Templo de Debod** was a gift from the Egyptian government in appreciation of Spanish archeologists who helped rescue a series of monuments from advancing waters near the Aswan Dam. The temple is a golden-brown building fronted by a horseshoe-shaped pool with two arches in the center. In the back, a fountain moistens the view of expanding urbanization and rolling green hills beyond, most appealing when softened by the sunset. (Open Tues.-Fri. 10am-1pm and 4-7pm, Sat.-Sun. 10am-1pm. Admission 5ptas. Metro: Ventura Rodríguez or Plaza de España. Buses #1, 25, 33, 39.)

The *terrazas* (outdoor cafes) along nearby **Paseo de Rosales** provide a perfect place to collapse in the shade of evenly spaced trees. In the vicinity you can catch the cable car up to Madrid's largest park: the **Casa del Campo.** (*Teleférico,* or cable car, one way 185ptas, round-trip 260ptas.) The Casa del Campo features woods, shaded lanes, a municipal pool, an excellent zoo, and an amusement park. This vast expanse of green will make you feel like you have left the city far behind. (Metro: Lago or Batán. Bus #33 or 21.)

Coming back toward Parque del Oeste, you'll find, on Paseo de la Florida near the river, the **Ermitaño de San António de la Florida.** The frescoed ceilings in this small church are attributed to Goya. The cupola depicts the miracle of St. Anthony in a natural, vibrant vision of common people and customs. The artist, except for his head, is buried here. (Open Tues.-Fri. 10am-2pm and 5-9pm, Sat.-Sun. 10am-2pm; in off-season Tues.-Fri. 10am-2pm and 5-8pm., Sat.-Sun. 10am-2pm. Free.) Next door is the **Iglesia de San António,** a pretty white chapel where people flock during the festival of the church's namesake (June 1-17). It is said that if you light a candle in the chapel during the festival, you are sure to fall in love—soon, if not immediately. Don't light two candles unless you want your life to become *very* complicated. (Open daily 8am-1:30pm and 5:30-9pm. Free. Metro: Norte.)

Other Sights

Madrid Antiguo (Medieval Madrid)

When Felipe II decided to make the village of Madrid into the capital of his empire, most of the town was located between today's Plaza Mayor and the Palacio Real, flanked on the northern side by the Teatro Real and on the southern side by Pl. Puerta de Moros. Before that, the Catholic monarchs had ordered the walls built by Muhammed I to be torn down, which later facilitated the city's rapid expansion. Only a handful of buildings from that period remain, but the layout of some of the backstreets is distinctly that of an old Moorish medina.

Right at the heart of what was medieval Madrid is **Plaza de la Villa.** Legend has it that Francisco I was held prisoner following his capture at the Battle of Pavia in the **Torre de los Lujanes,** a fifteenth-century structure on the eastern side of the plaza. The tower is the sole remnant of the once lavish residence of the Lujanes family. Note the original horseshoe-shaped Gothic door on C. del Codo. The Mudéjar tower of **San Nicolás de los Servitas,** west of Pl. de la Villa, on C. de San Nicolas, is believed to date from the twelfth century. Its primitive minaret-type tower was transformed by the addition of a belfry topped by the typical Philippine spire prevalent in Madrid. This tower has a Mudéjar twin in the **Iglesia de San Pedro el Viejo,** south of Pl. de la Villa, on C. del Nuncio. (Metro: Latina. Buses # 31, 50, 65.) The tower at San Pedro, which is adjacent to a seventeenth-century church, leans away from its architectural companion, and its foundation had to be reinforced. (Both open daily 7am-noon and 7-9pm.)

One block south, on **Plaza de la Paja,** the city's main square before the Plaza Mayor was built, sits the imposing **Capilla del Obispo** (Bishop's Chapel), one of the few examples of architectural mannerism in Madrid. This highly elaborate style—a step in the direction of baroque—came into fashion at a time when Madrid was still an unimportant town and was not widely adopted by architects. The chapel was built in the early sixteenth century by Francisco de Vargas to house the remains of San Isidro, kept here from 1518 to 1544, when the chapel surrendered the saintly bones to its next-door neighbor, the **Iglesia de San Andrés.** The chapel is currently undergoing restoration, but you may be able to peer inside, where you'll see a magnificently carved polychrome altarpiece by Francisco Giralte, a disciple of Berruguete, and an equally impressive set of exquisitely detailed alabaster sculptures adorning the tombs of the Vargas family, also attributed to Giralte. At the time when the Vargas family was busy constructing the Capilla del Obispo, Hieronymite monks were also at work building a new monastery closer to town. With the help of the Catholic monarchs, they constructed the church known as **Iglesia de los San Jerónimos Reales** on a small hill that today overlooks the Prado. (Bus #10, 14, 15, 19, 34, 37, or 45.) The original Mudéjar brick construction was subsequently modified. King Alfonso XIII's royal wedding, the Oaths of the Princes of Asturias (heirs to the Crown), and even emergency parliamentary sessions have taken place here. There is not much remarkable about the interior of the church. (Open daily 6am-1pm and 6-8pm. The caretaker will kick you out promptly even if you're praying—or pretending to be.)

Madrid de los Austrias (Habsburg Madrid)

During the sixteenth and seventeenth centuries, when the Austrian dynasty ruled the Spanish empire, Madrid expanded explosively. In 1561 Felipe II moved his court here and turned the formerly peaceful hamlet into the labyrinthine heart of the vast bureaucracy that handled his ever-growing empire. By the time the Bourbons took possession of the Spanish throne, the city's surface area had doubled and its population increased as many as 10 times. The architectural legacy of the Habsburgs is certainly richer than the near-empty treasure coffers they left for their successors.

Madrid's cathedral and churches can't rival Barcelona's or León's, but some are nevertheless worthy of a visit. South of the Pl. Mayor, on C. de Toledo (metro: Latina; Bus #17, 23, 35, or 60), looms the mass of geometric angles known as the **Catedral de San Isidro,** a seventeenth-century church designed by Pedro Sánchez and Francisco Bautista, two Jesuit architects. In the gloomy interior, thin shafts of light squeeze their way through the small, stained-glass windows of the central dome, and the walls are covered with heavy gold leaf. The remains of San Isidro, the city's patron saint, finally came to rest here after being shuttled from church to church. Little is known about San Isidro except that he was a *labrador* (peasant). His lack of learning actually led to his becoming the new capital's patron saint: Conservative sixteenth-century Madrid frowned upon Jewish converts, who were associated with knowledge, and approved only of *cristianos viejos* (old Christians), who were generally considered uncultivated. (The church was reconstructed after it burnt down at the onset of the Civil War in 1936.)

Three other outstanding religious buildings of the period lie west of the Pl. Mayor. On your way to the post office, you may have admired the unusual, red-brown facade of the **Iglesia de Calatrava,** C. de Alcalá, 25. The church is all that remains of the huge Convento de la Concepción Real de Comendadoras. The Renaissance exterior contrasts sharply with the heavily baroque interior, which sports a cluttered altarpiece with polychrome statues, the work of Pablo González Velázquez. The type of cross that alternates with Carlos II's coat of arms as an ornamental motif is named after this church. (Open daily during Mass 7:30am-1pm and 6-8pm.) Much more impressive is the **Convento de las Descalzas Reales** at Pl. de las Desealzas Reales, west of Pl. Callao, between C. Mayor and Gran Vía (metro: Callao or Sol), a convent founded in 1559 by Juana de Austria, daughter of Emperor Carlos V. In the sixteenth and seventeenth centuries, the convent sheltered only women of royal blood, and thus acquired an exceptional collection of religious artwork—tapestries, paintings, sculptures, and liturgical objects. The 33 chapels of the upper cloister are especially rich, in particular the one by La Roldana, one of the few known women artists of the seventeenth century. The **Salon de Tapices** contains 12 tapestries based on drawings by Rubens. Other rooms hold paintings by Zurbarán, Breughel the Elder, Titian, and Rubens, as well as sculptures by Pedro de Mena. Mena's *La Dolorosa* is exceptional. Although cloistered nuns have inhabited the convent since 1559—residents have included such diverse personages as Empress Maria of Austria and Saint Teresa of Avila—the museum was opened to the public only in 1960. After four centuries, it deserves a look. (Open Tues.-Thurs. 10:30am-12:45pm and 4-5:15pm, Sat.-Sun. 11am-1:15pm. Admission 300ptas, students 225ptas.)

The art galleries of the **Convento de la Encarnación,** founded by Queen Margarita of Austria, harbor the historical painting, *Exchange of Princesses on the Bidasoa,* a depiction of the exchange on the Bidasoa River in the Pyrenees of Ana de Austria and Isabel de Borbón; Ana's hand had been promised to Louis XII of France and Isabel's to Felipe IV of Spain. The *relicuario* houses about 1500 relics of saints; the most famous one is the vial containing Saint Pantaleon's blood, which is supposed to liquefy every year on July 27. (Open same hours as Descalzas Reales. Admission with the same ticket.)

The needs of an expanding city prodded the authorities of early seventeenth-century Madrid to build a new home for the city hall north of Pl. Mayor on Pl. de la Villa. Architect Juan Gómez de Mora designed a graceful and elegant little palace in the baroque style then fashionable. The building, roofed with slate slabs and zinc plates, first doubled as the mayor's home and city jail. As Madrid kept growing, it became necessary to annex the neighboring **Casa de Cisneros,** a pleasant plateresque house built in the mid-sixteenth century. The elegant and sometimes gaudy interior of the **Casa de la Villa,** as the town hall is affectionately called, is now accessible to the public. Free guided tours (in Spanish) are offered every Monday at 5pm; they start at the Oficina de Información, Pl. de la Villa, 5. Farther north on C. Mayor, you will run into another example of Hapsburg *madrileño* architecture, the former **Palacio del Duque de Uceda,** also designed by Gómez de Mora. It is now the **Capitanía General,** occupied by the Army. This building is not open to the public; furthermore, overly nervous guards are uneasy about anybody staring at this military installation for too long. Southwest of the Pl. Mayor, on Pl. de la Santa Cruz, you will find a better, more accessible example of the Spanish Habsburg style, the **Cárcel de Corte** (Court Jail), which today houses the **Ministerio de Asuntos Exteriores** (Foreign Relations). Ask the guard to let you look inside. The precise, clear-headed harmony between the building's exterior and its internal design is remarkable. The Plaza Mayor is also a product of Habsburg Madrid. (See Major Sights.)

Madrid de los Borbones (Bourbon Madrid)

Carlos II's death marked the end of Habsburg rule in Spain. Felipe V, the first king of the French Bourbon family to rule Spain, was faced with bankruptcy, industrial stagnation, military incompetence, mercantile ruin, and widespread moral disillusionment. Madrid reflected all aspects of the empire's decline. Undaunted by the seemingly impossible task in front of him, Felipe V successfully applied a French-style plan of urban rejuvenation and reorganization that was continued with equal zest by his successors, Fernando VI and Carlos III, during the eighteenth century. Madrid as we know it today, from the Palacio Real on the west to the Museo del Prado and Parque del Retiro on the east, is the direct result of reforms effected by the Bourbons.

The majestic **Basílica de San Francisco el Grande,** at Pl. de San Francisco el Grande, down Carrera de San Francisco and a five-minute walk from the Pl. Mayor, is a late eighteenth-century neoclassical edifice built by Francisco Cabezas, Antonio Plo, and Francisco Sabatini during the renovating spree that marked the reign of Carlos III. The somber interior of the temple was largely created by the artists, including Goya and Zurbarán, who painted the seven interior domes. Tradition has it that St. Francis built an earlier convent on this site in the thirteenth century. (Open Tues.-Sat. 11am-1pm and 4-7pm. Admission with optional brief tour in Spanish. Metro: Puerta de Toledo or Latina. Bus #3, 60, C.)

The **Basílica de San Miguel,** on C. Sacramento, betrays the Italian training of its designer Guarino Guarini. A bas-relief portrays the Spanish saints, Justus and Pastor, while four large statues represent Charity, Strength, Faith, and Hope. Inside, light filters through the blue windows onto light blue marble, lending an ethereal air to the marble pillars and cherubim.

The Bourbon monarchs, striving to combine practicality with their aesthetics, set out to improve the gates and bridges to the city, creating some of modern Madrid's better-known landmarks. The wide **Puente de Toledo,** the beginning of the road to Toledo, lies at the end of C. de Toledo, beyond the Puerta de Toledo. It replaced a series of rickety bridges spanning the banks of the Manzanares River. Sandstone carvings on one side depict San Isidro rescuing his son from a well; on the other is a portrayal of San Isidro's wife, the equally saintly Santa María de la Cabeza.

The **Iglesia de las Salesas Reales,** at Pl. de las Salesas on C. Bárbara de Braganza, across from the Biblioteca Nacional, was built by Fernando VI at the request of his wife Doña Bárbara in 1758. The church's ostentatious facade and lavish interior were the target of sharp criticism by *madrileños* accustomed to more sobriety. Critics coined an acrimonious criticism of the building, playing with the double meaning of the queen's name in Spanish: "Barbaric queen, barbaric tastes, barbaric building, barbarous expense." Both Fernando VI and his barbaric wife are buried here. (Metro: Colon.)

The Puerta del Sol, Puerta de Alcalá, Fuente de la Cibeles, Fuente de Apolo, Fuente de Neptuno, and Palacio Real were all creations of Bourbon Madrid. (See Major Sights.)

Madrid del Siglo XIX (Nineteenth-Century Madrid)

The defeat of Napoleon's invading armies in 1808 gave Spaniards only a short-lived sense of power. Soon after Fernando VII was back on the throne, Spain lost most of its Latin American colonies and the country slid into a century of mediocrity. By the end of the nineteenth century, Spain had no overseas possessions except for Morocco, having lost Cuba, Puerto Rico, and the Philippines in the war of 1898.

Most of the notable buildings constructed in the nineteenth century attempted to recapture the grandeur slipping away from Spain. The majestic **Banco de España,** Alcalá, 50, just off Pl. de Cibeles, was built in 1891 by Adaro and Sainz de Lastra. Nearby, at Jovellanos, 3, between San Jerónimo and Alcalá, is the **Teatro de la Zarzuela,** home of the Spanish-style operetta genre. The theater's layout is an exact copy of Milano's La Scala. The **Royal Academy** of the Spanish language is housed in a nineteenth-century building between the Prado and Casón del Buen Retiro. They may let you peep inside, where the erudite members work on solemn dark wood tables and meet to decide what is correct Spanish and what ain't. Not far from here, on Paseo del Prado north of the museum, stands the **Obélico a los Mártires del 2 de mayo,** a memorial containing the ashes of the heroes of the 1808 uprising, who died fighting against Napoleon's troops. Juan Carlos I lit an eternal flame on the site. Right next to the memorial is the **Bolsa de Madrid,** the city's stock exchange. Like other buildings of this period, it was copied from a foreign design, that of the Vienna stock exchange.

The nineteenth century also witnessed the growth of several neighborhoods around the core of the city, north and northwest of the Palacio Real. Today, the area known as **Argüelles** and the zone surrounding **Calle San Bernardo** are a cluttered mixture of working-class and student housing, bohemian hangouts, and cultural activities. The best way to get a feeling for this area is to wander along its old cobblestoned streets. Argüelles was heavily bombarded during the Civil War, inspiring Pablo Neruda, then a resident, to write his famous poem *España en el corazón.* Be aware that the area around Pl. 2 de Mayo is Madrid's drug-dealing center and is dangerous at night.

Take time to check out the imposing **Cuartel del Conde Duque,** on C. Conde Duque, built in 1720 as headquarters for the Guard de Corps and later used by Franco's dreaded secret police. It is now undergoing extensive renovation; it should be open to the public within a few years. Part of the building is used for plays, ballet performances, and other exhibits. Behind the *cuartel* is the **Palacio de Liria,** C. Princesa, 20. The lovely estate of the Duchess of Alba, the palace specializes in fifteenth- and sixteenth-century painting. The Italian Renaissance collection is particularly noteworthy. (Closed for renovation. Call ahead. Metro: Ventura Rodríguez.)

Parks and squares extend north and east of here. In **Plaza de España,** the olive trees that surround the grandiose monument to Cervantes are perhaps the only aspect of the plaza the writer would have appreciated. Next to the square are two of Madrid's tallest skyscrapers, the **Torre de Madrid** and the **Edificio de España.** Both offer superb views of Madrid. You may have to buy a drink at the *edifio's* small cafe on the 26th floor, but the beautiful panorama is worth it. (Open noon to early evening.)

West of Pl. Colón are the sunny **Jardines del Descubrimiento.** In the gardens, huge clay and cement boulders are covered with inscriptions related to the discovery of the New World, including Seneca's prediction of the discovery, the names of all the mariners on board the caravels and quotations from Columbus's diary. The sheer size of the boulders, separated and connected by water, and the texts are inspiring. Below the gardens lies the **Centro Cultural de la Villa,** where concerts, lectures, plays, and other cultural events take place. On its front, facing a noisy and refreshing waterfall, a large map details the discoverer's voyages to America. A more traditional monument to Columbus stands directly above the Centro Cultural.

The **Ciudad Universitaria** extends to the northwest of Madrid beyond the Parque del Oeste. A battleground in the Civil War and a center of resistance during the fascist period, the university now enjoys a more placid pace. Its many schools and technical institutes are scattered throughout the large wooded campus.

In the 1860s Madrid's old walls were torn down to build a more modern district. The elegant **Barrio de Salamanca** was the result. The brainchild of the enterprising Marqués de Salamanca, its architecture is not as beautiful as that of Barcelona's Eixample (no bold art nouveau structures here), but its shady, boutique-lined streets—Serrano, Príncipe de Vergara, Velázquez, Goya, Ortega y Gasset—are Madrid's best answer to New York's Fifth Avenue. Here, you will find the finest in high fashion and hunting gear. Salamanca has a reputation for being Madrid's most *facha* (conservative) district.

Near Atocha train station in the southern corner of central Madrid is the new **Centro de Arte Reina Sofía,** C. Santa Isabel, 52. Formerly the Hospital Provincial, this pink, art deco building houses no permanent art collection, but features rotating exhibits. (Open Wed.-Mon. 10am-9pm. Admission 400ptas, students free. Art films in Spanish at noon and 4:30pm, 150ptas. Metro: Atocha.)

Other Museums

After extensive restoration of its building and artwork, the **Museo de la Real Academia de Bellas Artes de San Fernando,** Alcalá, 13, recently opened its doors to a public eager to see the most important collection of paintings in Madrid after that of the Prado. The fantastic wealth of canvases include works by such masters as El Greco, Goya, Velázquez, Rubens, Sorolla, and Zurbarán. Outstanding canvases include El Greco's *Saint Hyeronimus,* Tiepolo's *Old Man's Head,* and Ribera's disturbing *Ecce Homo.* The unbelievable Goya collection features the carnivalesque *Entierro de la sardina,* the eerie *Escena de inquisición,* a few self-portraits, and the last palette the artist ever used. (Open Tues.-Sat. 9am-7pm, Sun.-Mon. 9am-2pm. Admission 200ptas. Metro: Sol or Sevilla.)

North of Pl. de las Cibeles, near Pl. Colón, the **Biblioteca Nacional,** Paseo Recoletos, 20, displays treasures taken from monarchs' private collections including a copy of the first edition of *Don Quixote.* (Open Mon.-Sat. 9am-1:30pm and 4:30-7pm. Admission 25ptas. Metro: Colón or Serrano. Bus #1, 9, 19, 51, 53, or M-2.) In the same building, the **Museo Arqueológico Nacional** offers glimpses of Spain's distant past. A life-size reproduction of the prehistoric cave painting in Altamira lies in the garden. The rooms of Iberian antiquities are the most interesting; the mysterious, beautiful *Dama de Elche* is a B.C.E. Greta Garbo. Ashes of the cremated dead were deposited in the large *Dama de Baza,* a fourth-century statue found in a tomb in the province of Granada. The small, elaborately carved *Diosa Tánit* is a Carthaginian goddess. Other rooms house the votive crowns of Visigoth kings, ivories from Muslim Andalucía, Romanesque and Gothic sculptures, Celtiberian silver and gold items, and Roman and Greek art. (Open Tues.-Sun. 9:15am-2:45pm. Admission 200ptas, students free. Tickets valid for 2 days.) The entrance to the library is on Paseo de Recoletos, but you must enter the museum from the back at C. Serrano, 13.

The **Museo Lázaro Galdiano,** C. Serrano, 122, is housed in a turn-of-the-century palace that once belonged to a well-known patron of the arts. Its wonderful collections are perhaps Madrid's best-kept museum secret. Among its treasures are a twelfth-century French ivory Virgin, ancient jewels, Celtic bronze objects, and a bronze head attributed to Leonardo da Vinci. Paintings by Bosch, Cranach, Murillo, Claudio Coello, Rembrandt, and Van Dyck vie for attention. English art is well represented by Gainsborough, Reynolds, Hoppner, Constable, and Turner. (Open Sept.-July Tues.-Sun. 10am-2pm. Admission 150ptas. Metro: Serrano or Avenida America.)

Most of the **Museo de América,** Avda. Reyes Católicos, 4, near Avda. Puerta de Hierro and just north of the C. Princesa junction, is usually closed, but it does host frequent art expositions, usually well publicized by the media. If you're lucky enough to catch the museum when it's open, you're in for a treat of pre-Hispanic art. The collection draws mostly from Mexico and Peru. (Open Tues.-Sun. 10am-2pm Tues. free. Metro: Moncloa.) A few hundred meters down Avda. Arco de la Victoria, at Avda. Juan de Herrera, is the **Museo de Arte Contemporáneo.** A sculpture garden and refreshing fountain introduce this shiny modern building. Inside, you will find the unsettling talents of Picasso, Miró, and Dalí. Look for Picasso's series of three paintings entitled *El pintor y el modelo* (*The Painter and the Model*) for a fascinating study of the odd nature of this relationship. The museum also houses two of Dalí's important early works, *Muchacha de espaldas* (*Girl from Behind*) and *Muchacha en la ventana* (*Girl in the Window*), in which the eerie lighting contributes to a vaguely disturbing vision of the world. The collection includes many enthralling paintings by Miró, including *La Vieja ostrera* (*The Old Oyster Vendor*). Don't miss the work of José Solana and Julio González Pellicer. Among the many sculptors represented in the museum are Alberto Sánchez (see *El gallo y la gallina—The Cock and the Hen*), Eduardo Chillida, and Julio Hernández. (Open Tues.-Sat. 10am-6pm, Sun. 10am-3pm. Admission 200ptas, students free.) Downstairs, the smaller exhibition hall hosts temporary displays. (Open same hours. Free.)

The **Museo Romántico,** C. San Mateo, 13, depicts domestic life in nineteenth-century Madrid, including a decaying but quiet garden. Converted from a count's palace to a museum in 1924, the Museo Romántico houses not only an extensive collection of nineteenth-century painting, but also an exceptional collection of prints and lithographs of Madrid from the same period. Also worth seeing are the collection of photographs and the rare musical instruments. Domestic objects in the museum range from the extremely delicate and tasteful to the shockingly tacky, such as the velvet-lined, gold-filled, throne-like toilet *ensemble,* complete with a selection of bathroom readings. Look for the French screen fitted with movable illustrated glass panes, a predecessor of animation. (Open mid-Sept. to July Tues.-Sat. 10am-5pm, Sun. 10am-2pm. Admission 200ptas. Metro: Alonso Martínez or Tribunal.)

The **Museo Municipal,** C. Fuencarral, 78, houses works of art, models, and writings that trace the burgeoning of Madrid into an urban center. The ornate front doorway was designed by Pedro de Ribera. (Open Tues.-Sat. 10am-2pm, Sun. 10am-3pm. Free. Metro: Tribunal.)

The little-known **Museo Sorolla,** Paseo General Martínez Campos, 37, was the home and studio of the celebrated nineteenth-century Spanish painter from Valencia. Sorolla's seaside paintings, as well as his lovely garden, make for a refreshing break from the more crowded museums. Here, you can see some of his best works, including *Paseo a orillas del mar* (*Seaside Promenade*), and his studies of Spanish people and customs. The artist's *Joaquina la gitana* (*The Gypsy Joaquina*) combines a subtle sense of psychology with a careful portrayal of Spanish folk culture. (Open Sept.-July Tues.-Sun. 10am-2pm. Admission 200ptas, students free. Metro: Iglesia.)

The **Museo de Artes Decorativas,** C. Montalbán, 12, displays an interesting collection of ceramics, leatherwork, gold- and silverwork, tapestries, and rugs from many periods. (Open Tues.-Fri. 10am-5pm, Sat.-Sun. 10am-2pm. Admission 200ptas, students free. Metro: Banco de España.)

Nearby, the **Museo Naval,** C. Montalbán, 2, features maritime objects associated with the battle of Lepanto and the discovery of America. The map made by Juan de la Costa in 1500 was the first to chart North America. (Open Sept.-July Tues.-Sun. 10:30am-1:30pm. Admission 50ptas.) In a more militaristic vein, the **Museo del Ejército,** at C. Méndez Núñez, 1, near El Prado, contains war trophies, banners, insignia, and similar paraphernalia. As a sign that times have indeed changed in Spain, the boastful display of artillery in front of the museum has been quietly carted away. (Open Tues.-Sat. 10am-5pm, Sun. 10am-3pm. Admission 50ptas. Metro: Retiro or Atocha.)

There's a lot of bull at the **Museo Taurino,** C. Alcalá, 237, at Pl. Monumental de Las Ventas-Patio de Caballos. It's a remarkable collection of *trajes de luces,* capes, posters of famous *corridas,* souvenirs from the greatest *matadores,* some historical information on bullfighting, and a lot of *trivia taurina.* (Open Tues.-Fri. and Sun. 9am-2:30pm. Free. On bullfight days it opens 1 hr. before the *lidia.* Metro: Ventas.)

Ironically, the **Casa de Lope de Vega** is located at C. de Cervantes, 11. The prolific playwright of the Spanish Golden Age and the author of *Don Quixote* were the worst of enemies, and Lope de Vega would have abhorred the idea of his street being renamed after his archrival. His house is worth a visit not only because Lope de Vega wrote many of his works here, but also because it's a fine example of a typical seventeenth-century *madrileño* residence. (Open Aug. 15-July 15 Tues. and Thurs. 10am-2pm. Admission 75ptas. Metro: Antón Martin. Bus #10, 14, 24, 27, 37, 45, or M-6.)

Off the western corner of Pl. de España, you will find the engaging **Museo de Cerralbo,** Ventura Rodríguez, 17, a small palace with an eclectic collection of paintings, drawings, etchings, armor, coins, and a library of rare volumes. (Open Wed.-Mon. 9am-2pm. Admission 200ptas. Groups over 5 pay half-price. Metro: Place de España or Ventura Rodríguez. Bus #1, 2, 44, or C.)

Entertainment

Madrid lives by night. Every evening after work, *madrileños* go out to *dar una vuelta* or take an evening stroll. The tradition is most visible on Sundays from 7 to 9pm, when the boulevards (particularly Paseo del Prado and Gran Vía) are filled with elegantly dressed *novios* and lined with watchful older couples.

Late-night entertainment can mean whiling away long hours in one of the old-fashioned cafes or skipping from bar to bar for a *copa de vino*—a surprisingly social and sober experience. The *Guia del Ocio* (60ptas at any kiosk) provides complete entertainment listings—restaurants and clubs as well as movies, shows, and theater.

Boulevards

Madrid's boulevards provide the perfect setting for a favorite Spanish pastime: teeming crowds come to see and be seen while maintaining a most civilized, relaxed attitude: **Paseos del Prado, Recoletos,** and **Castellana** form a long tree-lined strip where *madrileños* go for an evening stroll, a drink, and some quiet—or not-so-quiet—conversation. These boulevards, with huge medians, are covered by increasing numbers of outdoor cafes, *terrazas,* or *chiringuitos,* as they are sometimes called. Generally, the closer you get to the Castellana, the more fashionable the spot. The "in" spots change every summer, and they vie for pedestrians' attention by hiring all sorts of entertainment. Walking along Recoletos, you'll see small five-piece bands playing *pasodobles,* young generic singers, flamenco guitarists, Spanish balladeers ruining romantic Latin American songs with their thick Castilian accents, jugglers, and—of course—mimes. But these streets don't have a monopoly on *terrazas.* **Plaza de Santa Bárbara** and **Calle Serrano** also enter the competition. At C. Alcalá, 43, is one of the best *terrazas,* outside the recently reopened **Círculo de Bellas Artes.**

At this beautiful, art deco building, aficionados gather to discuss the evening's bull-fight in sessions that may last all night or end in pugilistic endeavors.

Just off the south side of the Pl. Mayor, you will be lured to the **Rastro,** a monstrous flea market where antiques and second-hand goods abound—as do pickpockets and gypsy street shows. Individual side streets specialize in pets, household tools, and books. (Sun. and holidays 9am-2pm. Metro: Latina. From Pl. Mayor, take C. de Toledo to Pl. de Cascorro, where the market begins. It ends at the bottom of C. Ribera de Curtidores.)

Cafes

The cafes along **Paseo de Rosales, Paseo de Recoletos, Plaza de Santa Bárbara, Plaza de Santa Ana,** and the **Plaza Mayor** are particularly lively. Madrid's bars, *mesones,* and "pubs" are concentrated in the **Lavapies, Argüelles,** and especially on **Calle de las Huertas** and **Calle de Manuel y González** (metro: Sol or Antón Martín). If you are short on money, stock up in the wine department before the stores close. A nice bottle of *vino tinto* (red wine) won't set you back more than 300ptas.

Viva Madrid, C. Manuel Fernández González, 7 (tel. 467 46 45), next to Pl. de Santa Ana. Metro: Antón Martin. U.S. expatriate hangout. Wonderful tiles and animals carved in wood. Rafael Albertí drew an ink picture in honor of this place: Look for it behind the bar. *Canapés* 470ptas, *thé* 370ptas, juice 210ptas. Open Sun-Fri. noon-1:30am, Sat. noon-2am.

Café Central, Pl. del Angel, 10 (tel. 468 08 44), off Pl. de Santa Ana. Metro: Antón Montin or Sol. Free potato chips and olives. Live jazz music nightly 10pm-2am. Open Mon.-Thurs. 1pm-2am, Fri.-Sun. 1pm-3am. Cover charge Mon.-Thurs. 250ptas, Fri.-Sun. 300ptas.

La Fídula, C. de las Huertas, 57 (tel. 429 29 47), near Paseo del Prado. Quiet place to relax and listen to live classical music. Coffee 215ptas, wine 200ptas. Cover for musical performances (11:30pm) 175ptas. Open Sun.-Thurs. 7pm-1:45am, Fri.-Sat. 6:30pm-2:45am.

Café-Bar Hidria, C. de Jesús, 14. Always packed with a local crowd. Loud music blasts from speakers. Open nightly 7pm-3am.

Champañería Gala, C. Moratín, 24, at Costanilla de Desamparados. Metro: Antón Martin. A classy place to sample champagne at 180ptas per *copa.* Open daily 7pm-3am.

Albatros Glu Glu, C. de las Huertas, 65 (tel. 429 56 64), next to the Prado. Metro: Antón Martin or Atocha. Upwardly mobile *madrileños* come here to sip sangria and relax on the comfy couch in a smoke-filled room in back. Non-alcoholic drinks 175ptas, mixed drinks 300ptas. Open nightly 7pm-2am.

El Oso y el Madroño, C. de la Bolsa, 4 (tel. 522 13 77). A hand organ and old photos of Madrid. Try the potent *Licor de Madroño,* a berry-flavored Spanish liquer. Open daily 8pm-midnight.

Café Gijón, Paseo de Recoletos, 21. Metro: Colón. Choose between a breezy terrace and a smoky bar-restaurant. Long a favorite of the literati, now filled with bankers. People bring their books here to study and their friends to talk. Open daily noon-midnight.

Café Comercial, Glorieta de Bilbao, 7 (tel. 531 34 72). Metro: Bilbao. Traditional cafe with high ceilings and huge mirrors. A/C. Frequented by artists and Republican aviators alike. Under Franco, protests started here. Frequent *tertulias* (gatherings of literati and intellectuals). Sandwiches from 150ptas. Beer only 70ptas. Open daily 11am-midnight.

At night, the area around **Malasaña** and **Plaza 2 de Mayo** (metro: Bilbao) is one of Madrid's unsafest: Come here accompanied and hold your belongings tightly. In recent years, this area has become a center of drug deals and thefts. At the same time, however, this section of the city becomes a nightly playground for street musicians, hippies, intellectuals, and bohemians. The following places will allow you to join in the fun.

Bodegas el Maño, C. Jesus del Valle, 1. This enchanting place dates from 1890. The owner is friendly and the ancient wine casks fascinating. Try the *fino* (125ptas). Open daily 7pm-1:30am.

Tetería de la Abuela, C. Espíritu Santo, 19, off Pl. 2 de Mayo. Metro: Noviciado. Herbal teas to cure anything (100-150ptas). Crepes and tarts as well. Open daily 7:30pm-1:30am.

Manuela, C. San Vicente Ferrer, 29 (tel. 531 70 37). Metro: Bilbao or Tribunal. Intellectuals seem to live here. Attractive, with mirrors and live music—usually folk songs. Wine 200ptas. Cover for performances 300-400ptas per table. Open daily 6:30pm-3:30am.

Fashionable *terrazas de verano* include **Amnesia,** Castellana, 93, for the more sophisticated crowd; a no-name establishment at Castellana, 21, for the post-mod squad; **El Chiringuito de la Bolsa,** in front of the Stock Exchange Building; **Paseo del Prado,** for a varied assortment of *madrileño* youths; and **El Espejo,** Recoletos, 31, featuring a little orchestra and mixed-age clientele. The action usually starts around 10:30pm. **Ella's,** San Dimas, 3, on the corner of Palma (metro: Noviciado) is a *terraza* popular with lesbians. Gay men can try **Elle et Lui,** Traversía de Parada, 6, on the corner of San Bernardo near Gran Vía (metro: Callao or Pl. de España).

Theaters

Madrid seethes with cultural activities. In summer, the city sponsors free movies, plays, and concerts. The *Guía del Ocio* (75ptas from newsstands) and the *Villa de Madrid* (100ptas from bus-ticket kiosks) list all these activities. In July and August, free movies are shown nightly at 11pm in the **Parque del Retiro.** The **Plaza Mayor, Plaza de Lavapiés, Plaza Villa de París,** and others all host frequent concerts and plays. For foreign films, check the **Filmoteca,** C. Princesa, 1 (tel. 247 16 57; metro: Banco de España). Tickets run 400ptas. Also try **Alphaville,** C. Martin de los Heroes, 14 (tel. 248 45 24; metro Pl. de España), which often features English-language films with Spanish subtitles. (Admission 400ptas.) Films advertised as "V.O." (*versión original*) are screened in the original language with Spanish subtitles. Most movie houses have three showings per day: at 4:30pm, 7:30pm, and 10:30pm. In general, tickets are 350-475ptas.

Teatro Español, C. Principe, 25 (tel. 429 03 18; for hours and tickets 429 62 97). Metro: Sevilla. Classical plays. Tickets 700ptas.

Teatro Maravillas, C. Manuela Malasaña, 6 (tel. 447 41 35). Metro: Bilbao. Plays. Tickets 600ptas, 900ptas, or 1100ptas.

Sala Olimpia, Pl. de Lavapies (tel. 227 46 22). Metro: Lavapies. Plays. Tickets 700ptas.

Teatro de Círculo de Bellas Artes, C. Alcalá, 42 (tel. 221 18 34). Metro: Banco de España.

Teatro María Guerrero, C. Tamayo y Baus, 4 (tel. 419 47 69). Metro: Banco de España. Plays. Tickets 900ptas.

Cine Gran Vía, Gran Vía, 66. Metro: Callao. Popular U.S. and Spanish films. Tickets 450ptas.

Music

Classical music concerts frequently occur in the **Teatro Real,** Carlos III (tel. 248 38 75; metro: Opera). The **Fundación Juan March,** C. Castelló, 77 (tel. 435 42 40; metro: Núñez de Balboa), usually holds free weekly concerts. The **Conservatorio Superior de Música,** Pl. Isabel II, near the Palacio Real, often presents free student performances, professional traveling orchestras, and celebrated soloists. For opera and *zarzuela,* go to the **Teatro de la Zarzuela,** C. Jovellanos, 4 (tel. 429 12 86; metro: Banco de España). For tangos, try **Cambalache,** C. San Lorenzo, 5 (tel. 410 07 01; metro: Manso Martínez or Tribunal). You can find live tangos, Argentinian food, and drinks at the bar daily from 10pm to 5am for no cover charge.

Flamenco in Madrid is tourist-oriented and expensive, but often fun. Try **Arco de Cuchilleros,** C. Cuchilleros, 7 (tel. 266 58 67; metro: Sol), just off the Pl. Mayor, which features some emotive guitarists and stamping dancers with beautiful dresses. The seating area is smaller than most, making the show very intimate. The 1600ptas cover includes the show and one drink; subsequent drinks, both alcoholic and non-alcoholic, are 700ptas. (Two shows per day at 10:30pm and 12:30am. No dining.) *Madrileños* say that the most authentic flamenco show takes place at **Torres Bermejas,** C. Mesonero Romanos, 11 (tel. 532 33 22 or 531 03 53; metro: Callas). The cover is 2300ptas. Three dinner *menús* (5500ptas, 6500ptas, and 7500ptas) are avail-

able for the earlier of the two shows. (Open 9:30pm-2:30am.) You can also witness
this Andalusian tradition at **Café de Chinitas, C.** Torrija, 7 (tel. 248 51 35; metro:
Santo Domingo) for 3000ptas, for 8000ptas you can have dinner as well. (Open
Mon.-Sat. 10:45pm-2:30am.)

Discos are popular but hard on the budget. There are so many of them in Madrid
that there just isn't enough money around to keep them full every night. Many discos have "afternoon" sessions (usually 7-10pm, cover 250-700ptas) and "night" sessions (11:30pm-3:30am, cover up to 1200ptas). Men are usually charged 200ptas
more than women. The *entrada* sometimes includes a drink. Be warned that in many
of the *discotecas,* and in even more of the *salas de fiesta,* the dancing alternates with
"shows" during which you are supposed to take a seat and watch. These can range
from stand-up comics to poor magicians to "sex shows" (plays in the nude). After
dancing 'til the wee hours (you'll be considered a party-pooper if you leave before
5am), Spanish tradition requires that you go out for *churros* (tube-shaped pastries)
and chocolate (thick and served in a cup to dip your *churros* in). One popular
churros-chewery is on C. Atocha, next to the disco Joy Eslava.

> **Joy Eslava, C.** Arenal, 11 (tel. 266 37 33 or 266 54 69). Metro: Sol or Opera. Where *ma-*
> *drileños* go. A 3-tiered theater turned disco. 3 bars, laser lights, videoscreen, and live enter-
> tainment. Young crowd, disco music. Cover 1500ptas. Open daily 7-10pm and 11:30pm-
> 5:30am.
>
> **Pacha, C.** Barcelo, 11 (tel. 446 01 37). Metro: Tribunal or Bilbao. Come here to rub shoulders
> with the jet set; hope your wallet is as thick as theirs. Cover 2500ptas. Open Sun.-Thurs.
> evenings, Fri.-Sat. afternoons and evenings.
>
> **Titanic, C.** Atocha, 125 (tel. 228 76 27). Metro: Atocha. 3 dance areas, each with different
> music, videos, bar, and pub. Open Thurs.-Sat. 6pm-midnight, Sun. 6-11pm.
>
> **Oba-Oba, C.** Jacometrezo, 4 (tel. 221 97 59). Metro: Callao. Brazilian music and tropical
> drinks. Try the *caipirinha.*
>
> **Bocaccio, C.** Marques de la Ensenada, 16 (tel. 419 10 08). Metro: Colón. Intellectuals dance
> flamenco here late at night. Open Sun.-Thurs. 7-10pm and 11:30pm-4:30am, Fri.-Sat. 7-10pm
> and 11:30pm-5am.

Toros

Bullfights—and bullfighters—are loved or loathed. If the crowd thinks the matador is a man of mettle, they will exalt him to the level of Juan Carlos. If they think
him a coward, they'll whistle cacophanously, chant "Váyate" (Leave!), throw their
seat cushions (40ptas to rent) at him, and wait outside the ring to stone his car.
A top *matador* may receive over three million pesetas per bullfight (US$25,000).
But a bullfighter's coffer cannot shield him from critical reviews in the next morning's *El País.* A bloody killing of the bull, instead of the desired swift death-stab,
can upset the career of even the most renowned matador.

Corridas (bullfights) are held during the Festival of San Isidro and usually every
other Sunday during the rest of the year. If you can stomach the killing of six beautiful *toros bravos* (and occasionally a reckless matador), keep your eyes open for posters advertising upcoming fights in bars and cafes (especially on C. de la Victoria,
off Carrera San Jerónimo), or inquire at either ticket office listed below. **Plaza de
las Ventas, C.** de Alcalá, 237, northeast of central Madrid, is the biggest bullring
in the country. (Metro: Ventas. Bus #21, 53, or 110.) Even if you leave by metro
or bus 1½ hours before the fight, you'll have a rather asphyxiating trip. Tickets
are usually available on the Saturday before and the Sunday of the bullfight. Typically, there are two bullfights, one in the afternoon and one in the early evening.
Ticket outlets are located at C. de la Victoria, 3, off Carrera San Jerónimo, east
of Puerta del Sol (metro: Sol), and Pl. de Toros, C. de Alcalá, 237 (metro: Ventas).
A seat in the monumental bullring runs 225-6600ptas. To give this unparalleled
spectacle a fair chance, go with someone who can tell you a bit about what's going
on in the ring. Beware of ticket scalpers outside the plaza, although they are sometimes the only source of *entradas* for a good *cartel* (seat).

From mid-to-late May, the **Fiestas of San Isidro** bring a bullfight each day with top *toreros* (bullfighters) and brawny bulls. The festival is nationally televised; if you don't have a ticket, slip into a bar. Aficionados hang out at **Bar El Pavón,** C. de la Victoria, 8, at C. de la Cruz (metro: Sol); **El Abuelo,** on C. Núñez de Arce, where *fanáticos* (fans) reportedly brandish the restaurant's famous shrimp during arguments over bullfighters' *parar* (style); and **Bar Torre del Oro,** Pl. Mayor, 26 (tel. 266 50 16; metro: Sol or Opera; open daily 10am-2am).

Festivals

Madrid's **Carnaval,** prohibited during Franco's dictatorship, has resurfaced as never before. Recent scholarship suggests that the *carnaval* was inaugurated by Christians in the Middle Ages. From late February to early April, street fiestas with dancing and processions dot the city. The celebration culminates with the "Burial of the Sardine." In late April, the city comes alive with the famous **Festival Internacional de Teatro.** The month-long **Fiestas de San Isidro,** in honor of Madrid's patron saint, bring concerts and parades, and attract Spain's best bullfighters. The fiestas kick off a slew of lesser celebration in May. In summer, the city sponsors the **Veranos de la Villa,** an outstanding variety of cultural activities, including free classical music concerts, movies in open-air settings, plays, art exhibits, an international film festival, opera and *zarzuela,* ballet, and sports. In August, there is a flurry of typical *madrileñismo,* as the quintessentially local *barrios* of **San Cayetano, San Lorenzo,** and **La Paloma** celebrate their own festivities with renewed zest. Don't miss the processions, street dancing, traditional games, food, and drink; when combined with breakdancing, home-grown hard rock, and political slogans, they form a multifaceted microcosm of the new *"Madrí."* In October, the **Festivales de Otoño** (Autumn Festivals) also bring an impressive array of music, theater, and film to the city.

For information on future fiesta attractions, write to Patronato Municipal de Turismo, Sres. de Luzón, 28103 Madrid. The brochure *Las Fiestas de España* offers historical background and general information.

Near Madrid

Sierra de Guadarrama: Cercedilla

A pine-covered mountain range halfway between Madrid and Segovia, the Sierra de Guadarrama is perhaps the most beautiful area in central Spain. Particularly attractive are the town of Cercedilla and the breathtaking mountain pass of Puerto de Navacerrada; it's fairly easy to visit both on a daytrip from Madrid.

Cercedilla is a town of picturesque alpine chalets and cows peacefully grazing on the surrounding hillsides. If you're weary of museums, you'll be pleased to discover that Cercedilla monuments and possesses not even one Romanesque church; the most exciting event in the town's history is a cursory mention in Quevedo's seventeenth-century picaresque novel *El Buscón.* Come here for a respite from high art, but be advised that on summer weekends most of Madrid will join you.

Orientation and Practical Information

Cercedilla is about 90 minutes from Madrid on the Madrid-Segovia line (430ptas). To get to town from the train station, walk uphill and follow the signs to *Centro Urbano.* It's a 12-minute walk, but travelers with luggage may prefer to catch a cab since it's uphill.

Post Office: C. Marquesa Casa Lopez, 9 (tel. 852 05 91). A tiny building tucked away below the road. Go down the stairs from the road and turn left. Open Mon.-Fri. 9am-2pm, Sat. 9am-1pm.

Telephones: Payphones on the Pl. Mayor, across from the police station. **Telephone Code:** 910.

Train Station: Estación RENFE, C. Emiliano Serrano (tel. 852 00 57). Open daily 5:30am-11:30pm. To Madrid (13 per day, 1 hr., 290ptas), Segovia (11 per day, 1¾ hr., 460ptas), Los Cotos (11 per day, 15 min., 80ptas), and Puerto de Navacerrada (11 per day, 10 min., 60ptas).

Bus Station: Avda. Jose Antonio, 2 (tel. 852 02 39).

Taxis: At Estación RENFE (tel. 852 03 24).

Hospital: Carretera Las Dehesas (tel. 852 12 04).

Police: Ayuntamiento, Pl. Mayor, 1 (tel. 852 02 00 or 852 04 25). Call here for an **ambulance.**

Accommodations and Camping

IYHF Youth Hostel (IYHF)(tel. 852 14 23), located on one of the slopes. Climb the hill behind the train station and look for it on the mountainside. Well equipped—comfortable, paneled rooms, a bar, and a disco. 450ptas, ages over 26 530ptas. Full pension 1100ptas, ages over 26 1200ptas. Sheets 150ptas.

Hostal Longinos, Avda. del Generalíssimo, 3 (tel. 852 15 11), across from the train station. Run by a popular couple with 2 cute kids; it's a favorite gathering spot for *copas* and *naipes* (cards). Cozy rooms, many with views of the mountains. The place is shining. Bar/TV lounge with reasonably priced breakfasts and snacks. Singles 1200ptas, with bath 2200ptas. Doubles with bath 2800ptas. Suites 4000ptas.

Campground Las Dehesas is located about 4km outside town.

Food

The few restaurants here offer fine food, but there is not quite enough competition to keep prices down. If you're short on pesetas, **Supermercado Hermanos Ruz,** C. Docta Cañados, 2 (tel. 852 00 13), is your best bet. (Open Mon.-Sat. 9:30am-1:30pm and 5:30-9pm, Sun. 9:30am-1:30pm.) Numerous meat, fruit, produce, and bread stands line the same street.

Restaurante La Maya, Travesía del Señor, 2 (tel. 852 12 67), off Avda. del Generalísimo. Popular bar and restaurant where locals come to watch TV and catch up on town happenings. Hamburgers and *platos combinados* 450-550ptas.

Restaurante La Cazuela, Carretera Las Dehesas, 4 (tel. 852 02 71), 1km from the town center, up the road from the train station. Large windows offer picturesque alpine views. Terrace outside. Owners are proud of their *judiones Cazuela*—lima beans stuffed with chorizo, bacon, and pig's feet, served in a clay jug with a ladle (550ptas).

Meson-Restaurante "Helio", Cuesta de la Estación (tel. 852 13 45). Rather expensive, but convenient if you're staying at Hostal Longinos. Varnished log cabin decor and starched white tablecloths. Downstairs bar and restaurant features a TV and a motorcycle ride for kids. Head upstairs for a more formal atmosphere. 4-course *menú* with bread and wine 1100ptas. A la carte entrees 600ptas. Open in summer daily 10am-11pm; in off-season Mon.-Fri. noon-4pm, Sat.-Sun. 10am-11pm.

Sights and Entertainment

From the train station in Cercedilla, you can board a little red train to **Puerto de Navacerrada** (11 per day; 10 min.; one way 60ptas, round-trip 90ptas), a mountain pass where Old and New Castillas meet. The train ride up passes through pine forests laced with mountain streams. In summer, Puerto de Navacerrada is popular with backpackers who climb the peaks reaching 180m for a view of the Castilian plains below. Weather here can be wild; dress warmly even in summer. In winter, the town becomes a ski resort frequented by *madrileños*. Skiing aficionados also head to **Los Cotos,** a popular spot accessible to Cercedilla by train (11 per day, 15 min., one way 80ptas, round-trip 120ptas). The town of **Rascafría** in Los Cotos has two ski stations that are well regarded by locals, **Valdesqui** (tel. 852 04 16) and **Valcotos.** (Both open in winter roughly 10am-5pm.) In summer, go to Rascafría for a swim in **La Laguna de Peñalara,** a lovely lagoon nestled in a valley below the commanding mountain peak. Cercedilla's own *piscinas* (ponds), set below amidst cascading waterfalls, are a popular summer attraction. (Open July-Aug. daily 10am-8pm. Admission 100ptas.) The bridge overlooking the Río Guadarrama is yet another pretty spot. Unfortunately, neither site is accessible by train or bus.

In late summer, Cercedilla comes to life with festivals and fairs. Try to visit during the **Semana Cultural de Cercedilla,** an art festival held during the last week of August. Aspiring Madrid artists flock to town to showcase their creations. The Iglesia de San Sebastian hosts chamber music concerts, and photography, painting, ceramics, and tapestry exhibits sprout up all over the place. On the heels of Semana Cultural, the **Fiestas de la Virgen de Natividad's** week long celebration begins on September 8 with a parade to Iglesia de Santa María. Bullfights and dances on the Plaza Mayor follow. Games and sports competitions pit local families against each other.

Aranjuez

The nicest thing about Aranjuez, 47km south of Madrid, is the amount of greenery and tranquility so close to the capital; the worst thing is that the national highway passes right through the central square. Just look both ways before crossing, and enjoy the now vacant eighteenth-century **Palacio Real.** No longer the Bourbon's summer retreat, having lost out to Mallorca, the royal grounds today seem to belong to anyone willing to linger along the abandoned pathways. Don't daytrip here on a Tuesday, when nearly all sights are closed.

Construction of the palace began under Juan de Herrera, known for designing El Escorial, but Santiago Bonavía and the Italian architect Sabatini carried out most of the plans. Room after opulent room displays a collection of finely worked Vatican mosaic paintings in natural marble, sixteenth-century chandeliers from the La Granja crystal factory near Segovia, Flemish tapestries, Chinese points, and magnificent clocks. Most notable are the Oriental porcelain room with Italian rococo ceramic work that looks like three-dimensional wallpaper, and the Mozarabic smoking room (a gaudy copy of the Alhambra). (Open 10am-1pm and 3:30-6:30pm; Oct.-April Wed.-Mon. 10am-1pm and 3-6pm. Admission 300ptas.)

If you follow the bank of the Tajo River from the smaller gardens outside the palace, the **Jardines de la Isla** and **Jardín del Parterre,** you'll come to the huge park of **Jardines del Príncipe,** created for the youthful amusement of the future Carlos IV. This park contains the **Casa del Labrador,** a so-called laborer's cottage that is actually a miniature continuation of the palace. Its three neoclassical floors were destined for courtly galas and the queen's private quarters and contain further interesting knicknacks such as Roman mosaics from Mérida and views of contemporary Madrid embroidered in silk. (Open daily 10am-sunset. Admission 100ptas.) Also within Jardines del Príncipe, the **Casa de Marinos,** once the quarters of the Tajo's sailing squad, houses splendid royal boats. (Open Wed.-Mon. 10am-1pm and 3:30-6:30pm. Free.) Nearby is the **embarcadero** (dock) from which the royal family set sail on the swampy river. If you wish to do the same, cross the precarious footbridge to the bar **Arboleda** on the other side, where paddle boats are rented for 275ptas per hour.

Aranjuez has been known for centuries for its delicious **strawberries.** In fact, the very first Spanish train, which ran from Madrid to Aranjuez on February 9, 1851, was dubbed the "strawberry train." Queen Isabel II was one of the esteemed passengers, and was seen off by over 100,000 Spaniards. The "strawberry train" continued to be popular in subsequent decades, bringing Aranjuez strawberries to Madrid and *madrileños* to Aranjuez for weekends. The steam-engine train, reinaugurated in 1987, now provides excursions for tourists. (Inquire at the tourist office for more information.)

The **tourist office,** in the center of Pl. de Rusiñol (tel. 891 04 27), has a small leaflet on Aranjuez and tons of imformation on Madrid. (Open Mon.-Sat. 10am-2pm and 4-6:45pm.) About 2 blocks away on C. de Stuart, municipal bus N-Z picks up passengers headed to the **train station** (tel. 891 02 02), about 1km out of town. Due to the erratic bus schedule, you may be best off on foot (a 15-min. walk). Frequent trains run to Toledo (40 min., 250ptas) and Madrid (50 min., 275ptas). Direct lines are also available to Andalucía. The **bus station,** C. Infantas, 8 (tel. 891 01 83), serves Madrid seven times per day for 300ptas. The **post office,** at C. Peña Redonda (tel. 891 12 56), is open Monday to Friday from 9am to 2pm. To reach the **police** dial 891 00 22; for medical assistance, contact the **Cruz Roja** (Red Cross), C. Capitán, 10 (tel. 891 02 52).

Clean and cheap rooms, with an airy inner patio and TV room are found at **Hostel Rusiñol,** C. San Antonio, 26. (Tel. 891 01 55. Singles 800ptas. Doubles 1500ptas.) If Rusiñol is full, try **Hostal Infantas,** C. Infantas, 4 (tel. 891 13 41), which charges similar prices. On the highway to Andalucía, about 1km out of town, **Camping Soto del Castillo** (tel. 294 13 95) is one of the most delightful campgrounds in Spain. This site has all imaginable facilities, including a swimming pool. (Open April-Sept. 350ptas per adult, per tent, and per car. 225ptas per child.)

Avoid emptying your wallet at Aranjuez's tourist-trap restaurants; a mediocre meal here averages 1000ptas. Head to the **mercado** instead, an outpost of small stores selling fresh produce, breads, and deli foods, between C. del Gobernador and C. de Abastos. A number of less expensive bars and restaurants also line this area. But if your legs are tired and you want to dine with a view of the palace gardens, try **El Jardin de Isabel II** (tel. 891 63 31), an outdoor terrace restaurant on C. Gobernación. Their 800ptas *menú* brings small portions. (Open March-Nov. daily 11am-1am.)

On May 30, Aranjuez launches into its **Fiestas de Primavera** (Spring Festivals) with bullfights, arts and crafts shows, and an agricultural-industrial fair. The **Feria de Septiembre** brings concerts, expositions, and a bull fair.

Castilla/La Mancha

Lacking Galicia's green exuberance, Catalunya's attractive coast, and Andalucía's flowery orchards, Castilla nonetheless possesses its own beauty. The windswept plateaus around Burgos, the Romanesque belfries of León and Valladolid, the cliff dwellings of Cuenca, and the high mountains surrounding the walled city of Avila emblazon themselves as images not only of Castilla, but also of all Spain.

The concept of a unified Spain took root and flourished in this province. The Spanish language, frequently referred to simply as *castellano,* originated here. At the turn of the century, Spanish writers and intellectuals, appalled by their country's defeat in the Spanish-American War, turned to Castilla's landscape and traditions in search of the essence of Spain.

Make sure you try some of the hearty Castilian specialties. *Sopa castellana* is a soup made with garlic bread, ham, and eggs; the Castilian version of the *sopa de ajo* (garlic soup) made all over Spain also includes egg. *Cocido castellano* is a stew made with beef, ham, potatoes, *chorizo,* carrots, and garlic. Both pork and mutton are popular in Castilla and prepared in various succulent dishes.

Toledo

Toledo is mobbed with tourists only because it is a treasury of Spanish history and culture. Don't be discouraged by the crowds. The city downplays traditional Castilian austerity. For Cervantes, Toledo was that "rocky gravity, glory of Spain and light of her cities," and to Cassio it was "the most perfect epitome, the most brilliant and evocative summary of Spain's history."

If you compare the map Turismo gives you to the one held by El Greco's son in the painting *View and Map of Toledo* at the House of El Greco, you'll discover that little has changed in 400 years. With no room to sprawl on the naturally moated promontory, the city's monuments crowd together in a dizzying blur of periods and styles, held together in a medieval matrix of sagging houses. Emblematic of the cultural blend and *convivencia* (the centuries of coexistence and cooperation among Spain's three main ethnic groups) are the numerous churches, synagogues, and mosques that retire in the alleyways. Alfonso X El Sabio (the Wise), King of Castilla in the thirteenth century, founded the renowned Escuela de Traductores de Toledo (Translators School). Besides producing the first bilingual edition of the Scriptures, the school's scholars, most of them Jewish, translated Arabic texts into Spanish for a Christian king. Toledo was for a long time one of the great cultural centers of medieval Europe. The city was famous for its swords and knives, and for *damascene,* the ancient craft of inlaying gold on a black steel background, now used to decorate everything from sabres to ashtrays and picture frames.

Orientation and Practical Information

Buses depart frequently from Madrid's Estación Sur de Autobuses, at the Palos de Moguer metro stop (31 per day, 1½ hr., 410ptas one way). Trains leave only from Estación de Atocha (10 per day, 1½ hr., 420ptas one way). Skip the 20-minute uphill jaunt; the bus marked "Santa Bárbara" or "Polígono" goes right to central Pl. de Zocodover (45ptas).

No Castilian city is as labyrinthine as Toledo. Make sure to request the large poster map (with an El Greco monk on the back) at Turismo; it's worlds better than the small one in the Toledo brochure, also available at the tourist office.

Most points of interest are near or atop the central hill, pinpointed by **Plaza de Zocodover.** Main arteries such as **Calle del Comercio,** leading to the cathedral, and **Cuesta del Alcázar** radiate from the plaza. The second-greatest concentration of sights lies on the western edge of town in the **Judería,** the old Jewish quarter. Unless otherwise noted, offices, stations, accommodations, restaurants, and sights listed below are inside the walls of old Toledo.

Tourist Office: Tel. 22 08 43. On the north side of town, just outside the Puerta de Bisagra. Very friendly; some English spoken. Up-to-date maps and information. Ask for the poster map in addition to the brochure. Open Mon.-Fri. 9am-2pm and 4-6pm, Sat. 9am-1:30pm.

Student Travel Office: Oficina de Información Juvenil, C. de la Trinidad, 8 (tel. 21 20 62), right by the cathedral. Student travel information, rail passes, bus and plane tickets. No English spoken. Open daily 9am-2pm and 5-6:30pm.

Post Office: C. de la Plata (tel. 22 36 11). Open Mon.-Fri. 9am-2pm and 4-6pm; Lista de Correos Mon.-Fri. 9am-2pm. **Telegrams:** Tel. 22 20 00. Open Mon.-Fri. 9am-2pm and 4-6pm, Sat. 9am-2pm. **Postal Code:** 45001.

Telephones: C. de la Plata, 18. Open Mon.-Sat. 9am-1pm and 5-9pm. **Telephone Code:** 925.

Train Station: Paseo de la Rosa (tel. 22 30 99), across the new Puente de Azarquiel. To Aranjuez (8 per day, 45 min., 400ptas) and Madrid's Atocha Station (10 per day, 1½ hr., 700ptas). No direct line to Avila (connection in Madrid) or Andalucía (connection in Algodor or Aranjuez, depending on destination). **RENFE,** C. de la Sillería, 7 (tel. 22 12 72).

Buses: In the Zona Zafónt (tel. 21 58 50), just northwest of the Puente de Azarquiel outside the old city. **Continental/Galiano** (tel. 22 29 61) to Madrid (12 per day, 2 hr., 420ptas) and Cuenca (1 per day, 2½ hr., 450ptas).

Taxis: C. Cuesta del Alcázar (tel. 21 23 96).

Car Rental: Avis, Paseo de Miradero (tel. 21 45 35).

Laundromat: Juan Pascual, C. Azacanes, 3 (tel. 22 16 03), a tiny street on the right side of C. Gerardo Lobo as you walk from Pl. Zocodover to the tourist office. 5kg washload for 850ptas. Open daily 9:30am-1:45pm and 4:30-7:30pm; in off-season daily 9am-1:45pm and 5-8pm.

Medical Emergency: Casa de Socorro, C. General Moscardó (tel. 22 29 00), behind the Alcázar. **Ambulance: Cruz Roja** (Red Cross), C. Moscardó, 6 (tel. 22 29 00).

Police: Municipal, Pl. de Zocodover, 1 (tel. 21 34 00). **Emergencies:** Tel. 091.

Accommodations and Camping

Though most tourists opt to return to Madrid instead of spending the night in Toledo, the scarce supply of rooms makes finding a bed difficult and potentially expensive. You'd be wise to call ahead and reserve a room. Otherwise, arrive in the late morning or early afternoon when guests are checking out and rooms are more likely to be available.

Residencia Juvenil "San Servando" (IYHF), Castillo San Servando (tel. 22 45 54), uphill on the left from the train station and across the Puente Viejo from the center of town (about a 15-min. walk). A castle from without and a palace from within. Beautiful pool, comfy TV room, and modern bathrooms. 96 rooms, each with 3 bunk beds, many with views. An *albergue* around the corner has 64 rooms, but no view. No toilet paper. Women returning alone at night should take a cab. Curfew 12:30am (loosely enforced). Bed and breakfast 500ptas. Half-pension 800ptas. Full pension 1250ptas. Ages over 26: bed and breakfast 650ptas. Half pension 100ptas. Full pension 1500ptas.

Hostal Residencia Labrador, Juan Labrador, 16 (tel. 22 26 20). Near Fonda Lumbreras. Large place with hotel-like atmosphere. Well-kept rooms, some quite spacious, with bright bedspreads. Elevator and TV room. Singles 1200ptas, with shower 1400ptas. Doubles 2100ptas, with bath 2500ptas.

Hostal Las Armas, C. Armas, 7 (tel. 22 16 68), to the right of Pl. Zocodover. 200 year-old home with the lushest patio you'll ever see. Regress to childhood in the small rooms with flowered wallpaper and firm mattresses; they resemble a nursery. Singles 1300ptas. Doubles 2400ptas.

Fonda Segovia, C. Recoletos, 4 (tel. 21 11 24), just off C. de la Sillería (off Pl. de Zocodover). Clean, refreshingly quiet rooms with balconies. Motherly owner. Doubles 1300ptas. Triples 1950ptas.

Hostal Residencia Los Guerreros, Avda. de la Reconquista, 8 (tel. 21 18 07), northwest of the old city, outside the walls on the same street as the Roman theater. Very comfortable rooms and an extremely friendly management. A bit far from some of the sights and a bit more expensive than the rest. Singles 1800ptas. Doubles 2750ptas. Triples 3750ptas.

Pensión Descalzos, C. de los Descalzos, 30 (tel. 22 28 88), just inside the southern walls, east of Pl. del Tránsito, near the Casa del Greco. Brand-new and spacious. Friendly owners. Nostalgic amenities like soft toilet paper, liquid soap, and truly hot showers. One fly in the *ungüento:* Rooms in front resound with traffic at night. Singles 800ptas. Doubles 1500ptas, with bath 2500ptas.

Fonda Lumbreras, C. Juan Labrador, 9 (tel. 22 15 71), 2 blocks from Pl. Zocodover. Run-down place with a batty but sweet owner. Be careful not to trip over the cat. Singles 750ptas. Hot shower 150ptas.

Three nearby campsites charge 300ptas per person, per tent, and per car. **Circo Romano,** Avda. Carlos III, 19 (tel. 22 04 42), just outside the old city, has a great swimming pool and tennis courts. Entrance to the pool costs 450ptas (550ptas on weekends) and 1-hr. rental of the tennis courts costs 400ptas, whether or not you're staying at the campground. (Open March-Sept.) **Camping El Greco** (tel. 21 35 37) is 1½km from town on the road to Madrid (N-401). **Toledo** (tel. 35 80 13) is 5km out of the city. (Open April-Sept.)

Food

Food in Toledo is tough on the budget; take advantage of the *platos combinados* and *menús del día.* Seek out and sample the delicious *marzipán,* made with almonds and fruit.

Restaurante La Cubana, Paseo de la Rosa, 2 (tel. 22 00 88), across the river in front of the Puente Viejo de Alcántara, down the road from the youth hostel. Choose between the wooded, tavern-like restaurant and the outdoor *terraza* with overhanging grapevines. Try the gazpacho (250ptas) and *pollo al ajillo* (garlic chicken; 550ptas). Open daily 1-4pm and 7:30-10:30pm.

Restaurante Chirón, Puerta del Cambrión, 1 (tel. 22 01 50), off Paseo de Recaredo on the west side of Toledo. To get there from center of town, follow C. de los Reyes Católicos through the Puerta. Try the Navarra trout, garnished with artichokes, tomatoes, and peppers (550ptas). From the balcony, you can see the Taso river slithering through the Sierra. Open Sept.-June daily 10am-11pm; July daily 10am-4pm and 8pm-midnight.

Bar-Restaurante Bisagra, C. Real del Arrabel, 14 (tel. 22 06 93), just within the Puerta de Bisagra, about 2 blocks from Turismo. Informal atmosphere upstairs with wooden booths and TV. Head downstairs for privacy and tablecloths. *Platos combinados* 350-675ptas, *menú* 600ptas. Open Sun.-Fri. 1-4pm and 8-11:30pm

El Nido, Pl. de la Magdalena, 5, just south of Pl. de Zocodover. Fixed-price *menú* for 700ptas includes pork chops. Main dishes in the 400-550ptas range. A really lively place. Open daily 1-4pm and 8-11pm. **Bar-Restaurant Casino,** across the street, has another fine *menú del día* for 675ptas; *menú especial* 775-875ptas. Open daily 1-4pm and 8:30-11pm.

Restaurante Hierba Buena, Cristo de la Luz, 9 (tel. 22 34 63), up the street from the Mezquita. Lovely patio restaurant with marble floor. High prices (780-1200ptas). Open Mon.-Sat. 1:30-4pm and 9pm-midnight, Sun. 1:30-4pm.

Restaurante-Bar Mariano, Paseo de Merchan (tel. 21 13 34), down the boulevard from Turismo. Indoor and outdoor seating. Excellent *platos combinados* 500-600ptas. A generous salad with eggs and tuna 390ptas. Open daily 1:30-3:45pm and 8:15-10:45pm.

Restaurante Sinaí, C. de los Reyes Católicos, 7 (tel. 22 56 23), across from the Sinagoga de Santa María la Blanca. Run by an amicable English-speaking Moroccan who claims to be the only resident Jew in Toledo since the 1500s. He invites Christian *madrileños* and *toledanos* to a Passover feast every year. A la carte dishes and combination plates 600-800ptas. Open Wed.-Mon. 1-4pm.

Sights and Entertainment

The **cathedral** is a rich banquet of styles that will take you at least two hours to consume. The second largest in Spain (after Sevilla), this cathedral is suited to extended exploration and appreciation of its variety of architectural styles (from thirteenth-century Gothic to late baroque) and the storehouse of artwork within. The sanctuary is an imposing structure with a huge retable inspired by the life of Jesus. Directly behind it in the ambulatory is Narciso Tomé's *Transparente,* an eighteenth-century composition executed in stone and dependent on sunlight from above for its fanciful, glowing effect. Beneath the dome is the Mozarabic Chapel, the only one in the world where the ancient Mozarabic ritual (followed by the Visigoths) is still enacted. The *tesoro* (treasure) flaunts the worldly accoutrements of the church, including a 400-pound sixteenth-century gold monstrance carried through the streets in the annual Corpus Christi procession.

The *coro* has beautiful choirstalls carved in a secular theme (vanquished Granada); the graceful smiling Virgin by the entrance was made in France in the fourteenth century. The ceiling of the chapter house is Mudéjar, and the paintings (including two by Goya) depict all the archbishops of Toledo. The small Kings' Chapel was built to house the tombs of several Trastamara monarchs who ruled in Castilla during the fourteenth and fifteenth centuries.

A glimpse of the **sacristy** alone is worth the price of admission. Among its holdings are 27 paintings by El Greco. The **Casa del Tesorero,** in the northern part of the cathedral (entrance on C. Sixto Ramón Parro), contains recent acquisitions such as an unusual El Greco sculpture in polychrome wood of *La Apariencia de la virgen a San Ildefonso* and works by Bellini and Caravaggio, among others. (Cathedral open daily 10:30am-1pm and 3:30-7pm; Sept.-June daily 10:30am-1pm and 3:30-6pm. Admission to the *tesoro, coro,* chapter house, King's Chapel, and sacristy 250ptas. No shorts allowed.)

Domenico Theotocopuli, alias El Greco, is partly responsible for Toledo's image as an entrancing, mysterious place. Although born in Crete (hence his popular name, "The Greek"), the painter spent most of his life as a Toledan, and his tempestuous skies and expressive, almost tortured portraits have come to be identified with this city. The visitor expecting to see El Grecos at every turn will not be disappointed—many of his paintings have not left Toledo since he painted them in the sixteenth century. The modest Mudéjar **Iglesia de Santo Tomé** houses El Greco's masterpiece, *El Entierro del Conde de Orgaz* (*The Burial of Count Orgaz*), a transcendent meeting of heaven and earth. (Open Tues.-Sat. 10am-2pm and 3:30-7pm, Sun. 10am-2pm; in off-season Tues.-Sat. 10am-1:45pm and 3:30-6pm, Sun. 10am-1:45. Admission 85ptas.)

The so-called **Casa del Greco** (House of El Greco), at C. Levi, 3, stands at best only close to where the painter lived. Nevertheless, it is a fine example of Toledo's sixteenth-century secular architecture. The decorations and furnishings in the various rooms show the way people lived four centuries ago. The place rapidly fills up with tourists, so come as early as possible. The museum upstairs houses an excellent collection of paintings, including a replica of *Vista y Mapa de Toledo* (*View and Map of Toledo*). (Open Tues.-Sat. 10am-2pm and 4-6pm, Sun. 10am-2pm. Admission 200ptas.)

Two **synagogues** are all that remain of what was once the largest Jewish community in Spain. The Jews were expelled from Spain in 1492, but not before they established themselves as a major cultural and economic force on the Iberian Peninsula. After centuries of living outside of Spain, in places as far away as Yugoslavia and Greece, Jews of Spanish ancestry still speak Ladino, a patois that preserves echoes of fifteenth-century Castilian. Some have even kept the keys to their houses in Toledo and passed them on as heirlooms. Both synagogues are in the Judería on the west side.

The **Sinagoga del Tránsito** was built in the fourteenth century by Samuel HaLevi, treasurer to Pedro I of Castilla. The simple building has wonderful Mudéjar decorations and an *artesonado* ceiling. Three rooms house the **Museo Sefardí**, with a good collection of manuscripts, lids of sarcophagi, inscriptions, and amulets. Many of the objects exhibited here belong to Sephardic Jews. (Open Tues.-Sat. 10am-2pm and 4-6pm, Sun. 10am-2pm. Admission 200ptas.) The nearby **Sinagoga de Santa María la Blanca** was built to function as a synagogue, looks like a mosque, and for many years was a church. Especially appealing are the capitals of the columns, with decorations that look like pine cones. (Open daily 10am-2pm and 3:30-7pm; in off-season daily 10am-2pm and 3:30-6pm. Admission 50ptas.)

The **Monasterio de San Juan de los Reyes** was built by Fernando and Isabel to commemorate their victory over the Portuguese in 1476. Although the site was originally intended to serve as their burial place, after the reconquest of Granada in 1492, these plans were abandoned and the royal couple was eventually interred in the city where they had achieved their greatest military victory. The cloister has an *artesonado* ceiling decorated with the F and Y of their names—Isabel was spelled with a Y in the fifteenth century. (Open daily 10am-2pm and 3:30-7pm; in off-season daily 10am-2pm and 3:30-6pm. Admission 75ptas.)

The **Alcázar** is Toledo's most formidable landmark. Little remains of the original thirteenth-century structure, which has been restored on several occasions. During the Spanish Civil War, 538 people sought refuge here. According to Francoist historians, when Colonel Moscardó, the man in charge of the Alcázar, was ordered by the Republicans to surrender or suffer the assassination of his son, he chose the latter. The supposed telephone conversation between Moscardó, the Republicans, and his son is posted in 19 languages in the Colonel's former office, where it took place. Evidence has since surfaced to refute the entire incident. The Alcázar was shelled sometime later. No longer architecturally remarkable, it is now a distressing museum of Fascist superiority in the Civil War. You can visit the dark, windowless refuge where women and children lived for weeks. The museum houses such sobering exhibits as books punctured by bullets. For Spaniards, the Alcázar is above all a painful reminder of the Civil War's atrocities. (Open Tues.-Sun. 10am-2pm and 4-7pm. Admission 125ptas.)

The **Museo de Santa Cruz**, M. Cervantes, 3, off Pl. de Zocodover, in a beautiful plateresque building, is one of Toledo's finest museums. Its holdings are first-rate and well-organized, and, fortunately, it's not as tourist-infested as the cathedral sacristy or El Greco's house. Don't miss the large, fifteenth-century *Astrolaba* tapestry on the first floor, woven in Flanders and representing the zodiac. (Open Tues.-Sat. 10am-6:30pm, Sun. 10am-2pm, Mon. 10am-2pm and 4:30-6:30pm. Admisssion

200ptas, students free. Ticket also valid for the Museo de los Concilios y de la Cultura Visigótica.)

More reminders of the Islamic presence in Toledo are visible near the **Puerta del Sol,** a fourteenth-century Mudéjar gate. Throughout its long history, the **Mezquita del Cristo de la Luz** has been both a Muslim and a Christian place of worship. The tenth-century mosque was built on the site of a Visigothic church. It is Toledo's only intact building from the pre-Christian era. The Visigothic columns support arches inspired by the mosque at Córdoba. The church of **Santiago del Arrabal,** an outstanding Mudéjar temple, is nearby.

Outside the handsome **Puerta Nueva de Bisagra** on the road to Madrid is the **Hospital de Tavera,** a private museum that displays five El Grecos as well as works by Titian and Ribera. Titian's huge *Portrait of Carlos V* hangs in the dining room. The hospital itself is a fine Renaissance building of the sixteenth century. (Open daily 10:30am-1:30pm and 3:30-6pm. Admission 150ptas.)

Toledo was the seat of Visigothic rule and culture for the three centuries prior to the Muslim invasion of 711. The **Museo de los Concilios y de la Cultura Visigótica,** on C. San Clemente, is clear evidence that the importance of Visigothic culture in Spain has been grossly overstated. Ironically, the museum is housed in a thirteenth-century Mudéjar church where the Visigothic exhibits can't compete with the surrounding architecture and frescoes. Come to see the votive crowns if you haven't been to Madrid's Museo Arqueológico, but don't expect any masterpieces. (Open Tues.-Sat. 10am-2pm and 4-6:30pm, Sun. 10am-2pm. Admission 100ptas, students free. Ticket also valid for the Museo de Santa Cruz.) Apart from the museum, this part of town is worth a visit since its streets are untouched by commercial frenzy.

On the eastern side of the cathedral, the **Posada de la Hermandad,** C. de la Hermandad, 6, was used as a prison during the Inquisition. It now exhibits torture instruments employed throughout the ages: Don't come here on a full stomach. All objects are meticulously described in four languages, although often a glance is explanation enough; about half of the items are replicas. (Open Mon.-Fri. 10am-2pm and 4-9pm, Sat.-Sun. 10am-9pm; in off-season Mon.-Fri. 10am-2pm and 4-8pm, Sat.-Sun. 10am-8pm. Admission 300ptas, ages under 14 200ptas.)

Every Tuesday from 9am to 1:30pm Toledo's outdoor **El Martes** market is held in the shaded area behind the Convento Concepcionistas, east of Pl. de Zocodover. A lot of clothing and music tapes are sold here, and very little food. Boxed pastries, however, can be bought at a low price. Hold on tight to your belongings.

Since most of Toledo's nightspots cater to tourists, nightlife tends to wander down sidestreets and get lost. Still, you can find congregations of young people consuming *tapas* and beer along **Calle de Santa Fe,** behind Pl. de Zocodover, and **Calle de la Sinagoga,** north of the cathedral. For dancing try **Gris** or **María Christina.**

Corpus Christi is an impressive feast in Toledo, celebrated starting the Thursday after the eighth Sunday after Easter. On this day, the gold monstrance kept in the cathedral treasure is paraded through the street, and people don costumes straight out of an El Greco canvas. Observed in honor of the Virgen del Sagrario, the **August feasts** occur during one of the month's middle weeks.

Near Toledo: La Mancha

Southeast of Toledo is La Mancha, a land of seemingly endless sun-scorched plains, occasionally interrupted by white *molinos de viento* (windmills), which were the imaginary foes of the immortal **Don Quixote.** The region is renowned for its rich *queso manchego* (Manchegan cheese), abundant olive groves, dense vineyards, and excellent hunting, particularly of birds and rabbits. If you liked the marzipan in Toledo, then try *sopa de almendra,* a soup also made with almonds.

Most towns in La Mancha are accessible by bus from Toledo. But schedules tend to cater to townspeople traveling into Toledo rather than tourists visiting La Mancha. Inconvenient bus departure times may force you to spend a night where you only want to stay several hours. For greater flexibility (at greater expense), consider renting a car and using Toledo as a base for excursions into this region.

Today in La Mancha, one can retrace the steps of Cervantes and his most famous creations, Don Quixote and faithful squire, Sancho Panza. Cervantes met and married Catalina de Palacios in the main church in **Esquivias** in 1584. It is supposed that he began writing his masterpiece in the Cueva de Medrano (Medrano Cave). It was in **El Toboso,** 100km southeast of Toledo, that the noble Quixote first glimpsed and fell in love with Dulcinea—to all other eyes a frowsy farm girl. The so-called **museo de amor,** C. Jose Antonio (tel. 19 72 88), marks the spot where he met his fair damsel. This typical Manchegan house contains a rather dull collection of old housewares. (Open Tues.-Sun. 10am-2pm and 4-6:30pm. Admission 100ptas.)

Of all Manchegan villages, tiny **Consuegra,** with its whitewashed adobe houses and nearby mountain crowned by nine *molinos* (windmills) and a Roman castle, most echoes Quixote's imaginary adventures. The castle, which lies partly in ruins, is called the "Crestería Manchega" by locals. It was first a Roman fortress, then an Arab one, and was finally reconquered by Alfonso VI. The only son of El Cid, Diego, died in its stable. (Castle open erratic hours, but you can enter by climbing up a mound of dirt and over the wall in back.)

Consuegra makes an easy daytrip from Toledo. **Samar buses** (tel. 22 39 15) depart from Toledo's Zona Safón (4 per day, 380ptas). Returning to Toledo, buses depart from C. Castilla de la Mancha (4 per day). Tickets can be purchased on the bus from the driver. Consuegra's **post office** is at C. Florinda, 5, in the town center. (Open Mon.-Fri. 9am-2pm, Sat. 9am-1pm.) In case of **medical emergency,** dial 48 13 12. The municipal **police** station is at Pl. de España, 1 (tel. 48 10 05 or 48 09 11).

Hostal de las Provincias (tel. 48 03 00), on the Carretera Toledo-Alcázar de San Juan, is the only hotel in town. With its spacious rooms, friendly management, and inviting swimming pool, it's hardly a sacrifice to stay here. From Pl. España, follow Carretera de Tuleke; it's across the street from the gas station. (Singles with bath 1050ptas. Doubles with bath 1700ptas.)

The selection of restaurants in Carsuegra is also limited. Small *tapas* bars are plentiful. Tasty *conejo con tomate* (rabbit with tomato), a local speciality, can be found at **Los Faroles,** Pl. España, 10 (tel. 48 13 34). At 425ptas, it is one of the better buys in town. The tortillas run 200-250ptas. (Open Wed.-Mon. noon-4pm and 7pm-midnight.)

Cuenca

No wonder Cuencans felt so secure in the Middle Ages: This hilltop town is by nature nearly impregnable. Cliffs drop to swift-flowing rivers on three sides, and mountains protect the fourth. Buildings compensate for the lack of space by rising high, crowding close, and actually hanging over the cliff top.

Orientation and Practical Information

Modern-day Cuenca, less concerned with security, has overflowed its hill and trickled, like the Huecar River, into the valley below. The new city is the site of cheap accommodations and food, but the old city remains the stronghold of Cuenca's charm. Municipal buses (every ½ hr., 25ptas) run from outside the tourist office uphill to the Pl. Mayor in the old town.

Tourist Office: C. Dalmacio Garcia Izcara, 9 (tel. 22 22 31), 2 blocks from train station. Friendly, but hesitant to provide more than basic information. Be sure to ask for the glossy *Castilla-La Mancha* book. Open Mon.-Fri. 9am-2pm and 4:30-6:30pm, Sat. 9:30am-1pm.

Post Office: Parque de San Julián, 18 (tel. 22 40 16; for telegrams 22 20 00). Open for stamps Mon.-Fri. 9am-2pm and 4-6pm, Sat. 9am-2pm. Open for **telegrams** Mon.-Fri. 8am-10pm, Sat.-Sun. 8am-8pm. **Postal Code:** 16000.

Telephones: C. Cervantes, 2, near Pl. del Generalísimo. Open Mon.-Sat. 9am-1pm and 5-10pm. **Telephone Code:** 966.

Train Station: Avda. de la Estación, in the new city. As you exit, turn left and follow the signs to the town center. To Madrid (8 per day; 2½-3 hr.; *ter* 1380ptas, *automotor* 880ptas), Valencia (5 per day; 2¾-3¾ hr.; *ter* 1380ptas, *automotor* 880ptas), and Toledo (1 per day, 3 hr., 795ptas).

Buses: No central station, but Turismo has a complete listing of companies and their services. **Auto-Res,** C. de Tervel (tel. 22 11 84), near the train station. To Madrid (4 per day, 2½ hr., 805ptas). **Alsina** (tel. 22 04 96), off Avda. Reyes Católicos near the bullring. To Valencia (4 per day, 4½ hr., 1090ptas).

Hospital: Residencia Sanitaria Virgen, de la Luz, Carretera de Madrid, km 81 (tel. 22 42 11.)

Police: C. Martinez Kleiser (tel. 22 48 59). **Emergency:** Tel. 091.

Accommodations

Cuenca is most appealing as a pit stop between Madrid and Valencia. There's no need to stay the night unless you're train- or bus-weary. Turismo can offer additional accommodation suggestions.

Fonda Victoria, C. Fray Luís de León, 38 (tel. 22 54 15), off Pl. Calvo Sotelo. Ignore the creaky wooden staircase and climb upstairs to enormous rooms. Friendly owners will make sure you don't oversleep. Singles 1000ptas. Doubles 1500ptas. Truly hot showers 200ptas.

Fonda La Mota, Pl. Calvo Sotelo, 7 (tel. 22 55 67). Clean rooms in a modern office building, as well as a filling 550ptas *menú* for guests. Disorganized owners are sometimes unsure whether they have a vacancy. Singles 800ptas. Doubles 1500ptas.

Pensión Central, C. Alonso Chirino, 9 (tel. 21 15 11). Decent rooms with a little dirt. The hallway creaks.

Hostal Residencia Posada de San José, C. Julián Romero, 4 (tel. 21 13 00), in the old town just up from the main cathedral. Blow your savings and enjoy this 17th-century building that sits right on the cliff. From some rooms, you can look over the gorge and beyond. One of the owners speaks English, and the rooms are immaculate. Singles 1400ptas, with shower and view 2400ptas. Doubles 2600ptas, with bath 3800ptas. Triples 3100ptas, with bath 4300ptas. Stylish pajamas included.

Food

Food is cheaper in the new city. The morning **market** is held in Pl. de los Carros, behind the post office, and low-priced eateries can be found along **Calle Cervantes** and **Calle República Argentina.**

Casa Aparicio, C. Cervantes, 7 (tel. 22 08 00). Don't look at the food—just eat it. *Casa* means "home," which is exactly what this tasty food will remind you of. Lots of potatoes in the 450ptas *menú.* Open daily 1-4pm.

Cafeteria Reyes, C. República Argentina, 2 (tel. 21 38 38). Assorted, flavorful *platos* 450-600ptas. Open daily 7am-2am.

Mesón Juanjo, C. Fray Luís de León, 16. Overcooked food, but where else can you create your own *platos combinados* for 300-400ptas? Open daily 8am-midnight.

Bar Cueva Clot Tío Serafín, built into a cave across from Hos de Huescar, with a lair-like interior to match. Great for *tapas* and *bocadillos* (175-300ptas).

Sights

The attraction of Cuenca lies in the airy setting of its **old town,** where you can walk through winding streets and underneath covered ways. Along the town's edge, the view sweeps across the deep valley to the opposing cliff wall, and on the Huecar River side, to the **Iglesia de San Pablo.** The old section can be reached by walking up C. Palafox. The road ends, after 10 minutes, at the **Plaza Mayor.** Built into a baroque arch at the plaza's southern end, the **Ayuntamiento** dates from the eighteenth century, while the **cathedral** dominates the other side. A group of little known architects began construction of the cathedral in 1183, six years after Alfonso VIII of Castile conquered the city. Perhaps influenced by the king's English wife, Leonor Plantagenet, they built what would become the only Anglo-Norman-Gothic cathedral in Spain. A Spanish Renaissance facade and tower were added in the sixteenth and seventeenth centuries, only to be ripped off after they were deemed inappropriate. In 1724, fire cut short another attempt at building a front, leaving the current exterior incomplete. (Open daily 9am-1:30pm and 4:30-7:30pm. Free.) From here, follow C. Obispo (down the stairs) to the **casas colgadas** (hanging houses), which dangle over the riverbanks as precariously today as they did six centuries ago. The footbridge 60m above the river affords a grand view of the old houses huddled high on the cliffs, the new city as it spreads into the green fields beyond, and the waters rushing beneath your feet. Inside one of the *casas,* at Pl. de la Ciudad de Ronda, is the **Museo de Arte Abstracto,** with a collection of modern Spanish works. (Open Tues.-Fri. 11am-2pm and 4-6pm, Sat. 11am-2pm and 4-8pm, Sun. 11am-2pm. Admission 150ptas, students 75ptas.) The nearby **museo arqueológico** exhibits an interesting collection of Roman mosaics, ceramics, coins, and other finds from local excavations. (Open Tues.-Sat. 10am-2pm and 4-7pm, Sun. 10am-2pm. Admission 200ptas.)

For a great vista of the town high above, go for a walk along either of the two roads that surround the old part of Cuenca: **Hoz del Jucar** and **Hoz del Huecar.** The best view of the valley is from the side of Hoz del Huecar opposite the *casas colgadas.* Follow the winding road around the first two bends and the *hoz* (literally "gorge") opens its gigantic jaws to greet you. It's a 5-kilometer walk to the end; be careful in the heat. The *hoces* are also beautifully illuminated after dark.

Castilla/León

El Escorial

Were it not for Felipe II's huge Monasterio de San Lorenzo de El Escorial, the small, unremarkable village of San Lorenzo de El Escorial wouldn't be much more than a quaint summer resort in the Sierra de Guadarrama. Built in fulfillment of a promise to St. Lorenzo for Spain's victory in the Battle of San Quentin, El Escorial is a huge complex that includes a monastery, two palaces, a church complete with two pantheons, museums, and some of the most splendid architectural and artistic creations in the world.

Orientation and Practical Information

El Escorial lies 50km northwest of Madrid. There's a lot to see, so if you're making a daytrip, get here early. In summer you'll be competing with mobs of tourists pushing their way through the monastery. Some sections limit the number of visitors allowed in at the same time, so you might have to wait up to 15 minutes before you can enter certain rooms. Because the guided tours (in Spanish) are rushed and irritating, you may wish to leave your group after the first rush through the royal palaces to wander around by yourself. Don't come on a Monday, when the whole complex and most of the town shuts down.

Buses from Madrid and the local train station drop you off on **Calle Reina Victoria,** near the town center. This street connects **Plaza San Lorenzo,** a garden in front of the main entrance to the monastery, with **Plaza de la Constitucion,** a tree-less square uphill. **Calle Floridablanca,** the main street parallel to C. Reina Victoria and 1 block downhill, runs along the front of the monastery.

Tourist Office: C. Floridablanca, 10 (tel. 890 15 54), up a staircase partially hidden by trees. They've got the only town map. Open Sun.-Fri. 10am-2pm and 3-5pm, Sat. 10am-1:30pm.

Currency Exchange: Caja Madrid at C. General Mola and at C. General San Jurgo, 26 (tel. 890 17 14). Both open Mon.-Fri. 8:30am-2pm.

Post Office: C. Juan de Toledo (tel. 890 26 90), at the end of C. Floridablanca. Open Mon.-Fri. 9am-2pm, Sat. 9am-1pm. Open for **telegrams** Mon.-Fri. 9am-8pm, Sat. 9am-1pm. **Postal Code:** 28200.

Telephones: International calls may be placed from phone booths, from **Motel Victoria Palace,** C. Juan de Toledo, 1 (tel. 890 51 11), or from **Hotel Miranda Suizo,** C. Floridablanca, 20 (tel. 890 47 11). The latter two charge hefty commissions. **Telephone Code:** 91.

Train Station: Tel. 890 04 13. Located about 2km outside the town center. Herranz buses meet all trains and provide shuttle service (60ptas). **RENFE** runs trains to Madrid's Atocha Apeadero and Chamartín stations (28 per day, 1 hr., 250ptas) and Avila (11 per day, 1 hr., 290ptas).

Buses: Autocares Herranz, C. de la Reina Victoria, 3 (tel. 890 41 22). Information open 7:45am-1:30pm and 2:30-5:30pm. To Madrid (11 per day; 1 hr.; one way 235ptas, round-trip 410ptas), Valle de los Caídos (1 per day; 15 min.; one way 250ptas, round-trip 350ptas), and Sierra de Guadarrama (6 per day, 20 min., 150ptas). In Madrid, their office is at C. Isaac Peral, 10 (tel. 243 36 45 or 243 81 67).

Taxis: Stands at C. Floridablanca, 1 block down from the bus station on the corner (tel. 890 02 78; open daily 8am-10pm), and at Pl. de la Constitución (tel. 890 40 01; open daily 8:30am-10pm).

Lost Property: Cuartel de la Guardia Civil, Carretera de Guardarrama (tel. 890 26 11). Open 24 hours.

Bookstore: Libreriá Arias Montano, C. Joaquín Costa, 1 (tel. 890 33 94). Small selection.

Swimming Pools: Club de Golf, Tel. 890 59 04. Open in summer daily 11am-7pm.

Hospital: Hospital de la Alcadesa, C. San Pedro Regalado, 1 (tel. 890 54 44). Call here for an **ambulance.**

Police: At the Ayuntamiento, Pl. de la Constitución, 1 (tel. 890 36 44 or 890 36 94), up the street from the post office.

Accommodations and Camping

In summer, accommodations are neither cheap nor easy to come by. El Escorial is popular with Spanish families on their ritualistic *veraneo* (summer vacation), and Spanish youth groups often fill the hostels. Trying to find a room in July and August without reservations might prove impossible. Call ahead to ensure a bed, or at least get here early in the morning. Vacancies abound in the off-season, though you may have to bargain prices down to their true *temporada baja* (low season) levels.

Albergue Juvenil Santa María del Buen Aire (IYHF), C. Herrera (tel. 890 36 40). Walk down C. Floridablanca past the monastery and take the 1st right at the sign to the Casita del Príncipe; follow the road for 1½ km. Picturesque *finca* (farm) with open fields, cows, and a beautiful view of the monastery. Rooms accommodate 4-8 people. 92 beds. Make reservations a few weeks in advance. No curfew. Members only. 450ptas, ages over 26 530ptas. Breakfast included. Full pension 1100ptas, ages over 26 1200ptas. Hot showers 150ptas. Sheets 150ptas.

Albergue Juvenil La Villa de María Paz Unciti (IYHF), C. Rosario Muro, 4 (tel. 890 56 01 or 890 36 40), at C. Maestro Alonso. From C. Floridablanca, walk 2-3 blocks to Pl. Santa Joaquina de Verdura, and go up the hill along C. Maestro Alonso for 2 blocks. The 2-story stone building is set back from the road and concealed by trees; look for the small fountain with stairs on either side. It's an old Spanish house with arches, tiles, woodwork, patio, and flower gardens. Dining and recreation rooms. 29 beds. Call or write for reservations and keys since there is no permanent staff here. No curfew. 450ptas, ages over 26 530ptas. Breakfast included. Full pension 1100ptas, ages over 26 1200ptas.

Hostal Vasco, Pl. Santiago, 11 (tel. 890 16 19), 4 blocks up and 3 blocks to the right from Pl. San Lorenzo via C. San Francisco. Charming, 19th-century building with a terrace on the plaza. Lounges on each floor; restaurant on 1st floor. Clean, spacious rooms, some with excellent views of the monastery. Singles 1000ptas. Doubles 1900ptas, with shower 2100ptas, with bath 2200ptas. Triples 2600ptas. Breakfast 300ptas. *Pensión completo* available.

Hostal Malagón, C. San Francisco, 2, 2nd floor (tel. 890 15 76), at C. Mariano Benavente. Helpful owners. Comfortable rooms with high ceilings. Small dining room. Singles 1100ptas. Doubles 1700ptas. Triples 2200ptas. Showers 150ptas. *Pensión completo* 2600ptas.

Hostal Cristina, C. Juan de Toledo, 6 (tel. 890 19 61). Excellent location, next to a park with rose gardens and a fountain, overlooking the mountain range. Garden terrace. Clean rooms have modern wood furniture and tile floors. Doubles with bath 2800ptas. Triples with bath 3300ptas. Restaurant open daily 1-2:30pm and 9-10:30pm.

Camping la Herrería (tel. 890 56 17), 2km out of town on Carretera Robledo de Chavela on the Finca de Merrería. Scheduled to reopen in 1989. Open June-Sept. 225ptas per person.

Caravaning El Escorial (tel. 890 24 12), 15km away on Carretera de Guadarrama a El Escorial. 350ptas, ages 3-9 300ptas. 325ptas per car and per tent. Electricity 250ptas.

Food

El Escorial is no paradise for the hungry budget traveler—seriously consider picnicking or going on a hunger strike. For those who reject these options, **Mercado Publico,** C. General Sanjurjo, 9, 2 blocks off C. Floridablanca, offers a large selection of fresh produce, deli meats, cheeses, and other staples. (Open Mon.-Sat. 9am-2pm and 6-9pm. Closed Thurs. morning.) Several good *panaderías* (bakeries) are on the same street; shop at the supermarket farther down if you can't deal with pigs dangling from huge hooks. A number of inexpensive but nondescript bars and cafes lie at the end of C. Reina Victoria, near the bus and train drop-off point from Madrid. For a light lunch, try one of the kiosks along C. Floridablanca.

Restaurant Madrid-Sevilla, C. de Benavente, 4 (tel. 890 15 19), off Pl. de Animas. Family-run, with crisp tablecloths and comfortable wooden booths. Enormous 4-course *menú* 800ptas. Open daily 1-4pm and 9-11:30pm.

Meson-Taberna La Cueva, C. San Antón, 3 (tel. 890 15 16). Built in 1768 by the same architect who designed the Prado. Home to refugees of the French invasion and, beginning in 1961, home of the hungry. Historical decor and traditional Spanish dishes. *Menús* 900ptas and 1800ptas. *Plato turístico* (soup, fried veal, desert, bread, and wine) 1000ptas. Open daily 1-4pm and 9pm-midnight. For drinks and *tapas,* go the tavern downstairs, with its appropriate mural of Spanish men ogling pretty women. *Copa de vino* 75ptas, mixed drinks 175ptas. Open daily 10:30pm-2am.

Cerveceria-Marisquería la Real, C. del Rey, 25 (tel. 890 44 56). The black-and-white checked floor, fancy woodwork, and marble make this an upscale place, but the prices are down with the best of 'em. *Platos combinados* 400ptas. Open daily 8:30am-3am.

Cafeteria-Restaurante del Arte, C. Floridablanca, 14 (tel. 890 15 20 or 890 17 21). Bland coffee shop atmosphere. Central location, efficient service. Sandwiches 300-400ptas. *Platos combinados* 800ptas. One of few restaurants open early and late. Open daily 8am-midnight.

Restaurante Cubero, C. Don Juan Deleyra, 3 (no phone), a block up and to the right of Pl. San Lorenzo. After the tablecloths and a relaxed, low-key environment, you'll be ready for an afternoon of jostling with the other tourists. Open Tues.-Sun.

Sights

The **Monasterio de San Lorenzo de El Escorial** was Felipe II's gift to himself and to the populace, commemorating his victory against the French at the battle of St. Quentin on August 10, 1557. The site was chosen in 1561, construction began in 1563, and the monastery was finished in a remarkable 21 years, accounting for the uncommon unity of style. The complex, which includes a royal palace and pantheon, was a Herculean creation, as Felipe, the "Prudent King," knew full well: He oversaw much of the work, according to legend, from a chair-shaped rock 7km from the construction site. That stone is now known as **Silla de Felipe II** (chair), and the view is still regal. The Hieronymite order was chosen to inhabit the monastery because of its Spanish origin.

Juan de Toledo (trained in Italy as a classicist) was the first architect. Upon his death in 1567, Juan de Herrera took over. The monastery is Herrera's greatest work and the embodiment of his ideas: Architecture should be integrated with the materials, stylistically consistent, and functional as well as beautiful. Take time to walk around and inspect the structure from every possible angle. Artists and artisans from Italy and Spain all worked on the monastery—its unity is all the more astounding.

The **Palacio Real** is actually two dwellings in one—Felipe II's austere sixteenth-century apartments and the more luxurious, eighteenth-century rooms of Carlos III and Carlos IV. The latter kings, like the other Bourbon monarchs, weren't that fond of El Escorial and preferred the new palace at La Granja.

The palace tour begins with a 20-minute assault on astoundingly beautiful tapestries. Copies of works by Goya, El Greco, and Rubens worked in intricate detail and brilliantly colored wool yarn are literally used as wallpaper—every inch of wall is covered by them.

The two palaces are joined by the long **Sala de Batallas.** The huge fresco here depicts some of Castille's and Spain's greatest victories: Juan II's triumph over the Muslims in 1431 at Higueruela (notice the fleeing women and children), Felipe II's two successful expeditions to the Azores, and the battle of St. Quentin.

In the modest Habsburg palace, the small rooms of Princess Isabel Clara Eugenia belie the status of Felipe II's favorite daughter, who would later become regent of the Netherlands. Felipe II's apartments are devoid of self-indulgence. The studies, lined with blue and white tiles, are furnished in a dignified, simple manner. A copy of Bosch's painting *Los pecados capitales* (*The Cardinal Sins*) hangs on one wall and watercolors attributed to Dürer line the others. Note the two luxuries Felipe allowed himself, a clavichord and a theological library.

The **Nuevos Museos** alone are reason enough to visit El Escorial. Flemish and German paintings from the fifteenth and sixteenth centuries hang in Room I. Coxcie (1497-1592) is represented in Room II. Note the difference in his treatment of the human figure and palette between his *Death of St. Felipe* and *Birth of Christ.* Works by Titian, who became court painter to Carlos V in 1533, dominate Room III. The hay in Jesus' cradle doubles as a halo in Zuccaro's *Adoration of the Shepherds.* More works by Titian, and paintings by Veronese, Tintoretto, and other Italian artists grace Room V; the Spanish painter Ribera is also well-represented here. Veronese's *Annunciation* is especially beautiful. The most impressive room features several masterpieces by El Greco. They include *The Dream of Felipe II, Saint Peter,* and two paintings of St. Francis. To get to the El Greco room, go past the architecture exhibit and up the stairs near the exit sign.

The **basílica,** the center of the huge complex, was consecrated in the presence of Felipe II on August 30, 1595. Marble steps lead up to an altar graced by two groups of elegant sculpture by Pompeo Leoni. The figures on the left represent Carlos V accompanied by his wife Isabel (mother of Felipe II), his daughter María, and his sisters María (Queen of Hungary) and Leonor (Queen of France). On the right are figures of Felipe II, accompanied by three of his four wives and his son Carlos. To illuminate the altar, buy a 100ptas token from the attendant at the entrance. The retable is a splendid four-level alternation of deliverance (birth of Christ), suffering (stoning of Stephen), deliverance (joy of heaven), and suffering (Christ on the cross). Be sure to see the **Coro Alto** (High Choir), with its amazing frescoed ceiling depicting heaven filled with choirs of angels. The cloister contains Titian's gigantic fresco of the Martyrdom of St. Lawrence.

The convent's **Escalera Principal** (staircase) was frescoed by Luca Giordano in seven months and has a different animal hidden in each corner. It's a tribute to perspective; the tiers of people (mortal to angelic) achieve a dome-like effect by growing smaller as they approach the central brilliant light of heaven.

The **Panteón Real** was the brainchild of Felipe II, who did not live to see the project finished; nevertheless, he is buried here with his father Carlos V and most of their royal descendents. The stairway leading to the crypt is elegantly faced with black and red marble and jasper. Of the 26 gray marble sarcophagi, 23 contain the remains of Spanish monarchs, and three are still empty. All kings are buried here (except Felipe V and Fernando VI, who preferred to be interred elsewhere), but only those queens whose sons became monarchs are admitted. The nearby **Panteón de las Infantas** is intended for the other queens and for men of the royal household who didn't attain the throne. Don Juan's tomb has a statue of him in uniform (even though he didn't die in battle), and he still receives kisses from female visitors. His fingers are covered with rings to protect his hands from the harsh metal mesh gloves that lie at his feet.

The **Salas Capitulares** (chapter houses) are the least interesting part of a visit to El Escorial. They contain a fine collection of ecclesiastic garments and some interesting paintings, but no masterpieces. The **Biblioteca** on the second floor was made into one of the most important in Europe by Felipe II, its founder. Today, its corpus of Arabic manuscripts is unsurpassed, and its holdings are priceless despite several fires that have thinned the collection. The exhibits in the center of the room include such masterpieces of book art as Alfonso X's *Cántigas de Santa María*, the Book of Hours of the Catholic monarchs, Saint Teresa's manuscripts, a Koran that belonged to a Moroccan monarch, the gold-lettered *Aureus Codex* (by German Emperor Conrad III, 1039), and a *Commentary on the Apocalypse* by Beato de Liebana. The paintings by Tibaldi on the vaulted ceilings represent the liberal arts, one art per vault of the ceiling.

Outside the monastic complex near the train station is the **Casita del Príncipe**, commissioned by Carlos, Prince of Asturias, who later became Carlos IV. Here you'll find a splendid collection of objets d'art, including chandeliers, lamps, rugs, furniture, clocks, tapestries, and china. The French severely damaged the *casita* during the Napoleonic invasions, and many rooms were redecorated later by Fernando VII in the then-popular Empire style. The **Casita de Arriba** was commissioned by Gabriel de Borbón, Carlos's brother, at about the same time. Although not as sumptuous as the Casita del Príncipe, it offers some splendid views of the surrounding countryside. To get here, walk or hitch 3km down the road toward Avila. (All sights open April 15-Oct. 15 Tues.-Sun. 10am-1:30pm and 3:30-6:30pm; Oct. 16-April 14 Tues.-Sun. 10am-1:30pm and 3-6pm. Last admission to palaces, pantheons, and museums ½ hr. before closing, 15 min. for the Biblioteca and the *casitas*. Admission to all sights 500ptas, to the monastery alone 350ptas, to the *casitas* alone 150ptas each. Reduced ticket to the Basílica, pantheons, and the Biblioteca 150ptas, sold 1 hr. before closing.

Entertainment

Several nightspots service the mainly tourist population. **Cafe Cerveceria La Jara**, C. Floridablanca, 34 (no phone), is a mod bar with a loud, youthful crowd. (Open daily until 12:30am.) Nearby, at #28, **Cerveceria El Ancla's** fresh seafood *raciones* (400ptas) draws many vacationers. The *copa* (40ptas) is among El Escorial's cheapest. (Open daily until midnight.) Sangria pitchers (600ptas) at **El Gurriato**, C. Leandro Rubio, 3 (tel. 890 47 10), fill the space between the funky, green wood walls. (Open daily until 3am.) Late night (or early morning) rockers should head to **Disco-Pub Que Maz Da**, C. Santiago, 11. There is no cover charge and beer costs only 125ptas. (Open Fri.-Sat. 8pm-4:30am, Sun.-Thurs. 8pm-midnight.)

August 10-20 brings the **Festivals of San Lorenzo.** Parades of giant figures line the streets as fireworks fill the sky. Folk dancing contests and horse-drawn cart parades mark **Romeriá a la Ermita de la Virgen de Gracia**, the second Sunday in September. Ceremonies are also held in the forest of Herriá.

Near El Escorial: El Valle de los Caídos

Eight kilometers from El Escorial, in an untouched valley of the Sierra de Guadarrama, the overpowering monument of **Santa Cruz del Valle de los Caídos** (Valley of the Fallen) stands on a rocky crag. The massive granite cross measures 150m and spreads its arms 46m. The cross and the blue-and-white tiled plaza behind it honor the victims of the 1936-1939 Spanish Civil War; many other victims died quarrying and hauling the huge slabs of rock. Francisco Franco is buried inside the mausoleum. (Open daily 10am-6pm.) **Autocares Herranz,** in El Escorial, runs one bus here per day (bus leaves at 3:15pm and returns at 5:30pm, 15 min., round-trip 300ptas).

Segovia

Rising above the dusty and rocky countryside, Segovia represents Castilla at its best—beautiful golden churches, twisting alleyways filled with the smells of *sopa castellana* and *lomo de cerdo,* and a people fiercely and justifiably proud of their city and province.

Segovia was an important settlement as early as Celtiberian times. In addition to the famous aqueduct, the Romans established a city mint—proof of Segovia's prominence within the Empire. At the meeting point of two vital Roman roads, the city remained important until captured by the Visigoths and later the Muslims. Segovia regained its privileged position in the eleventh century, following the reconquest of Toledo by the Christians. In the fifteenth century, Juan II and Enrique IV, kings of the House of Trastamara, set up their courts here and embellished the town with new monuments. Isabel the Catholic was proclaimed Queen of Castilla here in 1474. After Segovian nobles clashed with Emperor Carlos V, the city fell into decline until the Bourbons built the Palace of La Granja 11km away.

Orientation and Practical Information

On the far side of the Sierra de Guadarrama, 88km northwest of Madrid, Segovia is close enough for a daytrip. Seeing all its sights and the magnificent Palace of La Granja will, however, require an overnight stay. To get to the tourist office from the bus or train station, take bus #3 (50ptas) to the **Plaza Mayor** (Pl. de Franco on the maps), next to the cathedral. Only masochists would contemplate the 20-minute, mountainous walk up Paseo Conde de Sepulveda and right onto Avda. Fernández Ladreda. Segovia is impossible to navigate without a map.

Tourist Office: Pl. Mayor, 10 (tel. 43 03 28), in front of the bus stop. Complete information on and prices for accommodations, intercity bus routes, trains, and sights are posted outside the door. Friendly, English-speaking staff. Open Mon.-Fri. 9am-2pm and 4-6pm, Sat. 9am-2pm.

Post Office: Pl. del Dr. Laguna, 5 (tel. 43 16 11), up C. Lecea from Pl. Mayor. Open Mon.-Fri. 9am-2pm and 4-6pm, Sat. 9am-2pm. Open for Lista de Correos Mon.-Sat. 9am-2pm. **Postal Code:** 40006.

Telephones: C. Sargento Provisional, 8 (tel. 22 20 00), in Pl. de los Huertos down C. Cronista Lecea. Open Mon.-Fri. 9am-3pm. **Telephone Code:** 911.

Train Station: Paseo Conde de Sepulveda (tel. 47 07 74), a 20-min. walk southeast from the town center. To Madrid (3 per day, 2½ hr., 500ptas) and Valladolid (1 per day) via Medina del Campo (3 per day, 2¾ hr., 600ptas).

Bus Station: Estacionamiento Municipal de Autobuses, on Paseo Conde de Sepulvedra at Avda. Fernández Ladreda (tel. 42 77 25), on the highway to Avila. To La Granja (9 per day, 25 min., 80ptas), Madrid (3 per day, 1½ hr., 490ptas), Avila (2 per day, 350ptas), Valladolid (4 per day, 2½ hr., 540ptas), and Aranda de Duero (2 per day, 2½ hr., 505ptas).

Taxis: Pl. Mayor (tel. 43 66 80) and Pl. del Azoguejo (tel. 43 66 81).

Skiing: Segovia province's ski station, **La Pinilla,** can be reached via the Madrid-Burgos RENFE line (get off at Riaza) or La Castellana buses. Ski rentals, lift tickets, tennis courts, and low-priced *hostales.* Inquire at Segovia's tourist office.

Hospital: Hospital de la Misericordia, Dr. Velasco, 3 (tel. 43 08 12). **First Aid: Casa de Socorro,** Arias Dávila, 3 (tel. 43 41 41). **Ambulance:** Tel. 43 01 00.

Police: C. Perucho, 2 (tel. 42 51 61). **Emergency:** Tel. 091.

Accommodations and Camping

Finding a place to stay should be a problem only in late August. Check the accommodations list outside the tourist office. Most places are on the **Plaza Mayor** or nearby side streets.

IYHF Youth Hostel, Paseo Conde de Sepulveda (tel. 42 00 27), halfway between the train and bus stations. Uncrowded. Friendly management. A gym and luxurious common rooms with a piano and TV make this the best place to stay in town. No curfew. 450ptas, ages over 26 550ptas. Sheets 150ptas.

Hostal Victoria, Pl. Mayor, 5 (tel. 43 57 11). Classier than its neighbors, Aragon and Cubo. Modest but clean rooms, some with great views of the cathedral. Run by a friendly family. TV lounge and restaurant. Singles 1200ptas, with shower 1350ptas. Doubles with shower 2675ptas, with bath 2850ptas. Breakfast 200ptas. Lunch or dinner 900ptas. Full pension 1700ptas. Reservations accepted one week in advance.

Hostal Sol Cristina, C. Obispo Quesada, 40 (tel. 42 75 13), near Pl. Mayor. Clean, bright rooms match owner's disposition. Singles 1100ptas. Doubles 2000ptas. Showers 200ptas. Breakfast 185ptas. Lunch or dinner 750ptas. Full pension 1432ptas. No reservations.

Casa de Huéspedes Aragón, Pl. Mayor, 4, 1st floor (tel. 43 35 27), across from Turismo. The location and prices can't be beat, but you get what you pay for: Cramped, dark rooms are concealed behind a gloomy hallway. Singles 700ptas. Triples 1600ptas. Hot showers 200ptas.

Hostal-Residencia El Postigo, Pl. del Seminario, 2 (tel. 43 66 33). Modern building is as safe as you can get; next door sits the police station. Singles with shower 1265ptas. Doubles with bath 1900ptas. Breakfast 185ptas. Lunch 735ptas. Dinner 525ptas. Full pension 1228ptas.

The second-class **Camping Acueducto,** Carretera Nacional, 601 (tel. 42 50 00), is 1km out of Segovia towards La Granja. (Open June-Sept. 300ptas, children 275ptas. 275-425ptas per tent and 225ptas per motorcycle.)

Food

Eating in Segovia can be a lesson in fine Castilian cooking—without your having to pay a high tuition. Unless you can part with about 1100ptas for a meal of *cordero asado* (roast lamb), wander away from Pl. Mayor and steer clear of the establishments with credit-card stickers in their windows on Plaza de Azoguejo. True pesetapinchers can shop at the **supermarket** at the end of C. Isabel la Católica. (Open Mon.-Fri. 10am-2pm and 4-7pm, Sat.-Sun. 10am-2pm.)

Méson del Campesino, C. de Infanta Isabel, 12 (tel. 43 58 99), off Pl. Mayor. Wooden beam ceiling and bar. Youngsters sit at the high tables, while their elders stand at the bar. Combo plates 200-500ptas. *Menú* 600ptas. Open Fri.-Wed. 11am-4pm and 8pm-midnight.

Restaurante La Oficina, C. Cronista Lecea, 10 (tel. 43 16 43), off Pl. Mayor. Over 100 years old, and it's easy to taste why. A superb *menú* (850ptas) in an atmosphere full of Castilian cookware and pictures of suckling pigs past. Open daily 12:30-4.30pm and 7:30-11:30pm.

Meson Candido, Pl. de Azoguejo, 5 (tel. 42 81 03). Money shouldn't be a concern if you're planning to eat here. Famous throughout Spain for its authentic *menú* (2500ptas). *Cochinillo asado* (roast suckling pig, a Segovian specialty) 1300ptas. Open daily 12:30-4:30pm and 7:30-11:30pm.

El Bernadino, C. Cervantes, 2 (tel. 43 32 25 or 43 17 41), uphill from Pl. del Azoguejo. Come here for a huge, inexpensive meal. You get tons of food with the regular *menú* (900ptas). *Menú* with *cochinillo asado* 1790ptas. Open daily 1-4pm and 7:30-11:30pm.

Bar El Túnel, Santa Columba, 3, off Pl. del Azoguejo and up the stone steps. Cheap fare with a view of the aqueduct. Add your key chain to the hundreds above the bar. *Platos* 250-500ptas. Meals served noon-3:30pm and 7:30-11:30pm.

Sights

Segovia's most famous monument is also its most ancient. The imposing **Roman aqueduct** is about to enter its third millennium of existence and use—it still carries water to the town. No mortar was used in constructing its 167 stone arches. The most impressive view is from **Plaza del Azoguejo** (in front of and to the right of the aqueduct), where the aqueduct reaches its maximum height of 30m. Here it frames the Castilian landscape in a series of unrivaled arches, which also serve as great private parking places for local businessmen. Climb the steps on the left side of the plaza for a diagonal view. If you continue to the top, you can climb over the small wooden fence and see the inside of the aqueduct.

The city's position at the confluence of the rivers Eresma and Clamores has led people to compare Segovia to a sailing ship, with the **Alcázar** as its majestic bow. Although the Alcázar looks like an archetypal late-medieval castle, much of the effect actually derives from an inspired and faithful reconstruction after a fire in 1862. It is poised at the tip of a sheer precipice overlooking a lush valley. Recent excavations have found granite analogous to that of the aqueduct in the foundations, leading historians to believe that a fort has occupied the spot since Roman times.

The Gothic-Mudéjar decorations inside were in place during the great fiestas of Juan II, recorded by the poet Jorge Manrique. Don't miss the **Sala del Solio** (Throne Room), with its beautiful handcrafted ceiling. The **Sala de las Piñas** (Room of Pineapples) also sports an interesting ceiling; it's decorated with small pineapples made of gold and it features a beautiful stained-glass window. The **Sala de Armas** houses cannons, bows, and barbed weapons from Carlos II's eighteenth-century artillery academy. There are numerous anecdotes about the Alcázar's royal residents. Perhaps the most tragic tells of Prince Pedro, son of King Enrique IV, who slipped from his nurse's arms on the balcony and plunged over the ramparts to his death. Out of desperation the nurse leapt after the child and ended her own life. Before leaving, climb the **tower** for a fabulous view of Segovia and the surrounding valley. The building was used as a prison in the sixteenth century, but you may find the dark, steep, and narrow staircase torture enough. (Open April-Sept. daily 10am-7pm; Oct.-March daily 10am-6pm. Admission 150ptas, students 75ptas.)

The **cathedral** is new by Spanish standards. Carlos V ordered its construction in the sixteenth century, when the old cathedral near the Alcázar was destroyed during the revolt of the Comunidades. Like Salamanca's new cathedral, it is a massive edifice in the late Gothic style. The main altar, designed in 1768 by Francisco Sabatini, shines with brass and marble. Though the cupola is oddly placed and the retable difficult to see, the rococo chapels behind the altar are a fun change of pace. The first chapel on the right of the entrance houses a touching *Entombment* by the sixteenth-century sculptor Juan de Juni. The characters' emotional gestures are tempered by the strict geometric arrangement. The beautiful cloister was brought over from the old cathedral. A fine **museum** houses a fine collection of Brussels tapestries (in the chapterhouse) and some interesting paintings. (Open April-Sept. daily 9am-7pm; Oct.-March Mon.-Fri. 9:30am-1pm and 3-6pm, Sat.-Sun. 9:30am-6pm. Succinct history 50ptas from a tape machine opposite the entrance. Admission 100ptas, students 75ptas.)

Segovia is encrusted with more Romanesque churches than any other Spanish town of its size. The **Iglesia de San Esteban** is a beautiful example; its tall square tower and the portico surrounding part of its facade are typical of Romanesque religious architecture in Segovia. Built in the thirteenth century, the church houses a calvary from the same period. **San Martín,** on Pl. San Martín off C. Juan Bravo, dates from the tenth century and combines Mozarabic and Romanesque elements. **San Justo,** not far from the aqueduct outside the wall, contains a stunning collection of frescoes in its main apse, and **San Juan de los Caballeros** features a portico with remarkable capitals. There is a splendid view of **San Andrés** from small Plaza de la Merced. Unfortunately, these churches can be visited only during services. The only exception is San Juan de los Caballeros, which houses the **Museo de Daniel Zuloaga,** dedicated to the ceramicist, who died in 1921. (Currently closed for renovation.)

Secular architecture also flourished in medieval and Renaissance Segovia. The most fanciful example is the **Casa de los Picos,** its facade decorated with rows of diamond-shaped stones.

From the tower of the Alcázar, you will spy three interesting buildings across the Eresma River, outside the city proper. The **Monasterio del Parral,** founded by Enrique IV, looks most impressive from afar, but it does have an interesting polychrome altarpiece. (Open Mon.-Fri. 9am-1pm and 3-6:30pm. Free.) The facade of the **Iglesia del Convento de los Carmelitas Descalzos** (Barefoot Carmelites) is flanked by young cypresses that are especially attractive on sunny afternoons. St. Juan de la Cruz, the great mystic, friend of St. Teresa, and author of some of the most beautiful poems in Spanish literature, is buried here. The tomb itself is grandiose, but the small **museum** is rather disappointing. The most interesting exhibit is the manuscript of *Cántico Espiritual,* a poem on the soul's mystical search for Jesus. (Open daily 10am-1:30pm and 4-7pm. Free.) The 12-sided **Iglesia de La Vera Cruz,** nearby, appears like a specter on the dusty road to Zamarramala. Most likely built by the Knights Templar in the early thirteenth century, it was inspired by Romanesque churches in Northern Italy, most notably Bologna's Church of the Holy Sepulchre. The two rooms in the middle were supposedly used by the Templars to perform their secret ceremonies. (Open April-Sept. Tues.-Sun. 10:30am-1:30pm and 3:30-7pm; Oct.-March Tues.-Sun. 10:30am-1:30pm and 3:30-6pm. Admission 50ptas.)

Entertainment

Nighttime activity focuses on Plaza Mayor and surrounding side streets. Great pubs line **Calles Infanta Isabel** and **Isabel la Católica** (nicknamed "the streets of the bars" by locals). At Pl. Mayor, **Pub Oja Blanca** and **Café Jeyma** are good watering holes. High schoolers hit **La Planta Baja Bar,** on C. Infanta Isabel, while intellectuals congregate at **Bar Basilico,** on C. de Herrera off C. Cronista Lecea. Cool down in the pastel decor of the **Oasis Bar,** 50m down C. Isabel la Católica.

The most colorful **feasts** near Segovia are those of Santa Agueda (St. Agatha), held in **Zamarramala** on the second Saturday and Sunday in February. For one day, women symbolically take over the town's administration, dress up in beautiful, old-fashioned costumes, and parade through the streets. Married women are led by the mayor's wife, who carries the scepter of authority, and later there is a banquet for women only—except for the priest. Origins of this festival date back to an attempted sneak attack on the Alcázar based in Zamarramala. The women of the town tried to lull the castle guards with wine and song, but the guards remained vigilant, and the attack was thwarted. Zamarramala is 1km from Segovia and is visible from the Alcázar.

There's dancing and a running of the bulls in **Cuéllar,** 46km north of Segovia, on the last Sunday in August. Take the Valladolid bus to get there. Segovia's **Week of Chamber Music** usually takes place in July.

Near Segovia: La Granja de San Ildefonso

The royal palace and gardens of **La Granja de San Ildefonso,** 11km from Segovia, are frequently called the Versailles of Spain, but don't come here expecting another French extravaganza. In the early eighteenth century, the Bourbon dynasty began its reign in Spain following the War of the Spanish Succession. French-born King Felipe V, grandson of Louis XIV, commissioned La Granja out of nostalgia for Versailles. Although parts of the gardens and buildings suffer from lack of care, this is a worthwhile daytrip if you have a taste for palaces. Many of the rooms have marble floors; windows are framed by original, 250-year-old lace curtains; and elegant, crystal chandeliers dangle from ceilings painted in false perspective.

In 1918 a fire destroyed the living quarters of the royals and their servants. The rubble was rebuilt to house one of the world's finest collections of *tapices flamencos* (tapestries). Segovia was selected by preservationists as the optimal site for the tapestries because of its cool, dry climate. The works, some covering entire walls, date from the sixteenth and seventeenth centuries. All were crafted in Brussels and then acquired by the Spanish Crown under the Habsburg Kings Carlos V and Philip

II. They depict various biblical, historical, and mythical themes of the time. The most famous scenes include *Honors and Virtues* (1520), *Apocolypse of San Juan* (c. 1540), and the tapestry of *San Jeronino.*

The domed **church** next to the palace is faced with red marble and decorated with elaborate gilded woodwork. In a side chapel, the bones of various saints and martyrs make a gruesome display. The **gardens,** with their 26 fountains and statues, were designed by René Carlier and Esteban Boutelon. The surrounding forest conceals statues of children and animals. Jean Thierry and René Fremin designed the **Cascadas Nuevas** (cascades), an ensemble of pools representing the continents and the four seasons. The tourist office in Segovia can tell you when they will be turned on—in summer usually after 7pm. (Palace open Mon.-Fri. 10am-1:30pm and 3-5pm. Admission 300ptas.)

The town of La Granja itself hosts a **crystal factory** where much of the crystal used at the royal palaces here and in Madrid was made. The original crystal factory is undergoing renovation to convert it into a museum exhibiting crystal-making equipment and works of the eighteenth and nineteenth centuries. In a modern factory, the production of lavish chandeliers has given way to more practical projects. For a tour of the factory, call 47 00 00 (Mon.-Fri. 7am-3pm).

Frequent buses leave Segovia for La Granja (9 per day, 25 min., 100ptas).

Two little towns near Segovia that merit daytrips of their own are Coca and Pedraza. Both have splendid castles and offer the visitor a glimpse of life in a Castilian hamlet. **Coca,** 32km to the northwest of Segovia, dates back to Roman times. Nevertheless, its well-preserved castle, built in the fifteenth century on the orders of Bishop de Fonseca, is flamboyantly Gothic. A visit here requires an overnight stay (unless you come by car), since the only bus leaves Segovia at 5pm and does not return until 9am the following morning (285ptas). Accommodations can be arranged in a private house for about 600ptas—ask in the bars.

Pedraza, thought to be the birthplace of the Roman Emperor Trajan, is dominated by its castle on an enormous crag nearby. Restored in 1430 by Don Pedro Frenández de Velasco, the walls and machicolations are still in perfect shape. Thirty-seven kilometers northeast of Segovia, Pedraza can be reached by train (4 per day, 1 hr., 224ptas).

Avila

Avila is a near-perfect, eleventh-century walled city framed by the snowcapped ridge of the Sierra de Gredos. Within the walls, little carved images of bulls and hogs dot the town, mute reminders of a Celtiberian culture much older than the surrounding medieval fortifications. The cathedral, actually embedded in the battlements, brings to mind the long, turbulent centuries of the Reconquista, when war and religion went hand in hand, and Avila was anything but its present tranquil self.

The most durable Avilian institution after the walls is **St. Teresa de Jesús,** a mystic and a writer as well as a reformer of monastic life. Teresa of Avila, born in 1515, left an autobiography that recounts her mystical experiences—her casual conversations with Jesus, her bliss resembling sexual rapture but provoked by asceticism, as well as her utter despair, caused by the belief that her transports were the work of the devil. If you think that RENFE and the hot Castilian sun make traveling in Spain excruciating, read her *Book of the Foundations,* an account of the perils and misadventures she encountered on her convent-founding perambulations from Soria to Sevilla. The people of Avila refer to her simply as *la Santa,* and everything from pastries to driving schools are named after her.

Orientation and Practical Information

Just west of Segovia and northwest of Madrid, Avila is an easy daytrip from either city. From the bus station, cross the street and walk down C. del Duque de Alba, keeping the small park to your right. Follow the street to Pl. Santa Teresa, just outside the walls. From the train station, follow Avda. José António to C. de Isaac Peral, bear right, and turn left on C. del Duque de Alba, continuing to Pl. de Santa Teresa 15 min.). Municipal buses also pass 1 block in from the train station and will take you to **Plaza de la Victoria,** the central square within the walls.

Tourist Office: Pl. de la Catedral, 4 (tel. 21 13 87), in front of the cathedral. Helpful English-speaking staff. Open Mon.-Fri. 9am-3pm and 5-7pm, Sat. 9am-1:30pm; in off-season Mon.-Fri. 9am-3pm and 4-6pm, Sat. 9am-1:30pm. Afternoon schedule may vary.

Post Office: Pl. de la Catedral, 2 (tel. 21 13 54; for telegrams 22 20 00). Open Mon.-Sat. 9am-2pm. Open for **telegrams** Mon.-Fri. 8am-9pm, Sat. 8am-7pm. **Postal Code:** 05001.

Telephones: Pl. de la Catedral (tel. 003), next to the post office. Open Mon.-Sat. 10am-1pm and 5-11pm. Accepts Visa for a 500ptas min. **Telephone Code:** 918.

Train Station: Avda. Portugal, 17 (tel. 22 01 88 or 22 65 19 for information; 22 07 81 for office), at the end of Avda. José António on the northeast side of town. To Madrid (2 hr., 530ptas), Segovia (2 hr., 610ptas), and Salamanca (4 per day, 2 hr., 470ptas). For Toledo, transfer at Madrid's Atocha Station.

Bus Station: Avda. Madrid at Avda. Portugal (tel. 22 01 54), on the northeast side of town. To Madrid (3 per day, 2 hr., 585ptas), Segovia (2 per day, 1½ hr., 350ptas), and Salamanca (2 per day, 550ptas).

Taxis: Pl. de Santa Teresa (tel. 21 19 59). Open daily 8am-10:30pm. Also at the train station (tel. 22 01 49). Open daily 6am-2am. Fare from train station to Pl. de Santa Teresa 280ptas plus 20ptas per piece of luggage.

Hospital Provincal: Tel. 22 16 00 or 22 16 50. **Ambulance:** Tel. 21 12 20.

Police: Avda. José António, 3 (tel. 21 11 88). **Emergency:** Tel. 091.

Accommodations

Inexpensive accommodations abound both within and outside the walls. Not surprisingly, those within the walls are more expensive.

Residencia Juvenil "Duperier" (IYHF), Avda. de la Juventud, Ciudad Polideportiva (tel. 22 17 16). Past the Convento de Santo Tomás and the cinema, next to the municipal swimming pool (closed). Be sure to call before making the 20-min. hike from the train station—there are only 10 beds. Doubles with bunkbed, desk, and small wooden closet. 450ptas, ages over 26 550ptas. Full pension 1050ptas, ages over 26 1400ptas.

Hostal Continental, Pl. de la Catedral, 6 (tel. 21 15 02), next to the tourist office within the walls. This century-old hotel has seen better days but retains elegance and charm. Excellent location and friendly management. Rooms are large and come with private phones. Incredibly strong hot showers, even late at night. Singles 1500ptas. Doubles 2350ptas. Breakfast 150ptas. Lunch or dinner 450ptas. Meals served at Hotel Valderramos, 10m away and run by the same owners.

Fonda La Abulense, C. Estrada, 11 (tel. 21 14 95), between Pl. de Santa Teresa and Pl. de Italia, just outside the wall. Homey place with wood floors, old-fashioned wallpaper, and pleasant owners. The rooms are bare, but some of the doubles are extremely large. Singles 1000ptas. Doubles 1800ptas. Showers 150ptas.

Fonda San Francisco, Trav. José Antonio, 2 (tel. 22 02 98), just off Avda. de José António, between the train and bus stations and Avda. del 18 de Julio. Beds take up most of the small rooms. Singles 1200ptas. Doubles 2000ptas. You may be able to bargain prices down 300ptas late in the day. Showers 200ptas.

Hostal Residencia Elena, C. Marques de Canales y Chozas, 1 (tel. 21 31 61). 4 doubles, 2 of which are huge, with full bath. Nice owner. Doubles 1900ptas.

Food

The city is famous for its *ternera de Avila* (veal) and its *mollejas* (sweetbread). The *yemas de Santa Teresa* or *yemas de Avila,* local confections made with egg yolks, are also tasty, though tourist demand makes them expensive. Be sure to try the smooth regional wine, *vino de Cebreros;* it has a high alcohol content. Seek out cheap eats in and around **Plaza de la Victoria,** though even here the atmosphere and prices are tourist-inspired. Also try **Mercado de Abastos,** on C. Comuneros de Castilla near Pl. de la Victoria. (Open daily 9:30am-2pm and 4-7pm.) **Mercado Gimeco** is on C. Jardin de San Rogue. (Open daily 9:30am-2pm and 4:30-7:30pm.) Every Friday from 9am to 2pm, there is a *mercado típico* in Pl. de la Victoria, where local food, flowers, and crafts are sold.

Bar/Restaurante Palomar, C. Vara del Rey (tel. 21 31 04), at C. Tomás L. de Victorias. A local favorite for *cochinillo asado* (roast suckling pig) at 900ptas. *Menú* 800ptas. Open daily 1:30-4pm and 8-10pm; in off-season daily 1:30-4pm. Bar open daily 7:30pm-midnight.

Bar-Restaurant Casa Felipe, Pl. de la Victoria, 12 (tel. 21 39 24). A small place with outdoor tables facing the plaza. Quick and courteous service. *Platos combinados* 500-600ptas. Chocolate-lovers will get a buzz from the *chocolate caliente* (100ptas), the thickest and richest hot chocolate you've ever tasted. Open daily 7:45am-midnight.

Restaurante El Ruedo, I. Enrique Carreta, 7 (tel. 21 31 98), off the beaten path within a stone's throw of the wall. A tranquil place to catch a superb regional feast. Great gazpacho 295ptas. *Menú* 795ptas. Open Wed.-Mon. 1:30-5pm and 9pm-midnight.

Mesón el Rastro, Pl. del Rastro, 4, at C. Cepadas and C. Caballeros at the southern wall. Huge portions of regional specialties. Try the *Judias del Barco de Avila* appetizer (450ptas) and the *truchas del tormes* (700ptas). *Menú* 1000ptas. Open daily 1-4pm and 9:30-11pm.

El Molino de La Losa, Basada de La Losa, 12 (tel. 21 11 01), outside the western walls. Cross the Puente del Adaja and turn right. Come to this water mill/restaurant not for the food but to sip their rum-powered sangria (9-glass pitcher 450ptas). Sit on the outdoor terrace above the river along with Avila's small yuppie crowd. Open for meals daily 1-4pm and 9-11pm. Bar open daily 10:30am-midnight.

Sights and Entertainment

Avila in its entirety has been declared a national monument, and the perfectly preserved **medieval walls** played no small role in the attainment of this status. Construction began around 1090 by the order of Raimundo de Borgoña, and Mudéjar architectural features reveal that Muslim slaves must have shared in fortifying Christian Avila. Ninety massive towers and eight gates create a sense of completeness rare in other European walled towns. The **Puerta de San Vicente,** at the end of C. de López Núñez in the midst of a park, is particularly beautiful. The best view of the walls and of Avila itself is from the **Cuatro Postes,** a tiny four-pillared structure past the River Adaja on the highway to Salamanca, 1½km to the northwest of the city. For a more intimate encounter with the old stones, climb the walls along the Parador Nacional in Pl. Concepción Arenal; enter through the garden, worthy of a picnic or a siesta.

Some believe that the view of Avila's **cathedral** looming over the watchtowers inspired St. Teresa's metaphor of the soul as an interior castle. In any case, the cathedral is radiant. Construction started in the early twelfth century, when three Romanesque naves were erected; at its completion two centuries later, Castilla possessed its first Gothic cathedral, owing to a series of alterations to the original project. The sixteenth-century altarpiece, a beautiful depiction of scenes from the life of Jesus, is by Pedro Berruguete, Juan de Borgoña, and Santa Cruz. Behind the chancel is the alabaster tomb of Cardinal Alonso de Madrigal; an Avila bishop known as El Tostado because of his dark complexion. The small **cathedral museum** has a fine collection of gold and silver work, sculptures, and paintings from the twelfth to eighteenth centuries including a small work by El Greco. (Cathedral open May-Sept. daily 8am-1pm and 3-7pm; Oct.-April daily 8am-1pm and 3-5pm. Free. Museum open May-Sept. daily 10am-1:30pm and 3-7pm; Oct.-April daily 10am-1:30pm and 3-5:30pm. Admission 100ptas.)

Casa de los Deanes, the building in Pl. Nalvillos with a Renaissance facade, houses Avila's **Museo Provincial.** The museum displays a collection of Celtiberian objects excavated in the area, Spanish paintings, and ceramics. The collection includes a bullfighting exhibit preserving the heads of the most fearsome *toros* to have pounded across Avila's plains. (Open Tues.-Sat. 10am-2pm and 5-8pm, Sun. 10am-2pm. Admission 200ptas, students free.)

For a town its size, Avila has an exceptional quantity of first-rate religious architecture. The **Basílica de San Vicente** is a large Romanesque and Gothic building dedicated to Vicente, Sabina, and Cristeta, three martyred saints buried beneath the church. Walk around to the west portal to view the remarkable sculptures of Jesus and 10 of his apostles. (Open daily 10am-1pm and 4-6pm. Admission 25ptas.) The Dominican **Monasterio de Santo Tomás,** outside the walls at the end of C. de Jesús del Gran Poder, was the summer palace of the Catholic monarchs. King Fernando and Queen Isabel initiated its construction in 1482. *Granada* (pomegranate) motifs recall the monarchs' triumphant 1492 capture of Granada, the last Moorish kingdom in Spain. (Open Mon.-Sat. 10am-12:30pm and 4-7pm, Sun. 4-6pm. Admission to museum 50ptas, to the cloister 50ptas. Mon. free.)

Three buildings are closely linked to the life of St. Teresa. The **Monasterio de Santa Teresa** was built in the seventeenth century on the site of her parents' home. The church's restrained baroque facade offers no hint of the extravagant decoration of the chapel that was built over the spot where Teresa is said to have been born. (Open daily 8am-1pm and 3:30-9pm. Free.) Many of Teresa's mystical experiences took place during the 30 years she spent in the **Monasterio de la Encarnación.** Visit her cell to see the comfort she was rebelling against when she initiated the reform of the Carmelite order. Upstairs is an interesting museum with a collection of furnishings, letters, and other personal effects. (Open daily 9:30am-1pm and 4-6pm. Obligatory tour in Spanish 40ptas.) The first convent Teresa founded was the **Convento de San José,** also known as the **Convento de las Madres,** at C. de las Madres, 3, off C. del Duque de Alba. Although the 1608 building can't be visited, the small **Museo Teresiano** exhibits the saddle she used while traveling all over Spain establishing convents, the drum she played at Christmas, and a letter written in her elegant, educated hand, which alone merits a trip here. (Open daily 10am-1pm and 3:30-6pm. Admission 25ptas.)

Secular architecture is also well represented in Avila. The **Palacio de los Polentinos,** on C. de Vallespín, presents a beautiful Renaissance facade. (It's now an army facility.) To get an interior view, ask one of the armed guards out front to escort you into the majestic blue-and-white tiled courtyard, the upper story of which is supported by seemingly weightless escutcheoned pillars. The **Palacio de los Dávila,** in Pl. Pedro Dávila, has Gothic doors and windows. (Entry is prohibited.)

Together with the cathedral, the Gate of San Vicente, and the Monasterio de Santo Tomás, Avila's walls are illuminated most summer nights from 10:30pm to midnight; Saturdays, Sundays, and holidays in off-season from 8pm to midnight; and daily from 8pm to midnight during **Teresa's Feasts** (Oct. 8-16) and Christmas (Dec. 22-Jan. 7). Go to Cuatro Postes for the best view.

Every year from October 8 to 16, the city goes crazy for a week in Teresa's honor, with fairs and parades of *gigantes y cabezudos* (figures with large heads). From mid- to late July, the **Fiestas de Verano** (Summer Celebrations) are held with exhibits, folk singing, dancing, pop groups, fireworks, and a bullfight. Procure a calendar of events from the tourist office.

Salamanca

For centuries the "hand of Salamanca," inherited from the Moors and traditionally found on the doors of this city, has welcomed students, scholars, rogues, princes, and saints. In the old city, golden sandstone has been forged into almost every architectural style from Romanesque to baroque, creating a harmony common to few other cities. The Plaza Mayor, in the center of the city, was built by Felipe V in the eighteenth century and is considered by many to be the most beautiful plaza in Spain.

Salamanca is known primarily for its university. Founded in 1218, it's the oldest in the country. After almost two centuries of decline, it is now striving to be worthy once more of the prestige it enjoyed in medieval times, when it was considered one of the four great western centers of learning along with Bologna, Paris, and Oxford. Many outstanding Spanish intellectuals have come to Salamanca. Nebrija, who put together the first grammar of Spanish—indeed of any modern language—in 1492, taught here for a while but left appalled by his fellow professors' scarce knowledge of Latin. A professor of Greek and a university rector, Miguel de Unamuno wrote most of his novels and essays here, and was arrested here for objecting to fascism.

The streets of Salamanca are lively year-round. If you're interested in studying in Spain, consider the university's well-organized summer program for foreigners. Though Salamanca can't boast Santander's beaches or Madrid's big-city bustle, its student *movida* is second to none.

Orientation and Practical Information

Whether you arrive by bus or train, you will be 20 minutes from the town center. The **train station** lies northeast of the center. Either catch the bus that goes to Pl. Mercado (next to Pl. Mayor), or, with your back to the station, turn left down Avda. Estación Ferrocarril to Pl. de España, and walk down C. Azafranal to Pl. Mayor. From the **bus station,** either catch the bus to Pl. Mercado or walk down C. Filber to C. Villalobos across Avda. Alemania, and continue down C. Ramón y Cajal (which becomes C. Prior) to Pl. Mayor.

From **Plaza Mayor** the heart of the city continues south, encompassing the monumental zone. Anything you want—including cheap food and accommodations—can be found in this area. Since Salamanca is small, you can easily get around on foot; tangled streets, however, make a map indispensable. **Rua Mayor** connects Pl. Mayor with the university and cathedral. **Calle de España** (better known as **Gran Vía**) runs almost parallel to Rua Mayor and connects the Pl. Mayor with Pl. de España and the newer section of town, including the main business district.

Tourist Office: National, C. de España, 39-41 (tel. 24 37 30). English spoken by a helpful staff. Open Mon.-Fri. 9:30am-2pm and 4:30-7pm, Sat. 9:30am-2pm. **Municipal,** Pl. Mayor (tel. 21 83 42). More of an information booth—go to the national office for a better map and information on all of Spain. Open Mon.-Fri. 10am-1:30pm and 5-7pm.

Student Travel Office: TIVE, Pl. de la Constitución, 1 (tel. 24 61 29). Budget travel information and discounts. The lines are long, so get here early. Open Mon.-Fri. 9am-2pm. Also **Viajas Juventus,** Pl. de la Libertad, 14 (tel. 21 74 07), and **Viajes Zarco,** Cuesta del Carmen, 27 (tel. 24 61 29).

Post Office: C. de España, 25 (tel. 24 30 11), 2 blocks from the national tourist office toward Pl. España. Open for stamps and information Mon.-Fri. 9am-2pm and 4-6pm, Sat. 9am-2pm. Open for Lista de Correos Mon.-Fri. 9am-2pm. Open for **telegrams** Mon.-Sat. 9am-9pm. **Postal Code:** 37008.

Telephones: Pl. Peña Primera, 1, off C. de Torres Villarroel. Open Mon.-Sat. 9am-1pm and 5-9pm. **Telephone Code:** 923.

Airport: Aeropuerto Aeródromo de Matacán, 20km down the road to Madrid. Private flights and charters available.

Train Station: Avda. Estación de Ferrocarril (tel. 22 57 42), northeast of town. To Madrid (3 per day, 3½ hr., 1100ptas), Avila (4 per day, 1¾ hr., 550ptas), Valladolid (6 per day, 1½ hr., 1000ptas), Barcelona (1 per day, 3690ptas), and Oporto (1 per day, 41/3 hr., 1825ptas).

Bus Station: Avda. Filiberto Villalobos, 79 (tel. 23 67 17 or 23 22 66). To Zamora (roughly hourly, 300ptas), Madrid (14 per day, 4 hr., 1100ptas), Avila (3 per day, 1¾ hr., 500ptas), Sevilla (2 per day, 4 hr., 2439ptas), Barcelona (2 per day, 4 hr., 4190ptas), Oporto (4¾ hr., 1625ptas), and León (450ptas).

Taxis: Tel. 25 44 44 or 25 00 00.

Car Rental: Hertz, Avda. Portugal, 131 (tel. 24 31 34). **Avis,** Pl. del Campillo, 4 (tel. 22 98 66 or 25 86 11). **AutoLux,** Paseo de la Estación, 2 (tel. 23 30 43).

Lost Property: Edificio Lasalle, Avda. de Lasalle (tel. 21 51 08). The National Police (tel. 091) may also offer assistance.

English Bookstores: Librería Cervantes, Pl. Hermanos Jerez (tel. 21 86 02), off C. de José António. Out-of-date bestsellers. **Portonaris,** Rua Mayor, 33, opposite the House of Shells. Salamanca's most renowned bookstore. Penguin classics and all of Hemingway's Spanish classics. Open Mon.-Fri. 9:45am-1:30pm and 4:30-8pm, Sat. 9:45am-1:30pm

Summer Courses: Secretaria de los Cursos de Verano, Universidad de Salamanca, Patio de Escuelas Menores, Salamanca (tel. 21 66 89). Courses offered year-round. Tuition about 33,000ptas per month.

Laundry: Lavandería la Glorieta, C. de Torres Villarroel, 61 (tel. 23 57 27), on the north side of town. Walk north from Pl. Mayor on C. Zamora to Pl. del Ejército, then continue in the same direction on C. de Torres Villarroel (15 min.). Cheap and run by friendly people. Wash, dry, and fold 375ptas per 5kg. **Lavandería Soap,** Avda. Italia, 29 (tel. 25 32 57 or 21 53 93), closer to the center of town. Self-service. Open Mon.-Sat. 10am-9pm, Sun. 10am-2pm.

Swimming Pool: Las Torres, Carretera de Madrid (tel. 21 90 97), across the river from the university (20 min.). A bus runs from C. de España near Pl. de España every hr. The most accessible pool of the nine or more around town. Open in summer daily 11am-8pm. Admission 300ptas.

Medical Services: Hospital Clínico, Paseo San Vicente, 23 (tel. 23 22 00 or 23 30 62). **Prusa España,**N Edificio España, in Pl. de España, 4th floor (tel. 22 20 29 or 24 91 76; weekends 20 09 07). A private medical clinic at quite a price. The staff speaks fluent English, French, German, and Japanese. Foreign medical insurance accepted.

Police: Policía Municipal, Carretera Ciudad Rodrigo (N-620, tel. 21 51 05). **Emergency: Municipal Police,** Tel. 092. **National Police,** Tel. 091.

Accommodations and Camping

Between Plaza Mayor and the University

With its large, transient student population, the university area of Salamanca has no shortage of hotels and pensions. There are plenty of inexpensive *fondas* on the side streets off the Pl. Mayor, especially on **Calle Meléndez,** just south of the plaza. Rooms run about 600ptas per person.

Pensión Barez, C. Meléndez, 19 (tel. 21 74 95). You'll want to call this place home. Sparkling clean, with owners who will treat you like one of the family. Balcony rooms with a view of San Benito. Singles 650ptas. Doubles 1300ptas. Showers 125ptas.

Pensión Marina, C. Doctrinos, 4, 3rd floor (tel. 21 65 69), between C. de la Compania and C. Prado. One of the best deals in Salamanca. Immaculate rooms with brand-new mattresses. Most rooms open onto the street, with views of Iglesia la Purísima. Gigantic bathroom. Plush TV lounge. Outgoing owners. Singles 700ptas. Doubles 1500ptas.

Hostal Tormes, Rua Mayor, 20 (tel. 21 96 83), next to the university. Long, white halls lead to clean, airy rooms. TV lounge. Singles 950ptas, with shower 1200ptas. Doubles 1700ptas, with shower 2150ptas. Showers 150ptas. Breakfast 150ptas.

Fonda Lisboa, C. Meléndez, 1 (tel. 21 43 33). Cramped and damp, but renovations are underway. Prices will rise. Singles 500ptas. Doubles 1000ptas. Showers 125ptas.

Fonda Lucero, C. Meléndez, 23 (tel. 21 55 41). A good deal if you can get an airy front room; others are cramped or windowless. 600ptas per person. Hot showers 200ptas.

North of Plaza Mayor

As you move farther north from the Plaza Mayor, prices and quality escalate, though not always at the same rate. The density of *fondas* decreases and gives way to more expensive *hostal residencias* near Pl. de España.

Hostal Residencia la Esperanza, C. Concejo, 4 (tel. 21 35 33), just north of Pl. Mayor. Dark entrance conceals comfortable rooms with patterned wallpaper and lots of light. Singles 900ptas. Doubles 1600ptas, with shower 1800ptas. Showers 200ptas.

Hostal Los Hidalgos, Paseo de Canalejas, 14-16 (tel. 24 20 41), near the above. Noisy since it's off a major intersection, but rooms are beautiful, modern, and clean. Parking garage for guests. Singles 1200ptas. Doubles with shower 1800ptas, with bath 2200ptas.

Hostal Carahela, Paseo de Canalejas, 10-12 (tel. 24 22 61), off Pl. de España. Like its neighbor it tends to be noisy, but the rooms are impeccable. Friendly management. Singles 1300ptas, with bath 2000ptas. Doubles 1800ptas, with bath 2300ptas.

There are several campgrounds near Salamanca. **Regio** (tel. 20 02 50), 4km out of town on the road to Madrid, has a nice pool. (275ptas per person, per tent, and per car.) **Don Quixote,** 4km out of town on the road to Aldealengua, is a bit cheaper. (Open July-Sept. 250ptas per person and per tent.)

Food

Plaza Mayor is lined with inexpensive cafeterias and restaurants, many with tables outside when the weather permits. This is the place to come to see and be seen; locals and tourists alike flock here to scope.

A slew of very cheap bar/restaurants line **Calle Meléndez,** where a full meal will set you back no more than 500ptas. These places are smaller and don't offer outside tables, but they are also popular hangouts and are less touristy. Don't miss the *jeta,* a local *tapas* specialty of fried skin from the mouth of a pig—not surprisingly, it tastes like bacon. For groceries, go to the daily **market** (8:30am-2pm) at Pl. del Mercado to the east of Pl. Mayor, or to the **Supermercado** on C. Iscar Peyra, 2 blocks from Pl. Mayor (open daily 9:45am-3:30pm and 5-8pm). For really cheap meals, visit the **Comedor Universitario,** the university dining hall open to the public. Meals are 325ptas and less. (Open Oct.-May.)

Cafeteria-Restaurante Roma, V. Ruiz Aguilera, 8 (tel. 21 72 67 or 21 75 64). Italian villa decor, but the menu consists of *salmantino* specialties. After a few bottles of the wine they keep putting on the table, it will all make sense. Large portions, cheap prices, and friendly service. *Menú* 600ptas, *chanfaina* (rice with chunks of lamb, seasoned with lamb's blood) 290ptas. Open daily 1-4pm and 8-11:30pm.

Mesón Cervantes, Pl. Mayor, 15, 1st floor (tel. 21 72 13). A likeness of a stoic Cervantes keeps an eye on the bar and reminds students of their work. Fight for the one wooden table that looks out over the plaza. Run by young people and full of students. *Platos* 400ptas, sandwiches 300ptas. 75ptas more if you eat at the terrace tables in the Pl. Mayor. Open for meals daily noon-4pm and 8pm-midnight. Drinks served at almost any hour.

Restaurant El Bardo, C. Compania, 8 (tel. 21 90 89), behind the Casa de Conchas and in front of the Clerecía. Classy place with newspapers to read if you're bored of the background music. Vegetarian and classic *menús* (550ptas) served only at midday. A la carte at night runs 600ptas. Open Tues.-Sun. 11am-4pm and 7pm-midnight.

Bar Restaurant La Luna, C. Libreros, 4, down the street from the university facade. Wood and plaster interior, a student crowd, and mood music. The restaurant serves Salamanca's cheapest, largest *menú* (500ptas); a la carte runs 600ptas. Open Mon.-Thurs. 10:30am-1:30pm, Fri.-Sun. 10:30am-3am.

Restaurante Casanova, C. Meléndez, 19 (tel. 21 52 41). You could have a love affair with this family-run place; it serves delicious home-cooked meals. 4-course *menú* 575ptas, combination plates 300-400ptas. Open daily 1-4pm and 8-11pm.

Aleko's, Rua Mayor, 26 (tel. 21 73 68). Imaginative McDonald's impersonation: kiddie-proof booths, monkey posters, and a huge trophy collection on the wall. Hamburgers 300ptas, pizza 350ptas, combination plates 400ptas. Open daily 11:30am-11:30pm.

Imbis, Rua Mayor, 31, across from Aleko's. Boring rows of plain wood tables. Large selection of *tapas.* Combination plates 375ptas. Open daily 8am-midnight.

Restaurante Vegetariano El Trigal, C. de Libreros, 20 (tel. 21 56 99), near the cathedral and the Patio de las Escuelas. Meager portions and nonalcoholic wine called *mosto.* The only place in Salamanca offering strict vegetarian fare and a smoke-free atmosphere. *Menú* 600ptas. Open daily 1-4pm and 8:30-11pm.

Sights

Salamanca is an architectural tapestry woven in sandstone. Although there are excellent examples of Roman, Romanesque, Gothic, Renaissance, and even baroque structures, the golden stone itself is a thread of continuity and harmony. Nowhere is the golden glow more apparent than in the **Plaza Mayor.** Begun in 1729 during the reign of Felipe II, the plaza was constructed by various artists until its completion in 1755. Until a hundred years ago, it was often used for bullfights; audiences stood on the three floors of balconies surrounding the plaza. Between the arches—almost 100 of them—are medallions with bas-reliefs of famous Spaniards from El Cid and Cervantes to Franco. The facade of the **town hall,** designed by Andrés García de Quiñones, is partially balanced by the **Pabellón Real** by Alberto Churriguera to its left.

The **university** was founded by Alfonso IX of León in 1218, predated in Europe by only Paris, Oxford, and Bologna. Enter from the **Patio de las Escuelas,** off C. Libreros. The statue here represents Fray Luis de León, one of the top names in literature of the Spanish Golden Age. A Hebrew scholar as well as one of the best Spanish stylists, Fray Luis was condemned by the Inquisition for translating Solomon's *Song of Songs.* After four years in prison, he returned to his chair at the university and started his first lecture with a phrase that shook all Salamanca: "*Decíamos ayer . . .* " ("As we were saying yesterday . . . "). Upon graduation, students used to paint their initials on the walls surrounding the patio, using a mixture of bull's blood, olive oil, and herbs to produce the reddish ink. Facing the patio, the university's plateresque facade depicts King Fernando and Queen Isabel, the Catholic monarchs. Just above them, a pope addresses his cardinals, and Hercules and Venus try to figure out why they are included. A small frog carved on a skull in the facade's plaster symbolizes the dankness of prison life, but students allege it brings them good luck on exams. A more dangerous tradition holds that you'll get married in one year if you can spot it without help.

Inside, you can visit some of the old lecture halls. The **Aula Fray Luis de León** (lecture room) still has its original benches and the professor's pulpit. If you can read Spanish, don't miss the plaque bearing Unamuno's poem on love and the students of Salamanca. The **Paraninfo** contains baroque tapestries and a portrait of Carlos IV attributed to Goya. Fray Luis is buried in the eighteenth-century chapel. (Open Mon.-Fri. 9:30am-1:30pm and 4-7pm, Sat. 9:30am-1:30pm and 4:30-7pm, Sun. and holidays 10am-1pm. Admission 100ptas, students free with university ID but not ISIC.)

The **Escuelas Menores,** also on the Patio de las Escuelas, is another university building with a plateresque facade. Its arcaded patio is an escape from the constant motion of the Pl. Mayor. On the ceiling of the **Sala Calderón de la Barca,** you'll find the famous *Cielo de Salamanca* (*Sky of Salamanca*), a fifteenth-century fresco depicting the signs of the zodiac. (Open same hours as the university. Admission with the same ticket.) The nearby **Casa de Alvarez Abarca** belonged to Fernando Alvarez Abarca, physician to Queen Isabel. This beautiful fifteenth-century building is now the seat of the **Museo Provincial de Bellas Artes.** In Room II, the handsome lid of a sarcophagus depicts a reclining Knight of Malta. Spanish paintings predominate, but the Italian, French, and Dutch schools are represented in Room IV. The first floor shelters an interesting collection of modern art as well as the works of regional artists. (Open Mon.-Fri. 9:30am-1:30pm and 4-7pm, Sat. 9:30am-1:30pm and 4:30-7pm, Sun. 10am-1pm. Admission 100ptas.)

Salamanca flaunts two adjacent cathedrals. The **new cathedral** was begun in 1513 to accommodate the growing tide of believers and was constructed gradually (as coffers permitted) until 1733. The basic structure is late Gothic, with Renaissance and baroque elements. Alberto Churriguera fashioned the lovely cloister, with its Renaissance and baroque flourishes. Cherubic faces contrast sharply with the ornamental patterns and shields that decorate most of the massive cathedral. In the Sagrario Chapel is the *Cristo de las Batallas* carried by El Cid in his campaigns. The facades of the cathedral incorporate beautiful sandstone friezes depicting Jesus' birth and his ride into Jerusalem. If you have the chance, see the cathedral at night: Dozens of storks blend into the architecture as they perch eerily on each one of the church's spires.

Begun in 1140, the Romanesque **old cathedral** features heavy lines that are a welcome break from the Gothic madness next door. Assorted ghouls and gremlins stare down from the capitals of the thick columns marking the aisles. The central altarpiece narrates the story of the Virgin Mary in 53 scenes painted by Nicolas Florentino. Inside the cupola, apocalyptic angels separate the sinners from the saved. The oldest part is the Chapel of San Martín, with brilliantly colored frescoes from 1242. Off to one side is the twelfth-century cloister, rebuilt after the earthquake of 1755. Some of the side chapels around the central courtyard hold intricately carved alabaster tombs. One of the most interesting is the Talavera chapel, with a Gothic Mudéjar dome similar to the one in the mosque in Córdoba. The Chapel of Santa Barbara, also called the "Degree Chapel," was once the site of final exams for those wishing to graduate from the university. The **museum** features a paneled ceiling by Fernando Gallegos, Salamanca's most famous painter, and houses the Salinas organ, named for the blind musician to whom Fray Luis dedicated an ode. (Both cathedrals open June-Sept. daily 10am-1:30pm and 4-7pm; Oct.-May daily 9:30am-1:30pm and 3:30-6pm. Ticket sales end 20 min. before closing. Admission to old cathedral, cloisters, and museum 100ptas. New cathedral free.)

Plaza de Anaya, outside the new cathedral, is a beautiful, grassy square, flanked by elegant golden buildings. It's a favorite hangout for street musicians and students even during the hot siesta hours; no distracting bars or restaurants ruin the setting.

One of the city's most famous landmarks is the **Casa de las Conchas** (House of Shells). This fifteenth-century house of golden sandstone is decorated with several rows of scallop shells chiseled out of sandstone. Shells such as these were worn by the pilgrims who journeyed to Santiago de Compostela as a token of their visit to St. James the Apostle's tomb. The owner of this house, a knight of the military and religious order of Santiago, wanted to create a monument to the renowned pilgrimage site. (Closed to the public.)

The **Clerecía** or **Real Colegio del Espíritu Santo,** built under the orders of Felipe III, is a splendid baroque building under the care of the Jesuits. It houses a church, a *colegio* (school), and the community's living quarters. Unfortunately, its wonderful facade can't be properly appreciated because of the Casa de las Conchas across the street. In fact, a few wealthy believers once offered a large sum of money to have the Casa demolished in order to clear the way for admiring viewers. (Closed to the public.)

The **Convento de San Esteban,** downhill from the cathedrals, is one of Salamanca's most imposing monasteries. Seen in the afternoon, its monumental facade becomes a solid mass of light depicting the death of the martyr St. Esteban and the crucifixion of Jesus. The beautiful **Claustro de los Reyes** (Kings' Cloister) is both Gothic and plateresque. The huge central altarpiece, crafted in 1693 by José Churriguera, is a baroque masterpiece with intricate golden columns decorated with grapevines. The statues of Santo Domingo de Guzmán and St. Francis are attributed to Carmona, and the *Martyrdom of Saint Stephen,* above, is by Claudio Coello. The chancel contains classic, unadorned stalls by Alfonso Balbas (17th century), and a large allegorical fresco by Palomino representing the victory of the church over vice and sin through the Dominican order. (Open daily 9am-1pm and 4-8pm. Admission 50ptas.)

The nearby **Convento de las Dueñas** was formerly the Mudéjar palace of a court official. The elegant cloister was a later addition, explaining why its five sides are of unequal length. The elaborate capitals on the first floor are nearly joined together by the decorations that form arch-like structures. The cloister, with its elegant medallions, is perhaps the most beautiful in Salamanca. (Open 10am-1pm and 4-7pm. Admission 40ptas. There's a good candy shop inside the convent on the 1st floor.)

In the center of the **Puente Romano,** a 2000-year-old Roman bridge spanning the Tormes, stands the **Toro Ibérico,** a huge granite bull—minus its head. The bridge was part of an ancient Roman road called the Silver Way that went from

Mérida, in Extremadura, to Astorga, near León. The old Celtiberian bull made it into literature in one of the most famous episodes of *Lazarillo de Tormes,* a classic sixteenth-century picaresque novel, and from these pages butted its way onto the town shield. The view from across the Puente Romano is breathtaking: The cathedral presides like a monarch over its sandstone subjects.

Entertainment

The **Plaza Mayor** is the center for people-watching and just hanging out in Salamanca. If you're lucky, you may run into La Tuna de Salamanca or one of the local high school *tunas.* A *tuna* is a group of men whose role is to entertain. Dressed in traditional black costume, they woo women in the audience with song and dance. Look for them in the plaza and restaurants, carrying guitars, mandolins, *bandurrias,* and tambourines. When the show is over, they make excellent drinking partners.

Café Novelty, on the northeast corner of the Pl. Mayor, is the oldest cafe in Salamanca and a place where students and professors often meet. Miguel de Unamuno was a regular here. **Cafe El Corrillo,** Pl. Mayor by C. Juan del Rey, is another popular place, crowded day and night. Bars (without dance floors) are also popular. **El Puerto de Chus,** at Pl. San Julián, is known as one of the best late-night spots. Various bars along **Calle Meléndez** belt out assorted music, including vintage hard rock and Spanish new music, until the wee hours. For drinking, try the **Big Apple** on Pl. San Julian, east of Pl. Mayor.

Some of the most frequented discos (really bars with dance floors) line **Calle Iscar Peyra.** Try **Titali,** with primary colors galore, or black-and-silver **La Nuit. Limón y Menta** posts ads around town for their special theme nights. **Camelot,** a medieval-castle-turned-disco, and **Frescas,** its more modern rival, are other local favorites. **Bar Coppelia,** C. Consuelo, 9, near Pl. del Mercado, attracts both gay and straight clientele. All discos have evening (7-10pm) and late night/early morning (11pm-4am) sessions. For music in a different vein, **Mezcal,** on Cuesta del Carmen, offers live jazz shows nightly at midnight and 1:30am in a laid-back environment.

Pick up a copy of *Ambiente,* a small pamphlet available at the municipal tourist office, for listings of movies, nightspots, and special events. Also read the posters at the **Colegio Mayor** (Palacio de Anaya) for university events, free films, and student theater. Avoid the southwest section of town after dark unless you're accompanied by a friend or two.

In summer, the city sponsors the **Verano Cultural de Salamanca,** a series of events including silent movies, contemporary Spanish cinema, pop singers, and theater groups from Spain and abroad. On July 12, in celebration of San Juan de Sahagún, there is a **corrida de toros.** From September 8-21, the town indulges in festivals, bullfights, and expositions for no apparent reason other than to have a good time.

Near Salamanca: Zamora

A one-hour bus ride away from Salamanca, Zamora has a number of interesting monuments from the days when it was controlled by Carthage and Rome. Viriatus, the renowned "terror of the Romans" who wore eight streamers to recall his eight victories over the consuls, was born here. In 1476, King Fernando inadvertently created the city's famous emblem by adding an emerald streamer to the eight red ones to honor Zamorans' courage in the Battle of Toro, which helped to consolidate Spanish unity. The town's medieval works are well worth the quick excursion from Salamanca.

Zamora's foremost monument is its **cathedral,** begun in 1135 by Alfonso VII and completed 36 years later. Its most salient feature is its Serbian-Byzantine dome, which sits like a bulb waiting to burst, surrounded by small cupolas with an oriental flair. The scaly stone roof makes the slender pillars seem ready to collapse. Inside the cloister, the **cathedral museum** houses a collection of art, documents, and fifteenth-century tapestries. The tapestries are the most distinctive part of the exhibit. A gift from the sixth Count of Alba de Aliste in 1608, the tapestries are among the world's best given their size, composition, drawing, and coloring. Don't miss the depiction of the Battle of Troy. (Open daily 11am-2pm and 4-7pm. Admission to museum 50ptas.)

Examples of Romanesque architecture are as abundant as Zamora's many churches: San Cipriano (1025), Santa María de Nueva (the original structure dates back to the 7th century), San Juan de Puerta Nueva (13th century), Santiago del Burgo (12th century), San Vicente, San Ildenonso, Santo Tome, San Esteban, Santa María de la Horta, San Claudio de Olivares, and the Iglesia de la Magdalena together have earned Zamora its nickname of "Romanesque museum."

Ruins are as omnipresent. The remains of the San Francisco, San Jeronimo, Dueñas de Cabañales, and Corpus Christi monasteries are all here, recalling the strong influence of monastic life on the city during its medieval years. The city's most impressive ruins, behind the cathedral in the castle, were once part of the city's formidable **walls.** The remains of the walls are mainly Roman gates scattered about town, the most famous of which is the "Traitor's Gate," near the castle. Here the treacherous Sancho II died during his attempt to take over Spain. Also worth a look is the **house of El Cid,** where he and Doña Urraca were both tutored in their youth by Governor Arlas, and the **Iglesia de Santiago de Caballeros,** where El Cid is said to have been knighted.

Most of Zamora may be seen in a day. If you decide to stay overnight, however, try **Hostal San Carlos,** Carretera de Tordesillas (tel. 52 24 42; singles 850ptas; doubles 1400ptas). The helpful **Turismo** is on C. Santa Clara, 20 (tel. 51 18 45; open Mon.-Fri. 9am-2pm, Sat. 10am-1pm). The **post office** is nearby on C. Santa Clara, 15 (tel. 51 33 71; open for stamps, Lista de Correos, and **telegrams** Mon.-Sat. 10am-1pm and 5:30-7pm). The **bus station** is at C. Condes de Alba de Aliste, 3 (tel. 52 12 81 or 51 12 82). To reach the Turismo, walk left out of the station, turn left on Ronda de San Torcuato, continue straight through Pl. de Alemania onto Avda. Alfonso IX, and take a right on C. Santa Clara (10 min.). Only slow-moving **automotores** run to Zamora. The **RENFE** office is at C. Ramon Alvarez, 6 (tel. 51 36 18). For **train information,** call the train station (tel. 51 14 56). The **municipal police** are at C. San Vicente, 5 (tel. 52 18 46); **first aid** is available at Pl. de San Esteban (tel. 51 14 44).

Valladolid

About 30 years ago, the French car company Renault opened a factory near Valladolid. Since then a huge influx of workers has boosted the city's population to three times that of León, the province's second largest city. As always, the economic explosion proved a mixed blessing: The new boom town was chosen to be the capital for the Junta de Castilla-León, the provincial governing body, but thoughtless urban planning heavily polluted the Rió Pisuerga. Rapid economic growth combined with unchecked construction have also accelerated the old quarter's deterioration. The city has shed its nickname, "Facha-dolid" (read Fascist-dolid), by electing a socialist mayor and abolishing Franco-related street names.

Valladolid's challenge, then, has been to move forward while remembering its historic past. The pristine beauty of the Campo Grande park and the elegant Augustine monastery (still in use) are promising landmarks. The hurry of shoppers and students at the foot of the cathedral seems to best represent the city's balanced coexistence with its glorious past.

Orientation and Practical Information

Valladolid lies in the middle of the quadrilateral formed by León (133km), Burgos (122km), Salamanca (114km), and Madrid (186km). The Río Pisuerga marks the periphery of the city. The train and bus stations will leave you on the southern edge of town.

Tourist Office: Pl. de Zorrilla, 3 (tel. 35 18 01). From the train station, walk up Avda. Recoletos (formerly Gen. Franco) to Pl. Zorrilla. The friendly manager can provide maps and information on the city's museums. Open Mon.-Fri. 9am-2pm and 4-6pm, Sat. 9am-2pm.

Student Travel Service: TIVE, located in the Servicios Mutiples Edificio, on C. José Luis Arrese. After crossing the river on C. Calvo Sotelo, it's the first, huge municipal building on your left. Open Mon.-Fri. 9am-1pm and 5-8pm, Sat. 9am-1pm.

Post Office: Pl. de la Arrinconada (tel. 33 06 60), between Pl. Mayor and San Benito. Open Mon.-Fri. 9am-2pm and 4-6pm, Sat. 9am-2pm; for Lista de Correos Mon.-Fri. 9am-2pm. **Telegrams:** (tel. 22 17 42). Open Mon.-Fri. 8am-9pm, Sat. 9am-7pm. **Postal Code:** 47001.

Telephones: C. Gondomar, 2. Open Mon.-Fri. 9am-1pm and 5-9pm. **Telephone Code:** 983.

Airport: Villanubla Airport (tel. 25 68 92). A 1100ptas taxi ride or a 15-min. Linecar ride from the bus station (tel. 23 00 33; two per day). Daily service to Gijón and Barcelona.

Train Station: Estación Campo Grande (tel. 22 33 57), at the end of Campo Grande Park. To Madrid (13 per day; *tranvía,* 4½ hr., 1090ptas), Palencia (9 per day, 1 hr., 220ptas), Bilbao (3per day, 1340ptas), Burgos (1 per day, 2½ hr., 525ptas), Salamanca (4 per day, 550ptas), and León (8 per day, 2¼ hr., 735ptas). Information open daily 7am-11pm.

Bus Station: Puente Colgante, 2 (tel. 23 63 08). From the train station, turn left and stick close to the railroad tracks for the 10-min. walk. To Madrid (2 per day, 2½ hr., 995ptas), Palencia (1 hr., 250ptas), León (2 per day, 685ptas), Barcelona (2 per day), and Salamanca (550ptas).

Bookstores: Librería Miñón, C. Fuente Dorado, 17 (tel. 30 02 66). About 40 Penguin titles, and 40 Grafton and Oxford titles. Open Mon.-Fri. 9:30am-1:30pm and 5-8pm, Sat. 9:30am-2pm.

Public Library: Biblioteca Publica de Chancilleriá, on C. Chancilleriá between Paseo de Ramón y Cajal and C. Real de Burgos. Open Mon.-Fri. 9am-1pm and 4-6pm.

Swimming Pools (Picinas Municipales): C. Delicias Rondilla, across the river where C. Garciá Morato crosses the bridge. Indoor. Open daily 9am-9pm. Admission Mon.-Sat. 225ptas, Sun. 250ptas. For outdoor swimming June-Sept., head to **Piscinas Deportivas,** located next to the river, off Paseo de Isabela Católica, near the Puente del Poniente. Admission 260ptas. Open daily 11am-8pm.

Lost Property: In the Ayuntamiento in the Pl. Mayor. Open Mon.-Fri. 9am-2pm.

Hospital: Policlínica 18 de Julio, C. Gamazo, 13 (tel. 22 23 27). **Ambulance:** C. San Blas, 3 (tel. 25 40 50).

Police: Felipe II, 10 (tel. 25 33 44).

Accommodations

Before the university closes at the end of June, you may have problems finding accommodations during the week. Students usually room in the city on weekdays. If you're in a bind, try looking in the triangular area formed by **Avenida Recoletos** (formerly Gen. Franco), **Calle Miguel Iscar,** and **Calle Gamazo:** This area is removed from the university hub.

Río Esqueva Albergue Juvenil (IYHF), Carretera Cementerio (tel. 25 15 00). Take the #1 or #8 bus from the Pl. Mayor. Get off the #1 at the Esqueva River (really a stream) and walk across the park on your right. Get off the #8 at the river. By foot, proceed down C. de Chancilleriá, which turns into C. Madre de Dios and finally into C. del Cementerio. No curfew. Open July-Sept. 450ptas, ages over 26 550ptas. Sheets included.

Fonda Villa Segovia, Calle del Perú, 11 (tel. 20 74 39), off Avda. Recoletos, a 10-min. walk from the train station. New management/family bends over backwards to take care of the place. Big, clean rooms with bedside lamps. Singles 750ptas. Doubles 1400ptas. Showers 100ptas.

Fonda Florez, C. Marina de Escobar, 10, 4th floor (tel. 30 81 38), near Fonda Segovia. Immaculate, quiet rooms. Singles 636ptas, doubles 1272ptas. Showers 150ptas. On the 1st floor of the same building, **Fonda Los Charros** (tel. 22 90 55) offers rooms of the same quality. Singles 800ptas. Doubles 1200ptas. Showers 150ptas. Disabled access.

Pensión Madrid, C. Gamazo, 11 (tel. 30 03 91), between Pl. Colón and Pl. de España. Lovely decor with arched doorways and beautiful ironwork. Doubles 1400ptas.

El Greco, C. Val, 2 (tel. 35 61 52), centrally located near the Pl. Mayor and Mercado del Val. A stately grandfather clock guards the draped doorway. Spotless rooms with desks. Singles 920ptas. Doubles 1620ptas. Showers 170ptas. Also in this building, **Hostal Vuelta** rents satisfactory rooms. Singles 1000ptas. Doubles 1700ptas. Showers 200ptas.

Pensión Bautista (no phone), and **Fonda Tordesillas** (tel. 30 56 79), at Pl. Solanilla next to Santa Mariá La Antiqua Church. The noisy neighborhood is a bit run-down, but the inside is better than the outside. Singles 700ptas. Doubles 1400ptas. Triples 2100ptas.

Food

Valladolid is a university town, so cheap eats are never far away. Explore **Plaza de la Universidad,** near the cathedral, for *tapas.* The **Mercado de Val** on C. Sandoval, in Pl. de Val, is full of vegetable, meat, and fruit stands. (Open Mon.-Sat. 9am-2pm.)

El Bolinche, C. Encarnación, 2 (tel. 33 38 74), behind San Benito. The place has been making waves ever since it started making fruit-veggie drinks 12 years ago. Banana-orange, avocado-orange, and carrot-apple juice are served freshly squeezed (about 250ptas). Much of the food is vegetarian, including banana-cheese-apple and hot asparagus, lettuce, and tomato sandwiches (about 250ptas). Open daily 1-4pm and 8-11:30pm.

Sidrerrá Asturiana, Pl. del Portugalete, 7 (tel. 39 68 82), to the left of the cathedral as you face its front. Nautical decor and a stuffed turtle surround the 50-ft. bar. Order a bottle of *sidra* at the bar and marvel at the bartender's Asturian style of pouring: The server holds the bottle over his head and the cup near his crotch. *Platos combinados* 450ptas. Open daily 11:30am-3pm and 5:30-11:30pm.

Restaurante Lope de Vega, C. del Perú, 5 (tel. 30 20 59), off Pl. de España. Modern interior filled with locals who stay for the after-hours poker games. *Platos* 325-500ptas, *menú* 600ptas. Open daily 11:30am-4pm and 6-11:30pm.

Cafeteriá El Chicote, C. Tarandona, 4 (tel. 33 00 63), Pl. de Val, near the market. The bright orange counter and blue vinyl may remind you of a hometown diner, but the food won't. ½-chicken, french fries, and salad 425ptas. *Filete* (steak) and eggs 400ptas. Open Thurs.-Tues. 10am-4pm and 7-12pm.

Restaurant Bar Castilla, Pl. de España, 2. Home of delicious *sopa castellana* and other regional specialties, but a full meal runs as high as 1000ptas. Excellent service. *Menú* 800ptas. Open daily 1-4pm and 8-11:30pm.

Sights and Entertainment

Although Vallodolid is known for its churches, its museums are also esteemed. The **Museo Nacional de Escultura Policroma,** in the **Colegio de San Gregorio,** contains what is considered the best collection of multicolored sculpture in the world. Alonso Berruguete is perhaps the most famous artist represented here, but don't miss Juan de Juni's elegant and moving *Entombment* or his *Saint Anne,* a beautifully realistic depiction of old age. Pedro de Mena's *Mary Magdalene,* starkly contemplating a sculpture-within-a-sculpture of the Crucifixion, has captivated generations. (Tel. 25 03 75. Open Tues.-Sat. 10am-2:30pm and 4-6pm, Sun. 10am-1:30pm. Admission 200ptas.) The facades of San Gregorio and its neighbor, **San Pablo,** are attributed to Simon de Cologne, although some question the identity of San Gregorio's designer. Regardless, the buildings exemplify the best of the plateresque school, and, true to the meaning of *"platero,"* resemble complex, silver patterns. Organic motifs fill San Gregorio's ornate entrance. The **patio's** interwoven masonry is hypnotizing and worth the three-minute walk north from the cathedral.

Tucked away in the basement of the **Real Colegio Padres Agustinos Filipinos,** Paseo Filipinos, 7, an unexpected treasure awaits. The **Museo Oriental** houses Spain's best collection of Asian art. Throughout their four centuries of missionary work, the fathers were accumulating the collection, comprised mostly of Chinese and Philippine works. Bowls in the **porcelain room** date from the second century B.C.E.; the seventeenth-century vases are newer additions to the room. The **Sala**

de Numismática displays over 1300 coins. Don't overlook the Taoist paintings on rush wood, the ink drawings on delicate rice paper, or the 15-inch ship crafted from cloves by a patient Filipino artist. (Tel. 30 69 00. Open Mon.-Sat. 4-7pm, Sun. 10am-2pm. Admission 125ptas. Located near the train station, on the south side of Campo Grande.)

The cold, cavernous **cathedral** is not surprisingly the work of Juan de Herrera, who also designed Felipe II's monumental El Escorial. Herrera never finished the building. In the eighteenth century, Alberto Churriguera decorated the upper portion of the imposing facade in the extravagant baroque style named after his family. The **Museo Diocesano** is worth a look for its interesting jewelry and wooden polychrome statues of John the Baptist. (Tel. 30 43 62. Open Mon.-Fri. 10am-2pm and 5-8pm, Sat.-Sun. 10am-2pm.) Behind the cathedral, the Romanesque tower of **Santa Mariá La Antiqua** tops mostly Gothic underparts. Up C. San Blas and C. Heroes de Tervel, the **Iglesia de San Benito el Real** boasts a gigantic portico, under which an entire tank unit could park with ease. Inside, the dark wooden choir stalls are decorated with scenes from Jesus' life.

From the fountains of **Pl. de Zorrilla** (named after the popular author of *Don Juan Tenorio*), a beautiful park fans out towards Paseo de los Filipinos; **Campo Grande's** paths are favorites for afternoon strollers. Nearby, *Don Quixote's* creator spent his final days in the **Casa de Cervantes**. (You might conclude that he died of boredom.) There's an amusing collection of old books and furniture, but the medieval bed-warmer is the real highlight. (Tel. 30 88 01. Open Tues.-Sat. 10am-6pm, Sun. 10am-2pm. Admission 200ptas.)

As you'd expect in any sizable university town, Valladolid's nightlife doesn't disappoint. In the early evening after classes, the grass near the cathedral is a popular hangout. Be sure to bring your liter bottle of San Miguel *cerveza* (beer) so you don't stick out. Later, the flocks migrate from the bars near the university to **Plaza Cantarranas,** 2 blocks east. On your way over, make sure to visit Valladolid's most famous bar; **El Penicilino,** Pl. de la Libertad. Cristina, the proprietor, will tell you about the medical student who used to request a special concoction which others found so delicious that the bar now bottles the mixture. "Penicilino" was named in honor of the antibiotic discovered at the same time. (Tel. 30 50 32. Open Thurs.-Tues. 11:30am-2:30pm and 6-11pm.)

Semana Santa (Holy Week) in Valladolid ranks with Sevilla's as one of Spain's most interesting religious festivals. It is a solemn affair, enriched by the rituals of *cofradías* (brotherhoods) and religious orders. Palm Sunday begins with veiled women dressed in white carrying palm fronds through the city. Ash Wednesday is marked by high masses, while on Holy Thursday, huge polychrome floats from the seventeenth century are carried through the streets. On Good Friday, all the orders march in total silence except for the beating of a lone, mournful drum, accompanied by statues and religious images. The week of September 21 marks the **Fiesta Mayor** celebrations, featuring bullfights, carnival rides, and parades. The first week of April belongs to the city's **film festival;** in May, **theater** companies from all over the world converge on Valladolid to perform.

Palencia

Sandwiched by León, Santander, Valladolid, and Burgos, the province of Palencia extends from the ochre-colored Castilian plain to the green foothills of the Cantabrian Mountains. The capital city and sleepy surrounding *pueblos* carefully guard some of Spain's most important Romanesque and Visigothic monuments.

Known as "La Bella Desconocida," the **cathedral** in the capital city of **Palencia** is the pride of its citizens; but as long as there are *palentinos* to sing its praises, the fourteenth-century landmark will never truly be a "forgotten beauty." Judging from its battered exterior, the city's foremost historical sight seems neglected, but inside the *trascoro's* impressive plateresque and Gothic lines are quite well-preserved. Next to the *trascoro,* a stairway leads into the **San Antolín Crypt,** an eerie seventh-century

Visigothic sepulchre. The **Museo de la Catedral** contains enormous Flemish tapestries, El Greco's *San Sebastín,* and silver liturgical instruments. (Cathedral and museum open Mon.-Sat. 10am-1pm and 4-6pm, Sun. 10am-1pm.)

While none of Palencia's other churches is considered to be an architectural masterpiece, several are worth a visit for their oddities. The **Iglesia de Santa Clara** is the resting place for a singularly different Jesus, shown floating on the sea after a Christian naval victory over the Moors. This corpus bears a chilling resemblance to a well-preserved mummy. Blackened fingernails, decomposed toes, and a gaping mouth, seemingly frozen in *rigor mortis,* promote fantastic rumors. Señora Mariá, the relic's self-appointed curator, explains with absolute sincerity that medical experts are baffled by this man-God-corpse; after reciting the chronology of its long voyage to the church, she will shuffle away to say a rosary for you. The church is 2 blocks from Pl. de San Lorenzo, which is on Avda. de Casado del Alisal. (Church open Mon.-Fri. 9am-1:30pm and 3pm-sunset, when who-knows-what happens in that glass sarcophagus.)

The ogival tower of the **Iglesia de San Miguel,** 1 block from Rió Carrión, is a local landmark, giving the church a fortress-like appearance. The facade of the **Iglesia de San Pablo,** opposite the train station, is a sixteenth- century predecessor of Spanish-American mission architecture. Two Renaissance sepulchres sit inside the building, to the right and left of the *capilla mayor,* and a plateresque retable rests on the main altar. (San Miguel and San Pablo open daily 9am-1pm and 7-8:30pm. Time your visits to avoid interrupting Mass.) A 35-minute walk from town on the highway to Santander leads to an ostentatious little monument dubbed **El Cristo del Otero.** Here, towering over the plain around Palencia, an art-deco Jesus sports a streamlined gown and appears hands-up, as if to say "Don't shoot!" The mildly strenuous trek up the *cerro* (hill) is rewarded by a splendid view and possibly a cool breeze.

Palentinos' renewed interest in their churches (most have been partially or completely renovated in the past 150 years) accompanies the beautification of the city itself. **Los Jardinillos** near the train station, **La Huerta de Guardiaán,** and the new *paseo* (walk) by the river are all small, well-groomed parks, where townspeople stretch their legs.

Accommodations are difficult to find. The safest choice is **Casa Eduardo,** C. Valentín Calderón, 5 (tel. 74 29 48). A gloomy, green staircase arrives at narrow bedrooms with nightmarish wallpaper. (Singles 1000ptas. Doubles 1500ptas. Showers 200ptas.) **El Salón,** on Avda. República Argentina (tel. 72 64 42), is a pleasant alternative on the opposite side of town. Run by a pleasant, older couple, the place features a spotless white interior, large bedrooms, and even a few chandeliers. (Singles 1000ptas. Doubles 1500ptas. Showers 200ptas.) The **Alberga Juvenil: Campo de la Juventud (IYHF),** Cardinal Cisneros, 12 (tel. 72 04 62), just off Avda. Valladolid, is due to open in October 1988.

There are few ways to avoid the 600ptas *menús* scattered around town. Either hit the **mercado,** just off Pl. Mayor (open Mon.-Fri. 9am-2pm and 4-6pm, Sat. 9am-2pm), or dine with every male pensioner in town at **Restaurante La Carronesa,** Pl. Mayor, 16. *Menús* are the 600ptas norm. *Platos combinados,* like half-chicken and salad, cost425ptas. **Restaurante Tuchar,** C. Valentín Calderón, 21 (tel. 74 22 46), serves a 650ptas *menú* and a tasteful *menestra,* a stew with peas, mushrooms, artichoke and ham (400ptas). The brave will be rewarded for trying a delicious plate of *sesos,* pig's brains (350ptas).

Palencia can be reached by train from Burgos (7 per day, 1¼ hr., 380ptas), Valladolid (25 per day, 45 min., 205ptas), León (17 per day, 1½ hr., 510ptas), and Santander (2 per day, 6 hr., 895ptas). The **train station** is across the Jardinillos park near Pl. de León and the end of the C. Mayor. The **bus station** is nearby, to your right as you walk out of the train station. **Turismo** (tel. 72 07 77), at the end of C. Mayor, #153, provides information on sights in the city and outlying area. (Open Mon.-Fri. 9am-2pm and 4-6pm, Sat. 9am-2pm.) For information on the entire province, check with the **Diputación Provincial,** C. Don Sancho, 3. (Tel. 74 11 00. Open Mon.-Fri. 9am-1:30pm.) **Telephones** are located at C. Berruguete, 8.

(Open Mon.-Fri. 9am-2pm.) Public **swimming pools,** open in July, are near the Polideportivo, close to the river. The **hospital** is on Avda. San Telmo (tel. 72 82 00); the **police** are in the Pl. Mayor (tel. 74 97 00). The **post office** (tel. 71 15 80) can be found in the Pl. de León. (Open Mon.-Fri. 9am-2pm and 4-6pm, Sat. 9am-2pm.)

Near Palencia

The city of Palencia's greatest virtue, as its tourist office will gladly tell you, is its proximity to the oldest and most numerous Romanesque ruins in Spain. From this gateway, you can easily explore the Camino de Santiago (Road to Compostela), and earlier ruins including Visigothic chapels and Roman villas. Palencia is the best place for bus and train connections to some of these remote areas.

Paredes de Nava offers a simple existence on the Castilian plain: a church, a plaza, two *fondas,* three bars, and fewer than three thousand people. Only 20km from Palencia, but at least a century and a half away, it's the first stop on the railroad north and the birthplace of the painter Pedro Berruguete, the sculptor Alonso Berruguete, and the poet Jorge Manrique.

Other than cloud-watching in the plaza, the thing to do in town is to visit the **Iglesia de Santa Eulalia** and the **Museo Parroquial** inside. Only the twelfth-century Romanesque tower was spared when the church was enlarged in the fifteenth century. Pedro Berreguete painted the scenes of *The Restoration of the Virgin* for the main retable in 1485, while Esteban Jordan, married to one of the master's daughters, designed the architecture. Along with more Berruguete paintings, some Mudéjar relics, vestal garments, and an enshrined rib from St. James, the museum houses a collection of retables in the Berruguete style. Take a look at the one attributed to Juan González, also married to a daughter of Berruguete. The two distinct styles show that he probably had help from his father-in-law. (Museum open May-Sept. daily 11am-2pm and 4-7pm; Oct.-April daily 11am-2pm and 4-6pm. If the building is locked, ask around for the priest or call 83 00 98 to receive a personal tour. Donations appreciated.)

Only five trains per day connect Palencia with Paredes de Nava (135ptas). Check the schedule; departures are erratic. For a 600ptas *menú* which could stuff half the human race, chow down at **Fonda Sofía,** down C. Santa María from the church and behind the Ayuntamiento.

Pass through another time-warp from Palencia to **Baños de Cerrato** to see the perfectly-preserved Visigothic **Basílica de San Juan Bautista.** Recesuinto raised the basilica in 661 C.E. as a monument to his favorite martyr. With its short, squat lines, it is the oldest Christian temple still standing in Spain. Try to read Recesuinto's inscription above the altar, and find the impression of his hand on the floor.

Reaching the basilica is at least half the fun, especially if you enjoy dodging cowchips and lunatic tractor drivers. Take the train 9km from Palencia to **Ventas de Baño** (every 40 min., 75ptas). Turn left at the station entrance and keep walking; Baños de Cerrato is the town visible 2km down the road. The basilica is on the far side of this farming community; don't mistake it for its brick-walled impostor at the center. The caretaker and his extremely large keys reside at C. San Juan de Baños, just up from the basilica—ask for Sr. Antonio. (Basilica open Tues.-Sun. 9am-1pm and 5-7pm.)

Right on the Camino de Santiago, 32km north of Palencia sits **Frómista,** home of the **Iglesia de San Martín.** Considered by many to be the masterpiece on which later Romanesque churches were styled, San Martín was built in 1066 and restored in 1904. Pilgrims used to stop and make an offering at the monastery that once surrounded the church. The building's unique symmetry and small exterior sculptures (called corbels) make it an exceptional Romanesque church. Only six of the original capitals have been replaced. (Open Wed.-Fri. 10am-2pm and 5-8pm, Sat.-Sun. 10am-2pm and 4-8pm.) Elsewhere, **Santa Mariá del Castillo,** a late Gothic church with a Renaissance portico, is closed for restoration. Five trains per day leave Palencia for Frómista; the 45-minute ride costs 150ptas. From the train station, walk into town; the **tourist booth** is the first thing you'll see and the church is just 1 block away.

A 45-minute bus ride from Palencia brings you to **Carrión de Los Condes,** most famous for the **Iglesia de Santa Mariá,** a twelfth-century temple. The portal on the south side supposedly represents the tribute of 100 maidens that Carrión extended to its Moorish conquerors. Miraculously a stampede of bulls crushed the would-be kidnappers. Time has carved its own ideas on the wall; the 40 miniature figures lining the arch are indistinguishable. The better preserved frieze above the arch depicts the Adoration of the Magi. Inside the building, original and reconstructed parts share a rather uneasy coexistence. The rounded vault over the side naves, for example, gradually develops a distinctive point toward the front of the church, as if the seventeenth-century rebuilders felt the need to correct the simplicity of its original design. The church sits behind the **tourist office** and the plaza where the bus leaves you. (Church open daily 8am-2pm and 7-9pm.) If the entrance is locked, ring the bell at the priest's house next door.

The **Iglesia de Santiago,** now closed for repairs, features a beautiful frieze which runs the width of the building and shows Jesus, surrounded by the apostles, doling out blessings. On the other side of the Rió Carrión looms the now unpopulated **Monasterio de San Zoilo.** The Renaissance cloister is the only part open to the public: The faces of saints, popes, and skeletons peer out from its ornate, crossing arches. A moving, life-size statue of Jesus stands tied to a tree. The garden within the cloister is now an overgrown weed patch, but as you leave try to sneak a peak at the more recently abandoned seminary garden, where roses still bloom. The guard will show you to tombs of the Carrión de Los Condes, the unfortunate evil-doers of the Poema del Cid who married El Cid's daughters only to abandon them in the middle of nowhere. (Open Tues. and Fri. 10am-1pm and 4-6pm; during summer, it may open daily. Check the Diputación Provincial in Palencia for details.)

Carrión's hidden treasure is the **Convento de Santa Clara,** 2 blocks from the bus stop (also known as Café España). The *repostería,* or bake shop, serves delicious, homemade cookies. Just 450ptas will buy a meat or fish *empanada* (pie with a flaky crust). Since the nuns are cloistered, all food-money exchanges are expedited by a revolving cabinet: They peer out from behind two iron gratings to speak to their customers. Sr. Antonio may faciliate your purchase and then show you (for 50ptas) the recently inaugurated **museum** of the convent. The rich fourteenth-century fabrics of the bishops' frocks seem almost new. Be sure to take a look at the shepherd's nutcrackers and ask Sr. Antonio to tell you about the statue of the infant Jesus with a toothache. (Open Tues.-Sun. 10:30am-12:30pm and 5-7pm; in winter Tues.-Sun. 10:30am-12:30pm and 4-6pm.)

The only **campground** (tel. 88 01 85) in the area north of Palencia is 2 blocks from the Ayuntamiento in Carrión de los Condes, next to the river. (Open May-Sept. 160ptas per tent.) Three buses daily connect Palencia to Carrión, and three travel in the reverse direction. The 45-minute trip costs 175ptas.

León

Had that grave medieval predecessor of modern guidebooks, the *Codex Calix-tinus,* employed a rating system, the attractive city of León would certainly have received five shining stars. The budget-traveler-*cum*-monk author enthusiastically writes (in Latin) of "the court and royal city of León, brimming with all kinds of felicity." Happily, León is still a remarkably beautiful town—and not just because of its splendid Romanesque and Gothic buildings. The lofty Gothic cathedral is as radiant as ever, but the fountains, parks, and avenues in the newer part of town also shine.

The Roman camp of the Seventh Gemina Legion at the juncture of the Torío and Bernesga Rivers was the predecessor of the city of León. Indeed, the city's name represents a vulgar version of the Latin *legio* (legion); the lion which you see emblazoned all over postdated the naming of the city. Formerly the seat of the Asturian-

Leonese Kingdom, León still proudly reminds the world that it had 24 kings before Castilla even had laws. It was here that the Reconquista began.

Today, *leonéses* mine the rich deposits of iron and cobalt found throughout the province. Regional pride still shows in popular slogans like "¡ Castilla, no! ¡ España, si!" While certainly not in danger of erupting into nationalistic violence, as has occurred in Euskadi and Cataluña, León insists on affirming its own unique cultural and historical identity. The reorganization of Spain's provinces earlier in this century upset *leonéses*. More pressing concerns lay with the destruction of old villages, near the Picos de Europa, in order to make way for a new dam. "¡Riaño, crimen del año!" ("Riaño, crime of the year!") is a local line that bemoans the first town to be razed. Like most of Spain, León faces problems of modernization, including damage inflicted on regional culture and geography; however, the capital of the province still manages to display a careful harmony between industry and art.

Orientation and Practical Information

The newer area of León, across the river from the train station, intersected by the **Avenida de Ordoño II, Plaza de Santo Domingo,** and **Plaza de Calvo Sotelo,** forms the city's center for shoppers and drivers alike. At Pl. Santo Domingo, **C. del Generalisimo Franco** replaces Avda. Ordoño II and splits the old section in two, with the cathedral and San Isidoro on one side, the Ayuntamiento and **Plaza Mayor** on the other.

Tourist Office: Pl. de Regla, 3 (tel. 23 70 82), right in front of the cathedral. A busy location because of its proximity to the city's number 1 monument. City guide pamphlets available in English. Open Mon.-Fri. 9am-2pm and 4-5:30pm, Sat. 10am-1pm.

Student Travel: TIVE, C. Conde de Guillén, 2 (tel. 23 83 73), the Delegación de Cultura Building off Avda. de la Repúbluca Argentina. Open Mon.-Fri. 9am-2pm.

Post Office: Jardín San Francisco (tel. 23 42 90), down Avda. de la Independencia, opposite the park of St. Francis. Stamps and Lista de Correos. Open Mon.-Fri. 9am-2pm and 4-6pm, Sat. 9am-2pm. **Telegrams:** Open Mon.-Fri. 8am-9pm, Sat. 9am-7pm. **Postal code:** 24001.

Telephones: C. de la Torre, 13, 1 block down from San Isidoro. Open Mon.-Sat. 9am-2pm and 5-10pm. **Telephone Code:** 987.

Train Station: Avda. de Astorga, 2 (tel. 22 37 04), across the river from Pl. de Guzmán el Bueno. To Madrid (8 per day; *rápido* 1750ptas, 5 hr.; *talgo* 3400ptas, 4 hr.), Barcelona (2 per day, 10 hr., *electrotren* 4800ptas), Valladolid (3 per day, 21/3 hr., 740ptas), Oviedo (5 per day, 1½ hr., 600ptas), La Coruña (4 per day, 7 hr., 2050ptas), Palencia (8 per day, 12/3 hr., 550ptas), and Astorga (7 per day, 45 min., 250ptas).

Bus Station: Cardenal Lorenzana, 2 (tel. 32 62 00), off Avda. de Roma. To Madrid (3 per day, 5 hr., 1730ptas), Valladolid (3 per day, 2 hr., 715ptas), and Salamanca (3 per day, 4 hr., 1320ptas).

Taxis: Tel. 24 24 51 or 25 00 00.

Car Rentals: Hertz, Avda. Sanjurjo, 23 (tel. 23 25 54). Ford Fiesta 3010ptas per day plus 23ptas per km. Insurance 900ptas. **Avis,** Avda. de la Independencia, 7 (tel. 20 65 12), in the lobby of Hotel Conde de Luna. Similar rates.

Baggage Check: Mon.-Sat. 7:30am-8pm, Sun. 8-10am and 5-6pm. 25 ptas per article.

English Bookstore: Pastor, Pl. de Santo Domingo, 4 (tel. 22 58 56) or C. Sanjurjo, 7 (tel. 22 17 12). Penguin classics. Both open Mon.-Fri. 10am-1:30pm and 4-8pm, Sat. 10am-2pm.

Laundromats: Lavasec, C. Pérez Galdós, 1 (no phone), off Avda. de Quevedo, 3 blocks from the San Marros Bridge. 290ptas per load, 100ptas to dry. Open Mon.-Fri. 10am-1:30pm and 4-7:30pm, Sat. 10am-1:30.

Swimming Pool (Piscinas Municipales): In the Polideportivo, Paseo del Ingeniero Saenz de Miera. Cross the arched foot bridge between the bullring and the old veterinary school. Open daily July-Sept. Admission 100ptas.

Hospital: Clínica San Francisco, Carretera Marqués de San Isidro (tel. 20 21 11), at the corner of C. Arcipreste de Hita. **Ambulance:** Tel. 25 25 35.

Police: Villa Benavente (tel. 25 26 08). Lost and found items usually end up here. **Emergency:** Tel. 091.

Accommodations

Budget accommodations aren't scarce in León, but soldiers on leave fill most of the *fondas* and *casas de huéspedes* during holidays and weekends in late spring. For a start, look on **Avenida de Roma**, the left branch leading into the new town from Plaza Guzmán El Bueno, right across the river from the train station.

Residencia Juvenil Infanta Doña Sancha (IYHF), C. de la Corredera, 2 (tel. 20 22 01), 2 blocks past the Jardín San Francisco on the right. A clean dormitory, used by university students during the academic year. Open in July for hostelers. Singles, doubles, and triples available for 450ptas per person, 550ptas ages over 26. Showers and sheets included. Breakfast 100ptas.

Consejo de Europa (IYHF), Paseo del Parque, 2 (tel. 20 02 06), off Pl. de Toros. The newly opened hostel offers fully renovated accommodations. New sports facilities to open in 1989. No curfew. Open July-Sept. 15. 450ptas, ages over 26 550ptas.

Fonda Condado, República de Argentina, 28 (tel. 20 61 60), the right branch into town from the plaza by the river. Spotless, two-toned rooms with an ever-smiling owner. Out of traffic. Singles 800ptas. Doubles 1400ptas.

Hospedaje Suárez, Avda. de Gen Franco, 7 (tel. 25 42 88). Big, clean rooms, dusted from top to bottom by the well-dressed *señora de la casa*. Doubles 1500ptas. Triples 2000ptas. Showers 200ptas.

Hostal Residencia Londres, Avda. Roma, 1 (tel. 22 22 74), at the end of Avda. Roma off Pl. de Calvo Sotelo. Friendly management and comfortable rooms, some with great views. Exquisitely tiled bathroom. Singles 1375ptas. Doubles 2000ptas.

Hostal Oviedo, Avda. Roma, 26 (tel. 22 22 36), next to Pl. de Guzmán el Bueno. Spotless establishment run by the grandparents you always wished you had. Singles 1300ptas. Doubles 2000ptas. Showers 250ptas. **Hostal Europa,** downstairs (tel. 22 22 38), is run by a compulsively clean *señora*. 1000ptas per person. Showers 200ptas.

Hostal Residencia Guzmán el Bueno, C. López Castrillón, 6 (tel. 23 64 12). Walk up C. Generalíssimo from Pl. Santo Domingo, and turn left on C. del Cid; López Castrillon is a pedestrian street on the right. A large, comfortable splurge in a central location. Singles 1200ptas, with bath 1800ptas. Doubles 2200ptas, with bath 3000ptas. Showers 250ptas.

Pensión Jalisco, Avda. Roma, 18 (tel. 22 64 44). Newly renovated and painted. The *señora* is proud to show off the rooms—even in her bathrobe. Elevator in the building. Singles 800ptas. Doubles 1400ptas. Showers 100ptas.

Food

The rich countryside around León provides great milk, cheese, butter, meat, and trout. For inexpensive restaurants, try the area around Plaza Mayor and **Plaza San Martín.** For do-it-yourself menus, shop at **Mercado Municipal del Conde,** Pl. del Conde off C. General Mola. (Open Mon.-Sat. 9am-2pm.) The Pl. Mayor also holds huge **vegetable markets** on Wednesdays and Saturdays.

Bar Restaurante Real, C. Mariano D. Berrueta, 7 (tel. 25 70 15), off C. del Gen. Franco near the cathedral. Traversing the dining room's labyrinth-layout will pique your appetite for the 500ptas *menú*. Open Tues.-Sun. 1-4pm and 8-11:30pm. **Casa Lorenzo** (tel. 25 44 57) at #9 and **La Cepedana** (tel. 25 60 59) at #11 offer smaller *menús* for 450ptas. Lorenzo closed during July. Both open daily 1-4pm and 8-11:30pm.

Bar-Restaurante Gijón, Alcázar de Toledo, 15 (tel. 22 22 83), between C. San Augustín and Avda. Ordóno II. House specialties are *carne guisada* (stewed meat) for 475ptas, *callos* (tripe), and loin of pork. *Menú* 600ptas. A sentimental photograph of the owner's destroyed hometown, Riaño, hangs on the wall. Open Mon.-Sat. 10am-5pm and 8-12pm.

Restaurant Fornos, C. del Cid, 8 (tel. 23 69 21), off C. del Generalíssimo. Family-run and large. Excellent food and service. A good place to escape from the chaotic atmosphere of *bares-restaurantes*. Meat dishes 450-900ptas, but you can eat a delicious full meal for about 700ptas. Open Tues.-Sat. 1:30-4pm and 8:30-11:30pm, Sun. 1:30-4:30pm.

Mesón San Martín, Pl. San Martín, 8 (tel. 25 60 55), a winding block from Pl. Mayor. A bit expensive—and prices go up if you go down to their basement. Assorted daily specials include *menestra* (440ptas), green beans and ham (675ptas), and *cocido* (an untranslatable stew: boiled sausages, carrots, lettuce, chickpeas, and other meat) for 875ptas. Cheaper specialties include *alubias* (stewed white beans) and *paella.* Closed part of July. Open Mon. 1-4pm, Tues.-Wed. 1-4pm and 8-11:30pm, Thurs. 1-4pm, Fri.-Sun. 1-4pm and 8-11:30pm.

Cortijo Susi, C. López Castrillón, 8 (tel. 23 60 46), on the same pedestrian way as Hotel Guzmán, off C. El Cid. The pleasant owners speak English (as the sign over the bar reminds you) and serve a heaping *menú* for 575ptas. The combinations include *paella* and lamb stew, cold cuts and fish, and chicken with rice and beef stew. Open Mon.-Sat. 1-4pm and 9-11:30pm.

San Román Bar and Restaurante, C. Recoletas at C. Castrillón (tel. 23 93 94), off C. El Cid. Their specialty is *molleja* (gizzard). The faint-hearted may prefer to try the 450ptas *menú.* Closed Aug. 15-Sept. 15. Open daily 1:30-3:30pm and 9-11pm.

Dos de Mayo, C. Rúa, 5 (tel. 25 71 86), off C. Gen Franco. Crowded at midday with local shopkeepers and families. Try the *pulpos a la gallega* (Galician-style octopus, 575ptas) or the *merluza a la romana* (hake, 400ptas). *Menú* 550ptas. Open Sun.-Fri. 11am-4pm and 8-11pm.

Sights and Entertainment

Though León's monuments are comparatively few, you'll soon realize that the emphasis is on quality rather than quantity. The **cathedral** is a Gothic masterpiece, a harmonious ensemble of light, color, and stone. The extremely varied facade includes everything from a smiling statue of *Santa María la Blanca* to a no-nonsense depiction of hell. Nothing you've heard about Gothic cathedrals will prepare you for the glorious stained-glass windows. They occupy so much of the wall-space area that the building suffers from a lack of solid rock support. The huge rose window covering much of the main facade is a resplendent example of late medieval stained-glass art. You'll find even more stained glass in the cathedral's chapels. Bach and Mozart resound throughout the interior. This is one place to spend money on a cathedral guidebook (700ptas), because the stained glass tells a story that's hard to decipher on your own. The **museum** has an extensive collection of Romanesque sculpture showing the style's evolution in the province of León. Four more rooms have been opened recently, housing a collection of pre-medieval artifacts. (Museum open Mon.-Sat. 9:30am-1pm and 4-6pm, Sun. 10:30am-1pm. Admission 150ptas.)

The **Basílica de San Isidoro** was dedicated to San Isidoro of Sevilla, whose remains were brought to León during the Muslim rule in the South. Much of the original 1063 C.E. building was redone in the twelfth century. Look for the distinctly Muslim arches whose small lobes form a larger arch. Many members of León's royal family are buried in the impressive **Panteón Real.** The real treasures here are not below your feet, but above them. Remarkably colorful, tempara frescoes cover two crypt ceilings. The vibrant frescoes depict scenes from the New Testament (an innovative step at the time), including the Pantocrater surrounded by the four evangelists. The artists chose to paint the head of the animal normally associated with each evangelist instead of showing Matthew, Mark, Luke, and John next to their beastly counterparts as was the convention at the time. Specialists have been trying to prevent the 800-year-old paintings from peeling; they have also taken protective steps against the sun's harmful intrusion into the vault. Admission to the panteón allows you to view the rooms of treasure and ancient books. Doña Urraca's famous chalice, comprised of two Roman cups set in gold and jewels, is the focal point of the treasury room. A tenth-century handwritten Bible is certainly the library's highlight. (Museum open Mon.-Sat. 9am-2pm and 3:30-8pm, Sun. 9am-2pm; Sept.-June Tues.-Sat. 9am-1:30pm and 4-7pm, Sun. 9am-1:30pm. Admission 150ptas.)

Once a resting place for pilgrims on their way to Santiago de Compostela, the **Monasterio San Marcos** is now Spain's only five-star hotel with a plateresque facade. The **museum** in the adjacent Gothic church houses objects from Roman and medieval times. Among its treasures are the eleventh-century *Carrizo Crucifix,* which displays unmistakably Byzantine features, and a Mozarabic cross decorated with jewels. (Open Tues.-Sat. 10am-1pm and 4-6pm, Sun. 10am-noon. Admission 150ptas. The doorman may stop you from entering the hotel.)

Divinely inspired or mentally unbalanced (depending on your point of view), architect Antonio Gaudí designed few buildings outside his native Catalunya. The **Casa de los Botines,** near Pl. de Santo Domingo, is a rare exception. The building lacks the sensuous, organic curves of his unfinished cathedral in Barcelona, but the design has still provoked enough violent criticism to merit a spiked fence protecting it. On the facade, *Saint George Killing the Dragon* displays a most enthusiastic dying dragon that looks more like a crocodile. (The building now houses a bank; so look like you are making a deposit as you try to sneak in.)

Leon's **Roman walls** are nicely preserved by the cathedral and San Isidoro. The Pl. Mayor perks up for market days on Monday and Thursday, and book day on Sunday. The long *paseos* extending from San Marcos to the bullring cut through well-tended gardens, but **Parque Quevedo,** right across the San Marcos Bridge, is livlier.

The **Feasts of St. John** (June 24) and St. Peter and St. Paul (June 29) are celebrated with bullfights. At the end of September and beginning of October, León hosts an **International Organ Festival.** The cathedral windows set the mood for some divine concerts.

Near León

If you've been to Barcelona and fallen in love with the work of Antonio Gaudí or found yourself intrigued by the Casa de los Botines in León, by all means visit **Astorga.** Though not a pretty town, its monuments make it a worthwhile daytrip. The fairy-tale **Palacio Episcopal** (Bishop's Palace) is one of Gaudí's most brilliant and fanciful creations. The original residence of Astorga's bishop burned down in 1886 and Gaudí was commissioned to design a new one. Working in cahoots with the bishop, a friend and fellow Catalan, Gaudí set about creating a neo-Gothic fairy castle and temple. No expense was spared in the construction since the bishop controlled the purse strings. However, the Obispo Reus' demise put a halt to Gaudí's extravaganza; he soon quit after disagreements with the chapter. For twenty years, the building remained unfinished. When Ricardo Guereta finally completed the project in 1913, no bishop felt comfortable living in the lavish building since the surrounding parish was so poor. The structure's first floor now houses the **Museo de los Caminos.** Inside, spiky capitals and tiled ogival arches underscore Gaudí's willingness to improvise on traditional Gothic forms. The museum's holdings range from thirteenth-century polychrome sculptures to the *Crucifijo de Miguel Angel,* a seventeenth-century cross possibly made by the great Florentine artist himself. (Open daily 10am-2pm and 4-8pm; Oct.-April daily 11am-2pm and 4-7:30pm. Admission 150ptas; 250ptas includes the Museo Diocesano in the cathedral.)

Astorga is an easy 45-minute train ride from León on the line running northwest to Galicia (7 per day, 250ptas). Autocares Alvarez runs eight buses per day from León (235ptas). The bus stop is in sight of the cathedral; just keep walking uphill from the train station until you can see the two buildings to your right. Cheap combo plates (250-400ptas) can be eaten at the nameless **Bar Restaurante** at Pl. del General Santoclides, 17. **Hostal Norte** (tel. 61 66 66) has fairly clean rooms. (Singles 1000ptas. Doubles 1800ptas. Showers 200ptas.) **Turismo** is in the Ayuntamiento on Pl. de España. (Open summer only.)

Although **Sahagún,** to the southeast of León, houses superb examples of Mudéjar architecture, it is an otherwise unremarkable town. The twelfth-century **Iglesia de San Tirso** is an impressive brick church; stones were not readily available when it was built. You can see how the main apse was begun with stone, before the builders changed their minds. The building's famous tower and its arched perforations stand out, but the inside is where the Mudéjares (Muslims living in reconquired Christian Spain) left their trademarks. Horseshoe arches in front of the three altars provide this building with its Eastern flavor. Prominently positioned before the altar is a three-foot Star of David, intertwined with the floor brickwork. The piece symbolizes the coexistence of the three Iberian religions in the early Christian kingdoms. Up a small hill near San Tirso sits the **Iglesia de la Peregrina.** The exterior of this twelfth- and thirteenth-century building boasts Muslim stonework, as the arch over the side entrance indicates. The building's glory hides off the main nave in a small chapel lined with delicate geometrical reliefs. The eye-straining patterns of the molded weaves may appear repetitive, but in fact, each design is unique. Discovered only seven years ago, this Eastern-influenced artisanship may lead to other surprises still hidden under the limestone of the main chapel. (Both open Tues.-Sat. 10:30am-2pm and 5-8pm, Sun. 10am-3pm; Oct.-May Tues.-Sat. 10:30am-2pm and 4-7pm, Sun. 10am-3pm.) If the door of either is locked, walk over to the other; one *señor* holds the keys to both sights. From the train station, go right and walk to Pl. de Gen. Franco, about 10 minutes away; walk out C. Flora Flórez and turn right on C. de San Benito. San Tirso is off to the left.

The **Iglesia de San Lorenzo,** on C. Alhóndigo, is similar to San Tirso. The brick tower and rounded apses mimic those of its earlier counterpart. To enter entails launching a manhunt for the local priest. The ruins of the **Monasterio de San Benito** allow you to see several centuries of architectural design merged. The **town hall** (tel. 78 00 01) is on Pl. Mayor; the **civil guard** (tel. 78 00 45) is housed in a restored part of the San Benito monastery. The **consultorio médico** (tel. 78 01 00) is a block from the police. Two hundred meters past the **Red Cross** (tel. 78 01 45), on the other side of the Roman bridge, is **Camping Pedro Ponce** (tel. 78 11 12). (Open June 15-Sept. 15. 185ptas per person, 150ptas per tent.) Trains leave for Sahagún eight times per day (290ptas; 40 min.).

Burgos

Tranquil, conservative Burgos is one of Spain's finest treasures of Gothic art and architecture. Well-trimmed roses and tidy plazas seem omnipresent. Burgaleses pride themselves on the purity of their spoken Spanish—the best in all Castilla, they'll tell you. Rodrigo Díaz de Vivar, El Cid, Spain's real-life epic hero, wasn't born in Burgos, but some of his most celebrated achievements took place here. The people of Burgos remember his and their own former grandeur—and at times, nothing else. The cathedral, the river, and the statue of El Cid—these are perhaps what Burgos is still all about.

Orientation and Practical Information

Burgos lies on both sides of the **Río Arlanzón.** In front of the centrally located cathedral is **Plaza Santa Mariá,** and beside it **Plaza del Rey San Fernando,** which you enter as you come from the river. Tree-lined **Paseo del Espolón** runs along the river.

Tourist Office: Pl. de Alonso Martínez, 7 (tel. 20 31 25 or 20 18 46). From Pl. del Rey San Fernando beside the cathedral, start down C. Paloma and continue to Pl. Alonso Martínez. Helpful and well-staffed, but the map is hopelessly out of date. Open Mon.-Fri. 9am-2pm and 4:30-6:30pm, Sat. 9am-2pm. When the office is closed, lists of hotels and sights are posted in the window.

Student Travel: Viajes TIVE, in the Casa de Cultura on Pl. San Juan (tel. 20 98 81). Turn left once inside. Helpful tips and literature on discount travel, lodging, and museum prices. Student IDs (250ptas) and IYHF card (1800ptas). Open Mon.-Fri. 9am-2pm.

Post Office: Pl. Conde de Castro, 1 (tel. 26 27 50), across the river from Pl. Primo de Rivera. Stamps and Lista de Correos open Mon.-Fri. 9am-2pm and 4-6pm, Sat. 9am-2pm. Telegrams open Mon.-Fri. 8am-9pm, Sat. 9am-7pm. **Postal Code:** 09000.

Telephones: C. de San Lesmes, 18, off Pl. España. The entrance is actually on the side of the building on C. Hortelanos. Open Mon.-Sat. 9am-1pm and 5-9pm. **Telephone Code:** 947.

Train Station: At the end of Avda. Conde Guadalhorce (tel. 20 35 60), across the river from Pl. Castilla. Quite a big junction. Information open daily 7am-11pm. **RENFE,** C. Moneda, 21 (tel. 20 91 31). Open Mon.-Fri. 9am-1pm and 4-7pm, Sat. 9am-1pm. To Madrid (9 per day, from 2200ptas), Barcelona (3 per day, 3700ptas), Bilbao (6 per day, 815ptas), Irún/Hendaye on the French border (12 per day, some continue to France, 1130ptas), Salamanca (2 per day), Valladolid (3 per day), and La Coruña (3 per day).

Bus Station: C. Miranda, 4-6 (tel. 26 28 00), across the river from the Santa María Arch off Pl. Vega. To Madrid (4 per day, 1245ptas), Barcelona (2 per day, 1 on Sun., 2935ptas), Bilbao (8 per day, 4 on Sun., 880ptas), Donastia (2 per day, 1185ptas), Santander (2 per day, 930ptas), León (1 per day Mon.-Sat.), Salamanca (1 per day Mon.-Sat.), Palencia and Valladolid (3 per day Mon.-Sat.). International lines to Paris (4 per week, 11,350ptas) and London (4 per week, 10,500ptas).

Car Rentals: Azteca, Avda. General Vigón (tel. 22 38 03), near the Servicio Lanza car dealer. Seat Pandas for 2650ptas per day plus 20ptas per km. Open Mon.-Fri. 9am-2pm and 4-8pm, Sat. 9am-2pm. **Hertz,** C. Madrid, 10 (tel. 20 16 75). Ford Fiestas from 3010ptas per day plus 23ptas per km. Must be 20 with a major credit card.

Hitchhiking: Walk south along C. Madrid from Pl. de Vega until you reach highway N-1. To Madrid and Bilbao.

Baggage Check: In train station (100ptas). Open 24 hours. In bus station (50ptas per day for backpacks, 35ptas for other pieces). Open Mon.-Sat. 9am-7:45pm.

English Bookstore: Librería Hijos de Santiago Rodríguez, Pl. José Antonio, 22 (tel. 20 14 43). A fair selection of fiction upstairs. Open Mon.-Fri. 9:30am-2pm and 5-8pm, Sat. 9:30am-2pm.

Public Library: Casa de Cultura, Pl. San Juan (tel. 26 13 22). Mostly Spanish works. Open Mon.-Fri. 10am-1pm and 5-8:30pm, Sat. 10am-1pm.

Swimming Pool (Piscinas Municipal): El Plantió (tel. 22 00 01), to the east along the river. Before jumping in the river, ask about the non-polluted and safe areas for swimming. The Arlanzón has some sudden and treacherous drop-offs despite its apparent shallowness. Admission 200ptas. Open in summer daily 11am-8pm.

Medical Services: Casa de Socorro, Conde de Vallellano, 4 (tel. 26 14 10), at C. Ramón y Cajal near the post office. For 24-hour pharmacy, check listings in *El Diario de Burgos*. Signs listing the all-night pharmacies are posted daily in every pharmacy.

Police: Policía Municipal, C. Merced, 11 (tel. 091 or 20 21 38). **Lost and found** items are sent here.

Accommodations and Camping

Hostile to El Cid during his exile, the people of Burgos are much friendlier to tourists. It's a pleasure to stay here, since there are a number of clean, modest *hostales.* The nicer ones are north of the river around Pl. José António, but the cheaper ones lie south of the river, around Pl. de Vega. The week of June 29 can be difficult for hostelers, since the city fills up to celebrate the *fiestas* of Paul and Peter.

Residencia Juvenil "Gil de Siloi" (IYHF), C. General Vigón (tel. 23 03 62), on the northeast side of town. Walk out Avda. de los Reyes Católicos and turn left on General Vigón. The hostel, in a modern *colegio,* is on your right (50m). IYHF membership required. Dormitory-style sleeping in groups of 4 to 6. Reception open 8-10:30am and 6-10pm. Strict curfew and lights out at 11pm. Open July-Sept. 15. 550ptas, ages over 26 650ptas. Breakfast and sheets included.

Hostal Hidalgo, C. Almirante Bonifaz, 14 (tel. 20 34 81), 1 block up from Pl. José Antonio. Big rooms with high ceilings and wide beds. Something any *hidalgo* (a hard-up, lowly Spanish noble) would be pleased with. The hostal has about 45 rooms so it's unlikely to fill. Singles 100ptas. Doubles 1600ptas. Showers 200ptas.

Hostal Victoria, C. San Juan, 3 (tel. 20 15 42), off Pl. Alonso Martinez near the tourist office. Clean and comfortable, though the young proprietors often make more noise than their guests. Singles 800ptas. Doubles 1300ptas. Showers 150ptas.

Hostal García, C. Santander, 1 (tel. 20 55 53), near Pl. de Santo Domingo. Run by a soft-spoken, friendly woman and her family. Sunlit rooms are small, but not cramped. The beds are suffering a mid-life sag. Doubles 1400ptas. Showers 100ptas.

Fonda Fontaneda, C. Concepción, 14 (tel. 20 80 35), near Pl. de Vega. Low ceilings, but solid beds in rooms of moderate size. Singles 750ptas. Doubles 1400ptas. Showers 125ptas.

Hostal Moderno, C. Queipo de Llano, 2 (tel. 20 72 46), in between Pl. José Antonio and Pl. de Santo Domingo. Bright rooms, half with a view of Pl. José Antonio. Singles 1300ptas. Doubles 1900ptas. Showers 100ptas.

Fonda Boston, C. San Pablo, 13 (tel. 26 13 41), 1 block away from the Puente de San Pablo. Small, tidy rooms with whitewashed walls and fake wooden tiles. Toby, a sweet, black dog, welcomes guests by playfully nibbling at their shirtcuffs and prancing underfoot. The *señora* is more reserved in her salutation. Singles 800ptas. Doubles 1500ptas. Showers 125ptas.

Hostal Joma, C. San Juan, 26 (tel. 20 33 50), beyond C. Santander near Pl. San Juan. Some comfortable rooms, but those without a street window become stuffy in hot weather. Singles 800ptas. Doubles 1200ptas. Showers 175ptas.

Several kilometers out of town in Villafría you can camp at **Río Vena** (tel. 22 41 20), a second-class site. (Open May-Oct. 200ptas per person, 190ptas per tent.) Take the bus from C. General Sanjurjo near the river to highway N-1. **Camping Fuentes Blancas** (tel. 22 10 16) is nicer and only 3½ km outside Burgos, near the Cartuja de Miraflores. (Open April-Sept. 225ptas per person, 175ptas per tent.) Buses marked "Fuentes Blancas" leave hourly 11am-9pm from Pl. Primo Rivera (40ptas) during July and August. During the other months, take the Eladio Perlado bus (#10) and ask the driver to let you off at the pedestrian bridge near Fuentes Blancas. Cross the river and walk east for about 1km. The campgrounds are next to the river.

Food

Land-locked Burgos has created some fine meat dishes. The area's roast lamb is especially famous. Try *picadillo de cerdo* (finely chopped pork) and Burgos's own soup, which contains bits of lamb and crawfish tails. *Burgalés* butchers consider their verson of *morcilla* (blood sausage) to be the best: The rice and spices will wow your tastebuds. Snails are bountiful in this area and taste delicious when prepared well, so don't allow crawling *caracoles* in the market stands to turn you off.

Burgos has two markets, **Mercado Norte** near Pl. España and the smaller **Mercado de Miranda** on Miranda opposite the Museo Arqueológico. Fresh fish is brought down from the northern coast daily. (Markets open Mon.-Sat. 7am-3pm. Mercado Norte has late hours Fri. 5:30-8pm.)

Health food stores have blossomed in Burgos during the past decade. These stores offer whole wheat products, herbal medicines, and health drinks. Nearest to the center of town is **Los Tilos,** at Yagüe, 6, 1 block from Pl. España. (Open Mon.-Fri. 10am-2pm and 4:30-8pm, Sat. 10am02pm.)

Bodego Riojana, Pl. de Alonso Martínez, 9 (tel. 26 07 19), on the corner of C. San Juan. The young owners have given *tapas* a fun twist: They serve their *calamares* and *picadillo* in *cazuelitas* (miniature casseroles). Sandwiches are also available. Three *cazuelitas* will fill you up, but be sure to ask for them (150ptas) and not *cazuelas* (400ptas), bigger servings. Open daily 10am-3pm and 7-10:30pm.

Restaurante Casa Ojeda, C. Vitoria, 5 (tel. 23 35 40), off Pl. Primo de Rivera near the river; the back opens onto Pl. Calvo Sotelo. Simply an institution—everyone comes here, from schoolteachers to the town's bigwigs. Absorb some atmosphere over a 600ptas *combinado* in the downstairs bar/cafeteria (open daily until midnight), but the exquisite food is served in the upstairs restaurant (tel. 20 90 52), a definite splurge. *Cordero asado* (roast lamb) is the house specialty (700ptas). Many other entrees for 800-1200ptas. Royal *menú* 1500-2100ptas. Open Mon.-Sat. 1-4pm and 9:30-11:30pm, Sun. 1-4pm.

Restaurante La Riojana, C. Avellanos, 10 (tel. 20 61 32), off Pl. Alonso Martinéz. The 630ptas *menú* includes salad, *pimientos rellenos* (stuffed peppers) and your choice of water or wine. ½-chickens (340ptas) and pork loin (450ptas) are cheaper alternatives. Open Tues.-Sat. 10am-4pm and 7-11pm, Sun. 10am-4pm.

Bar La Flor, Avellanos, 9 (tel. 26 60 52), across the street from La Riojana. You may feel caged by their enclosed dining area, but the meal will compensate for any claustrophobia. The menú (625ptas) includes *paella,* chicken, dessert, and wine. For 400ptas and under, you can get one of their *combinados* like *tortilla* (omelette), *croquetas,* and *lomo* (pork) all on one plate. Open daily 10:30am-5pm and 6:30-11pm. Closed second week of July.

Restaurante Cafeteria Mannis, C. de San Cosme, 22 (tel. 20 15 50), just over a block from Pl. de Vega. Simple and straight: One *menú* each day and that's it. *Menús* sometimes include *platusa,* a flounder relative, salad with tuna chunks, or kiwi pie. The owner/waitress is pleasant and businesslike as is the decor. Open Mon.-Sat. 1-4pm for lunch.

Bar La Moneda, C. Moneda, 13 (tel. 20 59 31). The next best thing to going to the supermarket. Hot dogs 75ptas. *Bocadillos de patatas* 75ptas. Spicy *patatas bravas* 40ptas. Open daily until 11pm.

Sights and Entertainment

Burgos' most famous landmark, its **cathedral,** is also a monument to the wealth of its citizens in the thirteenth century when construction began. The city was at the heart of Castille, when sheep owners created an unprecedented amount of commerce. The Mesta, a powerful group of gentlemen sheep farmers, legislated and brought prosperity to Burgos by selling their extraordinary Merino wool at home and abroad. The cathedral's ornate exterior was designed to demonstrate the city's wealth and, of course, to worship God. By the time the building was complete two centuries later, the Mesta's glory days were over, but the exterior of the cathedral is still a vivid reminder of the prosperity these men oversaw.

Inside, El Cid's bones rest alongside those of his wife, Ximena, in the *capilla mayor,* giving *burgaleses* another reason to be proud of their monument. The *coro* features wooden reliefs depicting biblical scenes as well as some graphic moments in the lives (and deaths) of early Christian martyrs. The artisans who crafted the wood seem to have recreated their wildest fantasies in the less conspicuous, non-religious carvings.

Behind the altar, the octagonal **Capilla del Condestable** (Constable's Chapel) contains the richly carved tomb of Hernández de Velasco, Constable of Castilla in the late fifteenth century, and his wife. Above, the sun shines through an eight-point glass skylight set into the vaulting. More glass than stone, the main crossing is even more impressive. Use your ticket to gain access to the iron-caged, central part of the nave, then stand in the center and tip your head back to look up—it's easy to imagine the heavens directly above.

It took 34 years to finish the impressive Renaissance altarpiece; the silver Virgin weighs in at 69kg. Each of the many chapels surrounding the cathedral contains its own treasures, and the excellent **museum** of religious art and liturgical objects, located in the cloisters, is especially rich.

In the **Capilla de Santo Cristo** near the main entrance, a particularly mangled Jesus hangs on a cross. Welts line his arms and his neck is bloated. An incongruous, regal skirt replaces the conventional loin cloth. Before leaving the cathedral, look for the *papamoscas* (fly catcher), which peeks out of a window high up near the main door in the central aisle. As it strikes the hours, this strange creature opens its mouth, just like the crowds gawking at it below. (Cathedral open daily 10am-1:30pm and 4-6:30pm. Free, but you need a ticket to visit any of the chapels or museum, which should be bought in the sacristy to your right as you enter. Tickets 200ptas, students 125ptas.

The **Iglesia de San Nicolás** lies across Plaza de Santa Mariá and up the stairs. The interior of this dwarfed neighbor of the cathedral seems awkwardly unfinished. The stones are clear antecedents of modern cinderblock, and half a tumbler of concrete appears to have spilled near the wall opposite the door. But when you see the altarpiece, you'll gasp: The elaborately carved *retablo* shows off about 50 scenes from the lives of saints. The small details near the upper reaches will test your vision. (Open Mon. 9am-2pm and 5-9pm, Tues.-Fri. 6:30-8pm, Sat. 9am-2pm and 6:30-8pm, Sun. 9am-2pm and 5-6pm.)

The people of Burgos claim El Cid as their greatest hero. Cab drivers will tell you how they've named their first born Rodrigo (the Cid's real name); Jimena (the Cid's wife) is a popular choice for girls. The impressive **statue of El Cid** in Plaza

General Primo de Rivera reflects the glory attached to this famous figure. The inscription in Spanish reads "his death caused the most severe mourning among Christians and great joy among his enemies." Contrary to popular myth, the Cid's close Muslim friend Abenamar probably mourned the legend's death as much as his dreaded Christian enemy the Count of Barcelona celebrated it.

The **Arco de Santa María,** across Plaza del Ray San Fernando near the cathedral, houses statues of Burgos' greatest heroes in its niches: Diego Porcelos, founder of the city in the ninth century; Carlos V (an honorary, rather than native, *burgalés*); and of course, El Cid. The **Puente de San Pablo,** 1 bridge east of the Arco de Santa Mariá, supports the great literary weight of eight characters from the Cantor del Mió Cid: Jimena, the Archbishop of Valencia, a Moorish King, and Alvar Fáñez, one of the few *burgaleses* who stood by El Cid when he was banished, are all represented here.

Just up C. Santander, the **Casa del Cordón,** Burgos' most recently renovated building, glows in the sunshine. The Caja Municipal de Ahorros spent millions to restore this building where Columbus met with King Fernando and Queen Isabel after his second trip to America, and where Felipe el Hermoso (the Handsome) expired after a trying game of *pelota,* leaving his wife Juana la Loca (the Mad) utterly insane. The building's mundane use today—it is a bank—belies its remarkable historical significance.

An intelligent remodeling of the **Monasterio de San Juan** left untouched the remaining walls of a destroyed church, while fully renovating and enclosing the cloister. Rich landscape scenes and portraits of Marceliano Santa Mariá, an accomplished *burgalés* artist who died in 1952, lie within. (Open Tues.-Sat. 10am-2pm and 5-8pm, Sun. 10am-2pm. Admission 25ptas.)

Across the river on C. Miranda, the **Museo Arqueológico** resides in the Casa de Miranda, a lovely example of Spanish Renaissance architecture. The museum's rooms house a fair share of prehistoric artifacts, but also some real gems in its medieval section, like the Gothic tomb of Juan de Padilla and an eleventh-century Moorish ivory casket. Roman artifacts from the nearby town of Clunia have been transferred here. The large mosaic just inside the entrance reflects the egalitarian beliefs of this Roman community, as a porcupine gets a ride from a gazelle and a leopard kisses a horse. (Open Tues.-Sat. 10am-1pm and 4:45-7:15pm, Sun. 11am-1pm. Admission 200ptas, students free.)

Four blocks from El Arqueológico stands a rebellious, modern church, which defies its Gothic grandparents across the river. **Nuestra Señora del Carmen** is a combination of unsightly concrete and industrial-grade bricks shaped like a pie wedge. A sickly, yellow light filters through a foodgrater ceiling, illuminating a 15-foot high crucifixion. The building is a refreshing contrast to the Gothic conventions of the cathedral. Cross the pedestrian bridge west of the Arco de Santa Mariá and look for the factory-type building on C. de la Merced. (Mass held at 8am, 10am, 5:30pm, 7:30pm, and 8:30pm. The church opens 15 minutes earlier.)

A brief walk from the cathedral on Fernán González brings you to **castle ruins** sitting on the city's highest point. The view here invites both evaluation of the city's design and appreciation of the lovely hills and fields which surround it.

People-watching is almost a sport in this otherwise quiet city, and the prime playing field is the elegant **Paseo del Espolón** along the river. Enjoy its quiet beauty during siesta because in the evening it fills up with hundreds of *burgaleses* of every age. Well, almost every age—most of the young crowd hang out on **Plaza Huerto del Rey,** which is lined with pubs and bars. It's 1 block behind C. Paloma and C. Laín Calvo, by the cathedral. Later, the party moves to the newer part of town, on the other side of the Monasterio de San Juan. Bars along **C. las Calzadas** become popular after 10pm, especially **Vía Lactea** at #4 and **Cafe-Bar Raul** at #13. A fun place to dance with your reflected image is **Pub Panorama,** Pl. Bernardas, 5, which plays good, loud music.

On June 29, Burgos holds *fiestas* in honor of its patron saints, Peter and Paul. Castilian reserve is set aside as the town comes to life with traditional dance, song, and bullfights. The day after Corpus Christi, the *Pendón de las Navas,* a banner captured from the Moors during the Battle of Las Navas de Tolosa in 1212, is paraded through town.

Near Burgos

Extremely close to Burgos are two impressive examples of medieval architecture. One kilometer west of the city, the **Museo-Monasterio de las Huelgas Reales** was once a summer palace of Castilian kings but later became a convent for Cistercian nuns. The abbess here had many of the privileges of a bishop and wielded immense power for a woman in her time. The bishop's staff now residing in the church by the abbess's seat is only symbolic; her powers were revoked by the pope in the nineteenth century. The Huelgas Reales also served as a royal pantheon, but most of the tombs were desecrated by Napoleon's troops. The church is in the form of a Latin cross. The Gothic cloister has a badly damaged ceiling but you can still see some classic Islamic motifs such as the peacock tail and stars. Several rooms around the smaller and prettier Romanesque cloister are also the work of Muslims. The contents of the one unsacked tomb, that of Fernando de la Cerda (1225-1275), oldest son of Alonso el Sabio, have been put on display in the **Museo de Teles** that has reopened after years of restoration. You can see practically his whole wardrobe, including billowing silver-threaded smocks and elaborately embroidered shirts. The only way to visit the museum and the monastery is with a tour in Spanish; it's worth it even if you don't understand a word. (Open Tues.-Sat. 11am-2pm and 4-6pm, Sun. 11am-2pm. Admission 300ptas, students 50ptas, everyone free on Wed.) You can walk to the monastery (beyond the train station) or take the "Barrio del Pilar" bus (every 40 min., 40ptas) from Pl. de Primo Rivera. (Admission and tour 100ptas, students free.)

The **Cartuja de Miraflores** is a Carthusian monastery that houses the ornate tombs of King Juan II and Queen Isabel of Portugal, and of Don Alfonso, the queen's brother who died as a child. Historians still debate whether Alfonso's untimely death was the result of evil machinations by the nobility or merely bad health. Regardless, Alfonso's demise cleared the way for his sister, Queen Isabel the Catholic's eventual ascendance and felicitous marriage to Ferdinand. Sculptures of Alfonso in prayer and his parents reclining were rendered by Gil de Siloé upon Isabel's bequest. To get here, take the "Fuentes Blancas" bus (July-Aug. only, 35ptas) or walk east along the Paseo de La Quinto for 3 km. (Open Mon.-Sat. 10:15am-3pm and 4-6pm, Sun. and holidays 11:20am-12:30pm, 1-3pm, and 4-7pm. Free.)

La Rioja

Tucked away in the northeastern tip of Castilla-Leon, less than 130km from tip to tip, **La Rioja** boasts some of northern Spain's most fertile lands. While the western section of the region benefits from its proximity to the rainy hills of the País Vasco, irrigation has assured that even the dry regions near Aragon produce bumper crops. Most people attribute the name "La Rioja" to the Ebro River tributary Río Oja. The hearts of wine connoisseurs skip a beat when the name Rioja crops up. Since the twelfth century, the grape-squeezings of this *vega* (fertile plain) have delighted humble and refined palates alike.

Haro

The town of Haro, on the northwest border, has some of the best known *bodegas* (wine cellars) in Spain. Clustered like plump grapes on the vine, thirteen famous wine-makers overwhelm the tiny town of 8000, drawing international merchants and acclaim to the otherwise sleepy region. If the wines of Rioja have whetted your curiosity while quenching your thirst, you may want to meet the exact 1800-liter barrel that once hosted your nectar. **Bodegas Muga,** on Avda. Vizcaya near the RENFE station (tel. 31 04 98 or 31 18 25), offers tours of their wine cellars. (Open Mon.-Fri. 10:30am-1pm.) The thick stone walls of the mansion ensure that the *vino* is kept at a steady 17°C year-round. The guide speaks only rapid-fire Spanish and can smell a greenhorn a mile away; either do your homework before descending to the stockrooms or nod your head knowingly. Squeezed grapes are first fermented in monstrous barrels 15 feet high. The wine is then aged for at least two years in more standard-size barrels. The clarification process next requires a transfer back to the huge barrels where egg whites are poured through the containers. Twenty-five days later, the final product is bottled. Muga uses all oak barrels (the guide will show you where they're made by hand), but other companies sometimes use stainless steel tanks. One such facility, **Cune** (tel. 31 06 50), is downhill from the RENFE station, near the bridge into town. **Rioja Alta** (tel. 31 03 46), uphill from Muga on the same side of the road, seems especially excited about showing off their process. (Open Sept.-July Mon.-Fri. 11am-1pm.) Other companies that open their cellars to the public include **Bodegas Ibaiondo,** near the bridge over the Río Tizón, and **Bodegas Carlos Serres,** Santo Domingo, 40 (tel. 31 02 79), on the other side of town. Since none of these companies has full-time personnel leading tours, it's important to call a day or two ahead of time. If you show up unannounced, do so by 11am; *bodegas* are shown in the mornings only. The **Centro de Iniciativas Turisticas** (CIT), on the ground floor of the Banco de España, C. Conde de Haro (tel. 31 27 26), arranges free group visits to a different *bodega* every Saturday at 10:45am and 12:15pm. From Semana Santa to September 30, they are also available to answer questions. (Open Tues.-Sat. 10am-1pm and 7-9pm, Sun. 10am-1pm.)

On June 29, to cap off the 5 days of the town's **Fiesta Mayor,** the townspeople migrate to a nearby hermitage. At 10am, they wage **La Batalla del Vino,** in which they drench themselves and their neighbors with wine, hoping some will make it into anxious mouths.

Restaurante La Parra, Pl. Juan García Gato (tel. 31 08 72), off Pl. de la Paz, keeps customers plump with their 560ptas *menú.* **Hostal Aragón,** C. de Vega, 9 (tel. 31 00 04), offers the town's only economical rooms for 850ptas per person. Although the heavy odor of olive oil wafts about persistently, and the spiral staircase is amazingly narrow, the rooms are comfortable and clean. For **medical emergencies,** contact the **Cruz Roja** (Red Cross), C. Siervas de Jesús, 2 (tel. 31 18 38), or the **police** (tel. 31 01 25). Haro is accessible from Logroña by bus (5 per day, 225ptas) and train (6 per day, 250ptas).

Logroña

Logroña, capital of La Rioja, lies on the road to Compostela. While the town maintains a handful of monuments from its days as a rest stop for pilgrims (including the long stone bridge across the Ebro), it focuses more attention on riding Spain's industrial wave. As a consequence, the historic neighborhood is quite run-down and witnesses frequent thefts. **Plaza del Espolón's** beautiful trees and fountains act as magnets, attracting half the city out for an afternoon *paseo.* The **Iglesia de Santa María del Palacio,** 5 blocks from the Espolón toward the river, is crowned by a thirteenth-century pyramidal tower; the **Iglesia de San Bartolomé's** Gothic Pantocrator guards the doorway, surrounded by beheaded and badly damaged saints and apostles. The city's **cathedral** offers a bland, eighteenth-century facade that precedes an eerie interior. Poor lighting and a few narrow windows have left the upper reaches of the vault in almost complete darkness. The etching of Calvary, behind the main altar, may be the work of Michelangelo.

Calle de San Juan, parallel to the Espolón, provides the only oasis for budget travelers. **Hostal Residencia Sebastián,** at #21 (tel. 24 28 00), offers modern, spotless rooms and crisp white bed sheets. (Singles 1500ptas. Doubles 2000ptas.) **Habitaciones Daniel,** run by the sister of the Sebastián *señora,* charges similar prices. Near the Iglesia de Santiago, **Pensión El Revellín,** C. Norte, 50 (tel. 22 02 31), also has adequate rooms. (Singles 900ptas. Doubles 1700ptas.)

You can eat at **Restaurante Revellín,** C. San Juan, 21 (tel. 23 07 75), for 700ptas if you stay at Hostal Sebastián. The owner suffers from an aversion to backpacks, but his wife cooks a mean *merluza à la romana* (batter-fried hake). **Bar Beronés,** at #24 (tel. 25 88 28), serves a 450ptas *platos combinados.* Try their specialty, *pulpitos à la plancha* (baby octopus on the grill), for 300ptas. (Open Wed.-Mon. 1-4pm and 8:30-11pm.) The **post office** (tel. 22 00 66) is in Pl. San Agustín. (Open Mon.-Fri. 9am-2pm and 4-6pm.) The **telefónica,** Portales, 77, is not far away. (Open Mon.-Sat. 9am-1pm and 5-9pm.) The **tourist office,** on the Espolón, C. Miguel Villanueva, 10, distributes guides to many of La Rioja's sights (tel. 25 54 97; open Mon.-Fri. 9am-2pm). If you need the **police,** call 25 60 60; the **Cruz Roja** (Red Cross) answers at 22 52 12.

RENFE trains from Logroño run to Donostia (2 per day, 3½ hr.), Madrid (1 per day, 2400ptas), and Barcelona (4 per day, 1070ptas). The **bus station,** 2 blocks up Avda. de España, sends buses to Madrid (2 per day, 1700ptas), Burgos (3 per day, 560ptas), and Pamplona (4 per day, 495ptas).

Soria

The serene town of Soria offers neither splendid Gothic cathedrals nor wide tree-lined boulevards. Yet the people wearing black berets or carrying loaves of the excellent local breads give this town of reddish-brown Romanesque churches a warm appeal. In contrast to most Castilian towns, Soria receives very few foreigners, so it is a good place to rest after heavy sight-seeing. Just outside the city is the Duero River, bordered by the melancholy elms, poplars, and oaks that captivated Antonio Machado, one of Spain's greatest twentieth-century poets (author of *Campos de Castilla*) and resident for many years of "martial, mystical Soria."

Orientation and Practical Information

Soria is a small place. Principal points of orientation include the **Parque Alameda de Cervantes** on the west end of town and the **Río Duero,** which bounds Soria to the east. The center of town is formed by the interconnected plazas **Ramón y Cajal** and **General Yagüe,** both at the tip of the park. From here, **Calle de Collado** runs past several more plazas to the **Plaza Mayor.** In general, all useful things are closer to the park, the sights toward the other end of town.

Tourist Office: Pl. Ramón y Cajal (tel. 21 20 52), across from the entrance to the Parque Alameda de Cervantes. Warmly run, some English spoken. The updated map is considerably better than the old one. Open Mon.-Fri. 9:30am-2pm and 5-7pm, Sat. 10am-1pm.

Post Office: Paseo de General Yagüe, 4 (tel. 22 13 99), close to the tourist office, on the north side of the park. Open for stamps Mon.-Fri. 8am-6pm, Sat. 8am-3pm; for Lista de Correos Mon.-Fri. 9am-2pm, Sat. 9am-1pm. **Telegrams** (tel. 22 20 00) open Mon.-Sat. 8am-9pm. **Postal Code:** 42000.

Telephones: C. de Aduana Vieja, 2, between Pl. San Esteban and Pl. San Clemente. Open Mon.-Fri. 9am-2pm and 5-10pm, Sat. 9am-1pm and 5-9pm. **Telephone Code:** 975.

Train Station: Estación Cañuelo (tel. 22 28 67), about 1½ km (20 min. on foot) from Pl. General Yagüe, by the park. Start at C. Alfonso VIII and continue out Avda. Mariano Vicen; when you come to the highway, veer right (downhill). From the station, follow the "Centro Ciudad" signs up the hill or take the bus (30ptas) that meets each train and goes to General Yagüe. To Madrid (4 per day, 3½ hr., 1000ptas), Pamplona (2 per day, 2½ hr., 850ptas), and Zaragoza (3 per day, 1½ hr., 675ptas). Tourist office has reliable schedule information.

Bus Station: Avda. Valladolid at C. Gaya Nuño (tel. 22 51 60), a 10-min. walk from Pl. General Yagüe. **Continental** to Madrid (4 per day, 2 express, 1085ptas). **Conda** to Pamplona (3 per day, 2 express, 975ptas). **Martínez** to Logroño (3 per day, 600ptas). **Linecar** to Valladolid (2 per day, 845ptas) and Zaragoza (1 express per day, 635ptas). **Renfe Iñigo** to Barcelona (1 per day, 2480ptas) and Salamanca (1 per day, 1725ptas) Other lines cover other routes. The schedules can be confusing—even to the local tourist office.

Hitchhiking: To Madrid: Walk south along C. Alfonso VIII and continue on Avda. Mariano Vicen until you hit the highway. North (Logroño): Walk up C. Numancia to C. de las Casas.

Swimming Pool: Pabellón Polideportivo de la Juventud, at the far end of C. Nicolás Rabal (tel. 22 13 00), near Pl. de José Antonio and the municipal park. Open in summer daily 11am-8:30pm. Admission 200ptas.

Medical Service: Casa de Socorro, C. Fuentes, 1 (tel. 21 20 30), off Pl. Mayor. **Ambulance,** tel. 22 61 54. **Hospital General,** Paseo de Santa Bárbara.

Police: C. Nicolás Rabal, 11 (tel. 21 12 89). **Policía Municipal,** tel. 21 18 62.

Accommodations

Supply and demand works perfectly in Soria. There are just enough spots for the number of visitors, and none of the beds is especially cheap. If you do have trouble finding a reasonably priced room, the tourist office can advise you. During the last week of June, reservations are necessary.

Casa Diocesana, Dio XII, C. San Juan, 5 (tel. 21 21 76). From Pl. General Yagüe walk up C. de Collado 3 blocks; C. San Juan is on your right. Your satanic invocations will be thwarted by all the crucifixes on the walls of this church-operated inn. The only cheap rooms in town—and worth more than what you pay. Clean and comfortable, with large bathrooms, although the hall bathrooms are cramped and antique. Singles 980ptas, with bath 1457ptas. Doubles 1600ptas, with bath 2077ptas. Sept.-June: Singles 795ptas, with bath 1272ptas. Doubles 1293ptas, with bath 1770ptas.

Residencia Juvenil Juan Gaya Nuño (IYHF), Paseo de San Francisco (tel. 22 14 66). Walk out C. Nicolás Rabal and cut left on C. Santa Lucía de Marillac (at the Casa de Cultura) to San Francisco. Near Pl. José Antonio. A modern, clean college dorm that becomes an IYHF hostel July 4-Sept 15. Mostly doubles and quads. Curfew 10pm. Members only, 400ptas.

Hostal-Residencia Ruiz, C. Numancia, 49 (tel. 22 67 01). Small with no frills except wall-to-wall carpeting. Locked after 11pm, so ask for a key. Singles 1696ptas. Doubles with bath 2650ptas.

Hostal-Residencia Viena, C. García Soller, 5 (tel. 22 21 09). Follow Avda. Valladolid from Pl. General Yagüe to large intersection; C. García Soller is to the right. How can you go wrong with a name like this? Friendly owner maintains clean and modern rooms complete with phones and clock radios. Unfortunately, *sachertorte* is not included. Singles 1325ptas. Doubles 1908-3074ptas. Oct 7-June 25: Singles 1007ptas.

The nearest campground is **Camping Fuente de la Teja** (tel. 22 29 67), 1½km from town on Carretera de Madrid (223km). It has a pool. (265ptas per person. 212ptas per tent, per car, and per motorcycle.) There is no bus, so you must walk or hitch.

Food

Soria is a wonderful place to try such Castilian specialties as *sopa castellana* (soup made with bread, garlic, eggs, ham, and *chorizo*) and *migas pastoriles* ("shepherds' bread crumbs," bread with garlic, and *chorizo*). Soria's bread and butter enjoy a distinguished reputation throughout Spain. The **market** is at Pl. de Bernarda Robles. (Open Mon.-Sat. 8am-2pm.) Soria's restaurants seem to have conspired to establish 600ptas as the lowest price for a *menú del día*. **Calle D.M. Vincente y Tutor** has a high concentration of restaurants.

Restaurante Palafox, C. D.M. Vincente y Tutor, 4 (tel. 22 00 67). The best one on this stretch. *Macarones* and *escalope* are specialties on the 600ptas *menú*. Members of the family, representing 3 generations, bring fresh food into the kitchen every 5 min. Huge TV in corner. Open daily 12:45-4pm and 8:45-11pm.

Bar Brasil, C. San Clemente, 2 (tel. 21 14 43), 1 block off C. de Collado. A small, uncrowded restaurant hides upstairs in a building already tough to find. Zesty soups. Open daily 1-4pm and 9:30pm-midnight.

York Pastelería, C. de Collado, 14 (tel. 21 27 84). You can spread fresh butter on a sweet *tostada* or settle for *churros con chocolate*. Breakfast menu (140ptas) changes daily. Open daily 9am-10pm.

Sights and Entertainment

Soria's most important sights are its many churches, convents, and monasteries. Don't miss the **Monasterio San Juan de Duero,** whose partially destroyed cloister combines Romaneseque and Moorish elements to an extent unusual even in Spain. The cavernous interior, once home to the Templar Order, now houses a small museum devoted to bits and pieces of similar structures from the province that have fallen victim to the traditional disregard for such masterpieces. To reach the monastery, cross the bridge over the Duero River and turn left after the bank. (Open Wed.-Sat. 10am-2pm and 4-7pm, Sun. 10am-2pm. Admission 200ptas.) Downstream you'll find a peaceful park in the middle of the river. Crossing the two red and green bridges and then following the path parallel to the river will take you to the impressive **Ermita de San Satuario,** named for the patron saint of Soria and concealing a frescoed, natural cave-chapel. This 3-kilometer walk was a favorite of Antonio Machado. (Open daily 10am-2pm and 4:30-9pm; Oct.-April Wed.-Mon. 10:30am-6:30pm. Free.)

Eight kilometers from Soria are the meager ruins of **Numancia,** a Roman city built over a Celtiberian town. Numancia is famous for its heroic inhabitants, who completely destroyed the town and starved themselves rather than surrender to the Romans. Buses to Logroño pass by here; however, they are infrequent and Numancia can be seen in 15 minutes, so you might be stuck here for hours unless you hitch or walk back. (Open daily 10am-2pm and 4:30-9pm; Oct.-April Wed.-Mon. 10:30am-6:30pm. Free.) The province of Soria is also known for its well-preserved **castles,** examples of those which once dotted all Castilla.

Soria's **festival** starts the first Thursday after St. John's Day (June 28) and lasts until the following Monday. Celebrations include bullfights, regional costume displays, and dancing in the streets. Sunday is the most exciting day. The performing arts also thrive in Soria; in summer, highbrow entertainment usually finds its way to the Instituto Antonio Machado.

Cantabria and Asturias (Cantabrian Coast)

The Cantabrian coast denotes the part of northern Spain wedged between Euskadi (the Basque Country) in the east and Galicia in the west. Politically, the coast is divided into two autonomous regions, Cantabria (the province of Santander) and the Principado de Asturias (the province of Oviedo). Cantabria is the richer of the two regions, having long been a summer retreat of the Spanish elite as well as possessing numerous industrial centers and prosperous dairy farms. The decline of the mining industry and the harsh conditions of the rugged countryside have prevented Asturias from matching its neighbor in economic growth.

Cantabria has its own peculiar identity problems: Historically part of the kingdom Castilla-Léon, Cantabria's ethnic and cultural roots are distinct from those of the Basques and the Celtic Asturians, yet its geographic separation created by the Picos de Europa mountain range has ignited the desire for political autonomy from the central government. Asturias (the titular fiefdom of the heir to the Spanish crown, the Príncipe de Asturias) on the other hand, has for centuries possessed a strong regional character. In the years following the Moorish invasion of Iberia in 711, Asturias became the mountain stronghold of the Christian resistance. It was here in Covadonga that the first major uprising against the Moors was won in 722, signalling the beginning of the Reconquista. Perhaps the most vivid demonstrations of the Asturian's resistance to outside authority were the bloody miners' strikes before and during the Civil War. Motivated by the ideal of establishing an independent workers' state in Asturias, the miners resisted first Republican and then Fascist attempts to subjugate them. Franco's troops finally quelled the rebellion, but half of Oviedo was demolished in the process.

Unlike much of Spain, both Cantabria and Asturias are luxuriously fertile: Their hilly and often mountainous countryside remains cloaked in rich tones of green throughout the year. These natural paradises offer hikers, fishers, and other outdoor enthusiasts a remarkably unspoiled environment in which to escape the banal terrors of industrial civilization.

If it's beaches you're after, Cantabria's spectacular coastline is dotted with resort towns and a few isolated sandy coves. The Atlantic currents might be colder than what you'd expect (or prefer), but there's real surf and fewer beach-mobs than in the south. Visit unspoiled Orinon, 70km from Santander. Its broad, find sand beach suffers no other development than a campground; the lovely village of Castro Urdiale, with one of the most important cathedrals in Cantabria, is nearby. Closer to Santander, some of the better beaches are Liencres, Noja, and Laredo, Cantabria's current boom town.

Santander

The capital of Cantabria, Santander is a favorite seaside resort among the Spanish, perhaps outdoing rival Donostia (San Sebastián). An enormous fire in 1941 gutted Santander and much has been rebuilt along modern lines. Santander's basilica is the one major medieval edifice to have survived the blaze (even so, it is half in ruins), and aside from that, very little is spectacular about the city's architecture. Cultural festivals and the presence of the Universidad Internacional Menéndez Pelayo also serve as magnets for renowned artists, scholars, and overseas students who come to attend summer sessions here. Despite this certain measure of sophistication and its gorgeous beaches, Santander never indulges in civic puffery. Too bad the prices aren't equally modest.

Orientation and Practical Information

Santander is a long, narrow city built on the northwestern tip of the mouth of a bay. **Plaza Porticada** is at the city's heart; **Avenida Calvo Sotelo,** which becomes **Paseo de Pereda** to the east, runs along the waterfront. Buses and trains arrive at **Plaza de Estaciones,** about 6 blocks west of Pl. Porticada. Hotels and beach activity are in the residential neighborhood of **El Sardinero,** around the Península de Magdalena at the end of town, as is the university, along Avda. de los Castros. Buses #1, 2, or 7 (also #3 and 4 in summer) will take you there. Get off at Pl. de Italia or Brisas. Buses cost 45ptas and run until 10:30pm (#1 until midnight). Route #7 circles the town, and almost all buses run along the stretch Calle de San Fernando-Calle de Burgos-Paseo Pereda through downtown. Be sure to board double-section buses at the rear.

Tourist Office: Pl. Porticada (tel. 31 07 08). From the stations, walk 6 blocks to C. Alfonso XIII and turn left. Young staff provides helpful regional and local information. The Santander booklet with maps is detailed, but you may go blind searching for street names. Open Mon.-Fri. 9am-1:30pm and 4-7pm, Sat. 9am-1:30pm. Another office 2 blocks away in the Jardines de Pereda (tel. 21 61 20) provides the same services. Open Mon.-Fri. 9:30am-1:30pm and 4:30-7:30pm.

Student Travel: Viajes TIVE, C. Canarias, 2 (tel. 33 22 15), in the development off C. de Vázquez Mella at Avda. de General Camilio Alonso Vega. This lies roughly north of the building, near Pl. de Cuatro Caminos; walk 20 min. or take bus #5 or 6 (direction Complejo Deportivo). Useful for student travel discounts, and the only people in Santander who will agree to find you a *casa particular.* Open Mon.-Fri. 8am-3pm, Sat. 9am-1pm.

American Express Travel Representative: Viajes Altair, C. Lealtad, 24 (tel. 31 17 00), near the cathedral. All the usual services, including personal check cashing for members. Open Mon.-Fri. 9am-1:30pm and 4-7:30pm, Sat. 10am-1:30pm.

Post Office: Avda. de Alfonso XIII (tel. 21 26 73), overlooking the Jardines de Pereda at the waterfront. Open for stamps Mon.-Fri. 9am-2pm and 4-8pm, Sat. 9am-2pm; for Lista de Correos Mon.-Fri. 9am-2pm and 4-6pm, Sat. 9am-2pm; for **telegrams** Mon.-Fri. 8am-9pm, Sat. 9am-7pm. **Postal Code:** 39000.

Telephones: C. Hernán Cortés, 37, near Pl. José António. Open Mon.-Sat. 9am-1pm and 5-9pm. **Telephone Code:** 942.

Airport: In Maliaño (tel. 25 10 07), 7km away, across the bay. Daily flights to Madrid and Barcelona. Accessible only by taxi (800ptas). **Iberia,** Paseo Pereda, 18 (tel. 22 97 00). Open Mon.-Fri. 9am-1pm and 4-7:30pm, Sat. 9am-1pm.

Trains: Pl. de las Estaciones, on C. Rodríguez. **RENFE station** (tel. 21 02 88). To Palencia (8 per day, from 920ptas), Valladolid (5 per day, from 1130ptas), and Madrid (4 per day, from 2175ptas). **FEVE station** (tel. 21 16 87). To Oviedo (3 per day, 4 hr., 1250ptas) and Bilbao (4 per day, 2½ hr., 585ptas). Commuter trains to Torrelavega leave on the ½-hr. (140ptas). **RENFE ticket office,** Paseo Pereda, 25 (tel. 21 23 87). Open Mon.-Fri. 9am-1pm and 4-7pm, Sat. 9am-1pm.

Buses: All but **Turytrans** leave from the modern bus station in Pl. de las Estaciones. Information open daily 8:30am-9:00pm. **Continental** (tel. 22 53 18) drives to Madrid (2 per day, 5 hr., 2165ptas), and Burgos (2 per day, 3 hr., 930ptas). **Intercar** (tel. 22 10 41) goes to Oviedo (5 per day, 5 hr., 1500ptas), León (1 per day, 6 hr., 1485ptas), and La Coruña (2 per day, 12 hr.). **La Cantábrica** (tel. 22 08 22) connects to Santillana del Mar (5 per day), Comillas, and San Vicente. **ALSA** (tel. 22 10 41) reaches London (10,500ptas, students 9300ptas). 3 blocks down C. de Castilla from the station (then a left), at C. Federico Vial, 8, **Turytrans** (tel. 22 16 85) departs for Bilbao (6 per day, 590ptas), Torrelavega (5 per day, 145ptas), Oviedo (4 per day, 1040ptas), Pamplona (2 per day, 1405ptas), and Donostia (4 per day, 1405ptas).

Ferries: Brittany Ferries, Muelle del Ferry, near the Jardines de Pereda. To Plymouth, England (2 per week, 24 hours, 10,600ptas). Tickets sold by Modesto Piñeiro, S.A. (tel. 21 45 00), at the ferry station. Reserve 2 weeks in advance in summer. Year-round service, weather conditions permitting.

Taxis: Tel. 37 62 62, 33 33 33, or 23 23 23.

Baggage Check: At the FEVE station. Open daily 7am-11pm. 100ptas. Also in the basement of the bus station. Open Mon.-Fri. 8:30am-1pm and 3:30-7pm, Sat. 8:30am-1pm.

English Bookstore: El Estudio, C. Calvo Sotelo, 21 (tel. 37 49 50). A good selection of Penguin classics and best sellers. Open Mon.-Fri. 9:30am-1pm and 4:30-8pm, Sat. 9:30am-1pm. **La Estilográfica,** C. Hernán Cortés, 1 (tel. 23 21 07). A cramped stationery store with a small but varied selection of foreign books.

Public Library: C. Gravina, 4. Open Mon.-Fri. 9am-2pm and 5-8pm.

Laundromat: Lavomatique, C. Cuesta de la Atalaya, 18 (tel. 31 38 19). 300ptas per wash load. 50ptas per 12 min. drying. Open Mon.-Fri. 9am-1:30pm and 4-8pm, Sat. 9am-3pm.

Swimming Pool: Piscina Municipales in the sports complex Albericias. Take bus #6 to the end of the line.

Lost Property: In the Ayuntamiento, Pl. de Gen. Franco (tel. 22 04 64).

Center for Women: Instituto de la Mujer, Pasaje de la Puntida, 1 (tel. 31 36 12). Information on gatherings, exhibitions, and speeches.

Rape Crisis: Asociación de Asistencia a Mujeres Violadas, C. Santa Clara, 5, 3rd floor in the Comisiones Obreras Building (tel. 21 95 00). English spoken.

Medical Services: Casa de Socorro, Escalantes (tel. 21 12 14). **Medical Center,** Avda. de Valdecilla (tel. 33 00 00). **Ambulance:** Tel. 27 30 58.

Police: Policía Municipal, in the Ayuntamiento, Pl. del Generalísimo (tel. 21 12 31 or 092). **Guardia Civil,** C. Alta, 81 (tel. 22 11 00).

Accommodations and Camping

No one in Santander is bashful about charging what the market will bear, meaning—with a few exceptions—about 1200-1300ptas per person in July and August, perhaps 100-200ptas less in winter. *Casas particulares* do exist; ask at Viajes TIVE.

Expect to pay 1200ptas per person, maybe a shade less for groups of two or more. You can also inquire in bars, but the city is a little too large to make this a very effective method. One alternative to the generally unappealing *hostales* in the city center are the hotels along **Avenida de los Castros** in El Sardinero; this modern, residential neighborhood is close to the beach though a bus ride away from downtown. The **Alberque Juvenil "Bien Aparecida,"** an IYHF youth hostel, at C. Gomez Oreña, 5 (tel. 22 70 31), near Pl. José Antonio, is scheduled to reopen in early 1989.

Fonda María Luisa, C. Rodriguez, 9 (tel. 21 08 81), right by the train station. Shipyards obscure the view of the water, but the owner is very friendly and rooms are clean and spacious. Doubles 2300ptas. Singles 1100ptas if there are any unfilled doubles.

Pensión Puerto Rico, C. Isabel II (tel. 22 57 07). Large, comfortable rooms, maintained by a bubbling and hard-working *señora.* Some windows look out onto the market stalls across the street. Doubles 3000ptas. Showers 200ptas. **Hostal Botín,** in the same building (tel. 21 00 94), has doubles (3000ptas) large enough for a gymnastics competition. Showers 200ptas.

Fonda Millán, C. Pedrueca, 13 (tel. 22 63 90), 2 blocks from Pl. José Antonio. Clean, well-furnished rooms. Fun proprietor. Doubles ostensibly 1600ptas; you may pay 1800-2000ptas, but it's still a deal. Showers 150ptas.

Hostal Magallanes, C. Magallanes, 22 (tel. 37 14 21), near Museo de Bellas Artes. Green carpeting, white walls, and tidy pleasant rooms. Singles 1300ptas. Doubles 2300ptas.

Hostal-Residencia Luisito, Avda. de los Castros, 11 (tel. 27 19 71). The best choice of the establishments at El Sardinero. Doubles from 2000ptas. If no room is left, the friendly proprietor will send you to a nearby alternative; reasonably priced options are at #9, 17, and 19 on the same street.

About 3km up the coast from the Playa de la Magdalena is a scenic bluff called the Cabo Mayor. Planted back to back are two **camping** sites. **Bellavista** (tel. 27 10 16) charges 200ptas per person and 140ptas per tent. **Cabo Mayor** (tel. 27 35 66), open only June through September, has a swimming pool and tennis courts. Prices are 275ptas per person and 250ptas per tent. Take the "Cueto-Santander" bus in front of the Jardines de Pereda to reach the Cabo Mayor. Another possibility is **Playa de Somo** (no phone), on the beach in Somo, across the bay by boat (see below). (Open June-Oct. 160ptas per person. 125ptas per tent.)

Food

The most interesting eating experiences you'll have in Santander will likely be in the **Barrio Pesquero** (fishing quarter). Abandoned warehouses sit on one side, freight cars on the other. Don't let getting there scare you off. Most restaurants cluster around **C. Marques de la Ensenada;** from the station, walk 8 blocks down C. de Castilla and turn left on C. Heroes de la Armada.

You can find a few reasonable *menús* in the center of town. The market also offers a cheap alternative; **Mercado Pl. de Esperanze** is on C. Isabel II, near Pl. Gen. Franco. (Open Mon.-Fri. 8am-2pm and 5-7pm, Sat. 8am-2pm.)

Bar-Restaurante Casa José, C. Mocejon, 2 (tel. 22 20 09), in the *barrio pesquero.* Same management as that of the chic, expensive El Vivero, around the corner on C. Marqués de la Ensenada. Excellent seafood but zero atmosphere. Try *rabas fritas* (fried squid) or the *menú del dia* (550ptas). Open daily 9:30am-midnight.

Las Peñucas, right on C. Marqués de la Ensenada (tel. 22 94 45), in the *barrio pesquero.* Great fish in what looks like some patched-together mobile homes. Lots of locals. Try *bonito* (fresh tuna) for 500ptas. The menu usually includes fish soup and a scrumptious stew of different kinds of squid. Open Mon.-Sat. 12:30-3:30pm and 7:30-midnight. Next door, **La Cueva** (tel. 22 20 87) serves *chipirrones encebollados* (baby squid fried in onions), and *pulpo* (octapus) for 500ptas.

Bodega Flor de Potes, C. San Simon, 10 (tel. 22 10 34), above Pl. Cañadio (in the city center). Be ready for a hostile greeting but a fine meal: The locals are onto a good 600ptas *menú* and may resent your taking 1 of the 7 tables. Bar open daily for drinks and snacks 9am-8:30pm. Dinner served 8:30pm-midnight.

El Pajar de Güelo, C. Peña Herbosa, 11 (no phone), in the same part of town. Also smoky, but more of a restaurant, less a bar—racks of wine hang perilously overhead. *Menús* for 550ptas, but the a la carte seafood is good too. Open for snacks and drinks 9am-midnight, dinner after 8:30-9pm.

Bar-Restaurante Bus Fradejas, C. Guevara, 12 (tel. 31 42 99), at the corner of C. Quevedo. Look for the big red bus facade. *Merluza,* chicken, and stuffed peppers rotate on the cheap *menú* (450ptas). Open daily 11am-2am.

Bar Franvi, C. Santa Lucía, 6 (tel. 22 83 73), near Pl. Cañadío. 1 daily *menú* (500ptas) and that's it. Fish soup, *glubias blancas* (white beans), and pork loin are typical entrees.

Restaurant Self-Service, C. Calderón de la Barca (tel. 31 02 61), by the train station. *Cocido* (similar to a New England boiled dinner), meatballs, or *paella* are featured on different *menús* (500ptas). Self-service section open daily 1-4pm and 8-11:30pm.

Sights and Entertainment

The city's beaches are truly spectacular. **El Sardinero,** at the end of town, is the classic choice and sees some pretty strong waves. But a whole series of fine, less crowded beaches lies across the bay: **Playas Puntal, Somo,** and **Loredo.** Los Reginas (tel. 21 66 19) runs boats across to Pedreña from the Santander side from Embarcadero, by the Jardines de Pereda (in summer, every 15 min. 10:30am-8:30pm, 180ptas round-trip). The same company also offers 80-minute excursions around the bay in summer (2-6 per day, 500ptas).

Near the Ayuntamiento, the **Museo de Bellas Artes,** C. Rubio, 4 (tel. 23 94 87), houses a hodgepodge of sixteenth- through eighteenth-century paintings. Some landscapes by Riancho and other local painters may catch your eye, but the real gems are Goya's portrait of Fernando VII and a 1937, seventh edition of his gristly *Disasters of War.* The understated captions for these prints contribute to their shock value: If you don't speak Spanish, tote your dictionary along and work out the pithy phrases. (Open Mon.-Fri. 10am-1pm and 5-8pm, Sat. 10am-1pm.)

For a glimpse of some of our finned friends, walk past the *puerto chico* (old part) to the **Museu Maritimo.** In addition to the aquarium (be around for the noon-time feeding), the museum exhibits traditional fishing boats and artifacts collected in marine salvage expeditions. (Open Tues.-Sat. 11am-1pm and 4-7pm, Sun. 11am-2pm; Sept. 27-June 25 Tues.-Sat. 10am-1pm and 4-6pm, Sun. 11am-2pm.)

Serious students of archeology and cave-man buffs alike will be fascinated by the **Museu Regional de Prehistoria y Arqueologia,** C. Casimiro Sainz, 4. Skulls and paleolithic tools unearthed from sites in Cantabria abound. Its most important exhibit is a display of artifacts and photographs of the famous Cuevas de Altemira. Since you probably won't be able to see the real thing, check out the exhibit here instead. (Open Mon.-Sat. 9am-2pm.)

Santander's **cathedral basilica,** the city's oldest building, also deserves a visit. The original construction housed a hermitage in the twelfth century. As a result of the 1941 fire, the cathedral's exterior isn't much to see. Inside, however, you can admire the unusually low Romanesque vaulting and examine the remains of the earlier church through a glass section in the floor.

No walking tour of Santander is complete without a hike to the **Peninsula de la Magdalena** and the **palacio** that crowns its cliffs. Jutting into the sea between the Sardinero beaches and the port, the peninsula boasts a pretty public park and stupendous views from its rocky heights. The *palacio* ia a magnificent neo-medieval creation of the early years of this century. Originally the summer residence of Alfonso XIII, the palace is now municipal property, functioning as a classroom building and dormitory for the Universidad Internacional Menéndez Pelayo. (Peninsula open daily 7am-10pm. The *palacio* does not have visiting hours, but a polite request at the door may gain you entrance.)

As night falls, Santander turns from the beaches to the bars. The area around **Plaza Canadio, Calle Pedruecu,** and **Calle Daoíz y Velarde** is popular with both residents and students—any number of small bars crowd the streets here. **Zeppellin,** a popular spot on the chic Paseo de Menéndez Pelayo, near C. Santa Luciá, starts hopping after 1am; the scene at **El Sardinero,** with tourists and students mixing, gets going later and lasts all night. **Plaza de Italia** and nearby **Calle Panamá** are the center of the action, ranging from people-watching cafes to heavy-duty discos. Two popular examples of the latter are **La Real** and **Rebecca's,** both on C. Panamá. Right on Pl. de Italia is the **Gran Casino,** an imposing white elephant perfect for an evening of *belle-epoque* gambling. (Open daily 7pm-4am. Admission 400ptas. Passport and proper dress required.)

During August, many natives of Santander stay put instead of migrating like other Spaniards; they hope to watch the spectacular **International Festival** unfold. Recent festivals have brought the London Symphony Orchestra and the Bolshoi Ballet to Santander. Tickets, priced accordingly, are sold in a booth on Paseo Pereda and in the Pl. Porticada. (For information, call 31 48 19.) In addition, the town hosts an annual **Jazz Festival,** featuring some of the world's best musicians.

Near Santander

Since only a handful of people each day may sneak a peek at Altamira's caves (and this group has probably been on a 4-month waiting list), many speleologists spelunk in the lesser-known caves of **Puente Viesgo,** about 25km south of Santander. The **Cuevas del Castillo, de las Mondedas, de la Pasiega,** and **de las Chimeneas** offer paintings almost as well preserved as those in Altamira. (Open Tues.-Sun. 10am-12:15pm and 3-6:45pm; Nov.-March Tues.-Sun. 10am-2:15pm. 400 admitted per day.) Admission varies by cave; Castillo is most expensive at 225ptas.) For information, call 59 84 25. Continental buses stop in Puente Viesgo on the way from Santander to Burgos (2 per day, 275ptas).

Santillana del Mar

This remarkably well-preserved village has been declared a medieval national monument for good reason: Some of its stone houses and streets date from as far back as the ninth century, and only a few homes were built after the eighteenth. Today the town thrives on cows and tourists; on a stroll down the main *camino* to the church of San Juliana, you may have to step aside for either a tourist bus or a horse-drawn cart laden with hay.

Heraldic shields above the doors of virtually every home proclaim the rank and honor of the *hidalgos* (petty nobility) who once inhabited Santillana. **La Casa de les Villa,** near the bus stop, boasts a shield which proudly proclaims the glory of an honorable death. Other shields, most large and ornate, praise family lineages and the eligibility of sons and daughters. The present humbler inhabitants of these houses don't seem to mind the gawkers and photographers; in fact, half the entrances have been converted into food stands selling local sweet milk and *biscocho* (sponge cake) at inflated prices.

Virtually every building in Santillana is a museum, right down to the barbershop. More official, however, is the **Museo Diocesano.** Religious art and artifacts are spread throughout the halls of the old Regina Coeli Monastery, a building with a Romanesque cloister and corridors rivaling the museum's 200 sculptures for three-dimensional grace and coherence of form. (Open daily 9am-12:30pm and 4-7:30pm; Sept. 16-June 14 Thurs.-Tues. 9am-12:30pm and 4-7:30pm. Admission 100ptas.) At the other end of C. Santo Domingo sits the **Colegiata de Santa Juliana,** a twelfth-century Romanesque church. The **cloister** provides the true delight of this visit. Small, tranquil, and ivy-covered, it features capitals of Jesus and his disciples, and Daniel in the lion's den among other biblical scenes. Much of the ornamentation on these double pillars displays not religious figures, but vegetal patterns and intertwining straps. (The twelfth-century Cistercian reform prohibited the representation of any human form on capitals.) The remains of the virgin martyr St. Juliana lie inside the church. Although she subdued the devil (he's on a leash behind her),

her evil captors eventually won out as the reliefs and paintings show. (Cloister is open same hours as the Museo Diocesano. Admission with the same ticket.)

Staying in Santillana is expensive. Of the town's hotels, only **Hostal Castillo** (tel. 81 80 33), near the tourist office, even remotely approaches budget prices, but with only four rooms, it's likely to be full. (Doubles 2800ptas.) You're much better off allowing the friendly woman in the tourist office to set you up in a *casa particular;* you can get a double for around 2000ptas. If you're in town when she's not, cast an eye on a few windows—many have *"habitaciones"* signs. The thickest concentration of private rooms lies along the first kilometer or so of the road to the Altamira caves (follow the signs). Less than 1km away, on the road to Comillas, **Camping Santillana** (tel. 81 82 50) provides an excellent site with a view of the town. A pool, mini-golf area, and tennis courts are available for an extra charge. (220ptas per person. 200ptas per tent.)

Eating cheaply in Santillana isn't easy. A wafer-thin piece of *biscocho* can set you back 50ptas. The most economical *menú* in town is surprisingly near the colegiata; for 650ptas, **Casa Cossio** delivers a filling, possibly greasy, plate of *lomo* (pork loin) or *costillas* (ribs), together with a salad.

Santillana's **tourist office,** run by a remarkably friendly woman who will be happy to stow your backpack while you look around, is on the town's main square, Pl. de Ramón Pelayo. (Tel. 81 82 57. Open Mon.-Fri. 9:30am-1pm and 4-7pm, Sat. 9:30am-1pm; in winter daily 10am-1pm and 4-6pm.) The **post office** is next door. (Open Mon.-Fri. 9am-2pm, Sat. 9am-1pm.) The **postal code** in Santillana is 39330.

By far the easiest way to reach Santillana is by bus from Santander, 30km away. In fact, Santillana makes a fine daytrip from Santander, particularly if you've already fought for a room there. **La Cantabrica** has five buses per day (180ptas) that depart from Pl. de las Estaciones; ask at the tourist office for an exact schedule or call 72 08 22. It's also possible to take a FEVE train to Torrelavega (railpasses invalid), and then a bus the remaining 5km to Santillana. The last bus leaves Santillana from a stop at the beginning of the Altamira road at 8pm.

Near Santillana del Mar

Altamira Caves

The "Sistine Chapel of Primitive Art," the **Cuevas de Altamira** are celebrated by historians, archeologists, and artists alike. Exceptionally well-preserved prehistoric paintings cover the ceiling with some 30 roaming or resting bulls. To see them requires a written petition from the **Centro de Investigación de Altamira,** Santillana del Mar, Cantabria, Spain (tel. 81 80 02). Only 10 people per day get to make the 15-minute tour, and they book months in advance for the summer. If you can't visit in off-season and haven't written ahead, you can still see the dramatically illuminated stalagmites and stalactites in the other caves and wander through the museum of prehistory. (Open Mon.-Sat. 10am-1pm and 4-6pm, Sun. 10am-1pm. Free.)

To reach the caves, get off the bus at Santillana del Mar and follow the signs along the pleasant 2-kilometer path. From the road, you can see the abandoned and overgrown **Iglesia de San Sebastián.** Make a detour through the streets of tiny Herran, and turn right into the corn field at the wooden barrier on the other side of town. The church is a great picnic site.

Comillas

Comillas is an understated resort town favored by Spain's noble families, who retain modest palaces here along with their anachronistic titles. As one of the only places in historically leftist northern Spain where people can refer to themselves as count or duchess with a straight face, Comillas exudes a conservative elegance that is diluted by the thousands of young people tracking sand through the streets every summer. The wide **Playa Comillas,** haunt of the betitled, ends in a small pleasure port. **Oyambre,** 2km away, stretches out twice as long and has half as many tourists.

The many small palaces and the enormous Jesuit **colegio** that rises in Gothic splendor above the sea and town are offset on clear days by a view of the Picos de Europa. The Marqúes de Comillas is responsible for the looming **palacio** outside of town, now open only for occasional art exhibitions. It's up for sale along with the neo-Gothic steepled chapel out back—both can be yours for 60,000,000ptas. The nearby **El Capricho** (The Caprice), a tiny stone palace designed by Gaudí, is also for sale. Comillas is crowded during the weekend of July 15 when the **fiestas** begin. Have a go at greased pole-walking, goose chases, and dancing in the plaza. Vacationing residents of Madrid and Barcelona dance the rest of the summer at **El Bote.** Closed at least three times by the Guardia Civil, it's right on the sand at the end of the parking lot.

Near the neighboring town of **Ruibola** (a 30-min. walk) is the **Convento de Ruibola,** where cloistered nuns sell hand-painted ceramics. Just ring the bell and the merchandise will appear on a lazy-susan in the rock wall, installed to protect the sisters' secret identities. Just be sure to stick to the road; the apparent shortcut through the fields is anything but.

If you stay in town, plan on camping or paying a little more for generally comfortable accommodations. **Hostal Esmeralda,** C. Fernandez de Castro, 6 (tel. 72 00 97), has rooms with windows that reach from the hardwood floors to the molded ceilings, as the talkative owner will repeatedly point out. (Singles 1500ptas.) A few rooms are available above **Mesón el Torreón** in Pl. de los 3 Caños (tel. 72 07 38), in the oldest building in town. (Doubles 2500ptas.) The **restaurant** is good if overpriced, and the night bartender is friendlier and more informative than the tourist office staff. **Camping de Comillas** (tel. 72 00 74) is a first-class site right on the water, with space for 800. (Open July-Aug. 250ptas per person, per tent, and per vehicle.) It's cleaner and more convenient than **El Rodero** at Oyambre, a sad third-class site. (Open June-Oct. 160ptas per person.)

Eating in Comillas, like sleeping, is worth the few extra pesetas. As its name suggests, **Restaurante los Mellizos,** on C. Constanillo de la Cruz, is run by twins. The long-haired one makes an inspired sangria (the rum's the secret), and the *mariscadas* (shellfish) are the spiciest and best in town. Comillas takes its *tapas* seriously, and at **Bar Artico,** Paseo Garelly, you can get a great *marmitacos,* a Cantabrian fish-and-potato specialty that is a meal in itself. The best restaurant of all, however, is in **Ruibola.** Without name or menu, it's a family-run place with a daring cook. Hopefully you'll hit a day when they serve *carne con manzana* (meat with spiced apple).

The **tourist office,** C. La Aldea, 2 (tel. 72 07 68), is low on information about the town itself but has bus and excursion information and can supply a list of *casas particulares.* (Open Mon.-Sat. 10am-1pm and 4-7pm.) The **post office** is on C. Luis Lopez, 6. (Open Mon.-Sat. 9am-1:30pm.) In July and August a long distance **telephone** shack is set up in front of the church. (Open daily 9am-2pm and 4-10:30pm.)

The only way to reach Comillas is by bus or thumb, although you can take the train as far as Torrelavega and catch the bus from there. Only 18km from Santillana del Mar and 49km from Santander, Comillas makes an easy daytrip.

San Vicente de la Barquera

San Vicente is a rapidly growing resort, a jigsaw puzzle of modern hotels and older houses. Situated in a marshy wedge between two rivers, 12km west of Comillas and 52km from the Picos de Europa, San Vicente's only advantage is that it's accessible by train—almost. The station is actually 4km away in La Acebosa. The expansive sands of **Playa Merón** are visible on the other side of the river but are a good 2-kilometer walk.

The **Barrio Pesquero** is modern and uninteresting, but the twelfth-century church-fortress, **Santa María de los Angeles,** boasts a handsome Romanesque portico. The delightful Renaissance tomb of Antonio Corro, an infamous sixteenth-century Grand Inquisitor, is inside. San Vicente comes alive for **La Folia,** held on the first Sunday after Easter. The torch-lit, maritime procession coincides with the high tide, and the costumed Virgen de la Barquera is paraded through the streets. There's dancing in the evening in the plaza.

Casas particulares run about 1400ptas for a double; a cheap alternative is **Camping El Rosal** (tel. 71 02 63), on the other side of the Maza Bridge (1km away). A second-class site with its own spit of sand, it fills up quickly. (250ptas per person, per tent, and per vehicle. Hot showers 80ptas.)

In San Vicente, try **Fonda Liebana** on C. Ronda (tel. 71 02 11), at the top of the stairs off Pl. el Canton. Rooms cost 950ptas per person, and inexpensive hot meals (*menús* at 550ptas) are served in a friendly, local atmosphere. Most restaurants along C. Generalísimo Franco are generic and overpriced, but at least the seafood's always fresh. **Bodega Marinera,** Pl. el Catón, 10, serves a substantial *paella* for 700ptas, and there's outdoor seating until midnight.

The **tourist office,** on the main street, Avda. António Garelly (tel. 71 07 97), deals mainly with accommodations information. (Open June-Sept. 15 Mon.-Sat. 11am-1pm and 5-7pm.)

Picos de Europa

Stretching across the provinces of Oviedo, León and Santander, the Picos de Europa crown the Cantabrian Mountain Range in rugged splendor. Only 25km from the ocean, these immense corkscrews of rock and snow rise sharply through the mist and clouds to heights of over 2400m. While other mountains in Europe may surpass the Picos in altitude, few can match the savage beauty of the *sierra's* jagged profile.

Unless you're camping, you may often find yourself with nowhere to stay during the busy months of July and especially August. To avoid shutouts, you should contact hostals or pensions in June or earlier, confirming a date and price. In a jam, the tourist office can help you spend a few hours calling private residences in search of extra beds. Plan your daytrips carefully: Buses may run through town here only twice per day.

When camping in this area, pack warm clothes and raingear as sudden temperature drops and rainstorms are frequent. For safety, tell someone your planned hike route.

Those interested in hiring a climbing instructor or mountain guide have many choices. **CAREX,** C. San José, 43 (tel. 38 63 05), based in Gijón, is the largest. **Compañia de Guiás de Cangas de Onís,** C. Emilio Laria, 2 (tel. 84 89 16), and **Compañiá de Guiás de Picos de Europa** (tel. 84 51 78), in the **Camping Bulnes** near Arenas, also offer guides. Most guide companies will take you anywhere in the Picos. Guides are easy to find in any town. They charge 3000-500ptas for a half-day excursion; since this price doesn't vary with the number of hikers, the more the cheaper.

Potes

The most convenient base for exploring the southeastern and central Picos is the town of Potes, built along the Río Deva. Linked by bus to León in the southwest and to Santander in the northeast (3 per day, 2 hr., 540ptas), Potes leads a double life: In winter it sits quiet and snow-bound, removed from the popular ski station, but in summer, cosmopolitan climbers on their way to the heights hang out in the squares and cafes. While you're here, take a quick look at the **Torre del Infantado:** Though not as tall or rugged as surrounding peaks, it is not bad for an artificial mountain.

Several *hostales* and *pensiones* line the road through town. **Casa Gómez** (tel. 73 02 81), where the bus for Santander loads, offers clean, cheerless rooms. (Doubles 2000ptas.) The restaurant downstairs serves a reasonable 700ptas *menú*. **Casa Cuba** (tel. 73 00 64) sits on a nameless cobblestone road behind the buildings where the main street turns into pedestrian passageways. This relatively run-down local beer joint is paneled with slabs of meat and canned goods. Rooms have sagging beds;

if they're full the owner and his brother-in-law will keep you laughing while they hunt up a *casa particular* for you at about the same price. (Rooms 1000ptas per person in August, 800ptas per person in off-season.) Homestyle bean soup and fresh trout top the menu in the dining room off the bar; meals run 700-850ptas. **Casa Cayo** (tel. 73 01 50) rents singles for 900ptas and doubles for 1800ptas that get snatched up in peak periods. **Hostal La Serna** (tel. 73 01 52), near the tourist office, has tired-out but acceptable doubles for 1400ptas. **Hostal Rubio's** (tel. 73 00 15) clean singles for 1200ptas and doubles for 2765ptas are another option. Calling or writing ahead to any of these places is a good idea.

There's no official camping in Potes, but a 4-kilometer walk or hitch west to Turieno brings you to **Camping La Isla.** (Open April-Oct. 235ptas per person. Tel. 73 08 96.) Camping sites in San Pelayo (tel. 73 05 97), 8km west, and **El Molino** (tel. 73 04 89), 9km south in La Vega, are also available.

The **tourist office** on Pl. Jesús del Monasterio, near the church, has general information about the region and sells a reasonably good map of the surrounding towns and trails for 250ptas. Ask here for the locations of the free mountain *refugios.* (Open Mon.-Fri. 10am-1pm and 4-8pm; Oct.-May Mon.-Fri. 10am-1pm.) More detailed maps and guidebooks are available at **Bustamante,** a photo shop in the main square that's an invaluable resource center about the Picos. The maps published by the *Instituto Geográfico Nacional* and the *Federación Española de Montañismo* are the best, though serious mountaineers may find them inadequate (30ptas). Pick up some of the small brown guidebooks on specific areas of the Picos, too; these offer valuable hiking information (in Spanish only) and topographical maps. The friendly staff will answer any questions, though English is not their forte.

Excursions

If you want to experience these mountains without going out on a ledge, you can wander down several footpaths and four-wheel-drive tracks in the area. **Peña Sagra** is a two-hour walk from the towns of Luriezo or Aniezo, and from the summit you can survey all the Picos and the sea 51km away. On your way down, be sure to visit the **Iglesia de Nuestra Señora de la Luz,** the isolated home of the simply and beautifully carved patron of the Picos. Known affectionately to locals as *Santuca* (tiny saint), the Virgin is celebrated on May 2, when mountainfolk gather to sing in the spectacular setting. The **Monasterio de Santo Toribio de Liébana,** 3km west of Potes, has preserved some of its fine Romanesque and Gothic architecture, and claims to hold part of the original cross. A ninth-century Mozarabic church sits 11km north of Potes in **Lebeña.** The horseshoe-shaped arches are telltale signs of the Muslim influence on the building's Christian architects.

Hitch or catch a bus out of Potes (2 per day, 230ptas) to **Fuente Dé.** Here the government completed an ambitious, tri-partite project in 1966—building an astonishing 800-meter *teleférico* up the sheer mountain face, installing a fancy *parador,* and connecting these two new creations with a paved road from **Espinama,** 4km away. The lift leads to a breathtaking view of the surrounding peaks. There are usually huge lines in the middle of the summer; arrive early. (Open daily 10am-8pm; Sept.-June daily 10am-6pm. 375ptas one way, 550ptas round-trip.) Once at the top, if your knees aren't jellied from the trauma of ascent, you can walk 4km to the **Refugio de Aliva** and grab a meal or a room in the modern buildings. The rooms are almost always full; inquire at the cable lift in Fuente Dé or in the Ayuntamiento in Potes about vacancies. (Doubles 2000ptas.) The rolling meadows that abruptly cut the rock faces near Aliva have earned this area the nickname "La Luna" (the moon). For your return, you can either retrace your steps to the *teleférico* or walk the three-hour route to Espinama. On July 10, a rowdy **festival** at Aliva brings horse racing and dancing to the mountaintop.

Another interesting hike begins at the town of **Mogrovejo,** 10km west of Potes. The trail winds down to **Pembes** and then back to the road near Espinama; this is about 15km, or four hours, from start to finish. Less strenuous is the route between **Lon** and **Brez,** which begins 7km west of Potes, 1km off the main road.

Cangas de Onís

Off the road from Oviedo to Santander, the picturesque hill town of Cangas de Onís is a gateway to the Picos de Europa. The town was the site of the first capital of Spain, established after the Christian victory over the Moors at Covadonga in 725. Today it serves as an excellent base for excursions to Covadonga (and from there hikes into the western Picos) and as a rest stop before Arenas, 24km away and directly to the north of the central Picos.

Getting to Cangas is easy: EASA runs **buses** from Oviedo (13 per day, 1½ hr., 430ptas). From Santander and Panes buses (2 per day) drive across the northern edge of the Picos on Hwy. C-6312; Cangas is their final stop. Across the street from the bus stop is the new **Residencia Juvenil Rey Pelayo** (tel. 84 84 78), owned by the Ayuntamiento and run by four energetic mountain climbers. The spotless facility houses 140 guests in rooms of eight to ten. (700ptas, with your own sleeping bag 400ptas. Their anticipated admission to the IYHF in 1989 should lower prices. Reservations recommended for the busy summer months.) At **Fonda El Chofer,** C. Emilio Laria, 10 (tel. 84 83 05), a handful of doubles may be available for 2000ptas. From the bus stop, walk 1 block toward Puente Romano and turn left. **Hostel El Sella** (tel. 84 80 11) offers clean doubles from 2200ptas. The true budget option is **camping.** Either pick a secluded meadow by the river and sequester yourself, or obey the law and camp at the second-class site **Soto-Cangas de Onís,** about 5km up the road toward Covadonga by bus (5 per day). (Tel. 84 88 97. Open June-Sept. 260ptas per person and per tent.)

A *menú* in Cangas runs 650-700ptas. **Restaurante El Casín,** Avda. Castilla, 2 (tel. 84 83 31), serves *fabada* (pork and beans, Asturian style), *calamares en su tinta* (squid in its ink), and veal stew as alternating *platos* on its 700ptas *menú.* In the restaurant part of **Fonda el Chofer,** a heaping plate of *fabada* is available for 550ptas.

Modest by modern standards, Cangas was the capital of Asturias during the period after the legendary battle of Covadonga. The **Capilla de Santa Cruz,** a Romanesque chapel, was built over Cangas's oldest monument, a Celtic **dolmen** or prayerstone that dates from the Bronze Age. (The chapel may be open to visitors; if closed, obtain the keys at the tourist office.) Having paid your respects at the druidic shrine *cum* Christian chapel, saunter over to the **Puente Romano,** a misnamed Romanesque bridge, which spans the Río Sella on the northern edge of town. The chief attraction here, however, is not the bridge but the **river.** Clean, deep in spots, and fast-flowing, it is the perfect place for an afternoon dip. Enjoy **diving** from the rocks at the bridge's base or shooting along with the current farther upstream.

Other important sites in the area include the **Iglesia de Santa Eulalia** in **Albamia** (11km away), a Romanesque church where King Pelayo and his wife were buried, and the **Cueva del Buxu** (5km away), whose walls display primitive paintings about 15,000 years old. Only 25 people are admitted each day, so arrive early. (Open Tues.-Sun. 10am-12:30pm and 4-6:30pm. Admission 100ptas, free on Tues.) Both attractions are less than a two-hour walk, or an easy hitch, from Cangas.

The **tourist office** is on the second floor of the Ayuntamiento. (Tel. 84 80 05. Open daily 10am-2:30pm and 4-7pm.) Hikers and mountaineers are better off visiting the **Compañia de Guías de Montaña,** C. Emilio Laria, 2 (tel. 84 87 99). The staff should have a list of of mountain refuges and a collection of maps. (Open daily 10am-2:30pm and 4-7pm.)

Covadonga

"*Nuestra esperanza está en cristo; y este pequeño monte que ves será la salvacíon de España.*" ("Our faith is in Christ; and this little mountain you see will be the salvation of Spain.") So prophesied King Don Pelayo to his Christian army, gesturing to the rocky promontory in the Asturian Mountains that was to be the site of the first successful rebellion against the incoming Moors—**Covadonga.** It was here that, according to legend, the Virgin interceded with God on behalf of Don Pelayo's renegade forces, creating an invisible shield and ensuring them a victory against the Moorish host. In reality a pin-prick to these new Iberian inhabitants, the victory was ever afterward romanticized by proponents of a traditionally monolithic, Christian Spain.

The **Santa Cueva** (Sacred Cave) is the most important religious and historical site in Covadonga. A boulder's throw from the bus parking lot, it was here that Don Pelayo prayed to the Virgin. Throngs of pilgrims and tourists crowd into the sanctuary at all hours, so don't expect to have much time or room to look around. The imposing **basilica,** a neo-Gothic edifice of pinkish stone constructed by German architect Roberto Frasinelli in the late nineteenth century, incarnates a romanticized notion of the past. (Open daily 10am-2pm and 4-7:30pm.)

Directly across the square from the basilica is the **Museo del Tesoro.** This little museum houses a fascinating collection of religious objets d'art and also displays models of traditional Asturian farmsteads. The priceless *Corona de la virgen* is a dazzling crown of gold and silver studded with no less than 1109 diamonds. It is reputedly the most valuable artwork of its kind in the world. (Open daily 10:30am-2pm and 4-7:30pm. Admission 30ptas.)

Covadonga makes a fine half-daytrip. Should you stay, lodgings are cheaper the farther away you walk from the basilica. **Hospederia del Peregrino** (tel. 84 60 47) offers sizable doubles for 2100ptas. **Buses** stop on La Esplanada, a square just to the west of the basilica, traveling to Cangas (5-6 per day, 75ptas), continuing to Oviedo (515ptas). Two buses per day leave Covadonga for the **Lagos de Enol y de la Ercina,** a pair of alpine lakes, 1500m above the **Parque Nacional de Couadonga.**

The 12-kilometer ride into the mountains is spectacular itself, and during the summer you can swim in the surprisingly warm lake. On July 25, the shepherds of Covadonga celebrate their annual **festival** with tree-climbing competitions and folkloric song and dance. You can **camp** at either of the official sights (1 per lake) or stay in the **Refugio de Pastories,** near the lakes. (Contact the Compañiá de Guías de Onís (tel. 84 89 16) for more information.) Those wishing solitude can hike to the **Refugio de Villaviciosa** (3½ hr.; contact the Federación Asturiana de Montañismo in Oviedo for information) or the **Refugio de Vegarredonda** (2 hr.; contact Regugios de Montaña de Asturias (tel. 84 89 16) with questions). Nobody will stop you from finding your own spot away from the often crowded campsites, though the grazing cattle might object to your intrusion on their pastures.

Arenas de Cabrales

Between Cangas and Panes on the road skirting the northern Picos, the small town of **Arenas** provides a home base for two extraordinary daytrips. By thumbing or walking 5km from Arenas to **Poncebos** you arrive at the beginning of perhaps the most splendid—and certainly the most famous—hike in the Picos, the **Ruta del Cares** (Cares Gorge). Hewn and blasted out of mountain and sheer rock faces, the tidy 12-kilometer trail was built by the government as part of an effort to monitor a man-made channel of water. But today hikers outnumber the rarely seen maintenance personnel on the path from Poncebos to Caín. At points, the Cares River gurgles 500 feet below the trail; the walls of the gorge often become vertical, allowing you to see your shoes, the trail, and a tiny stream far beneath you. The trail crosses the gorge twice, ending in Caín, a town only recently hooked to civilization by a paved road. The walk takes about three hours, and the only way back is by foot. Although the drop-offs are dramatic, the path is perfectly safe. Another hike from Poncebos leads east to the villages of Bulnes and La Villa. A pristine mountain community, **Bulnes** only recently employed electricity; the hike here takes one-and-a-half hours.

Arenas has a surprising number of accommodations. **Hostal Naranjo de Bulnes** (tel. 84 51 19) offers singles for 1300ptas and doubles for 2300ptas. The two stars on the door are well-deserved: Rooms are immaculate, and the owner is courteous and a fine cook. She whips you up real *comida casera* (homecooking) for her 700ptas *menú.* **Pensión Anselmo** (tel. 84 51 55), **Pensión Fermín Cotera** (tel. 84 51 66), **Pen-**

sión el Castañeu (tel. 84 52 63), and **Pensión Casa Pachín** (tel. 84 51 46) are all small village enterprises with rooms from 900-1200ptas per person, depending on each owner's mood. Reservations are strongly recommended for the month of August. **Camping Naranjo de Bulnes** (1km toward Panes; tel. 84 51 78) provides a safe housing alternative and is the home of a mountain guide company. The **tourist office** (tel. 84 52 84) in Arenas is small but helpful for planning local hikes. Several quality maps are available. (Open Tues.-Sat. 9:30am-1:30pm and 4-7:30pm; Oct.-May Tues.-Sat. 10am-12:30pm and 4-7pm.)

A potently aromatic cheese has brought Arenas and the surrounding Cabrales region as much fame as their fine view of the Picos; *queso de Cabrales* has long been praised and gobbled by gourmets worldwide. Galdós, choosing ambiguous terms, described the cheese as a "pestiferous fragrance." Aged in nearby caves, the cheese is wrapped in leaves and sold in all the towns of Cabrales. With the proper license, you can fish for trout and salmon in the Cares River.

Oviedo

In 1934, General Franco responded to a miners uprising in Oviedo with brutal repression. Over 1500 insurgents were summarily executed. This hate-hate relationship between the city and Nationalist Spain continued during the Civil War and, as a consequence, a large portion of Oviedo was destroyed. Today, Oviedo is an attractive, modern city, the capital of the Principado de Asturias. The city's fine examples of the pre-Romanesque art form called Asturiano, and its recent efforts to reinvigorate Bable, a native language, reflect Oviedo's desire to reclaim a neglected heritage.

Orientation and Practical Information

The new city lies to the north and west of the beautiful **Parque de San Francisco,** the old city to the south and east. **Calle de Uria,** which becomes C. de Fruela in the old city, is the city's primary artery. The tourist office is a 15-minute walk from the train station: Walk straight up C. de Uria, past the Parque de San Francisco, and turn left on C. de San Francisco. You'll bump into **Plaza de Alfonso II** 3 blocks down.

Tourist Office: Pl. Alfonso II (tel. 21 33 85). English spoken. In addition to bus and hostel information, the office has ambitiously mounted an exposition gallery with shows on important buildings and folkloric costumes. Also advice on travel in the Picos de Europa. Open Mon.-Fri. 9am-2pm and 4-6pm, Sat. 9am-2pm.

Student Travel Office: TIVE, C. Asturias, 9 (tel. 23 60 58). Open Mon.-Fri. 9am-1:30pm.

Post Office: C. Alonso Quintanilla (tel. 21 26 72). Open for stamps and Lista de Correos Mon.-Sat. 9am-2pm and 4-6pm. **Telegrams:** Open daily 8am-9pm. **Postal Code:** 33070.

Telephones: Pl. de Porlier. Open Mon.-Sat. 10am-2pm and 5-10pm. **Telephone Code:** 985.

Trains: RENFE, C. Uria (tel. 24 33 64). Best serves points south of León. Make sure to check on the kind of train you take: Slow locals through the mountains can double your travel time. To Madrid (4 per day, 6½ hr., 3400ptas), La Corúna (2 per day, 3000ptas), Salamanca (4 per day, 1800ptas), and León (4 per day, 3½ hr., 590ptas). **FEVE,** 2 stations: C. Económicos (tel. 28 01 50), 2 min. from RENFE, to your left as you exit. To Santander (2 per day, 4¼ hr.), Llanes (4 per day, 2¼ hr.), and Bilbao (1 per day, 7 hr.). C. Jovellanos, 19 (tel. 21 43 97). To points west in Asturias like Pravia and Collanzo.

Buses: ALSA, Primo de Rivera, 1 (tel. 28 12 00), in the lower level of a shopping arcade. To La Coruña (2 per day, 7 hr., 1945ptas), León (7 per day, 2 hr.), and Madrid (6 per day, 5½ hr.) **International:** To London (1 per week, 11,190ptas), Paris (9 per week in summer, 4750ptas), and Rome (1 per day in summer, 16,990ptas). **Turytrans,** on Jerónimo Ibrán (tel. 28 50 69), opposite the FEVE station. To Donostia (4 per day, 8¼ hr., 2310ptas), Bilbao (7 per day, 7¼ hr., 1690ptas), and Santander (8 per day, 4¼ hr., 1140ptas). **EASA,** C. Jerónimo Ibrń (tel. 22 28 44). To Cangás, de Onís (13 per day, 1½ hr., 430ptas) and Covadonga (5 per day, about 500ptas).

Taxis: Tel. 25 00 00 or 25 25 00.

Car Rentals: Hertz, C. Victor Chavarri, 25 (tel. 21 54 12). **Avis,** C. Ventura Rodríguiz, 12 (tel. 24 13 83). **Asturcar,** C. Foncalada, 17 (tel. 21 36 30).

Hiking Information: Federación Asturiana de Montañismo, Melquiades Alvarez, 16 (tel. 21 10 99). From the RENFE station, walk 2 blocks down C. Uria and turn left. Good collection of trail maps and mountain guides. Staff can inform you about the best hiking routes and weather conditions. Open Mon.-Fri. 6:30-7:30pm.

English Bookstore: Cervantes, C. Doctor Casal, 3 (tel. 21 24 55). Penguin classics. Open Mon.-Fri. 9:30am-1:30pm and 4-7:30pm, Sat. 9:30am-1:30pm.

Public Library: Pl. de Fontán, near Pl. Mayor. Open Mon.-Fri. 10am-1:30pm and 4-6pm.

Lost Property: Tel. 24 03 00.

Hospital: General de Asturias, J. Claveria (tel. 23 00 50).

Police: C. General Yagüe, 5 (tel. 21 19 20).

Accommodations and Camping

The cheap places in the old city around the cathedral look ready for the demolition squad: dirty, cramped, and perhaps dangerous. Accommodations are much newer and cleaner in the new city, especially on C. Uria and C. Campoamor, both near the train station.

Resuidencia Juvenil "Asturias," C. Hermanos Pidal, 5 (tel. 24 47 04), near Pl. de América and **Residencia Juvenil "Ramón Menéndez Pidal,"** C. Julián Clavería (tel. 23 20 54), across from hospital. Welcome alternatives to a rather touch-and-go hostel and *pensión network*. Open July-Sept. Both 450 ptas, ages over 26 550ptas.

Pension Montreal, C. Campoamor, 18 (tel. 22 05 56). Yellow, floral wallpaper and chandeliers. Singles 800ptas. Doubles 1100ptas. Showers 200ptas.

Fonda Menéndez, C. Rosal, 26, 2nd floor (no phone), 1 block southeast of the park. Somewhat dorm-like, but the rooms are adequate. Singles 900ptas. Doubles 1600ptas. Hot showers 125ptas.

Pensión La Armonía, C. Nueve de Mayo, 14 (tel. 22 03 01), 1 block up C. Uria from the trains and then 2 blocks to the left. Groovy tile floors and clean bathrooms. Toddlers underfoot. Singles 800ptas. Doubles 1900ptas.

The closest camping is in Gijón, 28km away at the end of the train line. **Camping Gijón** (tel. 36 57 55) is a second-class site located near the coast with foothills in the background (160ptas per person, 125ptas per tent).

Food

Oviedo's proximity to the seashore and the mountains allows you to enjoy both seafood and hearty country dishes. The specialty is *fabada*—a filling blend of sausage, tomatoes, and beans. The **mercado municipal** is on Pl. del Fontan, ½ block east of C. Rosal. (Open Thurs.)

Mesón la Caleya, C. de la Lila, 7 (tel. 22 01 15). The delicious specialty of the house is *cebollas rellenas,* onions stuffed with ham and eggs. Lean on the tile bar with the drinkers, or take a wicker seat for the 550ptas *menú.* Open daily noon-3:30pm and 6:30-10pm.

Casa Muñiz, C. de la Lila, 16 (tel. 22 30 77). Farther down the same street but in another world. Packed with locals who love the cheap a la carte and the family who runs the place. "Joint" is the best description. They'll fix whatever you want at almost any hour. Open Thurs.-Tues.

El Muiñeira, C. Gascona, 7 (tel. 29 09 37), 3 blocks from the cathedral. The *menú del día* (550ptas) includes Galician specialties like *chipirones* (baby squid) and *trucha* (trout). Open Tues.-Sun. 1-4pm and 8:30-11:30pm

Restaurante Gran Taberna, Pl. de Porlier, 1 (tel. 22 44 52), just off Pl. de Alfonso II. Best place in town to sample local fare. Try *pinchitos* (finger sandwiches) of *chorizo* or *queso ca-*

brales, a pungent sheep's cheese. 3-course *menú del dia* is 400ptas at the bar. Refreshing *sidra* (fermented apple cider). Open daily 1-4pm and 8:30-11pm.

Sights

If you visit Oviedo's **cathedral** (finished in 1388), note the fine baroque bas-relief over the central doorway, which depicts the Transfiguration. Take time to climb the 80-meter tower for the striking panorama of the city. In the north transept is King Castro's Chapel with the King's Pantheon, designated by Alfonso II as the official bone-site for the Asturian kings. The most interesting of the chapels is the **Capilla San Pedro,** which exhibits a peculiar work of metal relief depicting Simon Magus being dropped from the sky by hideous demons. While the event was undoubtedly instrumental in the conversion of Rome to the Christian faith, records do not indicate whether poor Simon survived his fall. (Cathedral open daily 8:15am-1pm and 4-6pm.)

Behind the cathedral stands the **Cámara Santa,** a shrine to medieval pilgrimages containing the Cross of Los Angeles and the Cross of Victoria. (Open daily 10am-1pm and 4-6pm; in summer daily 10am-1pm and 4-8pm. Admission 20ptas.) Be sure to visit the **museum** and **Cloister of San Vicente,** adjoining the south transept. The cloister contains a graveyard of pilgrims who never made it to Santiago and back; the museum contains ho-hum but historically important examples of pre-Romanesque art. (Open Mon.-Sat. 10am-1:30pm and 4-6:30pm., Sun. 11am-1pm. Free.) Also in the cathedral square are the **Casa Palacio de la Rúa,** whose fifteenth-century facade is the oldest in town, and the **Palacio de Composagrad,** now the home of the provincial court.

Near Oviedo

Ramiro I, one of the ninth-century kings of the young Asturian nation, chose the best real estate in the area for his summer hunting escapades. High above Oviedo, strategically placed on **Monte Naranco,** sit two quite noteworthy examples of Asturian pre-Romanesque architecture: **Santa Marí´del Naranco,** a former palace, and **San Miguel de Lillo,** a royal chapel. **Santa María,** a miniature church with its tidy masonry and rough-hewn capitals, exudes a down-to-earth warmth. You almost expect the king himself to lay down his chisel and come shake your hand. The decorative lines around the windows look like an after-thought, whereas the ridges in the columns were coarsely executed. The masterful arches and vaulted ceiling demonstrate design techniques ahead of their time. The more weathered **San Miguel de Lillo** rests 500m from Santa María. Fifteenth-century "remodeling" left the full-length church looking like a stubby hermitage. But you can still see the fine lines of reliefs over the inside doorway; outside, the gingerbread-style window vents pose as stone sunflowers. (Both churches open daily 9:30am-1pm and 3-7pm; Oct. 16-April Mon.-Sat. 10am-1pm and 3-5pm, Sun. 10am-1pm. Admission 100ptas, children 50ptas.)

A 300ptas taxi ride from the RENFE station or a 45ptas bus ride (#6, Naronco-Marqués de Vidal, leaving from the intersection of C. Uria and C. Gil de Jaz) will hoist you up the mount. A 45-minute walk will also bring you to the top. Walk down C. de Independencia, to your right as you exit the RENFE station. Turn right on C. Coronel Tejeiro, across the train tracks, and hang another right on C. Ramiro I. The rest is all uphill.

Euskadi (Pais Vasco, Basque Country)

As you travel north from the sizzling plains of central Spain, the Basque provinces will light upon you like a breath of spring. The rain in Spain does *not* fall mainly on the plain: The rugged hills and mountains—and, unfortunately, the sandy beaches as well—get more than their share of precipitation. The green and forested Basque Country remains for the most part unspoiled, despite the heavy industrialization on the peninsula around Bilbao.

Culturally, the Basques are a people apart. Linguists still disagree on the origin of Euskera, the Basque language, which has no relation to Spanish or French and seems related to inner Asian tongues. It is called (by some other Spaniards) *la lengua del diablo* (the devil's tongue). Over a half-million Euskera-speaking Spaniards have created a linguistic stronghold, however, and after years of stubbornly destroying highway signs in the "foreign" language of *castellano,* they've been conceded official bilingualism.

The Basques' cultural separation from most of Spain has meant centuries of tense relations with the central Spanish government. The three territories of Gipuzkoa (Guipúzcoa), Bizkaia (Vizcaya), and Alaba (Alava) were finally restored to the status of an autonomous community in 1979, a state of affairs that had not existed since 1876. Navarre, another region with Basque cultural roots, may one day join the community. But Basques are so fiercely proud of their independence and tradition of representative government, historically and symbolically centered in Gernika (Guernica), that even these measures have proven inadequate.

Euskadi Ta Askatasuna (ETA), the Basque Liberation Movement, has carried on a militant struggle for over 30 years, although it came into full force only in the early '70s. In 1973, the group assassinated Admiral Carrero Blanco, Franco's probable successor. Whether or not they approved of the technique of elimination, many Spaniards breathed a sigh of relief since Blanco's style of leadership was more dreaded than the Generalísimo's. If Basques were proud of the old ETA, however, much of Euskadi has distanced itself from the new ETA, responsible for a Barcelona department store explosion in 1987 that killed over 20 shoppers and the assassinations of Basque industrialists who refused to pay extortion fees. The idea of a separate homeland continues to appeal to many *Euskaldunak* (Basques), but only a small minority currently support the techniques that have come to dominate this struggle. To avoid the limited danger that the situation presents to tourists, steer clear of all political demonstrations (2-3 individuals carrying a banner counts as such) and any concentrations of police.

Other areas of Basque divergence from the Spanish mainstream are more peaceful. *Pelota,* or jai-alai, was born here; to the Basques, this lightning-fast sport is a passion that rivals the *corrida.* Its popularity is such that churches and government buildings are forced to prohibit play against their dignified walls. Other less sophisticated sports have not spread beyond the region, such as boulder hefting, deadweight drags by oxen teams, and between-the-legs log chopping.

Few places can match the energy and gusto brought to the Basque table. *Bacalao a la vizcaina* (salted cod in a tomato sauce), *a la vasca* (in a delicate parsley-tinted white wine sauce), and *chipirones en su tinta* (cuttlefish in their ink) are now eaten throughout the peninsula, and Basque cuisine has gourmet outposts as far away as New York.

Donostia (San Sebastián)

Donostia—San Sebastián in Castilian—is what Walt Disney might have created if he'd been God instead of an ambitious American. Donostia entertains its visitors with a profusion of bars, clean beaches, grassy parks, and elegant buildings. The term "bar-hopping" takes on new meaning as you carouse in the *barrio viejo* (old quarter), where every doorway beckons you with colorful *tapas* and glasses of wine lined up on the counters. By day, people flood La Concha, the half-moon beach that fronts the city, where sunbathing gives way to soccer on the sand as the sun goes down. On either side of this giant playground, two mountains rise on the edge of the sea.

While Gernika is the political and emotional center of Euskadi, Donostia frequently flares up as the region's trouble spot. Political graffiti assaults almost every wall, statue, and rock; often the mild-mannered students with whom you enjoy *tapas* will scream obscenities at the city's nervous national police. The lazy mood on **Plaza de la Constitución** during Sunday and Wednesday **flea markets** gives way to angry expressions of Basque pride at evening **folk festivals**. Tranquil Alameda del Boulevard marks the spot where two men on a motorcycle dropped a bomb on the roof of a general's car.

As a tourist, perhaps your greatest danger is falling in love with the city and consequently going broke. Spanish nobility first sniffed out the pleasures of this seaside resort over 100 years ago; the city's prices still reflect this exclusive origin.

Orientation and Practical Information

The **Río Urumea** splits the city; across the peninsula, tipped by **Monte Urgell,** is the **Bahía de la Concha.** The *barrio viejo,* or old city, lies toward the northern end of the peninsula. Beneath it, **Alameda del Boulevard** and **Avenida de la Libertad,** Donostia's main avenues, cut the peninsula in half east to west. Just south of the *avenida* rises the cathedral. Since addresses are often written in Euskera, it may be difficult to locate places by their Castilian street names. Refer to the bilingual street index on the city map provided by the tourist office. Donostia is small enough to be negotiated on foot.

Tourist Offices: Oficina del Gobierno Vasco, C. Andia, 13 (tel. 42 62 82), on C. Miramar at Pl. de Cervantes on the beach. Helpful and patient. English spoken. Information for all Euskadi, and transportation schedules. If you're desperate, perhaps some discreet accommodations assistance. Open June 15-Oct. 30 Mon.-Fri. 9am-1:30pm and 4-7pm, Sat. 9am-1pm; Oct. 31-June 14 Mon.-Fri. 9am-1:30pm and 3:30-6:30pm, Sat. 9am-1pm. **Centro de Atracción y Turismo,** C. Reina Regente (tel. 42 10 02 or 41 31 80), in the Victoria Eugenia Theater next to the 1st bridge over the river. This municipal office is less helpful, but they do keep a list of *casas particulares.* Open Mon.-Fri. 9am-2pm and 3:30-7:30pm, Sat. 9am-2pm.

Student Travel: Viajes TIVE, Avda. Ategorrieta, 9 (tel. 27 69 34), across the river. Student IDs and discount fares. Open Mon.-Fri. 9am-2pm, Sat. 9am-noon.

Post Office: C. Urdaneta, 9 (tel. 46 49 14), facing the rear of the cathedral. Open for Lista de Correos Mon.-Fri. 9am-1pm and 4-6pm, Sat. 9am-2pm. Open for stamps Mon.-Fri. 9am-8pm, Sat. 9am-2pm. **Postal Code:** 2000.

Telephones: Avda. de la Libertad, 26. Open Mon.-Sat. 9am-1pm and 5-9pm. **Telephone Code:** 943.

Airport: Near Hondarribía (tel. 64 22 40), about 25km away. Bus "Fuenterrabía" leaves C. Oquendo, 16, near the Zurriola Bridge, every 15 min. 7am-11pm (45 min., 110ptas). Tourist office at airport (same phone) open Mon.-Fri. 10am-2pm and 5-7pm, Sat. 10am-2pm. Aviaco flights to Madrid (3 per day, 9950ptas), and Barcelona (1 per day, 10,570ptas).

Train Stations: RENFE, Avda. de Francia (tel. 28 35 99), across the river. Information (tel. 28 30 29) open daily 7am-11pm. To Madrid (4 per day, 7½ hr., from 2835ptas), Barcelona (2 per day, 8½ hr., 3040ptas), Salamanca (1 per day, 7¾ hr., 2290ptas), La Coruña (1 per day, 16 hr., 3625ptas), and Lisbon (1 per day, 16½ hr., 5180ptas). Two private lines run trains out of **Estación de Amara,** to the west at Pl. Easo. **Vascongadas** (tel. 45 01 31) has a lumbering line to Bilbao (about 5 per day) with connections to Guernica and Bermeo. Next door, **Topo** (tel. 45 01 31) offers *tranvías* to Hendaye (the French side of the border at Irún) twice per hr. (130ptas). Both lines are expensive and do not accept railpasses. To Bilbao, the bus is much more convenient; to Irún, take RENFE or the bus.

Bus Station: Most buses leave from the platforms at Pl. de Pio XII. Walk along the river on the *paseo*. From the beach, walk up C. Easo until you hit Avda. de Sancho el Sabio. Sort out which company goes where at the tourist office. To Bilbao (1¼ hr., 620-650ptas), Pamplona (4 per day, 1½ hr., 450ptas), Burgos (3 hr., 1185-1470ptas), Logroño (3½ hr., 775ptas), Madrid (6½ hr., 2415ptas), and Salamanca (82/3 hr., 2770ptas). **Viajes Abril** (tel. 45 26 88) will book you for Paris (in summer daily, 6050ptas) and Brussels (8200ptas). A French company, **ATCRB**, serves Biarritz and Bayonne (3 per day, about 700ptas); buy tickets aboard their buses. **Intercar** runs to Galicia along the coast (1 per day Mon.-Sat., 5050ptas)—get your tickets at Bar O'Galego, Avda. Felipe IV, 13 (tel. 45 08 01). Green buses to Irún (95ptas) and Fuenterrabía/Hondarribía (110ptas) leave every 15 min. or so 7am-11pm from C. Oquendo, 16, near Alameda del Boulevard.

Taxis: Radio Taxi Easo, Tel. 46 76 66. Stands on Avda. de la Libertad.

Car Rentals: Hertz, C. Marina, 2 (tel. 46 10 84). **Avis,** C. Triunfo, 2 (tel. 46 15 56). **Europcar,** C. San Martín, 60 (tel. 46 17 17).

Bicycles: Mini, C. Escolta Real, 10 (tel. 21 17 58), in Antiguo. 1-speeds 500ptas per day. 10-speeds 1000ptas per day. Open Mon.-Fri. 9:30am-1pm and 3:30-7pm.

Hitchhiking: Avda. de Carlos I, between Pl. de Pio XII and the main highway. For all but the nearest destinations. Not a snap, but worth a try. **Tandem,** Paseo de Salamanca, 7 (tel. 42 11 33), is a new service; you call them, and they try to hook you up with someone going your way, usually for a small fee. Office open 11am-2pm and 6-7pm, or leave a message.

Hiking Information: Club Vasco de Camping, San Marcial, 19 *bajo* (tel. 42 84 79). Organizes excursions and provides information. **Club de Montaña Kresala** (tel. 42 09 05).

English Bookstores: Librería Lagún, Pl. de la Constitución, 3 (tel. 42 20 07). Penguin novels. Open Mon.-Sat. 10am-1pm and 4-8pm.

Laundromat: Lavomatique, C. Iñigo (Kalea Enego), 12 (no phone), in the old city. Self-service. Wash 275ptas per 4kg (33 min.). Dry 25ptas per 7 min. Soap 25ptas for a small quantity (you'll need two or three). Open Mon.-Fri. 10am-2pm and 4-8pm, Sat. 10am-2pm, Sun. 11am-2pm.

Swimming Pools: Piscina La Concha, Indoors at Paseo de la Concha. Open Mon.-Fri. 7am-9pm, Sat. 7am-1:30pm. Admission 450ptas. **Piscina de Tenis Ondarreta** (tel. 21 81 36) has a 20-m outdoor pool next to the tennis courts bordering Pl. de Ondarreta. Admission 490ptas. You can also swim at **Piscinas de Anoeta** (tel. 45 29 70), next to the youth hostel, for 250ptas.

Medical Services: Casa de Socorro, C. Easo, 39 (tel. 46 41 20). **Ambulance:** Tel. 27 22 22.

Police: Municipal, C. Larramendi, 10 (tel. 092 or 45 00 00). **Comisaría de Policía,** Pl. Pio XII (tel. 091), in the Gobierno Civil building.

Accommodations and Camping

Lodgings are expensive, and desperate backpackers are often forced to scramble for rooms during the August crunch. If you spend 1200ptas per night on housing, consider yourself lucky. Singles aren't available for love or money. If you arrive in the late afternoon of a hot August day, keep cool, obtain a list of cheap accommodations from the tourist office, and start plugging away. The local IYHF fills up early in the day. Many people sleep on the beach. La Concha is a favorite because you can move under the covered walkway if it starts raining. Fear no hassles from the local police: They actually patrol the beach all night to maintain the safety of the sand-sleepers.

Youth Hostel "Anoeta" (IYHF), Ciudad Deportiva Anoeta (tel. 45 29 70), all the way south. Walk 20 min., or catch the Amara-Anoeta bus, which originates along Alameda del Boulevard and runs down C. de Urbieta (50ptas). The orange-roofed hostel is behind the track. Plumbing was recently redone. Reserve a room for the next day even if it's full or if you plan to stay more than 1 night; groups sometimes arrive to displace lodgers. 10-bed rooms. Curfew 2am. Reception open 10am-noon and 4-7pm. Lockout 10am-6pm. Baggage check available. Members only, 625ptas. Breakfast included. Sheets 190ptas. Meals 450ptas. All slightly more for ages over 26. IYHF cards 1850ptas.

Pensión La Perla, C. Loyola, 10 (tel. 42 81 23), 1 block north of the cathedral. From the train station, cross the bridge and walk to the front entrance of the cathedral; Loyola begins across the street. A friendly and well-run establishment. Spacious, clean rooms with high ceilings. Single 1400ptas. Doubles 2500ptas.

Pensión Urkia, C. Urbieta, 12 (tel. 42 44 36), 1 street over. Mirrors cover much of the walls. Bathroom floors sparkle. Doubles 2400ptas.

Pensión Donostiarra, C. Easo, 12 (tel. 46 79 45), 1 block over from C. Urbieta. Sagging mattresses. Some rooms have sofas. 1 single, never available, 1400ptas. Doubles 2200ptas. **Pensión Josefina** (tel. 46 19 56), upstairs, offers competitive prices.

Hostal Residencia Easo, C. San Bartolomé, 24 (tel. 46 68 92), 4 blocks from the cathedral. Big, modern rooms in a freshly scented environment. Owner will help you find *casas particulares* if the place is full. Doubles 3000ptas; in off-season 2500ptas.

Hostal Comercio, C. Urdaneta, 24 (tel. 46 44 14), at C. Easo. Some rooms are small, but all are clean. 3 floors and lots of beds, so it may not fill up as early as other places. Singles 1700ptas. Doubles 2750ptas.

Hostal Oscariz, C. Fuenterrabía (or Hondarribia Kalea), 8 (tel. 42 53 06), 1 block before the cathedral coming from the train station. Handsome wood floors and high ceilings. Friendly management. Doubles 2900ptas.

Pensión Alemana, C. San Martín, 53 (tel. 46 48 81), at C. Lersundi. Huge, airy rooms. Beautiful decorations dot the old ceilings, but the harried owner doesn't have time to stop and look at them. Doubles 3100ptas, with bath 3500ptas. Breakfast included.

Pensión Lizaso, C. San Vicente, 7 (tel. 42 29 77), in the *barrio viejo* near Monte Urgull, next to the Iglesia San Vicente. The conscientious *señora* and the crisp white linen on the beds make this one of the best bets in the old town. Doubles 2400ptas.

Pensión San Lorenzo, C. San Lorenzo, 2 (tel. 42 55 16), also in the *barrio viejo.* If this hardworking and friendly owner doesn't have room for you in her small and comfortable *pensión,* she'll give you names of people who might have a bed in a *casa particular.* Doubles 2500ptas.

Fonda Arsuaga, C. Narrica, 3 (tel. 42 06 81), perpendicular to the boulevard that borders the *barrio viejo.* The owners are a cheery couple who meticulously maintain their tidy and fresh rooms. Singles 1200ptas. Doubles 2400ptas.

Hostal Estrella, C. Sarriegui, 8 (tel. 42 09 97), in the *barrio viejo.* Walk north toward the isthmus and cross Alameda del Boulevard; it's 1 block inside the old quarter. Spacious rooms with wood floors, some with balconies. Singles 1500ptas. Doubles 3000ptas, with shower 3500ptas.

Fonda Vicandi, C. Iparraguirre, 1 (tel. 27 07 95), across the Santa Catalina bridge near the intersection with C. Secundino Esnaola and C. Miracruz. Quiet, old-fashioned rooms are kept clean by a quiet, old-fashioned man. Its distance from the hub makes this place less likely to fill as early as other establishments. Doubles 2500ptas. Showers 200ptas.

Casa de Huéspedes Oñate, C. Matía, 19 (tel. 21 52 15), 2 blocks from the main entrance to the Palacio Miramar, near Pl. de Ondarreta. The *señora* offers four simple, small doubles for 2000ptas per room. Upstairs, **Casa de Huéspedes Mercedes** (tel. 21 67 18) has several more doubles at the same price. This location ensures more vacancies later in the day.

If you want to camp, bear in mind Donostia's changeable weather; you'll probably encounter a shower or two. **Camping Igueldo** (tel. 21 45 02) is 5km west of town. The site's amenities include hot showers. (Open May-Sept. 295ptas per person and per car, 190ptas per tent.) The bus to Barrio de Igueldo leaves 13 times per day Monday through Saturday, five times per day Sunday, from Alameda del Boulevard, 22; the last bus is at 10pm (53ptas).

Food

Donostia has turned the national institution of *tapas* into something like a religious observance—consider making a roving meal of them. The bars in the old city spread an array of enticing tidbits held together with a toothpick. These are often referred to as *pinchos* (spikes) or *banderillas* (after the colorful darts that are stuck into the bull at the *corrida*). Try them with the strong regional wine *Txacoli.* Many small places in the harbor serve tasty sardines with cider, and *señores* sit outside selling small portions of *gambas* (shrimp) in eggcups and *caracolillos* (periwinkles) in paper cones for 100-200ptas. Beyond this, however, Donostia may be seafood heaven, but its prices are a budget traveler's hell. Expect to pay about 950ptas for a three-course meal that usually includes a minimal amount of seafood, some sort of unexciting cutlet, and dessert.

The closer you get to the sea, the more outrageous seafood prices become. The only establishment on the *puerto* that a budget traveler can gaze on without gasping is **Mariscos Kaia el Puerto,** at #1 (tel. 42 71 44), which sells cooked and prepared seafood, especially shellfish, by the kilo. They're understandably crowded. (Open 10am-2pm and 5-9:30pm.) Two **markets** are in large buildings on Alameda del Boulevard at Narrika Kalea and between C. Loyola and Urbieta a block north of the cathedral; they're patrolled by pickpockets. (Both open Mon.-Fri. 7:30am-2pm and 5-7:30pm, Sat. 7:30am-2pm.)

La Barranquesa, C. Larramendi, 21 (tel. 45 47 47). The 550ptas *menú* remains a local miracle. This is a smoky, basement, neighborhood restaurant. Down-home specialties include *lengua en salsa* (cow's tongue in sauce), *cabeza de cordero* (lamb's head), and *txiperones* (squid in its own ink). Open Mon.-Sat. 11am-2pm. Open for meals 1:10-6:30pm and 8:30-11pm.

Bar Etxadi, C. Reyes Católicos, 9 (tel. 46 07 85), near the cathedral, a block from the above. House specialties are *anchoas al ajillo* (400ptas) and *gambas al ajillo* (anchovies and shrimp with garlic, 500ptas). *Conejo* (rabbit) also 500ptas. *Menú* 750ptas. Open Tues.-Sat. 1:30-3:30pm and 9-11:30pm.

Restaurante Bar La Maitia, C. Easo, 31 (tel. 42 79 64), also in the cathedral neighborhood. *Platos combinados* include fried *merluza* (hake) and salad. *Calamares fritos* (fried squid) 500ptas. Daily *menú* 600ptas. The small dining room hangs in a loft over the bar. Open Mon.-Sat. 1-3:30pm and 8:30-11pm.

Restaurante Oquendo, C. Oquendo, 8 (tel. 42 07 63), near the Victoria Eugenia Theater. Hearty meals for vegetarians—pasta and pizza 650-700ptas, salads around 400ptas. Modern, comfortable atmosphere. Open Sun.-Thurs. 1-3:30pm and 8-11pm, Fri.-Sat. 1-3:30pm and 8-11:30pm.

Restaurante Morgan, Narrika Kalea, 7 (tel. 42 46 61), in the *barrio viejo*. Frequented by Basque gourmets. Perfectly seasoned soups and meat pastries covered with delicious sauces. *Menú* at lunch 675ptas, at dinner 1200ptas. Open Oct. 16-Sept. 30 daily 1:30-3:30pm and 9-11:30pm.

Restaurante Egosari, C. Fermín Calbetón, 15 (tel. 42 82 10). Avoid the expensive meals or you may be doing dishes during your entire stay in the city. The *tapas* are a delight; at 80ptas per *pincho,* they're reaonably priced. Open Fri.-Tues. 1-4pm and 8-11:30pm.

Bar Restaurante Alotza, C. Fermín Calbetón, 7 (tel. 42 07 82), a few doors down from Egosari. The *pinchos* are served with a smile and the tasty deep-fried seafood morsels (65-80ptas) are a house specialty. Open Tues.-Sun. 10am-11:30pm.

Sorkunde Jatetxea, C. 31 de Agosto, 28 (tel. 42 08 40). Enter on Pl. Don Alvaro de Lersmundi. The food may not be prepared with TLC, but you're not going to find a cheaper 3-course meal in the *barrio viejo*. *Menú* 700ptas, *chipirones* (baby squid) 500ptas, a hefty chunk o' chicken 375ptas. All available a la carte. Open daily 1:30-3:30pm and 9-11:30pm.

Self-Service Aurrera, C. Urbieta, 12 (tel. 42 31 82). An array of colorful and tasty food. Trout 300ptas. 700ptas *menú* includes *paella* and a delicious *pastel de merluza*. Open Mon.-Sat. 1-3:30pm and 8:30-11pm, Sun. 1-3:30pm.

Sights

The most spectacular sight here is Donostia itself and the green mountains and thundering ocean that surround it. The top of **Monte Igueldo,** at the far side of the bay, provides the best view. From here you can see the hilly Basque countryside meet the Atlantic in a long line of white and light blue surf. The city spreads out in a jumble of solid buildings around its fan-shaped bay. The view of the bay—from anywhere—is especially spectacular after dark, when the entire base of Santa Clara Island is lit by banks of floodlights so that it seems to float on a ring of light. The summit of Monte Igueldo holds an amusement park with bumper cars, miniature trains, and donkeys for hire. To reach the funicular that climbs to the top, take the "Igueldo" bus from Alameda del Boulevard or walk along the beach and turn left just before the tennis courts. (Funicular runs daily 10am-10pm, in off-season daily 11am-6pm or 8pm depending on the weather; every 15 min.; 50ptas.) At the other end of the curved beach, **Monte Urgull** provides the walker with a gentler ascent as gravel paths wind upward through cool, shady woods. Reminders remain of Donostia's tumultuous past: Halfway up the mountain, facing the sea, is the **Cementerio Británico,** a huge monument and tomb for the unknown British soldiers who died in 1813 defending the fortress at the top. A more jarring monument to a fallen hero is the unmarked, white-plaster blob on a rock near the *paseo* as it rises above the aquarium. A member of the ETA accidentally blew himself up here trying to plant a bomb.

Circling the base of Monte Urgull, **Paseo Nuevo** lets you get close enough to the untamed waves for a gentle saltwater shower. At one end, the **aquarium** (tel. 42 19 05) maintains only a few live fish, but its displays on seafaring history are more thorough. (Open daily 10am-1:30pm and 3:30-7:30pm. Admission 150ptas.) At the other end of Paseo Nuevo (you can cut through the *barrio viejo* by Pl. de la Trinidad if you don't want to walk around the whole *monte*), the **Museo de San Telmo** remains curiously ignored by tourists. It houses a fascinating array of Basque artifacts and a collection of Spanish art reaching back several centuries. The former Dominican monastery rests in Pl. Zuloaga, a quiet corner of the old city. The peaceful, overgrown cloister is strewn with Basque funerary monuments. Upstairs, the galleries display several schools of Spanish painting. El Greco's *El Salvador* gazes heavenward, his eyes brimming with saintly tears. Nearby, Antonio Echagüe's *Mujeres de Tafiladet* (Women of Tafiladet) peer out from behind their Moroccan garb, exposed only above the cheeks. Inside the adjoining old church, the walls blaze with the gold and sepia murals of José María Sert, painted in 1931. The soaring walls of the interior are well suited to his epic depictions of Basque life and culture. (Open Mon.-Sat. 9:30am-1:30pm and 3:30-7pm, Sun. 9:30am-2pm. Free.)

In 1845, Queen Isabel II journeyed to Donostia. After the strong-willed, somewhat capricious monarch took a liking to the place, the court and aristocracy coincidentally began to spend their summers in the town also. Reminders of these glory days abound. Even the railings on the boardwalk and the grandiose street lamps hearken back to the time when only a wealthy elite enjoyed this jewel of the Cantabrian coast. **El Palacio de Miramar,** built on the land that splits Pl. de la Concha and Pl. de Ondarreta, housed Regent Maria Cristina's court in 1893. Although the palace itself is closed for renovations, the expansive lawns and colorful flower beds remain open. (Open daily 11am-2pm and 4-8pm.) A 30-minute walk from the cathedral up Cuesta de Aldapeta or a 50ptas bus ride (#19 to Avete from Pl. de Gipuzkoa) brings you to another regal getaway, the **Palacio de Ayete.** Again, the residence itself is closed to the public, but the lush forest trails of the summer house grounds are worth a stroll.

Back in town, at the end of the boardwalk near Pl. de Ondarreta, *El Peine del Viento* (The Wind Comb) is a stark mesh of manmade art and environment. Designed by Basque artist Chillida, three clusters of twisted iron girders sprout from huge boulders, where the waves meet land. The wind and sea have readily incorporated this humble gift and the regular baths they provide are rusting the combs to a rich red hue.

Fierce fighting in 1813 destroyed the old city. The rebuilt old quarter, *barrio viejo* (*barrua erri* in Euskera), centers around **Plaza de la Constitución,** a square surrounded by buildings with covered walkways and balconies. The plaza is often a focus of Basque nationalism; the government buildings at one end are plastered with Basque slogans. Attempts by the government to plant trees have failed because local residents keep peeling the bark off in protest. Nearby stand the eighteenth-century baroque **Iglesia de Santa María,** with its highly ornamented concave portal (look for the vividly ghoulish statue of St. Sebastián, killed by archers), and the sixteenth-century Romanesque **Iglesia de San Vicente,** now covered with Basque slogans. Be careful at night in this area, especially on Basque holidays—the Guardia Civil are likely to put down demonstrations with tear gas and rubber bullets.

Entertainment

Beaches made Donostia famous and they continue to draw hordes of sun-worshippers. **Playa de la Concha** curves from the port to the **Pico del Loro,** the beak-shaped butt on which Palacio de Miramar sits. As the tide rolls in, sunbathers retreat to the beach's center since its edges are gradually swallowed up by the surf. At the shorter **Playa de Ondarreta,** bodies jam close; the main attraction here is the windsurfing school and rental stand. (Private lessons 3000ptas per 2 hr. Rentals 600ptas per hr.) Pedal boats are also available (500ptas per hr.) Both beaches face **Isla de Santa Clara,** in the center of the bay—a great spot for picnics. A motorboat leaves from the port daily every half-hour until 8:30pm (round-trip 150ptas). You can also rent rowboats at the port (675ptas per hr., 2-hr. min.) for two people. On Sunday you must rent for a half-day (1500ptas, 4 people) or more. Both services operate from the six-sided kiosk by the port.

As the sun goes down, the *barrio viejo* sucks in everyone. **Calbetón Kalea** becomes virtually impassable; the human wall is thickest in front of **Bar Uraitz,** at #26, and next door at **Bar Eiboytarra.** Those in search of some air should retreat to **Bar Colchonería,** Sant Vicente Kalea, 9, where bright modern art and small tables make for more intimate conversation. **Akerbeltz,** Koroko Andra Mari, 10, near the port, gleams with shafts of light and a sleek black bar inside a cave-like *bodega* (wine-cellar).

Fifteen turns forty and leather goes suede as you move to the streets around the cathedral. **Bar Udaberri-Beri,** C. de los Reyes Católicos (or Errege Katolikoen Kalea), 8, passes drinks through a window to the crowds on the sidewalks and blocked-off streets. If your sweet tooth suddenly acts up, **Chupi,** right around the corner, sells candies and dried fruit until the wee hours. On the other side of C. Easo, **C. San Bartolomé** jumps with a younger, beer-drinking crowd. Bisected motorscooters hang on the walls and mod music blares at **El Cine;** next door at #21, **La Prima Pury** offers an even more energetic clientele to help keep the good times rolling. The eclectic crowd quietly escapes to the other side of the Rió Urumea. Down the *paseo,* past Playa de Gros, the hip trudge through a muddy parking lot to listen to the latest Smiths and The Cure and to sip a large variety of British ales at **El Muro.**

At about 2am, Donostia's small but active disco scene starts thumping. **La Perla** on Paseo de la Concha, packs mobs onto a large floorspace and zaps them with neon and strobes. (Cover 600ptas. Open until 5:30am.) Nearby at **Bataplań,** the action sinks beneath the boardwalk, where the small, steamy dance floor looks out on the beach. (Cover 1000ptas. Open until 6am.) **Komplot,** C. Pedro Egaña, 7, off C. Easo, is an after-hours haven for those who just want to keep drinking. (Open until 5am.)

Donostia's **Jazz Festival** has hosted such giants as Art Blakey, Wynton Marsalis, Dizzy Gillespie, and Gerry Mulligan. For information about this year's festival, which will take place during the third week of July, contact Jazzaldia, Reina Regente (tel. 42 10 02). Local jazz artists perform once or twice a week at the **Be Bop Bar,** Paseo de Salamanca, 3. On certain Wednesdays the stage opens for anyone who wants to play. Around August 15, **Aste Nagustia** (Big Week) is celebrated with sports events, concerts, movies, and an international fireworks display on all six nights. The end of September brings an **international film festival** that attracts well-known directors and actors from all over the world. With all this international activity swamping a once-humble fishing village, the people of Donostia have set aside two days to honor their own past. January 20, **El Diá de San Sebastián,** is marked with cultural dances and festivities. On August 31, a candlelit procession slowly makes its way down C. 31 de Agosto, a poignant reminder of the 1813 fire that consumed the city.

Near Donostia: Hondarribía (Fuenterrabía)

At Hondarribía, the Spanish border hits the sea. This well-kept beach town lures artists and rich, vacationing Spaniards. The town also hosts flocks of French tourists who want to keep their eye on a patch of France. Historically, the proximity to France has made the place popular with smugglers and fugitives who were good swimmers.

Cobbled streets twist inside Hondarribía's ancient city walls, lined with structures that seem to compete in their profusion of elaborately carved and brightly painted balconies. Atop this jumble, visible from afar, the **Portuko Eliza** is an oft-remodeled Gothic church; Louis XIV of France was married off by proxy here to the Spanish Infanta María Teresa. Not two streets away, the cold stone box of the **Karlos V. Gaztelua** has been converted from a castle into an expensive *parador*. From the popular, wide *beach* along the estuary, it's possible to swim over to France with a little discretion, but there are also beaches directly on the Atlantic. A short distance down the coast toward Donostia, the scenery shifts to sun-warmed boulders and fewer people. Hondarribía also offers painting classes to travelers who've wearied of eyeing museum greats and want to try their own hand. Head for **Estudio Arrecubieta,** Gipuzkoa Plaza, 2 (tel. 64 25 39), where you can take your choice of drawing, painting, or decorating instruction.

Scrambling for rooms in this expensive town might be worthwhile if Donostia, with beautiful beaches and more lodgings, weren't so close. Hondarribía is best visited as a daytrip. There is no tourist office. For lodgings, try the modern and attractive **Juan Sebastián Elcano Hostel (IYHF),** Carretera del Faro (tel. 64 15 50), which is perched on a hillside overlooking the sea. From the town center, head to the beach, or take the bus marked "Playa." Turn left where the road forks right near the beach entrance (also where the bus turns around) and follow the signs to the hostel. If you're lucky, or have called ahead, you may find space in this four-bedroom house. Flexible curfew 11pm. 3-day max. stay if full. Members only, 450ptas. Sheets 300ptas. You can camp in the field below the hostel or in one of two nearby camp: **Jaizkebel** (tel. 64 16 79) and **Faro de Higuer** (tel. 64 10 08), 2km down the road. The former is closer, the latter newer. (Both charge 260ptas per person, 170ptas per tent or motorcycle.) A bit of camping seems to be tolerated on the wild grassy fields by the beach (beyond the soccer field and basketball courts).

Buses run to Donostia and Irún (every 20 min., 110ptas) from Zuloaga Kalea. Most restaurants, along with an **artisan's market,** can be found around **San Pedro Kalea.** At the other end of town, where the two car streets meet at a traffic circle, **Bar-Restaurante Emilio,** Harresilanda Kalea, is an honest, simple place frequented by locals who gather beneath the huge tree in front. (800ptas *menú.* Open daily 1-4pm and 7:30-11pm.) The **post office** is at the intersection with the traffic circle. (Open Mon.-Fri. 9am-2pm, Sat. 9am-noon.) If you need an **ambulance** in Hondarribía, call 27 22 22; the **police** are at 64 23 40.

Lekeitio (Lequeitio)

Lekeitio is as good an example of an unspoiled Basque fishing village as you'll find in modern Spain. At the turn of the century, the bounty of the sea was so abundant that fishing boats barely left shore to haul in loads of sardines and anchovies; whales swam within view of land. Now, the number of boats has diminished greatly, and *pescadores* traverse the deep seas for up to 15 days to pull in *bonito* (tuna) and anchovies. But modern boats and fishing techniques haven't spoiled the delicate harmony between village and ocean. During the late afternoon, the bay fills with the clumsy oars and primitive, wide-body boats of rowing teams churning the water at the mouth of the river that still empties into the sea.

Lekeitio's observance of traditions takes on less picturesque qualities during the **Antzar Eguma** (Goose Festival). On a selected weekday (usually Sept. 5) during the **Jaiak San Antolín** (Sept. 1-8), seven to nine unlucky geese get their necks greased; one at a time each is strung up across the harbor. Young men standing in rowboats try to yank the geese heads off while the living *piñata* is raised and lowered, causing some contestants to make a real splash. The winner receives a prize, his picture in the paper, and presumably, possession of his trophy. On September 8, an impressive candlelight march winds through the streets with everyone dressed in white to mourn not the noble geese but the end of the fiesta.

The **Feast of San Pedro** (June 29) marks the day when the statue of St. Peter is taken from its niche and paraded down to the wharf. The bearers menacingly lean the statue toward the water, threatening it with the wrath of the ex-fisherman apostle, lest the sea not cooperate with Peter's modern-day counterparts. The statue fell in the water a few years ago, though nobody knows how this accident affected the fishing industry that season. The inanimate Peter is accompanied by a very animate president of the fishermen's brotherhood, who dances the Kaxarranka on top of his society's venerated coffer while other fishermen tote it on their shoulders. In the week immediately following this spectacle, Lekeitio sometimes remembers its artistic and cultural roots with **Euskal Zinema Bilera** (Basque Amateur Film Festival). Inquire at Turismo about whether it will be held. Some surprisingly informative and entertaining 8mm films of political, humorous, or artistic nature are shown here at little or no cost. The first week of August also brings the **Itxas Soinua** music festival to the Church of Santa María (tickets 300ptas, students 150ptas). Be sure to peek inside the church; the incredible altarpiece looks like an entire Gothic city of saints and churches thrown against a towering stone wall and spray-painted gold.

Most of what looks like Lekeitio's bay at high tide turns into a very wide sandy beach when the water recedes. The farther out around the point you go, the colder and fresher the water. At low tide you can wade out to **Saint Nicholas Island** and rummage around the ruins of the old Franciscan convent. Keep an eye on the tide, however, unless you're looking for about 12 hours of privacy. A drier excursion starts opposite Santa Mariá, on the other side of the road to Ondarroa. The small road Eusebio Erkiada ends at the cemetery, but at the gates, a trail winds away to the right. Cutting behind the graveyard and sandwiched between the stone walls of the tiny gardens and backyards, **Paseo de Lumentza** climbs the mount of the same name. Simple stone crucifixes, life-size and numbered, tick off the Stations of the Cross on the way up. At the top, the view lets you see the meeting of mountain and sea from an altered perspective.

The paucity and expense of lodgings in Lekeitio are real incentives to make this a daytrip. Since the last bus to Donostia leaves at 5pm, you may end up staying the night. The two-year old **Hotel Piñupe** has doubled the number of hotels in Lekeitio. Opposite the bus stop, on Avda. Pascual Abaroa, 10 (tel. 684 29 84), it offers spotless modern singles (2100ptas) and doubles (3400ptas), all with full bath. You might want instead to camp on a dry spot of the **Campo de Marearrota** swamp beyond the bridge leading out of town to Ondarroa. Creatures of comfort on a budget should consider staying at the official **Camping Endai** (tel. 684 24 69), 3km toward Ondarroa. (Open June 15-Sept. 15. 155ptas per person, 125ptas per tent.)

Tucked away around town are a few good, moderately priced restaurants, but you'd be foolish to eat anywhere besides **Restaurante Egaña,** on the upper side of town at C. Santa Catalina, 4 (tel. 684 01 03). There is something unethical about getting so much good food for so little money. In the large, cool dining room, you'll be well-served and stuffed to the gills if you order the 600ptas *menú*. (Open daily 1-4pm and 8-11pm.) The food at **Restaurante Txalaparta**, Avda. Abaroa, 22 (tel. 784 23 66), may not be as rich as Egaña's but it's still cheap and plentiful. A salad, chicken, and fries cost 400ptas; no *plato combinado* is over 500ptas. The friendly owners have also been known to help people find *casas particulares* during the summer crunch. (Open Nov.-Sept. daily 1-4pm and 8:30-11pm.)

Avda. Pascual Abaroa (Paskval Abaroa Etorbidea) is the main street along the upper edge of town. The exceptionally friendly and helpful **tourist office** is down toward the waterfront, at Arranegiko Zabala, 10. (Tel. 684 22 72. Open Mon.-Sat. 10am-1:30pm and 5-8pm, Sun. 10am-1pm; Oct.-May Mon.-Sat. 9am-2pm and 4:30-

7:30pm.) Not only will they give you names of *casas particulares,* they'll call around until they find one for you. Expect to pay 1500ptas if you're alone, 1500-2000ptas with a companion. If you arrive when the tourist office is closed, ask at Restarante Egaña, or Hotel Piñupe.

Gernika (Guernica)

On April 26, 1937, mass aerial bombing of undefended civilian populations made its European debut in Gernika. Nazi dive-bombers, at the request of the Spanish Nationalists, unleashed volley after volley of explosives on this small town just as its inhabitants had gathered for the market. More than 2000 people died, and the town was left in ruins. The world reacted with shock, and Pablo Picasso painted his great rendition of the event, *Guernica.* Ever since, Gernika has been etched into the Spanish consciousness as the scene of one of the most brutal atrocities of the Civil War.

Gernika was a center of the Basque nation during the Middle Ages, and the **Arbola Zaharra** (tree) still grows on the site where feudal lords once gathered. There are actually three trees now standing next to the **Juntetxea,** the former Basque Parliament building. The remains of the old oak, its age estimated at a couple thousand years, stands beneath the eight-pillared dome. The oak's offspring, an august tree of 128 years, grows next to the building, behind the grillwork fence. The grandchild tree, about 26 years old, rises right behind it. Basque families like to have their pictures taken next to the trees, which remain symbols of Basque nationalism. The Juntetxea may be visited without charge daily from 10am to 7pm; there is a small documentary museum as well. To reach the area from the train station, walk up C. Urioste and across the carefully tended flower beds on the hillside to a large plaza. Behind the buildings to your left rises a stone staircase that becomes a small amphitheater—walk up these steps.

The main street, arcaded **Artekale,** runs through Foruen Plaza, a harmonious group of official buildings. Gernika's single hotel, **Hotel Boliña,** Barrenkale, 3 (tel. 685 03 00), 2 blocks from the plaza, is a one-star affair. (Singles 2000ptas, with bath 2500ptas. Doubles 3000ptas, with bath 3200ptas.) The **tourist office,** which has a list of *casas particulares,* is at Artekale, 7. (Tel. 685 35 58. Open June 15-Sept. 15 Mon.-Sat. 10am-1:30pm and 4-7pm, Sat. 10am-1:30pm.) The **post office** is around the corner on the plaza. (Open Mon.-Fri. 9am-2pm, Sat. 9am-1pm.) For **medical help,** call 685 08 80; the **police** are at 685 05 54. Gernika's **telephone code** is 94.

Vascongadas trains go to Bermeo (10 per day, 80ptas), Bilbao (11 per day, 175ptas) with an occasional change in Amorebieta, and Donostia (3 per day, 440ptas) with a change in Amorebieta. Dial 685 11 82 for train information. **Buses** stop in the train station parking lot and journey to Lekeitio (4 per day, 40 min., 135ptas), and Bilbao (4 per day, 40 min., 170ptas). Call 433 12 79 for bus information.

Bilbao (Bilbo)

Two forces conspire to give Bilbao a bad rap: the pollution in its outlying areas (visible from incoming highways) and the nasty brown of its river which cuts the old and new *barrios* into separate chunks. While there's no denying the problems which heavy industrialization has brought to Bilbao, the city's unique charm and tremendous energy also remain unchallenged. The wealth generated by iron factories and mining was well spent; the wide tree-lined avenues and elegant turn-of-the-century architecture reflect tasteful city-planning. Start from the center of the new section, **Plaza de Moyúa,** and any *avenida* you follow will offer a pleasant *paseo.* Activity in the *casco viejo* (old town), on the opposite side of the river, centers around the **Siete Calles,** the seven streets starting at Somera and ending at Barrencalle Barrena.

You would have to spend at least a day at the **Museo de Bellas Artes de Bilbao** to fully appreciate the wealth of artwork on display. Spanish Romanesque and Gothic paintings hang in the first galleries. El Greco's languid and sultry characters appear in five of his paintings, and farther on you'll see paintings by other Spanish greats, including an elegant portrait of Felipe IV by Velazquez and scathing portraits of Carlos IV and Queen María Luisa by Goya. In gallery 19, Gauguin's *Lavanderas en Arles* catches the misty morning light which hovers over white sheets and flowing water. Upstairs, 12 rooms hold paintings by Basque artists; Arteta's colorful paintings create a friendly mood recognizable in Basque coastal villages. The large contemporary art section contains mostly international abstract art. *La Fabrica* by the Basque artist Agustin Ibarrola Goicetxea depicts the worker reduced to square shapes under the towering and dominating pipes of the factory. The museum is on the edge of the Parque de Doña Casilda de Iturriza, on the northern side of the new part of the city. (Open Mon.-Sat. 10:30am-1pm and 3:30-7pm, Sun. 10:30am-1pm. Closed for half of Aug.)

The **Euskal Arkeologia, Etnografia eta Kondaira-Museoa** (Basque Museum of Archeology, Ethnology and History), C. Santa Cruz, 4, houses a confusing arrangement of artifacts pulled from prehistoric sites in Euskadi. A keen eye and trained mind may discern the function and evolution of the stone tips, shards, and bone utensils, but don't expect much help from the explanations on the walls. In the ethnology section on the first floor, there is an amusing collection of pistols, some predating the revolutionary Colt; you can also see nineteenth century *pelota* equipment, including the wicker *remontes* used to hurl the ball at frightening speeds. On the top floor, patient topographers are assembling a 7 by 10-meter relief of Euskadi, with every village, mountain, hill, and dale represented. (Open Tues.-Sat. 10:30-1:30pm and 4-7pm, Sun. 10:30am-1:30pm. Free.)

The **Basilica de Nuestra señora de Begoña** sits atop the hill overlooking the *casco viejo* (old quarter). Inside, the strangely sloping floor leaves the altar perched above the congregation. The *patrona* of the province, dressed in a long flowing robe, shines brightly inside the dimly lighted building. To reach the basilica, you can walk up the long set of stairs starting at Pl. Unamuno, but it's more fun to take the elevator from C. Esperanza, 6 (Open daily 7am-9pm; 12ptas). The upper walkway has a view of the city which extends to Bilbao's port, the largest in Spain.

Bilbao's shoppers come in two breeds: those who favor expensive stores lining wide avenues in the area around Plaza de Indautxu, and those who prefer cheaper buys on the narrow streets of the *casco viejo*, near the Catedral de Santiago. At the riverside end of the Siete Calles, the **Mercado de Atxuri** sells daily catches of fish, as well as meat, fruit, and veggies. (Open Mon.-Sat. 8am-2pm.)

If you want a meal made for you, **Bar Eisko Etxea**, C. Somera, 15, serves *merluza* (hake) in tomato sauce or fried sardines as part of their 550ptas *menú*. (Open daily 1-3:30pm; *menú* Mon.-Fri. only.) Just down the street from Spanish writer Miguel de Unamuno's birthplace (#10), **Herriko Taberna**, C. de la Ronda, 20 (tel. 416 16 90), has no sign; just look for the interior plastered with political posters and photographs of Basque detainees. The friendly and outspoken cooks make an amazing *paella*. (*Menú* 475ptas. Open Sept. 15-Aug. 15 daily 1-3:30pm.)

Prices for lodgings in Bilbao are quite attractive. You shouldn't have to pay much more than 700ptas per night to stay in the old town. Señora Rosario, owner of **Hospedaje Serantes,** will practice her English with you if she sniffs out an anglicized Spanish accent. When she's not taking piano lessons or classes in parapsychology, she mothers young travelers and maintains an immaculate house at C. Somera, 14 (tel. 415 15 57). Doubles cost 1200ptas; singles are 600ptas if she splits a double for you. (Closed in July.) If her rooms are full, walk over to **Hospedaje de la Fuente,** C. Correo, 11 (tel. 416 99 89), where a nice but somewhat stern man keeps clean rooms with shiny wooden floors and colorful bedspreads. Some rooms overlook the bustling street below. (Singles 900ptas. Doubles 1200ptas.) **Pension Residencia Manoli,** C. Libertad, 2 (tel. 415 56 36), is located next to Pl. Nueva and has a large and modern bathroom. (Singles 900ptas. Doubles 1300ptas. Showers 100ptas.)

The **tourist office** (tel. 424 48 19) isn't in a hurry to send anyone anywhere, but if you can command their attention, they can be helpful. From the Abando train station, walk over 1 block to El Corte Inglés and turn right on Alameda Urquijo, which becomes Avda. de Mazarredo. The office, 6 blocks down, is unnumbered on the righthand side. (Open Mon.-Fri. 9:30am-1:30pm and 4-6pm.) **TIVE** (student travel) has an office at Gran Via, 50, seventh floor. (Tel. 441 42 77. Open Mon.-Fri. 9am-1pm.) The **United States Consulate** is on Avda. del Ejército, 11 (tel. 435 83 00); the **British Consulate** is on Alameda Urquijo, 2 (tel. 415 76 00). The **post office** is at Alameda Urquijo, 15. (Tel. 432 05 08. Open Mon.-Fri. 9am-1pm and 4-6pm, Sat. 9am-1pm.) **Telephones** are at C. Barroeta Aldamar, 2 blocks from Pl. España. The **Hospital Civil de Basurto** (tel. 441 88 00) is on Avda. de Montevideo. For the **police,** dial 092; for an **ambulance,** call 444 62 56.

Estación de Abando, Pl. España, 1 (tel. 423 86 36), is the **RENFE** terminal serving Barcelona (2 per day, 3805ptas), Madrid (3 per day, 2580ptas), La Coruña (2 per day, 3920ptas), and Salamanca (2 per day, 2040ptas). **FEVE** trains depart **Estación de Portugalete** and **Estación de Santander** (tel. 423 22 66; both are in one building) for Santander (4 per day, 580ptas), and León (1 direct per day, or make connections at Valmoseda). On the other side of the river, south of the old town, **Ferro carriles Vascos** trains (tel. 433 00 88) leave **Estación de Atxuri** for Gernika (13 per day, 165ptas), and Donostia (4 per day, 440ptas). **Transportes PESA** buses (tel. 416 46 10) zip out of C. Urazurrutia, 7, for Donostia (9 per day, 1¼ hr., 650ptas). **Vascongadas,** Pl. Encarnación, 7 (tel. 433 12 79), travels to Lequeitio (6 per day, 320ptas), and Gernika (12 per day, 175ptas). **Turytrans,** from Pl. de Arriaga next to the Teatro Municipal, will get you to Santander (8 per day, 590ptas), Oviedo (4 per day, 1690ptas), and Donostia (9 per day, 620ptas). The **airport** (tel. 453 08 51) hosts both domestic and international flights; take the Munguia bus from Paseo de Arenal (130ptas).

Navarre

Many of Navarre's inhabitants quietly embrace the Basque customs and language practiced so vociferously in Euskadi today. While the Basque independence party Herri Batasuna retains the support of the radical few who editorialize with posters everywhere, most citizens deplore the violent tactics employed by extremists. The spirited Navarrese have been politically active since expelling Charlemagne from Spain in 778 in the famous battle of Roncesvalles. Fernando el Católico took away the area's independence in 1512, incorporating it into the kingdom of Castilla. Further subjugation came during the Carlist wars, when Navarre was converted into a province. Democracy has since restored some of this past independence.

Pamplona

The ancient capital of Navarre performs a spectacular quick-change act for the **Fiesta de San Fermín,** better-known to English-speakers as the Running of the Bulls, Spain's wildest festival and Pamplona's only irresistible attraction. The week of July 6-14, bunting streams from every building and barricades rise along the streets. Each morning, as bystanders cheer from balconies, doors, and windows, the *encierro* begins: Six frenzied bulls charge down an 825-meter course toward Plaza de Toros, joined by thousands of half-crazed young men and women. Pamplonians complain that the influx of tourists has spoiled the fun, but the running of the bulls remains as undiluted and gripping an expression of lunacy and joy as ever careened down a city street. Even if you do not run, the weeklong revelry is still worth the trip. While the older generation may mutter that *las mujeres* are only permitted to watch, more and more women run in each fiesta. Coming to Pamplona any other time of the year is like visiting Santa's village in August. The trampled flower beds and color photos posted around town will remind you of what you missed.

Orientation and Practical Information

About 200,000 people live in Pamplona, most of them in the city's concrete suburbs. This urban conglomeration centers around **Plaza del Castillo.** The narrow, slightly confused streets of the old quarter extend from three sides of the plaza; to the south, the grid-like avenues of the new town take over. The **Río Arga,** surrounded by parks and swimming clubs, cuts across to the north. **Plaza de Toros,** the bullring, lies just east and south of Pl. del Castillo. You'll find most restaurants and *hostales* in the old part of town, and most services in the new. From the train station, take bus #9 to the end of the line, Paseo de Sarasate, to reach the town center (every 15 min., 40ptas).

Tourist Offices: C. Duque de Ahumada, 3 (tel. 22 07 41), off Pl. del Castillo. Suffers from an understandable siege mentality during the Fiesta, but otherwise quite helpful. Bus and train information posted. During Fiesta, make contact with locals offering *casas particulares* here. Open Holy Week-Sept. 15 daily 9am-9pm; in off-season Mon.-Fri. 9am-2pm and 4-7pm, Sat. 9am-2pm. **Municipal Information Office,** in the rear of the Ayuntamiento, (tel. 22 12 00), off the plaza by the *mercado.* Not a tourist office, but provides a good map of the city. During the Fiesta, you can pick up the helpful publication **BIM,** which lists many of the town's services. Open Mon.-Sat. 8am-2pm.

Student Travel: Viajes TIVE, Avda. de Carlos III, 36, 3rd floor (tel. 23 37 22), near C. Gorriti. Student IDs 225ptas. Discount travel fares. Open Mon.-Fri. 9am-2pm.

Currency Exchange: During the Fiesta, banks are open only 9:30-11:30am. Some travel agencies will keep you in pesetas outside of these hours, as will the Hotel los Tres Reyes, C. Jardines de la Taconera. Expect a criminal exchange rate and a commission of at least 500ptas.

Post Office: Paseo Sarasate, 9 (tel. 22 12 63; in off-hours 944 24 20 00). Lista de Correos. Open Mon.-Fri. 9am-2pm and 4-6pm, Sat. 9am-2pm; during the Fiesta closed afternoons and Sat. Open for **telegrams** Mon.-Fri. 8am-9pm, Sat. 9am-7pm. **Postal Code:** 31000.

Telephones: C. Amaya, 2, at C. Cortes de Navarra around the corner from the tourist office. Open Mon.-Sat. 9am-1pm and 5-9pm. **Telephone Code:** 948.

Train Station: Estación de Rochapea (tel. 12 69 81), off Avda. de San Jorge. Take bus #9 from the end of Paseo Sarasate (40ptas). Information open Mon.-Fri. 10am-10pm. To Madrid (2 per day, 6 hr., 2560ptas), Donostia (4 per day, 1700ptas), Barcelona (3 per day, 6½ hr., 2550ptas), and Zaragoza (6 per day, 2½ hr., 950ptas).

Bus Station: C. Conde Oliveto, 4 (tel. 21 36 19), 1 block off Pl. del Príncipe de Vianda. **Conda** (tel. 22 10 26) to Madrid (2 per day, 5½ hr., 2060ptas) and Zaragoza (5 per day, 31/3 hr., 1025ptas). **Burundesa** (tel. 22 17 66) to Bilbao (4 per day, 3½ hr., 925ptas) and Santander (2 per day, 4¾ hr., 1405ptas). **Roncalesa** to Donostia (5 per day, 2¾ hr., 450ptas). **Estellasa** to Estella (4 per day, 1¼ hr., 270ptas) and Logroño (4 per day, 2½ hr., 495ptas). **Veloz Sangùesa** (tel. 22 69 25) to Sangùesa (5 per day, 45 min., 250ptas) **La Montañesa** to Burguete (1 per day, 2½ hr., 405ptas). **Hispano-Ansotana** to Jaca and Huesca via Yesa (2 per day, 550ptas).

Baggage Check: In the bus station (tel. 22 38 54). Open daily 6:15am-9:30pm. Backpacks 100ptas per day. Other baggage 75ptas.

English Bookstore: Libreriá Gomez, Pl. del Castillo, 28 (tel. 22 67 02). Penguin novels.

Laundromat: Lavomatique, C. de Descalzos, 28 (tel. 22 19 22), in the old part of town. Self-service. Wash 225ptas. Dry 25ptas per 10 min. Open Mon.-Fri. 10am-2pm and 6-8:30pm, Sat. 10am-6pm. Cleaner, less hassle, and probably cheaper is the laundry service at the **public baths** on C. Eslava, 9bis. 350ptas for wash and dry. 2-hr. service. Open Tues.-Sat. 8am-8:30pm, Sun. 8am-2:30pm. **Lost Property:** In a booth at the bus station during the Fiesta. Go to the municipal police any other time of year.

Public Bathrooms: C. Conde Oliveto, 4 (tel. 22 88 26), in the bus station. Open daily 8am-9pm; during Fiesta 24 hours. Also on C. Jaravta.

Swimming Pool (Piscina Municipal): In the bend of Río Arga below the old city. Walk out C. Carmen, through the Portal Zumalacárregui, and continue towards Puente de San Pedro (15 min. from Pl. del Castillo). Open June-Sept. daily 10:30am-9pm. Admission 80ptas, during Fiesta 235ptas.

Ambulance: Tel. 26 12 12. **First Aid: Casa de Socorro,** C. Tudela, 2 (tel. 22 18 76), near the bus station. The **Cruz Roja** (Red Cross), C. Yanquas y Miranda, 3 (tel. 22 64 04), also sets up stations at the bus station and the *corrida* during the Fiesta.

Police: Policía Municipal, C. Monasterio de Irache, 12 (tel. 11 11 11). **Emergency:** Tel. 091.

Accommodations and Camping

It would take months of advance planning, an extraordinarily charismatic personality, or divine grace to find a bed in Pamplona during the first few days of the *encierro.* In most cases, you must reserve about two months in advance and pay rates two to three times higher than those listed below. Check at Turismo for *casas particulares,* which run at least 1500ptas per person, plus 100ptas for showers. Later in Fiesta week, some accommodations become available. If you sleep in parks here, be careful: Sleep on top of your belongings if you can. Avoid Pl. del Castillo, where the hordes snooze. This square is not only filthy from Fiesta refuse, but dangerous too. Any of the parks that surround old Pamplona is more hospitable, particularly **Parque Media Luna.** This area is right next to the bullring, so you won't have to worry about sleeping through the *encierro.* You can shower and wash your clothes not far away at the municipal swimming pool (not to be confused with the *Club de Natación*) below the *corrida,* on the other side of the river.

Another alternative is **Camping Ezcaba** in Oricain (tel. 33 03 15), 7km outside of Pamplona on the road to Irún, a second-class facility. (Open June-Sept. 275ptas per person, 195ptas per tent, 275ptas per car.) The La Montañesa bus to the site leaves Pamplona from C. Arrieta in front of the bullring four times per day during the Fiesta, with three additional departures at other times of the year. The last bus leaves at 8:30pm—see the schedule posted at Turismo.

The other 51 weeks of the year, you should have little trouble finding accommodations in Pamplona. **Calle San Nicolas,** off Pl. del Castillo, and its continuation, **Calle San Gregorio,** have lots of *fondas* and *habitaciones,* but some tend to be run-down; a little effort will ferret out a good deal.

Fonda La Montañesa, C. San Gregorio, 2 (tel. 22 43 80). Clean rooms with overpowering wallpaper. From the 4th floor, you hear every church bell within 3 blocks chime every quarter-hour. 800ptas per person.

Hostal Bearán, C. San Nicolas, 25 (tel. 22 34 28). Large rooms with comfortable beds. Friendly owners. Singles 1000-1300ptas. Doubles with bath 2400ptas. Triples 3000ptas.

Casa Huespedes Santa Cecilia, C. Navarreria, 17 (tel. 22 22 30), 1 block from the cathedral. Although the splendid entryway is sadly run-down, rooms are elegant with high ceilings. 1000ptas per person.

Hostal Otano, C. San Nicolás, 5 (tel. 22 50 95). A modern, comfortable choice over a hopping bar and restaurant. Some rooms lack interior ventilation. Booked solid during Fiesta. Singles 1000ptas. Doubles 1850ptas.

Casa Marceliano, C. Mercado, 7-9 (tel. 22 14 26), behind the Ayuntamiento and market. Small rooms up a wooden staircase. Many have washbasins built into old commodes. 1000ptas per person, less if you eat in the restaurant downstairs.

Hostal Ibarra, C. Estafeta, 85 (tel. 22 06 06 or 22 21 72), just 100m from Pl. de Toros. Reasonable rooms, some with balconies that overlook the route of the *encierro.* The owner isn't the friendliest. Doubles 1800ptas.

Food

Restaurants around Pl. del Castillo in the Casco Viejo pay the year's overhead with their Fiesta prices. Venture into the side streets instead. **Calle Navarrería,** near the cathedral, has lots of small bars and restaurants. At #14, **Bar Elaleman** (tel.

22 51 93) serves a profusion of *bocadillos* and quick meals for 150-300ptas. Food and sandwich stands sprout everywhere for the week of celebrations, and although expensive, these are your best alternatives besides the supermarket. At any time, look for restaurants along **Calle Estafeta, Calle Mayor,** and **Calle San Nicolas** (though the last is longer on crowds and alcohol than solid food). Pamplona's **markets** are in the old city by the Ayuntamiento and in the new city between C. Amaya and C. Olite at C. Gorriti. (Both open Mon.-Sat. 8am-2pm.)

> **Bar-Restaurante Lanzale,** C. San Lorenzo, 31 (tel. 22 10 71), near the end of C. Mayor. A truly satisfying way to blow 550ptas. Say "buenos días" to your neighbor across the table (seating is tight), and prepare for a hearty 3-course meal with *alubias blancas* and *merluze a la romana* (batter-fried hake). Open Mon.-Sat. 1-3:45pm and 9-11pm.

> **Bar La Papa,** C. Estafeta, 46 (tel. 22 52 58). Yummy creative pizza combinations and pasta dishes 400-490ptas. *Platos combinados* 475-525ptas. Open daily 11am-midnight; during the Fiesta, the friendly owner gets into the spirit by staying open for the entire weeklong party.

> **Casa Garciá,** C. San Gregorio, 12 (tel. 22 38 93). Tasty food in a bright, modern dining room. The 600ptas *menú* offers a huge range of entrees, from *lomo* (pork) to baked ham. Open Mon.-Sat. 1-4pm and 9-11pm.

> **Self-Service Estafeta,** C. Estafeta, 57 (tel. 22 16 05). Get here early, when the food is hot and fresh. 600ptas *menú* or a variety of cheaper dishes. Open Thurs.-Sat. and Mon.-Tues. noon-4pm and 8:30-11:30pm, Sun. noon-4pm.

> **Restaurant La Viñá,** C. Descalzos, 8 (no phone), near the Iglesia de San Saturnino and C. Mayor. Half-chicken and fried clams keep locals coming back for the 600ptas *menú*. Open Mon.-Sat. 1-3:30pm and 9-11pm.

Los San Fermines

Judging by the number of casualties, the **Running of the Bulls** is the best party in Europe. In its profane fashion, this weeklong orgy of bull worship celebrates Pamplona's patron saint, San Fermín, who was martyred by being dragged through the streets by bulls. For seven days, thousands of Pamplonians clad in white clothes and red sashes carouse through the city streets, accompanied by equal numbers of foreigners. They dance, sing, parade, and drink 24 hours per day. The activity is punctuated only by brief cat-naps and even briefer heroic moments spent running away from the bulls that rampage through the barricaded streets of **Santo Domingo, Mercaderes,** and **Estafeta** every morning.

Hemingway immortalized the festival in his first novel, *The Sun Also Rises,* a story of 1920s expatriates who come down from Paris for the party. The book's vivid descriptions have drawn thousands to the extravaganza, but perhaps more instrumental in the mushrooming of the festival was its international promotion by the still influential Manuel Fraga, a member of Franco's cabinet. Locals complain, however, that their festival has been ruined by the influx of greenhorns and argue that the sort of tourism it generates does little to enrich the general populace.

The festival is exhausting and continuous. Parades jam the streets, bullfights draw blood, parties souse the mind, fireworks tingle the senses, and rock-and-roll roars through Pl. del Castillo until dawn. You must rise early to catch the most important part of the Fiesta, the actual running of the bulls at 8am every morning. Runners crazed with a lust for their own blood dart in front of the bulls along the streets leading to the *corrida*. The idea is to run alongside a bull for a few yards without letting it gore you. Six steers accompany the six bulls, but they have horns too. The best places to witness the madness are at the Santo Domingo stairs and inside the bullring itself. Be there by 7am.

Before you decide to run, remember that severe wounds and even deaths are not uncommon. Once you watch an *encierro,* however, you'll be amazed that only 12 bull-related fatalities have occurred since 1926. (Party-related fatalities are a bull of a different breed.) Watch an *encierro* before participating, and avoid running in the dangerous traffic jams on the weekends; there's usually a lot of pushing and shoving, and bodies have a curious tendency to pile up in the flow of taurine traffic.

Traditionally less crowded, Mondays and Tuesdays are the best days to run. Make sure to carry a rolled newspaper. Even if you don't use it to taunt the bulls or divert them from some trapped reveler as the locals do, you can always raise it high during the hymn to San Fermín that opens and closes each *encierro*.

At the firing of a rocket, the first pair of horns charges from the pen. The bulls begin their 825-meter dash through Cuesta de Santo Domingo and run through Pl. Consistorial, Carrer Mercaderes, and Carrer Estafeta to Pl. de Toros. A second rocket marks the exit of the last bull, and a third explodes once all the bulls have reached the end of the course. Rarely do more than two minutes separate the first and final rocket, and a safe, clean *encierro* is usually accompanied by the quick succession of the first two. A delay means the bulls are scattered; an isolated bull is more likely to wreak havoc in his search for company. Try not to cower in a doorway; a lonely bull might drop in and you'll have no back door. Three out of the 12 deaths were caused by one such rampaging bull.

The scene inside the bullring provides more than enough thrills for those who would rather participate vicariously. For an hour, the tense and energetic crowd packs both the free seats of the lower part of the stadium and the 600ptas seats above. As 8am approaches, the clapping spectators gradually drown out the band, until finally the first rocket goes off. All bodies rise, necks crane toward the bull entrance, and a slow-moving stream of people begins to flow into the stadium—many of these wish merely to claim they ran, while others tote movie cameras. As the bulls come in, their horns are only inches away from the runners' backs, and spectators stand on tip-toe to see if anyone has been gored. Some running also takes place in the stands: Some fans bring large vats of sangria to the stadium to pour on their neighbors; flour is then dumped on the fruity victim.

The fun, however, has only begun. The next 20 minutes, heifers are periodically unleashed on the crowd that has collected in the bullring. The animals burst through the human wall in front of the bull chute and charge wildly about, slamming their sawed-off horns into as many humans as possible. It's actually safer to receive them head on (you can dodge to the side) than to turn your back and offer the brawl-crazed beast your kidneys. When a heifer starts to tire, the crowd will taunt it and pull its tail. On weekdays, these fun games are followed by a mini-*encierro*, with calves, for the kiddies.

After this taurine track-and-field event, the party moves into the streets, gathering more and more steam until it explodes at nightfall. Come darkness, all restraints imposed in the name of civilization dissolve in waves of alcohol. There is singing in the bars, dancing in the alleyways, and an unbelievable party in Pl. del Castillo. Everywhere, red-and-white garbed locals stumble about, joined by foreigners keeping one eye on their backpacks and two fists around their drinks. Every nook claims its passed-out partisan, and every square becomes an open-air dance floor. At 11pm fireworks rip the sky, at midnight rock-and-roll heats up the central plaza, and all night long, the dirt, grime, and vomit seem as trivial as your search for a night's resting place. The truly inspired partying takes place the first few days. After that, the crowds thin out, putting a few extra beds on the market, but by that time the casualties strewn about town may be grisly. Try to make it early in the week, before the delirium is reduced to decadence, and the locals become impatient with tourists sleeping in their gardens.

Nearby towns sponsor more unspoiled *encierros* in summer. **Tafalla**, for example, holds one August 15, and Estella (see following section) holds one the first week of August. Altogether, over 90 *encierros* with bulls are held across Spain each year. In addition, photographs in the windows of every camera shop in Pamplona record the event and stay on display (and for sale) weeks afterwards. At any time of year, the pathetically stunted and mutilated trees in Pl. del Castillo (and the stains on the pavement) bear witness to the running.

Sights and Entertainment

When it's not being trampled on by half-ton bulls, Pamplona reverts to a quiet existence. Pretty plazas and a maze of medieval streets enclose more modern buildings. The **cathedral's** uninspiring facade is more appropriate for a municipal courthouse than a house of worship, but behind this unfortunate eighteenth-century addition, the Gothic interior is lined with graceful, ogival arches, simple ornamentation, and the alabaster tomb of Carlos III. The **cloister** will easily justify your visit. (Cathedral open daily 10am-1pm and 6:30-8pm. Cloister open daily 10am-1pm.)

The most beautiful sight in Pamplona is the facade of the **Ayuntamiento.** The darkly exuberant baroque wall stands out like a black sheep from the surrounding buildings. As you stare up at the building, waiting for the beginning of the Fiesta, notice the ironic allegory of prudence on the front door. The attractive **Museo de Navarra** houses the province's few artistic treasures. The second floor provides a chance to inspect more fourteenth- and fifteenth-century murals than you ever dreamed existed. The third floor contains luxurious nineteenth-century furniture, and a special room displays a roped-off Goya portrait of a haughty count. (Closed for renovations.) When **Plaza del Castillo** is not being used as a communal bedroom during the Fiesta, its elegant, tree-lined *paseos* and outdoor cafes offer a cool respite. To completely escape the city's streets, relax in its large and spacious parks: **La Taconera,** with a few deer, elk, and playful rabbits, and **La Ciudadela,** enclosed within remnants of the ancient city walls.

The city's third set of walls, built between the sixteenth and eighteenth centuries, rises behind the cathedral. Charlemagne dismantled the first walls in the ninth century; area residents responded by killing his nephew Roland. The second collection of walls was destroyed by the Duque de Alba when he took the city in 1512. You can exit the old city at one of two gateways, **Portal de Francia** or **Portal de Guipúzcoa,** and stroll along the **Río Arga,** gazing at the walls from the bases. These impressive walls humbled the French: When they arrived to occupy the city, they were so awestruck that instead of attacking the city, they staged a snowball fight among themselves in front of the gates. When Spanish sentries decided to join in, Napoléon's troops gained entry to Pamplona through the door, *not* over the walls.

Those who feel trapped by the narrow streets of San Gregorio and San Nicolás escape to the more refined nightlife of **Barrio San Juan,** beyond Hotel Los Tres Reyes on Avda. de Bayona. Here, the flashing disco lights and neon beacons guide many midnight sailors into port. Right on the *avenida,* about 3 long blocks past Hotel Los Tres Reyes, **Bar Convoy** choo-choos into the wee hours behind its elaborate locomotive #9 facade. **Desigual** and **Casablanca** are tucked away on a pedestrian side street, Travesía de Bayona, farther down the *avenida.* Farther into the icy *barrio nuevo,* **Más y Más** provides thumping rhythms and plenty of floorspace to dance the night away. You can take bus #9 to the *barrio.* The last bus leaves at 10:30pm.

Estella

In 1090, King Sancho Ramírez decided to give his economy a boost by allowing several merchants to set up a commercial village along the Road to Compostela. **Estella,** the result of his promptings, became the second largest market town in Europe by the thirteenth century. The city still bears traces of its days as a segregated, multi-ethnic metropolis with Jewish, Frankish, and Navarrese quarters. More recently, both nineteenth-century revolutions by arch-conservatives were headquartered here. Indeed, regularly scheduled Carlist revolts are still held. About 15 years ago, tempers flared among rival factions and one person died in a shoot-out. This incident effectively extinguished the final manifestations of a once-powerful political force in Spain.

Today, tranquil Estella boasts the **Iglesia de San Pedro de la Rúa,** which sits above the main street of the original commercial center. The early Gothic church has a Romanesque baptismal font and a simple but poignant wooden carving of Jesus in the left apse. Behind the building, a 100-foot cliff rises above the Romanesque cloister. If you squint and use the tourist map's detailed explanations, you may be able to distinguish scenes from the New Testament and the lives of saints in the capitals. Across the *rúa* from San Pedro, on the capitals of the twelfth-century **Palacio de los Reyes de Navarra,** the oldest stone Roland in the world jousts with the Moor Farragut. (The real Roland once served as a stalwart defender of the Christians.) Visit the **Casa de Cultura** to view the inside of its handsome sixteenth-century palace. Patient builders lay thin stones in star-shaped mosaics on the main patio floor; plateresque columns wind around the interior galleries. (Open Mon.-Sat. 7-9pm.) At the end of the street, a monstrous Satan swallows the damned by the mouthful in an amazing fourteenth-century depiction of the Last Judgment on the archway of the **Iglesia del Santo Sepulcro.**

Blown up in 1873 during one of Estella's frequent rebellions, the **Puente de la Cárcel,** which spans the Rió Ega, was rebuilt a century later. The new architects outdid themselves, raising the pointed arch in the middle of the bridge twice as high as the original. No car can pass over it without getting stuck at the top like the moving plank of a see-saw. Residents joke about this and other examples of overblown grandeur, such as the time the Ayuntamiento went into bankruptcy to properly attire every citizen for the visit of King Felipe III, at which the elaborate fireworks prepared for the occasion refused to go off.

Estella may be small, but neighborhood rivalries have always run strong. The area along **Calle Mayor** sprung up in the twelfth century to challenge the Frankish merchants across the Ega. At its center, the **Iglesia de San Miguel's** five-arch doorway with well-preserved capitals of the baby Jesus' tribulations is quite impressive. (Church undergoing renovation—should reopen in 1990.) While the **Iglesia de San Juan,** on Pl. de los Fueros, can't compete with the glory of the two older churches, the arcades and pretty pavilion of the plaza provide an appropriate center for socializing.

Las Fiestas de la Virgen del Puy y San Andrés begins the Friday before the first Sunday in August and lasts for one week. Estella has its own *encierro* with heifers, smaller and less ferocious than the *toros* that run in Pamplona. Women run with official consent here.

After a slump during the economic crisis of the '70s, Estella is finding new ways to survive in the '80s. Record numbers of pilgrims have passed through in the past decade. Since nearby Santiago has been recognized as an international monument, the government of Navarra has poured huge sums of money into restoring Estella's streets and buildings. At C. de la Rúa, 20, a local craftsman recreates the unique wood-carved furniture and implements of Navarra. *Templetas* and *argisaiolas* are two elements of the medieval heritage that this woodcarver is reviving. The former are wooden knockers used to clack the hours of Mass during Lent, when no bells could be rung; the latter are human-shaped pieces of wood bound by thin wax wicks. *Argisaiolas* originated in Navarrese witch rituals and were later used by the clergy during wakes. Founded almost 900 years ago to exploit the market created by Jacobean pilgrims, Estella once again seems to be banking its future on a vigorous interest in El Camino a Santiago, this time traversed by millions of tourists.

The extremely friendly owners of **Fonda San Andrés,** Pl. de Santiago, 50 (tel. 55 04 48), have just finished redoing their establishment. The new rooms with white tile floors cost 1200ptas per person, while the older, nonrenovated rooms run 800ptas per person. The equally pleasant owners of **Hotel San Andrés,** C. Baja Navarra, 1 (tel. 55 07 72), duplicate not only their competitor's name, but also their prices and cleanliness. (1200ptas per person.) **Fonda Joaquín,** Paseo de la Inmaculada, 15 (tel. 55 06 80), offers another clean alternative. (800ptas per person.) During the Fiesta, all three places are likely to be full.

Outrageously fresh *trucha* (trout), fried with a piece of ham between the gills, is the house specialty at **Casa Cachetas,** C. Estudio de Gramática, 2 (tel. 55 00 10), 3 blocks off Pl. de la Fueros. The 600ptas *menú* also includes other dishes. **Fonda**

San Andrés offers a 700ptas *menú* for lunch and dinner in their large dining room. (Meals 1:30-3pm and 9-10:30pm.)

The helpful new **tourist office** (tel. 55 44 08) is on the ground floor of the Palacio de los Reyes de Navarra, across the main bridge from the bus station side of town, on Paseo de la Inmaculada. (Open Mon.-Fri. 10am-1pm and 3-7pm, Sat. 10am-1pm.) The **police** (tel. 55 08 13) are in the Ayuntamiento, on Paseo de la Inmaculada by the river. The **post office** sits up the street at Paseo de la Inmaculada, 5 (tel. 55 17 92; open Mon.-Fri. 9am-2pm, Sat. 9am-1pm). Poor Estella used to have a train station, but RENFE dismantled it. The **bus station** on Pl. de la Coronación runs 11 buses per day to Pamplona, six on Sunday (1 hr., 260ptas). For **medical assistance,** the **Casa de Socorro** of Hospital Comarcal (tel. 55 16 00) is at C. Santa Soria, 22. Call 55 10 11 for an **ambulance.**

Twenty-one kilometers east lies **Puente de la Reina** (not to be confused with Puente La Reina near Jaca), where the main pilgrim routes from France join up for the westerly haul to Compostela at the famous six-arched bridge. Set into the pillars of the enormous arches above the Arga River are a series of smaller arches that allow rising floodwaters to pass through and pilgrims to pass by.

Olite sits in the flat lands 42km south of Pamplona on the right bank of the Cidacos River, a trickle given the benefit of the doubt. The **fortress** here was built in the fifteenth century. Although it has endured considerable intrigue, sieges, and sabotage by Aragonese, Castilian, and Napoleonic forces, its soaring stone walls and solid battlements still rise impressively from the arid plains. Take a walk across the river at night, when the castle is at its floodlit finest. If you're inside the courtyard, ask yourself how in the world Carlos III managed to stage bullfights in such a space. Many residents of this fortress lived and died tragically, including Carlos II, who died without a son to take his throne, and Doña Blanca, his daughter, who gave birth to three children by a new marriage after being widowed: Don Carlos, Prince of Viana; Doña Blanca; and Doña Leonor. The first was detested by his father, the second divorced by her husband, and the third hated the second and had her poisoned. While in town, don't miss the splendid fourteenth-century facade of **Santa María la Real.** La Tafallesa runs three buses per day from Pamplona to Olite, but none on Sunday (165ptas).

Navarrese Pyrenees

All along the valleys of the Río Arga and Río Aragon, east of Pamplona, "green Spain" meets "brown Spain" as the upland mountain valleys swoop down to the dusty red desert. Along the base of the mountains is the huge, artificial **Embalse de Yesa** (Yesa Lake), ringed by several historic monuments. Only 10-20km uphill, dramatic peaks surge over romantically isolated hamlets set in valleys that are not just geographic divisions but individual cultural and political entities. Each village has as much history as the once-great kingdom of Navarre itself. The entire land, mountains and plains alike, is crossed by **El Camino a Santiago,** or **St. James' Road,** the famous pilgrimage route that led from France to Santiago de Compostela. The road scaled the Pyrenees through Navarre's passes and then descended to the river valleys. The thousands of pilgrims who made this trip during the eleventh and twelfth centuries left a rich heritage of religious art in their wake. The life-threatening landscape that hindered medieval pilgrims now allows for spectacular hiking. There is something awe-inspiring about negotiating the passes where Roland and Charlemagne once fought. Hitching is relatively good, at least up and down the valleys, since sympathetic drivers will often rescue tired-looking hikers. The **telephone code** for the entire area is 948.

The large and austere **Monasterio de Leyre** hides itself high up against the cliff face of the Pyrenees, overlooking Yesa Lake. Isolated among scrub hills and dry forests 50km east of Pamplona, the weathered-stone monastery was a center of power and wealth, the favorite charity and residence of the kings of Navarre during the late Middle Ages. The eleventh-century building was one of the first instances of the Romanesque style in Spain. Today the building looks much as it did then; it was fully restored by Benedictine monks 25 years ago. As you enter the cold, dark **crypt,** strain your eyes to see the high arches and curiously carved columns against the thin beams of sunlight that squeeze inside, or insert 25ptas for a five-minute illumination. The **church** stands above the crypt, but you'll have to go down the passageway and out into the courtyard to get there. This structure is distinguished by its lack of ornamentation, as well as the remarkably off-center arch that leads to its choir (25ptas for light). The wooden casket behind iron grillwork (on the left as you enter) holds the remains of the early kings of Navarre—all 10 of them, from Sancho Carlos, whose rule commenced in 804, to García Sánchez IV el Trémulo, whose reign ended in 999. As you leave, cast a glance at the portal, where angels, hobgoblins, weird faces, and snakes writhe above the holy entrance. Vespers held in the church at 7pm are quite moving. Outside the monastery, follow the path to the **Fuente de San Virila.** On the way, the monastery, its well-kept grounds set against the far-away blue-green lake of Yesa, and the sharp, dry countryside of Navarre all come into view. The fountain sits on the site where the abbot of San Virila was supposedly put into a 300-year trance by the singing of a little bird. The abbot had been attempting to determine the nature of heaven. When he awoke, 300 years later, the shock put him to rest for good.

You can stay overnight in the monastery's **hostel** (tel. 88 41 00; singles with bath 1900ptas; doubles with bath 3800ptas; breakfast 350ptas; full board 2250ptas). Knock on the door marked "hospedería." Single men can get much cheaper rooms in the monastery proper (650ptas; tel. 88 40 11); knock at the door marked "portería." To reach the monastery, it's easiest to hitch or take a bus to **Yesa,** a roadside village on the main Pamplona-Huesca road 4km below the monastery. Little more than a crossroads, Yesa has three hotels; **Hostal Arangoiti** (tel. 88 40 03) is the cheapest, though it may be closed for renovations. Yesa also has a small **tourist office** (tel. 88 40 00), open only in summer. Hispanio-Ansotana's buses from Pamplona to Huesca (2 per day Mon.-Sat.) stop in Yesa, and La Tafallesa runs a bus at 5pm Monday through Saturday to Yesa (260ptas), continuing to Javier Castle (280ptas) and Tiermas (305ptas) before going on to Isaba. **Tiermas** is an abandoned town on the shore of Yesa Lake, about 5km away. Once a way station on the Santiago road, it makes for wonderful exploring.

The walls of bulky little **Javier Castle,** just a couple kilometers south of Yesa, yield as little as did the sturdy faith of the saint born inside them: Francis Xavier, Apostle of the Indies and Japan, grew up in this unforgiving fortress before becoming a missionary to the Far East in the sixteenth century. The castle is now the site of a Jesuit College. There are guided tours of the thirteenth-century fort. The guide speaks only Spanish, but has the keys that unlock the doors, so follow along and enjoy the intricacies of castle architecture. Note the special slits for pouring boiling oil on attackers. (Castle open daily 9am-1pm and 4-7pm.) At 10:30pm on Saturday and Sunday from June through September, the Jesuits put on a **sound and light show.** The castle is lit, and the story of Xavier's adventures in the Far East are told (100ptas). You can stay right next to the castle at **Hostal Xavier** (tel. 88 40 06), with dark though clean rooms and appropriately medieval facilities. (Singles 1272ptas. Doubles 2120ptas. Breakfast 250ptas. Full board 1974ptas.)

Sangüesa

The **Iglesia de Santa María** in Sangüesa boasts one of the most extraordinary collections of Romanesque sculpture on any church exterior in Spain, according to Padre Vicente. Not many towns in the Pyrenees are lucky enough to have a full-time, self-appointed curator for their artistic treasures, but the 78-year-old retired priest is just that. With three books about the town already published and three more in the works, he knows virtually every stone in Sangüesa on a first name basis. Grabbing your hand, he'll show you the only hanged Judas Iscariot ever carved out of stone in Spanish Romanesque. In the same impressive archway, the central relief depicts the Day of Judgement with fanged devils casting the damned into the cavernous mouth of Lucifer. Pagan symbolism creeps into the upper corners of the right relief as an ironsmith pounds out a vicious sword on an anvil, while above him, Siegfried thrusts the same weapon into a dragon. A bizarre depiction of lust shows a woman nursing a toad on one breast and a snake the other.

The front of the **Iglesia de Santiago** has a unique statue of the patron saint of Spain: Saint James stands on top of a large conch. Painted on the wall behind him, two pilgrims kneel in reverence, garbed in characteristic cloaks, with their staffs and cockleshells. Saint Francis himself is supposed to have stopped in Sangüesa during his pilgrimage to Compostela, and founded the first Franciscan hermitage outside of Italy in the town. The **Convento de San Francisco de Asís** now stands on the spot of the original building. The **Palacio de Vallesantoro** now houses the Casa de Cultura; wood carvings—of horses riding humans who in turn are mounted piggyback on wizened old men—support the caves. (Open Mon.-Sat. 7-9pm, Sun. noon-2pm.) Many houses in Sangüesa have retained their Gothic arched doorways, and coats-of-arms still hold the place of honor on the walls of otherwise simple abodes.

Pensión Las Navas (tel. 87 00 77), near the bus stop, offers the most economical lodgings. Rooms are modern and clean. (Singles 1050ptas. Doubles 2100ptas.) The 750ptas *menú* in the restaurant downstairs is the only reasonably priced meal in town; for anything cheaper, scour around for *tapas* in local bars. The **tourist office,** around the corner from the Ayuntamiento, opens whenever the person who runs it feels like showing up (usually Mon.-Fri. 10am-1pm). A better source of information is Padre Vicente. Veloz Sangüesina **buses** leave Pamplona for Sangüesa four times per day (45 min., 250ptas).

A 4-kilometer hitch or hike from Sangüesa brings you to the town of *Liédana.* Two kilometers outside of town, along an old train route that has been poorly paved over and passes through a pitch-black tunnel, you'll enter the **Hoz de Lumbier.** This impressive gorge, centered on the Rió Irati, has 150-foot walls lining its 2-kilometer extension. Griffin vultures find the harsh combination of cliff and fast-flowing waters rather appealing; the *hoz* is a protected reserve for the birds, who were once hunted and killed to extinction-threatening extremes. About 2km from the opposite mouth of the gorge sits the town of *Lumbier;* a 12-kilometer ride from here brings you to **Iso** and the mouth of an even more impressive gorge, the **Hoz de Arbayún.** There is no blazed trail or train path through this 4-kilometer *garganta* (throat). If the River Salazar is low enough in late summer, you can wade, swim, and hike your way through the gorge. At other times of year, swimming is dangerous and the water petrifyingly cold; try a raft or a canoe. Check on conditions with locals in Iso before attempting any expeditions; what appear to be manageable waters could actually be dangerously swollen.

Valle de Roncal

As you move west through the Spanish Pyrenees, each valley becomes a bit more green and moist. The town of **Roncal,** which lends its name to both the valley and the cheese, sits near the bottom of the impression, straddling the Río Esca. As you travel north from here into the *valle,* Spain's Arabic-style roof tiles disappear, giving way to flatter stone shingles. Roofs also take on a more acute, alpine slant as area snowfalls increase drastically at the altitude of Roncal. During the mild summer, *roncaleses* complete silently to place the most colorful and numerous geraniums on balconies overlooking the streets.

Roncal wins the prize for the fewest bars per capita in Spain, but compensates by being the hometown of the famous opera tenor Julian Gayarre. Roncal has decorated itself with sculptures and monuments honoring the international singer and Basque hero. The town outdid itself with Gayarre's **tomb,** an ornate flourish of mourning cherubs and weeping muses. The tomb is located in the town's cemetery, 1km along C. Castillo, which runs behind the *pelota* court. Along the way, you'll pass the **Casa de Junta de Valle,** where you can see a display of the town's traditional garb, worn during festivals. If the wrought iron door won't let you pass inside, go back to the Casa Consistorial on the main road and ask to see the display.

There's only one *hostal* in Roncal, **Hostal Lopez-Sanz** (tel. 89 50 08), across the river from the *pelota* court, over Bar Zaltua. It offers clean rooms and a nice terrace lined with geraniums. (Singles 1000ptas. Doubles 1800ptas. Full board 1785ptas.) You can also ask around for a *casa particular*. Free camping is permitted in the valley but check with the Ayuntamiento or Guardia Civil (tel. 89 50 05) before you head out. Toward the northern end of town is the **post office** (open Mon.-Sat. 10am-2pm); across the street, **Banco Central** will change your money (open Mon.-Fri. 8:30am-2pm). The town's **postal code** is 31415.

Seven kilometers north of Roncal, **Isaba's** tranquil pastures have hosted pastors from the French side of the mountains since 125 B.C.E.; their livestock come to the Navarrese side to nibble tender green shoots. Over the years, squabbles over grazing rights have actually caused bloodshed. More civilized relations or the huge decline in the number of sheep have reduced tensions. Today, the only vestige of the feuding is a playful ritual enacted every July 13. Pastors from France give three cows to the pastors of Roncal. Placing their hands on top of each other, the mayors and pastors from both sides of the valley solemnly pray for peace as the bovine harbingers of peace switch nationalities.

A group of young locals opened **Albergue Oxanea,** C. Bormapea, 47 (tel. 89 31 53), a renovated stone house with a beautiful pine interior. They supply mattresses and blankets and charge 500ptas per night. They also happen to be good cooks, brewing a hearty beef stew that will fill you up for a couple days. (Lunch 700ptas. Dinner 600ptas. Both are worth it.) To get there, walk by the Centro de Salud on the main street and up the staircase on your left. The *albergue* is the second building on your left. **Fonda Tapia** (tel. 89 30 13), down the street from the Centro de Salud, also offers clean and comfortable rooms. (875ptas per person.) The daily *menú* at the restaurant downstairs costs 850ptas, but you can order **trucha con jamón** (trout with ham) for 475ptas. **Camping Asolaze** (tel. 89 31 68), 6km toward the French border, offers a restaurant and a store. (Open June-Sept. 260ptas per person and per tent. 1200ptas to rent a tent.) Eight kilometers farther north is the **Valle de Belagua.** Since many weekend mountaineers from Pamplona drive to the tip of the valley, hitching shouldn't be difficult. The view is magnificent; as you round a bend, the entire valley suddenly opens before you. A **refugio** operates near the valley. (Open June-Sept. 1200ptas per person.)

The **Centro de Salud** can be reached at 89 32 52 and the **Guardia Civil,** just up the hill from the *albergue,* at 89 30 06. La Tafallesa buses go to Roncal and Isaba (Mon.-Sat. at 5pm) from Pamplona (425ptas), and they return early the next morning.

Ochagavía

Forty kilometers from Pamplona (or a draining 90-km bus ride), Ochagavía is the largest town in the **Valle de Salazar.** Although the town is small nonetheless, the valley's traditional dance group uses it as a home base. If you're in town September 7 or 8, you'll get to observe their strange, warlike prancing and the intricate stick-dance in which groups of four men manage to bang two wooden cudgels off their neighbor's cudgels apparently without smashing any fingers. The annual pilgrimage to the **Hermita de Musquilda** also occurs at this time, but you can take the 30-minute hike to the rebuilt sixteenth-century hermitage year-round. About 20km north of Ochagavía is one of Europe's biggest beech and hemlock forests, second only to Germany's Black Forest. Near the entrance to the woods is the modern **Hermita de las Virgenes de la Nieve.**

Hostal Orialde's doubles go for 2300ptas (tel. 89 00 27). Farther upriver, **Hostal Laspalas** (tel. 89 00 15) offers doubles for 2150ptas. Both places are clean and pleasant; the second strives to maintain a mountain rusticity. A **tourist office** will open in 1989 on the main street in the old school building. (Tentatively open Mon.-Fri. 10am-3pm.) For the **police,** call 89 00 39. The **post office** is on the side of the river opposite the church. (Open Mon.-Fri. 10-11:45am, Sat. 11am-noon.) La Salacenca runs one bus per day from Pamplona to Ochagavía (Mon.-Sat. at 6pm, 450ptas). The return bus leaves Ochagavía at 7am. You can also hitch laterally from Burguete or Isaba, but don't walk; it's a long haul.

Roncesvalles

No bus, no train; nothing but a cold, stone monastery and thick mountain forests. The Valley of Thorns is 48km from Pamplona and 20km from the French border, but centuries outside reality. For more than a thousand years, pilgrims, poets, and romantics have been drawn by the tragic legend and spiritual shrine planted in the rugged slopes of **Puerto Ibañeta.** Here, Roland supposedly fell at the hands of the Moor Marsilio. A fourteenth-century cross marks the spot, just before the descent into the plain of Burguete. It was actually the Navarrese who finished off Charlemagne's nephew, angered at the emperor's razing of Pamplona's walls, and now it seems that the battle might not have taken place in Roncesvalles at all but in Hecho, a couple of valleys over. Little matter; the valley is magic and the cluster of monastic buildings is infused with medieval restfulness. The Augustine abbey has made a concession to the realities of mountain climate and is roofed in corrugated fiberglass, but more romantic structures stand nearby. The so-called **Capilla de Sancti Spiritus,** heavily restored, stands under a new roof and over the remains of an ossuary, where the bodies of fallen soldiers and pilgrims were deposited. This is supposedly the spot of Roland's unanswered call for help. Next door is the tiny twelfth-century **Capilla de Santiago.** If you peer through a window in the door, you can just make out a dark religious statue highlighted against an alabaster window. The bell in the gable once hung at the pass, 3km away, where it rang to guide pilgrims lost in fog and blizzards.

Inside the **Colegiata,** the tombs of King Sancho the Strong and his French bride sit in solitary splendor, lit by huge stained-glass windows. The massive arches at the cloisters, with their intricate stone pavement, are just outside. But the monastery's jewel is its Gothic church, endowed by the dead king and consecrated in 1219. Its elegant vaulting and luminous stained glass, recalling Chartres and Sainte-Chapelle in Paris, were totally alien to thirteenth-century Spain. Beneath a soaring canopy, the Virgin de las Lácrimas (Virgin of Tears), a gold- and silver-covered image, presides. The few monks who live in the monastery hold Mass daily around 7pm. The deep organ and monotonous chanting will take you back a couple hundred years. Outside the building, a small **museum** houses various religious artifacts. (Open daily 11am-1:30pm and 4-6pm.)

The monastery offers free lodging to those on their way to Santiago, as Roncesvalles is a popular starting point for Spanish pilgrims. If you plan to undertake the Camino a Santiago, just go in the door to the right as you face the front of the monastery. Other cheap beds can be found at **Hosteria Casa Sabina** (tel. 76 00 12); unfortunately, the beds are often occupied. (Singles 800ptas. Doubles 1550ptas.) The restaurant in this cozy *hostal,* however, is a good place to fill up on delicious meals (lunch 725ptas, dinner 625ptas). You can camp 3km south in Espinal at **Camping Urrobit** (tel. 76 02 00). Bring a tent—rain showers often pass through. (225ptas per person, per tent, and per car.) About 1km up the road from the monastery is the **Puerto Ibañeta** (1057m), marked by a small church and a stone decorated with a sword and two mules, in honor of Roland's death in 778. When it is not shrouded in a hummus-like fog, the view of both valleys may suck you into a metaphysical time warp, especially when the mist covers the mountaintops and the wind sweeps the sounds of far-away goat bells to your ears.

Roncesvalles is best reached by La Montañesa's bus to Burguete, which leaves Pamplona Monday through Saturday at 6pm (290ptas). From Burguete, it's a pleasant 2½-kilometer walk through upland forests to Roncevalles. To continue to Valcarlos, try to get a ride (although once you're over the pass 1km away, it's all downhill).

Valcarlos

"Caution: Cattle on the loose" says the sign as you descend into the valley to Valcarlos, just 3km from the French border and 17km north of Roncesvalles (16 of these head almost straight down toward the center of the earth). The town has an inordinately large number of former California residents, mostly Basques who chose Bakersfield as the Promised Land when they abandoned Franco's Spain en masse after the Civil War. Now returned to their homeland, these one-time autonomists are more vocal than their untraveled cousins on the subject of Basque independence and are happy to show off their English as well. The relatively modern **church** is notable for its fascinating, purely Christian retable, depicting St. James in his popular incarnation as Santiago el Matamoro (the Moorslayer). The saint sits on a white horse and aims a saber at a falling *moro* wearing a crescent moon, Spain's version of the black hat.

A friendly but reticent crowd runs **Hotel Maitena,** C. Elizaldea (tel. 76 20 10), on the main road below the *panadería.* Spotless doubles with wooden furniture cost 1900ptas. Downstairs, the 750ptas *menú* is quite good. The church, next door, does its best to keep you awake at night with its punctual and loud bells. You can also ask around for a *casa particular.* Start at the bar with the Ene Sort Lekua sign next to the *pelota* court.

The **tourist office** has the biggest sign in town, but it hasn't been open in a while. Walk down the street to the Ayuntamiento (tel. 76 20 07), where a friendly man will give you an antiquated pamphlet of the area and ask you lots of questions. (Open Mon.-Fri. 9am-1pm and 4-6pm.) At the other end of town, the **Guardia Civil,** slightly nicer than the ferocious German shepherd that sits outside, will help you in case of an **emergency** (tel. 76 20 44).

If you're coming to Valcarlos from France, you'll have to hitch across the border from St-Jean-Pied-de-Port, 10km away. From the Spanish side, the bus from Pamplona gets you as far as Burguete, 20km away, from which you'll have to hitch or hike to Valcarlos.

Aragon

As the kingdom of Castilla grew to dominate the western half of Iberia, Aragon gained supremacy on the peninsula's eastern section. Aragon's pivotal location may have played a role; it is positioned on the edge of *los Pirineos* (Spanish Pyrenees) and the dry, flat plains of Castilla. The region's natural and architectural diversity is tremendous. Towering peaks covered with lush vegetation roll into the barren flatlands of the south. While landlocked Zaragoza often suffers from searing summer heat, such natural wonders as the Monasterio de Piedra and the cool Pyrenean valleys in Huesca offer some relief from the sizzling interior. In the far reaches of the mountains, the slow-paced lifestyle offers a stark contrast to the bustling activity of Zaragoza.

Out of the fusion of Christian and Muslim cultures in places such as Aragon developed the Mudéjar style of brick architecture, evident in many older buildings in Zaragoza and Teruel. In the north, the Roman architecture of Huesca, sprinkled throughout the mountain villages, exhibits another facet of Aragon's diversity. However, wordly acclaim stems not from the varied architecture but from fine, full-bodied red and white wines from the area around Cariñena. While culinary novelties are not its strongpoint, Aragon cooks up hearty meals with *judías blancas* (white beans), a rib-sticking favorite, which can be served alone or with potatoes, *chorizo* (heavy sausage), or rice. Other specialties include fried trout from northern rivers and fresh vegetables from the Ebro basin.

Zaragoza

The Romans founded the town of Caesar Augusta in 24 B.C.E. as a retirement home for war veterans. Overrun during the subsequent Visigothic and Moorish invasions, the city did not rise to importance until, in 1118, the triumphant Christians made it the capital of Aragon. Imprints of these diverse cultures remain throughout the city, although the smog of a bustling modern metropolis is leaving its own distinctive mark. Despite Zaragoza's importance in modern Spain, tourists have not yet discovered its offerings, leaving its sights unspoiled by crowds.

Orientation and Practical Information

The center of Zaragoza is **Plaza de Paraíso,** where six long, tree-lined avenues converge. To get there from the train station, walk across Avda. Clave and take a right on María Agustín. A right on Paseo Pamplona will take you to Pl. Paraíso. Avenida de la Independencia will take you to **Plaza de España,** which is on the edge of the old part of town. **Plaza Pilar** (officially Plaza de Nuestra Señora del Pilar) sits on the edge of the Ebro, farther to the north. The university quarter lies at the other end of town, across the train tracks.

If you plan to explore the city thoroughly, the extensive **bus system** (40ptas) will be quite helpful. Complete summaries of all the lines are found on nearly every bus stop sign.

Tourist Office: Torreón de la Zuda, Glorieta de Pio XII (tel. 23 00 27), off the western or upriver end of Pl. Pilar. If you are too inquisitive, you may leave with more pamphlets, maps, and posters than you can fit in your bags. Open Mon.-Fri. 8:30am-2:30pm and 6-7pm, Sat. 9am-2pm. The new **municipal tourist office** in the center of Pl. Pilar (no phone), in a postmodern Roman templette with a broken column in front of the entrance, is much better. Friendly and bustling with energy. English spoken. Open Mon.-Sat. 10:30am-1:30pm and 5-8pm, Sun. 9am-2pm. Branch of the national office at the **train station** is also very helpful and enthusiastic. Open daily 9am-7pm; Nov.-March daily 9am-2pm and 2:30-7pm.

Student Travel: Viajes TIVE, Residencial Paraíso, Local 40 (tel. 21 83 15). Inside the large shopping plaza between Paseo de Sagasta and Paseo de las Damas, off Pl. de Paraíso and beyond El Corte Inglés. Charter flights on Iberia to major European cities, as well as student IDs and IYHF cards (2 photos, passport, 1800ptas). The office is useless for domestic travel arrangements. The staff suggests using a regular travel agency, though you may not receive a student discount. Open Mon.-Fri. 9am-2:45pm.

Post Office: Paseo Independencia, 33 (tel. 22 26 50). Open for information Mon.-Fri. 9am-2pm and 4-6pm, Sat. 9am-1:30pm; for Lista de Correos, Mon.-Fri. 9am-2pm and 5-6pm, Sat. 9am-1:30pm; for stamps Mon.-Fri. 9am-8pm, Sat. 9am-1:30pm. **Telegrams:** Tel. 22 20 00. Open Mon.-Fri. 8am-9pm, Sun. 9am-2pm. **Postal Code:** 50000.

Telephones: C. de Castellano Tomás, just behind the post office. Open Mon.-Sat. 9:30am-1:30pm and 6-10pm. **Telephone Code:** 976.

Airport: Tel. 34 90 50. Buses run between the airport and Pl. de San Francisco starting at 1:30pm (60ptas). **Iberia,** C. Canfranc, 22-24 (tel. 21 82 59 for information; tel. 21 82 50 for reservations), near the Puerta de Carmen. Open Mon.-Fri. 9:30am-2pm and 5-7pm, Sat. 9:30am-1:30pm.

Train Station: Estación Portillo, Avda. Claré (tel. 21 11 66). Information open daily 6am-10pm. To Madrid (13 per day, 4 ½hr. and longer, from 1420ptas); Barcelona (15 per day, 4½ hr. and longer, from 1505ptas) via Lleida or Tarragona, Valencia (3 per day, 6 hr. and longer, 1270ptas), and Pamplona (3 per day, 2½ hr., from 755ptas). **RENFE,** in the town office at C. San Clemente, 13 (tel. 22 65 98), just off Paseo Independencia. Open Mon.-Fri. 9am-2pm and 5-7pm.

Bus Stations: Buses of various companies depart from assorted locations. None of the tourist offices around town has schedules for buses operating outside the province. To minimize hassle, take the train, which costs about the same. If you must take a bus, call ahead as the offices maintain irregular hours. Some companies are the following: **Agreda Automóvil,** Paseo María Augustín, 7 (tel. 22 93 43), near Puerta del Carmen; **Conda,** Avda. de Navarra, 77 (tel. 33 33 72), beyond the Aljaferia, about 5km from the center of town. Catch city bus #25 along Paseo Constitución (direction Miralbueno) or 26 along Paseo Independencia (direction Parque Ebro) and look for the "Estación Cinco Villas" sign on your left; **La Oscenca,** Paseo María Agustín, 84 (tel. 29 47 61), at the end toward the river; **Autobuses Bajo Aragón,** C. Calatayud, 3 (tel. 22 98 86), off Avda. de Goya. To Andorra.

Baggage Check: In the train station. Buy tokens in *equipaje* office (100ptas). Open daily 7am-10pm.

Swimming Pool: Piscina Las Palmeras, at Parque Primo de Rivera (tel. 27 31 39), on the south side of town. Take bus #35 (direction Barrio Oliver) from Paseo Independencia to Pl. Carlos V, then walk through the park along Avda. San Sebastián.

Medical Emergency: Casa de Socorro, Paseo de la Mina, 9 (tel. 23 02 91 or 22 39 15).

Police: Policía Municipal, C. Domingo Miral (tel. 49 91 76). **Emergency:** Tel. 092.

Accommodations and Camping

Except during early October when Zaragoza celebrates La Virgen del Pilar, you won't encounter much difficulty finding a room. The area around Pl. Pilar and **Carrer Don Alfonso I** has the highest concentration of cheap places; rooms here should cost you fewer than 1000ptas.

Hostal Gijón, Pl. Lanuza, 40 (tel. 22 46 89), next to the huge *mercado* adjacent to the upriver end of Pl. Pilar. Spotless, bright rooms with balconies and comfortable beds. Singles 950ptas. Doubles 1800ptas. Showers 150ptas.

Fonda San Miguel, C. Prudencio, 23 (tel. 21 55 42), the first right as you walk away from Pl. Pilar. Small and hidden, but widely known to many Zaragozans as the nicest *fonda* in town. Large, fairly clean rooms, but the walls are run-down, and you must ask the manager to let you in each night. 800ptas per person. Hot showers 150ptas.

Fonda Satué, C. Espoz y Mina, 4 (tel. 22 55 94). The huge double stairway twists upward through the gloom, deserted and echoing like some post-cataclysmic remain. The place itself is better lighted and the manager welcoming. Though clean, parts of the room are in disrepair. Singles 600ptas. Doubles 1100ptas. Showers 150ptas.

Hostal Montaña, C. Castillo, 10 (tel. 43 57 02). From the train station, turn left on Avda. de José Anselmo Clavé, which runs into Paseo de María Agustín after 1 block. Keep going on María Agustín until you pass Avda. de Madrid; C. Castillo is the next on your left (10 min.). Dingy neighborhood. Holes in the sheets, but the rooms are big and sinks have hot water—a miracle. Singles 900ptas. Doubles 1600ptas. Breakfast 175ptas. Lunch and dinner 1175ptas.

You can camp near Zaragoza at **Casablanca,** Paseo Canal, 175 (tel. 33 03 22), a first-class site. Take bus #36 from Pl. Pilar or Pl. España to the suburb of Valdefierro. When all the streets begin to be named after constellations, it's almost time to get off, but wait for the corner of Vía Láctea and C. Estromboli. The prices are stiff, but good facilities include a pool. (Open April-Oct. 15. 350ptas per person, per tent, and per car.)

Food

While Zaragoza seems to have every kind of eatery—from a bar with *tapas* to a *restaurante* with three-course meals—none of them is cheap. Even a plate of *tapas* can cost almost 300ptas. The neighborhood bars around Don Alfonso offer an inexpensive alternative, but most of the people congregate at bars and restaurants on and around Paseo Independencia. Zaragoza does, however, have a colorful *mercado* (Avda. César Augusto; open Mon.-Sat. 9am-2pm) where you can buy anything edible from fruits and vegetables to cow's tongue and live squid.

Cafetería-Restaurante Aragón, C. Don Alfonso I, 38 (tel. 21 38 77), just off Pl. Pilar. Entrance covered with menus and announcements. Get bombarded by 80 different platters; specialties change daily. Try the thirst-quenching *granizados*. Mini-*combinados* 475ptas, the full-fledged thing 695-790ptas. Also a *menú* for 675ptas. Open daily 12:30-4pm and 8-11pm.

Tres Hermanos, C. San Pablo, 45 (tel. 44 10 85). A couple blocks off César Augusto. The sign out front says, "Economical meals." They are as good as they are cheap. The 450ptas *menú* has a dish of Spanish-style *macarones* (with chunks of meat, light on the tomato sauce) and baked chicken. You have to pass through the bar to get downstairs to the restaurant. Open daily 1-4pm and 8:30-11pm.

Casa Colas, C. Mártires, 10 (tel. 22 32 84). Your eyes will bulge to the size of the animals' piled in the window after you've eaten an entire one for lunch. The 725ptas *menú* features *paella valenciana* followed by a ½-chicken. Open daily 8:30-11:30pm.

La Nata, Pl. de la Independencia, 24-26 (tel. 21 13 62), in a shopping center accessible from Paseo Independencia or C. Cádiz. Serves all sorts of crepes, from pâte to chocolate. Other light fare is available.

Sights

The seventeenth- and eighteenth-century domes and towers of the **Basílica del Pilar** pierce the city skyline. The domes, which cap the cavernous interior, are decorated with frescoes by Goya, Velázquez, and Bayeu, none of whom evidently worked best in a prone position. The basilica houses the pillar that, according to legend, remains as proof of the Virgin Mary's appearance in 40 C.E. Mary is said to continually protect the city, having helped its inhabitants defend the city from the French (1808-1809) and from bombing in the Spanish Civil War. Thousands of pilgrims kiss the pillar each year in homage to the Virgin; they also come to see the chapel, where two of the three bombs dropped on the basilica during the Spanish Civil War now hang. The Gothic-Renaissance altarpiece of polychrome alabaster is the masterwork of Damian Forment; it now entirely encloses the pillar except for one small circle worn down by many centuries of lips. The **Museo del Pilar,** in the middle of the side closest to the river, displays the glittering *joyero de la Virgen,* which adorns the bi-pillared *Virgen* in times of celebration, and a collection of Goya's sketches that help you see the detail of the ceiling frescoes. (Museum open daily 9am-2pm and 4-6pm. Basilica open daily 6am-9:30pm. Free.) Before leaving, take the elevator to the top of the towers for an unhindered view across the river and plains. Go out the door at the end of the basilica nearest the tourist office and by the river; the entrance is outside. (Open daily 9:30am-2pm and 4-7pm. Admission 75ptas.)

A fourteenth-century Gothic extravaganza, the **Catedral de la Seo** sports a bit of Renaissance, plateresque, and even baroque. Undergoing a much-needed renovation, the building remains closed to the public. The **Lonja,** between the basilica and the cathedral, is the old commercial exchange. The building's majestic interior now houses exhibits of local artists. (Hours vary. Free.)

The **Museo Provincial de Bellas Artes,** located on Pl. de los Sitios, preserves the early remains of Roman Zaragoza with reconstructed mosaics and sculptures. Along with an extensive collection of Aragonese paintings the museum holds a series of portraits by Goya, including a self-portrait and one of Carlos IV and his wife. (Open Tues.-Sat. 9am 2pm. Admission 200ptas, students free.)

Much more charming, however, is the **Museo Pablo Gargallo.** The sculptor Pablo Gargallo was born in Maella, Zaragoza, in 1881, but spent most of his life in Barcelona and Paris, where he became one of the most innovative and influential figures in the '20s art world. The small but exquisite collection of his works, housed in the graceful Palacio de Argillo, a national monument, features a wonderful room filled with comical *faunos* and *faunesas* in copper and iron, modernist pieces from the '20s, and, surrounding the inner courtyard, a few dozen bronze figures with great facial expressions—especially the look of indulgence on the girl of *Baño de Sol* or the slightly smug face of *El Joven de la Margarita.* (Open Mon. 10am-1pm, Wed.-Sat. 10am-1pm and 5-9pm, Sun. 11am-2pm. Free.)

Following the Moorish conquest of the Iberian Peninsula in the eighth century, a dispute over succession caused the established kingdom to divide into factions, called *taifas.* The **Palacio de la Aljafería,** between the train station and the river, remains as the most predominant relic of Aragon's *taifa* kingdom, established by the Benihud in the eleventh century. While the ground floor exhibits a distinctly Moorish flavor with its intricately carved capitals and its *musallah* (private mosque) of multi-lobed arches and geometric and floral tracery, the second floor is flamboyantly Gothic and dates from the time of the Catholic monarchs. Recent renovation, however, has removed much of the building's charm. (Open Tues.-Sat. 10am-2pm and 4:30-6:30pm, Sun. 10am-2pm.)

Entertainment

Zaragoza erupts for a week of unbridled partying during the fiestas in honor of La Virgen del Pilar, beginning October 12. The activities include everything from sporting events to performances of the regional dance, *la jota,* to the finale at the end of the week when the *Rosario de Cristal* procession moves through town illuminated by 350 carrriage-borne lanterns. The tourist office at Torreón de la Zuda has copies of the schedule of events.

Should you miss this wild fiesta, Zaragoza's many bars do their best to simulate the *Pilar* festivities. The most rambunctious crowd, including American soldiers from the nearby army base, congregates on the streets around **Carrer Doctor Cerrada,** where **Picasso,** Laguna de Rios, 7, blares out dance music. The jet set tends to hang around the bars on **Carrer Léon XIII,** while the more bohemian crowd wanders down to **Calle Temple,** near Pl. Pilar where **Corte Maltés** and **La Recogida** are popular with Spanish *jóvenes.* For late-night dancing try **Papagallo,** C. San Ignacio de Loyola, 4, or **Discoteca Laser** around the corner at C. de General Suiero, 41. Most weeknights you can dance for free; on weekends, the cover charge is 500ptas.

Atuaire, Contaminada, 13 (tel. 21 37 34), remains a popular club for gay men with an uncrowded, relaxed atmosphere as does **Master's,** C. de Fita, near C. Doctor Cerrada.

The municipal tourist office distributes information on special events around town, including the **Sol de Verano** festival in May, which brings concerts to the amphitheater Rincón de Goya in the Parque Primo de Ribera (see directions to swimming pool). Other feast days are those of San Valero (Jan. 29) and San Jorge (April 23), patrons of the city.

Near Zaragoza

Goya fans can head for the **Cartuja de Aula Dei,** a sixteenth-century Carthusian monastery 12km from Zaragoza in Montañana. Here the young Goya completed one of his first major works, a series of 11 tableaux depicting the life of Mary. If you have the time and wish to follow in the footsteps of the Spanish master, travel south about 50km to **Fuendetodos,** Goya's birthplace. His house is now a museum that has been left as it was when he lived in it, except for an interesting display of transparencies of his works. Buses to the Cartuja are run on weekdays by **Autocares Teodoro Marrón,** C. Reconquista, 11 (tel. 29 59 90), near Pl. de los Sitios (220ptas).

Wine-lovers will gurgle with delight at the prospect of traveling the **wine route,** which lies about 43km to the southwest of Zaragoza, around the town of Cariñena. Pick up a guide at the tourist office or just follow your quivering liver. The route, if followed in its entirety, also passes through **Muel,** home of the world-renowned Muel pottery, and, in the extreme south of the province, **Daroca,** an ancient walled town surrounded by 100 fortified towers, give or take a few. **Agreda Automóviles** runs buses through the area, terminating in Daroca (3 per day, 465ptas).

Calatayud

According to some, this city was founded by Kalat-al-Yeud, a Jew who established what is now the *Judería* (Jewish Quarter). Others contend that it was founded by Kalat-Ayub, a Moor who conquered this area of Castilla. Whatever the truth, you'll find in Calatayud a mixture of varying artistic and religious influences. Mudéjar towers and moldings give the town a distinctly Moorish flavor. The remains of the castle that Kalat-Ayub built wind across the hills surrounding the city. In the twelfth century, its walls held back the attacks of El Cid, but now they crumble into the dry Aragon plain.

Orientation and Practical Information

Calatayud sits snugly under two hills to the north. As you leave the train station, turn right and follow the street until you reach the center of town, **Plaza del General Franco.** The older part of the city lies between here and the hills to the north. There is no tourist office, but the **Ayuntamiento,** Pl. de España, 1 (up C. Dato and right on C. Goya), supplies a map of the city with information about hotels and restaurants.

Post Office: Avda. de San Juan el Real, 2 (tel. 88 11 52). Open for stamps Mon.-Fri. 9am-2pm, Sat. 9am-1pm. **Telegrams:** Tel. 88 12 41. Open Mon.-Fri. 9am-3pm. On Sun., call 22 20 00 to place telegrams through Zaragoza. **Postal Code:** 50300.

Telephones: Paseo Ramón y Cajal, 2 (tel. 88 14 12). Open Mon.-Fri. 9am-2pm. **Telephone Code:** 976.

Train Station: At the end of Paseo Sixto (tel. 88 12 12), 10 min. from Pl. de Franco. To Madrid (12 per day, 5 hr. and longer, from 1045ptas), Zaragoza (9 per day, 1 hr. and longer, from 490ptas), and Barcelona (3 per day, from 1845ptas).

Buses: Automóviles Zaragoza, Paseo Ramón y Cajal, 2 (tel. 88 21 40 or 88 19 75). 1 block west of Pl. del General Franco. To Zaragoza (3-4 per day, 1¼ hr., 475ptas), Monasterio de Piedra (Tues., Thurs., and Sat. at 11am, 150ptas). If you're going to Zaragoza, take the bus; it's shorter, cheaper, more convenient, and you can watch movies on TV.

Hospital: Hospital Municipal, San Juan el Real, 4 (tel. 88 19 14), next to the post office.

Police: Municipal, Pl. España, 1 (tel. 88 15 20). **Emergency:** Tel. 091.

Accommodations and Food

Most accommodations can be found around Pl. del General Franco, especially along C. Luis Guedea and C. San Antón. **Hostal Gimeno,** Luis Guedea, 9 (tel 88 35 59), has clean rooms with a sink and a hall shower (no hot water in summer). (Singles 1060ptas. Doubles 1908ptas.) The talkative owner will tell you about the best sights in town. **Fonda El Comercio,** Dato, 33 (tel 88 11 15), past Pl. España, might turn you off with its grubby exterior, but the interior is clean and has the cheapest rooms in town. (Singles 600ptas. Doubles 1200ptas. Triples 1800ptas.) **Fonda Sixto,** San Antón, 9, may be the only affordable place left after Calatayud's meager hotel space fills. The walls are crumbling faster than Kalat-Ayub's castle, and the mattresses and pillows will make you feel like you are sleeping on a bed of flan. Only the price is right. (Singles 900ptas, if you pay in advance 700ptas.)

Restaurants where you can get a cheap meal are scarce in Calatayud; the bars, however, are not. If you're looking for a meal, try **El Mesón,** López Landa, 5 (tel. 88 25 25), off the end of Paseo de Calvo Sotelo. The 550ptas *menú* has a good *paella valenciano* and *lomo a la Riojana* and will fill you up with all the wine you can drink. For good *bocadillos,* find **Las Tortillas,** Paseo Nicolás de Francia (no phone). You'll smell the cigarette smoke from blocks away. Try also **La Perla,** San Antón, 17 (tel. 88 13 40) for a *menú* around 500ptas.

Sights and Entertainment

Most of the sights are concentrated in the old part of the city. On C. Dato, the Gothic **Iglesia de San Pedro de los Francos,** the tower of which leans precariously over the street, offers a good example of early Mudéjar architecture with its small, dark windows. The next left on C. de Obispo Arrué will take you to the **Colegiata de Santa María,** where intricate brickwork on the octagonal belfry decorates the tower with different patterns all the way to the top. Notice the intricate scrollwork on the door, characteristic of plateresque style. Taking a right on C. Unión will bring you to **La Parroquia de San Andrés,** whose elegant Mudéjar brickwork challenges the originality of Santa María. Follow your sense of direction (the Ayuntamiento's map is no help) through the *morería* (original Moorish town), up the hill to the castle. Here you will face a magnificent view of the town and surrounding plains to reward your trek through the scorching sun. The winding paths could take forever, but scampering directly up the hillside will get you to the ruins in under ten minutes.

Calatayud has plenty of bars, most of which get hopping only during the weekends. The younger generation flocks to the area below Calvo Sotello, especially **Calle Justo Navarro** and **Madre Puig.** The wall-to-wall bars in the *paseo* off Madre Puig blare music into the streets, but around the corner at **Pub Jocha,** Glen Ellyn, 5 (tel. 88 05 30), you can find a quiet place to talk and take in contemporary music. Later on, you can dance away the rest of the night at **Discoteca Vidrio's,** Madre Rafols, 8 (tel. 88 25 05).

Near Calatayud

An oasis of waterfalls, grass, and trees springs out of the dry Aragon plain in Nuévalos around the **Monasterio de Piedra,** 40km southwest of Calatayud. The monastery itself was founded by an order of Cisterian monks from Tarragona in 1195. Abandoned under government orders in 1835, a hotel occupies what is left of the monastery today. The **Torre del Homenaje,** built in the twelfth century, still stands strong overlooking the valley, and is the only part of the existing building that hasn't been restored.

The main attraction of the area is not the monastery but rather the **park** that surrounds it. The **Río Piedra** plunges down a valley, creating numerous waterfalls and lakes. A path leads you through, under, and over segments of this watery paradise. Starting out early is essential if you wish to enjoy the path before it becomes claustrophobic with other hydrophiles. Following the red arrows inside the park takes you first to the **Mirador de la Cola del Caballo,** so named because the 53-meter waterfall looks like a horse's tail. As you descend, take the **Baja de Gruta,** which leads underneath the large waterfall. Proceeding up the valley takes you to the **Lago del los Patos** and **La Caprichosa,** a cascade whose mist sprays the path and cools in the hot Castilian sun. If you brought a picnic, find a place in the **Parque de Pradilla** where you can sit in thick grass and drink the supposedly therapeutic waters. **El Lago del Espejo,** a placid lake which reflects the high, precipitous mountains alongside, awaits you at the bottom of **La Cola del Caballo.** Watch for trout in all the streams, but leave them alone—no fishing allowed. (Park open daily 9am-8:30pm. Admission 300ptas. The route takes about 1½ hr. on foot.)

Nuévalos, 2km from the park, is an extremely small town, with just one paved street and a few services. **Automóviles Zaragoza buses,** leaving Calatayud or Zaragoza (see Calatayud Practical Information), pass by on their way to the Monasterio de Piedra. The closest **train station** is 17km away in Alhama de Aragon. From other cities, contact a travel agent for tours to the monastery.

If you want to spend the night in Nuévalos, try **Hostal del Río Piedra** (tel 84 90 07), 2km down the road from the monastery. A friendly family runs this well-furnished country inn, where doubles are 1265ptas. The manager has a schedule of the buses that stop by. You can eat here a la carte (*trucha aragonesa,* trout, 650ptas) or go to the restaurant at the monastery (not the hotel), whose *menú* includes two dishes, wine, bread, and *postre* for just 650ptas. (Open April-Oct. daily 9am-8:30pm.)

Jaca

Once the capital of the Kingdom of Aragon, Jaca was one of the few regions south of the Pyrenees to resist the tide of Islam after the Moorish conquest. Pilgrims to Santiago recuperated from the treachery of the Pyrenees at this first major stop on their route. Today the pilgrimage has reversed directions; most now head through

Jaca *toward* the dreaded Pyrenees for the spectacular hikes and skiing. Only 29km from the French border, Jaca is a good base for excursions into the Aragonese Pyrenees. The town still preserves an important monument from its medieval days: Several hundred students at the army's Escuela de Montañismo (Mountaineering School) fill Jaca's streets and bars when not clinging to nearby rock faces.

Orientation and Practical Information

Most activity occurs within the area encompassed by **Avda. Primo de Rivera** and **Avda. de la Jacetania. C. Mayor** cuts through the middle of this neighborhood. **Avda. de Juan XXIII** leads south from the train station into town.

Tourist Office: Avda. Regimiento Galicia (tel. 36 00 98), just south of the park in front of the fortress. Very friendly and English-speaking. Some information on skiing and mountain climbing (ask for the pamphlet *Ski Aragon*), and a list of *casas particulares.* Open Mon.-Fri. 9am-2pm and 4-8pm, Sat. 9am-2pm and 5-7pm; Sept. 16-June Mon.-Fri. 9:30am-1:30pm and 5-7pm, Sat. 10am-1pm.

Travel Agent: Viajes Abad, Avda. Regto. Galicia, 19 (tel. 36 10 81). Has the only bus to San Juan de la Peña (July-Aug. at 9:30am; 810ptas). Also, Ordesa (July-Aug. Thurs. at 9:30am; 1000ptas).

Post Office: Avda. Rgto. Galicia (tel 36 00 85), on the main north-south avenue 1 block from Turismo. Open for stamps Mon.-Fri. 9am-2pm, Sat. 9am-1pm. **Telegrams:** Open Mon.-Fri. 9am-3pm. Lista de Correos is in same building but access is down Avda. R. Galicia; open Mon.-Fri. 9am-2pm. **Postal Code:** 22700.

Telephone Code: 974.

Train Station: At the northeast end of C. Juan XXIII (tel. 36 13 32), about a 20-min. walk from the center of town. To Madrid (1 per day, 2150ptas), Zaragoza (2 per day, 750ptas), and Huesca (3 per day, 485ptas). The only trains into the Aragonese Pyrenees service Canfranc/Puerto de Somport (3 per day), where RENFE connects with SNCF (French railroad). In July and Aug., a shuttle runs between the bus and train stations, timed to arrive about 15 min. before major departures.

Buses: Avda. Jacetania (tel. 36 00 88), across plaza from rear of cathedral. To Zaragoza (2 per day, 870ptas), Huesca (2 per day, 375ptas), and Pamplona (1 per day, 510ptas; take bus to Ansó and transfer at Puente la Reina, where the bus from Huesca picks up passengers for Pamplona). To Hecho and Ansó (Mon.-Sat. at 5pm) and Biescas (Mon.-Sat. at 8am and 6pm). Almost no buses run Sun.

Taxis: Pedro Juanín, Avda. Rapitán, 17 (tel. 36 32 95 or 36 18 48). Roughly 1000-1500ptas per hour.

Car Rental: Aldecar, Avda. Jacetania, 60 (tel. 36 07 81 or 36 11 70), sign says "Rent A Car." Open Mon.-Fri. 9am-1pm and 3:30-7:30pm.

Hitchhiking: Exceptionally difficult. Try near the gas station at the end of Avda. Regimiento Galicia for Huesca, Pamplona, and the San Juan de la Peña monastery.

Hiking Club: Española de Guias de Montaña, in Biescas (tel. 48 53 58). Organizes excursions throughout the Pyrenees for a price. Also information about the Pyrenees.

Laundromat: Lavomatique, Avda. Escuela Militar de Montaña, 1 (tel. 36 01 12); the door is on side street C. Huesca. Wash and dry around 470ptas. Open daily 10am-10pm.

Swimming Pool: Behind the skating rink below the town, off Avda. Perimetral (CC-134, or Travesia Exterior). Also tennis courts here. Open June-Sept. daily 10am-8pm. Admission 225ptas.

Ski Conditions: Tel. 22 56 56. Call also the ski stations themselves.

Medical Assistance: Cruz Roja (tel. 36 11 01). **Hospital Municipal,** C. Hospital, 4 (tel. 36 11 22).

Police: Policía Municipal, C. Mayor, 24 (tel. 36 02 00), in the Ayuntamiento.

Accommodations and Camping

Rooms are readily available except at the end of July and the beginning of August in years when the Folklore Festival is held (see Sights). *Casas particulares* in Jaca are comfortable, but only a budget option for two or more people as the average price runs about 1500ptas per room. Most *hostales* are sprinkled between **Carrer Major** and the cathedral.

Albergue Juvenil de Vacaciones, Avda. Perimetral (tel. 36 05 36), by the skating rink. From C. Major, turn down C. Ramón y Cajal, then take C. Ferrenal to the end. You'll be able to see the cluster of white buildings with bright red shutters from the top of the stairs. Run by a friendly and forthright man. Doubles and quads with thin walls. Open Jan.-Sept. 700ptas per person. Full pension 1500ptas.

Hostal Villanúa (IYHF), Camino de la Selva (tel. 37 80 16), in Villanúa, about 15km north of Jaca. Buses and trains to Canfranc stop here. Open July-Aug. Mostly for groups so call ahead. 3-day maximum stay. Members only, 500ptas. Breakfast 200ptas; dinner 400ptas.

Habitaciones Martínez, C. Mayor, 53 (tel. 36 33 74). Simple rooms run by a very accommodating *señora*. Check in at the family bar downstairs. 800ptas per person. Showers 150ptas.

Pensión Vivas, C. Gil Berges (tel. 36 05 31), off C. Mayor. Friendly residence. 6 rooms often full. Singles 750ptas. Doubles 1200ptas.

Hostal Galindo, C. Mayor, 45 (tel. 36 37 43). Over restaurant of the same name. A bit expensive, but decent rooms. Singles 1200ptas. Doubles 2300ptas.

Hostal el Abeto, C. Bellido, 15 (tel. 36 16 42). Very friendly owner rents modern, though dark, rooms. Singles 1400ptas. Doubles 2400ptas.

Hostal Paris, Pl. San Pedro, 5 (tel. 36 10 20), near the cathedral. Colorful bedspreads brighten the somewhat gloomy rooms. Singles 900ptas. Doubles 1700ptas. Breakfast 150ptas.

The best campsite is **Peña Oroel** (tel. 36 02 15), 3½km down the road to Sabiñánigo. Wooded grounds feature high escarpments in the background, and facilities are first-rate. (330ptas per person, per tent, and per car. Theoretically open from March through October.) The second-class **Camping Victoria** (tel. 36 03 23), only 1½km away on Highway C-134, has a panoramic view of the Pyrenees. (250ptas per person and per car, 200ptas per tent.)

Food

Jaca's *mesones* (tavern-style restaurants) flame broil *costillas de cordero* (lamb chops) and *longanizas* (short, spicy sausages). Given the conspicuous presence of many young military conscripts, women, especially those traveling alone, may find unwanted attention around the bars along C. Mayor, particularly at night.

La Fragua, C. Gil Berges, 4 (tel. 36 06 18), right off C. Mayor. A local favorite that cooks up chicken, beef, and lamb in an old blacksmith's forge. This is a meat 'n' potatoes joint; stay away from the seafood. Huge mixed grill plate with 2 kinds of sausage, pork chops, and a pile of fries (500ptas). *Potaje de garbanzos* (250ptas). *Menú* 650ptas. Open Thurs.-Tues. noon-3:30pm and 7-11:30pm.

Bar Restaurante Vital Aza, C. Mayor, 8 (tel. 36 26 21). The house specialties sit behind the glass counter on the bar: Different *tapas* are featured daily. *Champiñones rellenos* (deep-fried stuffed mushrooms) and *albóndigas* (meatballs) are regular favorites. A hearty 700ptas *menú* awaits those who make it past the *tapas* to the dining room upstairs. Open Wed.-Mon. 9am-11pm; meals served 1-3pm and 8:30-10:30pm.

Bar La Cuba, C. Gil Berges, 10 (tel. 36 10 02). Put on your sad face and shuffle past the solitary pensioners who know a good deal when they see it. *Arroz cubana* (fried eggs on rice coated with tomato sauce) and chicken are sample entrees on the filling 500ptas *menú*. Open daily 1-4pm and 9-11:30pm.

Pollo Guay, C. Huesca (tel. 36 40 93), at the corner of Avda. Francia. It sounds like a disco (the name means "Groovy Chicken"), and you have to eat at a breakfast counter, but the roasted ½-chicken (300ptas) is delicious. Order the *chorizos* and *longanizas* (two kinds of sausage) one-by-one until you're stuffed (110ptas each). Open daily 10am-1am.

Casa Martínez, C. Mayor, 53 (tel. 36 33 74). Italian-looking checkered tablecloths in the small dining room above the bar and beneath the pension. The *señora* cooks a mean *merluza* (hake) as part of the 500ptas *menú*.

Mesón El Cobarcho, C. Ramiro I, 2 (tel. 36 15 97), near the old Torre del Reloj. A fantastic fake cave inside, complete with imitation prehistoric wall paintings. A great place for a drink, *tapas,* or lamb chops (650ptas). Open daily noon-4pm and 6pm-midnight.

Sights

Jaca's Romanesque **cathedral,** built in 1063, influenced every artist and craftsman who entered Spain to work on other churches along the Jacobean route. Ignore the clashing baroque altarpieces and the ornate, ribbed vaulting (not part of the original construction). The numerous sculptures by the eaves and the capitals in the south entrance changed the way architects perceived churches. The **Museo Diocesano** inside the sealed cloister has curly-cue ironwork from thirteenth-century cathedral gates and Romanesque wall paintings from chapels and churches. Many of the pieces have been damaged over the centuries, but you can still discern in some the wide eyes, heavy facial lines, and disproportionate bodies of Jesus, his saints, and his apostles. (Open daily 11:30am-1:30pm and 4-6pm. Admission 100ptas.)

Felipe II, a king of austerity, ordered the construction of Castillo de San Pedro, a pentagonal fortress, frequently referred to as **La Ciudadela.** The deer roaming around in the moat of Jaca's most famous landmark seem oblivious to the military importance of the well-preserved citadel. Even today, 90 servicemen are stationed inside. (A well-mannered soldier shows the interior to groups daily 11am-noon and 5-6pm. Free.)

Roughly every odd-numbered year at the end of July and beginning of August, folks from all over the world dance around town for a week during the **Festival Folklorico de los Pirineos.** Traditional dance groups and bands come from the five continents to perform the typical folkloric celebrations of their respective countries wearing grass skirts, kilts, and patchwork skirts. It's a giant party for an entire week. Jaca's **Palacio del Hielo** (ice-skating rink), Spain's largest, stays open all summer (tel. 36 10 32). It's right below the town on Avda. Perimetral—walk down the steps at the end of C. Ferrenal. (Open daily 7:30-10pm; Sept.-June Mon.-Fri. 7-9:30pm, Sat. 6:30-9:30pm, Sun. 4:30-7:30pm. Admission 200-300ptas.)

It's difficult to reach, but the **Iglesia de San Juan de la Peña** is a worthwhile excursion. The church, about 23km from Jaca, has been wedged into its mountainside for nearly 1000 years; Aragonese kings chose this spot to rest their bones. The cloister, with detailed, well-preserved capitals, touches the mountain face. You could waste a day trying to hitch to the church; save yourself the time and energy by contacting the Abad travel agency (see Practical Information). They run buses from Jaca to San Juan during July and August.

Near Jaca

In the eleventh century, King Sancho Ramírez contructed a castle to protect himself and his court from the Moors' attacks. **El Castillo de Loarre,** 5km from the town of Loarre, seems impenetrable: It rests on top of a solid rock mount, protected by sharp cliffs at its rear and 400m of thick walls on its vulnerable eastern exposure. The design provides the castle with unique aesthetic as well as defensive properties. The outer walls of the building, for example, follow the turns and angles of the rock so closely that at night an attacker might only see the silhouette of an awesome stone monolith.

As you climb the steep staircase entering the castle, a crypt opens on the right. The remains of Demetrius were stored here after the French saint died in Loarre. A narrow staircase leads off the crypt and into the magnificent **chapel.** You'll be stunned by the size of this chamber (that is, if you're not stunned by the huge hatch door that some playful youngster might close on your head as you exit the staircase pit). Several dozen capitals line the apse, and a strip of checkered masonry curves directly above them. A maze of passages and chambers line the rest of the castle, making its relatively small extension seem surprisingly complex. You can climb up to the battlements of both towers; the only access designed for the larger of the two is a narrow, arched footbridge from the smaller tower. Attackers needed to gain control of the first tower in order to cross to this final retreat, but given enough time, the castle's defenders could dismantle the footbridge. If you climb the steel rungs to the roof, be careful: A few suffer from an unnerving wobble. Use equal caution descending into the **dungeon.** Though this dark, doorless chamber was probably used to horde supplies in case of attack, it's far easier to imagine prisoners being thrown through the hole in the ceiling (20 ft. above) and left to rot here. (Castle open Tues.-Sun. 10am-2pm and 4-7pm. Free.)

Reaching **Loarre** isn't easy. You have to love castles to set aside the minimum half-day necessary for an excursion to the monument. By **train,** the closest town is **Ayerbe,** 7km from the village of Loarre. Three trains from Jaca (leaving at 6:30am, 2:30pm, and 5:20pm; 1½ hr., 375ptas) pass through Ayerbe; three trains from Huesca (30 min.) also stop in Ayerbe. From Ayerbe, you can walk to Loarre (about 2 hr.), or you can walk to Bar Pirineos on the main plaza and call Miguel the *taxista* (about 500ptas to Loarre). The **bus** from Huesca to Ayerbe passes through Loarre (2 per day, departing Huesca at 1:30pm and 7pm; returning bus stops in Loarre at 7:45am). You can **camp** near the castle in the lovely pine forests, or stay at Señora María's in town, a *casa particular* run by a kind woman (800ptas per person). The castle is 5km from the town via a very circuitous road; the more direct walk from Loarre takes 45 minutes.

Aragonese Pyrenees

The dry, bumpy countryside north and east of Jaca folds and rises into the lush valleys and snow-capped peaks of the Pyrenees. The Aragonese Pyrenees are one of the most attractive natural regions in Spain, featuring five major ski resorts: Astún, Cerler, Panticosa, Candanchú, and Formigal, where the King and Queen of Spain spend their winter holidays. The pamphlets *Ski Aragon* and *El Turismo de Nieve en España,* free at tourist offices, offer complete information on the ski resorts; also ask at the office in Jaca about local mountain-climbing and fishing clubs.

The somewhat placid town of **Huesca** provides a convenient stopover before heading into the Aragonese Pyrenees. Huesca's **tourist office,** Coso Alto, 23 (tel. 22 57 78), has reams of information on the mountains. (Open Mon.-Fri. 8:30am-2:30pm and 4:30-8pm.) If you plan to stay overnight, most accommodations can be found to the east of Plaza Navarra, 1 block from the bus station. At C. San Orencio, 10, you'll find **Hostal San Lorenzo** (no phone; 750ptas per person). Hitchhiking out of Huesca doesn't work too well, but four **trains** per day head north to Jaca (530ptas) and Sabiñanigo, where you might be able to make the bus connection to Torla and Ordesa (sometimes the bus leaves early if it fills up before the train arrives). Buses also leave daily from C. del Parque, 3 (tel. 22 70 11) to Jaca and Sabiñanigo.

Ordesa National Park

Gold country for Spanish nature-lovers lies a little over 60km northeast of Jaca. Ordesa Park cuts deeply into the highest mountains of the Pyrenees, rising from a valley etched in stone by the **Río Arazus** toward the most magnificent peaks in the country. Poplar forests traversed by turbulent mountain streams cover a canyon flanked by towering cliffs that rise 1000m above the valley floor. Soon the park will also encompass the verdant Valle de Vío to the south.

Ordesa Park is a perfect base for hikers of all levels, from summer strollers who prepare a picnic basket to daredevil alpinists who pack a pickax before a toothbrush. Hiking boots are a must for almost all the well-marked trails. The best time of year to visit the park is from mid-July through the end of August, when the storms have cleared and the weather is almost perfect. Try to arrive by 7am or 8am to avoid the crowds.

Although camping is prohibited, the many *refugios* (mountain huts, usually without facilities) allow overnight stays. **Refugio Góriz,** about four hours from the parking lot, has 120 beds for a few hundred pesetas; food is also available. A restaurant sits near the parking lot, with a decent *menú* for 650ptas, but if you're planning a walk of any duration then buy provisions in town first. A **ranger station** at the end of Rte. C138, next to the parking lot, distributes information on trails and weather conditions. A make-shift **tourist office** opens in a separate shack from mid-July to mid-September. The best way to learn about the park, however, is to buy the red *Cartographic Guide to Ordesa, Vignemale, and Monte Perdido* (200ptas in local bookstores). This little booklet comes in Spanish, but the finely detailed map needs no translation. It shows all trails and *refugios* for the park and surrounding area.

The adventure begins way before Ordesa, as buses go only as far as **Torla,** a gorgeous stone village 9km from the park. Buses leave from **Sabiñanigo,** a town that lies on the railway between Jaca and Huesca, Monday through Saturday at around noon (supposedly waiting for the train from Huesca); the return bus leaves from Torla at around 4:30pm. A bus may eventually connect Torla to the parking lot at Ordesa, but until that day, it's still a two-hour walk away.

Torla is chock-full of accommodations. **Hostal Bella Vista,** Avda. de Ordesa, 6 (tel. 48 61 53), has nice mountain views. (Open in summer. Doubles 2200ptas.) **Fonda Ballarín,** C. Capuvita, 11 (tel. 48 61 55), just up from the post office, is a little cheaper. There are two campsites about 2km from Torla toward Ordesa. **Camping Rio Ara** is a third-class site down by the river. (Tel. 48 62 48. 250ptas per person, per tent, and per car.) **Camping Ordesa** (tel. 48 61 46) is a first-class site with a swanky hotel on the property; it's on the main road to Ordesa. (Open June-Sept. 250ptas per person, per tent, and per car.) Food is expensive in Torla; expect to pay 700-800ptas for a good *menú.* A ski club just up from **Hotel Vinamela** offers group rates for both downhill and cross-country skiers.

The Soaso Circle

The Soaso Circle walk will initiate you into the wonders of Ordesa without making you leap tall cliffs in a single bound or travel much faster than a moseying mountain goat. This smooth, satisfying trek circumscribes much of the park's boomerang-shaped eastern half, which is by far the most interesting side. The trail passes thick forests, thundering waterfalls, great cliffs, alpine plateaus, and vantage points with outstanding views. Take a hearty lunch, since the walk lasts about six or seven hours. You can complete the Soaso Circle either by following the gently sloping Río Arazas eastward or by crossing the river and heading directly up the mountainside to the Refugio y Mirador Calcitarruego. The latter route includes a steep, two-and-a-half-hour ascent that may tire you out for the rest of the walk; at the top is a beautiful view that's best saved for last. Check with the ranger station about weather forecasts before starting out, and remember that in the winter heavy snow can make the trail impassable.

If you arrive early, the sun will have only just begun illuminating the upper reaches of the canyon, leaving the valley cold and damp for a while. After about an hour, the path reaches the surging **Cascada del Abanico,** where the river roars over the rocks. For a splendid, close-up view, cross the bridge a few minutes upstream and come back down to the observation point on a huge rock. Continuing toward Soaso, you'll pass more thundering falls until the path leaves the forest behind. Past the **Gradas de Soaso** (stepped waterfalls), the valley broadens and flattens until it seems you're inside a great bowl with a mountainous rim. The fan-shaped **Cascada de Soaso** at the far end of the valley spews forth from between two cliffs. Intrepid types will continue from here to the Refugio Góriz to ascend **Monte Perdido** and **Pico de Añiselo,** while those with a greater talent for self-preservation will head for lower ground. As you commence the last leg of the excursion, you'll encounter jutting rocks with trees pirouetting nervously at their tips. As the path clambers onto these ledges, watch your step; at a number of points, a slip could send you tumbling hundreds of meters into a pile of boulders. When the parking lot comes into view—impossibly far below—the best and the worst of the trail still lies ahead.

The cliff-hugging section of the trek ends at the Refugio y Mirador Calcitarruego. Then it is down, down, and down again. Here the trail tumbles abruptly, as its numerous graded turns and interminable length put the Burma Road to shame. While the path intermittently doubles as a rock slide, you are incessantly teased with views of the parking lot, an unbelievable hour below.

Other Hikes

Consult the topographical map, know your own limits, and select your trails accordingly. The **Torla-Ordesa** trail is a beautiful, easy, two-hour hike that winds through valley and forest. Cross the bridge below Torla (Puente de la Glera), and follow the trail marked *"Camino de Turieto."* It takes you directly to the information shack. The **Circo Cotatuero** and the **Circo Carriata** are two pleasant four-hour hikes. The first starts at the parking-lot restaurant and goes to the Cotatuero and Copos de Lana (Tufts of Wool) waterfalls. The second winds up a steep and narrow mountaineering peg track that offers some nice views, ending at the 100m-high Carriata waterfall.

If you feel more energetic, you might undertake the **Torla-Gavarnie** hike, at least a six-hour haul to the French town of Gavarnie. Follow the valley, turn left at the river fork, and continue along the Río Ara for about an hour and a half until you come to the hamlet of **San Nicolás de Bujaruelo.** The trail then proceeds straight up into the mountains, crosses through the 2257-meter **Puerto de Bujarelo** (about 2 hr. later), and descends straight to Gavarnie. For still more beautiful views of the Pyrenees, hike the **La Valle de Ordesa-Sierra Custodia Valle de Vío** triangle. Only experienced hikers should attempt this trek, which winds past thundering waterfalls, through pine forests, and across alpine valleys. The same applies to the **Ordesa-Gavarnie** hike, which takes a minimum of 10 hours. The trail starts near the Ordesa information hut and shoots straight up the Circo de Salarons, a steep gorge that rises over 1000m. The trail then ascends even higher, crossing glaciers at the Brecha de Rolando at an altitude of 2804m before descending abruptly into the valley of Gavarnie. An even more rugged climb begins at the Refugio Góriz and climbs **Monte Perdido,** an altitude of 3355m. Count on eight hours there and back. If you're unprepared for strenuous hikes, inquire about the mule rides around Ordesa valley.

Valle de Hecho

The **Río Aragón Subordán** tumbles down this unspoiled, craggy valley that slices into the Aragonese Pyrenees roughly 20km west of Jaca. Each July and August the town houses and feeds artists from around the world during the **Simposio de Escultura y Pintura Moderna.** In past summers, the surrounding hills have been transformed into an exquisite open-air museum. A few dozen modern sculptures are scattered for about a ½ mile up the hillside in a park that incorporates both field and forest. An enormous party kicks off the symposium in the first week of July, during which villagers come down from the hills to feast on roast lamb and fried bread.

Frequently visited but rarely overwhelmed, the tiny, cosmopolitan town of **Hecho** makes an excellent retreat. Most houses have been restored with glistening varnished windowsills and carefully pruned plants sitting in the balconies, but the sloping roofs, some resembling Chinese pagodas, reveal their real age. The shepherd still lives in the mountain for days at a time, and women dry their wool on the village streets, moving their future yarn when the buildings cast a shadow. The tangled streets of Hecho lie between the main road and the river; the best way to find the center of town is to follow the signs to "Correos" on Plaza Alta, above the tall, wooden modern art sculpture. While many people pass through the town to absorb the flavor of this Pyrenean village, few stop at its **Museo Ethnologico,** which displays old photographs of valley residents and the meanest-looking collection of farming implements you've ever seen. (Open daily 11am-2pm and 5-8pm. Admission 50ptas.)

Hecho has two *hostales;* there's usually room available, even during the symposium. **Hostal Blasquico,** on Pl. Palacio near the lower end of town (tel. 37 50 07), is certainly the best place to stay. Its gracious, charming proprietor cooks fantastic meals. (Singles 1300ptas. Doubles 2200ptas. Full pension 3000ptas per person. Lunch or dinner 900ptas.) The building is on the same square where the daily bus stops; the official street signs call it Plaza de la Fuente—it's behind the row of plants and shrubs, next to Bar Subordan. **Hostal de la Val** (tel. 37 50 28), on the main road at the other end of town, runs a close second, and some of the rooms have a full view of the valley. (Open in summer. Doubles 2000ptas. Full pension 2740ptas per person.)

An afternoon bus runs from Hecho to Jaca (260ptas); the bus continues to Ansó and returns to Hecho and Jaca the following morning. Hecho's **post office** is next to the church in the center of town. Call 37 50 04 for the **Guardia Civil.**

North of Hecho, the narrow road winds along the hillside, affording great views of the high Pyrenean massif: majestic, rocky, and speckled with snow. Three kilometers north along this road, before the valley begins to narrow into a mass of great peaks, the tiny stone village of **Siresa** rises on its knoll, dominated by the ninth-century **Inglesia de San Pedro de Siresa,** built under Charlemagne. If it's locked, ask for the key at the white house around the corner and opposite the bar. The caretaker, almost as old as the church itself, is quite deaf, so you might try yodeling up the stairway to get her attention.

The quiet **Pensión Navasal** (tel. 37 51 13) in Siresa has clean rooms and comfortable beds; if you stay in the building up the hill, you'll probably get a room with a balcony facing a field of wildflowers. (Full pension 2500ptas.) You can take the Hecho bus up to Siresa if it is too hot to walk the 2km up valley; it arrives in Hecho at about 6:25pm Monday through Saturday.

Between Hecho and Siresa, carved wood signs mark the beginning of trails to Picoya, La Reclusa, Lenito, Fuente de la Cruz, and Ansó. These are not shown in the cartographic guide to the area, which is just as well—the latter should be attempted only if you have a death wish. Although not particularly difficult, they are overgrown with brambles, eroded in places, covered with rocks, infested by flies, and scorched by the sun.

From Siresa, the road weaves up the valley, passing through a number of tunnels, as well as **La Boca del Infierno** (The Mouth of Hell) rock formation. After about 9km, you'll reach the **Valle de Oza,** a crescent of meadows where you'll find the first-class **Camping Selva de Oza.** (Tel. 37 50 32. Open June-Sept. 285ptas per person, per tent, and per car.) The site is well equipped with hot showers, a store, and even a restaurant. You can swim and fish in the river that flows nearby.

Trails up into the mountain leave from near the campsite; go prepared with the red *Guía Cartográfica de las Valles de Ansó y Hecho.* The guide is stocked by several stores in Hecho (try **Cabanas** on Rincón de Lo Fraile; 250ptas). The campsite arranges excursions, but you'll probably have more fun being a rugged individualist. North of the site, you can hike along the peaks that form the French border, from **Pic Rouge** (2177m) to **Pico Lariste** (2168m) to **Pic Laraille** (2147m), which has a stupendous view of the **Ibon de Acherito,** a glimmering lake framed by alpine bush. If you follow the guidebook and take a car part of the way, the actual hiking time for these should be around three hours to the summit. To climb **Castillo de Acher** (2390m), a square-topped mountain that resembles a castle in the sky, follow the forest road toward the **Torrente de Espata,** amble along the path by this stream, cut up the mountainside on the zigzag path to the ridge, follow the ridge past the **Refugio Forestal,** and go left at the fork. The steep ascent to the summit is only two more hours and several narrow paths away. Plan to spend most of the day making the journey from the campsite and back. For a real hike, consider scaling **Bisaurin,** the highest peak in the neighborhood. From the rocky, snow-capped peak there's an amazing panorama of Old Aragon, including the jagged **Peña Forca** (2391m), the lonely **Pico Orhy** (2015m), and the fortress-like **Castillo de Acher** (2390m).

Valle de Ansó

Ansó, a collection of white plaster and stone houses where wrought-iron balconies balance colorful garden boxes, presides over its very own valley and makes yet another good base for mountain excursions. The town lies 50km from Jaca, 11km from Hecho, and 940m above sea level. Ansó was incorporated into the Kingdom of Aragon at the end of the tenth century but has always led an isolated existence; even today some of the villagers speak a dialect peculiar to the valley. The town also provides an extreme example of the collapse of the mountain economy and way of life with the onslaught of modernization. In 1900, the town boasted 1700 residents; it now claims 500. Ansó's **Museo de Etnología,** inside its church, displays costumes, candlesticks, spinning wheels, weaving looms, costume jewelry, wood carvings, religious books, and whatever else valley residents over the centuries cleaned out of their attics. (Open daily 10:30am-1:30pm and 3:30-8pm. Admission 75ptas.)

Few travelers spend the night in Ansó, but those who do are treated with mountain hospitality. **Hostal Estanés,** Paseo Chapitel, 9 (tel. 37 01 46), usually fills up first. It's on the main road as you enter town and run by an ebullient family. (Singles 1200ptas. Doubles with bath 2500ptas. Full pension 2800ptas—a delicious bargain.) Around the corner, a more earthy and laid-back crowd runs the **Posada Magoria,** C. Chapitel, 8 (tel. 37 00 49). Everyone sits at the same long table to eat delicious vegetarian meals, and the walls and furniture of the rooms glisten with bright varnish. (1200ptas per person; you might get to double up with someone if you're alone. Meals 850ptas.) Sra. Carmen Perez runs a luxurious *casa particular* called **Casa Chimena,** where the rooms and hallways are decorated with antique furniture, including a pedal-powered Singer sewing machine. You can ask around town for directions (it's at the end of the street on your left going down C. Mayor, just before Pl. Domingo Miral), or ask at **Hostal Aisa,** Pl. Domingo Miral, 2 (tel. 37 00 09). The latter has reasonable, but less charming, rooms for 1000ptas per person. (Full pension 2600ptas for meals of a generous portion.) The **post office** next door might stick to its schedule. (Open Mon.-Fri. 9am-1pm and Sat. 9am-noon.) The one bus per day to Ansó from Jaca fills quickly (leaves at 5pm, 285ptas; 75ptas from Hecho or Siresa).

Hikers head 15km north to **Valle de Zuriza.** At the bottom of the valley, **Camping Zuriza** (tel. 37 00 60) provides a perfect base for mountain hikes. (Open June-Sept. 15. 285ptas per person, per tent, and per car.) From the campsite, make a day hike to the **Mesa de los Tres Reyes,** a series of peaks by the borders of France, Navarre, and Aragon. From Zuriza, travel north to the **Fountain of Linza,** then east to the **Collado de Linza,** a break between two smaller peaks. Here the terrain dips toward the **Hole of Solana,** then rises (steeply at times) to the summit of **Escoueste,** and even more steeply to the kingly peaks. From Zuriza, you can also make the arduous hike to **Sima de San Martín** on the French border. If you're uninterested in trail hikes, walk 2km south of Ansó to the fork in the road. Just above the tunnel toward Hecho, you can see the weird, weather-sculpted rock formation called **The Monk and the Nun.** In the other direction, the road from Ansó leads into Navarre and to Roncal and Isaba.

Valle de Benasque

If Ordesa's throngs of hikers disconcert you, the Valle de Benasque will prove a welcome relief. The area is often overlooked by tourists fearing its serious mountaineering reputation. But the gorge dug out by the Río Esera, the surrounding, glorious peaks, and the astounding variety of mountain landscapes make a visit to the valley rewarding.

The charming town of **Benasque** sits at the valley's center; use it as a supply stop and base for day hikes. Climb northeast into the valley along the paved road. Peaks covered in snow rise 2500m and line the fields of the valley; cascades shoot down the sides of pine-covered hills. **Tres Hermanas,** three sisterly peaks, guard the valley. If you start early from Benasque, you can hike 8½km down the valley road, cross the river on the camping area bridge, and climb up, up, and up following the falls of the Río Creguena. Four exhausting hours later you will reach **Lago de Creguena** (2657m), the largest and (you won't doubt this) highest lake in the Maladeta massif.

There is no shortage of housing in Benasque, but avoid the nearby ski resort of Cerler, where inflated prices are the year-round rule. The newly refinished, but still unnamed *hostal* of Señor Gabas Solana has comfortable doubles for 1500ptas and singles for 800ptas. Go down C. Castillo to the house next to the Red Cross. **Fonda Barrabes,** near the bus stop, offers bright, large doubles for 1900ptas. Campers undoubtedly get the best view in town, with 200-meter rock faces replacing their bedroom walls. **Camping Aneto** and **Camping Ixeia** (both tel. 55 11 41) sit next to the river, off the valley road, 3 and 3½km out of town. (Open Holy Week-Sept. 250ptas per person and per tent.) **Camping Valero** (no phone) is 5km further toward the Plan del Hospital. (300ptas per person and per tent.) You can also pitch your tent in the wild, open spaces for a maximum of two days except in the Plan del Hospital, Plan d'Estany, Estós, and Vallibierna.

Eating is an expensive urge in Benasque; if you insist on a three-course *menú,* head to **Barrabes** underneath the hostel or **Salvaguarda,** C. San Marcial, 3-5 (tel. 55 10 39), where at least the expensive eats (about 950ptas) are well-prepared.

Watch (or ignore) the real pros lug supplies and equipment up the steep, 30-minute trek (from the end of the paved road) to the **Refugio de la Renclusa** (tel. 55 14 90 or 55 12 37). These experts often plan a 5am start for their journey to the **Aneto** (3404m), the highest peak in the Pyrenees. Should you choose not to join them, head downhill to the road and follow signs to **Forau de Aiguallts.** This tranquil pond, 50 minutes from the *refugio* trailhead, at the end of a waterfall, never seems to fill up as hundreds of gallons pour in every minute. The explanation takes the form of two, gaping black holes (*foraus* in Aragonese) which suck the water underground, later spitting it out in Valle d'Aran. A more strenuous hike from the *refugio* leads to the peak of **Sacroux** (2675m). Even if snow prevents you from reaching the top and peering into France, the rush of the **Torrents de Gorgutes** and the sight of Lake Gorgutes will make the four-hour climb worthwhile. (*Refugio* open March-Oct. 12. 700ptas per person. Breakfast 375ptas. Lunch and dinner 1100ptas. No showers; use the hose.)

Buses leave Huesca for Benasque at 10am and 4:45pm, returning to Huesca at 6:30am and 2:45pm (3½ hr., 785ptas). There is no tourist office in town, but the Ayuntamiento has a low-key **information center** (2 blocks off the main road from Restaurant Sayo). (Tel. 55 12 89. Open Mon.-Fri. 9am-2pm.) The **Guardia Civil** responds at 55 10 08; call 55 12 54 for an **ambulance.** The **Cruz Roja** (Red Cross) is best prepared for mountain emergencies (tel. 55 12 85). Don't even think of hiking off the valley road without a topographical map of the area or a professional guide.

Catalunya (Catalonia)

The Catalan mentality is often described as *seny,* a Catalán word, meaning something like shrewd, perspicacious, or sensible. Luck is certainly a factor in the region's success as Spain's wealthiest. The area was blessed with the peninsula's richest resources. But Catalans toiled to make their land yield valuable crops. The sayings "El Català de les pedres fa pa" ("A Catalan can make bread out of stones") seems only a slight exaggeration.

The region survived a tumultuous history, fighting for regional autonomy often, feeling a sense of regional pride almost always. Rapid industrialization and the development of a solid middle class in the nineteenth century confirmed Catalunya's position as a financial powerhouse. More recently, despite Franco's moves to homogenize the country by outlawing regional languages and autonomous governments, Catalan was carefully maintained, away from the watchful eyes of the Guardia Civil. Franco's death in 1975 led to the flourishing of the submerged Catalan culture, which the government has taken very seriously. Thanks to *seny* during the region's darker times, Catalan is today taught in local schools and is officially recognized, as is the autonomy of this region. The prosperity also continues, though militant separatism has caused understandable concern among area residents.

Catalunya's famous artists have become regional folk heroes. Antonio Gaudí, the father of *modernismo,* parallel to art nouveau in France, designed various buildings and sculptures throughout the region, and Joan Miró, who died in 1983, splashed the world with bright primary colors in his paintings. If you've never seen Miró's work, you will here—the ubiquitous blue starfish logo of "la Caixa" is taken from a Miró tapestry commissioned by the bank. Famous surrealist Salvador Dalí is ensconced on the Costa Brava. Other high points of Catalan culture are the region's annual festivals. On the **Fiesta de Sant Jordi** (April 23), loved ones exchange books and roses. On September 11, Catalans celebrate **Diada, La Fiesta Nacional de Catalunya,** when the region reaffirms its political autonomy.

Barcelona

On a rainy October night in 1986, elated, slightly tipsy Mayor Pascual Maragall climbed a platform in front of Montjuïc, raised his arms victoriously, and shouted "*Hem guanyat!*" ("We've won!"). For Barcelona, after years of enduring Franco's repression, being chosen to host the 1992 Summer Olympics was a chance to enhance its reputation as a cosmopolitan city and an opportunity to slide out from under the spectre of Madrid.

After the Carthaginians named the area Barca in the third century B.C.E., the Romans began the development of the port in 201 B.C.E. By early Christian times, the population had grown to 5000. Variously occupied by Moors and northern barbarian tribes, Barcelona bounced back to become capital of a world-class kingdom. In the thirteenth century, Jaume I the Conquerer extended the city's rule over much of the Mediterranean basin. One hundred years later under Pere III, Barcelona acquired a maritime empire that extended as far east as Greece. The discovery of America brought the first signs of decline, as trade routes shifted from the Mediterranean to the Atlantic. Ironically, it was here that King Fernando and Queen Isabel welcomed Columbus upon his return from the New World.

Towards the end of the nineteenth century, Barcelona began to regain its former prestige. With the industrial revolution came huge textile factories and economic success brought about by the Catalan Renaixença at the turn of the century. Catalan artists and architects enjoyed the support of a thriving bourgeoisie. Mass manufacture, however, also brought mass unemployment and the rise of anarchism. By May of 1917, the CNT, the anarchist labor union, was the largest labor union in Spain, and by the outbreak of the Spanish Civil War in 1936, it claimed over 55% of Barcelona's workers.

During the war, Barcelona was a funnel for the International Brigades and home to the Second Republic after it moved from Madrid in November of 1936. However, the city's effectiveness in the struggle against Franco was impaired by internal strife. The breaking point came in 1937, when Barcelona erupted in chaotic street fighting. The anarchists holed up in the *telefónica* building on Plaça de Catalunya, and the socialists hid in Hotel Colón, opposite the cathedral. Bullets scattered throughout downtown Barcelona. By the end of the month, the socialists gained control of the city, and anarchism has never regained its strength, although certain motorists practice their own form of anarchy on the wide avenues of the Eixample.

Now, feisty *barcelonins* have joined forces and undertaken an extensive modernization project. Over 50 buildings, including Casa Batlló, have been renovated,

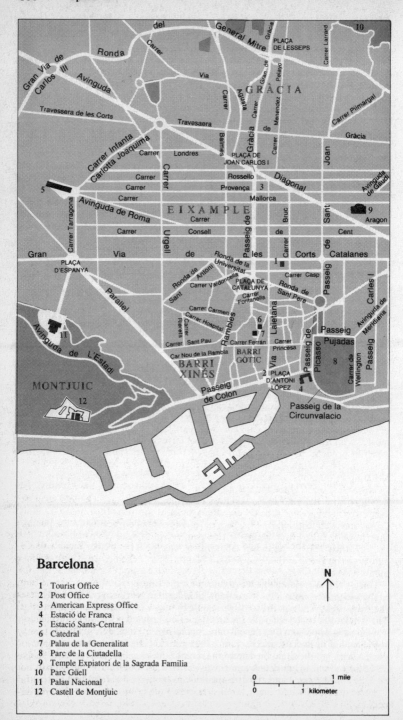

Barcelona

N

0   1 mile

0   1 kilometer

parks have been created, and streets, such as Avinguda Gaudí above the Sagrada Familia, have been turned into pedestrian walkways. Passeig de Colom, on the edge of the port, has seen one of the most impressive changes—a little-used duty dock metamorphosed into a pleasant park with palm trees and benches. As the city gears up for the 1992 Olympics, more changes will come, including the construction of the Olympic Village in the Barceloneta area.

You'll also find, however, a myriad of treasures from Barcelona's past: Roman remains, the narrow and sculpted streets of the Barri Gòtic, the elegant palaces on Carrer Montcada, and the enchanted *modernista* buildings of the Eixample. According to an old Catalan saying, *"Barcelona és bona si la bossa sona; com si sona com si no sona, Barcelona és bona."* (Barcelona is good if your pocket is full of coins; if it's full or even if it's not full, Barcelona is good.)

Orientation and Practical Information

Until Estación de Francia reopens in 1990, most train travelers will arrive at **Estació Sants-Central,** connected by metro to major parts of the city. From the **airport,** catch bus EA (every ½-hr. 6:45am-8:35pm, 100ptas) to Pl. Espanya, or hop on RENFE's shuttle, which takes you by train to Sants-Central (every 20 min. 6:15am-11pm, 125ptas). If you're stuck at the airport after 11pm, the EN bus runs until 2:30am along the same route as the EA (100ptas).

The exhaustive and useful public transport system will carry you just about anywhere in the metropolitan area. Plaça de Catalunya is the hub of the **metro,** with four lines. The system operates until 11pm, Sat.-Sun. until 1am (50ptas per ride, Sun. 55ptas). Buses (55ptas, Sun. 60ptas) are easy to use; routes are listed at each stop. They may often be more convenient, especially for getting up to Parc Güell and parts of Pedralbes and Sant Gervasi. There are also late night routes until 4:30am. (For information on money-saving, multiple-ride cards, see Municipal Transport below.) **FFCC commuter trains,** originating at Pl. de Catalunya and Pl. de Espanya, extend the transportation network to Barcelona's suburbs.

Barcelona cleaves neatly into distinct neighborhoods, so it's easy to keep your bearings. The hub of the city is **Plaça de Catalunya,** covered with pigeons and surrounded by elegant banks and flashing neon signs. From its southern corner, the tree-lined **Rambles** stretches a mile toward the port, ending near the ferry station at the Columbus monument. If you walk in that direction, the **Barri Gòtic,** centered around the cathedral and Pl. Sant Jaume, is to your left. Just beyond the Plaça Sant Jaume and roughly parallel to the Rambles, **Via Laietana** cuts through the medieval quarter; the post office, Cercaniás train station, and the Barceloneta district lie at its foot. **Carrer Ferràn,** which runs through Pl. Sant Jaume to Via Laietana, becomes **Carrer Princesa** on the other side of the *via*. At the end of Princesa sits **Parc de la Ciutadella.**

From the northern corner of Pl. de Catalunya, **Passeig de Gràcia** runs through the **Eixample,** which is bordered by **Gran Via de les Corts Catalanes** (1 block north from the *plaça*) on the south and **Avinguda Diagonal** on the north. **Ramble de Catalunya,** parallel to Passeig de Gràcia, also originates at the *plaça*. Don't confuse this Rambla with the Rambles described above. Farther uphill lies **Gràcia.** Farther north are the parks of **Tibidabo; Montjuïc** rises to the south.

A note on personal safety: Travelers should be wary of "helpful" people. Barcelona is full of crafty types who will do anything to get your money and belongings. They'll take the jacket off your back or pick your pocket with wicked efficiency. Avoid people who claim they can give you a good rate of exchange; save your money for the bank. The area around Pl. Sant Jaume remains safe because of the municipal police offices, but the situation deteriorates quickly as you approach the port. People go to Plaça Reial to get drunk and rowdy, as well as to sell hash and unload hot items. While the *plaça* and the area nearby can be fun, be careful and distrustful of people around you. At night, women traveling alone should avoid the area entirely.

Barcelona is officially a bilingual city, and you may encounter directions in Catalán. Normally the two languages do not differ to the point of irrecognizability. *Let's Go* uses such popular Catalán and Spanish names as Rambles/Ramblas interchangeably.

Tourist Offices: The Patronat of Barcelona operates four information offices where you can get a transit map and detailed map of the city; ask for the larger one with museum listings and suggested itineraries. **Estació Sants-Central** (tel. 410 25 94). Open daily 8am-8pm. **Plaça Portal de la Pau** (tel. 317 30 41), at the Columbus monument. Open daily 9am-9pm. **Pueblo Espannõl** (no phone), on Montjuïc. Open daily 10am-8pm. **Airport** office (tel. 325 58 29). Open Mon.-Sat. 9:30am-8pm, Sun. 9:30am-3pm. The Patronat also sends out two pairs of *casaques vermelles* (red-shirted officials) to patrol the Barri Gòtic and the Rambles, providing maps and information to tourists. **Municipal Information Office** (tel. 010), on the ground floor of the Ajuntament on Pl. Sant Jaume. Not a tourist office but a great place to investigate cultural events. Open Mon.-Fri. 8am-8pm, Sat. 8am-2pm. The Generalitat, Catalunya's autonomous government, maintains its own **tourist office,** Gran Via de les Corts Catalanes, 658 (tel. 301 74 43), 2 blocks from Passeig de Gracia. They carry most of the same material on Barcelona as the Patronat's offices. Ask for the hotel list that includes prices, not the short version. Open Mon.-Fri. 9am-7pm, Sat. 9am-2pm.

Student Travel: TIVE—Oficina de Turisme Juvenil, Carrer de Gravina, 1 (tel. 302 06 82), a block from Pl. de la Universitat off Carrer de Pelai (Pelayo). Come here first. Great new office with lots of services. Eurotrain tickets, cheap buses (London 10,395ptas, Paris 7185ptas, Rome 9975ptas), flights (round-trip to Palma de Mallorca 9850ptas, London 20,600ptas, Athens 30,000ptas), student IDs (225ptas), IYHF cards (1800ptas). Helpful, but often a line. Open Mon.-Fri. 9am-1pm and 4-5:30pm. **Centre d'Informació de l'Area de Joventut,** C. Avinyó, 7 (tel. 301 12 21), maintains an excellent library of travel guides. They don't sell tickets, but will help you investigate your travel options. Open Mon.-Fri. 10am-2pm and 4-8pm.

Consulates: U.S., Via Laietana, 33, 4th floor (tel. 319 95 50). Open Mon.-Fri. 9am-12:30pm and 3-5pm. **Canada,** Via Augusta, 125 (tel. 209 06 34). Open Mon.-Fri. 9am-1pm. **U.K.,** Avda. Diagonal, 477 (tel. 322 21 51). Open Mon.-Fri. 9am-1pm and 3:15-4:15pm, Sat. 9:45am-noon.

Currency Exchange: Caja Madrid and **Banca Catalana** charge a commission of 250ptas or 1%, whichever is more. For better exchange rates, avoid banks altogether. **El Corte Inglés,** Pl. de Catalunya, charges a 2% commission on traveler's checks at its travel center on the top floor. Open Mon.-Sat. 10am-8pm. Travel agencies often offer acceptable rates; **Viajes Marsans,** on the Rambles ½ block from Pl. Catalunya, charges a 2% commission. Open Mon.-Fri. 9am-1pm and 4-7:45pm. On Sunday, you can change money at bank exchange booths on the Rambles, at Sants train station, and in the Cercaniás train station on Avda. Margués de L'Argentera near the port.

American Express: Passeig de Gràcia, 101 (tel. 217 00 70), around the corner on Carrer Rosselló. Metro: Diagonal (L3, L5). 2% commission on their own traveler's checks and on personal checks cashed for cardholders. Mail held 1 month for card and check holders free of charge. Open Mon.-Fri. 9:30am-6pm, Sat. 10am-noon. **Postal Code:** 08008.

Post Office: Pl. d'Antoni López (tel. 318 38 31), at the end of Via Laietana near the port. Open for stamps (in basement) Mon.-Sat. 8:30am-10pm, Sun. 10am-noon. Open for Lista de Correos (window #17) Mon.-Fri. 9am-9pm, Sat. 9am-2pm. Open for **telegrams** Mon.-Sat. 8am-10pm. Go to Via Laitana, 1 (tel. 322 20 00), to send emergency telegrams when post office is closed. Open Mon.-Fri. 10pm-midnight, Sat.-Sun. 8am-10pm. Most neighborhoods also have post offices; a useful one near the city center is at Pl. de Urquinaona, 6. Open Mon.-Fri. 9am-2pm and 4-6pm. **Postal Code:** 08002.

Telephones: Carrer de Fontanella, 4, off Pl. de Catalunya. Open Mon.-Sat. 8:30am-9pm. Also at Estació Sants-Central. Open daily 7:45am-10:45pm. International collect calls can be made only at the first location. **Telephone Code:** 93.

Airport: El Prat de Llobregat (tel. 370 10 11), 10km from the city. The easiest and fastest way to get there is by train (every ½-hr. from Sants-Central 6am-10:30pm, 20 min., 125ptas). Bus EA takes longer and departs from Avda. Parallel next to Pl. d'Espanya (100ptas). To Madrid (every ½-hr., 10,820ptas). Decent connections to Spanish cities, the Balearics, and major European destinations. **Iberia,** Passeig de Grácia, 30 (tel. 301 39 93; for national reservations 301 68 00; for international 302 76 56). Open Mon.-Fri. 9am-1pm and 4-7pm, Sat. 9am-1pm. Several branch offices, including C. Mallorca, 277. Open same hours.

Train Stations: Estació Sants-Central (tel. 322 41 42), uptown at Pl. Païso Catalans (metro L3, L5), where all long-distance trains depart. **Estació França-Termino,** Avda. Margués Argentera, is closed for renovations until 1990, but the terminal next door, **Cercaniás,** handles local trains that run along the coast to the north. At Sants-Central, the **RENFE** information counter (tel. 322 41 42) is open daily 6:30am-10:30pm; **tourist information** (on the other side of the counter) with a map of the city is open 8am-8pm. Telephones next to tourism open daily 7:45am-10:45pm. To Paris (2 per day, 9650ptas), Valencia (1500ptas), Alicante (2500ptas), Sevilla (2 per day, 4125ptas), La Coruña (1 per day, 4500ptas), and Madrid (6 per day; *rápido* 3100ptas, *talgo* 5200ptas). The **Ferrocarrils de la Generalitat de Catalunya (FFCC),** or Catalan State Railways, with main stations at Pl. Catalunya and Pl. d'Espanya, is indispensable if you're going to Montserrat. Intersections with the metro are marked by a double-arrow symbol; the line towards Tibidabo charges the same as the metro and you can use a T-1 or T-2 pass card (see Municipal Transport); beyond Tibidabo, however, fares go up.

Long-Distance Buses: Iberbus, Paral-lel, 116 (tel. 242 33 00). Metro: Parallel L3. To London (11,000ptas), Paris (8100ptas), and Amsterdam (10,775ptas). **Auto Transporte Julia,** Pl. Universitat, 12 (tel. 317 04 76), is a madhouse best avoided. To Lisbon (8700ptas), Rome (11,725ptas), Zaragoza (1850ptas), and Montserrat. Office open daily 9am-7pm. **Alsina Graells,** Ronda Universitat, 4 (tel. 302 40 86), has service to Andorra (2 per, 1390ptas), Lleida (3 per day, 1020ptas), and Burgos (2975ptas). Office open Mon.-Fri. 9am-1pm and 4-7pm, Sat. 9am-1pm. Buy tickets aboard the bus on Sun. **Sarfa,** Pl. Duc de Medinaceli (tel. 318 94 34), near the harbor, has 12 departures per day (9 on Sun.) to towns along the Costa Brava.

Municipal Transport: Tel. 360 00 00. Get a hold of a *Guia del Transport Públic,* free at tourist offices and the **transport information** booth at Pl. Catalunya. Open Mon.-Fri. 8am-7pm, Sat. 8am-1pm. This map clearly indicates the city's bus and metro routes. Bus rides cost 55ptas, at night and on weekends 60ptas. The metro is 5ptas less at all times. A T-1 pass is good for 10 rides on bus and metro for 360ptas; a T-2 pass allows 10 rides on the metro only for 300ptas. Passes can be bought at the information booth, any metro entrance, or any bank.

Tourist Bus: Bus 100 runs a continuous loop to the 12 most visited tourist sights in Barcelona. Ticket (500ptas per 1 day, 1000ptas per 3 days) also lets you ride the *teleférics* and funicular on Montjuïc. Operates June 24-Sept. 18 daily 10am-7pm. Bus every ½-hr.; tickets available at the transport booth in Pl. Catalunya, the University metro stop, Patronat tourist offices, and El Corte Inglés.

Ferries: Trasmediterránea, Via Laietana, 2 (tel. 319 82 12). Extensive service to the Balearics. To Mallorca, Menorca, and Ibiza (all 4550ptas). Open Mon.-Fri. 9am-1pm and 5-7pm, Sat. 9am-noon. On the day of sailing, tickets are available until ½-hr. before departure at Estació Maritima (tel. 301 25 98), on the wharf that begins near the Columbus monument. **Saemar,** Rambla de Catalunya, 18 (tel. 318 21 58), represents Adriática for passage to Greece and Egypt.

Taxis: Tel. 300 38 11, 330 08 04, or 358 11 11. The 1st 6 min. or 1.9km costs 200ptas; then it's 50ptas per km (Mon.-Fri. 6am-10pm) or 70ptas per km (Mon.-Fri. 10pm-6am and Sat.-Sun. 24 hours).

Bicycle Rental: Bicitram, Tel. 204 36 78. Bikes 275ptas the 1st hr. plus 200ptas per additional hr. Open Sat.-Sun. 10am-7pm. Outlets also at Avda. Margués Argentera, near Parc Ciutadella; C. Sant Miquel, 71, in Barceloneta; and C. Aragón, 19, in Parc Escorxador.

Moped Rental: Vanguard, Carrer Londres, 31 (tel. 239 38 80). Vespas 3500ptas per day. Mopeds 2500ptas per day. Open Mon.-Fri. 9am-1:30pm and 4-7:30pm, Sat. 9am-1:30pm.

Hitchhiking: Barnastop, C. Pintor Fortuny, 21 (tel. 794 22 74), matches drivers with riders. Commission 1.5ptas per km. Open Mon.-Fri. 10am-2pm and 4-7pm, Sat. 11am-2pm. **Comparco,** C. Ribas, 31 (tel. 246 69 08), provides a similar service. To hitch to France, take the metro to Fabra i Puig, and take Avda. Meridiana to reach A-7. A-7 also leads south to Tarragona and Valencia; take bus #7 from Rambla Catalunya at Gran Viá or ride the green line to Zona Universitaria, at the southern end of Diagonal. The *autopista* access lies near here. With the proper sign, this approach should also put you on the A-2 to Zaragoza, the beginning of the trek to Madrid. Hitching on *autopistas* (toll roads) themselves is illegal; they are marked with the letter A. Hitching is permitted, however, on national (N) highways.

Lost Property: Objetos Perdidos, on the ground floor of the Ajuntament, Pl. de Sant Jaume (tel. 301 39 23). Open Mon.-Fri. 9:30am-1:30pm.

Baggage Check: On the far side of Sants-Central Station. Lockers 100ptas per day. Open daily 7am-11pm. Also at Alsina Graells bus station. 50ptas per item. Open daily 8:30am-8:30pm.

English Bookstore: Try the newsstands along the Rambles and Passeig de Gràcia. **Librería Francesa,** Passeig de Gràcia, 91, has a good selection, including *Let's Go* guides. Open Mon.-Fri. 9:30am-1:30pm and 4:30-7:30pm, Sat. 9:30am-1:30pm.

English-Language Library: Instituto de Estudios Norteamericanos, Via Augusta, 123 (tel. 227 31 45). Take the FFCC commuter train to Pl. Molina. Lots of American newspapers and periodicals, as well as a strong reference section. Open Sept.-July Mon.-Fri. 11am-1:30pm and 4-8pm. **Biblioteca Central,** C. Carme, 47 (tel. 317 07 78), next to Hospital de Santa Creu off the Rambles. Open Mon.-Fri. 9am-8:30pm, Sat. 9am-3pm. Many branches.

Laundromats: Lava Super, C. del Carme, 63. Wash and dry 650ptas per 5kg. Open Mon.-Fri. 9am-2pm and 4-8pm. **Lavanderiá Autoservicio,** at #114B, charges similar rates. Open Mon.-Fri 9am-2pm and 4-8pm, Sat. 9am-2pm. Farther up toward Pl. de la Universitat, **Lavanderiá Rambles,** C. de les Ramelleres, on Pl. Vicenç Martorell, offers wash and dry for 675ptas. Open Mon.-Fri. 8am-2pm and 4-8pm, Sat. 8am-2pm; July-Sept. mornings only.

Public Showers and Bathrooms: Carrer dels Carders, 32, off Via Laietana, but close to Parc de la Ciutadella. Showers 170ptas, baths 400ptas, towels 30ptas. Also in Pl. Urquinaona, underneath the triangular island in the center of the plaza. Open daily 8am-8pm.

Swimming Pools: Swim where the Olympians will in 1992. **Piscina Picornell** (tel. 325 92 81) is on Montjuïc near the main stadium. Open June-Sept. 15 daily 10am-5pm. Adults 150ptas. **Piscina Les Corts,** Trav. de les Corts (tel. 239 41 78), 6 blocks from Sants. Same hours and admission. The booklet *Guia di Esports d'Estiu* provides information on pools and other sports facilities.

Gay and Lesbian Association: Front d'Alliberament Gai de Catalunya (FAGC), Villarroel, 62 (tel. 254 63 98). **Grup de Lesbianes Feministes de Barcelona,** Pl. Berenguer Gran, 1 (tel. 319 60 29 or 319 79 41).

Crisis Services: Informacions i Urgencies de Les Dones, C. Comerç, 44 (tel. 319 00 42), is a social services department that helps women who have been battered or raped. English-speaking personnel can be of help in obtaining medical and legal services.

24-Hour Pharmacies: After-hours duty rotates among the city's pharmacies. Consult newspapers or check the sign posted on every pharmacy window for the night's pharmacy.

Medical Services: Hospital Clínico, Carrer Casanova, 143 (tel. 323 14 14). **Hospital Evangelico** Alegre de Dalt, 87-93 (tel. 219 71 00), in Gràcia. English-speaking. For an **ambulance,** call 302 33 33. For a **doctor** at any time, call 219 71 00. **Medicos de Urgencia,** Carrer de Plai, 40 (tel. 317 17 17). **VD treatment,** Departament de Sanidad, Passeig Lluís Companys, 7 (tel. 256 79 02).

Police: Jefatura Superior, Via Laietana, 49 (tel. 091) and C. Ample, 23. **Municipal police,** underneath Pl. Catalunya (tel. 092). The municipal police are usually helpful and receptive to questions. They wear blue uniforms.

Accommodations

Rooms in Barcelona form a beggar's banquet—there's lots of variety at little cost. Though the city gets many visitors, it absorbs them fairly well; you'll always find something with a little digging. If you are turned away, be sure to ask the owner for suggestions. The free booklet *Hotels, Campings, Apartamientos* is available at the Turismo on Gran Viá and is helpful.

Hostels

Barcelona's hostels offer everything from aristocratic living to shabbier environs. While establishments outside the city center suffer from obvious disadvantages, they're safer and they offer neighborhood living.

Hostal de Joves (IYHF), Passeig Pujades, 29 (tel. 300 31 04), across from Parc de la Ciutadella. Metro: Arc de Triomf or Marina (L1)—avoid Ciutadella, which is at the far end of the park. Barcelona's municipal hostel is a friendly urban-style set-up, and close to everything. The 70 beds fill quickly, so arrive early in summer. Low-key management. Unisex bedrooms (most with 4-6 beds) and showers (7-9:30am and 3-10pm). As always, watch your possessions. 5-day max. stay. Curfew midnight. Lockout 10am-3pm. Reception open daily 7-10am and 3pm-midnight. 435ptas. Sheets 225ptas, blankets included. Breakfast 90ptas. Snack bar open 3-11pm. Kitchen facilities. The place may close permanently in Sept., 1989.

Hostal Verge de Montserrat (IYHF), Passeig de la Mare de Deu del Coll, 41-51 (tel. 213 86 33), beyond Parc Güell off Avda. República Argentina. Take bus #28 from Pl. de Catalunya or Metro L3 to Plaça Lesseps, then bus #25; either stops in front of the door. The green metro drops you at Vallcaraca; from here, walk up Avda. República Argentina and across C. Viaducte de Vallcarca. Well worth the 30-min. commute. In a renovated neo-Moorish villa, with an atrium full of brightly colored tiles and a stained-glass skylight as well as a new wing of 4-6 bedrooms and sparkling showers. A great view. 5-day max. stay. Reserve for Aug., when large groups swarm the place. Curfew midnight, but door opens at 1am for the late-night crowd. Reception open daily 7:30-9:30am, 1:30-3pm, 5-8pm, and 9-11pm. Members only. 425ptas, ages over 26 550ptas. Sheets 225ptas.

Albergue "El Studio," C. Duquessa d'Orleans, 56 (tel. 205 09 61), in Sarrià. Take the FFCC to the Reina Elisenda stop and walk up the street. Alternatively, get off bus #22 or 64 on Passeig de Bonanova near Pl. de Sarrià and walk down to the FFCC stop entrance. This friendly, 40-bed hostel is in a modern dormitory used by university students during the year. All rooms are triples, each with shower. 3- to 4-day max. stay. No curfew. Open June 13-Sept. 875ptas. Breakfast included.

Hostal Pere Tarrés (IYHF), Carrer Numancia, 149-51 (tel. 230 16 06). Metro: Les Corts (L3). Small and not very close to anything except Estació Sants-Central. If you arrive there, this hostel may be worth a try—walk out the station toward the city, cross the square, and turn left up Carrer Numancia (15 min.) Kitchen facilities. 3-day max. stay. No curfew. Open daily 8-10am and 4-11:30pm. 550ptas, nonmembers 630ptas. Breakfast included.

Hotel Kabul, Pl. Reial, 17 (tel. 318 51 90), off the Rambles. Unsafe at night; almost anyone can stroll in and out at anytime. Despite all warnings, young travelers mob the place in summer. Open 24 hours. 500ptas per person.

Barri Gòtic and the Rambles

Barcelona's ancient streets brim with action, some of which you'll do best to avoid. However, the area offers loads of cheap places to stay, right in the heart of Barcelona, where you can eat and drink cheaper than anywhere else in the city. Since there is quite a selection to choose from in this area, be picky.

Casa de Huéspedes Mari-Luz, Carrer Palau, 4 (tel. 317 34 63). Metro: Jaume 1 (L4) or Liceu (L3). 1 block from Pl. Sant Jaume, Carrer de l'Ensenyança runs toward the harbor; after 150m, it becomes Carrer Palau. Clean, well-run, popular establishment on a quiet street. Mari-Luz will let you use the refrigerator, the stove, the sun on her roof, and let you place collect calls (200ptas). 2 new showers and a full renovation underway. 900ptas per person.

Hostal Bienestar, C. Quintana, 3 (tel. 318 72 83), between C. Ferrán and C Boqueríó. High ceilings and the lovely flower garden on the main patio recall days of grandeur. The friendly owners keep the place guarded all night. Singles 850ptas. Doubles 1600ptas. Showers 100ptas.

Hostal Lepanto, C. Rauric, 10 (tel. 302 00 81), parallel to C. Quintana. Big rooms with wardrobes and desks. Ignore the street sign boasting singles for 600ptas; it's 10 years old. Singles 800ptas. Doubles 1600ptas. Rates drop 100ptas if you stay more than 3 days.

Hostal Canaletas, Rambla de Canaletas, 133 (tel. 301 56 60), off Pl. de Catalunya. Cool tile floors on the top floor with a friendly manager. Singles 800ptas. Doubles 1400ptas. Cold showers 50ptas, hot showers 100ptas.

Hostal Noya, Rambla de Canaletas, 133 (tel. 301 48 31), below the above. A bit nicer. Some singles are small and dark, but other rooms look over the Rambles. Singles 800ptas. Doubles 1500ptas. Showers 100ptas.

Hostal Dalí, C. Boqueríá, 12 (tel. 318 55 80), off the Rambles. Not too abstract and not too modern. Comfortable rooms maintained by a business-like owner. Singles 700ptas. Doubles 1400ptas.

Pensión Venecia, Carrer Junta de Comerç, 13 (tel. 302 61 34), 2 blocks in from the Rambles off Carrer de Hospital. Dark hallway, but clean and simple rooms. Be careful outside. 800ptas per person. Showers (sometimes hot) 100ptas.

Hostal Rey Don Jaime I, Carrer Jaume I, 11 (tel. 315 41 61), on the other side of Pl. Sant Jaume, near Via Laietana—a safe, well-lit street. The location and safety are worth the prices. The manager is helpful and eager to speak English. Singles with shower 1600ptas, with bath 1800ptas. Doubles with shower 2600ptas, with bath 3200ptas. Extra bed 700ptas. Breakfast 250ptas.

Between Via Laietana and Parc de la Ciutadella

While the streets around Santa María del Mar are fun to explore during the day, they are deserted and dangerous at night. The *pensiones,* while tending to have larger rooms, are not as nice as those in other parts of the city. To get here, take the metro to Jaume I (L4).

Hostal-Residencia Pintor, Carrer Gignás, 25 (tel. 315 47 08), on the other side of Via Laietana near the main post office. Large, well-kept rooms with balconies overlooking the street. Singles 900ptas. Doubles 1500-1700ptas.

Hostal-Residencia Lourdes, Carrer Princesa, 14 (tel. 319 33 72). Clean but boring. Likely to have a vacancy. Singles 800ptas. Doubles 1300ptas. Showers 100ptas.

Near Plaça de Catalunya

Though a bit more expensive than in the Barri Gòtic, accommodations in this area are more modern, safer, and usually more peaceful, though you may be trading people noise for traffic noise in some cases. The metro stop is Pl. de Catalunya (L1, L3), though Universitat (L1) is just as close to most of these establishments.

Hostal-Residencia Lausanne, Avda. Porta de l'Angel, 24 (tel. 302 11 39), opposite the Galerías Preciados department store and overlooking a pedestrian mall often lined with street musicians. Great rooms and a great manager. Singles 1000ptas. Doubles 1600ptas, with shower 2000ptas. Breakfast 190ptas.

Residencia Australia, Ronda Universitat, 11 (tel. 317 41 77). Run by Sra. María Lorenzo, who cares about her guests: wooden boards under the mattresses, a spotless bathroom, and heat in winter. She speaks perfect English, having lived in Australia for 18 years. Singles 1340ptas. Doubles 2000ptas, with bath 2460ptas.

Hostal-Residencia Sena, Ronda Universitat, 29 (tel. 318 90 97). Clean and spacious, with pleasant management. Singles 1250ptas. Doubles 2000ptas, with shower 2100ptas. Reserve with deposit.

Pensión L'Isard, Carrer Tallers, 82 (tel. 302 51 83), off Pl. Universitat. Spotless rooms, some with alcoves next to a balcony. Great location that quiets down at night. Singles 1100ptas. Doubles 2200ptas. Triples 3150ptas.

Pensión Santa Anna, C. Santa Anna, 23 (tel. 301 22 46), just beneath Pl. Catalunya off the Rambles. On a relatively quiet pedestrian street, it has vacancies later in the day than other places. Light green rooms, high ceilings, and big beds. Some interior singles have poor air circulation, but rooms are clean. 800ptas per person. Showers 200ptas.

In the Eixample

The most beautiful *hostales* are found here. Most have huge entryways with colorful tiles and funky wooden neo-modernist elevators that take you up the stairwells. Furthermore, the wide *avenidas* in the area are particularly safe.

Hostal-Residencia Palacios, Gran Via de les Corts Catalanes, 629bis (tel. 301 37 92), across from the main tourist office. The *hostal* has a beautiful, newly painted entrance. Well-furnished rooms, if a little dark. Singles 1410ptas, with shower 1800ptas. Doubles with shower 2300ptas. Triples with shower 3000ptas. Breakfast 200ptas.

Hostal-Residencia Oliva, Passeig de Gràcia, 32, 4th floor (tel. 317 50 87), 1 block from metro: Passeig de Gràcia (L4, L3). A wooden elevator with painted windows carries you up. Owned by a friendly family, this immaculate place has lots of character and bright, spacious doubles. Singles 1300ptas. Doubles with shower 2600ptas.

Hostal Colón, C. Aragón, 281 (tel. 215 47 00), near Passeig de Gràcia. Big rooms in an old-fashioned *pensión.* Singles 1150ptas. Doubles 1900ptas.

Pensión Vicenta/Hostal Lider, Rambla Catalunya, 84 (tel. 215 19 23), on one of Barcelona's most expensive shopping streets. Spartan rooms in a grand old building. Singles can be claustrophobic, but the sheets are always fresh. Singles 1000ptas. Doubles 2000ptas.

Hostal-Residencia Montserrat, Passeig de Gràcia, 114 (tel. 217 27 00), near Pl. de Joan Carles I on the north side of Diagonal. Metro: Diagonal. Some rooms have nice views of the *plaça.* Singles with shower 1300ptas. Doubles with bath 2400ptas. Triples with bath 3200ptas. Breakfast 250ptas.

Pensión Alcázar, C. Valencia, 292 (tel. 215 36 88), at C. Pau Claris. Dark interior and rather unexcited owners. Safe location. Doubles 1500ptas. Showers 100ptas.

In Gràcia

The area above Diagonal, Gràcia offers relaxing neighborhood living where you can mingle with families as a respite from fellow travelers. Quaint neighborhood bars and *pastelerías* remain "undiscovered," and you might even get a feeling for what it would be like to live in Barcelona.

Hostal Bonavista, Carrer de Bonavista, 21 (tel. 237 37 57), 1 min. from the end of Passeig de Gràcia. Metro: Diagonal. Simple, well-kept rooms in a quiet neighborhood. Friendly management. Doubles 1750ptas. Extra bed 800ptas. Hot showers 200ptas.

Hostal Mozart, C. Mozart, 15 (tel. 218 37 41), 2 blocks off Gran de Gràcia near Pl. Rius i Taulet. A friendly woman oversees the small, tidy rooms, each with a desk, chair, sink, and concert piano. Doubles 1500ptas. Showers 200ptas.

Hostal Abete, Gran de Gràcia, 67 (tel. 218 55 24). Moderately sized rooms with balcony shutters; those overlooking the street can be noisy during early morning traffic. Doubles 2000ptas.

Pensión Norma, Gran de Gràcia, 87 (tel. 237 44 78). The mattresses are still wrapped in their factory plastic, and you may have to put the toilet seat in its place, but rooms are clean and have full-size dressers and tables. Views of the large neighborhood patio in back and the noisy main street in front. Singles 1000ptas. Doubles 2000ptas. Cold showers 150ptas, hot showers 200ptas.

Pensión Alberdi, C. Menéndez y Pelayo, 95, 5th floor (tel. 217 30 25), near Pl. del Sol. Simple rooms. Singles 900ptas. Queen-size bed for 2 1500ptas. Doubles 1700ptas. Showers 200ptas.

Pensión San Medín, Carrer Major de Gràcia, 125 (tel. 217 30 68), towards Pl. Lesseps. Metro: Fonta (L3). Rooms not as nice as the manager, but clean and inexpensive. Singles 1000ptas. Doubles 1800ptas. Triples 2450ptas. Cold showers 150ptas, hot showers 200ptas.

Camping

There is no camping in Barcelona. However, efficient inter-city buses (100ptas) can get you to all the following locations in 20-45 minutes. The campground nearest to the city is **Camping Barcino,** C. Laureano Miro, 50 (tel. 372 85 01). Take the CO or BI bus from Pl. Espanya; the blue-line metro (V) to Can Vidalet will also put you nearby. The site boasts a swimming pool, bar, and restaurant. (375ptas per person and per tent.) **Cala-Gogo-El Prat** (tel. 379 46 00) is toward the airport in Prat de Llobregat. This is a first-class site with plenty of trees and its own beach. Take bus #605 from Pl. Espanya; at the end of the run in Prat, board bus #604 to the beach. (Open Feb.-Dec. 15. 375ptas per person, 450ptas per tent.)

Gavá, the town before Castelldefels south of Barcelona, has several campgrounds, all accessible by UC and L90 bus from Pl. de la Universitat. **Albatros** (tel. 662 20 31) is a first-class campground on the beach. (415ptas per person, 500ptas per tent.) **Tortuga Ligera** (tel. 662 12 29) is another first-class site on the beach. (375ptas per person and per tent.) Both sites are near the "Tortuga Ligera" bus stop. **Tres Estrellas** (tel. 662 11 16) is 2km closer to town, one stop past "Ballena Alegre." (390ptas per person, 450ptas per tent.) **Camping Gavá** (no phone) is the cheapest of the four campgrounds. (220ptas per person and per tent.)

North of Barcelona, **Camping Don Quixote** (tel. 389 10 16) is a second-class site near the beach. (295ptas per person and per tent.) Take a RENFE local train from the Cercanías station. Get off at Monsolis, one stop past Mongat, about 15 minutes from the city.

Food

Just about every block in Barcelona has four or five places to eat. They range from local bars with *tapas variadas* to luxurious restaurants serving sorbet between courses. You'll find expensive but delicious *pastelerías* and cafes in the Eixample, where people eat under the shade of the trees on the wide *avenidas*. Closer to the port, the bars and cafes get more crowded and more hurried. In Barri Gótic, your moneybelt will cheer at the omnipresent 450-500ptas *menús,* but your body will thank you for exhibiting some discrimination in your choice of grub. If you have any doubts, stay away from seafood dishes; they're probably not fresh. Catalan specialities include *faves a la catalana* (lima beans with herbs), *butifarra con judias blancas* (sausage with white beans), and *escudella i carn d'olla* (a pork and chicken broth).

For night owls, **Les Puces del Barri Gòtic,** Carrer Montesió, 7 (tel. 317 19 91), above Pl. Nova, is open until 3:30am (and claims to be more than 400 years old). **Drugstore David,** Carrer Tuset, 17-19 (tel. 209 69 58; metro: Diagonal), between Travessera de Gràcia and Avda. Diagonal, serves great bocadillos until 2am.

Go to **Barceloneta** for fresh fish, though it tends to be expensive. Nonetheless, you may find some specials if you walk along the Passeig Nacional, depending on the day's catch (metro: L4 to Barceloneta or bus #45).

The adventurous or gregarious can also take the metro to **Ciutat Universitaria,** where the student cafeterias of the Autonomous University of Barcelona serve reasonably priced fare from October to May.

"La Boqueria," officially the **Mercat de Sant Josep,** off Rambla Sant Josep, is Barcelona's best market, with the freshest fish and produce in the city. The packed food stalls offer everything from dead squid to live calves. (Open Mon.-Sat. 7:30am-3pm and 6-8pm.)

Barri Gòtic and around Carrer Montcada

Menús for less than 500ptas abound in the narrow and dark streets between the cathedral and the port. Avoid empty restaurants, and order whatever is most popular because it's more likely to be hot and well prepared. Calle de Avinyó runs through the middle of the *barri,* between C. Ample and C. de Ferran; it's called Calle dels Gegants at its intersection with the latter.

Casa José, Pl. Sant Josep Oriol, 10 (tel. 302 40 20), a 2-min. walk from Pl. Nova, between Carrer del Pi and Carrer Boqueria. Casa José has wowed budget travelers for years with its incredibly cheap *menús* (350ptas and 500ptas). While fame hasn't spoiled the place, it has made it a bit sloppy (e.g., overused frying oil). Stick to the hefty *paella* (400ptas), chicken dishes, and *butifarra* plates. Open Mon.-Sat. 1-4:30pm and 8pm-midnight.

Bar El Tropezón, C. Gignás (tel. 315 34 04), at C. Regomir. The name means the "big tumble," which is what tipsy clients take on the ridiculously narrow staircase on the left. *Patatas bravas* (fried potatoes with *all i oli* and spicy sauce, 125ptas) and *pinchos* (pork on skewers, 200ptas) are 2 popular *tapas.* The *bomba* (140ptas), the bar's invention, is an overgrown *croqueta,* the size of a tennis ball. Open daily noon-midnight.

Restaurante Self-Naturista, C. Santa Anna, 11-13 (no phone), near Pl. de Catalunya. A cafeteria-style vegetarian restaurant with a 450ptas *menú.* Meatless *paella* and eggplant *croquetas.* The line to get in moves fast. Open Mon.-Sat. 11:30am-10pm.

Meson-Gallego, C. D'Avinyò, 29 (no phone). 3-course *menú* 500ptas, with *gallego* specialties. Good shellfish soup. Open Mon.-Sat. 1:30-4:30pm and 7:30pm-midnight.

Restaurant Agut, C. Gignas, 16 (tel. 315 17 09). This local favorite continues to offer traditional Catalan cuisine at reasonable prices after many years of popularity. *Butifarra amb mongetes* (sausage with white beans) 350ptas. Open Aug.-June Tues.-Sun. 1-4pm and 8pm-2am.

Restaurant Pitarra, Carrer d'Avinyó, 56 (tel. 301 16 47). Founded in 1890. Slightly expensive—800ptas *menú*—but popular regional specialties like *butifarra* and *merluza.* Open Mon.-Sat. 1-4pm and 8-11:30pm.

O'Nabo de Lugo, C. d'Avinyó, 58 (no phone), next to the above. Galician specialties and a filling 500ptas *menú.* Open daily 1-4pm and 8-11pm.

Bodega La Plata, C. Merced, 28 (tel. 315 10 09), near the post office. People crowd the bar and overflow into the street, chugging beers and eating *sardnas fritas* (fried sardines, 100ptas), the bar's most popular *tapa.* Open Mon.-Sat. 11am-5pm and 7-11pm.

Can Conesa, Llibreteria, 1 (no phone), on the corner of Pl. S. Jaume. Some of the best hot *bocadillos* in Barcelona. Toasted buns and melted cheese. Bacon and cheese 160ptas, *lomo* 200ptas. Open Mon.-Sat. 8am-9:30pm.

Bar Carmen, Carrer Montcada, 2 (tel. 310 15 49), between Carrer de la Princesa and Carrer dels Corders. Cheap place in a picturesque, secluded location. *Paella* 530ptas, *bacalao* 400ptas. Open Tues.-Sat. 1-4pm and 5-11:30pm, Sun. 1-4pm.

Al Primer Crit, Banys Vells, 2 (tel. 319 10 97), near Museo Picasso. Good cold foods at reasonable prices. Pasta 375ptas, paté 450ptas, *amanides* 375-390ptas. Hot food is expensive. Open Tues.-Sun. 8pm-midnight.

Between the Rambles and Ronda de Sant Antoni

Students and workers fill this area at lunch. The area around Carrer Talleres and Sitges, just a block off Rambla de Canaletas, is packed with cheap places, some of which advertise a special on a chalkboard outside. Stay away from Barri Chino, which begins roughly below Carrer de l'Hospital and caters to a different sort of appetite. Good *gallego* food can be found off Carrer de la Luna and Carrer de Joaquín Costa.

Restaurante Biocenter, C. Pintor Fortuny, 24 (tel. 302 35 67), behind the store of the same name off the Rambles. A delightful vegetarian restaurant for all. The place is small and friendly; the food tasty. Help yourself to the salad bar or order a hot entree (440ptas). The 640ptas *menú* includes rice salad and a spinach pastry. Open Mon.-Sat. 1-5pm.

Sitjas, C. Sitges, 3 (tel. 317 29 22), 1 block in from Rambla de Canaletas. You need to see it to believe it: The owner/waiter scrambles to serve 30 people at once, confirming your order from halfway across the restaurant and juggling beer bottles as if they were tennis balls. The food is surprisingly good and at 375ptas, no one complains. Open Mon.-Sat. 1-4pm and 8-11pm.

Can Maxim, Carrer Bonsuccés, 8 (tel. 302 02 34), just off Rambla de Canaletas. Hard to find a seat, but worth the wait. 575ptas *menú* with *pescadillos* and delicious rice salad (lunch only). *Platos combinados* 500ptas. Open Mon.-Sat. 1-4pm and 8-10:30pm.

Restaurante Nuria, Rambla de Canaletas, 133 (tel. 302 38 47), off Pl. de Catalunya. A great, bustling institution. You may have trouble choosing from all the delicious food displayed on the counter. Great *bocadillos* 100-190ptas (hot and to go), *menú* with strong gazpacho, rabbit, and fresh melon 700ptas. Open daily noon-1am.

Pizzeria Rivolta, C. de l'Hospital, 116 (tel. 329 34 15), 7 blocks in from Rambla de Sant Josep. Gets cranking late at night with Catalan rads and rockers. Large pizzas from 350ptas, *caña de cerveza* 125ptas. Open Tues.-Sat. 1-4pm and 8pm-1am, Fri.-Sat. later.

Bar Muy Buenas, Carrer del Carme, 63 (tel. 242 50 53), off Rambla Sant Josep near the market. An example of how Gaudí's *modernismo* influenced commercial architecture. Wavy wood and stained glass welcome you into this old-fashioned bar, with a huge marble sink almost as big as a bathtub. 2-course *menú* 400ptas. Open Sept.-July Mon.-Sat. 10am-9pm.

Restaurante Club Taurino, C. Xuclà, 5 (tel. 302 40 32), a dark, narrow street between C. Fortuny and C. del Carme. An Andalusian restaurant dedicated to the famous *toreadores* of Spain. The walls are reverently covered with photos of bullfighters. The 500ptas *menú* includes *macarrones* and veal. Avoid the fish dishes. Open Sun.-Fri. 1-4pm and 8:30-11pm.

Restaurant Super Pollo a l'Ast, Carrer de Santa Pau, 100 (tel. 242 44 79), in front of Sant Pau del Camp Church. The scent of spicy roasted chicken drifts down the street. Take-out whole chickens 550ptas, ½-chicken 280ptas. Good seafood: *pulpitos a la marinera* (little octopi) 350ptas, *merluza* 300ptas.

Restaurant Cal Ton, Elisabets, 9 (tel. 302 40 14). On the continuation of Carrer Bonsuccés, off the Rambles and a block below Pl. de Catalunya. Full of locals. Traditional dishes like *faves a la catalana* 495ptas. *Menú* 775ptas. Open Mon.-Sat. until 5pm.

In the Eixample

Restaurants in the Eixample tend to be more expensive than those in older Barcelona, but here you'll find a relaxing atmosphere for a meal in one of Barcelona's neighborhoods.

Restaurant Les Corts Catalanes, Gran Via de les Corts Catalanes, 603 (tel. 301 03 76), a block from Passeig de Gràcia. Behind the awnings that say "Vida Sana" is a great vegetarian restaurant and delicatessen, serving everything from interesting vegetable lasagna to *empanadas* (turnovers) with cheese or spinach (160ptas). Open daily 9am-4pm and 8-11pm.

El Viejo Pop, Gran Via de les Corts Catalanes, 635 (tel. 302 75 62), near the tourist office. Filled with young people who come for the pizza and sandwiches (325-400ptas) or 500ptas *menú.* Open Mon.-Thurs. 8am-1am, Fri. 8am-2:30am, Sat. 11am-1:30am.

Bar Stop, Carrer de Consell de Cent, 324 (tel. 301 82 47), between Carrer de Pau Claris and Passeig de Gràcia. Good for a quick bite. *Bocadillo blanco y negro* (pork and black sausage) with a *caña* of beer or wine 200ptas. Open Mon.-Sat. 8am-9pm.

Pizzería Argentina El Ceibo, Carrer Mallorca, 279 (no phone), a block from Passeig de Gràcia. South American specialties such as *empanadas* (meat turnovers, 80ptas) and assorted pizzas (375-425ptas). Open Mon.-Sat. 8:30am-1am.

Milano Pizzería, C. Provença, 292 (tel. 216 06 38), near Passeig de Gracia. A new restaurant with a glitzy facade to draw *turistas. Platos combinados* 425-600ptas, pizzas 395-550ptas. Open Sun.-Thurs. 8am-11pm, Fri.-Sat. until 2am.

Bar-Restaurante Can Segarra, Ronda San Antonia, 102 (tel. 302 44 22), off Pl. Universitat. Not really in the Eixample, but close enough. Affiliated with Pensión L'Isard. Lively atmosphere with many young people and a 450ptas lunch *menú.* Open Fri.-Wed. 8am-1am; meals served 1-4pm.

In Gràcia and Nearby Neighborhoods

Eating in Grácia is different: Most of the diners will speak Catalán, not English, French, or German. Away from the city center, these areas are less touristy. While some *crêperies* and vegetarian restaurants are a tad overpriced, you can still find good eats here for 500-750ptas.

El Glop, C. Sant Lluís, 24 (tel. 213 70 58), at C. Montmany. *Bona cuina catalana* (good Catalan cuisine) at affordable prices in an attractive, sunlit, dining room. Along with standbys such as *butifarra* (300ptas), they also prepare *conill* (rabbit, 425ptas) and *torrades* (big slices of toasted Catalan bread with tomatoes smeared across them, accompanied by cheese or sausage; 100-295ptas). Come early: After 10pm, the wait may top 45 min. Open Sept. 7-Aug. 20 Tues.-Sun. 1-4pm and 1pm-1am.

Restaurante Pas de la Virreina, C. Torrijos (tel. 237 51 09), at Carrer de L'Or, next to Pl. Virreina. A friendly, basement restaurant with a well-prepared 475ptas *menú* (650ptas on Sun.). *Bistec* and *lomo* 350ptas. Open daily 10am-5pm and 8pm-midnight.

La Crêperie Bretonne, C. Balmes, 274 (tel, 217 30 48), outside of Gràcia by about 5 blocks, next to Pl. Molina. Delicious crêpes at reasonable prices (chocolate 150ptas, chicken and bechamel 295ptas). Open late Aug.-July Tues.-Sun. 5am-2pm.

Sights

"Barcelona, posa't guapa" ("Barcelona, make yourself beautiful") was one of the exhortatory slogans plastered all over the city after it was chosen to host the '92 Olympics in October, 1986. The city has heeded the call, unleashing a seemingly endless wave of new construction and urban facelift projects. From Montjuïc, where the 1929 World's Fair site is being renovated, to the parks and plazas of Sants, Gràcia, and the Sagrada Familia area, Barcelona is pumping new blood into its ancient veins. For those intrigued by the new architecture, the Ajuntament publishes the multilingual brochure *Espais Urbans (Urban Spaces),* which maps out recent, public rebuilding projects. The tourist office stocks copies.

Barcelona's modernist buildings are now treated like venerable *grande dames.* The facade of Gaudí's Casa Batlló was cleaned in 1986 (no easy task, as one look at the building reveals) and, in 1988, the "Pedrera" was cloaked with scaffolding as workmen delicately began undoing the damages of air pollution and natural erosion. For a thorough look at Barcelona's modernist heritage, check out *Modernisme and Catalunya,* a free brochure available at the tourist office on Gran Vía. Barcelona's older architectural treasures have not been overlooked. Santa María del Mar, the finest example of Catalan Gothic in Barcelona, will see its roof rebuilt this year. Excavations on the old Roman colony underneath Pl. del Rei are speeding along.

As you stroll from one monument to another, keep your eyes open for hidden treasures: a beautifully carved doorway, a stained-glass window, the molding on the edge of a building, the lamps and tiles on Passeig de Gràcia.

Barri Gòtic

Strictly speaking, the **Barri Gòtic** is the area surrounding the cathedral, the Ajuntament (City Hall), and the Generalitat, but the name also extends to the area between the Rambles and Via Laietana. While streets such as **Carrer de la Pietat** and **Carrer del Paradis** have managed to preserve their medieval charm, most of the Barri Gòtic has been taken over by cheap pensions, souvenir stands, and bars. This intrusion of modernity, however, gives the area a liveliness—as well as a livelihood—it would otherwise miss. For some people, livelihood entails tourists parting with wallets, purses, cameras, and other valuables. Don't be caught off-guard: Don't leave your knapsack sitting next to you in an outdoor cafe unless you have a hand or foot on it.

There's no way you can miss the **cathedral;** you'll see either its high-flying spires or the numerous tourists that flock to smallish **Plaça de la Seu** in front of it. The facade was finished only in the nineteenth century by architect José Mestres, who took over the project begun by Charles Galtés (also known as Carlí), a fifteenth-century French architect. Archeological excavations have unearthed the remains of a fourth-century paleo-Christian church that was despoiled by the Muslim despot al-Mansur in the late tenth century. The present cathedral, begun in 1298, is an excellent example of Catalan Gothic architecture. Unlike the French builders of the Middle Ages, who were obsessed with height, Catalan architects, like the Italians, had the amplitude of the basilica on their minds. This ideal, perfectly rendered in Girona's cathedral, is defeated here by the otherwise beautiful *coro* (chancel), the church's geometric center. The elegant upper pews inside the chancel were designed by Pere Ça Anglada in 1399. Among the coats of arms painted on them are those of the kings of France, Portugal, Hungary, Denmark, and Poland, who came to Barcelona in 1519 to participate in a gathering of the Order of the Golden Fleece summoned by Carlos V. The marble choirscreen in the chancel illustrates the death of Barcelona's patron saint and martyr, St. Eulália. Nowadays, St. Eulália spends her time in a fourteenth-century alabaster sarcophagus in the church crypt. The cathedral's **cloister** is one of the most beautiful sights in Barcelona. Magnolias grow in the middle and fat white geese waddle around inside the iron fences, protected from the prodding tourists. The setting is especially beautiful in early evening. The small **museum** off the cloister houses religious treasures and the fifteenth-century *La Pietat,* painted by Bartolomé Bermejo. (Cathedral and cloister open daily 7:30am-1:30pm and 4-7:30pm. Museum open daily 11am-1am. Admission 25ptas. Ask a guard to let you see the *coro* for 25ptas.)

As you descend the cathedral steps, you'll see **Plaça Nova** to your left. Two cylindrical Roman towers, rebuilt in the twelfth century and recently restored, face the *plaça* and the facade of the modern **Collegi d'Arquitectes,** designed by Picasso.

Near the cathedral, on Carrer dels Comtes, is the **Palau Reial** (Royal Palace) of the counts of Barcelona, who later became kings of Aragon. The palace now houses a museum and several exhibit rooms. The **Museu Frederic Marés** is the first you reach if you arrive from Pl. de la Seu. Roman busts and Iberian stone figurines fill the first rooms, but the largest display here features twelfth- and thirteenth-century religious sculpture, carved and painted on wood. After the image of Jesus on a cross has become fixed in your mind (and it will after you've seen it 75 different ways), escape to the crypt, where a simple but poignant series of reliefs depicts Adam and Eve. (Open Tues.-Sat. 9am-2pm and 4-7pm, Sun. 9am-2am. Free.)

Also on Carrer dels Comtes, the beautiful **Palau del Lloctinent** (Lieutenant's Palace) boasts a pleasant courtyard and fountain. Notice the impressive carved wood ceiling as you ascend the principal stairway. The building now houses the **Arxiu de la Corona d'Aragó** (Archives of the Kingdom of Aragon), one of the major repositories of medieval documents in the world. Behind it is an imposing ensemble of buildings that form **Plaça del Rei.** The Renaissance tower, the square's landmark, was designed by Antoni Carbonell. Pause to look at the stairway, where a rebellious peasant tried to assassinate King Ferdinand the Catholic. Next to the *plaça,* you can again enter the Royal Palace, this time through the **Museu d'Historia de la**

Ciutat, on C. Verguer. Visit the ruins of the Roman colony in the basement; some well-preserved floor mosaics and villa walls are all that remain. Sixth-century Visigoths buried the Roman ruins to make rooms for their cemetery; their buildings, in turn, were scrunched under medieval structures. Only this century saw the ruins excavated. From the upper floors of the museum, you can enter **Capilla de Santa Agueda,** built to house the king's holy relics, just like the Sainte-Chapelle in Paris. Continue to the spacious, unadorned **Saló del Tinell,** where Ferdinand and Isabel received Columbus after his first trans-Atlantic jaunt. (Museu d'Historia and chambers of the royal palace open Tues.-Sat. 9am-8pm, Sun. 9am-1:30pm, Mon. 3:30-8pm. Free.)

The handsome **Plaça de Sant Jaume** was given its present form in 1823, but has served as the city's main square since Roman times. It is dominated by two of Catalunya's most important buildings: the **Palau de la Generalitat** and the **Ajuntament** (Town Hall). The palace houses the executive branch of Catalunya's autonomous government. Don't get too excited about the beautiful patio of orange trees inside; you aren't allowed entrance. The building does open to the public one day per year, April 23. The Ajuntament is also closed to the public. By the summer of 1989, however, visitors may be permitted in both buildings.

Spain's first museum of holography, **Holoscope,** is off Pl. Sant Jaume at C. Jaume I, 1. The collection isn't big, but it's fun to crouch and twist your body in front of about 40 holograms, reaching out in a deluded stupor to touch caged birds and other vivid images. (Open Tues.-Sat. 11am-1:30pm and 5:30-8:30pm. Admission 100ptas.) Also off the plaza at C. Paradis, 10, are mammoth Roman columns. Walk in the door to the CEC mountaineering club, and you'll see the remnants to your right, behind an iron fence.

Museo del Calzado, Pl. Sant Felip Neri, down C. Montjuïc del Bisbe and opposite the outside doorway to the cathedral's cloister, tries hard. Started by the shoemakers guild, this one-room institution features slave sandals from the first century, shepherd shoewear from the third century, unbelievably narrow satin shoes that tortured feet 300 years ago, Pau Casal's walkers, and even the boots of Catalunya's first climber of Mt. Everest. The museum is currently assembling a collection of shoes of famous people. The *cofradía* (guild) of shoemakers has existed since the thirteenth century; they even had a stone boot laid on the exterior of the cathedral walls during its construction. You can still see the boot on C. dels Comtes. (Museum open Tues.-Sun. 11am-2pm. Admission 10ptas.)

Plaça del Pi (Pine Tree Square) and adjacent **Plaça Sant Josep Oriol** are popular spots to enjoy snack and conversation. Saturday from 11am to 8pm and Sunday from 11am to 2pm, a group of local artists set up stands and sell their works. The two plazas are off the Ramblas along C. Cardenal Casañas. Nearby, Calle Petritxol is famous for its *chocolaterías,* where people dip *churros* (fried dough) in thick hot chocolate.

Around Santa María del Mar

This lively, picturesque area, part of the old city, was separated from the Barri Gòtic proper by the construction of Via Laietana in 1907. The area centers around the beautiful **Santa María del Mar,** closely associated with Barcelona's development as a major sea power during the Middle Ages. Construction began in 1329, just after the return of King Alfons III from his conquest of Sardinia. A hundred years earlier, as Jaume I embarked on his Mediterranean campaign, he vowed to build a church in honor of St. Mary (who was invoked by Catalan sailors in their battlecry). Santa María del Mar is perhaps the most perfect of all Catalan Gothic churches, with its horizontal lines, eight-sided towers, and numerous, large, unadorned surfaces. Inside, square elements predominate in the arches of the principal nave. Spaciousness was achieved by placing the columns 13m apart, a distance unusual at the time. (Open daily midnight-noon and 5-8:15pm, but occasionally closed Sun. for concert preparations.)

Secular architecture is well-represented by the monumental palaces on **Carrer de Montcada.** Especially interesting is the **Palau Agüilar,** at #15. Its elegant courtyard is so similar to that of the Palau de la Generalitat that both have been attributed to the same architect, Marc Safont. The Palau Agüilar is now home to one of Barcelona's greatest tourist attractions, the **Museu Picasso,** where you can follow the artist's development from his early textbook doodlings to his last exhibition posters. Its 30 rooms of paintings and drawings include masterpieces such as the *Maids of Honor* series (1957), Picasso's reinterpretation of the famous *Las Meninas* by Velázquez in the Prado. Lithographs and early works comprise a large part of the collection. Picasso's ceramic work (1947-65), which includes brightly painted plates and jugs shaped like bulls, is especially warm and unpretentious. (Open Tues.-Sun. 10am-7pm. Free.)

Almost across the street, you'll find the **Museu Tèxtil i d'Indumentària,** Carrer Montcada, 12-14. The museum houses some marginally interesting civilian clothes from the sixteenth century, when men's vests had 12 buttons and gold stitching. A fourteenth-century palace, the building is itself more interesting, with its gracious patio, intricate molding, and the wooden ceilings on the second floor. (Open Tues.-Sat. 9am-2pm and 4:30-7pm, Sun. 9am-2pm. Free.)

Fierce fighting and damage to the city convinced Felipe V to construct a large citadel in 1716 on what is now Passeig de Picasso. Citizens left homeless by the fires that ravaged Barcelona were relocated here, and the fortress became a symbol of the Bourbon king's strict treatment of Catalan insurgents. **Parc de la Ciutadella,** with its pretty promenades, replaced the fortress after it was razed in 1868. Site of the 1888 Universal Exposition, the park now houses the **Museu d'Art Modern's** collection of paintings and sculptures, most crafted by Catalan artists in the last 100 years. *Plein Air* by Casas is a masterful example of Parisian influence on Spanish painting. Josep Llimona's sculpture *Desconsol* (life-size version outside and on a reduced scale inside) seems romantic, while the tormented old man and his child in *Els Primers Freds* (*The First Chills*) by Blay Fabregas symbolizes human suffering. Isidre Nonell spent a number of months gaining the trust of a few gypsy communities in Catalunya; his dark, evocative paintings of the *gitanas* are among the museum's finest works. (Museum open Tues.-Sat. 9am-7:30pm, Sun. 9am-2pm, Mon. 3-7:30pm. Free.)

The **Museu de Zoologia,** at the corner of the park formed by Passeig de Picasso and Passeig de Pujades, is an amusing reminder of the antiquated stuff-and-tag approach to museum displays. Almost everything that once swam, crawled, flew, or knew how to have a good time now stares at visitors from behind glass cases. (Open Tues.-Sun. 9am-2pm. Free.) Nearby, the **Museu de Geologia's** rock displays are geared toward those who already understand a good bit of geology. (Open same hours as the zoological museum. Free.) Despite rumors to the contrary, Snowflake (Copita de Nieve) still lives. The albino gorilla is still the main attraction at Barcelona's **Parc Zoològic,** near the Museu d'Art. A horde of playful monkeys on a jungle gym also keep visitors amused, as do the dolphin and whale shows (5 per day). (Zoo open daily 9:30am-7:30pm. Admission a steep 550ptas.)

Around the Rambles

W. Somerset Maugham called it the most beautiful street in the world, and indeed the **Rambles** attracts more people than anything else in Barcelona. The wide boulevard, actually made up of five distinct segments, runs from Pl. de Catalunya to the Monument a Colon at the park. It's lined with exotic birds, chalk renditions of famous paintings, sprawling newsstands, and towering trees. The destination of many a *paseo,* the Rambles bustle with urban activity: families strolling amidst sleazy money-changers, fortune-tellers surprising young women, beggars holding out their hands, tourists rewinding their cameras, old men gazing silently, couples cooing over an afternoon drink, and policemen eyeing the scene with skepticism. Superstitious and sentimental tourists gather around the **Font de Canaletes** at the top of the Rambles near Pl. de Catalunya. Once you've drunk from this elegant fountain, tradition says, you'll return to Barcelona at least once in your life.

As you descend the Rambles, hash pushers and pickpockets become more common. The area to the right of Rambla Santa Mònica and Rambla de Caputxins is known as the **Barri Xinés,** or **Barrio Chino,** Barcelona's Red Light District. **Plaça Reial,** to the left off Rambla de Caputxins, continues bafflingly to exert its siren-like charm on naive tourists. While the architecture and palm trees are attractive, the open drug dealing and poverty should be warning signs: Watch your bags, cameras, and other valuables. Avoid the plaza at night. The safest time to visit is Sunday from 10am to 2pm, when the stands of stamp collectors line the porticoes.

Escape the hustle and bustle by ducking into one of the several museums in the area. The **Palau de la Virreina,** at Rambla, 99, houses temporary art exhibits on its first two floors. (Open Tues,-Sat. 10am-2pm and 4:30-8:30pm, Sun. 10am-2pm, Mon. 4:30-8:30pm. Admission 250ptas, students free.) Upstairs, the palace contains the **Gabinet Postal,** an interesting stamp musuem. (Open Sept.-July Mon.-Fri. 10am-2pm. Free.)

About halfway down the Rambles, you'll see the **Gran Teatre del Liceu,** Rambla, 61, on your right as you face the port. On opening night here in 1892, an anarchist launched two bombs from the upper balcony into the crowd of aristocrats on the bottom floor, killing 22 and wounding many more. After executing five others for the crime, authorities finally found the real culprit, who cried *"Viva la anarquía"* before being hanged. The place has calmed down since then, and you can tour the beautiful opera hall Monday or Friday from September through June. (Tours at 11:30am and 12:15pm. Admission 100ptas.) Inexpensive seats or standing room for performances can set you back as little as 750ptas.

Between C. del Carme and C. del Hospital, off the Rambles, is the **Hospital de Santa Creu,** the oldest hospital building in Barcelona. Art students and library-users have replaced the infirm in the tranquil patios of the complex. Walk around and gaze at the richly tiled walls of the central courtyard.

At the far end of C. de Sant Pau, near the Ronda de Sant Pau, sits Barcelona's oldest Romanesque church. The **Iglesia de Sant Pau** enjoys fame more for its age than its architectural excellence. The small, intricately decorated cloister with lobu-lated arches is a pleasant surprise in this otherwise unremarkable building. (No regular hours, but there's normally someone in the building next door Mon.-Fri. 6-8pm.)

The **Museu de l'Art de l'Espectacle,** Carrer Nou de la Rambla, 3-5, has a fine collection of nineteenth- and twentieth-century theater memorabilia. The **Palau Güell,** where it's housed, is the only Gaudí building in Barcelona you can actually enter (the Sagrada Família has no real interior). When Gaudí started construction in 1886, his design stirred great controversy with its reinterpretation of Moorish architecture and its free use of the parabolic arch. Both innovations are evident in the *sala d'actes.* (Open Mon.-Sat. 11am-2pm and 5-8pm. Admission 100ptas.)

A cast of surprisingly life-like characters awaits you at the **Museu de Cera de Barcelona,** Rambla, 4-6. In a nineteenth-century building, the museum houses over 300 wax figures, including a luscious Cleopatra, various political figures, and the cast of *Star Wars.* (Open Mon.-Fri. 11am-2pm and 4:30-8pm, Sat. 11am-2pm and 4:30-8:30pm. Admission 360ptas.)

At the end of the Rambles, near the port, is the towering **Monument a Colom,** erected in 1886. Be sure to see it at night, when the busy design benefits from some skillful lighting. (Elevator to the top open July-Oct. Tues.-Sun. 9am-9pm; Nov.-June Tues.-Sun. 10:30am-2pm and 3:30-6:30pm. Admission 150ptas.) The **Museu Marítim,** Pl. Porta de la Pau, 1, recounts Barcelona's maritime history by displaying old maps and compasses as well as a reproduction of the *Real,* the galley that Don Juan de Austria commanded in the Battle of Lepanto (1571). The museum fills the old *drassanes,* the only extant example of a medieval shipyard in Europe. (Open Tues.-Sat. 10am-2pm and 4-7pm, Sun. 10am-2pm. Admission 150ptas, students free.) In the harbor is a reproduction of the *Santa María,* the caravel in which Columbus sailed to America. (Open daily 9am-2pm and 3pm-sunset. Admission with ticket from Museu Marítim.) Nearby boats will take you out to the breakwater, giving you a chance to watch Barcelona's busy harbor. (Open for rides daily 10am-9pm. ½-hr. ride 150ptas.)

The Eixample

The **Eixample** ("Broadening" in Catalán) was the natural result of the nineteenth century's optimism. In 1859 the old medieval walls were torn down, and a year later Ildefons Cerdà's checkerboard design for a new Barcelona was implemented. As in most U.S. cities, the streets of the Eixample intersect at right angles. They don't form perfect squares, however; the corners, called *chaflanes,* have been cut, so that each block of buildings forms an octagon. **Avinguda Diagonal,** as its name suggests, is the only street to traverse the Eixample. Some of Barcelona's major arteries are part of the checkerboard. At the turn of the century, elegant **Passeig de Gràcia** was the utmost in residential chic but has gradually yielded to consulates and scores of banks. **Gran Via de les Corts Catalanes** is Barcelona's longest street, and the **Rambla de Catalunya** is filled with outdoor cafes and restaurants. Though the Eixample has become the city's financial hub, it's still pleasant to stroll along these attractive, tree-lined boulevards.

During the Catalan Renaixença at the turn of this century, the Catalan bourgeoisie commissioned many *modernista* architects to build their houses, making a *modernista* museum of the Eixample. Gaudí led the movement, with his bold dismissal of traditional plane geometry. Nature served as the model for his wavy horizontal lines, flowery ornamentation, and fluid surfaces. Even his methods were unconventional: He designed some buildings by first making a small-scale model, turning it upside down, and then hanging sand bags from key stress points to make sure it was properly balanced. He gave the craftsmen who worked on his buildings latitude for their own artistic instincts, resulting in the carefully detailed work evident in the ironwork and chimneys on the Casa Milà, for instance. Contemporaries of his include Luis Domènech y Montaner, architect of the Palau de la Musica Catalana and known for his Gothic reinterpretations, and José Puig y Cadafalch, architect of Casa Amatller, Passeig de Gràcia, 41.

Most astonishing among Gaudí's works is the **Temple Expiatori de la Sagrada Família,** on Carrer Marina between Carrer de Mallorca and Carrer de Provença. Francesc de Paula del Villar began the church in 1882 in neo-Gothic style, but Gaudí took over in 1891 and transformed it. For 43 years he worked on the Sagrada Família, and from 1914 to his death in 1925 (he was killed by a trolley), he even inhabited a small room here. Even had he lived, however, he would not have seen his project completed; he claimed it would take at least 200 years to finish. The church's three facades were to symbolize Jesus's nativity, passion, and glory; only the first is finished. Its three doors symbolize hope, faith, and charity, and are associated with Mary, St. Joseph, and Jesus. Be sure to take the elevator (open daily 10am-1:45pm and 3-7:45pm; admission 75ptas) or walk up the stairs to wander among the towers, bridges, and crannies of the facade, a unique art nouveau experience. Since 1926, construction has progressed erratically, with the latest bout (since 1979) of activity along the side toward Carrer Mallorca. In the crypt is a model of the completed structure, as well as various artifacts relating to the construction. There is also a fair 12-minute slide show for 100ptas. (Open daily 8am-9pm; in off-season daily 8am-7pm. Admission 250ptas.)

The odd-numbered side of Passeig de Gràcia between C. de Aragò and Consell de Cent, called *la manzana de la discordia* (block of disagreement), contains three buildings built during the peak of the Catalan *modernista* movement. The bottom two floors of the facade of **Casa Lleó Morera** (1905), by Domenech i Montaner, was destroyed to house a commercial establishment, but the upper floors seem to sprout flowers, and winged monsters snarl on the balconies. Puig i Cadafalch opted for a cubical pattern on the facade of the **Casa Amatller** (1900) at #41. Next door, Gaudí's fluid balconies and bright tile work on the **Casa Batlló** (1905) make the building look like something designed to entrap Hansel and Gretel. To see the interior, you need a letter of permission from Catedra Gaudí, Avda. Pedralbes, 7 (tel. 204 52 50; open Mon.-Fri. 8am-2pm). The letter will allow you to enter the *principal* (main apartment) owned by Iberia Seguros insurance company; don't be freaked out by the bending, swelling wooden doors and the mushroom-shaped arch in front of the main fireplace. The conference room ceiling is a magnificent twirl of plaster resembling a gigantic snail shell. Visits are permitted from 8 to 10am. No permission is required for just a peek into the building's entrance.

Popularly known as La Pedrera (Stone Quarry), **Casa Milà,** Passeig de Gràcia, 92, seems about to melt into the sidewalk because of its lack of straight lines. Notice the intricate ironwork around the balconies and the diversity of the front gate's egg-shaped window panes. Scaffolding along parts of the facade (restoration work is underway) has not prevented tours from showing visitors the rooftop and permitting a closer look at the spiral chimneys. While you're at this vantage point, you may get your only chance to see what the Eixample's design was all about: Look at the huge, interior patio in the block of apartment buildings next door. The preservation of open spaces was a key concept behind the Eixample's construction—the space permits light and air to reach what used to be the darkest part of buildings. (Rooftop tours Mon.-Fri. at 10am, 11am, noon, 4pm, and 5pm; Sat. at 10am, 11am, and noon; 1st and 3rd Sun. of each month at 11am and noon. Free.)

The **Museu de la Música** occupies the Casa Vidal-Quadras, Diagonal, 373. While its collection of odd and antique instruments is certainly worth a look, the most impressive art here is the building designed by Puig i Cadafalch. Sculpted heads jut from the plasterwork of the foyer walls and a richly inlaid roof and mosaic floor form the entrance. The second floor contains a stunning living room with neo-Arabic motifs on the ceiling. (Museum open Tues.-Sun. 9am-2pm. Free.) The Casa Terrades, Diagonal, 416, commonly knows as **Les Punxes,** with its spiky towers and triangular garrets, resembles an enchanted castle from a fairy tale. Walk through the unique archways and ask the doorman to see the elevator. Its mirrored walls and wood-stained seats look like they're out of an episode of *Mastepiece Theatre.*

The **Pau Casals Monument,** on Avda. de Pau Casals near Pl. de Francesc Macià, is a beautiful memorial to a notable Catalan. The great cellist went into exile after the Spanish Civil War and founded the prestigious Festival Casals in San Juan, Puerto Rico, where he died. This sculpture-cum-garden boasts an imposing *Allegory of Music,* which stands behind a realistic, low-key statue of the maestro.

Those interested in further exploring this area and its unique architecture might want three useful guides: *Modernism in Catalunya,* a newspaper-style brochure with short descriptions of important buildings and their architects; the large map of Barcelona distributed by the Patronat tourist offices, suggesting itineraries for seeing the most buildings in the least amount of time; and the colorful handout on Gaudí, describing his works in Barcelona. (All free from tourist offices.)

Montjuïc

In Barcelona's history, whoever controlled this mountain ruled the city. Its strategic location allows close surveillance of both the sea and the interior up to the Tibidabo; consequently, fierce battles have been fought for its domination. In the 1640s, *barcelonins* could not stave off the troops of Felipe IV in their makeshift fortress near the top. Later in the century, the current building was erected. The repressive Bourbon king Felipe V snatched the building away from the defiant Catalans in 1714. The unfortunate association of the castle with despotic rulers continued even in this century; the Generalísimo made this one of his local interrogation headquarters. Somewhere in the structure's dark bowels, his *beneméritos* ("honorable ones," a.k.a. the civil Guard) strangled Catalunya's former president, Lluís Companys, with their own execution device in 1941. Only in 1960 did Franco return the fortress to the city for recreational purposes. This act was commemorated with a huge stone monument expressing Barcelona's thanks to the generous dictator. The ironic reminder of enforced gratitude is still visible from the castle battlements.

Today, the mountain is a symbol of Barcelona's resiliency and rejuvenation; here, in 1992, the Summer Olympics will fulfill the city's collective dream. Montjuïc's main stadium, neglected for years, and exhibition halls, site of commercial fairs, are being readied for use as sports facilities. Pre-Olympian visitors to Montjuïc will not lack entertainment. In addition to its legendary view of Barcelona and the Mediterranean, the mountain offers several museums, lovely gardens, and a large amusement park. The best approach is from Pl. de Espanya, along Avda. Reina María Cristina. At the end of the esplanade are the **Fuentes Luminosas,** a string of fountains designed by Carlos Buigas and illuminated at night. One of Barcelona's most impressive sights, the fountains are especially enchanting when the light, water, and music interact in a mesmerizing, hour-long "concert." (Illuminated June to mid-Sept. Thurs. and Sat.-Sun 9pm-midnight; music show at 10pm; mid-Sept. to May Sat.-Sun. 8-11pm, music show at 9pm.)

At the end of the avenue, a stamina-testing staircase ascends to the **Palau Nacional,** the huge building that was the Spanish Pavilion during the 1929 International Exhibition. It now houses the **Museu d'Art de Catalunya,** one of the world's best Romanesque art collection. As humidity and foreign art collectors began to devour Catalunya's medieval painted chapels, teams of specialists carefully removed the works of art from their walls. Among the masterpieces exhibited are twelfth-century frescoes and Catalan Gothic paintings. In the same building, the **Museu de Cerámica's** collection spans the history of Spanish ceramics—from primitive Balearic pots to modern works. (Both museums open Tues.-Sun. 9am-2pm. Free.)

Following the road uphill to the right from the base of the fountains, you will come to the **Pavelló Mies van der Rohe,** the pavilion designed by the famous architect for Germany's exhibitions in the 1929 World's Fair. The simple lines and layout caused an uproar; defenders praised its innovations, while attackers compared it to the emperor's new clothes. (Open daily 10am-6pm.) From here, walk across the hillside to the **Poble Espanyol,** Barcelona's attempt to dissuade you from bothering to visit the rest of Spain. Built for the International Exhibition, it is a model town that displays architecture from every Spanish region. It boasts a Plaza Mayor (with a self-service cafeteria), a Calle de la Conquista, a Plazuela de la Iglesia, and so on. Go to the *barrio andaluz* if you think you won't make it to Andalucía, but beware that the fake walls of Avila are no substitute for the real thing. While prices here are expensive, you won't get another chance in Barcelona to see glassblowers and potters plying their trades. (Open daily 9am-8pm. Craftsmen close shop an hour early. Admission 350ptas, students 275ptas.)

The **Museu Arqueològic,** on the other side of the mountain on Carrer de Lleida, is worth a visit for its fine collection of Carthaginian art from Ibiza. There are numerous jewels and miniatures and several rooms are dedicated to relics found in the excavation of the Greco-Roman city of Empúries near Girona. Room XVI is especially interesting. The *Portrait of a Roman Lady* is a sensitive study of old age; a bronze bust of another Roman woman displays the curious "beehive" hairstyle of the first century. (Open Tues.-Sat. 9:30am-1pm and 4-7pm, Sun. 9:30am-1pm. Admission 100ptas, students 50ptas, Sun. free.) Up the street, the **Museu Etnològic** holds temporary exhibits on Asian cultures. (Open Tues.-Sat. 9am-8:30pm, Sun. 9am-2pm, Mon. 4-8:30pm. Free.)

Between museums, be sure to visit some of Montjuïc's many gardens. The **Jardín Botánico,** behind the Palau Nacional, nurtures a variety of exotic plants. (Open Mon.-Sat. 9am-2pm and 3-7pm.) A little up the road are the **Jardins Joan Maragall** and their sculptures. (Open Sun. 10am-2pm.) From there, you can visit the **Fundació Miró,** along the street on the way to the top. Designed by the famous Catalan architect Josep Lluís Sert after an international competition in 1975, the white concrete building commands a spectacular view of Barcelona. The permanent exhibit contains work from all periods of Joan Miró's life, including a 35-foot tapestry that explodes with brightly colored yarn. Two new wings provide more space for Miró's voluminous sculptures, including a rooftop patio with pieces resembling Play-Dough monsters from a psychedelic nightmare. The foundation also has a library and well-stocked art bookstore. (Open Tues.-Sat. 11am-7pm, Thurs. until 9:30pm, Sun. 10:30am-2:30pm. Admission 300ptas, students 150ptas.)

The end of the park closest to the sea contains a popular amusement park and the Montjuïc Castle, with its military museum. From the Fundació Miró, you can walk down the street and catch the *teleferique* (cable car) to the top. (Open daily 11:30am-2:30pm; in off-season Fri.-Sun. 11:30am-8:30pm. Fare 125ptas halfway up,

250ptas to the castle at the top.) If you come from Barcelona, you can ride the funicular from the Parallel metro stop (L3) to the bottom of the cable cars. (Operates daily 11am-9:30pm. Fare 55ptas.) The **Parc d'Atracciones** is at the cable car's mid-station. It flashes with rides of every description, including bumper cars and a roller coaster. (Open June 24-Sept. 10 Tues.-Fri. 6:15pm-12:15am, Sat. 6:15pm-1:15am, Sun. noon-12:15am; Sept. 11-June 23 Tues.-Sun. noon-9pm. Admission 250ptas; with use of rides 875ptas Tues.-Fri., 975ptas Sat.-Sun.)

Farther uphill is the historically rich **castle.** Since Franco turned it over to the city, the moats have become tidy flower beds, and amateur archers practice on a field in front of the walls. Enjoy the tremendous view of the busy port, the hazy city, and the blue Mediterranean. The **Museu Militar** inside contains an extensive collection of arms from the Spanish army and some paintings by Catalan artists. (Open Tues-Sat. 10am-2pm and 4-7pm, Sun. 10am-8pm. Admission 50ptas.)

Below the castle, off Avda. de Miramar, are the **Mossèn Costa i Llobera,** a splendid cactus garden, and **Mossèn Cinto Verdaguer.** From the tip of the park another *teleferique* crosses the harbor to deposit passengers on the breakwater. (Open July-Sept. 15 Mon.-Sat. noon-8pm, Sun. noon-9pm; Sept. 16-June Sat.-Sun. and holidays noon-5:30pm. One way 400ptas, round-trip 500ptas.)

Tibidabo

Come to Tibidabo for an amazing view of Barcelona. The mountain was actually named after the Latin words for "I shall give thee," which appear in St. Matthew's Gospel: *Haec omnia tibi dabo si cadens adoraberis me* ("All these things will I give thee, if thou wilt fall down and worship me"). The scene in which Satan tempts Jesus by offering him the world below could easily have taken place here. You can see Tibidabo's huge Temple del Sagrat Cor from several places in Barcelona. The church itself has little of artistic merit; indeed, the souvenir shop and pay telescopes tucked away in the building's spires might lead you to believe that its use for religious purposes was only an afterthought. Take advantage of the building's exploitation and ride the elevator to the top (round-trip 50ptas). From there, you can climb to the statue of Jesus, where the view can't get any better. Wander through the serene pine forests—on a clear day you can see Montserrat and the Pyrenees. There's another **Parc d'Atraccions,** but it's not nearly as good as Montjuïc's. (Open March 20-Sept. 15 Mon.-Fri. 10:30am-8:30pm, Sat.-Sun. 10:30am-9:30pm; Sept. 16-March 19 weekends and holidays only. Admission with rides 800ptas for an afternoon, 1000ptas all day.)

Designed to appeal to all ages and interests, the **Museu de Ciéncia** has become one of Barcelona's most popular museums. Only by twisting knobs, hitting vibrating surfaces, and observing can the visitor learn anything—so states the museum's official philosophy. Exhibit topics range from optics to wave motion. If you can't understand the Catalán and Spanish instructions stand back and let the first-graders show you the ropes. (Open Tues.-Sun. 10am-8pm. Admission 260ptas, students 160ptas. Admission to museum and ½-hr. planetarium show 475ptas, students 320ptas.) An FFCC train or bus #17 from Pl. de Catalunya can take you to Avda. del Tibidabo. From here, walk 2 blocks up the *avenida,* and turn left on C. Teodor Roviralta; the musuem is at the end of the street up a flight of stairs (10 min.). Follow the arrows that clearly mark the turns. To reach the mountain top, either wait 15 minutes for the *tranvía blau* (blue streetcar) or walk up Avda. Tibidabo in the same time. At the top of the street, you have to take a funicular. (Operates daily 7:30am-9:30pm. Round-trip 250ptas.)

Gràcia

Gràcia, absorbed by Barcelona in the construction of the Eixample, was not affected by the street-widening and the creation of airy open patios. Its narrow streets and numerous plazas confuse even *barcelonins* from outside the *barri.* Visit popular **Plaça Rius i Taulet.** The tower here is the **Torre del Reloj,** a symbol of revolution and change in the 1870s. **Plaça del Diamant,** on nearby Carrer d'Astúries, is a poetic landmark. Here, the heroine of popular novelist Merceè Rodoreda's novel, *La Plaça* *del Diamant,* falls to her knees and feels the sky closing in over her. Today she might find herself in the middle of a neighborhood basketball game.

Art nouveau did not leave Gràcia untouched. Carrer d'Astúries has such excellent examples as the beautiful facades of #13 and 15. One of Gaudí's youthful experiments, the **Casa Vicens,** is at Carrer de les Carolines, 24-26. Built for a local merchant, the house incorporates audacious variations on Islamic motifs. To get to Gràcia, take the metro to Fontana (L3).

Parc Güell

One of Antoni Gaudí's more ambitious plans was to create a park of 60 houses, incorporating his ideals of city planning. Lack of funding forced him to abandon the idea, and the land was turned into what is now **Parc Güell,** near Pl. Lesseps on Carrer Olot. (Take bus #24 from Passeig de Gràcia.) Inside the park, an elegant white staircase, lined with patterned tiles and a frightening multicolored salamander, leads you to a forest of pillars—86, to be exact—that support the pavilion that was to be the community's marketplace but is now just a good place to learn to ride a bike. Toward the back of the park, sweeping elevated paths, supported by columns shaped like palm trees, swerve through the park's large hedges and prehistoric plants. The **Casa-Museu Gaudí,** designed by Gaudí's associate Francisco Berenguer, has an eclectic *modernista* collection of designs, sensual furniture, and a few portraits. (Museum open Mon.-Thurs. 11am-1:30pm and 4:30-7:40pm, Fri. 11am-1:30pm, Sun. and holidays 10am-2pm and 4-7pm. Admission 100ptas. Park open May-Aug. daily 10am-9pm; Sept.-Oct. daily 10am-8pm; Nov.-Feb. daily 10am-6pm; March-April daily 10am-7pm. Free.)

Sarrià

Sarrià is an eminent residential district in uptown Barcelona. In the last century, before the Eixample was built, rich families came here from the city to spend the summer in their graceful villas. Nowadays, Sarrià's well-to-do residents still talk about "going down to Barcelona." A walk through the quarter's shady, peaceful streets reveals elegant mansions with manicured gardens, and a host of exclusive art nouveau *colegios* (private schools).

One of these schools, the **Colegio-Convento de Santa Teresa,** Carrer Ganduxer, 85, was designed by Gaudí in the 1880s. The brick facade is composed of high windows elongated by rows of his distinctive parabolic arches. Inside is a courtyard flanked by a corridor also built with these arches.

Two other works by Gaudí grace this area. The villa of **Bellesguard,** at Carrer Bellesguard, 46, is a good example of Gaudí's interpretation of Gothic Revival. The walls surrounding the villa used to belong to the royal summer residence of Margarita de Prades, wife of Martin I, King of Aragón. The **Finca Güell,** on Avda. de Pedralbes, 7, near Paseo de los Tilos and Paseo de Manuel Girona, sports an iron gate encrusted with a Gaudí dragon.

Off Passeig de Bonanova, the **Planetarium Barcelona,** C. Escoles Pies, 103, offers shows on the stars. (Shows Mon.-Fri. at 9:30am, 10:30am, 11:30am, 3pm, 4pm, and 5pm; Sun. at noon, 1pm, and 4:30pm. Admission 325ptas, students 250ptas.) **Museu Clarià,** C. Calatrava, 27, was home to Catalan sculptor Josep Clarà until his death in 1958. The building contains dozens of the artist's technically perfect, though somewhat cold, busts and nude studies. (Open Tues.-Sun. 9am-2pm. Free.) The planetarium and Museu Clarà can be reached by taking bus #22 from Passeig de Gracia or bus #64 from C. Aribau near the university.

In the first quarter of this century, the city of Barcelona built a summer residence for King Alfonso XIII in Sarrià. **Palau Pedralbes** was crafted after the style of the *palazzi* of the Italian Renaissance and is set in a large, peaceful garden. The spacious rooms inside contain the Colección Cambó, a small but impressive assortment of paintings by Raphael, Botticelli, Zurbarán, and El Greco. (Open Tues.-Sat. 10am-1pm and 4-6pm, Sun. 10am-1pm. Admission to the palace 200ptas, to the carriage museum nearby 100ptas, to both 250ptas. Metro: Palau Reial.)

The **Monastir de Pedralbes,** at the end of Passeig de la Reina Elisenda, has a fine three-story cloister from the fourteenth century. The three wings of the convent include huge kitchen hearths, an airy dining room, and the nuns' old infirmary. But the real artistic treasure is in the chapel of San Miguel. Ferrer Bassa's murals depict Mary's seven joys coupled with some of her low moments. The monastery recently received an excellent private collection of paintings from the famous collector Thyseen-Bornemisza. (Open Tues.-Sun. 9am-2pm. Free.)

Beaches

Dredging and sand-cleaning have made the **Barceloneta** an acceptable *playa.* It is accessible by foot, or take red-numbered bus 45 or 59. **Playa Mar Bella,** in Poble Nou, boasts somewhat cleaner waters, and is just a short ride from the city center (metro: Poble Nou, L3, or yellow-numbered bus 36 from Passeig Colón or red-numbered 141 from Pl. Universitat). If you take your beaching seriously, there's no reason to stay in Barcelona. Trains and buses can transport you to **Sitges** or **Sant Pol** in an hour or less. (See Near Barcelona.)

Entertainment

Every evening at about 5pm, a man sets up a box in the middle of Carrer Porta de l'Angel before the Galerías Preciados and, as a crowd gathers, sings opera, interspersing voluble commentary with his arias. Nightlife in Barcelona starts then and there, and winds up about 14 hours later. The city offers a perfect combination of exuberance and variety—if you leave without taking advantage of it, slink to the border in shame.

The daily papers *La Vanguardia* and *El País,* and the weekly *Guía del ocio,* an indispensable booklet, will be your best sources of information (60ptas at newsstands). *L'Informatui* is a monthly list of events put out by the Area de Joventut, C. Avinyó, 7. *Vivir en Barcelona,* a monthly guide to what's new in the city, incudes a small section for English visitors during July and August (350ptas at newsstands). Call 010 for information on doings in the city.

Concerts, Theater, and Film

Barcelona is, proudly, the only city in Spain to support a house devoted solely to opera, with a small concession made to ballet. The **Gran Teatre del Liceu,** Rambla de Caputxins, 61 (tel. 318 92 77), founded in 1847, is one of the world's leading stages. Its season lasts from September through July, when the box office is open from noon to 3pm and 5 to 10pm. (Metro: Liceu, L3.) Most classical music is performed at the **Palau de la Música Catalana,** an incredible brick art nouveau building, cleverly tucked away on Carrer Amadeu Vives, off Via Laietana near Pl. Urquinaona. You should see the building even if no tickets are available. Concerts cover all varieties of symphonic and choral music, and tickets run 500-14,000ptas. In winter, ask about free Tuesday night concerts. (Box office open June-July Mon.-Fri. 5-8pm.; Sept.-May Mon.-Fri. 11am-1pm and 5-8pm.) A music festival is organized during October. The **Conservatorio,** Carrer Bruc, 112, in the Eixample, is the city's one indoor classical music venue that remains in operation during the dog days of summer.

Theatrical offerings in Barcelona are no less satisfying, for those who understand Catalán. Fame of the first rank belongs to the **Teatre Lliure** (Free Theater), which has won respect with years of innovative productions. It's at Carrer Leopold Alas, 2 (tel. 218 92 51), in Gràcia. (Metro: Fontana, L3.) The company is often on tour in summer. The **Teatre Poliorama,** or Teatre Català de la Comèdieu, offers light theater, dishing up productions such as *Cyrano de Bergerac.* Look for it at Rambla Estudis, 115 (tel. 317 75 99).

Barcelona doesn't shut up its stage doors when summer arrives, however, the theater simply moves outdoors, primarily to the **Teatre Grec,** on Montjuïc, the Jardins de l'Hospital (Carrer Hospital, 56, in the Barri Gòtic), nearby Plaça del Rei, Parc de la Ciutadella, and the Poble Espanyol, for the fabulous *Grec* season. *Grec* (named for the Greek theater) offers music, theater, dance, films, folklore and a special program for young adults (Grec Jove). Prices start at 250ptas for the Banda Municipal concerts on Pl. del Rei (behind the cathedral) and go up to 1600ptas for concerts at the Poble Espanyol, which feature famous jazz and rock musicians. You can buy tickets at the door or at the Palau de la Virreina, Rambla, 99 (tel. 318 85 99; Mon.-Sat. 10am-7pm, Sun. 10am-2pm). You can also pick up a schedule of events here. Tickets for monster rock concerts held in the main soccer stadium or the sports palace are available in the booth on Gran Viá at C. Aribau, next to the university. (Open daily 10:30am-1:30pm and 4-7:30pm.) Other events can hardly hope to compete, but the suburban community at L'Hospitalet offers a respectable **L'Estiu a Ciutat** festival, with 440-700ptas tickets. Take the FFCC trains from Pl. d'Espanya.

Films are popular in Barcelona, and the theaters are immaculate. Besides Spanish and Catalán fare, you should be able to find a Hollywood classic or the hottest new flick in English. In the *Guía del Ocio,* "V.O." means "original version," with Spanish subtitles. It's customary to tip the usher who shows you to your seat 5-10ptas. Also check the offerings of the **Filmoteca**, Travessera de Gràcia, 63 (tel. 201 29 06), which screens classic, cult, exotic, and otherwise exceptional films. Tickets are only 200ptas. (Metro: Fontana, L3.) The end of June and beginning of July bring a **film festival** to Barcelona. For information and tickets, head to Rambla Catalunya, 57. (Open daiy 10am-2pm and 4:30-9pm.)

Discos, Clubs, Bars, and Dance Halls

Barcelonins take time to get revved up. The *paseo* starts in the early evening and is actually divided into two shifts: first the post-siesta burst of energy (around 5-7pm), then a second post-dinner wave (perhaps 9-11pm). The later stages of this *paseo* blend into the beginnings of a drink around 10 or 11pm, but only in a pub, cafe, or bar—not in a club or discotheque. Entrance to these chic establishments is delayed by the truly fashionable until 1 or 2am, though less image-conscious people do show up at midnight. Depending on your style of dress and hairdo, you may or may not get into the swanker bars and discos. Doormen may also invent a cover charge for men to prevent their numbers from overwhelming the *señoritas.*

Where to take your *paseo* is a decision in itself. Foreigners, prostitutes, and many *barcelonins* stalk the Rambles between Pl. de Catalunya and the Columbus monument. It's a unique show, but put your wallet in a front pocket, don't carry a purse, and stick to the center of the street. The pedestrian zone along **Carrer Porta de l'Angel,** between Pl. Nova and Pl. de Catalunya, is a nice, safe place to walk and watch, but chic *chicos* and *chicas* stick to **Rambla de Catalunya,** in the Eixample, and nearby streets, all of which are lined with trendy, exotic, and upwardly mobile places to eat and drink. The recent opening of the **Moll de la Fusta** on Passeig Marítim has brought five fancy bars to the former lumber dock.

Duetto, Carrer Consell de Cent, 294 (tel. 302 31 81), in the Eixample. One of the better discos, though the bouncer can be rude. Cover with 1 drink 800ptas. Open nightly 6pm-dawn.

La Gasolinera, Carrer Aribau, 97 (tel. 254 35 70). The gas pumps out front marks this bar of choice for the well-dressed and the young, who often book tables in advance. Drinks around 400ptas. Open Sun.-Thurs. until 2am, Fri.-Sat. until 3am.

Bikini, Avda. Diagonal, 570 (tel. 230 51 34), a 5-min. walk form Pl. Francesc Macia. Big-name musicians from Spain and abroad play here. Salsa, jazz, or rock are live Tues.-Thurs. Mini-golf in back for the young at heart. Cover starts at 500ptas.

Sisisi, Avda. Diagonal, 442 (tel. 237 56 73). Slick. Plexiglass floors illuminated by white lights from below. Open 7pm-dawn.

El Velódromo, C. Muntaner, 213, almost at the corner of Diagonal. An old-fashioned poolhall with a 2nd-floor loft where you can watch the action below. TV blares. Open Mon.-Sat. 9pm-1:30am.

Bar Bodegueta, Rambla Catalunya, 100 (tel. 215 41 94). This low-key wine and champagne cellar is a favorite with business people relaxing after work. Cramped quarters and small tables, but the overhead fans and walls lined with bottles will pry your attention away from the human squeeze. Champagne bottles from 500ptas; have a glass (150ptas) and *tapas.* Open Mon.-Sat. 7pm-1am.

Ebano, Carrer Roger de Flor, 114 (tel. 232 89 17), between Carrer Casp and Gran Via de les Corts Catalans. The crowd here, mainly in their 30s, enjoy dancing to African and Spanish music with a smattering of American hits. Bar serves a lethal concoction called "African cocktail." Cover 600ptas. Open Sept.-July Tues.-Sun. until 5am.

La Barretina, Carrer Sagristans, 9 (tel. 302 41 96), near Pl. Nova. Funky music alternates with astrology, seances, and fortune-telling at this bar/restaurant. *Menú* 650ptas. Open daily 1-4pm and 8pm-midnight for food, later for sorcery.

La Paloma, Carrer del Tigre, 27 (tel. 325 20 08). Somewhat less fancy, this dance hall attracts a friendly group—usually from nearby towns—that turns into a community by the end of an evening. Open Wed.-Sun. 11:15pm-2:30am, Fri.-Sat. 11:15pm-3am.

Bodega Bohemia, Carrer Lancaster, 2 (tel. 302 50 61). Another tradition: part-cafe, part-dance hall. All sorts of people come to dance to all sorts of music. Open nightly 10:30pm-early morning.

Harlem, C. Comtessa Sabradiel, 8 (tel. 310 07 55), off C. de Avinyó. A new jazz club with live performances Thurs. and Sun. No cover. Shows start around 10pm. Closes at 3am.

Studio 54, Avda. del Paral-lel, 64 (tel. 329 54 54), on teh opposite side of Barri Xinés from the Rambles. Unlike the New York disco, this has lost neither its popularity nor its pizazz. Famous rock groups sometimes play here. Open Fri.-Sun. midnight-dawn; cover 700ptas. Early sessions Sat.-Sun. 6:30am-10pm; cover 300ptas.

La Cova del Drac, Carrer Tuset, 30 (tel. 217 56 42). Popular with avant-garde jazz musicians. Shows start at 10:30pm. Cover 300-800ptas. Open Wed.-Sun.

Members, C. Seneca, 3 (tel. 237 12 04). Everyone is happy, and everyone is a member. This is one place where your clothes or haircut won't prevent you from hitting the cramped dance floor and having a blast. When the Communards play, the walls nearly crumble. No cover. Open nightly until 3am.

Monroe's Gallery-Bar, Carrer Lincoln, 3 (tel. 237 56 78). Gay people will find this a subdued place for a drink. Marilyn's face gazes at the low-key surroundings from various spots on the wall. Open daily 7pm-3am.

Zeleste, C. Almogavers, 122 (tel. 309 12 04), a 15-minute walk from Passeig Lluis Companys, or take the NL bus (11pm-4:30am). Located in an old warehouse, this dance club has rooftop terraces, video rooms, and live performances by well-known new wave acts. Despite its distance from the city center, it takes off at 2:30am, when the dance floor fills up. Cover around 900ptas.

666, C. Llull, 145, on a street parallel to Zeleste's. A multi-level nightspot with necrophiliac decor on one floor and more conventional scenery upstairs. Open until hell freezes over.

Bullfights, Sardanas, and Fiestas

While few Catalans are aficionados of bullfighting, Barcelona does maintain **Plaça Monumental,** a modernist bullring on Gran Vía at Passeig Carles I. Spain's best matadors don't risk their entrails in a Barcelona show, so go to Madrid, Sevilla, or Córdoba for better action. If you don't mind a green bullfighter, obtain tickets at Carrer Muntaner, 24 (tel. 253 38 21), near Pl. Universitat. (Open Thurs.-Sun. 10am-1pm and 4-8pm. Tickets start at 1300ptas. Tickets also sold at the box office before the start of the *corrida.* Bullfights normally take place on Sundays at 5 or 6pm; the season runs from June to October. The bullring also houses a **museum** of bullfighting history. (Open daily 10am-1pm and 3:30-6pm.)

One of Barcelona's most beautiful sights is the *sardana,* Catalunya's regional dance. Teen-agers and grandparents join hands to dance in a circle in celebration of Catalan unity. The dance's steps are intricate and precise; all the circles of people pop up at the same time. You can see the *sardanes* in front of the cathedral Saturday at 7pm and Sunday at noon or on Avda. Portal de l'Angel at noon on Saturday. Dances are also held in Pl. de Sant Jaume on Sundays at 7pm and in other locations throughout the city on Tuesday, Thursday, and Friday. Times change, and some dances are not held in August, so consult papers for current information.

Fiestas are as abundant as everything else in Barcelona. Before Christmas, **Santa Lucía Fair** fills Pl. de la Catedral and the area around Sagrada Família with stalls and booths. **Carnival** is celebrated wildly, and soon thereafter comes **St. George's Day,** April 23, the feast of Catalunya's patron saint and Barcelona's answer to St. Valentine's Day. Men give women a rose, and women reciprocate with a book. On May 11 is the **Feast of Saint Ponç;** the traditional market of aromatic and medicinal herbs and honey is set up in Carrer Hospital, close to the Rambles. On June 23, the night before **Día de Sant Joan,** there is dancing and a bonfire on Montjüic. Gràcia's **Festa Major** is one of Barcelona's biggest bashes (Aug. 15-21). The plazas and streets are draped in lights; rock bands and latin groups play all night.

During September, the **Feria de Cuina i Vins de Catalunya** brings wine and *butifarra* producers to the Rambla de Catalunya. For one week you can sample fine food and drink for a small ticket price. When the patron saint of Barcelona, **Verge de la Mercé,** is celebrated on September 24, the city erupts in fireworks and bustles with *correfocs,* insane parades of people dressed as devils, whirling around with pitchfork-shaped sparklers; buckets of water are thrown at the demons from balconies overlooking the fiery streets. During November, a **jazz festival** swings the city's streets and clubs.

Shopping

Everything you want but can't afford can be found in the elegant shops along Passeig de Gràcia and the Rambla de Catalunya, while things you probably can afford but may not want jam the tacky tourist traps along the Rambles. A great place for souvenirs is the **Centre Permanent D'Artesania,** Passeig de Gràcia, 55 (tel. 215 54 08), though it's not particularly cheap. Here Catalan artisans display and sell their beautiful crafts, from wicker baskets to clay bowls. (Open Mon.-Fri. 9am-2pm and 4-7pm, Sat. 11am-2pm and 5-7pm, Sun. 11am-2pm.) For antiques, try **Carrer Banys Nous** in the Barri Gòtic—it's lined with tiny shops, but prices and quality vary widely. Painters gather in Pl. del Pi to sell their creations. (Sat. 11am-8pm, Sun. 11am-2pm.) An antique market is held on Thursday from 9am to 8pm in Pl. Nova, and the famous **Els Encants** flea market takes place every Monday, Wednesday, Friday, and Saturday from 9am to 8pm on C. Consell de Cent at C. Dos de Maig, near Pl. Les Glòries. (Metro: Glòries, L1.) Philatelists and numismatists will love the market held Sunday from 10am to 2pm in Pl. Reial; a coin and book market is held at the same time in the Mercat de Sant Antoni.

Of the several department stores in Barcelona, **El Corte Inglés,** on Pl. de Catalunya (tel. 302 12 12), deserves mention. It is huge, crowded, well-stocked, and staffed by multilingual salespeople. The rooftop cafeteria commands an excellent view, but it's expensive. **Galerías Preciados,** a department store on Carrer Portal de l'Angel, runs a cafeteria on the roof, as well as a pet shop with a wonderful collection of birds (including a toucan) and a feisty monkey. (Both stores open Mon.-Fri. 10am-8pm, Sat. 10am-9pm.) **VIPS** may have only a fraction of the floor space, but it crams books, records, a food store, and a cafe into its late-night locale on the Rambla Catalunya, above Pl. Catalunya. (Open Sun.-Thurs. 8am-1:30am, Fri.-Sat. 8am-3am.)

Near Barcelona

Sitges and Castelldefels

While a resort for the tan-hungry chic, **Sitges** has managed to retain its charm through its vibrant Spanish population, old streets, and whitewashed houses, decorated brightly with flowers and ceramic tiles. Also home to a strong international gay community, Sitges buzzes with activity year-round.

In summer, the main beaches get crowded, but you can walk to less crowded areas to your right, where you'll also find nude sunbathing about 45 minutes away. Walk along the shore to the Solarium Club (on your right), then over the hill or through the train tunnel and left. The beach is mixed stone and sand with some surf. Over another hill is the largely gay area of the beach.

If you can tear yourself away from the golden sands, Sitges has several museums, reminders of a nineteenth-century attempt to turn the village into an artists' colony. Just behind the church on Carrer del Fonollar is the **Museu Cau Ferrat,** which contains works by Miguel Utrillo, Santiago Russinyol, and El Greco. The **Museu Maricel del Mar,** in an annex next door, has a good collection of medieval paintings and sculpture. (Both open Tues.-Sun. 10am-1pm and 5-7pm, Sun. 10am-1pm. Admission 150ptas.) The **Museu Romàntic** (Can Llopis), on Carrer San Josep, is an eighteenth-century bourgeois house filled with period pieces, including working music boxes and the Lola Anglada Collection of seventeenth- to nineteenth-century dolls. (Open Tues.-Sat. 10am-1pm and 5-7pm, Sun. 10am-2pm. Admission 125ptas, students free.)

Sitges is most beautiful during the spring **Fiesta of Corpus Christi,** when hundreds of thousands of flowers carpet the streets in fantastic patterns. This dazzling display of color and design lasts only one day on the Thursday following the ninth Sunday after Easter. For more raucous fun, visit during the **Festa Major** (Aug. 23-26).

A resort town, Sitges is not a cheap place to stay or eat. A good place to spend the night is the **Terminus Hostal,** Avda. de les Flores, 7 (tel. 894 02 93), across the train tracks. The hotel has a friendly owner (1200ptas per person). Slightly more expensive but more conveniently located is **Hostal Residencia Lido,** Carrer Bonaire, 16 (tel. 894 48 48). The large rooms are just 30m from the beach (1500ptas per person). While you won't find anything incredibly inexpensive to eat in Sitges, **Joan,** Carrer Nou, 13 (tel. 894 11 70), has two *menús*—500ptas and 700ptas—with surprisingly good food; the *merluza* is fresh and tasty. (Open Mon.-Sat. 1-4pm and 8-11pm.) **El Superpollo,** on Carrer Marquez de Montroig, serves *pollos para llevar* (½-chicken, 320ptas).

The **tourist office** tries to hide itself at the corner of the "Oasis" shopping mall, Passeig Vilafranca (tel. 894 12 30). From the train station, turn right and go downhill until you see Oasis signs on the right. (Open Mon.-Fri. 9am-9pm, Sat.-Sun. 10am-1pm and 5-8pm; in off-season Mon.-Sat. 10am-1pm and 4-6pm.) Should your belongings get stolen—one woman walked back to Barcelona in her bikini last year—call the **municipal police,** Pl. Ajuntament (tel. 894 00 00). You can get **medical attention** at the hospital on Carrer Hospital (tel. 894 00 03). The **post office** is on Pl. Espanya. (Open Mon.-Fri. 9am-2pm.) To get to this village, take the RENFE train from Barcelona (2 per hr., 50 min., round-trip 300ptas).

Castelldefels is another resort on the same train line. There's a bit more grit and less glitter here, but the beach is enormous and it's only 20 minutes from Barcelona (get off at Platja de Castelldefels). When commuting to either beach, try to head out in the morning and return in early afternoon or late evening; train cars are often packed. You can also take the UC bus from Pl. Universitat in Barcelona to Castelldefels.

Terrassa

Inland from Barcelona, Terrassa (Tarrasa) is a rather unattractive industrial town that does, however, showcase a few excellent monuments and museums. If you arrive by RENFE train (35 min., round-trip 250ptas), walk down Carrer del Mas Adey across from the station and turn left on Carrer de la Creu Gran. Across the narrow cobblestoned bridge rises the impressive Romanesque-Visigothic complex of **Sant Pere d'Egara,** a National Monument, built on the site of the Roman city of Egara. The Carolingian baptistry dates from the sixth century B.C.E. and has eight Roman columns of different diameters supporting a central dome. (Open May-Sept. Tues.-Sat. 9:30am-1:30pm and 3:30-7:30pm; Oct.-April Tues.-Sat. 9:30am-1pm and 3-6pm.)

Behind the church compound is Parc de Vallparadís, an overgrown, untended park where people park their cars. However, if you go up the other side, you'll come out on Carrer de Salmerón right by the **Museu Tèxtil,** one of the best of its kind in the world. The museum has important collections of Coptic, Byzantine, and Hispano-Arab textiles. (Open Tues.-Sat. 10am-1pm and 5-8pm, Sun. 10am-2pm. Admission 60ptas, students free.) If you're bored by displays of cloth and costumes, visit the **Castell-Cartoixa de Sant Jaume de Vallparadís** next door. This twelfth-century monastery encloses the small municipal art museum. (Open Tues.-Fri. 4-7pm, Sat.-Sun. 10am-2pm. Free.) The **Casa-Museu Alegre de Sagrera,** on Carrer de la Font Vella in the town center, contains a collection of Chinese art and has a lovely turn-of-the-century garden in back. (Museum open Sun. 10am-2pm. Gardens open Tues.-Sat. 10am-2pm and 5-7pm, Sun. 10am-2pm.)

Terrassa offers little in the way of restaurants or accommodations, since most visitors come just for the day. A convenient place for lunch is **Cafeteria Catalonia 2,** Passeig Comte d'Egara, 13-15 (tel. 783 37 27), near the main square across the bridge at the end of Carrer Salmerón, with good three-course *menús* for 600ptas and 750ptas.

Montserrat

Like huge bubbles of frozen steam, the boulders of Montserrat burst out of the Llobregat Valley, an arid agricultural region that gives no hint of its geological treasure. Amidst this natural wonderland resides *La Virgen de Montserrat,* Catalunya's spiritual leader. Each year thousands of pilgrims come to the mountain's monastery to worship the virgin's wooden image.

Founded in 1025 by Oliba, abbot of Ripoll and bishop of Vic, the monastery grew quickly, attracting so many fervent pilgrims that by the thirteenth century the Romanesque buildings had to be enlarged. Expansion continued, making the monastery a splendid conglomeration of architectural styles, but the work of generations was reduced to rubble by Napoleon's army in 1812. The present buildings—heavy and somewhat cold—date from the late nineteenth century, though two wings of the old Gothic cloister survive just left of the monastery. Some 80 Benedictine monks now occupy the site, tending the shrine, working in the ceramics and goldsmithing shops, and distilling *aromas de Montserrat,* an herbal liqueur that you can sample at the snack bar.

The most important buildings cluster around **Plaça Santa María.** The **basilica,** whose lovely original facade was relegated to an inner courtyard following construction of the modern facade in 1968, is dark, cavernous, and ornate, glowing with the flicker of dozens of suspended votive lamps, each one the gift of a different city or organization. Above the altar hangs a crucifix that combines a sixteenth-century ivory figure of Jesus with a modern metal cross. In the balcony beyond it stands the twelfth-century polychrome figure of Mary and child, affectionately called *La Moreneta* (literally "the brown one"). Access to the statue is through an outside door to the right of the basilica. (Open daily 6-10:30am and noon-6:30pm.)

The **Museu de Montserrat,** on the *plaça,* was also reconstructed after Napoleon's rampage. The antiquity section, by the Gothic cloister, contains religious paintings by El Greco and Caravaggio. You'll also find the Virgin's crown, a gift from the people of Catalunya upon accepting her as the *patrona* of the region, and various artifacts from biblical lands, including a mummified crocodile more than 2000 years old. The modern section, under the *plaça* in front of the monastery, contains a collection of Catalan paintings from the Renaixença movement, including several beautiful portraits downstairs by Ramón Casas. *El Viejo Pescador* (1895) by Picasso hangs upstairs. (Antique section open daily 10am-2pm and 3-6pm. Modern section open daily 10:30am-2:30pm and 3:30-6pm. Admission 175ptas, students 100ptas.)

Some make a different kind of pilgrimage to Montserrat: From the *plaça,* you might be able to hear mountain climbers hammering petons into the sheer walls that jut into the sky. Covered with lush vegetation and rarely without a cool, clear breeze, the mountain makes a perfect place for a hike. The adventuresome can head straight up the valley, away from the *plaça,* to find a quiet spot for a picnic. Most pilgrims, however, follow the many walkways that lead to shrines or old hermitages, all of which command amazing views of the surrounding valleys.

You can reach two of the hermitages with the help of a funicular. The one to **Sant Joan** takes you uphill for a beautiful view of the monastery and shrine. From there, you can walk 15 minutes to the hermitage along a path that overlooks the valley. (Funicular operates April-Oct. every 20 min. 10am-6:40pm. One way 300ptas, round-trip 480ptas.) The other funicular takes you down to **Santa Cova,** where the image of the Virgin was supposedly found. The road to the shrine is lined with religious works by famous Catalan artists such as Gaudí and Puig i Cadafelch. The seventeenth-century building has the shape of a cross and a reproduction of the Virgin's image. (Chapel open April-Oct. daily 9am-6:30pm; Nov.-March daily 10am-5:30pm. Funicular runs April-Oct. 10am-7pm. One way 115ptas, round-trip 180ptas.) You can also walk down to Santa Cova, taking a path that starts near Pl. de la Creu.

Some of the best views, however, can be reached only on foot. You can follow the path that starts between the two funicular stations and follows the tree-shaded contour of the mountain. A 20-minute walk will bring you to a lookout from which you can see Barcelona on a clear day. Even more spectacular sites can be seen from the route to the hermitage of **Sant Jeroni,** which starts near the hermitage of Sant Joan. The path provides some of the better views of Montserrat's famous rock formations—enormous domes and serrated outcroppings that often bear an eerie resemblance to human faces. From the chapel, a flight of stairs leads to the **Peak of Sant Jeroni,** the area's highest at 1235m. On a clear day, you can see a large segment of the coast, the Balearic Islands, and the eastern Pyrenees in all their grandeur. Just 500m down the road from this lower station is the former **Monastery of Santa Cecilia.** The attractive church dates from the tenth century, but the apses, with their distinctive Lombardic arches, were added a century later.

To visit other shrines, try **Via Crucis,** which starts behind Pl. de l'Abat Oliba, or **Via del Magnific.** The latter will take you near the **Escoliniá,** the residence and school of Montserrat's famed boys' choir. The choir sings the *Salve Regina* and the *Virolai,* Montserrat's hymn, daily at 1pm, and the Montserratine *Salve* with the monks at 7pm, but the choir is on vacation in July.

If you wish to spend the night, inquire at the building that says **Despatx de Celles** (Tel. 835 02 51, ext. 230; open daily 9am-1:20pm and 3-6pm). They can set you up with a monastically simple cell. (774 ptas per person. Reservations recommended. No singles Nov.-March.) Just up the hillside beyond the Sant Joan funicular there is a **campground** with cold showers (185ptas per person and per tent). Food on the mountain—either at the self-service restaurant or in one of the shops—is expensive and dull. More appealing, though no less expensive, is the tiny morning **market** in the square. Every day merchants from the farms trundle up, bringing fruit, nuts, and dairy products to tempt the hungry hordes. Try some clotted curds with honey; they sound much better in Catalán: *mel i mató.*

For more details on how to navigate your way through the mountains, go to the **information booth** on Pl. de la Creu (tel. 835 02 51, ext. 186), where the staff speaks English. (Open Mon.-Sat. 10am-7pm; in off-season 10am-2pm and 4-5pm.) Their *Official Guide to Montserrat* is especially useful. It contains maps, schedules, pictures, history, and detailed descriptions of various walks in the area. If this can't sell you on the region, check out the free, 14-minute **audio-visual presentation** around the corner, shown at 11am, 11:30am, noon, 12:30pm, 3:30pm, 4pm, 5pm, and 5:30pm. Just up the street from the tourist office is the **post office.** (Open Mon.-Fri. 9am-1pm and 2-5pm, Sat. 9am-1pm.) You can change money next door at "La Caixa." (Open Mon.-Fri. 9:15am-2pm.) For an **ambulance** or mountain rescue team, call 835 02 51 (ext. 162). The **Guardia Civil** in the main plaza can be reached at 835 00 85.

Montserrat makes a good daytrip from Barcelona. **Auto/Transporte Julia,** Pl. Universitat, 12 (tel. 318 72 38), runs two buses per day at 8am and 9am; they return at 5pm and 6pm. (One way 300ptas, round-trip 600ptas.) It's more fun, however, to take the **Ferrocarrils de Catalunya** trains from Pl. Espanya (Manresa line). There are 5 trains per day and the 875ptas round-trip fare (railpasses not valid) includes the ride up by cable car from the station at **Aeri de Montserrat**—be sure not to get off early at Olesa de Montserrat. The first cable car up leaves at 10:20am, and the last one down is at 6:45pm in summer. Be sure to look at the train schedule carefully before deciding when to descend: the cable car trips are coordinated with arriving trains, but less so with departures. If you've arrived by car to the station, the ticket up in the cable car costs 266ptas, round-trip 532ptas.

Tarragona

In Roman times Tarragona was considered one of the empire's finest foreign creations; its buildings were elaborate and extensive, its population large, and its wine world-renowned. The settlement of Tarraco, founded in 218 B.C.E., was raised to the status of a province by Julius Caesar in 45 B.C.E., and its name inflated correspondingly to Colonia Julia Urbi Triumphalis Tarraconensis, a change that must have left local schoolchildren sobbing in their togas. Present-day Tarragona has preserved the remains of this Roman settlement, sprinkled throughout its wide avenues and bustling streets. The predominantly family crowd here spends less time in discos than strolling down the street for a *paseo*. On Sunday afternoons Passeig de les Palmeres is packed with families gazing out over the azure Mediterranean.

Orientation and Practical Information

The older part of the city sits on a hill around the cathedral overlooking the sea. **Ramblas Nova** and *Vella* run parallel to each other and perpendicular to the shore halfway down the hill. The Rambla Nova, divided by a wide tree-lined walkway, marks the boundary between the old and new parts of town. From the sea end, you can gaze straight through the city to the mountains behind it. Farther down, the grid-patterned streets of the newer part are home to the train station. To reach the center of the old part from the train station, take a right and walk up to the stairs parallel to the shore. The second street after reaching the top of the stairs is Rambla Vella; your third right off the street will take you to **Plaça de la Font,** a center of activity. Bus #1 ("Catedral") will also bring you to this part of town, albeit several blocks farther up the Rambla (40ptas, on Sun. 45ptas.).

Tourist Office: Carrer Fortuny, 4 (tel. 23 34 15), off Rambla Nova, 5 blocks from the ocean end (to your left as you walk away from the ocean). A bit mum. The indexed map is a real help. Open Mon.-Fri. 8am-3pm, Sat. 9am-2pm. **Municipal Tourist Office,** just below the cathedral steps at Carrer Major, 39 (tel. 23 89 22). Often more helpful, especially on cultural events. Open July-Sept. Mon.-Fri. 9:30am-1:30pm and 4-7pm, Sat. 9:30am-1:30pm. The **Ayuntamiento,** on Plaça de la Font, has piles of handouts on the province and local beaches and may be more reliable than the municipal tourist office. Open Tues.-Fri. 9am-2pm and 3-6pm, Sat. 9am-1pm and 4-7pm.

Post Office: Plaça de Corsini (tel. 21 01 49), 2 blocks below Rambla Nova. Open for stamps, Lista de Correos, and certified mail Mon.-Fri. 8am-9pm, Sat. 9am-7pm. **Telegrams:** Same address and hours. **Postal Code:** 43000.

Telephones: Rambla Nova (#74) at Carrer Fortuny. Open Mon.-Sat. 9am-10pm. **Telephone Code:** 977.

Train Station: Plaça de la Pedrera (tel. 23 36 43), on the waterfront at the base of the hill. Information office open daily 6am-10pm. English spoken. To Madrid (4 per day, 8 hr., 2510ptas), Barcelona (32 per day, 1 hr., 420ptas), Zaragoza (6 per day, 3½ hr., 1090ptas), Lleida (4 per day), and Córdoba-Málaga-Sevilla (3 per day). **RENFE,** Rambla Nova, 40 (tel. 23 28 61). Tickets and inquiries. Open Mon.-Fri. 9am-1pm.

Bus Station: Plaça Imperial Tarraco (tel. 22 91 26). To Valencia (1 per day, 3 hr., 1400ptas), Alicante (5 per week, 8 hr., 2505ptas), Málaga (3 per week, 8½ hr., 5450ptas), Lérida (3 per day, 2½ hr., 560ptas), and Barcelona (18 per day, 1½ hr., 490ptas).

Car Rental: Auto Sport, Edificio Hotel Imperial Tarraco (tel. 23 77 28), at the beginning of Rambla Vella. Open Mon.-Fri. 9am-1pm and 4-8pm, Sat. 9am-1pm.

English Bookstore: Librería Adsera, Rambla Nova, 94*bis* (tel. 23 58 15). A wide variety of books on every subject, including English-language novels. Open Mon.-Fri. 9am-1pm and 4-8pm, Sat. 9am-1pm.

Medical Emergency: Casa Socorro, Rambla Vella, 14 (tel. 23 50 12). **Protección Civil,** Pl. Imperial Tarraco (tel. 006), handles any kind of emergency.

Police: Comisaria de Policía, Pl. d'Orleans (tel. 23 33 11). **Emergency:** Tel. 091 or 092.

Accommodations and Camping

Most of Tarragona's cheap places to stay are full of boarders and tend to stay that way. If you can't get into the youth hostel, try Plaça de la Font, but cheap singles may still be hard to find.

Residencia Juvenil Sant Jordi (IYHF), Carrer de Marqués de Guad-El-Jelu (tel. 21 01 95). At the end of Rambla Nova, cross the traffic circle to Avda. Prest. Lluis Companys and take a right after 2 blocks. Hovers on the outskirts of Tarragona, but the price is unbeatable, and the facilities well-kept and well-lighted. Large TV screen attracts boisterous local crowd. 5 days max. stay (more if there are vacancies). Reception open 7-8pm. Check-out 9:30am. Curfew 11pm, but negotiable. Members only, 525ptas.

Pensión Planelles, Rambla Vella, 31 (tel. 23 81 15). Clean rooms, freshly painted in shiny colors. Tantalizing ice-cream shop downstairs. 850ptas per person.

Pensión Marsal, Plaça de la Font, 26 (tel. 22 40 69). Another simple, slightly ragged place, but the location is great. Clean, quiet rooms. Singles 700ptas. Doubles 1300ptas.

Hostal la Unión, Carrer de la Unio, 50 (tel. 23 21 41). Homey rooms scattered about a fairly clean apartment. You might end up sleeping in the same room as someone else, but the price is right: 600ptas per person.

Fondas Acuario, Carrer Granada, 1 (tel. 23 43 01), in the old quarter near the cathedral. Sign proclaims this a "paradise of tranquility," but the owner's yapping lap dogs seem determined to prove otherwise, and the fly-infested building is desperately in need of renovation. Not likely to have vacant rooms in the summer, but worth a try in the off-season. Singles 550ptas. Doubles 950ptas. Triples 1250ptas. Quads 1450ptas.

Camping is fairly convenient in Tarragona. Several sites line the road toward Barcelona (Via Augusta or CN-340) along the beaches north of town. To reach any of them, take bus #3A or 3B from Plaça de Corsini, opposite the *mercado* (every 20 min., last bus 10pm, 45ptas, 50ptas on Sun.). The closest is **Tarraco** (tel. 23 99 89), 2km away at Platja Rabassada. (Open June to mid-Sept. 350ptas per person and per car; 240ptas per tent.)

Food

While Tarragona's prices tend toward the expensive, the large and active port makes seafood-eating a treat. If your energy and budget are up to it, search out a local dish called *el romesco,* which consists of fish prepared in a sauce of local wine, special pepper, Tarragonan hazelnuts, and breadcrumbs. For do-it-yourself meals, visit Tarragona's excellent **indoor market** at Plaça Corsini by the post office. Both food and many other wares (goldfish, plants, baby ducks, hard candy) are offered, and merchants spill outdoors onto the plaça. (Open Mon.-Fri. 7am-1pm, Sat. 7am-1pm and 7-9pm.)

Restaurante El Plata, Carrer August, 20 (tel. 23 22 23), between Rambla Vella and Rambla Nova, in the pedestrian zone. You can choose to sit at their outdoor tables (near the fountain) or eat in their carved-wood dining room with its view of the kitchen (where the cooks assemble your meal practically from scratch). Inexpensive for the area. *Combinados* from 425ptas, *menú* 700ptas. Open daily 1-4pm and 8-11pm.

Mesón El Caserón,, Trinquet Nou, 4 (tel. 23 93 28), just off Plaça de la Font. Casual, family atmosphere. Delicious, plain food. Roast chicken 275ptas, *paella* 475ptas, *menú* 675ptas. Open daily 8-11pm.

Bar Turia, Plaça de la Font, 26 (tel. 22 40 69). Well-cooked fish. Huge salads with the 550ptas *menúú.* Open Mon.-Sat. 1-3:30pm and 9-10:30pm.

Lina Pizzeria, Carrer de la Unió, 41*bis* (no phone). A large selection of crisp pizzas makes this place a local Sun. night favorite. Ignore the credit card decals on the window. Pizzas 320-450ptas. Open daily 10am-midnight.

Sights

Tarragona's sights span centuries, but the city is especially rich in Roman and medieval remains. The most ancient of these lie on the city's edges. East of the Balcón del Mediterráneo are the ruins of a Roman **amphitheater,** built using the sea as a backdrop and the hill as a natural slope for the tiers. A bishop and two deacons were martyred here in 259. Recent excavations have unearthed traces of an ancient Christian church erected to commemorate their deaths. Today a small park encircles the site, a cool refuge from the afternoon heat.

Climbing up to Passeig Sant Antoni and turning right will bring you to the crooked streets of the old town. Monuments and museums sprout up on every other corner. The **Museu Arqueològic** boasts a fun collection of statues, friezes, ancient utensils, and mosaics, including the wonderful *Head of Medusa*. (Open Tues.-Sat. 10am-1pm and 4:30-8pm, Sun. 10am-2pm; in winter Tues.-Sat. 10am-1:30pm and 4-7pm, Sun. 10am-2pm. Admission 100ptas, students free. Tues. free.) The museum adjoins the **Pretori Romà**, a palace that housed Tarragona's governors in the first century B.C.E. Tradition has it that Pontius Pilate was born here during his father's term of office. Tunnels linked the palace with the Roman circus, and the vaults were used as dungeons, a function they again served during the Spanish Civil War.

Nearby, you will find the Gothic **cathedral** built on the site of the Roman Temple of Jupiter. The altarpiece, carved in about 1430, dedicated to the city's patron Santa Tecla, dominates the apse. Nineteen chapels line the north and south aisles. Of particular interest are the Capilla de Nuestra Señora de Montserrat and its fifteenth-century altarpiece, and the baroque Capilla de Santa Tecla. The large cloister (center at back on the left) was built in the twelfth and thirteenth centuries. It displays beautiful handiwork on the capitals, portals, and arches; just to the left of the church door you can see the whimsical relief, the *Procession of the Rats*. Notice that the arches and geometric decoration are clearly Romanesque (smooth, curved arches), while the vaulting is Gothic, coming to a point above the walkway. Set into the west wall is a tenth-century Muslim *mihrab*, most likely a trophy captured in battle. The **Museu Diocesà**, in the east gallery, contains an important collection of Roman and Iberian pottery, religious images from medieval and Renaissance times, and valuable tapestries that stretch to the ceiling and depict scenes of medieval life. (Cathedral open Mon.-Sat. 10am-12:30pm and 4-7pm; in winter Mon.-Sat. 10am-12:30pm and 4-6pm. Admission 100ptas.)

Above the cathedral, wrapping around the old town stretches an archeology buff's paradise. **Passeig Arqueològic** reflects aspects of all ages of Tarragona's history, from foundations laid long before the Roman invasion to a twentieth-century statue. The imposing ruins of the ancient city walls date from the third century B.C.E. and were erected on an even older base—massive cyclopean stones put into place by the city's founders early in the first millennium B.C.E. The ramparts were restructured in the Middle Ages and again in the seventeenth century; now Moorish and Catalan towers guard the ancient gates, and rusting cannons stand near Roman statues and pillars. The walkway around the rampart's base is attractive, passing through flower gardens and providing a pleasant view of the surrounding countryside. (Open Tues.-Sat. 9am-1:30pm and 4-7pm, Sun. 10am-1:30pm; in winter Tues.-Sat. 10am-1:30pm and 3-5pm. Admission 100ptas.) In July and August the walls are illuminated at night, and free performances of Catalan dances occur on Saturdays at 10:30pm.

Tarragona was a city of two forums; one for local commerce and government, the other devoted to administering the affairs of the province. Though some remains of the provincial forum are preserved (just down the street from the cathedral, at Plaça del Fòrum), the **Fòrum Local** is more impressively maintained, on a site now halved by a street, but connected by footbridge. The ruins form an open-air museum in the center of the city that is especially attractive in late afternoon when the light falls softly on the ancient golden-brown columns. The entrance is on Carrer Lleida, near the post office. (Open Tues.-Sat. 10am-1pm and 4-7pm, Sun. 10am-1pm. Free.) Farther out of town on Passeig Independència are the **Necròpolis** and **Museu Paleocristià.** This enormous early Christian burial site has yielded a rich variety of urns, tombs, and sarcophagi, the best of which are on display in the museum at its center. (Museum open same hours as Museu Arquelògic; same admission fee or use the same ticket. Necropolis free.)

A bus from Carrer Christòfor Colom to San Salvador (every 15 min., 40ptas, on Sun. 45ptas) and a walk 1km back toward Tarragona, or a 4-kilometer hike from town through the woods, will bring you to the perfectly preserved **Roman aqueduct** called the *Puente del Diablo* (Devil's Bridge). The aqueduct's two tiers of weathered arches stretch for 217m through a peaceful pine forest.

For a break from history and a fishy assault on your nostrils, visit **El Serrallo,** Tarragona's fishing district, next to the port. Long, thin streets wind through the *barrio,* brightly colored fishing boats line up neatly at dock, and plenty of seafood restaurants charge plenty of money. You can take bus #1 ("Náutico") or walk. From the station, go down Carrer Comerça and take a long right on Carrer Reial (which starts as A. Clavé) until you reach Carrer Pere Martell; take a left for 1 block, then duck under the bridge. The best time to go is in late afternoon, when the boats return and the fish are auctioned.

The rather well-hidden access to **Platja del Miracle (beach),** directly below town, is along Baixada del Miracle, starting off Pl. Arce Ochotorena, beyond the Roman amphitheater. **Platjas Rabassada, Sabinosa,** and **Llarga,** north of town, are larger beaches—to reach them, take bus #3A or 3B from Pl. Corsini (40ptas, on Sun. 45ptas). These uncrowded beaches make for great walking.

Entertainment

Around *paseo* time (7pm or so), local sources have it that the only cool place to perch is under the awnings of **Moto Club Tarragona,** Rambla Nova, 53 (tel. 23 22 30), near Carrer Comte de Rius (open daily 7am-midnight). Judging from the crowd, it's true. You can listen to outdoor music on Carrer D'August on Sunday nights outside the Dastelería Granja at #30. People park the street and sing along to upbeat music. A little later in the evening, one of the most unusual spots in town is **La Cova del Swing,** Trinquet Vell, 4. Built into the hillside beneath Carrer Major, it's a dank retreat with loud, good music and a friendly clientele. Also enjoyable, if a little more sedate, is **La Canela,** Carrer Sant Magí, 6 (tel. 21 76 00), off Carrer La Unió. The converted warehouse has lots of space, dance music, and gets going a little later than La Cova. (Open daily 7pm-2:30am.) Real discotheques or dance clubs are scarce in Tarragona, mostly because they're all in **Salou** and **Torredembara,** two beach resorts about 10km south and north, respectively. Salou in particular is fun and easy to reach by Plana bus, but you'll need to find a ride back if you're just hitting the nightlife (last bus returns at 10pm). The cafes along Rambla Nova play host to many of the city's late-night visitors.

Bullfights take place in Tarragona's Plaça de Toros on Sundays in July and August. The lowest-priced tickets cost 1200 to 2200ptas; buy them at the kiosk on the corner of Rambla Nova and Carrer Canyelles (open most days 10:30am-1:30pm and 5:30-9:30pm). July and August also bring a **cultural festival** to the Auditori Camp de Mart near the cathedral. Surprisingly good offerings cover rock, jazz, dance, theater, and film. Buy tickets for the 10:30pm performances in a booth on Rambla Nova. (Tel. 23 46 64. Open Mon.-Sat. noon-2pm and 6-9pm.) On a Sunday in mid-August every other year (including 1989), Tarragona's sailors gather at around 10am to compete for the title of "Master of the Romesco," the local fish specialty. There's a big cookoff in El Serrallo and the entrees are then auctioned. The local festivals on August 19 and September 23 include traditional music and dancing in the streets, particularly in the provincial town of **Valls,** where colorfully dressed natives build human towers several layers high.

Near Tarragona: Poblet Monastery

While Montserrat is known for its setting, Poblet Monastery is celebrated for the architecture itself. Poblet was plundered in the early nineteenth century as well, but its buildings were lovingly restored, and today they form a splendid medieval monastic complex.

The monastery was founded in 1151 by Ramón Berenguer IV in thanksgiving to God for the recapture of Catalunya from the Moors. The first 12 Cistercian monks came from Fontfroide Abbey near Narbonne, France. The community rapidly increased in size and became a favorite stop for the kings of Aragon on their journeys between the capitals of Zaragoza and Barcelona. The monastery benefited greatly from the royal patronage, and finally was selected as the site for the royal pantheon. Although the buildings were abandoned during the Constitutional period (1820-1823) when religious orders were suppressed, a community of monks was re-established in 1940 and remains today.

The complex is surrounded by a series of three walls. The outer perimeter, 1 mile long, protected the peasants and workmen connected to the abbey. A second wall surrounds the conventual annexes, and the innermost wall protects the monastery itself. Guided tours pass through the most historic quarters, showcasing the twelfth-century kitchens and refectory, the cloister and adjoining lavabo with 30 Cistercian-style water taps, the chapter house, and the thirteenth-century library.

The large church exudes a majestic yet austere grandeur; its most remarkable ornaments are the immense low arches in the cross vault that support the tombs of the kings of Aragon. The sixteenth-century alabaster altarpiece is also of note. The four-tiered retable glorifying Jesus and Mary was executed in 1527 by Damián Forment, who also crafted the wonderful altarpiece in the Basílica del Pilar in Zaragoza. (Open daily 10am-12:30pm and 3-6pm. Admission 300ptas.)

Forty-eight kilometers from Tarragona, Poblet is a stop along the bus route to Lleida. (See Tarragona Practical Information.) The trip takes about one hour.

Lleida (Lérida)

Since the Celts used Ilerda as one of their last strongholds against the advancing Romans, the city's geography has continued to serve strategic purposes. Lleida is the capital of Catalunya's only land-locked province, stretching from the Pyrenees to the central plain.

Orientation and Practical Information

Lleida lends itself to walking; the city has even made the major shopping area a pedestrian walkway, a street decorated with Catalan flags and colorful tiles. You can walk in rhythm to the classical music coming from loudspeakers in the mornings.

Lleida's center encircles the Seu Vella and hugs the Segre River. **Rambla de Ferran** starts at the train station and splits into Avinguda de Blondel and Avinguda de Madrid. These two run into Avinguda de Catalunya. From there, **Rambla d'Aragón** and Carrer de Balmes will take you to **Plaça de Ricard Vignes.** Buses skirt the old city along these avenues (every 5 min. 8am-10pm, 45ptas, book of 10 for 300ptas).

Tourist Office: Arc del Pont (tel. 24 81 20), just inside the remaining gate to the old city, between Pl. Sant Joan and the Pont Vell over the Segre. From the train station, walk straight down the Rambla ahead of you; from the bus station, walk upriver (5 min. from either). Small, but helpful and well-supplied. English spoken. Open Mon.-Sat. 9am-7pm, Sun. 9:30am-1:30pm.

Post Office: Rambla de Ferran, 14 (tel. 23 64 49). Open for stamps Mon.-Fri. 9am-2pm and 4-6pm, Sat. 9am-2pm; for Lista de Correos Mon.-Sat. 9am-2pm. **Telegrams:** Mon.-Fri. 8am-9pm, Sat. 9am-7pm. **Postal Code:** 25000.

Telephones: Down the street at Rambla de Ferran, 37, at the corner of Carrer Democracia. Open Mon.-Sat. 9am-1pm and 5-9pm. **Telephone Code:** 973.

Train Station: Pl. de Berenguer IV (tel. 23 74 67), at the end of Rambla de Ferran, 15 min. from Pl. Sant Joan. Information window open daily 7am-9pm. To Barcelona (13 per day, 3 hr. and longer, from 780ptas) and Zaragoza (12 per day, 4 up the dead-end track to Pobla de Segur, 3 hr. and longer, from 740ptas).

Bus Station: Between Avda. de Madrid and Avda. de Blondel at C. Saracibar by the river (tel. 26 85 00). To Barcelona (6 per day, 2 on Sun., 2½ hr., 1020ptas), Huesca (4 per day, 2½ hr., 670ptas), Zaragoza (4 per day, 2½ hr., 691ptas), and La Seu d'Urgell (2 per day, 3½ hr., 805ptas). On Sun., buy tickets aboard buses.

Baggage Check: In the bus station. Open Mon.-Fri. 8:30am-8:30pm, Sat. 8:30am-7:30pm.

Swimming Pool: Huge municipal pool next to the campground (see directions below). Open daily June-Aug. Admission 85ptas.

Medical Assistance: Cruz Roja, Avda. Balmes, 2 (tel. 20 70 11). **Ambulance:** Tel. 26 66 66.

Police: Carrer Salmerón (tel. 23 43 40).

Accommodations and Camping

Lleida crawls with *fondas* and *casas de huéspedes,* most of which are crawling with things, too. Though there are any number along Carrer Cavallers's other side streets, most are not sanitary. **Carrer Anselmo Clavé,** off to the right from the train station, harbors several decent one-star *hostales* and *habitaciones.* The places listed below, however, are all good, clean, and in slightly more convenient locations.

Alberg Sant Anastasi (IYHF), Rambla d'Aragón, 11 (tel. 26 60 99). Take the bus from the train station (the one heading straight down the Rambla), or walk. Used as a *hostal* as well as a student residence. Bright, spacious, and clean. Members only, 500ptas. 225ptas extra if you don't have a sleep sack. Breakfast included.

Hostal-Residencia del Sol, Pl. Sant Joan, 9 (tel. 24 14 24). Bright, clean, and friendly, though bathrooms need renovation. Most rooms overlook plaza. Singles 750ptas. Doubles 1300ptas, with shower 1600ptas.

Habitaciones Racó, Pl. Sant Joan, 1 (tel. 21 21 94), hidden in the corner. The golden exception to Lleida's mediocre rule—clean rooms run by a friendly family. Curfew midnight. Singles 600ptas. Doubles 1100ptas. Triples 1300ptas. Quads 1600ptas. Warm showers 100ptas.

Residencia Rexi, Avda. Blondel, 72 (tel. 27 07 00 or 27 06 89), near the bus terminal. Definitely a first-rate place—nicely furnished rooms, friendly management, and a large TV lounge. Singles 874ptas, with shower 1139ptas. Doubles 1669ptas, with bath 1880ptas.

Habitaciones Brianso, Carrer de Pi i Margal, 22 (tel. 23 63 39), at the foot of the hill near the train station. Some rooms look up at the Seu Villa; all are run by a congenial family. Large, well-kept rooms ranging from quads to singles. 700ptas per person.

You can **camp** a few kilometers out of town at **Las Balsas** (tel. 23 59 54), along the road to Huesca. Take the municipal bus labeled either "piscinas" or "Las Balsas" (every ½-hr.) from the *plaça* on Carrer Prat de la Riba. (Open April-Oct. 275ptas per person, per tent, and per car.)

Food

The *comarca* (county) of El Segrià prepares a varied and interesting cuisine. For a hearty meal, try the peasant dish known as *la cazuela*—a conglomeration of potatoes, tomatoes, onions, bacon, and snails—or else *perdiz con coles,* a partridge specialty. No one area of the city is particularly saturated with restaurants, but a smattering of cheap places line the small streets of the old city, including Carrer Cavallers.

If you want to take a picnic to the park, the active **market** (open roughly Mon.-Sat. 9am-2pm) is located at Pl. dels Gramàtics and has fruits and vegetables at negotiable prices, especially if you're buying small amounts.

Casa Manuel, Carrer Cavallers, 37 (tel. 26 61 91), two-thirds up the hill from Carrer Mayor. A neighborhood favorite with a cheap but tasty a la carte. Be careful not to drown in one of their huge bowls of soup. *Lomo* 235ptas, *macarones* 115ptas. Open Mon.-Sat. noon-3pm and 8-11pm. **Casa Demetrio,** Carrer la Parra, 6 (no phone), off Carrer de Sant Joan, near the fork. Another local favorite, but while you eat you'll have to listen to a blaring black-and-white TV. The food, however, is well-cooked, fresh and cheap—425ptas for the *menú del día.* Open for meals daily noon-3pm.

Restaurante Studio 21, Rambla d'Aragón, 21 (no phone), 1 block up from the hostel. A sizable student clientele gives this place a lively atmosphere. *Combinados* 295ptas, choice of *menús* 600ptas. ¼-chicken with fries and wine 295ptas. Open daily 1-4pm and 8-11pm.

Marisquería Bar Lugano, Pl. Ricard Vignes, 10 (tel. 23 52 57). The *plaça* is at the intersection of C. de Balmes and Avda. Prat de la Riva. A great selection of *tapas* and all kinds of shellfish for 160-325ptas. Seafood plates 375-410ptas, sandwiches 175-200ptas. Indulge in a seafood delight, *gambas fritas* (fried shrimp) 325ptas. Open Mon.-Fri. 8am-1pm, Sat. 8am-4pm, Sun. 10am-3pm.

Sights and Entertainment

A tour of Lleida properly begins where the **Pont Vell** (Old Bridge) crosses the Río Segre's broad bed, just before the ancient city gate. Here stands the **monument to Indíbil and Mandonio,** heroes of the Iberian resistance to the Roman Empire. Just through the portal, sits **Plaça Sant Joan,** the city's major shopping area. Eventually it will be possible to hop an elevator from here to the hilltop, but for now, just follow Carrer de Cavallers up to the top and take a right at the *mercado* to the site of Lleida's highest glory. Here is the **Seu Vella** (Old See), one of Catalunya's greatest architectural monuments. The cathedral was founded in 1149, shortly after the Muslims had been driven back out of Lleida. Construction on the present-day basilica began in 1203, and was completed in only 75 years. The five-apsed building, designed by Pere de Coma, displays little of the heaviness usually associated with Romanesque architecture—its interior is a grand, well-lighted space. The somewhat later **cloister,** attached to the western end of the church, is distinctly Gothic and breathtakingly large; its elaborate stone tracery (even if most of it is reconstructed) is wonderfully imaginative—no two windows are alike. Look for the pattern that incorporates the Star of David. Above rises the 60-meter, fourteenth-century tower, **El Campanar.** Restoration of the church began in 1949 to undo the damage done when Felipe V used it as a fortress during the Spanish War of Succession. Pre-restoration photographs are displayed in some of the side chapels. Don't forget to walk around to the southern facade (looking toward the river) to see the grand Porta dels Fillols. (Open daily 9am-2pm and 4-8pm; in winter daily 10am-2pm and 4:30-6pm. Admission 100ptas.)

Just above the cathedral some even older blocks of history have maintained their tenacious grip on the hilltop. These are the remains of the **Zuda,** the ancient palace of the kings of Aragon, built on a site that goes back to Moorish times. There's little to see but some eroding masonry and one intact turret, but clamber up for the breeze, the view, and the history. The entire grounds on the hilltop are open daily until 8pm.

If you follow the road down from the hilltop, you'll pass through two gateways before coming to the broad staircase. At the bottom, a right turn on Carrer Sant Martí will bring you to the **Església de Sant Martí,** a little lump of late twelfth-century Romanesque architecture. If you'd like to examine the tiny interior with its semicircular apse, ring the doorbell of the rectory (by the side entrance), but respect the hours the pastor has posted. As you pass Plaça de Cervantes, notice the **Església de Sant Llorenç,** off Rambla d'Aragón, an almost contemporary and almost equally modest example of Lleida's typical late Romanesque-early Gothic religious architecture. Sant Llorenç, probably designed by Pere de Coma just before he built the Seu Vella, has suffered a good deal over the course of time, but the interior contains several notable Gothic altarpieces, especially those dedicated to Sant Llorenç, Sant Pere, Santa Llúcia, and to Santa Ursula and the 11,000 virgins.

To see the inside of Sant Llorenç, ask the pastor to unlock the door (the rectory is on Pl. Sant Josep, on the lower side of the church).

The low-lying portion of Lleida near the river contains two secular buildings of historic importance. **La Paeria,** on Carrer Major, is an extremely interesting structure of the thirteenth century, though subsequent remodelings (and work intended to reverse them) have reduced its features somewhat. Originally built as a private structure, the town government took possession of it in 1383. A nineteenth-century architect turned the riverfront facade into a neoclassical mess, but the courtyard and the elegant triple windows of the street front, with its massive entrance arch, remain intact. The first floor now houses archives and a **museum** of local history and prehistory. (Open Mon.-Fri. 10am-2pm and 6-8pm. Free.)

Down the street, a fountain splashes in the courtyard of the **Antic Hospital de Santa Maria,** a lovely, airy Gothic building. The University of Lleida now owns the building and uses it for special exhibits, but a visit to the building to see the fifteenth-century patio is worth a trip in itself. (Open daily noon-2pm and 6-9pm. Free.) For green relief, stroll through the **Camps Elisis** gardens just across the river. Pause as you cross the bridge (especially toward sunset) to enjoy the view of the Seu Vella.

For the older generation, nightlife in Lleida consists mostly of an evening *paseo* around Plaça de Richard Vigñes or **Plaça de Sant Joan,** where some of the town's nicer cafes are located. Cinemas can be found on Carrer Major and on C. Cavallers. The younger crowd heads to the area around **Pl. Ricardo Viñes.**

During the Festa Major de Lleida in May, thousands of people descend on the banks of the river for the **Aplec del Cargol,** an annual snail-eating orgy. September sees the local celebration in honor of the *Virgen Blanca.*

Catalan Pyrenees

Catalunya's mountains are less imposing than their Aragonese neighbors. Catalan climbers were the first Spaniards to scale Mt. Everest, but much of their preparation took place in Aragon, where snow covers the peaks year-round. Nevertheless, the Catalan Pyrenees are splendid in their own right, lined with rich green and yellow fields, wide valleys, and small, undiscovered villages. The area's upland valleys are more forgiving to the wobbly legs of the inexperienced or out-of-shape hiker than the central mountains.

You'll find some of the most beautiful scenery in the Pyrenees in the northwest of Catalunya. The *comarca* of Val d'Aran contains the popular ski-resorts of Baqueira-Beret and Tuca-Betrén, while the spectacular Parc Nacional d'Aigüestortes i Estany de Sant Maurici straddles the border between Pallars Sobirà and Pallars Jussà, also home to some of Catalunya's finest Romanesque architecture. For each Catalan *comarca,* the Department of Commerce and Tourism puts out pamphlets with information on local winter sports or areas of scenic grandeur. Skiers will find the English-language guide *Snow in Catalonia* (free at tourist offices) especially useful. Bikers should ask for the map *Valles Superiores del Segre/Ariège,* which covers the High Urgell, Cerdanya, and the Ribes Valley. Editorial Alpina publishes a series of excellent topographical maps bound in red booklets that are indispensable for hikers.

Besides Catalan and Spanish, inhabitants of the Catalan Pyrenees often speak French as well, while people in the Val d'Aran speak Aranese, a variant of the Gascon spoken in the Comminge region of France. French influence can also be found in some of the region's gastronomic specialties—pâtes, civets, and crêpes (*pasteres* or *pescajüs*)—but these give way to heartier peasant dishes like *trinxat amb rosa* (creamed spinach and salt pork) in areas farther from the French border.

La Seu d'Urgell

La Seu is small, unpretentious, and content to allow bus loads of shoppers to zip through on their way to Andorra. The surrounding countryside contains hundred of Romanesque churches, both intact and ruined, reminders of the region's medieval heyday. Cross-country skiers, hikers, and kayakers alike fan out from town to do their thing.

Orientation and Practical Information

La Seu d'Urgell is connected by Rte. 1313 with the rest of Spain and by Rte. 1 with Andorra. Both roads meet on the northern edge of the city. Avenida Pau Claris begins at their intersection and ends after a 10-min. walk in **Plaça Catalunya,** the nucleus of the town. To the left is the old quarter, defined by the austere cathedral and the L-shaped, arcaded **Carrer Major.** To the right, Carrer Sant Ermengol cuts into the modern neighborhoods. Directly in front lies **Passeig de Joan Brudieu,** with its three rows of trees, each watered by a burbling trickle that runs in a trough under the green park benches.

Tourist Office: Avda. Valira (tel. 35 15 11), on the road to Barcelona/Lleida, 1 block from Avda. Pau Claris. Well-stocked with information on Romanesque churches (ask for *Romanesque routes* brochure) and the nearby parklands of Cadí Moixeró. Open Tues.-Sat. 10am-2pm and 5-8pm, Sun. 9am-2pm.

Post Office: C. Josep de Zulueta, at the corner of Avda. del Salònia (tel. 35 07 24). Open Mon.-Fri. 9am-2pm, Sat. 9am-1pm. **Postal Code:** 25700.

Telephone Code: 973.

Buses: Alsina Graells, Passeig de Joan Brudieu, 15 (tel. 35 02 20), monopolizes most service to and from La Seu d'Urgell. Open Mon.-Fri. 10am-1pm and 4-7:30pm, Sat. 10am-1pm. To Barcelona (2 per day, 1245ptas), Lleida (2 per day, 805ptas), Puigcerdà (3 per day, 285ptas). All fares rise slightly on Sun. **La Hispano-Andorrana,** same office, runs buses to Andorra (Mon.-Sat. 8 per day, Sun. 5 per day, 185ptas). Because of traffic, service not very punctual on return trip. **Hispano-Igualadina** buses operate a daily Tarragona-Andorra-Tarragona run that passes through La Seu d'Urgell. For information inquire at Bar Quiosc, on Passeig de Joan Boudieu in La Seu d'Urgell; call 213 72 in Andorra; or call 21 10 51 in Tarragona.

Baggage Check: At the bus office. In bus stop. Open daily 10am-1pm and 4-7:30pm. 75ptas per item.

Medical Services: Cruz Roja, Avda. Vall d'Andorra, 1 (tel. 35 00 30), at intersection of Avda. Pau Claris.

Police: In the Ayuntament on Pl. del Oms (tel. 35 04 26), behind the cathedral.

Accommodations and Camping

You should have little problem finding a place to stay except during the Fiesta Mayor at the end of August. The medieval quarter, with its narrow, arcaded streets and unharried atmosphere, has the cheapest places; expensive hotels line Avda. Pau Claris.

Fonda Bernada, C. Sant Ermengol, 14 (tel. 35 10 33), near Pl. Catalunya. A mini-desk, mini-bedside table, and mini-dresser are in every well-kept room. A serious man and his friendly daughter run the large place, which rarely fills. 650ptas per person; queen-size bed 1200ptas. Showers 100ptas.

Fonda Urgell, C. Capdevilla, 34 (tel. 35 10 78), north of the short stretch of Carrer Major. A friendly place with cute, small rooms ideally located for eavesdropping on family discussions in the street. Doubles 1500ptas.

Fonda Bertrán, C. dels Estudis, 8, off Pl. Catalunya. Newly redone rooms managed by an enthusiastic couple. 750-800ptas per person.

Hostal Ignasi, C. Capdevilla, 17 (tel. 35 10 36), down the street from Fonda Urgell. Run by a friendly Catalan family. Cheery rooms with plaid bedspreads. Singles 800ptas. Doubles 1600ptas. Triples 2250ptas.

En Valira (tel. 35 10 35) is the nearest **campground.** Walk up Avda. Pau Claris until you reach the main highway, and then walk five minutes in the direction of Lleida (left). You can't get wet in the fenced-off river nearby, but the large pool will keep you cool. (230ptas per person, per car, and per tent. Hot showers 100ptas.) If you feel like you've just moved to the suburbs, try camping discreetly by the river downstream a bit.

Food

Not many people go out to eat in La Seu, and those who do usually go to the expensive restaurants in the many starred hotels along Avda. Pau Claris. Head to Carrer Major for the makings of a sumptuous picnic. (Market held Tues. and Fri.) **Casa Eugene,** at #58, offers some of the region's cheeses, including *cadí,* made from the milk of the cows you see munching away on the hillsides. (Open Mon.-Sat. 9am-2pm and 4:30-8pm.) You'll find good *tapas* at **Bar Les Arcades,** C. dels Estudis, 2 (tel. 35 19 07), which displays a tempting array of succulent snacks at the counter. (Open Thurs.-Tues. 8am-2am.)

> **Restaurante César,** C. Estret (tel. 35 28 58), just off C. del Jueus. A hearty 3-plate 700ptas *menú* with *butifarra* and other Catalan specialities like *crema catalana* (custard with melted sugar on top) for dessert. Open Thurs.-Tues. 1-4pm and 9-11pm.

> **Fonda Urgell,** C. Capdevilla, 34 (tel. 35 10 78). Runs a close second with an active kitchen that sends alluring smells into the street. 700ptas *menú* comes with a giant salad. Open daily 1-3pm and 8:30-10:30pm.

> **Bar Restaurant Jové,** Carrer dels Canonges, 42 (tel. 35 02 60), parallel to Carrer Major and 1 block away. The pleasant family members who run the place spend half their time getting in each other's way; but when they deliver, the home cooking is fresh and cheap. *Menu* 600ptas. Open Mon.-Sat. 1-3:30pm and 9-11pm.

> **Bàmbola Pizzeria-Crêperia,** C. Capella, 4 (tel. 35 09 30), just off Passeig de Joan Brudieu. The crust isn't thick and chewy, but the pizza toppings are delicious. Dare to try the *pica-pica* with garlic, anchovies, and olives (from 350ptas). Crepes start at 200ptas. Open Tues.-Sun. 1:30-3:30pm and 8:30-11:30pm.

After you eat, retire to the **Xocolateria-Xurreria Montse,** C. Major, 24 (right at the bend), with black-laquered chairs and marble topped tables for some delicious pastries. Also, roam Passeig Joan Brudieu for some still-hot fried dough.

Sights and Entertainment

La Seu's thirteenth-century **cathedral** suggests an elegance that has left the rest of the city behind. The facade is completely symetrical; inside, high, small windows throw a reddish light below. (Open Mon.-Sat. 9am-1pm and 4-7pm, Sun. 10am-2pm.) In the cathedral, three of the **cloister's** original galleries remain intact. The carved capitals show narrow-eyed men performing yoga while intertwined with fierce lions. (Kinky.) The 100ptas for admission must go to the gardener. Entrance to the cloister also allows you to see the **Church of San Miguel,** a simple chapel with Lombard arches on the exterior and bare walls within.

The **Museo Diocesano,** around the corner from the rear of the cathedral, contains the vividly illustrated, tenth-century manuscript of a work by Beato de Liébana. The fourteenth-century *Retaule de la Verge d'Abella de la Conca* depicts six of the Virgin's seven joys. Statues of the Madonna and child along with fragments of Romanesque paintings also fill the museum. (Open Mon.-Sat. 10am-1:30pm and 5-8pm, Sun. 10-1:30pm. Admission 200ptas.)

The Church of San Miguel hosts two classical music concerts in the first half of July. The **Festival de Música Brudieu** takes place in August, bringing three concerts to the cloister of the cathedral and the patio of the seminary. The **Retaule de Sant Ermengol,** in the second half of August, recreates the life of the patron saint in stained glass images come to life. Lights and music fill the cloister while actors move and pose, but rarely speak.

Near La Seu d'Urgell

On the outskirts of town, off the road to Lleida, two *castells* located strategically to protect the town in times of conventional warfare now lie in ruins. A road that starts behind this eroding hill leads across fields and past irrigation ditches up the valley toward Andorra and the miniscule farming hamlet of Anserall, with the **Monastery of Sant Sernì de Tavèrnoles** about 3km away. The **Parc Natural Cadí Moixeró** stretches from La Seu to Puigcerdà, along the southern area of the highway between the two. A 30-kilometer hike connects La Seu to **Pedraforca,** a giant rock formation resembling a molar. In the winter, cross-country skiers dominate the area.

The Segre Valley provides numerous other activities. Both the Segre and the Valira are known for their challenging white-water canoeing. An international canoeing and kayaking week occurs every year at the beginning of July, and the Valira has been chosen as the sight for kayaking in the 1992 Olympic Games. Organyà and Coll de Nargó lie downstream from Seu d'Urgell; they can be reached by a Graells bus (Mon.-Sat. 1 per day, 150ptas). The first document known to have been written in Catalán, the twelfth-century *Homilies d'Organyà* was discovered in the narrow valley of **Organyà.** A monument commemorates the lucky find—the manuscript had been lying in the local presbytery.

Puigcerdà

Less than 3km from the French border, Puigcerdà sits atop an abrupt hill, commanding its *comarca* Cerdanya. In summer, the town is a good starting point for hikers headed for the nearby mountains; in winter, cross-country skiers can head across the plains, and ice hockey fans congregate to watch the town's champion team annihilate other Spanish contenders.

Orientation and Practical Information

The narrow streets of Puigcerdà's center are boxed in by **Plaça de l'Ajuntament** to the west, **Plaços de Santa María** and **Dels Herois** to the north, and **Passeig 10 d' Abril** to the east. **Calle Alfons I** cuts through town. The **tourist office** (tel. 88 05 42) is at C. Querol, 1. (Open July-Sept. 15 Mon.-Sat. 10am-1pm and 4-7:30pm, Sun. 10am-1pm; Sept. 16-June 30 Mon.-Sat. 10:30am-1pm and 4-7pm, Sun. 10:30am-1pm.) The staff is helpful and can provide tips on nearby hikes. Puigcerdà's **post office** is across town on Carrer Colonel Molera. (Open Mon.-Fri. 9am-2pm and Sat. 9am-1pm.) For **police** assistance, call 88 01 29; their office is below the intersection of Avda. Segre and Highway CN-152 (toward Llivia). For **medical aid,** contact the Cruz Roja (Red Cross), at Avda. Segre, 9 (tel. 88 05 47). **Casa Opel** (tel. 88 12 52) rents bikes (500ptas per day); they are located 1km from the intersection of highways N-152 and C-1313, toward La Seu d'Urgell. (Open Mon.-Sat. 10-1pm and 4-8pm.) An extensive selection of guides and maps is available at **Palau 3,** C. Mayor, 13 (tel. 88 06 99).

Puigcerdà lies almost at the end of the **RENFE** line from Barcelona; about a dozen tired *tranvías* (glorified streetcars) rumble down this line each day (690ptas to Barcelona). Three **buses** per day connect Puigcerdà to Seu d'Urgell (290ptas, Sun. and holidays 310ptas), where you can catch the bus to Andorra. Trains pull into the RENFE station (tel. 88 01 65); buses do their business in front. Either way, you'll have to climb the hill to the center of town, which you can see with distressing clarity above. Go right on Avda. dels Pirineus, turn left a block later at the first plaza you hit, and follow the cobblestones of C. Rabadans. Turn left, climb a staircase, then head left along Carrer dels Monges to the final set of stairs. At the top is Plaça de l'Ajuntament.

Accommodations and Food

Since most visitors stay only a day, you should have no problem finding a room, though it won't be cheap. A scruffy but friendly man owns **Pensión Domínguez,** C. Mayor, 39 (tel. 88 14 27), where the clean rooms sport hardwood floors. (900ptas per person. Showers 100ptas.) You'll have to pass through a bar where old men debate politics to get to your bed in **Hostal Cerdanya** (tel. 88 00 10), in C. Ramon Cosp at C.M. Bernades. The rooms are bright, if a bit dusty. (1000ptas per person, with bath 1200ptas. Showers, sometimes hot, included.) Most likely to have a double (2000ptas), **Hostal-Residencia La Muntanya**, C. Coronel Molera, 1 (tel. 88 02 02), on Pl. de Barcelona, has a friendly manager and comfortable rooms. The Generalitat (Catalan government) runs a well-kept **IYHF youth hostel** (tel. 89 20 12) on Carretera de Font Canaleta just 500m from the La Molina RENFE stop in Alp. The slopes are only 1km away, and they have 170 beds. (Members only, 425ptas.)

Puigcerdà's streets are lined with the largest profusion of bakeries, markets, and delis ever beheld by the eyes of weary backpackers. Head straight for **Gourmet Cerdà**, C. Alfons I, 9 (tel. 88 14 85), for some take-out fare. (Open Mon.-Sat. 9am-1pm and 3:30-8pm, Sun. 9am-2pm.) Then head next door to the **Forn de Pa** for some fresh bread to make a giant *bocadillo*. The cheapest place in town for a full meal can be found at **Hostal Cerdanya** (see above), whose owners cook up a hearty 600ptas *menú* with a half-chicken and fresh fruit. (Open daily 1-3pm and 9-11pm.)

Sights and Entertainment

Although most of the town dates from the twentieth century, Puigcerdà has managed to preserve a few structures of architectural merit. The most obvious is the **campanar**, the octagonal bell tower in Plaça de Santa María. Only this 42-meter-high tower remains of the church of Santa Maria, destroyed by Spanish Civil War fighting in 1936. The base dates from the twelfth century, but the rest of the ruins are from the eighteenth century. Along Passeig 10 d'Abril, off Pl. Héroes, is the thirteenth-century **Convent de Sant Domènec**, whose large-scale renovation will bring a regional museum, library, and archives to the town this year. Next door stands the **Església de Sant Domènec**, the largest church in Cerdanya. The most interesting items inside are the Gothic paintings, presumably by Guillem Manresa, and considered some of the best of their genre. On the outskirts of town, spanning the Riu Querol, is the **Pont de Sant Martí d'Aravó**, with a Romanesque base and a Gothic superstructure. The two arches were constructed between 1326 and 1328.

Low-key sports fans can watch swans chase paddle boats around the **Estany**, the tree-lined lake up Avda. Pons i Guasch from Pl. de Barcelona. More active athletes head to the **Poliesportiu** sports center (tel. 88 02 43) in the northeast corner of town. Here you can skate (300ptas, skate rental 200ptas; open in winter daily 9:30am-2pm and 5-9pm; in summer daily 7-9pm) or swim (300ptas; open in summer daily 11am-9pm). In winter, Puigerdà's hockey team plays inspired games here. Call the rink for a schedule of games.

Festa de l'Estany, usually held the penultimate Sunday of August, begins with a parade of floats, a concert, and some folkloric activities, and culminates at night with a beautiful fireworks display over the lake. A few weeks later, on September 8, the town once more comes alive, this time for the **Festivitat de la Verge de la Sagristia**, when the townspeople dance *sardanes* in the square. In summer, *sardanes* are also held every Thursday at 10pm in one of the squares.

Near Puigcerdà

Six kilometers from Puigcerdà lies the little town of **Llívia**, a Spanish enclave in French territory. It owes its status to a 1659 treaty in which 33 villages in Cerdanya were ceded to France; since Llívia was considered a town, it remained Spanish. The town has picturesque old streets, a fortified church with a thirteenth-century defense tower, and the small **Museu Municipal de Llívia** across the street. The **Farmàcia Antiga** inside preserves an interesting collection of early apothecarian equipment and a complete nineteenth-century drugstore. (Open July-Aug. daily 10am-1pm and 3-7pm; Sept.-June daily 10am-1pm and 3-6pm. Admission 50ptas, students free.) To spend the night here, try **Fonda Restaurante Cerdanya Can Marcel·lí**, C. Frederic Bernades, 7 (tel. 89 63 94; doubles 2000ptas).

Other diversions lie along the valley in the direction of Seu d'Urgell. Hikers wander across the landscape above the small town of **Meranges**, which includes an ascent to **Estany de Malniu,** just below the glaciers along the Andorran border. In winter, this is cross-country skiing territory. There is a well-equipped **refuge** at Meranges. **Bellver de Cerdanya,** 20km down the Segre, is well-known for its Romanesque structures, both religious and secular. The tourist office provides useful information on winter sports and *Valles Superiores del Segre/Ariège,* an invaluable map that suggests several hiking trails. Bookstores stock the more authoritative *Guía de Cerdanya* by Editorial Alpina.

Nùria

Catalunya's love affair with downhill skiing blossomed in this isolated mountain valley over 50 years ago. Near the French border and just north of Ripoll, Nùria was already famous for its religious shrine and monastery, but major change came with the installation of a second-hand *funicular,* left over from the 1929 World's Fair in Barcelona. By 1934, a luxurious lodge had been erected at the top of the new cable ride. After the Civil War, Nùria enjoyed about 20 years of fame for its international ski competitions, but as bigger mountains were exploited and longer lifts sprung up nearby, the town declined. A 1962 fire gutted its lodge, marking the end of an era for the valley.

Nùria is now flying high once again, thanks in large part to the opening of Catalunya's newest youth hostel on the site of the legendary lodge. **Pic de L'Aliga** (tel. 73 00 48) is a three-story, modern establishment with fancy wooden floors and some of the former lodge's original furniture. Make reservations. (Members only, 425ptas. Sheets 225ptas.) **Hotel Nùria** (tel. 73 03 26) provides the only other lodgings in the valley. (Singles 2500ptas. Doubles 3200ptas.) Free **camping** is permitted near the hotel; shower and bathroom access is available for a nominal fee. There is a **food shop** near the hotel, but it isn't cheap.

The train ride up the valley (the only access to Nùria except by foot) proves an outing in itself; it cuts through the gorge of Cremal, climbing 800m.

The **Cremallera** train (literally, "the zipper"), part of the Catalan rail system, connects Nùria to the **RENFE station** in Ribes de Freser (9 per day, 45 min., 725ptas).

The lake near the shrine hosts picnickers and *señoras* in their Sunday best. Climbers prefer the popular four-hour hike to **Puigmal** (2913m). In 1988, eleven ambitious mountaineers climbed the peak on 6-foot stilts, setting a new world record. No one knows why they did this. **Pic d' Eina** offers a shorter but equally strenuous hike. You can also walk down the gorge that the train traverses, photographing the impressive rock walls and yellow mountainflowers that you saw on the way up.

Skiers whiz down the slopes at the **Estació de Muntanya Vall de Nùria** when there's good snow. For ski conditions, call 302 73 45 in Barcelona or 73 07 13 in Nùria. Only the "Super Mulleres" trail would challenge an expert; the one main lift and two small t-bars lead to mostly intermediate and easier trails. Weekend lift tickets cost 1000ptas, weekdays 800ptas.

In case of an **emergency,** call the Guardia Civil in Ribes de Freser (tel. 72 70 38); there is also a **hospital** in Ribes (tel. 72 70 72).

Ripoll

A visit to Ripoll to see the magnificent portal of the **Monestir de Santa María** can be disappointing. While the importance of this ambitious stone poem is not disputed—it is one of the most elaborate Romanesque archways in Spain—Mother Nature and Father Time have done their harm. What the wind and water didn't do, man's deliberate abuse and neglect did. At one time, the detail on this giant biblical story book was breathtaking. For eight centuries, the archway *was* the Bible for thousands of illiterate peasants. The **cloister** dates from the twelfth century; you'll probably be so cross-eyed after viewing the portal that you won't want to decipher the capitals and vault keystones, but the pleasant garden makes a nice escape from the sun. The interior of the church, the result of a nineteenth-century restoration, seems clumsy; the stone walls bear an uncanny resemblance to the artificial plasto-masonry used in amusement-park haunted houses. (Church and cloister open Tues.-Sun. 9am-1pm and 3-7pm. Admission to cloister 50ptas.)

To the left of the church and up a long spiral staircase, is the **Museu-Arxiu Folk-lòric,** which contains exhibits on Ripoll's industrial history and is not as boring as it sounds. While towns nearby were busy feeding their cows and mowing the fields, Ripoll manufactured many of Europe's guns and most of Spain's nails during the sixteenth to eighteenth centuries. Both these industries are well-represented. Also on display is the *porrón* (wine dispenser) with what must be the world's longest spout, unexploded bombs from the Spanish Civil War, and an exhibit paying homage to the pastor. If you've made it to the monastery, this funky museum is worth the trip. (Open Tues.-Sun. 9am-1pm and 3-7pm. Admission 75ptas.) You can reach the museum and monastery by walking up Carrer de Sant Pere from Plaça de Sant Eudald, which is right off Plaça Gran. Gaudí fans will enjoy the tiny **chapel of St. Miguel de la Roqueta,** built by Joan Rubió, a disciple of the modernist mystic. The interior is normally closed, but the exterior can be viewed by walking down C. del Progrés from the train station. Turn right on C. Lleida and then left on C. Industria.

Ripoll's **Festa Major** falls on May 11; on the following Sunday, the **Festa de la Llana** entertains the town as indignant sheep are sheared in Pl. del Ajuntament. In July, the **Festival de Música** brings seven evenings of classical music to the cloisters. Montserrat Caballé, Spain's foremost diva, frequently makes an appearance. Concert tickets run 300-700ptas; for more information, call 70 23 51.

Ripoll doesn't have many places to sleep, since most tourists stay only long enough to squint at the church portal. **Hotel Residencia Payet,** Pl. Nova, 2 (tel. 70 02 50), offers clean, moderate-sized rooms. (Singles 1000ptas. Doubles 1700ptas.) **Hostal Ripollés,** Pl. Nova, 11 (tel. 70 02 15), is cheaper as area fleas well know. (600ptas per person. Showers 150ptas.) You can camp 2km south of town at **Solana del Ter** (tel. 70 10 62), Carretera Barcelona, in Colonia Santa María; follow the road from Pl. Gran, since there is no bus. (Open Dec.-Oct. 325ptas per person and per tent.)

Restaurante El Recò, C. Pare Francesa Coli, 7 (no phone), is popular with Ripoll's younger crowd. Veggie sandwiches, pizzas (350ptas), and *platos combinados* (from 450ptas) fill the bill of fare. (Open daily noon-11pm.) **Hostal Ripollés** whips up a hardy 850ptas *menú* that successfully packs the place with swarms of local families on Sunday afternoons. (Open daily 1-3pm and 8-10pm.) Near the monastery, try **Hostal Cala Paula,** C. Berenger, 4 (tel. 70 00 11), which serves 700ptas *menú.* (Open same hours as Ripollés.) A good place to enjoy *tapas* or a *horchata* is **Cafe-Bar Sayol,** Pl. Gran, 20. (Open Mon.-Sat. 9am-11pm.)

The same trains that run to Ribes de Freser and Puigcerdà stop in Ripoll. From the station, turn left along Carrer del Progrés to reach town; on the way, you'll pass the **post office** at #21. (Open Mon.-Fri. 9am-2pm, Sat. 9am-1pm.) At Carrer d'Olot, turn left again and cross the tracks and river to Carrer de Macià Bonaplata; continue until you hit Pl. Gran. Pl. Nova is a block away. From here you can follow the *plaças* and Carrer de St. Pere around to the monastery and **tourist office** (tel. 70 23 51), both on Pl. de l'Abat Oliba. The tourist office, under the sundial on the facade, is friendly but not terribly useful. (Open daily 10am-1pm and 4-7pm.) Call the **Creu Roja** (Red Cross; tel. 70 04 71) for medical attention; the **municipal police** (tel. 70 06 00) are located in the Ajuntament, next to the monastery.

Near Ripoll: Sant Joan de les Abadesses

In the ninth century, the same Count of Barcelona who established the first monastery at Ripoll also set up a convent 10km away. By a strange coincidence, his daughter became the first abbess in a 300-year line. The current monastery in Sant Joan de les Abadesses dates from the twelfth century and houses a seven-piece sculpture that makes a visit here worthwhile. The **Santíssim Misteri,** about 700 years old, exquisitely depicts the descent from the cross. Why the statue of Jesus had a trapdoor built into its forehead has never been fully explained. The interior capitals of the building are well-preserved. Admission to the church and cloister (100ptas) allows you to visit the **museo,** where you get a good look at some richly embroidered cassocks, a gigantic mortuary cloth crafted for a bishop, and some humorously carved, sixteenth-century choir stalls.

Near the other end of the Rambla from Sant Joan, the **ruins of Sant Pol** greet most drivers passing through town. The bits of trash underneath the intact apses betray the cool picnic spot. If you prefer to be served, go to **Restaurant Nati,** C. Pere Rovira, 3 (tel. 72 01 14), near Sant Pol. The 650ptas, three-course *menú* will stuff you with *canelones,* salad, and *merluza* (hake). (Open daily 1-3:30pm and 9-11pm.) The **Centro de Iniciative Turística (CIT)** (tel. 72 00 92), on the Rambla, will give you a guide and a map, though you really won't need either. (Open daily 9-1:30pm and 5-7pm.) Nine buses per day connect Ripoll and Sant Joan de les Abadesses (20 min., 75ptas).

Parc Nacional d'Aigüestortes i Estany de Sant Maurici

The water is everywhere: ice-cold mountain lakes, violently gushing waterfalls, streams crossing trails. Hikes are gentle here. The park has a few challenging peaks; but most are enjoyable for the whole family. The park is divided in two by a 2500-meter range. Informally, the eastern half is considered the Estany de Sant Maurici (referring to the central lake), and the western half is the Aigüestortes section. The whole park can be traversed in an eight- to 10-hour hike. Don't rely on the stream-lined freebie maps from the information windows; the red Editorial Alpino guides, one for Montardo and Valle de Boí, the other for Sant Maurici, are better.

Estany de Sant Maurici

The giant lake of Sant Maurici greets motorists at the end of the road from Espot. At the edge of the parking lot, wooden signs point toward two of the park's four *refugios.* **Refugio E. Mallafré,** 15 minutes away, costs 400ptas per person; over-priced meals run 1200ptas, but you can always chug a beer (150ptas) and grab a *bocadillo de jamón* (ham sandwich; 400ptas). Walk an hour and a half in the other direction around the northeastern tip of the lake to **Chalet-Refugio de Amitges.** (Open June 17-Sept. 800ptas per person. Meals 1050ptas.) For the third *refugio* in the Sant Maurici area, turn off the road before you arrive at the lake. As you reach the first information shack, about 3km before Sant Maurici, a well-marked trail cuts left and three hours later brings you to **Refugio JM Blanch** (same prices and dates as Amitges). The two latter places are run by the Centre Excursionista de Cataluña in Barcelona (tel. (93) 315 23 11); both require sleeping bags. No camping is permitted in the park.

Avoid entering the park on the Sant Maurici side unless a one-day walk appeals to you. **Residencia Casa Pagés Felip** (tel. 63 50 93) will make your stay pleasant and clean for 800ptas per person. To reach there, walk across the main bridge in **Espot** and turn left after 2 blocks. **Camping Mola** (tel. 64 50 08) lies about 5km from the bus stop before Espot. (Open July-Aug. 275ptas per person and per tent.) **Camping Sol i Neu** (tel. 63 50 01), a little closer to Espot, copies its neighbor's prices and dates. Your best bet in Espot for food is to snack at a hamburger or pizza joint such as **Bar Barbacoa,** before the town bridge, which serves simple *platos combinados* from 500ptas.

Hike Information (tel. 63 50 93) is available in the white building on your left as you exit town at the Super Espot crossroad. A free slide show at 11:30am and 5pm offers ideas on areas of the park to visit. (Open June-Sept. daily 9am-1pm and 4-8pm.) An Alsina Graells **bus** will drop you off on highway C-147, about 7km from Espot. Buses leave Barcelona Monday through Saturday at 8am from Ronda de la Universitat, 4 (tel. 302 65 45, in Barcelona), and cost 1750ptas one way. Return trips leave at 5am and 1:15pm. Buses also leave Lleida from the bus station at 4pm (about 975ptas). Both buses stop in La Poble de Segur, which RENFE serves. In an **emergency** call 63 50 71.

Aigüestortes and Valle de Boí

Gentle inclines in the western half of the park attract more cows and casual strollers than the Sant Maurici side. To compare yourself, take the main trail up Valle de San Nicolau in Aigüestortes to the **Portarró de Espot,** the 2400-meter gateway between the two sides. The descent to Estany Sant Maurici is steep and covered in patches of snow at the higher altitudes. This six- to eight-hour hike crosses the whole park, passing the **Estany Llong,** a long lake indeed. Near its western tip, the park's fourth *refugio,* **Estany Llong,** charges 425ptas per person. (Open June 15-Oct. 12, Feb., and some weekends March-May. Breakfast 330ptas. Lunch or dinner 1000ptas.) Near the end of the paved road as you enter Aigüestortes, sneak a peak at the pine groves circled by winding streams; this tranquil sanctuary of twisted waters is the park's namesake.

Entering the park from its western side isn't much easier than the eastern approach. You have to cover 11km from **Boí** to the start of the trails. At least the bus from Lleida drops you off in a functioning community (not an empty stretch of highway like the Torrassa strip, 7km from Espot). Boí's 140 inhabitants live among stony streets that loop through stony archways and wind around stony houses. Until the completion of a nearby ski resort, the village and surrounding valley will probably maintain their mountain charm. **Casa Guasch** (tel. 69 60 42) will provide you with a queen-size bed (1400ptas) or a single (800ptas). **Casa Cosán** (tel. 69 60 18) charges 800ptas per person. These kind folk will provide clean sheets, and let you share their houses and kitchen facilities. One alternative is **Hostal Residencia Pey**(tel. 69 60 36), next to the bus stop. Generic and clean hotel rooms will run you 750ptas (in their old building across the plaza) to 950ptas per person.

Pont de Suert, 17km south of Boí, offers most emergency services. The **Creu Roja** (Red Cross) can be reached at tel. 69 02 85 for an ambulance; the **Guardia Civil** at tel. 69 00 06 will dispatch the Spanish Mounties or a St. Bernard if you need some help. The 8am bus from Lleida, which drops you off 1km from Boí, permits you to make the three-hour walk to the park by sundown. Land rovers from Boí to Aigüestortes cost 4000ptas and seat eight. The 3pm bus from Lleida pulls into Boí at 6:30pm. Leave Boí on a 9am bus to Lleida or walk down to the crossroad for the 2:30pm bus headed south.

Girona (Gerona)

Few travelers know what they're missing when, on their way from Barcelona to France, they bypass the ochre alleyways of Girona. Few Iberian towns possess as rich an artistic and historical heritage as the capital of Spain's northeastern province. Girona boasts one of the most original cathedrals in Europe, several noteworthy ruins from its Roman and Arab past, and the bewildering streets and gray dwellings of the Call (the Jewish quarter). The city was home to the renowned *cabalistas de Girona,* who for centuries managed to preserve and spread the mystical teachings of Judaism in the West. Despite its historical allure, however, Girona fills only on cloudy days, when crowds flock in from the resorts on the Costa Brava to view its impressive monuments.

Orientation and Practical Information

All trains going to Barcelona from the French border stop in Girona. Buses run regularly from Girona to the beach towns of the Costa Brava.

The **Riu Onyar** splits the city in half, the old part lying to the north, the commercial district to the south. To get to the center from the train and bus stations, take a left on **Carretera de Barcelona** and a right on **Carrer Nou,** the center of the commercial district. Across the Pont de Pedra lies **Rambla de la Llibertat,** which is lined with cafes and perfect for an evening *paseo.* **Carretera de França** is the other major thoroughfare.

Tourist Office: Rambla de la Llibertat, 1 (tel. 20 26 79). Infinitely patient staff will help you find your way around with a detailed map of the old city. Open Mon.-Fri. 8am-8pm, Sat. 9am-1pm. Branch office at the train station (tel. 21 62 96). Open Mon.-Sat. 9am-2pm.

Student Travel: Generalitat, C. Juli Garreta, 14 (tel. 20 15 54). C. Juli Garreta lies 1 block from C. Carretera de Barcelona across from the train station. Go to the door on the right of the building and ring the buzzer marked *joventut.* Railpasses, cheap buses to Europe, IYHF cards (1800ptas), and ISICs (225ptas). Information on area youth hostels. Open Mon.-Fri. 9am-1pm and 4-6pm; in off-season Mon.-Fri. 9am-2pm.

Post Office: Avda. Ramon Folch, 2 (tel. 20 32 36), near Pl. Independència. Open Mon.-Sat. 9am-2pm; for stamps only Mon.-Fri. 4-6pm. **Telegrams** upstairs. Open Mon.-Sat. 9am-9pm. For Lista de Correos, enter around the corner on C. Jeroni de Real de Fontclara. 2nd floor. Open Mon.-Fri. 9am-2pm. **Postal Code:** 17070.

Telephones: Gran Vía de Jaume I, 58. Open Mon.-Sat. 9am-9pm. **Telephone Code:** 972.

Train Station: Pl. d'Espanya (tel. 20 70 93). To Barcelona (2 per hr., 440ptas; get a *rápido*), Port Bou (2 per hr., 110ptas), and Figueres (2 per hr., 195ptas). Information open Mon.-Sat. 9am-1pm and 3-7pm.

Bus Station: Behind the train station (tel. 21 23 19). **Sarfa** is the cheapest company to Costa Brava. To Tossa de Mar (2 per day, 300ptas) and Palafrugell (15 per day, 250ptas), where you can make connections to Begur, Llafranc, Calella, and Tamariu. **Fills de Rafael Mas** runs buses to Lloret de Mar (3-5 per day, 360ptas). **Teisa** goes to Olot (8 per day, 325ptas), Ripoll (4 per day, 590ptas), and Sant Feliu (15 per day, 225ptas).

Hospital: Hospital de Girona Alvarez de Castro, Avda. de França, 60 (tel. 20 27 00).

Police: Policía Municipal, C. Bacià, 4 (tel. 20 45 26). **Emergency:** Tel. 092.

Accommodations

The Generalitat is taking its time renovating the building near Pl. del Vi that will become a new youth hostel. Singles can be hard to find in Girona, but doubles and triples never seem to fill since most visitors don't stay the night.

Habitaciones Perez, Pl. Bell-lloch, 4 (no phone), around the corner from the tourist office. Friendly owner keeps clean rooms. An annex around the corner may have more rooms if Perez is full. Singles 700ptas. Doubles 1300ptas.

Fonda Barnet, C. Santa Clara, 16 (tel. 20 00 33), off C. Nou near Pont de Pedra. Small rooms above the family's busy bar and restaurant. Doubles 1450ptas.

Hostal Residencia del Centro, C. Ciutadans, 4 (tel. 20 14 93), near Pl. del Vi. Enter through a majestic carriage doorway. The tilework and high ceilings of the spacious rooms enhance the impression of former glory. May be full of boarders Oct.-July. Singles (lots of them) 1100ptas. Doubles 2000ptas.

Hostal Residencia Reyma, Subida Rey D. Martin, 15 (tel. 20 02 28), near the cathedral on the bank of the Riu Galligans. Large, well-furnished rooms in a cozy atmosphere. Doubles 2000ptas, with bath 2800ptas.

Food

Partly because of its small tourist population, Girona's restaurants serve authentic and inexpensive Spanish meals. There are plenty of restaurants on **Plaça Independència** and a score of cafes along **Rambla de la Llibertat.** Every morning except Sunday, there's a **market** in Pl. Calvet i Rubalcaba, not far from Pl. Catalunya. Shop here for fruit and vegetables.

Bar-Restaurante Los Jara, C. de la Força, 4 (tel. 21 52 60), down the street from Pl. de la Catedral. Incredibly industrious waiter carries 5 plates up a spiral staircase to a dining room above the bar. 3-course dinner *menú* an especially good deal at 500ptas, including steamed mussels and delicious chicken. *Menú del día* 750ptas. Open Mon.-Sat. 1-4pm and 8-11pm.

L'Anfora, C. de la Força, 15, just up the street. 750ptas *menú* includes gazpacho, huge salad, and fresh melon. 550ptas *menú de la noche* is just as filling. Open Tues.-Sun. 1-4pm and 8-10pm.

Restaurant Felix Lloret, Pl. Independència, 14 (tel. 21 36 71). Cheapest *menús* (600ptas and 800ptas) in this popular area and tasty a la carte choices like *butifarra* and rabbit. Open Mon.-Sat. 1-4pm and 8-11pm.

Sights and Entertainment

Most of what you'll want to see in Girona is in the old city across the Riu Onyar from the train station. Ubiquitous arrows indicating all the major sights make navigation easy.

Girona's large **cathedral** proudly overlooks the city. When construction on the imposing building ended in the sixteenth century, only the southern tower had been completed, and the lone tower looks like a flag in front of an army. The single window of the Catalan baroque facade gazes down as you climb the 90 steps to reach the building, which has a single nave instead of the usual three. The architect, Guillem Bofill, decided to build only one after a Council of Architects had voted in favor of three and the lateral outside walls had already been built. As a result, the cathedral has the widest Gothic nave in the world with enough floor space for the entire soccer field of Barcelona's main stadium. Only the Renaissance nave of St. Peter's in Rome is wider—by only 3m.

A door on the left leads to the tranquil cloister and its forest-like double row of columns. The capitals' friezes depict biblical scenes in a candid, moving style. The cloister's trapezoidal shape was determined by the city's medieval wall, which borders it at an odd angle. The treasury (entrance near the cloister) boasts several masterworks of medieval art, including seven sculptures by the fifteenth-century Mercadante de Bretaña and a tenth-century illuminated manuscript of Beato de Liébana's *libre de l'Apocalipsi* (*Commentary on the Apocalypse*). The unique Tapis de la Creaciò (Tapestry of the Creation) hangs in Room IV; this alone would make a trip to Girona worthwhile. Probably woven in the city in the eleventh or twelfth century, its lovely depiction of humans and animals in the Garden of Eden contrasts with Beato's pessimism. (Open June-Nov. daily 9:30am-8pm; Dec.-Feb. Sat.-Sun. 9:30am-1pm; March-May daily 9:30am-1pm and 3:30-6pm. Admission 150ptas, students free.)

Girona's **Museu d' Art,** next to the cathedral, houses a large collection of twelfth-century Romanesque religious wood sculpture. Each page of the fifteenth-century book, *Martirologi,* is adorned with five delicately painted depictions of martyrs being abused. On the fourth floor, moody landscapes at sunset and the portraits of Catalan farmers are bunched together in the exhibit of modern Catalan painters. (Open Tues.-Sat. 10am-1pm and 4:30-7pm, Sun. 10am-1pm. Admission 100ptas, students free.)

The Romanesque **banys àrabs** (Arab baths), off Pujada del Rei Martí, resemble the public baths (actually vaporiums) still used in Islamic cities. Dating from the thirteenth century, each of the four rooms was kept at a different temperature to permit the gradual heating-up and cooling-down experience necessary for salubrious bathing. (Open Tues.-Sat. 10am-1pm and 4:30-7pm, Sun. 10am-1pm. Admission 100ptas, students free.) Running along the medieval wall, the **Passeig Arqueològic** (archeological promenade) is a partly stepped street lined with cypresses, pine trees, and flowers. The view is wonderful—it's a cool and fragrant place for a drink or a picnic. The **Museu Arqueològic,** in the Church of Sant Pere de Galligants on Pl. de Santa Llúcia, is the final resting place for the medieval Jewish tombstones that once marked graves on a nearby burial hill. The small section dedicated to artifacts from Empùries, the Greek trading colony, boasts *anforas,* ceramic containers from the second century B.C.E. The discovery of identical containers in France and Rome is proof of the great distances that early Greek merchants were able to cover as exporters of wine and oil. (Open Tues.-Sat. 10am-1pm and 4:30-7pm, Sun. 10am-1pm. Admission 100ptas, Catalan students free, but an ISIC may do.)

The **Museu d'Historia de la Ciutat,** on Carrer de la Força, which used to be the main road to Rome, contains Roman and Gothic artwork from Barcelona's Museu de Arte de Catalunya while it's being renovated. The museum downstairs, which used to be a Capuchin convent, houses a **mummification workshop,** one of only three known sites in the world. The room was used to dry out dead bodies, which were placed sitting up in the small stalls that line the room. Totally dehydrated, the mummies were then taken to another room and placed next to each other in chairs to meditate about the surrounding community. (Open Tues.-Sat. 10am-2pm and 5-7pm, Sun. 10am-2pm. Admission 150ptas, students free.)

In 1492, Queen Isabel and King Ferdinand ordered the expulsion of all Spanish Jews who would not accept Christianity. This ruthless attempt to ensure a homogenous Catholic Spain damaged Spain's economy as it entered its colonial period. The Inquisition was inaugurated to verify—by severe measures—the acceptance of the new faith by converts. Though the tragedy grew to larger proportions in the south of Spain, nowhere is it more poignantly evoked than in the Girona of today. **Carrer Força** and its perpendiculars, **Carrer de San Llorenç** and **Carrer de Cúndaro,** are the only remaining streets of the original *aljama,* or Jewish neighborhood. A Jewish presence has been recorded here as far back as the ninth century. A great influx of immigrants later swelled the population of these *calls* (narrow passageways). Girona became a leading center for the study of cabala, a set of concepts attributing life to the inanimate and seeking to understand God beyond the words of the scriptures. Intellectual endeavors of interpretation and study, however, often resulted in desperate struggles for self-preservation. In 1391, for instance, after accusing the Jews of everything from deliberately spreading the plague to draining the community's economic resources, Girona slaughtered 40 residents of the Jewish quarter. Recently, the Ajuntament acquired the house of **Isaac el Cec,** on C. St. Llorenç, probably the last site of the community's synagogue. While the building's sparse interior reflects the destruction or loss of most of its Jewish artifacts over the centuries, there is an informative video in English, Catalán, and French in the basement. Explanatory posters and photographs document the area's history. (Open Tues.-Sat. 10am-2pm and 4-7pm, Sun. 10am-2pm. Admission to videos 100ptas.) The town hall's reawakened interest in Girona's Jewish past has also led to efforts to open sealed passageways in the old quarter, such as C. de Hernàndez.

Girona takes its evening *paseo* seriously. The pedestrian walkways around Rambla de la Llibertat fill with well-dressed families. A good place to stop is **Cafeteria L'Arcada** at #38 (tel. 20 10 15); you can sit outside and watch people walk by or stay inside amidst the old town atmosphere. (Open daily 8am-2pm.) To indulge a sweet-tooth, go around the block to **Xocolateria Antiga,** Pl. del Vi, 8 (tel. 21 66 81). Marble-topped tables and ceiling fans complement the delicious pastries. (Open Mon.-Sat. 7:30am-10pm.) **L'Arc,** Pl. de la Catedral, 9 (tel. 20 30 87), is a nice place for a drink. The outdoor tables have a lovely view of the cathedral's facade, and the owner is an existentialist Catalan separatist. (Open Mon.-Sat. 9am-3am, Sun. 6pm-3am.) Of Girona's four discotheques, the best is **Boomerang,** in the Barrio del Pont Major on the outskirts of town (tel. 20 18 56), but it's open only on weekends.

In May, a **flower competition** opens the normally-closed church of St. Domènec; several private patios in the old neighborhood are also involved. From mid-June to late July, Girona hosts a **Festival Internacional de Música.** Six concerts, given either in La Mercé or the Teatre Municipal, feature classical musicians. (Tickets are 800-1200ptas and available at tourist offices.) In July, the Rambla bops to the beat of live music every Wednesday at 10:30pm.

Costa Brava

In winter, a bitterly cold wind comes screaming down from the Pyrenees across the flatlands of the Empordà, the region that encompasses Costa Brava. The *tramontana* sometimes blows at 45 miles per hour for four days straight. But the warm sun and cool sea breezes of summer quickly melt the frozen memories of February, just in time for thousands of tourists to descend upon the sand and rock that compose the rugged, *brava* (wild) coast. The RENFE rail heads inland at Blanes, the southernmost town on the Costa Brava, to avoid a potentially perilous route. Buses provide the area's only means of transportation, although the occasional hitchhiker gets around.

Vacations typically end in August. In September, the water is still warm, the beaches are half-empty, and hostel owners actually face the prospect of room vacancies; this is the perfect time to visit the area. Although bus service is drastically reduced in winter, this beautiful coastline can still prove quite rewarding in off-season.

Tossa de Mar

In Tossa, a popular beach resort on the lower part of the Costa Brava, year-round inhabitants entertain their guests with a small-town sincerity quickly lost in the larger resort towns. The first written record of Tossa appears on a Roman mosaic from the fourth century B.C.E. The ancient community has held tight since then in the Vila Vella, a small community of houses on the peninsula to the right of Tossa's friendly beach, where on Sundays fishermen spread out their nets to mend and dry them.

Orientation and Practical Information

Avenida de Ferran Agulló runs parallel to the coast from the bus terminal and becomes the highway to Sant Feliu de Guixols. **Avenida de la Costa Brava,** the main street, runs perpendicular from Agulló toward the beach. Avda. de la Costa Brava runs into Calle Pou de la Vila, which ends up in a tangle of alleys that lead to the Vila Vella, perched on a promontory overlooking the beach. **Paseo del Mar** curves from near the end of Avda. de la Costa Brava along the banks of the usually dry Riera de Tossa, beyond which lies the beach.

> **Tourist Office:** At the bus terminal on Carretera de Lloret (tel. 34 01 08). Their helpful map includes an indexed list of accommodations, campsites, and restaurants. Open Mon.-Sat. 9am-8pm, Sun. 10am-1pm and 4-7pm; in off-season Mon.-Sat. 10am-1pm and 4-7pm.
>
> **Post Office:** C. Bernats (tel. 34 04 57). Open for stamps and telegrams Mon.-Fri. 9am-2pm, Sat. 9am-1pm (urgent telegrams only). **Postal Code:** 17320.
>
> **Telephones:** C. San Sebastian, 1. Open Mon.-Sat. 9am-2pm and 5-10pm.
>
> **Bus Station:** Cruce de Carretera de Lloret (tel. 34 09 03). **Transportes Pujol** provides service to Lloret (every ½-hr. 8:15am-8:45pm, 85ptas), while **Transportes Sarfa** goes to Girona (2 per day, 270ptas) and Barcelona (7 per day; 475ptas, Sun. 545ptas).
>
> **Ferries:** The only direct way to Sant Feliu and other points immediately north of Tossa, since buses must first travel inland to Girona. **Cruceros** (tel. 34 03 19), on the main beach, goes to Sant Feliu (4 per day, round-trip 1100ptas).
>
> **Hospital: Centre Medic,** C. de la Iglesia, 5 (tel. 34 14 48). **Creu Roja** (Red Cross) sets up a first-aid stand on the main beach near Club Naútico June-Sept.
>
> **Police: Policia Municipal,** C. Iglesia, 4 (tel. 34 01 35). **Guardia Civil,** Carretera a Sant Feliu (tel. 34 03 29).

Accommodations and Food

Rooms in Tossa are far from cheap, and many *hostales* are rented for the entire summer by travel agencies. During July and August, reservations are a must. Still, if you look hard enough, you'll find lurking in the heart of the old section a few *fondas* and *pensiones* that miraculously maintain low rates. **Pensión Nadal,** C. Sant Telmo, 1 (tel. 34 00 50), is cute but simple with friendly management. (800ptas per person.) **Pensión Montserrat,** around the bend at #12 (tel. 34 01 48), offers larger doubles for 800ptas, but the owner isn't as friendly. **Fonda Lluna,** C. Roqueta, 20 (tel. 34 03 65), has modern, clean rooms in a cozy corner of the old city. (1000ptas per person.) Another option is **camping** in one of the five sites within a 6km radius of town, but their rates are also quite high. **Cala Llevado** (tel. 34 03 14) is one of the prettiest, surrounded by pines and right on the sea, 3km from Tossa on the road to Lloret. (Open May-Sept. 475ptas per person, 480ptas per tent.) **Caravaning**

Camping Pola (tel. 34 10 83) is 4km from town on the road to Sant Feliu. (440ptas per person and 550ptas per tent.)

For cheap food, avoid Avda. Agulló and the other main streets. Local families love **Restaurante Turin**, C. de Pola, 21, for its *calamares a la romana* (315ptas) and quarter chicken with salad (280ptas). (Open daily 1-2:30pm and 7-9pm.) **Can Paset**, C. Portal, 11 (tel. 34 10 48), near the old walls, serves *butifarra* for 450ptas and rabbit for 545ptas. (Open daily noon-4pm and 7-11pm.)

Sights and Entertainment

The enchanting **Vila Vella,** a National Artistic Monument, dazzles visitors with its high, golden-hued walls and towers and narrow alleys. On a high part of the walled town stand the ruins of the **Esglesia de San Vincent,** built in the thirteenth century. Outdoor concerts are given here in July, featuring jazz and classical musicians. (Admission 800ptas.) Also inside the walls, on tiny Plaza del Pintor J. Roig y Soler, the **municipal museum** occupies a wonderful old house with low, arched doorways, split-level floors, and stairs going every which way. It displays paintings and sculptures by the many artists who used to frequent Tossa in summer, making it known as "the Babel of the Arts." Marc Chagall and Spanish artists such as Serra, Sisquella, Creixams, and Benet are among those represented. The basement contains artifacts excavated at the nearby **Villa Romana,** including the fourth-century B.C.E. Roman mosaic that constitutes Tossa's first written record. Other mosaics and the foundations of the buildings themselves can be seen at the site off Avda. del Pelegrì. (Museum open Mon.-Sat. 10am-1pm and 3-8pm, Sun. 11am-1pm. Admission 150ptas. Villa Romana is unenclosed and free.)

Tossa itself has three **beaches,** all sheltered from the wind and waves: La Playa Grande, Mar Menuda, and Es Codolar. **Ely,** C. Pola, 10, and **Paradis,** Passeig de Mar, 13, are the currently fashionable discos, but you'll find merrymaking in all the streets after dark. Local festivals take place on January 20 and 21, when the townsfolk reenact the 42-kilometer **pilgrimage** from Tossa to Santa Coloma in honor of St. Sebastian. This is followed on January 22 by a **winter fair** celebrating the Feast of St. Vincent, Tossa's patron saint. A **summer fair** is held on June 29 in honor of St. Peter. The **Sant Grau outing,** a traditional picnic in the hills, takes place on October 13.

Near Tossa: Lloret de Mar

If you hate unspoiled beach towns, you'll love Lloret de Mar. This town of 14,000 people, 12km south of Tossa, bloats to 180,000 in July. Three-foot sombreros and a sunburn are all you'll take away from Lloret. At least there's a booming social life: 25 discotheques, 27 dance clubs, and five gay bars promise after-dark fun. **Platja de Lloret** is big, cleaner than you'd expect, and the best (if not only) sight in town.

Lodgings in Lloret aren't cheap or easy to find. Conduct your housing search between 10am and noon. Be warned that many people reserve summer rooms as early as March. **Hostal-Residencia Montserrat** (tel. 36 44 93) has clean and well-maintained rooms. (Singles 1155ptas. Doubles 2100ptas.) **Casa de Huespedes Alegría,** C. Migdia, 12 (tel. 36 74 72), offers simple, small rooms for 900ptas per person. For reasonably priced eats, try **Zur Wildsau,** C. Lleó, 8. Their 495ptas *menú* includes such foreign fare as *Gemüsesuppe, Bayerischer,* and a particularly tasty *Fleischkase.* If you find the dish names incomprehensible, you're not alone. To buy your own food, go to the central **mercado,** on Carrer Sènia del Rabic at Carrer Sant Roc. (Open Mon.-Sat. 8am-2pm and 6-9pm.) **Cafeteria-Bar "Mary,"** Carrer Sant Pere, 70, serves good *combinados* for 325-550ptas.

There are plenty of ways to get out of Lloret; the quickest is to go to the **bus station** on Carretera de Blanes (tel. 36 44 76), where you can catch buses to Blanes (3 per hr. 8am-9:15pm; 55ptas to town, 60ptas to RENFE station), Barcelona (12 per day, 410ptas, Sat.-Sun. 470ptas), and Girona (5 per day, 250ptas). In Lloret, the main **tourist office** is at Plaça de la Vila, 1 (tel. 36 47 35; open 9am-9pm); the branch office is at the bus terminal (tel. 36 57 88; open 9am-1pm and 4-7pm). If you're determined to stay, both offices can hook you up with an indexed map and list of accommodations. The **post office** is on C. Vincenç Bou. (Open Mon.-Fri. 9am-2pm, Sat. 9am-1pm. **Postal Code:** 17310.) For the municipal **police,** call 092. For a **medical emergency,** call the Creu Roja (Red Cross), Carretera de Blanes (tel. 33 03 36).

Palafrugell

Palafrugell lies smack in the middle of the Costa Brava. The town sits on a small bump several kilometers inland and contains little of interest except the sixteenth-century **Church of Sant Martí.** Without museum or theater to its name, it's a surprise that such a cultural desert actually engendered the renowned Josep Pla, Catalunya's literary master. Palafrugell's greatest fame, though, stems from the three nearby beach colonies that form part of its municipality. **Calella** and **Llafranc** attract the most tourists; **Tamariu** and the nearby rocky inlet of Aigua Xelida are just as beautiful and slightly less crowded. Calella, still a fishing port, offers a string of tiny sand beaches with interesting names: Port-Bou, Port-Pelegrì, El Golfet, Mala Espina, and Canadell. It's also horribly hectic and expensive. Llafranc, about 2km away, is more serene. Whitewashed houses cascade down the hillside, multi-colored boats bob in the harbor, and a double row of coniferous trees shades seaside Passeig de Cipsela. Tamariu's waters are crystal-clear, its village is small and charming, and its indented coastline is perfect for sailboat excursions.

The town congregates on Plaça Nova every Tuesday and Thursday night in July and August for a dance that lasts from 10pm until well into the wee hours. Friday's evening *paseo* also ends up at the *plaça,* where young and old join hands to dance a weekly *sardana* at 10pm. However, the town's biggest party occurs on July 20 and 22, when its citizens celebrate their **Festa Major** with live rock and roll and dancing until dawn. Calella celebrates on June 29 in honor of Sant Pere, Tamariu on August 15, and Llafranc on August 30 in honor of Santa Rosa. During Calella's **Cantata de las Habenaras** (1st Saturday in July), anglers spend the whole day singing old seafaring songs, scaring away most of the fish.

From the bus stop in Calella, a 45-minute walk brings you to the **Castell i Jardins de Cap Roig.** After fleeing his homeland during the revolution, Russian colonel Nicolas Woevodsky settled in Spain, where he constructed a castle overlooking the sea for his wife and himself. Gardening was more than a hobby for the couple; through years of careful pruning they created a splendid maze of paths and flower beds. Be sure to see the cactus garden near the edge of the estate; from here it's possible to discreetly zip down to the rocks below and go for a swim. (Open daily 8am-8pm. Admission 100ptas.) From Calella, walk down Avda. Costa del Sol, which becomes Avda. Costa Daurada as it curves around. Follow the arrows when the *avenida* ends in a residential neighborhood.

Accommodations on all three beaches are expensive—some one star *hostales* charge up to 4000ptas for a double in high season. Palafrugell, however, is a little more affordable and makes a good base from which to explore the area. **Pensió Ramirez,** C. Sant Sebastià, 29 (tel. 30 00 43), 2 blocks off Pl. Nova, has small but comfortable rooms with tile floors for 900ptas per person. Across the street at #34, **Hostal Plaja** (tel. 30 05 26) rents very simple rooms. (1000ptas per person, in off-season 950ptas per person.) **Fonda L' Estrella,** C. Caritat, 61 (tel. 30 00 05), is nestled by a lovely patio with a garden. (1000ptas per person.) To be near the beach in Llafranc, try **Hostal Garbí,** C. Isaac Peral (tel. 30 04 31); bed and breakfast run 1500ptas per person. You can also camp in Llafranc at **Kim** (tel. 30 11 56), which gets quite crowded in summer. (425ptas per person and 450ptas per tent.) At **Camping Moby Dick** (tel. 30 48 07) in Calella, you'll have a whale of a good time. (370ptas per person and 395ptas per tent.)

Palafrugell does offer cheap eats. **Restaurant Cepu,** C. Pi i Maragall, 31 (no phone), serves a half-chicken and fries for 400ptas or *butifarra* and white beans for 350ptas. A friendly couple at **Piscolabis,** C. Pi i Maragall, 18 (no phone), make hot sandwiches such as *sabrassada y queso* (Catalan sausage and cheese) for 175-250ptas. (Open daily noon-11pm.) The daily **fruit and vegetable market** near Pl.

Nova attracts people from nearby towns; the **mercado** on Pi i Maragall is open Monday through Saturday. In Llafranc, head for **Restaurante La Bodega,** C. de Pere Pascuet, 2 (no phone). Cool breezes and lively blue-and-white checked tablecloths brighten the dining "room" (more like a patio). You can get an individual pork chop for 275ptas, a quarter chicken for the same price, or special *platos combinados* for 525-800ptas. (Open daily for meals 1-11pm; 1pm-2am for drinks.)

To get to Palafrugell, take the Sarfa **bus** from the terminal in Girona (13 per day, 50 min., 250ptas). The terminal in Palafrugell is at C. Torres Jonama, 33 (tel. 30 06 23). From there, buses leave for Tamariu (July-Sept. 6 per day, 55ptas) and for Calella and Llafranc (July-Sept. 20 per day, Oct.-June 6 per day; 55ptas). Buses also leave four times per day for the beach of Bagur, Barcelona (July-Sept. 9 per day, Oct.-June 6 per day; 720ptas), and Sant Feliu de Guíxols (9 per day, 125ptas). Llafranc is a 3-kilometer walk from Palafrugell; the two other beaches are 25 minutes from Llafranc. **Bicicletas Domínguez,** C. Torres Junamo, 57, will rent you a bike. (650ptas per day. Open Tues.-Sun.)

Palafrugell's **tourist office** is at C. Carrilet, 2 (tel. 30 02 28), on the outskirts of town. (Open daily 10am-1pm and 5-9pm.) It operates summertime offices in Calella (C. Les Voltes, 4; tel. 30 36 75), Llafranc (Pl. Roger de Llùria; tel. 30 50 08), and Tamariu (Carrer Riera; tel. 30 50 07). (All open Mon.-Sat. 10am-1:30pm and 5-8:30pm, Sun. 10am-1pm.) The **post office** in Palafrugell is on C. Torres Jonama, 16. (Open Mon.-Fri. 9am-1pm, Sat. 9am-1pm. Open for **telegrams** Mon.-Fri. 9am-3pm, Sat. 9am-1pm.) The **postal code** is 17200. Summertime **telephone kiosks** are set up in Plaça Camp d'en Prats in Palafrugell and on Carrer Chopitea in Calella. (Open daily 9am-10pm.) To reach the **police,** call 30 02 42; call the **Creu Roja** (Red Cross) at 30 19 09 or 30 24 52.

Empúries and L'Escala

What began over 2500 years ago as an ambitious trading outpost on an island along the northeast coast of the Iberian peninsula was later expanded on the mainland. Emporion, literally "the market place," peaked in the first century B.C.E.; Roman merchants chose an area just uphill from the Greek colony to build an even larger city. **Empúries,** the name of these collective ruins, refers (in the plural) to the two markets that once existed at different times in this same area. The sea has since receded, uniting the former island with the mainland.

Archeologists continue their excavation of Spain's most important Greek ruins, begun only in the last century. Although only building bases remain in what was the Greek colony, you can easily envision the society that once thrived here with a little imagination and the help of the tour map from the admission gate. The only floor mosaic fully recovered indicates that many professions thrived in Emporion: "sweet coitus" reads the Greek welcome inscription on one doorway. While less work has been done in the Roman area, the ruins of excavated houses, an amphitheater, and an area of the forum indicate a huge city that would easily have dwarfed its Greek neighbor. The **museum** located next to the Greek ruins helps recreate the ambience with a collection of ceramics and artifacts from the necropolis. By the third century C.E., continuous attacks on Empúries and decaying frontiers elsewhere had diminished the Roman presence. Of the Visigoths who later settled on the site, all that remains are the ruins of a paleo-Christian basilica. By the ninth century, the area had fallen prey to the elements. (Grounds and museum open June-Sept. 15 Tues.-Sun. 10am-2pm and 3-7pm; Sept. 16-May Tues.-Sun. 10am-1pm and 3-5pm. Admission 150ptas.)

Two kilometers south of Empúries, **L' Escala** is a town that fully exploit sits touristic potential. Beaches surround the town; as you move closer to the ruins, they become smaller and condo-free. Every Wednesday *sardanes* in the plaza next to La Platja, the town's main beach, remind visitors and locals alike that they are still in Catalunya. Classical music concerts take place every Tuesday. For information on local happenings, consult the exhaustive list compiled by the tourist office.

Finding a room in L' Escala is challenging; many cheap *pensións* require full board of their summer guests. Miracle workers and people who make reservations months in advance may find room at the **IYHF youth hostel** (tel. 77 12 00). If this strategically located hostel got any closer to the ruins of Empúries, it would be declared a national monument. (Members only, 425ptas per person. Sheets 225ptas.) **Hostal Xic, C.** de Empúries, 3 (tel. 77 00 00), is run by a friendly woman and her mother; the clean rooms have weird sheets and holiday-colored bedspreads. (1000ptas per person.) **Hostal Marina, C.** de Gracia, 2 (tel. 77 01 13), offers larger rooms; breakfast and lunch or dinner are required. (1635ptas per person.) **Restaurante La Vinya,** Avda. Girona, 10 (tel. 77 03 46), offers a filling, three-course *menú* with steamed mussels and fried fish for 550ptas.

The **tourist office,** on Pl. de Les Escales (tel. 77 06 03), provides a helpful map and a list of accommodations. (Open daily 10am-1pm and 4-7pm.) The **post office** (tel. 77 16 51) is next door (open Mon.-Fri. 9am-2pm, Sat. 9am-1pm); the **postal code** is 17130. The **telephone center** is on Avda. Ave María near the waterfront. (Open daily 9am-1:30pm and 5-10pm.) Contact the **police** at C. Massanet, 24 (tel. 77 00 86); for an **ambulance,** call 75 92 02.

Sarfa **buses** depart from Avda. Ave María near the tourist office for Figueres (4 per day, 145ptas), Palafrugell (3 per day, 165ptas), Girona (2 per day, 265ptas), and Barcelona (2 per day, 885ptas).

Sant Feliu de Guíxols

One of the most beautiful and dangerous roads on the Costa Brava twists its way north between golden cliffs and frothy blue sea from Tossa to Sant Feliu, 23km up the coast. Sant Feliu, with the largest year-round population on the Costa Brava, has seen its cork export economy surpassed by the growing tourist industry, which the town manages to absorb without losing its identity. Locals still dominate the town's center, and the side streets are home to boatbuilders and kids kicking balls under cars.

You can't see much of Sant Feliu's history in its buildings; knocking down medieval monuments was a favorite hobby of the city's various invaders. However, bunched together in Pl. del Monestir is a significant patchwork of architecture, demonstrating the church's determination always to rebuild on the same spot. Oldest are the **Roman walls** running along the side of the church. A pre-Romanesque archway, the **Porta Ferrada** at the church's entrance dates back to the tenth century; its delicate horseshoe curves exemplify Arabic influence. The **Torre de Fum** served as a lookout tower, and smoke signals originated here when pirates threatened the town. The monastery next to the church and the museum within are undergoing reconstruction, scheduled to be completed in 1990.

After you've had your fill of history, you'll probably want to go to Sant Feliu's **beach,** but arrive before 11am or you'll have a hard time wading through the bodies to get to the water. For a new strip of sand, make the 20-minute walk to **Platja de Sant Pol.** A green Viñolas bus also runs every 30 minutes from Passeig Marítim to Sant Pol (55ptas). The cove opens right to the ocean because there's no marina or commercial docking, and brightly colored fishing boats bob up and down in the bay. Next to Sant Pol, the owner of a five-star hotel installed a 2-kilometer *paseo* along the rocky walls of the sea. As you walk this path with its stunning views of tiny coves and overbearing mansions, you will understand why this stretch of coast is considered *brava,* or untamed. At the end of the walk, **La Conca** is another popular beach.

On the Sunday before or the Saturday after July 16 (whichever falls closer), fishermen dress their ships as part of the **Processió de la Verge del Carme.** The **Festa Major** brings more *sardanes* to Sant Feliu in early August.

Staying in Sant Feliu isn't cheap, but there's normally something available. Many owners will reduce their prices if you stay five days or more. **Fonda Alga,** C. Algavira, 16 (tel. 32 10 33), offers smallish doubles with bright curtains, bedspreads, and a shower in each room (1900ptas). Also try **Amparo Escobedo,** Carrer de la Notería, 20 (no phone); the friendly owner offers only doubles and charges 1000ptas per person. Clean and centrally located though a bit spartan, **Hostal Bib-Cal,** on Carrer Sant Pere (tel. 32 10 10), rents rooms for 900ptas per person.

Eating cheaply is like finding the beach empty in summer, but **Chic Bar,** Rambla Portalet, 6 (tel. 32 10 23), will feed you heaping *combinados* for 375-525ptas. The main market is next to Pl. Espanya. (Open Mon.-Sat. 8am-2pm.) Across the street, at C. Anselm Clavé, 5, you can buy delicious roasted chickens for 550ptas. For a unique drinking experience, head down Passeig del Mar to Rambla Portalet. You can't miss **Nou Casino.** This puzzling modernist eruption resembles a mosque gone beserk; after you walk through the Arabic archway, you'll be surrounded by old men playing checkers and sipping beers, in an atmosphere similar to that of a bingo hall. Attempts to raze this architectural freak were violently opposed by citizens fond of their unique drinking hole.

The **tourist office,** Pl. d'Espanya, 6-9 (tel. 32 03 80), is packed with information about the cost of the Costa Brava, but has little more to offer about its own city than a map. (Open Mon.-Sat. 9am-2pm and 4-9pm, Sun. 9am-2pm; in off-season Mon.-Sat. 8am-2pm.) The Guiá del Sardanista will inform you about which *cobla* (*sardana* group) is playing each Wednesday night at 10:15pm. The tourist office also compiles a monthly list of events. The **post office** is at Carrer Girona, 15 (tel. 32 11 60; open Mon.-Fri. 9am-2pm, Sat. 9am-1pm). You can make collect **telephone calls** at Rambla Vidal, 44. (Open Mon.-Fri. 9am-1:30pm and 5-10pm.) The helpful municipal **police** are located at Pl. d'Espanya, 6-9 (tel. 32 42 11), in the same building as the tourist office. For **medical emergencies,** call the hospital, Carrer Hospital, 27 (tel. 32 43 14).

Sant Feliu is well connected to the rest of the world via **buses** and boats. Compañia de Ferrocarril de San Feliu de Guíxols a Girona runs the quickest bus to Girona, which leaves Pl. del Monestir (15 per day, 50 min., 225ptas). Sarfa, Carretera Girona, 35 (tel. 32 11 87), will take you north to Palafrugell (10 per day, 40 min., 145ptas) and south to Barcelona (10 per day, 605ptas). To journey south by sea, catch a ride with Cruceros's ocean-going vessels. **Boats** leave from the beach at the end of Rambla D'Antoni Vidal (tel. 32 00 26) to Tossa (4 per day, 1 hr., 550ptas), Lloret (4 per day, 1½ hr., 700ptas), and Blanes (4 per day, 2 hr., 800ptas).

Figueres (Figueras)

Figueres was a forgotten child of Spain's great tourism boom until its most famous son, Salvador Dalí, chose to let his imagination run wild in the town's ruined theatre. The **Museu Dalí** has since become one of Spain's most popular art institutions. The exhibit includes his erotic and nightmarish drawings, extra-worldly landscapes, and even personal rock collections, elements of which resemble human forms. For surrealist fun that kids will also enjoy, go straight to the black Cadillac with a 5-foot hood ornament and drop a coin in the slot; what follows is pure Dalí. (Open July-Sept. daily 9am-9pm; Oct.-June Tues.-Sun. 11:30am-5:30pm. Admission 300ptas, students 100ptas.) The same ticket will get you into the **Museu de l'Empordà,** a few blocks away on the Rambla. The museum houses some mildly interesting Roman remains and a collection of paintings from the Catalan *Renaixença.* (Open Tues.-Sat. 11am-1pm and 4:30-8pm, Sun. 11am-2pm and 4:30-8pm.)

The **Museu de Joguets,** Rambla, 10, hordes old toys, including miniature Singer sewing machines that really worked when tiny hands turned their crankwheels. Along with the permanent collection of tin soldiers and dollhouses, the museum also hosts temporary exhibits. One recent display highlighted toys designed for blind children. (Open July-Aug. daily 10am-12:30pm and 4-7:30pm; Sept.-June Wed.-Mon. only. Admission 200ptas.)

If you wish you were at the beach, you'll have to settle for the municipal **swimming pool,** C. Cusi i Fortunet (tel. 50 93 39), just behind the municipal park. (Open Mon.-Fri. 8am-2pm and 3-10pm, Sat. 9am-1pm and 3-7pm, Sun. 9am-2pm. Admission 100ptas.) On May 3, Figueres celebrates **Fires i Festes de la Santa Creu** with local competitions, cultural events, and expositions of drawings, paintings, and commercial machinery. The **Feast of Saint Peter,** the town's patron saint, is an occasion for revelry June 28-29.

Because so many visitors pass through without spending the night, finding a room should be no problem, except at the beginning of May, when the town celebrates its fiestas. The cheapest place to stay is the newly renovated **IYHF youth hostel,** C. Anicet de Pagés, 2 (tel. 50 12 13), a block from Pl. del Sol. Hot showers and French television make this place a popular stop-over. All rooms have three bunk-beds, except one with eight. (Lock-in 11pm-6:30am. Lockout 1-5pm. Rooms locked 10am-6pm. 425ptas; nonmembers (only when they're not crowded) 725ptas, 300ptas of which go toward 1/6 of an IYHF card. Sheets 225ptas.) If you want a little peace and quiet, stay at **Pensión Alay,** C. de la Jonquera, 15 (no phone). The owner runs the clothing store downstairs and fits her rooms with beautiful curtains and bedspreads. (700ptas per person.) **Pensión Rosa,** C. de la Rosa, 12 (tel. 50 90 19), 2 blocks from the Rambla, offers clean doubles off dark corridors for 1400ptas.

Try **Restaurant-Cafeteria Chappy,** C. Vilafant, 26 (tel. 51 08 03), for a 500ptas *menú* that includes simple but well-prepared tortillas, gazpacho, and chicken. (Open daily 1-4pm and 8-10pm.) **Brindis Snack,** C. de la Muralla, 12 (no phone), is run by a friendly Catalan woman who will feed you fried eggs, salad, and *butifarra* (500ptas) 'til you're full. (Open daily 1-4pm and 8-11pm.)

The **bus** and **train station** are next to each other at Plaça Estació. Sarfa buses (tel. 50 01 59) go to Cadaqués (3 per day, 220ptas), while Teisa buses go to Olot (3 per day, 285ptas), where you can make the connection to Ripoll. RENFE trains run to Port Bou (1 per hr., 140ptas) and Barcelona (1 per hr., 690ptas). The **tourist office** is on Pl. del Sol (tel. 50 31 55). They have a good map of the city and information on the Costa Brava. (Open Mon.-Sat. 9am-1pm and 3-6pm.) Also on Pl. del Sol is the **post office** (tel. 50 54 31) and the **phone kiosk** (open Mon.-Sat. 9am-2pm and 5-10pm). From the stations, the most direct route to Pl. del Sol is straight up C. Llàtzer (which becomes C. Collegi halfway up) to the Ronda de Barcelona. Turn right, and you'll hit the plaza in 2 blocks. The town's **postal code** is 17600. You can contact the **Creu Roja** (Red Cross) on Ronda de Barcelona (tel. 50 56 01). The **municipal police** (tel. 51 01 11) share the same building with the tourist office.

Cadaqués

The beautiful cluster of quiet, whitewashed houses around a small bay has lured artists to Cadaqués like sailors following a siren's song. However, its popularity may eventually prove Cadaqués's demise. Ever since Dalí built a house nearby in Port Lligat, this once-quiet fishing town has grown trendy beyond belief. Despite its development as a center for artists and musicians, however, condos and giant buildings have somehow been kept out of Cadaqués. The town's true pride, its "profile" painted from the southern tip of the bay, is as persuasive as ever.

The **Museu Municipal,** C. Monturiol, houses works donated by local artists, most of whom work under the influence of Dalí's surrealism or the area's rocky coastline. (Open Tues.-Sat. 10am-1pm and 4-8pm, Sun. 11am-1pm. Admission 100ptas.) The **Museu Perrot-Moore,** C. Vigilant, near the center of town, contains much Dalí memorabilia, including the doodles in his chemistry book, pictures of him as a young whippersnapper, and lots of lithographs and posters of his work. (Open Mon.-Sat. 11am-1pm and 5-9pm, Sun. 10am-2pm. Admission an inflated 200ptas, students 100ptas.)

Classical music concerts captivate the town for one month beginning at the end of July. The **Festival Internacional de Música** consists of nine concerts, two of which are given by student musicians. (Tickets 600-900ptas; the one contemporary music concert is free. For more information, call 25 83 15.) During the rest of the summer, people dance *sardanes* in the street every Saturday at 10pm and move to live rock every other Thursday. The **market** is held on Monday mornings. The beaches are covered by dark, pebbly sand. Those determined to catch some rays can try the **Platia Gran,** near the town center, or, even better, **Sa Concha,** to the south of town.

People come and go in Cadaqués so you should be able to find a room, though your choices are limited. **Hostal Marina,** just off Pl. Frederic Rohola (tel. 25 81

99), offers fine rooms smack in the center of town for 1000ptas per person. Next door at **Hostal Cristina** (no phone), equally satisfactory doubles go for 2500ptas. **Hostal Ubaldo**, C. Unió, 13 (tel. 25 81 25), offers fancier doubles for 2900ptas. Many people head straight for the campground, a few kilometers north of Cadaqués off Carretera Port Lligat. Since it's the only one in the vicinity, **Camping Cadaqués** (tel. 25 81 26) can charge a lot—330ptas per person and 430ptas per tent. (Open April-Oct.) The good part is that the beach is only ½km away.

The **tourist office,** Carrer Cotxe, 2 (tel. 25 83 15), just off Pl. Frederic Rahola opposite the *passeig,* provides lots of information about local events and the usual pictures of the Costa Brava. (Open in summer Mon.-Sat. 10am-1pm and 4:30-8pm, Sun. 10am-noon; in off-season fewer hours.) For **medical attention,** call 25 80 97. The more-than-helpful **local police** (tel. 25 81 94) are located at the Ayuntamiento on Es Baluart, the point to the right of the main beach. The **post office** can be found on an alley of Passeig Caritat Serinyana. (Open Mon.-Fri. 9am-2pm, Sat. 9am-1pm.) The town's **postal code** is 17488. To get around Cadaqués, you can rent bikes (350ptas per 2 hr., 750ptas per day) and mopeds (1200ptas per 2 hr., 2000ptas per day) at **Motos Cadaqués,** C. Tortola (tel. 25 87 35; open daily 10am-1pm and 3-8pm.)

Three **buses** per day run to Cadaqués from the bus station in Figueres; the first one leaves at 9:15am and the last one back leaves at 5pm (225ptas). Sarfa runs buses to and from Barcelona (July-Sept. 15 4 per day, Sept. 16-June 2 per day). The buses drop you off at the junction of Carretera Port Lligat and Passeig Caritat Serinyana; take the latter to get to the town center.

Port Bou, Llançà, and Sant Pere de Roda

Peaceful **Port Bou** metamorphosed into one big train station cafe about a hundred years ago upon the opening of the Barcelona-Port Bou-Cerbère railroad. Once a small fishing community, Port Bou now caters to the one-day tourists who flow through the town on their way somewhere else. It also sports a large beach that's usually crowded near town, but you may escape the throngs if you walk around to the left. There isn't much else to do in town, except have a drink in one of the many cafes along Passeig Marítim.

If you do get stuck in Port Bou, the town offers plenty of lodging options. **Hostal Plaza,** Carrer Mercat, 15 (tel. 39 00 24), on your left as you walk down from the train station, has smallish, marginally clean rooms; doubles cost 1750ptas. Closer to the beach you'll find **Hostal Juventus,** Avda. de Barcelona, 3 (tel. 39 02 41), with doubles for 1800ptas.

The most helpful **tourist office** in Port Bou is at the RENFE station (tel. 39 05 07; open daily 5:45am-2pm and 7-11:30pm). The **municipal police** can be found next door at Passeig de la Sardana, 11 (tel. 39 02 07). The **Centre Local de Salut** (clinic) is in the same building; in an **emergency,** call 39 06 06. For RENFE information, call 39 00 99 (open 7am-2pm and 4-11pm). Trains leave at least once per hour for Barcelona (735ptas) and Cerbère.

Some 7km from Port Bou, **Llançà** is the first major resort of the Costa Brava, with many beaches and coves as well as a smattering of historical sights. Platja del Port (beach) opens onto a protected harbor great for windsurfing or learning how to sail. Outside town lies the eleventh-century chapel of **Sant Silvestre de Valleta i del Terrer.** A beautiful Romanesque building with simple, narrow windows, the hermitage is the site of the town's yearly festival. To get there from town, take a right from the train station onto Carretera de la Bisbal. Cross the river on a bridge opposite the soccer field and continue on the path up the hill. Near the top take the left fork for the hermitage (1 hr.). The right fork leads to the dump.

Llançà's **Habitacions Can Pau,** C. Afora, 22 (tel. 38 02 71), is your best bet for lodgings in summer. Simple, clean doubles (1400ptas) and singles (not many at 900ptas) sprout out of a steep, narrow staircase. You'll have to run from landing to landing to be near the light switches because the *señora* keeps 10-second automatic timer-makers in business. From Pl. Mayor, walk down C. Salmerón; turn left on C. del Norte and wind your way up to C. Afora. **Hostal Gran Sol,** C.

Figueres, 4 (tel. 38 01 51), rents doubles for 2300ptas. **Restaurante El Puerto,** C. Castellar (tel. 38 00 44), has the cheapest *menú* around (625ptas) and serves good seafood, such as *merluza* and squid.

The mobbed staff in the **tourist office,** Avda. Europa, 17 (tel. 38 08 55), on the road to the port, will provide you with a terrible map, useful from town to the port, but not through the tiny streets near Pl. Major The **Creu Roja** (Red Cross) is on Carretera à Portbou (tel. 38 08 31). The **Guardia Civil** is near Pl. Major, (tel. 38 01 22). About 10 RENFE trains per day run to Llançà from Figueres (15 min., 80ptas) and Port Bou (10 min., 50ptas). To get to the town center from the station, cross the highway onto Avda. Europa and take a right when it curves to the left. To get to the port and the beaches, follow the curve to the left and walk about 1km.

The spectacular ruins of the monastery **Sant Pere de Roda** lie 9km south of Llançà. This Benedictine monastery was constructed during the tenth and eleventh centuries, and was unassailable thanks to the defense walls around the buildings. The monastery was abandoned in the eighteenth century, but the church remains fairly well preserved. (Open Mon.-Sat. 10am-2pm and 4-7pm. Admission 75ptas.) The monastery offers a spectacular view of the coastline; on a clear day you can easily see Port Bou to the north and Cadaqués to the south. If you don't have a car, it's an adventure getting there. **Autocares Estarriol** (tel. 38 74 55) leaves from the train station in Llançà and goes to Port de la Selva, 20km south. Catch this bus (6 per day, 45ptas) and ask to be dropped off at the road to the *monastir.* From there, you can try your luck at hitchhiking or make the hour-long hike, for which you will be supremely rewarded.

Andorra

The tiny principality of Andorra, with just 468 square kilometers of land to its name, sits in the middle of the French and Spanish Pyrenees. Once an undiscovered natural refuge, this tiny state has become a giant supermarket. Governed jointly by the Bishop of Urgell and the French head of state, Andorra imposes very low import taxes, making merchandise relatively cheap. Consequently, thousands of eager shoppers cross the border each week to stock up on cigarettes, liquor, and electronic equipment.

Hiking trails lead to unspoiled areas for great summer camping, and during the winter the state becomes an alpine skier's paradise with five different ski areas all accessible by the morning's bus from Andorra la Vella. Despite its natural beauty, Andorra's glut of bargain-seeking shoppers renders it an unappealing destination. If you do choose to visit Andorra, avoid the tourist-lined stores of its main city, and head instead to the tranquil and unpopulated countryside.

Balearic Islands

Tourism has become the main industry of this wealthy archipelago. The province's most important islands are Mallorca, Menorca, Ibiza, and Formentera. Thousands descend upon these sun-soaked islands each summer, making the residents some of Spain's richest citizens. Those islanders not running a restaurant or *pensión* might be working in the blanketing olive, fig, and almond groves. Since the Moors introduced the practice of growing cereals along with fruits, wheat or barley fields usually lie beneath these groves. The islands also produce delicious citrus fruits, exported to the peninsula and the rest of Europe.

Mallorca, with the province's capital Palma, attracts the most visitors. The beautiful Serra de Tramontana, with its jagged limestone cliffs, lines the north coast, while large, lazy bays scoop into the rest of the coastline. However, most of Mallorca's sandy beaches lie somewhere underneath layers of foreign flesh. Package tours dominate the island, as do beach condominiums and apartments. Ibiza, once a haven for Europe's hippies, follows a close second in luring tourists to this Mediterranean playground. Its whitewashed houses and endless condominiums house the most trendy of Europe's rich, who have come to flaunt their fashions and full-body tans. While the proper and upright shop in Palma, Ibiza's shoppers plunge into the enchanted world of the androgynous. Menorca offers a sobering contrast to this chaotic inundation of foreign visitors and remains the most genuine of the islands. Wrapped in green fields and strings of stone walls, Menorca's treasures are easily found: empty white beaches and mysterious Bronze Age remnants that befuddle the modern archeologist.

Reservations are highly recommended in July and August, when Mallorca and Ibiza are saturated with visitors. You can probably find a room at the last minute, but try to reserve by mail with one night's deposit and follow up with a confirmation. At the least, telephone for reservations a day or two ahead of time. You can always camp, but there is only one official campgrounds on Mallorca, and all the others are on Ibiza; and even campsites may be reserved. Many sites on all the islands, especially in the southeastern part of Mallorca, seem to invite illegal camping. If you travel before July or after mid-September, you should have your pick of rooms and rates anywhere in the archipelago. You'll find the best weather in autumn and spring anyway; summer days, while often blessed with a northeasterly wind, can be hot and humid, and winters can be quite cold.

The invention of mayonnaise catapulted Maò, the capital of Menorca, onto the culinary map. *Pa-amb-oli* (literally "bread with oil," usually served with ham, tomato, or egg) makes a great snack between meals, especially during a *paseo* before dinner. More substantial gastronomical specialties include *sopa mallorquina*, a heavy vegetable soup ladled over a hunk of brown bread, and *escaldums,* a savory chicken dish. If you're feeling adventurous, try *lenguas de cerdo con salsa de granada,* pigs' tongues in pomegranate sauce. Soft spicy sausages, such as *camaiot, sobressada,* and *botifarrons,* are great for picnics. While the islands do produce some good dry wines, better-known are the gin and sweet liqueur distilleries on Menorca.

Getting There

By Air

Charters are the cheapest and quickest means of round-trip travel. They are usually difficult to find and reservations must be made at least a month in advance. Charters leave from Barcelona (round-trip to Palma, 8000ptas). Most travel agents can book these flights and offer package deals, for instance, seven nights in a hotel near Palma and transportation to and from the airport for 14,500ptas. Student travel offices will have also reserved some spots on these charters, and you can make reservations if you show an ISIC.

If nothing seems to be available, try going to the airport: If an unscheduled flight (usually on Spantax or Aviaco) is not full a few hours before departure, the remaining seats may be sold to non-package customers. To procure such a seat, travelers must usually deal with tour company representatives rather than with airlines.

Scheduled flights are easier to book, with frequent departures from Barcelona, Madrid, and Alicante, as well as regular flights from Paris, London, and other European capitals. Iberia handles all flights from the Iberian Peninsula to the islands. However, prices are not low. From Barcelona, a one-way ticket to Palma costs 6725ptas; Valencia to Palma runs 7090ptas; Madrid to Palma 12,100ptas. Another option is the *tarifa-mini* fare. This discounts round-trip tickets by 40%, but only five or six seats are available per flight, and they are almost always sold out up to six months beforehand. It's still worth checking; any travel agent can make the reservation for you.

By Water

You can almost always go to the Balearics at the last minute by boat, and the fares are about as low as those for charter flights. The trip takes a little longer, but there's a disco and small swimming pool aboard. In addition, an overnight ferry saves you hotel costs.

Transmediterránea used to rule the waves between the peninsula and the islands. Their ships depart from Barcelona (office at Via Layetana, 2; tel. 319 82 12) and Valencia (office at Avda. Manuel Soto Ingeniero, 15; tel. 367 65 12); any travel agent in Spain will also book a seat for you. Ships sail from both ports to Palma, Maò, and Ibiza City. All connections are direct except Valencia-Maò, a painful 18-hour trip via Palma. Ships run with the following frequencies in summer (winter figures in parentheses): Barcelona-Palma, 10 per week (10); Barcelona-Ibiza, eight per week (4); Barcelona-Menorca, five per week (2); Valencia-Palma, nine per week (7); Valencia-Ibiza, four per week (2). The journey lasts 7-9½ hours, and the standardized fare is 4550ptas one way for a *butaca* (airplane-style seat). Reservations made a few days in advance are helpful, but tickets are often available until an hour before departure.

Flebasa (a.k.a. ISNASA) challenges Transmediterránea in the Ibiza market. The trip takes only three hours, and their boats serve Porto San Antonio rather than Ibiza City, departing from Denia on the peninsula. Denia lies on the FEVE rail line between Valencia and Alicante. In conjunction with **Ubesa Buses**, they offer free feeders from the bus stations in both of those cities, timed to match their seven departures per week (in summer). A one-way ticket from Madrid costs 6200ptas. From Valencia, Alicante, or Denia, the trip costs 4700ptas. Offices are located at the ports of Denia (tel. (965) 78 40 11 or 78 41 00), Valencia (tel. (96) 340 09 55), Alicante (tel. (965) 22 21 88), and San Antonio (tel. (971) 34 29 71 and 34 28 71). Travel agents can also book for this company.

Getting Around

The friendly skies provide the best means of island-hopping. Transmediterránea connects Palma with Ibiza City (2-3 per week, 4½ hr., one way 3600ptas) and Maò (1 per week, 6½ hr., one way 3600ptas), but the airlines are quicker, cheaper, and more fun. **Iberia** flies from Palma to Ibiza (3-4 per day, 20 min., one way 3360ptas) and Maò (2-3 per day, 20 min., one way 3360ptas). If you fly to Menorca, however, remember that no bus connects the airport to the city; you'll have to hitch or take a taxi (600ptas) into Maò. The planes fill a couple days in advance in summer, so be sure to make reservations. If you're flying round-trip, ask if the *tarifa-mini* fare is applicable. Mallorca, Menorca, and Ibiza all operate cheap and extensive **bus** systems. Mallorca also has two narrow-gauge train systems that don't accept Eurailpass. Traveling anywhere on Mallorca, Menorca, or Ibiza should never cost more than 300-400ptas. Since many of the islands' most beautiful areas, especially beaches, are inaccessible without wheels, you may also want to take advantage of the countless rental agencies for cars, mopeds, and bikes. A full day in a car such as a SEAT Panda should cost around 3600ptas, including insurance; on a Vespa or moped 1500-1800ptas, and on a bicycle about 350-400ptas. Hitching is quite safe and relatively easy on all three islands.

Mallorca (Majorca)

Many peoples have invaded this largest of the islands since the Bronze Age, and now more visit Palma, its largest city, than any other Spanish city. Once you emerge from the urban decadence of endless condominiums and expensive boutiques, you'll find an enchanting island with a variety of landscapes. The **Jagged Edge** of **Serra de Tramontana** stretches along the island's northwestern coast, hiding its isolated beaches of white sand and frothy water. Lemon groves and 1000-year-old olive trees cling to the hillsides in their terraced plots. To the east, you'll find expansive beaches, some as long as 6km, that open onto peaceful bays. The southeastern coast hides its beauty underground in giant caves that dangle menacing stalactites over your head. While the coast supports Mallorca's booming tourist industry by housing the thousands who flock here on package tours, the inland plains, dotted with windmills drawing water up for the almond and fig trees, are the agricultural heartland of a thriving economy.

Buses go to virtually every corner of the island, and hitchhiking is a snap. Be sure to try the island's favorite snack, the *ensaimada*—a light pastry with powdered sugar, and its fresh fruit. The well-informed and friendly tourist offices in Palma can lead you to wide open countryside for hiking or town centers for cultural expositions.

Palma

Palma is by far the largest and busiest of Balearic cities. You cannot arrive in Mallorca without passing through this urban mixmaster, where the first five people you bump into will each speak a different language. Most of them will glow like a boiled lobster. Shops sell leather coats and bags, designer clothes of every fashion, jewelry, silverware, and fancy car stereos. Amidst this chaotic consumption, the *mallorquines* go about their business, most of which concerns getting your money. Ironically, Palma itself has no beaches; they lie to the north and south of the city, where condo-crazed foreigners have lined the shore with apartments.

Orientation and Practical Information

To get to the town center from the airport, take bus #17 to Pl. España (every 25 min. 6:30am-10:30pm, 120ptas). From the ferry dock, walk outside the parking lot and turn right on Paseo Marítimo. Take bus #1 (60ptas) to **Plaza de la Reina.** Passeig des Born/Paseo de Borne leads away from the sea to **Plaza Pio XII. Avenida Rey Jaume III,** the main business drag, continues to the left. To the right, Carrer de la Unió leads after some stairs to the **Plaza Major,** the center of the pedestrian shopping district. **Plaza España,** where you will go sooner or later to catch a bus, lies off the end of Carrer de San Miguel, which starts at the Pl. Major.

Tourist Offices: National, Avda. Rey Jaime III, 10 (tel. 71 22 16), off Pl. Pio XII. Excellent information about all the islands in English—everything from accommodations to bus schedules. During the real crunch (mid-July to Aug.), they'll be reluctant to abandon you and will provide emergency help looking for rooms. Open Mon.-Fri. 9am-1:30pm and 3-8pm, Sat. 9am-1pm; in off-season Mon.-Sat. 9am-8pm, Sun. 9am-2pm. Branch office at the **airport** (tel. 26 08 03). Open Mon.-Sat. 9am-9pm, Sun. 9am-2pm; in off-season Mon.-Sat. 9am-8pm, Sun. 9am-2pm. **Municipal,** C. Santo Domingo, 11 (tel. 72 40 90 or 71 57 41), just as helpful and English-speaking. Many additional useful publications, including the monthly *A Palma,* with information about cultural events. Open Mon.-Fri. 9am-8:30pm and Sat. 9am-1:30pm. The **information booth** in Pl. España (tel. 71 15 27) is a branch of this operation. Open Mon.-Fri. 9am-8pm, Sat. 9am-1pm.

Student Travel: Viajes TIVE, C. Venerable Jeronimo Antich, 5 (tel. 71 17 85), near Pl. Obispo Berenguer de Palon toward Pl. España. Transalpino tickets, student IDs, IYHF cards, and mainland flights (call a few days in advance). Go elsewhere for inter-island travel. Open Mon.-Fri. 8:30am-2:30pm.

Consulates: U.S., Avda. Rey Jaime III, 26 (tel. 72 26 60). Open Mon.-Fri. 4-7pm. **U.K.,** Pl. Major, 30 (tel. 71 24 45), through the arcades off one corner. Open June-Oct. Mon.-Fri. 9am-1:30pm, Sat. 9:30am-12:30pm; Nov.-May Mon.-Fri. 9am-1pm and 4-6pm, Sat. 9:30am-12:30pm.

American Express: Viajes Iberia, Passeig des Born, 14 (tel. 72 67 43). Only a representative office, so it can't accept wired money. Open Mon.-Fri. 9am-1:45pm and 4-6:45pm, Sat. 9am-12:45pm.

Post Office: C. de la Constitució, 6 (tel. 22 18 67). Stamps and parcels (in basement) open Mon.-Sat. 9am-2pm. Poste Restante, upstairs at window #24, open Mon.-Fri. 9am-8pm, Sat. 9am-2pm. **Postal Code:** 07000.

Telephones: Avda. Rey Jaume III, 20. Open Mon.-Sat. 9:30am-1:30pm and 5-9pm. Also at C. de la Constitució, 2. Slow and inefficient. Be prepared to wait even if there's no line. Open

Mon.-Sat. 9:30am-1:30pm and 4:30-6:30pm, Sun. and holidays 10am-2pm. **Telephone code:** 971 for all the Balearics.

Airport: Aeropuerto Son San Juan, Tel. 26 46 24. Catch bus #17 inside the bus station at Pl. España (every ½-hr. 6:30am-10:30pm, ½ hr., 120ptas). **Iberia,** Passeig des Born, 10 (tel. 28 69 66 or 46 34 00 for reservations). Open Mon.-Fri. 9am-1:30pm and 5-7pm, Sat. 9am-1:15pm. Gets crowded in the afternoon. **Spantax** Tel. 26 77 00 or 28 50 08. **Aviaco,** Tel. 26 50 50.

Train Stations: Ferrocarril de Sóller, C. Eustebio Estada, 1/6 (tel. 25 20 28), off Pl. España. 6 per day over the 30km to Sóller (270ptas). Avoid the 10:40am "tourist-train"; prices are inflated to 375ptas for the privilege of a 10-min. stop in Mirador del Pujol d'en Banya. To Port Sóller (75ptas). **FEVE,** on Pl. España (tel. 25 22 45), goes inland to Inca about once every 40 min., on weekends once per hr. (140ptas). **RENFE** does not offer service, but maintains an information/bookings office at Pl. España (tel. 75 88 01).

Buses: Buses service virtually all points on the island. Fares 100-350ptas, typically 2-8 buses per day. Many buses depart from the bus station in Pl. España (tel. 25 22 24), near the Terminus Hotel. Even if this station doesn't handle your bus, chances are that it departs from somewhere near the plaza and that you can buy tickets on board. The tourist office provides a list of all services to and from Palma.

Ferries: Trasmediterránea, Muelle Viejo, 5 (tel. 72 67 40). Bus #1 runs along the Paseo Marítimo to the Muelle de Pelaires. Tickets sold Mon.-Fri. 8am-1pm and 5-7pm, Sat. 9am-noon. All travel agents charge the same prices. Ferries actually dock at the Muelle de Pelaires (a bit around the bay south of the city), where tickets may also be bought until shortly before sailing. To Ibiza in summer Wed. and Fri. at 9am and Sat. at 11:45pm; in off-season 2 per week (4½ hr., 3600ptas). To Mahón (Menorca) Sun. at 9am (6½ hr., 3600ptas). For schedules to the mainland, see the Balearic Islands Introduction.

Taxis: Tel. 25 54 40 or 40 14 40. The fare to the airport—one of the longer rides you're likely to take—is about 1500ptas, but the bus is painless.

Car Rental: Atesa, C. Antonio Ribas, 33 (tel. 24 04 04), east of downtown and parallel to, though somewhat inland from, the coast. A day often means 8am-9pm. Rentals of more than 3 days get discounts, as do those in off-season.

Bike or Moped Rental: Bom, C. Jabeque, 10 (tel. 26 68 84), in C'an Pastilla. Take bus #15. Many places that rent mopeds also rent bikes, but the bikes are usually not much cheaper. You need a cycle license for the more powerful mopeds.

English Bookstores: Maxine's Anglo-American Library, C. Teniente Mulet, 36, beyond Pl. Gomilia. A great selection of used novels and paperbacks. Open Mon.-Fri. 10:30am-1:30pm, Sat. 10am-1pm. Many bookstores closer to town have a token stock of English books.

Laundromat: Espartero, C. Espartero, 15 (tel. 45 35 20), near Pl. del Progreso. Friendly but expensive. 575ptas per machine. Wash and dry 700ptas. Open Mon.-Tues. and Thurs.-Fri. 10am-2pm and 5-8pm, Wed. 10am-2pm and 7-9pm.

Medical Assistance: Casa de Socorro, Pl. Santa Eulalia (tel. 72 21 79), near Pl. Cort. **Centro Médico,** Paseo Maritimo, 16 (tel. 23 00 23). Emergency (but private) medical care.

Police: Municipal, Avda. San Fernando (tel. 28 16 00). **Emergency:** Tel. 091.

Accommodations

Palma is the easiest place to find a room in the Balearics. If you plan to arrive during the peak summer rush, however, make reservations. The best places to look are around **Passeig des Born** and **Place Mayor,** but if you don't have any luck here try the **El Terreno** section to the west.

Alberg Juvenil Platja de Palma (IYHF), C. Costa Brava, 13 (tel. 26 08 92), in El Arenal. Take bus #15 from Pl. España (70ptas). Canned music in hallway speakers, canned sardines in rooms, but immaculate and only 2 blocks from the beach. Curfew 11:30pm. 500ptas, nonmembers 600ptas. Open Dec.-Oct.

Hostal La Paz, C. Salas, 5 (tel. 71 50 10), near the center. From Avda. Rey Jaime III, turn left onto C. Protectora then right onto C. Salas. Green, clean, and not at all mean. Poor maid service. Singles 1000ptas. Doubles 1500ptas. Shower included. Breakfast in bright dining room 225ptas.

Hostal Gual, C. Marina, 4 (tel. 71 20 39). From Pl. de la Reina, go down C. Mar and take a right on C. Boteria, which becomes C. Marina after a block. Small but cute rooms. 2 min. stay. Singles 1000ptas. Doubles 2000ptas.

Hostal Borne, San Jaime, 3 (tel. 71 29 42), off Pl. Pio XII. Shady rooms with a quiet patio in back. A little expensive, but palatial for the budget traveler. Its great halls and rooms give you a sense of Palma before the tourist invasion. Usually packed; make reservations. Singles 1340-1462ptas. Doubles 2194-2681ptas.

Hostal Goya, C. Estanco, 7 (tel. 71 21 34), off Passeig des Born. Simple, clean rooms. Singles 800ptas. Doubles 1300ptas.

Hostal Residencia Pons, C. General Barceló, 8 (tel. 72 26 58). C. General Barceló is at the end of C. Apuntadores, which starts at Pl. de la Reina. A pretty *hostal* with a living-room atmosphere. No 2 rooms are alike. Singles 700ptas. Doubles 1200ptas. Showers 150ptas. Up the stairs to the right is **Hostal Residencia Palma** (tel. 72 44 17), run by two friendly nuns and just as pretty. Singles 800ptas. Doubles 1200ptas. Showers (sometimes hot) included.

Pensión Brondo, C. Brondo, 1 (tel. 72 38 04), off Pl. Pio XII. Breezy but small rooms in a central location. Bring bugspray since the courtyard is a popular hangout for mosquitoes. Singles 1000ptas. Doubles 1500ptas. Showers 150ptas.

Food

Part of the fun of eating in Palma is seeing how many languages the menu comes in. German, French, and English, along with Catalán and Spanish, are common, although some places go to such linguistic extremes as Finnish or Swedish. Only the truly bold dispense with Spanish and Catalán altogether. Such tourist-oriented restaurants aren't, however, great bargains. Your best bet for a filling lunch is to stick to the *tapas variadas* of a small bar, Or buy the makings of a meal at the **market,** in Pl. del Olivar, near Pl. Espaañ, and across town by Pl. de Navegación. (Open Mon.-Sat. mornings.)

Restaurant Yate Rizz, Passeig des Born, 2 (tel. 72 62 46). This neon-front restaurant's 425ptas *menú* and friendly service are a pleasant contrast to the expensive, impersonal places around it. Open daily noon-3:30pm; in off-season Mon.-Sat. noon-3:30pm.

Cowboy Bar, C. Miguel Rossello Alemany, 2B (tel. 40 55 57), in Cala Major. Take bus #3, 20, 21, or 22 and get off near the Nixe Palace Hotel on the left. Alemany goes uphill to the right. *The* exception to the rule of sticking to local cuisine. The Mexican food here is fresher, tastier, and of better quality than much of what is offered in Mexico. The chili may be the best in the world. Popular hangout for U.S. seamen.

Casa Julio, C. Prevision, 4 (no phone), on a pedestrian street near Pl. Cort. Rather boring 500ptas *menú,* but the a la carte menu offers many rice dishes and some interesting Mallorcan specialties, such as *espinagrada* (peppers and greens rolled in pastry). Open Mon.-Sat. noon-4:30pm.

La Viña, C. General Barceló, 8 (tel. 72 11 45). The kind of restaurant you'd expect in a less touristed city. Full of locals who've come for a hearty meal. 375ptas *menú* includes large salads and fried *mallorquín,* a local fish. Open Mon.-Sat. 12:30-4pm and 8:30-11pm.

Bodega Casa Payesa, C. de Molineros, 3 (no phone), in an alleyway off C. San Miguel. This tiny place serves a large selection of *bocadillos* (around 100ptas), a *menú* for 400ptas, and simple meals for 280-350ptas. Open daily 8am-8:30pm.

El Jardín, C. Joan Miró, 57 (tel. 45 49 73), in the El Terreno area. Large salads under 500ptas, but most meals are more expensive. When you smell the outdoor grill, you'll want to break your budget. Open daily 8pm-3am; in off-season Mon.-Sat. 8pm-3am.

C'an Joan de S'aigo, C. Sans, 10 (tel. 71 07 59), near Pl. Coll. This old-fashioned ice cream and pastry parlor is a tradition. An indoor fountain and caged songbirds make it a pleasant retreat from the tourist crowds only a few blocks away. Order anything and everything; it's all inexpensive and all scrumptious. Open Wed.-Mon. until 9:15pm.

C'an Miguel Gelateria, Avda. Rey Jaime III, 6. Scoops out such bizarre flavors as Roquefort, shrimp, and gazpacho, using absolutely no chemical additives in their homemade ice cream. Open daily until 9:30pm.

Sights

Chances are that you've come to Palma to find the perfect beach, but those nearby won't fit the bill. The beach at **El Arenal** (bus #15) is probably the best one close to Palma. Other nearby beaches include **Palma Nova** and **Illetes** (buses #21 and #3, respectively), usually packed with people. Even that can't take away all the beauty of water so clear you can still see the bottom after you can no longer touch it.

If you get sick of tan sprints, head for Palma's **old quarter,** by the seafront, for a look back into history. The huge Gothic **cathedral** sits proudly on top of the hill that overlooks Palma and its bay. Started in 1230, the cathedral wasn't finished until 1601, partly because it is one of the largest Gothic cathedrals in the world. Antonio Gaudí, the architect of the Sagrada Familia in Barcelona, modified the interior in 1902 and designed the ornamentation that hangs from the ceiling over the altar. The south door opens to a lovely vista of the ocean, and on either side stand impressive statues of St. Peter and St. Paul by the fifteenth-century architect Guillermo Sagrera. The **treasury** contains relics of St. Sebastian, Palma's patron saint, and what are said to be pieces of the True Cross. The tombs of the last two Mallorcan kings and of Clement VIII, one of the Avignon popes, are also here. (Cathedral and treasury open Mon.-Fri. 10am-12:30pm and 4-6:30pm, Sat. 10:30am-1:30pm. Free.) The **Museo Diocesano,** in back of the cathedral, is wonderfully eclectic: Among its fifteenth-century statues and tableaux are an alligator killed and stuffed in 1776; the autographs of Napoleon Bonaparte, Emperor Maximilian of Mexico, Queen Victoria, and Louis Philippe D'Orleans; and a collection of American quarters. (Open Mon.-Sat. 10am-1pm and 3-7pm, Sun. 10am-1pm. Admission 150ptas.)

The **Baños Arabes** (Arab sauna baths), in the same area on C. Serra, are the only well-preserved and unrestored remnant of Moorish times on the island. (Open daily 9am-6:30pm. Admission 75ptas.) Also in the Barri Gòtic is the graceful **Lonja,** on Paseo Sagrera near the waterfront, a fifteenth-century stock exchange designed by Guillermo Sagrera. When it houses an exhibit, you can go inside to see the palm-tree columns. **Palacio Sollerich,** a few blocks away at C. San Cayetano, 10, displays contemporary art and sponsors frequent exhibits. (Open Tues.-Sat. 11am-1:30pm and 5-8:30pm. Free.)

In the heart of the old quarter, the church of **San Francisco** stands on the plaza of the same name. The thirteenth-century Gothic structure consists of a seventeenth-century half-plateresque, half-baroque facade; polychrome wood ceilings; and the alabaster tomb of Ramón Llull, a thirteenth-century reformed libertine, pacifist, preacher, and martyr. (Open Mon.-Sat. 9:30am-1pm and 3:30-7pm, Sun. 9:30am-1pm.)

Outside of town, the doughnut-shaped **Castillo del Bellver,** temporary residence to many centuries of distinguished and involuntary guests, overlooks the city and bay—it's floodlit at night. Take one of the buses out C. Joan Miró before walking up. The **municipal museum** inside the castle contains archeological displays. (Castle and grounds open daily 9am-sunset. Museum open Mon.-Sat. 9am-sunset. Admission 150ptas.) Also a little outside of town is Palma's **Poble Espanyol,** a smaller reproduction of its parent in Barcelona, with scaled-down samples of Spanish architecture. Buses #4 and 5 pass nearby along C. Andrea Doria. (Open daily 9am-8pm. Admission 225ptas.)

Entertainment

In *Foundation,* Isaac Asimov describes Terminus, a planet entirely covered with buildings. The **El Terreno** area of Palma, centered around Pl. Gomilia and along C. Joan Miró, is a Terminus of nightclubs, though there are some good bars and pubs in the area. The fashionable place to be for Spaniards hoping to avoid tourists (maybe you can change their minds) is **Minim's,** off Pl. Gomila. The place gets moving earlier in the evening than most clubs.

Palma's biggest dance-factories lie farther out in Cala Major along **Calle Joan Miró;** take buses #70, 21, or 22. Here, you'll probably be assaulted by English-speaking bouncers trying to convince you to come to their nightclubs. If you show up early enough, you should be able to get free passes or at least a two-for-one drink card. Without a pass, many of these slimy discos are not worth their cover charge. One that is popular with foreigners is **Liberty.** (Laugh at the gaudy, plastic statue. Cover 500ptas.)

Less flashy, the **Es Jonquet** area along C. San Magin offers more mellow bars, but these don't fill until 11:30pm or midnight. Particularly popular for late night dancing is **Abraxas** (your first left off C. San Magin as you come from Avda. Argentina) and the louder and glossier **Clan.**

Even if you just want a quiet drink, Palma has a trick or two in store for you. **ABACO,** C. San Juan, 1 (tel. 71 59 11), in the Barri Gòtic near the waterfront, is an eclectic fantasy, like a Salvador Dalí canvas gone baroque. Drinks are served amid elegant furniture, cooing doves and white ducks, piles of fresh fruit and flowers, and hundreds of dripping candles, all to the accompaniment of some light background music, like the *Messiah* or Mozart's *Requiem.* Be sure to explore upstairs. Fruit nectars cost 500ptas; cocktails 800-900ptas. (Open nightly 9pm-2:30am.) If a quiet drink is really what you want, the teeny bar called **Orient Express,** C. Marina, 6A, can slake your thirst amid old trunks and brass lanterns. (Open Mon.-Sat. 1:30-4pm and 9pm-12:30am.)

One of Palma's gay bars is **Sombrero,** C. Joan Miró, 26 (no cover charge, open nightly 9pm-3am), while **Baccus,** around the corner on C. Luis Fábregas, 2, attracts a lesbian and gay crowd (also open till 3am).

Often, the nightspots offer less entertainment than the city itself; residents will use just about any occasion as an excuse to throw a party. One of the more colorful bashes, **Día de San Joan** (June 24), involves a no-expense-spared fireworks display the night before, followed by singing, dancing, and drinking in the **Parc del Mar** below the cathedral. The publication *A Palma,* available at the municipal tourist office, includes a monthly list of concerts, exhibits, and sports events. For a more up-to-date listing, the *Daily Bulletin* (in English, 60ptas) prints a schedule each day of events in Palma.

Western Coast

The westernmost end of Mallorca, punctuated by the afterthought of the **Isla Dragonera,** plunges abruptly into the water from the Sierra de Tramontana range, which runs along the island's upper coast. The tortuous coastline of Mallorca's southwestern tongue curls around capes and coves. Stone walls stitched across the slopes support terraced olive groves, and villages hide in protected pouches. This district is perilously close to Palma, and many areas between the Bahia de Palma and the western extremity of Cabo Tramontana have suffered heavily from development.

Explore **Cabo de Cala Figuera** on foot. Playa del Sol runs buses from Pl. España in Palma that go as far south as the town of Magalluf, about 8km from the tip of the cape. Palma's only official nude beach, **Playa del Mago,** is near the tip of the cape, about 5km south of Magalluf near Portals Vells—best reached by foot or moped.

Buses from Eusebio Estada, next to the Sóller train in Palma, also reach **Andraitx** and **Puerto de Andraitx,** 5km apart and about 30km from Palma (Mon.-Sat. every ½ hr., Sun. every hr.; 130ptas), which, except for a smattering of Gothic residences, offer little to see. They do, however, make a handy base for exploring the many capes between Cabo d'es Llamp and the tip of the island. Boats for the Isla Dragonera also leave from the port (1 per day, round-trip about 700ptas), which is the site of an impressive maritime procession every July 16 in honor of the feast of La Virgen del Carmen.

A trip up the coast to **San Telmo** will give you a seaside view of the sharp cliffs that plunge into the water, outlining isolated beaches (4 buses per day, round-trip about 500ptas).

To escape the mobs of tourists, you might as well head straight for the northwestern coast. If you just want to get out of the city for a day, you'll waste the least time in transit this way; if you're planning to make a tour of the island, it's also the logical place to begin your circuit. The road to **Banyalbufar** twists and curves through the southwestern end of the Serra de Tramontana. The terraced hills, held up by mortarless stone walls, are dotted with olive and citrus groves. Moorish watchtowers gaze over the landscape; one of the more accessible ones can be seen just off the main road, overlooking the sea south of Banyalbufar.

The quiet town itself is a perfect place to escape the tourist hordes. Its wonderful hills are ideal for walking and offer breathtaking views. A small, uncrowded beach sits below. **Hotel Barronia,** on the main road (tel. 61 01 21), has cool, relaxing rooms and overlooks the sea. (Singles 1400ptas. Doubles 2180ptas, with shower 2650ptas. Open April-Oct.) Banyalbufar is also known for Malvasía, its answer to sherry.

On the way to Banyalbufar lies the country estate of **Sa Granja,** now a crafts, arts, and farming exhibit preserving ancient Mallorcan ways of life. A tour by a guide in traditional costume, all the *buñuelos* (doughnuts) you can eat, and all the homemade wine (7 kinds) you can gulp cost 275ptas. Every Wednesday and Friday between 3:30 and 5:30pm, the oasis comes alive with folk dancing, eating and drinking, and general merrymaking, all for 500ptas. (Open April-Oct. daily 10am-7pm; Nov.-March daily 10am-5:30pm.) Buses to Banyalbufar leave twice per day from Bar Rio, C. Archiduque Luis Salvador, 24, near Pl. España in Palma (140ptas); they pass La Granja on the way. Around September 10 feasts in honor of the town's patron saint occur.

Valldemosa (Valldemossa)

Eighteen tortuous kilometers from Banyalbufar, Valldemosa's weathered houses huddle in the midst of the harsh but beautiful Serra de Tramontana. Today, the cool, quiet streets of this ancient village hint at little of the passion that shocked the townsfolk in the winter of 1838-9, when tuberculosis-stricken Chopin and his companion George Sand (with her 2 children in tow, no less) stayed in the **Cartuja Real,** flouting the monastic tradition of celibacy. The monastery's museum has collected innumerable Chopin memorabilia, including a picture of the famous hands and the piano upon which they played. You will also find the living quarters for some of the monks who lived here, a sixteenth-century printer, and an eighteenth-century pharmacy with beautiful glass bottles made on the island. Next door you can visit the **Palacio del Rey Sancho,** a Moorish residence converted into a palace by the *mallorquín* kings. The **Musco Municipal** is inside the monastery; its collection documents the royalty who once lived in the town. (All open Mon.-Sat. 9:30am-1pm and 3-6:30pm. Admission to everything 375ptas.)

The whole town can be seen in less than an hour, but buses to Palma (5 per day, 105ptas) are not that frequent. While you're waiting, enjoy a fine lunch at **Sa Costa,** C. Jovellanos, 1, below the monastery. Try the vegetable soup for a first course and wash down the fish with a bottle of Callet, a local red wine. (Open at 1pm.) Half a block away, **Bodegas C'an Gotxo,** Blanoverna, 11, offers free samples of assorted Balearic liquors and wines.

Try to make it to Valldemosa for the lively **Festival of Santa Catalina.** On the night of July 28, the *carro triumfal* (triumphal cart) rolls through the town's streets, carrying a local girl dressed as the little saint. The festivities end on the last Sunday in July with a piano concerto by a world-famous pianist in the Chopin reclusory. Among those who have played the Steinway are Aaron Copland and Arthur Rubinstein. Valldemosa lacks many basic services (no tourist office, for example), but you can find the **post office** at C. Uetam, 1 (tel. 61 20 57), down the hill from the **monastery.** (Open for stamps Mon.-Fri. 9am-2pm, Sat. 9am-1pm, for telegrams Mon.-Fri. 9am-3pm.)

Near Valldemosa, on the bus route to Sóller, sits **Deià** (Deyà). Tourists frequent its overpriced restaurants for lunch; all are on the main road. Off this beaten track, you can find some charming walks through an unspoiled small town and surrounding countryside.

Sóller

Another 30km up the coast, Sóller and Port de Sóller hum with tourists all day long because they are directly connected to Palma by rail. There's not much to see in Sóller except its **cathedral,** whose tall, tan towers resemble a sand castle. The **Museu de Sóller,** C. Mar, 9, has amassed a somewhat random collection of tools and plates made on the island. (Open Mon.-Sat. 11am-1pm and 4-7pm.) The **tourist office** is in the town hall on Pl. de la Constitució (tel. 58 58 64); they'll give you a map of the area and suggest some beautiful hikes through the valley's citrus and olive orchards. One manageable route takes you to **Fornalutx,** about an hour up the valley. (Open Mon.-Fri. 9:30am-1:30pm and 4-6pm, Sat. 9:30am-1:30pm.) For **train information,** call 63 01 30. The **post office** is on C. de Crostobal Piza at C. de la Rectoria, about 2 blocks from Pl. de la Constitució. (Open Mon.-Fri. 9am-2pm, Sat. 9am-1pm.) Call the **police** (Guardia Civil) at 63 02 03, the **Red Cross** at 63 08 45.

Sóller offers few places to stay, but 2km down the road toward the port, you'll find **Restaurante Monumento** (tel. 63 01 18), where you might find a cheap room. (Singles 1600-1950ptas. Doubles 2200-2350ptas.) If you do stay in town, make sure it's for the **Ferias y Fiestas de Mayo.** Starting on the Friday closest to the second day of May, the Christians cream the Moors in a reenactment of the 1561 battle that involved the landing of seacraft, the sacking of homes, and much fighting in the streets. Everyone dresses up, dances wildly, and makes up for it at a high Mass the next day. The celebration ends the following Monday, but concerts and un-choreographed pillaging continue throughout the month. Sóller's patron **San Pedro** is celebrated with marching bands and festivities on June 26. In the middle of August, Sóller hosts an international **folkdance festival.** The half-hour walk from the town to the port is pleasant, but many prefer to take the narrow gauge trolley (75ptas).

Port de Sóller lies at the bottom of the valley and absorbs most of the tourists. The beach curves around in a semi-circle on the inside of the small bay, across which windsurfers zip back and forth. The **tourist office** is at C. del Canoningo Oliver, a block in from the trolley's last stop (open daily noon-3pm). The only places to stay that are not saturated by German or English package tours seem to be **Hotel Mare Nostrum,** Marina (tel. 63 14 12), and **Hotel Generoso,** Marina, 4 (tel. 63 14 50). The former has earned a two-star rating for its service and cleanliness; every room has a terrace and bathroom. (Singles 1555ptas. Doubles 2585ptas.) At the Generoso, rooms also come with terrace and bath. Just like Grandma's: Everything is so artificially clean that it looks like it's covered in plastic. (Singles 1650ptas. Doubles 2640ptas.)

Most local restaurants offer little more than expensive tourist fodder, but **La Casa Belga,** C. Canonigo Oliver (tel. 03 37 15), 1 block from the sea behind Hostal Miramar, offers refreshing 595ptas and 695ptas *menús* that begin with light and creamy *tostadas.* (Open after 12:30pm.)

You can continue exploring the coast by **boat.** Round-trip excursions leave for Sa Calobra (5 per morning, 1000ptas), Cala Tuent (Sat.-Sun. at 10am, 1000ptas) Cala Deia (Tues. at 10am and 3pm, 700ptas), and San Telmo (in summer Sun., 1700ptas). **Buses** connect Port de Sóller with Palma via Valldemosa (5 per day, 240ptas) and Port Pollença via Lluc (2 per day).

Sa Calobra and Lluc

If your mother saw the road to Sa Calobra, she'd never let you go. This terror drops 1000m to the sea over 10 hairpin kilometers, twisting back underneath itself in the process. The delicate of stomach should take the boat from Port de Sóller; in fact, everyone should, since there is no organized bus service into Sa Calobra. However, if you hop on the Sóller-Pollença bus and ask to be let off at the top of the Sa Calobra road, you should have little trouble getting a ride down: Drivers will be too glassy-eyed to refuse. Sa Calobra's tiny inlet shelters several overpriced restaurants—bring your own food. A five-minute hike through tunnels cut in the stone cliffs brings you to the **Torrent de Pareis,** a pebble-strewn canyon ending in a sandy beach. In winter, this becomes a river, but in summer it makes a super beach, with water so clear you can see the shadows of boats on the bottom.

The **Monasterio de Lluc** lies 20km inland, tucked into the serene mountains and peacefully removed from the frenetic activity of the coast. This is the home of the 700-year-old image of *La Virgen de Lluc,* whose carved wood has turned a dark brown over the years, hence its nickname *"La Moroneta."* It is now hidden in a room behind the main altar in the basilica. If you manage to get to the monastery in off-season, you can hear the choir boys of Lluc sing each day at 11am. Behind the monastery, Via Crucis takes you around a hill where you can survey the valley dotted with olive trees and jingling with the sound of goats with bells hopping down the hills. Antonio Gaudí designed the monuments depicting the stations of the cross that you'll find lining the path. The monastery's **museum** contains a collection of somewhat interesting prehistoric remains, fifteenth-century ceramics and fourteenth-century religious treasure. (Open daily 10am-6pm. Admission 150ptas.)

The monastery (tel. 51 70 25) makes a great place to stay since you'll be left alone with the monks, a few pilgrims, and the quite mountains after the last tour bus has gone. Singles 850ptas. Doubles 1375ptas. If you stay three or more nights, rates drop to 650ptas and 1050ptas, respectively.) The monks will also tell you where you may camp nearby. Though prices at the monastery's restaurant are a bit stiff, there is also a small food store where you can purchase your own groceries.

Northern Gulfs

Two peninsulas of land, pointing towards Menorca, form beautiful, large bays on the northern edge of Mallorca. These bays and beaches are overrun by package tours and condo developments, but patient exploration will expose a secluded cove and striking scenery. A highway connecting Palma to the eastern shore stretches directly across the flat plain, just to the south of the Serra de Tramontana, passing through the inland Inca and ending at Alcúdia.

Pollença (Pollensa)

Pollença seems the work horse of the region, with a strong native population and many practical services. Ascending 337 steps takes you to the top of **El Calvario,** where you can look down into the northern gulfs, straight beyond Porto de Pollença into the bay, and even into Alcúdia and the bay beyond. At the bottom of the stairs you'll find the **Ayuntamiento** (open Mon.-Fri. 9am-1:30pm), where they'll tell you everything you need to know about the area. **Museu Miguel Costa Llobera,** C. Llobera 9, is the artist's birthplace. (Open Tues., Thurs., and Sun. 10am-noon.) The **post office** is at C. Sant Josep, 3. (Open Mon.-Fri. 9am-2pm and Sat. 9am-1pm.) There's a **pharmacy** at Carretera Alcúdia, 7 (tel. 53 00 63), 1 block from the bus station. (Open Mon.-Sat. 9am-1:30pm and 5-8:30pm.)

The only place you'll find a room is at **Hostal Juma,** Pl. Major, 9 (tel. 53 00 07), which offers doubles with bath for 1400ptas. Down the hill, **Autocares Villalonga,** C. San Isidro, 4 (tel. 53 00 77), will take you to Port de Pollença (8 per day, 60ptas).

Port de Pollença's long beaches and short strip of residential development make for a relatively uncrowded beach of fine white sand. The water stays shallow quite a ways out into the bay and makes for great swimming. Toward the ocean side of the waterfront, you can browse in the **Colección Anglada Camarassa,** Paseo Anglada Camarassa, 87, to get out of the sun for a while. The museum displays many paintings and drawings by the renowned Catalan painter, but the collection has just been sold, and the new owner plans to move it to Palma within a few years. (Open Mon.-Tues. and Thurs.-Sat. 4-7pm. Free.) The area also hosts a **music festival** July to September. In the port, tickets are available at **Casa Peña** (tel. 53 11 56).

Pensión Rivoli, Passeig Saralegui, 12 (tel. 53 12 07), run by a friendly German family, offers impeccable lodgings. All rooms are bright and some have terraces and views of the port. (Open April-Oct. 1000ptas per person. Hot showers 150ptas.)

Meals tend to be expensive, but just a block inland, **Bar-Restaurante Mibar,** Carretera de Formentor, 18, offers cheap a la carte specialties and a 625ptas *menú.*

The **tourist office** will help you weed through the piles of bus schedules and send you off on an excursion or two. It's on Passeig Saralegui. (Open Mon.-Fri. 9:30am-1pm and Sat. 9:30am-1pm.) The **post office** is behind the museum on C. de Llevant, 15. (Open for stamps Mon.-Fri. 9am-2pm and Sat. 9am-1pm, for **telegrams** Mon.-Fri. 9am-3pm and Sat. 9am-noon.) **Motos Formentor,** C. de Llevant, 17, near the post office, rents bikes (400ptas per day, 1500ptas per week). Right on the beach, a summertime **telephone kiosk** is equipped to handle international calls. (Open daily 10am-1pm and 4:30-9pm.)

Following **Cabo Formentor** to its end, *miradores* (lookout towers) peer out over spectacular fjords. Before the final twisting kilometers, the road drops down to **Formentor Beach,** where a canopy of evergreens runs almost to the edge of the water. Here the sand is softer, the water calmer, and the crowds smaller than at Port de Pollença. The cape's beautiful, semi-isolated beaches can be reached by boat or bus, both from Port de Pollença. Buses leave the port (4 per day except Sun., 55ptas) and return from Formentor along the same route (last one at 4:30pm). **La Gaviota** (tel. 53 38 14) runs boats from the marina in Port de Pollença, behind Restaurante Stay, to Formentor (5 per day; one way 300ptas, round-trip 550ptas; last boat back at 5pm).

Alcúdia

A 10-minute bus ride (70ptas) south along the coast will bring you to Alcúdia, a sensible place to settle down and explore for a couple days. The town itself is encircled by ramparts from the fourteenth-century, and Roman amphitheater remains line the road to the port. The ancient Roman city of **Pollentia** was located near the amphitheater, and you can walk around what's left of it. Loops of isolated coves and beaches string their way around the point of Alcúdia, and here, in the Bon Aire section of town, you'll find Mallorca's only IYHF youth hostel outside of Palma. Signs to the **Albergue Victoria,** Carretera Cabo Pinar, 4 (tel. 54 53 95), lead you east from the town center; it's on the right of the road up on a hill 4km from Alcúdia (taxis run 450ptas). If heaven slept eight to a room, this would be it. It's only 100m from an empty beach on the Bahía de Pollença and tucked underneath some beautiful hills waiting to be climbed. Totally removed from the hoards of fleshy families who infest Alcúdia and its port, this clean and breezy youth hostel begs you to stay the maximum five days allowed. (Open mid-June to Sept. Members only 595ptas. Breakfast included. Call ahead because school groups often invade the entire place.) A long hike from the youth hostel will take you to the spiritual center of Alcúdia, **Ermita de la Victoria,** tucked away in a pine grove. The town also has an **archeological museum** of note, next to the church. (Open Tues.-Sat. 10:30am-1:30pm and 3:30-6:30pm, Sun. 10:30am-1:30pm.)

Port d'Alcúdia has more accommodations, which are considerably more expensive. **Hostal Vista Alegre,** C. V. Moreno, 22 (tel. 54 69 77), overlooks the port and offers clean rooms with kind owners. (1000ptas per person.) At C. Teodoro Canet, 41, **Hostal Calma** (tel. 54 53 43) offers breakfast with its rooms. It's best to reserve well in advance for the summer. (Open mid-March to mid-Dec. Singles with bath 1940ptas. Doubles with bath 2750ptas.) Toward town on your left, **Calle Hostaleria** has a few good restaurants with 600ptas *menús.* You can sit beneath palm fronds and keep cool at **Restaurante El Ancla,** or on the terrace at **Mallorca Bar Restaurante,** where you can get a huge serving of *paella* for 700ptas.

The **tourist office** is on the waterfront at C. V. Moreno, 2 (tel. 54 63 71). They offer friendly advice in English. (Open April-Sept. Mon.-Sat. 8:30am-6pm.) A bit down the waterfront, near Club Náutico, is the summertime **telephone kiosk.** (Open daily 10am-1pm and 4:30-9pm.) Bikes can be rented from **Reina Bike Rental,** C. Teodoro Canet, 27 (tel. 54 55 72). The bikes might squeak and complain, but they'll get you where you're going for 400ptas per day. (Open in summer daily 9am-8pm.) **Medical attention** in Port Alcudia is available at Casa del Mar, C. Ciudadela (tel. 54 59 68).

Buses for Alcudia and Port Alcudia leave Pl. España in Palma. (10 per day Mon.-Sat., 4 per day Sun.; 340ptas.) The bus between the Alcudias and Port de Pollença runs reliably every 15 minutes, and some buses continue on to Cabo Formentor. Bus service to the south goes only as far as C'an Picafort. All buses in Port Alcudia pass along waterfront C. Vicealmirante Moreno and through the center of Alcudia proper. Call **Alcanda,** Plaza Carlos V, 5 (tel. 54 52 42), for bus information. (Open Mon.-Fri. 9am-1pm and 4-7pm.)

Eastern Coast

The eastern coast of Majorca is the only part of the island that is both overrun and underrun by tourists. Not only do they swarm over the small coastal towns in ever-increasing numbers, but they storm their way underground as well, down to the eerie subterranean landscapes of the region's many caves. Buses connect most of the major towns and beaches.

In the northern end lies the dreary town of **Artá,** which offers a dull little **museo regional,** a Gothic church, and the **castle fortress** Almudaina, where Jaume I overpowered the Moorish forces in 1202. Fortunately, the magnificent **Cuevas de Artá,** Mallorca's best caves, are just 10km away. The labyrinth of vaulted chambers with towering stalactite and stalagmite formations is far less exploited than the Cuevas del Drach and exudes a macabre and mysterious beauty. Tours operate daily from 10am to 6:30pm (earlier in winter), cost 400ptas, and are blessedly free of the Cecil B. DeMille syndrome, which afflicts the island's other caves.

Buses leave Pl. España in Palma for Artá (Mon.-Sat. 4 per day, 340ptas) and continue to Cala Ratjada (60ptas more), with the same number of return trips.

Playa and **Costa de Canyamel,** just south of the Cuevas del Artá, are part of a classy German beach development; the hotels are expensive here but the magnificent sites on the seaside hilltops tempt unofficial camping. The fortress of Torre de Canyamel once protected peasants from pirate attacks but really doesn't merit a visit. The small fishing village of **Cala Ratjada,** 13km to the north, has become a popular hangout for German tourists, with a beautiful but bustling beach and a pleasant fishing and sailboat port. If you come in summer, rest assured that a luxurious blanket of white sand stretches beneath the roasting tourists. Forget about staying, though, since travel agencies have cornered the summer hotel market, and there's not a hovel to be had. The **Turismo,** on C. Bustanante, provides an impressive list of lodgings that comes in handy in off-season.

Porto Cristo and its famous **Cuevas del Drach,** lie 25km south. The port contains nothing but excursion buses, tired tourists, a crowded beach, and many restaurants serving hamburgers and fries. You can take a cruise up to Cala Millor in a boat (700ptas) or just float around looking through a glass bottom (1 per day at 11:15am; 1 hr.; 400ptas, ages under 10 200ptas).

Porto Cristo's **aquarium** is just off the road to the caves. (Open daily 9:30am-6pm. Admission 350ptas, ages 4-8 175ptas.) Inside is one of the most extensive marine-life collections in Spain; outside are some of the gaudiest murals. Both the aquarium and the Cuevas del Drach can be reached by bus or easily on foot; at most, they're a kilometer outside of Port Cristo. The **Cuevas del Drach** (Caves of the Dragon) are fairyland stalactite caverns where towering white cities, forests, angel wings, and coral reefs emerge from stone. If you can't get here early, be prepared to lose the magic in the multilingual drone while being pumped through with the polyglot masses. Tours last one hour and include a boat concert on the subterranean lake featuring music by Chopin. If you have to wait for the next tour group, take a stroll through the surrounding gardens, where peacocks screech as loudly as the tourists. (Tours daily on the hr. 10am-4pm, except 1pm. No 10am tour on Sat. Admission 500ptas.) The **Cuevas del Ham,** outside Porto Cristo on the road to Manacor, are best avoided: Though they are much less impressive, the gaudy, misleading billboards attempt to trick inattentive tourists into thinking these caves are the Cuevas del Drach. (Open daily 10:30am-1:20pm and 2:45-4:20pm. Some tours spare you the concert, some do not. Admission 450ptas.)

Aside from the port, there's a real town here. You can stay at **Pensión Orient,** Pl. del Carmen, 3, where you'll find a newly renovated room with hot showers. (Doubles 1500ptas.) **C'an Marti,** C. del. Puerto, 96 (tel. 57 07 48), serves a 500ptas *menú* with hot soup and *albóndigas* in an unbeatable sauce.

The **tourist office,** C. Gual, 31 (tel. 57 01 68), has a map of the town and a list of its scrumptious restaurants (open in summer daily 10am-3pm.) The **post office** is at C. Zanglada, 10 (tel. 57 07 64), at C. Navegantes. A **telephone kiosk** awaits you near the bus stop by the waterfront. (Open daily 10am-1pm and 4:30-8:30pm.) For **medical attention,** call 57 00 14. **Buses** connect Port Cristo with **Ca'n Picafort** (2 per day), Palma via Manacor (4 per day, 350ptas), and various beaches nearby, including Cala Ratjada (2 per day Mon.-Sat.). For more information, call 57 00 08, or go to the ticket booth at the port.

Southeastern Mallorca

The eastern coast of Mallorca's southern third is a scalloped fringe of bays and caves. Many harbor the island's most recent resort developments, where the new hotel towns at least try to maintain some architectural integrity. A walk of 1-2 km, however, should put plenty of sand between you and the thickest crowds. Buses leave Cafetería Alcalá, Avda. Alejandro Rosselló, 32 (tel. 46 35 27), in Palma, for **Santanyí,** an inland town whose Porta Murada testifys to the dangers of piracy the region once faced (3 per day, 308ptas); **Cala d'Or,** an inlet surrounded by pinewoods and massive boulders (3 per day, 378ptas); and **Porto Petro,** on the beach (2 per day via Cala d'Or, 367ptas). Try to make it to Santanyí when the *poble* erupts for the yearly patron saint feasts on July 25.

Rounding **Cabo de Salinas,** Mallorca's southernmost point, the long leg of coastline back to Palma begins. Miles of inaccessible and isolated sand lie between here and **Cabo Blanc,** beyond which ill-humored, rocky cliffs fend off Palma's southern suburbs. Buses and vacation resorts have yet to take this region seriously. They may have missed their chance, since the area has recently come under the protection of the state, but determined developers are doing their best to reverse the decision. Furthermore, the entire southeastern interior of Mallorca is in the hands of Joan March's grandsons (March was the Spanish banker infamous for the horrible exchange rate offered by his banks); they are not soon likely to sell off the land to hungry developers.

Es Trenc and **Sa Ràpita,** two of the island's most beautiful, deserted beaches, stretch 4km between Colonia Sant Jordi to the south and La Rápita to the north. Es Trenc is also Mallorca's de facto nude beach, especially below Ses Covetes, about 2km from Sant Jordi or 1km from La Rápita. Camping, although illegal, does occur in the woods behind these beaches. Buses run daily from Cafetería Alcalá in Palma to Colonia Sant Jordi.

From Colonia Sant Jordi, you can take a boat excursion to **Cabrera,** a 30-square-kilometer island that is the largest in a small archipelago of 17. Uninhabited except for a small military installation, it has a gruesome history. Besides the many ships that have gone down (wrecks are still visible on the ocean bottom), 8000 French prisoners-of-war died here during the War of Independence in 1809; they were abandoned on the island with no food and with only one freshwater well. A monument to the dead stands near the port; nearby is a fourteenth-century fortress used as a refuge by pirates. The boat excursion leaves the port at Sant Jordi (May-Oct. Tues.-Wed. and Fri.-Sun. at 9:30am, return at 6pm, 1½ hr.). Tickets are available at Restaurante Miramar (tel. 64 90 34) in Sant Jordi.

An excursion to the island also leaves from Palma on Sunday, departing at 8:45am; call 71 71 90 for more information. You may wish to bring your own food as there is only one (expensive) restaurant on the island.

Inland

The interior landscapes of orchards, vineyards, and wheat fields remain Mallorca's heartland. Ancient stone walls, crumbling and overgrown, parcel the inland valleys into individual farms, where windmills and sloppy haystacks dot chunks of hillside lined with fig, olive, and almond groves. The pastel almond blossoms flourish in February, their petals covering the island like fragrant confetti.

Manacor

Manacor rises out of this panoramic landscape as the industrial backbone of inland Mallorca. In order to lure the masses away from the beaches and lacking interesting sights of its own, Manacor has developed a booming artifical pearl industry. The pearls are made by repeatedly dropping a nucleus crystal into a shiny liquid made from synthetic and natural pigments (anchovy and sardine scales are used to make the latter). The factories are open for visits and the purchasing of pearls. The largest, **Perlas Majorca,** is on the road to Palma on the edge of town. (Open Mon.-Fri. 9am-1pm and 3-7pm, Sat.-Sun. 10am-1pm. Free.) Closer to town, **Perlas Orquídea,** on Pl. de Ramón Llull, can also be visited for free. (Open Mon.-Fri. 9am-7pm, Sat. 9am-1pm, Sun. 9:30am-1pm.) There's not much else to see except for the turreted Gothic **cathedral** and adjoining **archeological museum.** (Open Mon.-Sat. 10am-1pm.)

If you really want to spend the night, try **Hostal Jacinto,** next to the cathedral on C. Weyler, 1 (tel. 55 01 24; singles 875ptas), but rooms are scarce because of Manacor's large migrant worker population. For a drink, try **Bar Ramon,** in Pl. Ramon Llull. A smoky den with Spanish renditions of '50s music, it's a favorite place for solitaire or *tute,* a Spanish card game that's a mix of War and Gin Rummy.

The **post office** is at C. Nueva, 14. (Open Mon.-Fri. 9am-2pm, Sat. 9am-12:30pm.) Buses leave from Pl. José Antonio, 4 (tel. 55 07 30), for Palma (4 per day, 2 per day on weekends and holidays; 245ptas) and Porto Cristo (8 per day, 70ptas).

Near Manacor

Not far away is **Petra,** the hometown of Fray Junipero Serra, the man responsible for the Spanish presence in California. The house of this Franciscan, who founded a chain of West Coast missions—seedlings of San Francisco, Monterey, and San Diego, among others—is now a museum. A one-hour walk into the hills around Petra will bring you to **Hermitage de Bonany,** built in 1604. This "cathedral of the mountains" is empty and unadorned, but the simple setting and splendid view are lovely. July 21 brings the patron saint's feast to Petra. The town gathers together and celebrates Santa Práxedes. The town also commemorates the birth of Sena on the Sunday closest to November 24.

About 15km to the south of Manacor, on route C714, lies the city of **Felanitx** and its sixteenth-century convent of San Antonio. The town lies at the foot of the Puig de San Salvador, at the top of which is the **Santuario de Nuestra Señora de San Salvador** and the **Castillo de Santueri.** The monastery (tel. 58 06 56) overlooks the southern coast, the island of Cabrera, and the Bay of Alcudia. Some accommodations are available and the hostelry serves a simple but hearty lunch.

Should you take a liking to the sequestered life, only 30km east of Palma is another monastery, the **Sanctuario de Nuestra Señora de Cura** (tel. 66 09 94). The brothers know their way around a kitchen, but should you decide to stay, you can prepare your own meals in the large fireplace. If you don't have a car or motorbike, you'll have to take a bus to Lluchmajor and then hitch, hike, or take a taxi.

Inca

Inca lies just south of the Serra de Tramontana range, begging for the moisture that the mountains trap. Halfway between Palma and Alcúdia and at the end of a railway, it attracts many visitors with its inexpensive leather goods and bustling Thursday-morning market. The main streets parallel to the railroad tracks—**Calle de Colon** and **Calle de Vicente Enseñat**—are lined with factory outlet leather shops, where you can buy everything from books and combs to whips and chains. While quality isn't guaranteed, some real bargains can be found.

As you're exploring, make sure you find the *galletes d'oli,* cookies for which Inca is famous (at least among islanders); they resemble overgrown American goldfish crackers. If you want to stay, try **Pensión España,** Avda del Bisbe Llompart, 5 (tel. 50 07 09); from the train station, follow the road perpendicular to the tracks, and look to your right when the road starts going uphill. (500-800ptas per person.) **Hotel Victoria,** C. Rubi, 5 (tel. 50 01 05), behind the **Ayuntamiento** on Pl. España, also offers a few rooms, and you can get a hearty meal for 700ptas. (Doubles 1200ptas.) **Restaurante Moreno,** C. de la Gloria, 103, behind Pl. España, serves some of the largest *combinados* in Spain, complete with wine, bread, and dessert for 600ptas. It is worth trying to find.

Inca lies 35 minutes by train from Palma. Twenty trains per day connect the two, 16 on Sunday (140ptas). Five buses per day connect the city to Alcúdia.

Menorca (Minorca)

The most northerly and authentic of the major Balearic Islands, Menorca's sloping countryside remains blanketed by green pastures laced by stone fences, avoiding Mallorca's and Ibiza's condominiums and luxury hotels almost entirely. Its 224km of coastline cradle the province's most untouched beaches, some of which can be reached only by foot or by boat. Its Bronze Age visitors left over 200 stone monuments; *talayots, taulas,* and *navetas* dot the island, any of which make an ideal destination for a hike.

Maò (Mahón)

Maò's whitewashed houses and mellow inhabitants provide a welcome contrast to the other islands' buzzing cities. From atop a steep bluff, the city overlooks a harbor that now serves partly as a submarine base for the Spanish navy. The British occupied this capital city for almost a century in the 1800s and have left behind colorful Georgian doors, bright brass knockers, and wooden shutters. They introduced the gin distilleries that industrialized the production of indigenous liqueurs, such as *calent,* a sweet drink made from anise, cinnamon, and saffron.

The British never relinquished the area as a vacation spot; they seem to outnumber natives in summer. There is a relaxed elegance here: Tourists do not hustle about, but rather blend in with the scenery. The island's extensive bus service fans out from Maò, making the city a convenient base and the perfect backdrop for a peaceful vacation.

Orientation and Practical Information

To get to the center of Maò from its port, climb the path directly across from the ferry station. Most of the restaurants and sights will be on the streets to your left. To reach **Plaça de l'Esplanada,** continue on Carrer Rector Panedes to **Plaça Bastió.** From the southwest corner, follow Carrer de sa Comedia (C. San Bartolome) 1 block to Carrer de la Lluna, which leads to Carrer de ses Moreres (C. Dr. Orfila). Two blocks to the right is the plaza; the tourist office is on the far side. Many streets retain their Spanish spellings or names. We give both if there is any confusion.

Tourist Office: Pl. de l'Esplanada, 40 (tel. 36 37 90), near the corner across from the bus station. Friendly and helpful, but short on printed material about the island besides maps of Maò and Ciudadela—evidence of the dearth of tourists. English spoken. Open in summer Mon.-Fri. 9am-2pm and 5-7pm, Sat. 9:30am-1pm.

Consulate: U.S., C. del Bonaire, 16 (tel. 36 16 24), in Villacarlos. Take the bus.

Post Office: C. del Bonaire, 11-13 (tel. 36 38 92), at C. de l'Església. Open Mon.-Fri. 9am-2pm, Sat. 9am-1pm. **Postal Code:** 07700.

Telephones: The building on C. Ramon i Cajal is only a business office. In Maò proper, you'll have to try a phone booth, a public bar, or at a pension. A summertime **telephone shack** on the beach in Cala'n Porter (tel. 36 13 66), about 13km from Mahón, is equipped for international calls. Take the hourly bus (about 50ptas). The 2 private offices in town will not let you call collect or use a credit card. If you're desperate, try **Autos Calain Porter,** C. de Sant Roc, 27. Open Mon.-Sat. 9:30am-10pm. Also **Hallo,** C. Cós de Gracia, 9. Open Mon.-Fri. 9:30am-1:30pm and 5-10pm. Both are expensive.

Airport: 7km out of town (tel. 36 01 50). Main airport office open daily 7:15am-9:30pm. To Palma (4 per day, 20 min.) on Aviaco or Iberia. Any travel agent issues tickets—in summer, advance booking is essential. Also flights in summer to Barcelona and Madrid (see Balearic Islands Introduction). No buses run between the airport and the city, so you'll have to hitch or take a taxi. **Aviaco,** Pl. Esplanada (tel. 36 15 77). Open Mon.-Fri. 9am-1:30pm and 4-7:30pm, Sat. 9:30am-1pm.

Bus Station: Transportes Menorca (TMSA), C. José M. Quadrado, 7 (tel. 36 03 61), just off of Pl. Esplanada. To Alaior (6 per day, 79ptas), Es Mercadal (6 per day, 124ptas), Ferreries (6 per day, 163ptas), and Cirdadella (6 per day, 252ptas). Other lines to the beaches and to Villacarlos (50ptas) leave from Pl. Esplanada. **Autocares Fornells,** Pl. Esplanada. To Fornells (3 per day Mon.-Sat., 2 on Sun.) and other points. Be at the bus stop a few minutes early; the buses fill quickly and you're not allowed to stand in the aisles. No service in winter.

Ferries: Transmediterránea, at the Estación Marítima along Andén de Poniente (tel. 36 29 50). To Barcelona (5 per week at noon, in off-season 1-3 per week; 9 hr., *butacas* 4550ptas). To Palma (Sun at 4:30pm, 6½ hr., 3410ptas), continuing to Valencia (9 more hr., 1050ptas more). Consider flying instead. Open Mon.-Fri. 8am-1pm and 5-7pm, Sat. 8am-noon, Sun. 3 hr. before departures.

Taxis: Tel. 36 12 83 or 36 28 91 for the taxi stand; 36 71 11 to reach the radio taxi. You can also easily hail one around Pl. Esplanada.

Moped and Bicycle Rental: Motos Menorca, Cuesta del General, 18-20 (tel. 36 73 09), opposite the ferry station below town. Bicycles 350ptas per day, 2700ptas per week. Mopeds and motorcycles 900-2750ptas per day, insurance included. Open Mon.-Sat. 10am-1:30pm and 3:30-7:30pm, Sun. 10am-1pm; in off-season Mon.-Sat. 10am-1:30pm, Sun. 10am-1pm. **Gelabert,** Avda. J.A. Clavé, 12 (tel. 36 06 14), off Pl. Esplanada. Bicycles 400ptas per day. Mopeds and motorcycles 1400-2200ptas. Open similar hours.

English Books: English-Language Library, C. Deya (Costa d'en Ga), 2 (tel. 36 27 01), off Pl. Reial. Sells a few paperbacks but mostly lends anything you'd like to read. Open Mon.-Sat. 10am-1pm.

Laundromat: Lavandería Auto-Servicio, Mártires d'Atlante, 30, by the club Marítimo de Mahón. Open daily 8am-8pm.

Medical Assistance: Hospital Municipal, Cós de Gràcia, 26 (tel. 36 12 21).

Police: Municipal Police, Pl. Constitució (tel. 36 39 61). **Guardia Civil,** Carretera Sant Lluis (tel. 36 58 88). **Emergency:** Tel. 091.

Accommodations

Few *pensiones* can get by on the slack trade, and there are few *pensiones*. Try to make reservations. In July and August, singles are particularly scarce. Some places close in winter, but the following are open year-round.

Hostal Orsi, C. Infanta, 19 (tel. 36 47 51). The hard-working English owner keeps this bright *hostal* clean and friendly, and eagerly provides helpful information about the island. Schedule your trip around vacancies here; call ahead. Usually full in summer. Singles 1166ptas. Doubles 1908ptas, with bath 2385ptas. In off-season 40% less.

Hostal Reynés, C. del Comerç, 26 (tel. 36 40 59). No sign out front. A peaceful *hostal* with lots of plants inside. Clean rooms, some a little dark. Typically booked solid June-Sept. Singles 943-1313ptas. Doubles 1526-2024ptas.

Hostal-Residencia Jume, C. de la Concepció, 6 (tel. 36 32 66), near Plaça de la Miranda. Nice rooms, each with shower. Singles 1166-1272ptas. Doubles 2173-2385ptas.

Hostal Noa, Cós de Gràcia, 157 (tel. 36 12 00). Formerly the El Paso. Every room undergoing major renovation in 1988. Singles 1325ptas, with shower 2385ptas. Doubles 1961-3498ptas.

Hostal-Residencia Sa Roqueta, C. Verge del Carme, 122 (tel. 36 43 35). A bit far away and a little expensive. Moderately clean rooms in a homey atmosphere. Singles 1272ptas. Doubles 2014ptas; in off-season 1590ptas.

Casa Huéspedes Company, C. del Rosari, 27 (tel. 36 22 67), near Pl. de la Constitució. Singles usually full, but the doubles are brighter and more comfortable anyway. No toilet seats and gruff owner. Singles 900ptas. Doubles 1600ptas.

Food

Menorcans like to eat well but not inexpensively. Most economical meals will be found at bars around Plaças de la Constitucio and de l'Esplanada, most of which serve filling *combinados* for 200-400ptas. The **market** off Plaça del Carmen sells fruits, vegetables, and sandwich meats, but prices, again, are not low. You might try *formatge maonès* (a local cheese), *sobrassada* (a typical sausage), *crespells* (home-made biscuits), and *rubiols* (pastry turnovers filled with fish or vegetables). For a treat, seek out the delicious lobster stew *caldereta de llagosta*.

La Huerta, Carrer de Joan Ramis, 64 (tel. 36 28 85), a block from the tourist office. The only place you'll get a full meal without going broke—*menú* 625-675ptas. Popular lunchspot for local workers. Open Mon.-Sat. 1-10pm.

Majestic Café, Pl. del Princep, 5 (tel. 36 85 70). A quiet cafe with marble tables and serious eaters. Well-prepared, large salads 425-700ptas. *Combinados* and brochettes under 500ptas. Open in summer Mon.-Fri. 9am-3:30pm and 7-10pm, Sat. 9am-3pm; in off-season hours vary.

The Mad Hatter, Moll de Ponent (Andén de Poniente), 62 (no phone). Cheap, simple meals in a plain setting. Eggs, bacon, and beans 250ptas. British owners also bake fresh apple and lemon meringue pies. Open Mon.-Sat. 8am-6:30pm.

Trattoria Pizzeria, C. de Sant Roc, 25 (tel. 36 48 24), up the street from Pl. de la Constitució. A nice atmosphere, buzzing with conversation. Pizza 350-650ptas. *"Dolce Vita"* 900ptas. Open Mon.-Sat. noon-4pm and 8-11:30pm, Sun. 7-11:30pm.

Sa Plaçeta, Pl. del Bastió (no phone). Owned by a friendly, attentive family who won't let you go hungry with their generous *combinados* (490-690ptas). Open Thurs.-Tues.

Sa Parada, Pl. de l'Esplanada (tel. 36 52 13). Aptly named The Bus Stop, this restaurant catches tourists as they unload from coaches right in front of the door. You can sit outside, eating a 3-course *menú* for 600ptas or full a English breakfast for 600ptas. Mini-meals 350-375ptas. Open daily 9:30am-8:30pm.

Bodega Victoria, C. del Rosari, 4 (tel. 36 89 41), smack in the center of town. Great place for a drink and *tapas,* but no meals served. Open Mon.-Fri. 10am-3pm and 6-11pm, Sat. 10am-3pm.

Sights and Entertainment

The **Esglèsia de Santa Maria la Mayor,** founded in 1287 and rebuilt in 1772, testifys to Menorcá's many centuries of civilization. The church also houses an immense organ, built by Maese Juan Kilburz in 1810 with 51 stops and 3006 pipes. A **music festival** in August and early September was inaugurated to showcase this instrument. Festival concerts take place Tuesday and Thursday at 10pm; seats are free, but the sound carries into the surrounding streets, so you can also listen from a nearby cafe.

Just up Carrer de Sant Roc, the **Arc de Sant Roc** straddles the streets and reminds those who pass under it of the fortifications necessary to defend the city from marauding pirates. Closer to Pl. de l'Esplanada, you can look at some of the maps those pirates might have used at the **Ateneo Científico, Literario y Artístico,** C. Conde de Cifuentes, 25, a private cultural society. While the sign outside says "members only," you're welcome to admire their collection of old maps, books, stuffed birds, pickled Spanish professors, and preserved fish. (Hours vary. Free.) For the live version, head down to the waterfront, Andén de Poniente, 73, where you'll find a small **aquarium** of saltwater fishes. (Open Mon.-Fri. 10am-7pm, Sat. 9:30am-2pm, Sun. 11am-1pm. Admission 300ptas, ages under 12 200ptas.)

Unfortunately, the **Museo Arqueológico Provincial de Bellas Artes,** with its Catalan ceramics from Alcora and Talavera and remnants of Aztec, Mayan, and

Roman cultures, was moved to the cloister of the Church of San Francisco. The building is undergoing extensive renovations and will remain closed until 1990 or 1991.

You can pay 500ptas for an hour **boat tour** of the harbor, which isn't very interesting because you can see everything from the top of the hill anyway. (Tours leave daily at 3:30pm; 600ptas, children 300ptas; buy tickets at the Mad Hatter, Andén de Poniente, 62.) A more satisfying trip takes you out of the harbor to the island beach **Illa d'en Colom.** The steep 1800ptas price gets you lunch on the boat with wine and a taste of Menorcan gin. Ships leave at 10am and return by 5pm, but days vary. For information and reservations, call 35 05 37 or check at the aquarium.

The famous distillery **Xoriguer** brews its magic on the waterfront at Andén de Poniente, 93. Visiting it allows you to watch the huge copper vats on top of wood fires. You can sample the famous Menorcan gin here, but down-home liqueurs dominate; taste the 15 local brews, and it won't matter what you're tasting by the end. (Distillery and store open daily 8am-7pm; in off-season daily 9am to 2pm.)

Plaça de l'Esplanada fills with a *mercado* every Tuesday and Saturday from 9am-2pm in summer. Artisans from all over the island come to sell their wares: pottery, clothing, wooden carvings, and jewelry.

Most of the nightlife is in Villacarlos. **Fliston,** C. Sant Jordi, 10 (tel. 36 36 26), is a popular pub-disco. (Open nightly from 9pm.) Also in Villacarlos is **Tonic,** on Avda. Son Vilar (tel. 36 53 06), which often charges a 500ptas cover. Closer to town, **Lui** (tel. 36 63 68) is something of an institution. It's a 15-minute walk along the road that leads to Villacarlos (or hop the bus), overlooking the port. Also known as El Costell, it opens nightly at 11pm for dancing (cover with 1 drink 500ptas). Jazz may be found—after a search—at the **Jazz Club El Casino** in San Clemente every Tuesday evening at 9:30pm as well as Saturday in summer. San Clemente is on the bus line to Cala'n Porter and lies about 4km out of town; unfortunately, the last bus leaves shortly after 8pm, so you'll have to befriend someone who'll give you a ride back to town. Many students in town hang out at the bars along the port, across from the ferry, particularly at **Baixamar,** which has a pool hall upstairs.

Maò's **Fiesta de Nuestra Señora de Gracia** takes place September 7-9, and the **Virgen del Carmen** celebration, July 16, brings a colorful flotilla of decorated boats into the harbor.

Ciutadella (Ciudadela)

One-time capital of the island, Ciutadella retains an air of importance and dignity. It's an attractive city 40km from Maò, and its arcaded streets, picturesque port, stately aristocratic residences, and fourteenth-century Gothic cathedral make it a pleasant base for excursions to nearby sites and beaches. Buses leave from Pl. d'Artrutx for coastal points (fares around 100ptas), including the lovely beaches of Cala Blanca, Cala Bosch, and Cala Santandria, a sheltered beach near some caves that served as shelters during the Bronze Age. Cala'n Morell, 8-9km to the north, also has some interesting prehistoric caves that were once used as burial grounds. Boat excursions also run along the coast; boats leave the city's port Tuesday, Friday, and Sunday at 10am and return at 5pm.

Only 6km inland from Ciudadela lie the archeological sites of **Torre Trencade** and **Torre Llafuda,** which preserve various Bronze Age remnants. Perhaps the most important prehistoric site on Menorca, however, lies only 4km from the city. The oldest building in Europe, the **Naveta dels Tudons** was used for burials. Thanks to some cosmetic restoration, the ruins are today the most complete among the numerous similar community tombs on the island.

You can find a few places to stay around the bus station, but **Bar Ses Persianes,** Pl. Cabrisas i Caimaris, 2 (tel. 38 14 45), offers clean doubles close to the town center. (Doubles 1800ptas; in off-season 1600ptas.) If you're lucky, there will be room for you at **Pensión Ibiza,** Carrer Eivissa, 4 (tel. 38 39 05). Extremely friendly, Sra. Anglade has attic singles for 450ptas. (Other singles 600ptas. Doubles 1100ptas.

Showers 150ptas.) Pensión Juana, located next door at #8, has less character but cheap rooms. (550ptas per person.)

Most eateries in Ciutadella are fairly fancy, but **Restaurante El Horno,** C. del Horno, 10 (tel. 38 07 67), has some cheap a la carte offerings, including a *tortilla con queso* for 250ptas. (Open Mon.-Sat. noon-3:30pm and 7-11:30pm.) Some of the restaurants along Carrer Ses Voltes, the street that runs toward the waterfront from Pl. Nova, offer 600-700ptas *menús* and serve some cheaper a la carte choices. If you decide to eat with the seagulls down at the waterfront, be prepared to pay premium prices—the view is great, though, and half your table hangs over the water.

Six **buses** per day, fewer in off-season, connect Ciutadella with Maò (226ptas). The buses drop you off at the Transportes Menorca station, C. Barcelona, 8 (tel. 38 03 93).

For tourist information, go to the **Ayuntamiento,** on Pl. Borne, where the staff behind the door marked "*museo*" (tel. 38 07 87) will try to help. (Open Mon.-Fri. 11am-1pm.) The Ayuntamiento also houses the **police** office (tel. 38 07 87). The **post office** (tel. 38 00 81) lies across the square. (Open Mon.-Fri. 9am-2pm, Sat. 9am-1pm.) Call the **Creu Roja** (Red Cross) at 38 19 93 for medical assistance. **Motos Manolo,** Avda. Conquistador (Avda. Conqueridor), 86 (tel. 38 50 50), rents bikes and mopeds at a somewhat inflated rate. (Open Mon.-Sat. 9am-1pm and 4-7pm, Sun. 9am-noon.)

Excursions

Islanders sometimes say that Maò's interior bears more resemblance to Ireland than to the rest of Spain. Maò gets more precipitation than the other Balearic Islands because it is so far north and has no ridge of mountains to trap the southerly fronts. Thus, rolling green hillsides, crisscrossed by old stone walls and punctuated with clusters of whitewashed houses, dominate Maò's countryside. Much of the land remains unpopulated and ideal for hiking. You can buy excellent **topographical maps** (180ptas) surveyed by the Spanish military, at **Cos 4,** C. Cos de Gràcia, 4 (tel. 36 66 69), in Maò. The maps mark all the houses on the island as well as the known archeological sites, and they make finding that perfect, isolated beach of your dreams a reality.

Some of the more popular beaches are easily reached by bus from Maò. **Es Grau** is a large sandy bay about 8km north of the town. Once there, you can catch a boat out to the **Illa d'en Colom,** with more beaches (500ptas; ask in any bar at Es Grau). Buses leave from Pl. Esplanada (4 per day, 6 on Sun.; 90pt). **Punta Prima,** to the south, is a wide beach, also serviced by bus (6 per day, 60ptas). Buses will also carry you to the pretty **Platges de Son Bou,** a string of beaches on the southern shore (3 per day Mon.-Sat., 155ptas). If your interests extend beyond a suntan, visit the fifth-century Christian **basilica** in the settlement nearby. Here, primitive religious ardor, no matter how isolated, still managed three naves and a stone baptismal font.

Nine kilometers south of Ferreries, you'll find the narrow beach of **Cala Santa Galdana,** from which you can walk to **Cala Macarella,** about an hour to the west. Neither of these beaches can be reached via public transportation; thus they are two of the most natural beaches on the island. Closer to Maò and easily accesible by bus, **Calan Porter's** huge bluffs protect the open beaches that curve underneath them. The **Cuevas d'en Xoroi,** spooky prehistoric dwellings, also gaze down on the sea, and some are fun to explore.

On the island's northern shore, **Arenal d'en Castell,** a sandy ring around calm water, is sealed off by a thin barrier of pine trees, perfect for unofficial camping (though there are hotels nearby). While at the beach, try exploring the coastal ravines and cliffs that hide caves where the island's prehistoric residents lived and were laid to rest. Buses to Castell leave from Pl. Esplanada. (3 per day Mon.-Sat., 2 on Sun.)

For those who have had their fill of lying languidly on Menorca's many beaches, the island's interior lends itself to hikes. **Monte Toro,** the island's highest peak, is capped by a small chapel dedicated to Menorca's saint. At the foot of the road leading to the shrine lies **Es Mercadal,** a town of brilliant white and a departure point for the road to **Fornells,** a port situated on a rocky cove on the northern part of the island. Es Mercadal is on the bus route to Ciutadella (one way 107ptas), while Autocares Fornells runs buses (which also stop in Es Mercadal) to Fornells from Pl. Esplanada in Maò. (3 per day, 2 on Sun.) TMSA runs frequent buses to Ferreries (167ptas) and Sant Cristòfol (125ptas).

Prehistoric settlements rise from the grassy slopes like monumental rock gardens. These are built around *talayots,* great mounds of stone that may have covered burial sites and probably were the base for a superimposed structure of wood, and *taulas,* massive stone slabs that form capital T's of undetermined significance. The megaliths occasionally reach a height of 10m. Try to visit near dusk, when these cities of archaic civilization are most eerily evocative. The most impressive is the **Torre d'en Gaumes,** 14km from Maò off the route to Son Bou. A variety of structures, including a perfectly preserved *taula,* three *talayots,* caves, and a stone-pillared hall compose this prehistoric city. To get there, hike or take the Son Bou bus. Closer to **Trepuco** is the most accessible site, a 20-minute walk from the town center, off the road to Villacarlos.

Ibiza

A magnet for tourists of all types, Ibiza has lost any culture or charm of its own to the sea-breezes and currency exchange rates. Overcrowded, overpriced, and overrated, this is the one island in the Balearics to skip. One thing makes Ibiza noteworthy: its location directly en route to Formentera.

The island has three major towns: Ibiza (Eivissa), the capital and home of the fashion-conscious; Santa Eulàlia, the origin of many beach-bound buses; and San Antonio Abad (Sant Antoni Abat), where people migrate after the sun has set.

Ibiza City (Eivissa)

Ibiza perches atop a hill. Since it's the commercial and industrial center of the island, you probably won't want to spend your whole visit in Ibiza proper. Do, however, check out the waterfront's bustling activity and walk through the *d'alt vila* to the cathedral.

Orientation and Practical Information

Ibiza City breaks down into three parts: **La Marina,** the business district east of Paseo Vara de Rey, the long promenade 1 block in front of the harbor; **Sa Penya,** the one-time fishing village of whitewashed houses stretching from Estación Maritima along the waterfront to the old walls, now the heart and soul of the city; and the **d'alt vila** (high city), which lies up and behind those old walls. The ferry drops you off on the edge of Sa Penya; take a right at the end of the dock to get to the town center. From the bus station, walk down Avda. Isidoro Macabich, which turns into Avda. Bartolomé Roselló.

Tourist Office: Avda. Ignacio Wallis (tel. 30 43 04). Unhelpful, but they'll give you a useful map showing hotel locations. Open July-Sept. Mon.-Fri. 8am-12:30pm and 5-6pm, Sat. 9am-12:30pm; Oct.-June Mon.-Fri. 9am-12:30 and some afternoon hours.

Post Office: C. Madrid, 23 (tel. 30 02 43), off Isidoro Macabich. Open for stamps and Lista de Correos Mon.-Fri. 8:30am-2pm. Open for **telegrams** Mon.-Fri. 8:30am-8:30pm, Sat. 9:30am-8:30pm; or call 30 10 96. **Postal Code:** 07800.

Telephones: C. Aragon (tel. 30 10 97). This is only a business office. **Telephone kiosks** for collect international calls are located on the waterfront at the end of C. Carlos II and at Playa Figuertas. To get to the latter from Paseo Vara de Rey, walk 7 blocks on Avda. España and turn left. Both open June.-Oct. daily 10am-1pm and 4:30-9pm.

Airport: Tel. 30 03 00. Buses to the airport run every hr. 7am-10pm from Avda. Isidora Macabich, 20. Buses leave the airport on every ½-hour (45ptas). To Palma (5 per day, 20 min., 3360ptas), Madrid (2 per day, 1 hr., 12,010ptas), and Barcelona (5 per day, ½ hr., 6725ptas).

Iberia, P. Vara de Rey, 15 (tel. 30 09 54 or 30 13 68). Open for tickets and reservations Mon.-Fri. 9:30am-1pm and 4:30-7pm, Sat. 8am-12:30pm. Iberia's airport booth is open daily 7am-11pm.

Bus Station: The 2 main bus stations are both on Avda. Isidoro Macabich, one at #42, the other in front of #20. However, there are more than 2 companies, and their decentralized schedules are impossible to decipher. Go to #42 for San Antonio (every ½-hr. 7:30am-10pm, 90ptas), Sta. Eulalia (every ½-hr. 8am-9pm, 90ptas), Portinatx (6 per day, 175ptas), San Mateo (1 per day, 40ptas), and San Miguel (2 per day, 90ptas). Go to #20 for the airport (every hr. 7am-10pm, 45ptas), Salinas (9 per day, 45ptas), Playa en Bossa (roughly on the ½-hr., 40ptas), Talamaca and Cala Llonga (9 per day, 85ptas), and Can Misses (8 per day, 40ptas).

Ferries: All boats except Flebasa's leave from Estación Maritima (tel. 30 40 96), at the end of Avda. Bartolomé Rosello. **Trasmediterranea,** Bartolomé Vicente Ramón, 2 (tel. 31 16 50), at C. Lamiñe y Cayne. To Barcelona (6 per week in summer, 4550ptas), Valencia (5 per week in summer, 4550ptas), and Palma (4 per week in summer, 3410ptas). **Flebasa** (tel. 34 28 71) runs boats to Denia (1-2 per day, 3 hr., 4700ptas). From Puerto San Antonio, accessible by bus from Ibiza City (see above). **Marítima de Formentera** runs boats to Formentera (9 per day in summer, 1½ hr., 500ptas).

Taxis: Tel. 32 00 52.

Laundromat: Master Clean Lauanderiá Autoservicio, C. Felipe II, 12 (tel. 31 07 36). Wash and dry 650ptas per day. Takes about a day. Open Mon.-Sat. 9am-9pm.

Medical Services: Policlínica Nuestra Sra. Del Rosario, Via Romana (tel. 30 19 16). **Emergency Medical Clinic,** Paseo Vara de Rey, 18 (tel. 30 31 31).

Police: C. Madrid (tel. 30 11 31). **Guardia Civil,** C. Aeropuerto (tel. 30 11 00).

Accommodations

Most of what the city offers lies near its center, off **Avenue Bartolomé Rosellé.** You might also try the more expensive **Playa Figueretas.** If you don't have reservations during the summer crunch, try to arrive in the early morning; otherwise you'll find yourself one of many desperate room-seekers roaming the streets at dusk. The following are open year-round; rates given are for the summer high season.

Hostal Residencia Sol y Brisa, C. B.V. Ramón, 15 (tel. 31 08 18). Pleasant owners, sparkling facilities, and 2 tiny courtyards filled with plants. Singles 1100ptas. Doubles 2000ptas. Hot showers 200ptas.

Hostal Marina, Andenes del Puerto, 4 (tel. 31 01 72), across from the Estación Maritima. In a great location, so show up early. Clean rooms and a beautiful view for 1200ptas per person.

Casa de Huéspedes Hospedajes Muñoz, C. Bartolome Vicente Ramón, 3. Comfortable rooms in a homey atmosphere. Singles 1100ptas. Doubles 2000ptas.

Hostal España, C. B.V. Ramón, 1 (tel. 31 13 17), next door and overlooking the harbor. June 15-Sept. 15 singles 1350ptas; doubles 2650ptas. Sept. 16-Oct. 15 and April 2-June 14 singles 1150ptas; doubles 2250ptas. Oct. 16-April 1 singles 1000ptas; doubles 1950ptas. Breakfast 250ptas.

Casa de Huéspedes Sol-Paris, C.V. Cuervo, 8 (tel. 30 48 97 or 30 78 82), around the corner. Clean, with an agreeable owner. Singles 1000ptas. Doubles 1700ptas.

Hostal Las Nieves, C. Juan de Austria, 18 (tel. 31 58 22), and **Hostal Juanito,** C. Juan de Austria, 17. Run by the same management and virtually identical. Escape from the bright Ibiza sun into the clutches of deepest darkness, no matter what the time of day. Rooms are large and clean, but they often don't fill up until late because the owner is rarely present; try just before lunch. Singles 900ptas. Doubles 1800ptas. Showers 250ptas.

The island's **camping** facilities, located near San Antonio Abad and Santa Eulàlia, are listed in those sections.

Food

The restaurants here run the gamut. The expensive, swanky variety will put you outside on the main drag with cotton tablecloths, candles, and exquisitely prepared food. If your pockets are jingling with their last pesetas, however, try the **mercado** on Pl. Constitución (try to pick your own produce—the quality varies). At **Chicken Park,** Avda. Ignacio Wallis, 15, you can take out delicious whole chickens, and the **supermercado** on Avda. Rosello stocks a wide range of sandwich meats. (Open Mon.-Fri. 9am-2pm and 5-8pm, Sat. 9am-2pm.)

> **Fonda Sport,** Avda. Bartolomé Ramón y Tur, 3 (tel. 31 16 25). Fills with chic locals who would rather spend their money on expensive sunglasses. Basic bargain basement *menú* 550ptas. Open Mon.-Sat. 1-3pm and 9-11pm.

> **Restaurante Victoria,** C. Riambau, 1 (tel. 30 58 19). Service is a bit slow, but this no-frills restaurant churns out quality omelettes and fish—mussels 315ptas, sole 400ptas. Open Mon.-Sat. 1-4pm and 9pm-midnight.

> **Restarante California,** C. Carlos V, 22 (tel. 31 08 59), with a pastel sign out front. *Estofados* (stews) and other cheap dishes. *Menú* 600ptas. Open daily 1-4pm and 8-10pm.

> **Restaurante Fonda Cán Costa,** C. Cruz, 19 (no phone), down the street. Home cooking over a wood fire. Chicken or pork chops 375ptas. Open Mon.-Sat. 12:30-3pm and 8-11pm.

> **Pinocchio,** C. Mayor, 18 (tel. 31 01 76). Free tickets to the fashion show passing by. Tasty pizzas, too (350-640ptas). Open daily 12:30pm-1am.

> **La Casa de los Helados,** Luis Tur Palau, 18 (tel. 30 76 17), in the *d'alt vila* near the old gate. The rude French owners will charge you a fortune to satisfy your craving for their delicious ice cream concoction (450-575ptas). Open daily 10am-2pm.

Sights

Climbing the *d'alt vila*'s narrow, twisting streets to what seems like the top of a skyscraper is the best way to orient yourself. The view from the **cathedral** spans 360 degrees, taking in the whitewashed neighborhood you've just weaved your way through, the boats puffing out to sea, Playa Figueretas, Formentera clouded by salty vapor, the business district and the randomly placed houses and fields beyond. The cathedral's huge thirteenth-century belfry crowns this panoramic view.

Entertainment

Every morning in summer, an exodus of sun-hungry beach prowlers swarms to the nearby tanning grounds. One of the closest and cleanest beaches is in **Salinas** (9 buses per day, 45ptas). Buses also leave to the hippie hangout **Cala Llonga** (9 per day, 85ptas) and other beaches nearby, such as **Cala Olivera** and **Playa Talamaca.** You can also take a boat to Talamaca from the Estación Marítimo (every 15 min. 9am-10pm, 90ptas). **Aiguas Blancas,** 10km north of **Santa Eulàlia,** hosts the island's only official nude beach.

When the crowds return to Ibiza City, it comes alive with flashing bodies and bright lights. **Carrer Major** lets your imagination run wild and then shocks it with reality. Traditional notions of gender-based dress lose their meaning in the barrage of fashions that assails you on the cobblestoned street. Signs like "The Language of Clothes" hang outside bars and clothing stores throb and pulse like late-night discos. Take a look into **Loco Mia Bar** at Carrer Major, 46. The owners wear shoes with six-inch-long toes, making them look like intergalactic stewardesses. The bar also sells clothes. If you're not interested in living out your sartorial fantasies, go to **The Tavern Ibiza,** C. de La Virgen, 20, for 100ptas beers and strong, 250 drinks. (Open Mon.-Sat. 7pm-3am, Sun. 9pm-3am.)

At the other end of **C. de la Virgen,** gay men will find a couple of good bars. At #69, **Bar D'Jango** has a small terrace in the back looking over the harbor. **JJ's,** at #79, comes alive a little later with music.

If you're out early in the evening, look as hip as you can—you're bound to get a free pass to one of the city's discos, which start to fill around midnight. **Angel's,** Paseo Maritimo, attracts a slick crowd (open 11pm-3am). **Disco Ku,** on the road to San Rafael, attracts just about everyone. During the day, keep your eyes open for posters announcing special events around town, especially at **Glory's,** near San Rafael at Hipódromo C'an Bufí.

San Antonio Abad (Sant Antonio Abat)

San Antonio's huge half-moon beach, quiet harbor, and accessibilty to nearby beaches makes this town, 16km from Ibiza City, a popular hangout. Add to all that an inspired nightlife, and you've got a rocking beach resort.

During the day it's too hot to be anywhere but the **beach.** The crescent-shaped beach on the San Antonio bay fills up quickly, so many people take a bus or boat to beaches nearby. All buses and boats leave from the central part of the waterfront, C. Balanzat at C. Progrés. They go to **Cala Bassa,** a sandy beach on a spit of land (8 buses per day, on the ½-hr., 55ptas; 7 boats per day, on the ½-hr., 175ptas); **Cala Conta,** a slightly rocky beach (bus 60ptas; boat 200ptas); and **Cala Tarida,** a protected inlet at the base of forested hills (9 buses per day, 55ptas; roughly 1 boat per hr. in summer, 250ptas). Boats are also available to Portinatx (3 per week, 1000ptas) and Formentera (1 per day, 500ptas), while a round-the-island cruise leaves every morning (2300ptas). Buses connect several times per day to Cala Gra- ció (50ptas), Port des Turrent (50ptas), and Santa Eulàlia (140ptas).

For a break from the beach, head for the national monument on the outskirts of town. The underground **Capilla de Santa Inés** haunts visitors with its eerie reli- gious feel. Ask about tours of the church at the **tourist office** (tel. 34 33 63), in the park at the beginning of Passeig de Ses Fonts. (Open Mon.-Fri. 9:30am-1pm and 4:30-7pm, Sat. 9:30am-1pm.) The office can also lead the way to the **Cueva de Ses Fontanelles,** where the walls are covered by faintly colored paintings supposedly dating from prehistoric times.

By far the most interesting attraction in San Antonio is, however, the nightlife. People dance with their neon shadows, wearing little more than they wore all day long at the beach. The night dissolves into two stages: the bar scene and streetside drinking near Calles Vara de Rey and de la Mar, where people jockey for free passes (just ask around—in any language—for a free *entrada*), and, about midnight, the flood of dancers into the discos. The really fashionable head to **Es Paradis,** off Avda. Dr. Fleming (tel. 34 28 93), where white pillars, bushy plants, and bright lights sur- round the dance floor, where men remain on one side and women on the other. (Cover 500ptas.) **Extasis,** Avda. Portmany, which gives out passes that waive the 1000ptas cover, is a typical area disco, attracting mostly over-sunned, blond-haired foreigners. The most popular place in town, **Idea,** Avda. Dr. Fleming, charges no cover and is set up outside, so it never gets hot and stuffy. The smaller **Char Mol** attracts a full house, including a sizable group of gay people. More mellow types head for the cafes that line **Calle Balanzat** and sip cool drinks while watching the parades pass by.

If you plan to stay in San Antonio, head up Carrer del Progrés, which runs per- pendicular to the waterfront up the hill from the bus station. **Hostal Roig,** at #38 (the 3rd #38 up the hill, about a block after the 1st one and after #40), offers large, bright rooms with big balconies. (Singles 1378ptas. Doubles 2226ptas. Hot showers 250ptas. The friendly owner is fond of giving discounts. **Casa de Huéspedes Progres,** Carrer del Progrés, 40, has simple but clean and bright rooms for about 700ptas per person. **Hostal Mari,** at #36 (tel. 34 01 24), is booked through 1989 but offers a pleasant English breakfast for 275ptas. **Camp at San Antonio** (tel. 34 05 36), 2km out on Carretera Ibiza-San Antonio. (Open April-Sept. 380ptas per person, 350ptas per tent.) **Cala Bassa,** in San Antonio at Cala Bassa, is another camping option. (Open May-Oct. 430ptas per person, 430ptas per tent.)

If you are looking for a good meal, head for the neighborhood on the other side of the hill up C. Progrés. Take a left on C. Soldat, and walk 4 blocks to **Bar Nevada.** They serve a great *menú* for 600ptas, and you can chow down with all the workers from the apartment construction sites. Also try the centrally located **Sa Clau,** C. Balanzat, 8 (tel. 34 07 34), where half a roast chicken, fries, and salad cost 500ptas in the cafeteria (not in the more expensive restaurant upstairs). *Combinados,* includ- ing selections from the grill, run 450-775ptas.

The last week of June and first week of July bring the **Sun Festival,** with rock concerts in the park at night. The town's patron Saint Bartolomé not Antonio is celebrated with a cultural festival on August 24; sports events are also part of the festivities.

If you burn too badly or drink too much, you'll need **Centro Médico,** C. del Faro (tel. 34 11 34), which offers emergency medical care around the clock. The **post office** is on C. del Mar at C. de Sant Rafael. (Open Mon.-Fri. 9am-2pm, Sat. 9am-1pm.) Should some drunken slob steal your stamps before you've had a chance to lick them, tell the **police,** Avda. Portus Magnus (tel. 34 39 11). For **international phone service,** go to the kiosk on the beach across from the tourist office. (Open daily 10am-1pm and 4:30-9pm.)

Santa Eulàlia des Riu (del Rio)

Some of Ibiza's most popular beaches hide in the northeast corner of the island, just north of Santa Eulàlia. Ibiza's only river flows into the sea just south of town.

Many boats and buses connect Santa Eulàlia to the northern beaches. Buses leave from **Calle Mariano Riquer Wallis,** and boats leave from the waterfront near the edge of the boat basin. **Cala Llonga,** a long sandy cove, actually lies 5km south (10 buses per day, 40ptas; boats every ½ hr. 9am-6pm, 150ptas). Five kilometers north of town lies **Es Caná,** whose white, sandy beach and weekly market of arts and crafts each Wednesday attracts backpackers and families alike (buses and boats every ½-hr. 8am-9pm, 150ptas). **Cala Nova** and **Cala Llenya** might be a little less crowded (4 buses per day, 60ptas, get on the Figueral bus; 5 boats per day, 200ptas). Locals say **Aigues Blanques** (Aguas Blancas) is the most beautiful, but the word has spread (4 buses per day, 60ptas). Boats run to Formentera once per day at 9:30am (round-trip 1100ptas) and Ibiza City (6 per day, round-trip 600ptas).

The **tourist office,** Carrer de Mariano Riquer Wallis, 4 (tel. 33 07 28), proudly displays two gold-lettered awards received by the town for excellence in tourism. (Open Mon.-Fri. 9:30am-1:30pm and 5-8pm, Sat. 9:30am-1:30pm.) The **medical emergency** center is next door at #6 (tel. 33 24 53). The **municipal police** are on San Jaime, 2 (tel. 33 08 41). The **post office,** sits on Avda. General Franco. (Open Mon.-Fri. 8:30am-2pm.) The **telephone kiosk** wanders around from time; ask the turismo. (Open daily 10am-1pm and 4:30-9pm.)

You can camp at **Es Cana,** between Sta. Eulàlia and Es Cana. (Open May-Oct. 350ptas per person, 350ptas per tent.) The most beautiful site, however, is pine-canopied **Florida,** beyond Sta. Eulàlia, between Playa Es Cana and Punta Arabi right on the beach. (Open April-Oct. 300ptas per person, 275ptas per tent.)

The town's two-star *hostal* is worth its rating. Run by a stern but friendly woman, **Hostal Rey,** C. San Jose, 17 (tel. 33 02 10), offers singles for 1060-1431ptas and doubles for 1908-2862ptas (showers 250ptas). **Hostal Central,** C. San Vincente (tel. 33 00 43), serves a fantastic breakfast uncommon in Spain—eggs, salami, bread with three kinds of marmelade, and lots of coffee. Its rooms are bright. (Doubles 1749-2650ptas. Breakfast 300ptas.) Local sources say there's just one place to eat—**Restaurante Ca'n Miqul,** C. San Vincente, 49 (tel. 33 03 29). The 500ptas *menú* includes two well-prepared courses. (Open Mon.-Sat. 1-4pm and 8:30-11pm.) Sta. Eulàlia is a fine place to catch up on your sleep, since not much goes on after 11pm.

Formentera

The most southern of the Baleares, Formentera lies 18km south of Ibiza. The Romans named the island "Frumentaria" (*frumentum* is Latin for wheat) because it exported so much agricultural produce. It remains relatively tranquil and un-crowded compared to its sister islands.

You'll arrive in **La Sabina,** the island's main port. You'll have to take the bus or rent wheels to get to the nearest beach, 3km east in **Els Pujols.** Buses leave the port to Cala D'es Pujols (4 per day, 40ptas). Bicycles can be rented more cheaply here than in Ibiza; one day costs 300ptas, less if you rent for longer. Mopeds cost

1000ptas per day. **Moto Rent La Sabina** (tel. 32 02 84) operates an outlet right on the dock where the boat lets you off (deposit 1000ptas).

The longest beach on Formentera, **Platja de Migjorn** lies on the south side and has many places to spend the night or have a drink. **Es Caló** lies farther to the east. Nude sunbathing is common at the east end, where the beach gives way to a coral reef. Other beaches, including isolated **Cala Saona** to the west and **Platja de ses Illetas** to the north, can be reached only by dirt roads or motor boats.

Most of the hotels on the island are not only expensive, but also booked through summer. **Hostal Bahia** (tel. 32 01 06), at the port in La Sabina, usually has some vacancies. (Open June-Sept. Singles 1749ptas. Doubles 2215ptas. Showers 250ptas.) Probably the cheapest place on the island, their restaurant serves chicken with french fries for 430ptas. Otherwise, your most economical option is to head for one of the island's many markets. **Hostal Costa Azul** (tel. 32 00 24), on Platja de Migjorn, has a great view and a cool, relaxing garden. (Doubles with bath 2968-3292ptas.)

Services on the island are somewhat spread apart. The island's only **telephone kiosk** is in Sant Francesc Xavier. (Open Mon.-Fri. 10am-1pm and 5-10pm, Sat. 6-10pm.) Here you can also catch a **taxi** at Pl. de Sant Francesc Xavier or call (tel. 32 00 52). The **Cruz Roja** (Red Cross) is on the road to La Sabina (tel. 32 00 61). The **post office** (tel. 32 02 43) is in Sant Francesc Xavier. The only **tourist office** greets you as you get off the boat at the port. (Open Mon.-Fri. 10am-1pm and when the boats arrive.) They have a map of the island and can direct you to the interesting sights.

Try to make it to Formentera for the wild **Fiesta de San Juan,** which explodes on the night of June 23. The entire island congregates in El Pilar Church for *buñuelos* (a delicious fried pastry) and sangria. Fireworks and dancing until 4am end the night's festivities.

Valencia

Song describes Valencia as the land of water, light, and love. But today, many of its rivers run dry, the capital lies under a dark cloud of smog, and even love has become more difficult in summer when you haven't booked ahead. Fortunately, you can still see the friendly region of old if you travel inland or get off the train or bus between resort areas, where the community works together to convert what water it still has to maintain the famous orange groves and geometrically patterned vegetable orchards, known as *huertas.* The countryside is segmented by ancient irrigation canals built by the Moors and Romans. Similarly ancient, the Tribunal de las Aigües governs the distribution of the water, using an intricate set of rules to decide each grove's allotment. Each Thursday at noon, the tribunal congregates in the capital by the Apostle's Door of the cathedral in Plaça de la Mare de Déu.

Before its annexation to Castilla, Valencia formed a confederation with Catalunya and Aragon. Thus, its main language is not *castellano* but *valenciano,* a dialect of *catalán.* The dialect was all but stamped out under Franco, but there has since been a resurgence of *valenciano* language and customs, particularly in the countryside. Residents speak the official language as well.

Valencia

Spain's third-largest city has served many masters. Originally Greek, the city later passed into the hands of the Carthaginians, the Romans, the Visigoths, and the Moors. For a short time around 1080, it was actually independent, but in 1092 it was captured by the Moorish leader Tarik. The Catholic hero El Cid battled off an enormous flotilla of Moorish reinforcements to occupy the city, halting a pro-

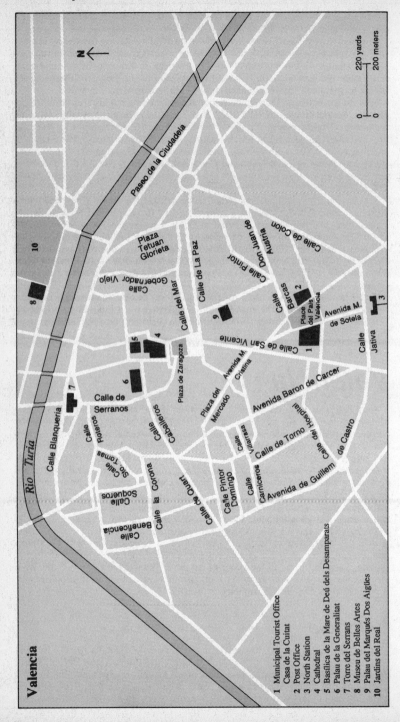

Valencia

1 Municipal Tourist Office
  Casa de la Ciutat
2 Post Office
3 North Station
4 Cathedral
5 Basílica de la Mare de Deú dels Desamparats
6 Palau de la Generalitat
7 Torre del Serrans
8 Museu de Belles Artes
9 Palau del Marqués Dos Aigües
10 Jardins del Real

posed Muslim invasion of the eastern coast in 1094. He later died defending the city. Falling back to the Moors in 1102, Valencia remained the capital of an important kingdom until 1238, when James I of Aragon retook it. During the seventeenth-century War of the Spanish Succession, the region sided with the Habsburgs, only to see Felipe V de Borbón implanted on the throne and much of the surrounding countryside ravaged. Used as a base by the Stalinists in the Spanish Civil War, Valencia was the last city to hold out against Franco's armies.

The cathedral houses the Holy Grail, attracting large crowds during Holy Week. But the most exciting time to visit Valencia is mid-March, when the city celebrates **Las Fallas** (see Entertainment). Otherwise, come to see the churches, palaces, towers, bridges, and gardens that line the city's wide avenues and ancient streets.

Orientation and Practical Information

It's most convenient to arrive in Valencia by train since North Station is close to the town's center. Simply walk up Avda. M. De Sotelo to **Plaza del Ayntamiento,** where the municipal tourist office is located. If you come by bus, city line #8 will take you to the same plaza. From this central hub, the interesting sections of the city fan north to the Turia River in three directions: along **Calle Barcas, Calle Pintor,** and **Calle Juan de Austria,** a commercial area that encompasses many expensive hotels and restaurants; along **Calle de San Vicente,** which leads to Plaça de Saragossa (site of the cathedral); and along **Avenida M. Cristina,** which leads to the bustling center of the huge central market, close to the older parts of the city. Affordable accommodations and eateries, historic sights, and municipal services abound here. Use the tourist office's excellent map, or purchase the indexed Bayarri map at a newsstand (350ptas). The municipal bus network connects the main parts of town, but it only runs until 1:30am. At night, buses run about a half-hour apart.

Tourist Offices: Municipal, Pl. del Ayuntamiento, 1 (tel. 351 04 17). Helpful but brusque. Keep asking for information or you'll get only a map. Open Mon.-Fri. 9am-1:30pm and 4:30-7pm, Sat. 9am-1:30pm. Branch at train station hands out a useful map. Erratically open Mon.-Fri. 9am-1:30pm and 4:30-7pm. Branch on Avda. Catalunya, 1 (tel. 369 79 32), for motorists coming from the north. Open Mon.-Fri. 9am-1:30pm and 4:30-7pm. Branch at the airport (tel. 153 03 25). Open Mon.-Fri. 10am-2pm and 4-7pm.

Student Travel Office: Viajes TIVE, C. Mar, 54 (tel. 352 28 01), between Pl. San Vicente Ferrer and Pl. Tetuán. The latest information on student discounts on planes, trains, and buses, as well as tips on local nightlife. Several English-language travel handbooks. BIJ and Transalpino tickets. Open Mon.-Fri. 8am-3pm, Sat. 8am-1pm.

Consulate: U.S., C. de Ribera, 3 (tel. 351 69 73). Open Mon.-Fri. 10am-1pm. There are no Canadian, British, Australian, or New Zealand consulates in Valencia.

American Express: Viajes Meliá, C. Paz, 41 (tel. 352 26 42). Cannot accept wired money or cash travelers checks. Will check for mail, sell checks, and exchange cardholders' personal checks for traveler's checks. Open Mon.-Fri. 9:30am-1:30pm and 4:30-8pm, Sat. 9:30am-1pm.

Post Office: Pl. del Ayuntamiento, 24. Helpful information office and stamps open Mon.-Fri. 9am-2pm and 4-6pm, Sat. 9am-2pm. Lista de Correos open Mon.-Fri. 9am-8pm. **Telegrams** (tel. 352 26 00, in off-hours). Open Mon.-Fri. 8am-midnight, Sat.-Sun. 8am-10pm. **Postal Code:** 14600.

Telephones: Pl. del Ayuntamiento, 27 (tel. 003). Open Mon.-Sat. 9am-1pm and 5-9pm. **Telephone Code:** 96.

Airport: 15km southwest of the city (tel. 153 02 11). Take bus #15 from the bus station (hourly, 90ptas). **Iberia,** C. de la Paz, 14 (tel. 352 97 37). Open Mon.-Fri. 9am-1:30pm and 4-7pm, Sat. 9am-1:30pm. To Madrid (8010ptas) and Palma de Mallorca (7090ptas).

Trains: North Station, C. de Xàtiva, 15 (tel. 351 36 12). Information open daily 7am-10:30pm. **RENFE,** Pl. de Alfonso el Magnanimo, 2, near the AmEx office. Open Mon.-Fri. 9am-1pm and 4-7pm, Sat. 9am-1pm. To Barcelona (9 per day; 4-6 hr.; *talgo* 2715ptas, *rápido* 1895ptas), Madrid (7 per day; 5-7½ hr.; *ter* 3650ptas, *rápido* 2555ptas), and Málaga (9 per day, 9 hr., 4095ptas).

Buses: Central Station, Avda. de Ménendez Pidal, 13 (tel. 349 72 22), across the river, about a 25-min. walk northwest of the town center. Take bus #8 from Pl. del Ayuntamiento. To Madrid (15 per day; 5 hr.; 1780ptas, express 2625ptas), Barcelona (8 per day, 5 hr., 1650ptas), and Málaga (4 per day, 11 hr., 4015ptas). **Municipal,** in the red shack on Pl. del Ayuntamiento. Information and tickets. 1 ride 60ptas, 10 rides 400ptas.

Ferries: Trasmediterranea (Aucona), Avda. Manuel Soto Ingeniero, 15 (tel. 367 07 04). To the Canary and Balearic Islands. To Palma de Mallorca (Mon.-Sat. at 11:30pm, 9 hr., 4550ptas). You can also buy tickets (on the day of departure only) at the port office, Estación Marítima (tel. 367 39 72). Take bus #3 or 4 from Pl. del País Valencià. Consider asking travel agent for ISNASA (tel. 340 09 05) ferry schedule leaving from Denia (3-hr. bus to Denia included in 4700ptas ticket).

Taxis: Tel. 370 36 00 or 370 32 04. Expensive.

Car Rental: Expensive if you want a car that moves in more than just spurts. **Flycar,** C. San José de Calasanz, 3 (tel. 326 71 55), and **Furgocar,** C. Linares, 12 (tel. 326 55 00), rent cars for as little as 3000ptas per day.

Laundromat: C. Balmes at C. Viana, just off C. Pie de la Cruz south of the Mercat Central. Coin-operated machines. Bring change and your own detergent. Wash 250ptas. Dry 25ptas per 6 min. Open Mon.-Sat. 8am-8pm.

Pharmacy: 24-hour duty rotate daily among the city's parmacies. Check the schedule posted outside any pharmacy for that night's location.

Hospital: Provincal, Avda. Cid con Tres Cruces (tel. 37 91 600). **First Aid,** Pl. de América, 6 (tel. 322 22 39).

Police: Jefatura Superior, Gran Vía de Ramón y Cajal, 40 (tel. 351 08 62). **Emergency,** Tel. 091.

Accommodations

Some of the cheapest rooms in town are concentrated in the area west of **Plaça del Mercat,** but with the savings comes a neighborhood that is unsafe at night. For a few duros more, there are somewhat more hospitable rooms all over town, particularly northeast of Pl. del Ayuntamiento or along student-oriented **C. Conde de Montornes,** between Plaça Tetuán and Plaça de San Vicente Ferrer.

Youth Hostal Colegio "La Paz" (IYHF), Avda. del Puerto, 69 (tel. 369 01 52), nearly halfway between town and the port. Take bus #19, and ask the driver when to get off. Forbidding, fortress-like structure. Curfew 10pm. Members only, 450ptas. Reception and dorm rooms closed 1:30-4:30pm. Breakfast included.

Near Plaza del Ayuntamiento

Hostal-Residencia Universal, C. Barcas, 5 (tel. 351 53 84), conveniently located off Pl. del Ayuntamiento. 3 floors of spacious rooms with ornate, high ceilings and friendly owners. Top floors are furnished with lifelike hunting trophies. Singles 1060ptas. Doubles 1696ptas. Hot showers 150ptas.

Hostal-Residencia Universo, C. Vilaragut, 5 (tel. 351 94 36), 2 blocks north of C. Barcas behind Hotel Asturias. Not a bargain, but a homey atmosphere with sunny balconies and a sweet proprietor. Singles 1696ptas. Doubles with shower 2332ptas.

Hostal-Residencia El Cid, C. Cerrajeros, 13 (tel. 332 23 23), 1 block from Pl. Redonda. Clean, quiet rooms in a central location. Singles 742ptas. Doubles 1696ptas, with shower 1908ptas.

Hostal Moratín, C. Moratín, 15 (tel. 352 12 20), off C. Barcas. Neat rooms, sweet owner. Singles 1190-1590ptas. Doubles 1850-2350ptas.

Habitaciones Cofrentes, C. Pérez Pujol, 4 (tel. 351 03 91), south of C. Barcas. Musty, dusty rooms, but the price is right. The 3rd floor doesn't look that high from outside, but you may give up while climbing the stairs. Singles 600ptas. Doubles 1200ptas. Showers 200ptas.

Near Plaça Tetuán

Habitaciones Australia, C. Conde Montornés, 16 (tel. 332 37 74), a hike up Paseo de Colón from the train station. Just about the cheapest rooms in town; they're small but reasonably maintained. 600ptas per person. Showers 100ptas.

Habitaciones Gran Glorieta, C. Conde Montornés, 22 (tel. 352 78 85), down the street. Nice owner, neat rooms, nasty cat. Singles 700ptas. Doubles 1200ptas. Cold showers 75ptas, hot showers 175ptas.

Near Plaça del Mercat

Hostal del Rincón, C. Carda, 11 (tel. 331 60 83), past Pl. del Mercat. Gruff but kind management offers a great value for the price. Rooms over a garage that's sometimes noisy during the day but quiet for siesta. Singles 700ptas. Doubles 1375ptas. Hot showers 185ptas.

Hospederiá El Comercio, C. Botellas, 7 (tel. 331 62 27), around the corner from the above. The spongy beds will swallow you up and the management won't bother to look for you afterward. Singles 630ptas. Doubles 1200ptas. Showers 125ptas.

Food

Valencia is the birthplace of *paella,* a traditional saffron-flavored rice dish, and claims to be the only town that serves the real thing. Today, *paella* is garnished with succulent seafood in restaurants and enjoyed with beans and even snails. Legend has it that men should cook the *paella* and that conversation should be about crops or bullfighting while eating it. When novelist Blasco Ibañez was asked about Schopenhauer over a *paella,* he replied "Shut up and eat, man; shut up and eat."

Another Valencian specialty is *arros a banda,* a rice dish of humble origins that often contains Rascasse fish. Valencians cook the fish with garlic, onion, tomatoes, and saffron, and then use the stock to cook the rice. The fish and rice are then served in a *banda* (large pot). Valencians also revere *all i pebre* (eels fried and served in a soupy sauce with oil, paprika, and garlic) and *horchata de chufa* (a sweet, milky white drink made from pressed earth-almonds). Around Easter, a gift of **mona de pascua,** a spongy bun capped with eggs, is a sign of love.

Most of the best restaurants are in the old city. Avoid the mediocre and over-priced eateries around Pl. del Ayuntamiento. Fresh fish, meat, fruit, and cereals are available in endless quantities at the **Mercat Central** on Pl. del Mercat. Prices are low, and you can even buy toys here. (Open Mon.-Thurs. 7am-2pm, Fri. 7am-2pm and 5-8:30pm, Sat. 7am-3pm.) For a respite from sight-seeing, stop off at Pl. de la Mare de Deú for a drink in one of the several outdoor cafes. For an ice cream binge, try **Horchatería de Santa Caterina,** Pl. Sta. Catalina, 6, off Pl. Saragossa south of the church of the same name and decorated with beautiful, intricate tiles that depict scenes from the saint's life.

Near Plaza del Ayuntamiento

Freiduría Duero, C. Xátiva, 12, near the train station. This cholesterol capital of Valencia is packed with locals who come for the *bocadillos de calamares* (squid, 160ptas), the wide range of *platos combinados* (400-550ptas), and the fresh gazpacho. Roast chickens to go 500ptas. Open daily noon-4:30pm and 7pm-midnight.

Bar La Rotonda, C. Derechos (tel. 332 32 21), at Pl. Rotonda in the old city a block south of the Church of Santa Caterina. A breezy place with windows that open onto the plaza and a terrace under an arch. Sizzling hot food. Cheerful pink tablecloths and an equally cheerful 600ptas *menú.* Open daily 1-4pm and 8:30-11:30pm.

Casa Eliseo, C. Conde de Montornes, 9, down from Pl. San Vicente Ferrer. A slightly grimy but popular dining room. If you don't mind some curious (though not unfriendly) stares, you can get very full very cheaply. *Menú* with *paella* 375ptas. Open Mon.-Sat. 1-4pm and 8:30-11pm.

La Utielana, C. Dels Transit, 2 (tel. 352 94 14), a block off Pl. del País Valencià off C. Barcas. Cramped local hangout. Ask for the inexpensive daily *menú* (500ptas) rather than the more expensive a la carte option. Good food, poor service. Open daily 1-4pm and 9-11pm.

Restaurante La Taula, Pascual y Genis, 3 (tel. 352 36 49), near C. Barcas. Save up some money so you can sample Valencian specialties as they were meant to be eaten at this 1st-class restaurant. Tranquil, relaxing environment. *Menú* 1000ptas. Gazpacho 325ptas. Thick, properly made *paella* 700ptas. Avoid the house wine. Open daily 1-4:30pm and 8:45-11:30pm. Reservations are recommended.

Salvas 12, Salvas, 12, alongside the university in a cool outdoor garden. Enjoy a range of food options including thick, fresh sandwiches (160-220ptas) and a *menú* of exotic local dishes (750ptas). Open daily noon-4pm and 9-11:30pm.

Cervecería Alberic, C. Cervantes, 27, 4 blocks west of the train station. Cheerful owner carefully prepares each meal himself. *Menú* with *paella* 450ptas. Owner says the place is open whenever you want to eat.

Near Plaça Mercat

Comidas El Canto, C. Muro Zeit, 1, on the diagonal street between the end of C. Murillo and C. Bolsería. Plastic furnishings accentuate the one redeeming quality here: cheapness. *Menú* with *paella* 550ptas. Open daily 1-3:30pm and 9-11pm.

Restaurante El Dintel, C. Murillo, 15 (tel. 322 38 91). Gourmet home-cooked meals in a pleasant setting. Green and white gingham tablecloths suit the disposition of the friendly owner, as does the Muzak. Try the *pollo a limone*. Widely varied *menú* 750ptas. Open daily 1:45-4pm and 9-11:30pm.

Sights

Valencia, is a cross-section of history, art, and architecture. The city's monuments are close to each other and make an easy walking tour. Beginning in the north and working your way south will allow you to finish the day at a hotel or restaurant in the town's center, where you can put up your feet.

A Valencian proverb says "I'll do anything but hurry." After seeing the city's many beautiful gardens you'll know why. The **Jardí Botànic** is somewhat distant (across the river from the bus station), but it displays trees and plants from around the world as well as a collection of exotic birds and fish. (Open daily 10:30am-7pm. Free.) Not quite as far from the town's center, the neoclassical **Jardí Monteforte** blends geometric hedges, orange trees, sculptures, and flower beds to make a perfect setting for a picnic. (Open daily 10am-sundown. Free.) A 1-block walk will bring you to the banks of the now dry **Turia,** where local landscaper Ricardo Bofill has planned and begun one of the world's biggest gardens.

The **Jardins del Real,** on the north bank next to the **Museu del Belles Arts,** houses a small zoo where bears, lions, yaks, and flamingos take continual siestas, perhaps to protest their shabby cages. (Open daily 8am-sundown. Free.) The museum, on C. Pio V, displays excellent Valencian "primitives" (14- to 16-century religious art) and works by later Spanish masters. The early paintings illustrated saints' lives in comic-strip fashion for medieval churchgoers, who were mainly illiterate. In one, an imposingly Wagnerian *Santa Caterina* steps on an unbeliever, only to get hers later in a beheading scene. Look closely at the details (jewels, flowers) of the Flemish-influenced primitives and you will see the beginnings—centuries ahead of time—of impressionism. Notable works by Spanish masters include Velazquez's self-portrait, a forlornly spiritual *San Juan Bautista* by El Greco, Ribera's *Santa Teresa,* and a number of portraits by Goya. Disregard the main character in Goya's *Doña Joaquina Candado,* but don't miss the spunky pooch in the corner. (Open Tues.-Sat. 10am-2pm and 4-6pm, Sun. 10am-2pm. Admission 200ptas, students free.)

Across the river, a few blocks west, you'll pass the **Torre dels Serrans** (Watchman's Tower), an arch-like structure built in the sixteenth century by Pedro Balaguer as a fortified entryway in the city. Heading down C. de Serranos, you'll find the **Palau de la Generalitat** (Valencian Community Governmental Palace). Although you can enter its courtyard, you must make an appointment to see the gilded, Asian-Renaissance blend of its famous ceilings. (Visits free by appointment Wed. 9am-2pm, Fri.-Sat. 9am-2pm. Call 332 02 06. Courtyard open Mon.-Sat. 9am-2pm.)

Nearby, on Pl. Virgen, stand Valencia's two most sacred buildings. The **Basílica de la Mare de Deú dels Desamparats** (Basilica of Our Lady of the Forsaken) is an elliptical edifice with a dark interior and a dirt-obscured fresco by Palamino. The altarpiece's gilded statue of Our Lady is much-venerated by Valencians. Next door, the Aragonese began the **cathedral** shortly after the Reconquest. They transferred many of their religious treasures to it including, in 1437, the Holy Grail, which had been floating around northern Spain for more than a thousand years.

The **Museu de la Seu** (Cathedral Museum) packs a great many treasures into very little space. In the first room are myriad statues, religious figurines, and paintings of the birth of Jesus. The second room shatters the tranquility with sorrow and horror on every wall. Note the two ghoulish murals by Goya. (Open June-Sept. Mon.-Sat. 10am-1pm and 4-7pm, Sun. 10am-1pm; March-May and Oct.-Nov. Mon.-Sat. 10am-1pm and 4-6pm, Sun. 10am-1pm; Dec.-Feb. daily 10am-1pm. Free.)

The facade of the cathedral, rising at an angle to Plaça Saragossa, incorporates a weathered tympanum that nevertheless exhibits an exuberant and expressive Valencian style. The refreshingly clean textures of the interior complement the high Gothic arches. From the *micalet* (the chapel's tower), Victor Hugo counted 300 bell towers in the city. He was probably suffering from a spell of dizziness at the time: There are actually no more than 100. (Tower open Mon.-Sat. 10:30am-12:30pm and 5-7:30pm, Sun. 10:30am-12:30pm. Admission 75ptas, students 50ptas.)

Heading toward the train station, you'll find the **Ayuntamiento** in the plaza of the same name. The modern facade was built in 1925 and features the gruesome little bat that *valencianos* regard as a good luck symbol. As you enter, the lavish, cool beauty of the marble staircase is striking. On your left is the **Saló de Festes,** where gatherings of dignitaries are still held. This beautiful room features an ornate ceiling and two huge but perfect chandeliers. In the older part of the building, the **Museu Historic** holds the 30-kilogram shield of James I and a portrait of Alfonso XIII, grandfather of Juan Carlos. Also displayed is the first map of the city, charted by a monk who explored Valencia's streets day and night, leaving an accurate record of his journeys. Even if you aren't interested in the history, the beautiful building and parlors themselves are worthwhile. (Museum open Mon.-Fri. 9am-1:30pm. Free.)

In a passageway next to the bullring rests the **Museo Taurino** (Bullfighting Museum), opened in 1929 as the first of its kind. Among the various displays of bulls' heads and matador equipment are several gory photos of the death of Manuel Granero, last of the great Valencian fighters, killed in the Madrid ring in 1922. (Open Mon.-Fri. 11am-1pm. Free.)

While walking through the city, look up from time to time through the smog to see some exciting architecture. The **train station,** on C. Játiva, and the **marketplace,** on Pl. Mercat, both boast colorful exteriors. Nearby, the **Llotja de la Seda** (Silk Exchange) is no longer used. Behind its handsome, twisted pillars, the upper chambers house a masterfully sculpted ceiling, which you can reach by a staircase in the Orange Court. (Open Tues.-Fri. 10am-2pm and 4-6pm, Sat.-Sun. 10am-1pm. Free.)

Overdone but eye-catching, the **Palau del Marqués de Dos Aigües,** a few blocks east, now doubles as the national **Museu de Ceràmica,** with ceramic pottery, statues, and tiles from all over Spain. The interior of clashing Italianate marbles, Valencian tilework, and rococo murals makes this an impressive monument to bad taste. The fanciful eighteenth-century carriages on the ground floor are worthy of Cinderella. No wonder Hipólito Rovira, the designer of most of this madness, went insane. (Open Tues.-Sat. 10am-2pm and 4-6pm, Sun. 10am-2pm. Admission 200ptas, students free.) Two blocks farther, the museum adjoining the lovely sixteenth-century **Església Patriarca** houses a rich display of paintings by El Greco, Moralto, Caravaggio, and others. (Open daily 11am-1pm; in off-season Sat.-Sun. 11am-1pm. Admission 50ptas.) Next door stands the old **university.** At the **Iglesia Parroquía de San Esteban,** above the cathedral, the Cid married off his daughters. Valencia is also proud of its brand new **Palau de la Mùsica,** in the middle of the Turia between the Aragón and Angel Custodio bridges.

Entertainment

Valencia's greatest entertainment is undoubtedly **Las Fallas** (March 12-19). The city's neighborhoods compete to build the most elaborate and satirical papier-mâché effigy; over 300 such *ninots* are erected in the squares and streets of the city. Parades, bullfights, fireworks, and street dancing enliven this annual excess, and on March 19, all the *ninots* are simultaneously set ablaze in one final, clamorous celebration. According to tradition, the inferno acts as an exorcism of social ills and starts the agricultural season off on the right foot.

Don't come to Valencia for the nightlife in summer: Much of it consists of prostitution, sex shows, and small knots of students wandering down empty streets in search of a bar or disco where something—anything—is going on. Beaches generate most summer entertainment. **Platja del Saler** is the most exciting, but it's 14km away. Buses stop running at 9pm, although you can always try hitching back; rides can be plentiful, since everyone's going the same way. For beachfront nightlife closer to the city, take bus #1 or 2 from Pl. de la Glorieta to **Platja de la Malva-Rosa.** Disco bars line the seaside avenue (which is also lively in winter), and buses run until 1:30am.

In winter, students gravitate around the pubs on **Pl. Xuques,** off Avda. Blasco Ibáñez in the new city, or the less wild **Pl. Cánovas del Castillo,** on Gran Vía Marqués del Turia. For jazz, try **Club Perdido,** C. Sueca 17, past the train station. For gay men, **Balkiss** at C. Dr. Monserrat, 23, is a good place to dance or drink. Lesbians can try the **Carnaby Club** at Poeta Liern, 17, for dancing and drinks. It is also a favorite hangout for local youths.

During **Semana Santa** (Holy Week), various brotherhoods of colorfully attired monks ride on platforms that depict biblical scenes sculpted by famous Valencians. In the streets of the city, children act out the miracle plays of St. Vincent Ferrer. The festival of **Corpus Christi** (beginning the Thurs. after the 8th Sun. after Easter), features the *Rocas,* magnificently intricate coaches that serve as stages for religious plays. The **Fira de Juliol** (July Fair, July 15-31) offers fireworks, cultural events, and a **Batalla de Flurs**—a real "flower war" in which girls on passing floats throw flowers at the populace, who hurl them back.

Near Valencia

The Second Punic War was declared on account of **Sagunto,** 25km north of Valencia. Spaniards are still proud of the city's Roman inhabitants, who, in the third century B.C.E., held out against the besieging Carthaginian army led by Hannibal until they starved. The town is rich in Roman ruins, most of which lie on the hill just above it. The **Museu Arqueològic** showcases a small collection of sculptures, friezes, and coins. One of Spain's more notable and well-preserved Roman theaters, the **Teatro Romano** is built into the slope a little higher up. The distant sea still acts as backdrop for occasional performances. At the hilltop, the ramparts of a medieval **castell** extend for an entire kilometer across the ancient acropolis. Traces of houses and temples built one on top of the other by Iberians, Romans, Visigoths, Arabs, and the French are visible everywhere. The superb view from the ramparts extends over the huddled town, the dark green *huerta,* the rolling sea, and the mammoth steel works. (All 3 open Tues.-Sat. 10am-2pm and 4-6pm, Sun. 10am-2pm. Admission to castle 200ptas, students free. Museum and theater free. The castle officially has longer hours in summer, but the caretaker often goes home early, locking the gate begind him. He boasts about the people he has caused to spend unplanned nights camping inside the walls.)

The **Turismo,** Pl. Cronista Chabret (tel. 246 22 13; open Mon.-Sat. 8am-2pm and 4-6pm) can answer any questions. When you're tired of touring, head for the **beach** by the port 4km away. Buses leave from outside the Turismo (every ½-hr., 45ptas). The port is a dirty, brown town with industrial smokestacks spewing foul black billows, but the beach is wide, sandy, and enjoyable if you ignore the industrial pier protruding into the sea. In summer, a number of nameless restaurants set up shop on the beach along Avda. Mediterani. One, opposite C. Claveles, serves a particularly refreshing *paella* for only 450ptas. You can catch the bus back to Valencia outside Bar Chamari (every 1½ hr., 165ptas).

The **beaches** closer to Valencia, **Levante** and **Las Arenas,** are too close to the city to have escaped pollution and overcrowding, but the **Salér** bus (from Pl. Porta del Mar by Glorieta Park on C. General Palanca) will take you to a beautiful, pine-bordered strand of the same name, 14km from the center (2 per hr., 200ptas). The beach is long and sandy, and Valencia is visible in the distance. As it is the only decent beach close to Valencia, it can get extremely crowded in summer. Many cafeterias and snack bars line the shore, with shower and bathroom facilities nearby. For some shade, try the pinewoods in the back. The sandy ground is great for a midday siesta.

For **camping,** try **Municipal "El Salér"** (tel. 367 04 11), right behind the beach (270ptas per person, 160ptas per tent, 320ptas per car). For beautiful scenery, take a bus from Salér village to lovely **Albufera,** Spain's largest lagoon, separated from the sea by a thin strip of sand. Rice fields rim the edges while fish and wild fowl populate the waters. In the nearby village of **El Palmar,** try the local *all i pebre* (eels fried in garlic and served with pepper sauce). Toward evening, the sun over the lagoon sets nature ablaze.

Játiva (Xàtiva)

Once the second most powerful city in the region, Játiva has been ravaged by a succession of conquerors. With an imposing mountainous backdrop and land that lends itself equally to *huertas* and to vineyards, it's no wonder so many civilizations have inhabited and fought over Játiva. It is a wonder that tourists don't come to enjoy the quiet charm of this out-of-the-way town.

The city is known as the birthplace of José Ribera (1591-1652), the painter whose dramatic, *chiaroscuro* portraits of saints show a grim attention to sometimes gory details. Ribera moved to Naples, where he was nicknamed Lo Spagnoletto, "The Little Spaniard," for his diminutive stature. The two Borja popes Calixtus III and Alexander VI also hail from Játiva. Memorials to these three historic figures abound in the city. Játiva also prides itself on being the first European producer of paper, manufactured here as early as the eleventh century from straw and rice.

Orientation and Practical Information

Játiva is an inland town 64km south of Valencia and 102km north of Alicante and is easily accessible by rail. The town is divided into two distinct parts: the old village, at the foot of the hill at the castles, where ancient walls of the Romans, Arabs, and Christians still remain; and the modern village, separated from the old section by Avda. de Jaume I.

When traveling to Játiva, make sure to bring your passport or student ID; the caretakers of the various sights like to prove to the government that foreigners do indeed visit by recording ID numbers.

Tourist Offices: The Ayuntamiento, Avda. Jaume I (tel. 227 65 97), and the **Policía Municipal,** downstairs, provide walking-tour maps.

Post Office: Avda. de Jaume I, 4 (tel. 288 25 78). Stamps and Lista de Correos open Mon.-Sat. 9am-2pm. **Telegrams** open Mon.-Fri. 9am-3pm, Sat. 9am-1pm. **Postal Code:** 46800.

Telephone Code: 227.

Train Station: RENFE, Avda. Cavaller Ximen de Tovia (tel. 288 34 11). To Valencia (hourly, 2 hr., one way 250ptas, round-trip 370ptas), Madrid (1 per day), and other destinations.

Bus Station: Next to RENFE.

Hospital: Tel. 227 24 00. **First Aid,** Tel. 288 19 59.

Police: Baixada del Carmen (tel. 227 55 61). **Emergency,** Tel. 227 20 82.

Accommodations and Food

As in the region's capital city, cuisine here features *paella* and other rice-based dishes; Játiva even has its own version, known as *el caldero*. This specialty can be had for 350ptas at **Café-Bar San Remo,** Avda. Jaume I, 52 (tel. 227 30 14), run by an extremely friendly family. They serve fresh, flavorful food and homemade ice cream in their outdoor cafe in the heart of town. *Platos combinados* (including a fresh seafood platter) run 375-800ptas. Many of the economical eateries in town double as *fondas*. For example, **El Margallonero,** on colorful Plaça del Mercat, 42 (tel. 288 30 06), offers a *menú* with scrumptious *paella* for 700ptas. Their cool, clean pension is often full, but there are a few other *fondas* (though of lesser quality) on or near the *plaça* if you get stuck. (Singles 1000ptas. Doubles 1800ptas.)

Sights and Entertainment

The striking ramparts that bristle atop the hill in back of town lead to two outstanding castles: the **castell machor** (larger castle) and **castell chicotet** (smaller castle). The former was in use from the thirteenth through sixteenth centuries, and, though it bears the scars of many seiges and an earthquake (1748), you can still walk inside the arched stone prison that has held many famous prisoners, including King Ferdinand the Catholic, freed by his grandson, Emperor Carl V, in 1522 and the Conde de Urgel, would-be usurper of the Aragonese throne. Referred to in Verdi's *Il Trovatore,* this man spent his final decades here before being buried in the castle's chapel (1433). A Borja and an advisor to the rebel Don Carlos (subject of another Verdi opera) continue the list chiseled in stone next to the doorway. The top of the castle walls provide a view across the plain to the sea. You can also see the town below and how the original city layout grew according to the contour of the countryside. The *castell chicotet* is in better shape, but it's actually older—the original stone and clay foundation was laid in pre-Roman times by Celto-Iberians. (Open Tues.-Sun. 10:30am-2pm and 4:30-8pm; in off-season Tues.-Sun. 10:30am-2pm and 3-6pm. Free.)

The walk to the castles is long but worth it. Follow the signposts from Pl. del Españoleto up the hill from the town center. The trek is enhanced by the cool, dark **Englésia Sant Féliu** (Church of St. Felix), a cavernous Romanesque structure with a magnificent altarpiece. Rap on the window to have the caretaker open up. (Open Tues.-Sun. 10am-1pm and 4-7pm. Free.)

The **Museu Municipal** (Municipal Museum) holds several works by Ribera; here the townspeople have avenged Felipe V's destruction of the town in 1707 by hanging his portrait upside-down. (Open Tues.-Fri. 11am-noon and 4-6pm, Sat.-Sun. 11am-noon. Admission 100ptas, students free.)

From August 15 to 21, the **Fira** (fair) brings street theater, bullfights, and fireworks to Játiva. Every Tuesday and Friday a **mercat** (open market) bustles on Plaça Mercat. Though a small town, Játiva is filled with young people who love to party. Enjoy an *agua de Valencia* (O.J., champagne, gin, and whatever else the owner feels like throwing in) at **Pub Tulay,** C. Obispos, 2 (tel. 227 14 33). The owner can tell you a lot about the area. For dancing, try **La Nit,** C. Padre Claret, in the evening (cover 150ptas), and **Elite** at night (cover 200ptas). During the day, people tend to congregate in the small park between the post office and the Ayuntamiento, along Avda. Jaume I.

Gandía

The main town of a verdant agricultural region called **La Safor,** Gandía has slowly shed its troubled past as the silk industry gave way to the sugar cane, then the mulberry tree, then the groves of orange trees of today. The fertile land caused many Muslims to stay behind after James I conquered the region in 1240; their descendants, the *moriscos,* were expelled in the seventeenth century. This led to the abuse of new immigrants by the feudal lords that precipitated the Second Germanic War in 1693.

Today, Gandía's main attraction is the **beach,** 4km away. This expanse of clean, fine sand, several food-fest-tables-wide between the sea and the adjoining tiled *paseo,* stretches from the docks of the colorful port for several kilometers to the end of the onshore apartments. Distinctive orange trees dot the roadside walk, their simple beauty untouched by the relaxed summertime crowds that never quite manage to fully blanket the sand.

To relive some of Gandía's former glory, visit the **Palau de Sant Duc** (Palace of the Sainted Duke), a mix of Gothic, Florentine, and baroque styles that reflects the successive reconstructions and renovations from the fourteenth to the seventeenth centuries. The palace was once inhabited by the Borja family, as well as doña Constanta, the aunt of King James II. (Open Mon.-Sat. 11am-noon and 5-6pm. Admission 75ptas.)

Accommodations aren't tough to find as long as you don't mind a little healthy dirt. The tourist office can give you a list of generally shabby *fondas* in town, as well as a lengthy leaflet on the overpriced and usually full beachside beds. The best bargains are found in the port, on the other side of the docks from the beach. There, **Habitaciones Constantia,** C. Levante, 21 (tel. 284 02 65), offers bright quarters (some face the port) with a friendly owner. (Doubles 1700ptas.) Down the road, **Hotel Europa,** C. Levante, 12 (tel. 284 07 50), rents clean rooms, but the bathrooms are a little shabby. (Doubles 2250ptas.) Three campgrounds lie near the beach; **Camping Ros,** 4 blocks up Carrer Armada Española from about the middle of the beach, is the closest to the sand. (Open June-Sept. 250ptas per person and per tent.)

The **tourist office,** C. Marqués de Campo (tel. 287 45 44), across from the train station, can help with accommodations. A branch at the beach (tel. 284 24 07) is open May to September only. (Both open Mon.-Fri. 10am-1pm and 4:30-7:30pm, Sat. 10:30am-1pm.) Shuttle buses (60ptas) leave from next to the tourist office for the port and the length of the beach every 20 minutes. The **post office** is in town on Plaça Jaume I, a few blocks behind the Ayuntamiento. (Open for stamps and Lista de Correos Mon.-Fri. 9am-2pm, for **telegrams** daily 8:30am-8:30pm.) The municipal **police** can be reached at 287 19 35; in an **emergency,** call 091. For **first aid,** either go to the shack on the beach or call 286 25 59. Frequent **buses** and trains (265ptas) connect Gandía with Valencia. Buses leave for Madrid from the Paseo Marítimo Neptuno, 55, along the beach (6 per day; 6 hr.; one way 2065ptas, round-trip 3815ptas).

Costa Blanca

As you venture south from Valencia, the beaches become sandier, and orange groves give way to vineyards bordered by a few lonely palms. The "White Coast," which extends from Denia down to **Torrevieja,** is reputedly named for the color of its sand, although some locals feel it also applies to the complexions of its summer colonists—mainly English, Germans, and Belgians—when they first arrive. Alongside the tourist spots are areas of great natural beauty, but developers are slowly snatching up these vacant parcels. A rail line out of Alicante, not operated by RENFE, connects most towns, as does an extensive bus service.

Denia

Primarily a family resort, Denia lies 100km down the coast on the promontory that forms the Golfo de Valencia, halfway between Valencia and Alicante. Named by the Greeks for Diana, the goddess of the hunt, the town is now visited by bronze tourists who stalk the sun and wander the tiny streets and palm-lined promenades. The multi-kilometer sweep of *playa* is interrupted only by a few brightly colored rowboats; the first stretch as you head north is disappointing, but as apartments become villas, you'll come upon sandy coves swarming with small fish.

While you're in Denia, climb up to see the eighteenth-century **castle** in the town's center; it's poorly preserved but the dungeon is fascinating. (Entrance off C. San Francisco. Open daily 10am-2pm and 5-8pm. Admission 25ptas.) Denia holds a mini **Fallas festival** of its own March 16-19. The burning of images takes place at midnight on the 19th. During the first half of July, the **Fiestas de la Santísima Sangre** (Festivals of the Holy Blood) feature street dances, concerts, and mock battles culminating in a wild fireworks display over the harbor. From August 14 to 16, don't miss the colorful parades and staged invasions reenacting past struggles between Christians and Moors.

Unfortunately, Denia is no haven for the budget traveler; the few affordable hotels are usually full in summer. Try **Hostal Maribel**, C. Templo San Telm, 28 (tel. 578 09 13), across from the tourist office off Pl. de Jorge Juan. Rooms are comfortable and attractive. (Doubles July-Sept. 2600ptas; Oct.-June 2000ptas.) There are also several campgrounds in the area. **Camping Eden del Sol** (tel. 578 12 53) is a second-class site by the beach on Carreterra Les Marines. (280ptas per person and per tent.) Eating is also expensive; try the restaurants along C. Marques de Campo for less costly fare. The morning **market** is on C. de Magallanes, 1 block north of C. del Marqués de Campo.

The **Turismo**, C. P. Ferrandiz (tel. 78 09 57), near Pl. de Jorge Juan, is helpful. (Open Mon.-Fri. 9am-1pm and 4-7pm, Sat. 9am-1pm.) The **post** and **telegraph office** is at C. Patricio Ferrandiz, 59, west of the tourist office. (Open Mon.-Fri. 10am-2pm and 4-7pm, Sat. 10am-2pm.) The **train station,** down the road at C. Calderon, runs trains to Alicante (6 per day, 2 hr., 560ptas). A **telephone** service operates next to the train station in summer. (Open daily 9am-2pm and 5-9pm.) The **bus station** is at Pl. del Archiduque Carlos and services buses to Valencia (5 per day, 650ptas) and Alicante (4 per day, 645ptas).

Denia serves as the embarkation point for several ferries to the Balearic Islands. Many companies combine their services with bus departures from Alicante and Valencia at no extra cost—ask any travel agent for details. **Flebasa** (tel. 578 40 11) serves Ibiza (April 9-June 15 and Oct. 16-Nov. 8 3 per week, June 16-July 15 and Sept. 16-Oct. 15 daily, July 16-Sept. 15 2 per day; 3 hr.; 4700ptas.) **Maritima de Formentera** (tel. 578 60 11) serves Formentera (3 per week, 4600ptas) and also operates inter-island service.

Nine kilometers farther down the coast, **Jávea** (Xàbia) hides in a protected cove. To its south, the fine sand turns to hard rock and intriguing caves, culminating in **Cabo de la Nao,** from which, on a clear day, you can see as far as Ibiza. Around the bend, the old fishing village of **Moraira** has been protected from centuries of pirates by a castle and watchtower. These structures have failed, however, in their battle against the area's developers. Fortunately, some of the area's old quaintness remains.

Calpe (Calp)

The first thing you'll notice about Calpe, 10km south of Moraira and 62km northeast of Alicante, is the imposing **Peñón de Ifach,** an enormous protrusion of rock that resembles a Dalí landscape. It rises some 327m above sea level. Wear sneakers and at least the top half of your bikini if you climb it, and don't take anything along. The hike should take just over an hour, less if you scramble up the rock-strewn faces on the far side. Although the path to the summit is accessible by a short tunnel at the base of the sheer face, you may want to make this hike strictly a daytime excursion; legend tells of goat-shaped ghosts that haunt the rock and butt unwary travelers over the cliff at full moon. If the ghosts don't get you first, you'll notice that Calpe is not as crowded, though just as beautiful, as neighboring resorts. **Playa Levante,** a white beach with lovely surroundings, offers plenty of room and windsurfing. Call the **Turismo** on Avda. Ejércitos Españoles, 66 (tel. 583 12 50; open Mon.-

Fri. 9am-1pm and 4-7pm, Sat. 9am-1pm), between the old town and the beach, for information about other beaches near Calpe.

Unfortunately, inexpensive lodging is at a premium in Calpe. Up the steep incline in the older **pueblo,** you'll find the most reasonable inns and restaurants; avoid the bland food and high prices at the seaside. **Fonda Pati,** Avda. Gabriel Miró, 34 (tel. 83 17 84), looks like a miniature, semi-enclosed row of cabanas. (Singles 800ptas. Doubles 1500ptas. When business is brisk in July and August, you'll either get doubles for 1600ptas or nothing at all.) **Hostal-Restaurante Larios,** C. José Antonio, 44, up the steep slope, charges 700ptas per person. They serve a *menú del diá* for 450ptas and a truly luxurious *menú especial* for 700ptas, featuring a mean *zarzuela de pescados*—all sorts of fish swimming around in a stew. There's also **Camping La Merced** (tel. 83 00 97), a second-class site just 400m from the beach (275ptas per person; in off-season less).

Calpe can be reached from Alicante by frequent buses (305-400ptas) and trains (1¾ hr., 380ptas). Municipal buses (50ptas) meet each incoming train to start the long journey downhill through the old town to the beach.

Benidorm

At Benidorm, an ugly city 42km northeast of Alicante, the skyscrapers huddle even closer together than do the tourists on the beach. Quasi-attractions include an offshore island that resembles a half-sunken ship and a checkerboard pentagon imposter of a castle that hangs by the edge of the sea. If you decide to stay, prepare to pay. Accommodations are scarce and expensive. If you insist, try the run-down **Hostal Garita,** C. Antonio Ramos Carratalá (tel. 585 01 95; singles 1462-1961ptas; doubles 2019-2576ptas). On **C. Maravall,** there are several cheap *casas de huéspedes,* but chances are good that they will be full. Although most sites are crowded, camping in one of the six campgrounds is a good idea: **La Torreta** (tel. 585 46 68) is only 1km up from the beach (320ptas per person). The **market** is off C. Mercado, north of the old quarter; otherwise, you're stuck with fish and chips or large quantities of canned *paella.*

The **Turismo** is a few blocks east of the castle off the beach at Avda. Martínez Alejos, 16 (tel. 585 13 11; open Mon.-Fri. 10am-1:30pm and 5-8pm, Sat. 10am-1:30pm). The **police** can be reached at tel. 585 02 22, and **first aid** at tel. 585 40 59. Frequent buses run between Benidorm and Alicante (275ptas), as do trains (260ptas).

The fortress village of **Guadalest,** lies 27km away from Benidorm. This small town offers tremendous views of the surrounding countryside. One bus per day leaves from C. de la Circumvalación. Ten kilometers to the south, **Villajoyosa** (La Vila Joiosa) remains unspoiled. The town is full of relatively low buildings, friendly natives who are not used to seeing foreigners, and lots of ice cream and chocolate joints. Trains run hourly to Alicante (195ptas); the bus also makes the trip (210ptas).

Alicante (Alacant)

Despite all the tourists, Alicante remains unspoiled. Beyond the polished pedestrian thoroughfares, inlaid with festive red tiles and cleaned meticulously, lies the old city—a snarl of lively streets at the foot of the dominant *castillo.* Grittier than their counterparts in Alicante's new quarter, these streets are full of local color and good, inexpensive eateries.

Orientation and Practical Information

The Esplanada de España stretches along the waterfront between two large jetties. Behind it, the old quarter is a maze of small streets and *plaças,* where nearly all services and points of interest (except the *castillos*) can be found. To get there from the RENFE station, walk 1 block toward the sea on Avda. Salamanca, turn left on Avda. Maisonnave, and continue until its conclusion. From the bus station, turn left onto C. de Italia and cross wide Avda. Dr. Gadea.

Tourist Office: Esplanada de España, 2 (tel. 521 22 85). Open June 15-Sept. 15 daily 9am-8pm; Sept. 16-June 14 Mon.-Fri. 9am-2pm and 5-7pm, Sat. 9am-1pm. There's also an **Oficina de Información Turistica** by the bus station at C. Portugal, 17 (tel. 522 38 02). Open Mon.-Fri. 9am-1pm and 4:30-7:30pm, Sat. 9am-1pm. Each office provides different information, so check both for the full scoop. The **provincial office,** on Pl. de l'Ajuntement near the waterfront, distributes the most comprehensive map of the city.

Consulate: U.K., Pl. Calvo Sotelo, 1 (tel. 526 66 00).

Post Office: Pl. de Gabriel Miro (tel. 520 55 91). Open Mon.-Sat. 8am-3pm and 4-6pm. **Telegrams:** Tel. 522 20 00. Open Mon.-Fri. 8am-9pm and Sat.-Sun. 9am-7pm. **Postal Code:** 03000.

Airport: Aeropuerto Internacional de El Altet, Tel. 528 50 11. Bus to city (12 per day, 45ptas). **Iberia,** C. F. Soto, 9 (tel. 521 85 10).

Telephones: Avda. de la Constitución, 10 (tel. 004). Open daily 9am-10pm. **Telephone Code:** 96.

Train Stations: RENFE, Estación Término, Avda. Salamanca (tel. 522 01 27). Most destinations require you to transfer trains. Direct to Murcia (14 per day, 1½ hr., 410ptas), Valencia (4 per day, 3 hr., 815ptas), Barcelona (3 per day, 11 hr., 2340ptas), and Madrid (7 per day, 9 hr., 1925ptas). **RENFE, Oficina de Viajes,** Esplanada de España, 1 (tel. 521 13 03). Open Mon.-Fri. 9am-1pm and 4-7pm, Sat. 9am-1pm. **FEVE, Estación de la Marina,** Avda. Villajoyosa (tel. 526 27 31), quite a walk from town. Take bus C-1 from Pl. de España. Local service along the Costa Blanca to San Juan (60ptas), Villajoyosa (195ptas), Benidorm (260ptas), Calpe (380ptas), and Denia (560ptas). Railpasses not accepted. Hourly departures 7am-10 or 11pm from each end of the line.

Bus Station: C. Portugal (tel. 522 07 00). Capitalism in full flower; different companies compete on the same routes. Frequent service to Elche (125ptas), Villajoyosa (210ptas), Benidorm (275-280ptas), Calpe (305-400ptas), Jávea (330-365ptas), Denia (330-645ptas), Gandía (405-745ptas), Valencia (430-1265ptas), Murcia (1½ hr., 455ptas), and Madrid (5-6 hr., 2230-3200ptas). International destinations are also served.

Ferries: Trasmediterranea (Aucona), Esplanada de España, 2 (tel. 520 61 09). To Ibiza (4 per day, 2¾ hr., 5500ptas). **Marítima de Formentera.** To Ibiza (2 per week, 7 hr., 4600ptas) and Formentera (2 per week, 10 hr., 4600ptas). **Flebasa** offers service from Denia, including bus from Alicante. To Ibiza (1 per day, 3 hr., 4700ptas).

Hospital: Hospital Provincial, C. General Elizaicín (tel. 520 10 00). **Ambulance:** Tel. 521 17 05.

Police: Commisará, C. Médico Pascual Pérez, 33 (tel. 521 13 13). **Municipal,** Fdo. Madroñal, 2 (tel. 528 47 65). **Emergency:** Tel. 091.

Accommodations and Camping

While there seems to be a *pension* or *casa de huéspedes* on every corner in Alicante, the number of rooms that are clean, crime-free, and not frequented by prostitutes whittles the number down considerably. Try the streets around **Calle San Francisco, Calle San Fernando,** and **Rambla Mendez Nuñez,** and arrive early for a good room, especially in summer. Quality plummets (as do prices) the closer you get to the Church of Santa María.

Youth Hostel "Lucentum" (IYHF), Avda. de Orihuela, 97 (tel. 528 12 11), 2km from town, on bus B or E toward Madrid. 8-bed rooms in a building that used to be a prison; fortunately, the hostel has responded to rehabilitation. Curfew midnight. 550ptas. Showers and breakfast included. Lunch 150ptas. Lunch and dinner 650ptas.

Pensión Castillo, C. Baron de Finestrat (tel. 521 25 52). Immaculately kept by extremely friendly, English-speaking owners who will recognize your well-thumbed *Let's Go.* Fresh sheets and bright rooms, but cramped. Bathrooms and plumbing need work, but there is no better place in town. Curfew 1am, negotiable on weekends. June-Sept. singles 650ptas, doubles 1200ptas. Holy Week-May and Oct. singles 600ptas, doubles 1100ptas. Hot showers 100ptas. Hot showers 100ptas. Complete pension available.

Residencia la Milagrosa, C. Villavieja, 8 (tel. 521 69 18), across from Iglesia de Santa María. Fragrant, breezy rooms with a view of the church. Singles 900ptas. Doubles 1700ptas.

Hostal Ventura, C. San Fernando, 10, 5th floor (tel. 520 83 37). Don't despair—there's an elevator. Large, well-furnished rooms watched over by a friendly family. Singles 1166ptas. Doubles 1696ptas, with bath 2438ptas.

Casa Miguel, C. Quintana, 4 (tel. 520 78 55), by the large and lively covered market. The shabby exterior gives way to a polished if plain interior. Likely to have vacancies in summer. Singles 1000ptas. Doubles 1500ptas.

Camping Bahia (tel. 526 23 32) is a second-class site 4km away on the road to Valencia. (Take bus C-1.) (Open March-Oct., 265ptas per person.)

Food

Restaurants along the main pedestrian thoroughfares cater mainly to tourists, a fact betrayed by their multilingual, expensive menus. Instead, try the smaller family-run establishments in the old city (between the cathedral and the steps to the castle) and on side streets around town, where most restaurants offer as many as three dishes.

For food to take to the beach or just to gawk, check out the bustling **market** near C. Alfonso el Sabio, which features fresh fish, meats, and produce as well as sandwich meats and bread. Appealing *tapas* bars liven up C. Mayor. For the less bold, there's a standard *supermercado* on C. del Cid at C. de Valdés.

Pension Castillo, C. Baron de Finestrat and C. de Bailen (tel. 521 25 52), off Rambla M. Nuñez. Friendly atmosphere and good home-cooking. Mostly hotel guests. Reservations required. *Menú* 600ptas. Open Holy Week-Oct. daily 2-3pm and 9-10pm.

Mesón La Chuleta, C. de Sanjurjo, 22, off Pl. San Cristóbal. One of the only places in town where the food is not drier than the air. Filling *menú* 550ptas. Open daily 1-4pm and 7-10pm.

Comidas Rafaela, Pl. de Sta. María, off C. Mayor. Bright interior with a pretty view of Sta. María. Fresh vegetarian *menú* (550ptas) and a great salad bar. Uninspiring *menú* 625ptas. Cook works topless. Open daily 1-3:30pm and sometimes for dinner.

La Madrileña, C. San José, 4 (tel. 21 82 21). Thick and chewy *churros* baked fresh all day. Open daily 8am-10pm.

Restaurante El Tunel, C. Jorge Juan, 4 (tel. 520 24 80), at C. San Telmo. Dry food and tiny glasses. *Menú* 600ptas. *Paella* variations 625ptas. Open Mon.-Sat. 1-4pm and 8-11pm.

Sights and Entertainment

Complete with drawbridges, tunnels, secret passageways, and dungeons, the **Castillo de Santa Bárbara** is not just another castle. Even if the fortress (most of it reconstructed since 1950) doesn't overwhelm you, the tremendous view might. Rising 200m above the city, the castle site was first occupied by the Carthaginians, who arrived around 400 B.C.E. Be sure to walk around in the dry moats and investigate the ammunition storerooms and dungeon. The castle can be reached by a paved road from the old section of Alicante, or use the elevator by the beachfront (75ptas). Also at the top is the tiny **Museu de les Fogueres de Sant Joan** (St. John), a small collection of statuettes of the famous martyr. (Castle open mid-June to Sept. Mon.-Fri. 9am-9pm, Sat. 9am-2pm; Oct. to mid-June Mon.-Fri. 9am-7:30pm, Sat. 9am-2pm. Museum open Tues.-Fri. 10am-1pm and 5-7pm, Sat. 10am-1pm.)

The **Catedral de San Nicolas de Bari,** 1 block north of Méndez Núñez on C. San Isidro, reflects the sober, often severe, Renaissance architectural style of Agustin Bernadino, while the lavish communion chapel is prototypically baroque. Examine the intricate wood carvings on the door leading to the cloister. For a sharp contrast, visit the **Iglesia de Santa Mariá,** built on top of the ruins of an Arab mosque. A successful hodgepodge of architectural styles, it features a Gothic nave, a baroque facade, and a Renaissance baptismal font of Carrara marble. The best time to visit is when it is open for Mass on Saturday afternoon and all day Sunday.

Inside the neoclassical **Provincial Council Palace** is an **archeological museum** that houses coins and paintings from excavations throughout the province. (Open Tues.-Sat. 9am-2pm and Sun. 10am-1:30pm.) Most impressive is the **Museo Colección "Arte de Siglo XX"** (Art of the Twentieth Century), at the east end of C. Mayor. Housing a collection that includes sculpture by Calder, paintings by Miró, and drawings by Picasso and Braque, the museum provides a delightful break from the beach. (Open Tues.-Sat. 10am-1pm and 5-8pm, Sun. 10am-1:30pm. Free.)

When you tire of Alicante's considerable offerings and sardine-can beach, either hop onto bus C-1 in Pl. de España or board the Alicante-Denia train for the 6-kilometer beach of **San Juan.** If the crowds here have occupied every square inch—a distinct possibility in August, try the more peaceful **Playa del Saladar.** Buses to Urbanova make the 35-minute trip three times per day (June 21-Sept. 21). The island of **Tabarca** has beautiful beaches and makes a fine daytrip. Boats leave from in front of the Esplanada de España three times per day in summer, daily in winter (round-trip 710ptas).

From June 21 to 29, Alicante bursts with the bacchanalian celebration of the **Festival of San Juan,** complete with *fogueres,* symbolic or satiric effigies that Christianize the primitive agricultural rites. The figures are burned in a *crema* on the 24th, but celebration continues with breathtaking nightly fireworks. The **Virgen del Remedio** takes place on August 5, with a pilgrimage to the monastery of Santa Faz the following Thursday.

In summer, nightlife centers around the **Playa de San Juan,** about 20 minutes north by bus C-1, with its many discos and pubs. Unfortunately, you'll probably have to hitch or drive back, since buses run only until around 11:30pm. Especially popular discos in San Juan include **Donde Noche, Copity,** and **Va Bene** along Avda. de Condomina. Pubs also dot the beachfront; **Voy voy** and **Caligula** are highly rated. In Alicante itself, most discos charge a 1000ptas cover and are not worth it. **Copy-Club,** in the Hotel Melia, is free, but open only in winter. In summer, the tradition is to drink from 11pm to 12:30am or so at bars along C. San Fernando, and then go dancing. Gay men might enjoy **Jardineto** on C. Baron de Finestrat; for dancing, ask for directions to the sometimes gay disco **Memphis,** or try **Rosé,** on C. San Juan Bosco. While there are no lesbian discos, it is common for women to dance together in straight clubs.

Near Alicante

Though most residents spend their days making shoes, **Elche** (Elx) is best known for its half-million palm trees that supply all of Spain with fronds for Palm Sunday. The *Dama de Elche,* Spain's finest example of pre-Roman sculpture (now in the national archeological museum in Madrid), also comes from here.

The best reason to visit is to witness the **Misterio de Elche,** a medieval play performed annually August 11-15, with celebratory fiesta **Nit de l'Alba** on August 13. During even years, you can also catch it October 31 and November 1. Of the several parks and public gardens that fill odd corners of the city, the most beautiful is the **Huerto del Cura** (Orchard of the Priest). Here, colorful flower beds are shaded by magnificent trees, including an eight-armed Imperial Palm said to be a century and a half old.

The **Oficina de Turismo** is at Pl. Alfonso XII, Parque Municipal (tel. 45 27 47; open Mon.-Fri. 10am-1:30pm and 4-6:30pm, Sat. 10am-1:30pm). The **post office** is in Parque Projecto (tel. 44 69 11), near the Puente de Canalejas. The **central train station,** Estación Parque, is at Pl. Alfonso XII, but there's also the Estación Carrus on Avda. de la Llibertat. The **bus station** is also on Avda. de la Llibertat services Alicante (on the hour, 125ptas), 23km away. The **police station** is in Parque Projecto (tel. 44 70 70), and **first aid** is available at C. Reina Victoria, 6 (tel. 444 45).

Only 24km north of Alicante lie the spectacular stalagtasmagorical caves, **Cuevas de Canalobre.** With their candalabra-like formations, these caves are considered one of Europe's great speleology centers. Located 700m above the tiny village of **Busot,** the caves offer a splendid view of the coastline. Buses run from Alicante several times per day. (Caves open April-Sept. 10:30am-8:30pm; Oct.-March 11am-6:30pm. Admission 250ptas.)

If you have a car, visit the **Nougat factory** in Jijona, 13km away, and sample their goods free of charge. (Open daily 9:30am-1pm and 4-8pm.) Also consider detouring to **Agost,** 15km northwest of Alicante, to visit the pottery museum and factory, where you can see *bojitos* (white clay jars) being made. (Open Tues.-Sat. 11am-2pm and 5-8pm; in off-season Tues.-Sat. noon-2pm.) Only 5km from Alicante, in the **Monastery of Santa Faz,** lies a piece of the controversial Holy Shroud of Saint Verónica, on which an imprint of the face of Jesus is supposedly preserved.

Murcia

Sitting atop vast mineral resources, the region of Murcia has seen one nation after another fight over its mines. Each successive victor has cultivated the soil, making the ground above as rich as that below with the vast produce that permits the region to refer to itself as "la Huerta de Europa" (the Orchard of Europe). During the Middle Ages, rule over the region passed back and forth between local Christian lords and Andalusian Moors; thus, Murcians speak a dialect of Spanish akin to Andaluz, not the Catalán of their northern neighbors.

Murcia, the capital city, sits near the eastern border, surrounded by agricultural villages. The city is irrigated by a complex system of canals and produces vast quantities of vegetables. Yecla and Jumilla to the north are known for their wine vineyards. In the south, the Costa Cálida stretches from uncrowded Aguilas on the western end through industrial and historic Cartagena to the Mar Menor, a 170-square-kilometer sea cut off from the Mediterranean by a thin strip of land dubbed La Manga. The region prides itself on colorful Holy Week celebrations, which include long marches from town to town.

Murcia

Compared to most Spanish cities, Murcia seems an afterthought, not founded until the ninth century, when Abderraman II built a small town in the midst of the region's orchards. The town did not gain importance until the thirteenth century, when the Moors and then the Christians declared it the capital of the area. For this reason, Murcia does not have a castle at its center, has few monuments, and only opened its university after World War I. The city attracts few tourists, mostly those in transit to Cartagena and the coast, making it an excellent place to avoid summer crowds for a day.

Orientation and Practical Information

Most places of interest are scattered around the periphery. The train station is across River Segura, at the southern edge of the city, a 15-minute walk from the tourist office. The bus station is an equal distance away at the western edge. A municipal **bus system** of 33 routes connects just about everything, including other towns within 15km (45ptas, book of 10 tickets 300ptas).

Tourist Office: C. Alejandro Seiquer, 4 (tel. 21 37 16). Not used to seeing foreigners. Open Mon.-Sat. 9am-2pm and 5-8pm.

Student Travel Office: TIVE, C. Manresa, 4 (tel. 21 32 61). Open Sept.-July Mon.-Fri. 8am-3pm; Aug. Mon.-Fri. 9am-2pm.

Post Office: C. Villacis (tel. 26 10 73). Open for stamps Mon.-Fri. 9am-2pm and 5-8pm, Sat. 9am-2pm. **Telegraphs** open Mon.-Fri. 8am-9pm, Sat. 9am-7pm.

Telephones: C. San Lorenzo, 16, 1 block up C. Alejandro Seiquer from Turismo. Open daily 10am-2pm and 5-9:30pm. **Telephone Code:** 968.

Airport: In San Javier on the Mar Menor. No direct bus service. **Iberia,** Avda. Alfonso X el Sabio, Edificio Velázquez (tel. 24 00 50).

Train Station: Estación del Carmen, C. Industria (tel. 26 37 36). Take bus #11 to the town center. To Alicante (12 per day, 1½ hr., 340ptas), Barcelona (1 per day, 11 hr., 2635ptas), Madrid (3 per day, 7 hr., 1925ptas), Cartagena (4 per day, 1½ hr., 290ptas), and Lorca (5 per day, 1 hr., 290ptas). The train line connecting Lorca to the Almería-Granada line was cut a few years ago, making transit to Andalucía by train long and arduous. Consider the bus. **RENFE,** C. Barrionuevo, 4 (tel. 21 19 63 or 21 28 42).

Bus Station: Sierra de la Pila (tel. 29 22 11), behind the Salzillo Museum. To Valencia (3 per day, 1016ptas), Almería (2 per day, 1345ptas), Granada (3 per day), Sevilla (1 per day), Málaga (1 per day, 4055ptas), Cartagena (every hr., 245ptas, limited service on weekends), Lorca (every hr., 350 ptas, limited service on weekends), and Yecla (4 per day, 485ptas) via Jumilla (350ptas).

Hospital: Ronda de Garay (tel. 25 69 00). **Emergency:** Tel. 23 75 50.

Police: Municipal, Glorieta de España (tel. 26 02 46). **Nacional,** Tel. 091.

Accommodations

Murcia offers few places to stay, and the few that fit the budget bill are far from everything. It should not be hard to find a room at any time of year; high season lasts only from mid-July through August. Unfortunately, there are no campgrounds near Murcia.

Hostal-Residencia Pacoche, C. González Cebrián, 9 (tel. 21 76 05). From the train station, head right 1 block and take a left on Po. Marqués de Corvera to the park; Cebrián is the 2nd street on the left. This feels like full-fledged hotel with its lobby, full-time reception, and large, clean rooms with phones, spacious bathrooms, and enveloping towels. Holy Week and July 15-Sept. 15 singles 1050ptas, with shower 1350ptas; doubles 1850ptas, with shower 2325ptas, with bath 2825ptas. Sept. 16-July 14 singles 925ptas, with shower 1150ptas; doubles 1625ptas, with shower 1975ptas, with bath 2325ptas.

Hostal Legazpi, Avda. Miguel de Cervantes, 8 (tel. 29 30 81), out in the boonies. From the train station, bus #11 stops about a block away, at the end of Ronda Norte. Bright but cool rooms in an institutional environment. Singles 1000ptas. Doubles 2000ptas, with bath 2400ptas.

Hostal-Residencia Bimher, Avda. Marqués de los Vélez, 16 (tel. 23 42 60), near Pl. Circular. Clean rooms, but bring waterproof clothes: Showers are set up in the middle of the rooms and there's no place to hang a curtain. Get a room without a shower, even though the hall showers are a little seedy. Holy Week and July 27-Sept. 25 singles 1100ptas, with shower 1210ptas; doubles 1815ptas, with shower 2175ptas. Sept. 26-July 26 singles 975ptas, with shower 1025ptas; doubles 1510ptas, with shower 1815ptas.

Food

Murcians fill their dishes with the produce that pours in from the surrounding countryside. Sample the regional harvest at the **market,** on C. Veronicas near the river. (Open Mon.-Sat. 9am-1pm.) Murcia also hosts a fair number of inexpensive restaurants spread throughout the city.

Mesón el Corral de José Luís, Pl. Santo Domingo, 23 (tel. 21 45 97). The smell of wood in the room is old, but the vegetables are fresh from Murcia's *huertas.* Try the shish-kebob (*pinchón*). *Menú* 650ptas. Open Sun.-Fri. 1:30-4pm and 7:30pm-midnight.

La Parranda, C. Ceballos, 7 (tel. 21 32 82), near the post office. A la carte items are justifiably expensive. The quality *menú* is a steal at 550ptas. Open daily 1:30-4pm and 8:30-11pm.

El Tío Sentao, C. la Manga, 12 (tel. 29 10 13), a couple blocks from the bus station. Large platters of specialty meats and some seafood for under 250ptas. Full *menú* 500ptas. Open 9am-11pm.

Sights and Entertainment

Begun in the fourteenth century, Murcia's medium-sized **cathedral** took more than four hundred years to complete. The result is a confusion of architectural styles: a baroque facade, Gothic entry, and Renaissance tower. Similarly diverse elements lie inside, including a temple built to imitate the mosque that once occupied this site. Almost of greater religious significance to Murcians, however, is the **Museo Salzillo,** which contains almost wood sculptures by local, eighteenth-century sculptor Francisco Salzillo. Note the touching facial expressions on the apostles in the *Last Supper.* Holy Week processions originate here. (Open Mon.-Sat. 9:30am-1pm and 4-7pm. Sun. 10am-1pm. Admission 100ptas.)

The **archeology museum** is one of the most complete in Spain, chronicling the province extensively from pre-historic times. (Open July-Aug. Mon.-Sat. 9am-2pm; Sept.-June Tues.-Fri. 10am-2pm and 6-8pm, Sat.-Sun. 11am-2pm. Admission 75ptas.) The **Museo de Bellas Artes** contains works by little-known Spanish artists of the nineteenth and twentieth centuries. (Hours and admission same as at archeology museum.)

During Holy Week, Murcia's streets fill with processions of colorful costumes and floats. On the day before Easter, the **Exaltación Huertana** brings a weeklong celebration of the crops that includes jazz and theater performances in the already crowded streets. On other nights of the year, students gather at around 11pm in the bars that dot the area south of the university, before heading to discos along **Gran Vía Alfonso X el Sabio.**

Cartagena

The Carthaginian general Hasdrubal organized small villages into Qart Hadas (New Carthage) in 223 B.C.E. to govern Carthage's possessions in Spain. It fell to the Romans 14 years later and was quickly established as the important port and naval base it remains today. Coveted for both its port and nearby mines, the city passed in and out of the hands of Visigoths, Byzantines, more Visigoths, Moors, Castilians, and Berbery pirates before its final incorporation into Spain in 1503. Even the British held it for more than a decade at the beginning of the eighteenth century.

The city is known for its Roman ruins, scattered throughout the port. Remains of an **amphitheater** are visible under the **bull ring** of the last century, and a few preserved streets lie nearby in the old town. Next to the amphitheater stands the **Castillo de la Concepción,** an ornate building constructed between the fourteenth and eighteenth centuries. It rises above a Roman wall augmented in the mid-eighteenth century when the neo-classic **Antiguo Hospital Militar** was built alongside. Below, on the esplanade that runs along the port, sits the first electric-powered submarine, a puny tub designed by Cartagena-born Isaac Peral in 1888. Heading back into town, you'll pass the **old cathedral,** built in the thirteenth century out of building parts already on the site, including Roman pillars, a Byzantine column, and parts of a mosque. Renaissance and baroque chapels were later added.

Cartagena also sports a number of twentieth-century modernist buildings, such as the **Palacio Consistorial,** built by Tomás Rico between 1900 and 1907, a block from the cathedral; the ornately painted **Casa Maestre,** Pl. San Francisco; and **Palacio de Aguirre,** Pl. Merced. In the new part of town, Cartagena's **archeology museum,** C. Ramón y Cajal, 45, houses an important collection of ancient artifacts from prehistoric times through the Roman era. (Open Tues.-Fri. 10am-1pm and 4-6pm, Sat.-Sun. 10am-1pm. Admission 100ptas.)

Quality budget accommodations are scarce in Cartagena. The nearby campgrounds actually require you to rent an entire parcel of land at ridiculous rates. Try **Pensión de Liarte,** Muralla de Tierra, 5 (tel. 50 69 75), on the edge of the Monte Sacro, for cheap but run-down rooms for 500-600ptas per person. Fortunately, tasty, inexpensive food is relatively easy to find. Plaza del Ayuntamiento and Calle Mayor, which leads north from the plaza, serve as the old town's central arteries. Good seafood is served in this area at places such as **El Mejillonero,** C. Mayor, 4, which offers fresh seafood plates for 90-190ptas. The specialty mussels run 170ptas. (Open daily 10am-11pm.)

Cartagena proper has no beaches, but **FEVE** provides service every 40 minutes to coastal spots as far away as **Los Nietos,** on the shores of the Mar Menor (95ptas). FEVE's station is at the near end of Pl. Bastarrede; **RENFE** is at the far end. Their trains run to Murcia (4 per day, 1½ hr., 290ptas), three continue to Madrid (7 hr. more, 2215ptas). **Buses** leave every hour for Murcia from C. Angel Bruna and Pasio de Alfonso XIII (1 hr., 245ptas). Cartagena's **post office** is on Paseo San Francisco (open Mon.-Sat. 9am-2pm), and **telephones** can be found on C. Caño (open Mon.-Sat. 9:30am-2pm and 6-11pm). In an emergency, you can reach the **police** on Angel Bruna at 092 and the **hospital** at 50 48 00.

Lorca

Huertas (orchards) never took root in Lorca because its strategic position along an ancient trade route earned it frequent attacks over the years. As a Byzantine outpost, Lorca successfully withstood the Visigoths for nearly a century, and the Visigoths, in turn, held out against the Moors until the end of the eighth century. On the eastern border of the Muslim monarchy of al-Andalus, the Christians deemed Lorca vital in their plan to surround the retreating Moors but could not take the city until 1243. Thereafter, the Moors continually tried to regain the city without success. Each conquering force augmented Lorca's defenses, leaving a large, historically diverse **castle** on its central hill. Its two towers have recently undergone renovation. The Moors built the **Torre Espolón** shortly before the city fell to Alfonso the Wise of Castile, who ordered another tower, the **Torre Alfonsina,** constructed. The Gothic interior was not completed until the fifteenth century. The ruins of Lorca's first church, the **Hermitage of San Clemente,** sit at the castle's eastern edge. (Open daily 9am-7pm. Free.)

Once Granada fell, the population could turn its attention from defenses to elaborate peacetime structures. A number of churches and residences from this period have been preserved. In the sixteenth century, nearly the entire population of Lorca moved to the bottom of the slope, leaving behind three idyllic churches, **Santa María, San Juan,** and **San Pedro.** The structures fell to ruins on the road leading down from the castle in favor of six new monasteries and the **Colegiata de San Patricio,** with its proto-baroque facade and Renaissance interior. Of the private residences, **Casa de Guevarra's** curving pillars and intricate carvings typify the architectural flair of the period. The interior remains closed to the public pending its conversion into a museum.

A walk through the town reveals a landmark on every corner. Note the **Columna Miliaria** on Pl. San Vicente, which marked mileage on the Roman road to Cartagena. Unfortunately, Lorca's historic buildings have been allowed to deteriorate; most are only walls crumbling into the dry landscape. The government is now belatedly restoring the most important sights, but most will not survive the passage of time.

Both **Restaurante Barcas Casa Cándido,** Santo Domingo, 13 (tel. 46 70 02; open daily 1:30-4pm and 8:30-11pm), and the popular bar **Mesón Lorquino,** Avda. Juan Carlos I, 15 (tel. 46 74 05; open Sun.-Fri.), offer a 500ptas *menú.* The former rests on a cool corner in the historic area; the latter on the main highway. Both garner high praise from locals. For lighter, more economical fare, try **Mesón Segoviano,** C. General Terrer Leonés, 12 (no phone), down from Casa de Guevarra. If you choose to stay overnight, **Rincón de los Valientes,** at the end of C. Nogarte (tel. 46 64 59), has clean rooms, uncommon in run-down Lorca, for 800ptas per person. You can probably bargain the price down. **Hostal-Residencia Ciudad del Sol,** C. Galicia, 9 (tel. 46 78 72), is a little more dirty, but its rooms have bathrooms. (Singles 911ptas. Doubles 1749ptas.)

The **tourist office,** in Casa de Guevarra on C. Lópes Gisbert (tel. 46 61 57), provides an informative map. (Open Mon.-Fri. 10am-2pm and 5-7pm, Sat. 10am-2pm.) The **post office** is across the street on C. Musso Valiente. (Open Mon.-Fri. 9am-2pm, Sat. 5-6pm.) The **police** are on the ground floor of the Ayuntamiento on Pl. de España (tel. 46 60 62), and **first aid** is on C. Abad Los Arcos (tel. 46 60 79). The **train station,** Estación Sutullana (tel. 46 69 98), is 1 block from town at the end of C. Poeta Carlos Mellado, off Avda. Juan Carlos I. Trains leave for Murcia (8 per day, 1 hr., 290ptas) and Aguilas (3 per day, 30 min., 150ptas). Hourly **buses** leave for Murcia from in front of the station (1½ hr., 350ptas).

Like the capital, Lorca is known for its colorful Holy Week processions. On Good Friday, religious groups combine for a massive staging of bible stories in true baroque style.

Andalucia

With its dramatic bullfights, feisty flamenco dancers, and sun splashed villages, Andalucía exudes an intoxicating charm. The Andalusian *duende* (spirit) grows out of the Muslim, Christian, Jewish, Roman, and Gypsy traditions, all of which flow through the region's fascinating past.

Centuries after Europe's first hunter-gatherers emigrated from Africa to Andalucía, the lost kingdom of Tartessos grew wealthy on the Sierra Nevada's rich ore deposits. Later, the Romans made Andalucía part of their expanding empire, maintaining control until they were bumped off by Vandals from the north. Arab invaders overwhelmed the Vandals in the eighth century and managed to hang on for 800 years, leaving behind a Moorish tradition that strongly influenced the later Christian culture. Andalucía even owes its name to the Arabs: It's an amalgam of Arabic words meaning "Vandal's house."

Andalucía's Moorish heritage survives in the extravagant trio of the Alhambra in Granada, the great mosque in Córdoba, and the Alcázar in Sevilla. Centuries of a powerful Christian culture have contributed Sevilla's cathedral (the largest in Spain) and Ubeda's delicate churches. The modern residents of these historic cities have preserved and perfected the fine art of celebration. Nightly they throng the cobbled streets for evening *paseos,* and gypsies at *romerías* clap, sing, and dance well into the night. Sevilla's Semana Santa (Holy Week) festivities rival even Pamplona's big celebration.

Far removed in spirit, though only hours away by train, the Costa del Sol on the Mediterranean coast hosts a crush of frenetic sun-worshipers almost year-round, while on Andalucía's Atlantic shores, the formerly untouched Costa de la Luz is now catching the resort fever.

The pace of Andalusian life in the **Pueblos Blancos** (White Villages) is gentler. Workers in the parched fields pause under the midday glare for a slug of wine; others take refuge from the sun beneath the shade of an olive tree. Stone bridges span precipitous gorges, tile roofs cap whitewashed walls, and black grille windows peer upward at castle ruins and lead inward to green courtyards. The *pueblos* on this route roughly form a triangle whose vertices are San Pedro de Alcántara, Tarifa, and Sanlúcar de Barrameda.

Regional cooking relies heavily on olive oil. The excellent Andalusian stew, *cocido andaluz,* is often served as a main course. Gazpacho is a specialty here, too, and extremely refreshing on a hot afternoon. Order it *con guarnición,* and the waiter may spoon the vegetables right at your table. You'll find *paella valenciana* widely featured as well, but this dish may be better prepared elsewhere in Spain.

Almería

If the dusty crags and dry gulches of the province of Almería look familiar, there's a logical explanation—you've probably seen them in the background of a B-movie shoot-out. Thanks to its resemblance to America's western badlands, the area has been a popular backdrop for filming spaghetti westerns. There's even a tiny ghost town you can spot from the highway to Alicante called **Pequeño Pueblo del Oeste.**

Almería, despite its location, does not receive many tourists; it's easy to see why. The city swells with seedy areas and accommodations that also resemble scenes from a bad movie. It's difficult to believe that, at its peak as a supplier of silk products—around the eleventh century, Almería was the second-wealthiest city in Europe after Constantinople. The city soon declined, and when its Moorish population was expelled in the fifteenth century, its remaining residents turned to smuggling as a prime source of income.

The city does have one sight worth seeing: its eighth-century Arab fortress, the **Alcazaba,** covering some 14 acres of hilltop and offering an impressive view of the coast. An attractive garden graces the first perimeter; art and music festivals take place here in August. (Open daily 10am-2pm and 4-7pm. Admission 75ptas, illegible map 15ptas.) Do not attempt a visit unless you are in a large group since bands of thieves prowl the lone stairway, even during the day.

Basing yourself in Almería city is the easiest way to hit the surrounding *playas*. The **old quarter,** bordered by the Alcazaba and the port (at the opposite end of town from the train and bus stations), captures best the mystery and lost grandeur of the city, but finding a room here may be difficult. **Casa La Francesa,** C. Narvaez, 18 (tel. 23 75 54), off C. de la Almedina, is neatly kept by a kindly, French-speaking owner. While the bathrooms look harmless, the tap water tastes like sea water, and the showers are tempermental. (Singles 600ptas. Doubles 1100ptas. Showers 100ptas.) If full, inquire about other lodgings in the area. When all else fails, try the twilight zone around **Plaza Purchena,** the center of the new part of town. On the plaza, **Casa Universal,** Pta. de Purchena, 12 (tel. 23 55 57), shows signs of former luxury, but reeks of time's unstoppable onslaught. Funny smells and noises emerge from the sink, the rooms are dark, and payment may be requested in advance. Prices depend on the mood of the owner and your bargaining skills. (Approximately 650-800ptas per person. Showers, if you're charged, 250ptas.) Forget about eating a full meal in Almería. The inhabitants often think it's too hot to cook, so they don't. Where you can get a meal, you'll pay for it dearly.

The **tourist office** is on C. Hermanos Machado, 4 (tel. 23 06 07), through the side entrance of the large, white Edificio Administrativo. (Open Mon.-Fri. 9am-2pm and 5-7pm, Sat. 9am-1pm.) The **post office** (tel. 23 72 07) is at Pl. J. Cassinello, 1. (Open Mon.-Fri. 9am-2pm.) The **postal code** is 04070. **Telephones** are on C. Navarro Rodríguez, 9. (Open Mon.-Sat. 9am-1pm and 5-9pm.) The **bus station** is in Pl. de Barcelona (tel. 22 10 11). Buses run to Murcia (2 per day, 4 hr., 1345ptas), Barcelona (2 per day, 14 hr., 4540ptas), and Málaga via the Costa del Sol (2 per day, 5½ hr., 1255ptas). **RENFE** (tel. 25 11 35) is opposite the bus station, with trains to Granada (2 per day, 920ptas), Madrid (2 per day, 2340ptas), Barcelona (1 per day, 3905ptas), and Sevilla (1 per day, 2130ptas). The **police station** is on Avda. del Mediterráneo (tel. 22 37 04), and the **hospital** is on C. Hospital (tel. 23 06 04). Almería's **telephone code** is 951.

Near Almería

Some excellent **playas** lie a short distance from the city. **Roquetas de Mar,** 25km away, disproves the claim that the Costa del Sol is overdeveloped. The government strictly controlled the urbanization of this multi-kilometer gravel beach, forcing high-rise hotels to stay well back from surfside. The result is a classy resort with intricate gardens and exquisite huts lining the beachtop *paseo*. To avoid the northern European crowds that flock here each summer, hop off the bus north of town or walk north to find an empty stretch. Cheap accommodations are out of the question. Shuttle buses connect Almería and Roquetas (hourly; last bus each way Mon.-Sat. 10pm, Sun. 8pm; 150ptas). Buses stop in **Aguadulce** (60ptas), a more crowded resort 10km outside of Almería.

The Cabo de Gata (Cape of the Cat) forms the western boundary of the Bahía de Almería. The desolate crags and undisturbed beaches provide an isolated haven for the wandering beachbum and wasteland connoisseur. If you attempt a car-free tour of this area, be prepared to sack out on a few beaches—accommodations are scarce. This is legal provided you spend no more than one night on any particular beach, and the police do check.

Heading east from Almería, villages dwindle until only scrub and desert remain. Thirty kilometers from the capital, the town of **El Cabo de Gata** marks the first sandy beach of the coast. This second-rate beachtown can boast only a few bars on the shore and a scattering of whitewashed houses, but the inviting sand stretches southeast for 5km until the cliffs of the Gabor mountain range abruptly terminate it. The road, after bordering the beach, winds up the mountains for 3km before descending to the lighthouse complex at the tip of the peninsula and the stunning **El Faro** beach nearby, enclosed by two sheer walls of rock.

San José, across the windswept range on the other side of the peninsula, plays its role as the cape's tourist capital grudgingly. A small bay with a semicircular beach bordered by vertical rock, San José hasn't yet decided whether it wants to become a full-fledged resort. Adobe apartments are sprinkled along the cliffs, and construction elsewhere continues intermittently, but the beach is wide and empty. **Camping La Tau,** on the beach, charges 260ptas per person and is open from June through September. **Huespedes Costa Rica,** on the main road (no phone), offers sparkling rooms with a *menú* of *paella* and *pescado* for 500ptas in their restaurant. (Doubles 1900ptas, with bath 2650ptas.)

The road north along the peninsula wanders among the inland gullies before retreating to the town of **Escullos,** where the ruins of an old Arab fort make up a fourth of the structures that preside over the clear, still waters of the beaches nearby. **Café-Bar Emilio** offers a few beds (booked July-Aug.) and serves a stomach-stretching *menú* for 450ptas, topped with fresh watermelon. Two kilometers north is the fishing village of **La Isleta del Moro,** where the main square is used for washing clothes and mending nets. **Hostal Isleta del Moro** (tel. 86 63 13) rents clean rooms that overlook the colorful fishing fleet. (Singles with bath 800ptas. Doubles with bath 1400ptas.)

Las Negras, 11km north of La Isleta, is even more dominated by the surrounding crags than its neighbors. The beach is composed of coarse gravel and is home to a large contingent of fishing boats, but the town is noteworthy for the large number of *casas particulares* and apartments to rent.

To reach El Cabo de Gata by road, head out of Almería on C. de Granada and follow the signs for the airport; the cape lies straight past it. Public transportation schedules make daytrips impossible. Four private companies run to El Cabo de Gata at 1pm and 7:30pm, returning at 7am and 3pm; to San José at 1:15pm and 6:15pm, returning at 6am and 3pm; to Escullos and La Isleta on the same schedule as San José; and to Las Negras at 5:30pm, returning at 7am. Buy tickets for most of these on the bus at the station in Almería.

Costa del Sol

Once a landing point for Phoenician, Greek, Roman, and Arab ships, the Costa del Sol now caters to a lucrative international tourist market. Artifice now covers once-natural charms, as chic promenades and hotels seal off whitewashed towns from the shoreline. North of Málaga, the hills dip straight into the ocean, and the road coils around splendid vistas of surf pounding against rock face. To the more convenient south, water washes almost entirely against concrete. Nothing can cast a shadow, however, on the coast's major attraction—abundant sunlight that gives the region four months of summer and eight months of spring per year.

Although the Costa del Sol officially extends from Tarifa in the southwest to Cabo de Gata east of Almería, the name most often brings to mind the resorts from Marbella, in the province of Málaga, to Motril, in the province of Granada. Most of these areas are flooded with sun-seekers in July and August—be prepared to search for accommodations. If you do find something, be prepared to pay: Prices double across the board in high season. Make reservations. Some travelers sleep on the beaches (women traveling alone or in pairs should be cautious), a practice that seems to be winked at on the outskirts of less elegant areas. Alternatively, ask around for *casas particulares.* June is the best time to visit, when summer weather has come to town but the hordes of vacationers haven't. Remember that the farther northeast you go, the more unspoiled your environment is likely to be.

Trains will get you as far as Málaga, Torremolinos, or Fuengirola, but connections along the coast itself are supplied by private bus lines. Railpasses are not valid, but prices are reasonable. Hitchhiking can be relied upon—with a little patience—to transport you from town to town early in the day.

Nerja

Nerja, 50km east of Málaga, has avoided much of the raw commercialism of other Costa del Sol resorts despite the attractiveness of its setting against the deep blue Mediterranean and its charming, narrow streets. This elegant town has maintained an appealing old quarter, some fine beaches, and a lively nightlife, all with a minimum of hype and glare.

Nerja's focal point is the **Balcón de Europa,** a clifftop promenade that looks out over 14km of coastline. At night the terrace becomes a lively *paseo* where you can watch and be watched. Below the cliff is a series of small coves and long **beaches,** mostly of gravel or coarse sand. As usual, the best lie some distance away. To reach them from the Balcón, cut through town westward to the new Playa Torrecilla apartments; from there you can follow the shoreline. After 15 minutes, you'll begin to see sand appear beneath the human carpet. Much closer but even more crowded is **Playa del Salón,** accessible through an alley off the Balcón, just to the right of Restaurante Marissal. **Playa Burriana** is a large, sandy beach a short hike to the east. From the tourist office, follow C. Hernando de Corabeo to a dirt road behind a few newly constructed apartments. There's less glamor here than on the main beaches, but there's also more room to spread your blanket.

The best strategy for finding **accommodations** in high-priced Nerja in July and August is to arrive early in the day and inquire in bars about *casas particulares.* You might also ask the local women as they wash down their doorsteps in the morning. Several rent a room or two or will lead you to a neighbor who does. They charge about 600ptas per person. The **tourist office,** on the left as you approach the Balcón de Europa, can suggest a few *hostales* on the outskirts of town, but don't expect much more from them. In off-season, accommodations are a beggar's banquet. Try the reasonably clean and convenient **Hostal Florida,** C. San Miguel, 35 (tel. 52 07 43), up the street as you leave the bus station. (Singles 1300-2000ptas. Doubles 2000-2300ptas.)

The **mercado municipal** is 2 blocks up C. San Miguel from the bus stop. Locals creep out at 9pm, after the foreigners have already dined, and head for **Marisquería La Familia,** Diputacíon Provincial, 17 (tel. 52 00 46), west of the Balcón. Their fresh fish dishes run 600-800ptas. (Open daily 1-3:30pm and 6:30-11pm.)

Nerja can be reached by fairly frequent **buses** from Málaga (10 per day, 1½ hr., 295ptas), less frequently from Almería (2 per day, 3 hr., 960ptas), and Granada (1 per day, 625ptas). The **Oficina de Turismo** (tel. 52 15 31) is at Puerta del Mar, 4. (Open July-Sept. Mon.-Fri. 11am-1pm and 5-8:30pm, Sat. 10am-2pm.) From October through June, address your inquiries to the **Ayuntamiento,** C. Carmen, 1 (tel. 52 09 45). The **post office** (tel. 52 17 49) is at C. Almirante Fernandiz, 6. (Open Mon.-Fri. 9am-2pm and Sat. 9am-1pm.) The town's **postal code** is 29780. The **telephone kiosk** is next to the Ayuntamiento. (Open Mon.-Fri. 10am-2pm and 5-9pm, Sat. 10am-2pm.) The **police** are located in the Ayuntamiento building (tel. 52 15 45). For **first aid,** call 52 09 35. The **Book Center,** C. Granada, 30, where secondhand English books are bought, sold, and swapped, has a bulletin board with lots of useful information. (Open Mon.-Sat. 10am-1:30pm and 5-9pm.)

Just 5km east of Nerja lie the tremendous, cathedral-like **Cuevas de Nerja,** former haunts of primitive civilizations. The cave is a huckster's paradise, with piped-in music and photographers snapping your picture for sale at the exit (400ptas each). At your first glimpse of the cave's main chamber, however, you'll forget all that. The sheer size of the caves is staggering. They're filled with weird rock formations created over millions of years by deposit and erosion; one even has the world's largest stalactite (65m). The caverns themselves consist of large chambers winding around a huge column of limestone. One has been converted into an amphitheater where music and ballet performances take place in July and August. Recently, a new section of caves was discovered, reputedly four times as large as the already existing one. Now in the process of being illuminated, the additions are expected to open sometime this year. Also look for the archeological exhibit of primitive art and tools in the cave. (Caves and exhibit open May-Sept. 15 daily 9:30am-9pm; Sept. 16-April daily 10am-1:30pm and 4-7pm. Admission 150ptas, ages 6-12 100ptas.) Buses run to and from Nerja (every hr., 50ptas).

Just before the cave is **Maro,** an unspoiled speck of a village whose lack of attractions is a relief and a blessing in itself. There's not even a *casa de huéspedes,* but you can spend the night in *casas particulares.* Paths from the town lead to nearly empty rocky beaches and coves.

Five kilometers north of Nerja, the tiny village of **Frigiliana** sits atop a hill. Thus far, only two small gift shops have put down their tourist-hungry roots in this village of glistening white buildings and patterned, cobblestoned streets. It's laid out according to an Arabic design; sayings and proverbs advise visitors from the tiled walls. Frigiliana is surprisingly accessible from Nerja by foot or bus (5 per day, 50ptas).

If you head west on the coastal road toward Málaga, you can clamber down the rocks for some excellent swimming at almost any point. As you approach the city itself, however, the beaches deteriorate into narrow, rocky strips, exposed to the roar of the traffic above.

Almuñécar

A steadily growing town that has not yet expanded beyond human dimensions, Almuñécar lives quite happily off its fish and its tourists. A lively, labyrinthine center makes up for the high-rises in the background, and gaily colored boats still moor alongside the sunbathers. The first-century **aqueduct,** 1km to the west off the highway, served the ancient Roman town and its salt manufacturing industry. Almost 8-kilometers-long, it is, along with that of Segovia, one of the only aqueducts in Spain still in use. The **Castillo de San Miguel** began as a Greek village, was enlarged by the Romans, Arabs, and Renaissance kings, and is now Almuñécar's cemetery. Closed to the public, the site affords its occupants one of the few quiet spots on the entire coast in summer.

The town's **beaches** are extensive but not overly impressive—mostly a mixture of gravel and coarse sand. Nonetheless, something about them seems more cozy than the glitzy resorts west of Málaga. The two main beaches in town are **Puerta del Mar** and **San Cristóbal,** split by the **Peñon del Santo.** Farther down Paseo Puerta del Mar to the east lies **Playa de Velillá.** You can also try the town of **La Herradura,** 4km west along the main road to Málaga and accessible by five buses per day. The sand isn't dramatically different, but the landscape is lovely—a beautiful blue bay enclosed by two rocky outcroppings.

You can find accommodations off Pl. de la Rosa, off the *paseo* overlooking Playa Puerta del Mar. **Fonda Casa Ruiz,** C. San José, 9 (tel. 63 11 52), in an alleyway between Pl. Rosa and the Ayuntamiento, offers clean rooms, passable bathrooms, and live music from across the street every evening. (800ptas per person. *Pensión completa* 1800ptas.) **Fonda Santa Teresa,** C. de la Aduana Vieja, 10 (tel. 63 05 64), has spacious rooms, some with large windows and balconies. The hot water, however, can be intermittent. (1000ptas per person.) **Hostal Gamez,** C. Cerrajeros, 8 (tel. 63 01 65), through the end of C. Columbia, is clean, stark, large, and noisy. (July-Sept. singles 850ptas; doubles 1650ptas. Oct.-June singles 700ptas; doubles 1350ptas.)

Many restaurants line Paseo Puerta del Mar, where you can enjoy the day's catch from a terrace overlooking the coast. Try **Restaurante Mediterráneo** (tel. 63 10 29), where a solid, widely varied, quality *menú* costs 795ptas. Locals favor **Restaurante Casa Paco,** across the *paseo* from Playa Velillá, 2km east around the point. The walk is more than worth it, as their 750ptas *menú* is surpassed only by their heaped mound of *paella* for two at 1400ptas. (Open 2-4pm and 7:30-11pm.) Several bars near the post office serve scanty *menús* for around 500ptas. To stock up on fruit and cheese, head north into the old town and follow the smell of the fresh fish to reach the **mercado** on C. Lonja. Also sample the exotic fruit in Almuñécar—*chirimoyas* (custard apples), papayas, and *nísperas* (Japanese medlars) are grown on nearby plantations.

The **tourist office,** on the beach at the Paseo del Altillo (tel. 63 11 25), is not particularly helpful and will only supply a poor photocopy of a map. (Open Mon.-Fri. 10am-1pm and 5-8pm, Sat. 10am-1pm.) The **post office** (tel. 63 04 59) is on Pl. Liury Gargan, 2. (Open Mon.-Fri. 9am-2pm, Sat. 9am-noon.) In a medical emergency, call the **municipal hospital,** Carretera de Málaga (tel. 63 05 16). The **police** can be reached at 63 03 33. Buses make frequent calls to Granada (5 per day, 2½ hr., 520ptas), Almería (2 per day, 3½ hr., 690ptas), and Málaga (2 per day, 2 hr., 480ptas) from the Alsina Graells station (tel. 63 01 40), off Carretera de Almería.

Salobreña

If you're tired of the sleek, the chic, and the carefully bronzed, this is the place for you. Despite the apartments springing up on the coast to the east, Salobreña the town remains "typically Spanish." Its small, whitewashed houses emerge from green fields, and mules plod through its streets, laden with tools and sugarcane stalks. Mountains rise up in the background, and the beach—a long stretch of coarse sand—is only a 10-minute walk away.

Like many Spanish towns, Salobreña is crowned by a **castle.** Its ramparts and turrets are well restored and its shaded walkways are enhanced by fragrant flowers. Concerts and theater take place here in July; ask at the tourist office. (Open 9am-sunset. Admission 25ptas.) A patio at the castle's base provides a wonderful place for a picnic; here you can enjoy an excellent view of the sea and surrounding hills while palm trees offer much-needed shade from the heat.

There are only a few places to stay in Salobreña, but since most visitors rent nearby apartments in summer, rooms aren't too difficult to find. Several options sit at the bottom of the hill, 1 block in from the street that connects the bus stop and the beach. Walk down this road to the first intersection, across from Mesón Don Quijote, and double back to the right. This street, **C. Fabrica Nueva,** and its continuations curve through town. **Pensión Arnedo,** C. Nueva, 15 (tel. 61 02 27), uphill off C. Fabrica Nueva, offers comfortable rooms and great views of the town, the mountains, and the coastline. (800ptas per person.) The owner is friendly at **Pensión Palamares,** C. Fabrica Nueva, 28 (tel. 61 01 81), where a trail of urns leads you to essentially clean rooms. (Singles 1000ptas. Doubles 1900ptas. Bargaining may do the trick.) In July and August, **Camping Peñón** (tel. 61 02 07), across from the beach, may be packed. Its hot showers, small store, cafe, and peacocks will cost you 250ptas per person and per tent. (Open April-Oct.)

The **tourist office** operates out of a shack on the beach next to the **Red Cross.** (Tourist office open Mon.-Fri. 9am-2pm and 5-8pm, Sat. 9am-1pm. Red Cross open daily 10am-8pm.) **Ambulance** services and the **police** can both be reached at 61 10 59. **Buses** stop just off the highway at the top of the road from the beach. Destinations include Almuñecar (6 per day, 30 min., 85ptas), Málaga (2 per day, 2½ hr., 570ptas), and Granada (5 per day, 2 hr., 270ptas).

Málaga

Trapped between the mountains and the ocean, Málaga has been forced to extend its concrete arms down the coast. Though its center city provides an abundance of shady trees, a fashionable promenade, and even a handful of impressive historic buildings, most people consider the city merely a convenient stopover in their search for the large, touristy beach resorts to the east and west. Indeed, Málaga has become the transportation hub of the entire Costa del Sol.

Orientation and Practical Information

A good way to get a feel for this city is to walk the length of palm-lined **Paseo del Parque,** which will take you below the **Alcazaba,** a Moorish palace whose fortified walls enclose fragrant gardens and an archeological museum. To get to the town center from the train station, take bus #3 or 4 from the park opposite the station to Paseo del Parque and get off at **Plaza de la Marina.** Alternatively, walk down C. de Cuarteles, cross the bridge and take **Alameda Principal** to Pl. de la Marina (15 min.). The bus station is behind the train station.

Tourist Office: C. Marqués de Larios, 5 (tel. 21 34 45), to the left of Pl. de La Marina on the right as you come from Alameda Principal. Look carefully; the signs are not very visible. Efficient English- and French-speaking staff can get you a long list of *fondas* and a guide to the city's *centro histórico.* Open Mon.-Fri. 9am-2pm, Sat. 9am-1pm.

Student Travel: Viajes TIVE, C. Huescar, 3 (tel. 27 84 13), next to El Corte Inglés. Books international plane, train, and bus tickets. Open Mon.-Fri. 9am-2pm.

Consulates: U.S., C. Ramón y Cajal, Edificio El Ancla, Apto. 502 (tel. 47 48 91), in nearby Fuengirola. **Canada,** Pl. Malagueta, 3 (tel. 22 33 46). **U.K.,** Duquesa de Parcent, Edificio Duquesa (tel. 21 75 71).

American Express: Viajes Alhambra, C. Especería, after #8, near C. Nueva. Accepts wired money. Open Mon.-Fri. 9am-1:30pm and 5-8pm, Sat. 9am-2pm.

Post Office: On Avda. de Andalucía, a tall building just over the bridge from the city center. Open Mon.-Fri. 9am-2pm and 4-6pm, Sat. 9am-2pm. Open for Lista de Correos Mon.-Fri. 9am-2pm. Open for **telegrams** Mon.-Fri. 8am-9pm, Sat.-Sun. 9am-7pm. **Postal Code:** 29070.

Telephones: C. Molina Larios, 11, next to the cathedral. Open Mon.-Sat. 9am-9pm, Sun. 10am-1pm. **Telephone Code:** 952.

Airport: Tel. 33 20 00. **Iberia,** Molina Lario, 13 (tel. 22 76 00). Open Mon.-Fri. 9am-7pm. Buses run from the cathedral and the airport every ½-hr. roughly 6:30am-11:30pm (55ptas). Train service to the airport and back is just as frequent 6:30am-10:30pm (45ptas). To Madrid (7-10 per day, 45 min., 10,165ptas), Barcelona (3 per day, 1½ hr., 14,480ptas), and other destinations.

Train Station: C. Cuarteles (tel. 31 25 00). **RENFE,** C. Strachan, 2 (tel. 21 31 22), is a less crowded, more convenient place to obtain tickets and information. Open Mon.-Fri. 9am-1:30pm and 4:30-7:30pm. To Madrid (4 per day; *expreso* 3280ptas, *talgo* 4705ptas), Barcelona (2 per day, 5195ptas), Córdoba (3 per day, 815ptas), and Sevilla (1 per day, 1150ptas). Trains to Granada and Sevilla must change at Bobadilla on the Córdoba line.

Bus Station: Málaga has just completed an enormous central bus station on Paseo de los Tilos, behind RENFE. To Granada (9 per day, 1¼ hr., 845ptas), Antequera (7 per day, 1 hr., 440ptas), Ronda (11 per day, 3 hr., 655ptas), Sevilla (5 per day, 3½ hr., 1435ptas), Madrid (3 per day, 7-9 hr., 2435-4440ptas), Barcelona (3 per day, 18 hr., 5960ptas), Almería (3 per day, 4½ hr., 1265ptas), with local stops along the Costa del Sol, Córdoba (2 per day, 2½ hr., 905ptas), and Valencia (1 per day, 11 hr., 3916ptas). **Municipal buses** charge 55ptas. Book of 10 tickets 370ptas.

Baggage Check: At the train station. 125ptas per day.

Medical Emergency: Tel. 22 44 00. **First Aid:** Tel. 29 03 40 or 22 64 98.

Police: Tel. 21 50 05. **Emergency:** Tel. 091 or 092.

Accommodations and Camping

Málaga is not a haven for the budget traveler; its affordable rooms are run-down and overrun. This may explain why few visitors remain long. Many *pensión* owners frequent the train station in hopes of enticing travelers to rent one of their rooms. If the price seems high (over 1000ptas for a single), you can often bring it down by bargaining. Be sure you know where the place is located before agreeing to anything. Many budget establishments cluster north of **Paseo del Parque** and **Alameda Principal**. Alameda Principal is the tree-lined avenue to the right as you exit the bus station. To get there from the train station, walk northeast along C. Cuarteles and take a right across Puente Tetuán. Singles may be difficult to find in July and August. To make matters worse, the city's IYHF hostel has closed for a few years.

Hostal Residencia Chinitas, Pasaje Chinitas, 2 (tel. 21 46 83), on an alley off Pl. de la Constitución. Wild, eclectic reception area with fish tanks, VCRs, and mirrors. Clean, basic rooms, one of which can be turned into a quadruple. Perhaps the only acceptable budget accommodation in town, but run by a disorganized family. Make sure they write your name down clearly if you reserve, or you may not have a room upon arrival. Singles 1300ptas. Doubles 2400ptas.

Hostal Residencia Lampérez, C. Santa María, 6 (tel. 21 94 84), off Pl. de la Constitución. Preferable to most places in town, but a dump nevertheless. At least the beds are large and clean. Singles 700ptas. Doubles 1500ptas. Poor showers (only after 8:30am) 150ptas.

Hostal Fali, C. Marqués, 4 (tel. 22 02 15), a couple blocks north of the market. Nice beds, but rooms are dark and spooky. Singles 800ptas. Doubles 1400ptas. Showers 150ptas.

Pensión Rosa, C. Martinez, 8 (tel. 22 72 68), above Alameda Principal. Clean enough to pass in Málaga, but stale. Singles 1300ptas. Doubles 2400ptas. Showers 200ptas.

Pensión Ramos, C. Martinez, 8 (tel. 22 72 68), next door. Not particularly clean bathrooms and a harsh owner. It will do in a pinch. 1000ptas per person. Showers 100ptas.

Camp at **Balneario del Carmen,** 3km from the center on Avenida Juan Sebastián Elcano (tel. 29 00 21). They charge 320ptas per person, per tent, and per car.

Food

Plenty of inexpensive restaurants are tucked away in the *pasajes* of the older section of town around **Plaza de la Constitución** and **Calle Granada.** More budget dining can be found on the streets behind **Paseo Marítimo.** The currently popular place for dinner is on the beachfront in **Pedregalejos,** near the eastern edge of town, where a row of crowded and inexpensive restaurants serve the day's catch. (Take bus #11 from Paseo del Parque.) Local cuisine is rich in both fish and meat dishes, so experiment. Try *arroz a la marinera* or *choto* (goat meat prepared with oil, vinegar, garlic, and almonds). Málaga is also known for *malagueño* and *moscatel,* its sweet wines.

El Tormes, C. San José and San Agustín, off C. Granada and to the right. Lively, local favorite. Enormous *menús* full of well-prepared Andalusian specialties: appetizer, 2 entrees, salad, dessert, bread, and drink 750ptas. Or subtract an entree and pay only 650ptas. The large photographs of Salamanca on the walls seem a little out of place. Open daily noon-3pm and 8-11pm.

La Cancela, C. Denis Belgrano, 3 (tel. 22 31 25), off C. Granada. Outdoor tables on a pleasant alley. Small *menú* for a small price (425ptas), but a good meal if the fish is fresh. Interesting pink gazpacho 160ptas. Open Thurs.-Tues. 11am-11:30pm.

Casa Matías, C. Duende, 4 (tel. 21 79 31), in an alley off C. Nueva. Main dishes such as tortillas and fried fish 300-400ptas. Open Sun.-Fri. noon-9pm.

La Tarantella, C. Granada, 61 (tel. 22 85 41). Pleasant, air-conditioned interior with paintings depicting smurf-like creatures in a wild bacchanalia. The best part of the meal is the complimentary, savory, homemade, after-dinner concoction made of amaretto, port, sugar, and other secret ingredients. A wide selection of pizzas (380-525ptas) and *pinchos* (small kebabs, 150ptas). Full meal for 2 about 1500ptas. Open daily noon-11pm.

Sights and Entertainment

Although people don't usually hang around long, there *are* things to do in Málaga. Stroll down **Paseo del Parque,** a pretty avenue with many palms and tropical plants. Toward the end of the street, you'll pass below the imposing **Alcazaba,** a fortified palace built for Moorish kings and now containing a museum of Roman and Moorish art. The approach winds through castle walls, past flowering purple blossoms, palms, and cacti. When you get to the top, catch the view of Málaga from the ramparts. (Open Mon.-Sat. 10am-1pm and 5-8pm, Sun. 10am-2pm. Admission 20ptas.)

For an even better view and a more strenuous climb, amble up the crumbling walkway at the side of the Alcazaba to lofty **Gibralfaro Castle,** another Moorish construction. From its walls you can see the concrete coastline of the Costa del Sol and most of Málaga's urban sprawl, including the bullfight ring and the cruise ship docks. The imposing, parched mountains of Granada form the backdrop. Thieves and other scurrilous types prowl the castle walls at night, so it's not the best place for an evening stroll. The castle is also accessible by microbus H, every hour from the cathedral. (Open daylight hours. Free.)

Málaga's **cathedral,** built on the site of a medieval mosque, is also worth a stop. This pastiche of Gothic, Renaissance, and baroque styles is known as "the little lady with one arm" because the complement to its single 65-meter tower was never completed. The carved seventeenth-century choir stalls are especially beautiful. The arches behind the altar have also been left open, exposing the colorful chapels behind and enhancing the transcendental feel of the pews in the main hall. (Open Mon.-Sat. 10am-1pm and 4-7pm. Free.) The **Museo de Bellas Artes,** San Agustín, 6, in the old palace of the Counts of Buenavista, houses a wealth of mosaics, sculptures, and paintings, including works by Murillo, Rivera, and native son Picasso. (Open 10am-1:30pm and 5-6pm. Admission 250ptas, EEC students under 21 free.)

The city itself has no particularly nice beaches; the most popular one is to the east at Pedregalejos. (Take bus #11.) After dinner in one of the restaurants along the beach, the student crowd heads for the bars a few blocks down. Those slightly older move inland to **Calle Juan Sebastian Elcamo** in the **Echevarria** district, where all crowds meet at around 1am, when the discos open. Buses stop running at midnight, so you may have to take a cab back to town (about 400ptas).

Near Málaga: Torremolinos and Fuengirola

South of Málaga lie infamous Torremolinos (13km) and Fuengirola (30km), the nearest alternatives to Málaga's lousy beaches.

If you've heard anything positive about **Torremolinos,** forget it. This monstrous tourist torture chamber proves that you can go to hell without dying. Just hop on the train from Málaga, and you'll soon find yourself in a nightmare landscape of overpriced kiosks, concrete high-rises, and pretentious boutiques. By late morning (in season), the sand on the stretch of unappetizing beach disappears beneath a carpet of eternal-beach-leach bodies. At sundown, the plastic nightlife takes over, and Torremolinos becomes torrid with pulsating disco and flamenco that lasts until 4am.

One relatively cheap place to stay in Torremolinos is **Hotel-Residencia Manila,** C. Manila, 3 (tel. 38 10 50; singles 950ptas; doubles 1700ptas; showers 150ptas). A little cleaner and in better condition is **Hostal Residencia Guillot,** Pasaje Pizarro (tel. 38 01 44), on a small alleyway off the main street. Its large rooms are maintained by a friendly owner. (Singles with bath 1500ptas. Doubles with bath 2000ptas.) Try **Taberna Pepe López,** Pl. de la Gamba Alegre (tel. 38 12 84), off C. San Miguel, for some decent flamenco music. (Cover with 1 drink 2000ptas. Shows start at 10:30pm.) Restaurants in town are substantially overpriced, so it's best to avoid eating here. But breakfast at the student-run **Bar El Castel,** Avda. Imperial, where fresh *churros* and thick chocolate cost 130ptas.

For a list of other reasonably priced hotels and eateries, stop by the **tourist office,** 1517 Nogalera (tel. 38 15 78), ½ block south of the train station. Call the **police** at 38 99 99 and **first aid** at 38 64 84.

The coastal development seems to go on forever, and 30km farther south of Málaga, **Fuengirola** strives to become Torremolinos II. Huge skyscrapers overwhelm a packed, unattractive beach smothered beneath hordes of sunbathers. This town has just completed a glitzy new fake harbor. The **tourist office** is at Pl. España (tel. 47 61 66); for the **police,** call 091; for **first aid,** 47 29 29. Both Fuengirola and Torremolinos can be reached easily by train every half-hour from Málaga's Fuengirola-Torremolinos train station, outside and beneath the main station. (To Torremolinos 75ptas. To Fuengirola 150ptas.) Bus service connects Málaga to Torremolinos (every 15 min., 70ptas) and Fuengirola (every 30 min., 140ptas).

Marbella

Marbella lies hidden beneath kiosks, boutiques, and beachside chairs. This resort has one function: the fleecing of the crowds of Swedes, Germans, French, British, and Americans who descend upon it each season. Marbella will relieve you of your pesetas quickly, efficiently, painlessly, and in five different languages.

Orientation and Practical Information

Marbella lies 56km south of Málaga, and buses connect the two cities every half-hour (330ptas). To get to the town center from the bus station, take a left on Avda. Rocardo Soriano until it becomes Avda. Ramón y Cajal. The old town is on the left; the beach lies to the right.

Tourist Office: Avda. Miguel Cano, 1 (tel. 77 14 42), opposite C. Huerta. English spoken. Ask for the indexed map and guide to Marbella. Open Mon.-Fri. 9:30am-1pm and 5-7:30pm, Sat. 10am-1pm.

Post Office: C. Alonso de Bazán, 1. Open Mon.-Fri. 9am-2pm, Sat. 9am-1pm. Open for **telegrams** Mon.-Fri. 8:30am-8:30pm, Sat. 9am-7pm. **Postal Code:** 29600.

Telephones: Kiosks are set up every couple of blocks along the beach. Open June-Sept. daily 10am-3pm and 5-10pm. **Telephone Code:** 952.

Bus Station: Avda. Ricardo Soriano (tel. 77 21 92). To Málaga (every ½-hr., 1½ hr., 330ptas), Fuengirola (every ¼-hr., ½ hr., 140ptas), Puerto Banús (every ½-hr., 15 min., 50ptas), Ronda (4 per day, 1½ hr., 310ptas), Gibraltar (1 per day, 1350ptas), Granada (4 per day, 2½ hr., 1030ptas), Sevilla (2 per day, 2½ hr., 1080ptas), Cádiz (3 per day, 3 hr., 1180ptas), Madrid (3 per day, 8-11 hr., 2695-4300ptas), and Barcelona (2 per day, 20 hr., 6100ptas) via Valencia (13 hr., 4206ptas).

Medical Emergency: C. Trapiche, 5 (tel. 77 94 45). **Hospital:** Tel. 77 42 00.

Police: C. Serenata (tel. 77 31 94). **Emergency:** Tel. 092.

Accommodations and Camping

If you don't have reservations here, especially during the second half of July and in August, you'll have to arrive early and hope. The people at bars often know of *casas particulares:* The lively **English Pub** and **The Tavern,** face to face on C. Peral (in the old section behind Avda. Ramón y Cajal), can give you advice in English. The area is loaded with little *hostales* and *fondas,* all of which fill up quickly. Several cheap guest houses line **Calle Ancha** and its continuation, **Calle San Francisco.** Even more lie on **Calle Aduar,** parallel to and 2 blocks west of C. Ancha, and on **Calle Caballero.**

Albergue Juvenil "Africa" (IYHF), C. Trapiche, 2 (tel. 77 14 91), just above C. San Francisco. A beautiful place with a pool, palm trees, and a well-tended garden, but maintenance has ignored the rooms. No reservations. Strict curfew 11pm. 420ptas. Breakfast 130ptas.

Hostal del Pilar, C. Mesoncillo, 4 (tel. 77 13 41), in a sheltered alley behind the English Pub. A small piece of England in Spain. Management is friendly, efficient, and British. Rooms scrubbed spotless everyday, and the busy maids never seem to take breaks. Singles 1500ptas. Doubles 2400ptas. Triples 3000ptas. Alternately scalding and freezing showers.

Casa Huéspedes Aduar, C. Aduar, 7 (tel. 77 35 78), up from C. Peral. Positively overflowing with roses in summer; the manager is friendly as long as you tell him exactly when you're leaving. 1st floor rooms on cool courtyard; upstairs they sport balconies. All are clean and refreshing. Singles 1200ptas. Doubles 2000ptas. Showers 150ptas.

Pensión Luisa, C. San Francisco, 6 (tel. 77 08 40). Big, clean beds. Doubles 2000ptas. Hot showers 200ptas.

Camping Marbella is a second-class site, 2km east on N-340. (Open June 6-Oct. 10. 325ptas per person and per tent.)

Food

Bar El Gallo, C. Lobatas, 46. Serves Marbella's cheapest *menú* (450ptas), with simple Spanish specialties running 150-350ptas. The birds in the cage are as intent on watching the TV as the customers. Open daily 1-4pm and 8-11pm.

Bar Taurino, toward the top of C. San Francisco. Boisterous local crowd inspired by bullfighting posters. A slew of great tortillas under 300ptas, but not much else. Open March-Sept. daily 10am-11pm.

Restaurante Sol y Sombra, C. Tetuán, 7. Not particularly inexpensive, but this popular hangout's fresh fish dishes (300-1200ptas) are a great deal when the occasional *menú del día* comes around. Open daily 1-4pm and 8-11pm.

Restaurante El Pilar, C. Mesoncillo, 4, beneath the hotel. Well-prepared English food. Fish and chips with salad 450ptas, juicy sandwiches 200-250ptas. Breakfast 125-450ptas. Open all day.

Restaurante La Trucha, C. Anduar, 22. Filling *menús* (550ptas) in bright and airy atmosphere.

Sights and Entertainment

Marbella is primarily as a resort town for sun-starved, fat-walleted tourists. Aside from some third-century **baths** at the western city limits, don't look for much in the way of historical excitement. Shaded by lush plants, **Plaza de los Naranjos** is an especially pretty square where you can sit and sip drinks to the soothing roar of a fountain. The eastern section, just up from the church, is also worth exploring. A massive Arab wall once protected the town, but now numerous houses huddle against its crumbling remains. Peer through their doorways; many conceal beautiful courtyards.

Unfortunately, Marbella has built a chic promenade over the beach, leaving its most valuable asset skinny and overcrowded. If you're looking for more tranquility, hop on the Fuengirola bus and get off at **Playa de las Chapas,** 10km east, and walk in either direction to find an open stretch.

If it's ritzy nightlife you're seeking, take the bus to **Puerto Banús,** 7km west. This international yacht harbor crawls with bars, discos, and the jet set. For an American atmosphere, try **Jo's Bar.** Popular discos include **Zelius Beach,** at Lindavista Baja, and **Impanema,** on the highway. Discos do not charge at the door, but drinks, even in the adjacent bars, run a steep 700ptas and up. Public transportation ends at 10:30pm, and a cab back to town costs 1000ptas; a night here can be quite expensive. If you choose to stay in moderately-priced Marbella for the evening, head down to the **Puerto Deportivo,** where crowds fill the bars from 1am on. To relax a bit, try the pubs along **Calle Peral,** such as the **English Pub, The Tavern,** and **Friendly.** For Spanish neon disco, visit **Old Vic,** Avda. Ansol, 2. The **19th Hole,** across Avda. Ricardo Soriano on C. Calvario, attracts lots of locals and offers dancing and piano music.

The **Feria y Fiestas de San Bernabé** (June 9-17) is the big event of the year, with fireworks, concerts, and, of course, bullfights.

Until recently, **San Pedro de Alcántara,** 10km west of Marbella, was an unspoiled fishing village; then the crowds arrived. **Estepona,** another 15km away, has also lost its charm. To see what this area used to look like, try **Casares,** 25km past Estepona. Buses from Marbella run to San Pedro every half-hour (50ptas) and to Estepona every 20 minutes (135ptas). Only two buses per day connect Estepona to Casares (110ptas).

Gibraltar

Timeless, resolute, severe: The peninsula of Gibraltar juts its mountainous profile out of the Mediterranean, guarding the gateway to the Atlantic. "The Rock" commands a breathtaking view of the Straits of Gibraltar all the way to the Moroccan coast. Known affectionately as "Gib" by the locals, this British dependency is a microcosm of modern Britain, complete with bobbies, fish 'n' chips, a changing of the guard, and punk rockers. Unlike their counterparts in London, however, Gibraltarians can whimsically switch from speaking The Clash's or the Queen's English to Andalusian Spanish.

The Ancients considered the Rock of Gibraltar one of the Pillars of Hercules, marking the very end of the world. After the Moorish invasion of Spain in 711, Gibraltar was strongly fortified as an important strategic base, a role it has continued to play. After they recaptured the Rock from the Moors in 1462, the Spaniards also inundated the peninsula with military wares to ward off Barbary pirates and Moorish attacks. England considered Gibraltar strategically important, letting troops storm its shores after the War of the Spanish Secession. The Treaty of Utrecht (1713) officially confirmed Britain's dominance in the region. Gibraltar today is one of the last vestiges of Britain's colonialism.

The Rock remains a bone of contention between Spain and England. In the '60s, the Spanish government tried to bring the Rock down by imposing strict restrictions. By 1969, General Franco had sealed off the border and explicitly forbidden any contact between Spain and Gibralter. After a decade of negotiations and nearly 20 years of isolation, however, the border was reopened at midnight on February 4, 1985. Now tourists as well as residents can cross the border freely. Although the Spanish government is far from relinquishing its claim to *El Peñón,* the people of Gib remain optimistic about their eccentric enclave.

Orientation and Practical Information

Buses run to La Línea from the Empresa Comes station, behind Hotel Octavio, in Algeciras on the hour and on the half hour, (2/3 hr., 135ptas). From the bus stop on the Spanish side, walk directly toward "the Rock." The border is a 10-minute walk. After passing through Spanish customs and Gibraltarian passport control (a painless process), pick up an excellent guide and map from the **frontier tourist office** stand. (Open mid-June to mid-Sept. Mon.-Fri. 8am-2:30pm, Sat. 10am-2pm; mid-Sept. to mid-June Mon.-Fri. 9am-4:30pm, Sat. 10am-2pm.) Walk across the airport runway, and cross the overhead pedestrian bridge to get to the left side of the street.

To reach downtown, continue until Winston Churchill Ave. turns to the right to Corral Lane, then go up to your left through **Landport Tunnel.** After the large public car park, turn left onto Gibraltar's **Main Street,** which rocks with the frenzied activity of British commercialism. Most of the public offices and hotels are located only a few blocks away. Shops keep modified Spanish hours, closing during the afternoon for a short siesta and staying open until early evening. Tourists will want to change their currency into Gibraltar pounds or British pound sterling (the two are equivalent). Even though pesetas are accepted everywhere (prices are posted in both pounds and pesetas), you'll find prices slightly more favorable in pounds. For larger purchases (£5 and up), the difference might be substantial.

Tourist Office: Piazza John Mackintosh (tel 764 00) facing Main street. Excellent maps and informative brochures. Information on the famous Gib taxi tour. Open mid-June to mid-Sept. Mon.-Thurs. 8am-5:30pm, Fri. 8am-5pm, Sat. 10am-2pm; mid-Sept. to mid-June Mon.-Thurs. 9am-6:30pm, Fri. 9am-5pm, Sat. 10am-2pm. The main office at Cathedral Square keeps shorter hours.

Currency Exchange: Prata Bureau de Change, 137 Main St. (tel. 78 07 01). Look for the yellow awning. Better rates here than at banks. Open Mon.-Fri. 9:30am-2pm and 3-7pm, Sat. 9:30am-5pm, Sun. 9:30am-1:30pm.

Post Office: 102 Main St. Sells Gibraltar stamps in sets for collectors. Open Mon.-Fri. 9am-3:15pm, Sat. 10am-1pm.

Telephones: In the basement of City Hall, just behind the *piazza.* Open daily 8am-12:30pm and 2-8pm. **Telephone Code:** (010) 350.

Bookstore: Stock up on books in English while you're here. **The Gibraltar Bookshop,** 300 Main St. (tel. 718 94), stocks an excellent collection of classics. Open Mon.-Fri. 9:30am-7pm, Sat. 9:30am-5pm.

Foreign Newspapers: Sacarelo News Agency, 96 Main St. (tel. 787 23). The widest selection of papers and magazines. Open daily 9am-7pm.

Hospital: St. Bernard's Hospital, on Hospital Hill (tel. 797 00).

Police: Irish Town St. (tel. 725 00).

Accommodations

Unfortunately, it's no longer possible to camp in Gibraltar. Great Britain runs a tight ship: The new laws against unofficial camping are strictly enforced. To compound the problem, budget accommodations are nearly nonexistent. The less expensive places fill quickly from mid-June through August, so make reservations or start looking as soon as you set foot on the peninsula.

Algeciras, only a bus ride away, makes an excellent base from which to explore Gibraltar because of its cheaper lodgings. Ask around the restaurants near the bus station in La Línea for information on rooms for rent in private homes.

Toc H Hostel, Line Wall Rd. (tel. 734 31). Walk south along Main St., and turn right just before the arch at Referendum Gate, then left in front of the Hambros Bank; the entrance is through the small blue hut with an orange door. The only inexpensive bed on the Rock. A bohemian place with shack-like lodgings. Small aviary adds to the outback feel. Rooms on a weekly basis only, £10 per person. Cold showers only.

Miss Serruya Guest House, 92/1a Irish Town (tel. 732 20). From Main St., turn onto Tuckey's Lane and then make a left before the stairs. Living space is cramped, but clean. As always, calculate your bill carefully. Singles £7. Doubles £10. Shower and bath included. Breakfast £1.50. Call ahead to make sure there's room.

Queen's Hotel, 1 Boyd St. (tel. 740 00), facing the cablecar station. Game room, sun deck, friendly management. Comfortable rooms with quality lighting, fine furnishings, and wood floors. Sparkling white bath. Singles £18, with bath £21. Doubles £30, with bath £35. Breakfast £3-4.

Bristol Hotel, 10 Cathedral Sq. (tel. 768 00). The place is huge, so rooms are usually available until late in the day even in July and Aug. Live in the lap of luxury: Modern, spacious rooms with shower, carpeting, and color TV. Swimming pool across the street. Singles £21.50, with bath £23. Doubles £32. Breakfast £2.50.

Food

English, Irish, Spanish, Moroccan, Indian, Italian, Chinese, and French cuisine can be enjoyed, but few places cater to the budgetarian.

Smith's Fish and Chips, 295 Main St. (tel. 742 54). Still the budget traveler's friend in Gibraltar. Run by a cheerful fellow who dishes out generous portions. Note the photograph of Prince Charles and Princess Di's motorcade passing in front of the shop during their honeymoon. Prawn curry £3.05, fish and chips £1.95, hamburger and chips £1.55. Open Mon.-Fri. 11am-11pm, Sat. noon-4pm.

Mac's Kitchen, 245 Main St. (tel. 711 55), down the street from Smith's. Fiercely competing for the affection of the impecunious. Inexpensive and tasty fast-food. Hamburgers 75p, cheeseburgers 85p, and eggburgers 95p. Jumbo pizzas £4.25. Open Sun.-Thurs. 11am-2am, Fri.-Sat. 11am-4am.

Uptown Chicago, 10 Cannon Lane (tel. 789 51), right off Main St. Recently renovated with a romantic ice-cream parlor decor. A little bit of America on the Rock. The only place that serves Southern fried chicken (with chips, £1.85). Try the "Chicago Special," a ¼-lb. patty topped with bacon, egg, and cheese with fries and a salad (£2.90). Open Mon.-Sat 9am-10pm.

Ye Olde Rock, Mackintosh Sq. (tel. 718 04), near the tourist office. If it's a place with local atmosphere you're searching for, look no further. Colorful British pub with beer mugs hanging from the rafters. Hot pies £1.95, sandwiches 65p. Open daily 10am-11pm.

Hong Kong Chinese Restaurant, 11-13 Market Lane (tel. 773 13), just off Main St. If a craving for *moo goo gai pan* suddenly strikes, satisfy the pangs here. Many entrees under £2.50. Beef with mixed vegetables, chicken noodle soup, and fried rice with egg £4.10. House-favorite butterfly prawns £3.10. Open daily noon-3:30pm and 6-11:30pm.

Sights

Known as the **Top of the Rock,** the soaring northern tip of the monstrous massif offers a spectacular view of Spain and the Straits of Gibraltar. Sheer walls on three sides drop along the white cliff to the turquoise Mediterranean rippling far below. This natural barrier is the source of Gibraltar's historic military significance. Ever since the Spanish cut off mainland access to the peninsula, freshwater has been in short supply; along one side of the rock face a great water catchment system has been constructed to trap rain.

Cable cars carry visitors between the southern end of Main St. and the Top of the Rock, making a stop at Apes' Den (every 15 min. Mon.-Sat. 9:30am-5:15pm; one way £1.80, round-trip £3; get the one-way ticket if you want to take the panoramic walk down).

The ruins of a Moorish wall crumble near the cable car station and down the road to the south, the spooky, subterranean chambers of **St. Michael's Cave** wind downward into the rock. Giant clusters of stalactites drip from these eerie ceilings, enhanced by colored lights and soft music. Thought by the Romans to be a bottomless cavern, the cave was outfitted as a hospital during the bombardments of 1942 but has since been converted into an auditorium. If you're lucky, you might catch a rock concert in this cool, damp chamber. The first Neanderthal skull discovered (now in the British Museum) was unearthed here. To reach St. Michael's from the Top of the Rock, take St. Michael's Road, a gravel road heading downhill, and stick to your right. Do yourself a favor and wear a comfortable pair of walking shoes. (Open daily 10am-7pm; in off-season daily 10am-5:30pm. No entrance 15 min. before closing. Admission £1.) Next door, a cafe with a view sells soft drinks for 80p.

Take a U-turn down to Queen's Rd. to reach the **Apes' Den,** which houses a colony of wild Barbary primates who clamber dexterously about the sides of the rock. The tailless apes have inhabited Gibraltar at least since the invasion of the Moors. Legend has it that the British will control the peninsula only as long as the animals survive. In 1944, when the ape population came dangerously close to extinction, Churchill ordered reinforcements from North Africa. Today, the community flourishes, nurtured by Gibraltar's authorities and thousands of affectionate tourists.

Instead of taking the cable car down from Apes' Den, consider walking north along Queen's Rd. (take Upper Town Rd. at the fork) to catch Gib's newest attraction, aptly named **The Gibraltar Laser Experience.** Housed in the vast rock tunnels used in World War II, the Experience highlights Gibraltar's long military legacy with a movie/laser spectacle. Decorated with army paraphenalia and World War II posters, the entire cave complex kindles a nostalgic feeling that is compounded by the highly informative movie that both sounds and looks like a '40s newsreel. (Open Mon.-Sat. 11am-5pm. Performances every 35 min.)

A majestic presence over the city, the **Moorish Castle** (now proudly flying the Union Jack) stands just below the batteries of the Experience. The castle was built in 1160 by the Moors, who were sweeping their way across the Iberian peninsula.

The fortress has always been the symbol of power in Gibraltar. The British first hoisted their flag in 1704, and it has remained ever since. (Open daily 10am-7pm; in off-season daily 10am-5:30pm. Admission 20p.) A labrynth of steep stone alleyways through Gibraltar's **Old Town** brings you back to bustling commercial activity on the northern end of Main Street.

In town, catch the **Changing of the Guard** in front of the Governor's Residence on Main St. (every Tues. at 10:20am). The **Gibraltar Museum** on Bomb House Lane houses nearly everything of interest in Gib's history and displays a set of lavish, fourteenth-century **Moorish baths.** (Open Mon.-Sat. 10am-6pm. Admission 50p.) Proceed from here toward the port and poke about the **public markets** on Fish Market Rd.

At the southern tip of Gibraltar, **Europa Point** commands a nearly endless panorama of the straits guarded by three machine guns and a lighthouse. On a clear day you can see all the way to the North African coast. Take bus #3 from Line Wall Rd, just off Main St., all the way to the end (every ½-hr. 9:30am-9:30pm, 20p).

Tucked at the foot of the great, white cliff on the northern end of the peninsula, **Catalan Bay** is a white, fine-grained *playa* full of British tourists. Several seaside cafes and grocery stores offer a variety of snacks and beverages. A short hike up the road brings you to **Sandy Bay Beach,** smaller and slightly less crowded. The most spacious crescent of sand is **Eastern Beach,** accessible by foot from Catalan Bay. To reach the beaches, take bus #1 from Line Wall Rd. toward Sandy Bay (every 15 min. 8:45am-8:45pm, 20p).

In the evening, visit one of the countless, lively, local **pubs** along Main St. (½-pint of beer 45-55p), or catch an English-language feature at the **Queen's Cinema** (Mon.-Thurs. at 9:30pm, Fri.-Sun. also at 7pm. £2 stalls), near the Queen's Hotel across from the cable car station. If you're feeling lucky, tempt fate at the **Casino,** just up the hill from the cinema—minimum bet £1.50.

Algeciras

About the only thing to do in Algeciras itself is to admire the excellent view of the **Rock of Gibraltar.** Most visitors, however, venture to the unattractive southern extremity of the Iberian peninsula solely for ferries and hydrofoils to Ceuta and Tangier. Rather than spending the night in Algeciras, consider stopping in the neighboring town of Tarifa or farther north in Vejer de la Frontera.

If you do stay in this grimy port-town, venture into the city, where life and atmosphere dramatically improve as you move away from the constant calls of dope-sellers at the port. The old city possesses a certain decayed charm that may just cause you to reverse your initial impressions of Spain's gateway to Africa.

Orientation and Practical Information

With its many banks, hotels, and restaurants, **Avenida Virgen del Carmen** stretches along the coast. As you approach the port, the name of the street changes to **Avenida La Marina,** at the mouth of the entire port/harbor complex, jutting out into the Bay of Algeciras.

All services necessary for international transit are clustered conveniently around the port, accessible by a single driveway (marked by a red and yellow flag). Be wary of fake guards who approach and try to sell you bogus ferry tickets. You'll need about 30 minutes to clear customs and board, 90 minutes if you have a car. Customs control slackens significantly in off-season. Tickets can be purchased at the port immediately prior to departure; there is no need for advance purchase. Leave your Dramamine behind; these ferries resemble mini-cruise ships and do not dance to the motion of the ocean. For a less harrowing introduction to Morocco, take the ferry to Spanish Ceuta instead of Tangier.

Tourist Office: C. Juan de la Cierva (tel. 60 09 11). From the port, stick to the left sidewalk until you come to the traffic lights on Avda. La Marina. Cross the railroad tracks, and turn right after 1 block onto the street with the Casa Alfonso restaurant. English-speaking staff.

Helpful map. Many color brochures on Spain (none on Morocco), principally Andalucía. Get directions to the beach if you plan to extend your stay. Open Mon.-Fri. 9am-2pm, Sat. 9am-1pm.

Student Travel: No office, but many of the travel agencies sell BIJ tickets. Try **Tourafrica,** Avda. La Marina (tel. 65 22 20). Open daily 8am-10pm.

Currency Exchange: To change your money into pesetas, go to a bank around Plaza Alta. The travel agencies offer abominable rates. To change into dirhams, use the branch of the Bank of Morocco at the port, to the right of the stairs that lead up to the embarkation area. Open Mon.-Fri. 9am-2pm and 4-6pm; Ramadan Mon.-Fri. 9am-2pm.

Post Office: C. Ruiz Zorrilla (tel. 66 32 76), inconveniently located uptown. Open Mon.-Sat. 9am-2pm. **Postal Code:** 11080.

Telephones: To your left as you exit the port terminal building. **Telephone Code:** 956.

Train Station: RENFE (tel. 66 36 46), all the way down C. Juan de la Cierva and its connecting street, C. San Bernardo. To Granada (at 4pm, 2000ptas; 11:30pm, 1270ptas), Sevilla (at 4pm, 2250ptas; 11:30pm, 1470ptas), Málaga (at 4pm, 1440ptas; 11:30pm, 1050ptas), and Madrid (at 8:30am, 4300ptas; 10pm, 4080ptas).

Buses: Empresa Portillo, Avda. Virgen del Carmen, 15 (tel. 65 11 55), 1½ blocks to the right as you leave the port complex underneath Banco de Bilbao. To Málaga (11 per day, 775ptas), Granada (2 per day, 1505ptas), Almería (1 per day, 2015 ptas), and Madrid (1 per day, 3015ptas). **Empresa La Valenciana,** Viajes Travimar, Avda. de la Marina (tel. 65 36 61). To Sevilla (1255ptas) and Jerez (3 per day, 795ptas). **Empresa Comes** (tel. 65 34 56), under the Hotel Octavio on C. San Bernardo, the continuation of C. Juan de la Cierva. To Cádiz (8 per day, 795ptas), La Línea (for Gibraltar, 135ptas), and Tarifa (135ptas). Buses leave on the hr. and ½-hr. daily 7am-9:45pm. **Empresa Bacoma,** at the Tourafrica office on the port. To Barcelona (at 1pm and 8:45pm, 6725ptas; 2:30am, 5000ptas). Schedule is shortened on weekends and holidays.

Ferries to Ceuta: late June to mid-Sept. Mon.-Fri. 12 per day 7am-9pm, Sat. 10 per day 7am-9pm, Sun. 5 per day 10am-9pm; mid-Sept. to late-June 9 per day 8am-9pm; 11/3 hr.; 1140ptas per person, 4580-5730ptas per car, 1140-1790ptas per motorcycle.

Ferries to Tangier: April to mid-Sept. Mon.-Sat. at 9am, 1pm, and 6pm; Nov.-March Mon.-Sat. at 12:30pm and 8pm; 2½ hr.; Class A 3290ptas per person, Class B 2250ptas per person. 7500ptas per car, 2400ptas per motorcycle. 50% discount for children, 20% with Eurail pass, 30% with InterRail. No cars and no service on board in stormy weather. Limited service on Sun.

Ferries from Tarifa to Tangier: 1 per day at 9am, 1 hr., 2550ptas.

Baggage Check: In the port complex, by the stairs of the embarkation platforms. Bags must be locked or well secured. 25ptas per small, 45ptas per medium, and 70ptas per large bag.

Foreign Newspapers: On. C. Juan de la Cierva across from Turismo next door to the Casa Alfonso Restaurant.

Pharmacy: on C. Cayetano del Toro at C. Tarifa. Open Mon.-Fri. 9:30am-1:15pm and 5pm-8:30pm. **First Aid,** Tel. 66 20 54.

Police: Tel. 66 01 55.

Accommodations

Convenient *casas de huéspedes* and *hostales* (a mostly bureaucratic distinction) are bunched around **Calle José Santacana,** parallel to Avda. La Marina and 1 block inland, and **Calle Duque de Almodóvar,** 2 blocks farther up from the water. Rooms on C. José Santacana fill up quickly in summer. Do not confuse C. José Santacana with C. E. Santacana.

Consider asking for a back room, as Vespa vigilantes cruise the narrow streets at ungodly hours. Note that the beach in Algeciras is not the best place for camping. Police patrol the waterfront and unsavory types hang out there at night.

Hostal Levante, C. Duque de Almodóvar, 21 (tel. 65 15 05). From the port, follow the railroad tracks, and take the 4th street to the right. A good deal, with clean, modern bathrooms and cozy, well-lit rooms. Restaurant downstairs. Singles 900ptas, with bath 1100ptas. Doubles 1400ptas, with bath 2000ptas.

Hostal Residencia González, C. José Santacana, 7 (tel. 65 28 43). Modern, immaculate rooms with new wood furnishings. Spotless bathrooms and attentive managment. Singles 800ptas, with bath 1000ptas. Doubles 1600ptas, with bath 2000ptas.

Casa de Huéspedes Dora, C. José Santacana, 6 (tel. 65 57 48). Cruddy exterior belies the elegant rooms inside. Fine tile walls and hanging glass lamp add a touch of class. June-Sept. singles 1100ptas; doubles 2200ptas. Sept.-March singles 700ptas; doubles 1400ptas. March-June singles 900ptas; doubles 1800ptas. Cold showers 150ptas, hot showers 300ptas.

Hostal Vizcaíno, C. José Santacana, 9 (tel. 65 57 56). Helpful management, well-scrubbed rooms. Restaurant downstairs serves all three meals, but they'll cost you an arm and a leg. June-Sept. singles 900ptas, with shower 1000ptas; doubles with shower 1500ptas. Oct.-May singles 750ptas, with shower 850ptas; doubles with shower 1350ptas.

Hostal Continental and **Hostal Residencial Pérez,** C. Santacana, 16 (tel. 65 63 01). Run by the same management. Street rooms a bit noisy. Singles 700ptas. Doubles 1200ptas. Showers 100ptas.

Food

One thing Algeciras has going for it is its selection of budget eateries. Relax with your final plate of *paella,* or welcome yourself back from Morocco with a *medio pollo asado,* sold in many places along **Avenida Virgen del Carmen,** near the port.

Casa Alfonso, C. Juan de la Cierva (tel. 60 27 54), near the tourist office. For no-nonsense eating with the people who run the port. *Paella,* steak, vegetables, bread, beverage, and dessert 500ptas. Assemble your own *menú* by choosing items from three groups (450ptas). Open daily noon-10pm.

Casa Montes, C. Juan Mórrison, 27 (tel. 65 69 05). From the Carretera a Málaga, turn right on C. Castelar then left on Juan Mórrison. A wholesome, family atmosphere. Huge, delicious 4-course meals around 650ptas. Open daily noon-5pm and 7pm-midnight.

Casa María, C. Castelar, 38 (tel. 65 47 02), not far from C. Santacana. Varied a la carte menu. A satisfying meal of *gazpacho,* fried mullets, pork cutlets, bread, wine, and dessert 700ptas. Open daily 8:30am-midnight.

Restaurant Casa Sánchez, Avda. Segismundo Moret, 6 (tel. 65 69 57). Lively local joint. *Menú del día* with salad, 2 courses, fruit, bread, and wine 550ptas. *Gazpacho andaluz* 175ptas. Open daily 8am-midnight.

Sights

Some of the Spaniards forced to leave Gibraltar in 1704 settled in Algeciras around what is now **Plaza Alta,** the nicest place to hang out in town. Some older buildings surround an open square with a handsome blue- and gold-tiled fountain. Many outdoor cafes and *heladerías* line nearby **Calle Regino Martinez,** the main *paseo.*

If you have a car or are willing to exercise your thumb, the nicest **beach** around is next to the tiny village of **Getares** (not marked on most maps), 5km south of Algeciras off the main road. The milelong stretch is relatively uncrowded, catering mostly to local families. It features a great view of Gibraltar.

Advertised with great pomp and circumstance throughout Andalucía, the **Fiesta de Algeciras** rocks the town with fairs, carnival rides, and dancing the last week of June. The final evening features a fireworks extravaganza. Follow the crowd to see some of the traditional costumes.

Near Algeciras: Tarifa

A 45-minute bus ride from Algeciras (135ptas) brings you to Tarifa, which is, contrary to popular knowledge, more than just a hydrofoil port. It is the most southern city in continental Europe, and, on a clear day, its view of the north African coast can be spectacular. Since the town lies off the beaten track, you can expect to find long stretches of deserted beach and uncongested, clean, cobbled streets.

Plaza San Mateo is the main square. In addition to housing a long, tiled walkway complete with palm trees and a playground, the plaza hosts a number of fine restaurants and cafes. At the bottom of the square, you'll find a statue of Guzmán el

Bueno, the town's hero. The stone monstrosity to your left is the **Castillo de Guzmán el Bueno.** In the thirteenth century, the Moors, in an attempt to recapture parts of Andalucía, kidnapped Guzmán's son and threatened to kill him if Guzmán didn't surrender the castle. Guzmán chose his *patria* (country) over his son. The castle is not open to visitors, but you can look out from its ramparts onto the straits for the area's best view of Morocco. To get to this section of the castle, follow the street on your left from the entrance and climb the medina-like stairs through the lovely gardens of **Plaza de Santa María.**

Cool off in the afternoon by walking 10 minutes west along the port road for a dip in the **Playa Chica,** a small, sheltered beach between the harbor and the military base. The **Playa de Lances** is an especially beautiful, 5-kilometer stretch of beach beginning 200m north of the Playa Chica. Be careful of the high winds and the undertow.

Relatively cheap lodgings can be found a block north of the central plaza at **La Casa Concha,** San Rosendo, 4 (tel. 78 49 31). The beds are large and the rooms and bathrooms are spotlessly clean. (Singles 800ptas. Doubles 1700ptas. Hot showers 120ptas.) Tarifa's high season is in August, so if you visit then, call ahead or arrive early. There are a number of official **campgrounds** on the beach, a few kilometers to the north. The police seem remarkably tolerant of short-term, unofficial camping closer to town.

There is no tourist office, but the staff at the **Ayuntamiento,** on Pl. de Santa María, will hand out brochures and advise visitors. (Open Mon.-Fri. 8am-2pm; in off-season Mon.-Fri. 8am-3pm.) The **post office,** C. Colonel Moscardó, 9 (tel. 68 42 37), is near the town center. (Open Mon.-Fri. 9am-2pm, Sat. 9am-1pm.) The **postal code** is 11380.

Vejer de la Frontera

Vejer de la Frontera is the quintessential Andalusian village, with its whitewashed houses scattered at the base of a handsome Moorish castle, an elegant church standing atop an imposing rock spike, and flower-adorned patios. Best of all, its inland location has allowed the village to remain almost entirely tourist-free although it lies on the Ruta de los Pueblos Blancos (Route of the White Towns).

Vejer de la Frontera can be easily reached by convenient hourly buses from Cádiz (360ptas) and Algeciras (445ptas). Some buses do not climb up to Vejer itself, but let you out by the highway at **Barco de Vejer.** Taxis charge 400ptas to take you up the hill, a fee that can be split among several passengers. It's money well spent, since the walk up can be murderous with a back pack. Leaving Vejer, you won't have to walk downhill as all buses come up to a stop on the **Corredera,** the main road running on and along the mountain.

Señora Luisa Doncel offers extremely clean and homey rooms in her nameless pensión on C. San Filmo, 12 (tel. 45 02 46). (An excellent deal at 600ptas per person. Hot showers 50ptas.) From the Corredera, follow the signs indicating the *iglesia* (church) onto La Pazuela, a small square. Take Molinos de Viento, on your right, and go up the steep walkway at the curve. Turn right on C. San Filmo, which is clearly marked with a sign. If *doña* Luisa is not around, ask at #10, or stop any passerby. Should she have no available rooms, *doña* Luisa will direct you to a comparable *pensión*. More expensive, but just as clean and very luxurious, is the modern **Hostal La Janda** (tel. 45 01 42), all the way up Avda. da Andalucía. Follow the directions for the pensión, but instead of going up the stairs at the curve, pass 2 more blocks before turning right. (Singles and doubles 2000ptas. Both with bath.)

For a spectacular view of the countryside while you eat or sip your drinks, try **La Ratonera,** along the Corredera near the bus stop. Sit along the esplanade to view the sunset or to watch *The Flintstones* in Spanish. Later at night, try some of the colorful bars that cluster around **Plaza de España** and the **Mercado de Abastos.**

Take some time to amble around Vejer's maze of cobbled streets and admire the view from the edges of town. The **Moorish castle** offers the usual assortment of heavy stone battlements and crenelated walls, along with an excellent view of the town's glowing white houses. Erected on the foundations of a mosque, the **Iglesia del Divino Salvador** is a peculiar mix of Romanesque, Mudéjar, and Gothic styles. It's worth staying overnight in Vejer just to see the castle and the church illuminated.

The village is known for its traditional fiestas. As soon as the wild **Corpus Christi** celebrations end (beginning the Thurs. after the 8th Sun. after Easter), Vejer celebrates the **Candelas de San Juan.** The highlight is a huge bonfire over which a mannequin filled with firecrackers is hung and burned. In Plaza de España, amid much pomp and ceremony, a committee reviews the mannequins prepared by the village children and selects the most charming for the toasty honor. A marching band then escorts the winning entry through the village. In spring, the **Semana Santa** and **Feria de Abril** celebrations are delightfully delirious, with dancing in the streets and a running of the bulls. Here, the bulls' horns are padded with rubber.

Although Vejer has no tourist office, information about the town and the surrounding area can be found at the **Ayuntamiento** (tel. 45 02 38), on Pl. de España. (Open Mon.-Fri. 8:30am-2:30pm; in off-season Mon.-Fri. 8am-3pm.) The **post office** (tel. 45 02 28) is located at C. Juan Bueno, 22. (Open Mon.-Fri. 9am-2pm, Sat. 9am-1pm.) The **postal code** is 11150. The closest beach is at **Los Caños** (14km), accessible only by private wheels or a public thumb.

Costa de la Luz

Although the coast from Ayamonte to Tarifa can't compete in attractiveness and popularity with the Costa del Sol or the Portuguese Algarve, there are some long, sandy beaches where weary travelers en route between Portugal and Morocco can soak up Spanish sun. Unfortunately, the most accessible shoreline is marred by heavy winds and, near Huelva, by heavy industrialization. However, you can swim at Rota, Chipiona, and Sanlúcar de Barrameda. Foreigners seem to prefer flashier resorts, so most of the tourism on the Costa de la Luz is native.

Prices here are also lower than on the Costa del Sol, but in July and August hotels and restaurants may charge 15-25% more than in the off-season. Don't be prompted by the high prices, however, to camp unofficially by the ocean: Thieves frequent this region, and the police tend to equate thrifty backpackers with drug smugglers. During your visit, be sure to sample the tasty sea creatures caught by the shores' large fishing industry: *Chocos,* a local variety of squid, are especially delicious.

Cádiz

Founded by Phoenician merchants over 3000 years ago (perhaps upon the base of an earlier, Tartessian settlement), the commercial port of Cádiz, linked to the mainland by a sandy isthmus, is one of Spain's oldest cities, if not the oldest. Hannibal lived in Cádiz, and the Romans under Caesar traded salt fish here.

When Rome fell, so did Cádiz: For centuries it suffered invasions from Visigoths, Arabs, and Normans. With the discovery of America, Cádiz regained prominence as the "City of the Explorers" and headquarters of the Spanish treasure fleets. In cutthroat competition with the merchants of Sevilla, Cádiz gained a monopoly over trade in the Americas that made it the wealthiest port in Western Europe. This prosperity also made Cádiz the target of foreign powers. In 1587 Sir Francis Drake torched the Spanish Armada as it lay at anchor, and the port was invaded by the British navy several times during the seventeenth century.

Ironically, Cádiz played a crucial role in the granting of independence to the colonies from which it had profited for centuries. When Napoleon seized Fernando VII and occupied Spain, Cádiz resisted militarily and politically, proclaiming a provisory *junta* to rule the country, which prompted Latin American creoles to similarly resist Bonapartist domination. Latin America didn't stop with resistance to Napoleon, however, and eventually it revolted against Spain. Most of the colonies liberated themselves in the 1810-1825 period. With the loss of the colonies, Cádiz declined, but its liberal tradition continued: In the Civil War, the city was a bastion of anti-Franco republicanism, and today its inhabitants vote consistently for leftist parties. Despite economic problems, Cádiz retains its position as southern Spain's foremost commercial port.

Practical Information

Cádiz is accessible by both bus and train from Sevilla, Jerez de la Frontera, and Algeciras.

Tourist Office: C. Calderón de la Barca, 1 (tel. 21 13 13). From the bus station (Pl. de la Independencia), cross over to Pl. de España and walk straight uphill along C. Antonio López. Office is directly across Pl. Mina on the corner of C. Calderón de la Barca. From train station, follow Avda. del Puerto north all the way to Pl. de España, then follow directions above. Open Mon.-Sat. 9am-2pm.

Post Office: Pl. de las Flores (tel. 21 39 45). Open daily 9am-7pm. Open for Lista de Correos Mon.-Fri. 9am-3pm. **Telegrams:** Open Mon.-Sat. 9am-8pm. **Postal Code:** 11080.

Telephones: Avda. Andaluciá (tel. 27 53 62 or 27 66 06). Open Mon.-Fri. 8:30am-1:30pm. **Telephone Code:** 956.

Train Station: Avda. del Puerto. **RENFE information** (tel. 25 43 01).

Bus Stations: Transportes Generales Comes, Pl. de la Hispanidad, 1 (tel. 21 17 63 or 22 42 71). To Sevilla (8 per day), Málaga (3 per day), Córdoba (1 per day), Granada (1 per day), Jerez de la Frontera (11 per day), and Arcos de la Frontera (4 per day). **Transportes Los Amarillos,** Avda. Ramon de Carranza (tel. 28 58 52), across from Jardines de Canaleja. To Sanlúcar and Chipiona (8 per day, ½-hr., 200ptas), Arcos de la Frontera (2 per day), and Prado del Rey (2 per day).

Taxis: Tele-Taxi (tel. 27 69 69).

Medical Emergency: Casa de Socorro, C. Benjumea, 11 (tel. 21 10 53) or Avda. López Pinto (tel. 23 10 80).

Police: National, Avda. Andaluciá, 28 (tel. 28 61 11). **Municipal** (tel. 22 17 63). **Emergency:** Tel. 092.

Accommodations

You can find many inexpensive *hostales* near the harbor and the area around **Plaza San Juan de Dios,** on Avda. del Puerto, a 20-minute walk from the bus or train station.

Pensión Marqués, C. Marquéz de Cádiz, 1 (tel. 28 58 54), just off Pl. San Juan de Dios. Cool, green and white interiors, plant-filled patio. Clean, spacious rooms with high ceilings. Singles 1000ptas. Doubles 2000ptas.

Hostal Barcelona, C. Montñés, 10 (tel. 21 39 49), just off Pl. de la Candelaria. Plain place, but rooms are large and well-scrubbed. Singles 1000ptas. Doubles 1700ptas.

Camas Cuatro Naciones, C. Plocia, 3 (tel. 25 73 94). Clean, nautical blue rooms—those facing the street recieve lots of light. Flirty sailors line the street. Cubicle-size bathrooms; cubicle-size prices. Singles 700ptas. Doubles 1400ptas. Cold showers 100ptas, hot showers 150ptas.

Huéspedes La Aurora, C. Sopranis, 8 (tel. 25 33 52). Cramped rooms. The shy may object to the bathroom's location—in the middle of the reception room. Singles 800ptas. Doubles 1400ptas. Cold showers 100ptas, hot showers 150ptas.

Food

For cheap meals, the area around **Pl. de San Juan de Dios** also offers your best opportunities. Cádiz is famous for *pescado frito* (fried fish). You can buy 'em by the bagful at any *freiduría*.

Restaurante Andaluz, Pl. San Juan de Dios, 9 (tel. 28 52 54). The plain decor hides one of Cádiz's best and cheapest restaurants. Huge *menú* 350ptas. Quick service. Open daily 1-4:30pm and 8-11pm; Oct.-June Sat.-Thurs. 1-4:30pm and 8-11pm.

Restaurante Fanny, C. Barrocal, 2 (tel. 29 59 51), at the corner of C. Urguinoana. For 600ptas you get *paella*, a ¼ chicken, fries, and dessert. Classy white tablecloths and friendly service. Open Mon.-Sat. 10am-2:30pm and 8-11pm.

Restaurante La Economica, C. San Fernando, 2 (tel. 28 69 52). Framed photographs of northern Spain on the walls belie owner's nostalgia for home. Large selection of entrees and *menús del día.* Other *menús* 375-475ptas. Open Mon.-Sat. noon-4pm and 7-11:30pm.

Restaurante El 9, C. San Fernando, 4 (tel. 27 86 81) next to the above. The place to come if you're really pinching pesetas. *Paella de mariscos* (seafood *paella*) 125ptas, combination plates 300ptas, *menú* 350ptas. Open Fri.-Wed. noon-4:30pm and 8-11pm, except Sun. afternoons.

Sights

The most scenic portion of town is the **Old City,** situated on a tiny peninsula. Its winding, cobbled streets form a labyrinth of seaside honky-tonks and tiny shops. Right across from Turismo on Pl. de la Mina, the **Museo de Bellas Artes y Arquéologico** contains a fine collection of Murillo, Rubens, and Zurbarán canvases. (Open Mon.-Sat. 9am-2pm. Admission 250ptas.) To the south along C. Sagasta is the **Municipal Historical Museum,** which features a fascinating eighteenth-century ivory and mahogany model of the city. (The museum, following restoration work, is scheduled to reopen in 1989.) Around the corner and 2 blocks downhill on C. Rosario, you can see canvases by Goya, Cavallini, and Camarone at **El Oratorio de Santa Cueva.** (Open Mon.-Fri. 10am-1pm and 5-7pm, Sat. 10am-1pm. Admission 50ptas.) Continue down C. Rosario and turn right on C. Padre Elejarde to reach the eighteenth-century **cathedral.** Its gold dome and baroque facade are somewhat dilapidated but still imposing; its treasury houses an eye-opening collection of silver and jewels. (Open Mon.-Sat. 10am-1pm. Adults 150ptas, children 75ptas. No shorts or bare shoulders allowed.)

Cádiz also offers a balustraded, seaside **promenade** that commands a view of the vast Atlantic oceanscape and the neighboring **public gardens**—full of exotic trees, fancifully sculpted hedges, and even a couple of chattering monkeys. To reach the nicest part of the beach, catch local bus #1 (toward Cartadura) at Pl. de España or points east. Get off at "Balneario," and turn right on C. Glorieta Ingeniero La Cierra. If you prefer to hike to the beach (about a ½-hr. from Pl. de España), walk east to Pl. de la Constitución and continue along Avda. Cayetano del Toro.

Rota

Rota is a small, oceanside town with a long, sandy beach, about a half-hour from Chipiona and Sanlúcar de Barrameda, an hour from Jerez. It's inadvisable to advertise U.S. citizenship here: Brash military manners at the American naval base have not endeared Uncle Sam to the Spaniards.

Cheap accommodations are a problem in this beach town. **Hostal la Española,** C. Charco, 9 (tel. 81 00 98) has cramped rooms, but the price is right. (Singles 750ptas. Doubles 1400ptas.) Fork over a little more and live it up at **Hostal Florida,** Avda. de Sevilla, 32 (tel. 81 05 96). Rooms are clean, have primitive showers, and entitle you to relax on the pleasant outdoor patio. (Singles 2000ptas. Doubles 2750ptas.)

Some of the least expensive food in town is served at **Restaurante 2001,** Avda. de Sevilla, 11, where veal, fried eggs, green peppers, and fries cost 400ptas and ocean view is free. Moderately priced restaurants along Avda. de Sevilla have excellent entrees and lovely terraces near the beach. Try the grilled swordfish (650ptas) at **Bar Yola,** Avda. Sevilla, 21. Be careful: The food around here is good. Pancakes, pizza, and other American *haute-cuisine* dishes can be sampled at the many fast-food restaurants patronized by U.S. servicemen.

Buses connect Rota with Jerez (5 per day), and Chipiona, and Sanlúcar de Barrameda. Come in May for the Spring Fair and Festival. While in town, be sure to see the ruins of medieval walls and the **Castille de Luna** (Castle of the Moon), dating from the thirteenth century. Also head to the **beaches,** renowned for their fine sand. La Costilla, Punta Candor, and Almandraba are especially beautiful.

Chipiona

In the winter, Chipiona is a quiet town with pretty garden patios lining its streets. From June 15 to September 1, the beaches are packed and the pensions overflowing with Spanish families. Legend has it that the waters of the spa have special curative powers. The capacities of the fountain water in the recently renovated **Iglesia de Nuestra Señora de Regla** are believed to be particularly exceptional. The town's two beaches beckon swimmers and beachcombers.

Orientation and Practical Information

Tourist Office: Pió XII, off C. Isaac Peral.

Post Office: C. Padre Lerchundi, next to Pl. Pio XII. Open Mon.-Fri. 9am-2pm, Sat. 9am-1pm.

Telephones: Pl. de Juan Carlos I (tel. 37 19 87). Open daily 8:30am-12:30am. Friendly staff. Postcards and birdseed for doves in the plaza on sale.

Bus Stations: Los Amarillos, Avda. de Regla (tel. 37 02 92). **La Valenciana,** Pl. San Sebastián (tel. 37 12 83). To Sevilla, Jerez de la Frontera, Cádiz, and Sanlúcar de Barrameda.

Taxis: Tel. 37 00 18 or 37 11 20.

Medical Emergency: Cruz Roja (Red Cross), Avda. Cruz Roja (tel. 37 04 81). **Ambulance:** Tel. 37 17 04.

Police: Pl. General Franco (tel. 37 10 88).

Accommodations

During July and August, accommodations may be difficult to find. Head for the bus station where women will approach you with the question "*Habitaciones?*" These people are local scouts for the *hostales* and the most knowledgeable room-hunters in town. They will bring you to a bed in exchange for a small tip. Otherwise, try for one of the excellent *hostales* near the beach.

Hostal Nuestra Señora de la O, C. Isaac Peral, 4 (tel. 37 07 29). As close to the church as you can get. Pretty patio. Singles 1500ptas, with bath 2500ptas. Doubles 2500ptas, with bath 4000ptas. *Media pension* (breakfast and lunch or dinner) 975ptas.

Hostal Gran Capitan, C. Fray Baldomero Gonzalez, 7 (tel. 37 09 29), off Pl. Juan Carlos I. Lovely old Spanish home with antique furniture and knickknacks. Impeccably kept. Open April-Oct. Singles with bath 1600ptas. Doubles with shower 2300ptas, with bath 2600ptas.

Food

Chipiona's daily catch is for sale fresh from the nets at the **public market,** Avda. de Huelva, 82. More formal dining options are also possible. Cheap restaurants line the Cruz del Mar beach, at the end of C. Isaac Peral. Also try the area around Pl. de las Palomas and Pl. Pio VII for inexpensive food. Order a glass of *vino moscatel,* the local wine to conceal your tourist identity. **El Quinto,** near the market, will grill the fish of your choice; incredible portions come with a salad and beer for 700ptas.

Bar Paquito, C. Isaac Peral, 36 (tel. 37 01 05), in Pl. Pío VII. Tasty *tapas* (100ptas) and seafood *raciones* (500ptas). Beers 70ptas. Open daily 8am-2am.

Restaurante El Gato, C. Pez Espada, 9-11 (tel. 37 07 87). Worshiped by locals as Chipiona's best. Specialties include local seafood and Bellota ham dishes.

Sights and Entertainment

The **Iglesia de Nuestra Señora de la O,** constructed in 1640, stands in Pl. Juan Carlos I. Gothic architecture buffs may prefer the **Santuario de Nuestra Señora**

de Regla, still the site of daily Mass. In July the town celebrates both the **Festival de la Virgen del Carmen** and the **Festival del Moscatel.**

Sanlúcar de Barrameda

The best way to approach Sanlúcar de Barrameda is by sea: An old harbor protected by stone breakwaters flanks a comparatively uncrowded sandy beach. Unfortunately, you'll be approaching from the other side, so be prepared for an initial disappointment. Once you're past the industrialized outskirts, you'll find that the streets of the old town display a rugged charm. In 1519, Magellan embarked from here for his round-the-world journey. Columbus also used this port on his third trip to the New World. Today, Sanlúcar is primarily known for *manzanilla,* the local sherry that can be savored at any of the *bodegas* (wine cellars) in the old city. Seafood enhances the town's fame. Don't miss a heaping plate of fried *mariscos* accompanied by a glass of *manzanilla.* Residents affectionately refer to the two as "best friends."

Orientation and Practical Information

Running parallel to the beach, but a dozen blocks inland, is the main street, **C. San Juan. Pl. de San Roque** and **Pl. Cabildo** are town gathering spots.

Tourist Office: Calzada de Ejército, Paseo Maritimo, 1 block from the beach.

Post Office: Avda. del Cerro Falón (tel. 36 09 37). Open Mon.-Fri. 9am-2pm, Sat. 9am-1pm.

Bus Stations: Los Amarillos, Pl. de la Salle (tel. 36 04 66). **La Valenciana,** C. San Juan, 12 (tel. 36 01 96). To Cádiz, Chipiona (10 per day), Jerez de la Frontera (11 per day), and Sevilla (2 per day).

Taxis: C. San Juan (tel. 36 11 02); C. San Jorge (tel. 36 00 04).

Ambulance: Tel. 36 02 69.

Police: Juan de Argüeso, 11 (tel. 36 25 26). **Municipal,** Cuesta de Belén (tel. 36 01 02 or 36 40 43).

Accommodations

Hostal La Blanca Paloma, Pl. Pinto Pacheco, 9 (tel. 36 36 44). Spacious, clean rooms; those facing the street have gigantic balconies. Singles 1200ptas. Doubles 2500ptas.

Hostal Andalucía, C. Torno, 8 (tel. 36 01 40). Stunning old Spanish home with carved wooden doors and an elegant, tiled patio. Bathrooms are *sans* modern comforts, but clean. Singles 1115ptas, with shower 1317ptas. Doubles 1815ptas, with shower 2420ptas.

Hotel Los Helechos, Pl. Madre de Dios, 9 (tel. 36 13 49 or 36 14 41). Lots of perks await if you decide to treat yourself. Refurbished Spanish home retains its old charm, and boasts modern conveniences. International cable TV, lounge, patio, bar/restaurant, and parking garage. Singles with bath 2300ptas. Doubles 4500ptas.

Food

Inexpensive bar restaurants serving *tapas, raciones,* and *tascas* line El Barrio, the area between San Nicolás, Bolsa, Rubiños, Barrameda, and San Antonio o Pirrado streets. For sit-down meals, the side streets off **C. San Juan** are your best bet.

Bar Restaurante El Cura, C. Amargura, 2 (tel. 36 29 94). Old-fashioned fans and a huge Picasso print set the tone. Combination plates 325ptas, *paella* 225ptas, fried seafood dishes 300-500ptas. Open daily 7am-2am.

Bar-Restaurante La Parada, Pl. de la Paz, 4-5 (tel. 36 11 60). Always crowded with locals. Long *tapas* menu on the wall (200ptas). Waiters total your bill on the counter with chalk. Open daily noon-5pm and 8pm-12:30am.

Restaurante Mi Tate, near C. San Juan. Tasty meals are a steal at 300-400ptas. Outside tables in warm weather.

Sights

Sanlúcar is home to a number of historic sites, including the **Palacio Infantes Orleans,** a resplendent nineteenth-century palace built by the Infantes and the Bourbons. (Closed indefinitely for restorations. Call 36 03 41 for information.) The town sports more glorious architecture in the **Palacio de los Duques de Medina Sidonia,** a fifteenth-century edifice of Portuguese design. The palace houses an important archive collection of the Casa Ducal. Cathedral lovers will feel drawn to the **Iglesia de Nuestra Señora de la O;** contructed in the fourteenth century, the building was crafted in an interesting mix of Gothic, Renaissance, and Mudéjar styles. The stately Renaissance exterior of *Santo Domingo* appears more traditional. The sixteenth-century edifice was contructed exclusively out of *canteriá.*

Sanlúcar hosts numerous festivals throughout the year, a testimony to *san-luqueños's* fame for merry-making. May's Appel Fair and June's Corpus Christi celebration force visitors to have a good time. In August, there is horseracing on the beach and the **Festival of the Exaltation of the Guadalquiver River,** which livens up the streets with a flamenco competition, popular dances, and bullfights.

Doñana National Park, one of the most important natural reserves in Europe, extends north of Sanlúcar. You can reach the Doñana beach by boat from the northern end of the Sanlúcar beach (100ptas). For tours, call 40 61 40; short tours are free. For those who call well in advance, **Cooperativa Marismas del Rocio** (tel. 43 04 32) offers a more extensive guided tour that lasts for four hours (1600ptas). Yet another way to visit Doñana is to approach the park from Sevilla, taking a bus that passes through the picturesque towns of **Almonte** and **El Rocío.** From El Rocío you can stand by the railings of an immense esplanade, and stare out across the endless expanse of marshes that in winter becomes Western Europe's largest lake. Millions of birds pass through in winter on their maintain south to Africa. (Park open Tues.-Sun., closed during the festival of Romeria del Rocío.)

Huelva, the northern provincial capital of the Costa de la Luz, is an industrial wasteland, best avoided unless you want to catch a train for the Algarve. Three trains per day run from Huelva to **Ayamonte,** where a ferry crosses the Río Guadiana into Portugal. (70ptas per person, last ferry at 8pm.)

Jerez de la Frontera

One of Andalucía's least touristed cities, Jerez de la Frontera is a modern commercial center best known for some of the world's finest sherry. The production of these famous wines is largely controlled by English families, some of whom have been in the business since the reign of Henry VII, when *jerez* first became popular in England. Today, you can still visit the *bodegas* (warehouses storing wine barrels), where the stuff ferments.

Orientation and Practical Information

The main street, **Calle José Primo de Rivera** runs north-south through the center of the city, and **Calle Fermín Aranda** is almost perpendicular to it. **Plaza Reyes Católicos,** off C. Corredera, is a local focal point. On the eastern end of C. Fermín Aranda is the train station; to the west, halfway to the city center, lies the bus station.

Tourist Office: C. Alameda Cristina, 7 (tel. 33 11 50 or 33 11 62). Open 8am-2pm and 5:30-7:30pm; Oct.-April 14 9am-3pm and 5-7pm.

Post Office: C. Ceron, 1 (tel. 34 22 95), off C. Fermin Aranda. Open for stamps and Lista de Correos Mon.-Fri. 9am-2pm and 4-6pm. **Telegrams:** Open Mon.-Fri. 8am-3pm. **Postal Code:** 11000.

Telephones: Located at Pl. del Banco and C. José Primo de Rivera, 4. **Telephone Code:** 956.

Airport: Carretera Jerez-Sevilla (tel. 33 56 86). Connections to Barcelona, Madrid, Zaragoza, Valencia, Tenerife, Las Palmas, and Palma de Mallorca. No international flights. **Iberia,** Pl. Reyes Católicos (tel. 34 27 40 or 34 99 65). **Aviaco,** at the airport (tel. 33 22 10).

Train Station: Pl. de la Estación (tel. 34 96 12 or 33 66 82), at the eastern end of C. Fermin Aranda. **RENFE information,** C. Tornería.

Bus Station: C. Medina, at the corner of Madre de Dios. To Arcos de la Frontera (5 per day, ½-hr., 200ptas), Ronda (5 per day, 3 hr., 700ptas), Sanlúcar (9 per day, ½-hr., 135ptas), and Cádiz (13 per day, 1½ hr.).

Taxis: Tel. 34 48 11 or 34 48 60.

Car Rental: Hertz, C. Sevilla, 29 (tel. 33 55 20 or 34 74 67). **Avis,** C. Sevilla, 25 (tel. 34 43 11 or 30 60 86). **Europcar,** C. Honda, 18 (tel. 30 34 66 or 33 48 56).

Medical Emergency: Cruz Roja (Red Cross), Avda. de la Cruz Roja (tel. 34 74 54). **Casa de Socorro,** C. Diego Fernandez Herrera, 5 (tel. 33 13 31).

Police: C. Ingeneiero Antonio Gallegos (tel. 34 35 43). **Emergency:** Tel. 091 or 092.

Accommodations

Finding accommodations in Jerez is easy, even during July and August. Look around near the west end of **C. Fermin Aranda** or along **C. Medina,** near the bus station.

Residencia Juvenil Jerez, Avda. Carrero Blanco (tel. 34 28 90). A favorite of the tourist office. 400ptas. *Pension completa* 1000ptas.

Hostal Las Palomas, C. Higueras (tel. 34 37 73), 3 blocks from the bus station down C. Medina. Sparkling clean and very comfortable. Modern bathrooms. Patio with plants, TV, and singing canaries. Lounge on every floor. Singles 1000ptas. Doubles 1800ptas.

Pensión los Amarillos, C. Medina, 39, 3 blocks from the bus station. Convenient location. Singles 700ptas. Doubles 1400ptas.

Hostal Jerezana, C. Arcos, 11 (tel. 34 56 03). A last resort: The street is noisy, and though the rooms are reasonably clean, they are bare and run-down. Singles 800ptas. Doubles 1500ptas.

Food

Unless you don't mind bar food, eating out cheaply is notoriously difficult in Jerez.

Restaurante Economico, C. Fontana, 4 (tel. 33 40 00), to the right of C. Medina as you leave the bus station, toward Pl. de Angustias. The sign says it all: "Come here to eat well and cheaply." Frequented by raving capitalists. 4-course *menú* 450ptas. Open daily 1-4pm and 8-11pm.

Restaurante El Colomado, C. Arcos, 1 (tel. 33 76 74). You'll forget the decor, but remember the food. Try *Urta a la Roteña,* a fish dish prepared with tomatoes, peppers, and onion sauce (1000ptas). *Menú* 750ptas. Bar open Mon.-Sat. 8am-midnight, Sun. 8am-4:30pm; restaurant open Mon.-Sat. noon-4:30pm and 8-11:30pm, Sun. noon-4:30pm.

Pizzeria, Pl. Reyes Católicos. Outside tables sit beside the fountain. Limited selection of a la carte items, but reasonable prices. Pizzas 400-600ptas, omelettes 300ptas, sandwiches 300-400ptas.

Sights and Entertainment

Jerez's cache of *bodegas* (wine cellars) is its main drawing card. Mildly inebriated tour guides show you the sherry-making process from beginning to end. For most visitors, the highlight of the *bodega* comes with sampling more than enough of the free sherry to loosen eyeballs. The best time to visit is early September, when the annual bottling has just finished. Many of the *bodegas* close down for the harvest during August, so check with the tourist office. Maps showing the *bodegas'* locations are also available in many of the town's travel agencies. Group reservations for tours must be made at least one week in advance, so make sure to call ahead. Inquire at a travel agency or the tourist office for more complete listings.

Harveys of Bristol: C. Arcos, 53 (tel. 34 60 00). The only *bodegas* without a cover charge. No reservations required. English-speaking guide leads 2-hr. tour. Closed for the first 3 weeks of Aug.

Sandemán: C. Pizarro (tel. 33 11 00). Open Mon.-Fri. 9am-1pm. No reservations required.

Williams and Humbert, Ltd.: Nuño de Cañas, 1 (tel. 34 59 72). Open Mon.-Fri. 10:30am-1:30pm. Admission 280ptas. No reservations required.

González Byass: Manuel María González, 12 (tel. 34 00 00). Open Mon.-Fri. 11am-1pm. Admission 350ptas. Reservations required.

B. Domecq: San Ildefonso, 3 (tel. 33 19 00). Reservations required.

When you decide your liver needs a rest, go for a walk around town. Visit the monks in their sixteenth-century baroque **Iglesia de Santo Domingo** on C. Marques de Casa Arizon. (Open daily 8-11am and 7-9pm. Women prohibited to enter the monastery, and men must wear long pants.) From here, follow C. José Primo de Rivera south to the eleventh-century **Alcázar** fortress, the Moorish **Torre Octagóna** (Octagonal Tower), and the **Arab baths** of the Almohads. However, more interesting examples can be seen elsewhere in Spain. The **Zoologico Alberto Duran,** C. Taxdirt (tel. 34 33 97), is both a huge park and a zoo with botanical gardens, 144 species of animals, and 50 species of reptiles. (Open Tues.-Sun. 10:30am-6:30pm.)

Jerez also boasts some of Spain's top horse stables. Carthussian horses are bred here. From May 1 to 7, the Royal Andalusian School of Equestrian Art sponsors a **Feria del Caballo** (Horse Fair), featuring shows, carriage competitions, and races. The **Festival of Theatre, Music, and Dance** in August, celebrates flamenco dancing. Holy Week brings parades of beautiful statues, and during the second week in September, the town erupts in the **Fiestas de la Vendimia,** a celebration of the season's wines.

Arcos de la Frontera

A white labyrinth on a harsh promontory, **Arcos de la Frontera** seems an anomaly amid the soft, rolling fields of vines and sunflowers that surround the road from Jerez de la Frontera. The town is built on a giant spike undercut on three sides by the Guadalete River. The fascinating old city, a maze of alleyways, medieval ruins, and stone arches, has been declared a national historic monument. Its placid setting conceals a turbulent past when the town was once a formidable Muslim fortress, and later, a Christian garrison during the Reconquista.

Orientation and Practical Information

Arcos lies on the highway between Jerez (30km) and Antequera, accessible by bus from either city, as well as from Cádiz. To reach the center of town from the bus station, turn left on C. Corregidores and walk uphill to C. Josefa Morena. Continue uphill to Múñoz-Vásquez and turn right. Múñoz-Vásquez becomes Corredera after the rotunda, and that street leads you into the old quarter. Most of the town's restaurants are in the rotunda area, and the *pensiones* are off the **Corredera,** halfway up to the old quarter.

Tourist Office: C. Cuesta de. Belén (tel. 70 22 64), at the end of the Corredora. As you exit the bus station, turn left, left again at the end of the street; walk uphill on the Corredora 10-15 min. Open Mon.-Sat. 10am-2pm.

Post Office: C. Sevilla, 5 (tel. 70 15 60), in the new part of town. Open Mon.-Fri. 9am-2pm, Sat. 9am-1pm. **Telegrams:** Open Mon.-Fri. 9am-3pm, Sat. 9am-2pm. **Postal Code:** 11630.

Telephone Code: 956.

Bus Station: C. Corregidor (no phone), about a 15-min. walk downhill from the old quarter. To Jerez (every 15 min. 8am-7pm, 250ptas), Cádiz (5 per day, 2 on Sun., 400ptas), and Sevilla (2 per day). More frequent connections to Cádiz and other cities can be made in Jerez.

Taxis: Tel. 70 13 55 or 70 00 66.

Medical Emergency: Cruz Roja, (Red Cross) (tel. 70 03 55) or call 70 04 98. **Ambulance:** Tel. 70 05 55.

Police: Tel. 70 16 52.

Accommodations

The cheap lodgings in Arcos lie in the newer section of town. The Parador Nacional is the only hotel in the old quarter, and you'll have to empty your wallet to stay there.

Fonda Las Cuevas, C. Alta, 1, across the street and up from Banco de Vizcaya on the Corredera. Typical, white Andalusian home. Outdoor terrace filled with potted plants. Rooms are spartan but clean, many with lovely views. Singles 600ptas. Doubles 900ptas.

Fonda del Comercio, C. Debajo del Corral (tel. 70 00 57). Rooms open off a long hall with a high-beamed ceiling and antique furniture. Recently remodeled, all rooms have fresh paint, new wood furniture, and bright bedspreads. Singles 800ptas. Doubles 1500ptas.

Casa de Huéspedes Galvin, off the Corredera across from the Caja de Aborros de Ronda bank (tel. 70 05 54). Singles 1000ptas. Doubles 1600ptas. Primitive bath/shower 100ptas cold, 250ptas hot.

Food

You can chance upon some little bars in the old quarter, but most of the good eateries lie at the bottom end of the Corredera, by the rotunda.

Meson Camino del Rocio, C. Debajo del Corral, 8 (tel. 70 19 16). An Egyptian-Spanish couple serve the unexpected: Arab and Spanish dishes. Felafel and lamb shish kebab 400ptas. Andalusian *menús* 525-795ptas.

Cafe Bar El Faro, Debajo del Corral, 16 (tel. 70 00 14). A retreat with A/C and color TV that serves surprisingly cheap, filling meals. Try *filete de cerdo* (pork chop with fries, 400ptas). Large salad and beer 320ptas.

Freiduria la Parada, across the street from El Faro (tel. 70 07 02). More of a bar than a restaurant; there are no tables. Buy a bagful of *chocos* (fried squid) at 250ptas per ¼ kg. Open Mon.-Sat. 9am-midnight.

Sights

A walking tour of Arcos de la Frontera should begin in **Plaza del Cabildo,** a rectangular esplanade hanging over the cliff that suspends Arcos over the Guadalete River. With your back to the majestic vista of olive groves and low hills, you can see a privately-owned **Moorish castle** rising on the left and ahead the late Gothic facade of the **Iglesia de Santa María.** Built in 1732, the church's unique interior represents a melange of Gothic, Renaissance, and baroque styles. It houses a number of paintings and other art works including the resplendent baroque image of the *Virgen de las Nieves* (Virgin of the Snows), the patron saint of the town. (Due to recent robberies, the church is closed. Make arrangements to see it by calling the tourist office, which schedules tours, or by attending the daily, 7:30pm Mass. No photography, shorts, or tank tops allowed.) From here, wander through the twisting street and alleys of the old quarter taking special note of the heraldic emblems over the entrances of what used to be medieval *palacios,* or noblemen's dwellings. On the northern edge of the old quarter lies another late Gothic structure, the **Iglesia de San Pedro,** which was built on the site of an old Arab fortress. Inside, baroque works by Murillo, Zurbarián, and Rivera, as well as two canvases by Pacheco are among the pieces on display. (Closed due to thefts. Call the tourist office to make arrangements or attend the daily, 7:30pm Mass.) The tourist office can also make arrangements for you to tour local convents built between 1529 and 1650.

When the monuments start to all look the same, give yourself a break at **Parador de Arcos Nacional,** Pl. del Cabildo (tel 70 05 00), in the heart of the old quarter. Sit on the patio, order a drink, and enjoy the spectacular views without having to pay the ridiculous guest fees. **Mirador de Abades,** a large outdoor terrace, also offers enjoyable views. For local *artesanía* (arts and crafts), visit **Galeria del Arte Arx-Arcis** on C. Magdalena Amaya (tel. 70 06 81), which exhibits and sells local paintings, pottery, and leatherwork. (Open Mon.-Fri. 10am-2pm and 4-7pm.) On C. Maldonado, you can visit a thirteenth-century *alfombra* (rug) factory and observe the careful weaving on a loom from the same period.

If you are continuing east of Arcos along the *Ruta de los Pueblos Blancos* (Route of the White Villages), stop for a dip in the fresh-water lake at **Bornos,** another hillside hamlet. At the foot of the village, a tributary of the Guadalete River widens into a cool basin. To get here, climb down the hill and turn left on the dirt road; at the very end a bar is cleverly disguised as a straw hut. Swim only in the area directly in front of the bar, since other parts of the lake have dangerous whirlpools.

Ronda

The German poet Rainer Maria Rilke, whose residence is commemorated by a statue, settled in Ronda in search of inspiration. He chose well: The town is perched on a rocky massif split by a thousand-foot gorge that channels the Guadalevín River. Ronda's old city is separated from the new part by the gorge **El Tajo,** a natural fortress formed by an earthquake, now graced by remnants of the civilizations that thrived here. The city's halves are connected by three bridges: one Roman, one Moorish, and one known as the "new bridge" dating from 1735. The last was as much of an architectural achievement for its time as the Brooklyn Bridge—one head architect died in the collapse of a scaffold, while another is said to have committed suicide in order never to have to build another such bridge in his life.

Ronda's history runs as deep as El Tajo. Pliny and Ptolemy mention it as Arunda (literally "surrounded by mountains"), a southern enclave of the Celts. During Muslim occupation, Al Mutadid ibn Abbad annexed the city for Sevilla by asphyxiating the former lord in his bath. Fernando's troops conquered the city in 1485, as did Napoleonic troops in 1808. Ernest Hemingway was a frequent visitor, and most recently, Orson Welles's ashes were buried on a bull farm outside of town.

Orientation and Practical Information

About 125km southeast of Sevilla, 60km northwest of Marbella, 75km west of Antequera, and 98km north of Algeciras, Ronda consists of three district neighborhoods: **La Ciudad,** the old city, which developed around the Arab fortress; **El Mercadillo,** the new commercial district across the gorge; and **Barrio de San Francisco,** a small residential neighborhood on the other side of the old city. **Carrera Espinel,** the main *paseo* of the city, runs perpendicular to **Calle Jerez,** a long street that extends east-west and connects the old and new parts of the city at the **Puente Nuevo.**

Both the train and bus stations are on the western side of the Mercadillo. To reach the tourist office and the center of town, walk along Avda. de Andalucía until just before its end, take a left on Calle Jevez, and follow this past the Alameda del Tajo (city park) and Plaza de Toros to reach **Plaza de España.**

Tourist Office: Pl. de España, 1 (tel. 87 12 72). Staff knowledgeable about Ronda, but little help for surrounding towns. Open Mon.-Fri. 10am-2:30pm and additional hours if staff is available.

Post Office: C. Virgen de la Paz, 20 (tel. 87 25 57). Open for stamps and Lista de Correos Mon.-Fri. 9am-2pm, Sat. 9am-1pm. **Telegrams:** Open Mon.-Sat. 8:30am-8:30pm. **Postal Code:** 39400.

Telephones: At the post office. **Telephone Code:** 952.

Train Station: Avda. Andalucía (tel. 87 16 73). To Sevilla (2 per day, 4½ hr., 1050ptas), Algeciras (6 per day, 2 hr., 525ptas), Málaga (2 per day, 2 hr., 650ptas), and Granada (2 per day, 4 hr., 860ptas). Change at Bobadilla for destinations other than Algeciras. **Ticket office,** C. Infantes, 20 (tel. 87 16 62). Open Mon.-Fri. 10am-2pm and 5-7pm, Sat. 10am-1:30pm.

Bus Station: Avda. Concepción García Redondo, 2. **Empresa los Amarillos** (tel. 87 22 64). To Sevilla (4 per day, 3 hr., 850ptas) and Málaga (2 per day, 770ptas). **Empresa Comes** (tel. 87 19 92). To Jerez de la Frontera (4 per day, 800ptas) and Cádiz (2 per day, 920ptas). **Costa del Sol** (tel. 87 22 62) to Marbella (6 per day, 560ptas). **Ferron Coin** handles most local connections, also cheapest route to Málaga (3 per day, 490ptas).

Car Rental: Ignacio, C. Lorenzo Borrego. Also a branch at C. Los Remedios, 26.

Hitchiking: To Sevilla, Jerez, and Cádiz, follow C. Sevilla out of the Mercadillo. To Granada, walk up Carrera Espirel and take the third right after the tree-lined Avda. Martínez Stein. To Málaga and the Costa del Sol, take the highway leading downhill out of Barrio de San Francisco.

Baggage Check: At the bus station. 50ptas. Open daily 8am-7:45pm.

Laundromat: Lavandería Andaluza, C. Almendra, 23. 150ptas per item. Open Mon.-Fri. 9:30am-2pm and 5-8:30pm, Sat. 9:30am-2pm.

Medical Services: First Aid (tel. 87 97 73). **Clinica Comarcal,** Carretera del Bulgo (tel. 87 15 40).

Police: C. Espinel, 39 (tel. 87 13 70). **Emergency:** Tel. 091.

Accommodations

Almost all accommodations are in the Mercadillo, along the streets running perpendicular to Carrera Espinel. Since a lot of the tourist crowd are daytrippers from the Costa del Sol, finding a place should be difficult only during the Feria de Ronda in September.

Fonda La Española, C. José Aparicio, 3 (tel. 87 10 52), on a side street around the corner from Turismo. An incredible deal. Sparkling clean place with spacious rooms, modern bathrooms, and a sundeck view of El Tajo. 750ptas per person.

Hostal Morales, C. Sevilla, 51 (tel. 87 15 38), near the intersection with C. Lauria. Kept spotless by friendly management. Well-lighted rooms with a pleasant, tiled courtyard and fresh woodwork. Modern bathrooms. Singles 1000ptas. Doubles 1800ptas.

Hostal Ronda Sol, C. Cristo, 11 (tel. 87 44 97), near the intersection with C. Sevilla. All-new wood furnishings. Worth the bit of extra dough. Singles 1000ptas. Doubles 2000ptas.

Fonda Nuestra Señora de Lourdes, C. Sevilla, 16 (tel. 87 10 32), right off Carrera Espirel. Huge Virgin in courtyard. Very quiet but somewhat run-down, so be selective about your room and make sure the neighboring bathroom functions. 600ptas per person. Showers 200ptas. Crowded dining room with 575ptas menú.

Pensión La Purísma, C. Sevilla, 10 (tel. 87 10 50), next to the above. Modern bathrooms, airy hallways, and solid beds. A bargain if you can get a room away from street. Singles 800ptas. Doubles 1400ptas. Showers 200ptas.

Hostal El Tajo, C. Cruz Verde, 7 (tel. 87 62 38), off Carrera Espinel. Very clean place, comfortable rooms. Your tired feet will love the elevator. Singles with shower 1700ptas, with bath 2000ptas. Doubles with shower 2700ptas, with bath 3300ptas.

Food

Ronda possesses a number of good, inexpensive restaurants, almost all offering a *menú* or *platos combinados* for 550-600ptas. Most eateries are conveniently located near the center of town around **Plaza España.**

Snack bars and bakeries line **Carrera Espinel,** near Pl. de España. For dessert, nibble a sumptuous pastry at **Gestoria Harillo,** at #36, or sample the delicious ice cream at **Heladería La Ibense,** next door. **Café Alba** at #44 has three-foot *churros* (delicious curlicues of fried dough) in the morning.

Ronda's well-stocked **mercado** is near the end of Carrera Espinel on Avda. Martínez Stein. (Open Mon.-Fri. 9am-2pm and 4-7pm, Sat. 9am-noon.)

Cervecería Marisquería "El Patio," C. Espinel, 100 (tel. 87 10 15). As the name suggests, the patio here is an attraction; it overflows with flowers. The perks continue in the colorful dining room. *Menú* 600ptas. Open Thurs.-Tues. noon-4pm and 8pm-1am.

Las Cañas, Avda. Duque de la Victoria, 2 (no phone), off Pl. del Socorro. Excellent food, reasonable prices, and local flavor. *Callos* (diced tripe and chickpeas in tomato sauce) 200ptas. *Platos combinados* 275-500ptas. *Menú* 500ptas.

Todo Natural, C. Marina, 1, on a passage off Pl. del Socorro. A vegetarian delight: fresh vegetables, brown bread, *muesli,* hummus. Large variety salad plate or *menú* with dish of the day (both around 400ptas). A trip to Ronda is not complete without the orgasmic chocolate and orange mousse (150ptas). Open Mon.-Sat. noon-10:30pm.

Mesón Santiago, C. Marina, 3 (tel. 87 15 59), just off Pl. del Socorro. Delicious food at moderate prices. *Platos combinados* 675ptas. *Menú* 850ptas. Sit on a vine-covered terrace in the summer or by a cozy fireplace in winter. Open daily 1-4pm.

Cafetería Doña Pepa, C. Marina, 5 (no phone), next to the above and run by the same management. The same food at much cheaper prices. No-frills atmosphere. *Platos combinados* 300-475ptas. *Menú* 650ptas. Save room for *flan de la casa* (225ptas). Open daily for dinner.

Sights

Ronda's most dramatic sight, the precipitous gorge chiseled from the rocky Guadalevín River, is spanned by three stone bridges. The most impressive of these, the eighteenth-century **Puente Nuevo,** is suspended nearly 100m high and connects the city's old and new quarters. Clamber down the stairway for a spectacular upward view of the cliffside houses. To the left across the bridge, a colonnaded walkway leads to the **Casa del Rey Moro** (House of the Moorish King), which, notwithstanding its name and Moorish facade, dates only from the eighteenth century. From the gardens in back, 365 steps descend to *la mina,* a spring that originally served as the town's water supply. The 400 Christian prisoners who performed the arduous task of drawing water were turned over to Fernando el Católico when the city was recaptured. (Interior closed for restoration indefinitely.) Across the street, behind a forged iron balcony and a stone facade portraying four Peruvian Incas, stands the eighteenth-century **Palacio del Marqués de Salvatierra.** The palace floor sparkles with ceramic tiles. (Open Mon.-Wed. and Fri.-Sat. 11am-2pm and 4-6pm, Sun. 11am-2pm. Tour every ½-hr., minimum 6 people. Admission 150ptas.)

Cobbled steps descend from the turn-off to the Puente San Miguel to Ronda's **Arab baths.** The roofs are punctured with star-shaped holes and capped with skylights, making the baths look more like an extraterrestrial vehicle than a set of medieval washing chambers. Surprisingly, however, you'll find the fourteenth-century saunas still functioning. For now you'll have to bathe elsewhere; they're currently undergoing restoration. Enter through the unmarked brown door under the dilapidated plaster wall at the bottom of the street; a yellow sign says "Ministerio de Cultura Monumento en Restauración." (Open Tues.-Sun. 10am-2pm and 4-7pm. Free.)

To the right on the way back up the cobbled steps appear Ronda's second and third bridges: the seventeenth-century **Puente Viejo** (rebuilt over an earlier Arab bridge) and the Roman **Puente San Miguel.** Calle Marquis de Salvatierra leads into Ronda's old quarter. Follow it to the end to reach the **Iglesia de Santa María,** an impressive cathedral crowned by a Renaissance belfry. Just inside the entrance, a small arch, all that remains of a former mosque on the site, frames nuns decorated with Nazarite arabesques and inscriptions. Inside the cathedral is a moving *Virgen de los Dólores* by Martínez Montañez; the rest of the interior is unremarkable. (Open daily 10am-7pm. Knock on the door and the caretaker will admit you for 50ptas.) The balcony on the tower side of the church overlooks Plaza de la Ciudad, former parade grounds of the castle in which bullfights were held. Back toward the new city, the **Minaret of San Sebastián** is part of a former mosque converted into a church after Ronda was recaptured in 1485. Nearby, toward the Puente Nuevo, sits the **Palacio Mondragon,** formerly owned by Don Fernando Valenzuela (not of the Los Angeles Dodgers), one of Carlos III's ministers. The baroque facade, bracketed by two Mudéjar towers, hides fifteenth-century Arab mosaics. (Open daily 8am-2pm; in off-season daily 8am-3pm.)

Across the gorge in the Mercadillo stands Ronda's **Plaza de Toros,** vying with that of Sevilla to be considered the heart of bullfighting in Spain. Ronda's is definitely older, inaugurated in 1784. The **Museo Taurino** inside can take you through the history of two dynasties of Ronda: that of Pedro Romero, inventor of the *muleta* (red cape) and founder of modern bullfighting, and Cayetano Ordóñez, immortalized as the role model for the matador in Hemingway's *The Sun Also Rises.* (Open daily 10am-8pm; Oct.-May daily 10am-2pm and 4-6pm. Admission 200ptas. Tickets sold in souvenir shop to the right of the entrance.)

Perhaps the most pleasant and certainly the coolest place in town is the green and shady **Alameda del Tajo** on C. Virgen de la Paz. Complete with drinking fountains, flowery gardens, street lamps, and a view of the gorge, the park houses ducks, swans, canaries, doves, roosters, and pheasants. A park with a better view of the gorge is the **Paseo de Blas Infante,** at the bottom of C. Espinel by the bullring.

Entertainment

Possibly the best place to enjoy an Andalusian sunset is from the Puente Nuevo, where the cliffs glow a soothing orange and red. Ronda's nightlife is similarly calm, mostly families and friends sitting in the Alameda or going for a *paseo* down Carrera Espinel. Some excitement can be found in the discos and pubs near Pl. de España. Try **Café Tenorio,** C. Tenorio, 1, to the right of the bridge in the old quarter; it plays rock music at night in a rustic bar with an exquisite pool table. Farther into the old city, the basement of the Iglesia de Santa María—of all places—becomes a lively tavern called **Las Catacumbas.** (Open only at night, when godfearing folk have gone home.) **Pub Galera XXI,** C. de las Tiendas, 12, has live jazz nightly. The place doesn't usually fill up until around 11:30pm.

In early September, crowds flock to **Plaza de Toros,** where *corridas goyescas* (bullfights in costumes *a la Goya*) and flamenco contests are held as part of the **Feria de Ronda** celebrations. The **Corpus Christi** festivities (beginning the Thurs. after the 8th Sun. after Easter) revolve around the Alameda del Tajo and Calle Virgen de la Paz.

Near Ronda

Cuevas de la Pileta

The Cuevas de la Pileta is a subterranean, prehistoric museum complete with stalactites, stalagmites, bones, and paleolithic cave paintings. The caves are located about 25km west of Ronda along the road to Ubrique. Discovered in 1905 by José Bullón Lobato, grandfather of the present owner, the caves extend for nearly a mile into the side of a stony cliff. They are thought to have been inhabited 25,000 years ago. Traces of the oldest pottery in Europe were found within. The cave interiors are both spooky and spectacular. Rock formations and dripping waters come together in vaguely recognizable shapes, here resembling a *Venus de Milo,* there a gorilla. Your guide will probably conjure up fanciful names for the natural sculptures. The chambers within soar to heights over 20m. Look closely at the prehistoric markings and paintings of animals on the cave walls. The highlight of the expedition is the "Chamber of the Fish," named after a strange enormous drawing. Although gas lanterns are provided, bring your own flashlight if possible. Dress warmly—even in the summer the caves are a natural refrigerator—and avoid wearing sandals. The tour takes over an hour.

To reach the caves from Ronda, take the train to Benojáon (4 per day, 100ptas—the 6:10am is highly preferable to the next one at 11:35am, since it will spare you the midday heat on the hike) and prepare yourself for the grueling 7km uphill hike to the cave entrance. From the station, take the wide dirt road leading uphill to town. At the rotary in the middle of town, bear right. Cut back uphill just outside of town on the road to the caves—it's only 4.5km from here. Ask for directions in town, since signposts are few. Drivers should take highway C-339 north (Carretera a Sevilla heading out of the Mercadillo). About 13km out of town is the turn-off to Benojaón and the caves, in front of an abandoned bar-restaurant. The road winds through the town of Montajaque on its 13km route to Benojaón; the turn-off to the caves is just outside of town. Don't leave valuables in your car during the tour. Whether afoot or on wheels, the approach through the barren stone massifs of the Serrania de Ronda is stupendous. Upon arrival, climb to the mouth of the caves to see if the guide is inside or if others are waiting. If no one is about, head down to the farm below to rouse the owner, who will make appropriate arrangements. (Open daily 9am-2pm and 4-7pm. Admission 200ptas.)

Serrania de Ronda

The Serrania de Ronda is a rocky mountain range south of Ronda that extends east to west. With the exception of the area between Ronda and Ubrique, where wind and rain have created a polymorphic landscape, the terrain is composed of mountainous brown rock and sparse vegetation. Spend a few days exploring by car or by bus the mountain roads that fan out from Ronda.

Of the narrow, winding roads that traverse the range, the one from Ronda south to San Pedro de Alcántara is most spectacular: The southern stretch climbs up along a fantastic coast overlooking the valley of the Guadalmedina River. Other routes are worth exploring as well. The highway toward Málaga features the **Mirador de Guardia Forestal** lookout point. The road toward Jerez and Sevilla winds among the Serrania foothills, passing through the lovely village of **Zahara de la Sierra,** dominated by the imposing **Iglesia de Santa María de la Mesa.** Highway C-341 toward Algeciras offers not only beautiful scenery but three delightful *pueblos blancos:* **Benadolid,** with its handsome, cliffside Moorish castle; **Algatocín,** which sports an eighteenth-century stone bell tower; and **Gaucín,** wrapped around a giant rock scattered with the ruins of a Moorish castle. On clear days the North African coast is visible.

Olvera and Setenil de las Bodegas

Majestic, moving, magical—these words only begin to describe the beauty of **Olvera,** about an hour outside Ronda. Washing up a hill crested by a twelfth-century Moorish castle, this wave of white houses breaks upon the green and gold of the surrounding farmlands. Rows of houses with orange roofs sweep down the hillside, while two belfries tower above. Horses and mules are still popular means of transport here.

The key to the **Castillo Arabe** can be procured from the caretaker, María, who lives on Pl. de la Iglesia, 2, directly to the left of the castle gate. She also has the keys to the seventeenth-century church across the plaza (donations expected). Climb to the top of the castle for a fabulous view of the whitewashed town set against acres of olive groves. The best place to stay—and you may want to stay for a long time—is **Pensión Maqueda,** C. Carbarios, 35 (tel. 13 07 33). The sundeck and glass hallway overlook the town's rooftops. (750ptas per person.) **Pensión Olid,** Llana, 13 (tel. 13 01 02), offers immaculate rooms, friendly management, and an architecturally remarkable shower curtain. (Singles 950ptas. Doubles 1800ptas. Showers 150ptas.) **Bar-Restaurante Manola,** in Pl. de Andaluciá between the hotels and the castle, serves a *menú* for 650ptas and a la carte dishes for 500-700ptas.

To or from Ronda, the bus (5 per day, 150ptas) will stop at the village of **Setenil de las Bodegas,** perched on a mountain marked by numerous caves. The first inhabitants of Setenil were troglodytes; facades were added later to the grottos, and then free-standing houses were erected. Today, long rows of chalk-white houses built into the hillsides under common rock roofs mingle with new constructions. The village stretches along a dramatic gorge cut by the waters of the sparkling Guadalporcun River. The riverside streets are called *cuevas* (caves) because they burrow under the gorge's cliff walls, creating long, covered passageways. **Cuevas Sombra, Cuevas del Sol,** and **Cuevas de Cabrerizos** are among the most striking. Climb up the huge rock to the fifteenth-century **Iglesia de la Incarnacíon** for a marvelous view of the village below. You'll find an equally splendid panorama along with the best fare in town at **Bar Las Flores,** at the top of the other side of the village from the church. Try the broiled lamb and fries (325ptas). In August, fairs and folkdancing enliven the streets.

About a half-hour east of Olvera and Setenil, the unspoiled village of **El Gastor** is surrounded by rocky ravines and a ruined dolmen known by the villagers as the **Sepulcro del Gigante** (Giant's Tomb). The community expresses its botanical passion annually in the wonderful **Corpus Christi** celebrations (beginning the Thurs. following the 8th Sun. after Easter), during which streets and buildings are carpeted with greenery. The party rages all day.

Ferron-Coin buses serve Olvera, Setenil, and El Gastor, but they are not too kind to the would-be daytripper. The buses stop in Setenil. Drivers should start out from Ronda on Calle Sevilla to reach C-339 north. To reach Olvera and Setenil, you can take either the turn-off for El Gastor or the longer route by the dramatic outcrop of the village of **Zahara.**

Antequera

Broiling silently in a valley below a Moorish fortress, the whitewashed houses and occasional church towers of Antequera give way to the foothills of the Torcal Mountains. Although named by the Romans, civilization here began much earlier—*dólmenes* (funerary chambers built from rock slabs) constructed 5000 years ago dot the outskirts of town. Antequera is chiefly of interest as a base for forays into the surrounding mountains and expeditions to the spectacular Chorro Gorge, but a sunset captured through the mountains from the top of the Moorish fort might change your view of this peaceful town.

Orientation and Practical Information

Antequera lies at the crossroads of Córdoba, Granada, Sevilla, and Málaga (rail travelers, however, will notice that RENFE has made Bobadilla the major switching point). The train station leaves you a 10-minute hike up a long, slow, shadeless hill from town. The bus station sits atop a neighboring hill. If you don't like climbing with luggage on sweltering days, arrive by bus and leave by train—or just take a cab (about 200ptas; agree on the fare before you get in). **Plaza San Sebastián** is the town center. The main street, **Calle Infante Don Fernando,** leads west to **Alameda de Andalucía.**

Tourist Office: Pl. Coso Viejo (tel. 84 18 27), just inside the Museo Municipal, off C. Nájera. Map is helpful, staff is not. No information about surrounding countryside. Open Tues.-Fri. 10am-1:30pm, Sat. 10am-1pm, Sun. 11am-1pm.

Post Office: C. de Nájera (tel. 22 20 00), down the street from the tourist office. Open Mon.-Fri. 9am-2pm, Sat. 9am-1pm. **Postal Code:** 29200.

Train Station: Avda. de la Estación (tel. 84 23 30). To Sevilla (2 per day, 3 hr., 875ptas), Algeciras (1 per day, 4 hr., 920ptas), and Granada (3 per day, 2 hr., 560ptas). Take any train not going to Granada to Bobadilla for a number of connections (60ptas).

Bus Station: Paseo Garcia del Olmo, near the Parador Nacional. To Granada (4 per day, 760ptas), Málaga (3 per day, 440ptas), Sevilla (6 per day, 1355ptas), Córdoba (2 per day, 1120ptas), and the Bobadilla train station (5 per day Mon.-Sat., 105ptas).

Hospital: Hospital Municipal San Juan de Dios, C. Infante Don Fernando (tel. 84 44 11).

Police: Municipal, Tel. 84 11 91. **Emergency:** Tel. 091.

Accommodations

Most establishments lie between the museum and the market. All are inexpensive, and most serve meals.

Pensión Toril, C. Toril, 5 (tel. 84 31 84), off Pl. de Abastos. Clean, well-lighted rooms with windows. Charming English-speaking proprietor will tell you everything you want to know about the area. Sun deck. Singles 700ptas. Doubles 1300ptas.

Hostal Madrona, C. Calzada, 31 (tel. 84 00 14), down the hill from the above. Clean and well kept. Friendly management. Singles 850ptas. Doubles 1600ptas.

Hostal Manzanito, C. Calvo Sotelo, 5 (tel. 84 10 23), on Pl. San Sebastián. Clean and central. All rooms, some newly renovated, have showers. Mosaic walls and odd layout make the place mazelike. Singles 1060-1410ptas. Doubles 1908-2756ptas.

Food

Located mostly in *hostales,* the restaurants serve a variety of Andalusian specialties for reasonable prices. Stop by the **mercado** on Pl. de Abasto for succulent *queso de cabra* (goat's milk cheese). (Open daily 8am-2pm.)

Pensión Toril, C. Toril, 5 (tel. 84 31 84). A local favorite with larger-than-life *menús* (500ptas) and generous drinks (50ptas). Open daily 1-4pm and 8-10pm.

Restaurante la Madrona, C. Calzada, 31 (tel. 84 00 14), under the hotel. Excellent fare, with a blaring TV at lunch. Limited *menú* (550ptas), but affordable a la carte dishes. *Gazpacho con guarnición* 200ptas. Open daily 11am-4pm and 8-11pm.

Restaurante Chaplin, San Augustín, 3 (tel. 84 30 34), off C. Infante Don Fernando. Huge terrace and outdoor bar. Extensive wine list. When you see the bartender, you'll realize where the name comes from. *Platos combinados* at the bar 350-400ptas, *menú* in the restaurant 825ptas.

Sights

Antequera's three ancient **dolmen caves** are the oldest and best-preserved prehistoric tombs in Europe. Crudely cut slabs of rock form the entrance, antechamber (where all the deceased's possessions were stored for the afterlife), and burial chamber. The actual remains and artifacts are kept in museums in Málaga and Sevilla. **Cueva de Menga** dates from 2500 B.C.E. Its roof is a gargantuan 180-ton monolith, supposedly dragged over 5 miles to the burial site. The three figures engraved on the chamber walls are typical of Mediterranean Bronze Age art. The elongated **Cueva de Viera,** of 2000 B.C.E. and discovered in 1905, is of equally monstrous proportions. Bring a flashlight to explore the dark recesses, or ask to borrow the caretaker's. The interior walls of **Cueva de Romeral,** which date from 1800 B.C.E., were constructed with small, flat stones in order to create the circular walls and domed ceiling. The entrance was reconstructed in 1940—note the two different types of rock.

To reach the Menga and Viera caves, follow the signs towards Granada until the edge of town (a 10-min. walk from the market), or catch the bus (30ptas) and watch for a small sign on C. Granada next to the gas station. To reach the Romeral cave from the Menga and Viera caves, continue on the *carretera* to Granada for another kilometer or so. Just past Almacenes Gómez, the last warehouse after the flower-lined intersection, a gravel road cuts left and runs into a narrow path bordered by 30-foot-high fir trees. Take this path across the train tracks to reach the cave. (All caves open daily 9:30am-1pm and 3:30-7:30pm. Free. Small tips appreciated.)

Back in town, all that remains of the **Arab Castillo Santa María** are two towers and the wall stretching between them. Climb to the top of the wall to soak up the beautiful view of farmland capped by the soaring promontory of a neighboring mountain. The hedges of the fortress gardens, trimmed into exotic shapes, act as surrogates for the castle's original interior. Down the hill along a shady, cypress-lined stairway is the Renaissance **Iglesia de Santa María.** (Open only during Mass on Sun. and holidays.) Near the edge of town past Pl. del Carmen, the **Convento del Carmen's** interior is enclosed in crumbling walls. Mudéjar woodwork covers the nave's ceiling, leading to three impressive baroque altars that compete for attention. The convent epitomizes the baroque aspiration to infuse movement into stationary art, but unfortunately it's closed for renovations. Try knocking on the side door and persuading the priest who answers to let you in.

Near Antequera

Torcal Mountains

The spooky landscape of the Torcal Mountains resembles a science fiction rendition of purgatory: A gigantic and desolate rock garden of wind-sculpted boulders encroaches from all sides. The towering pillars seem to be a tribe of frozen people who might at any moment thaw and begin waving their jagged granite appendages.

The central peak of **El Torcal** dominates the horizon, soaring to a height of 1369m. Close to the summit, two circular trails await your well-shod feet. The path marked with yellow arrows takes about an hour and is 2½ km long; the path marked with red arrows takes over two hours and is 4½ km long. Both feature spectacular vistas and rock formations. Beware that the trails are hot in summer (though sandals are inadvisable) and cold in winter. Don't be deterred if the summit is smothered in clouds. The trails' extra-galactic ambience is enhanced when its weird rock formations are shrouded in mist.

Both paths begin and end 16km from Antequera, at the *refugio* at the base of the mountain. Two-thirds of the 16km can be covered by bus: From the station in Antequera, take any bus headed for Villanueva de la Concepción, and ask the driver to let you off at the turn-off for El Torcal (110ptas). Buses leave Antequera only at 1pm and 6pm; the return bus leaves Villanueva de la Concepción at 3pm. Spend the night on the mountain or try hitching back to Antequera. Hitchhiking back can be easier if you make friends with tourists in the bar of the *refugio*. (Open in summer at the owner's whim.) If this fails, descend the mountain to the road. There are no towns or turnoffs before Antequera, so anyone heading east is going all the way.

Chorro Gorge

In a country of remarkable geological formations, the Chorro Gorge, 70km southwest of Antequera, is one of Spain's premier natural wonders. Suspended above a clear, green river, a raised passageway clings to the edge of a towering cliff wall that forms the narrow partition of one of Europe's largest limestone massifs. Even more amazing than the physical proportions of the gorge is the extent to which it is neglected by travelers. True, the gorge is difficult to reach, the entrance to the walkway hard to find, and the route somewhat dangerous; those susceptible to vertigo or frightened of walking through functioning train tunnels are guaranteed to be scared stiff. But if none of this dampens your appetite, bring sturdy footwear (and some rope, if possible) and prepare for one of the adventures of your life.

Finding the safer part of the **Camino del Rey,** the walkway through the gorge, is a bit tricky. Half of the walkway is unsturdy, full of holes, and liable to collapse at any moment. The other half is accessible only via narrow, forbidding train tunnels and bridges. Fortunately, the prudent search undertaken with the *Guía RENFE* in hand takes you through some of the more beautiful scenery this planet has to offer.

The train station overlooks a modern dam complex, fed by water issuing from the slit of the gorge, also visible from the station. The bartender at the station can tell you a number of ways to hike the 2km to the gorge, but the easiest route starts along the gravel road leading up from the station. Cut off onto the path up the steps between two houses. The path turns to gravel; take the downhill split after the last of the eight-odd houses in town to follow a winding construction road up the hill to the train tracks. Follow the tracks through a short tunnel, a concrete bridge, and another tunnel to reach the outermost side of the gorge. On the other side of an iron bridge, the dilapidated end of the Camino del Rey begins, but the suspended path soon crumbles away.

To safely enter the widest end of the gorge, follow the tracks through a short series of tunnels until you can see, at the base of the gorge, a peaceful meadow next to a wide and deep section of luminescent green water, a wonderful spot for a picnic or dip. Several paths down are on the other side of the next tunnel, whose opening rock-wall face is a favorite for intermediate to advanced rock climbers. Skirt the edge of the next bridge and tunnel by the old signal post to catch a glimpse of the natural wonders to come—the foot bridge to the safe half of the walkway is at the end of this last tunnel, at the start of the gorge's narrowing. Be extremely careful when crossing: The bridge, though sturdy, is only about 4 feet wide, and the wind can gust so violently through this 100-foot dropoff that it can hit the second harmonic on an open bottle top.

The *camino* is extremely dilapidated in spots, and it lacks handrails in more spots. It is reasonably safe if treated with respect. Large groups should spread out to avoid overburdening the platforms. If you have rope, tie it around each person's waist as a security measure. This surviving portion of the walkway proceeds through the most breathtaking part of the gorge. Amorphous masses of rock, sculpted by water and wind, poise 300 feet over the trickling stream at bottom. Near the end, a staircase with green railings leads down for a better view of the fish swimming at the bottom. The path ends at a small power station at the mouth of the gorge, a two-hour hike from the train station.

Public transport schedules make it difficult to spend a full day at El Chorro. From Antequera, take the 6:15am bus toward Málaga (Mon.-Fri.) and get off early in Alora (200ptas). Then take the 9:20am train from Alora to El Chorro (60ptas). The return train to Antequera (with a change in Bobadilla) leaves El Chorro at 6:32pm (175ptas). Late risers can spend a short afternoon in the near end of the gorge by taking the 2:42pm train from Antequera (220ptas).

Drivers following signs to El Chorro will reach the dam by the train station. To reach the *camino* at the other end of the gorge, follow the signs for 8km to the **Pantano de Galtanejo.** You'll come to a pair of artificial reservoirs next to the mouth of the gorge, near the shimmering lake of **Conda de Guadalhorce.** Just before the highway reaches the reservoirs, it passes through a rock-hewn tunnel. The dirt road leading off the right immediately before the tunnel leads to a small power station by the mouth of the gorge. A footpath leads from the left of the locked entrance to the station, then to the right away from the small dam, and finally to one extreme of the Camino del Rey.

The nearest town to El Chorro is tiny **Alora,** 13km away. If you're stuck in the area, the only inexpensive lodgings are available at a nameless **pensión,** C. Camino Nuevo, 1. (750ptas per person.) The best place to eat, **Bar La Reja,** C. Soto Mayor, 11, near the fountain in the main square, serves a delicious meal for about 650ptas.

Granada

> Give him alms, woman
> for there is nothing in life, nothing,
> so sad as to be blind in Granada.
> —*Francisco de Icaza*

As the Moors retreated from the Christian Reconquista, they concentrated their efforts on building up Granada, the capital of their southernmost Iberian stronghold. They constructed layers of protective fortification and made the area as lavish as possible for the multitude of Muslim refugees still on the peninsula. After King Boabdil surrendered the city's keys in 1492, the Catholic monarchs had much of the lower city—and all the mosques—burned, but the Spanish Renaissance replaced

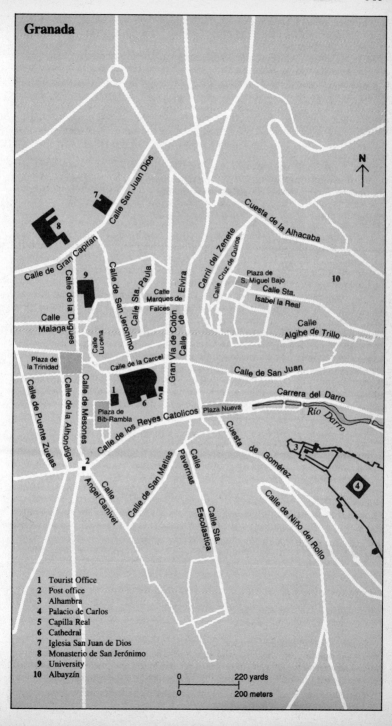

Granada

1   Tourist Office
2   Post office
3   Alhambra
4   Palacio de Carlos
5   Capilla Real
6   Cathedral
7   Iglesia San Juan de Dios
8   Monasterio de San Jerónimo
9   University
10   Albayzín

0   220 yards
0   200 meters

this lost beauty with towering, ornate monuments. The hills overlooking the city remained relatively unscathed. Sprawled across one today sits the Alhambra, perhaps Spain's most famous attraction. The intricate design and elaborate architecture of this complex benefited most from Granada's expenditures during its last couple hundred years of Moorish control.

Other prominent signs of Granada's Arab ancestry lie on two neighboring hills across the Darro River. On one sits the ancient Arab quarter, a maze of Moorish houses and twisting alleys known as **Albayzín;** this is the best-preserved Arab settlement in Spain and the only part of the Muslim city that escaped destruction during the Reconquest. On the other hill, Sacromonte, are the footpaths of the Gypsy quarter and, higher up, its cactus-trimmed caves. The remains of Arab city walls dot the top of the hill.

Spanish university students have adopted Granada since the time of Yusef I, and made it one of the liveliest provincial capitals, equaled only by Salamanca and Santiago for the prominence of its student community.

Orientation and Practical Information

The center of Granada is **Plaza Nueva,** framed by a handful of handsome Renaissance buildings. The surrounding group of hotels and restaurants range from the economical to the astronomical. Pl. Nueva is just north of Pl. de Isabel la Católica, which sits at the intersection of the city's two main commercial arteries, **Gran Vía de Colón** and **Calle de los Reyes Católicos.**

Municipal buses (50ptas, book of 10 320ptas) run to nearly all areas of town; bus #11 connects a number of major streets, including Carretera de Madrid, where hitchhikers can pick it up,; the train station; all bus stations; and the town center. From RENFE and all buses except Alsina Graells, you can also walk into town by following Avda. Calvo Sotelo to Gran Vía de Colón and turning right (15-20 min.). From Alsina Graells, make a right on Camino de Ronda and a left 3 blocks later onto C. Recogidas, which runs into C. Reyes Católicos at Puerta Real. A shuttle bus (175ptas) connects Granada to the airport. Since the Alhambra, Albayzín, and Sacromonte hills are all near each other and the town center, the best way to get from one to another is on foot. Avoid the small streets at the foot of the Albayzín northeast of Pl. Nueva after dark.

Tourist Office: C. de Libreros, 2 (tel. 22 10 22 or 22 59 90), in a passage between the southwest corner of the cathedral and Pl. Bib-Rambla. Everything you could ever want to know is posted on the bulletin boards in the window when the office is closed. Cramped and crowded, but patient, multilingual staff answers all questions. Open Mon.-Fri. 10am-1pm and 4-7pm, Sat. 10am-1pm. This office is scheduled to move sometime in 1989. If no one is here, call the Patronato, Pl. Mariana Pineda, 10 (tel. 22 59 59). Ignore the location marked on the government's official city brochure; no office has been there for years.

Student Travel: Viajes TIVE, Martínez Campo, 21 (tel. 25 02 11). BIJ tickets and assorted travel information. Open Mon.-Fri. 9:30am-2pm.

American Express: Viajes Bonal, Avda. de Calvo Sotelo, 19 (tel. 27 63 12), at the north end of Gran Vía de Colón. Traveler's checks in exchange for cardholder's personal checks. Holds mail. Open Mon.-Fri. 9:30am-1:30pm and 5-8:30pm. Office is open Sat., but AmEx services aren't.

Post Office: Puerta Real (tel. 22 48 35), at the western end of C. de los Reyes Católicos. Open for stamps and Lista de Correos Mon.-Fri. 9am-2pm and 4-6pm, Sat. 9am-2pm. Open for telegrams Mon.-Fri. 8am-9pm, Sat. 9am-7pm, Sun. 9am-2pm. **Postal Code:** 18070.

Telephones: C. de los Reyes Católicos, 55, 1 block towards Pl. Nueva from Pl. Isabel la Católica. Open daily 9am-1pm and 5-9pm. **Telephone Code:** 958.

Airport: Tel. 20 33 22. 17km from city. **Iberia,** Pl. de Isabel la Católica, 2 (tel. 22 75 92). Pick up a shuttle bus schedule. To Madrid (2 per day, 40 min., 9400ptas) and Barcelona (1 per day, 1 hr., 12,900ptas). Open Mon.-Fri. 9am-1:15pm and 4-7:15pm.

Train Station: Avda. Andaluces (tel. 23 34 08), off Calvo Sotelo. To Madrid (3 per day; *talgo* 7 hr., 3650ptas; *expreso* 8½ hr., 2555ptas), Sevilla (2 per day, 5 hr., 1350ptas), and Bobadilla

(3 per day, 2 hr., 625ptas) for additional connections. **RENFE,** C. de los Reyes Católicos, 63 (tel. 22 34 97). Open Mon.-Fri. 9am-1:30pm and 4:30-7pm.

Bus Stations: Alsina Graells, Camino de Ronda, 97 (tel. 25 13 58), near C. Emperatriz Eugenia. To most places in Andalucía, including Almería (4 per day, 4 hr., 1040ptas), Córdoba (5 per day, 3½ hr., 1115ptas), Málaga (11 per day, 2½ hr., 730ptas), and Sevilla (7 per day, 4-5 hr., 1735ptas), as well as service to Granada's Costa del Sol and Alpujarras. **Bacoma,** Avda. Andaluces, 12 (tel. 23 18 83). To Barcelona (3 per day, 5195ptas), Valencia (4 per day, 3220ptas), Alicante (4 per day, 2200ptas), and Madrid (5 per day, 1865-2775ptas). **Autedia,** Rector Marin Ocete, 10 (tel. 28 05 92), off Avda. de Calvo Sotelo, near the Comedor Universitario. To Guadix (10 per day, 1½ hr., 355ptas), Baeza (7 per day, 2½ hr., 640ptas), and neighboring villages. **Autocares Bonal,** Avda. de Calvo Sotelo, 34 (tel. 27 31 00). Tour bus to Veleta in the Sierra Nevada (410ptas), which leaves from Hotel Zaida in front of the Fuente de las Batallas at 9am in Aug. only.

Car Rental: Atesa, Pl. de los Cuchilleros, 1 (tel. 22 56 65). **Avis,** Airport and C. Recogidas, 31 (tel. 25 23 58). **Gudelva,** Pedro António de Alarcón, 18 (tel. 25 10 80). **Hertz,** C. Braille, 7 (tel. 25 16 82).

Bike Rental: Taller Manolo, C. Manuel de Falla, near C. Pedro Antonio de Alarcón, about 6 blocks west of Puerta Real.

Hitchhiking: Tourist office has information on buses to good hitching spots out of town. **Mitzfahrzentrale,** C. Elvira, 85 (tel. 29 29 20), 1 block east of Gran Vía, is an unofficial agency that can help arrange rides with at least two days notice.

Baggage Check: The dilapidated shack with the Camas sign to the right of the exit of the train station will store your bags until 10pm for 100ptas; you decide.

English Bookstores: Atlantida Librería, Gran Vía de Colón, 5 doors north of the cathedral. Excellent collection of guidebooks and maps, including hard-to-find map of the Sierra Nevada (350ptas). Open Mon.-Fri. 10am-1:30pm and 4-7pm, Sat. 10am-1:30pm. **Librería Dauro,** Zacatín, 5 (tel. 22 45 21), just off Pl. Bib-Rambla, has Penguin classics. Open Mon.-Fri. 9:30am-1:30pm and 4:30-8pm.

Foreign Newspapers: Newsstands at Pl. Nueva on C. Elvira, and in front of the cathedral on Gran Vía de Colón.

Laundromat: Lavandería Autoservicio, C. Duquesa, 24 (tel. 28 06 85), just north of Pl. de la Trinidad. Wash and dry 560ptas per kg. Open Mon.-Fri. 9:30am-2pm and 4:30-9pm.

First Aid: Clínica de San Cecilio, Carretera de Jaén (tel. 28 02 00).

Police: Municipal, Pl. del Carmen (tel. 092). **Guardia Civil,** Tel. 25 11 00. **Policía Nacional,** Tel. 091.

Accommodations and Camping

Except during Semana Santa in April, Granada always has an ample supply of accommodations starting at 700ptas per person, and a few that are even less expensive.

Residencia Juvenil Granada (IYHF), Camino de Ronda, 171 (tel. 27 26 38), down the street from the Alsina Graells station. From the other bus station and RENFE, head away from town on Avda. Calvo Sotelo, continuing on C. de Málaga. Camino de Ronda starts on the left and goes over the tracks. The sign over the arch reads "Junta de Andalucía Instalaciones Deportivas." The hostel is the white building across the field on your left. If the gate is locked, go around to the back. A swimming pool (open June-Aug.), only passable rooms, music blaring over hallway speakers, and room keys left unguarded on entryway table. Curfew 11:30pm. Office open 9-10:30am and 7-11:30pm. 420ptas.

Along Cuesta de Gomérez

The most scenic and conveniently located budget hotels are just off Plaza Nueva, the street that leads to the Alhambra. The area fills quickly in summer, and the noise of tour buses ploughing up to the Alhambra commences in early morning. To reach this area, take bus #11 from the train or bus station, and get off at the cathedral. The cathedral isn't visible from a bus window; either count stops or look for the purple signs pointing to the entrance at each stop.

Hostal Residencia Britz, Cuesta de Gomérez, 1 (tel. 22 36 51). Friendly owner keeps place tidy and nicely decorated. Firm, bouncy beds. Some rooms with a beautiful view of Pl. Nueva. Singles 1000ptas. Doubles 1650-2250ptas.

Huéspedes Gomérez, Cuesta de Gomérez, 2, 5th floor (tel. 22 63 98). Fairly clean, cool, and comfy. Some rooms have balconies overlooking the plaza. Ask for a key if you wish to return after midnight. Singles and doubles 1200ptas. Hot showers 125ptas.

Hostal Residencia Gomérez, Cuesta de Gomérez, 10 (tel. 22 44 37). Kept sparkling clean by a young, multilingual, calculator-toting proprietor. Watchdog sleeps in the doorway. Singles 725ptas. Doubles 1250ptas. Hot showers 110ptas.

Hostal Navarro-Ramos, Cuesta de Gomérez, 21 (tel. 22 18 76). Once you can figure out the elaborate rope mechanism that unlocks the door, you'll discover clean, airy rooms. Singles 742ptas. Doubles 1378ptas. Hot showers 125ptas, cold showers 100ptas.

Hostal California, Cuesta de Gomérez, 37 (tel. 22 40 56), just below the entrance to the Alhambra. Clean, tiled rooms, though a bit cramped. You can check out anytime you want, but you can never leave. Hospitable management works out of kitschy souvenir shop in the reception area, and can change money in a pinch. Singles 800ptas. Doubles 1600ptas. Triples 2400ptas.

Near the Cathedral

The area just west of the cathedral and the Capilla Real is also one of the city's busiest commercial centers, where you can find everything from toys to horse saddles. It buzzes with activity during the day, but calms down in the evening. Inexpensive *hostales* and *casas de huéspedes* abound. A string of cheap *casas de huéspedes* (around 700ptas per person) lines **Calle Lucena,** northwest of Pl. de la Trinidad, but they're usually full when the university is in session. Take bus #11 from the train or bus station to reach the cathedral; follow the directions above.

Hostal-Residencia Lisboa, Pl. del Carmen, 27 (tel. 22 14 13), across C. Reyes Católicos. The same management that owns the Britz runs this place with the same high standards of cleanliness. Some rooms overlook the plaza. Singles 1000ptas. Doubles 1840ptas.

Huéspedes Romero, C. Sillería, 1 (no phone), overlooking Pl. de la Trinidad (not to be confused with the C. Sillería off Pl. Nueva), at the end of C. de Mesones. Gruff matron keeps rooms clean and kitchen pots steaming. 700ptas per person. Showers 125ptas.

Huéspedes Capuchinas, Capuchinas, 2 (tel. 26 53 94), off Pl. de la Trinidad. Elaborate plateresque foyer. Rooms, though old, are reasonably clean. 700ptas per person. Showers 100ptas.

Huéspedes Muñoz, Mesónes, 53 (tel. 26 38 19), east of Pl. de la Trinidad. Rooms are better maintained than the entrance. 700ptas per person.

Hotel Residencia Los Tilos, Pl. Bib-Rambla, 4 (tel. 22 75 40). Spacious rooms with balconies overlooking Pl. Bib-Rambla have a great view of the cathedral. More expensive than others in the area. Singles with bath 1802ptas. Doubles with bath 3206ptas.

Off Calle San Juan de Dios

This is the area closest to the train station. From the station, head straight along Avda. Andaluces, turn right onto Avda. de Calvo Sotelo, follow it to the end, and turn right again onto C. San Juan de Dios (10 min.). This is the seediest area of the three, but still perfectly safe.

Hostal Residencia San Joaquin, Mano de Hierro, 14 (tel. 28 28 79). Built in the 15th century, this former count's estate sports 3 beautiful patios and tapestry-lined stairways. Be choosy about your room and the neighboring bathroom—some rooms are better than others. Since sprawling premises make supervision difficult, leave your valuables at the front desk. 1000ptas per person. 1200ptas per person with bath. Dinner with *mucho vino* 500ptas.

Huéspedes Saliente, C. Cardenal Mendoza'll (tel. 28 22 76). Take the 3rd left off C. San Juan de Dios from Calvo Sotelo. Clean and well kept, but a tad small. Pleasant living rooms smell like home. Singles 850ptas. Doubles 1500ptas.

Hostal las Cumbres, C. Cardenal Mendoza, 4 (tel. 27 23 52). Forbidding, small, and shabby, yet pleasant enough. Singles 1000ptas. Doubles 1600ptas.

Elsewhere

Hostal América, Real de la Alhambra, 53 (tel. 22 74 71). The cheapest place in the Alhambra. The hilltop is wonderful when the daytime crowds disappear. Book as far in advance as possible. Singles 3429ptas, with shower 3790ptas, with bath 3922ptas. Doubles with bath 6360ptas.

There are five campsites within 5km of Granada. **El Ultimo,** Camino Huétor Vega, 50 (tel. 12 30 69), has a free swimming pool. (250ptas per person, per tent, and per car.) **María Eugenia** is on the Carretera de Málaga (tel. 20 06 06), km 4.36. (290ptas per person, per tent, and per car.) **Los Alamos** (tel. 27 57 43) is next door at km 4.39. (Open April-Oct. 250ptas per person and per car. 200ptas per tent.) **Regina Isabel** (tel. 59 00 41) lies in nearby Zubia. (275ptas per person, per tent, and per car.) The best is **Sierra Nevada,** on the Carretera de Madrid (tel. 27 09 56), which is not the Sierra Nevada. (Open March-Oct. 300ptas per person, 175ptas per tent, 275ptas per car.) Buses run from Granada to all five places; check the departure schedules at the tourist office.

Food

As in the rest of Andalucía, the accent in Granada is on fresh, usually fried, fish. Following the *rutas de las tapas* (the shortest distance between two bars) helps you develop an appetite while sampling the best each place has to offer: See if you can hit all the bars on **Campo del Príncipe** (several blocks south of Pl. Nueva) or **Plaza de la Trinidad** (west of the cathedral down C. Capuchinas). If you do this late in the evening, you'll be accompanied by almost all of Granada. A heady glass of *vino "la costa"* washes everything down superbly.

Morning *chocolate y churros* are the best at **Café Alhambra,** on Pl. Bin-Rambla. Ice cream fanatics should head to the mirrored walls of **Heladería Walther,** 2 blocks east of Puerta Real off Pl. de las Batallas, or the increasingly popular **Veneciano** (commonly called "Los Italianos"), Gran Vía, 4, where ice cream creations run 50-300ptas. The **mercado municipal** overflows from its building onto C. San Augustin, 1 block west of the cathedral just off Gran Vía. (Open Mon.-Sat. 9am-2pm.)

The site of gypsy caves lends its names to the *tortilla Sacromonte,* an omelette composed of ham, shrimp, and many green vegetables. You may (or may not) want to try other *platos típicos: sesos a la romana* (calves' brains fried in batter) and *rabo de toro* (bulls' tail).

Near Plaza Nueva

La Nueva Bodega, C. Cetti Merién, 3 (tel. 22 24 01), on a street perpendiular to Gran Vía de Colón and leading away from the cathedral. Flavorful *menús* 525-1200ptas, munchable *bocadillos* 100-150ptas. Prices much cheaper at the bar. Open daily 11am-midnight.

Restaurante-Bar-Café Boabdil, C. Corpus Christi, 2 (tel. 22 81 36), 2 blocks west of Pl. Nueva. Popular with locals, this place serves everything, including drinks, *tapas,* and a wide variety of *platos combinados* from 557ptas. A/C. *Menús* from 769ptas. Meals served daily noon-11pm.

La Riviera, C. Cetti Merién, 5, next to La Nueva Bodga. Ask about their special *menú: paella, merluza,* salad, and dessert (700ptas). Try the delicious peach sangria. House wine mediocre. *Platos combinados* 440-465ptas. Open 1-4pm and 8pm-midnight.

Restaurante Alcaicería, Pl. de la Enmita (tel. 22 43 41), west of the cathedral. Considering that it's one of the most highly regarded eateries in town, it's surprisingly easy on the wallet. Guitar music and great fruity house wines. Service is good humored but rushed. Overflowing *menú* 952ptas. Open 1-3:30pm and 8-11:30pm.

Restaurante-Bar León, C. Pan, 3 (tel. 22 51 43), 1 block west of Pl. Nueva. Comfortable atmosphere. Tasty meals from 500ptas. Open daily 1-3:30pm and 7:30-11pm. *Tapas* at bar anytime.

Resaurante El Farol, Cuesta de Gomérez, 10 (tel. 22 97 57). It's fun to sit by the window and watch exhausted tourists descend from the Alhambra. Decent food. *Menús* 583-901ptas. Open daily 1-4:30pm and 8pm-midnight.

In the Albayzín

El Ladrillo, Placeta de Fatima (tel. 29 54 05), off C. Pagés, the eventual name of the main street, which winds up the hill. A sea of outdoor tables buzzing with local families. A great evening hangout. Enormous servings of fresh, fried seafood: flounder 350ptas, *calamares* 400ptas, *gambas* (shrimp) 600ptas. You'd be foolish not to order the mountainous *media barca* (half-boat), a fried fish platter for 2 for 800ptas. *Ensalada* 300ptas.

Mesón Mexuar, C. Pagés, 33. Friendly, prompt service. Upstairs terrace affords good view. Mostly seafood platters from 350ptas, including the local favorite—*gambas fritas* (fried shrimp, 500ptas). For dessert, try melon, flan, strawberries, or ice cream (125-300ptas). *Menús* 300-650ptas.

Elsewhere

Restaurante Casa Rosa, C. San Juan de Dios, 54 (tel. 20 00 06), at Cardenal Mendoza. Simple and clean, with no-frills food. Faded chef outside advertises 450ptas *menús.* Open daily 1:30-4pm and 8-11:30pm.

Restaurante Vegetariano Raices, C. Prof. Albareda, 11 (tel. 12 01 03), a bit far from center, across the Río Genil and a 10-min. walk east of Puerta Real. Bus #11 eventually makes its way to C. Prof. Albareda. The only authentic vegetarian restaurant in town. Full *menú* only 550ptas. Open Mon.-Sat. 1:30-4pm and 8:30-11pm.

Sights

The crenelated towers of the Arab monarchs' royal palace still reign over the Andalusian plains, framed by the silvery backdrop of the Sierra Nevada. Named by the Moors, the **Alhambra** (red castle) is a haunting combination of beauty and bloodshed, the foremost tribute to the turbulent eight-century Moorish occupation of Spain. The Alhambra's layers of walled fortifications encircle several square kilometers of manicured gardens and intricately designed, lavish palaces, comprising four areas: the Alcázar, or royal palace, surrounded by the lush Partal Gardens; the sixteenth-century Palace of Carlos V; the Alcazaba, the oldest portion of the fortress; and the Generalife, or summer palace.

Enter the Alhambra through Granada Gate, off Cuesta de Gomérez, and climb to the well-marked main entrance. If you're driving, there's plenty of parking at the top. Whatever your mode of transport, ignore (or run over) the pushy gypsies who line the route: The flower they present you as a gift will cost more than you expected if you later discover your wallet missing.

The best way to see the complex is to wander, stopping now and then to admire an intriguing room or garden and to pull out your water bottle. (Bring plenty of water as the refreshment stand at the top of the Partal Gardens is open only sporadically.) Although up on a hill under the beating Spanish sun, the grounds remain cool due to Moorish architecture and design, which utilizes plenty of fountains, channels of running water, large trees, and thick walls.

The sheer beauty of the **Alcázar** (Royal Palace) has conjured up tales of romance and intrigue for centuries (Washington Irving's *Tales of the Alhambra,* for example). Legend has it that Abdul Hachach Yusef I was murdered in an isolated basement chamber, leaving his son Muhammad V to complete the structure. Raised between 1333 and 1391, the enchanting myriad of chambers and corridors sparkle with stalactite ceilings, painted tiles, and carvings of astounding intricacy. Much of the **Mexuar,** a pillared entranceway, needed massive restoration after an explosion in a nearby gunpowder mill in 1590. A bubbling fountain reflects elaborate carvings in the original fourteenth-century wood of the adjoining **Fachada de Serallo.** Foliated horseshoe archways of successively diminishing width open onto the **Sala de Oro,** commanding a fine view of the valley below. Overhead, the starry wooden ceiling is meticulously inlaid with ivory and mother-of-pearl.

From here, a path winds into a court of myrtle trees, where a lacy colonnade overlooks a pool teeming with hungry goldfish. The **Galería de la Barca** (Boat Gallery) flanks the north side of the courtyard, its ceiling crafted from the hull of a boat. King Fernando and Christopher Columbus are said to have discussed the route to India in the adjoining **Sala de los Embajadores,** whose ceiling is crafted from thousands of pieces of Lebanese wood. Housed in the **Torre de Comares,** the hall is interrupted on three sides by rounded windows that reveal spectacular vistas in all directions. Crumbling fortifications vanish into the distance over the ridge of the Albayzín.

The opulence continues in the **Patio de los Leones,** the most photogenic haunt in the palace and once the center of the sultan's domestic life. A stunningly symmetrical procession of archways, horseshoe arches, and alternating paired and single columns border the courtyard. Spouting tenth-century lions surround the twelve-sided fountain in the center. As you enter through the **Galería de los Mozárdos,** note the contrast between the stucco Moorish walls and the sixteenth-century ceiling added by Fernando and Isabel after a fire destroyed the original. Above the sultan's bed, in the **Sala del Rey** at the far end of the court, hangs a fifteenth-century painting attributed to one of the Christians employed by the sultan before the Reconquista. South of the fountain of irons, the **Galería de Abencerrajes** is the chamber in which the ruthless Sultan Mulay Abdul Hassaon piled the heads of the sons of his first wife so that Boabdil, son of his second, could inherit the throne. Sixteen stucco windows line the arcade of the gallery's honeycombed, eight-pointed cupola. On the northern side of the patio, the splendid **Sala de las Dos Hermanas** was named for the twin marble slabs embedded in the chamber's pavement. A frosty, stalactite cupola crowns the interior, giving way to a secluded portico overlooking the **Jardines de Daraxa,** where geometrical shrubbery echoes the shape of a bubbling central fountain.

Passing the room where Washington Irving resided, a balustraded courtyard leads to the **Baños Reales.** The center of court social life, Yusus I ordered their construction in the fourteenth century. Light shining through star-shaped holes was once refracted through steam to create indoor rainbows here. Between the courtyard and the gardens just outside, a small doorway allows a peek at the baths of the royal harem. In the **Jardines del Partal** just outside the Alcázar, lily-studded pools drip from level to level beside terraces of roses shadowed by the soaring **Torre de las Damas** (Ladies' Tower).

Although considered the most beautiful Renaissance building in Spain, the **Palacio de Carlos V** seems out of place given the Moorish splendor of its environs. The bulbous brickwork of the facade elbows in visibly over the intricate Alcázar; within it maintains a certain dignity. Ringed with two stories of Doric colonnades, it is the only surviving effort of master architect Pedro Machuca, who studied under Michelangelo.

In the **Alcazaba,** the oldest portion of the Alhambra, climb up the **Torre de la Vela** (watchtower) for the finest view of Granada and the Sierra Nevada. When the Alcázar was constructed, the Alcazaba was a separate palace. Its massive battlements were later transformed into a guard house and palace garrison. Napoleon stationed his troops here, but before leaving made sure to blow up enough of the fortifications to ensure that the palace could never again be an effective military outpost. Poke about the remaining fortress walls before exiting through **Puerta del Vino** (wine gate), where wine was sold to the inhabitants of the Alhambra tax-free. Unfortunately, this practice has been abandoned.

The **Generalife,** spacious summer retreat of the sultans, sits atop a rise to the northeast of the Alcázar. It blooms with exotic gardens and overflows with fountains. As you retrace your steps past the main entrance to the Alhambra and up the hill, you'll pass through **Callejón de las Cipresas** and the shady **Callejón de las Adelfas** and come to the lush palace greenery. The highlight of the Generalife is the **Corte del Canal de Agua,** a narrow pool fed by dramatic fountains that form an aqueous archway. To the east, the Corte de las Cipresas is bordered by myrtle ledges around a central stone fountain. According to legend, the wives of Sultan Boabdil took advantage of its seclusion to court their lovers here. Climb the steps to enjoy the terraces of the well-trimmed Generalife gardens, and return via a staircase lined with rushing water. (Alhambra open May-Aug. Mon.-Sat. 9am-8pm, Sun. 9am-6pm; Sept.-April Mon.-Sat. 9:30am-6pm, Sun. 9:30am-5:30pm. Admission 425ptas, but unused portions of the ticket are valid for return visits. Separate ticket required for illuminated nighttime visits. Wed. and Sat. 10pm-midnight.)

Granada's most outstanding Christian monument is the ostentatious **Capilla Real** (Royal Chapel), the private chapel of King Fernando and Queen Isabel. During their prosperous reign, they devoted almost one quarter of the royal income to the chapel's construction, and after the queen's death, its completion was supported by the royal estate. The monarchs' quest for immortality is imposing. Richly festooned with Gothic carving and gilded floral ornamentation, the chapel is a treasure of late medieval and early Renaissance decorative art. Behind an elaborate screen wrought by Bartolomé de Jaén repose the cool gray marble figures of the royal mausoleums, carved by sixteenth-century Italian sculptors. The figures of Fernando and Isabel recline to the right as you enter from the transept. Beside them lie their daughter, Juana la Loca (the Mad), and her husband, Felipe el Hermoso (the Fair).

Griffins, saints, and wild animals entwine themselves about the edges of the cenotaphs. The actual tombs lie in the crypt directly below, accessible by a small stairway on either side. Carved into the walls beside the monogram of the Catholic monarchs, dignified eagles of the Knights of St. John peer down. The north transept is hung with a triptych of the *Passion* by the Flemish master Thierry Bouts. The highlight of the chapel, Queen Isabel's private **art collection,** hides next door in the sacristy. The collection specializes in Flemish masterpieces of the fifteenth century, focusing on the early realism of Memling, Thierry, Bouts, and Roger van der Weyden; it also includes a minor work by Sandro Botticelli. The paintings' rich colors are complemented by the glittering **royal jewels** on display in the middle of the sacristy. Beside the queen's golden crown lie her scepter and jewel box, as well as the king's sword. (Open March-Sept. daily 10:30am-1pm and 4-7pm; Oct.-Feb. daily 10:30am-1pm and 3:30-6pm. Admission 100ptas, Sun. morning free.) Facing the entrance to the Capilla Real is a fourteenth-century **Madraza,** or Arab school, through a marble horseshoe doorway. Directly across the patio you'll find a well-preserved and intricately carved Arabian Room.

The Capilla Real is dwarfed by the adjacent **cathedral,** the first purely Renaissance cathedral in Spain. Begun in 1523, 30 years after the Christians regained control of the city, construction was supervised by three architects: Enrique Egas (1523-28), Diego de Siloé (1528-1568), and Alonso Cano (1568-81). The most innovative architectural feature, masterminded by Siloé, is the **Capilla Mayor** (Great Chapel), a striking, domed rotunda skirted by an ambulatory and ingeniously linked to the nave in such a way that, from the rear of the church, it seems to be rectangular. Portraits of the Virgin by Alonso Cano grace the inner walls, where the gilded detail twinkles in the light. The cathedral's nave ascends to an impressive height, supported by massive Corinthian pillars and stone vaults. Arched windows illuminate the nave from all sides; as a result, the frosty white interior has the washed-out look of a slightly overexposed snapshot, while the seventeen chapels adjoining the nave remain lost in murky shadow. You can adjust the lighting yourself with tiny, coin-operated electric switches beside each chapel. Bring plenty of change: Lighting costs 25ptas per viewing. The **Capilla de Nuestra Señora de la Antigua,** at the northern end of the transept, contains a fifteenth-century icon of the patron saint, which the Catholic monarchs carried into battle during the siege of Granada. Your admission ticket also entitles you to visit the **treasury** and cathedral **museum.** (Same hours and admission as the Capilla Real, but different ticket.)

The seventeenth-century **Hospital Real** houses Andalusian *azulejos* in its inner quadrangle. Above the landing of the main staircase, the Moorish inlaid roof is reminiscent of its older cousins in the Alhambra. A series of semicircular arches encloses the festively painted patio nearby. Next door rise the twin, stone spires of the **Iglesia de San Juan de Dios,** an elaborately decorated monument that contains a superb Churrigueresque reredos. The fourteenth-century **Monasterio de San Jerónimo** is just around the corner; badly damaged by Napoleon's troops, it has since been restored. The courtyards have weathered well, accumulating Gothic, Mudéjar, and Renaissance elements. (All three sites are at the end of C. San Juan de Dios. Open daily 10am-1:30pm and 3-6pm. Admission 100ptas.)

The first residents of the **Albayzín,** Granada's old Arab quarter, were ejected from Baeza in 1227. After the Reconquista, the quarter remained inhabited by an isolated Moorish population until the sixteenth century. The labyrinth of alleyways is a rather tame version of an Arab medina. The best way to explore the neighborhood is to proceed along C. de Darro off Pl. Nueva, climb up Cuesta del Chapiz on the left, then wander aimlessly. You will encounter ramparts, cisterns, and gates that date from the Muslim period, as well as numerous *cármenes,* traditional Arab houses with large kitchen plots and enclosed gardens. You can also take bus #7 from beside the cathedral and disembark at C. de Pagés on top of the hill. From here, walk down C. Agua through the **Puerta Arabe,** an old gate to the city at Pl. Larga. The terrace adjacent to the **Iglesia de San Nicolás** affords the city's best view of the Alhambra. The view is most beautiful in winter, when the Sierra Nevada is covered with snow. The nearby **Iglesia de San Salvador,** built on the site of the Albayzín's most important mosque, preserves a *patio arabe.* The tourist office provides a detailed guide to the Albayzín on request. Be cautious here at night.

On the outskirts of Granada stands **La Cartuja,** an eighteenth-century Carthusian monastery. A marble with rich brown tones and swirling forms (a stone unique to nearby Lanjarón) lines the Sacristy of Saint Bruno. The baroque exuberance of the altar enhances the opulent atmosphere. On the other side of the serene courtyard await the refectory and its antechamber, both highlighted by ingenious *trompe l'oeil* wall paintings: Look from afar and you'll swear there's a wooden cross nailed to one wall and large stone columns emerging from another. To reach the monastery, take bus #8 from in front of the cathedral. (Same hours and admission as the Capilla Real and cathedral.)

If you have access to a car, you can visit the house in Fuentevaqueros, near the airport, where Frederico García Lorca was born. The building has recently been converted into a **museum,** housing photographs, manuscripts, and possessions of the poet, shot by right-wing forces near Granada at the outbreak of the Civil War. (Open to 15 people every ½-hr. April-Sept. Tues.-Sun. 10am-2pm and 6-9pm; Oct.-March Tues.-Sun. 10am-1pm and 4-6pm. Admission 100ptas.)

Entertainment

Avoid the **Cuevas Gitanas de Sacromonte** (gypsy caves). Once home to a thriving gypsy community, the hill today is a prosperous tourist trap. As you proceed up the hill to Albayzín in the evening, you will be accosted at the turn-off for Sacromonte by gypsies shouting "flamenco! flamenco!" and forcibly redirecting you. The disappointing performance takes place in whitewashed grottoes converted into theaters. As family members play guitars, castanets, or tambourines, or simply shake in rhythm to the music, the audience is expected to show appreciation by showering money on the performers.

Fortunately there's more in the **Albayzín.** Casual bars with good folk music abound, as do extravagant pubs such as **Casa Yanguas,** a fifteenth-century Moorish patio that must be the most romantic bar in Spain (take C. de San Buenaventura off Cuesta del Chapiz). It's hard going in, but pulling out with a new friend is easy. **Casa Arabe,** also in the Albayzín off C. Pages, provides a similar atmosphere and a small dance floor. Drinks aren't cheap.

On the other side of town, you can see a real flamenco show at **Jardines Neptuno,** on C. Arabial (tel. 25 11 12). (Cover with 1 drink 1900ptas.) The performance is highly regarded, so it's wise to reserve in advance. (Shows nightly at 10pm.)

Nearby, you can mingle with the university crowd in pubs and bars in the area bounded by **Calle Pedro Antonio de Alarcón, Callejón de Nevot,** and **Calle de Melchor Almagro.** The music is just as likely to be North American or British as Spanish. Discos tend to be overpriced and unpopular. If you're in Granada on a Sunday night, stop by the **Jardines del Triunfo,** where Calvo Sotelo meets Gran Vía, to see the illuminated polychromatic fountain.

Granada is famous for its **Corpus Christi** celebrations, which include processions and bullfights. (The fiesta begins on the Thurs. following the 8th Sun. after Easter.)

The **International Festival of Music and Dance** (June 15 to July 15) is another good time to visit the city. The festival features classical ballet and open-air performances in the gardens of the Generalife, as well as concerts in the Renaissance palace that Carlos V built on the Cerro del Sol. You can get inexpensive seats for most performances; write to Comisaria del Festival, Ancha de Santo Domingo, 1, Granada 18009 (tel. 22 52 01). If you're in town, contact their office at C. Gracia, 21 (tel. 26 77 42), or any travel agency (which will charge an additional fee). Travel agencies also have tickets to the **Conciertos Romaticos,** held in the Generalife by the Ayuntamiento from April to October on Friday and Saturday nights at 11pm.

Near Granada: Guadix

Contrary to popular belief, the cave-dwellers of **Guadix,** 55km east of Granada, are neither gypsies nor troglodytes. Most of the caves have whitewashed exteriors resembling those of more typical Andalusian houses and the bare, sand-colored mounds are crowned by TV antennae and spooky white chimneys punctured with circular "eyes" to let out smoke in winter. It's not difficult to strike up conversation with residents, and you may be invited inside to see the three- or four-room houses carved into the soft tufa stone of the hills. Due to the natural insulating quality of the walls, the caves are toasty in winter and cool in summer. Some of the structures date back more than one thousand years.

From the bus station, walk along Carretera de Almeria (which becomes Avda. de Medina Olmos) to the white arch of **Puerta de San Torcuato.** Uphill you'll find the stately **Plaza de las Palomas** (Dove's Square), which may take its name from the silly looking birds, resembling a cross betwen pigeons and chickens, that strut about like peacocks under the colonnade. Farther up, you'll come to the sixteenth-century **Iglesia de Santiago,** its imposing plateresque facade crowned by serveral decorative cannons. Atop the hill, poking its crenelated towers above the roofs of the old town, stands a ninth-century Moorish **Alcazaba.** Climb to the top for a superb view of the surrounding countryside and cave dwellings in Barrio de Santiago to the south. The Moors in this medieval stronghold communicated with neighboring outposts by building bonfires atop the fortress's main tower. Today a stikingly out-of-place, sculpted Madonna occupies the uppermost turret. Erected by Christian worshipers, she gazes westward, anticipating the site of the tall and thin sixteenth-century **cathedral.** Enter through the neighboring theological seminary (on C. Barrada), joined to the citadel grounds by a short walkway. To reach the entrance, follow the signs, climbing C. Villaita in front of the cathedral. (Open daily 9am-2pm and 4-7pm. Admission 50ptas.)

Guadix makes a fine daytrip from Granada, but if you wish to spend the night, stay at **Fonda García,** C. San Turcuato, 12 (tel. 66 05 96), just inside Peurta San Turcuato, with small but basically clean rooms. (700ptas per person. Hot showers 200ptas.) You might also try **Hostal Río Verde** (tel. 66 07 29), on La Cruce (the traffic circle where all the highways meet), which offers large, white rooms on the side of the building away from the noisy road. (Singles 900ptas. Doubles 1400ptas.) For grub, visit **Restaurante Accitano,** Jardín, 3 (tel. 66 00 07), on the corner across from Puerta de San Turcuato, with a hefty *menú* for 600ptas (served 1:30-3:30pm and 8:30-10:30pm). For breakfast or a snack, **Serrano** on the opposite corner will fry up *churros* (curlicues of dough) before your eyes (150ptas, with coffee or hot chocolate).

Guadix is accessible by **bus** from Granada (10 per day, 1 hr., 355ptas), Almeriá, Sevilla, and Jaén. The bus station is located at Urbanización Santa Rosa, near Carretera de Almeriá (tel. 66 06 57). The **train station** (tel. 66 06 25), a 20-minute walk down Carretera de Murcia, connects to Granada (3 per day, 1 hr., 245ptas), Almería (6 per day, 1½-2½ hr., 485-895ptas), Madrid, Sevilla, and Barcelona. Tourist information is available at the **Ayuntamiento,** on Pl. de las Palomas (tel. 66 01 15). The **post office** is also on the plaza (tel. 66 03 56; open Mon.-Sat. 9am-2pm). The **postal code** is 18500.

Purullena, 7km down the road from Guadix to Granada, harbors more cave domiciles and bizarre tufa landscape. It's an unbeatable place to buy Andalusian ceramics, brass, and animal hide souvenirs; try any of the shops that line the road. Shop around for price and variety. Granada-Guadix buses stop here, but make sure you're not stuck here for more than two hours. Hitching is easy.

Sierra Nevada

Jutting high above the sun-scorched beaches and plains of Andalucía, the desolate peaks of Mulhacén (3481m) and Veleta (3428m), the highest mountains of the Sierra Nevada range, glisten with snow most of the year. The nearby towns attract winter tourists, but they are fun to visit year-round. The most popular approach to the Sierra Nevada (Snowy Mountains) is to zoom straight up the highway from Granada to Veleta. The alternative is to come around from the south through the Alpujarras range. The first option is quick and easy; the second is time-consuming and circuitous, but ultimately even more rewarding. To escape the beaten track and enjoy the mountain air, head for the Alpujarras.

Veleta

Near the foot of the Alhambra, the highest road in Europe begins its ascent to the clouds. Beginning as a tranquil *camino* through the arid countryside, the highway climbs the face of the Sierra wall, ultimately topping one of the continent's highest peaks (3470m). At 410ptas round-trip, the **bus** to the top by **Autocares Bonal** (tel. 27 31 00) is Spain's greatest transportation bargain. The bus leaves Granada (from in front of the Hotel Zaida, by the Fuente de las Batallas in front of the Palacio de la Diputación) daily at 9am in August for the **cabin-restaurant,** which is a two- to three-hour hike from the peak. The bus returns to Granada at 5pm, arriving at 6pm. Be sure to buy your ticket at **Bar Sol-y-Nieve,** next to the bus stop, before boarding. This is one daytrip worth raving about.

During the ski season (Nov. to mid-May), a network of ski lifts operates from the cabin-restaurant to the peak and several intermediary points. An all-day lift ticket will set you back 1500-1800ptas. Equipment rentals are located in the Gondola Building and in Pradollano Sq. This is the sunniest and southernmost ski resort in Europe—don't forget your sunscreen and sunglasses. Check **conditions** through Federación Andaluza de Esquí, Paseo de Ronda, 78 (tel. 25 07 06). The cheapest of the area's accommodations is probably **Albergue Universitario,** Peñones de San Francisco (tel. 48 01 22; half-pension 2800ptas per person).

You can drive to the very top of Veleta only in late summer. Buses run year-round to as high as they can get, in heavy snow up only to Prado Llano (19km from the peak). From mid-June on, however, the road is clear up to an altitude of at least 2700m, leaving you a snowy, treacherous, three-hour hike to the peak. Under clear skies, the view extends all the way to the Rif mountains of Morocco. When the snow has melted, you can drive or walk over the peak to Capileira in the southern valley of the Alpujarras. This hike is a good 25km among rock-strewn meadows where wild goats and birds provide the only company. Even in summer, the wind is severe and temperatures drop considerably at night, so plan your hike as a daytrip. The most detailed, inexpensive **hiking map** is printed by the Federación Española de Montañismo and costs 350ptas in bookstores in Granada. Before you go, call to check on **road and snow conditions** (tel. 48 01 53 in Spanish and English) as well as hotel vacancies.

The entire resort community of **Prado Llano** closes in summer. Look for the turn-off just after the 2500-meter mark. Europe's highest tennis court commands a million-dollar view in the background.

Las Alpujarras

The small, white houses of the Alpujarras, secluded villages on the southern slopes of the Sierra Nevada, huddle together as if to protect themselves from the harshness of nature. Colonized by mountain Berbers in the Middle Ages, they utilize an architectural style found only here and in the Algerian and Moroccan Atlas. The beauty and innocence of these settlements can be attributed to their isolation; until the '50s, travel to them was possible only on foot and by mule. While in the Alpujarras, make sure to try their local *especialidades,* including *sopa alpujarreña* (broth with eggs, croutons, and ham) and *plato alpujarreño* (ham, fries, eggs, sausages, and salad).

At the base of the range, **Lanjarón** distinguishes itself mainly through its mineral water, consumed throughout Spain. Not far off the highway connecting Granada to the coast, it sees more curious tourists than its sister villages. If you're stuck here overnight, try **Hotel El Sol,** Avenida, 30 (tel. 77 01 30), which has new firm beds, scrubbed marble floors, and maids who sparkle more than the water. Upper floor rooms have balconies. (Singles 1200ptas. Doubles 1900ptas.) If you're driving, take the left-hand turn just before Orjiva. If you're on the bus to Ugijar via the main highway, you'll have to disembark here to take advantage of the tourist route.

As the road winds in serpentine curves up to **Pampaneira,** the lowest of the Alpujarras villages (1059m), the scenery suddenly becomes dramatic. The village's *fuente agria* spouts water that looks and tastes metallic due to the mineral wealth of the soil. If you can't resist stopping, you can find good food and lodgings at **Casa Alfonso,** José Antonio, 1 (tel. 76 30 02). The large, clean rooms, all doubles, are kept warm in winter with Mexican-style knit quilts and central heating. Local ham is the restaurant's specialty. (1400ptas per room. *Pensión completa* 2000ptas per person.) The snow-covered peaks of the high Sierra come into view as soon as you reach the picturesque village of **Bubión.** Ask around for private rooms (800ptas per person). You can dine in high style at the local favorite, **Casa Teide,** C. Francisco Pérez Garrión (tel. 76 30 37), where tables are placed around a lush rose garden (*menú* 500ptas). Potent gazpacho 90ptas, homemade whisky ice cream cake 250ptas.

Continue 3km up the road to the wonderful village of **Capileira,** a good base for exploring the region and the closest thing to a tourist center in the Alpujarras: You'll find two *hostales,* three restaurants, and a handful of foreign tourists. The cobbled alleys wind jaggedly up the slope amid ivy and chirping birds; on either side, Mulhacén and Alcazaba loom above while the Alpujarras valley plummets below. You can enjoy the latter vista from your bedroom window at **Mesón-Hostal Poqueira,** C. Dr. Castillo, 6 (tel. 76 30 48), with fresh, wooden rooms (600ptas per person). You can enjoy a hardy meal of lamb or chicken *asado* (roasted) for 550ptas at **Casa Ybero,** C. Parra, 1 (tel. 76 30 06).

The road through Capileira continues up the mountainside to Veleta, where it meets the highway from Granada. Unfortunately, it is passable only in late summer. By June, you may be able to drive far enough to make a two-hour climb to **Mulhacén,** Spain's highest peak and the ultimate vantage point. Always proceed with extreme caution when approaching the summit: The wind can be gusty, the snow very slick, and the drop to the other side sheer and sudden. To reach the trail, follow the signs marked "Sierra Nevada"; the well-marked fork for the road toward Mulhacén branches to the right after 20km. The hike from Capileira down to the gorge is also pleasant. There is no clearly marked trail and at times the going is rough, but a dip in the river is cool and refreshing in summer. For the most comfortable (and least direct) route, take the road to Bubión and the path from there to Pampaneira (3 times faster than the road); then walk upstream along the river to a sufficiently secluded spot.

At Capileira, buses back up and continue along the highway through the cozy cliffside hamlet of **Pitres.** Spain's highest official campground (1295m), **Balcón de Pitres** sits at the cliff's edge. (250ptas per person and tent, 175ptas per car.) The lookout points are spectacular, but avoid this stretch after a full meal if you're prone to car sickness. You can recover in the village of **Portugos,** at **Hostal Mirador de**

Portugos, Pl. Nueva, 5 (tel. 76 60 14), complete with swimming pool and magnificent view. The village of **Busquistar,** about 1½ km down the road, rests on an inclined ridge over a precipitous gorge. The highway stops at the township of **Trevélez** (1476m), Spain's highest community, renowned for its cured ham. For a wonderful view of the village, cross the stone bridge over the Río Chico de Trevélez and continue along the opposite side of the gorge. You can find a room at **Casa Alvarez** (tel. 76 50 03), near the entrance to town. Rooms are slightly run-down, but the balconies provide terrific views of the mountains. (Singles 1500ptas. Doubles 2000ptas.) Otherwise, rent a private room for about 600ptas per person; look for the *camas* signs.

On June 13, Trevélez celebrates the **Fiesta de San Antônio** with a costumed dramatization of the Moorish-Christian conflict. Despite the villagers' lack of equestrian experience, all mounted actors are required to rear their horses high onto their hind legs, often resulting in dramatic spills.

The final portion of the highway through the Alpujarras is less frequently served by bus and seldom visited. On a mountaintop outside Berchules, you'll find what is possibly the world's most scenic playground; **Yegen** offers marvelous panoramas and a nameless *pensión* with inexpensive lodgings; **Mecina-Alfahar** sits by a handsome dam on the Rio Nechite overlooking brown slopes, green fields, and gray rock. Thereafter, the road forks to the larger agricultural villages of Laroles to the north and Ugijar to the south. If you're driving, this eastern portion of the Alpujarras is most directly accessible by the somewhat dilapidated highway originating in the village of Lacalahorra near Guadix.

A **bus** line runs from the Alsina Graells station in Granada to all the major villages in the range (500ptas). Departing at 1:30pm and returning to Granada the next morning, it makes a stopover for the night at an inn in **Berchules** (700ptas per person). If you prefer not to spend the night, buy a ticket as far as Capileira or Trevélez, and hitch back. From July to September, Viajes Bonal (see Practical Information) provides a Sunday excursion from 9:30am to 7pm (2000ptas, midday meal included). Reservations are required. Unfortunately, this is the only form of public transportation between the villages. You can also thumb it. The locals, aware of the trasportation problem, will most likely pick you up.

Jaén

One of the few landlocked provinces in Andalucía, Jaén makes up for its lack of coastline with the sheer richness of its land; these fertile fields yield bushel after bushel of barley, hops, and wheat, and nurture countless vineyards and olive trees. The province is surrounded by mountains: the Sierra Morena and Valdepeñas to the north, the Segura and Cuzorla ranges to the east, and the Huelma and Noalejo ranges to the south. The west opens onto the plains that widen into the fertile Guadalquivir valley. The Moors called it Geen (caravan route), since this varied and rugged terrain was the crossroads between Andalucía and Castilla.

Light years off the beaten track, this province is a relaxing break from the hectic highlights farther south. Spaniards themselves come for the stunning mountain views and fine Andalusian architecture. What little hotel space exists is completely filled on weekends and holidays.

Jaén

Orientation and Practical Information

Everything smells or tastes funny in this provincial capital, yet some all-but-hidden gems lie beneath its humdrummery. The town is dominated by the **Castillo**

Santa Catalina, a 3-kilometer vertical crawl from the town center. The view from the outcrop in front of the castle is dizzying. From here, you can see **Paseo de la Estación,** the main artery of the modern area, connecting the train station in the north; **Pl. Contitución** in the south; the **barrio antiguo,** home to most points of interest, on the bottom of the slope; and the surrounding ring of mountains.

Tourist Office: Avda. de Madrid, 10A (tel. 22 27 37). Take a left and then a right from the bus station. Extremely friendly, helpful staff can tell you everything you might ever want to know about the city, province, and Andalucía. Open Mon.-Fri. 9am-1:30pm and 4-7:30pm, Sat. 9am-1:30pm.

Post Office: Pl. de los Jardinillos (tel. 22 01 12). Open Mon-Sat. 9am-2pm. **Postal Code:** 23071.

Telephone Code: 953.

Train Station: Paseo de la Estación (tel. 25 17 56). Since RENFE cut all southbound trains, it's difficult to go anywhere from Jaén. Two trains per day go to Madrid, a *rápido* in the morning to Chamartín (3½ hr., 2005ptas) and a *tranvía* at night to Atocha (5 hr., 1590ptas). Otherwise, go to Esperluy to connect to the Madrid-Sevilla line (3 per day, 30 min., 105ptas). To anywhere else in Andalucía, take another train from Esperluy to Linares.

Bus Station: Pl. Coca de la Piñera (tel. 25 01 06). To Ubeda (8 per day, 1 hr., 355ptas) via Baeza (45 min., 250ptas), Granada (10 per day, 2 hr., 580ptas), Madrid (7 per day, 4½ hr., 1285ptas), Málaga (1 per day, 4½ hr., 925ptas), Sevilla (5 per day, 5 hr., 1285ptas), and Barcelona (1 per day, 14 hr.) via Valencia (8 hr.).

Hospital: Hospital Provincial Princesa de España, Carretera de Madrid (tel. 22 26 50 or 22 27 08).

Police: C. Arquitecto Bergés, 13 (tel. 25 16 01). **Emergency:** Tel. 091.

Accommodations and Food

All of Jaén's budget accommodation options seem ready for the demolitión crew. Try the stark, new **Residencia Juvenil (IYHF),** Avda. de Andalucía, 10 (tel. 25 26 41), at Arjona, on bus line "Peñamifecete." (550ptas per person.) **Hostal los Cazadores,** Paseo de la Estación, 51 (tel. 25 21 42), offers basically clean rooms, though the pillows and mattresses are lumpy. (Singles 1100ptas, with shower 1200ptas. Doubles 1500ptas, with shower 1600ptas.) Go to **Fonda Martín,** C. Cuatro Torres (tel. 22 06 33), off Pl. de la Contitución, only as a last resort. (Singles 800ptas. Doubles 1350ptas. Showers 100ptas.)

Calle Nueva, a block north of Pl. de la Constitución, is lined with bars and restaurants to suit every taste and budget, including scads of seafood. **El Mesón,** C. Nueva, 10 (tel. 25 39 32), in an old wine cellar, is especially good, with *platos* for 350-450ptas at the bar. (Closed for renovations. Expected to reopen in 1989.) **Freiduría Pitufos,** inside Café-Bar Los Mariscos at #2, serves a tasty breakfast of *churros y chocolate* for 130ptas.

Sights

Dating from the eleventh century, Spain's largest **hamman** (Arab baths) have only recently been excavated and restored in Jaén. Public rather than private, they lack the ornamentation of the better-known *hamman* in Granada and Córdoba. Nevertheless, they are the most ambitious Muslim municipal architecture on the peninsula; they are so amazingly intact you can almost feel the steam rising from the vaporium, see sunlight streaming through the stars in the ceiling, and hear the conversation of bathers seated on the central rectangle of benches. Enter through the Renaissance **Palacio de Villadompardo,** soon to open as a **Museo de Arte Popular.** (Open Tues.-Sat. 10am-2pm and 5-8pm, Sun. 10am-2pm. Free. Informative booklet 100ptas.)

The **Catedral de Santa María,** a few blocks southwest of Pl. de la Constitución, features a remarkably intricate facade by Pedro Roldán, flanked by twin bell towers. The interior disappears under the weight of fluted Roman columns, but the **Museo**

de la Catedral, with its work by Martínez Montañés and Alonso Cano, provides less somber fare. (Cathedral open daily 8:30am-1pm and 4:30-7pm. Museum open Sat.-Sun. 11am-1pm. Admission to museum 50ptas.)

Between the bus and train stations, at Paseo de le Estación, 29, the **Museo Provincial** contains an impressive range of works, from prehistoric artifacts to expressionist paintings. The famous *Toro Ibérico de Poruna* and *Sarcófago Paleocristiano de Martos* are displayed here; they were discovered in a nearby Tartessian necropolis. (Open Tues.-Fri. 8am-3pm, Sat. 9am-2:30pm, Sun. 10am-2pm. Admission 250ptas, students free.)

While you can climb (or at least try to) the side of the mountain to reach the walls of **Castillo de Santa Catalina,** the interior remains closed for restoration. The southern half of the castle, once an Arab palace, now serves as a *parador.*

Baeza

Baeza is charmingly unaware of its allure. Despite the noteworthy monuments on every street corner and the winding, walled streets, accommodations are scarce, backpackers are considered an oddity, and the tourist director still isn't really sure when the bus leaves for the train station.

The cityout layout is a sight in itself, and you may find yourself pleasantly lost in a maze of sunny streets. The historic buildings are, however, worth finding. **Plaza del Pópulo,** at the entrance to the city from Jaén, is surrounded by the well-preserved town slaughterhouse and the former city hall, which is now the tourist office. Eroded stone lions guard the central fountain and the Iberian princess Imilce, wife of Hannibal, stands atop the fountain's pillar.

The greatest concentration of monuments lies straight uphill. Climbing the staircase to C. Conde de Ramones and past the Capilla del Santo Cristo del Cambrón, you'll reach the Renaissance **university,** where poet Antonio Machado taught French at the turn of the century. A few more buildings of the the period, including the ornate, pointy **Palacio de Jabalquinto,** line Cuesta de San Felipe on its way to the **Santa Iglesia Catedral,** a soaring, brightly colored work by Vandelvira on **Plaza de la Fuente de Santa María,** with its sixteenth-century fountain. The glint of gold in the cathedral's *retablo* is blinding. (Church open daily 10:30am-1pm and 5-7pm.) Across the plaza, the **seminary** bears the names of its graduates, along with a caricature of an unpopular professor, in bull's blood. Kids who have memorized the tourism brochure will run up to you and explain everything for the price of a soda.

If you're lucky, prices will not have gone up at the lavish, velvet-covered **Hostal Adriano,** C. Conde Romanones, 13 (tel. 74 02 00), where large, well-maintained rooms in an old mansion are a steal. (Singles 700ptas. Doubles 1300ptas, with shower 1700ptas.) **Hostal Residencia Comercio,** C. San Pablo, 21 (tel. 74 01 00), on the street leading to the bus station, has brass pots on the walls and plain rooms, some of which feature closets converted into showers. (Singles 860-1110ptas. Doubles 1540-2070ptas.) Decent meals cost 660ptas in their dining room. If you can fit your pack through the crowded bar, **Restaurante Sali,** on Pasaje Cardenal (tel. 74 13 65), serves generous *menús* for 800ptas, packed with the region's delicious vegetables. (Open daily 1-4pm and 8-11pm.)

Turismo, Pl. del Pópulo (tel. 74 04 44), around the corner from the wide end of the central square, is not overly helpful, but they hand out lots of brochures. (Open Mon.-Fri. 9:30am-1:30pm and 4:30-8pm.) The **post office** is on C. Julio Burell, 19 (tel. 74 08 39; open Mon.-Fri. 9am-2pm, Sat. 9am-noon). The **postal code** is 23440. The **bus station** is along Paseo de Elorza Sarat. To get to Sevilla or Madrid, first go to Ubeda (9 buses per day, 15 min., 150ptas). Four buses per day run to the Linares-Baeza train station, 16km away on the Madrid-Sevilla line (20min., 85ptas), and frequent buses run to Granada (830ptas). For the **police,** call 74 06 59; for an **ambulance,** 74 01 50.

Ubeda

For those with a low tolerance for tourists, Ubeda offers modest Andalusian attractions. Sitting on a ridge above the olive-bedecked Guadalquivir valley, this former battleground of the Spanish Reconquista features narrow, cobbled streets, remnants of medieval walls covered with vegetation, and a good number of old palaces and churches. Many have decayed or been put to a new use, but those still untouched attest to the imagination and virtuosity of Spanish Renaissance architecture.

Once a stop on an important trade route, the city had become the favored battleground for local skirmishes by the Middle Ages. It was avoided by travelers who came to prefer more prominent commercial routes, thus the origin of the Spanish expression "to go via the hills of Ubeda," meaning far out of the way or off the subject.

Orientation and Practical Information

In front of the bus station and to the left as you exit is **Calle Ramón y Cajal.** Most of this compact city's accommodations and restaurants lie on this street, which runs east to west. The historical district lies downhill.

Tourist Office: Pl. del Ayuntamiento (tel. 75 08 97), next to the Ayuntamiento. Head for Pl. de Andalucía, look for the sign, and follow C. Real to the bottom. Open Mon.-Fri. 10am-1:30pm and 6-8pm, Sat.-Sun. 10am-1:30pm.

Post Office: C. Trinidad, 1 (tel. 75 00 31). Open for mail and **telegrams** Mon.-Fri. 9am-2pm, Sat. 9am-1pm. **Postal Code:** 23400.

Bus Station: C. San José (tel. 75 21 57). To Linares-Baeza train station (9 per day, 200ptas), Baeza (7 per day, 150ptas), Jaén (8 per day, 355ptas), Córdoba (3 per day, 840ptas), Sevilla (3 per day, 1640ptas), Madrid (1 per day, 930ptas), and Barcelona (2 per day, 3985ptas).

Medical Services: Residencia Sanitaria (tel. 75 11 03).

Police: In the Ayuntamiento (tel. 75 00 23), next to Turismo.

Accommodations and Food

Despite Ubeda's isolation, lodgings are expensive. Your options lie either on or near C. Ramón y Cajal, the main drag, and include the plain and clean **Hostal Castillo,** at #16 and 20 (tel. 75 04 30), with an extremely friendly manager. (Singles 1100ptas, with shower 1200ptas. Doubles 1700ptas, with shower 2100ptas, with bath 2300ptas. Filling meals 660ptas.) **Hostal Sevilla,** at #9 (tel. 75 06 12), rolls out the red carpet in hallways leading to shining bathrooms but small rooms. (Singles 1100ptas. Doubles 1900ptas.)

Ubeda does not excel in fine cuisine, but there are plenty of places to try regional specialties such as *andrajos,* a soup made with ground chickpeas. *Pipirrana,* a mixture of pieces (or pieces of pieces) of tomatoes, peppers, onions, and eggs, is another local favorite. **Cafetería Neón,** on Pl. de Andalucía at C. Rastro, is popular with locals. Its friendly waiters love conversing with foreigners. There's dining outdoors, in the bar, or upstairs. Many *platos combinados* run 250-650ptas, and a wide array of tortillas cost 200-225ptas. (Open daily 1:30-4:30pm and 8-11pm. Do your shopping at the **market,** halfway down the hill on C. Cruz de Hierro at Corredera de San Fernando.

Sights

Carl V originally hired Diego de Siloé to build an enormous palace, but the architect died after drawing up the designs, leaving construction to his pupil, Adrés del Vandelvira, a developer of the Spanish Renaissance style. Vandelvira did away with superficial embellishments, concentrating instead on the structure's enormity and unity. The result is almost more Italian than Spanish. Unfortunately, only the **Sacra**

Capilla del Salvador and the main facade remain today. (Chapel open daily 9am-1pm and 5-7pm. If the front door is closed, go around the side and ring the sacristy bell.) The chapel sits at the narrow end of **Plaza de Vázquez de Molina,** whose stateliness and balance deserve contemplation. At the plaza's opposite end, the **Palacio de las Cadenas,** built by Vandelvira for Vázquez de Molina, has seemingly misplaced caryatids on top and an attractive, open-air courtyard below. To the south is the **Iglesia de Santa María de los Reales Alcázares,** with chapels enclosed by grilles crafted by Master Bartolemé. The exterior reflects a mixture of styles. Just as impressive is the Gothic **Iglesia de San Pablo,** on Pl. 1 de Mayo, with its overlapping, concave southern portal done in Isabeline style. Inside, head straight for the magnificent chapels with their intricate wrought-iron grilles. (Open daily 9am-1pm and 5-7pm. Free.)

Ubeda is a good starting point for forays into the Andalusian wilds. The mountainous countryside to the east and south hides numerous whitewashed villages with multicultural ruins. Most are accessible by bus or car. **Cazorla,** high in the hills, is notable for its two castles, marvelous pine-forested mountains, and rolling countryside. **Quesada,** to the south, is a place to relax among quaint, whitewashed houses and Roman, Islamic, and Christian ruins. **Orcera,** less than 100km east of Ubeda, is a traditional highland village devoted to the wood trade. These towns hide in the natural parks of the Sierras de Cazorla y Segura, unspoiled wilderness.

Córdoba

On the banks of the Guadalquivir River, Córdoba combines the traditions of Judaism, Islam, and Christianity with flamenco flair to create a mixture as surprising as it is charming. The city, one of the oldest on the Iberian Peninsula, has seen these three religious traditions meet in harmony and strife for centuries—an interaction preserved both in the variegated monuments and in the faces of Córdoba's people.

The first inhabitants of the area were Iberian natives who lived in the caves of the nearby Sierra Morena. In 206 B.C.E. Romans conquered the province of Baética, now southern Spain and Portugal. Just 54 years later Roman Praetor Claudius Marcellus, considered by many to be the founder of Córdoba, proclaimed the city capital of Roman Ulterior Spain. With its Romanization, Córdoba became a major cultural center, producing such renowned intellectual figures as the philosopher Seneca and poet Lucanus.

The Visigoths ended Roman rule in the late sixth century, but it was under the Arabs (711-1263) that Córdoba emerged as a seat of intellectual, cultural, and political power. During its peak in the tenth century (dubbed "The Golden Age"), Córdoba was home to many of Spain's most famous citizens, including Maimonides, Luis de Gongora, Bartolomé Bermejo, and Antonio del Castillo.

Although the Catholics reconquered Córdoba in the thirteenth century (and subsequently used it as a strategic base in planning their Reconquista of Granada), they did not entirely eliminate the city's strong Arab and Jewish traditions. On the anniversary of its construction, Muslims and Catholics still gather for joint services in the Mezquita. And every Sunday morning the Mezquita's courtyard bears witness to the eclecticism of Córdoba's young people, who are given to dressing up as punks much more than as flamenco dancers.

Orientation and Practical Information

Córdoba's train station is on Avda. América in the northernmost part of the city; the various bus companies also have depots in this area. The city's prime tourist attraction is the **Judería,** the old Jewish quarter. It lies south of **Plaza de las Tendillas** and extends to the banks of the Guadalquivir. In the Judería lie the Mezquita, the Alcázar, the palace of the Catholic monarchs of Spain, and the maze of narrow, winding streets for which Córdoba is famous. The more modern sections of the city stand to the north, on the other side of Pl. de las Tendillas, near the train station.

Tourist Offices: Provincial, C. Torrijos, 10 (tel. 47 12 35), on the western side of the Mezquita; enter the Palacio de Congresos y Exposiciones and turn right. Very helpful, not only with Córdoba, but with information on all of Andalucía. English spoken. Open Mon.-Fri. 9:30am-2:30pm and 5-7pm, Sat. 9:30am-1:30pm. Also **Municipal,** Pl. de Juda Levi (tel. 29 07 40), 2 blocks west of the Mezquita. Open Mon.-Fri. 8:30am-1:30pm.

Post Office: C. Cruz Conde, 15 (tel. 47 82 67), just north of Pl. de las Tendillas. Open for stamps and Lista de Correos Mon.-Fri. 9am-2pm and 4-6pm, Sat. 9am-2pm. **Telegrams:** Tel. 47 20 09 or 47 03 45. Open Mon.-Fri. 8am-9pm, Sat. 9am-7pm, Sun. 9am-2pm. **Postal Code:** 14001.

Telephones: Pl. de las Tendillas, 7. Open Mon.-Fri. 9am-1:30pm and 5-9pm. **Telephone Code:** 957.

Airport: 6km from the city. Domestic flights only. **Air Condal** (tel. 47 78 35) services Madrid, Barcelona, and Palma de Mallorca. **Iberia,** Ronda de los Tejares (tel. 47 12 27 or 47 26 95). Open Mon.-Fri. 9am-1pm and 4-7pm, Sat. 9am-1:30pm.

Train Station: Avda. de América (tel. 47 82 21 or 47 58 84). **Information:** Tel. 47 93 02. To Sevilla (13 per day, *talgo,* 1-2 hr., 1120ptas; *tranvía,* 625ptas), Madrid (5 per day, *talgo,* 4½-8 hr., 3330ptas; *tranviá,* 1940ptas), Algeciras (2 per day, 5½ hr., 1930ptas), Valencia (3 per day), and Málaga (5 per day, 3 hr., 950ptas). **RENFE,** Ronda de los Tejares, 10 (tel. 47 58 84). Open Mon.-Sat. 9am-2pm and 4:30-7pm.

Buses: Transportes Ureña, Avda. de Cervantes, 22 (tel. 47 23 52). To Sevilla (3 per day, 2-3 hr., 795ptas) and Jaén (5 per day, 3 hr., 575ptas). **Alsina-Graells Sur,** Avda. Medina Azahara, 29 (tel. 23 64 74). To Granada (5 per day, 3-4 hr., 1200ptas), Málaga (3 per day, 3½ hr., 1000ptas), and Cádiz (1 per day, 1415ptas). **Autocares Priego,** Paseo de la Victoria, 29 (tel. 29 01 58). To Madrid (1 per day, 6 hr., 2010ptas), Valencia (3 per day, 3085ptas), and Barcelona (1 per day, 4645ptas).

Taxis: Tendillas (tel. 47 02 91) or **Gran Capitán (tel. 41 51 53).**

Car Rental: Avis, (tel. 47 68 62). **Ciudad Jardin** (tel. 23 28 06). **Hertz** (tel. 47 72 43).

Baggage Check: Café Sagitarió, across from the train station. Holds luggage until 10pm for 100ptas.

Laundromat: Cordobesas, Dalmacia, 3 (tel. 26 98 54), visible on middle of C. Barros, midway between Tendillas and the Mezquita. 5kg washload for 785ptas. Open Mon.-Fri. 9:30am-1:30pm and 5-8:30pm, Sat. 9:30am-1pm.

First Aid: Casa de Socorro, Avda. Republica Argentina, 4 (tel. 23 46 46). **Hospital Cruz Roja** (tel. 29 34 11). **Ambulance:** Tel. 23 76 90.

Police: Campo Madre de Dios, 5 (tel. 25 14 14). **Guardia Civil** (tel. 23 37 53). **Emergency:** Tel. 091 or 092.

Accommodations and Camping

There are plenty of inexpensive lodgings in Córdoba, but the situation gets tight during the summer. An IYHF hostel is on the way; ask at the tourist office.

Near Plaza del Potro

It's a 20-minute hike from the train station, but this modest area is friendly, reasonably priced, and only 10 minutes east of the Mezquita. From the train station, walk 4 blocks down Avda. Cervantes, turn left on Ronda de los Tejares and right on José Cruz Conde. Cut diagonally across Pl. de las Tendillas, walk down Claudio Marcello, turn right on María Cristina, and go down the stairway on the left. Stretching downhill should be C. San Fernando.

Fonda Maestre, C. Romero Barros, 16 (tel 47 53 95), between C. San Fernando and Pl. de Potro. The closest thing Córdoba has to a youth hostel. Friendly owners. Clean rooms with windows and washbasins. Patio with gas stove. Sink and clothesline for washing clothes. Solar-heated showers. Singles 1050ptas. Doubles 1750ptas.

Hostal Lucano, C. Lucano, 1 (tel. 47 60 98). Almost palatial; bright, marble-floored patio and cheerful, clean rooms. Great buy. Singles with bath 1200ptas. Doubles 2000ptas, with bath 2500ptas. Triples with bath 2500ptas.

Fonda Augustina, Zapatería Vieja, 5 (tel. 47 08 72), off Cardenal González halfway between Pl. del Potro and the Mezquita. Old, stark rooms with dilapidated showers on the first premises. However, the adjoining premises at Cardenal González, 48 has clean rooms with modern bathrooms. Singles 800ptas.

In the Judería

Huéspedes Martínez Rücker, Martinez Rücker, 14 (tel. 47 25 62), just west of the Mezquita. Airy, plant-filled courtyard. Pretty furnishings and clean rooms. Don't overstay your welcome: Noon checkout is strictly enforced. Singles 900ptas. Doubles 1800ptas.

Hostal-Residencia Séneca, C. Conde y Luque, 7 (tel. 47 32 34), 2 blocks north of the Mezquita. Impeccably maintained. Breakfast in the patio, with a lively singing canary for company, is a treat. Singles 1325ptas. Doubles 2650ptas, with bath 3200ptas. Breakfast included.

Fonda La Milagrosa, C. Rey Heredia, 12 (tel. 47 33 17). Nice courtyard; clean, small rooms. Most clientele are local students, so rooms open up primarily in summer. Singles 800ptas. Doubles 1400ptas.

Fonda Rey Heredia, C. Rey Heredia, 26 (tel. 47 41 82), on a narrow street parallel to the northeastern corner of the Mezquita. High ceilings, large courtyard, and jigsaw puzzle decor. Modern bathrooms. 1000ptas per person.

Hostal-Residencia El León, C. Céspedes, 6 (tel. 47 30 21), on a street running north from the Mezquita, obscured by the tower on tourist office's map. Beautiful courtyard, but the bathrooms neeed renovating. Singles 1300ptas. Doubles 2600ptas. Breakfast included.

Hostal-Residencia El Triunfo, C. Cardenal González, 87 (tel. 47 63 76), on the Mezquita's southern street. Management runs the place with clockwork efficiency. Clean well-kept rooms. Not an inexpensive proposition. Singles with bath 2350ptas. Doubles with bath 3350ptas. Breakfast included.

Fonda los Leones, C. Saravia, 3 (tel. 47 02 94), off C. Barrosso, a few blocks north of the Mezquita. Don't come here first. Very dark and grim: wallpaper peeling off, walls about 3 feet thick. Caters mainly to soldiers. 750ptas per person. Showers 150ptas.

Near the Train Station

Hotels here tend to be inexpensive, but the rooms are more modern and sterile than in the Judería.

Hostal Residencia La Paz, C. Morería, 7 (tel. 47 37 88), near Pl. de las Tendillas, on a street connecting the plaza with Avda. del Gran Capitán. Friendly management, spacious rooms, hot water. Doubles 1713ptas, with bath 2330ptas. Showers 150ptas.

Hostal Perales, Avda. de los Mozárabes, 19 (tel. 23 03 25). Turn right down Avda. de América as you exit the train station, and go past the park until you reach Avda. de los Mozárabes and blue-white awnings. Cheap and clean, almost institutional; washbasins in each room. Singles 750ptas. Doubles 1500ptas. Showers 200ptas.

Hostal Las Tendillas, Jesús y María, 1 (tel. 23 30 29), on Pl. de las Tendillas. Not particularly distinctive, but rooms and bathrooms are in good shape. Bring a pair of earplugs to block out the plaza revelry. Singles 800ptas. Doubles 1600ptas.

Casa de Huéspedes Córdoba, Avda. de Cervantes, 22 (tel. 47 72 04), down the street from the train station. Friendly managament and wide rooms, but dark yellow halls suffuse gloom throughout. Singles 1000ptas. Doubles 1500ptas.

Camping is available at the **Campamento Municipal,** Avda. del Brillante (tel. 27 50 48). Buses run every 10 minutes from the campsite to monuments in the city. The campground also has a swimming pool. (225ptas, children 175ptas.) Three kilometers out of the city on the Madrid-Cádiz road is **Cerca de Lagartijo** (tel. 25 04 26), which also has a swimming pool. (Open June-Sept. 210ptas, children 110ptas. Cars 190ptas. Tents 220ptas.) If these campsites are full, try **La Campiña,** Carretera Aldea de Quintana a Santaella 11,500 (tel. 31 33 48), a smaller campground farther away, also with a swimming pool. (240ptas, children 180ptas. Car, tent 240ptas.)

Food

To eat in Córdoba without spending a bundle, stay away from the Mezquita. The famous sight attracts more high-priced eateries than Muhammed did followers. These restaurants do offer some of the best specialties, but if you're counting pesetas, branch out into the Judería. Many establishments here still offer *platos combinados* at a moderate 400ptas. For an afternoon beer, try the outdoor cafes along Pl. de las Tendillas. **Café Bar Coronas,** just south on C. Blanco Belmonte, gives a good taste of life in the Judería.

If you leave Córdoba without trying any regional specialties, you may be tormented and maladjusted for the rest of your life. High on any must-eat list are gazpacho (which Córdovans drink out of a glass over ice), *salmorejo* (a sauce version of gazpacho with hard boiled eggs on top), and *rabo de toro* (oxtail meat simmered in a tomato-based sauce). The nearby towns of Montilla and Moriles produce superb wines. There are four types: a light, dry *fino;* darker *amontillado;* sweet *oloroso;* and a fruity, dark wine, *pedro ximénez.* All can be bought for 350 to 450ptas. For an enjoyable diversion, taste the wine and read the famous signatures on the barrels at **Bodegas Campos,** in an alley off C. Lineros, east of Pl. del Potro. This establishment was founded in 1908 and has bullfight posters to prove it. (Open daily 11am-3pm and 6-11pm.) Córdoba is big on nonalcoholic drinks as well: *horchata de chufa, horchata de almendra* (made with almonds), and *granizados* (iced drinks). Try them all at **Helados Navarro,** Ronda de los Tejares, 11. For about 75ptas, you can indulge your sweet tooth in a light *Pastel Córdobés* (pastry shaped like a pie wedge) at any *confitería.*

Restaurant Lalala, C. Cruz del Rastro, 3 (tel. 47 15 30), on the river, several blocks east of the Mezquita. Highly recommended. Huge portions of fresh, carefully prepared food. Several *menús* 400-500ptas. Mixed salad, enough for 2 people, 175ptas. Jug of watermelon sangria (in season) 330ptas. Open daily 8am-4pm and 6-10:30pm.

El Extremeño, Pl. Benavente, 1 (tel. 47 83 14), just inside the old quarter, at the end of C. Conde y Duque. Extremaduran and Andalusian specialities. *Rabo de toro* 425ptas. *Platos combinados* around 400ptas. *Menú* a harsh 750ptas. Try their *pijama* dessert (apricot, pineapple, and cream) for 325ptas. Open daily 1-4pm and 8-11pm.

Mesón-Restaurante El Tablon, C. Cardenal González, 75 (tel. 47 60 61), about 3 blocks from the Mezquita. Outstanding *gazpacho con guarnición.* Just try to fit all the garnishes into your bowl. Ignore the service and enjoy the delicious food and cheap prices. *Platos combinados* 490ptas. *Menú* 600ptas. Open Mon.-Sat. 1-4pm and 8-11pm.

Bar Restaurante Carmona, C. Meléndez y Pelayo (tel. 47 31 10), 2 blocks west of Avda. del Gran Capitán, just south of Hipólito. No-frills atmosphere and food. Come here to fill up. Aesthetic dining dreams are best realized elsewhere. Large selection of *menús* 425ptas. Open daily 1-4pm and 8:30-11pm.

Bar-Mesón Rafaé, C. Buen Pastor, a few blocks north of the Mezquita. Proud of its *rabo de toro* (375ptas). Popular with budget-minded locals for cheap *raciones.* Open Wed.-Mon. 9am-10:30pm.

Restaurant El Caballo Rojo, C. Cardenal Herrero, 28 (tel. 47 53 75), in front of the mosque. Splurge city: They'll accept almost any credit card, but you may never be able to charge again. *Menú de la casa* 1300ptas. Open daily 1-4pm and 8-11pm.

Mesón Bandolero, C. Torrijos, 6 (tel. 41 42 45). Patio dining in imitation of its high-class neighbors, but *plato del día* only 500ptas. Open daily 1-4pm and 8-11pm.

Restaurante Cafetería Halai, C. Rey Heredia, 28. The last outpost of Islamic influence in Córdoba. 550ptas *menú* includes *couscous* and *harira.*

Sights

One is crenelated and buttressed, the other composed of tourist leeches and garish kiosks. But once you've dodged the horsebuggies-for-hire and beaten your way through the endless tour groups, you'll be rewarded by a sight that no crowd, no matter how enormous, could ruin. Situated next to the Juderiá, a 15-minute walk form the center of town, Córdoba's **Mezquita** is surrounded by two walls. The Mezquita was built on a site once occupied by a Visigothic church. Construction began in 785 under the reign of Abderraman I; it took almost two centuries to complete the golden-brown building that now covers an area equivalent to several city blocks. The **Patio de los Naranjos,** the front courtyard open to the public all day, consists of carefully spaced orange trees, palm trees, fountains, and covered archways. Inside, 850 marble, alabaster, and stone pillars—no two of the same height—support hundreds of red-and-white-striped, interlocking, double-decker arches, infusing the interior with a sense of immensity. At the far side stands the *mihrab,* or prayer niche. The opening to this small, intricately carved area resembles a keyhole; it sparkles with gold, pink, and blue marble mosaics that were gifts to the Córdoba caliphs from Emperor Constantine VII of Greece. Three domes supported by woven arches enclose the *mihrab;* the lighted central dome, with its ornate design and spider-web pattern, is stunning.

When Córdoba was conquered by the Christians in 1236, the mosque was converted into a church. Only in the early sixteenth century, however, was the Bishop of Córdoba granted permission to modify the building substantially. The result disappointed even the king who authorized it: The cathedral's Christian arches, huge gold and silver organ, and baroque mahogany choir stalls stand in rude contrast to the quiet elegance of the Islamic arches. This juxtaposition of styles is apparent from the outside as well; climb the tower to see exactly how the cathedral was planted in the middle of the mosque. (Open daily 10:30am-1:30pm and 4-7pm; Oct.-March daily 10:30am-1:30pm and 3:30-5:30pm. Admission 250ptas.)

Construction of the **Alcázar,** the palace of the Catholic monarchs, began in 1328 during the campaign for the conquest of Granada, and between 1490 and 1821 the palace served as headquarters for the Inquisition. Its walls surround a beautiful garden of manicured hedges, colorful flower beds, terraced goldfish ponds, multiple fountains, and palm trees. Inside, the museum contains some first-century Roman mosaics and a third-century Roman marble sarcophagus that resembles a large bathtub. (Open daily 9:30am-1:30pm and 5-8pm; Oct.-April daily 9:30am-1:30pm and 4-7pm. Gardens illuminated May-Sept. daily 10pm-1am. Admission 100ptas.)

The **Sinagoga,** a solemn reminder of the expulsion and genocide of Spanish Jewry in 1492, is tucked away on C. de los Judíos, marked by a statue of Maimonides. Mozarabic patterns and Hebrew inscriptions from the psalms decorate the walls of the quadrangular temple. The statue, based on an original portrait by a French artist that was later destroyed, was used as the model for the New Israeli Shekel. (Open Tues.-Sat. 10am-2pm and 5-7pm, Sun. 10am-1:30pm. Admission 75ptas.)

The **Museo de Bellas Artes,** in Pl. del Potro, now occupies the building that was once King Ferdinand and Queen Isabel's Hospital of Charity. Works by well-known Spanish artists such as Murillo, Goya, and Ribera as well as a collection of paintings by foreign artists are on display. (Open Tues.-Sat. 10am-2pm and 6-8pm, Sun. 10am-1:30pm; Oct.-April Tues.-Sat. 10am-2pm and 5-7pm. Admission 250ptas.) Also in the plaza, the **Museo Julio Romero de Torres** contains the major works of this anachronistic native artist whose favorite—in fact, only—subjects were beautiful women. He painted them all—his mother, the popular flamenco dancers of his day, and his servant's daughter—but never his own wife. (Open Tues.-Sun. 10am-1:30pm; Sept.-June Tues.-Sun. 10am-1:30pm and 5-7pm. Free.) The **Posada del Potro,** a fourteenth-century inn described by Cervantes in *Don Quixote,* is next door.

The **Museo Taurino y de Arte Cordobés,** at Pl. de Maimonides, devotes one little room to leatherwork, ceramics, and other crafts; the rest is dedicated to *la corrida,* with galleries full of the heads of bulls who killed matadors and other unfortunates. Rooms are devoted to the *tauromaquia* of the Cordovan matadors Lagartijo, Guerrita, and Manolete. A copy of Manolete's tomb is exhibited beneath the stretched hide of his nemesis, Islero. (Open Tues.-Sat. 9:30am-1:30pm and 5-8pm, Sun. 9:30am-1:30pm; Oct.-April Tues.-Sat. 9:30am-1:30pm and 4-7pm, Sun. 9:30am-1:30pm. Admission 100ptas.)

The **Monumento a Manolete,** in the Pl. Conde Priego, honors this local hero. The monument borders **Barrio de los Toreros,** where some of Spain's most famous matadors were born and lived. Continue from Pl. Conde Priego to Pl. Santa Marina and turn left on the Mayor de Santa Marina. Pl. de la Lagunilla is a few blocks down on the left. In the center of the tranquil public garden, a bust of Manolete overlooks the house where he spent a great part of his life.

Just southwest of the barrio, on C. Capuchinos in a small plaza of the same name, is the **Cristo de los Faroles.** Four large lanterns surround the crucifix, which is known for the anomalous two nails in the feet. This plaza, one of the most famous religious shrines in Spain, frequently hosts all-night vigils.

The **Museo Arqueológico** is on Pl. Paez, several blocks northeast of the Mezquita. Housed in a Renaissance mansion, the museum contains a chronological exhibit of tools, ceramics, statues, coins, jewelry, and sarcophagi, including interesting stone carvings of lions that date from 500 B.C.E. (Open Tues.-Sun. 10am-2pm and 6-8pm, Sun. 10am-1:30pm; Oct.-April Tues.-Sat. 10am-2pm and 5-7pm. Admission 250ptas.)

The townspeople take great pride in their traditional *patios,* many dating from Roman times. These open-air courtyards offer hidden, tranquil pockets of orange and lemon trees, flowers, and fountains in the otherwise crowded and noisy old quarter of the city. You'll find the most beautiful patios at the **Palacio del Marqués de Viana,** Pl. D. Gome (open Thurs.-Tues. 9am-2pm; Oct.-May Thurs.-Tues. 10am-1pm and 4-6pm. admission 150ptas); C. Basilio, 50; C. Cardenal Herrero, 16; and C. Badanas, 15. For the first two weeks of May, Cordovans celebrate the **Festival de los Patios,** with flamenco dances, classical music concerts, and a city-wide patio contest.

Entertainment

Entertainment in Córdoba assumes many forms: flamenco dancer, bull, *oopa,* or even guitarist. A **flamenco** performance here can be a delight, especially if you attend a performance of one of the flamenco groups that travel across Spain; ask at the tourist office if any are in town. Otherwise, follow your ears. Numerous performances take place in the restaurants in front of the Mezquita; **Restaurante Rafael,** for example, offers decent dance floor entertainment for about 800ptas per person. For a less formal performance, order a drink on C. La Luna, where the flamenco music at **Mesón La Muralla** entices local women to participate. This bar and **Mesón La Luna** share a large outdoor patio where students often gather to sing, play guitar, and dance flamenco. To reach these *mesónes,* take the first right after heading south from the Museo Taurino, and follow the winding street to its end. Bulls perform the flamenco during **bullfights** at the Las Califas bullring. Check at the tourist office for schedule.

Those in search of more peaceful fun may attend one of Córdoba's many **concerts.** Every Sunday the Municipal Orchestra gives a concert in the Alcázar. In the summer, the city's open air theater hosts concerts and festivals including the **International Guitar Festival** from July to October. (For information and tickets stop by the office at F.P.M. Gran Teatro, Avda. Gran Capitan, 3. Tel. 48 02 37 or 48 06 44. Tickets 400-800ptas.)

Nights come alive along **Calle de Osario** and **Calle de los Reyes Católicos,** both north of Pl. de las Tendillas. Most of the city's popular pubs and bars are located in this area. In addition, Pl. de las Tendillas and the area immediately north and west of C. Cruz Conde sport a large number of outdoor cafes and *terrazas.* Try **Bar Restaurante Siena** or **Bar Restaurante Boston** in Pl. de las Tendillas or **Bar Restaurante Oscar** in Pl. Carrillos.

For authentic local entertainment, visit Córdoba during a festival. **Semana Santa,** with its floats and parades, is the biggest. Late May brings the **National Contest of Flamenco,** and the **Feria de Nuestra Señora de la Salud** (Fair of Our Lady of Good Health), in which thousands of Cordovan women dress in traditional apparel.

Córdoba celebrates its patroness in early Ssptember with the **Feria de Nuestra Señora de la Fuensanta.**

Near Córdoba

Eight kilometers northwest of the city lies one of Córdoba's hidden treasures, the **Medina Azahara.** Constructed in the tenth century by Abderraman III as a gift to the favorite wife in his harem, the medina was considered one of the greatest palaces of its time. The structure, built into the Sierra Morena, was divided into three terraces; one containing the palace, another holding the living quarters for the thousands of servants and attendants, and the third enclosing the medina's gardens. The site was surrounded by almond groves because Azahara—the favorite wife—lived in Granada and loved the snow in the Sierra Nevada. When spring came, the almond groves turned white, reminding Azahara of her beloved snow. Interest in the medina as an archeological treasure is fairly recent; the site was first excavated in 1944, and only in the last two decades has the government attempted to preserve and restore it. Efforts are now moving at a faster pace.

The **Salón de Abd al-Rahman III,** the grand hall on the lower terraces, is almost completely restored to its original, intricate, geometrical beauty. Even with the rest of the palace in rubble, the structure retains its ancient grandeur and solemn immensity. (Open Tues.-Sat. 10am-2pm and 6-8pm, Sun. 10am-1:30pm; Oct.-April Tues.-Sat. 10am-2pm and 4-6pm, Sun. 10am-1:30pm. Admission 250ptas.)

Reaching Medina Azahara takes some effort. The Ayuntamiento in Córdoba runs a free tour bus that leaves from the Alcázar on Wednesday and Friday at 10am. (Check first with the tourist office or Ayuntamiento.) Otherwise, **Autotransportes San Sebastián,** C. de la Bogeda (tel. 47 04 28), runs five buses per day in that direction (150 ptas). Ask the driver to let you off near the medina; you'll find yourself about 2km from the ruins. To return to Córdoba, either flag down the same bus on its way back or hitch. Don't jump any brick walls in the area; Ramón Sánchez keeps his fighting bulls here.

Thirteen kilometers from Córdoba on the rail line to Sevilla, the impenetrable **castle** at **Almodóvar del Río** crowns a solitary, rocky mount. The castle is a remarkably well-preserved example of Gothic-Mudéjar architecture. On the second Sunday in May the town celebrates the **Romería de la Virgen de Fátima** with a parade from Cuatro Caminos to Fuen Real Bajo roads. Frequent trains run to Almodóvar del Río from Córdoba (8 per day, 18 min., 100ptas, last train back at 9:42pm).

Osuna

It's easy to imagine the Dukes of Osuna sallying forth from their mountaintop retreat to scourge the countryside for the *osunas* (bears) that once filled the land. No bears are around today, but Osuna's former status as a ducal seat is apparent in its handsome stone mansions.

Orientation and Practical Information

Halfway between Sevilla and Antequera, Osuna is a daytrip from either. Trains stop on the side of Calle Sevilla, a 15-min. uphill walk from the center. The bus stop is on Plaza Santa Rita—walk down C. Carrera to reach the **Plaza Mayor** (5 min.). Most of the sights are on the hilltop, accessible by the road leading up from the southeast corner of the plaza.

Tourist Office: Viajes Alharafe, Pl. Mayor (tel. 81 16 17). Helpful staff will store bags for the afternoon. Open Tues.-Sun. 10am-1:30pm and 4:30-7:30pm; in winter Tues.-Sun. 10am-1:30pm and 3:30-6:30pm.

Post Office: C. Carrera, 8, between the bus stop and the Pl. Mayor. Open for mail services Mon.-Sat. 9am-2pm; for **telegrams** Mon.-Fri. 9am-3pm, Sat. 9am-1pm. **Postal Code:** 41640.

Telephone Code: 954.

Train Station: C. Sevilla. To Sevilla (5 per day, 1½ hr., 450ptas) and Bobadilla (4 per day, ¾ hr., 140ptas) for additional connections.

Bus Stop: Pl. Santa Rita (tel. 81 01 46). Empresa Díaz Paz (tel. 41 52 58) runs buses to Sevilla (7 per day, 3 on Sun., 2 hr., 450ptas). Other *empresas* stop here for connections to Málaga (9:30am) and Granada (9am, 11am, and 5pm)—ask at tourist office for updates.

Medical Emergency: Hospital Comarcal (tel. 81 09 00).

Police: Municipal (tel. 81 00 50). **Guardia Civil:** Tel. 81 09 13. **Emergency:** Dial 91.

Accommodations and Food

More suited to daytrippers and careening carloads of touring Spaniards, Osuna has little to offer in the way of a budget bed. Those with a little pluck might try several of the loud, dirty bars with beds on C. Carrera between the bus stop and the Pl. Mayor. Otherwise, hike past the plaza to reach **Hotel Caballo Blanco,** at the corner of C. de Ecija and C. de Granada, for clean rooms. (Singles with bath 1100ptas. Doubles with bath 1900ptas.) The restaurant downstairs serves relatively inexpensive food. Try *los libritos,* a dish with *habas,* ham, and stuffed potatoes (600ptas). Across the street, **Hotel Las Cinco Puertas,** C. Carrera, 79 (tel. 81 12 43), has comfortable rooms, though they're a bit noisy from bar below. (Singles 725ptas, doubles with shower 1500ptas.) The restaurant is convenient, though prices are a bit stiff. The *gazpacho flamenco* (300ptas) or the *cocido* (650ptas) are safe choices.

For a meal that involves more exercise than a set of stairs, try **Restaurante Meson del Duque,** Pl. dde la Duquesa, 2 (tel. 81 31 01), on the road to the Museo Arqueologico and Iglesia Colegiata. The *menú* runs a whopping 850ptas, but it's tasty, and comes with a flower-filled view of the plains from an outdoor terrace. (Open Tues.-Sun. 1-4pm and 9pm-midnight.) For appetizers, *raciones,* and a la carte dishes, visit **Taberna Andaluza,** Alfonso XII, 61 (tel. 81 15 69). (Open Thurs.-Tues. 1-5pm and 9pm-midnight.)

True budget watchers will have to pick the oranges off the trees in the Plaza Mayor (very sour), or at least stop at the adjoining **mercado,** accessible through the iron gate to the left of the tourist office. (Open Mon.-Sat. 9am-2pm.)

Sights

Crowning the hilltop, the **Iglesia Colegiata** dominates the horizon, commanding a fine panorama of the community and countryside. Built in 1535, the church serves as a walking tour through the history of the ducal family. The third Duke of Osuna was for a time the protector of Ribera: To the left of the main altar hangs his stunning rendition of the Crucifixion, while the neighboring treasury holds a quartet of canvases portraying Saints Bartholemew, Peter, Sebastian, and Jerome. The dukes had their own private chapel built beneath the main one, complete with pulpit and choir. On the way to the depths one you'll pass a tiny plateresque patio and the sacristy, which includes a splendid *Ecce Homo* canvas by Morales. The neighboring sixteenth-century mausoleum holds the Duke of Osuna's impressive treasures. By far the most intriguing of the chambers is the **Panteón Ducal,** a darkly morbid sepulchre with low ceilings. Only three empty spaces await the remaining nobility. Among others interred here is Goya's protector. Goya painted a portrait of the ducal family for him that now hangs in the Prado. The only duke not buried here, a former Spanish ambassador to Russia, lies in a marble sarcophagus upstairs. Though he did lose most of the family's money, the real reason he lies apart from his ancestors is that his coffin could not fit through the sepulchre's entrance. (Admission 150ptas.)

Sharing the summit with the church is a sixteenth-century **palace** with handsome, pointed towers (now the local secondary school). Just downhill from the church's entrance rests the **Monasterio de la Encarnación.** One of the resident nuns will show you room after room of polychromatic wooden sculptures and silver crucifixes, but the sights not to miss are the eighteenth-century main retable with a touching statue of *Cristo de la Misericordia* in the adjoining baroque church and the typical Sevillan *azutelo* tiles in the shadow of the sun-filled patio. (Admission 150ptas. Homemade sweets 150ptas.)

The **Museo Arqueológico,** on the road to the hilltop, houses a collection of Roman artifacts found in the vicinity and replicas of pieces sent on to Madrid and Paris. Try not to awaken the attendant. (Free.) The Ducal Sepulchre, monastery, and museum hold the same hours. (Open Tues.-Sun. 10am-1:30pm and 4:30-7:30pm; in winter Tues.-Sun. 10am-1:30pm and 3:30-6:30pm.)

Sevilla

Sevilla's whitewashed grace, jasmined balconies, and exotic parks may convince you that romantic cities still exist. Site of a small Roman acropolis founded by Julius Caesar, thriving seat of Moorish culture, focal point of the Spanish Renaissance, and guardian angel of traditional Andalusian culture, Sevilla has never failed to spark the imagination of newcomers. Jean Cocteau included it (along with Venice and Peking) in his trio of magic cities. St. Teresa denounced it as the work of the devil's hand. The Moorish historian al-Saqundi proclaimed that even the milk of birds could be found here. *Carmen, Don Giovanni,* the *Barber of Seville,* Dostoyevsky's *Grand Inquisitor,* and Zorilla's play *Don Juan Tenorio* are only a few of the artistic works inspired by this metropolis. The city has lost none of this charm. Today, dexterous matadors still outwit raging bulls every summer Sunday. Clapping, tapping, and flamenco strumming echo through the night air, and pilgrims, zealots, and parade enthusiasts gather annually during Semana Santa and the Feria de Abril for both holy and unholy festivities.

Orientation and Practical Information

Throughout the past few centuries, the city has expanded, swallowing neighboring villages. These communities, now *barrios* of the city, have not lost their distinct characters. **Río Guadalquivir** flows roughly north-south through Sevilla, having been redirected by the extension of a peninsula from the east bank to the west some forty years ago. Most of the city, including the labyrinthine alleyways of the old **Barrio de Santa Cruz,** is on the east bank, while the **Barrio de Triana** and **Barrio de los Remedios**—where you'll find some of the most active nightlife and least expensive food—lie on the west bank. The **cathedral,** next to the Barrio Santa Cruz, defines Sevilla's center. If you have just arrived in town or ever lose your way, just look for the cathedral's conspicuous bell tower. In front of the cathedral runs **Avenida de la Constitución** with the tourist office, post office, banks, and travel agencies. Sevilla's **shopping district** lies north of the cathedral where Avda. de la Constitución fades into **Plaza Nueva,** bordered by a bustling pedestrian zone. **Calle Sierpes** is at the core of this cluster of arcades and culminates in the **Campana**—a busy intersection laced with inexpensive cafes and *cafeterías* that comprises Sevilla's commercial center. For other good, cheap restaurants and *pensiones,* try lesser-known areas such as **Barrio de la Puerta de la Carne** and **Barrio de la Puerta de Carmona,** contiguous with each other and northeast of the Barrio de Santa Cruz.

To reach Avda. de la Constitución from **Plaza de Armas (Córdoba) train station,** walk south along C. Arjona and then Paseo Colón, turn left on C. Santander, and follow it to Avda. de la Constitución. From the **main bus station** or the **San Bernardo (Cádiz) train station,** turn left on C. Menéndez y Pelayo, right on C. San Fernando, and right again onto Avda. de la Constitución. **Municipal transport** via buses (Sevilla gave up on its subway system because of embezzlement and the tilting of the cathedral) is extensive but only necessary when completely traversing the city. Most lines (55ptas) stop along Pl. Nueva, in front of the cathedral, or on Pl. del Duque de la Victoria.

A word of caution: Don't leave your belongings unattended either on the street or in a car. Sevilla lives up to its reputation as the Spanish capital of pickpockets

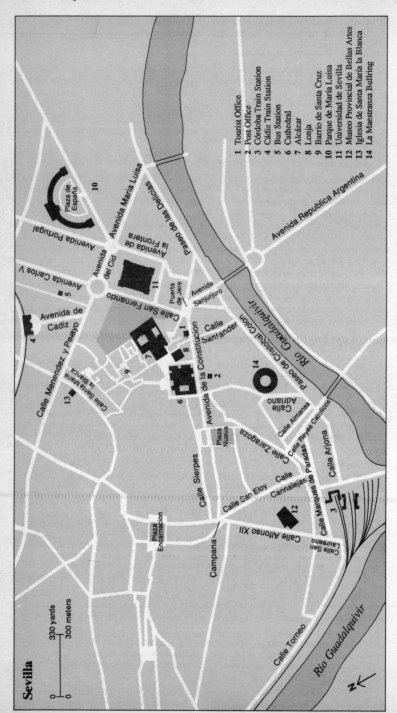

Sevilla

1 Tourist Office
2 Post Office
3 Córdoba Train Station
4 Cádiz Train Station
5 Bus Station
6 Cathedral
7 Alcázar
8 Lonja
9 Barrio de Santa Cruz
10 Parque de María Luisa
11 Universidad de Sevilla
12 Museo Provincial de Bellas Artes
13 Iglesia de Santa María la Blanca
14 La Maestranza Bullring

and car theft. To avoid trouble, dress neatly but inconspicuously, try not to carry large sums of money, and avoid dark and solitary places at night.

Tourist Office: Avda. de la Constitución, 21B (tel. 22 14 04), 1 block south of the cathedral (to the right facing the main facade). Helpful staff, English (usually) spoken. Excellent selection of city and regional information—get their map of Barrio de Santa Cruz. Open daily 9:30am-7pm; Oct.-May Mon.-Sat. 9:30am-7pm.

Student Travel Office: Viajes TIVE, Avda. Reina Mercedes, 53 (tel. 61 31 88). Helpful staff. Open Mon.-Fri. 9am-2:30pm, Sat. 9am-12:30pm.

Consulates: U.S., Paseo de las Delicias, 7 (tel. 28 18 84 or 28 18 85). **Canada,** Avda. de la Constitución, 30, 2nd floor, #4 (tel. 22 94 13). **Great Britian,** Pl. Nueva, 8 (tel. 22 88 75). Open Mon.-Fri. 9am-2pm. In emergencies, call Madrid for referral in Sevilla. In charge of **New Zealand** affairs, as well as **Australian** cases referred from Madrid.

After-Hours Currency Exchange: El Corte Inglés, on Pl. del Duque de la Victoria or next to Motel Lebreros (15 min. from the cathedral), offers exchange booths. 2% commission. Open Mon.-Sat. 10am-9pm.

American Express Representative: Viajes Alhambra, C. Coronel Segui, 3 (tel. 21 29 23), just north of Pl. Nueva. Long lines and a 2% commission: Change traveler's checks at a bank. Emergency check-cashing for cardholders. Open Mon.-Fri. 9am-1pm and 4-8pm, Sat. 9am-1pm.

Post Office: Avda. de la Constitución, 32 (tel. 22 88 80), across from Lonja Palace, and Avda. Molini (tel. 61 56 95). Open for stamps Mon.-Fri. 9am-9pm, Sat. 9am-2pm; for Lista de Correos Mon.-Fri. 9am-8pm, Sat. 10am-2pm. **Telegrams:** Tel. 22 20 00, national or 22 68 60, international. Open Mon.-Sat. 8am-9pm. After hours, telegrams can be sent from the back of the building on C. Tomás de Ibarra, Letra D. Open Mon.-Sat. 9pm-midnight, Sun. and holidays 8am-10pm. **Postal Code:** 41001.

Telephones: Pl. Nueva, 3. Open Mon.-Fri. 9am-1pm and 5-9pm, Sat. 9am-noon. **Telephone Code:** 954.

Airport: About 12km from town (tel. 31 61 11 or 51 61 11). **Iberia** at C. Almirante Lobo (tel. 22 96 39). Buses depart from Puerta Bar Iberia, C. Almirante Lobo, for the airport (10 per day 9am-10:20pm, 169ptas). To Madrid (5 per day, 9000ptas). Prices vary with season.

Train Stations: Estación Plaza de Armas (Córdoba), Pl. de Armas, 56 (tel. 22 88 17), just off C. Marqués de Paradas. To Córdoba (12 per day; *tranvía,* 2 hr., 610ptas; *talgo,* 1 hr., 10,140ptas), Granada (5 per day; *tranvía,* 5 hr., 1240ptas; *ter,* 4 hr., 1930ptas), Málaga (5 per day; *tranvía,* 3½ hr., 1050ptas; *ter,* 2½ hr., 1590ptas), and Madrid (6 per day; *tranvía,* 8 hr., 2500ptas; *talgo,* 6 hr., 4130ptas). Frequent trains to Bobadilla (2 hr., 690ptas) for additional Andalusian connections. *Estación de San Bernardo (Cádiz),* C. San Bernardo, 13 (tel. 23 22 55), just off C. Menéndez y Pelayo. Regional service to Cádiz (7 per day; *tranvía,* 2 hr., 750ptas; *rápido,* 1½ hr., 1250ptas).

Bus Stations: Ask at the tourist office for their list of major routes. Main station, C. José María Osborne, 11 (tel. 41 71 11), houses many carriers. **Alsina Graells** (tel. 41 88 11) serves Almería (2 per day, 3½ hr., 2500ptas), Córdoba (3 per day, 2 hr., 795ptas), Granada (5 per day, 4 hr., 1465-1735ptas), and Málaga (5 per day, 3 hr., 1215-1435ptas). **Transportes Comes** (tel. 41 68 58) travels to Cádiz (8 per day, 1¾ hr., 740ptas), Algeciras (3 per day), and Jerez (7 per day, 1½ hr., 595ptas). **La Unión de Benisa** (tel. 41 46 60) services Madrid (3 per day, 8 hr., 2760ptas), Valencia (3 per day, 10 hr., 3890ptas), Barcelona (1 per day, 18 hr., 5395ptas), and Ubeda (3 per day). **Los Amarillos** (tel. 41 52 01) runs to Ronda (2 per day, 3 hr., 800ptas) and Marbella (2 per day). In addition, **Estación de Empresa Damas,** C. Segura, 18 (tel. 22 22 72), serves the Huelva line.

Taxis: Dial-a-Taxi (tel. 62 04 61) or **Radio Taxi** (tel. 58 00 00). All cabs in Sevilla have meters. Fare should be 68ptas initial charge, 39ptas per km, 42ptas surcharge for Sun. and late-night service.

Car Rentals: Avis, Avda. de la Constitución, 15B (tel. 21 53 70 or 22 62 94), next to Turismo. Open Mon.-Fri. 9am-1pm and 4-7:30pm, Sat. 9am-1pm. **Ital,** C. República Argentina, 9. **Hertz,** Avda. Republica Argentina, 3 (tel. 27 88 87 or 27 07 98), and at the airport (tel. 51 47 20).

Hitchhiking: To Madrid and Córdoba, take bus #20 or 21 to the Avda. Pedro Romero and walk down C. Telasonica to the highway. To Granada and Málaga, take bus #23 to Canodromo and walk away from the park to the highway (about 20 min.). To Cádiz and Huelva, take bus #34 to Heliopolis and walk west to the bridge.

Baggage Check: At the main bus station. 45ptas per day.

English Books: Librería Vértice, C. Mateus Gago, 24A, just up from the cathedral. Open Mon.-Fri. 10am-2pm and 4-8pm, Sat. 10am-2pm. **Librería Pascual Lázaro,** C. Sierpas, 4 (just off the Campana). A good collection of tourist guides and glossy books on Andalucía.

Foreign Newspapers: Large newsstand at C. Sierpes and the Campana. Others with smaller selections are on Pl. Nueva. **Esteban,** C. Alemanes, next to the cathedral, has a good selection of daily newspapers, including the *Tribune* (135ptas) in addition to a rack of Penguin classics.

Laundromats: Lavandería Robledo, C. F. Sanchez Bedoya, 18 (tel. 21 81 32), 1 block across Avda. Constitución, in front of cathedral. Next-day service. Wash and dry 5kg for 850ptas. Open Mon.-Fri. 10am-2pm and 5-8pm, Sat. 10am-2pm.

Public Toilets: Off Avda. de la Constitución, between the cathedral and the Lonja Palace.

Swimming Pool: Piscina Municipal "Sevilla," Ciudad Jardin, 81 (tel. 63 58 92), west of Pl. de Armas station. Admission 200ptas. Open June-Sept. daily 11am-8pm.

Lost Property: C. Alamansa, 21 (tel. 21 26 28).

Women's Center: C. Mateus Gago, 9 (tel. 21 33 75).

Medical Emergency: Casa de Socorro, Jesús del Gran Poder, 34 (tel. 38 24 61). **Hospital Universitario,** Avda. Dr. Fedriani (tel. 37 84 00). English spoken.

Police: Pl. de la Gavidia (tel. 22 88 40). **Emergency:** Tel. 091.

Accommodations and Camping

Thanks to the local student population, Sevilla has plenty of inexpensive *hostales* and *casas de huéspedes.* Many proprietors treat even those who stay for a single night as their personal guests. During Semana Santa and the Feria de Abril, scavenging groups of backpackers will be tracking down the last few rooms at tripled prices. Reservations are a must to retain sanity, though sometimes rooms do appear during the last few days of each festival. If you're really stuck, ask in other *pensiones* or in bars for *casas particulares* that open up during the celebrations (abouts 1000ptas). With the exception of festival times, bargaining is the rule; don't accept the first price you are quoted unless places seem filled to the hilt.

Fernando el Santo Youth Hostel (IYHF), C. Isaac Peral, 2 (tel. 61 31 50), several kilometers out of town. Take bus #34 or walk. Crowded and noisy, housing mostly local students. Cheapest beds around, but not worth the inconvenience. 2 rooms per bathroom with 4 sinks and 2 showers. TV lounge. Recreation room. No curfew. 3 night max. stay. 470ptas, nonmembers 570ptas.

Albergue-Residencia Juvenil Alameda de Hercules, C. Peral, 16 (tel. 37 52 90). 1 common bathroom. 3 to 8 people per rrom. No dining room; it has been turned into a recreation room. Curfew 12:30am. 530ptas.

Barrio de Santa Cruz

Look here for charm as well as convenience. The streets are closed to motorists. Only those feeling extremely lucky should attempt to prowl this area during the first few days of the *feria.*

Hostal Residencia Monreal, C. Rodrigo Caro, 8 (tel. 21 41 66). From the cathedral, walk north on C. Mateos Gago to the 1st block on your right. A wonderful location and a lovely courtyard. Be prepared for some really rough edges: sloppy service, tempermental plumbing, and possibly an inflated bill. Bar and restaurant with TV open all day. Singles 1000ptas. Doubles 1900ptas, with bath 3900ptas. Hot showers a rip-off at 400ptas. Breakfast 350ptas. Dinner 750ptas.

Hostal Virgen de los Reyes, C. Alvarez Quintero, 31 (tel. 21 48 51), west of the cathedral's Moorish gate. A great deal. Whitewashed rooms with high ceilings, terraces, new bathrooms, kitchen facilities, bar, TV room, and laundry facilities. Singles 1100ptas. Doubles 2200ptas.

Hostal-Residencia Córdoba, C. Farnesio, 12 (tel. 22 74 98). Clean and run by a friendly family. Recent renovations mean modern bathrooms, but bland surroundings. Singles 1000ptas, with bath 1500ptas. Doubles 1800ptas, with bath 2700ptas.

Pensión Vergara, C. Ximénez de Encisco, 11 (tel. 22 47 38). From the cathedral, go north on C. Mateos Gago, east on Rodrigo Caro, and north on Pje. Andreu. Look for the tiny black *camas* sign above the doorway. Rather cramped with low ceilings and small bathrooms. Abundant knickknacks give it character. Singles 800ptas. Doubles 1600ptas.

Huéspedes Buen Dormir, C. Farnesio, 8 (tel. 21 74 92). Climb north from the cathedral on Mateus Gago, bear left on main thoroughfare, then turn right on Fabiola. Look for the alley across from #10. Colorful and economical, though some of the rooms are tiny. Sevilla's version of Dr. Doolittle—the chirping and barking of resident pets may prevent the *buen dormir*. 800ptas.

Barrios de la Puerta de la Carne/de la Puerta de Carmona

These old areas lack the distinction of Barrio de Santa Cruz, their neighbor to the southwest, but rates might be lower, and rooms during fiestas easier to find. Try the main thoroughfares of C. San Esteban, C. Santa María la Blanca, and Avda. Menéndez Pelayo, and the plazas Alfalfa, Pilatos, and los Curtidores.

Casa Saez, Pl. Curtidores, 6 (tel. 41 67 53). Spotless. Plainly furnished rooms with high ceilings. Singles 900ptas. Doubles 1700ptas. Showers 125ptas.

Hostal Pérez Montilla, C. Archeros, 16 (tel. 41 23 25) and Pl. Curtidores, 13 (tel. 42 18 54), around the corner off C. Santa María la Blanca. The lobby uncannily resembles an Arab bath. Spotless rooms range from threadbare to elegant. Singles 1000ptas. Doubles 1500ptas, with adjoining shower 1800ptas, with complete bath 2200ptas.

Hostal Bienvenido, C. Archeros, 14 (tel. 41 36 55), near the Pl. de Curtidores. Welcoming managers speak English. Simple, clean rooms. Lovely terrace upstairs for sunbathing or writing letters on tables under a thatched roof. Singles 900ptas. Doubles 1800ptas.

Casa Diego, Pl. Curtidores, 7 (tel. 41 35 52). Marble staircase leads to well-kept rooms with new furniture and modern bathrooms that shine as brightly as the *señora's* disposition. Singles 850ptas. Doubles 1700ptas. Showers 200ptas.

Hostal-Residencia Javier, C. Tintes, 22 (tel. 41 18 56). From Pl. Pilatos, take C. San Esteban north; Tintes is your 3rd right. You'll feel right at home; owner has strong maternal instincts. Singles 900ptas, with bath 2000ptas. Doubles 1900ptas. Showers 200ptas.

Hostal Bonanza, Sales y Ferre, 12 (tel. 22 86 14), in the depths of a labyrinth, but perhaps worth the hike. From Pl. Pilatos, head south on C. Aguillas to C. del Rey Don Pedro. Cross onto Alfalfa, take the 1st right, and go to the end of the block. Rooms are decorated with odd *Dating Game*-vintage furniture. Fun owner. Singles with shower 1800ptas. Doubles with shower 3000ptas, with bath 4000ptas. Discounts given for stays over one night.

Casa de Huéspedes San Esteban, C. San Esteban, 8 (tel. 22 25 49), just north of Pl. Pilatos. The proprietor has a great sense of humor. Some rooms are seedy—ask to see them. Singles 950ptas. Doubles 1900ptas.

Zona "El Centro"

Though less picturesque, this area is closer to the Pl. de Armas train station and the commercial district. Lodgings here will be noisier—watch for neighboring bars that may become raucous nightspots. From the train station, take a left as you exit and then a right on C. Marqués de Paradas. C. Canalejas, the first left, turns into C. San Eloy after 4 blocks.

Hostal La Gloria, C. de San Eloy, 58 (tel. 22 26 73). Bright and clean. Modest rooms in good shape. Singles 1200ptas, with bath 1500ptas. Doubles 2000ptas, with bath 2500-3000ptas.

Hostal Los Angeles, C. de San Eloy, 37 (tel. 22 80 49). The place itself is rather run-down, but the rooms are attractive, with tile floors, wood furniture, and ceilings high enough for any Celtic. Singles 1000ptas. Doubles 2000ptas. Triples 3000ptas.

Hostal-Residencia Generalife, C. Ternán Caballero, 4 (tel. 22 46 38), off C. San Elox. In need of some renovations, but very clean. Singles 1000ptas. Doubles 2000ptas.

Elsewhere

Hotel Simon, C. Garcia de Vinuesa, 19 (tel. 22 66 60), across Avda. de la Constitución from the cathedral. A renovated, eighteenth-century mansion with a beautiful inner courtyard and fountain. Laundry service available. Call ahead. Singles 1300ptas, with bath 2200ptas. Doubles 2500ptas, with bath 3500ptas.

Residencia Sevilla, C. Daoiz, 5 (tel. 38 41 61), 2 blocks from the Campana. Wonderful, sparkling clean, traditionally furnished rooms off a grand patio. Singles with bath 1750ptas. Doubles with bath 4505ptas.

The area has three **campsites,** each accessible by an airport bus. For **Sevilla,** take the bus to the Carmona stop; for **Club de Campo** and **Villsom,** get off at the Dos Hermanas stop. Sevilla, Carretera Madrid-Cádiz, km 534 (tel. 51 43 79), sits 5km out of town, near the airport. A happy medium, its close to the city, but unmistakably in the country with its acacia trees and gardens. The swimming pool is a plus. (Adults and vans 250ptas, children 200ptas, cars 250ptas, and motorcycles 175ptas.) Club de Campo, Avda. de la Libertad, 13-Ctra. Sevilla-Dos Hermanas (tel. 72 02 50), 15km out of the city, also boasts a pool. (Adults and cars 255ptas, children and motorcycles 180ptas, and vans 300ptas.) Closer to Itálica, Villsom, Ctra. Sevilla-Cádiz, km 554-8 (tel. 72 08 28), lies 18km out of the city. (Open Feb.-Nov. Adults and cars 275ptas, children 210ptas, vans 290ptas, and motorcycles 220ptas. Hot showers free.)

Food

Excellent restaurants serving typical Andalusian specialities abound in Sevilla, but food tends to be expensive by Spanish standards. Nonetheless, with some hunting you'll eat well at affordable prices. The cheapest places are the *bar-restaurantes* around the Pl. de Armas train station on **C. Arjona** and **Avda. Marqués de Paradas.** (Utter cheapness available at **Restaurante Juli,** C. Arjona, 7, with 325-350ptas *menús.*) Even in the central tourist and commercial areas, however, you should be able to find a full meal for 400-500ptas. After hours, your best bet is to look around the cathedral or the Campanas/C. Sierpes districts.

There is a **market** near the bullring on C. Pastor y Leandro, between C. Almansa and C. Arenal, but prices are cheaper at the **Mercadillo de Triana,** across the Puente de Isabel II and down the stairs to the right. (Both open Mon.-Sat. 9am-2pm.)

Barrio Triana is the best part of Sevilla for **tapas barhopping,** a fun and inexpensive alternative to full-course meals. Just spend the evening wandering and snacking. On or near C. Betis along the river, go from the **Río Grande,** with outdoor tables overlooking the river, to **El Morapio,** a friendly place with *toro* decor, to **La Primera de Puente,** to **La Tertulia,** and then to **Akela.** If you're near Pl. de la Encarnación, try **Taberna La Tahona,** C. Regina, 15. The old cast iron bread ovens are idle, but *pringas* (fried beef and bacon subs) are still served up for 225ptas.

Near the Cathedral

Restaurants close to the cathedral cater exclusively to tourists. If you must, shop around the streets just north of the church for the cheapest *menú* and watch your change wherever you go. Although these spots are good places to meet fellow travelers over a meal, better local flavor can be found at the outdoor cafes around the nameless plaza 2 blocks east of the bullring.

Cervecería Giralda, C. Mateus Gago, 1 (tel. 22 74 35), just east of the cathedral. Lovely Andalusian tiled walls and Moorish arches for doorways. Clientele is local, loyal, and progressive. Entrees and *platos combinados* 400-1000ptas. Open daily 9am-midnight.

Mesón La Barca, C. Santander, 6 (no phone), across C. Tremprado, up from the Torre del Oro. Green baseboards plastered with bullfighting posters. Ample portions at some of the cheapest prices around. Try a tough-to-find Andalusian specialty, *estofado de venado,* deer prepared with red wine, garlic, and vegetables (350ptas). Open daily 12:30-4pm and 8-11:30pm.

Restaurante El Baratillo, C. Pavia, 12 (no phone), on a tiny street off C. Dos de Mayo. You'd never know it existed if it weren't for the raving of locals. Small, informal place with great food. *Menú* 375ptas, *platos combinados* 350ptas. Open Mon.-Sat. 8am-10pm.

El Mesón, Dos de Mayo, 26 (tel. 21 30 75). Facing the post office, take the 1st right, continue through the golden archway, and proceed straight ahead. The specialty here is fighting bull steak, and it doesn't have to come far—Plaza de Toros is only 2 blocks away. If you can't stomach taking the bull by the loins, try the excellent *merluza vasco navarra,* piping hot in a delicious sauce with pear and red peppers (800ptas), or the *gazpacho con guarnición* (250ptas)—possibly the best in town. *Menú de la casa* 1500ptas. Food 15% cheaper at the bar. Open Tues.-Sun. 12:30-4:30pm and 8pm-12:30am.

Bar Pizzería El Artesano, C. Mateus Gago, 9 (tel. 21 38 58). Bright wood and tile decor drags in drinkers from the *bodega* across the street, but they get repeat business from their Spanish-style pizzas 300-500ptas. Try the namesake "Artesano," with *mejillones* and *champiñon* (550ptas). Open daily 12:30pm-1am.

Restaurante Las Meninas, Santo Tómas, 3 (tel. 22 62 26), across from the Lonja Palace. Come here for the outside tables and view of the cathedral. The *menú* is expensive (1000ptas), and the food nothing special. Ordering a pitcher of refreshing sangria (450ptas) and head elsewhere to eat. Bar open daily 8am-8pm; restaurant open daily noon-7pm.

Barrios de la Puerta de la Carne/de la Puerta de Carmona

Look here for budget restaurants and a more local crowd.

Casa Diego, Pl. Curtidores, 7 (tel. 41 58 83). Good food at great prices. The *sopa de picadillo,* an Andalucsían broth with eggs and bread (195ptas), or gazpacho (140ptas) makes a delicious prelude to the house specialty, *brochetas* (grilled meat or fish strips, 400ptas). *Menú* 550ptas. Open daily 1-4pm and 8:30-11:30pm; Nov.-March daily 1-4pm and 8-11pm.

El 3 de Oro, C. Santa María la Blanca, 34 (tel. 42 27 59), just down from C. Melendez y Pelayo. Self-service cafeteria with superb *paella* (600ptas) and a number of Andalusian dishes (500-700ptas). *Menú* 525ptas. Open daily 8am-4:30pm and 8-11:30pm.

Bar Las Filipinas, C. Maria Santa Blanca, 19, across from El 3 de Oro. Slot machines and obnoxious waiters, but prices can't be beat—neither can the waiters. *Platos* 250-400ptas, 50ptas more if served at outside tables. Open Wed.-Mon. 1-4pm and 8-11pm, Tues. 1-4pm.

Zona "El Centro"

Outside of the usual tourist haunts, this area swarms with businesspeople and shoppers during the day and young people on their *paseo* at night.

Rincón San Eloy, C. San Eloy, 24 (tel. 22 25 04). The barking of waiters can barely be heard above the crowds. Airy courtyard, old wine barrels, massive beer taps, and old bullfight posters. *Platos combinados* 450ptas, *menú* 475ptas. Open daily noon-4:30pm and 7-11:30pm.

Los Gallegos, C. Carpio, 3, (tel. 21 40 11) in an alley just off the Campana. More than a bit on the greasy side, but portions are generous and reasonably priced. The hearty fare is popular, especially with large families. Nice selection of vegetable dishes. *Menú del día* 560ptas. Open daily 1-4pm and 8-11pm.

Jalea Real, Sor Angela de la Cruz, 37 (tel. 21 61 03), near Pl. de la Encarnación. Excellent and varied vegetarian dishes in a Spanish version of a fern bar. Two-course *menú* with bread, wine, and dessert 650ptas. Open Mon.-Sat. 1:30-5pm and 8-11pm; Sept.-June Mon.-Sat. 1:30-5pm.

Bar-Restaurante Enrique Becerra, C. Gamazo, 2 (tel. 21 30 49). Serves superb vegetarian dishes, but at steep prices. *Platos* 450-1275ptas. Open Mon.-Sat. 1:30-4:30pm and 8:30pm-midnight, Sun. 1:30-4:30pm.

Barrio de Triana

This famous *barrio,* on the other side of Río Guadalquivir, was a separate village until it was absorbed by the burgeoning city. Local pride and ambience remain strong. You'll find many a *tapas* bar and *freiduría* (fried-fish vendor), as well as terrific sunsets along the river.

Casa Manolo, C. San Jorge, 16 (tel. 33 47 92). Crowded with locals, a madhouse during fiestas. Waiters try to outscream each other as they tally bills with chalk on the bar. Steep prices: *menú de la casa* 1025ptas, *pescada frita* (fried fish) 700ptas. Open daily 1pm-midnight.

El Puerto, 59 Betis (tel. 27 17 25). The setting is worth the expense: outdoor terrace, lush shrubbery, palms, vines, and a view overlooking the river. The seafood entrees are delicious; the cheapest selection is shrimp (625ptas). *Menú de la casa* 800ptas. Open Tues.-Sun. 1-4pm and 8:30pm-midnight.

Restaurante El Timón, C. Salado, 57 (tel. 27 46 43). Clean and green; nautical decor. *Platos* 250-450ptas, *raciones* about the same. The *caldereta* (300ptas) can easily make a light meal. Open daily 1-4pm and 8pm-midnight.

Café-Bar Jerusalem, C. Salado at Virgen de las Huertas. International atmosphere, and—they said it couldn't be done—kosher *tapas.*

Sights

Old City

Splendid, spacious, and majestic, Sevilla's crowning monument is conspicuous for a reason. Space was cleared for the **cathedral** in 1401, when victorious Catholics seized the city and razed the great Almohad Mosque to the ground. The conquerors demonstrated the extent of their religious fervor by constructing in its place a church so great that, in their own words, "those who come after us will take us for madmen." It took more than a century to build Sevilla's cathedral, the third-largest cathedral of any style (after St. Peter's in Rome and St. Paul's in London), and the largest Gothic edifice ever built. Black and gold coffin-bearers block the entrance, guarding one of Sevilla's most cherished possessions, the **Tumba de Cristóbal Colón** (Columbus's Tomb). The inscription at the base attempts to vouch for the authenticity of its contents. To the east lies the **chapter house,** a gilt oval chamber where green and gold floor tiles form a geometric pattern that mirrors the egg-shaped perimeter of the interior. Next door a collection of over-sized medieval hymn books awaits, each at least one meter high. Paintings by Murillo, Ribera, and Pedro de Campana grace the walls of the **Sacristía Mayor.** Note the enormous bronze candlestick in a corner across from an equally oversized silver monstrance designed by Juan de Arfe. Behind the wooden partitions on either side resides the **treasury,** with a locally sculpted disembodied head of John the Baptist. Also in the treasury are the two keys presented to the city of Sevilla by leaders of the Jewish community after King Fernando III ousted the Muslims in 1248. Art history enthusiasts will enjoy the neighboring **Sacristía de los Pintores,** hung with minor canvases by major masters, including Zurbarán, Goya, Valdés Leál, and Jordaens. The gem here is the *Cristo de la Clemencia,* reputed to be Montañés' finest sculpture. Walk back to the center of the cathedral to see the overwhelming golden mass in the transept of the largest *reredos* in Spain. Directly across hovers a colossal, baroque organ—the beneficiary of a windfall of valuable mahogany, by-product of the construction of a nineteenth-century Austrian railway. At the back of the cathedral facing Avda. de la Constitución stands the **main portal,** usually barred. To the north, the **Capilla de San Antonio de Padua** celebrates the Portuguese-born saint notorious for demonstrating his evangelical exuberance by preaching even to fish. Before stepping outside, stroll through the peaceful adjoining **Orange Court,** gardens located on the site of the main courtyard of the original mosque. The sturdy Almohad walls are still replete with intricate carvings and an imposing Moorish gate facing out onto C. Alemanes. Just before the exit, and filling the eastern wall, is the **Capilla Real** (Royal Chapel). Former kings and queens of Spain peer down from the ornate Renaissance dome. (Open Mon.-Sat. 10:30am-1pm and 4:30-6:30pm, Sun. 10:30am-1pm. Admission 200ptas. No shorts or tank tops allowed.)

In spite of their zeal, the triumphant Catholic armies lacked the audacity to topple the harmonious spire of Sevilla's **Giralda Tower.** Raised in 1184 by ruling Arabs, this tower and its twin in Marrakech are the oldest and largest surviving Almohad minarets. Though the tower no longer possesses its original gilded bronze apples, subsequent Christian generations have made only modest alterations to its Almohad profile. In 1565, the tower was crowned with a belfry of classical arches, regal statuary, and a bronze orchestra of 25 bells, later topped by an ostentatious weathervane in the shape of the Goddess of Faith. Its cumbersome gyrations inspired the minaret's modern name—the Spanish verb *girar* means "to rotate." A well-preserved stone ramp leads to the equally well-preserved tower and belfry; the wide ramp was built to permit ascent on horseback. The climb is sweetened by encouraging foretastes of the final panorama, a sweeping sea of whitewashed *barrios* punctuated by the barbed spires and buttresses of the cathedral roof. On the way up, be sure to return the glares of some of the grimacing gargoyles. (Open same hours as the cathedral; on same ticket. Entrance inside church.)

The imposing crenelated walls of the **Alcázar,** the city's fabulous fourteenth-century Mudéjar palace, face the south side of the cathedral. The decorative detail of its lavish interior echoes Granada's Alhambra. Traces of an earlier Almohad citadel still remain within the walls of the later Muslim fortress, though most of what's visible was completed during the reign of the Christian monarch, Pedro I. Today, the Alcázar has the distinction of being the oldest palace still used by European royalty; during his visits to Sevilla, King Juan Carlos lives here.

Court life in the Alcázar traditionally revolved about the misnamed "**maid's court,**" a spacious, colonnaded quadrangle ringed by golden, foliated archways and glistening tilework. The theme of overwhelmingly kaleidoscopic detail carries over into the chambers that open off the central patio. The giant, wooden doors are usually open in summer, while the smaller, carved entryways are used during winter months. Most mesmerizing is the **Corte de los Embajadores** with its overbearing golden dome; legend has it that Fernando and Isabel welcomed Columbus here upon his return from America. Portraits of the kings of Spain peer down from the upper walls, while the entrance is framed by the gaudy Peacock's Arch, a triple horseshoe gateway enameled in pink, gold, and turquoise. The nearby **Corte de las muñecas** contains the private quarters of the palace, adorned with the building's most exquisite carvings. The rooms open to the public on the ground floor display portraits of smug Spaniards after the defeat of the Arabs, a unique collection of hand fans, and a bed purportedly slept in by Queen Isabel. Stretching away from the residential quarters on all sides, the verdant **Jardines** are worth a stroll; don't miss the elaborate myrtle labyrinth. (Open daily 9am-12:45pm and 3-5:30pm. Admission 150ptas.)

Between the cathedral and the Alcázar stands the old city's most neglected attraction: the sixteenth-century **Lonja** (Palace). Designed by Juan de Herrera, architect of Castilla's El Escorial, this rectangular structure houses the **Archivo de Indias**(Archive of the Indies), a collection of over 30,000 documents relating to the discovery and conquest of the "New World." Highlights include the wildly inaccurate *Mapa Mundi* of Juan de la Costa and letters from Columbus to Fernando and Isabel arguing about the choice of his first mate. (Open Mon.-Fri. 10am-1pm. Free.) Modern art fans should head next door for the **Museo de Arte Contemporaneo,** C. Santo Tomaso, 5. The Mirós on the top floor are a well-earned reward after a climb up the stairs. (Open Tues.-Fri. 9am-2pm, Sat.-Sun. 11am-2pm. Admission 250ptas.)

On C. Tremprado, just off C. Santander, 2 blocks west of the Lonja, rests the **Hospital de la Caridad,** a compact complex of spacious patios and intricate chapels. Begun in 1645 by the craftsman of the cathedral, Pedro Sánchez Falcorete, due to lack of funds the church was not completed until 1721, under the direction of Leonardo de Figueroa. Its main attractions today are paintings by Murillo and Valdés Leál. On the far wall above the entrance hangs Valdés Leál's *Finis Gloria Mundi,* a particularly gruesome display of equality in death. The corpses of a peasant, a bishop, and a king are putrefying under a stylized depiction of Justice and amusing representations of the Seven Deadly Sins. Highlights of Murillo's work include the frenzied drinkers in *Moisés haciendo brotar el agua de la roca* and the drooling eaters in *La Multiplicación de panes y peces,* on the opposite wall. Though most of the wall space of the church is coated with these two artists' works, the ornate, almost

Churrigueresque **altar mayor** (main altar) of Pedro Roldán is worth a peek for the grisly, gray statue of Jesus. (Open daily 9:30am-1:30pm and 4-7pm. Admission to church 100ptas.)

The winding alleys of **Barrio de Santa Cruz** are packed so densely and run in such skewed directions that most city maps do not even attempt to reproduce them. It's best to leave your maps behind, hold your breath, and plunge in. You haven't found the essence of the Santa Cruz quarter until you've lost your way and allowed yourself to amble aimlessly through inner courtyards and secluded plazas. Every home, shop, and cafe in the medieval residential quarter seems to have a halo of geraniums, jasmine, and ivy. Once home to Sevilla's thriving Jewish community, the *barrio* later became popular with Spanish nobility. Traces of its former heritage linger: A tranquil covered alleyway straddling the Alcázar is still known as the **Judería,** and the thirteenth-century **Iglesia de Santa María la Blanca,** on the street of the same name, was originally one of the neighborhood's main synagogues.

While in the Barrio Santa Cruz, don't miss the **Casa Murillo** at the tip of the Jardines de Murillo. The lovely old home houses some of the painter's work, as well as some fascinating seventeenth- and eighteenth-century religious wood carvings. (Open Tues.-Fri. 10am-2pm and 4-7pm, Sat.-Sun. 10am-2pm. Admission 250ptas.) For more contemporary art, browse through the private galleries tucked away in Barrio de Santa Cruz. Among the most interesting are **Galería Juana de Aizpuru,** C. Canalejos, 10 (open Mon.-Fri. 11:30am-2pm and 5-9:30pm), and the **John Fulton Gallery,** Pl. de Alianza, 11, which displays a small collection of paintings and books by the only American ever to achieve the rank of matador in professional Spanish bullfighting. (Open Mon.-Sat. 11am-2pm and 4:30-7:30pm, Sun. and holidays 11am-2pm.)

To the north of Barrio Santa Cruz off Pl. de Pilatos stands the **Casa de Pilatos,** an extravaganza the scale of the Alcázar. It is said to have been modeled on the praeterium of Pontius Pilate in Jerusalem. Constructed in 1540 by the Marquis de Tarifa and currently occupied by the Duke of Medinaceli, the palace is an outstanding example of Mudéjar architecture, a dazzling combination of Moorish, Gothic, and plateresque styles. Turquoise *azulejos* sparkle in the reflection of the courtyard fountain that is supported by a quartet of carved marble fish. Busts of Roman emperors line the courtyard on all sides, gazing wistfully into the bubbling pool where a petulant turtle paddles about. Iridescent Andalusian tilework lines the white stucco walls of the interior rooms, culminating in a gleaming stairwell that leads to the mansion's most sumptuous chamber. (Open daily 9am-8pm; Oct.-April daily 9am-6:30pm. Admission 400ptas.) If you arrive during visiting hours and the gate is closed, tug on the metal bellpull.

New City

In 1929, elaborate plans were made for an Iberian-American world's fair to be held in Sevilla. When Wall Street crashed, so did the fair, but the event bequeathed the lovely landscapes of the **Parque de María Luisa** to the city. Innumerable courtyards, turquoise-tiled benches, and tailored gardens fill this expanse of manicured greenery. For a taste of Sevilla at its most romantic, amble about the paths in early evening—but don't come here if you're feeling lonely.

On the park's western edge, the distinctive twin spires of **Plaza de España** tower above the Sevillan skyline. The plaza's enormous colonnade, checkered with terra cotta tiles, curves toward the neighboring park in a broad semicircle, while a narrow moat, spanned by four bridges, encircles the pavilion. Colored mosaics representing the provinces of Spain adjoin the sides of the walkways just below their stately balustrades. The enclosed area is overlaid with a festive brickwork pattern, punctuated by a large fountain in the center. It now houses municipal government offices. Hop in a boat and row about the miniature canal (250ptas per hour, open until 10pm).

Sevilla's **Museo Arqueológico,** inside the park at Pl. de América, contains a collection of pre-Roman and Roman treasures excavated in the surrounding provinces. (Open Tues.-Sat. 10am-2pm. Admission 250ptas, Sat. free.) Nearby, across C. San Fernando, the new campus of the **Universidad de Sevilla** occupies Spain's second-largest historic building (El Escorial is the largest) and is the setting of Bizet's *Carmen*. (At the time of the opera's writing, this was the site of Sevilla's famous tobacco factory, although the recent movie version with Plácido Domingo was filmed in Ronda.)

On the other side of the town, the **Museo Provincial de Bellas Artes** houses an impressive collection of Spanish masters, notably Murillo, Leál, and Zurbarán, second only to the Prado in scope and beauty. The museum's focal point is Room VI, a converted church now presided over by Murillo's lofty *La imaculada concepción*. In Rooms VII and VIII, Murillo's images of beatitude contrast with Zurbarán's morbidity. The work of the Dutch master Jan Breughel shares the spotlight with a pair of captivating portraits by El Greco in Room V. To reach the museum, walk west from the Campana along C. Alfonso XII. (Closed for restoration. Scheduled to reopen in spring of 1989.)

Several blocks away lies the **Iglesia de San Lorenzo,** remarkable only for the occupant of the main altar. Inside a large shell stands Martínez Montañés's amazingly lifelike statue *El Cristo del Gran Poder.* Worshipers kiss Jesus' ankle through the opening in the bulletproof glass. The procession with this statue is the culmination of Semana Santa celebrations. (Open daily 8am-1:30pm and 6-9pm. Admission 25ptas.)

The thirteenth-century **Torre del Oro** (Gold Tower), on Paseo Cristóbal Colón, is a 12-sided crenelated tower constructed by Arab rulers to defend the city's harbor. A glaze of golden tile once sheathed its squat frame, but today a tiny yellow dome is the only reminder of its original splendor. At sunset, the medieval watchtower forms a striking silhouette against the river. For a sure-fire attack of claustrophobia, climb to the top and visit the **Museo Naútico** inside. (Tower and museum open Tues.-Sat. 10am-2pm, Sun. 10am-1pm. Admission 15ptas.) The inviting riverside esplanade, **Marquez de Contadero** stretches along the banks of the Guadalquivir from the base of the tower. Take a gander at the river, or stroll along the tiled boardwalk to **Plaza de Toros de la Real Maestranza,** considered by many the heart of bullfighting in Spain. Home to one of the two great schools of *tauromaquia* (the other is in Ronda), the plaza fills to capacity for the 13 *corridas* of the Feria de Abril and for fights every Sunday in summer. (Open to visitors April 24-Oct. 12 Mon.-Sat. on non-bullfight days at 4:45pm, 5:30pm and 6:15pm. Admission 100ptas.)

Entertainment

On spring and summer evenings there are often free open-air concerts in Santa Cruz and Triana as part of the *velás* (neighborhood fairs). Ask at the tourist office, or check the bulletin board in the lobby of the university (on C. San Fernando). The tourist office also distributes a free magazine on entertainment in Sevilla called *El Giraldillo,* with very complete listings on music, art exhibits, theater, dance, fairs, and film.

Flamenco

The lightning-fast footwork of Sevilla's flamenco *bailadores* dazzles the eyes, while the accompanying classical Spanish guitar, rhythmic handclapping, and wailing of the *cantadores* fill the ears. There are two ways to see flamenco: Go to a professional show or visit a local club where flamenco music is played and locals dance. The former is tourist-oriented and expensive, but the colorful costumes and expert performances are often worth it. The best show in town and the only one in which professional dancers appear is on the western edge of Barrio Santa Cruz at **Los Gallos,** Pl. Santa Cruz, 11. One drink is included in the 1900ptas admission. The first show begins at 9:30pm, the second at midnight; if you pay for the first, the second is free. Arrive early to find a seat where you can see the stage floor. Shows may also be seen at **El Arenal,** C. Rodo, 7 (tel. 21 64 92), where performances are given daily from 10pm to 1:30am, and **Patio Sevillano,** Paseo de Colón, 11 (tel. 21 41 20), which is open daily from 9:30pm to 2am.

If prices at these places are beyond your budget, don't despair: There are a number of clubs on C. Salado in **Barrio de los Remedios,** where local enthusiasts flock to dance flamenco *sans* costume. To reach the *barrio,* situated across the river, take bus #41. **La Garrocha, Las 3 Farolas** (tel. 27 97 86) and **Candela Pura** are the liveliest spots. Expect them to open nightly at about 10pm, closing only in the wee hours. Flamenco-hop and head to **Barrio Triana,** 10 minutes away; **El Ajoli,** C. Pureza, 118, and **La Portada de Feria,** on C. Castilla, usually sport similar *sevillana* music and dancing. Some locals even bring along their own guitars, tambourines, and, of course, boisterous buddies.

On most evenings, **Barrio de Santa Cruz** is also alive with the singing and strumming of flamenco. Follow your ears. Stop by with the university crowd at **Bodega Santa Cruz,** near the entrance to the *barrio,* then move on to **La Gitanilla,** C. Ximénez de Encisco, 11, a lively local hangout that inevitably bursts into folk music or flamenco before the evening is over. Even if no one happens to be performing at **Plaza de los Venerables** when you arrive, it's still a wonderful spot to enjoy the evening mood of the *barrio*—order a drink at one of the outdoor tables of **La Hostería del Laurel** or **Casa Romana.** Be wary of pickpockets and purse snatchers as the hour becomes late.

Other Music and Bars

Sevilla is replete with bars and clubs: Gear yourself for a fast-paced nightlife that rarely closes before 7 or 8am. For drinks, try **La Carboneriá,** C. Levies, 18, a couple of blocks west of C. Menendez y Pelayo, a combination art gallery-club-bar. Begun 30 years ago to encourage young artists and musicians whose work was censored during Franco's dictatorship, the place now functions as a popular nightspot, with jazz, folk, and other shows nightly (flamenco on Thurs.). **Los Chiringuitos** is a huge carnival of outdoor bars on the Recinto Ferial (fairground) in Barrio Los Remedios, where local festivals occur. Don't come here expecting cotton candy and roller coasters, though the rides can be bumpy; Chiringuitos is a definite pick-up scene.

For a quieter evening, head to **Abades** an eighteenth-century mansion-turned-bar at C. Abades, 15 (tel. 21 50 96). Sit in the elegant courtyard next to a fountain, or enjoy a drink in one of the comfortable dens while you listen to classical music. For a cozy setting with worn leather chairs and quiet music, visit **La Taberna,** C. Duarte, 3, near C. Betis, where one of the waiters stacks empty glasses 20 high and carries his precarious creation back to the bar. At **Casa Morales,** C. García de Binuesa, 11, 1 block from the cathedral, you can sit at small tables dwarfed by 5m-high barrels and sample regional wine for 40ptas per glass. Machiavellians may feel uncomfortable here. No *tapas* are served, so bring in some *pescada frita* from the stand next door. Jazz enthusiasts can try **Be Bop,** C. Sol, 40 (tel. 21 72 56), **Blue Moon,** C. Roldana, 5, or **Orfeo,** on C. Gerona. **La Alcaiceria** on C. Alcaiceria, offers folk music.

Dancing hot spots include **El Coto,** on C. Luis de Morales next to Hotel Los Lebreros (cover charge 800ptas), and **El Rio,** on C. Betis (cover charge occasionally). In the summer, people try to avoid the hot indoors by packing places such as **E.M.,** a small, outdoor disco on Avda. Garcia Morato, within walking distance of Los Chiringuitos (cover charge 300ptas), and **La Recua,** a romantic, tropical outdoor club with palm trees, thatched huts, and a huge swimming pool. (Club located on Carretera de Cádiz, in front of Hospital Miltar; no cover charge. Open Fri.-Sat. nights.) A gay/lesbian ambience can be found in a number of bars and clubs along C. Trastamara. **Tibus II,** C. Desealzos, and **Chandelier,** Luis de Vargas, 6 (both for women), or **Metal,** C. Jesús del Gran Poder (for men), are especially popular.

Los Toros

Several booths on C. Sierpes, C. Velázquez, and Pl. de Toros sell **bullfight** tickets. Prices depend on how shady your seat is and the reputation of the matadors. To avoid the scalper's 20% markup, buy tickets at the bullring. However, the booths might be the only source of tickets for a good *cartel.* Prices run from 7000ptas for a *barrera de sombra* (front row seat in the shade) to 1300ptas for a *grada dea sol* (nosebleed seat in the sun). *Corridas de toros* (bullfights) or *novillados* (cut rate fights with young bulls and novice bullfighters) are held nearly every Sunday in summer and on Corpus Christi, August 15, and the 13 days surrounding the Feria de Abril. Peak season is from April to mid-October. For information on dates and prices, go to **Plaza de Toros de Sevilla** or dial 22 31 52.

Festivals

During Sevilla's fiestas, the city swells with tourists. Accommodations become scarce and restaurants crowded, but the atmosphere is unparalleled. The world-famous **Semana Santa** (Holy Week) festival is designed to inspire even the most parade-weary sight-seer. Commencing on Palm Sunday, the celebration continues for a solid week, culminating on Good Friday with morning and afternoon processions. Scores of penitents in hooded gowns guide their jeweled floats through the streets. A central float carries a likeness of the city's patron, the *Virgen de la Macarena*. The masked paraders are members of ecclesiastical guilds, each of which venerates a different image of Jesus from one episode of the Passion. The oldest guild, the Brotherhood of Silence, was founded in 1356. In all, penitents march through the streets eight times during Holy Week, conducting 99 floats from their respective neighborhoods to the cathedral and back. Try to book your room well in advance of the festivities, and expect to pay at least double normal prices.

Two or three weeks after Semana Santa, the city rewards itself for its piety with the six-day **Feria de Abril** (April Fair; April 11-16 in 1989). Circuses, bullfights, and flamenco roar into the night. The fair centers in the grounds of the Prado de San Sebastian, on the southern side of Triana near the river. Hundreds of kiosks, tents, and pavilions are decked with a spectacular array of flowers and lanterns. Though most of the *casetas* (booths) are for private neighborhoods or organizations, if you wander around enough you can find a tent to enter whose party is overflowing into the street. Horsemen costumed in traditional garb gambol about the grounds, carrying *señoritas* in ruffled gypsy dresses. The festival originated at the time of a popular revolt against foreign influence in Spain during the nineteenth century, when Andalusians began to revive their local folk customs. The power output of Sevilla dwindles when the lights and the party are activated Monday at midnight. The activity on the fairgrounds runs from Tuesday to Saturday from around 9:30am to 2pm, with the party dispersing at night throughout Sevilla for the rest of the week.

Spain's biggest festival occurs 50 days after Easter at the Pentecost celebration (May 23 in 1989), **Romería del Rocío.** Caravans of pilgrims trundle over the Spanish countryside to converge on the tiny village of **El Rocío,** 60km west of Sevilla. They come to venerate the *Blanca Paloma,* a sacred image of the Virgin housed in the town's shrine. Guided by a silver wagon, a large contingent of pilgrims from the Triana quarter of Sevilla makes the annual procession. The activities at the sacred shrine extend from Saturday afternoon to Monday morning and include numerous candle-light parades as well as a joyous Mass featuring brilliant costumes, traditional dance, and general chaos. Buses run five times per day to El Rocío from Estación de Empresa Damas on C. Segura in Sevilla. Needless to say, you'll have trouble finding a seat during festival time.

Near Sevilla

Itálica

The ruins of the ancient Roman colony, Itálica lies only 9km northwest of Sevilla. Founded in 206 B.C.E. after the Romans' victory over the Carthaginians in the Battle of Ilipa, Itlica was the first significant Roman settlement on Iberian soil. P. Cornelio Escipción, the Roman general who orchestrated the victory and settlement, affectionately named it in memory of his beloved Italy. The Romans promptly became the town's aristocracy with two families wielding particular power, the Ulpios and Aelios. The reigns of Emperors Trajano and Ardiano from these families saw

Itálica become the Hispanic world's first monumental city. The city walls, Nova Urbs, and other edifices were constructed during this period (300-400 C.E.), subsequently dubbed the "*apogeo*" (apogee) period.

In the centuries that followed, Itálica's power declined; its monuments suffered serious disrepair. By the Middle Ages, the town was referred to simply as "Campos de Talica" (the countryside of Talica); and during the fifteenth and sixteenth centuries, bustling Sevilla had become the region's seat of power.

Archeological excavations, which began in the eighteenth century, continue today. The remarkably well-preserved **amphitheater,** one of Spain's largest, seats 25,000. Classical theater is still performed here; check Sevilla's *El Giraldillo* for schedules. A handful of colorful **mosaic floors** remain in some buildings. Some of the finest mosaics and other relics have been moved to Sevilla's Lebrija Palace and the Museo Arqeológico. (Site open Tues.-Fri. 9am-5:30pm, Sat.-Sun. 10am-4pm. Admission 250ptas.)

Take Empresa Casal's bus from C. Marques de Paradas in front of the Pl. de Armas train station toward the village of Santiponce, and tell the driver you want to go to Itálica (Mon.-Sat. every ½-hr. 6am-11pm, Sun. every hr. 7:30am-midnight, 200ptas).

Carmona

An hour's bus ride from Sevilla takes you to the ancient city of Carmona, once a thriving Arab stronghold and later the favorite fourteenth-century retreat of Pedro the Cruel, under whose rule Sevilla's Alcázar was built. Both Moorish and Christian monarchs left a lasting architectural imprint here: Faded Mudéjar palaces mingle with Renaissance mansions amidst a tangle of streets still partially enclosed by fortified walls. The most popular sight here is **Puerta Sevillana,** a horseshoe-shaped passageway burrowed through the ramparts. Other attractions include the upper and lower **Alcázares,** and some opulent baroque **private mansions.** Presiding over a vibrant Roman mosaic depicting a Medusa's head, the town hall doubles as the local **Museo Arqueológico.** Its artifacts were excavated just west of the town limits at the ruins of what was once the most important Roman necropolis in Iberia. Over a thousand tombs have been unearthed, including some pre-Roman burial mounds.

Carmona is an easy daytrip from Sevilla. Buses leave from the main station (17 per day, 165ptas).

Aracena

Aracena, 89km northwest of Sevilla, is a quiet Andalusian town built on a hillside that conceals the Gruta de las Maravillas (Grotto of Marvels), a natural wonderland of stalagmites, stalactities, and underground lakes.

Practical Information

Tourist Office: Pl. San Pedro (tel. 11 03 55), next to the Gruta. Newly opened office with enthusiastic staff eager to tell you all about their town. Open daily 10:30am-1:30pm and 4:30-7pm.

Post Office: C. Juan del Cid López (tel. 11 01 54), near the Gruta. Open Mon.-Fri. 9am-2pm, Sat. 9am-1pm. **Postal Code:** 21200

Telephones: Avda. de Andaluciá, 1, near the center of town.

Buses: Avda. de Andaluciá, 9 (tel. 11 01 96). To Sevilla (2 per day, 1 hr. 200ptas), and Huelva (1 per day). Make connections in Sevilla.

Medical Emergency: Tel. 11 00 86.

Police: Tel. 11 02 32.

Accommodations

Casa Carmen, C. Mesones (tel. 11 07 64), up the hill from the park at Pl. Pilat. From the bus station, turn right onto C. Jose Nogales, walk about 2 blocks until you hit C. Mesones, and turn right. Large, clean rooms. Plants and flowers fill the patio, nice place for writing postcards when you can't find anything else to do here—at night. Singles 600ptas. Doubles 1200 ptas.

Hostal Sierpes, C. Mesones (tel. 11 01 47), 2 doors up from the above. Rooms are well-kept, but the bathrooms aren't. TV lounge. Singles 1100ptas, with shower 1450ptas. Doubles with shower 2150ptas.

Food

Restaurante Carmen, C. Mesones, 15 (tel. 11 00 60). Next to Casa Carmen and run by the same family. The bar is a greasy spoon, but the homey restaurant tucked behind it is a local favorite. *Menú* 700 ptas. Open daily 1-5pm and 9-11pm.

Restaurante Sierra, C. Mesones, 9 (no phone), farther down the street. Pretty place with pastel curtains and tablecloths. Try the house specialty, *solomillo de cerdo Iberico,* grilled pork served with vegetables, ham, potatoes, and eggs (700ptas). *Menú* 900ptas. Open daily 1-4:30pm and 9pm-midnight.

Bar-Restaurante San Pedro, C. San Pedro, 36, near Turismo. Large place with cheerful red and white tablecloths. *Plato especial* 550ptas.

Bar El Casino (tel. 11 03 98), at the foot of C. Mesones. *Pinchitos* (skewered beef) are worth the 80ptas per serving; a plate of freshly cooked potato chips are 125ptas.

Sights

Aracena's main attraction, as signs all over town will remind you, is the *Gruta de las Maravillas.* Upon arrival at the bus station, walk to the right along Avda. de Andaluciá, which becomes Gran Viá, until you reach the "Grutas" sign pointing to the left. Piped-in piano music will accompany your descent into the grotto (the largest of its kind in the world) along a wet, dimly lit stone path. Created over millions of years by the accumulation of mineral deposits, these white, green, and orange rock formations have grown into myriad shapes: Giant, knotted, upside-down carrots and plain slabs are all mirrored in the shimmering lakes. Toss in a peseta, watch it sink to the bottom, and wish that all lakes were this clear. When a voice calls from the dark recesses, just say "cheese"; later you will be asked for 500ptas, but don't feel obliged to purchase the photo. (Open daily 10:30am-6:30pm; Oct.-May daily 10am-6pm.) Unless you're traveling with a group of a dozen or more, be prepared to wait as long as an hour for the guided tour (300ptas, children 200ptas). While waiting, study the displays in the lobby's **Museo Geologico-Minero.** The open-air **Museo de Arte Contemporaneo** outside exhibits modern sculptures, paintings, and other works. (Open 24 hours. Free.)

After your tour, climb the mountain to **Templars' Castle,** a thirteenth-century castle built by the occult Templar. Little remains of the castle today except ruins, but the **church** still stands and houses an interesting collection of art objects. (Open daily 9:30am-10pm. Free.) The road to the castle and church begins at the Church of the Asunción in Pl. Alta. As you ascend, cast a glance back at the town's chalk-white houses.

Extremadura

In Spanish, the very name of this region contains the adjectives that define it in the minds of many people: extreme, remote, and harsh. For some, Extremadura remains a synonym for poverty, backwardness, and isolation. Although there is more than a grain of truth in the stereotype, Extremadura is not at all unattractive.

Snowcapped mountains, wide rivers, healthy forests, and prosperous towns provide variety to its austere landscape. With their recently acquired autonomy, its people are regaining the pride and zest that was their trademark during the conquest of the New World.

The spell cast by Extremadura comes mainly from its rich history. For centuries it has been on the frontier, a strategic area successively conquered by Tartessians, Celts, Romans, Arabs, and Christians, all of whom left behind their monuments, bridges, and castles. From Extremadura came most of the *conquistadores,* men and women who crossed the Atlantic with cross and sword in pursuit of glory, wealth, and status. Some—such as Hernán Cortés and Francisco Pizarro, conquerors of Mexico and Peru—won *fama y fortuna* with their recklessness and cunning. Others, such as Pedro de Valdivia, who tried to vanquish the fierce Araucanians of Chile, perished in the attempt. Two great bodies of water were "discovered" by explorers coming from this land plagued by frequent droughts: Vasco Núñez de Balboa crossed the Panama isthmus to the Pacific, which he called *Mar del Sur,* and Francisco de Orellana came upon the Amazon River. An *extremeño,* the son of Diego García de Paredes ("The Samson and Hercules of Spain"), was able to defeat Lope de Aguirre, the maverick conquistador known as "The Wrath of God." Women from Extremadura also left their imprint on history. María Escobar was the first person to plant wheat in Peru, and Inés de Suárez saved Santiago del Nuevo Extremo (today Santiago de Chile) by chopping off the heads of captive Araucanians and displaying them in front of the attacking tribes. Many places in the New World were named by *extremeños* after their native towns, among them Trujillo, Mérida, Medellín, La Serena, Guadalupe, and Valdivia.

Just as Extremadura prospered during the expansion of the empire, its fortunes sagged as Spain declined. Many of the structures built during the city's apogee are now inhabited only by storks, and others have been converted into convents, cultural centers, and schools. Nevertheless, they retain a mysterious stateliness and grandeur.

Extremadura is administratively and culturally divided into the provinces of Cáceres (also known as Alta Extremadura) and Badajoz (Baja Extremadura). During the Spanish Civil War, the province of Badajoz (especially the capital, Badajoz) fiercely resisted Franco's troops, while Cáceres fell with virtually no fighting. Since the region became one more *autonomía* after Franco's death, most political differences no longer exist, leaving only soccer rivalries to divide *extremeños.*

The great variety of Extremaduran cuisine is worth investigating. The most traditional *extremeño* dishes come from the wild: rabbit, partridge, lizard in green sauce, wild pigeons with herbs, and codfish *a la Alcántara* are just a few examples. Soups are especially delicious in this region: Try the *cocido* (chickpea stew) in winter or the many varieties of gazpacho in summer. Consommes and tomato soup with figs are enjoyed year-round. In Cáceres, try *frite,* a lamb stew, and *migas,* a bread soup served mainly in colder weather. Ham from the town of Montánchez is renowned throughout Spain. In Badajoz, the food resembles that of Andalucía. The entire region enjoys remarkable melons.

Because tourists—both native and foreign—tend to skip the Extremadura's haunting landscapes and garrison towns, the artificial airs of tourist resorts are foreign to Extremadura, but tourist offices tend to be unorganized and inefficient (albeit enthusiastic), museum hours can be erratic, and budget lodgings can be scarce. Nonetheless its beautiful, ancient cities and unique cultural amalgamation make Extremadura an unusual and provocative detour. (Stick to buses in Extremadura, since trains tend to take long detours where they have service.)

Cáceres

A bustling provincial capital, Cáceres maintains a cool, green air despite the sweltering Extremadura sun. Its medieval city is one of the most architecturally harmonious in all of Europe. Superbly preserved Christian churches and palaces stand close to vestiges of the region's Roman and Arab past. Because of its central location, Cáceres makes a good base from which to explore the rest of Extremadura.

Orientation and Practical Information

The **medieval city,** by far the most interesting part of town, lies to the east of the **Plaza Mayor** (Pl. del General Mola on out-of-date maps). The plaza is 3km from the bus or train stations, across from each other on Carretera de Sevilla. Try taking erratic bus #1 from the bus station to the plaza (38ptas).

Tourist Office: Pl. Mayor, 33 (tel. 24 63 47). Pamphlets on Extremadura in the language of your choice. Open Mon.-Fri. 10am-2pm and 5-7pm.

Post Office: C. Miguel Primo Rivera, 2 (tel. 22 50 70). Open for stamps and Lista de Correos Mon.-Fri. 9am-2pm and 5-7pm, Sat. 9am-2pm. Open for **telegrams** Mon.-Sat. 9am-2pm. For 24-hour telegram service, dial 22 20 00. **Postal Code:** 10004.

Telephones: C. Antonio Reyes Huertas, 40 (tel. 004). **Telephone Code:** 927.

Train Station: Avda. Alemania (tel. 22 50 61), 3km outside the city. To Badajoz (1 per day, 21/3 hr., 540ptas), Mérida (3 per day, 1 hr., 350ptas), Plasencia (5 per day, 11/3 hr., 370ptas), Sevilla (1 per day, 5½ hr., 1500ptas), Madrid (6 per day; *expreso* 4½ hr., 2200ptas; *automotor* 6 hr., 1510ptas), and Lisbon (2 per day; *ter* 6 hr., 2175ptas; *expreso* 6½ hr., 1750ptas).

Bus Station: C. Gil Cordero (tel. 24 59 50). To Badajoz (2 per day, 1½ hr., 510ptas), Plasencia (6 per day, 1¼ hr., 450ptas), Guadalupe (2 per day, 3 hr., 750ptas), Trujillo (4 per day, 1 hr., 350ptas), Sevilla (6 per day, 4½ hr., 1500ptas), Madrid (6 per day, 5 hr., 1500ptas), and Mérida (4 per day, 1 hr., 350ptas).

Taxis: Pl. Mayor (tel. 24 84 44). Open 24 hours.

English Bookstore: Librería Quevedo, C. General Ezponda, 3 (tel. 24 98 73), 1 block from Pl. Mayor.

Medical Emergency: Casa de Socorro, C. Badajoz, 1 (tel. 24 30 38). **Cruz Roja** (Red Cross), Tel. 24 78 58. **Hospital Provincial,** Tel. 24 23 00.

Police: Comisaría de Policía, Avda. Virgen de la Montaña, 3 (tel. 22 60 00). **Emergency:** Tel. 091.

Accommodations

Cáceres's lack of tourists means there are few *hostales* from which to choose. In addition, many *extremeños* visit Cáceres on weekends—it's wise to call a day or two in advance. The best places to look are around the Pl. Mayor.

Fonda Carretero, Pl. Mayor, 22 (tel. 24 74 82). An old Spanish house kept in impeccable shape. Rooms have tile floors; high, wood-beamed ceilings; and views of either the plaza or the countryside. TV lounge. Singles 750ptas. Doubles 1400ptas.

Pensión Márquez, Gabriel y Galan, 2 (tel. 24 49 60), off Pl. Mayor. Pleasant and clean rooms, those on the plaza full of light. Owner has a fascination with the color yellow. Tiny bathrooms. Singles 800ptas. Doubles 1600ptas. Breakfast 100ptas. Lunch or dinner 500ptas.

Hostal-Residencia Adarve, Sanchez Garrido, 4 (tel. 24 48 74), off Pintores above the plaza. Decent rooms, but often noisy since it's above a bar. Singles with shower 1025ptas, with bath 1050ptas. Doubles 1750ptas.

Hostal Residencia Almonte, C. Gil Cordero, 6 (tel. 24 09 25 or 24 09 26), 10 min. from Pl. Mayor. All the amenities without high prices. Well-scrubbed rooms, all with private bath and telephone. TV lounge, parking garage, elevator, laundry service, and bar and restaurant. Singles 1600ptas. Doubles 2400ptas. Triples 3500ptas.

Food

Like accommodations, restaurants are scarce in Cáceres. Aside from smoky bars and cafes, few establishments serve respectable meals. On Wednesday, check out the market at Pl. Marrón, 2½ blocks north of the Pl. Mayor. The permanent local

market, Mercado de Abastos, is on C. de San José at C. de la Piedad. (Open Mon.-Sat. 8am-2pm and 4-7pm.)

El Pato, Pl. Mayor, 24 (tel. 24 87 36). A lively bar/restaurant with tables outside. Local hang-out. *Menú* 650ptas, *raciones* 500ptas, *platos combinados* from 350ptas. Open Fri.-Wed. 1-4pm and 8pm-midnight.

Donald, Pl. Mayor (tel. 24 97 63), next door. Just ducky. Similar fare at similar prices in a modern, cafeteria setting. *Bocadillos* 200ptas, *platos combinados* 450ptas. Open Wed.-Mon. 7am-1am.

Restaurante Jemy, C. Juan XXIII, 1 (tel. 22 25 08), near the bus station. Generous helpings and cheap prices make it worth finding. *Menú* 625ptas. Open Mon.-Sat. noon-4pm and 8-11pm.

El Adarve, Sánchez Garrido, 4 (tel. 21 35 26), off Pintores near Pl. Mayor. A stand-up bar, but the food is tasty and you can easily fill up on the no-frills *bocadillos* (150ptas), *tapas* (250ptas), and *raciones* (500ptas). Open daily 8am-3pm and 8-10:30pm.

Sights

The *barrio antiguo,* or old city, is one of the purest and best-conserved architectural ensembles in all of Europe. Surrounded by Almohad walls built on Roman foundations and later modified by the Christians, it encompassed churches, towers, ancestral mansions, and palaces. The best way to enter the old town is from the eastern side of the Pl. Mayor; you will be treated to a view of the **Torre del Horno** and **Torre de Bujaco,** constructed by Almohad king Abu-Jacob. The steps between these towers lead to **Arco de la Estrella,** an unusual, twisted stairway designed by Churriguera, and one of the citadel's main entrances. As you enter the citadel, note the star-shaped lantern atop the arches. Here, Queen Isabel the Catholic was obliged to swear that she would respect the *fueros* (city charters). An autonomous city governed by 12 elected men before Queen Isabel and King Ferdinand's monarchy, Cáceres greatly valued the legal code. Unfortunately local nobles resolved their disputes more often than not through violence, prompting Isabel and Ferdinand to remove all battlements and spires from local lords' houses.

In front of Arco de la Estrella, **Plaza de Santa María** is a sunny square of golden stone buildings. Overlooking the plaza, the dark **Catedral de Santa María** is surrounded by tombstones of the city's nobility. (Church open daily 8am-1pm and 6-8pm.) Look for the **statue of San Pedro de Alcántara,** one of Extremadura's two saints, near the church walls. Legend has it that rubbing or kissing his big toe will bring good luck.

Toward the western side of the plaza, the many palaces and ancestral mansions make it easy to imagine yourself in medieval Spain. The doorway of the **Palacio Episcopal** (Bishop's Palace) is engraved with sixteenth-century images of the Old and New World. The **Palacio de los Golfines de Abajo,** one of two palaces belonging to a prominent noble family, bears the coat of arms of Isabel and Ferdinand. Following a stay at the palace, the monarchs had their coat of arms engraved in gratitude for their hosts' hospitality. Farther uphill, by C. Olmos and C. Adarros de Santa Ana, the **Palacio de los Golfines de Arriba,** is the Golfino family's other palace. Here, on October 26, 1936, Francisco Franco was proclaimed head of the Spanish state and Generalísimo of its armies. Down the street to the right is the **Casa de los Toledo-Montezuma.** Local Juan Cáno acquired the means to build this place by marrying Aztec emperor Moctezuma's daughter.

Walk downhill to **Plaza Veletas,** where the **Palacio de las Cigueñas** (storks) and **Casa de las Veletas** (weathervanes) are located. Due to its owner's loyalty to Isabel, Las Cigueñas was one of the few palaces spared from the toppling of battlements. Storks collaborate to preserve the house's name by building impressive nests on its spires every spring. Cross the street to Casa de las Veletas, home to both weathervanes and the **Museo Provincial.** The museum's exhibits range from paleothic and medieval artifacts (check out the collection of Visigothic and Roman tombstones) to popular art objects, including regional embroidery and clothing. An extraordinary **aljibe** (cistern) from the Arab period was constructed in the eleventh century. Fed by rainwater caught by an intricately designed drainage system, it supplied the city with water as late as 1935. (Museum open mid-June to Sept. Mon.-Sat. 10am-1:30pm and 5-7pm, Sun. 11:30am-1:30pm; Oct. to mid-June Mon.-Sat. 10am-1:30pm and 4-6pm, Sun. 11:30am-1:30pm. Admission 200ptas.)

To conclude your tour of Cáceres's monuments, head to Pl. de Santiago, site of the **Church of Santiago Matamoros** (Saint James the Moorslayer). Here, the Friars of Cáceres harbored pilgrims on their journey to Santiago de Compostela. (Church open during Mass only.)

Trujillo

Birthplace of famed *conquistadores* Francisco Pizarro, the Conquerer of Peru, and Orellana, who discovered the Amazon River, Trujillo is one of Extremadura's most intriguing towns, encompassing palaces (some still owned by *conquistadores'* descendents), churches, and medieval fortresses bearing witness to a time when Trujillo was known throughout the world. Rising from a 517-meter-high granite hill, its edifices silhouetted against the horizon, Trujillo is today an important link to the characters who left their imprint on the New World.

Orientation and Practical Information

Trujillo is accessible by bus and car only. The bus station is at the foot of the hill, on the road to Badajoz. To get to the **Plaza Mayor,** the town center, take a left as you exit the station and go uphill on C. de Pardos, past small Pl. de Aragón onto C. de Romanos. Hang a right at the end of Romanos, where it meets C. de la Parra, and then take a left on C. de Hernando Pizarro (15 min.).

Tourist Office: Pl. Mayor (tel. 32 06 53), by the orange tree grove and the bank. A map charts the exploration of Trujillo's native sons who traveled (probably on an even smaller budget than yours) during the conquest. Hours are erratic; come in the morning. Open daily 11am-1:30pm and 5-8pm.

Post Office: C. Ruiz de Mendoza, Paseo 7 (tel. 32 05 33), 10 min. from the Pl. Mayor. Enter from C. Encarnación. Open for stamps, Lista de Correos, and **telegrams** Mon.-Fri. 9am-2pm, Sat. 9am-1pm. **Postal Code:** 10200.

Telephone Code: 927.

Bus Station: Carretera a Badajoz (tel. 32 12 02 or 32 01 36), near C. de la Encarnación. To Guadalupe (1 per day Mon.-Fri., 2 hr., 450ptas), Cáceres (4 per day, 40 min., 244ptas), Badajoz (5 per day, 2 hr., 752ptas), Plasencia (1 per day, 1½ hr., 375ptas), Mérida (5 per day, 1 hr., 512ptas), and Madrid (14 per day; 4½ hr., 1236ptas; *expreso* 3½ hr., 1800ptas).

Medical Emergency: Centro de Salud de la Seguridad Social, C. Ramón y Cajal (tel. 32 00 89). Ramón y Cajal is the road to Cáceras; the hospital is by the road to Montánchez.

Police: Ayuntamiento, C. Hernandez Pizarro, 2 (tel. 32 01 08 or 091). The policía municipal will store your backpack during the day in their little jail. Contact any agent on the Place Mayor.

Accommodations and Food

Trujillo's most convenient accommodations and eateries are on the **Plaza Mayor.** Explore **Calle de Sillerías,** where the signs to Portugal and Badajoz are posted, for a couple of *mesones* that offer the hearty foods of Extremadura in a quiet ambience. For groceries, try **Supermercado Natividad Garcia Arias,** C. Merced, 1 (tel. 32 05 81; open Mon.-Sat. 9:30am-2pm and 5-9pm, in off-season Mon.-Sat. 9:30am-2pm and 4-8pm).

Hotel Pizarro, Pl. Mayor, 13 (tel. 32 02 55). Terrific rooms, many with a nice view of the plaza. Singles 900ptas. Doubles 1800ptas.

Hostal Residencia Emilia, C. Gran Mola, 26 (tel. 32 00 83), a 10-min. walk from the Pl. Mayor. Across from a simple but lovely park. Shining clean—even the staircase is scrubbed daily. Spacious brown and white rooms. Singles 1300ptas. Doubles 2226ptas, with bath 2703ptas.

Restaurante Pizarro, Pl. Mayor, 13 (tel. 32 02 55). Some of the finest cuisine in all of Extremadura, but it's not inexpensive. Try the *extremeño* specialties: *gallina trufada Pizarro* (1000ptas) or *crema tostada nupcial* (a dessert, 250ptas). *Menú* 850ptas. Open daily 1-4pm and 9-11pm.

Meson-Restaurante La Troya, Pl. Mayor, 10 (tel. 32 14 65). Large place packed with locals. Bar designed as a facade of a Spanish house, a theme continued throughout the restaurant with red tiles, potted plants, and plates on the walls. You'll be hard-pressed to budge after the *menú:* salad, potato omelette, 3 courses, wine, and mineral water (950ptas). No a la carte. Open daily 1-4pm and 9-11pm.

Mesón La Cadena, Pl. Mayor, 8 (tel. 32 14 63). Modern decor. Expensive *menú* 1090ptas, but the *platos tipicos* (regional plates) are a good deal at 550ptas. Open daily 1-5pm and 9pm-midnight.

Restaurante Emilia, C. Gran Mola, 26 (tel. 32 00 83). Small and intimate, with booths and a fireplace. Enjoy drinks on the small patio with a fountain and plants. *Menú* 850ptas, a la carte dishes about 550ptas. Open daily 1-4pm and 9-11:30pm.

Cafeteria Nuria, Pl. Mayor, 2 (tel. 32 09 07). Come here for a simple meal and to watch TV. *Bocadillos* 225ptas, *raciones* 450ptas, *platos combinados* 500ptas. Open daily 8am-1am; in off-season daily 8am-11pm.

Sights

Presided over by the flamboyant **statue of Francisco Pizarro,** the **Plaza Mayor** resembles the one Pizarro had built in Cuzco, Peru, after he defeated the Incas: an ample, pleasant, stone-paved space with a fountain in the middle, surrounded by palaces and arched passageways, and flanked on one side by wide flights of steps. The statue, the gift of an American couple, was sculpted in 1927. At night the eerie clock tower of the church keeps vigil over the lit fountain and statue. On the southwestern corner of the plaza is the **Palacio de la Conquista,** built by Francisco Pizarro's brother and companion in arms, Hernando. (This is only one of the several casas de Pizarro found in Trujillo.)

As an illegitimate child of the Captain Gonzalo de Pizarro, Francisco was not allowed to be born in his father's house on C. de Ballesteros. The Pizarros' palace is not open to the public, since the owner, a descendant of the man who brought in half the gold Spain once had in its coffers, is now too punurious to repair the roof. On the northeastern corner of the plaza stands the **Iglesia de San Martín,** bedecked with stork nests; it houses the tomb of Francisco de Orellana, the first European to explore the Amazon. The church maintains no regular hours, but the caretaker will show you around. Across the street is the **Palacio de los Duques de San Carlos,** which was given by its owners to the few remaining Hieronymite cloistered nuns, who had to abandon their decaying convent. If you ring the bell, one of the two nuns with a special papal dispensation to serve as guide will show you around the patio and up an extraordinary winding staircase that has no visible support. One ancestor of the Duke was said to have climbed it on horseback. Emperor Carlos V stayed here a couple of times and allowed his coat of arms to be painted on the ceiling above the staircase. The seven smokestacks atop the house signify the different religions defeated by conquering Spaniards in the New World. (A small tip at the end of the tour is appreciated.)

Climb uphill to the northeast in order to reach the spectacular **castle** built by the Arabs on the site of a Roman bastion. The castle walls are in excellent shape, and you can climb up to its battlements and walk on its ramparts. On a clear day you can see all the way to the Sierra de Gredos. Inside the walls lie remnants of the castle's *aljibe* (cistern) and the entrance to the lower-level dungeons. A small image of Nuestra Señora de la Victoria, the town's patroness, is in a small chapel inside. Supposedly, the Virgin Mary appeared during the battle Fernando III led against the Moors here in 1232 and gave the Christians the strength to recover the city. For a dramatic view of the Extremaduran countryside, come here to catch the sunset. (No regular hours; your best bet is to visit 10am-2pm or 5-7pm.) On your way up to the castle, on C. de Ballesteros (Street of the Cross-bow Shooters), you will pass by the house of Pizarro's father, which is now a cultural center.

Heading straight west on C. de Ballesteros, you will hit the biggest church in town, the **Iglesia de Santa María,** an impressive Gothic building constructed upon the foundations of a former mosque. Ask around for Sra. Tomasa, the caretaker, who will show you the inside and point out the places assigned for Fernando and Isabel to hear Mass during their brief residence in the city. Pizarro is said to have been christened on a stone font here. And legend has it that Diego de Paredes, the Herculean soldier, picked up the fountain and carried it to his mother . . . at age 11. The giant was buried here after he twisted his ankle, fell, and perished. On the altar there is a beautiful 24-panel retable painted by Master Fernando Gallego; the floor is made of the tombstones of old *hidalgos.* (Open daily 10am-2pm and 4-7pm. Sun. Mass at 11am.)

Guadalupe

In 1300, cowherd Gil Cordero found his lost cow, apparently dead, on the banks of the Río Guadalupe. Just as he began to skin the animal, the Virgin Mary appeared and told him to return with the local priests, for under the stones on which the cow had died lay an image of the Holy Mother. The cow revived, the cowherd fled, and the pilgrims haven't stopped coming. After the Battle of Salado in 1340, when Alfonso XI invoked the Virgin's aid and triumphed against a superior Muslim army, he erected the great **Real Monasterio de Santa María de Guadalupe,** part church, castle, and fortress, on the site.

Guadalupe became more than just a shrine; the monastery and town came to unite all of *hispanidad.* Fernando and Isabel tied the name of Guadalupe to the New World by signing their contract with Christopher Columbus here. Columbus, in turn, named the island of Turugueira "Guadalupe" in 1493 and also brought the first Native American converts here to be baptized in 1496. The rest of the Extremaduran *conquistadores* who embarked for the Americas took with them their religious devotion, ensuring that Guadalupe would be the name the Virgin Mary received in America.

Today, Guadalupe is a small mountain town dependent on agriculture and the thousands of tourists who come to visit its monastery. During your visit, do the local economy and your tastebuds some good by sampling one of the town's many culinary specialties. *Migas* (bread spiced with pepper, garlic, and chorizo, fried and eaten with a spoon), *caldereta* (simmered goat and lamb), and the local gazpacho (prepared with raw eggs, *migas,* vinegar, and oil) are unique to the town.

Orientation and Practical Information

An hour and a half east of Trujillo and a three-hour bus ride southeast of Madrid, Guadalupe rests on a mountainside in the Sierra de Guadalupe. It's possible to rush through the monastery on a daytrip from Madrid, but from Trujillo bus schedules require an overnight stay.

Everything you need in Guadalupe is within 100m of the bus stop. The multipurpose Ayuntamiento lies on the other side of **Avenida Don Blas Pérez,** the town's main thoroughfare (better known as **Carretera de Cáceres**). Walk around the corner and down the hill to reach the restaurant-lined **Plaza Mayor,** fronted by the basilica of the monastery on one side and open to the mountains on the other.

Tourist Office: None. Direct questions to the **Ayuntamiento,** Avda. Don Blas Pérez, 2 (tel. 36 70 06; open Mon.-Sat. 10am-1pm); to the **Parador Nacional Zurbarán,** Marqués de la Romana, 10 (tel. 36 70 75), up the street to the right from the plazas; or to a monk at the monastery.

Post Office: Ayuntamiento, Avda. Don Blas Pérez, 2 (tel. 36 71 42). Open for stamps, Lista de Correos, and **telegrams** Mon.-Fri. 9am-2pm, Sat. 9am-1pm. **Postal Code:** 10140. **Telephone Code:** 927.

Bus Stop: By the grocery store across from the Ayuntamiento. Empresa Doalde to Madrid's Estación Sur (daily at 9am and 3:30pm, 3 hr., 1400ptas); S.A. Mirat to Trujillo (Mon.-Fri. at 6:30am and 4:30pm, 1½ hr., 410ptas).

Swimming Pool: Carretera de Cáceres (tel. 36 71 39), 3km downhill from town. Open June-Sept. daily 11am-8pm. Admission 175ptas, children 125ptas.

Medical Emergency: Contact one of the two town doctors (tel. 36 71 97 or 36 74 68), or the **Guardia Civil** (tel. 36 70 10). **Ambulance:** Tel. 36 71 95.

Police: Ayuntamiento (tel. 36 70 06).

Accommodations and Food

Everything lies on the Plaza Mayor. Trying to find a room is difficult only during Semana Santa.

Hostal Cerezo, Gregorio López, 12 (tel. 36 73 79 or 37 70 08), between the Ayuntamiento and the plaza. The hotel you've dreamed about. Friendly staff and immaculate rooms, many with lovely views. Strong, hot showers. Singles 1300ptas. Doubles 2200ptas. Triples 3000ptas. Restaurant-bar *menú* 675ptas, a la carte available.

Mesón Extremeño, Pl. Mayor, 3 (tel. 36 73 60). Clean, sparse rooms above a sometimes raucous bar, but you can't beat the prices. Singles 700ptas, with sink 800ptas. Doubles with sink 1500ptas. Classy bar-restaurant with tables inside and out. *Caldereta extremeña* (lamb stew) 550ptas.

Mesón Típico Isabel, Pl. Mayor, 18 (tel. 36 71 28). Modern rooms. Animal pelts serve as rugs or late-night footwarmers. Singles 800ptas. Doubles 1600ptas. Bar serves amazingly large *raciones* (350-400ptas) and delicious *caldereta* (450ptas).

Bar-Restaurante Guadalupe, Pl. Mayor, 32 (tel. 36 70 80). From Pl. Mayor, walk down the street farthest to the left. The patio dining area, with its fountain and lush ivy, is Edenic. Gazpacho 150ptas, *caldereta extremeña* 600ptas. Restaurant open daily 1-4pm and 7-10pm. Bar open daily 9am-midnight.

Restaurante Lujuan, C. Gregono Lopez, 21 (tel. 36 71 70), across from Hostal Cerezo. Rather bland, modern decor, but locals rate the food among the best in town. *Menú* 700ptas, *cordero asado* (roast lamb) 800ptas.

Sights

Twisted hallways, at times unnavigable even by tour guides, betray the numerous changes the **Real Monasterio de Santa María de Guadalupe** has undergone. Construction began in the fourteenth century, but haphazard renovations and additions continued through the eighteenth century. Despite the jumble of styles, from Gothic to baroque, the monastery projects power and majesty.

The **claustro Mudéjar** is the focal point of the complex. Surrounded by towers, the cloister combines Almohad arches in the surrounding arcade with an inspiring Gothic temple in the garden, raised in 1905 by a Hieronymite monk. Twenty Franciscan monks, who replaced the Hieronymites in 1908 after negotiation, live behind the green windows on the uppermost floor.

Just off the cloister, the **Museo de Bordados** (embroidery) displays intricately designed vestal garments in the old refectory of the monastery. All garments were woven by former friars and worn in liturgical ceremonies. Look for the gems and gold thread laced into the *Capa Rica* by the famous fingers of Friar Cosme in the fifteenth century. The tour's next stop is the **Museo de Libros Miniados,** home to more weighty subject matter. Each of the twenty-odd, four-foot-high tomes on display weighs about 50 kilograms and contains fifteenth-century Gregorian chants. The shortened shepherd's crook in the corner was used as a bookmark.

The **sacristía,** built between 1636 and 1645, is a breathtaking monument to the painter Zurbarán, whose portraits of Hieronymite monks capture the full emotion of their faith and mysticism. *Apoteósis de San Jerónimo* and *Los azotes en el juicio de Dios,* two of his greatest works, hang in the **Capilla de San Jerónimo,** at the far end of the sacristy.

In the **relicuario** are many of the gifts presented to the image of the Virgin through the centuries. Most amusing are the garments used to dress the icon; her clothes are changed several times a year for religious festivals. The Manto Rico de la Comunidad holds more jewels than all the cloaks in the Museo de Bordados combined. The statues of hands placed in the drawers along the walls of this sixteenth-century chapel are not real—merely casts of supposedly original saints' hands.

At this point, one of the Franciscan friars assumes control of the tour and leads the group up two flights to the incredibly rich baroque mansion of the **Camarín de Nuestra Señora.** The dense decoration took 40 years to finish after the rotunda-like construction was completed in 1696.

On her gold throne in a small chapel off the Camarín, stands the **Imagen de Nuestra Señora Santa María de Guadalupe.** Legends date the sculpture back to the first century C.E. and trace its path through the hands of Cardinal Gregorio in Constantinople in 590 and to the Sevillan monks who buried it near the river to prevent its capture by Muslims. However, modern technology has dated it at the end of the twelfth century. As with primitive wooden sculptures of the period, Mary is painted black, so that the light of God's glory can better reflect off her face onto the populace. The baby Jesus is on Mary's left arm; his right hand, made of silver, blesses viewers. The blue globe on the golden throne shows the ties of Guadalupe with the rest of Spain and with Hispanic America. If the crowds aren't too great, ask the friar to spin the throne around so you can see the intricate handpainted tiles on the back depicting various visitors to the shrine, among them Cervantes and St. Teresa of Avila. (Monastery open April-Sept. daily 9:30am-1pm and 3:30-7pm; Oct.-March daily 9:30am-1pm and 3:30-6pm. Admission 150ptas. You must wait until a small group has assembled; visitors are allowed only with guides.)

The **basílica** of the monastery fronts Guadalupe's **Plaza Mayor,** connected by a wide set of stairs. Inside the basilica, look for the severe multi-tiered Gothic retable from the eighteenth century, designed by Jorge Manuel Teotocópuli, El Greco's son. Ask someone at the door to the monastery to let you see the **coro.** Here lie the ornate wood chairs and magnificent ceiling painting of Juan de Flandes, out of sight from below. (Basilica open daily 9am-6pm. Free.)

Mérida

As a reward for services rendered, Caesar Augustus granted a group of his veteran soldiers the privilege of founding a city in Lusitania. The legionnaires chose a site surrounded by several hills on the banks of the Guadiana River and called the new settlement Augusta Emerita. Strategically located, Mérida became the capital of the province of Lusitania, which comprised Portugal and part of Spain. The nostalgic soldiers set out to adorn their "little Rome" with bridges, baths, aqueducts, temples, a hippodrome, an arena, and the famous amphitheater where plays are still performed.

Modern Mérida cannot match the splendor that made its Roman ancestor famous, but its ruins and new Roman museum are worth a stop. Come in June and July, when the Classical Theater Festival attracts some of Europe's finest classical and modern troupes. Attending a performance of a Greek or Roman classic under Mérida's starry summer sky is unforgettable.

Orientation and Practical Information

Mérida lies near the center of Extremadura, 73km south of Cáceres and 59km east of its provincial capital, Badajoz. To reach the tourist office, take a right out of the bus station and turn right onto C. Camilo José Cela; from the train station, walk straight uphill to reach this street and head left onto C. Cervantes, cross the small plaza to C. Juan Ramón Melida, and continue uphill to the end of the street. The **Turismo** will be to your right across the street, next to the entrance to the Teatro Romano. **Plaza de Espana,** the town center, lies near the Guadiana, down C. Valverde Lilo from the end of C. Camilo José Cela.

Tourist Office: C. P.M. Plano (tel. 31 53 53), next to the entrance to the *teatro.* Staff is well-meaning, but not especially knowledgeable. Schedules and tickets for plays in the *teatro romano.* Open June-Sept. Mon.-Fri. 9:30am-2pm and 5-7:30pm, Sat. 9:30am-2pm and 4-6:30pm; Oct.-May schedule varies.

Post Office: Pl. de la Constitución (tel. 31 24 58). Open for stamps and Lista de Correos Mon-Sat. 9am-2pm. Open for **telegrams** Mon.-Fri. 9am-8pm. **Postal Code:** 06800. **Telephone Code:** 924.

Train Station: C. Cardero. **RENFE** (tel. 31 20 05), next to Hotel Cervantes and across C. Marquesa de Pinares/Avda. de Extremadura (1 long street with 2 names). To Cáceres (4 per day, 1 hr., 400ptas), Badajoz (9 per day, 1 hr., 320ptas), Sevilla (1 per day, 4 hr., 1100ptas), and Madrid (5 per day, 6 hr., 3000ptas).

Bus Station: Avda. de la Libertad (tel. 25 86 61, 30 04 04, or 30 04 07), across the Puente Romano. To Cáceres (3 per day, 2 hr., 450ptas), Badajoz (8 per day, 1 hr., 390ptas), Sevilla (6 per day, 3 hr., 1100ptas), and Madrid (7 per day, 3¾ hr., 1688ptas).

Taxis: Tel. 31 91 67. 24-hour service.

English Bookstore: Librería Martín, Santa Eulalia, 56 (tel. 30 13 95).

Medical Emergency: Residencia Sanitaria de la Seguridad Social Centralita Tel. 31 03 50. **Ambulance,** El Madrileño (tel. 31 57 58 or 31 11 08).

Police: Ayuntamiento, Pl. España, 1 (tel. 31 50 11 or 30 08 07). **Emergency:** Tel. 092 (municipal police) or 091 (national police).

Accommodations

Hostales seem to be disguised in Mérida. The best place to look is **Plaza de España,** but you could spend days wandering the side streets without seeing any blue-and-white square signs.

Hostal-Residencia Guadiana, Pl. de Santa Clara (tel. 31 31 11). Enter through Hotel Emperatriz. Rooms are bare, but spacious and clean; all have a telephone. Singles 1500ptas. Doubles 2250ptas.

Hostal-Residencia Senero, C. Holgvin, 12 (tel. 31 72 07), a 5-min. walk from Pl. España. Spanish tile interior. Comfortable, clean rooms. Patio is cool in summer. Singles 1100ptas. Doubles 2300ptas.

Hostal-Residencia Bueno, C. Calvario, 9 (tel. 31 10 13). The cheapest of the lot. Singles 1000ptas, with shower 1300ptas. Doubles 1600ptas, with shower 2000ptas.

Food

There are plenty of restaurants in Mérida, but they tend to be expensive. For light meals and *tapas,* explore the areas around Pl. de España and Juan Ramón Melida near the Roman theater.

Hotel Emperatriz, Pl. de España, 19 (tel. 31 30 00 or 31 31 00). Expensive, but a great place to relax with a drink or light snack. Exquisite courtyard with fountain, arches, busts, and potted plants. Gazpacho 250ptas, *trucha* (trout served with ham and egg garnishes) 600ptas. *Menú* 1500ptas. Open daily 1:30-4pm and 9-11:30pm.

Restaurante "J. Pacheco" Moto Club, C. San Juan de Dios, 11 (tel. 31 54 06), behind Pl. de España off C. San Salvador. Tablecloths do exist behind the slot machines. Maps of the Spanish empire at its height in the *comedor.* Large *menú extremeño* 600ptas. Open daily 1:30-5pm and 8pm-midnight.

Bar Restaurant Britz, Féliz Valverde Lillo, 5. Try typical *extremeño* fare here. Excellent lamb stew 575ptas. Filling *menú* specializing in *callos* 700ptas. Open Mon.-Sat. 1-4pm and 8:30-11:30pm.

Sights

The fifth and tenth legions have left Mérida, but remnants of the former wealth of Lusitania remain. Coming from the north on the Cáceres road, you can see to the left the **Acueducto de los Milagros** and beyond, the bridge over the Albarregas River. Farther up the Albarregas rise the three remaining pillars of the **Acueducto de San Lázaro.**

Begin your Roman excursion at the **Museo Nacional de Arte Romano,** across from the entrance to the *teatro.* The museum is essential since no complete guidebook of Mérida's ruins exists. However, the architectural merit of the building itself almost steals the show from the wonders of the ancient Roman empire. The relics from the Roman theater, amphitheater, and circus, as well as detailed explanations and diagrams of each structure (in Spanish), are displayed in the sun-filled atrium of simple columns of brown brick. An old Roman road passes under and through the museum.

Among the sculptures housed here are the statue of Ceres that used to grace the theater and several bust portraits of Caesar Augustus. You will also find an interesting collection of tombstones. On one of them is a prayer to the goddess Proserpina to avenge the thefts endured by the supplicant in his lifetime, complete with an itemized list of the losses ("Tunics 6, linen capes 2, etc.). (Museum open Tues.-Sat. 10am-2pm and 5-7pm, Sun. and holidays 10am-2pm. Admission 200ptas, students with ID free.)

Across the street lies the **teatro romano,** a gift from Agrippa to the city, built to resemble stages in the metropolis. The semicircle of tiers with seating for 6000 spectators faces a *scaenaefrons,* an impressive marble colonnade built backstage. Seating is divided in three sections, originally used to separate social classes. In Roman times, theaters were used not only for shows but also for disseminating the emperor's ideology through short preambles to each presentation. Now only the performances of the *teatro clásico* take place here (mid-June to mid-Aug. nightly at 10:30pm). The ticket office is at the entrance; tickets run 550-750ptas.

Next to the theater is the 14,000-seat **anfiteatro romano,** in worse shape than its neighbor. Inaugurated in 8 B.C.E., the amphitheater was used for gladiator combat and *venationes,* gladiator combat versus wild animals. If you walk in the corridors at both ends of the ellipse, you can see the rooms in which men and animals waited before combat. (Theater and amphitheater open April-Sept. daily 8am-9:30pm, Oct.-March daily 8am-6pm. Admission 200ptas, students with ID free.)

Northeast of the theater complex lies the **circo romano,** or hippodrome. Though now resembling a large parking lot, this arena was once filled with 30,000 spectators cheering their favorite charioteers. Diocles, a Lusitanian racer who was considered the best of all time, got his start here and wound up in Rome with 1462 victories. (Hippodrome open whenever you want to open the gate and walk around. Free.)

On elegant Plaza de España, 2 blocks from the Guadiana, you can relax at one of the many *terrazas* before exploring the thirteenth-century **Iglesia de Santa María la Mayor.** Inside is a fascinating sixteenth-century chapel dedicated to the Virgin of the Guide. One block northwest of the plaza lies the **Museo Arqueológico de Arte Visigodo.** Housed in a seventeenth-century baroque mansion, the museum contains a treasure of artifacts from the Roman world. (Open Mon.-Fri. 10am-2pm and 4-6pm.) On the banks of the Guadiana, near Pl. de España, stands the **Alcazaba,** a Moorish fortress built to guard the Roman bridge. The Arabs made an interesting architectural mixture by using building materials left behind by the Romans and Visigoths. (Open April-Sept. Mon.-Sat. 8am-1pm and 4-7pm, Sun. 9am-2pm; Oct.-March Mon.-Sat. 9am-1pm and 3-6pm, Sun. 9am-2pm. Admission 100ptas.)

Badajoz

The capital of Baja Extremadura has been the quintessential frontier town since Roman times. It has witnessed invasions, counter-invasions, victory parades and surrenders, acts of bravery, betrayals, and massacres. More than 3000 are said to have been killed here by Franco's troops in the aftermath of one of the bloodiest battles of the Civil War, many of them executed in the old bullring. Involved in every major armed conflict since the Wars of Succession between Spain and Portugal, this low-key provincial capital is now beginning to prosper, happily forsaking its war-torn past.

Perhaps the only way to enjoy Badajoz is to wander around the old city in the early evening and enjoy the sight of its people unwinding in cafes, *terrazas,* arbored boulevards, narrow streets, and squares. In summer, the afternoon sun can be particularly ruthless on the stone-paved, whitewashed streets. The fortress-like **cathedral,** dating from the thirteenth century, looms over orange, tree-lined **Plaza de España.** Its austere facade was softened by the addition of plateresque and Manueline decorations. If the lighting inside allows it, you can admire a hand-carved wooden choir section in the middle of the central nave. Each of the 85 chairs sporta a carving, representing as many saints. Jerónimo de Valencia, the artist, was influenced by his master Berruguete. (Church open daily 8am-1pm and 7-8pm.)

The ruins of the **Alcazaba,** the Moorish castle at the end of C. de San Juan, dominate the lowlands of the Guadiana. Nearby hovers the **Torre de Espantaperros,** strangely nicknamed after the medieval occupation of shooing dogs away from public gatherings. Its octagonal shape is similar to the Torre de Oro over the Guadalquivir in Sevilla. The **museo arquelógico,** recently reopened. An ancient *mezquita,* its pieces include examples of Roman and Visigothic architecture. (Open Tues.-Sat. 11am-2pm and 4-7pm, Sun. 11am-2pm. Admission 100ptas.) Walk north from the Alcazaba and skirt the Carretera de Circunvalación to reach the old city gate known as the **Puerta de Palmas.** The gate stands in front of the sixteenth-century **Puente de Palmas,** a 582-meter bridge designed by Juan de Herrera as part of the city's defenses. For an encompassing view of the city, walk over the bridge toward the RENFE station and back, entering the city through its old gate.

Most *hostales* and restaurants lie around Pl. de España. Try **Hostal Tena,** Primo de Rivera, 15 (tel. 22 26 80), for Gothic wallpaper and a free bell concert by the nuns next door. (Singles 700ptas. Doubles 1150ptas. Triples 1650ptas. Showers 175ptas.) **Hostal Villa Real,** Donoso Cortés, 4 (tel. 22 34 16), rents nondescript rooms for a nondescript price. (Singles 950ptas. Doubles 1600-1700ptas, with shower 1800ptas.) Cheap eats are tough to come by, but **La Bellota de Oro,** Zurbarán, 5 (tel. 22 21 99), for a 575ptas *menú* in a lively, smoke-filled, local atmosphere. (Open daily 1-4pm and 8pm-midnight.) **Café Bar La Riú,** Pl. de España, 7 (tel. 22 20 05), is another popular hangout, with large *raciones* for 450-550ptas. (Open daily 1:30-4:30pm and 8-11pm.)

Plaza de España lies in the old town, across the Guadiana from the bus and train stations. Take bus #5 or 5bis from the bus station (60ptas), the hourly bus from the train station, or a taxi from either (no more than 300ptas). The **bus station** (tel. 25 70 07) sends buses to Sevilla (5 per day, 6½ hr., 2080ptas), Madrid (7 per day, 4 hr., 1100ptas), Mérida (6 per day, 1 hr., 410ptas), and Cáceres (2 per day, 1¾ hr., 350ptas). **Trains** run to Mérida (8 per day, 1½ hr., 290ptas), Cáceres (1 per day, 2½ hr., 620ptas), Lisbon (2 per day, 5½ hr., 1650ptas), and Madrid (2 per day, 5 hr., 1490ptas). The **Turismo,** off Pl. de España at Pasaje de San Juan, 1 (tel. 22 27 63), offers little information. (Open Mon.-Fri. 9am-1pm and 4-6:30pm, Sat. 9am-1pm.) The **post office** is at Paseo General Frans, 4. (tel. 22 23 09; for telegrams 22 26 56; open for stamps and Lista de Correos Mon.-Fri. 9am-2pm, Sat. 9am-1pm; open for **telegrams** Mon.-Sat. 9am-8pm.)

Plasencia

Alfonso VIII of Castilla founded this lively town in the twelfth century "in order to please God and men" and to establish a stronghold of Castilian influence in Extremadura. Its well-preserved sandstone buildings, the narrow streets overlooked by wrought-iron balconies, and the verdant park on an islet in the middle of the Jerte River all make Plasencia an amiable introduction—or farewell—to Extremadura.

Orientation and Practical Information

The Río Jerte forms a semicircle around the promontory upon which Plasencia is perched. From the **Plaza Mayor,** streets radiate toward what used to be the city gates. To reach the town center from the bus station turn left as you exit onto Avda. de la Vera. Continue past Avda. José Antonio until you reach the **Puerta del Sol,** where C. Sol begins. Follow this street to the heart of this animated town (15 min.).

Tourist Office: C. Trujillo, 17 (tel. 41 27 66), downhill from the plaza. Staff is helpful. Open in theory Mon.-Fri. 9am-2pm and 5-7pm, Sat. 9am-2pm.

Post Office: Avda. Alfonso VIII, 18 (tel. 41 23 77). Open for stamps and Lista de Correos Mon.-Fri. 9am-2pm, Sat. 9am-1pm. Open for **telegrams** Open Mon.-Fri. 8am-8pm, Sat. 9am-1pm. **Postal Code:** 10600. **Telephone Code:** 927.

Train Station: Estación de Palazuelo-Empalme (tel. 41 00 49), in Palazuelo, 5km from town. The hourly municipal bus is unreliable. Trains only to Cáceres (6 per day, 11/3 hr., 400ptas) and Madrid (4 per day; *expresso* 3½ hr., 1580ptas; *omnibus* 4 hr., 1100ptas).

Bus Station: Avda. de la Vera (tel. 41 45 50). To Cáceres (3 per day, 1½ hr., 450ptas), Salamanca (4 per day, 2½ hr., 790ptas), Sevilla (4 per day, 6 hr., 1900ptas), Madrid (4 per day, 6¾ hr., 2000ptas), and Valladolid (4 per day). For connections to the rest of Extremadura, go to Cáceres.

Taxis: Stops at Pl. de España (tel. 41 21 73), Puerta del Sol (tel. 41 13 77), and Puerta de Talavera (tel. 41 13 78).

Baggage Check: At the bus station. Open Mon.-Sat. 7am-9pm, Sun. 11:30am-3pm and 4:30-7pm. 30ptas per bag.

Medical Emergency: Puesto de Socorro (tel. 41 36 79). **Hospital Provincial** (tel. 41 31 00). **Ambulance:** Tel. 41 23 07 or 41 30 74.

Police: Policia Municipal (tel. 41 00 33). **Emergency:** Tel. 091.

Accommodations

You will have no problem finding a bed in Plasencia.

Hostal La Muralla, Berrozanas, 6 (tel. 41 38 74). Take the 2nd street to the left off C. de los Quesos. Large place, nicely maintained by a diligent manager. Well-lit, clean rooms and modern bathrooms with strong water pressure. TV lounge. Singles 800ptas. Doubles 1400ptas, with bath 1800ptas. Showers 150ptas. Breakfast 150ptas. Lunch or dinner 600ptas.

Fonda Salmantina, C. Trujillo, 15 (tel. 41 24 40), next to the tourist office. Rooms are rather dark, but they are clean and the mattresses firm. Cluttered bathroom. Singles 500ptas. Doubles 1000ptas. Cross the street to better-lit, elegantly furnished, and pricier rooms. But hold your nose in the bathrooms. Singles 800ptas. Doubles 1200ptas.

Fonda Salmantina, C. Talavera, 17 (no phone), off Pl. Mayor. Cramped and dilapidated, but reasonably clean and extremely cheap. Rooms next to the kitchen lack ventilation and seem to absorb kitchen odors. Singles 450ptas. Doubles 900ptas. Showers 1500ptas.

Food

Plasencia is famous for the remarkable number of bars per capita. The Plaza Mayor is literally surrounded by *mesones* that serve typical *tapas* and *bocadillos*. *Raciones* run around 450ptas.

Restaurante-Bar Mi Casa, C. Patalón, 15 (tel. 41 14 50). Homey place with unfinished wood furniture, crisp, white tablecloths, and fresh flowers. Gaze at the mural of Navaconcejo, a nearby town, as you enjoy the 550ptas *menú.* Try *cabrito al horno* (baby goat, 700ptas) or *cochinillo asado* (roast suckling pig, 700ptas), the house specialties. Open daily 1-4pm and 9pm-midnight.

Taberna Extremeña, C. Vidrieras, 6 (tel. 41 51 76), off the Pl. Mayor. Lively spot crowded with locals. Specializes in regional game cuisine. *Menú* 650ptas. Open daily 11am-2:30am.

Rincón Extremeño, C. Vidrieras, 6 (tel. 41 11 50), down the street from the above. Cozy atmosphere with rust-and-white-checkerboard floor, plaid tablecloths and curtains, and old-time wooden lanterns. *Menú* 600ptas. Open daily 1:30-4:30pm and 9-11pm.

Sights and Entertainment

As in the rest of the Extremadura, sight-seeing in Plasencia consists mainly of sitting in the plaza and watching the rest of the town sitting in the plaza. However, you can head down C. Trujillo and take a left at C. Blanca to one of the most unusual architectural clusters in Spain: the thirteenth-century Romanesque **old cathedral** and the Gothic **new cathedral,** begun in 1498. The two churches are connected by a door built in the common wall. The exquisitely decorated facade of the newer church was designed by some of the biggest names in architecture of the time, including Juan de Alava, Diego de Siloek and Gil de Hontañón. Master carver Rodrigo Alemán fashioned the choir stalls in the new cathedral. The backs and the lower parts of the front pews were decorated with scenes from the Bible on one side and daily life on the other. A few of these latter scenes have puzzled some and enraged others. While some claim the converted Jew took the opportunity to mock the Church with his grotesque and vaguely obscene carvings, legend has it that he was confined to the church by his impatient employers until he finished his work. In defiance, he is said to have tried to build a flying machine and to have jumped from the belfry to his death. The main altar displays the more traditional but no less inspired gilded and polychrome carvings of master Gregorio Fernández. Crossing the door in the right aisle, you will enter the earlier Romanesque part of the building, now transformed into the **Museo Diocesano.** A small collection of old bibles, vestal garments, and gold chalices can't compete with the simple, elegant lines of the old church, but a seven-foot statue of an unsaintly Santa Ana slaying Satan serves as a second course. (Museum open May-Sept. daily 10am-1pm and 4-7pm, Oct.-April daily 10am-1pm and 4-6pm. Admission 100ptas.)

In Pl. San Nicolas stands Plasenciá's other famous monument, the **Palacio de Marqués de Mirabel,** still used as a private residence by the *marqueses* when they visit town. The lovely garden **courtyard** and a **museum** are open to the public. On display in the first of its two rooms are deer heads from a former *marquese's* hunting adventures and a collection of European sculptures and paintings. The bust of Carlos V is said to be the creation of Italian sculptor Pompeye Leoni. Across the terrace, check out the medieval kitchen and pantry. The bed warming devices merit a look. (No regular hours. Ring the bell and the resident caretaker may give you a personal tour. A tip is appreciated. Best to come 10am-2pm and 5-7pm.)

The famous **Fiesta del Martes Mayor,** on the first Tuesday in August, celebrates the town's foundation. Not as well known, but just as much fun are the **carnivals** held in early June, with rides, bullfights, and music. You can sample a bit of local color year-round at the open-air **mercado** every Tuesday in the Pl. Mayor. Vendors journey from all over Extremadura to display their *artesanía* (arts and crafts).

Galicia

Galicia, frequently veiled by a misty drizzle, is a Celtic land where bleating *gaitas* (bagpipes) can still be heard in the rolling green hills. Here the narrow, pitted roads weave through dense woods, around plunging valleys patched with stone-walled farmsteads, and past slate-roofed fishing villages set beside long white beaches. Rivers wind through the hills, gradually widening into the famous *rías* (inlets or firths) that empty into the Cantabrian Sea and the Atlantic Ocean.

Galicia has been isolated from Spain in every sense. Until Columbus's voyage, **Cape Finisterre** was considered by many to be the western end of the earth. The

Swabians maintained a kingdom here for almost two centuries that had very little intercourse with the rest of Spain. And although the Moors attacked Galicia (once under the famous Moorish King Almanzor), this region felt little of the Moorish influence that shaped the rest of the peninsula.

Galicia has, however, been shaped by Celtic influence. Geographically it is similar to Ireland, and many villages preserve the same lore (superstitions to the uninstructed) about witches capable of curing ills, fairies that frequent certain fountains, and buried treasure hidden beneath the *castros* (ruins of ancient Celtic villages).

Modern day politics reflect the separatist character of this region. Although officially granted political autonomy by the post-Franco government, Galicians find subtle and not-so-subtle ways to complain about Madrid's control of the region. Political graffiti is abundant, and Galician citizens aren't shy when it comes to burning the Spanish flag at local fiestas. Regional identification is reinforced by widespread use of Gallego, a language more closely related to Portuguese than to Castilian. (For a cultural treat, try watching the American TV series *Falcon Crest* dubbed in Gallego.)

You'll have to rely on buses to reach the tiny coastal towns and haunting inland hillsides. They are generally quicker, though a bit more costly, than the trains, which adequately connect the main cities.

Sample the wonderful Galician specialties. All the bars serve *pulpo a la gallega* (octopus prepared with a slightly spicy seasoning). If you're less adventurous, try the excellent *empanadas* (bread-dough pies stuffed with tuna and tomato or meat and onion), the wide variety of shellfish, and *queso gallego,* a regional cheese shaped like a giant chocolate kiss. *Caldo gallego,* a vegetable broth, makes a fine start to any meal. The area's Ribeiro, served in white ceramic cups, is a tart, slightly cloudy, young wine that goes great with *tapas.*

Santiago de Compostela

In 813, a beckoning star revealed the earthly remains of the Apostle St. James the Elder and thereby escalated Santiago's position to that of Jerusalem and Rome as one of the three holy cities of the Catholic faith. Santiago Matamoros, or St. James the Moorslayer, occasionally appeared on a white charger to lead Christians into battle and pick off a few thousand infidels. By the twelfth century the field where the warrior-saint's bones were found had become the center of a vast pilgrimage. The Benedictines built monasteries to host the pilgrims around this site, creating perhaps the first major European tourist industry. The emotional appeal and morale boost provided by the saint swept Europe: Pilgrims descended on the Field of the Star for centuries and, although many came as true believers, an equal number followed the Way of St. James as a stipulation to inheritance, an alternative to prison, or a lucrative adventure, hoping to make money from all that ambulatory faith, hope, and charity.

Today pilgrims of every category still follow the superhighway (Carretera 120), but somehow Santiago de Compostela has remained an international spiritual center of extreme beauty and modest size. The all-granite old town (designated a national monument) is ringed and separated from the newer and uglier districts by a wide avenue that changes identity each time you finally discover where you are. Most of Santiago's 30,000 students live in the modern part of town where there are a good many restaurants and hotels and all of the city's club and disco life. If you don't have much time, or if you wish to experience the Santiago of history and legend, focus your sight-seeing on the old city.

Orientation and Practical Information

If you're coming from the interior, you'll probably arrive in Santiago de Compostela by train. As you leave the station, turn right at the top of the stairs, taking C. del General Franco to Plaza de Galicia. The old city lies straight ahead. From the bus station, take bus #10 to Pl. de Galicia (every 10-15 min., 45ptas). A circle of major streets, beginning with C. Calvo Sotelo, surrounds the old city, which sits higher than the new city.

Tourist Office: Rúa del Villar, 43 (tel. 58 40 81), in the old town under the arches of a colonnaded street. Generally helpful. Brochures and useful pamphlets with maps on Santiago and all of Galicia. Bus schedules and accommodations information. English and French spoken. Open Mon.-Fri. 9:30am-2pm and 4-7pm, Sat. 10am-1pm.

Student Travel Service: TIVE, on the university campus in the student service building (tel. 59 61 87). Sells train, bus, and plane tickets for destinations outside of Spain. ISIC and Inter-Rail sold. Open Mon.-Fri. 9am-2pm.

Post Office: C. de Franco (tel. 58 12 52), 2 blocks south of Rúa del Villar. Open for stamps Mon.-Fri. 9am-2pm and 4-6pm, Sat. 9am-noon; for Lista de Correos Mon.-Fri. 9am-2pm. **Postal Code:** 15700.

Telephones: C. do Bautizados, 13, in the old town off Pl. de Toral. Open Mon.-Fri. 10am-11pm, Sat. 10am-8pm, Sun. 11am-9pm. **Telephone Code:** 981.

Airport: Aeropuerto Nacional de Santiago de Compostela (tel. 59 74 00), 11km away on road to Lugo, connected by bus (8 per day, 100ptas). Good national connections and direct flights to London, Paris, Zurich, Amsterdam, and Frankfurt. **Iberia,** General Pardiñas, 24 (tel. 59 41 00). Open Mon.-Fri. 9:30am-2pm and 4-7pm, Sat. 9am-1pm.

Train Station: C. del General Franco (tel. 59 18 08 for information). To Madrid (2 per day, 11 hr., 4475ptas), La Coruña (11 per day, 1 hr., 310ptas), Vigo (9 per day, 1½ hr., 455ptas).

Bus Station: Estación Central de Autobuses, C. San Cayetano (tel. 58 77 00). Good service to Rías Bajas and Rías Altas. (See Rías Bajas and Rías Altas for details.) Also to La Coruña (hourly), Madrid (several per day), Barcelona (2 per day), and Paris (1 per day). Generally 15-20% more expensive than trains, but up to 50% faster for long distances and more scenic for coastal destinations.

Taxis: Tel. 58 24 50 or 58 07 17.

English Bookstore: Libraría González, Rúa del Villar, 52 (tel. 58 13 48). Open daily 9am-1:30pm and 3:30-8pm.

Laundromat: Lava-Express (tel. 59 00 95), in the new town at C. Alfredo Brañas and C. República Salvador. Self-service, up to 4½kg washed and dried for 475ptas. For 100ptas more, they'll do it for you. Open Mon.-Fri. 9:30am-2pm and 4-8:30pm, Sat. 9:30-2pm.

Medical Services: Hospital General de Galicia, C. Galeras (tel. 58 52 00). **Ambulance:** Carrera del Conde, 20 (tel. 58 82 11).

Police: Avda. Rodrigo del Padrón (tel. 58 11 10). **Emergency:** Tel. 091.

Accommodations and Camping

What was, in 1130, a pilgrims' hospital across from the cathedral is now a five-star luxury hotel that shamelessly keeps some of the city's finest Romanesque sculpture from the public. Fortunately for pilgrims and tourists alike, the old city is full of *pensiones* and *fondas.* **Rúa del Villar** and **Calle Raiña** are lined with numerous budget accommodations. Galicians are veterans when it comes to hanging around the local bus and train station in hopes of enticing travelers to stay at their particular *pensión.* Usually they run under-the-table boarding houses or just rent rooms in their own homes, so you can often bring prices down by bargaining (quality varies widely). Stay cool, and offer 700ptas or less for a single. *Fondas, hostales,* and their prices are listed at the tourist office.

Hospedaje Villa de Cruces, Patio de Madres, 16 (tel. 58 08 04), off Calvo Sotelo near Pl. Mazarelos. Clean rooms, nice proprietor, incredibly cheap. Old-fashioned pitchers and wash basins. 400ptas per person. Hot showers 100ptas.

Hospedaje Rodríguez, C. Pison, 4 (tel. 58 84 08), around the corner from Villa de Cruces. Immaculate. On a quiet street with purple flowers growing horizontally out of the stone walls. Singles and doubles 700-800ptas per person.

Hospedaje Meson do Arreiro, C. de la Raiña, 9 (tel. 58 10 77), 1 block south of Rúa del Villar. Sparkling, modern interior. Very safe. Singles with bath 1000ptas. Doubles with bath 2000ptas.

Hospedaje Ramos, C. de la Raiña, 18, 1st floor (tel. 58 18 59). Simple but comfortable. No charge for the fragrances from the restaurant below. Rooms with private baths are nicer and by far a better deal. Singles 800ptas, with bath 900ptas. Doubles 1500ptas, with bath 1600ptas.

Hostal Suso, Rúa del Villar, 6 (tel. 58 66 11). Sparkling place. Rooms are very comfortable, though plain. Friendly proprietor. Cafe below; historic arches before the entrance. Singles 1000ptas, with bath 1500ptas. Doubles with bath 2850ptas.

Camping As Cancelas, Rúa do 25 de Xullo, 35 (tel. 58 02 66), is on the northern edge of town. Take bus #6 or 9. (290ptas per person. 305ptas per tent and per car.) A much nicer site is the new, first-class **Camping Santiago** (tel. 88 80 02), about 5km from Santiago on the road to La Coruña, with pools, supermarkets, and buses to town. (Same prices.)

Food

Santiago looks after the hungry budget traveler by providing many restaurants with *menús* for about 550ptas. The highest concentration is in the old town near the cathedral, most notably on **Rúa del Villar, Calle del Franco,** and **Calle de la Raiña.** Galicians dine earlier than other Spaniards, so you can't wait until 11pm to go out for a bite.

The daily open **market** stretches from Pl. de San Felix to the Convent of San Augustín. The streets are lined with fruit and vegetable vendors; only meat vendors have stalls. The chickens and rabbits are fresh—in fact, they're still alive. (Open Mon.-Sat. 7am-3pm.)

Bar Rois, C. de la Raiña, 12 (tel. 58 24 44). Popular with locals. All entrees between 300-500ptas. *Chuleta de cerdo* (pork chops) 300ptas and *merluza a la gallega* (hake) 500ptas. Open daily 9am-midnight.

Asesino, Pl. de la Universidad, 16 (tel. 58 15 68). No sign. You're in luck, even though the horseshoe points down. Always full of students who know the owners by name. An excellent meal costs about 550ptas. Open daily 2-4pm.

Café-Bar El Metro, Rúa Nova, 12 (no phone). Friendly proprietor but dry atmosphere. Solid *menú* for only 500ptas. Other entrees 300-450ptas. Open daily 1-3pm and 7-10pm.

O' Sotano, C. del Franco, 8 (tel. 56 50 24). Wonderful basement restaurant that is extremely popular with locals. Hearty *menú* for 675ptas. Excellent seafood entrees 500-700ptas. Open daily 11am-4:30pm and 9:30-11:30pm.

Restaurante Abella, C. del Franco, 30 (tel. 58 29 81). Dining room in back with no-nonsense *menús* for 550-700ptas. *Empanadas* are a bargain at 175ptas. Also try *pollo asado* (roast chicken) for 375ptas.

Cerveceria Dakar, C. del Franco, 13. Not a place for a meal, but a pleasant little bar. Order the great *batidos*—a dessert that kicks. For 170ptas you can sip what resembles a milkshake but contains various liqueurs and nutmeg.

Sights

The **Catedral de Santiago de Compostela** is a religious shrine of poetic construction. Two outstanding baroque towers, adorned by eighteenth-century stone flowers from around the world, soar above the city. Four famous facades, each architecturally unique but harmoniously blended, surround the cathedral. The **Obradoiro** (Praza do Obradoiro), the main facade, flickers upward like a flame captured in stone, a fine example of Galician baroque. The **Azabacheria** facade (Praza da Immaculada) is a somewhat confused blend of styles with an unbalanced arrangement of towers and domes in the background. The **Platerías** facade (Praza de Praterias) is the oldest and contains beautiful rows of round archs, statues, and excellent bas-relief details. The **Quintana** facade (Praza de Literarios) contains the Romanesque **Puerta Santa** (Holy Door), open only in years of great significance. Above the door is a famous seventeenth-century statue of Santiago in civilian dress. His pilgrim's cloak, large hat, cockleshell, and staff are far preferable to the army of warring Santiagos that adorns the rest of the church. Try to catch the cathedral from each angle and in different light.

Santiago's finest architectural treasures are assembled in **Praça do Obradoiro.** To the left, the old **Colegio de San Jerónimo** impresses with its fifteenth-century Romanesque doorway of fine sculpted figures; directly opposite the cathedral, the long, elegant facade of the former **Palácio de Rajoy** radiates gold-accented balconies and simple columns. The amazing bas-relief of the Battle of Clavijo is a splendid neoclassic work. Once a royal hospital, the **Hostal de los Reyes Católicos** is now a luxury hotel. Its intricate doorway is a masterpiece of sculpture, characteristic of Galician architecture. Enter the cathedral, and linger just inside, by the **Pórtico de la Gloria,** one of the most outstanding ensembles of Romanesque sculpture in Europe. Executed by Maestro Mateo between 1168 and 1188, it includes a likeness of the sculptor. Pilgrims bow to the statue of St. James the Elder just above. Inside, organ pipes protrude from stone arches along the central aisle, resembling trumpet horns over the heads of the congregation. To the left of the altar are several domed side chapels decorated with Ionic columns. One contains the tomb of two archbishops, whose remains lie under what appear to be small Greek temples. However, the cathedral's best-known religious artifact is St. James's remains in a silver coffer immediately under the high altar. The stairs and terraces visible on top of the cathedral are unfortunately no longer accessible, but visit the **museum** and **cloisters.** (Cathedral open daily 10am-1:30pm and 4-7:30pm. Admission to museum and cloisters 200ptas.) Don't miss the *bota fumeiro,* a huge silver incense burner swung from end to end in the transept during high Masses and major liturgical ceremonies.

Santiago features some fine museums. The **Monasterio de San Pelayo de Antes-Altares** goes beyond the usual relics with a brilliant little statue of Mary holding Jesus and clubbing a demon. (Open Mon.-Sat. 10am-1pm and 4-7pm, Sun. 10am-2pm. Admission 75ptas.) The **Iglesia de Santo Domingo** is home to both the **Museo do Pobo Galego** and the **Museo Municipal,** which contain interesting exhibits on Galician culture, such as replicas of the ancient *castros.* Confusing but fascinating spiral stairways start at three separate points on the ground floor and twist their way to the top, never intersecting. (Open Mon.-Sat. 10am-1pm and 4-7pm. Admission to both 50ptas, students free.)

Located 1km from the cathedral is the **Colegiata de Santa María del Sar,** a church crumbling since the twelfth century. Inside, the pillars lean at unlikely angles, giving the impression that the whole thing is about to collapse into a pile of Romanesque rubble. (Open Mon.-Sat. 10am-1pm and 4-6:30pm. Admission 30ptas.)

Entertainment

Stepping out in Santiago's old town means making the rounds of the city's cellars. Bars and pubs, which close at 1am and 3am, line the medieval streets along C. Santiago de Chile. **Teteria,** on C. Algalia Arriba, is a beatnik teashop that plays solid American rock. **Modus Vivendi,** in Pl. de Feixoo, is an eclectic dungeon that alternates between Galician bagpipes and David Bowie. Near Pl. de Cervantes, **Poison** serves great local wines that are anything but poisonous in large glasses to a mostly student crowd. For discos, which don't really start bopping until midnight, try **Araguaney** on C. Montero Rios during the summer. Its slick neon interior features a Venus de Milo copy above the bar. **Discoteca Black** in the Hotel Peregrino, C. Rosalia de Castro, is also popular. All clubs are free for women, around 400-600ptas for men, and open roughly from 11pm to 4am, with action starting well after midnight.

Santiago's fiestas occur annually July 18 to 31. The climax is the bacchanalian **Féstival del Apóstol;** tension and parties mount for a week or more beforehand. Street musicians and performers set up shop in Pl. Imaculada, with elaborate figures worn by people on stilts parading through the streets. A famous one is a witch with a broom who literally sweeps pedestrians aside, clearing a path for an even older woman (also on stilts) who snatches hats with her gnarled fingers and keeps people at bay with loud fireworks. On July 25, the cathedral's facade is rigged with hundreds of fireworks.

Be sure to catch Santiago's *tuna* performances, held nightly in the Praza do Obradoiro and surrounding squares. A student singing-group *cum* comedy troupe, the *tuna* belts out ribald songs and serenades women. If a woman loves the singer, she gives him a long ribbon with the color of his professional school (or increasingly, hers) for his cape. The capes are elegant examples of wearing a heart on your sleeve, but the woman has the final say; if she doesn't like the song, she pours water on the head of the singer.

La Coruña (A Coruña)

La Coruña is a healthy city grown too big for its own peninsula. From the time the Roman navy landed here until the present day, the lighthouse has guided sailors safely into its port. Charles I marched through on his way to being crowned Emperor of Austria, as did Felipe II on his way to marry Mary Tudor, the daughter of Henry VIII and Catherine of Aragon. The Invincible Armada also departed from here on its way to defeat at the hands of Francis Drake in May 1589, but this departure is less well-remembered than the fatal wound Sir John Moore suffered here during the War of Spanish Independence.

The old town is lively and bustling, and what La Coruña lacks in monuments, it makes up for in energy, beaches, and good transportation to other places. It's big, but you can safely ignore all but a few areas of the city. La Coruña is a perfect base for exploring the upper estuaries and for catching transport to points south.

Orientation and Practical Information

La Coruña's prettiest quarter is, not surprisingly, the *ciudad vieja* (old city), which occupies the southern tip of the peninsula, overlooking the port area. The **Avenida de la Marina** leads past the tourist office into this section of town famous for its shaded streets and old stone buildings. The bus and train stations are a 20-minute walk south of the port area. If you decide not to take the bus in from the new part of town, follow your nose to the water and then turn left. The **municipal beach** (Playa del Orzán) is a 10-minute walk northwest from the tourist office at the other extreme of the peninsula's neck.

Tourist Office: Dársena de la Marina (tel. 22 18 22), on the south side of the isthmus connecting the peninsula and the mainland, near the waterfront. A bit gruff, but helpful if you have specific questions. Great color brochures on Galicia and the rest of Spain. Open Mon.-Fri. 9am-2pm and 4:30-6:30pm, Sat. 10:30am-1pm; Oct.-June Mon.-Fri. 10am-1:30pm and 4-6pm.

Consulate: U.S., Cantón Grande, 16-17, 8th floor (tel. 21 32 33). Open Mon.-Fri. 10am-1pm.

Currency Exchange: El Corte Inglés, Ramón y Cajal, near the bus station. Open Mon.-Sat. 8:30am-9pm.

American Express Travel Representative: Viajes Amado, C. Compostela, 1 (tel. 22 57 32). Open Mon.-Fri. 9am-1:30pm and 4-7:30pm, Sat. 9:30am-1:30pm.

Post Office: Alcade Manuel Casas (tel. 22 19 56), a few blocks toward the mainland from Turismo. Open for Lista de Correos and stamps Mon.-Fri. 9am-2pm and 4-6pm, Sat. 9am-2pm. **Telegrams:** Open Mon.-Fri. 8am-9pm, Sat. 9am-7pm, Sun. 9am-2pm. **Postal Code:** 15000.

Telephones: C. de San Andrés, 101, in the center of the isthmus. Open Mon.-Sat. 9am-1pm and 5-9pm, Sun. 10am-2pm and 5-9pm. **Information:** Tel. 003. **Telephone Code:** 981.

Train Station: Avda. de San Riego (tel. 23 03 09), in the new city. Bus #14 (55ptas) will take you from here to Turismo and the post office. To Santiago (10 per day, 1 hr., 310ptas), Vigo (5 per day, 2½ hr., 770ptas), Oviedo (2 per day, 10 hr., 2755ptas), Madrid, and León.

Bus Station: C. Caballeros (tel. 23 96 44), not far from the train station. Frequent service to the Rías Altas and Rías Bajas including Finisterre (4 per day, 785ptas). Also to Santiago (hourly, 400ptas), Vigo (5 per day, 925ptas), Oviedo (2 per day, 1945ptas), and Madrid (3 per day, 2330ptas).

Taxis: Tel. 22 96 00 or 28 77 77.

English Bookstore: Librería Colón, C. Real, 24 (tel. 22 22 06), parallel to the waterfront, a few blocks in from the tourist office. A good selection of classics and a few contemporary titles. Open Mon.-Fri. 10am-1:30pm and 5-9pm, Sat. 10:30am-2pm.

Laundromat: Lavanderia Glu Glu, C. Alcalde Marchesi, 4 (tel. 28 28 04), off Pl. de Cuatro Caminos. 5kg for 500ptas. Open Mon.-Sat. 9am-9pm.

Hospital: Hospital de la Seguridad Social "Juan Canalejo," Avda. Pasaje (tel. 28 74 77). **First Aid:** Carretera del Pasaje (tel. 29 79 05). **Ambulance:** Tel. 23 08 10.

Police: Avda. Alféres Provisional (tel. 22 61 00).

Accommodations

For a town with so much late-night street life and all-night discos, La Coruña has a surprisingly large number of places to sleep. The peninsula is full of *pensiones, casas de huéspedes,* and hotels. Summer, however, keeps the city booked, and finding a room can be rough, especially for those traveling alone. Start looking between late morning and noon. There are two **IYHF youth hostels** near La Coruña: **Marina Española** (tel. 62 01 18) is in Sada, a small town with a fine sandy beach, 20km away on the road to Betanzos; **Albergue Juvenil de Gandario** (tel. 79 10 05) is in Gandario, 22km away by bus, but it's often full with school groups, so call ahead. Buses to both towns leave about every hour from the bus station. Both cost 500ptas; you can probably find a better deal in town, where you can avoid the hassle of buses or midnight curfews (although the latter hostel is understanding if you wish to come home late). Best streets for starting your search are **Calle Riego de Agua,** and **Calle Real,** near the tourist office.

Hospedaje San Nicolás, C. San Nicolás, 23 (tel. 22 85 36), a few blocks in from Turismo above a fruit store near St. Nick's church. Bright and cheery with a friendly proprietor, but spongy beds. Singles 800ptas. Doubles 1500ptas.

Pensión Almar, C. Real, 81, 4th floor (tel. 22 60 62). The wonderful owner will set you up in a clean but small room. Singles 500ptas. Doubles 1000ptas. Hot showers 100ptas.

Pensión la Alianza, C. Riego de Agua, 8, 1st floor (tel. 22 81 14). Clean and likely to be full, but the friendly proprietor will recommend other well-run places. Rooms have balconies that look onto an active and sometimes noisy street. Singles 1200ptas. Doubles 1800ptas.

Fonda Maria Pita, C. Riego de Agua, 38, 3rd floor (tel. 22 11 87). Gruff but kind owner. Cheery rooms. Singles 600-700ptas. Doubles 1750ptas. There are 3 other clean, attractive *hostales* in this building.

Food

Eating in La Coruña on a budget is easy. Wonderful seafood and a slew of cheap cafeterias with good combination plates make things easy on your pockets. Though the non-seafood items are often cheaper, splurge a little and enjoy some delicious large scallops and octopus. **Calle Real** and **Calle de la Franja** have plenty of cheap, tasty eateries.

If you're looking for fresh fruit and vegetables, go to the big **market** held in the oval building on Pl. San Agustín, near the old town. (Open Mon.-Sat. 8am-12:30pm.) If you miss the morning vendors, buy your groceries in the supermarket below.

Taberna Maurel, C. de la Franja, 17 (tel. 22 47 52). Seafood entrees and *raciones* at reasonable prices. *Gambas a la plancha* 450ptas or meaty *chuleta de cerdo* 350ptas. Open daily 2-4pm and 8pm-midnight.

Casa Santiso, C. Franja, 26 (tel. 22 86 34). Very humble, with blaring TV, but cheapest place for a sit-down meal in the old quarter. *Menú del día* (no seafood) 525ptas. Open daily 9:30am-midnight.

A Vendimia, C. Franja, 53 (tel. 22 56 92). As a restaurant, it's in the 1000ptas range, but you can indulge inexpensively in seafood *tapas* washed down with local wines (white Ribeiro, rosé Rueiro, and sparkling Lubay). Open daily 11am-4pm and 7pm-midnight.

Cafeteria Piscis, C. de la Franja, 19-21 (tel. 22 61 07). Great variety of seafood, most in the 225-500ptas range, including the unsightly *chipirones en su tinta* (300ptas). Open daily 11am-11pm.

Cafeteria Delfos, C. Marina, 7 (tel. 22 08 35). Formal service; pink and gray decor. Huge *platos combinados* cost less than 500ptas; they're even cheaper at the bar. Open daily 7am-1:30am.

Sights and Entertainment

Although it has much less of an aged feeling than the old quarters of other Spanish cities, La Coruña's *ciudad vieja* is a pleasant place for a stroll. The granite streets here are well-kept, and most buildings have a fresh coat of white paint. The cobbled **Plaza de Maria Pita** is surrounded by simple arches and windows typical of La Coruña. The three red tile domes of the **Palacio Municipal** rise majestically. Explore the cobbled **Plazuela Santa Bárbara,** bordered by the fifteenth-century convent of the same name. Close by is the **Iglesia de Santa María del Campo.** Built between the twelfth and fifteenth centuries, it has a small Gothic doorway and granite columns that form the central aisles and lead to a pretty rose window. Jutting out into the bay on the southeast side of the peninsula is the sixteenth-century **Castillo de San Antón,** which now houses the **Museo Arqueológico.** Don't miss the bizarre fourteenth-century stone pig bearing a large cross on its back—it's only one of many unusual pieces in the collection. There are also Bronze Age artifacts, bones from the local Roman necropolis, and a reconstruction of a supposedly fourth-century wicker and skin boat. (Open daily 10am-2pm and 4-8pm; Oct.-May 10am-2pm. Admission 100ptas.) You can also walk along the ramparts for a view of the sprawling city beyond the port and the rolling Galician greenery abruptly meeting the Atlantic.

The opposite end of the peninsula holds Coruña's other famous tourist magnet, the **Torre de Hércules.** The only extant Roman lighthouse in the world, it dates from the second century and still throws out a nightly signal to ships from the westernmost point of the peninsula. Over 100m high, the tower provides a fine view of the sea and city. The original Roman construction is visible only from the inside. Legend has it that Hercules himself erected the tower upon the remains of his defeated enemy Gerión. (Open Mon.-Sat. 10am-1pm and 4pm until 1 hr. before sunset. Free.) Either walk the 2km along the Carretera de la Torre or take bus #9 or 13 (40ptas).

Lovers of Spanish literature can stop by the childhood home of the grand aristocrat and great nineteenth-century Castilian novelist, the **Condesa Emilia Pardo Bazán.** Her family's eighteenth-century mansion has been converted into the headquarters of the **Real Academia Gallega** (Royal Galician Academy), whose library contains 25,000 volumes on the subjects of Galician literature, history, and culture. The academy also maintains a rotating exhibit of modern and nineteenth-century Galician art. Next door, at C. Tabernas, 11, a small museum is devoted solely to the writing and houses both permanent collections and rotating exhibits of Galician art. (Open Mon.-Fri. 10am-noon. Free.)

The **Jardin de San Carlos,** in the old part of the city, was originally planted in 1843 on the site of the old San Carlos fort. It shelters the tomb of Sir John Moore, a British general who died in the Battle of Elviña during the Peninsular War. One of the most charming small city parks in Spain, it makes a nice picnic spot. The sandy beaches of **Orzán** and **Riazor** are both within easy walking distance on the northwest side of the isthmus.

Summer nightlife in La Coruña is perhaps the liveliest in all Galicia. If you want to take part, catch up on sleep in the afternoons because most of the action doesn't start until 2am. Visiting and local prodigals hang out at **Chaston,** C. Costa Rica, 4 (tel. 27 59 13), near Pl. de Galicia. Packed with young Spaniards, the club's kinky red felt walls and gold couches reverberate with Euro-dance music. (Open daily 8-10:30pm and 11:30pm-5am. Women 500ptas, men 700ptas.) Try also the disco and cafes on C. Juan Florez. **Piramide,** at #50 (tel. 27 61 57), plays great dance music. (Women 600ptas, men 700ptas.)

Rías Bajas and Rías Altas

The Rías are Galicia's estuary lands. The Rías Bajas, the seacoast indentations to the south of Santiago de Compostela, offer abrupt encounters of hill and ocean. Sequestered in quiet coves, the fishing villages here thrive on the commerce of the daily catch. The Rías Altas, north of Cabo Finisterre, are wilder, woolier, and usually wetter (better than Six Flags). Beaches here are just as stunning as their southern counterparts. Unfortunately, rarely a day passes north of Coruña without fog or low clouds, and there are barely enough sunny afternoons to support the few modest vacation colonies. The cleanest water is found closest to the ocean: While more inland sands higher up the estuaries may beckon with their beauty, confine your dips to beaches nearer the Atlantic. Beaches, however, are not what the Rías Altas are all about. No region in Galicia—or perhaps in all of Spain—has preserved its traditions so well. Granite barns, sturdy fences, and old *horreos* (corn cribs) decorate a hard, misty countryside in which Gallego is still spoken.

Count on buses for getting around—both for the view and the time saved. Trains hobble through the region, stopping for mail at each tiny town and spending half the trip in dark tunnels. From Santiago de Compostela there are daily bus connections (usually 3 or 4) to Vigo, Muros, El Ferrol, and Ortiguiera. La Coruña has more frequent connections to the preceeding as well as to Pontevedra, Finisterre, Viviero, Foz, and Ribadeo.

Túi

The town of Túi sits on the Portuguese border about 29km south of Vigo. The old section of the village is built on a rise overlooking the Miño River. Most people stop here to change trains. If you find yourself with a several-hour wait, take time to visit the **cathedral-fortress,** a twelfth-century monument to feudalism. Originally utilitarian Romanesque with crenelated battlements and towers, the blank exterior was gussied up in the thirteenth century with a few Gothic embellishments such as a fine portico. The **Museo Diocesano** next door is interesting only for its manuscript Bibles. (Open daily 10am-1pm and 4-8pm. Admission 75ptas.) Several *casas de huéspedes* surround the cathedral. The **tourist office** (tel. 60 07 57) in Túi is actually a kilometer away on the border and is geared more for regional and national rather than local information. (Open Mon.-Fri. 9:30am-1pm and 4-6pm, Sat. 9am-1pm.)

Vigo and Cies Islands

Vigo is a large, convenient gateway into the Rías Bajas and northern Portugal. The **tourist office,** Jardines de Elduayen (tel. 43 05 77), near the port, can provide accommodation information as well as schedules for free music and ballet performances in the park. (Open Mon.-Fri. 9am-1:30pm and 4-7pm, Sat. 9:30am-1:30pm.) To reach the office, take bus #14 from the **train station,** get off at Porta del Sol, and weave your way down to the right past the Ayuntamiento and the cathedral. Trains run to Pontevedra (17 per day, 125ptas), Santiago de Compostela (8 per day, 440ptas), Viana do Castelo (3 per day, 410ptas), and Oporto (3 per day, 665ptas).

Residencia Xuvenil Altamar (IYHF), Rúa Cesáro González, 4 (tel. 29 08 08), offers a clean housing option. (450ptas. Breakfast 100ptas. Breakfast and dinner 250ptas.) Take a taxi from the train station (250ptas) or walk along Gran Via to

Pl. de América (½-hr.). Near the station, **Calle Alfonso XIII** is jammed with cheap *hostales.* The best is **Hostal Residencia Madrid,** at #63 (tel. 22 55 23). Spotless, homey rooms run 1600ptas. The nearest campsite is the first-rate **Camping Samil** (tel. 23 21 98), 6km away at Playa Samil (275ptas per person, 250ptas per tent). For a bite, drop by **Cafeteria Jackie's,** Rua Marquez de Valladarez, 14 (tel. 43 35 00), for bargain combination dishes. (Open Mon.-Thurs. 7am-1:30am, Fri. 7am-3am, Sat. 7am-6pm.)

Although Vigo is now a modern industrial center, it retains signs of its humble origins: the dirty fishing quarter and some surprisingly good beaches. **Playas América** and **Bayona** can be reached by interurban bus, and **Samil** by municipal bus (#16 from Porta del Sol). However, for the whitest sands and deep blue-green water, take the ferry out to the **Cies Islands** (mid-June to mid-July 5 per day, 750ptas; mid-July to mid-Aug. 8 per day, 850ptas). Your only choice for accommodations is **Camping Islas Cies** (tel. 42 16 22), a third-class site. Spaces fill quickly, and clandestine camping is prohibited. There are no other accommodations on the island, so arrive early. (Open June-Sept. 1250ptas per person.)

If you want to tour the region near Vigo, hop a bus for **Moaña,** which offers great views from its Mount Jaján and Escula, **Cangas,** a picturesque fishing village, or **Redondela,** where majestic forests surround sunny beaches. Buses for Moaña and Cangas leave from in front of the Universal Hotel. A faster way to reach Moaña and Cangas is by ferry, just across from Turismo. Buses for Túi or Pontevedra leave from C. Uruguay, a few blocks west of the train station.

Pontevedra

The best base for exploring the Rías Bajas is Pontevedra, a beautiful city of stone on the Santiago-Vigo highway and train line. If the wind is blowing the wrong way, a peculiar stench may waft over from the paper mill. Don't let this mar your stroll through the granite alleys of the old town or along the wide Alameda, where the light from the fountains occasionally splashes over lovers. The *ciudad vieja* is dominated by the **Basilica Menor de Santa María.** Its plateresque portico changes from splendid to spectacular when bathed in golden floodlight.

The **tourist office,** C. General Mola, 3 (tel. 85 08 41), has a list of accommodations. (Open Mon.-Fri. 9:30am-1:30pm and 5-7pm, Sat. 9:30am-1:30pm; Oct.-May Mon.-Fri. 9:30am-1:30pm and 4-6pm, Sat. 9:30am-1:30pm.) If you strike out on your own, beware that finding a room, especially a single, is difficult unless you start looking between late morning and noon. **Calle Charino** and its parallel streets in the *ciudad vieja* have a number of very cheap *fondas;* look for signs in windows. **Residencial Xuvenil Atlántico,** Fernando de Olmedo, 3 (tel. 85 77 58), is a 10-minute walk from the city's center. The luxurious doubles all have private baths. (500ptas. Breakfast 75ptas.) Undoubtedly the best place to eat for your money is on C. Charino—**Bar As 5 Calles** has a well-prepared *menú* for 350ptas. **RENFE** has an office on C. Gondomar, 3 (tel. 85 13 13). The train and bus stations (tel. 85 19 61) are about 1km out of town on the Alféreces Provisionales.

Many Spaniards and other Europeans pass their holidays at **El Grove,** 34km west of Pontevedra. It's a nice ride past beaches, rocky caves, and small fishing villages such as **Combarro,** where the stony shore becomes a street and *horreos* (raised granite corn cribs typical of Galicia) line the water's edge. El Grove has a summertime **tourist office** located near the bridge to the neighboring island of **La Toja.** If you care to stay in town, try **Habitaciones María Aguino,** C. General Mola, 26 (tel. 73 11 87), near the last bus stop. The rooms are plain but pleasant. (Singles 1200ptas. Doubles 1600ptas. Showers 100ptas.) Camp nearby at **Camping Moreiras.** (Tel. 73 16 91. 185ptas per person.)

If you're in this area the first weekend in July, don't miss the **rapa das bestas** (round-up of the wild horses), a three-day long and five-century old festival held in **San Lorenzo de Sabucedo,** a small village between Pontevedra and La Estrada. Similar *rapas* take place in other towns throughout the summer months—inquire at any tourist office.

Cabo Finisterre

Once thought to be the end of the earth, Cabo Finisterre now shelters a number of small villages where this belief hasn't been totally dispelled. The best beaches, hidden behind pine trees, extend below the road along the coast between **Muros** and **Finisterre.** The bus from Santiago will take you along this stretch for around 500ptas, or you can make the killer-hitch. Near Muros is the second-class **Camping A Bouga** (tel. 82 60 25), 2.6km away on the road to Louro. (225ptas per person and per tent.) **Ezaro** (accessible by bus from Muros) is a typical beach town with the added allure of magnificent waterfalls and a picturesque lagoon 1km up the river behind the town. Although the nearby power plant ruins the effect, the sheer stone walls and deep pools beneath the two beautiful cascades are much warmer than the sea. There's even a small, natural waterslide leading from a small pool to a larger one. In town, **Hospedaje O'Farcado,** on the main drag (no phone), is the nicest place to stay. (Doubles 1200ptas.) **Bar Stop,** on the other side of the highway a few doors up, has cornered the market on singles. (Singles 800ptas. Doubles 1500ptas.) If the peace, quiet, and natural beauty get to you, hike 2km to **O'Pindo,** where a few bars and even a disco liven the scene. O'Pindo has a wide beach of its own, but a sardine canning factory is unfortunately upwind.

Finisterre itself is an unassuming fishing village better known for its geographical location than for anything else. Still, its gorgeous beaches and spectacular views attract thousands of tourists every summer, including the famous writer, Camilo José Cela (his villa is by the beach just outside of town). The actual "**end of the world**" is 2km away at a **lighthouse** perched several hundred feet above the crashing blue waters.

The rocky promontory that shelters Finisterre's harbor was once a sacred hill for Roman legionnaires and then Celtic settlers, and its cool caves became a hiding place for locals escaping the ravages of the Viking raids in the Dark Ages. The superstitious Vikings never dared enter these openings in the earth because they imagined that the sounds of subterranean life were the voices of local spirits. Now the surrounding beaches are prime spots for unofficial camping. Organized camping and more temperate water are on the opposite side of the isthmus connecting Finisterre with the mainland. **Camping Ruta Finisterre** is a second-class site right on the beach 2km east of the port. (265ptas per person, 300ptas per tent.) North of Cabo Finisterre lie the Rías Altas.

El Ferrol

Ferrol spoils an enchanting estuary with large shipyards and an ugly naval base. Birthplace of Francisco Franco, Ferrol once capitalized on its good fortune by acquiring important arsenals, industrial aid, and a boastful suffix. Until Franco's death in 1975, the town was known as El Ferrol del Caudillo, or "of the leader." The city is profoundly dull unless you have a sailor's sense of a good time. The nearest beaches are at **San Jorge** and **Cobas,** 10km away. Ferrol, however, is extremely well-connected, and you may find yourself passing through on your way to the misty Rías Altas north from La Coruña.

If you're stuck here overnight, head to **Pardo Bajo,** a street filled with bars, restaurants, and *pensiones;* follow C. Rochel from Pl. de España. Cheap though shabby accommodations are available for the asking: Go into any of the numerous bars along C. del Sol. **Casa Castro,** C. María, 90, just parallel to C. del Sol, has dingy but adequate rooms (650ptas). Kitchen-style eating downstairs is nothing to rave about, but it's all under 400ptas. Off C. Real, **Hostal Residencia Toki-Alzi,** C. Magdalene, 98 (tel. 32 86 15), provides sterile hospital beds. (Doubles 1400ptas. Triples 1800ptas. Quads 2600ptas.)

The tourist shack is permanently closed, but you can obtain a map and a brochure at the tourist office in La Coruña. If you're heading north to Ortigueira or Vivero, take the bus (400ptas). Although it takes a little longer, the bus follows the forested coastline past small coves perfect for clandestine camping. All buses leave from Pl. de España: to La Coruña (hourly, 375ptas) and Cabo Ortegal (4 per day, 390ptas).

Ortiguiera to Ribadeo

The coves and countryside between Ferrol and **Cabo Ortegal** present some dismal hitching, so once again buses are your best option. From Ferrol you can get as far as **Ortigueira,** a pretty hamlet on a small peninsula. From there you can hike out to Cabo Ortegal; hitching is practically impossible. Ortigueira itself makes a good base. Try **Hostal Monterrey** at Avda. Franco, 105. (Tel. 40 01 35. Singles 1000ptas. Doubles 1800ptas. Lower in winter.) Don't miss beautiful Morouzos beach.

The town of **Vivero,** at the head of the estuary of the same name, provides access to nearby beaches at **Covas** and **Abrela** and excellent views of the coast from **Mount San Roque.** In Covas, stay at **Hostal Villa Dolores,** Hnos. Perez Lambarta, 3 (tel. 56 00 87; singles 850ptas, doubles 1200ptas), or try camping in Viviero at **Camping Viviero** (tel. 56 00 04), 1km toward La Coruña. (Open June-Sept. 225ptas per person.) The Masma River pours into the Atlantic on the coast nearby at **Foz.**

On the estuary of the Eo River and surrounded by pretty Galician scenery, the town of **Ribadeo** lies 25km farther east. Ribadeo is a pleasant spot to while away a day. Hike up to the **Church of Santa Cruz,** about 3km outside of town on a hill overlooking the Eo estuary. If the climb doesn't take your breath away, the tremendous view of the surrounding countryside and ocean certainly will. A statue commemorating the *Gaiteiro Galego* (Galician bagpiper) stands behind the church. Take the 3-kilometer walk to the *faro* (lighthouse) near **Playa de Rocas Blancas**—also a lovely, small beach. You'll know you're on the right track when you pass the garbage dump that emits billows of smoke. Fortunately, the prevailing winds keep the stench away from the sands.

The budget traveler can sleep comfortably at **Hospedaje el Bueno Gusto,** C. San Roque, 36 (tel. 11 06 40). The rooms are tidy and cheerful. (Singles 1200ptas. Doubles 1600ptas. 100-150ptas less in winter. Hallway showers 200ptas.) More expensive, but also cleaner, brighter, and more comfortable is **Hostal Costa Verde,** Pl. de España, 13 (tel. 11 01 13), in the center of town. (Doubles 2000-2500ptas.) The nearest **campsite** is at **Reinante** (no phone; 175ptas per person), a beach 8km to the east. Take the bus toward Lugo or La Coruña, get off at the Reinante stop, and walk 1km to the beach. Ribadeo's **tourist office** (tel. 11 06 89), is in the center of town in Pl. de España. (Open Mon.-Sat. 9am-2pm and 5-7:30pm.) No maps are available and the staff is unhelpful, but if you're insistent, you may be able to obtain information on hotels.

Despite the fact that it is known as a gateway to Galicia, the town is surprisingly poorly connected by public transportation. Two **buses** per day make the trip west from here to La Coruña (3½ hr., 700ptas). The ride is slow, but the scenery is spectacular—hills, valleys, slate-roofed houses, and stone fences. If you're trying to reach the Cantabrian coast, you'll have to change buses in Oviedo (4 hr., 780ptas). The same goes for **trains,** which crawl along the same coastal route at an even slower pace (and at approximately equal cost). The travel agency **Proa,** across the square, is staffed by friendly and attentive folks who can give specific information on local bus and train connections.

Canary Islands (Las Islas Canarias)

From the snowy peak of Mount Teide to the fiery volcanic spectacle of Timanfaya, the Canary Islands have enchanted humanity since the time of the ancient Egyptians. Homer and Herodotus referred to their gardens of great beauty, and the lost civilization of Atlantis was said to have left behind these seven islands when it sank in the Atlantic Ocean. Their captivating beauty lies in the stark contrast between their lush, fertile valleys, the clear, blue ocean water, and the sand dunes resembling those of the Sahara. The climate can change drastically from island to island and at various altitudes. This climatic variability earned the Canaries their reputation as a "continent in miniature."

The Canary Islands were once inhabited by Guanches—light-skinned, blond troglodytes who practiced a complicated death ritual that included mummifiction. How these Stone Age cave-dwellers, unfamiliar with the art of navigation, ever reached the islands remains a mystery. One theory considers the Guanches to be descendants of people who came over from Egypt during the time of the pharoahs. Using clubs and sheer valor, the Guanches drew Spanish conquest of the islands out to nearly an entire century. Even today, remnants of Guanche culture still remain: *Lucha canaria* (Canarian wrestling), *gofio* (a grain staple used in many local dishes), and place names such as Tenerife, Timanfaya, and Doramas.

After the Spanish conquest in the fifteenth century, the economy of the islands boomed with both sugar and wine production. As the Spaniards set their eyes beyond this horizon to the New World, the Canary Islands served as an important transportation link. Christopher Columbus stopped in Gran Canaria before setting out on his now famous voyage of 1492. Before that time, the westernmost island, El Hierro, was considered the end of the world. Following Columbus's exploration, the Spaniards used the Canaries as a base for their colonization of the Americas. Many *canarios* emigrated to these new Spanish colonies. Their role as a bridge between the Old and New Worlds has engendered in the Canaries a cultural mix that is most pronounced in the people themselves. *Canarios* watch Spanish television and eat Spanish food, but their spoken Spanish resembles that of Cuba and Puerto Rico.

Canarios are experiencing a new self-arareness that has already had significant ramifications: Just recently, the islanders were granted autonomy by the Spanish government. Don't be surprised by graffiti proclaiming, "*Las Canarias no son España*" ("The Canaries are not Spain") and signs promoting independence.

Island geography may prove frustrating without a map, and the perplexing nomenclature only serves to confuse matters. The Canaries are made up of seven major islands divided into two provinces. From east to west, the three islands of Lanzarote, Fuerteventura, and Gran Canaria form the province of Las Palmas de Gran Canaria. Each of these islands is a major tourist destination. They are all dry and desert-like, but ideal for beachgoers. Tenerife, Gomera, La Palma, and El Hierro form the second province, Sant Cruz de Tenerife. With the exception of Tenerife, tourism has yet to overtake this province, due, in large part, to its lack of sandy beaches. The climate is cooler and wetter, and the islands are refreshingly green. Don't confuse La Palma (the island) with Las Palmas (capital of Gran Canaria) or its capital, Santa Cruz de La Palma, with Santa Cruz de Tenerife (capital of Tenerife and the province of the same name).

The Canary Islands have become a tourist haven for millions of Europeans escaping the cold weather of the continent with a do-or-die sense of beach urgency. Tourism is big business, but the tourist inundation has proved a mixed blessing: In resort areas such as Maspalomas (Gran Canaria) and Puerto de la Cruz (Tenerife), local *canarios* are almost non-existent. Entire communities complete with apartments and supermarkets have been built solely to accommodate the large number of German and Scandinavian tourists indulging in comfortable package tours. You must escape the German pubs, French cafes, and Finnish bars to see the true beauty of the Canaries.

Getting There and Getting Around

Iberia Airlines flies from Málaga and Madrid to Las Palmas and Tenerife (daily departures in summer, 3 hr.). Madrid to Las Palmas one way costs US$178, but you can receive a discount either by purchasing the flight as an addition to a transatlantic flight or by qualifying for a mini-fare. (Check with Iberia.) **Transmediterránea** connects Cádiz to the Canaries by ferry. From Morocco you can reach Gran Canaria on **Royal Air Maroc**. There are flights from Casablanca, Agadir, and Layoune.

Inter-island transportation is cheapest aboard **Transmediterránea** ferries. With round-trip, open-ended tickets, island-hopping need not be exorbitant. However, if you're determined to spend, **Iberia** flies between five of the islands, and a jetfoil links Gran Canaria and Tenerife for about 4000ptas (1½ hr.—less than ¼ the time it takes by ferry).

Gran Canaria

You will immediately shake away preconceptions about a lush tropical paradise when you see the amazingly dry and hilly terrain of Gran Canaria. Unfortunately, this feeling of being in a barren desert will remain with you. The sunshine works its magic on area beaches, but crowded and noisy. Tourism has overtaken this island, and you will be hard-pressed to find much local charm.

Las Palmas

Pleasure capital of the Canaries, Las Palmas is filled with fun-loving Europeans hell-bent on having a good time. The shopping streets bustle with all the frenzied commerce of a duty-free port where everything from cigarettes to sex is for sale; **Paseo de las Canteras,** on the western side, is especially lively. Gambling, ivory tusks, pornography, and hashish are all legal and popular here.

The touristic center of town lies around **Parque Santa Catalina,** not really a park but a square with cafes, bars, and kiosks. This area contains a tawdry district of touristy restaurants and sleezy *hostales.* Set up camp here, but spend your time in the more pleasant parts of town.

Practical Information

From the international airport at Gando, you can take green bus #60 (every 40 min., 125ptas) to the Hotel Iberia on Avda. Marítima. Turn right from the hotel and walk to the concrete Estación de Guaguas (bus station). Take bus #1 (50ptas) to Parque Santa Catalina, where you'll find the tourist office, post office, hotels, and numerous shops and cafes.

Tourist Office: Pl. Ramón Franco (tel. 26 46 23), across from Parque Santa Catalina. Look for the fountain. Well stocked with brochures, maps, and accommodations information, but unable to help with travel questions. Open Mon.-Fri. 9am-1:30pm and 5-7pm, Sat. 9am-1pm.

Consulates: U.S., C. José Franchy Roca, 5, 5th floor (tel. 27 63 40). Open Mon.-Fri. 10am-1pm. **U.K.,** C. de Luís Morote, 6, 3rd floor (tel. 26 25 08).

American Express: Viajes C.Y.R.A.S.A., C. Mayor de Triana, 114 (tel. 34 41 00), off Parque San Telmo. Open Mon.-Fri. 9am-1pm and 4-7pm, Sat. 9am-noon.

Post Office: Behind Turismo. Open Mon.-Fri. 9am-2pm, Sat. 9am-1pm.

Telephones: C. de Luís Morote, at the northern end of Parque Santa Catalina. Open Mon.-Sat. 9am-9pm. **Telephone Code:** 928.

Bus Station: Estación de Guaguas, across from Parque San Telmo. Bus #1 will take you practically everywhere you want to go. Green buses go to Maspalomas and other destinations outside Las Palmas.

Ferries: Transmediterrnea, Muelle (dock) de Santa Catalina (tel. 26 00 70), across from Parque de Santa Catalina. Service to all the islands including frequent, cheap ferries and expensive hydrofoils to Tenerife. To Arrecife and Puerto Rosario (both 3 per week, 9 hr., round-trip 3680ptas).

English Bookstore: Canary Books, C. Senador Castillo Olivares, 52 (tel. 36 05 25), near Pl. de Tomás Morales. Large selection of English classics and some guidebooks. Open Mon.-Sat. 9am-4pm.

Laudromat: Lava Sec, C. Joaquín Costa, 46 (tel. 27 46 17). Self-service washer and dryers. Open Mon.-Fri. 9am-1pm and 4-8pm, Sat. 9am-7pm.

Pharmacy: Parque de Santa Catalina (tel. 26 44 52). Open Mon.-Fri. 8am-1pm and 4-7pm. Pharmacies rotate night-shift duty.

Accommodations and Food

One block inland from the open-air African art stands and cafes in Parque Santa Catalina is a tawdry part of town where cheap but perfectly acceptable *hostales, residencias,* and *pensiones* abound. Family-run dives with doubles for as little as 850ptas per night front the side streets off pedestrian **Calle de Ripoche.** In high season (Nov.-April), expect a 20% increase.

Hostal Residencia Majórica, C. Ripoche, 22 (tel. 26 28 78). Clean rooms, all with baths. Cold showers only. Singles 1300ptas. Doubles 2200ptas.

Residencia Syria, C. de Luís Morote, 27 (tel. 27 06 00). A cut above the rest, but you pay for it. Balconies, phones, and good baths with hot showers. Singles 2000ptas. Doubles 2500ptas.

Hostal Duque, C. Ripoche, 14 (tel. 26 39 44). Check your room before accepting it: Some are much better than others. Singles 700ptas, with bath 800ptas. Doubles 1200ptas, with bath 1500ptas. Cold showers only.

Hostal Residencia Guacamayo, C. Dr. Miguel Rosa, 9 (no phone). Clean, windowless rooms. Bathrooms somewhat musty. Doubles 1200ptas.

Between Las Canteras and Parque Santa Catalina, there are many uninspiring tourist dive restaurants that offer everything from Chinese noodles to a Swedish smorgasbord. A rare Canarian restaurant is **La Cascada,** C. Tomás Miller, 46 (tel. 26 30 11). Classy red and white decor comes complete with a tropical, homemade waterfall. The *menú del día* (soup, main dish, dessert, and wine) is a good deal at 525ptas. (Open Mon.-Sat. 8am-2am, Sun. 8am-midnight.) Above all, avoid the buffet places on C. Tomás Miller. They serve more mediocre food than you can either stomach or pay for.

Sights

Inside the Pueblo Canario of Parque Doramos, a re-creation of typical Canarian architecture, is the **Néstor Museum** (tel. 24 51 35), which contains numerous paintings and personal belongings of Néstor de la Torre, an artist whose phantasmagorical and erotic works earned him the Catholic Church's disapproval. (Open Mon.-Tues. and Thurs.-Fri. 10am-1pm and 4-7pm, Sat. 10am-noon, Sun. 10:30am-1:30pm. Admission 50ptas.) Two weekly performances of authentic Canarian song and dance also take place in Parque Doramas. (Sun. at 11:45am and Thurs. at 5:30pm.)

The only collection of pre-Hispanic Canarian artifacts is housed in the **Canarian Museum,** C. Dr. Vernean, 2 (tel. 31 56 00). Look for the fine collection of ceramics and the large library. (Open Mon.-Fri. 10am-1pm and 4-8pm, Sat.-Sun. 10am-1pm. Admission 300ptas.)

Lanzarote

This unique isle is the oddest in the archipelago. It is the only place in Spain—possibly the world—where you can ride camels over fields of volcanic ash, view colored salt paintings, and watch farmers raise *cuchinillo* parasites.

Arrecife

The capital of Lanzarote, Arrecife is a good base for excursions to the rest of the island. All ferries arrive and depart from here for Fuerteventura and La Gran Canaria. From the port, you can take a taxi into town or hitch a ride with one of the many tourists from the ferry. **Calle León y Castillo** is the main drag.

Practical Information

Tourist Office: C. Dr. Rafael González, 100m west of C. León y Castillo on the coast. Staff speaks English and distributes a map of Lanzarote and various brochures. Open Mon.-Fri. 9am-noon and 5-7pm, Sat. 9am-noon.

Buses: Transportes Lanzarote, S.A., C. General García Escámez, 71 (tel. 81 15 46). Walk away from the coast on C. León y Castillo, then veer left on Hnos. Zenoro. Take the right-hand fork, which is C. Gen. García Escámez—the station is on the left. To Teguise (5 per day), Haria (3 per day), Guatiza (3 per day), Tinajo (4 per day), and Yaiza (3 per day).

Ferries: Transmediterránea operates service to Las Palmas (3 per week), Puerto Rosario in Fuerteventura (2 per week), and Cádiz (1 per week).

Car Rental: Many places lie along C. Dr. Rafael González.

Accommodations and Sights

There are only three places to stay for under 1500ptas per night, and they get crowded in spring. **España,** Gran Canaria, 4 (tel. 81 11 90), at the end of C. León y Castillo, and **Avenida,** Avda. Mancomunidad, 6 (tel. 81 16 00), offer doubles for 1200ptas. As a last resort, brave **Alespa,** on C. León y Castillo (tel. 81 17 56), offer doubles run 1000ptas.

The two castles that once defended Arrecife today house small museums. **Castillo de San José** (built under Felipe II) contains a museum of contemporary art and **Castillo de San Gabriel** (built under Carlos III) is now an archeological museum. (Both open daily 9am-1pm and 3-7pm. Tours in Spanish.)

North

Take the northern route from Arrecife toward Teguise via Tahiche and Nazaret. Former capital of Lanzarote, **Teguise** is a charming eighteenth-century village of manors and churches; worth visting are the **Spinda Palace** and the **Church of San Francisco.** Above a dead volcano stands the **Castle of Guanapay,** which defended Teguise from invading Berbers for centuries.

Only 9km north of Teguise, **Playa de Famara,** a fine, sandy beach ringed by cliffs, makes an excellent detour. **Los Valles,** a typical agararian village; **Haria,** set within an oasis of palms; and **Maguez,** another picturesque Canarian village, are conveniently situated along the road to **El Mirador del Río.** From the Mirador, you can catch a glimpse of the islet **La Graciosa,** but to actually visit La Graciosa you must arrrange for a ride in the fishing village of **Orzola.** Fishing boats from Orzola run regularly to **Caleta del Sebo,** the only village on the island. La Graciosa is practically surrounded by beaches, but the most famous (and most developed) is **Playa de las Conchas.**

Heading back south along the east coast of Lanzarote, you will pass two volcanic caves, **Cueva de los Verdes** and **Jameo de Agua.** Both caverns are home to the Munidopsis polymorpha, a 1-centimeter long albino crab species that has not been discovered anywhere else in the world. Farther along in **Mala** and **Guatiza** farmers cultivate the *cuchinillo* parasite. The red pulp pressed out of the bugs—*el rojo del cuchinillo*—is used to dye the finest carpets.

South

In **La Geria,** home of the Malvasia grape, viticulture has taken a strange twist. Here, the vineyards are grown in volcanic ash pits where lava, two or three feet below the surface, keeps the vines warm, while the ash walls of the pit protect the vines from the wind. Eleven kilometers southwest of La Geria, **Yaiza** is just another Canarian village en route to the **Janubio Salt Works.** At Janubio you must make a difficult choice: Head either south to the finest beaches on Lanzarote, **Playa Blanca** and **Playa del Papagayo,** or north to **Los Hervideros,** where lava flows have been eroded into seaside caves, and **El Golfo,** a volcanic crater breached by the sea that forms a green lagoon. **Timanfaya National Park,** north of Yaiza at the Islote de Hilario, is the site of the **Montañas de Fuego** (Mountains of Fire), which are circled by the **Ruta de los Volcanes** (Route of the Volcanos).

Fuerteventura

There are two reasons to go to Fuerteventura: the beach and the windsurfing. Those who know include it among the five best places in the world to windsurf.

Puerto del Rosario

Recently founded and rather bland, the island capital offers many services as well as the main port. The **tourist office** is at C. 1 de Mayo, 33, 2nd floor (tel. 85 10 24). Some English is spoken. Their maps and brochures orient you to the island. (Open Mon.-Fri. 8am-3pm and Sat. 9am-1pm.) The **post office** (tel. 85 04 12) is just up the street.

As in Arrecife, there are only three moderately priced *hostales,* and all fill quickly. **Tamasite,** León y Castillo, 9 (tel. 85 02 80), five minutes from the port, is the best (doubles 2000ptas). Across the way is **Roquemar,** Pl. Domingo J. Manrique, 2 (tel. 85 03 59; doubles 1200ptas). Finally, **Macario,** Almirante Fontan Lob, 12 (tel. 85 11 97), is a 20-minute walk from the port; it's a two-star *hostal* like the Tamasite with similar prices.

PORTUGAL

US $1 = 153 escudos ($)   100$ = US $0.65
CDN $1 = 127.42$ 100$ = CDN $0.78
UK £1 = 259.68$ 100$ = UK £0.39
AUS $1 = 123.19$ 100$ = AUS $0.81
NZ $1 = 101.72$ 100$ = NZ $0.98

Once There

Getting Around

Caminhos de Ferro Portugueses, Portugal's national **railway,** operates throughout the country, but aside from the service between Lisbon and the Algarve and on the Oporto-Coimbra-Lisbon line, it's best to go with the buses. The country's steam-operated trains are not known for their swiftness; they may reach speeds in excess of 20 miles per hour on steep downhill grades, but usually poke along at about 15 miles per hour. If this strikes you as romantic, remember that most of the cars will also be old and crowded. With a first-class Eurailpass, a supplementary fee, and an advance reservation, you can take the electric express trains and minimize your discomfort. The Portuguese national **bus** line, the Rodoviaria Nacional, provides faster and more frequent, though costlier, service. Express coach service between major cities is especially worthwhile. Rodoviaria's Lisbon office is located at Avda. Casal Ribeiro, 18. Within cities, public buses are cheap and run to even the smallest villages.

If you do decide to try the train, ask about the Cheque-Trem card, which provides a 15% discount on all tickets for an unlimited time span. There are "green period" discounts (*penodes verdes*), as well as Cartão Jovem and Cartão Família, which give you discounts for round-trip fares. To receive these discounts on international routes and some direct routes, you must make reservations. The return on round-trip tickets must be used before 3am on the following day. Ages under 4 always travel free; ages 4-12 pay half-price and receive their own seat; and ages over 65 can get a Gold Card, which gives you a 50% discount during non-rush hours. The Cartão Jovem provides a 50% discount for trips of more than 50km, but it's not good on *rápidos* or international routes. You must purchase a ticket for each ride; the fine for riding without without a ticket is at least 1250$.

Traveling by **car** in Portugal will either make your head turn or your stomach churn. Off the main arteries, you will encounter the unspoiled countryside that makes Portugal a picnicker's paradise. At the same time, the narrow, twisting roads may prove difficult to negotiate, especially when donkey carts mosey along beside you and villagers with piles of goods on their heads cross in front of you. Gas is expensive, parking in the cities is a pain, and Portuguese drivers live up to their reputation for rash and risky maneuvers. Avis, Hertz, InterRent, and other major companies operate offices in cities and at airports. Rates start at about US$120 per week plus gas, but check around—local companies may be significantly less expensive. An international driver's license is required and can be obtained through the Automóvil Club de Portugal (1600$).

Unfortunately, **hitchhiking** is difficult in Portugal. Auto insurance doesn't cover hitchhikers, and this coupled with Portuguese driving habits, makes the situation easy to understand. For short hops between country towns where the bus schedule is inconvenient, thumbing it may be worth a try, but don't count on longer rides or rides out of larger towns.

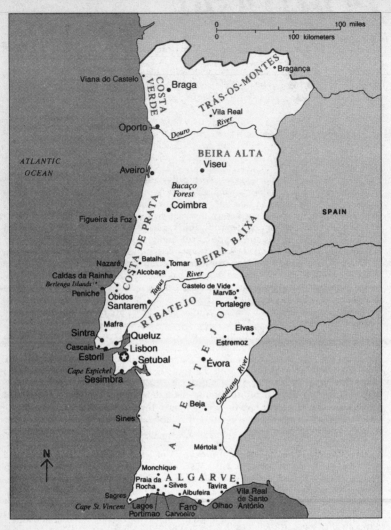

ATLANTIC
OCEAN

SPAIN

Viana do Castelo
COSTA VERDE
Braga
TRÁS-OS-MONTES
Bragança
Vila Real
River
Oporto
Douro
BEIRA ALTA
Viseu
Aveiro
Bucaço
Forest
Coimbra
Figueira da Foz
COSTA DE PRATA
BEIRA BAIXA
Nazaré
Batalha
Tomar
River
Alcobaça
Caldas da Rainha
Berlenga Islands
Castelo de Vide
Peniche
Marvão
Óbidos
Santarem
Portalegre
Tagus
Mafra
RIBATEJO
Elvas
Sintra
Queluz
Estremoz
Cascais
Lisbon
Estoril
Setubal
Évora
Cape Espichel
Guadiana River
Sesimbra
ALENTEJO
Sines
Beja
Mértola
N
Monchique
ALGARVE
Praia da
Rocha
Silves
Tavira
Albufeira
Vila Real
de Santo
Sagres
Lagos
Faro
Olhao
António
Cape St. Vincent
Portimão
Carvoeiro

100 miles
100 kilometers

Accommodations

The **Associação Portuguesa de Pousadas de Juventude,** Rua Andrade Corvo, 46, Lisbon (tel. 57 10 54), runs the country's IYHF **hostels.** These *pousadas de juventude* tend to be an even better bargain than those in Spain, although the *penão* rates are already low. Prices average 425$- 550$, with breakfast included and lunch or dinner running 400$ apiece. An IYHF card is obligatory and costs about 1700$. As a rule, there is a lockout from 10:30am to 6pm, with midnight curfews. Reservations can be made with booking vouchers available at American youth hostels.

Pensões will likely be your mainstay; they lie between hotels and the less expensive **residencias, albergarias,** and **casas de hospedes** in terms of amenities, and are only slightly more expensive than hostels. All accommodations are rated by the government and required to display prominently their category and legal price limits. *Pensões* are rated on a four-star system; hotels, on a five-star system.

Hotels are usually more expensive than they're worth. Turismos maintain lists of all recognized hotels, *residências,* and *pensãos,* but not *hospedarias* (the cheapest option). A good establishment usually includes showers and breakfast in the price. Generally, you must vacate your room by noon the following day. Be suspicious of any place except a hostel that enforces a curfew. Finally, bargain down your room charge in advance; the "official price" is merely the maximum allowed.

The **pousada** (resting place) is Portugal's version of the Spanish *parador,* a reasonably priced guest house run by the government. (Don't confuse *pousada* with *pousada de juventude.*) Often located in converted castles, palaces, or monasteries, *pousadas* are attentive to local craft, custom, and cuisine. They generally cost slightly more than hotels, except those near Lisbon and Oporto; most require reservations. **Estalgems** are the privately-owned equivalent of *pousadas.* For information on these establishments, contact ENATUR, Avda. Santa Joana Princesa, 10A, Lisbon (tel. 88 90 78).

If you're planning to spend a long time in Portugal, contact the **Turismo de Habitação Regional,** through which you can rent rooms or entire houses, many of them mansions. This practice is most common in the provinces north of the Ribatejo; it can be very affordable, especially for groups of travelers. You can also write to the regional and municipal tourist offices listed under individual cities for information.

Stick to official **campgrounds,** which are abundant. Arrive early; urban and coastal parks may require reservations. The great majority of campgrounds (*parques de campismo*) lie along the country's long Atlantic coast. Often situated on a picturesque site, campgrounds are usually equipped with toilet and electric facilities. An **International Camping Carnet** may be required, but can usually be purchased on the spot. An indispensable and thorough multilingual guide to all campgrounds, *Guidebook Roteira Campista* is easily obtainable. Write to the Federação Portuguesa de Campiso, Rua Voz do Operario, Lisbon (tel. 86 23 50). Some travelers camp unofficially on beaches or in public gardens; do not do this on beaches within 1km of an official campground or in government-defined "public zones."

Life and Times

History and Politics

Perched on a strip of land on the western edge of the Iberian peninsula, the Portuguese had nowhere to go but to sea, and in the fifteenth century they did this with a vengeance, eventually establishing an empire that circled the globe. Before this time, Portugal's history was a patchwork of ancient settlers and conquerers. Various peoples—Phoenicians, Celts, and Greeks—all established settlements before 500 B.C.E. Though the Carthaginians were Iberia's first true conquerers, the tide of the Roman Empire soon swept over Lusitania (the Roman name for Portugal). The Romans brought with them Latin (a variant of which later became Portuguese), and their religion, Christianity. After the twilight of Rome, the Visigoths moved in, only to be crushed by the powerful Moors in the eighth century. Evidence of four centuries of Moorish rule is found in the heavy stone castles throughout the country. With the help of the Crusaders, Dom Afonso Henriques eventually swept out the country's Moorish invaders. At the site of the first Christian victory in Guimarães, Henriques declared himself ruler of the Kingdom of Portugal in 1143.

The capture of Ceuta in 1415 took on symbolic importance as the beginning of the Portuguese age of exploration. Prince Henry, third son of King John, visited Ceuta and returned inflamed with visions of discovery. Henry the Navigator, as he came to be known, launched the famous school of navigation at Sagres, where explorers, shipbuilders, and cartographers came to refine their skills. Portuguese adventurers drove into Africa in search of wealth, glory, and the curious figure known as Prester John, the mythic leader of a lost Christian empire thought to be an earthly paradise in the African interior. But not every expedition was so quixotic. The Portuguese colonized Madeira, the Azores, and Guinea-Bissau before Bartolomeu Dias's pivotal voyage around the mysterious Cape of Good Hope. With that knowledge, Vasco da Gama discovered the first ocean route to India in 1498, and enabled Portugal to add numerous colonies along the African and Indian coasts to its empire. Portuguese explorer Pedro Alvares Cabral hit the jackpot of Brazil by accident. Half a century later, the Portuguese became the first Europeans to set foot on Japan. With riches pouring in from all around the globe, Lisbon blossomed into Europe's most magnificent city. King Manuel the Fortunate commissioned buildings and monuments adorned with symbols of conquest (the ubiquitous Manueline style), but good fortune was neither widespread (it benefited only a small commercial oligarchy) nor long lasting. By 1580, Portugal's Golden Age had begun to tarnish as the empire exhausted its resources and its royal line. Despite minimal resistance, Iberia was united under Castille's Habsburg monarch Felipe II.

During 60 years of Spanish rule, Portugal maintained much of its independence. Despite its antipathy toward the Spanish cause, Portugal sided with Spain in a number of wars and lost much of its empire as a result (although it still retained possession of enormous areas, including Brazil). The Portuguese rebelled in 1640, and the House of Bragança assumed the throne and formed an alliance with England; as part of the marriage dowry, Portugal handed Tangier and Bombay to England and in the next two decades ceded Ceylon and Malabar to the Dutch. Gold from Brazil financed the enlightened despotism of João V, who undertook enormous architectural projects in flamboyant foreign styles. The great earthquake of 1755 devastated the capital and killed as many as 50,000 people. The catastrophe, unparalleled in Portuguese history, shook European faith in both God and humanity. The dictatorial statesman Pombal led Lisbon's reconstruction, literally rebuilding the city from the ground up in the austere Queen Anne style of London.

In 1807 Napoleon's troops occupied Portugal, and the Portuguese royal family reigned in exile from Brazil. Although the British drove the French from the country, the family remained in Brazil, ruling Portugal by regent. Many interest groups, including the small commercial class and the military, resented rule from abroad and demanded a constitutional monarchy. For the next 90 years, the Portuguese monarchs and the legislature wrangled for executive authority. Meanwhile, Brazil declared its independence from Portugal in 1822 (in the New World's only bloodless revolution), and the old country turned its attention to its African territories.

As the Portuguese Empire crumbled further, political dissidence at home culminated in the assassination of the king and his heir in 1908, and in the institution of a parliamentary republic in 1910. Fraught with political instability, the new republic fell in a military coup in 1926.

Antonio Salazar, a conservative economist, led the country in 40 years of authoritarian rule. Although women obtained the vote for the first time, very little of the population qualified for enfranchisement. While improving Portugal's international economic standing, the Salazar government laid the cost of progress squarely on the shoulders of the working class and peasantry as well as on the peoples of Africa, who chafed under Portuguese colonial administration. A much feared secret police crushed all opposition. Stubbornly tenacious, Salazar quelled African rebellions in bloody battles that drained the nation's already feeble economy.

In 1974, a democratic left-wing government overthrew the Premier-for-Life in a swift coup. Civil and political liberties were established, as the revolution's rallying cry of "*25 de abril sempre!*" ("April 25 forever!") covered the nation in graffiti. A year later, Portugal's African colonies gained independence only to tumble into civil war. Hundreds of thousands of *crioulos* (overseas Portuguese) and Africans—most of whom had never set foot in Europe—streamed into the country, increasing the population by nearly 10% almost overnight and straining what was already an over-turned society and a collapsed economy.

Plans to nationalize large companies and estates prompted violent conflict; none-theless, socialist and coalition socialist governments remained in power until 1978, when the more conservative Social Democrats took over. Faced with the country's severe economic crisis (including a $13 billion foreign debt, 20% inflation, bankrupt state industries, and nearly 15% unemployment), Prime Minister Mario Soares quickly instituted his electoral promise of "100 measures in 100 days," designed to get Portugal back on its feet. These years of strict austerity imposed great strains on Soares's government and the Portuguese people. Heavy reductions of govern-ment subsidies, increased taxes, and the opening up of state industries to private investment (causing a relaxing of some laws protecting workers) meant sacrifices for everyone.

In a move that will undoubtedly change the future of the country, Portugal (along with Spain) joined the European Economic Community in 1986, collecting a prom-ise of US$700 million in aid over the next 10 years. The following year, a victory by the Social Democrats (145 of the 250 seats in parliament) made them the first majority party to rule since Portugal's return to representative government. How-ever, many economists attribute the victory not to any policy of the Social Demo-crats, but rather to the 4-4.5% growth rate since Portugal joined the EEC.

While Portugal's economic future may finally be looking up, the Portuguese still reminisce about the age of glory that dealt them a devil's hand. For five centuries Portugal exploited its colonies and neglected its own agricultural and industrial de-velopment; today it is paying the price. Because of its primitive farming techniques, Portugal must import 60% of its food and devote a quarter of its work-force to agriculture. Aid from the EEC will help modernize food production, but that mod-ernization will force many farmers off their land; they'll enter weak industrial job markets already flooded by waves of immigrants.

Language

The soft *j* (pronounced "zhe") will remind you of French, the flurry of "shhh" sounds Russian, the light inflections Italian, and the vocabulary Spanish: Portu-guese will remind you of almost every language you've ever heard. Often eclipsed by the umbra of Spanish, the Portuguese assert that their language is very different from Spanish. This is both true and false. Spanish is the closest linguistic relative to Portuguese, and the two languages share a wide vocabulary. With its tricky nasal-ization and slurring of vowels, however, Portuguese pronunciation proves much more difficult than the straightforward, staccato sounds of *castellano*. Familiarity with Latin, French, Italian, and especially Spanish will give you a head start. Most Portuguese have a fairly good, natural comprehension of spoken Spanish, but far fewer can actually speak it. You'll be able to ask directions or make reservations in Spanish, but unable to understand the response.

While a Portuguese word may look Spanish, it certainly won't sound it. The let-ters *o* and *a* at the end of a word or syllable are pronounced "oo" as in *moo* and "uh" as in *duh*, respectively. Thank you is *obrigado* (obri-GAH-doo) if the speaker is male, *obrigada* (obri-GAH-duh) if the speaker is female. The *s* at the end of a word is pronounced "sh." Of particular trouble to many foreigners are nasal vowels and dipthongs. To pronounce the "ão" sound in *não* (no), try saying the English *now* while pinching your nose and releasing it (seriously). Saying yes is a bit easier, *sim* (nasal, like *sing*).

Because French and English are required in schools, most young people can speak at least a smattering of both. A pleasant *Faz favor. Fala inglês?* (fahsh fuh-VOR. FAH-luh ing-GLAYSH; Excuse me, but do you speak English?) should start things on the right foot. Other useful phrases are *bom dia* (good morning), *boa tarde* (good afternoon), and *boa noite* (good evening). If asking the price of something, say "Quanto custa?" (KWAHNG-too HOOSH-tuh). Good-bye is *adeus* (uh-DEH-oosh).

Architecture and Art

Everywhere you venture in Portugal, Moorish-influenced buildings decorate the landscape. Although very little survives from the time of the occupation, the effect of this period on later architecture is pervasive; tile work, church ceilings, castle windows, and farmhouses all utilize Moorish elements. Even Portugal's "national style," called Manueline after King Manuel the Fortunate and in celebration of the explorations and expansions of his reign, is really a unique hybrid, combining the Mudéjar style (a blend of the Islamic and the Gothic) with Italian and north European influences and plateresque elements from Spain. This wonderful amalgamation found its greatest expression in the church and tower at Belém, now a suburb of Lisbon, begun in 1502 to commemorate the travels of Vasco da Gama. Many architects worked on the church, the most important being **Diego Boytac** and **João de Castilho.** Other major figures in developing the Manueline style were the brothers **Diego** and **Francisco Arruda.**

Azulejos are the Portuguese tiles that grace an extraordinary number of walls, old and new, around the country. Again the Moorish influence is present, infused with Italian and north European components. The oldest tiles were carved in relief; after 1600, when Portugal began to make its own *azulejos,* they became flat, with glaze designs. These days they are mass-produced.

The Age of Discovery linked Portugal with the trading countries of Renaissance Europe, and the Flemish had a decisive impact on Portuguese art. Early in the fifteenth century, the crowns of Portugal and the Netherlands united in marriage. The Flemish painter **Jan van Eyck** stopped off for a spell in Lisbon in 1428, while many Portuguese artists polished their skills in Antwerp. King Manuel's favorite, **Jorge Afonso,** was the premier painter of the High Renaissance in Portugal; his works demonstrate the period's penchant for order and its fascination with human anatomy. You'll find Afonso's best work at the Convento de Christo in Tomar and the Convento da Madre de Deus in Lisbon. **Domingos António de Sequeira** returned Portuguese art to prominence in the early nineteenth century with his portraits, allegories of the triumph of liberalism, and otherworldly religious works. Sequeira's later paintings may have inspired some of the impressionists.

More recent styles, such as impressionism, cubism, expressionism, and futurism, have all had their Portuguese adherents. But the Salazar government considered much modern art subversive. **Amadeo de Sousa Cardoso, Almeda Negreiros,** and **Maria Helena Vieira da Silva** are among the very few modern Portuguese artists to gain international recognition. The 1974 revolution removed Salazar's restrictions. **Alvaro Siza,** Portugal's most important contemporary architect, shows a concern for setting and tradition and, like his Manueline forebears, fuses diverse influences into an original style. You may encounter some of his houses in Oporto and in the Malagueira District at Evora.

Literature

Whether or not you find the Portuguese to be more lyrical than their Spanish neighbors, poetry has long held a distinctive place in Portugal's literary tradition. As early as the twelfth century, bards and balladeers entertained kings and queens, and it was the poet-king Dinis I who made Portuguese the region's official language.

Although many of the early songs survive, political developments, including the merger of the crown with Castilla through marriage, contributed to a short-lived decline in the use of written Portuguese. The era of exploration and expansion, however, brought with it a growing national awareness and opened Portugal to the influences of the Renaissance, especially at the court. Historians, among them **Fernão Lopes, Caspar Correia,** and **João de Barros,** were Portugal's most important prose writers of the fifteenth and sixteenth centuries, celebrating with great flourish and varying degrees of accuracy the exploits of the Portuguese discoverers. **Lúis de Camões** acquired his reputation as the greatest Portuguese writer of all time by celebrating the Indian voyages of Vasco da Gama in his *Os Lusíadas* (*The Lusitanians,* 1572). Other leading literary figures during the Renaissance were **Bernardim Ribeiro,** the poet and novelist, and **Gil Vicente,** the country's first known playwright, both of whom wrote sympathetically about the pastoral life, peasants, and nature. Shakespeare, Erasmus, and Cervantes are all said to have read Vicente's plays. **Almeida Garrett,** leader of the Romantic school, lyric poet, dramatist, politician, revolutionary, frequent exile, legendary lover, and dandy, led a resurgence of patriotic literature with his accounts of Portuguese heroism against Spain. His most famous play, *Frei Luiz de Sousa* (*The Life of Luiz de Sousa,* 1844), includes a scene in which the hero burns down his own palace when faced with the mortifying prospect of playing host to the Spaniards.

Portuguese modernism, despite its name, has not foresaken the tradition of lyric poetry; Portugal's greatest writers in the twentieth century have been poets too. **Fernando Pessoa,** who wrote in English as well as Portuguese, was so convinced of the multiplicity of the self that he wrote in four distinct styles under four different names: Pessoa, Alberto Caeiro, Ricardo Reis, and Alvaro de Campos. The Campos part of Pessoa's self is often credited with bringing free verse to Portuguese poetry. And for what it's worth, Pessoa carried forward the once common technique of writing while standing up. **José Regio,** a playwright and poet, drew parallels between the poet and Jesus, both made to suffer by the unenlightened. Regio then criticized himself for being so vain and criticized God for being hidden to the poet. Religious themes pervade his poetry, especially the collection *Poemas de Deus e do Diabo* (*Poems of God and the Devil*), and his plays, most notably *Jacob e o Anjo* (*Jacob and the Angel*). Modern Portuguese novelists particularly worth reading are **Ferreira de Castro, Fernand Namora, Aquilino Ribeiro,** and **Miguel Torga.**

Food

Portugal's kitchens offer fine produce, poultry, and game, as well as superb seafood. Olive oil and garlic figure prominently here as in Spain, but so do aromatic herbs, sea salt, and lemon juice.

Soups are hearty and filling: *caldo verde,* a potato and spinach or cabbage mixture with olive oil, is a national obsession. Also sample the equally famous *açorda,* a bread soup or porridge with garlic and herbs. *Grão* (chickpea soup) and gazpacho (especially in the south) are also worth a taste. *Sopa rice de peixa* (fish soup), *caldeirada a fragateira* (a chowder), *sopa de mariscos* (seafood bisque), and *Arroz de polvo* (literally octopus-rice, actually an orange soup) are equally scrumptious.

You'll find the country's fish, in general, to be quite fresh. Try some *peixe espada grelhado* (grilled swordfish). *Bacalhau* (cod, usually salted) is one of the country's staples, consumed by the Portuguese in astounding quantities. *Lagosta suada* (steamed lobster) or *mexilhões* and *amêijoas* (mussels and clams—served any way at all) are sure to please. Consider trying *lulas grelhades* (grilled squid), a Portuguese specialty often served with its insides intact. If you're set on meat, however, stick to pork. *Bife de porco à Alentejana,* made with clams in a coriander sauce, is a favorite. *Cozida à Portuguesa,* a beef and vegetable stew with token bits of pork, is staple fare at economy restaurants. As an alternative to the standard *frango assado* (chicken roasted on a spit), try *cordoniz* (quail), *cabrito* (goat), or *frango a carril* (curried chicken). You'll also find *presunto* (smoked ham), *leitão assado* (suckling pig), and *coelho* (rabbit) on the menu. In the country, *cabrito* is delicious and not much more expensive than more common dishes. *Frango no churrasco* (barbecued chicken) is the favorite Portuguese budget option. Succulent and fresh off the grill, it is usually served with a basting of melted butter and *piri-piri* (a mild hot sauce). The Portuguese learned to cook their chickens this way from Brazilian colonists.

Order *broa* to accompany your meal—it's a sweet cornmeal bread made with olive oil. Garnish it with some of the country's fine cheeses. *Serra* is soft ewe's milk cheese; *cabreiro* is made from goat's milk, and *alvorca* is a hard cheese alternately made from cow's, goat's, or ewe's milk. No matter where you go, you'll encounter *batatas* (potatoes), often served with more than one course per meal and prepared a hundred different ways though most of them familiar to college students.

Portuguese sandwiches are smaller than their Spanish counterparts—meat pastries make a better snack. Be careful when munching bread, butter, cheese, vegetable paté, and olives before your meal—all of these combined can raise your bill considerably, so ask the cost before you start to indulge.

Portugal's favorite dessert is the *doces de ovos* (egg pastries), but you'll also see flan and *arroz doce* (rice pudding) on the menu. *Peras* and bananas are bathed in sweet Port wine and served with a sprinkling of raisins and filberts on top. Melons, grapes, pineapples, oranges, peaches, and mangoes are all wonderful here. Marzipan is the special dessert of the Algarve.

Though you may not hear much about it from the rest of the world, you shouldn't leave the country without sampling Portuguese wine. You've probably heard of Port, pressed from the red grapes of the Douro Valley and fermented with a touch of brandy. It's a dessert in itself. Almost as well-known is Portugal's Madeira, but equally fine is *vinho verde,* literally "green wine"—the name refers to its youth, not its color. It's a sparkling variety that comes in both red and white. Try Gatão or Tres Marias. The white goes down smoother than soda and isn't very alcoholic. Other local wines worth sampling are the Colares and Dão red table wines, the white Bucelas, and the Mateur Rose. The *vinho de casa* (house wine) will rarely leave you disappointed.

If it's a brew you want, order Sagres. Bar and cafe terminology is specialized, and learning it is a sure way to endear yourself to the Portuguese: A small glass of draft beer is a *fino* or an *imperial,* while a mug of it is a *caneca* and a liter jug is called a *girafa.* A cup of that delicious black coffee is a *bica* (not to be confused with a *pica* which is a marijuana joint); *galão* is often used to mean *cafe com leite* (coffee with milk).

Portuguese eat earlier than Spaniards: The midday meal is served between noon and 2pm; dinner between 8 and 10pm. A good meal anywhere will cost you around 450$; in small towns or students' restaurants, a full meal runs 250-300$. If your appetite is small or your wallet running on empty, half portions (called *meia dose*) cost more than half-price but often are more than adequate. One entree will often suffice for two people. Although restaurant prices certainly won't drive you to the marketplace, concocting a meal from the outdoor food stalls is an experience in itself. Every town you visit is likely to have at least one open-air market per week. Prices are amazingly low, but bargain anyway.

Climate

Portugal isn't called the California of the Continent for nothing; its temperate climate and its status as the European country with the greatest number of sunny days per year earn its fine reputation. There are no drastic regional variations, although the north is cooler and more damp than the central and southern parts of the country. In summer, the Alentejo and inland section of the Algarve can be ruthlessly hot. Throughout most of Portugal, however, summer temperatures are comfortable, averaging in the mid-80s during the day and the low 60s at night. Winters in Portugal are quite mild, with temperatures from the low-50s to low-60s.

Festivals and Holidays

Community activity retains importance in Portugal. The festival, whether a celebration of a saint or a season, is a mainstay of life here. In almost every fishing village, the rowing in of the catch at dusk and the auction afterward are rituals that draw a crowd.

Mid-May and mid-October witness the two great events of the land, commemorating the appearances of Mary to three unsuspecting shepherds in 1917. Against an illuminated sky above the verdant hills of Fátima, she is said to have delivered her call for world peace along with the promise to return on the same day for the next half-year. Thus, great pilgrimages in honor of the first and last appearances of Our Lady of Fátima occur May 12-13 and October 12-13.

Holy Week (March 26-April 2 in 1989) enters with a burst of festivities. In Braga, which is famous for its processions, the crowds will be thinner than in Sevilla, but the fervor no less ardent. Easter Sunday marks the commencement of Portugal's bullfighting season, a less gory event than its Spanish cousin. Here, the bullfight is a bloodless display of skill and bravery: The bull is challenged by a bespangled horse and plumed rider before the *toureiro* takes his turn. And when he does, he merely dons a droopy red hat and jumps on the horns. Still very much alive, the bull majestically departs, surrounded by highly trained steers while the crowd cheers them from the ring.

Festivals in honor of local patron saints are called *romarías;* they're invariably accompanied not only by pilgrimages to the neighborhood shrine, but also by a village fair complete with livestock and homemade cheeses for sale.

The following dates are official public holidays: January 1 (New Year's Day), Carnival Tuesday, March 24 (Good Friday), Easter Sunday, April 25 (Liberty Day), May 1 (Labor Day), June 10 (*Camões,* or National Day), June 24 (*São João*), Corpus Christi, August 15 (Assumption), October 5 (First Republic Day), November 1 (All Saints' Day), December 1 (Restoration of Independence), December 8 (Feast of the Immaculate Conception), and December 24 and 25 (Christmas).

Lisbon (Lisboa)

Each black and white stone has been carefully tapped into the mosaic sidewalks. Pastel facades surround the squares. Armies of children and bands of stray dogs run screaming and barking through the alleyways, while trolleys comb cobblestoned streets and weathered fisherfolk peer out of smokey *adegas.* Salt air pervades the seven hills of Lisbon, where *Lisboetas* relax at irresistibly civilized outdoor cafes. The cynicism, impatience, and ethnocentricity of modern urban culture have yet to taint this modest metropolis at the mouth of the Tagus River.

While legend has it that the city was founded by Ulysses, historians and archeologists say that Lisbon was first settled by Phoenicians in the twelfth century B.C.E. and given the name "Alis Llppo." In 205 B.C.E., the Roman Empire engulfed Lusitania (Portugal) and elevated Olissapona to the status of a Roman municipality. Later, Lisbon fluorished as a center of trade under 300 years of Moorish rule; the Alfama section of the city hosted the Moorish aristocracy. Dom Alfonso III completed the Moorish expulsion in the Algarve, however, and made Libson the capital of the Kingdom of Portugal in 1255. Toward the end of the fifteenth century, Portuguese mariners developed advanced navigational techniques that permitted them to pioneer the exploration and charting of the "New World." Riches poured in from every corner of the globe, and the city entered the period of its greatest glory. Then, on November 1, 1755, a mammoth earthquake struck. Many *Lisboetas* were at Mass; hundreds were killed immediately as churches collapsed on their congregations. Those who fled to the Tagus were drowned by the tidal wave that engulfed the lower part of the city. Close to 50,000 died in the catastrophe that reduced Lisbon to a pile of smoldering rubble and shook Europe's faith in Divine Providence.

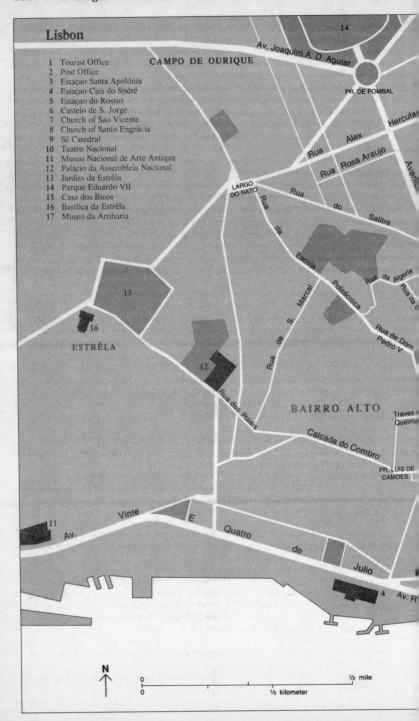

Lisbon

1 Tourist Office
2 Post Office
3 Estação Santa Apolónia
4 Estação Cais do Sodré
5 Estação do Rossio
6 Castelo de S. Jorge
7 Church of Sao Vicente
8 Church of Santo Engrácia
9 Sé Catedral
10 Teatro Nacional
11 Museo Nacional de Arte Antiqua
12 Palácio da Assembleia Nacional
13 Jardim da Estrêla
14 Parque Eduardo VII
15 Casa dos Bicos
16 Basilica da Estrêla
17 Museo da Artiharia

CAMPO DE OURIQUE

Av. Joaquim A. D. Aguiar

PR. DE POMBAL

Herculan

Rua   Alex

Rua Rosa Araujo

LARGO
DO RATO

Rua   do   Salitre

Rua da

Escola

Rua de S. Marcal

Politécnica

Rua da Algeria

Rua da G

Rua de Dom
Pedro V

ESTRÊLA

BAIRRO ALTO   Traves
                    Queima

Rua dos Poiais

Calcada do Combro

PR. LUIS DE
CAMOES

Vinte   E

Av.   Quatro   de

Julio

4   Av. R

N

0   ½ mile
0   ½ kilometer

Under the decisive leadership of the Prime Minister, the Marquês de Pombal, the city quickly recovered; magnificent new squares, palaces, and churches were erected.

When Mozambique and Angola won their independence from Portugal, hundreds of thousands of refugees streamed into the Portuguese capital. This, combined with the demise of the long-standing dictatorship, has restored a vibrant and cosmopolitan air to Lisbon.

Orientation and Practical Information

Lisbon's complex topography of hills and valleys makes some familiarity with the city's layout essential. The **Baixa,** or Lower Town, is Lisbon's old business district; it consists of a grid of small streets that begins at the **Rossio,** the city's main square, and ends at Praça do Comércio, near the Tagus River (Rio Tejo). The newer business district centers on the broad avenues that radiate from Praça Marquês de Pombal, many of which boast elegent art-nouveau buildings. Connecting these two commercial areas is **Avenida da Liberdade,** a broad, tree-lined boulevard that begins its uphill climb at Praça dos Restauradores just north of the Rossio. Connected to the Baixa by Eiffel's Ascensor de Santa Justa is Lisbon's Old World shopping district, the **Chiado,** which includes the must-see streets of Rua do Carmo and Rua Garrett. West of Rua da Misericórdia spreads the **Bairro Alto,** or Upper District, a populous working-class area of narrow streets, tropical parks, and baroque churches. Beneath the city's *castelo* (castle), the **Alfama,** Lisbon's famous medieval quarter, stacks its tiny whitewashed houses along a labyrinth of impossibly narrow alleys and stairways. **Belém** (Bethlehem), formerly a separate town and now absorbed by Lisbon, about 6km west of Praça do Comércio, contains the city's masterpiece of Manueline architecture, the Monastery of Jerónimos Abbey, as well as an array of museums and palaces.

If you arrive by train at the **Estação de Santa Apolónia,** take bus #9 or 9A from the water side of the station to **Praça dos Restauradores,** or take bus #59 to the Rossio. From the **Estação de Cais do Sodré,** the *praça* is a 15-minute walk or a short ride on bus #1, 2, 32, 44, or 45. Bus #17 connects Santa Apolónia with Cais do Sodré. The **Estação de Rossio** is in Praça dos Restauradores. If you come into **Lisbon Airport,** take local bus #8, 22, 44, or 45 to the town center, or take the faster *linha verde* (green line) express bus (20 min., 200$). A taxi from the airport to town costs 800-850$.

Buses provide frequent and convenient service throughout the capital and cost about 95$, depending on the number of zones you cross. Covering only part of the city, the clean and fast **subway** is ideal for connections between Lisbon's new business district and the Rossio (35$ per ride, book of 10 tickets 320$), not to mention getting from one end of Avda. da Liberdade to the other. Signs with the letter "M" indicate metro stops. **Trolley** enthusiasts will be thrilled by the extraordinary variety of streetcars, many of pre-World War I vintage. These brightly colored vehicles, emblazoned with whiskey, cigarette, and insect repellent ads, overflow with passengers hanging precariously from outside platforms as the cars climb the city's hills. Route #28 (Graça-Prazeres) offers beautiful views of the city's harbor and streets. In addition, three **funiculars** connect the lower city with the hilly residential areas. The one next to Palácio da Foz linking Praça dos Restauradores with Bairro Alto is especially useful.

If you plan to stay in Lisbon for any length of time, consider investing in a *bilhete de assinatura turístico* (tourist pass), good for unlimited travel on CARRIS buses, trolleys, funiculars, and the subway (1175$ for 7 days, 850$ for 4 days). The passes are sold in CARRIS booths (open daily 8am-8pm), located in most network train stations (try Santa Apolónia), the Rossio, and the Santa Justa elevator off Rua do Carmo.

Tourist Offices: Palácio da Foz, Praça dos Restauradores (tel. 36 33 14 or 36 36 43). Metro: Restauradores. No Portuguese hospitality here. Get your map and run, as other requests may be rudely rebuffed. Open Mon.-Sat. 9am-8pm, Sun. 10am-6pm. Busy branch offices at Santa Apolónia Station (open Mon.-Sat. 9am-7pm) and the airport (open 24 hours). **National Tourist Office Headquarters,** Avda. Antónia Ausgusto de Aguiar, 86 (tel. 57 50 15). Open Mon.-Fri. 9:30am-5:30pm.

Student Travel: Tagus, Praça de Londres, 9B (tel. 88 49 57). Metro: Alameda. Helpful. Open Mon.-Fri. 9am-1pm and 2:30-6pm.

Embassies: U.S., Avda. das Forças Armadas (tel. 72 56 00). **Canadian,** Rua Rosa Araújo, 2, 6th floor (tel. 56 38 21). **British,** Rua de São Domingo à Lapa, 37 (tel. 66 11 22). Will also handle **New Zealand** affairs. **Australian,** Avda. da Liberdade, 244, 4th floor (tel. 52 33 50).

Currency Exchange: At Santa Apolónia Station. Enormous lines on weekends here and at the branch at the airport. Both open 24 hours. The main post office also changes money. Open Mon.-Fri. 9am-7pm. Banks open Mon.-Fri. 8:30-11:45am and 1-2:45pm.

American Express: Star Travel Service, Avda. Sidónio Pais, 4A (tel. 53 98 71). Metro: Parque. Open Mon.-Fri. 9am-12:30pm and 2-6pm. The branch office at Praça dos Restauradores, 14, offers the same services and is more conveniently located.

Post Office: Correio, Praça do Comércio (tel. 36 32 31). Open Mon.-Fri. 9am-7pm. Poste Restante around the corner at Rua do Arsenal, 27. 27$ per item. Open Mon.-Fri. 8am-5pm. Also a branch at Praça dos Restauradores with central telephone exchange. Open daily 8am-10pm. **Postal Code:** 1100.

Telephones: Praça Dom Pedro IV, 68. Open daily 8am-11pm. For **telegrams,** call 32 98 11. **Telephone Code:** 01.

Airport: Tel. 80 20 60. Take local bus #44 or 45 to the town center (bus stops along the length of Avda. da Liberdade and Avda. República), or take the faster green line express bus, *linha da verde* (180$). Major airlines have offices at Praça Marquês de Pombal and along Avda. da Liberdade. **TAP Air Portugal,** Tel. 54 40 80; for reservations 57 50 20. To Faro (6600$), Funchal (13,800$), London (APEX round-trip £243), and New York (APEX round-trip US$708). **Iberia,** Tel. 56 20 16; for reservations 56 95 71.

Train Stations: Rossio for Sintra (105$) and western lines; **Santa Apolónia** for all international, northern, and eastern lines; **Cais do Sodré** for Estoril and Cascais (80$); and **Barreiro** for the Algarve and southern lines. To reach Barreiro, you must take a ferry across the Tagus (80$, free if you're coming from the south into Lisbon); boats leave from Praça do Comércio every 5-10 min. Accurate and friendly information is available at Rossio Station. Open daily 8am-11pm. To Lagos (5 per day; 1100$, *expresso* 1450$), Faro (6 per day, 1515$), Evora (6 per day, 500$), Portalegre (4 per day, 755$), Oporto (6 ALFA *expresso* 1900$; 4 others per day 1045-1450$), Paris (1 per day, 15,000$), Badajoz, and Spain via Elvas (4 per day, 975$).

Bus Station: Rodoviária Nacional, Avda. Casal Ribeiro, 18 (tel. 57 77 15), near Praça Salhanha. A ½-hr. walk to Praça dos Restauradores. Take bus #1, 21, 32 or 36 (95$) to the *Rossio*. Bus #1 will also take you to Cais do Sodré, or walk up Casal Ribeiro, turn left at the *praça,* and take the subway at Picoas. To Lagos (4 per day, 1125$), Faro (3 per day, 1000$), Evora (9 per day, 700$), Portalegre (3 per day, 875$), Oporto (2 *expressos* per day, 1000$), Coimbra (14 per day, 775$), and Braga (2 per day, 1185$).

Hitchhiking: Thumbing can be difficult since there's a lot of competition. To travel south toward the Algarve, take the ferry to Cacilhas from Praça do Comércio and start on the Setúbal road. To Oporto and the north, take bus #8, 21, 44, 45, or 53 to the Rotunda do Aeroporto, and get in line. To Spain, go to the Autoestrada do Porto; after 30km it links with the road to Badajoz.

English Bookstore: Livraria Clássica Editora, Praça dos Restauradores, 17. Wide selection of classics and best-sellers. **Livraria Britanica-The English Bookshop,** Rua São Marçal, 168A, between the Botanical Garden and Bairro Alto.

Laundromat: Lavatax, Rua Francisco Sanches, 65A (tel. 82 33 92). Metro: Arroios. Self-service wash only, 300$. 5kg washed, dried, and folded 555$. Open Mon.-Fri. 9am-1pm and 3-9pm, Sat. 9am-noon.

Medical Services: British Hospital, Rua Saraiva de Carvalho, 49 (tel. 60 20 20; at night 60 37 85). **Ambulance,** Tel. 115.

Police: Tel. 36 61 41, or 115 anywhere in Portugal.

Accommodations and Camping

You should have no trouble getting a single for around 1000$ or a double for 1300-1500$ in a *pensão* or hotel with decent bathroom facilities. Most establishments have only rooms with double beds and charge quite a bit more than half for single occupancy. The vast majority of hotels are conveniently located in the center of town on **Avenida da Liberdade** and adjacent side streets. Accommodations near the city's **castelo** (castle) and in the **Bairro Alto** will put you in quieter and more interesting locations for a price. Ask at the tourist office about your safety in an area before you take a room there. Be especially cautious in the Bairro Alto and the Alfama after dark; it's not a good idea to walk alone here.

The cheapest lodgings (for those with membership cards) are provided by the IYHF hostels. Beach aficionados with tents or lots of cash may want to make **Estoril** and **Cascais** their bases. They are 20 and 22km away from Lisbon and are mercifully free of the noise and smog of the capital. Be aware, however, that food and lodging prices here may be 50% higher than what you would find in the city. Cascais is the more pleasant of the two towns and has the cleanest beaches (see Near Lisbon).

Pousada de Juventude de Lisboa (IYHF), Rua Andrade Corvo, 46 (tel. 53 26 96), off Avda. Fontes Pereira de Melo. Metro: Picoas. Take bus #1 or 45 from the Rossio or Cais do Sodré. Not the homiest of hostels: drab, bare-wood floors in rooms that are crammed with beds and flooded in harsh fluorescent light. Strict rules and an impersonal staff. Cooking facilities. Come early to reserve a room in summer. Curfew 1am. Reception open 8-10:30am and 6pm-1am. July-Sept. 700$; Oct.-June 550$. Breakfast included. Nonmembers may purchase a guest card for 2000$.

Pousada de Juventude de Catalazete (IYHF), Estrada Marginal (tel. 243 06 38), outside Lisbon in the coastal town of Oeiras. Take a train from Cais do Sodré to Oeiras (20 min., 80$), and then exit the station by turning right under the sign "Praia" (beach). Follow the street as it curves downhill all the way to the beach (1000m). Turn left at the underpass, and walk through the INATEL tourist compound; the hostel is at the far end of the enclosed area. Perched right on the ocean, this excellent hostel boasts facilities and views that would be the envy of any resort. Intimate, relaxing atmosphere and a riveting social scene. Step out onto the patio for a moonlight view of crashing ocean waves. Curfew midnight. Reception open 9:30-10:30am and 6-11:30pm. 550$. Breakfast included. Lunch or dinner 350$.

Baixa

A slew of accommodations center around Praça dos Restauradores and the Rossio. Many are in pre-war buildings that appear decrepit outside and even in the stairway, but often contain renovated rooms. Quality varies greatly.

Residencial Florescente, Rua Portas de Santo Antao, 99 (tel. 32 66 09), 1 block from Praça dos Restauradores. A bit of class in the heart of Libson. Pretty *pensão* with cozy living rooms on each floor and a waterfall in the lobby. Great rooms and an immaculate bath make this far and away the best deal in town. Singles and doubles 1000-1200$, with shower 2600$.

Pensão Prata, Rua da Prata, 71, 3rd floor (tel. 36 89 08), 2 blocks up from Praça do Comércio. The sign is hidden by yellow awning. Bright, airy rooms in a peaceful apartment setting. Kind management. Singles 1500$. Doubles 1700$, with shower 2800$.

Pensão Beira Minho, Praça da Figueira, 6, 2nd floor (tel. 32 79 36), beside the Rossio. At the northern end of the *praça* through a flower shop. Ugly, ugly stairwell, but the renovated rooms are quite nice. Small, windowless singles are well lit and cheerful. Singles 1000-1600$. Doubles 1600-2100$, with bath 2300-2500$.

Pensão Residencial Estrela do Mondego, Calçada do Carmo, 25 (tel. 36 11 09), 1 block south of Rossio Station. Neat, carpeted rooms with big windows. The huge 3-man room is a veritable dance hall. The common bath is somewhat shabby. Singles and doubles 1800$, with shower 2800$.

Residência Mucaba, Avda. da Liberdade, 53 (tel. 36 56 47). Despite the warehouse-like surroundings, the decor inside is wonderfully modern. Spanking clean baths. Singles 2100$, with bath 3300$. Doubles 2200$, with bath 3400$.

Pensão Campos, Rua Jardim do Regedor, 24, 3rd floor (tel. 32 05 60), on the busy pedestrian street between Praça dos Restauradores and Rua Portas de Santa Antão. Cozy, well-furnished rooms and spotless bath. Run by a sweet family. Singles 2200$. Doubles 2500$.

In and around the Bairro Alto

Quieter than the Baixa, the Bairro Alto has a sense of community you will not find in the town center, but be careful walking alone here after dark—this area is known for muggings.

Pensão Londres, Rua Dom Pedro V, 53 (tel. 36 55 23). Take the funicular by the Palácio da Foz in Praça dos Restauradores. Facing away from the funicular, walk to the right (west) up to Rua Dom Pedro V. A pleasant location near parks and the city's best inexpensive restaurants. A bit gloomy, but the *pensão* has rooms of varying sizes on its 4 floors. Singles 1800$, with shower 3000$. Doubles 1800$, with shower 3500$.

Pensão Monumental, Rua da Gloria, 21 (tel. 36 96 07). Clean, modern rooms and friendly management. Singles 1300$, with shower 1500$. Doubles 1500$, with shower 1750$. 4 people in a room with 2 double beds and complete bath 3000$. In off-season, prices about 100-150$ less.

Hotel Suisso Atlántico, Rua da Gloria, 3-19 (tel. 36 17 13). A worthwhile extravagance with modern rooms and money-changing services for guests. Singles with bath 3500$. Doubles with bath 4600$. Breakfast included.

Pensão Globo, Rua Teixeira, 37 (tel. 36 22 79), on a small street parallel to Rua S.P. Alcântera at the top of the funicular. Small but pleasant doubles from 1600$.

Near the Castelo (Mouraria)

This neighborhood has lovely narrow streets, flowered balconies, and wonderful views. Nonetheless, the hilly streets can prove tortuous on the traveler with a heavy pack. Don't walk alone in this area at night.

Pensão Ninho de Águias, Rua Costa do Costelo, 74 (tel. 86 03 91). A long, winding stairway leads to the patio, where an aviary, flowering garden, and stupendous views of Lisbon unfold before you. Some of the best lodgings for the money in Lisbon and certainly some of the most popular. Make reservations. Singles with shower 1800$. Doubles 2800$, with shower 3500$, with bath 3900$. Breakfast included.

Pensão Residencial Brasil Africano, Travessa das Pedras Negras, 8, 2nd floor (tel. 86 92 66), off Rua Madalena. Conveniently located near the cathedral and Baixa. Spacious, comfortable rooms with balconies and funky wallpaper. Singles 1600$. Doubles 1800$, with shower 2000$.

Lisbon's municipal campground is called **Parque Nacional de Turismo e Campismo** (tel. 70 44 13). Take the bus to the Parque Florestal Monsanto. A swimming pool and a reasonably priced supermarket are on the grounds. (June-Sept. 276$ per person, 244-372$ per tent, 211$ per car; Oct.-May 179$ per person, 147-211$ per tent, 179$ per car.) You can also camp at **Costa da Caparica,** 5km out of Lisbon (take the bus from Praça de Espanha, 15 min.). You'll find beautiful beaches and plenty of shade here. Bungalows are also available.

Food

Lisbon has some of the least expensive restaurants in any European capital. You can have tons of delicious food, gallons of excellent beer and wine, and tempting desserts, often for less than 600$. As a port city, Lisbon specializes in seafood dishes. Try *ameijoas à bulhão pato,* a spicy meal of clams, or *crema de mariscos,* a seafood chowder with tomatoes.

If you're down to your last escudos, take bus #40 to **Mercado Ribeira,** a market complex on Avda. 24 de Julho outside the Cais do Sodré. (Open Mon.-Sat. until

2pm.) Or try the larger market in Cascais held on Wednesday morning (a 5-min. walk from the train station). These markets also supply those commodities more precious than food to some travelers—cheap, traditional **fishing sweaters.**

Baixa

The southern end of town, between Praça da Figueira and the port, is the best area to find cheap restaurants. Many places line **Rua Dos Correeiros,** parallel to Rua da Prata, and neighboring streets. One block from Praça dos Restauradores, on **Rua das Portas de Santo Antão,** many superb (and expensive) seafood restaurants thrive alongside a slew of cheap sandwich bars. Food here is generally less expensive than elsewhere, but the quality varies. It's worth moving off the tourist track to find one of the little-known gems common in this area. Beware that many of the Baixa's restaurants are not open on Sunday and close around 9pm or 10pm on weekdays.

Adega Popular 33, Rua da Conceiçao, 33 (tel. 87 94 72), 2 blocks up from Praça do Comércio. Small restaurant popular with locals. The most inexpensive good food on the block. Entrees 350-400$. Half-portions served. Open Mon.-Fri. 8am-9:30pm.

Adega do Atum, Rua dos Bacalhoeiros, 8D, off Rua da Madalena, 1 block north and parallel to Rua da Alfandega. A friendly place in a sun-splashed square not far from the port. Good fresh fish. Try their *lulinhas* (squid). Entrees 300-500$. Open Mon.-Sat. 7am-midnight.

O Baleal, Rua de Madalena, 277 (tel. 87 21 87), 1 block toward the Mouraria from Praça da Figuiera. Delicious seafood. Excellent *espada da Madeira* 595$. Other dishes 400-800$. Open Mon.-Fri. noon-10:30pm, Sat. noon-4pm.

Porto de Abrigo, Rua dos Remolares, 16-18 (tel. 36 08 73), near the Estação Cais de Sodré. One of the most popular of the riverside eateries. Try the *pato com arroz* (duck with rice and olives) for 525$. Other entrees 500-650$. Open Mon.-Sat. noon-3:30pm and 7-10pm.

Restaurante Chekiang, Rossio Station, Store #108 (tel. 32 69 57). Tasty Chinese cuisine in a quiet atmosphere. Try chicken with mussels (580$) or sweet-sour fish (490$). Sumptuous glazed fruit desserts. Open daily noon-3pm and 7-11pm.

Lua de Mel, Rua Santa Justa, 242-248 (tel. 247 10 88), beside the entrance to the Santa Justa elevator. Cute decor. Snack bar and A/C. Some of the freshest, most delicious pastries in Lisbon. Well worth every escudo. Sandwiches 90-150$. Wonderful fruit salads and ice cream sundaes 300$. Open Mon.-Sat. 7:30am-8:30pm.

Bairro Alto

West of Rua da Misericórdia, the Barrio Alto is slowly being gentrified, spawning some excellent restaurants whose late-night hours, offbeat clientele, and superb food make them extremely popular. Though more expensive than restaurants in the Baixa, they are definitely worth exploring, as are the small restaurants of the **Alfama. Calçada do Combro,** the neighborhood's main westward artery, has many a cheap haunt. Entrees at **Principe do Calhariz,** 30, run about 280$. On Rua do Loreto, which runs into C. do Combro at the easternmost end, **Casa da India,** 49-51, serves up tame curry for 250$ and other entrees for 250-400$. To find more interesting places, walk up **Rua da Misericórdia** to the adjacent side streets.

Cervejaria da Trindade, Rua Nova da Trindade, 20C, parallel to Rua Misericordia. This spacious restaurant was once a convent and still retains its beautiful tiled walls and garden. *Carne de porco à alentejana* (pork with clams) is a house specialty (1700$) that should be washed down with *mista* (mixed light and dark beer). Other tasty entrees 500-800$. Open Thurs.-Tues. 9am-10pm.

Bota Alta, Travessa da Queimada, 37 (tel. 32 79 59), on the other side of Rua da Misericórdia. Tasty entrees served with a smile. Outstanding *caldo verde.* Open Mon.-Fri. noon-2:30pm and 7-10:30pm, Sat. 7-10:30pm.

O Esturro, Travessa da Queimada, 13 (tel. 32 49 10), down the street from Bota Alta. Delicious, inexpensive meat and fish dishes. Try grilled squid (380$) or pork chops (390$). Open Mon. noon-3pm, Tues.-Fri. noon-3pm and 7pm-midnight, Sat.-Sun. 7pm-midnight.

Xêlê Bananas, Praça des Flores, 29. Walk down Rua de S. Marçal from Rua da Escola Politécnica; you'll find the restaurant in one of Lisbon's most pleasant little squares. Popular with *Lisboetas* willing to pay a little more for good food. Entrees 500-900$. Open Mon.-Sat. 11am-4pm and 7pm-midnight.

A Pérola do Bonjardim, Rua da Cruz dos Poiais, 95A (tel. 60 84 80), off Rua dos Poiais, a continuation of Calçada do Combro. This stuccoed and tiled restaurant in a charming neighborhood offers delectable entrees (420-650$) and *pratos do dia* (385$). Open Mon.-Sat. noon-3pm and 7-10pm.

Casa de Pasto de Francisco Cardoso, Rua do Século, 244, off Rua Dom Pedro V. Friendly, intimate atmosphere. Excellent homemade sangria and delicious cornbread. After dessert, take a look at the spreading cedar that shades the park across the street—it's a national monument. Entrees 380-650$. Open Mon.-Sat. noon-10pm.

Alfama

No stay in Lisbon would be complete without at least one meal in the Alfama. A number of inexpensive, colorful restaurants line **Rua São Pedro,** its main, medieval-looking street. The Alfama is an area known for theft. Come here by day, without handbags or cameras.

Mestre André, Calçadinha de Sto. Estevão, 6 (tel. 87 14 87), off Rua dos Remédios. A friendly, eclectically yet tastefully decorated place with old cinema and theater posters and photographs. Brazilian music in the background. Excellent food—their *lingua de ternera* (beef tongue, served with mashed potatoes and sauteed onions and carrots, 325$) has turned many people on to the great taste of tongue. Also try their *salada roxa,* a remarkable fish salad (380$). Open Mon.-Sat. noon-3pm and 7pm-midnight.

Os Minitotos, Rua dos Remédios, 31 (no phone), next to Mestre André. Less sophisticated than its neighbor, but good, simple food cooked on an outdoor grill. A ½-chicken with rice, potatoes, and olives 350$. Fresh *lulas* (squid) or grilled *trutas* (trout) 320-350$. Open Mon.-Sat. 11am-4pm and 7pm-midnight.

Dragão de Alfama, Rua Guilherme Braga, 8 (tel. 86 77 37), near the Church of São Estevão. Regional dishes and fresh fish entrees 350-550$. *Pratos do dia* 375$. Open Mon.-Fri. noon-4pm and 7pm-midnight, Sat. noon-4pm.

Belém

A 10-minute train ride from Cais do Sodré brings you to the delightful district of Belém. Several nice restaurants line **Rua de Belém** between the monastery and the coach museum.

Restaurante Casa Azul, Rua de Belém, 83 (tel. 63 61 16). Excellent grilled swordfish and other entrees 450$. Open daily 8am-midnight.

Adega Belém, Rua de Belém, 40 (tel. 63 62 46). White stucco walls and pretty blue *azulejos.* Equally attractive entrees 350-550$.

Pasteis de Belém, Rua de Belém, 84 (tel. 63 74 23). An old-fashioned coffee house famous for its *pasteis de Belém* (pastries sprinkled with cinnamon, 50$). Open daily 8am-8pm.

Sights

Old Center

The hub of Lisbon is the **Rossio,** or more properly, **Praça Dom Pedro IV,** the city's main square. Originally a cattle market, it later witnessed public executions, bullfights, and carnivals. Today, its sidewalk cafes attract crowds who sit placidly amidst dashing buses. Three sides of the *praça* are lined with the beautifully proportioned houses (note the way their tiled roofs curve up in a pagoda-like manner), built under the Marquis of Pombal after the terrible 1755 earthquake. On the fourth side, marking the former site of the Palace of the Inquisition, stands the stately **Teatro Nacional,** crowned with a statue of Gil Vicente, Portugal's first dramatist.

Atop a tall Corinthian column in the center of the *praça* reigns a stoic **Dom Pedro IV.** According to popular belief, the statue is actually a likeness of the Mexican Emperor Maximilian, purchased for a bargain price after the Austrian-born archduke was executed.

After the earthquake, Pombal created the **Baixa,** the grid of streets south of the Rossio, to facilitate communication between the town center and the river. In an age that prized rationality and order, its perpendicular, straight streets, each one designated for a specific trade, were considered the utmost in urban planning. Today the streets can no longer comfortably accommodate the crowds of people flocking to the numerous stores and offices, although the eloquence of the architecture—in the restrained "Pombaline" style of the Rossio—gives the Baixa a graceful air. Rua Augusta, lined with shops selling furs, shoes, and perfume, leads past a triumphal arch to **Praça do Comércio.** According to a Lisbon saying, "God gave the Portuguese the Tagus and in gratitude they made the Terreiro do Paço." Now known by its popular name, the Praça do Comércio boasts the huge statue of Dom José I, cast in 1755 from 9400 pounds of bronze. Unfortunately, the grandiose figure looks a little silly—he now oversees an enormous parking lot.

From the northwest corner of the square, Rua Alfandega leads to the late Gothic **Igreja da Conceição Velha.** Its portal, effusively decorated in the Manueline style, shows Mary protecting various clerics and royal personages with her mantle. The church's interior, redone after the earthquake, has a handsome Renaissance vaulted chancel and a statue (in the 2nd chapel on the right) of Our Lady of Rastelo, brought here from a small church in Belém where the great Portuguese navigators spent their last night in prayer before leaving on their journeys. The **Casa dos Bicos** (House of the Beaks), the area's prominent sixteenth-century landmark, once belonged to the family of the first viceroy of India and is now used to display temporary exhibits. (Open Mon.-Sat. 10am-noon and 2:30-6:30pm. Admission varies with the exhibit.)

New Center

North of the Rossio, **Praça dos Restauradores** commemorates the 1640 restoration of Portugal's independence from Spain with an obelisk that bears a bronze sculpture of the Genius of Independence on its south side. Here begins **Avenida da Liberdade,** once a green valley and today the city's most imposing boulevard. Its malls of flowering shrubs, palm trees, swan ponds, and fountains were at one time Lisbon's favorite promenade. Though this mile-long avenue has seen better days, a stroll here is still delightful. The avenue ends at **Praça de Pombal,** or **Rotunda,** where a proud Pombal leaning on a lion marks the entrance to one of the city's largest open areas, **Parque Eduardo VII,** named in honor of the English king's visit to Lisbon in 1903. At the upper end of the park, a terrace allows for an expansive view of the city as well as a glimpse of the **Estufa Fria** (greenhouse) and **Estufa Quente** (hothouse), the park's two tropical gardens, which stock a variety of exotic plants and birds. (Open Mon.-Sat. 9am-7:30pm. Free.)

A kilometer north, bordering Avda. António Augusto Aguiar and Praça de Espanha, is the **Gulbenkian Foundation,** a complex of gardens and museums. The **Museu Calouste Gulbenkian,** set in a modern, airy building, houses what was once the private collection of Calouste Gulbenkian, an Armenian oil millionaire who sought refuge in Portugal during World War II. You'll find among the treasures an exquisite Egyptian collection; a room devoted to Armenian art; Chinese porcelain vases; Persian miniature paintings; delicately carved French ivory triptychs dating from the fourteenth century; works of European masters such as Rubens, Rembrandt, Monet, and van Dyck; and some beautiful small sculptures by Rodin. This is a museum not to be missed. The adjacent complex, **Centro de Arte Moderno,** contains an extensive collection of modern Portuguese art as well as a temporary exhibit hall. Look for the 2.4-meter-tall *Skop,* by Emilia Nadal. The bright, shiny letters on the box boast "*New* detergent—ideological for brainwash." Even more interesting is the collection of Portuguese paintings and drawings from the '20s and

'30s. Check out the *Humoristas* section for a glimpse into a time of cultural and political effervescence in Portuguese art, exemplified by the work of António Almada Negreiros. The center hosts a jazz festival during the last week of July. Both buildings are air-conditioned in summer, with many a couch on which to escape the midday sun. You may wish to have lunch in one of the restaurants here—excellent entrees cost 200-300$. (Both museums open Tues., Thurs.-Fri., and Sun. 10am-5pm; Wed. and Sat. 2-7:30pm. Admission 40$, students free. Metro: Palhavã.)

Chiado and Bairro Alto

Boxed in a fanciful Gothic tower created by Eiffel himself, the **Ascensor de Santa Justa** connecting the Baixa to the Chiado is perhaps one of Lisbon's most beloved landmarks. (Rides 20$.) From the upper terrace, a narrow walkway leads under a huge flying buttress to the fourteenth-century **Igreja do Carmo,** largely destroyed in the 1755 earthquake. Though roofless, it still preserves dramatic Gothic arches. A ramshackle **archeological museum** here includes Dom Fernando I's tomb, still black from a treatment inflicted for photographic purposes. (Open Tues.-Sun. 10am-1pm and 2-5pm. Admission 100$.)

One block south, Old World coffee houses, bookstores, jewelry shops, and baroque churches line Lisbon's elegant Rua Garrett. **A Brasileira,** at #120-122, perhaps the most famous of the city's coffee houses, was the meeting place for such late-nineteenth-century Portuguese writers as Eça de Queirós. Two blocks south on Rua Serpa Pinto, the **Museu Nacional de Arte Contemporânea** offers an interesting collection of late-nineteenth-century Portuguese painting and sculpture. (Open Tues.-Fri. 10-12:30am and 2-5pm. Admission 150$, students free.)

Returning to Rua Garrett past a square guarded by two churches, a right turn on bustling Rua da Misericórdia leads to the plain facade of the **Igreja de São Roque,** begun in 1567. According to legend, the intervention of this saint saved the Bairro Alto from the devastation wrought elsewhere by the great quake. The church's interior contains a flat wooden roof painted to give the illusion of a series of domes, as well as the famous **Capela de São João Baptista** (4th from the left), which caused quite a sensation when it was installed in 1747. Rumored to be the costliest ever, the chapel was built in Rome by the architect of Caserta with agate, lapis lazuli, alabaster, *verde antica,* and mosaics, and brought to Lisbon aboard three ships. Particularly astonishing is the *Baptism of Christ,* a mosaic so fine that it's hard to believe it's not an oil. View the chapel in the morning when sunshine through the window lights up the precious stones and sets ablaze the gold and wrought silver censers. Adjoining the church, the small **Museu de São Roque** preserves a fine collection of gold and silver filigree work. (Open Tues.-Sun. 10am-noon and 2-5pm. Admission 25$, students free.)

A few streets over, flowery balconies and hanging laundry frame the view of the **Igreja das Mercês,** a handsome eighteenth-century travertine building. Its small *praça* offers an enticing view of the neoclassical **Palácio da Assembléia Nacional,** which looms above the district's orange-tiled roofs. Past the Parliament on Calçada da Estrela rises the **Basilica da Estrela** (1796), its exquisitely shaped dome poised in the air behind a pair of tall belfries. When the half-crazed Maria I gave birth to a male heir, she fulfilled a vow by building this church. Its richly decorated nave has narrow proportions that make the flood of light pouring in from the dome all the more spectacular. Be sure to ask the sacristan to show you the enormous tenth-century *presepio* (manger). (Open daily 9:30am-1pm and 3:30-7:30pm.)

Across from the church, the **Jardim da Estrela,** one of the loveliest of the city's many parks, stands in front of the **Cemitério dos Ingleses** (Englishmen's Cemetery), overgrown with tropical plants, cypress trees, and odd gravestones. (Ring the bell for entry.) Its musty, English-style chapel dates from 1885. The cemetery's most famous remains belong to the novelist Henry Fielding, who came to Lisbon in search of health in 1714 only to drop dead after a two-month sojourn.

An easy 15-minute walk downhill to the river brings you to Portugal's national museum, the **Museu Nacional de Arte Antiga** on Rua das Janelas Verdes. Here you'll see a fine collection of European paintings, from Gothic primitives to eighteenth-century French masterpieces. The museum's most prized possession is the six-panel polyptych of the *Adoration of St. Vincent* (Lisbon's patron saint) by Nuno Gonçalves, one of Portugal's greatest artists. Various people, including a lonely beggar and the king himself, pay homage to the red-cloaked figure of the saint. In the central panel on the left, Queen Isabel kneels while her mother, Isabel of Aragon, stands behind her. Prince Henry the Navigator in his wide-brimmed hat kneels behind the saint on the other side, and the artist himself is depicted in the upper left-hand corner. Other paintings worthy of note are the ghoulish sixteenth-century *O Inferno,* by an artist of the Portuguese school, and the small Breughel works in Room VIII. (Open Tues. and Thurs.-Sat. 10am-5pm, Wed. and Sun. 10am-7pm. Admission 100$, students and Sun. free.) To get back to the town center, take bus #40 or trolley #19 from the stop near the entrance, which will take you to Praça da Figueira next to the Rossio.

Lisbon's worst disaster since the earthquake of 1755, a fire in August of 1988 destroyed a 10-square-block area of the Chiado shopping district surrounding the Rua Do Carmo pedestrian mall. This area, which was jammed with department stores and lovely specialty shops, will likely be rebuilt quickly.

Alfama and Mouraria

The **Alfama** is Lisbon's oldest quarter and is situated over the hill from the Castelo de São Jorge, on the southern slope facing the Rio Tejo. Between the Alfama and the Bairro Baixa is a section of town known as the **Mouraria** because the quarter became the Moorish ghetto after the Moors were expelled by Henriques and the Crusaders in 1147.

The best way to enter this part of the city is from the street alongside the sixteenth-century **Igreja de Madalena,** at the eastern end of the Baixa's Rua da Conceição. Behind the Madalena rises the delicately proportioned **Igreja de Santo António da Sé** (1812), supposedly built over the saint's birthplace. The construction was funded with money collected by the city's children, who fashioned tiny altars bearing images of the saint to place on their doorsteps—a custom still re-enacted annually on June 13, the saint's feast day. By the entrance is a museum devoted to the saint's life and miracles. Ask the caretaker for the fascinating stories of the Franciscan's deeds. On Fridays at noon, Mass is sung in Latin with Gregorian chants.

Directly beyond the little church looms the stolid mass of Lisbon's sé (cathedral), built in the late twelfth century. Its unadorned facade has been likened to a cyclops silently guarding the town and bay. Inside, a Romanesque nave with a beautifully proportioned triforium leads to a baroque choir. Gothic chapels, pierced by elegant lancet windows, surround the choir and shelter medieval royal tombs.

The much-restored **Castelo de São Jorge,** used as a fortress in the time of Julius Caesar and later as a Moorish citadel, crowns a hill a few blocks up from the cathedral. From its windswept esplanade shaded by olive trees, you can look down upon Lisbon as though studying an open map. Open every night until sunset, its garden is replete with ducks, peacocks, albino deer (and sundry other victims of genetic manipulation), a perfect place for an evening stroll.

From here it's a short walk to the Alfama, Lisbon's famous medieval quarter. Originally a Visigothic settlement, the Alfama became the fashionable cultural quarter during the period of Saracen rule. Its elegance grew under the Arabs, who filled it with costly mansions. After the Christians took over, it became the noisy and popular residence of fishermen and sailors, and has remained so ever since. The town planners of the eighteenth century didn't dare try to sort out this turbulent brew of balconies, archways, terraces, and courtyards. Let yourself get lost here if you have some time.

From Largo das Portas do Sol, take the ramp or stairway down to Beco de Santa Helena and make a left on Rua do Castelo Picão, which will bring you to Largo do Salvador. At #22 stands a dilapidated sixteenth-century aristocrat's mansion. From here, Rua da Regueira descends to a small *praça* that adjoins a pair of interesting byways: **Beco do Carneiro** (Sheep Alley), which is so narrow that the eaves of the buildings on either side touch one another, and **Beco do Mexias,** where one doorway leads to a fountain in which the local women do their washing. Rua da Regueira ends at Rua dos Remédios. A right turn takes you past an open square to **Rua de São Pedro,** the principal trading street of the Alfama, where the smell of raw fish pervades. A small opening (to the right, midway down the street) leads to the **Igreja de São Miguel,** which houses a beautiful ceiling made of Brazilian jacaranda wood and a rococo gilt altar screen. (Ask the sacristan to turn on the lights.) Rua de São Pedro ends at Largo de São Rafael, enclosed on one side by the remains of an old Moorish tower. To return to Largo das Portas do Sol, climb up Rua da Adiça and keep going until you reach the top.

Before venturing farther east, stop at the **Fundação Espíritu Santo Silva,** Lisbon's splendid decorative arts museum bordering the Portas do Sol. Designed by a noble who appears to have had lots of free time, the collection is housed in a pre-earthquake palace that survived to become a veterinary hospital and later a home for 17 successive families. As noble houses go, it is an eccentric place, each room irregularly shaped and stocked full of furniture and decorations from the golden age of the aristocracy. Most of the tables and chairs date from the eighteenth century and were crafted out of Brazilian jacaranda wood by Portuguese artisans. The tapestries are especially beautiful—don't miss the sixteenth-century work of Flemish origin that depicts Vasco da Gama in India. (Open Tues.-Sat. 10am-1pm and 2:30-5pm. Free admission includes a tour in French, English, or Portuguese—it is customary to tip the guide 50$.)

Exit the museum to your left and follow the trolley tracks as they descend Travessa de São Tomé and emerge at the **Igreja de São Vicente de Fora** (1582-1627), dedicated to Lisbon's patron saint. The church's handsome, two-towered Renaissance facade (the dome collapsed during the earthquake) conceals a gracefully proportioned nave that sets off a sumptuous baroque high altar and organ. The adjacent cloister is decorated with a series of *azulejos* illustrating La Fontaine's *Fables,* barely distinguishable due to a botched attempt at restoration. Beyond it broods the **Panteón de Bragança,** containing the tombs of the later kings and queens of Portugal; an uncanny sculpture of a woman mourns over the dead Dom Carlos. Ask to see the deathly still *sacristia,* with fabulous eighteenth-century walls inlaid with marble from Sintra—perhaps the only part of the complex that makes the cloister visit worth the 75$ admission. (Open daily 10am-1pm and 3-6pm.)

The **Igreja de Santa Engrácia,** which lies a little farther east, took so long to build (1682-1966), that it gave rise to the expression, "endless like the building of Santa Engrácia." The church has been designated the Portuguese National Pantheon, to commemorate the "low-born" heroes of the country, in contrast to the aristocratic function of the Pantéon de Bragança.

Hop a trolley going east from Santa Apolónia Station for the short ride to the **Convento da Madre de Deus.** Founded at the beginning of the sixteenth century and heavily restored after the earthquake, the convent complex houses the excellent **Museu do Azulejo** (Tile Museum), as well as Lisbon's most baroque interior. (Open Tues.-Sun. 10am-5pm.) The interior of the church, reached through a fine Manueline doorway, is a riot of oil paintings, *azulejos,* and gilded wood. This same elaborate decoration continues in the *coro alto* (chapter house) and the **Capela de Santo António,** where *azulejos* and paintings depict the life of the saint. Two spaces offer refreshing respite from all this grandiosity: a Renaissance courtyard and a Gothic cloister embellished with brightly colored geometric *azulejos.*

Belém

Rising from the banks of the Tagus behind a sculpted garden worthy of a king, the **Mosteiro dos Jerónimos** stands as Portugal's most refined celebration of her age of Discoveries. Begun by Manuel I in 1502 to give thanks for the success of

Vasco da Gama's voyage (he set sail for India from Belém in 1497), the monastery is a superb example of Manueline architecture. Born of an exuberant age when Portuguese navigators rolled back the boundaries of the known world, this transitional style combines Gothic forms with early Renaissance details. Its most pervasive signature is the use of symbols inspired by the sea: sailor's ropes, anchors, coral, algae, and various navigation instruments.

Soaring to the full height of the facade, the south door of the church is a masterpiece of sculpture. On both sides of the central column, which supports a statue of Henry the Navigator (or, according to some, Vasco da Gama), figures of the 12 Apostles stand under carved canopies. In the vast interior, six octagonal columns spring open like palm trees to support an elaborately creased roof 82-feet high. Unlike the naves in most European cathedrals, this one is the same height as the side aisles, making for an extraordinarily delicate open space. Note how the columns, though alike in their early Renaissance decoration, become thinner as they approach the entryway, giving the interior a nervous energy rare in Western architecture. The pagoda-style tombs in the chancel and transepts, and the various fruit and vegetable encrustations throughout the church typify the exoticism of the Manueline style.

The symbolic tombs of Portugal's premiere poet, Luís de Camões, and navigator Vasco da Gama lie in two opposing transepts. Considered the Portuguese Shakespeare, de Camões had an unwitting, romantic flair that made him a Casanova among the ladies of the gentry and the bitter enemy among their self-important husbands. The writer died an exile in Asia, having chronicled Portugal's discoveries in lyric poetry; his body was never found.

Perhaps even more exuberant than the church's interior are the octagonal **cloisters,** some of the most monumental in Europe. They are vaulted throughout in two stories lavishly decorated with fantastic sculpture. The church is 40 minutes from Praça do Comércio by trolley, 10 minutes by train from Cais do Sodré Station. (Open Tues.-Sun. 10am-6:30pm, in off-season Tues.-Sun. 10am-5pm. Admission 150$, students free.)

Next door to the abbey, the **Museu de Marinha** houses an unspectacular collection of maps and replicas. (Open Tues.-Sun. 10am-5pm. Admission 100$, students 50$, Wed. free.) Across the small, sunny square, the **Planetário C. Gulbenkian** features astronomy shows on Saturday and Sunday at 4pm and 5pm in both English and French. There are also shows on Wednesday at 11am, 3pm, and 4:15pm in Portuguese.

The **Torre de Belém,** built to protect the seaward entrance of the Portuguese capital, stands majestically in the waters of the Tagus. The six-corner turrets, copied from originals in India, and the Venetian-like balconies and windows demonstrate the deftness with which Manueline architects combined a variety of styles. Climb the narrow, winding steps to the top of the tower for gusts of wind and a memorable panoramic view. (Open Tues.-Sun. 10am-6:30pm, in off-season Tues. Sun. 10am-5pm. Admission 150$, students free.)

Before leaving Belém, consider visiting the **Museu Nacional dos Coches,** which displays a collection of 74 carriages ranging from the gilded baroque coaches that brought the Portuguese ambassador from Rome in 1716 to the simpler carriages of the late eighteenth century. (Open June-Sept. Tues.-Sun. 10am-6:30pm; Oct.-May Tues.-Sun. 10am-5pm. Admission 150$.) As an antidote to the extravagance of the rich, stop at the **Museu de Arte Popular,** where folk art is displayed in a simple setting not unlike that of a big sales shop. (Open Tues.-Sun. 10am-12:30pm and 2-5pm. Admission 100$.) The **Palácio Nacional da Ajuda** is just a short bus ride away in the hills overlooking Belém. A royal palace constructed in 1802, its 54 rooms indulge in an opulent decadence that is truly astonishing, particularly in juxtaposition to the impoverished neighborhood. The palace is now used by the Prime Minister to entertain visiting dignitaries. (Open Tues.-Sun. 10am-5pm. Admission 85$.) Trolley #18 ("Ajuda") stops behind the palace and will take you back into town.

Entertainment

You can find a complete listing of concerts, movies, plays, exhibits, and bullfights in the newspaper *Sete;* buy it at any kiosk, or thumb through the copy kept at the desk in the Turismo. The **Teatro Nacional de Maria II,** at Praça Dom Pedro IV (tel. 32 37 46), stages performances of the most important classical Portuguese and foreign plays. (Tickets 300-2000$, 50% student discount.) Every night in June and less frequently during the rest of the summer, there are **folk concerts** and **dance performances** in the Congress Palace of Estoril. The Gulbenkian Foundation also sponsors classical and jazz concerts year-round. The opera season begins in late September and lasts through the middle of June with performances held at the **Teatro São Carlos,** Rua Serpa Pinto (tel. 36 86 64), the largest theater in Lisbon.

Fado

Symbolically named for "fate," *fado* are nostalgic ballads wailed to the accompaniment of a soulful guitar. These melodramatic tales of lost loves and faded glory are the trademark of the capital. Hauntingly moving, the songs alternately lull their listeners into silence and rouse them to slightly drunken chorusing. There is no night off for *fado*—something's always bound to be open. The **Bairro Alto** is usually the place to go for this. A popular if somewhat expensive *casa do fado* is **Arcadas do Faia,** Rua da Baroca, 54 (cover 1300$). The shows here often draw big crowds, so it's best to book in advance (tel. 32 67 42 or call the municipal tourist office). **Patio das Cantigas,** Rua São Caetano, 27, charges a cover of about 1000$. Outside the Bairro Alto in Madregoa, the **Sr. Vinho,** Rua do Meio a Lapa, 18, has some of the best *fado* in Lisbon (cover 1000$). Back in the Bairro Alto, **A Transmontana,** Rua Diario de Noticias, 139-141, has a seductive atmosphere complete with red-glowing lanterns. Try the *frango a angolana,* chicken sauteed in a spicy sauce. (Cover 1000$. Optional dinner from 800$.) You can hear more *fado* outside the Bairro Alto in the Alfama, but these houses are relatively new and have been created mostly for tourists. Try the **Parreirinha da Alfama** on Beco do Espírito Santo (tel. 86 82 09). Be careful in the Alfama after dark. Most *fado* starts around 9:30pm, but gets much better after 11:30pm once the tour groups begin to leave. The evening entertainment usually lasts into the early morning.

Nightlife

What nightlife? There is little in Lisbon. The capital, like most cities in Portugal, goes to bed by 10 or 11pm. Lisbon's handful of discos are mostly for members only, exclusive watering holes where Libson's *haut monde* go to pat each other on the back; this usually means no foreigners.

If an irrepressible case of dance fever strikes, your best shot is **Blue Ghost,** Rua Andrade Corvo, 27B (tel. 53 63 66), across from the youth hostel. The place opens as a pub at 5pm; the disco starts rocking at around 11pm with computerized light effects and a giant TV screen. Before you jump in line, be aware that entry is not guaranteed. The doorman has a habit of letting in "friends" and may charge you a ridiculous sum. For a fine gay disco with bar, try **Memorial,** Rua Gustavo de Matos Sequeira, 42A (tel. 66 88 91), in the Bairro Alto 2 blocks south of Rua da Escola Politécnica. The lights and Euro-dance music are in full tilt from 10pm to 4am, but the place doesn't get moving until after midnight. The 600$ cover charge includes one drink.

Lisbon's cafes generally close before midnight. For people-watching, try the **Pasteleria Suiça,** on the eastern side of the Rossio, a boisterous gathering place mobbed until closing at 11:45pm. Across the square, **Café Nicola,** famous as a meeting place for nineteenth-century Portuguese writers, has an Old World atmosphere. Likewise for **A Brasileira,** on Rua Garrett, which attracts a more bohemian crowd. A Brasileira is in a commercial district and closes at 9pm, so plan on coming here in the late afternoon or early evening.

Fairs

In May and June there is a three-week **book fair** in Parque Eduardo VII. In June, the **International Fair of Lisbon (FIL)** is held in Alcântara, while in July and August the **Cascais Sea Fair** and the **Estoril Handicrafts Fair** take place near the casino. If you buy, bargaining is the name of the game, and even if you don't, just looking is fun and the food is cheap. Don't miss the *fritadas* (Portuguese doughnuts) or the freshly baked bread from the 3-meter-square Portuguese oven.

For enthusiasts of second-hand goods, the **Feira da Ladra** (flea market) is held Tuesday and Saturday morning at Campo de Santa Clara (take bus #12 or trolley #28). The **Mercado Ribeira,** an open-air market just outside Cais do Sodre station, always seems festive. This is the place to buy "Sun of a beach" T-shirts and heavy fishing sweaters, as well as fresh fruit and cheap food. (Open Mon.-Sat. until 2pm.)

The **Feira Popular** is Lisbon's amusement park. Filled with Portuguese of all ages, this throwback to the '50s is open May through September nightly until 1am. So many *caracois* (snails) get consumed with beer here that you'll begin to think they're the Portuguese version of the pretzel. Try the *sardinhas assadas* (grilled sardines). Take the metro to Entre Campos—but remember that it stops running at 1am. (Admission to park 75$, rides about 50$.)

Near Lisbon

North of Lisbon, the town of Sintra is a delightful base from which to explore such localities as Mafra, Queluz, and the beach towns of Cascais and Estoril.

The **Serra da Arrábida** is a small mountainous area on the Setúbal Peninsula due south of Lisbon. With mountain scenery, sparkling beaches sheltered by white limestone hills, and a combination of small towns and countryside, this region has become a popular escape for urban Portuguese. The seaside village of Sesimbra is an important fishing center, while the larger city of Setúbal thrives on cement, salt, and shipbuilding. Farther south begin the sheltered beaches and lovely fishing villages of the **Costa Azul.**

Sintra

After Lord Byron dubbed it "glorious Eden" and sang its praises in his autobiographical poem *Childe Harold,* Sintra became a must for nineteenth-century English travelers taking the grand tour. Today, Sintra still retains the air of a fairytale city. Bordered by a thick magical forest and punctuated with assorted architectural fantasies, Sintra makes a delightful daytrip from Lisbon. Better yet, stay the night and enjoy the eccentric streets and cool climate. The best time to go is when the weather is clear—from one of Sintra's castles you can see across the plain to where the Tagus opens to the sea. Unfortunately, ocean mists often obscure the view.

Orientation and Practical Information

Sintra is connected by train to Lisbon (every 15 min., ½ hr., 105$). From the train station, it's a pleasant 10-minute walk to the town center.

Tourist Office: Praça da República (tel. 923 11 57), in the same building as the regional museum. Paintings on the ground floor and archeological exhibits on the upper floor. Friendly staff. Good map. Open Mon.-Fri. 9am-12:30pm and 2-5:30pm, Sat.-Sun. 9am-8pm.

Post Office: Across from Turismo (tel. 923 00 17). Open Mon.-Fri. 9am-noon and 2-6pm. **Postal Code:** 2710.

Train Station: Estação de Caminhos de Ferro, Avda. Dr. Miguel Bombarda (tel. 326 05), at the northern end of the city. To Lisbon (every 15 min, 105$). To Obidos, Figueira da Foz, and the northern beaches change trains at Cacém. No trains to Estoril or Cascais.

Bus Station: Rodoviária Nacional, across the street from the train station. To Cascais (12 per day, 250$) and Estoril (19 per day, 170$). **Mafrense** buses (green and white) depart from stops to the right of the train station as you exit. To Mafra (13 per day, 180$), with connections to points north.

Hospital: Largo Rainha Doña Amélia (tel. 923 34 00).

Police: Largo Dr. Virgilio Horta (tel. 923 07 61). **Emergency,** Tel. 115.

Accommodations and Camping

Pensão Adelaide, Rue Guilherme Gomes Fernandes, 11 (tel. 923 08 73). Turn left as you leave the train station and walk to the yellow *camara*. The *pensão* is around the corner to the left. Decent rooms and amiable manager. Singles and doubles 1500$, doubles with bath 2000$.

Pensão Nova Sintra, Largo Afonso d'Albuquerque, 25 (tel. 923 02 20), facing the square east of the train station. Charming terrace, clean rooms—some with stupendous views of the *castelo.* Singles 1700$. Doubles 2500$. Breakfast included.

Hotel Central, Largo da Rainha Doña Amélia (tel. 923 00 63), facing the Royal Palace. Treat yourself; this place is worth it. You will feel like a nineteenth-century hero here. Clean and wonderful rooms. Singles 4100$, with bath 4500$. Doubles 5400$, with bath 5700$.

The best camping facilities are at the nearby beach towns of **Azenhas do Mar** and **Praia das Maçãs,** both accessible by bus from town. (100$ per person, per tent, and per car.) **Camping Capuchos,** 10km southwest, offers primitive facilities (50$ per person, 50$ per tent).

Food

Restaurante Alcobaça, Rua das Padarias, 9 (tel. 923 16 51), on a street running uphill from the square in front of the tourist office. Best good-food-to-price ratio in expensive Sintra. Try scrumptious grilled swordfish (480$). Open daily 9am-midnight.

Casa Piriquita, Rua das Padarias, 5 (tel. 923 06 26). Wonderful bakery and cafeteria. Open Thurs.-Tues. 9am-noon.

Casa da Avó, Rua Monserrate, 44 (tel. 923 12 80), near the fire station. Cheaper entrees and fewer tourists than most local restaurants. Pork chops with fries and salad 475$. Open Mon.-Sat. 11am-11pm.

Sights

Between Sintra's train station and the town center stands a storybook village hall behind which rises the incoherent but fantastic mass of the **Paço Real** or **Palácio Nacional.** A royal country home since medieval times, it was built partly in Moorish and partly in Manueline style on the foundations of an early Moorish castle. Though not much to look at from the outside—its two huge conical chimneys give the look of a cement factory, the palace has a stunning interior decorated with the freshness of Moorish influence. Note the fabulous ivory pagoda in the exquisite Chinese room. Also impressive is the **Hall of Magpies.** Legend has it that Dom João I was surprised by his wife as he kissed one of the ladies of the court. Although he claimed that it was merely a gesture of friendship, the word got around among the other ladies of the court. To "punish" them, the king painted the entire ceiling with magpies in a geometric pattern. The bird motif is echoed in the **Hall of Swans,** the banquet hall where the ceiling is decorated with 27 swans, each in a different pose. (Open Thurs.-Tues. 10am-5pm. Tickets sold 10am-4:30pm. Admission 150$, students free.)

After the palace tour (1 hr.), you can begin the 3-kilometer ascent to the Castelo dos Mouros (Moorish castle) and the Palácio da Pena, which crowns one of the highest peaks in the Sintra range. Outside the palace, taxis (round-trip 1500$) and buses (May-Sept. daily at 10:45am, 3pm, and 4pm; one way 90$) will whisk you there and back. However, the quintessential forest wonderland of Sintra is best appreciated on foot. Before climbing, consider buying some food at the local market in the small square behind the buildings facing the palace. (Enter through Calçada do Pelourinho.)

Two roads ascend to the palace. The wider roadway that skirts the Parque das Merandas is longer and scenically less interesting. Instead, walk up Rua Monserrate and take the first right (signs point to Monserrate and Seteais); hang a left very shortly thereafter on Calçada dos Clérigos. Continue climbing a short distance past the small twelfth-century Santa Maria church until you see a sign for the **Castelo dos Mouros.** From here, follow the trail upwards through the dense forest. The *castelo,* built by the Moors in the seventh and eighth centuries, offers a wide panorama of the surrounding countryside with a particularly fine view from the tower. Returning to the fork in the forest path, take a right turn and walk along (10 min.) until the path exits onto a roadway where you can either continue the climb to the palace (10 min.) or make a slight detour down the road to a small park so lush it looks like a tropical rainforest.

The **Palácio da Pena** was built in the 1840s by Prince Ferdinand, the German-born consort of the queen, on the site of a seventeenth-century convent. No doubt nostalgic for his country, the prince commissioned an obscure German architect to design a palace that would combine the aesthetic heritages of both his homeland and his adopted country. The result is pure fantasy: a Bavarian castle embellished with Arab minarets, Gothic turrets, Manueline windows, and a Renaissance dome. The rooms inside contain the usual assortment of royal Portuguese, Indo-Portuguese, and Sino-Portuguese furnishings; they're definitely worth seeing if only for the cloister and chapel, the only remains of the original convent. (Open Tues.-Sun. 10am-5pm. Admission 200$, with ISIC free.)

To get back to town, take the narrow road straight down. You may want to make a 15-minute detour by climbing up a trail to your right along this road (look for a sign marked "Sta. Eúfemia"). The trail will lead you past a ruined convent up to a **chapel** built on a ridge to mark the miraculous appearance of St. Eúfemia in the eighteenth century. The view from here is incredible (Lisbon, the Río Tejo, Cascais, and the coastline are easily visible), but an even more panoramic scene can be enjoyed by continuing along the path to the **Cruz Alta,** a stone cross built on a rocky peak 520m above sea level. The wind here is indecently strong, so watch your hats and skirts. Returning to the road, continue down and visit the lovely **Igreja de São Pedro,** which preserves seventeenth-century *azulejos* of scenes from the Bible. From there, Rua do Trindade leads past a small convent and then rejoins the road you came up on.

Cabo da Roca, 11km from Sintra, the westernmost point on the continent, has spectacular views of the ocean crashing into the cliffs. The cape is accessible by a bus from Sintra and a 3-kilometer hike, or a bus from Cascais. On Sunday, the cape is mobbed.

Mafra and Queluz

In a country famous for its modest charms, **Mafra** comes as a complete surprise. An immense building whose facade alone is 260m long, it houses a hospital, a palace, a royal library, and a church of cathedral-sized proportions all under one roof. The building is so large that it took 50,000 workers 13 years (1713-1726) to complete its 2000 rooms.

Although modeled after Spain's El Escorial, Mafra's construction gave rise to the Mafra school, named after the many sculptors who worked on its embellishments. Dom João V, the king who ordered Mafra built in fulfillment of a vow, claimed to have said to the workers: "It will be enough for you to say you have worked in the building of Mafra to receive the reply, 'Here then, is a great artist.'"

The magnificent baroque **church** showcases elegant belfries and a sumptuous dome that speak of Bernini's unexecuted plan for St. Peter's in Rome. The church's interior is one of Portugal's finest, superbly proportioned and richly decorated with colorful marble, bas-reliefs, and statues in Carrara marble. The church-like **hospital,** where the rooms are arranged like side-chapels so patients can hear Mass, is a bizarre sight. (Note the slots placed between boards of the beds to make a night's sleep easier on the spinal cord.) The **trophy room,** furnished from chandeliers to chairs with the antlers and skins of stags, is one of the more macabre aspects of the tour. Vegetarians and ecologists may want to concentrate instead on the tricky use of fake painted doors and ceilings, where the perspective changes to create a mirror image.

There are buses to Mafra from Lisbon's Largo Martim Moniz (1½ hr.), Lisbon's Rossio Station (1½ hr.), and Sintra (1 hr.).

Queluz, 13km west of Lisbon, is famous for its **royal palace,** built between 1758 and 1794 as the residence for Queen Maria I (1734-1816). Although not quite the Portuguese Versailles, as many local residents claim, the building has a certain intimate charm that, along with its delightful gardens, makes a short daytrip worthwhile. (Open Wed.-Mon. 10am-5pm. Admission 125$.) Frequent trains leave from Lisbon's Rossio Station.

Estoril and Cascais

The reputations of these two towns as playgrounds for the rich and famous shouldn't deter you from spending a pleasant day at one of the area's many beaches. Though both Estoril and Cascais host their share of luxury hotels, their shorefronts in no way resemble the overbuilt circuses of Italy's Adriatic coast or Spain's Costa del Sol. Turn-of-the-century villas and tropical gardens still prevail in these pleasure havens only a half-hour west of Lisbon by train. (From Caís do Sodre Station 125$ and 150$ respectively.)

There's not much to do in **Estoril** except soak up the sun and spend money. The former activity can be easily pursued on the town **beach** or by strolling along the flowered paths of the **Parque do Estoril,** a magnificent public garden immediately visible from the train station. Kiss the money *Let's Go* has helped you save goodbye at Estoril's famous **casino,** reputedly the largest and most luxurious in Europe. The glass and marble game-palace stands just above the park and contains a restaurant, bars, a cinema, and a room full of one-armed bandits. Minimum bets in the main gambling room are 1000$. (Open daily 3pm-3am.)

If you really must spend the night here and forgo the cheaper *pensões* of Lisbon or the accommodations at the nearby Catalazete youth hostel, try **Pensão Costa,** Rua de Olivença, 2 (tel. 268 16 99; doubles 2600$), or **Pensão Maryluz,** Rua Maestro Lacerda, 13 (tel. 268 27 40; doubles 2500$). The **Turismo** on Arcadas do Parque (tel. 268 01 13), across from the train station, is helpful. (Open Mon.-Fri. 9am-8pm, Sat. 10am-6pm.) Between Estorial and Cascais is **Pensão Londres,** Avda. Gausto Figueiredo, 7 (tel. 268 15 41; singles 1800$, doubles 2200$).

Cascais is the more interesting of the two towns. The **Palace of the Court of Castro Guimarães,** set in the city's lush municipal garden, is an exotic setting for its fine collection of seventeenth-century Portuguese and Indo-Portuguese silver and furniture. Nearby, the small Manueline **Igreja da Assunção** boasts walls decorated with vibrant eighteenth-century *azulejos.* Stroll along Antiga Rua Direita, a few blocks inland from the waterfront.

Pensão le Biarritz (tel. 28 22 16) is relatively inexpensive but lies a long way up Avda. do Ultramar. From the train station, walk up Estrada Marginal to Avda. 25 de Abril; follow that road up to Avda. do Ultramar, then turn right. (Doubles 2400$. Breakfast included.) Turning left on Avda. do Ultramar will lead you to the more expensive but charming **Pensão Residêncial Casa Lena** at #389 (tel. 286 87 43; doubles with bath 4000$; breakfast included). The **Turismo** (tel. 286 82 04), in the Camara Municipal (town hall) on Praça de 5 de Octubre (a large square by the beach), may be able to help you find other lodgings.

Cascais is known for its seafood, but the **Jardim dos Frangos,** Estrada Marginal, 66 (tel. 28 06 75), serves up excellent barbecued chicken. Ask for *frango no churrasco com manteiga e piri-piri* (whole chicken with butter and hot sauce, 480$). Take the meal with you and eat it in the nearby **Alameda,** a small park. Slightly more formal meals can be enjoyed at the local favorite **Restaurante Pereira,** Rua Bela Vista, 30 (tel. 28 12 15), an uphill walk from the Alameda. (Open Fri.-Wed. noon-3pm and 7:30-10pm.)

About a kilometer west of town on the shore lies the **Boca do Inferno** (Jaws of Hell), a huge mouth carved in the rock by the incessant work of Atlantic waves. Unfortunately, the site is swamped with tourists. Relatively untouched, however, is the **Praia do Guincho,** an immense stretch of sandy beach that lies 8km to the west. Its dangerous undertow and cold water make it less than ideal for a swim, but it's good for a view of **Cabo da Roca.** Here, the Serra de Sintra ends abruptly in a sheer cliff 150m above the sea. A little farther from the Praia do Guincho, at a bend in the road flanked by small restaurants, a road leads to the **Praia do Abano,** well worth the 2-kilometer walk. Buses to Praia do Guincho leave from the station in Cascais hourly. A bus leaves for Cabo da Roca from in front of the Cascais train station; bus service is also available from Sintra.

Costa Azul (Blue Coast)

The Costa Azul is the seaside stretch between Lisbon and the Algarve. Tourists are scarcer here, and the traditional maritime lifestyle has been preserved remarkably well. Sandwiched between Portugal's two hot spots, the Costa Azul possesses neither the cosmopolitan sophistication of the capital nor the "sunburn-or-bust" lifestyle of the southern resorts. Instead, a certain authenticity permeates the scenic storybook landscape. Setúbal and Sesimbra in the north are both conveniently located near Lisbon, while the southerly city of Sines is an easy stopover on the way to or from the Algarve by bus or train.

Setúbal

Setúbal (pronounced with a heavy accent on the second syllable) is Portugal's third largest urban center after Lisbon and Oporto. On the edge of the **Serra de Arrábida National Park,** Setúbal has long depended on a strong fishing industry and on the sale of salt extracted from the marshes of the Sago River. Though not an attractive city, Setúbal's interesting churches and expanse of beach make either a daytrip or a stopover from Lisbon worthwhile.

The city's most famous building is the **Convento de Jesus,** a fantastic Manueline structure with twisted, spiraling columns and rope-like ribs. Their rhythmic motion, suggestive of the sea, gives the church a bizarre quality unique in Western architecture. Adjoining the church, the **Museu da Cidade** contains works by the brilliant sixteenth-century Portuguese painter known as the Master of Setúbal. (Open Tues.-Sun. 9am-12:30pm and 2-5pm. Admission 50$, students free.)

To sweeten your morning of sight-seeing, take one of the many ferries that cross the bay (actually the estuary of the Sado River) to the **Tróia Peninsula.** Though the northern end is now being developed into an ugly resort village, the southern portion offers miles of deserted beach lined with sand dunes and pine trees. Take the tractor trolley at the ferry terminal to the campground; from here you can venture south. (Ferry 30$ one way.)

Although Setúbal hosts a great many tourists (mostly Portuguese), it has very few *pensões.* Most people stay in the overcrowded **camping** area at the edge of town. The tourist office has a list of rooms in private homes that may be your best alternative. The cheapest *pensão* in town is **Residência Alentejana,** Avda. Luisa Todi, 124 (tel. 213 98), near the water and across from a military barracks. (Doubles around 1200$.) More central and expensive is **Residência Bom Regresso,** Praça do Bocage, 48. Eat at one of the restaurants by the docks or in the **Praça de Bocage.** Here, **Restaurante Bocage** has excellent entrees for about 600$. (Open Wed.-Mon. 11am-4pm and 7-11pm.)

If you're in need of advice, go to **Turismo** (regional office), at Largo do Corpo Santo (tel. 242 84). The **municipal office,** at Praça do Bocage (tel. 221 05), has an accommodations service. The **post office** is also at Praça do Bocage. (Open Mon.-Fri. 9am-noon and 2-6pm.) The **postal code** is 2900. The **bus station** is at Praça de Espanha, near Turismo. Buses for Lisbon leave every half-hour. The **telephone code** is 065.

Eight kilometers north of Setúbal is the hilltop town of **Palmela.** Its steep, cobbled streets lined with whitewashed houses are dominated by a large **castle** (open until 7pm), which commands a tremendous view extending from the city of Setúbal to the Troia Peninsula. Originally constructed by the Moors in the eighth century, the castle was rebuilt in 1172 for Portugal's first king, Dom Afonso Henriques. Buses run between Palmela and Setúbal every 20 minutes.

Sesimbra, Cabo Espichel, and Costa da Caparica

Residents of Lisbon and Setúbal often come to **Sesimbra** on a Sunday drive. This fishing village, equidistant from the two cities, is graced with a beach of transparent blue waters. Unfortunately, the stone walkway above is smelly and unpleasant. Recent construction of modern high-rises bodes ill for this area.

Camping is west of the center, at **Forte do Cavalo.** (Open Jan.-Oct.) Many inexpensive restaurants line Avda. da Liberdade. **Turismo** (tel. 223 19 26) is near the beach, across from the fortress. The **post office** is at Rua Cândido dos Reis, 61. The **bus station** is in the town center at Avda. da Liberdade, 21.

From Sesimbra you can take a bus (20 min., 100$) or hitchhike (there's a lot of local tourist traffic on weekends) to **Cabo Espichel,** where the southwestern corner of the Setúbal Peninsula comes to a point. The road passes by farm houses, fruit trees, and open fields. Some of the best beaches on the peninsula are north of Espichel: Try long, pristine **Meco Beach** at the base of an ominous cliff. (You may want to use the rickety stairs.) The beach is half-nudist. Beware at all times of the powerful undertow.

Just south of Lisbon across the Tagus River, **Costa da Caparica** offers a broad beach enclosed by dunes and wooded hills extending 22km down the coast to the cape. About a dozen different campsites dot the peninsular stretch. **Camping Orbitur** is on the main beach just outside the city. (Tel. 240 06 61. 286$ per person, 220$ per tent, 260$ per car. Hot showers 90$.) However, as with the beaches, locations farther south typically prove more peaceful.

Area beaches are extremely crowded on weekends, but a narrow gauge railway brings the more remote sections within reach. For nude bathing, get off at stop 19; the best time to go is on weekdays. Buses leave from Praça de Espanha (near the Palhava metro station) in Lisbon. On Saturday and Sunday lines start forming as early as 7:30am, and the wait may last three or four hours. You can also get there by taking the boat to Cacilhas from Praça do Comércio and taking a bus from there.

Sines

Situated halfway between Lisbon and Lagos, Sines is the historical and economic center of the southern Costa Azul. The city is best known as the birthplace of Portuguese navigator Vasco da Gama, who sailed around the Cape of Good Hope and "discovered" the Indian Ocean. A sign that the Age of Sail lies far in the past, however, is the presence of an oil refinery on the southern edge of town. Fortunately, this and other landmarks of progress since Vasco da Gama's day haven't spoiled the small fisherman's-village character of Sines.

Built upon a medieval foundation, the **castle** dominates the center of Sines and contains the **Paço dos Alcaides-mores** (Palace of the Governor), the very building where the city's famous son was born. While exploring the interior of the castle, taxidermy connoisseurs should visit the **Museu de História Natural,** which boasts a small but varied collection of stuffed animals (not the teddy bear kind). (Open daily 9am-noon and 3-5pm. Free.)

One of the cheapest places to stay in Sines is **Pensão Beira Mar,** Rua Luís de Camões, 70 (tel. 623 58), in the center of town. The large rooms surround a pleasant courtyard. (Singles 700$, doubles 1500$. Lukewarm showers.) From the bus station, follow the alleyway on your far right past the Centro Ciclista Sineénse and then take your first left. **Municipal camping** (tel. 621 44) is on the outskirts of town. (105$ per person, 90-120$ per tent, 150$ per car. Showers 40$.) Run by a warm father and son duo from China, **Dragão Dourado,** Largo Afonso de Albuquereque, 1 (tel. 63 30 56), next to the bus station, serves inexpensive Chinese dishes (most entrees around 450$). Fried noodles with shrimp (320$) will satisfy both your appetite and your palate. (Open daily noon-3pm and 7-11pm.)

The **tourist office** (tel. 63 40 12), with its friendly English-speaking staff, can provide you with detailed information for catching some serious rays in Sines and its nearby beaches. (Open Mon.-Fri. 9am-7pm, Sat. 9am-12:30pm and 2-5:30pm.) The **bus station** is near the town center in the Largo Afonso de Albuquerque. Six buses per day connect Sines to Lisbon (700$). To reach Turismo, turn left and walk 1 block until you come to the long Avda. Gen. Humberto Delgado. Make another left and continue up the avenue until you come to the modern blue and white **mercado** (market) building. The **train station** is 3 blocks northeast of the bus station on Avda. Gen. Humberto Delgado. Just turn right and walk up the avenue to Turismo. The **post office** (tel. 634 21) is on Praça Tomás Ribeiro in the old town (open Mon.-Fri. 8:30am-6pm); the **postal code** is 7520. **Telephones** are located in the post office.

Near Sines: Porto Covo

White-sand beaches line the coast from Sines all the way down to **Porto Covo,** a comfortably small resort noted for its heavy surf and colored cliffs. Just south of the fishing village is **Praia da Ilha.** From the shores of this popular but isolated beach, you can see the remains of a seventeenth-century fortress on nearby Ilha do Pesseguiro. *Pensões* in Porto Covo tend to be expensive, so opt for a room in a private home (1000$) or the **campsite** (tel. 931 36; 180$ per person, 150-220$ per tent, 160$ per car) if you plan to stay overnight. Better yet, base yourself in Sines. Porto Covo is easily accessible by bus from Sines, (4 per day, 140$ round-trip), so daytrips are possible.

Algarve

The Algarve is as wonderful as everyone says. Despite encroaching high rises and an exponential increase in tourism, the Algarve remains unique in Iberia. Here you'll find clear skies all summer, a steady breeze to keep temperatures bearable, and 200km of perfect beaches with long open stretches to the east, rocky coves and red cliffs to the west, and fine gold sand and crystalline water everywhere. The locals celebrate folk festivals with a gusto that reflects their determination to preserve tradition.

As investors buy up the coastline, the skyline at Praia da Rocha is slowly coming to resemble that of Miami Beach, and toy villages for the rich such as those around Vilamoura just west of Faro are sprouting like weeds. The rich have also brought their prices to the larger resorts, though they are by no means beyond the reach of budget travelers.

The tourist traffic, of course, has not spoiled everything. Especially to the west, you can still find your own secluded sandy cove. Between the resorts, there are some smaller villages where hardly a foreign language is spoken and prices are well-suited to budget beach bums. Try the area between Lagos and Sagres (Salema and Burgau are possibilities), or head for Olhão or Tavira to the east. Reaching the more remote beaches is not difficult, since Rodoviária Nacional has local bus service just about everywhere you'd want to go, with convenient schedules and low prices. Summertime hitching is an excellent, cost-saving alternative. For longer hauls, the train is cheaper than the bus but also less convenient, since it runs inland, connecting only major coastal cities.

The food, especially fish, is generally delicious. As an alternative to *sardinha assada* (grilled sardines), try *caldeira,* a chowder of fish and shellfish, potatoes, and tomatoes, all flavored with onion and garlic; *cataplana,* a combination of clams, ham, and sausage, flavored with onions and paprika and cooked in a double pan; *lulas* (squid), often cooked in its own ink; *carne de porco a Alentejana,* pork marinated in wine and cooked with clams in a coriander sauce; and *robalo* (bass), *peixe espada,* or *anchova* (anchovy) cooked a hundred different ways. The local wines, especially white, are cheap, full-bodied, and robust; Cartaxo is an inexpensive, dependable label. Unfortunately, some—not all—establishments run by English-speaking expatriates tend to bring their prices along with them, with disastrous results for the budget traveler. Keep your eyes open.

If you're staying for a month or more, look into renting an apartment. Rates have skyrocketed, and a four-and-a-half room apartment may cost up to 120,000$, but a determined search should yield something that (when split 3 or 4 ways) will be considerably less expensive and more comfortable than a hotel. If you stay only a week or two, remember that hotels and *pensões* are usually filled during the peak months of July and August; if at all possible, make reservations. The best solution for those heading to the Algarve in peak season without reservations is the reasonably priced *quarto* (a room in a private house to rent for short periods). Such accommodations abound in this region. Ask at tourist offices or bars, and keep your eyes open for signs. You can take chances with the room-pushers at bus and train stations who meet incoming travelers during peak seasons in an effort to round up business. Many proprietors are housewives who offer clean, pleasant rooms, though you may not always have such luck.

Pick up a copy of *The Algarve News* at tourist offices for 30$ or the *Algarve Magazine* for 100$. Both run articles on trendy clubs, local festivals, special events, nude beaches, and other fun things to see and do. A word about nude beaches: Topless nudism is the fashion in the Algarve, but bottomless (especially for women) is illegal, offensive to the locals, and can result in police arrest. Some get away with it on remote beaches.

In case of **emergency,** dial 115. Hospitals at Faro, Lagos, and Portimão have 24-hour emergency service.

Sagres

For perhaps the most mellow, relaxing time you'll have in the Algarve, head for beautiful Sagres in the extreme southwestern corner of Portugal. The spectacular sights here are works of nature; man's limited presence has preserved this sanctuary of incredible beauty in a region overwhelmed by beach-resort glitter. In a rare shift in the balance of power, good-natured backpackers far outnumber tour-bus visitors who swarm the fortress and then leave after claiming their prize—personalized certificates (no kidding!). If curiosity or dementia impels you, take a look at one in the tourist office.

Powerful Atlantic winds bring cooler temperatures and large rolling waves to Sagres's spectacular coastline. Leaving behind the gardens and whitewashed houses at the edge of the village, you'll pass through a field of windblown cactus and desert flowers. Suddenly, you'll reach the steep edge of a seemingly endless shelf of land supported by a sheer rock wall that towers 70m above the pounding waves of the Atlantic.

The approach to the **fortaleza** (fortress), built by Prince Henry the Navigator on the promontory, is awe-inspiring. From this cliff-top outpost the Prince formulated and executed his daring plan to chart the unknown. Within the walls, a round **windrose** (mariner's compass) 43m in diameter dominates the cobbled yard. The structure itself is made from stones and dates back to the Age of Discovery.

Once the school of navigation where Vasco da Gama, Magellan, Diaz, and Cabral studied, the fortress now houses the well-stocked **tourist office.** (Tel. 641 25. Open daily 9:30am-7:30pm; in winter daily 9:30am-6:30pm.) Here, too, is the **IYHF youth**

hostel (tel. 641 29), the center of activity for backpackers in the Algarve. The hostel's thriving social scene is well known. In fact, it may be Sagres' only social scene. (Office open daily 9am-noon 6-7pm and 8-11pm. 3-night max. stay during July-Aug. Members only, 900$. Breakfast and dinner included.)

Many windows display signs for **private rooms** in three or four languages, and prices range from 1000-1300$ for singles and doubles, and from 1300-1600$ for triples. Nevertheless, if you are an experienced haggler, rooms can be rented for as little as 500$ per night. Remember to do your best to look poor. The police tend to hassle anyone who attempts illegal camping on the beach or in the fields.

During the day, the youth hostel crowd hangs out at **Café Conchinha.** When the cafe closes at 8pm, the hostel crowd crosses the street to quaff a few at **A Lanterna,** a lively German-run restaurant bar always filled with young travelers. Another popular nightspot is **The Last Chance Saloon,** a far-west imitation overlooking the beach. English dance tunes are blasted through the speakers and the small bar gets crowded by curfew time.

Restaurante-Bar Atlántico, down the main street, is the best of the bargain restaurants in town. Try the generous portions of grilled swordfish (500$). **O Dromedário,** on the same street, serves delicious fruit shakes (160$), sandwiches, and original wholemeal pizzas (460$). Bicycles and mopeds can be rented from the GALP station at the roundabout. (Bicycles 150$ per hr., 700$ per day; mopeds 250$ per hr., 1300$ per day.) The **post office** (open Mon.-Fri. 9am-12:30pm and 2:30-6pm) and the **market** are down the street from the kiosk; turn left at Rua do Correio.

Many mercifully uncrowded beaches line the peninsula, but the two main beaches are close to Sagres. The most popular spot, **Mareta,** lies at the bottom of the road from the kiosk; rock formations jut far out into the ocean on both sides of this sandy crescent. **Tonel** is along the road to the cape. Despite its more isolated location, it's still popular. (In Sagres, this means there are about a dozen people.) You'll miss the gaudy Bermuda shorts of tourists if you visit during the afternoon when crowds attack the fortress.

At **Salema** and **Burgau,** between Lagos and Sagres, more good beaches await you. Both are served by direct bus from Lagos; there are several convenient buses per day between Lagos and Sagres. The trip takes about an hour and costs 260$. For hitching out of Sagres, the best spot from the GALP gas station near the entrance to town.

Near Sagres: Cabo de São Vincente and the Western Coast

Crowning the southwestern tip of continental Europe, **Cabo de São Vicente** (Cape St. Vincent) was once revered as *o fim do mundo* (the end of the world). To sail beyond the visible expanse of ocean, it was believed, was to plunge over the edge into nothingness. A more dramatic setting for the edge of the world could not have been created. Pools of frothing white foam churn below the cliffs while the ocean relentlessly collides with craggy headlands hundreds of feet down. Standing at the tip of the cape, the second most powerful **lighthouse** in Europe projects its beam 60 miles out to sea. (Ask at the gate for a tour.)

No buses connect the cape with Sagres. Nevertheless, transportation is really not a problem. Hiking the 6km along a paved road from Sagres takes only about an hour, and the walk is the best way to absorb the surrounding beauty. Another popular way to see the cape is by renting a bicycle or a moped (see Sagres). If you've been struck by an attack of lazy bones, you can always hitch a ride, though you'll miss several of Sagres's finest, secluded beaches along the way.

Halfway down the stretch of road between Sagres and the cape, **Beliche,** a seventeenth-century fortress with a dinky chapel, affords an excellent view of the coastline. To the right of the entrance, iron handbars lead the way down the rocky cove where fishermen board their small boats.

One of the Algarve's better-kept secrets remains the enormous, windblown crescent of sand at **Carrapateira,** 16km to the north of Sagres, where you can camp in the summer. To get here, take the road (turn-off at Vila do Bispo) or the bus for Aljezur to the small village of Carrapateira, and proceed 1km down the small dirt road to the coast. At the top of the road, marking the turn-off, you'll come to **Restaurant Corbrita,** where a feast of freshly caught fish grilled on an open-air barbeque is served. Try the *robalo* (bass) or *anchova.* Entree prices range from 300-650$.

A more distant yet equally well-kept secret is **Odeceixe,** 20km north of Carrapateira, which marks the northernmost beach in the Algarve. **Camping** is possible on the beach where the river meets the sea. Take the road by the edge of town at the bridge marked "camping"—it's a 4-kilometer hike. Hitching often works. Infrequent buses pass through town (1 per day each to Lagos and Sagres) and stop at the station across from the **post office,** Rua Estrada Nacional, 19. Rooms in the town center, **Largo Primero do Maio,** are well-advertised. (Doubles 800-925$.) The center also has many inexpensive restaurants. Try **Restaurant Pensão,** Rua do Rossio, 19.

Lagos

Lagos offers all the pleasures of a well-developed beach resort yet maintains a measure of local color that stems from its important fishing trade. Founded by the Romans as Lacobriga, it was renamed Zawaya by the Arabs and thrived under the Moors as the largest port between Portugal and North Africa. Evidence of the city's remarkable past is apparent in the remains of the Moorish fortifications that skirt the waterfront. During the Age of Discovery, Lagos shipyards built the caravels that traveled the globe, and it was from here that Gil Eanes set sail in 1434 for Cape Bojador, then the farthest known point on the west coast of Africa. In 1578, Lagos saw the departure of King Sebastião on his foolhardy and fatal Moroccan campaign. Capital of the Algarve for two centuries, the city soon became a key port in the slave trade. The decline that set in after the city was destroyed by the earthquake of 1755 has now been completely reversed by the swarms of European sun-worshipers who flock here every summer. The city's commercial center has been taken over by restaurants, bars, and hotels, but fortunately the historic center has been spared by encroaching cosmopolitanism. Narrow, cobble streets and dilapidated houses are reminders of the past. In spite of recent development, Lagos remains an agreeable city surrounded by some of the Algarve's most gorgeous beaches. The sheer cliffs of the western shore create secluded sandy coves connected by tunnels in the rock.

Orientation and Practical Information

Running along the length of the river, **Avenida dos Descobrimentos** carries traffic in and out of Lagos. Rua das Portas de Portugal is the gateway leading into **Praça Gil Eanes** and the town's glitzy tourist center. Most restaurants, accommodations, and services are centered around the *praça* and **Rua 25 de Abril.**

Tourist Office: Largo Marquez de Pombal (tel. 630 31), in the center of town, near Praça Gil Eanes, a 20-min. walk from the train station and a 15-min. walk from the bus station. Dispenses brochures with maps about Lagos and the entire Algarve region. Train and bus information also available. Open Mon. 9:30am-7pm, Tues.-Thurs. 9:30am-8pm, Fri. 9:30am-7pm, Sat. 9:30am-12:30pm and 2-5:30pm.

Post Office: Between Praça Gil Eanes and Avda. dos Descobrimentos, on Rua das Portas de Portugal (tel. 631 11). Always very busy. All services open Mon.-Fri. 8:30am-6pm. **Postal Code:** 8600.

Telephones: At the post office. **Telephone code:** 082.

Train Station: On the eastern edge of town across the river from the bus station. To reach the center, cross the bridge to the bus station, and follow the directions below. To Lisbon (5 per day, 1100-1450$), Vila Real de Santo Antónia via Faro and other coastal cities (11 per day, 700$), Evora (3 per day, 1000$), and Beja (3 per day, 700$).

Bus Station: Rodoviária Nacional, on the eastern edge of town. To reach the town center, follow the avenue by the water going west, then bear right on Rua des Portas de Portugal until you reach Praça Gil Eanes. To Lisbon (4 per day, 1125$), Portimão (10 per day, 180$), and Sagres (12 per day, 260$). Private companies also provide service.

Taxis: Tel. 624 69.

Laundromat: Lavandaria Luso-Britânica, Praça Gil Eanes, 11 (tel. 622 83). 4 kg washed for 460$, washed and dried for 840$. Open Mon.-Fri. 9am-1pm and 3-7pm, Sat. 9am-1pm.

Medical Emergency: Hospital, Rua do Castelo dos Governadores (tel. 630 34), next to Santa Maria Church.

Police: General Alberto Silva (tel. 629 30).

Accommodations and Camping

In the summertime, the *pensões* in Lagos are very expensive and usually full. Your best option is a room in a *casa particular* for 1000-1200$. For the most part, rooms are quite nice, and the spanking clean bathrooms have hot showers. You can try your negotiating skills with some of the housewives who wait at train and bus stations to offer rooms in their homes. Make sure the location is no more than 10-15 minutes from downtown. If you aren't approached with offers, ask for referrals at Turismo.

Os Reis, Rua Candido dos Reis, 54 (tel. 630 82), 1 block north of Rua 25 de Abril. No sign. Go up the stairs; it's the door on your right. The cheapest *pensão* rooms in Lagos. Very clean rooms with high ceilings. Small singles without windows 1300$, with windows and shower 1800$. Doubles 1800-2000$. If no one seems to be at home, go to the **Snack-Bar O Charco,** Rua 25 de Abril, 3 (tel. 630 87), a restaurant managed by the owner.

Residência Baia, Rua da Barroca, 70. Down Rua 25 de Abril and then left on Travessa da Senora da Graça. Cozy atmosphere with interesting furnishings. Primitive but clean private baths; common bath is the best. Some rooms with carpet. Great value for two people. All rooms 2000$.

Residência Marazul, Rua 25 de Abril, 13 (tel. 636 16), near Turismo. Quality establishment with elaborate wood interior. Immaculate, comfortable rooms, some with small terrace overlooking the street. Spotless baths. Access to luxurious glass lounge with wicker chairs. Great value off-season. June-Sept. singles 3300$, with bath 3850$. Doubles 5300$, with bath 5800$. Nov.-Mar. singles 1500$, with bath 1800$. Doubles 2000$, with bath 2500$. Prices higher during intermediate months.

Residencial Rubi Mar, Rua da Barroca, 70 (tel. 631 65), upstairs from Residência Baia. Run by Anglo-American couple. Beautifully decorated hallway and homey atmosphere. Airy, bright rooms are spanking white. Doubles 3000$, with private bath and balconies overlooking the ocean 4000$. Breakfast included.

Caravela Residencial, Rua 24 de Abril, 8 (tel. 633 61), on the main street. Musty rooms wrapped around a central courtyard. Hallways are dark and old. Singles 1900$. Doubles 2700$. Breakfast included.

Campgrounds near Lagos are crowded and expensive. The jam-packed **Parque de Campismo no Imulagos** (tel. 600 31 or 600 35) is in town. (495$ per person, 270$ per tent, 272.50$ per car.) At Praia Dona Ana, the more pleasant **Campo da Trinidade** (tel. 629 31) charges 160$ per person and per tent, and 150$ per car. (Showers 75$.) At the beautiful beach 4km west of Praia da Luz, the peaceful **Camping Valverde** (tel. 692 11) exacts 300$ per person, per tent, and per car; they charge 50$ for a shower.

Food

Most restaurants here cater to tourists, but some are still inexpensive. Look around **Rua Silva Lopes** or **Rua Soeiro da Costa.**

Restaurante A Capoeira, Rua 25 de Abril, 76. Lamb chops with mint sauce or steak and kidney pie (650$), comes with veggies and chips. Open Mon.-Sat. noon-3pm and 5-11pm.

Restaurante Ao Natural, Rua Silva Lopes, 29 (tel. 626 64). A new, Dutch-run, European-staffed veggie haven. Healthful foods that please the taste buds. Heavenly fruit cocktails, tasty entrees and appetizers. Try their sushi (495$) or mushroom quiche (450$). Fruit salad breakfast 195$. Tropical rooftop terrace with live music and bar. Open daily 10am-4pm and 6pm-midnight.

Costinho, Rua Soeiro da Costa, 6 (no phone). From Rua 25 de Abril, turn right at Jotta 13. A tiny, family-run, popular establishment that grills its fish outdoors. Most entrees 350-500$. Try the grilled sardines with salad (400$). Open Mon.-Sat. 11am-3pm and 6pm-midnight.

Restaurante-Bar Jutta 13, Rua 25 de Abril, 58 (tel. 623 19). Not the place to escape the tourist crowd, but the restaurant does serve regional dishes. Grilled sardines on charcoal with salad 400$. Tourist menu with Algarvean main dishes 700$. Open daily 10am-midnight.

Restaurante O João, Rua Silva Lopes, 15 (no phone). Dry atmosphere, but a decent variety of dishes, including grilled mackerel (500$). Open daily 10am-4pm and 6-midnight.

Sights and Entertainment

The statue marking the entrance to Lagos at **Praça Gil Eanes** resembles a pale northern tourist. In fact, it is a modern rendition (1973) of King Dom Sebastião, who inherited the throne as a child in 1557. The precarious reign of this dreamy and unfortunate king ended in 1578 when he set out from Lagos to conquer Morocco and never returned.

The 1755 earthquake destroyed many buildings in Lagos. The **Igreja de San António** still stands, however, and its wooden facade conceals an extraordinarily rich interior of gilded woodwork. The painted, vaulted ceiling has replaced one of framed paintings. See if you can spot the cow and dog in the upper balcony and the statue of the saint sporting a red sash worn by a British general in the Peninsula War. Adjoining the church, the **Museu Municipal** has a surprising variety of collections ranging from the usual costumes, weapons, and handicrafts to an odd collection of animal fetuses from the Algarve. (Both open Tues.-Sun. 9am-12:30pm and 2-5pm.) On either side of Praça da República, near the parish church Igreja de Santa Maria ou da Misericórdia, stands the **Antigo Mercado de Esravos,** the remains of Europe's first slave market.

The streets of Lagos are lively late into the evening. The area between Praça Gil Eanes and Praça Luís de Camões is filled with cafes. **Café Gil Eanes,** Praça Gil Eanes, 20, is especially popular. Every Saturday in the summer, posters all around the Algarve advertise a bullfight at Largo da Teira at 5:30pm, about a 15-minute walk from the town center. (Admission 2000$.)

The city's main attractions, naturally, are the crystal clear beaches surrounded by the ancient weathered cliffs. Follow Avda. dos Descobrimentos (the main waterside avenue) west until you reach a sign for **Praia de Pinhão.** Follow this to the shore and continue on the paths until you find a suitable cove. The rocks here afford tremendous views of the inlets and are great fun to climb. One of the loveliest spots is **Praia Dona Ana,** whose sculpted cliffs and grottoes are featured on at least half of all Algarvian postcards. The place is crawling with vendors and little kids during the summer. A motorboat leaves from here for a 45-minute grotto-viewing cruise (2000$, but up to 6 people can fit in 1 boat). Ask the captain to find you a secluded spot and pick you up in a few hours (watch out for rising tides, though).

Carvoeiro

An old fishing village, Carvoeiro has a tiny beach below spectacular cliffs, atop which sit small whitewashed villas. Overlooking the scene is a sunny *praça* filled with tables and chairs from nearby bars, where backpackers mingle with the local anglers. **Turismo,** on Largo da Praia (tel. 573 28) by the beach, can help you find a room, although the pickings are slim and expensive. (Open Mon.-Fri. 9am-8pm, Sat.-Sun. 9am-12:30pm and 2:30-5pm.) **Pensão Baselli** (tel. 571 59), on a terrace overlooking the beach, has only four doubles. (2500$. Large breakfast included.) **Le Mistral** (tel. 573 82), is about a seven-minute walk from the shore along the main road. (Doubles 2100$. Breakfast included.) Finding a room in a private house shouldn't be a problem; just ask in one of the many restaurants along the town's commercial street.

To reach Carvoeiro, take a bus to Lagoa from Portimão or Silves (100$), and then change for another bus to the beach. Service is infrequent, so consider taking a taxi from Lagoa (about 800$).

Silves

Originally known as Xelb, Silves was once the center of Moorish culture in Portugal. Its mosques outshone even those of Lisbon. Decline set in as silt closed up the river port, and whatever was left of the town was finished off by the 1755 earthquake. Though no longer "one of the most desolate and deserted places in Portugal" (as one nineteenth-century traveler described it), Silves is still a singularly cheerless place, hardly the attractive town depicted in its tourist brochures. You won't find any of the Algarve's glitz here; in fact you'll see quite the opposite. Aside from one or two streets in the center, the town is dominated by cobble streets and faded buildings with peeling paint. How Silves strikes you will depend on your mood; you may find its small-town earthiness refreshing.

An imposing **Moorish castle** dominates the town from its hilltop position. Huge castle cisterns, built by the Moors to store water during the endless sieges of the period, still supply the town. Below the castle stands a small city garden, a welcome addition of color to the drab old section of town. Nearby stands the town's other major landmark, the bulky **cathedral,** built on the foundations of an old mosque.

Silves is of most interest, however, for its famous **Festa de Cerveja** (Beer Festival) held every July for five consecutive evenings. Natives and tourists converge on the grounds of the Moorish castle to make merry and sample the different brands of Portuguese beer. Any tourist office can supply you with dates and times. The **Turismo** here is just up the steps from the town's main street, Rua Francisco Pablos, on Rua 25 de Abril, 26-28 (tel. 422 55). (Open Mon.-Fri. 9:30am-8pm, Sat.-Sun. 9:30am-12:30pm and 2-5:30pm; in off-season, Mon.-Fri. 9:30am-7pm, Sat.-Sun. 9:30am-12:30pm and 2-5:30pm.) Buses connect Sines with Portimão (170$) and Lagoa (100$). By the river, the **bus station** is on the main road running in and out of town, Rua da Cruz da Palmeira. To reach the tourist office, walk straight into town (perpendicular to the river) until you come to the stairs at the intersection of Rua Francisco Pablos and Rua Samora Barros. The city streets are windy (keep to your left), so don't hesitate to ask for directions. The **train station** is 2km from town and connected by bus (every ½-hr., 35$). The modern **post office,** Rua do Correio (tel. 421 11) is all the way down the street; **telephones** are inside. (Open Mon.-Fri. 9am-12:30pm and 2:30-6pm.)

Residencial Sousa, Rua Samoura Barros, 17 (tel. 425 02), a left turn at the bank before the stairs to Turismo, has grandiose rooms with ivory white walls and carpeting. Bathrooms are not quite up to the same standards as other aspects of this classy establishment, but they're clean. (Singles 1000-1500$, doubles 2000$; a bit more during the beer festival.) You'll enjoy the seafood dinner at **Marisqueira Central** across the street from the post office—try their *lulinhas* (squid) for 350$. On Rua Francisco Pablos, by the river, is the large, bustling **mercado** (market), open daily from 9am to 1pm.

Albufeira

As the largest seaside resort and tourist center of the region, Albufeira is often referred to as the St. Tropez of the Algarve. The comparison is apt: Like its French counterpart, it is overcrowded, overpriced, and overrated. But the beach here, however crowded, does have its merits. Everyone is hell-bent on relaxation. Come here to socialize, hang out in the bars, and enjoy the nightlife—less populated beaches and better prices can be found elsewhere in the Algarve.

The last holdout of the Moors in Southern Portugal, Albufeira has preserved and cultivated a heritage of graceful Moorish architecture still present in the old quarters of town. Especially noteworthy are the city's four churches: **Santana,** whose small dome decorated with tiny minarets has a Byzantine flavor; **São Sebastão,** which boasts an exquisite filigree doorway; **Misericórdia,** with its old Gothic portal; and **Matriz,** the town's municipal church, which bears a handsome barrel-vaulted interior.

Though the throngs of students who congregate here are gradually being priced out, Albufeira's fine beach, **Praia dos Barcos,** and rocky coves are still popular among younger crowds. The town's whitewashed homes sit on rugged yellow cliffs that overlook the coastline rendering a strange sense of seclusion and tranquility. The center of town—despite construction and commercialization—is undeniably cheerful. Local artisans vend crafts and souvenirs in the tropical park at **Largo Engenheiro Duarte-Pacheco.** Off to the side, there is an open-air fruit and vegetable **market.** Rua V de Outubro, 1 block away, is the main concourse; all essential services cluster here, near the tunnel blasted through the rocks to the beaches.

Accommodations at any price are almost impossible to find in the high season. Many places are booked solid in advance through travel agents. **Pensão Albufierense,** Rua da Liberdade, 18 (tel. 520 19), 1 block from the *largo* through Travessa V de Outubro, is a modern operation with a nicely decorated interior and comfortable rooms. Guests are permitted access to a great lounge area with TV. (July-Sept. singles 2000$, doubles 3500$; Oct.-June singles 1500$, doubles 2500$. Some rooms with private bath.) **Quartos** (private rooms) cost about 1200$ in high season, but the price varies with location (higher the closer to the center of town). **Camping Albufeira** (tel. 538 50) is a few kilometers outside town on the road to Ferreiras. More like a crowded shopping mall than a peaceful retreat, the place comes with four swimming pools, three restaurants, a supermarket, and an inflated pricetag. (380$ per person, per car, and per tent.) Unfortunately, the new campsite means that unofficial camping on nearby beaches is forbidden.

Albufeira is packed with restaurants; you will trip over cafe chairs as you walk through the streets. The restaurants near the old fishing harbor, east of the main beach, are the best for budget meals. **Sotavento** and A Taverna do Pescador both serve entrees for under 600$. The latter has a wide selection of fish grilled on the spot.

If it's a good, quick meal you're after, **Guionque,** on the corner of Rua de Outubro and Rua Padre Semedo Azevedo (tel. 556 94), 2 blocks from the tourist office, is the perfect place. This small, family-run establishment offers economical meals in a fast-food bar. Chicken and chips, to eat in or take out, costs 300$. (Open daily noon-midnight.) Watch for the chickens pointing the way.

The hottest dance spots in town, **Silvia's** and **Club 7 1/2,** sit across the street from each other on Rua de São Gonçalo de Lagos. The steep cover charge of 600$ includes one drink. One of the best places to meet people is the **Fastnet Bar** on Rua Candido dos Reis. Bands perform almost nightly on the outdoor stage in the *largo.* Grab a front row seat at one of the nearby cafes.

The **tourist office,** Rua V de Octubro, 5 (tel. 521 44) is helpful with *pensão* listings and names of people renting rooms. The office also has tickets for the weekly bullfight (Sat. at 5:30pm). (Open daily 9:30am-8pm; in winter daily 9:30am-7pm.) The **post office** (tel. 521 11) is right next to the tourist office. (Open Mon.-Fri. 8:30am-6pm.) The **postal code** is 8200. The **train station,** 6km inland, is connected to the center by a bus running every half-hour (60$). The **bus station** is at the entrance to town; walk downhill to reach the center. Dial 522 05 for **police,** 115 in an **emergency,** and 521 33 for the **hospital.** The **telephone code** is 089.

Faro

Faro is the Algarve's capital and largest city. Hundreds of northern Europeans begin their sun-splashed holidays here. If Faro remains unspoiled, it may be due in part to its size—the tourist population is more easily absorbed here than at smaller resort towns.

King Afonso the Wise composed a famous *cantiga* about the port before it was conquered by the Arabs in 714. After another Afonso (III) reconquered it from the Moors, Faro steadily grew in importance until the Count of Essex, a favorite of England's Elizabeth I, decided to sack and burn the city to the ground in 1596. The city was completely rebuilt only to be leveled again by the 1755 earthquake. Its tenacious inhabitants reconstructed Faro in time for the Napoleonic invasion of 1808; Faro was the first Algarvian city to defeat the French. Clearly, the place has a stout character, and it's unlikely to lose it in the face of the current invasion of tourists in search of the beach.

Orientation and Practical Information

Faro's touristy center surrounds **Doca de Recreio,** the small dock with all the empty fishing boats. The streets leading off Praça Doctor Francisco Gomes and the Jardim Manuel Bivar (the small city garden) contain most of the sights and services you'll need. **Rua D. Francisco Gomes** and **Rua de Santo António** are the main pedestrian thoroughfares.

Tourist Office: Rua da Misericórdia, 8 (tel. 254 04). Very helpful. If you're having trouble finding a place to stay, they will help. English spoken. Open daily 9am-8pm; Oct.-June Mon.-Fri. 9am-7pm, Sat.-Sun. 9am-12:30pm and 2:30-5pm. Ask the bus driver to let you off here.

American Express: Star Agency, Rua Conselheiro Rivar, 36 (tel. 251 25 or 251 26) off Praça D. Francisco Gomes. Mail pick up. Also authorizes personal checks to be cashed at local banks. Open Mon.-Fri. 9am-12:30pm and 2-6pm.

Post Office: Largo do Carmo (tel. 233 18), across from the Igreja de Nossa Senhora do Carmo. Telephones and Poste Restante services. Open Mon.-Fri. 8:30am-6:30pm, Sat. 9am-12:30pm. **Postal Code:** 8000.

Telephones: Rua da Misericórdia, 1 (tel. 206 38). Across from the tourist office. Air-conditioned, comfortable cabins for long-distance calls. Open Mon.-Fri. 9am-2:30pm and 3:30-7:30pm. Also try the post office. **Telephone Code:** 089.

Airport: Tel. 242 01. Bus #16 leaves for station every 45 min. 7:51am-7:51pm (75$). From station to airport, similar frequency, 7:38am-7:33pm.

Train Station: Largo da Estação. To get from the station to the tourist office or center of town, turn right when you walk out the door down Avda. da República. Cross Praça D. Francisco Gomes and the small adjacent park. Turismo is on your left next to the large arch. To Lisbon (6 per day, 1515$; *expresso* 1600$), Albufeira (5 per day, 260$), Vila Real de Santo António (12 per day, 355$), and Lagos (7 per day, 355$).

Bus Station: Avda. da República. Follow same directions to center as from train station. To Lisbon (3 per day, 1000$), Beja (4 per day, 650$), Albufeira (14 per day, 325$), Olhão (frequent departures, 130$), and Portimão (6 per day, 415$).

Laundromat: Sólimpa, Rua Letes, 43 (tel. 229 81). Go up Rua Primeiro de Maio and walk straight through the *praça*. Wash and dry 200$ per kg, 2kg minimum.

Hospital: Rua Leão Pinedo (tel. 220 11), north of town.

Police: Rua Serpa Pinto (tel. 220 22), 1 block from Largo do Carmo.

Accommodations and Camping

Rooms go quickly in high season (July-Aug.). With persistence and the tourist office's list of Faro's 20-odd *pensões,* you should be able to locate a bed. In the off-season, try bargaining with proprietors if business is slack, though many lower their prices anyway.

Pensão Residencial Algarve, Rua D. Francisco Gomes, 4 (tel. 233 46), 2 blocks from Turismo near the *praça*. Far and away the best housing option in Faro. Ideal location and well-lighted, spacious rooms with immaculate baths. Very comfortable set-up. Singles 1800$. Doubles 1800$, with two separate beds and complete service 3500$.

Residêncial Galo, Rua Filipe Alistão, 41 (tel. 264 35), around the corner off Rua Primeiro de Maio. Amiable proprietors. Well-decorated old wood interior with modern bath. Spacious, airy rooms. Kind owner. Large doubles 1800$.

Pensão Oceano, Rua Primeiro de Maio, 21 (tel. 233 49), off Praça D. Francisco Gomes. Plain, uninspiring rooms and apathetic management. No warmth or hospitality here. Singles 1500$, with shower 2500$. Doubles 2500$, with shower 3000$.

Casa Emilia, Rua Dr. Teixeira Quedes, 21 (tel. 233 52), a 5-min. walk up Rua de Santo António. Dark, empty hallways and solitary confinement await you here. The dim rooms are well-furnished but very poorly lighted. Singles 1000$. Doubles 1600$, with washbasin 1800$.

Residência Pinto, Rua Primeiro de Maio, 27 (tel. 228 20), on a street off Praça Doctor Francisco Gomes. Don't be fooled by the innocuous exterior and the attractive price. If you are condemned to this fate, be prepared to share your depressing bare floor and over-furnished room with ravenous bedbugs. They do bite. One filthy bath shared by the entire building. Stay away. Enter at own risk. Singles 1150$. Doubles 1500$.

Camping is at the beach, Praia de Faro (tel. 248 76). (75$ per person and 75-90$ per tent.)

Food

Try the almonds and figs for which the city is famous. Faro has some of the Algarve's most pleasant cafes, such as those on Rua D. Francisco Gomes.

Restaurante Snack-Bar Centenario, Largo Teneiro Bispo, on Rua Letes, 4-6 (tel. 233 43). Wide variety of fish (550$) and meat dishes (500$). Half-portion of the *prato do dia* 290$. Open daily 9:30am-midnight.

O Cozinheiro, Rua Filipe Alistão, 30 (no phone). Take a left at the end of Rua Primeiro de Maio. A low-key operation, dishing out excellent food in generous portions with a smile. Good grilled sardines and swordfish. *Doses e meias doses* 200-300$. Open Mon.-Sat. 8am-11pm.

Restaurant Fim do Mundo ("end of the world"), Rua Vasco da Gama, 53 (tel. 262 99), off Praça Ferreira de Almeida. Delectable roast chicken dinners (about 400$ or 700$ per kg for take-out). Open Mon. 11am-noon and 3-10pm, Wed.-Sun. 11am-10pm.

Restaurante Chelsea, Rua D. Francisco Gomes (no phone), on the pedestrian walkway. Elegant sidewalk cafe downstairs, restaurant upstairs with blue and white striped tile walls and Parisian movie posters. Hamburgers Chelsea style 450$, a complete meal about 600-700$. Open daily 8am-midnight.

Gelateria Ponto Frio, Rua Conselheiro Bivar, 4 (tel. 213 81), off Praça D. Francisco Gomes. New wave hangout with a whole lot of sweet stuff. Natural fruit juices (200$), delicious fruit shakes (150$), and huge triple scoop ice cream cones (150$). Ice cream sundaes and light sandwiches. Open Mon.-Fri. 8am-11pm, Sat.-Sun. noon-midnight.

Sights

Near the city's small harbor and public garden is the **Arco da Vila,** an impressive Renaissance archway. Beneath, a narrow roadway leads past Faro's elegant City Hall to the **sé** (cathedral), which sits forlornly in a deserted square. The church's truncated tower is all that remains of the original Gothic structure, severely damaged by the 1755 earthquake. Inside, a simple Renaissance interior shelters the Rosary Chapel (right) covered with seventeenth-century *azulejos,* a red Chinceiserie organ, and two friendly Nubians holding lamps. The city's **Museus Municipais** (diagonally across from the back of the church) has a varied and interesting collection of archeological remains from Roman and pre-Roman times, religious paintings, *azulejos,* and military memorabilia, all housed in light and airy rooms that wrap around a robust part-Gothic, part-Renaissance cloister. The prize piece, a 30-foot by 20-foot Roman mosaic found during the construction of a sewer line, now graces a room of its own. (Open Mon.-Fri. 9am-noon and 2-5pm. Admission 110$.)

Across from the old city, facing the huge and dusty Largo de São Francisco, stands the **Igreja de São Francisco,** with a plain facade that conceals a delicate interior. Note especially how the chancel has been extended to create a long, tunnel-shaped room that focuses on the intricate high altar. A central octagon between the chancel and the nave rises, its marvelous buoyancy stemming from the interplay of arches with the gentle curves of the jewel-like balconies in between. A macabre contrast to this church is the **Capela dos Ossos** (Chapel of Bones) in the **Igreja de Nossa Senhora do Carmo,** completely paneled with the bones and skulls of monks unearthed in the adjacent cemetery. (Open daily 10am-1pm and 3-5pm.) Nearby, the **Igreja de São Pedro** displays beautiful *azulejos* of St. Peter (in a rococo chapel to the right) and twin pulpits approached by curving stairs. For a good introduction to the folklife of the Algarve, go to the city's **Museu de Etnografia Regional,** which occupies a wing of the District Assembly Building. (Open Mon.-Fri. 9:30am-12:30pm and 2-5:30pm. Admission 20$.)

The **Maritime Museum,** on the top floor of the Departamento Marítimo do Sul (next to the Hotel Eva), has a carefully assembled exhibit of model wooden boats, sailor's nets, and handicrafts, all in a room painted with detailed pictures of local fish. Here you can see the history of Portuguese boats from the very earliest models built by Manuel Carvelhas of Lisbon. The boat used to discover the Zaire River in 1492, the largest galleon of the sixteenth century, and the vessel that alone defeated the Turkish navy in 1717, are all here. (Open Mon.-Fri. 9:30am-12:30pm and 2-5:30pm, Sat. 9am-1pm. Free.)

Numerous sidewalk cafes line the pedestrian walkways off the garden in the center of town. Come here in the late afternoon or early evening cool to watch people stroll by. For dancing, try the boisterous (and somewhat expensive) **Sheherazade,** in the Eva Hotel on Avda. da República. Folklore and *fado* nights are held on Thursday. Faro has a bustling **market,** where locals and gypsies buy and sell everything from baskets to fresh octopus. (Open Mon.-Fri. 9am-1pm).

Today's invading hordes are drawn to the marvelous **beach** on an islet off the coast. To get there, take bus #16 from the stop in front of the tourist office; it runs hourly until 9pm and costs 80$.

Eastern Coast

The region between Faro and the Spanish border is both the least developed and the least expensive part of the Algarve. If you're looking for beautiful beaches in quieter towns with fewer tourists, consider the towns of Olhão and Tavira.

Olhão

With access to some of the most heavenly beaches in Portugal, Olhão is hospitable and relatively untouched by tourist hotels or restaurants. Founded in the sixteenth century, Olhão prospered during the Napoleonic wars with a lucrative smuggling trade. Today it is the largest fishing port in the Algarve; its undaunted *pescadores* venture as far as Newfoundland to catch cod. Olhão recently gained the status of "city," and massive construction on the outskirts of town bodes ill.

Olhão is most famous for its brilliant white cube-shaped terraces and observation decks built onto the flat roofs of houses. Climb up to the top of the town's handsome **Igreja de Nossa Senhora do Rosario** (1681-1698) to appreciate the surrounding Moorish atmosphere. The church stands at the mouth of Olhão's main street, **Avenida da República.** The drab, modern buildings that line the avenue exemplify this "new" city's efficacy. However, the area between the church and the Ria Formosa (river) possesses infinitely more character.

Turismo is on Largo Sebastião Martins Mestre, an offshoot of Rua do Comércio. The helpful, English-speaking staff distributes a great map of the city and ferry schedules. (Open Mon. 9:30am-12:30pm and 2-8pm, Tues.-Thurs. 9:30am-8pm, Fri. 9:30am-12:30pm and 2-7pm, Sat.-Sun. 9:30am-12:30pm and 2-5:30pm.) From the bus station, turn right and walk down Rua General Humberto Delgado before making another right onto Avda. da República. The **post office** (tel. 720 13) is on Avda. da República (open Mon.-Fri. 8:30am-6pm); the **postal code** is 8700.

The city has two beautiful gardens along the river. Between the gardens are two robust, red-brick buildings that house the fresh produce **market.** Nearby sits the pier with ferries leaving for Olhão's true attraction—heavenly beaches spread across three islands. **Ilha da Armona,** the easternmost island, is home to a lively summer community that crowds around the ferry dock and the road beyond but otherwise leaves miles of oceanfront almost deserted. Bungalows and rooms in private homes can easily be rented here. (Ferries hourly, 110$ round-trip.) **Ilha do Farol** also has plenty of beaches; its lighthouse appears as a prominent offshore landmark from the town's harbor. (Ferries every 2 hr., 160$ round-trip.) **Ilha da Culatra,** an island fishing community, is legendary among a small group of backpackers and seafarers for its hospitality and fine bars. Its ocean beach, even more deserted than those of its neighbors, is great for camping. (Ferries every two hr., 125$ round-trip.)

To reach **Pensão Residencial Helena,** Rua Dr. Miguel Bombarda, 42 (tel. 726 34), go straight from the front door of Turismo, take the left road at the fork. The classic hallways are complete with flowered wallpaper; the dim, flame-shaped lights add a touch of antiquity. Rooms are spacious and comfortable. Be sure to see the richly furnished living room with chandeliers and paintings that typify the hidden grandeur of this *pensão.* (Singles 1500$. Doubles 2000$, with bath 2700$.) **Residencial Bicuar,** Rua Vasco da Gama, 5 (tel. 748 16), also offers luxurious rooms, most with small patios. (Doubles 1800$.) From the front door of Turismo, turn right onto Rua do Comércio and walk back toward the church, taking your first right on Rua de São Pedro; it's the first block on your left. A great place to chow is **Dionísio,** Praça Patrão Joaquim Lopes, 17-19 on Rua de "O Olhanense." (Main dishes and the works 450$. Open Mon.-Sat. 9am-10pm.)

Tavira

In Tavira, one of the Algarve's most enchanting cities, white houses line the estuary banks of the Gilão River, and festive baroque churches gaze down from the hills above. Founded in the pre-Roman era, today the city is an important fishing center; in mid-afternoon, men sit in small riverfront warehouses repairing nets while their empty boats wait nearby.

The seven-arched **Roman Bridge** leads from the center of town around Praça da República across the river to the fragrant Praça 5 de Outubro. A climb up the stairs at the opposite end of the square brings you to the imposing **Igreja do Carmo.** Its elaborately decorated chancel, where false perspectives give the illusion of windows and niches supported by columns, has a wildness akin to a late nineteenth-century opera set. Note the exquisite eighteenth-century benches lining the walls. On the other side of the river, steps opposite the tourist office lead to the **Igreja da Misericórdia,** which exhibits a superb Renaissance doorway decorated with a variety of heads and animals that sprout from twisting vines and candelabra. Just beyond, the remains of the city's **Moorish castle** (open daily 9am-5pm) now embrace a lovely garden.

At dusk, take a stroll down Rua José Pires Padinha, which runs along the river. The tree-lined park, with its cafes and shops, has a peaceful quietude. The sunset behind the leafy trees and the old fishermen's homes along the river casts a light reflection on the river, creating a picture-perfect village setting.

To reach Tavira's excellent **beach,** on an island 2km away, take the "Tavira-Quatro Aguas" bus from Praça da República. The ferry between Quatro Aguas and **Ilha da Tavira** runs until 8pm and costs 40$ round-trip (keep your ticket stub for the return). Many people bathe nude on this beach, but don't feel overdressed in your swimsuit; it's perfectly acceptable.

Tavira has one of the finest *pensões* in the Algarve, **Pensão Residencial Lagôas Bica,** Rua Almirante Cândido dos Reis, 24 (tel. 222 52), on the other side of the river. (Immaculate singles 1200$. Doubles 2000$, with bath 3000$.) Outdoor hand-laundering and drying facilities are available. The view of the city from the rooftop terrace is spectacular, and the indoor garden is lovely. Demand for space here is high, so try to arrive early. If the rooms are full, the owners, a congenial couple, will direct you to rooms in private homes; expect to pay about 1000-1500$ for one of these rooms. To reach the *pensão* from Praça da República, cross the bridge and continue straight down Rua A Cabreira; turn right and go down 2 blocks. A more expensive option is **Pensão-Residencial Castelo,** Rua da Liberdade, 4 (tel. 239 42), across the street from Turismo. These new rooms with wood decor are clean and have wonderful ventilation; some also feature patios and carpeting. The rooftop terrace has a great view of the castle and the entire town. (Doubles 2300$, with bath 3000$.) The city's **campsite,** with its entourage of snack bars and restaurants, is on the beach. (200$ per tent, 70$ per person.)

Restaurante Bica, underneath the *pensão,* serves excellent entrees from 300$. Equally reasonable cafes and restaurants can be found on Praça da República and opposite the garden on Rua José Pires Padinha. Tavira's **Turismo** is conveniently located on Praça da República, just up and across the street from the bus station. The *señora* doesn't speak much English, but can provide you with an excellent map. Bus schedules are also available. (Open Mon.-Fri. 9am-12:30pm and 2:30-5:30pm, Sat. 9am-12:30pm and 2:30-5pm.)

Vila Real de Santo António

At the mouth of the Guadiana River opposite the Spanish border, Vila Real de Santo António is a convenient transfer point to other destinations but offers little of interest to the visitor. The Marquês de Pombal founded the city in 1774 and planned its *praça* and streets after his design for the Baixa in Lisbon. While the town's square remains handsome, the rest of the city is a dreary grid of straight streets lined by nondescript buildings.

Turismo (tel. 432 72), at the exit of the border control station, will exchange money and help you get out of town as fast as possible. (Open daily 8am-11pm; Nov. to mid-May daily 8am-8pm.) They can send you off with a good map of the Algarve. There are **trains** to Lagos (6 per day, 530$) and Faro (8 per day, 255$); for train service to Spain, you must cross the river by ferry to **Ayamonte,** a delightful fishing town and art colony. During the summer, ferries run from 7:10am-1am and cost 65$ per person and 370$ per car. In Ayamonte, you can catch a bus in the main square to Huelva (hourly, 370ptas), where you can make a connection to Sevilla (8 per day in summer, 650ptas). Banks along the port in Ayamonte will change your money into pesetas; Turismo in Vila Real de Santo António can provide you with escudos. Don't forget that Spain is an hour ahead of Portugal in the summer. By 1990 a bridge will replace the ferry, connecting the Algarve to Ayamonte.

Bus service from Vila Real de Santo António to the rest of the Algarve is reliable and faster than trains, if more expensive. There are buses to Faro (9 per day, 345$; usually via Tavira, 225$) and Lagos (8 per day, 530$). Two daily express buses leave for Faro (400$) and Lisbon (1125-1700$). The last bus out of Vila Real leaves at 6:30pm for Faro. Buses leave from the esplanade to the right of the tourist office. While waiting to leave, it's well worth trying to hitch a ride within Spain or Portugal from all the international traffic disembarking from the ferry.

Ask at Turismo for directions to the **IYHF Pousada de Juventude,** Rua Dr. Sousa Martins, 40 (tel. 445 65). Decent quarters are available for 500$; breakfast is included. **Pensão Felix** (tel. 437 91), across from the tourist office, has clean rooms. (Doubles 1335$.) Two streets down, on Rua do Dr. Manuel de Arriaga, **Residência Baixa Mar** (tel. 435 11) rents singles for 1700$ and doubles for 2500$. If you arrive in Vila Real after 6:30pm in summer, you won't be able to leave town and may have difficulty finding a room. The police are lenient about letting people camp out in the municipal garden by the river, but do this only as a last resort. There are many inexpensive restaurants along the pedestrian Rua do Dr. Manuel de Arriaga. **Bar-Restaurante Princeza,** Rua da Princeza, 67 (the street above the river), is a little off the beaten track and offers very reasonable meals in an untouristed setting. The *prato do dia* costs 360$.

Planicies

Stretching from Tomar in the heart of the country south to the Algarve and from outside Lisbon east to the Spanish border, the Planícies ("plains") cover almost one-third of the country's total area. However vast, the region is Portugal's least populated and one of its poorest. Historical legacy and development around the region's larger towns have created islands of wealth in this struggling farming zone. Severe droughts, resistance to contour farming, and overplanting of soil-drying eucalyptus trees have severely affected much of its agricultural capacity (especially in the east). Many locals predict a grim future as the output of the under-mechanized farms here may have trouble competing with the products of the more technologically advanced EEC (Common Market) countries.

The Planícies region is comprised of the vast, rugged **Alentejo** province and the meadowlands of the smaller Ribatejo province. Except for the city of Beja, the population of the lower Alentejo resides principally on large farms and in whitewashed hamlets in the countryside, where olive and cork trees dot the countryside. Named Riba do Tejo (bank of the Tagus) by its first settlers, the richly fertile **Ribatejo** province is best-known in Portugal as a pastureland and a breeding ground for Arabian horses and great black bulls. The **Festa Brava,** the Ribatejo's great biannual celebration, occurs during the first week of July and the first week of October in Vila Franca de Xira (32km north of Lisbon). Festivities revolve around the countless bullfights and the *corrida,* the traditional running of the bulls; *campinos* in customary garb chase the enraged animals down the main street.

Mértola

High on a hill overlooking the confluence of the Guadiana and Oeiras Rivers, the town of **Mértola** sits 53km south of Beja in the midst of the burning hills of the Alentejo. A number of interesting sights make this a worthwhile stopover on your way from Beja to the eastern Algarve or the Spanish border (Ayamonte/Vila Real).

In the upper part of town, below the castle, excavations have recently revealed huge water **cisterns** built by the Romans and used in later times as storehouses for meats and grains. When the Moors seized Mértola in the eighth century, they transformed it into the capital of a *faifa* kingdom and built the *mezquita* (mosque). Look up at the airy vaulted ceiling supported by marble columns, each of which is topped by a different kind of capital. Though later converted into a church, this is the only mosque in Portugal with an extant *mihrab*—the niche in the eastern wall facing the holy city of Mecca. Climbing up the hill, you'll reach the thirteenth-century **castle** built on the remains of the Roman fortress. The castle is not as well-preserved as others in this region, but it serves as a marvelous point for viewing the valley and the town's white houses below. Both castle and mosque are locked; ask for the key at the caretaker's house, near the road going up the hill.

Also visit the **Museu Arqueologico,** on Largo da Misericordia (at the lower end of the Rua dos Combatentes da Grande Guerra, which begins below the mosque). The museum exhibits artifacts unearthed during the excavation of the castle grounds, some of which date back to Roman antiquity. It also has an especially fine collection of religious images, mostly baroque carvings rescued from the castle's chapel. (Open Mon.-Fri. 9am-1pm and 2-5pm.)

The cheapest and most pleasant place to spend a night is the unmarked **Pensão Ideal** (tel. 624 33). To arrange for a room, visit the bar on Rua Afonso Costa that doubles as the municipal Socialist Party headquarters (halfway to the town center from the river, on your right; look for the distinctive golden clenched fist on a red field placard). The man at the bar will escort you around the block to the *pensão.* (Singles 400$. Doubles 800$.) The bar itself is a good place to soak up some local atmosphere. When you can bear to divert your attention from the political arguments, admire the metal sign to the right of the bar which reads: "This bar exists for the purpose of serving militants of the Socialist Party and its sympathizers." Count yourself a "sympathizer" and one of the "militants" may buy you a drink! **Residêncial Beira Rio,** Rua Dr. Afonso Costa (tel. 623 40), near the river, has a clean, whitewashed interior. The bathroom is down the hall. Ask for a room with a view of the river. (Singles 700$. Doubles 1000$.)

For lunch, eat at one of the several restaurants along Rua Dr. Afonso Costa, the main road going into town, or choose among the few cafes near the tourist office. For a homecooked meal, you might try **Casa Maria Barbara Neves Gama,** Rua Alves Redol, 35 (follow the signs going toward Vila Real from the tourist office and bear left). The *prato do dia* costs 400$.

Turismo is in the center of town. (Open Mon.-Fri. 9am-12:30pm and 2-5:30pm.) Mértola is about an hour and a quarter by bus from Beja (275$), and about two hours from Vila Real de Santo António on the Spanish border. The town is an easy daytrip from either city and a fine place for a restful afternoon.

Beja

The remains of Beja's historic past bake quietly under the fierce Alentejo sun. Long known for its strong communist bent, Beja erupted into bitter disputes between landlords and farmers after the 1974 revolution. The farmers, angered by years of exploitation, occupied and confiscated many of the *latifundia* (large estates). Fourteen years later, political graffiti still covers Beja's buildings, but otherwise the city is serene. Winding narrow streets accommodate both old homes and modern shops lending an unimposing charm to this mini-metropolis. To ensure the town's recent pacification, a German military installation sits on the town's outskirts (courtesy of the NATO exchange program).

Orientation and Practical Information

Beja is connected by direct highways to Lisbon (193km to the northwest), Evora (78km to the north), and to the Spanish border at Ficalho (about 65km due east) for transit to Mérida and Sevilla. Transportation to the Algarve is definitely easier by bus than by train.

The train station is hidden in the eastern corner of town; the bus station lies at the southern edge. **Rua de Mértola** and **Rua de Capitão João Francisco de Sousa** mark the center of town, home of the largest concentrations of shops. Points of interest lie close to this area, while peaceful but uneventful residential neighborhoods spread outward. Winding streets are unmarked and confusing, especially in the center of town, but people are friendly, so don't be afraid to ask for help.

Tourist Office: Rua Capitão João Francisco de Sousa, 25 (tel. 236 93). Run by a friendly and helpful staff. Ask them to mark everything on their nameless map. Open Mon.-Fri. 9am-7pm, Sat. 10am-1pm and 3-7pm.

Post Office: Largo do Correio (tel. 221 11), down the street from Pensão Rocha. Mail and Poste Restante services open Mon.-Fri. 8:30am-5pm. **Postal Code:** 7800.

Telephones: At the post office. **Telephone Code:** 084.

Train Station: On the eastern edge of town. From here, walk down Rua Pedro Victor and continue to bear right through at least one change in street name until it becomes Rua Nuno Alvares Pereira; from the end of this street follow the signs to Turismo. To Lisbon (5 per day, 590$), Evora (1 per day, 380$), Faro (2 per day, 650$), and Vila Real de Santo António (2 per day, 825$).

Bus Station: Rua Cidade de São Paulo, at the roundabout on the corner of Avda. do Brasil. To reach the center of town, walk past the statue and turn left onto Avda. do Brasil for 1 block. Turn right at the open field and go straight past the post office and the curving street with Pensão Rocha. At the intersection, take a left on Rua Capitão J.F. de Sousa with a small pedestrian square; keep to your right and watch for Turismo. To Lisbon (6 per day, 1420$),

Evora (2 per day, 435$), Faro (3 per day, 635$), Vila Real de Santo António (2 per day, 590-700$), and Rosal de la Fronteira (1 per day, 475$) for connections to Spain and France.

Swimming Pools: Avda. do Brasil, near bus station and camping. Open Sat.-Thurs. 10am-8pm. Admission 40$, with shower 100$. Children under 12 ½-price.

Hospital: Estrada do Faro (tel. 221 33).

Police: Rua Nuno Alvares Pereira (tel. 220 22). **Emergency:** Tel. 115.

Accommodations and Camping

Almost all hotels (and restaurants) are within a few blocks of the tourist office and the bustling central pedestrian street. Cheaper looking *pensões* cluster around Praça da República.

Pensão Rocha, Largo D. Nuno Alvares Pereira, 12 (tel. 242 71), up the curving street from the post office. Run by a friendly middle-aged couple. Bathroom with hot showers down the hall or across the roof. Singles 800$. Doubles 1500$.

Pensão Tomás, Rua Alexandre Herculano, 7 (tel. 246 13). Turn right 1 block up from the intersection. Easy-going owner. Bare-floor, but bright rooms with comfortable furnishings. Somewhat drab interior. Old smelly bathroom with unreliable hot water. Singles 1000$, with bath 1900$. Doubles 1600$, with bath 2300$. Breakfast 300$.

Residência Bejense, Rua Capitão João Francisco de Sousa, 57 (tel. 250 01), down the street from Turismo. Worth every escudo. Luxuriously spacious rooms with carpeting. Lush interior with classical dining room and mirrored hallways. Access to kitchen and TV lounge. Singles 2000$, with bath 2500$. Doubles with bath 2800$. Breakfast included.

Camping is on the southwest side of town at the end of Avda. Vasco da Gama. (Tel. 243 28. 40$ per person and per car, 30-60$ per tent; use of swimming pool included.)

Food

Beja offers a number of inexpensive restaurants, most serving lunch from noon to 2pm and dinner from 7 to 10pm. The local specialty is *migas de pão,* a sausage and bacon dish cooked with bread.

Casa Saiote, Rua da Biscayinha, 45 (tel. 258 87), off the intersection of Sousa and Mértola. Small, family-run restaurant with limited menu. Cholesterol-lovers special: big pork steak and mounds of fries (350$). Try the banana pudding (65$) for dessert. Open daily 8am-midnight.

Restaurante Tomás, Rua Alexandre Herculano, 7 (tel. 246 13), right beneath the *pensão.* A stylish, award-winning restaurant offering fish and meat dishes for 500-600$. Wide variety of desserts. Open daily noon-3pm and 7-10pm.

O Beco, Rua dos Infantes (tel. 259 00), 1 block up from the museum. Enter through a vine-covered courtyard, and take your meal in a large room with a bar. *Prato do dia* from 500$, ½-portions available for under 400$. Terrific chocolate mousse 60$. Open Mon.-Sat. noon-3pm and 5-10pm.

Casa Frade, Rua da Biscayinha, 7 (tel. 223 10), down the street from Casa Saiote. A family-run dive with no atmosphere. Very cheap, somewhat greasy entrees start at 350$. Soup 40$. Open daily 7am-9pm.

Sights

Beja's main attraction is its outstanding **Museu "Rainha D. Leonor,"** housed in the former Convent of Nossa Senhora da Conceicão (Our Lady of the Immaculate Conception), built between 1459 and 1506. A nun here allegedly had a steamy affair with a French officer and wrote her story in *Letters of a Portuguese Nun* in 1669. Soon after publication, the letters were translated into French and became an immediate literary success. Questions have surfaced as to the real author of the poetry, but it still makes a nice story. For the romantically inclined, the museum has reconstructed the cell window through which the lovers exchanged secret vows of passion.

Upon entering the museum, you'll see a richly gilded church decorated with eighteenth-century *azulejo* panels depicting the lives of Mary and St. John the Baptist. Nearby are fine baroque marble altars done in intaglio, and panels of *talha dourada* (carved wood overlaid in gold). Moorish *azulejos* and a Persian-style ceiling embellish the chapter house, accessible through a beautiful fifteenth-century doorway. As a result, the whole room looks like a miniature mosque. The rest of the museum contains a miscellaneous collection that includes three paintings of saints attributed to the seventeenth-century Spanish master Ribera, some fine Roman sculpture, and colorful *azulejo* panels. Don't miss the nineteenth-century costumes on the second floor; they are all worn by mannequins that bear a striking resemblance to the young Bette Davis. (Open Tues.-Sun. 9:30am-1pm and 2:30-5:45pm; in winter Tues.-Sat. 9:30am-1pm and 2:30-5pm, Sun. 10am-1pm and 2:30-5pm. Admission 25$, students and Sun. free. Ask for a free English pamphlet.)

One block northeast of the convent stands the adobe-like **Igreja de Santa Maria** (thirteenth-century, rebuilt in the fifteenth century). Its corner column is emblazoned with a miniature bull—the symbol of the city. From here, Rua Dr. Aresta Branco leads past handsome old houses with wrought-iron balconies and stone-framed windows and doorways. At the end of the street looms the city's massive **castelo,** built around 1300 on the remains of a fourth-century Roman fortress. Though only a pale shadow of its former self, it still flaunts its enormous crenelated marble keep and large, vaulted chambers; the interior walls are covered with ivy. From the top of the parapet stretches a wonderful panorama of Alentejo landscape. (Open daily 10am-1pm and 2-6pm; Oct.-March daily 9am-noon and 1-4pm. Admission 30$.)

On your way back to the center of town, stop at **Praça da República,** a long square enhanced by a Manueline column. On one side stands the **Igreja de Misericórdia,** built in 1550 as a market hall. As you exit the *praça* to the southeast, you'll find **Rua do Touro** and **Rua Dr. Afonso Costa,** also known as **Rua das Lojas** (Street of Shops); note the aged grillwork on the balconies.

Evora

Whatever you do in Portugal, don't miss Evora. This medieval university town rises from a rolling plain punctuated by tough little cork and olive trees. Coveted by a succession of empires, its labyrinthine streets recall a long past with everything from a unique Roman temple to Portugal's largest and grisliest *capela de ossos* (bone chapel). The town's ornamental horseshoe arches suggest the long tenancy of the Moors, from the eighth to the twelfth centuries. Above all, however, Evora stands as Portugal's foremost showpiece of medieval architecture. The **Universidade de Evora,** whose cloister is open to visitors, flourished from 1559 to 1759. It wasn't reopened until 1979.

Orientation and Practical Information

Evora is easily accessible, with several trains per day from Lisbon and Faro. The town is also linked by train with Estremoz, Portalegre, and Elvas to the north. No direct bus connects the train station to the center of town, so if you'd rather not hike 700m up Rua do Dr. Baronha, treat yourself to a taxi (180$) or try flagging down bus #6, which crosses the tracks 2 blocks over (50$). Near the edge of town, Rua do Dr. Baronha turns into Rua da República, which leads to the main square, **Praça do Giraldo.** If you arrive by bus at the main station, proceed uphill to the *praça.* Most monuments and lodgings cluster in the area uphill from this square.

Tourist Office: Praça do Giraldo, 73 (tel. 226 71). Well-informed, English-speaking staff. Pick up a copy of their map complete with guided tour of Evora's monuments. Also has an exhibition gallery. Open Mon.-Fri. 9am-7pm, Sat.-Sun. 9am-12:30pm and 2-5:30pm; in winter Mon.-Fri. 9am-6pm, Sat.-Sun. 9am-5:30pm.

Post Office: Rua de Olivenca (tel. 233 11), 2 blocks north of Pr. de Giraldo. Exit the *praça* and walk through João de Deus, keeping to your right. Pass under the aqueduct and make an immediate right uphill; it's on your left. Mail, Poste Restante, and **telephone** services open Mon.-Fri. 8:30am-6:30pm and Sat. 9am-12:30pm. **Telegram:** Open Mon.-Fri. 8:30am-5:30pm and Sat. 9am-11:30pm. **Postal Code:** 7000.

Train Station: 1½km from town center (tel. 221 25). To Lisbon (6 per day, 500$), Faro (3 per day, 905$), Beja (3 per day), and Estremoz (7 per day, 355$).

Bus Station: Rodoviária Nacional, Rua da República (tel. 221 21), opposite Igreja de São Francisco. To Lisbon (4 per day, 700$), Faro (1 per day, 950$), Vila Real de Santo António (1 per day, 1125$), Beja (2 per day, 435$), and Elvas (4 per day, 625$).

Taxi: Tel. 286 66. Operates daily 7am-midnight.

English Bookstore: Nazareth, Pr. do Giraldo, 46 (tel. 222 21). Open Mon.-Fri. 9am-1pm and 3-7pm.

Swimming Pool: A splendid complex of 5 pools on the outskirts of town is open varying hours (tel. 323 26). Frequent bus service in summer (60$).

Hospital: Rua do Valasco (tel. 221 33).

Police: Rua Francisco Soares Lusitania (tel. 220 22). **Emergency:** Tel. 115.

Accommodations and Camping

Finding a room shouldn't be a problem—especially given the spacious youth hostel. In the *pensões,* try bargaining during the off-season.

Pousada de Juventude (IYHF), Rua de Corredoura, 32 (tel. 250 43). From Pr. do Giraldo, take Rua João de Deus next to the church on your right and pass under the aqueduct onto Rua de Aviz; Rua da Corredoura is the 2nd turn-off on your right. An excellent, clean, often empty hostel with laundry facilities. The warden and his wife are sweethearts. Bus and train schedules are posted at reception. If you aren't spending the night, the warden will store your bags, 100$ per item. Flexible curfew 11pm. Reception open daily 9-10am and 7-11pm; Oct.-April 9-10am and 6-10:30pm. 500$. Breakfast included.

Pensão Os Manueis, Rua do Raimundo, 35 (tel. 228 61), around the corner from Turismo and upstairs from a restaurant. Sunny, yellow hallways give this simple, clean establishment a spacious feeling. Sparkling white baths with decorative blue tiles. Singles 1500$. Doubles 2000$, with bath 2500$.

Pensão Residencial O Eborense, Largo da Misericórdia, 1 (tel. 220 31), 1st right as Rua da República turns left into the center of town. Ducal-mansion turned pension. Grandiose stone stairwell covered with plants leads up to a beautiful outdoor balcony. Rooms themselves don't match this grandeur; they are small and cozy with high ceilings and rugs. Open Dec.-Oct. Singles 1600$. Doubles 2800$. Much higher with bath.

Camping Orbitur (tel. 232 16), a two-star park on Estrada das Alcáçovas, charges 253$ per person, 190-253$ per tent, and 210$ per car. Hot showers cost 75$. (Open Jan. 16-Nov. 15.)

Food

Every weekday morning, a **public market** is set up in the small square in front of the Igreja de São Francisco and the public gardens. Produce and flowers are sold (delicious spring strawberries at 350$ per kg) as well as a wide assortment of local cheeses, including *queijo de cabra* (goat cheese).

Café-Restaurante A Grata, Avda. General Humberto Delgado, 2 (tel. 281 86), on the way to Praça de Touros. Go down Rua da República toward the train station and turn right at the end of the park. Follow your nose and look for smoke. This place is packed with locals—and for good reason. All the meats are cooked on a huge open grill. Mouth-watering *frango no churrasco* (barbequed chicken) buried under a heap of fries makes a satisyfing and filling meal for two (600$). Open Sun.-Fri. noon-2:30pm and 5-10:30pm.

Restaurante Faísca, Rua do Raimundo, 33 (tel. 276 35). Around the corner from Turismo, downstairs from Pensão Os Manueis. Serves regional specialties such as *costoletas do porco* *y fritas a Alentejana* (Alentejo-style pork chops and fries, 480$). Other basic entrees from 400$. Open Mon.-Fri. 8am-9pm, Sat. 8am-3pm.

Restaurante Repas, Praça Primeiro de Maio, 19 (tel. 285 40), near Igreja de São Francisco. Very cheap food in a bar-like atmosphere. Grilled lamb chops, fries, and rice 460$. Half-portions available. Open daily 7am-11pm.

Restaurante A Choupana, Rua dos Mercadores, 16-20 (tel. 244 27), off Pr. do Giraldo. Excellent and inexpensive with counter service. *Lulas* (squid), served with potato salad and rice, 500$. Open daily noon-10pm.

Sights

Evora lives up to its title of "museum city," with monuments that mark each stage of its history. **Praça do Giraldo,** the graceful plaza in the center of town, was named for the Christian knight who captured the city from the Arabs in 1165. White buildings decorated with pale yellow window frames lend the square an inviting, sunny atmosphere. At the northern end of the *praça* is the **Igreja Santo Antão,** a weighty example of regional Renaissance architecture. Its airy interior with vaulted ceilings contains robust columns reminiscent of an ancient temple. The floor is lined with wooden tombstones.

Rua de 5 d' Outubro leads from the east side of the *praça* to the colossal **sé** (cathedral), begun in 1186. Two heavy asymmetrical towers, one capped by a conical dome covered with tiles, the other encircled by a series of turrets, frame a deeply recessed porch. The statues of the 12 Apostles adorning the porch are masterpieces of medieval Portuguese sculpture. From the far end of the nave, the multi-colored and marble-faced baroque chancel looks like a precious jewel encased in a band of masonry; it was designed in the eighteenth century by the architect of Mafra. Between the nave and the chancel soars an octagonal tower supported by squinches—arches across the corners of the tower.

The **claustro** (cloister) of the cathedral (accessible by a small door to the right of the entrance) dates from 1325 and, though technically Gothic, exhibits the ponderous Romanesque style. Small circular openings with Moorish latticework pierce part of the area above the arcade. Look for the four Evangelists, who grace the corners of the inner arcades. Dark spiral staircases lead to the cloister's roof. The **Museu de Arte Sacra,** in a gallery above the nave, houses the cathedral's treasury, which includes an astonishing thirteenth-century ivory *Virgin and Child.* On the way up to the museum, admire the sixteenth-century choir stalls, above which are wood panels depicting the country life of the period. (Cloister and museum open Tues.-Sun. 9am-noon and 2-5pm. Admission 100$.)

Abutting the cathedral to the north is the **Museu d'Evora.** Housed in a sixteenth-century Episcopal palace, it contains a varied collection ranging from Roman artifacts found in the nearby countryside to sixteenth- and seventeenth-century European paintings. The archeological material, arranged around a central cloister, includes an exquisite Roman bas-relief of a dancer. Upstairs, the prize of the painting collection is a series of 13 canvases illustrating the life of Mary. (Open Tues.-Sun. 10am-12:30pm and 2-5pm. Admission 150$, students free.)

Across from the museum, outlined against the sky, stands Evora's most famous monument, the second-century **Templo de Diana.** It dates back to the time when the city, then called Liberalitus Julia, was one of the most important Roman towns in Iberia; for centuries it was used as a slaughterhouse. The temple is remarkably well-preserved, its slender Corinthian columns still supporting most of the original architecture. At dusk or dawn, this timeless setting is quite inspiring.

Facing the temple is the town's best concealed treasure, the **Igreja de São João Evangelista** (1485). Adjoining the Paço dos Duques de Cadaval, the church is still the private property of the Cadaval family. The caretaker next door, in the palace, will open the church (85$). The interior is covered with beautiful *azulejos* from 1711 that depict the life of St. Lawrence Giustiniani, patriarch of Venice; look for the *trompe l'oeil azulejo* window. After you've seen the interior, urge the caretaker to unlock the church's assorted hidden chambers—among other objects, you'll see a crypt filled with the bones of bygone monks, as well as a painting with eyes that always meet your gaze and feet that seem to move as you do.

Walking back past the front of the cathedral and down Rua de São Marcos, at #29 you'll come to the small **Casa de Garcia de Resende.** Once the home of the sixteenth-century poet and architect, the house retains its graceful Manueline windows. From here the street leads to **Largo das Portas de Moura,** one of Evora's most delightful squares, enhanced by an eclectic variety of buildings and sculpture. Beyond the spherical Renaissance **fountain** (1556), symbolic of Portugal's global adventures, stands the sixteenth-century **Casa Cordovil.** Its roof supports an elegant Moorish loggia graced by six delicate columns and crowned by a conical spire. The mansion is closed to visitors.

On the west side of the *largo,* down a flight of steps, lies the **Convento de Nossa Senhora do Carmo** (1665), enhanced by a baroque version of Manueline motifs that look like ribbons on a Christmas package. As you leave the square on Rua da Misericórdia, you'll pass the **Igreja da Misericórdia,** which displays a stunning 1767 rococo portal. Just down the street and to the left via a narrow passageway stands the sixteenth-century **Convento de Nossa Senhora da Graça.** On its cramped and ill-proportioned Renaissance facade perch four overscaled Michelangelo-esque figures with the look of startled Neanderthals. Not much remains of the original interior except three rear windows. Miniature ceiling coffers recede rapidly, providing an illusion of depth—a common Renaissance optical trick.

Nearby, on Praça Primero de Maio, the **Museu de Artesanato** contains an exhibit of local handicrafts, including brightly painted ceramic figures, local costumes, tools, and an intricately carved castle made entirely of cork, one of the area's major products. An excellent selection of crafts is sold here too. (Open Tues.-Sun. 10am-noon and 2-5:30pm. Free.)

Evora's second most famous (but, without a doubt, most arresting) attraction is housed down the street in the **Igreja Real de São Francisco,** whose undecorated bulk represents the finest example of Manueline Gothic architecture in Southern Portugal. The church is most notable for its perverse **Capela de Ossos** (Chapel of Bones). Above the door an inscription reads: "*Nos ossos que aqui estamos, pelos vossos esperamos*" (literally, "Our bones are here awaiting yours"; poetically, "Our bones here awaiting lie, your own bones and you to die"). The chapel was constructed with the bones of some 5000 monks and nuns as a slightly less-than-subtle reminder of human mortality. It offers an exercise in interior decoration at its most macabre: As you enter, rows of empty skull sockets are trained upon you, and every inch of wall space is neatly paneled with human bones. The top of one of the columns is adorned exclusively with coccyges. The bones of the three founding monks are not on display, but rest more privately in a large stone sarcophagus to the right of the altar. Other such chapels of bones exist in the Algarve, but this one is Portugal's most extensive. Outside the chapel wall, a collection of shorn human braids testifies to those who have paid their promises to the saint. (Church and chapel open Mon.-Sat. 8:30am-1pm and 2:30-6pm, Sun. 10-11:30am and 2:30-6pm. Admission to chapel 25$; 50$ more to take pictures.)

Just south of the church spreads the lush expanse of the **Jardim Público** (Municipal Garden). Covered with neatly trimmed plants and beautiful flowers, the park's rotunda and fountain (with a resident black swan) lend it an air of elegance. Within the garden is the sixteenth-century **Palácio de D. Manuel.** The former residence of the Aviz Dynasty, it now contains an art gallery. At the northeast end of the park, an exit leads to Rua do Raimundo, past the seventeenth-century **Igreja Conventual de Nossa Senhora das Mercês** (Church-convent of Our Lady of Mercy). The interior, lined with polychrome tiles, is now used as a museum of decorative arts. (Open Thurs. and Sat.-Sun. 10am-12:30pm and 2-5pm.) From here either continue onto Praça do Giraldo or explore the neighboring side streets, where the stone pavements, whitewashed houses, and connecting arches have changed little since the thirteenth century, when this was the old Jewish quarter of town.

Entertainment

Though most of Evora reverts to a sleepy little town at 11pm, **Xeque-Mate,** Rua de Valdevinos, 21, and **Discoteca Slide,** Rua Serpa Pinto, 135, keep the music blaring until 2am. Only couples and single women are permitted to enter, so men without partners are out of luck. Evora's most popular cafe/bar hangout is **Portugal,** Rua João de Deus, 55. Since unaccompanied women seldom go out for entertainment here, women entering alone will be conspicuous.

Evora's most famous festival, **Feira de São João** (June 18-July 2), celebrates the arrival of summer. It is a full-fledged fair—Portuguese style. You'll find the usual fair gimmicks—rides and pink cotton candy—but you'll also enjoy regional dances and pungent Portuguese meats and cheeses sold in stalls. Many bargains can be found in the mass of tents set up by local shops selling everything from fine porcelain to stuffed animals (you buy them, not win them). The Feast of São Pedro on June 29 is the climax; after a bullfight and fireworks display, the dancing continues until dawn.

Near Evora

Prominently situated on a hill 35km northeast of Evora, the tiny village of **Evora-monte** is dominated by its massive **castle.** Originally Roman, the castle was extensively remodeled in the fourteenth and sixteenth centuries, and now encloses three vaulted Gothic halls. From the top of its three-story keep there are magnificent views of the neighboring countryside; Estremoz is visible to the northeast. The town's only street, lined with whitewashed houses, leads to the small parish church. Evoramonte is famous in Portuguese history as the place where the liberal Dom Pedro IV secured for his niece the Portuguese throne after forcing his reactionary brother to abdicate. The house where the 1834 agreement was signed bears a commemorative plaque.

Though this hamlet is a lovely place to pass a few hours, you'll have to hitch back to town unless you have a car. A morning train or bus will take you there (215$; check at Turismo for the timetable), but no public transportation travels in the other direction.

Evora's most interesting neighbor, **Monsaraz,** overlooks the Guadiana Valley from a hilltop on the border between Portugal and Spain. Its extensive battlements command a breathtaking view of a wide stretch of Southern Portugal. Entering the town through a pointed gateway, the road leads to the main square. On the south side lies the **Municipio** with a three-arched veranda and a splendid coat of arms. The sixteenth-century **parish church,** surprisingly large for such a tiny town, contains the late thirteenth-century marble tomb of Gomes Martin, decorated with carved figures in a funeral procession. On Rua Direita, a virtually intact sixteenth-century street, the former **Tribunal** houses a recently discovered thirteenth-century fresco which portrays both a just and a corrupt judge. Before leaving town, stop at the eighteenth-century **Misericórdia Hospital,** opposite the parish church. It has a beautiful meeting hall and a chapel of very fine gilded baroque woodwork.

Round-trip public transportation is a problem here as well. An afternoon bus runs from Evora with a return trip the following morning (round-trip fare 320$). Either hitchhike back or take a room at **Estalagem D. Nuno,** Rua José Fernandes Caeiro, 6. (Tel. 551 46. Singles 2100$. Doubles 2800$. Breakfast included.) *Quartos,* rooms to let in private houses, are a less expensive option at 600-700$ per person. Turismo in Evora can give you details; remember to ask there before you depart.

Estremoz

Famous for its earthenware and ceramic figures, Estremoz lacks the aesthetic green surroundings of the region's other important cities. This old Alentejo town has changed little over time: Crumbling white houses with projecting chimneys still climb narrow streets to a fortified hill. (The castle has been converted into an elegant *pousada.* Mere visitors can glimpse the inside only briefly.)

Orientation and Practical Information

West of Elvas, north of Evora, and south of Portalegre, Estremoz is approximately one hour away from all three points by bus or train and needs no more than a few hours or a day to visit. The center of town is the mammoth dirt lot eloquently named **Rossio Marquês de Pombal.**

Tourist Office: Largo da República, 26 (tel. 225 38), 1 block south of the *rossio.* Free maps, as well as a list of accommodations, including rooms in private homes. No English spoken. Open Mon.-Fri. 9:30am-1pm and 3-6pm. The Turismo kiosk at the *rossio* (on your left as you come out of the bus station) offers the same materials plus an English-speaking staff. Open daily 9:30am-1pm and 3-6pm.

Post Office: Rua 5 de Outubro (tel. 221 11). Open Mon.-Fri. 9am-12:30pm and 2:30-6pm. **Postal Code:** 7100.

Telephone Code: 068.

Train Station: Avda. 9 de Abril. To reach Turismo kiosk, go straight onto Rua Condesa da Cuba. Turn left when you get to the *rossio,* and then make a right on Rua Mousinho da Albuquerque; walk past the bus station and the kiosk is at the corner on your right. To Evora (4 per day, 255$) and Portalegre (2 per day, 275$).

Bus Station: Rossio Marquês de Pombal. To Evora (3 per day, 325$), Elvas (6 per day, 305$), and Portalegre (with connection at Elvas, 3 per day, 380$).

Hospital: Rossio Marquês de Pombal (tel. 228 69).

Police: Rossio Marquês de Pombal (tel. 222 89). **Emergency:** Tel. 115.

Accommodations and Food

Pensão Residencial Carvalho, Largo da República, 27 (tel. 227 12), right next to Turismo. Enormous, clean, and cheerful rooms. Singles 1100$, with bath 2500$. Doubles 1750$, with bath 2850$. Breakfast included.

Pensão Mateus, Rua da Almeida, 41 (tel. 222 26), near the post office. From Turismo kiosk, go straight into Praça Luís de Camões and turn right on Rua 5 de Outubro. Turn left just before the post office and continue to Rua da Almeida. Dark, narrow hallways with gaudy pink walls. If you can tolerate the exterior, you'll find the airy, wood-tile rooms to be quite comfortable. Old bathroom. Singles 1000$. Doubles 1850$.

Miguel José Refeições Quartos, Travessa da Levada, 8 (tel. 223 26), turn right before Rua da Almeida. Only sign for "Quartos." Inquire at snackbar next door. Dreary rooms. Singles 750$, with bath 1000$. Doubles 1400$, with bath 1800$.

Fresh fruit and vegetables are sold daily at the stands on the *rossio.* **Café-Restaurante de Carlos Miguel Oliveira,** Rua Vitor Cordon, 14, off the southeast corner of the *rossio,* serves a plate of steaming *pescada* (whitefish), spinach, and boiled potatoes for 400$. On Wednesday, when this place is closed, you might want to try one of the restaurants on the *rossio* around the corner. **Café Central,** across from Turismo, is a good place for a light meal.

Sights

Most points of interest in Estremoz lie in the upper town around the impressive **Torre de Menegem,** which commands a view of the parched plain. Construction of the tower began in the thirteenth century and spanned the reigns of three kings. To reach the castle, follow signs for the museum from the *rossio* to Praça Luiz de Camões, cross the *praça* diagonally, and continue to follow signs for the museum, walking uphill. Dominating the hill is the thirteenth-century **keep** with its splendid vaulted chamber and, at its upper end, galleries supported by sizable brackets. Entry to the tower is through the *pousada,* a state-run hotel that occupies a restored eighteenth-century palace.

Across from the hotel, the small **Museu Municipal** exhibits a nice collection of ceramic figures, Roman pottery, religious art, and stone *estrelas* (symbolic stars used by various medieval religious and military orders). Upstairs, three rooms less-than-convincingly attempt to recreate a typical eighteenth-century Alentejo house. (Open Tues.-Sun. 10am-noon and 2-6pm.) The curator of the museum has the keys to the small **Capela da Rainha Santa Isabel** (Chapel of the Queen Saint Elizabeth) adjacent to the *pousada,* where *azulejos* illustrate the life of St. Isabel of Aragon. The false perspective of the tiny ceiling here is too cramped to be impressive, but the small "dome" over the doorway adds a cheerful note. (A 50$ tip per group is advisable.) The king's **Sala de Audiências de D. Dinis** (Audience Chamber), diagonally across from the *pousada,* stands behind a delicate Gothic porch that sports old mason's markings under the ogival arches. Inside is an exuberant, vaulted Manueline room, now an art gallery. Next door, the sixteenth-century **Igreja de Santa Maria** shelters a spacious interior with ceiling vaults supported by lofty Ionic columns.

The lower town seems spread out, but most of the monuments worth exploring are found around the *rossio.* The **Igreja de São Francisco** has a handsome Gothic interior that contains the exquisite Tomb of Vasco Esteves Gato, whose bearded head rests on three pillows while his feet rest on two dogs. Notice to the left of the altar the delicately carved wooden tree with the 12 apostles; the piece dates from the thirteenth century. **Misericórdia Hospital** occupies a former convent of the Knights of Malta, founded in 1539. It wraps around a marvelously uneven Gothic cloister so overgrown with wild greenery that the fountain is difficult to find. Just next door is the **Museu Rural,** which contains an educational presentation on *alentejanos* and their handicrafts. (Open Tues.-Sun. 10am-1pm and 3-5pm.) Dominating the square to the south, the **Câmara Municipal** (town hall) occupies a beautiful 1698 convent complete with a splendid staircase and *azulejos* illustrating the life of St. Philip Neri.

Elvas

Known throughout Portugal for its sugarplums, the walled city of Elvas has been fortified since the late medieval period. In the seventeenth and eighteenth centuries, the defenses were reinforced with imposing bastions that are now among the best-preserved in Portugal. Today it is an important market town for an agricultural region abounding in fruit orchards and olive groves. From behind the mammoth fortifications, Elvas preserves the Moorish air of its past, as well as a number of extraordinarily beautiful churches.

Orientation and Practical Information

Elvas is conveniently situated some 15km west of the Spanish border, making it an ideal stopover on your way to or from Badajoz (1 hr. by bus). Infrequent buses connect Elvas' train station to the town center. The bus station is on **Praça da República** (the main square), no more than a five-minute walk from the *pensões* and restaurants. Many stores and restaurants can be found along the busy **Rua da Cadeia** and the two streets perpendicular to it, **Rua da Carreira** and **Rua do Alcamin,** just south of the *praça.*

Tourist Office: Praça da República (tel. 622 36). Decent city maps and many color brochures. Helpful English-speaking staff. Open Mon.-Fri. 9am-7pm, Sat.-Sun. 9am-12:30pm and 2-5:30pm.

Post Office: Rua da Cadeia (tel. 621 11) at the end of the street. Open Mon.-Fri. 8:30am-6pm for mail and Poste Restante. **Postal Code:** 7350.

Telephones: At the post office. **Telephone Code:** 069.

Train Station: Fontainhas, 3km north of city, connected to Praça da República by local bus (every 2 hr., noon-10pm., 50$). To Lisbon (4 per day, 850$), Evora (2 per day, 620$), Portalegre (4 per day, 235$), and Spanish border at Rosal (connections to Badajoz, 2 per day, 75$).

Bus Station: Praça da República (tel. 628 75), next to Turismo. To Lisbon (4 per day, 850$), Portalegre (2 per day, 380$), Evora (3 per day, 525$) and Spanish border at Rosal (connections to Badajoz, 4 per day).

Hospital: Rua da Feira (tel. 622 25).

Police: Rua Andres Gonçalves (tel. 626 13). **Emergency:** Tel. 115.

Accommodations and Camping

Given Elvas' modest fame, it may come as a surprise to discover that inexpensive accommodations here fill up during the summer. As always, try renting a room in a private home. Politely and firmly bargain the price of a single down to 800$, and pay no more than 1500$ for two.

Casa de Hóspedes Arco do Bispo, Rua do Sineiro, 4 (tel. 634 22). From Pr. da República, go down Rua Andres Gonçalves until you reach the police station. The yellow-tiled *pensão* is before the small archway to your right. Small rooms, but all very clean and neat. Bathrooms impeccable. Singles 800$. Doubles 2000$.

Residência O Lidador, Rua do Alcamin, 33 (tel. 626 01). With your back to Turismo, turn the corner to your left, pass under an archway, turn left again onto Rua da Cadeia, and take Rua do Alcamin (1st street on your right). The bathrooms down the hall aren't terrifically clean, and you need a key to use the shower. Singles 875$. Doubles 1500$.

Camping is a few kilometers out of town at **Parque da Piedade.** (Tel. 637 72. 100$ per person and per car, 50-100$ per tent). Cold showers and water are available, and facilities are less than clean.

Food

Elvas has a slew of inexpensive restaurants serving quality food. You can really pamper yourself here (and you're worth it). There are markets along Rua da Cadeia. Every Monday, fresh produce is sold at an outdoor **market,** near the aqueduct.

Bar Os Elvenses, Rua de Evora, 2, follow Rua da Carreira (west of Rua do Alcamin) and bear left at the fork in the street. Filling meals for 350-450$ in a sun-drenched interior patio. *Prato do dia* 450$, *figado grelhado* (grilled liver) 375$. Open Thurs.-Tues. 10am-10pm.

O Vinho Verde, Rua do Tabolodo, 4 (tel. 691 69), around the corner from the above. Mellow place, a bar hangout for locals. Pork steak 300$. Open daily 8am-3pm and 5-9:30pm.

Canal 7, Rua dos Sapateiros, 16 (tel. 635 93), on a street just off the north end of Pr. da República. Good food served in a negative-frills ambience. Roast chicken 295$. Open Mon.-Sat. 11am-3pm and 5-11pm.

Sights

The most spectacular monument in Elvas is the **Aqueduto da Amoreira,** the colossal, five-tiered structure sitting at the entrance to the city. Its construction took 124 years and spanned three centuries. Proudly bearing the city seal, the aqueduct is the largest in Europe and deservedly considered the most beautiful.

The **Igreja de Nossa Senhora da Assunção** sits in front of the mosaic main square. Reconstructed in the sixteenth century in Manueline style, the church has a gracious interior decorated with abstract *azulejos* and covered by a beautifully ribbed and vaulted ceiling. In front of the marble chancel stands an eighteenth-century ivory crucifix and two candelabra made from imported Mozambique wood. Note the marble reliefs of saints and apostles embossed on the walls of the chancel as well as the magnificent eighteenth-century organ at the front entrance. Behind the cathedral and just uphill to the right is the **Igreja de Nossa Senhora da Consolação,** also known as **Freiras.** Ostensibly built in Renaissance style, the octagonal interior actually reveals a mosque-like atmosphere in its explosion of polychromatic abstract tiles. In the small, three-sided *praça* in front of the church stands another of the city's unique monuments. Built in the sixteenth century, the **pelourinho** is an octagonal pillory that culminates in a pyramid. From here, narrow streets lined with color-

ful houses bring you to the **castelo.** Enlarged in the fifteenth century, it was originally constructed by the Moors on the site of a Roman fortress. To the right of
the entrance, hidden behind some plants, is a stairwell leading up to the castle walls
where you can walk around the periphery and view the striking surrounding landscape.

Walking to the left as you leave the castle, follow the alleys skirting the city walls
and pass under the Arco do Miradeiro. As you head downhill, just after the **Cemetério dos Ingleses** (Graveyard of the Englishmen, so-named for the Protestant
Peninsular War soldiers buried there), you'll reach the **Ordem Terceira de São
Francisco,** also known as **Igreja dos Terceiros.** Ask the sacristan here to unlock
the cemetery gate for you. A delightful view of **Forte da Graça,** high on a hill north
of the city, extends from here. The church itself, built in 1741, has an extraordinary
interior including a richly gilded baroque high altar. Lost among all the gilding is
a fine statue of St. Francis, whose creed of poverty and simplicity seems ironically
out of place here. Ask the sacristan to show you the small garden in the back with
its *azulejo*-decorated altar and small well. (All churches and the *castelo* open daily
9:30am-12:30pm and 2:30-7pm; Oct.-April daily 9:30am-12:30pm and 2:30-
5:30pm.)

If time permits, stop at the **Museu Arqueológico e Etnológico,** around the corner
from Pensão Central on Largo do Colegio (the entrance is between the library and
a large church). Once a Jesuit convent, the building now houses life-size paintings
of various saints in its wide corridors. The museum rooms display, among other
articles, Roman mosaics and artifacts from Africa and the Portuguese east. (Open
Mon.-Fri. 9am-1pm and 3-6pm, Sat. 10am-1pm. Admission 50$.) About ½km to
the southeast of Elvas is **Forte de Santa Luzia.** Constructed in a star-shaped pattern,
it was designed to trap all aggressors in crossfire.

Portalegre

The upper Alentejo city of Portalegre lies in the foothills of the Serra de São
Mamede only 24km from the Spanish border. Once an important Moorish fortress
and later a thriving capital of the region's wool tapestry and silk industries, modern-
day Portalegre is now a sleepy, provincial urban center. Most of its inhabitants are
dependent on agricultural work or employment in a nearby chemical plant and cork
factory. Baroque mansions emblazoned with family shields are a common sight in
the old quarter, and the stern grey walls which enclose the **medina,** the Moorish
section, remind visitors and *portalegrenses* alike that the warriors of Islam had no
wish to yield to the Christians this gateway to the plains of the south. Some of the
values and skills of traditional Portalegre have also been preserved as the result of
modern commercial enterprise: A tapestry factory housed in what was once a Jesuit
monastery turns out masterpieces in cloth that may have taken two years to produce; a **cork factory,** originally set up by nineteenth-century English entrepreneurs,
is the inheritor of an ages-old industry of converting cork-oak bark into bottle-
stoppers and insulation material. Cork from this factory is partially responsible for
liveable temperature conditions on NASA spacecraft.

A quiet charm and rich history are perhaps secondary assets to Portalegre when
compared with the stark grandeur of the countryside that surrounds the city. The
craggy hills and cork-oak forests are home to boar, mongoose, and lynx. Lonely
little villages dot the landscape and some are easily accessible by foot through the
countryside. Portalegre's central location in this idyllic area makes it a perfect base
for weekend hikers and those who want to escape the tourist traps of the coast and
savor traditional Portuguese life.

Orientation and Practical Information

In the center of the new town, the *rossio* (roundabout) is the intersection of all
traffic going through Portalegre. The old, walled section of the city is located on

a gently sloping hill. Most sights and Turismo are located in this charismatic part of town.

Tourist Office: In the Convento de Santa Clara, Rua de Elvas (tel. 216 36). English-speaking staff can help you with train and bus schedules. For information about walks in the countryside, it is better to ask the youth hostel warden. (See Accommodations.) Open daily 9am-12:30pm and 2-5:30pm. A more convenient option is the Turismo kiosk (tel. 218 15) at the *rossio* in front of Banco Pinto & Sotto Mayor. A sketchy map of the city, but helpful directions and information. No English spoken. Open daily 10am-7pm.

Post Office: Avda. da Liberdade (tel. 211 11), across the long rectangular traffic island from the *rossio*. All services open Mon.-Fri. 8:30am-6pm. **Postal Code:** 7300.

Telephone Code: 045.

Train Station: 13km south of the city. Infrequent bus connections to the bus station (100$). To Lisbon (4 per day, 920$) and Estremoz (2 per day, 380$) with connections to Evora (420$) and Beja (630$).

Bus Station: Rua Nuna Alvarez Pereira, near the *rossio*. To reach the Turismo kiosk, turn right when you exit the station and cross the *rossio* diagonally. To Lisbon (4 per day, 7 Sat.-Sun., 875$), Estremoz (2 per day, 380$), Evora (2 per day, 520$), and Beja (2 per day, 680$).

Hospital: Avda. São Antônio (tel. 623 14).

Police: Pr. da República (tel. 215 47). **Emergency:** Tel 115.

Accommodations

Pousada de Juventude (IYHF), Pr. da República (tel. 235 68). From Turismo at the convent, walk up Rua de Elvas and turn right following the police sign onto Rua 19 de Junho. Walk under the archway and take the path on your left at the fork; the hostel is at the end of the road. Go through the gates to a sorry-looking building complex, and the hostel is on your left. This superb place is very clean and often completely empty. Hot showers aren't always working. Warden will enthusiastically help you discover the many treasures of the town and region. Kitchen facilities available. Open daily 8-10am and 6-11pm, though if the warden is around and awake at other hours, he'll gladly admit you. 500$. Breakfast included.

Pensão Nova, Rua 31 de Janeiro, 28-30 (tel. 216 05). Follow the signs from the *rossio*. Standard rooms. Singles 1200$, with bath 1400$. Doubles 1600$, with bath 2000$. Breakfast included.

Mansão Alto Alentejo, Rua 19 de Junho, 59 (tel. 222 90). 2 left-hand blocks up from the main office of Turismo. Pleasant, family-run *pensão* in heart of the old city. Homey rooms with typical Alentejano furniture painted with colorful floral designs. Singles 1550$, with bath 2050$. Doubles 2650$, with bath 3550$. Breakfast included.

Food

On Wednesday and Saturday from roughly 6am to 3pm, fresh produce, fish, and meat are sold at the **municipal market,** near the São Bernardo Convent. Bars around the *rossio* serve beer, *bicas* (small espresso coffees), and light meals to consume with the drinks.

Restaurante O Abrigo, Rua de Elvas (tel. 227 78), near Mansão Alto Alentejo. Delicious *açorda Alentejana* (regional soup) 80$. Entrees around 400$. Open Wed.-Mon. 10am-3pm and 5-10pm.

Restaurante "Stop," Rua Don Nuno Alvares Pereira (tel. 213 64), on the same street as the bus station. Tasty *lulas* (squid) in butter sauce 350$. Open Mon.-Sat. 12-2pm and 7-10pm.

Casa Capote, Rua 31 de Junho, 56 (tel. 217 48), in the old city. Come here if your pocketbook is nearly empty, or you're so hungry that atmosphere is just another dirty A-word. Bland ambience. *Bife a Capote* (steak, ham, eggs, fries) 250$. Other entrees 300-350$. Open Sun.-Fri. noon-3pm and 6:30-9pm.

Ponto de Encontro, Rua de Elvas, 8 (tel. 233 86), downhill from Turismo. A strangely charming atmosphere. Low-key operation. *Prato do dia* (a complete and filling meal) 400$. Other entrees (280-400$) may be ordered in ½-portions. Open daily noon-3pm and 6-9pm.

Sights

At the western end of Portalegre's old town stands the **sé** (cathedral), the city's most prominent landmark. Huge granite pilasters enhance a late-Renaissance facade recessed between two towers. The tower's deeply set window frames reduce the openings to narrow slits. Begun in 1556, the airy interior consists of five aisles where lofty columns support Manueline vaulting; the side chapels are connected to each other by narrow passages. In the second chapel on the right, a huge altarpiece depicts scenes from Mary's life. A terrace behind the **sé** (entered through an archway of the bishop's residence) looks out toward the Penha de São Tomé, a rocky hill with 289 steps leading up to a small church. (Open daily 8-11am and 3:30-6pm. Free.)

The **Museu Municipal,** across from the cathedral houses a fine collection of sacred art that once belonged to the city's convents. It's a delightful museum, definitely worth the one-hour guided tour (in Portuguese only), if only to see the stunning ivory reliefs illustrating the *Slaying of the Innocents* and the *Ascension of the Virgin.* Also beautiful is a miniature of Santa Anna holding a miniature Mary who in turn holds an even smaller Jesus. (Open Tues.-Sun. 9:30am-12:30pm and 2-6pm. Admission 50$.) A little farther north you'll find the **Palácio Amarelo** (yellow palace), now decaying but famous for its beautiful seventeenth-century wrought-iron grilles. All the way across the old section of town (near the youth hostel) stands **Casa Museu José Régio,** a home-turned-museum containing a collection of popular and religious regional art crafted by the poet himself. (Open Tues.-Sun. 9:30am-12:30pm and 2-6pm. Admission 50$.)

Near the *rossio,* a seventeenth-century Jesuit college is now the headquarters of **Fabrica Real** (Royal Factory), where paintings are authentically reproduced in woven cloth with 5000 shades of thread. Turn left off Rua 31 de Janeiro as you're walking uphill. (Open daily 10am-4pm.) Not far from the factory, the **Convento de São Bernardo** has a huge Manueline interior decorated with large, 1739 *azulejos* illustrating the life of St. Bernard. Although the convent is now a military installation, it is accessible to the public. Ask the guard at the gate to admit you.

Near Portalegre

One of Portalegre's greatest attractions is the countryside. Make every effort to amble outside the city among the cork trees, olive groves, terraced fields, pastures, and stone walls. Hitchhiking is fairly easy for short hops, and buses run between most towns once or twice per day on weekdays. On weekends schedules change or service stops entirely. Always check with Turismo for changes in the timetable. If you're in reasonably good shape, you'll find that hiking between towns is one of the best ways to explore the area. Footpaths between the villages are numerous. The warden at the youth hostel is a fount of information on jaunts in the hillsides and may even take guests out for daytrips.

Marvão

If you have time to visit only one hill town in Portugal, let it be Marvão. This border stronghold, 24km northwest of Portalegre and only 6km from Spain, preserves its full medieval character in a truly awesome setting. Still encircled by massive walls, the town was of great military importance during the Middle Ages. Inside, all has remained intact, just as it was hundreds of years ago. From the thirteenth-century **castelo,** which occupies the western edge of town, there is a spectacular panorama of the rugged Spanish mountainscape. Below the walls of the town, terraced fields and patchwork pastures bordered by stone walls stretch as far as the eye can see. The gentle tinkling of goat bells drifts upward as shepherds and their herds pass by below.

Marvão's **Turismo** is at Rua Dr. Matos Magalhães, 7330 (tel. 932 26), near the castle. (Open daily 9am-12:30pm and 2-5:30pm.) Stop here for information on the only inexpensive accommodations available in town—rooms in private houses. Free and unofficial **camping** is tolerated inside the castle walls during the summer as long as there is no more than a tent or two. The government-run **Pousada de Santa Maria** is beautiful but definitely a splurge. **Estalgem Dom Denis** (opposite Turismo; tel. 932 36) is a three-star hotel with stone floors and steps. (Comfortable doubles with bath 3200$. Breakfast included.) Among the town's good, inexpensive restaurants is the one at the end of Travessa da Praça. (No name—go through the door on the left off the large stone terrace at the end of the street.)

Marvão is a stop on the Madrid-Lisbon train line. The bus that meets incoming trains (be prepared to wait 1 hr.) will take you up to the town for 80$ and continue on to Castelo de Vide and Portalegre. Though stops in every intervening village make the ride rather slow, the rural scenery outside the windows compensates.

Castelo de Vide

Tiny white houses and a maze of streets and squares stretch along the top of a foothill of the Serra São Mamede to form the old town of Castelo de Vide, 27km due north of Portalegre and 15km west of Marvão. The town's **Judiaria** (Jewish Quarter), once one of the most concentrated in Portugal, still preserves its medieval flavor. Here, the windows and doorways of small houses are framed by Gothic arches, and there is a tiny one-story orthodox **synagogue.** Obtain the key from Turismo before you go. Just below this area, the **Fonte da Vila** (1586), a small granite fountain adorns an intimate square surrounded by venerable old houses.

In the center of town at Praça Dom Pedro V, the dominating **Igreja de Santa Maria** stands across from two seventeenth-century buildings, the baroque **Torre Palace** and the **Santo Amaro Hospital.** The church's barn-like interior, entered through an elaborate door, contains some fine wood carvings. The **castle** (for which the town is named—*vide* means "vine") offers fine surroundings from which to view the landscape below. Unlike those in Marvão, the residents of Castelo de Vide live inside the castle walls, where well-kept houses have ancient arches over their windows and door frames. Follow the signs from the center of town; it is not far from the synagogue to the castle.

Turismo (tel. 913 61) is in the center of town on Rua de Bartolomeu Alvara da Santa near the square. (Open daily 9am-12:30pm and 2-5:30pm.) The staff here can make arrangements for rooms to rent in private houses. Castelo de Vide can prove an inexpensive place to spend the night. Try **Cantinho Particular,** Rua Miguel Bombarda, 9 (tel. 917 51), on a street off the square opposite Turismo. This is a family-run *pensão* with about a dozen rooms and a homey atmosphere. (Singles 600$. Doubles 1000$. Breakfast included.) The ground-floor **restaurant** serves a homemade *prato do dia* for 450$.

Flor da Rosa

Built by the Knights Templar of Malta in 1356, the former monastery of Flor da Rosa rises 24km west of Portalegre. Even in its abandoned and semi-ruined state, it's an extraordinary complex of buildings that consists of a huge barrel-vaulted church, a Gothic cloister, and a splendid Manueline chapter house and refectory. The enthusiastic caretaker will act as guide, pointing out all the unusual features for 50$. Don't be surprised if he asks you to stay for lunch or dinner.

The nearest train station, at **Crato,** is 3km away. From here, you can either walk or hitch to the monastery. Buses from Portalegre also run to Crato, leaving in the early evening and returning the next morning. Check with Turismo in Portalegre for the timetable.

Tomar

Set between a lush park and a craggy hill, this tranquil Ribatejo medieval township graces the banks of the winding Nabão River. Tomar's claim to being the historical center of Portugal is no hype. While Roman and Visigothic remains are ubiquitous, most of Tomar's architectural monuments attest to its former status as the headquarters of the religious order, the Knights of Templar. These warrior-monks first set up residence here in the twelfth century, after helping the first king of Portugal, Dom Afonso Henriques, expel the Moors; however, it was not until the fourteenth century, when the order was persecuted throughout the rest of Europe, that the Templars made Tomar their center of operations. The rather gruff, unsophisticated men of the order soon fell into disfavor with the monarchy, and were replaced by the more noble Order of Christ, Ordem Militar dos Cavaleiros de Nosso Senhor Jesus Christo. Their famous convent-castle, one of the great masterpieces of Portuguese architecture, contains no less than seven cloisters and a window framed by an unusually exotic piece of architectural decoration.

In 1801, Tomar became a military headquarters during the *War of Oranges* with Spain, and troops were garrisoned in the castle. In 1810, the Napoleonic Army followed the Portuguese example with ruinous consequences: French soldiers were responsible for much of the damage done to the priceless paintings and sculptures inside the castle. The Knights of Christ were officially disbanded in 1834, thereby ridding Christian Europe of militant religious orders. Today, Tomar is an extremely pleasant town that hasn't overgrown its natural beauty and rich history. The Cross of Christ (symbol of the Order of Christ and Portugal's banner during the Discoveries) dominates the tile pattern along the modest main streets. Old arching bridges make the short stretch across the river, while families of ducks and swans pass rambunctiously underneath. A vivid dash of green on an otherwise brown canvas, **Mouchão Parque** is actually an islet in the River Nabão. Its fantastic and ancient **roda** (water wheel) still functions, testimony to Tomar's original reliance upon water power to achieve its prosperity.

Orientation and Practical Information

The **Nabão River** divides Tomar, but most accommodations and points of interest, as well as the train and bus stations, are on the west bank. The main drag, **Rua Serpa Pinto,** connects the Ponte Velha (old bridge) to the main square, **Praça da República.** Several blocks south and parallel to the street, **Avenida Dr. Cândido Madureira** runs from the roundabout in the center to the entrance of the Mata Nacional (national park), which is crowned by the convent-castle.

Tourist Office: Avda. Dr. Cândido Madureira (tel. 332 37), facing Mata Nacional dos Sete Montes Park. Open Mon.-Fri. 9:30am-12:30pm and 2-6pm, Sat.-Sun. 10am-1pm and 3-6pm; Oct.-May 9:30-12:30pm and 2-6pm, Sat. 10am-1pm.

Post Office: Avda. Marquês de Tomar (tel. 323 24), across from Mouchão Park. Open Mon.-Fri. 9am-7pm. **Postal Code:** 2300. If reconstruction work is still underway, the temporary office is at Rua João de Oliveira Casquilho, 32, near the bus and train stations.

Telephones: At the post office. **Telephone Code:** 049.

Train Station: Avda. dos Combatentes da Grande Guerra, at the southern edge of town. To reach Turismo, walk straight down the street in front of you until you reach Avda. Dr. Cândido Madureira; Turismo is down 2 blocks on your right at the corner. To Lisbon (11 per day, 500$), Coimbra (7 per day, 470$), Oporto (7 per day, 800$), and Faro (via Libson, 1210$).

Bus Station: Avda. dos Combatentes da Grande Guerra. To Lisbon (5 per day, 700$), Leiria (4 per day, 325$), Fátima (3 per day, 260$), Coimbra (3 per day, 475$), Oporto (via Leiria or Torres Novas, 900$), and Albufeira (1 direct per day, 1200$).

Hospital: Avda. Cândido Madureira (tel. 330 74).

Police: Rua Dr. Sousa (tel. 334 44). **Emergency:** Tel. 115.

Accommodations and Camping

Finding a place to stay isn't a problem unless you arrive during the grand Tabuleiros Festival.

Pensão Nuno Alvares, Avda. Nuno Alvares, 3 (tel. 328 73), 1 block to the right as you leave the bus or train station. Royal rooms, but those facing busy thoroughfare in front are extremely noisy. Singles 1000$, with bath 1500$. Doubles 1300$, with bath 2000$. Breakfast included.

Residencial Luz, Rua Serpa Pinto, 144 (tel. 323 17), near Pr. da República. Cheerful *pensão* with large rooms. Somewhat dim and overfurnished, but excellent location. Singles 1000$, with bath 1400$. Doubles 2500$, with bath 2900$.

Residencial União, Rua Serpa Pinto, 94 (tel. 328 31), down the street from the above. Fantastic rooms and sparkling baths. Singles 1500$, with bath 2250$. Doubles 2700$, with bath 3000$. Breakfast included. 20% discount Nov.-April.

Pensão Luanda, Avda. Marquês de Tomar, 13-15 (tel. 329 29). A pretty location next to a park and the river. Cool, modern interior with marble steps. Run by a hospitable family. Singles with bath 2000-2500$. Doubles with bath 3000-3200$. Breakfast included.

Pensão Tomarense, Rua Torres Pinheiro, 15 (tel. 329 48), 1 block up from Pensão Nuno Alvares. Noisy rooms patrolled by squadrons of biting ants. No hot water. If you arrive late, drop by here to pick up a map of Tomar—then find somewhere else to stay. Singles 1000$, with bath 1300$. Doubles with bath 1850$. Breakfast included.

You can **camp** at **Parque Municipal de Campismo** near the stadium. (Tel. 339 50. 110$ per person, 55-190$ per tent, 80$ per car.) Fourteen kilometers south of Tomar, **Castelo de Bode** (tel. (041) 942 44) lies alongside a 130m-high dam with a fine view of the Zêzere valley. (42$ per person, 35-50$ per tent, 30$ per car.)

Food

Take advantage of Tomar's green spaces by picking up picnic fixings at the **market** (Mon.-Sat. 8am-2pm), on the corner of Avda. Norton de Matos and Rua de Santa Iria on the other side of the river. A section of **Mouchão Parque** is set aside for picnickers. Friday is the big market day with everything from clothes to food on sale from 8am to 5pm.

Snack-Bar Tabuleiro, Rua Serpa Pinto, 140 (no phone), near Pr. da República. Dim, slightly seedy-looking place that serves surprisingly delicious meals. Mouth-watering *bitoque de porco* (375$) comes in an earthenware bowl topped with an egg and buried in a heap of fries. Open daily 9am-midnight.

Restaurante Piri-Piri, Rua dos Moinhos, 54 (tel. 334 94), joins Avda. Dr. Cândido Madureira and Rua Serpa Pinto. Simple but pleasant decor with long, flowing drapes. House specialty is *ensopado de coelho* (rabbit stew), an interesting culinary experience for 550$. Standard meat and fish dishes are also available for the less adventurous. Open daily noon-3:30pm and 7-10:30pm.

Restaurante A Bela Vista, Fonte do Choupo, 6 (tel. 328 70), across Ponte Velha on your left. Excellent entrees ranging from 450-850$. Sit on the vine-covered stone patio and take in a view of the river along with your meal. Open daily 8am-3pm and 6pm-midnight.

Paraíso, Rua Serpa Pinto, 127, near Pr. da República. Not a place for a meal, but this is a lovely old-fashioned coffeehouse, shadowy and cool in the best of Portuguese cafe tradition. Open daily 8am-10pm.

Sights and Entertainment

From its hilltop location, the **Convento de Cristo** dominates the city. It was established in 1320 as the Portuguese home for the disbanded Knights of Templar, who helped reconquer the country from the Moors. Entered through an effusively decorated doorway, the heart of the complex is the Byzantine-Romantic **Templo dos Templares** or **Charola.** Begun in 1162 and modeled after the Holy Sepulchre in Jerusalem, it contains an ornate octagonal canopy that protects the high altar. The knights supposedly attended Mass on horseback, each under one of the arches.

The sixteenth-century **coro** (choir), which extends north from the rotunda, is an outstanding example of Manueline architecture. Here you'll find all the exotic oceanic iconography associated with the style: seaweed, coral, sea chains, stretches of rope, and cork flats. On the west wall, the design culminates into two great windows, both masterpieces of Portuguese design. The circular rose window **Rosacea** has a thick rope border which spirals inward. The winding whirlpool this creates represents the danger of the seas. Below stands Portugal's most popular "window" (an unjustly plain word), an artistic condensation of the golden Age of Discoveries. The **Janela do Capítulo** (chapter window) contains more Manueline symbolism, such as sailor ropes, coral, artichokes (eaten by mariners to prevent scurvy), and an anchor. The modest spheres—a ring around the globe—on either side portray the ambitious aspiration for the ultimate status of grandeur, Portugal's marriage to and possession of the world.

To the south of the nave rises the main cloister, **Claustro dos Felipes,** constructed between 1557 and 1566. It is one of the outstanding masterpieces of Renaissance architecture in all of Europe. Its main feature, the Palladian arch, creates a bold three-dimensionality heightened by the layering of columns and the play of light stone against dark voids. Dramatically bridging the sides, the cloister's corners bulge outward, creating a theatrical effect intensified by the elegant swagger of the spiral staircases leading to the roof. In the center of the cloister, a graceful fountain rises from a Cross of Christ base; a monument to King Felipe II of Castile, who was crowned here as King Felipe I of Portugal during Iberia's brief unification, is also present. On the northeast side of the church is the Gothic **Claustro do Cemetério,** the only part of the complex that dates from the time of Henry the Navigator. Decorated with *azulejos,* stone slabs cover the tombs of Templar and Christ Order Knights that lie underfoot. Adjoining this cloister, through a Renaissance portal, the **Claustro do Lavagem** (Laundry Cloister) is where the monks of the order did their wash. Primitive Gothic arches surround the lower courtyard. Water was supplied by the **Aqueducto dos Pegões** (1593-1614), part of which you can see by leaving the convent and walking to the right, around the new chapter house and Renaissance cloister. As you leave the convent through the main door, you'll see the altars of two incomplete churches, one atop the other. Oddly enough, the altar on the bottom is younger than the one on the top. Apparently, the architect left the country without revealing how to install the key piece into the dome. (Complex open daily 9:30am-12:30pm and 2-6pm; Oct.-Feb. daily 9:30am-12:30pm and 2-5pm. Admission 100$, students free.)

On the way back into town you'll pass the **Capela de Noussa Senhora da Conceição** (Chapel of Our Lady of the Immaculate Conception, 1540-50), an excellent example of early Renaissance architecture. Inside, delicately carved Corinthian columns support a barrel-vaulted nave and a shallow dome in the form of a shell over Mary. The church is closed to the public, but you can borrow the key from Turismo in exchange for some form of ID.

On Rua do Dr. Joaquim Jacinto (or Rua da Judearia) is Portugal's only significant reminder of what was once one of the great Jewish communities of Europe. Now classified as a national monument, the **Sinagoga** or **Luso-Hebraic Museum** (at #73) was constructed in the fifteenth century. The synagogue was used as a temple of worship for only the first 30 years of its existence because in 1496 King Dom Manuel ordered the Jews to convert to Christianity or face expulsion. The Jewish community all but disappeared, at least in name. The synagogue was saved from destruction by its conversion into the village prison and later its reconsecration as a chapel. Only recently rediscovered by Jewish refugees during World War II, the cell-like museum, with its vaulted ceiling supported by four columns, now houses a modest collection of old tombstones, inscriptions, and donated pieces from around the world. (Open daily 9:30am-12:30pm and 2-6pm. If you arrive at other times, just ring at #104 and Mr. Vasco will be glad to open the synagogue for you.)

In keeping with the city's strong tradition, the **Feira Nacional de Artesanato** (National Handicrafts Fair) occurs for a week in either June or July and features handicrafts from the entire country, folklore, *fado,* and theater. But Tomar is most famous for its **Festa dos Tabuleiros** (Feast of Trays), when girls dressed in white parade down the streets. They actually carry huge willow baskets on their heads. Filled with 30 loaves of bread and stacked as high as the girls are tall, the baskets are held together by threads of reeds decorated with paper flowers. The festival recalls the "giving of bread to the poor," a custom begun by Queen (later Saint) Isabel in the fourteenth century. Thousands travel to Tomar for the festival, which is held every two or three years for four days in July. The festival was last held in 1987, so expect the next one in 1989 or 1990.

Santarém

Capital of the Ribatejo province and its major town, Santarém sits on a rocky hilltop overlooking the Tagus River. Along with Beja and Braga, it was one of the three main cities of the ancient Roman province of Lusitania. As a flourishing medieval center it boasted 15 convents. Today Santarém still preserves many of the buildings from its past.

Santarém takes its name from Santa Irene, the nun killed, according to legend, by an admirer who thought her pregnant by a monk (the monk, for some reason, had given her a drink to make her look pregnant). The poor woman was miraculously discovered the following day encased in a marble grave, but then the grave disappeared into the Tagus River.

Orientation and Practical Information

The core of this swiftly-growing town is formed by the densely packed streets between **Praça Sá da Bandeira** and the park **Portas do Sol.** The shallow but wide **Río Tejo** drifts past the park. An expanse of farmland falls away from the elevated town.

Tourist Office: Rua Capelo e Ivenes, 63 (tel. 231 40). Extremely helpful, English-speaking staff can provide you with information on the town's many festivals and local accommodations. Open Mon.-Fri. 9am-7pm, Sat.-Sun. 9:30am-1pm and 3-5:30pm, holidays 9am-12:30pm and 2-5:30pm.

Post Office: Travessa das Condinhas, 25A (tel. 221 01.) Turn right from the front door of Turismo; then make a right and a left. All services, plus **telegrams,** open Mon.-Fri. 8:30am-6:30pm. **Postal Code:** 2000.

Telephone Code: 043.

Train Station: Estação de Caminhos de Ferro (tel. 231 80), 2km outside of town with connecting bus service from the bus station every ½-hr. (70$). To Lisbon (2 per hr., 280$), Tomar (9 per day, 250$), Portalegre (3 per day, 520$), Elvas (4 per day, 640$), and Faro (2 per day, 975$).

Bus Station: Avda. do Brasil (tel. 220 01). To reach Turismo, walk straight ahead and cross the busy Avda. Marquês Sá da Bandeira. Turn right and take Rua Pedro Canavarro uphill, making a right on Rua Capelo e Ivens. To Lisbon (33 per day, 435-500$), Tomar (10 per day, 425-475$), Obidos (5 per day, 400$), and Faro (2 per day, 1125$).

Hitchhiking: To Lisbon, start out on west side of the city, on Rua Prior de Crato. To Oporto, take Rua Alexandre Herculano in the north of the city.

Hospital: Avda. Bernardo Santareno (tel. 270 61).

Police: Campo Sá da Bandeira (tel. 220 22). Emergency: Tel. 115.

Accommodations and Camping

Staying the night here can be expensive. During the Ribatejo Fair prices for rooms may increase 10-40%. Turismo will help you find a double room in a private house during the fair for 2000$ (1000-1500$ during the rest of the year). *Pensões* with amenities may cost a pretty penny (or rather an exquisite escudo), but they're often worth the extra money. True budget *pensões* here often leave plenty to be desired.

Hotel Central, Rua Guilherme de Azevedo, 24 (tel. 220 28), around the corner from Turismo. Large, airy rooms in a nice archaic setting. Comfortable common room with noisy pool salon downstairs. Clean baths have no hot water. Singles 1000$. Doubles 2000$.

Hotel Abidis, Rua Guilherme de Azevedo, 4 (tel. 220 17), down the street from the Central. A nineteenth-century conception of luxury complete with antique phones in each room. Well-decorated living room with fireplace. Singles 1650-1875$, with bath 3450$. Doubles 2800$, with bath 4700$. Breakfast included.

Residêncial Muralha, Rua Pedro Canavaroo, 12 (tel. 223 99) between Avda. Marquês Sé da Bandelra and Rua Capela e Ivens. Recently renovated rooms are extremely comfortable. All come with carpeting and a patio. Singles 2570$, with bath 3320$. Doubles 2750$, with private bath 3500$. Breakfast included.

Pensão Floresta, Largo Infante Santo, 5 (tel. 226 41), in the square across from the park. From the bus station, turn left and make a right at the end of the avenue. The *pensão* is hidden in a dingy storage area, but the seven rooms are quite comfortable. Singles 800$, with window 1000$. Doubles 1500$.

Pensão Coimbra, Rua 31 de Janeiro, 44 (tel. 228 16), opposite the Jardim da República. Spartan, claustrophobic, and reeking of old wood, but these large rooms are the cheapest in town. Consider only as a last resort. Singles 700$. Doubles 1200$.

Escaropim (tel. (063) 554 84), is a camping complex 30km south of town; its facilities include coffee shop, swimming pool, and various courts for sports. (Open Jan. 15-Dec. 13. 380$ per person, 35-50$ per tent, 30$ per car.)

Food

O Verdadeiro Chefe, Largo Terreirinho das Flores, 6, near the archeological museum. Sit at the strangely triangular bar table and feel the beat of English rock. Limited menu, but great *bitoque de porco* (pork steak) with salad, olives, and fries (260$). Open daily 8am-midnight.

O Ribatejano, Avda. do Brazil, 43, 1st floor (tel. 225 50), over the bus station. The atmosphere here may be bland, but the food certainly isn't. House specialties include such regional dishes as *espetadas à Ribatejano* (meat cooked over a skewer Ribatejo style, 500$) and *javali no tachinho de barro* (wild boar cooked in a clay pot). *Manjar do chefe* (120$) is a sinful cake and cream flambé. Open Sun.-Fri. noon-3pm and 7-11pm.

Restaurante Portas do Sol (tel. 231 41), in the municipal park. Breezy outdoor patio overlooks peaceful garden and fountain. *Lulas na brasa* (barbecued squid) braised in butter and lemon 600$. Open Tues.-Sun. 10am-11pm.

Restaurante Caravana, Rua Travessa de Montalvo (tel. 225 68), in the square off Rua Capela e Ivens. Entrees 300-600$. Kind locals at bar. *Frango corado* (ruddy chicken—don't ask) with fries 500$. Open Sun.-Fri. noon-3pm and 6:30pm-10pm.

Restaurante Solar, Largo Emilio Infante de Câmara, 9 10 (tel. 222 39), down the street from the post office. Fresh, high-quality food at affordable prices. Roomy place with family atmosphere. Grilled *lulas* (squid) in lemon and butter (350$), country-style lamb stew (400$). Extensive wine list.

Sights and Entertainment

Dominating **Praça Sá da Bandeira,** Santarém's main square, is the austere facade of the **Igreja do Seminário dos Jesuitas** (Jesuit Seminary Church). Stone friezes, fashioned as ropes, separate each of its three stories, and Latin mottos from the Bible embellish every window lintel and doorway. Some of the side chapel altars are quite handsome, especially the second one on the right with its Bernini-like drama of cooing cherubs floating around polychromatic marble columns. The building to the left of the church, the former **Escolas dos Jesuitas** (Jesuit School) conceals a lovely cloister shaded by two huge palm trees. Between them bubbles a small fountain. (Both open during hours of worship, generally 9am-noon.)

The **Capela de Nossa Senhora da Piedade** (Chapel of Our Lady of Piety), diagonally across from the seminario, was built in 1664 to commemorate a Portuguese victory over the Spanish; Latin inscriptions on the side doors recall the battle. The small domed interior is faced with blue-trimmed red marble. In the center of the *praça* is a statue of the Marquês Sá da Bandeira. Standing back-to-back with him, you will see two streets in front of you. To the left, Rua Serpa Pinto takes you to the wonderful **Praça Velha** (now called Praça Visconte de Serra Pilar), lined with beautiful *azulejos*. Centuries ago, this commercial area was the only place where Christians, Moors, and Jews mixed for social and business affairs. Inside the sixteenth-century **Igreja de Marvila** (Marvila Church) with its Manueline doorway, Moorish influence is evident in the lofty three-aisled interior completely embossed with abstract blue, yellow, and white *azulejos*. The church was built over the site of the first church in Santarém (1050).

Contrasting with this vibrant interior is the nearby **Igreja da Graça,** a Gothic structure built in 1388. Above the door rises a rose window, perhaps the finest in Portugal. Buried in the floor of the chapel to the right of the chancel are the remains of Pedro Alvares Cabral, the explorer who discovered Brazil.

Off Rua de São Martinho, opposite **Torre das Cabaças** (Tower of the Gourds) is the **Museu Arqueológico de São João do Alporão,** a former thirteenth-century church. Two short, squat stone Indo-Portuguese elephants guard its Gothic doorway. Amid an impressive collection of Roman and Arab pottery displayed in grocery-store fashion, you can see some truly extraordinary pieces, as well as many fossils dug up at the nearby site. Here, too, is the Gothic tomb of Dom Duarte de Meneses. This elaborately carved work, with swirling tracery and stone flames bursting forth from pointed arches, contains but one tooth of the poor man whose body was hacked to pieces so fiercely by the Moors that there remained nothing to bury but this meager relic. (Open Tues.-Sun. 10am-noon and 2-5pm. Admission 150$, students free.)

Just in front of the museum begins Avda. V de Outubro. From here you can follow the yellow and blue signs down the avenue leading to a splendid park, **Portas do Sol.** Come here for the view of the olive groves and fertile fields of the Tagus Valley below. Planted in the grounds of the old **castelo,** the grounds also offer an excellent view of the mammoth walls still surrounding Santarém. In addition, they boast a clock sculpted out of bushes which tells the date, month, and year. Nearby is a refreshing pond with fountains and black swans. Equally beautiful is the **Jardim da República,** just north of Praça Sá da Bandeira; it's a veritable island of tranquility amidst a congested sea of exhaust and traffic. Red and green beaches surround a cute candy-cane-striped rotunda sitting by a pond.

Before leaving Santarém, make the extra effort to visit the small **Capela da Nossa Senhora do Monte,** a lovely Romanesque church on the northwest side of town, embraced on two sides by an elegant loggia. On the eastern wall, framed in a Manueline niche, stands a sixteenth-century Madonna. To see the church's interior, illuminated by only two tiny openings, ask at #13 on the street that runs into the church off busy Rua Alexandre Herculano.

The town, however, is not known only for its exquisite churches and spectacular views, but also for its festivals. **Lusoflora '89** (April 4-8) features floral displays from all over the world as well as regional music, folk dancing, and a sailing exhibition. Bring your sweet tooth (and toothbrush) to the sweets fair featuring desserts from all over Portugal. From April 30 to May 7, Santarém plays host to an **International Film Festival** with films from more than 30 countries. A string of short films concerning agriculture and the environment are shown after midnight. A national agricultural exhibition, the **Ribatejo Fair** (June 2-11) is famous for its bullfights. Finally, in the fall the city hosts the **National Festival and Seminar of Gastronomy,** in which each region of Portugal has a day to prepare a typical feast and entertainment. Here you can stuff yourself for days on end (Oct. 21-Nov.).

Costa de Prata

An angry Atlantic foams below the lofty cliffs and the whitewashed fishing villages along the "Silver Coast." Mornings dawn cloudy and grey here, but because of peculiar weather conditions (the meeting of cold and warm fronts at the beach), the gloominess almost always disappears. In spite of the tourists drawn to the pleasant weather and the miles of silvery beaches, the people of Costa de Prata cling tightly to their traditions. Along the coast, this age-old culture thrives in such towns as Nazaré, Figueira da Foz, Peniche, and Barra, on the edge of the Aveiro lagoon. Inland, medieval strongholds and monumental monasteries remain at Obidos, Alcobaça, and Batalha.

Caldas da Rainha

A pleasant, almost tourist-free town of colorful streets, Caldas da Rainha is at the heart of one of Portugal's most interesting regions. Bursts of activity barely disrupt the overall lax pace dictated by the town's tranquil park. (Midday traffic along the narrow streets, however, is the notable exception.) Both a historical curiosity and a bastion of an important art form, Caldas manages to present its star-attractions in a modest, easily-absorbed package, forsaking the overwhelming grandeur attempted by so many Iberian towns.

Most famous for its sulfur springs, the town takes its name, "Baths of the Queen," from Queen Leonor, who in 1484 stopped here for a bath in the thermal springs. The queen then ordered the construction of the world's first **thermal hospital,** where victims of rheumatism, respiratory ailments, and skin afflictions could come to be cured or at least soothed. You can still come to Caldas for treatments. Baths are generally open Monday to Friday from 8am to 6pm. Towels cost 70$. You will be led to a small, private room with a deep stone tub where you can soak in the steaming, soothing, sulfurous, and somewhat smelly water. An hourglass times your allotted 20 minutes. To reach the thermal hospital, walk downhill on Rua da Liberdade from Praça da República, the town's main square. The hospital is at the bottom of the ramp on the left. Even if you don't need a bath, you can have a look at the hospital during the afternoon hiatus (2-4pm).

Caldas's artistic claim-to-fame lies in the town's long, unrivaled prestige in ceramics. Most art museums throughout the country house at least a few characteristic pieces from Caldas. The fine tradition is continued today by sculptors who combine flowing, modern forms with traditional techniques. You can watch artisans at work and view the finished products in an inpromptu workshop/gallery at the **Casa da Cultura.** (Open daily 10am-12:30pm, 2-6:30pm, and 8pm-midnight. Free.)

Across Largo Rainha D. Leonor is the old chapel of the thermal hospital, **Igreja de Nossa Senhora do Pópulo** (Church of Our Lady of the People). The church (like the hospital) was built in the late fifteenth century at the request of Queen Leonor. Most prominent in the early Manueline design are the Moorish tiles and arches. The simplistic, eight-petal flower dome overhead is certain to catch your eye. The **treasury** contains fanciful robes of the queen, a Gothic wood sculpture of São Silvestre, and a small collection of eighteenth-century silverware. (Open daily 9am-12:30pm and 2-5pm. Admission 100$.)

One of Portugal's most beautiful parks, **Parque Dom Carlos I** is a popular place for emersion in a peaceful setting. The focal point of the garden sanctuary is the small lake complete with its own idyllic islet. The calm waters constitute a training course for struggling rowers and lovers alike. Watch out for the crabs. Nearby, the **Museu de José Malhoa** houses an impressive collection of modern sculptures and ceramic pieces. One room of paintings contains landscapes by Fausto Sampaio; the subject matter spans the Portuguese empire from the boot in Sagres to a lazy afternoon in sub-tropical Macau. (Open Tues.-Sun. 10am-12:30pm and 2-5pm. Admission 150$, students with ID free.)

If you plan to stay overnight, try **Residencial Portugal,** Rua Almirante Cândido dos Reis, 30 (tel. 226 06), which has sparkling rooms and a restaurant worth trying even if you don't spend the night. (Singles 1500$, with bath 2000$. Doubles 2000$, with bath 3000$.) **Pensão Parque,** Rua de Camões, 63 (tel. 326 49), offers some of the town's cheapest and oldest beds. The neat rooms are large and carpeted, though the lighting is poor. (Singles 800$. Doubles 1500$.) Turn right as you enter Largo Rainha D. Leonor from Praça da República; the *pensão* is across the street from the park. **Orbitur** (tel. 323 67) has a convenient campsite in Parque Dom Carlos I. (253$ per person, 190$ per tent, 210$ per car. Hot showers 75$.)

Even if you don't want to buy any produce, visit the large **Mercado da Fruta** (Fruit Market). Everyday, Praça da República buzzes with color and activity as local vendors and shoppers amass in a frenzied morning of commerce. Inexpensive, no-frills meals can be had at **Churrasqueira Zé do Barrete,** Travessa da Cova da Onça, 16 (tel. 327 87), off the busy pedestrian shopping thoroughfare Rua Almirante Cândido dos Reis. An entire *frango no churrasco* (barbequed chicken) is just 400$. (Open Mon.-Sat. 9am-midnight.)

The **tourist office** (tel. 345 11) is centrally located in Praça da República. The staff can only dole out brochures and maps; no English is spoken. (Open Mon.-Fri. 9am-7pm, Sat.-Sun. 10am-1pm and 3-7pm.) The **post office,** Rua Heríos da Grande Guerra (tel. 321 56), is across the street from the bus station. (Open Mon.-Fri. 8:30am-6:30pm, Sat. 9am-12:30pm.) The **postal code** is 2500. The **train station** is located in the northwestern edge of town. To reach the *praça,* take Avda. Independência Nacional (straight ahead), which veers right and changes into Rua Dr. Miguel Bombarda. Continue straight ahead onto Rua Almirante Cândido dos Reis; both Turismo and the *praça* are at the end of the street. Six trains per day connect the town to Lisbon (440$). There is frequent bus service, to Obidos (14 per day, 65$) and Peniche (7 per day, 250$). The **bus station** is on Rua Heróis da Grande Guarra. Turn left as you exit the station and left again 2 blocks later onto Rua Almirante Cândido dos Reis.

Obidos

Inside medieval walls, colorful geometric patterns highlight Obidos's freshly painted white buildings. Long a favorite haunt of the Portuguese royalty, the town was once frequently chosen as the queen's dowry. Today, it is designated a national monument and tourists come to admire this remarkably well-preserved museum town. Despite its label as a "must-see" village—probably because of it—Obidos is an antiseptic, lifeless place. No tourist pamphlet can honestly claim that this town of fantastically clean streets, high-priced restaurants, and multilingual inhabitants is "typically Portuguese." Obidos is an exhibition piece, nothing more, and you should treat it as one: Appreciate its beauty, take some pictures, and after a few hours, leave. Cheaper lodgings can be found in other towns nearby such as Caldas da Rainha, and more fun can be had at the beaches around Peniche, 20km away.

As the bus makes its uphill approach and drops you off just outside the walls, Obidos looks attractive yet imposing. Portugal's first king, Dom Afonso Henriques, must have felt somewhat humbled when he tried several times to conquer the town from the Moors. Legend has it that the leader disguised himself with cherry branches (for which the town is still known) to penetrate the fortifications. Forces at the main gate diverted the attention of the Moorish guards, while the king's forces, in their cherry tree garb, approached the castle. Sitting at her window, the Moorish princess asked her father if trees walked. Of course the king replied no, but the princess insisted. By the time the king realized what was happening, the Portuguese had pushed down the castle door, later named Porta da Traição (Door of Betrayal).

Construction of the present city walls, built upon Moorish fortifications, began in the twelfth century. At that time, the Lagoa de Obidos came right up to the town walls. Today the lagoon is over 7km away. The main entrance has always been **Porta da Vila;** Dom Afonso Henriques had to pass through this very portal as you must today.

Built on the foundations of a Visigothic temple and later used as a mosque, the seventeenth-century **Igreja de Santa Maria** occupies a *praça* enhanced by a fountain bearing the arms of Queen Leonor. When her only son was killed in a riding accident, his body fell into the river and was returned by a fisherman who found it in his net. In memory of her son, the queen adopted the fishing net as her symbol. The church displays eighteenth-century *azulejos* near the entrance and Islamic *azulejos* at either side of the altar. In the middle, seventeenth-century *azulejos* with swirling patterns reach for a wooden ceiling painted with arabesques, flowers, and chubby cherubs. The work is by students of the seventeenth-century artist Josefa de Obidos, whose more graceful and vividly colored canvases fill the retable to the right of the main altar. At the far left, the exquisite Renaissance tomb of João de Noronha (1526-28) features a sculpted stone *Piedade* with St. John and Mary Magdalene. (Open daily 9:30am-12:30pm and 2:30-7pm; Oct.-May daily 9:30am-12:30pm and 2:30-5pm.)

Behind the church, the unimpressive **Museu Municipal** houses Portuguese paintings and religious Gothic sculptures from the sixteenth to eighteenth centuries. (Open daily 10am-12:30pm and 2-5pm. Free.) A left turn from the museum leads to another square and the **Igreja de São Pedro.** Built on the site of a Gothic temple that was razed by the earthquake of 1755, the church is crowned by a curious dome steeple. Inside, the arch standing near the entrance is the only reminder of the original temple. The high altar contains some interesting guilded woodwork. At the eastern end of Rua Direita stands Igreja de Santiago and the **castle walls.** Here, a staircase leads to the upper reaches of the walls where you can walk around the entire periphery (1½km). The ramparts command a beautiful view of Obidos's weathered orange roofs, whitewashed churches, square medieval castle, and ancient aqueduct—a toy-like structure, outside the walls, that dates from the twelfth century. One of Portugal's many windmills stands nearby, conveniently framed by a "window" carved out of the wall. You can see the windmill from Torre do Facho at the extreme western end of the walls.

The only slightly inexpensive place to stay is **Casa de Hóspedes Madeira,** on Rua Direita (tel. 952 12). The rustic rooms are decorated with a bonanza of traditional handicrafts. If you don't mind the souvenir-shop feeling, you may actually enjoy the forced charm. (Mid-July to mid-Aug.: Singles 2500$. Doubles 3000$. Mid-Aug. to mid-July: Singles 2000$. Doubles 2500$.) A **private room** in town costs 2000-2500$, not exactly a thrifty option; Turismo can help make the arrangements. Camping is your best alternative to the high-priced accommodations in Obidos. Despite promises from city hall, there is no official campsite near town. Therefore, authorities turn a blind eye to **unofficial camping** near the aqueduct. The olive trees and nearby cemetery can't be considered premium surroundings, but what do you want for nothing—wicker?

Obidos is no haven for the hungry budget traveler. The fact that locals aren't to be found in the restaurants tells you something about the prices for cooked meals. If you're making a daytrip, consider picnicking. Purchase your provisions at the **minimarket** near the town's main gate. Otherwise, **Café I de Dezembro,** on Largo San Pedro, serves entrees for around 500$. Before leaving Obidos, sample *ginga,* a sweet liqueur made from wild cherries. The local variety is smoother than that served in other parts of the country. Try a glass at the **Ibn Errik Rex Bar,** on Rua Direita.Thick metal chains and large rusty hooks hanging from the ceiling give the place a lot of atmosphere. Decanters of *ginga* top every table.

Turismo (tel. 952 31) is in an adobe house on the main street, Rua Direita, right before Praça de Santa Maria. The busy but knowledgeable staff is eager to help and extremely pleasant. (Open daily 9:30am-8pm; Sept.-June daily 9:30am-6pm.) The

post office (tel. 951 99) is nearby in Praça de Santa Maria. (Open Mon.-Fri. 9am-12:30pm and 2:30-6pm.) The **postal code** is 2510.

Obidos is an easy two-hour train ride from Lisbon's Rossio Station. You can either take a commuter train to Cacém and then change trains to Obidos (4 per day, 440$), or take a train directly to Caldas (6 per day, 440$). The train station is just outside the city, due north. There are frequent bus connections via Caldas da Rainha (12 per day, 65$) to Lisbon, Santarém, and Nazaré. The **bus stop** is down some stairs form the main gate.

Peniche and Berlenga Islands

Portugal's second-largest fishing fleet is based in **Peniche,** a busy town 24km from Obidos. On a rocky peninsula edged by rugged cliffs, Peniche is connected to the mainland by a narrow isthmus. Travelers often overlook the town as they hurry on to the Berlenga Islands, but a glimpse of its interesting monuments and two beautiful beaches might cause you to linger a while. Moreover, the workaday quality of this town comes as a relief after the tourist-oriented cities to the south (although women may be hassled by fishermen and other salty types). At night, walk along the dock area to see the crates of fish and crushed ice packed neatly into the awaiting trucks. The town's festivals, held the first weekend in August, bring arts and crafts, music, and a terrific temporary amusement park to Peniche.

Dominating the town are the high walls and bastions of the **fortaleza,** a sixteenth-century fortress that Salazar used as a political prison and that later became a camp for Angolan refugees. It now houses the **Museu de Peniche,** which contains local paintings and sculptures as well as a section devoted to the Anti-Fascist Resistance during the "New State" regime. (Open Tues.-Sun. 10am-noon and 2-7pm. Admission 50$.)

Churches are plentiful in this bustling port (women who suffer the lascivious leers of the seamen may feel the town has great need of them). Visit the baroque **Igreja da Ajuda,** at the end of a pleasant walk along **Parque do Murraçal,** at the opposite end of town from the fortress. Its biblical *azulejos* are placed above delightful pastoral scenes depicting classical ruins, medieval castles, and luxurious gardens. Be sure to look at the chancel's ceiling, where polychrome tiles reflect a strong Moorish influence.

The most impressive sights, however, are found just outside the town along the peninsula. The best way to savor the crude ocean atmosphere is to walk all the way around the peninsula (8km). Feel the strong winds and sniff the salty ocean air as waves pound against the cliffs below. Start your hike at **Papôa,** a small, rocky peninsula that juts out to the north of Peniche. Stroll out to the tip, where orange cliffs protrude from a swirling blue sea, affording fine views of the coast. On the eastern side, a windmill stands amidst farmers' fields, and nearby lie the ruins of an old fortress, **Forte da Luzo.** At the cove, fishermen standing perilously close to the cliffside bait their long lines. The **Santuário de Nossa Senhora dos Remédios** stands at the edge of a Portuguese ghost town. In this unusually tiny chapel, *azulejo* panels, decorating the walls and covering the cylindrical ceiling, glow in the semi-darkness. Only six pews fit inside the chapel proper while another six sit in the sun-lit anteroom. Inside, an aged stone nave to your left lies a glass coffin with a statue of Jesus. **Cabo Carvoeiro** and its lighthouse sit at the extreme western end of the peninsula. At the cape, enjoy the view of **Nau dos Corvos,** an odd rock formation popular as a bird roost.

For sun and surf, head to either of Peniche's two beaches. **Praia de Peniche de Cima,** along the northern crescent, is more beautiful and has warmer water, but watch out for the undertow. The beach connects with the great beach at **Baleal,** a small fishing village popular with tourists. The southern beach **Praia do Molho Leste** has considerably colder water, but is safer.

Pensões fill up quickly in July and August, so try to arrive early in the day. As an alternative, women and children roam the streets ready to connect you to a room in a private home. **Pensão Marítimo,** Rua Antonio Cervantes, 14 (tel. 728 50), 2 blocks inland from the fortress, offers luxurious rooms with elegant drapes, chandeliers, and modern baths. (Singles 1500$. Doubles 1800$, with bath 2000$.) A considerable drop in quality and price, **Pensão Aviz,** Largo Jacob Rodrigues Pereira, 2, is in the small square in front of the public garden. The rooms are painfully plain, and the bathroom is nothing to phone home about. (Singles 800$. Doubles 1300$.) The closest **IYHF youth hostel** (tel. 421 27; 550$ per night) is at Praia Areia Branca, 13km south. The hostel is accessible by the local bus to Lisbon (9 per day, 200$). An overcrowded **municipal campground,** (tel. 725 29), 1½km outside of town, fronts a beach. (60$ per person and per car, 100$ per tent. Hot showers 45$.)

For inexpensive meals, **Restaurante O Navegante** and **Casa Canhoto,** almost next to each other on Rua 13 de Infantaria, both serve delicious food grilled outside. At 475$, the *lulas grelhadas* (grilled squid) is especially good. Excellent and cheap restaurants also line Avda. do Mar.

Turismo, Rua Alexandre Herculano (tel. 722 71), is hidden in a garden. The kind, well-informed staff is one of the most helpful you'll encounter. (Open July daily 9am-9pm; Aug. daily 9am-10pm; Sept.-June daily 10am-12:30pm and 2:30-5:30pm.) The **post office,** Rua Arquitecto Paulino Montez (tel. 711 15), is around the corner from the bus station. (Open Mon.-Fri. 9:30am-12:30pm and 2:30-6pm.) The town's **postal code** is 2520. The **bus station** is on Rua Estado Português da India. To reach Turismo, turn left on Largo Bispo Mariana and left again at the public garden. Buses travel to Lisbon (9 per day, 575$) and Caldas (9 per day, 250$).

Rising out of the Atlantic Ocean some 12km northwest of Peniche, the **Ilhas Berlengas** (Berlenga Islands) present an awesome and rugged beauty that is also a bit terrifying. Consisting of one main island about a square mile in size and numerous reefs and isolated rocks, the archipelago is home to hundreds of screeching seagulls, wild black rabbits, and a small fishing community. A long flight of steps, cut into the cliffs, ascends to the island's grassy, treeless summit. The tiring trek to the top yields a spectacular view of the seventeenth-century **Fortaleza de São João Baptista,** which sits on an islet surrounded by the sea and connected to the land by a narrow causeway. The island, encircled by sparkling blue waters, is indented by deep gorges and rocky cones. One named the "Blue Grotto" has been justly compared to the better-known grotto of the same name on Capri. South of the castle, a spectacular 75-meter natural tunnel leads to a small rocky inlet. For 250$ to 350$ per person (in groups of 8-10), a motorboat will take you to explore some of the island's scenic wonders, but unfortunately you won't be allowed to swim. For a dip, you'll have to head over to one of the island's two protected **beaches,** one by the landing dock and the other by the castle.

Though you can camp on the island for free, the old castle, once a state-run *pousada,* is now a **hostel** (no phone) that rents spartan rooms for 350-400$ per person. You'll need to bring your sleeping bag. The hostel has a kitchen, but no cooking utensils. The small canteen carries basic food, and you can eat either in the *pousada's* former dining room or in one of the deep window ledges of the fortress. Check with Turismo in Peniche before setting out—reservations may be necessary. (Open June-Sept. 20.) **Pavilhão Mar e Sol** (tel. 720 31), the island's only good restaurant, is also the island's only restaurant. It also offers rooms with private showers for a hefty price. (Doubles with breakfast 4500$, with lunch and dinner 6000$.) Near the boat landing, there's a tiny **supermarket** as well as bathroom facilities.

In July and August, the **ferry** to Berlenga is so crowded that you may need to buy your ticket an hour or so in advance. From Peniche's public dock, boats make three trips per day to the Berlengas in July and August (9am, 11am, and 5pm, returning 10am, 4pm, and 6pm), and one per day in June (10am, returning 6pm) and September (10am, returning at 5pm). The charge is 500$ if you make the round-trip in the same day, 300$ each way if you stay on the islands overnight. Beware that the crossing can be very rough: Even the hardiest sailors should carry seasickness pills and sit in the back of the boat. No matter how green you turn, however, the one-hour journey is definitely worthwhile. If you intend to stay the night, bring a flashlight. The 15-minute walk from the bar near the boat landing to the hostel is illuminated only by periodic flashes from the lighthouse.

Nazaré

In spite of the numerous tourists who flock here every summer, Nazaré has miraculously maintained its traditional way of life. Above all, this village lives for the sea. The people spend the day going to sea, cleaning and salting the fish, taking it to market, mending nets, and preparing bait. They cling to their own particular form of dress unlike any other community in Portugal. The typical Nazaré fisher, barefoot with plaid pants rolled up to the knees, wears a black stocking cap in which he keeps tobacco, matches, hook and line, and, in the bulging hem, whatever money he may have. Women typically wear seven petticoats and a thick shawl. Large gold-colored earrings dangle from faces toughened by the hot summer sun. The boats, too, are ancient in design. Long, narrow, and brightly painted, the prow of each sturdy vessel curves to a delicate point.

In the midst of all this tradition simmers a veritable playhouse. Nazaré has a large sandy crescent, shielded in large part by a mass of beach tents arranged in a strangely pleasing manner. The beach-side promenade Avda. da República is always cluttered with fun-seekers carousing on the avenue at all hours of the day and night. Nazaré has acquired neither the touristic blandness that plagues the Algarve, nor the prices that usually accompany it.

Orientation and Practical Information

Nazaré is organized north-south along a long, populated, and wind-swept beach. On a cliff to the north of town lies the **Sítio,** the old town, which preserves a sense of calm and tradition less prevalent in the rapidly developing resort below. To get from the bus station to Turismo (a 10-min. walk), walk to Avda. da República, which lines the beach, and then turn right. Turismo is along the avenue between the two major *praças*. The nearest train station (Valado), 5km away on the Lisbon-Figueira da Foz line, serves both Nazaré and Alcobaça. Regular buses shuttle between the three points (65$).

Tourist Office: Avda. da República (tel. 521 94). New office along the beach. Pick up a practically useless map of the city. Open daily 10am-10pm; Oct.-June daily 9:30am-12:30pm and 2-5:30pm.

After-Hours Currency Exchange: Viagens Maré, Centro Comercial Maré, Store #10 (tel. 519 28), next to Hotel Maré in Praça Dr. Manuel de Arriaga. Open daily 9am-midnight.

Post Office: Avda. da Independencia Nacional (tel. 516 34). From Praça Dr. Manuel de Arriaga, walk up Rua Mousinho de Albuquerque, which veers to your right. Open Mon.-Fri. 9am-12:30pm and 2:30-6pm. Also a branch in a caravan along the beach. Open Mon.-Fri. 9am-12:30pm and 2:30-6pm, Sat. 10am-noon and 1-4pm and 5-8pm, Sun. 1-4pm. **Postal Code:** 2450.

Telephone Code: 062.

Bus Station: Avda. Vieira Guimarães (tel. 511 72), on a street perpendicular to Avda. da República. Express service to Lisbon (4 per day, 625$), Coimbra (5 per day, 575-600$), Oporto (3 per day, 825$), and Tomar (3 per day, 475$). Also regular service to Leira (6 per day, 260$), Alcobaça (15 per day, 110$), and Caldas da Rainha (8 per day, 250$) for connections to Obidos and Peniche.

Baggage Check: In the bus station. 35$ per bag.

Hospital: Tel. 511 16.

Police: Rua Subvila, 9 (tel. 512 68). **Emergency:** Tel. 115.

Accommodations and Camping

Any fears of not finding a place to bed down for the night will be dispelled as soon as you get off the bus: You'll immediately be accosted by housewives screaming "*Chambres, chambres!*" Although prices are lower than at *pensões,* a "room" may be anything from a comfortable bedroom with private kitchen and bathroom to a prison-like cell at an inflated price. Insist on seeing your quarters before settling the deal. As always, bargain, and never pay more than the lowest prices for a room in a *pensão.*

Pousada de Juventude (IYHF) (tel. 995 06). Located at the pretty but inconvenient site of São Martinho, about 5km south of Nazaré. Take the bus to Caldas da Rainha, and get off at São Martinho, then take either the direct bus to the hostel or the one to Alfeizerão and walk up the path (25 min.). Clean and rustic, with polished floors and acres of gardens. 500$. Breakfast included. Lunch or dinner 350$.

Residencial Marina, Rua Mouzinho de Albuquerque, 6A (tel. 515 41), off Praça Souza Oliveira. Cheery, spacious rooms with carpeted interior decked out in modern furnishings. Spotless baths. Gracious management. Singles 1000$, with bath 1200$. Doubles 1800$, with bath 2200$.

Pensão Nazarense, Rua Mouzinho de Albuquerque, 48 (tel. 511 88), up the street from the above. Clean and economical, even compares favorably with the *chambres,* but fills up early. Pricey restaurant below serves meals for 750$. Singles 800$, with breakfast 1000$. Doubles 1500$, with breakfast 1800$.

Pensão Europa, Praça Dr. Manuel de Arriaga, 23 (tel. 515 36), on a main square parallel to the beach. Small, cramped, bright rooms with high ceilings. Some rooms overlook the beach. Singles 1200$. Doubles 2000$.

Camping is available at **Orbitur** (tel. 511 11), about a 3-kilometer uphill climb from town. (253$ per person, 190$ per tent, 210$ per car. Hot showers 75$.) The site is shaded by pines, and bungalows are available. Bus service is infrequent; take a taxi if you arrive at night. A newer and closer site, **Vale Paraíso,** on Estrada Nacional, 242 (tel. 515 68), includes swimming pools, a restaurant/bar and a supermarket. (295$ per person, 265-300$ per tent, 245$ per car. 20% discount Oct.-May.)

Food

As long as you stick to fresh fish, you're going to eat well no matter where you are. But if your escudos are running low, remember that the tourist-filled restaurants along the beach and in the main square tend to be more expensive than the small places along the side streets, near the bus station, and around Praça Souza Oliveira. For fresh fruits and vegetables, shop at the large **market** across from the bus station. (Open daily 8am-1pm; in winter Tues.-Sun. 8am-1pm.)

A Casinha do Graça, Avda. Vieira Guimarães, 30L (tel. 522 11), across the street from the bus station. Cute atmosphere: Fresh flowers top every checkerboard picnic table, and you expect a family to step out of the little house. Delicious fish stew 500$. Other entrees 400-500$. Open daily 11:30am-3pm and 6-11pm.

Forno d'Orca, Largo das Caldeiras, 11 (tel. 518 14). From Praça Souza Oliveira, follow Travessa do Elevador toward the funicular. The pleasant outdoor patio is in the small square immediately on your right. Excellent and generous helpings of *lulas* (squid) or *ameijos* (clams) 550$. Open daily noon-midnight.

Casa Santos, Rua Dr. José Maria Carvalho Júnior, 19A, a narrow street 1 block toward the water from the bus station. Small place with a surprising touch of elegance. Pretty tablecloths and bright pink flowers top every wooden table. Sardines and salad (300$) served with a smile. Open daily 11am-9pm.

O Frango Assado, Praça Dr. Manuel de Arriaga, 20 (tel. 518 42). For perhaps the best and most unconventional meal you'll have in Portugal, pick up a heavenly barbecued chicken piri-piri (690$ per kg). Even though they'll cut the chicken, you'll still have to tear, rip, and peel caveman-style. Take-out only. Open daily noon-9pm.

Sights and Entertainment

Other than the living cultural spectacle the *nazarenses* put on themselves every-day, there isn't much to see in Nazaré. Do take the strange, stairway-shaped funicular (20$) up to the **Sítio**, all there was of Nazaré before the tourist boom. Here, the uneven cobbled streets and weathered buildings tell of a less refined quarter; the relative peace and solitude are a welcome change. The striking facade of the **Igreja de Nossa Senhora da Nazaré** (Church of Our Lady of Nazaré) fronts a large square, site of the annual festival dedicated to Nazaré's patron saint (2nd week in Sept.). The church itself, approached by a lantern-jaw staircase, rises from a hand-some portico that wraps around three sides of the building. Inside, pendentives dec-orated with a dense foliage of grapevines support an elegant, coffered dome. The motif is repeated on the twisted columns of the high altar. On the transept walls, *azulejos* illustrate scenes from the Bible.

On a side street leading off the *praça,* the **Museu Dr. Joaquim Manso** contains exhibits relating to the maritime lifestyle of the region. On display are miniature fishing boats and objects from the fishing industry. Religious paintings and objects of superstition round out this small museum's modest collection. (Open daily 9:30am-12:30pm and 2-6pm, in off-season Tues.-Sun. daily 9:30am-12:30pm and 2-6pm. Admission 100$, students and Sun. free.) In a corner of the square diago-nally across from the church stands the tiny, whitewashed **Ermida da Memória** (Hermitage of Memory). The closet-like room is covered from floor to ceiling with *azulejos.* Tradition has it that the hunter Dom Fuas Roupinho nearly plunged to his death while chasing a deer. As he was tottering on the edge of the abyss, Our Lady of Nazaré appeared and saved him. Dom Fuas then built the chapel to com-memorate the miracle. Beside the hermitage, a splendid panorama of the lower town's orange-tiled roofs fans out. The magnificent view of the town and coastline, 120m above the sea, is breathtaking.

In the **Praia quarter,** Avda. da República is infested with cars, tour buses, local vendors, and bronzing bodies trying to manuever through the traffic to the sanctity of the beach. Sure it's crowded, but you can always reserve a spot of sand for your-self underneath the virulent afternoon sun. Be certain to stay in the populated area if you do venture into the water, avoiding the dangerous waters on the far side of the Sítio. The nautically inclined may consider renting **windsurfs** at the **Watersport Centre Nazaré,** a grandiose name for the dinky establishment located in a beach cabin in front of the Avda. da República (2 blocks south of the bus station street).

At around 7:30pm, visit the **port** at the southern end of the Praia quarter to wit-ness the return of fishing boats through the surf. On the way back to the center of town, pause at the lively auction at the shorefront market. Here local restaura-teurs bid for the best-looking catches of the day as the unfortunate fish are rolled past in plastic tubs. After catching some rays with what seems to be all of Europe, join the continent at one of the bustling cafes in Praça Souza Oliveira and sip *bicas* until 1am. Of course, you might want to graduate to **Discoteca Jeans Rouge** (opens at 11:30pm), just up the street from the *praça,* and dance away the early morning. More folkloric entertainment can be seen every Tuesday and Friday at 10pm in the **casino,** on Rua de Rui Rosa, where a local group performs traditional dances called *viras.* (Admission 300$.) **Praça de Touros,** in the Sítio, hosts bullfights every other Saturday or Sunday in summer (seats from 600$); inquire at Turismo for de-tails.

Alcobaça

In a lovely valley watered by two rivers—the Alcoa and the Baça—stands the town of Alcobaça, which owes its very existence to the great Cistercian **Mosteiro de Santa Maria,** a strong candidate for the most beautiful building in Portugal. The town was founded in 1153 as an offering of thanks after the recapture of Santarém from the Moors.

Carved pinnacles decorate the three wide staircases leading up to the main front of the abbey; above them rises a handsome baroque facade, richly embellished with sculpture. Between two robust towers rests a carved niche framing a swooning Mary and crowned by two plump cherubs. Of the original Gothic structure only the main doorway and rose window remain.

The interior of the **church,** the largest in Portugal, is extraordinary for its clarity, austerity, and simplicity. Notice that there aren't many windows, but the church hall captures a lot of sunlight, which is a break from the usual solemnity of Portuguese churches. Two parallel rows of towering pillars stretch into the distance, capped by immense overarching vaults. To increase the impression of height, the pillars are placed close together, making for narrow, elongated bays. Note how the attached columns end about four-fifths of the way down the shafts, emphasizing bold three-dimensionality and providing extra space for the congregation. The surprising depth of the window niches indicates how thick the walls have to be to support the vaulted ceiling. From behind the choir radiates a series of chapels, each enhanced by one terra cotta sculpture of a saint; a vestibule leads to the sacristy and the Chapel of the Holy Sacrament. A chapel off the south transept shelters a beautiful eighteenth-century painted terra cotta *Death of Saint Bernard.* Though the work was severely damaged by Napoleon's troops, you can still admire the four angels playing musical instruments as Mary hovers on a cloud surrounded by the sad, fat faces of cherubs.

The most beautiful pieces of sculpture in the church, the fourteenth-century **tombs of Inês de Castro and Dom Pedro,** lie in the transept. Inês, the mistress and secret wife of Pedro while he was prince, was assassinated in 1355 by noblemen jealous of her influence. When the outraged prince became king some years later, he exhumed the body of his beloved, dressed her in royal robes, sat her on a throne, and made the court pay homage to her by kissing her decomposed hand. After the macabre ceremony was completed, she was reinterred in an exquisitely carved tomb in the king's favorite monastery, Alcobaça. The king had his own tomb placed opposite hers so that they could be reunited at the moment of resurrection.

Decorated with reliefs depicting scenes from the life of Jesus, the tomb of Inês rests on crouching figures in the north transept. Especially interesting, the *Last Judgment* (at the statue's feet) shows naked souls tumbling into the mouth of a dragon while, above, the saved serenely march toward Jesus. The stone sarcophagus of Dom Pedro, borne by six lions, is adorned with reliefs depicting the life of St. Bartholomew, the king's patron saint. A wheel of fortune stands at the head of the tomb, guarded by Vanna, while the king's dying moments are portrayed on the opposite side.

A doorway on the north side of the church leads to the monastic rooms which surround the two-story **Claustro do Silêncio** (Monastery of Silence). Of unequal size, the individual bays of the cloister are ornamented by discs whose tracery shows a Moorish influence. Delicate twisting columns support the bays overhead. From here you can see the layered baroque towers which contrast with the stark crenelated walls of the cathedral.

The monastic rooms have been so stripped of their ornamentation that wandering through them is a bit like wandering around the cold and spartan spaces of ancient catacombs. The chapter house, which opens off the east gallery, is now surrounded by enormous, colored terra cotta statues of saints and angels made by the monks in the seventeenth and eighteenth centuries. Huge fireplaces and chimneys that stretch all the way up to the ceiling dominate the kitchen. At the end of the room there is a curious fountain supplied with water by the town's two rivers; when the Cistercians were ready to prepare dinner, they would simply open a grille and allow fresh fish to flow into the basin, ready to be cooked. The finest of the abbey's rooms, the **refectory** has ribbed vaulting and a staircase built directly into the wall leading to a pulpit. The last of the chambers is the **Sala dos Reis** (Room of the Kings), embellished with seventeenth-century *azulejos* depicting the founding of the convent. Life-size statues of the kings of Portugal, sculpted by the monks themselves, look down from an upper ledge. Since many were damaged by Napoleonic vandalism, those of uncertain identity bear question marks next to their names. (Abbey open daily 9am-7pm; Oct.-March daily 9am-5pm. Admission 150$, students free.)

The **Museu Nacional do Vinho,** Portugal's national museum devoted to the history, production, and consumption of wine, lies about 1km outside of town on the road to Batalha. A meticulous, multilingual guide leads tours through the musty, warehouse-like museum, stopping at ancient wine presses and giant storage jars. The tour also passes resin-coated rooms that once served as enormous wine vats, each devoted to a specific wine-producing region. At the end you can purchase a bottle of the museum's subject matter (from 200$) or an old-fashioned ceramic mug from which to imbibe it. (Open Mon.-Fri. 9am-12:30pm and 2-5:30pm. Free.)

Cheerful and clean rooms can be found at **Pensão Corações Unidos,** Rue Frei Antonio Brandão, 39 (tel. 421 42), on a street leading away from the monastery's entrance. (Singles 1200$, with bath 1800$. Doubles 1800$, with bath 2500$.) **Pensão Mosteiro,** nearby on Avda. João de Deus, 1 (tel. 421 83), has bright and comfortable rooms, but a rather apathetic management. (Singles 1300$. Doubles 1800-2000$.) The budget traveler's haven in Alcobaça, however, is **Pensão Alcoa,** Rua Araujo Guimarães, 30, where an amiable couple offers simple accommodations amidst dark wood floors and ceilings. (Singles 600$. Doubles 1000$.) The *pensão* is just across the bridge and to your left as you approach Praça da República. Those in the know eat at **Restaurante Machado,** Rua Miguel Bombarda, 52 (tel. 410 52), which serves inexpensive meat and omelette combos for 280-350$; full entrees cost twice as much. You might want to forage for cheap eats at the **mercado municipal,** located just across the little green park north of the bus station. (Open Tues.-Fri. 9am-1pm.) Monday and Saturday are the town's big market days (8am-4pm).

Turismo (tel. 423 77) is in Praça 25 Abril opposite the monastery steps. (Open July-Sept. Mon.-Fri. 9am-7pm, Sat.-Sun. 10am-1pm and 3-6pm; Oct.-April daily 10am-1pm and 3-6pm; May-June daily 10am-1pm and 3-7pm.) The **post office** (tel. 415 11) is on an adjacent corner. (Open Mon.-Fri. 8:30am-6pm.) The town's **postal code** is 2460. The **bus station** is on Avda. Manuel da Silva Carolino, a five-minute walk from the center of the old town. To reach Turismo from here, turn left from the station exit, walk down the slope, and then turn left again. Follow Rua Dr. Brilhante across the bridge to Praça da República. Walk through the portal, and the sight of the monastery towers will guide you to Praça de Abril, a square in front of the monastery entrance. You can leave your pack at the station (50$). Buses travel to Nazaré (13 per day, 110$), Batalha (6 per day, 205$), and Leiria (6 per day, 300$). The **train station,** 5km away in **Valado dos Frades,** halfway between Nazaré and Alcobaça, is accessible to both cities by frequent buses (13 per day to Nazaré; 15 per day to Alcobaça, 65$).

Batalha

The town of Batalha is filled with architectural delights. The **Mosteiro de Santa Maria da Vitória** rises unexpectedly out of the fertile Lena Valley. Massive and elaborate in gold-hued stone, the *mosteiro* stands as stately testimony to an age in which religion and territory were the primary preoccupations of kings. Built by Dom João I to commemorate his victory against the Spanish in the 1385 battle of Aljubarrota, it remains one of Portugal's greatest national monuments.

Lacking strong vertical elements, the exterior of the **church** rests heavily on its many flying buttresses. At the center of the facade is a Gothic portal whose pointed hood reaches toward a large window of almost equal size decorated with swirling tracery. The tympanum of the doorway shows Jesus on the Throne of Majesty surrounded by the four Evangelists.

The church's interior soars upward, its pillars supporting ribbed vaulting divided into eight panels. Light reflecting through the stained glass windows creates colorful flower patterns on the heavy stone floor. Unlike the church at Alcobaça, this structure has an exterior support system that allows for thinner walls and large luminous windows. Note how the window frames are gently splayed to de-emphasize the thickness of the wall—an effect quite the opposite of the one at Alcobaça.

The **Founder's Chapel,** immediately to the right of the church's entrance and covered by an octagonal lantern, shelters the sarcophagi of Dom João I and his English-born wife, Queen Philippa. On top lie life-size marble effigies, their heads resting under intricately carved Gothic canopies. In the recesses of the south side of the chapel are the tombs of the royal couple's children, the most famous of which is the Infante Dom Henrique (1394-1460)—Henry the Navigator—who also rests under a Gothic hood. His tomb bears three emblems: the Cross of the Knights of Christ, the symbol of the Order of the Garter, and the royal heraldry belonging to a Prince of Portugal. On the west wall of the chapel lie the tombs of King Afonso V, King João II, and his son Afonso. (Open daily 9am-6pm; Oct.-April daily 9am-5pm. Admission 150$, students free.)

North of the church lies one of the great masterpieces of Portuguese architecture, the grand, royal **cloister of Dom João I.** Broad Gothic arches are filled with elaborate, dense Manueline tracery in which vegetables, ropes, cables, the armillary sphere, and the Cross of the Order of Christ are interwoven in unfathomably intricate patterns. Delicate columns support the bays, each column somewhat different in its carving and ornamentation. Fleurs-de-lis rest on the balustrade that crowns the cloister. Looking through the well house (in the northwest corner of the cloister) you'll enjoy an unforgettable view of the church and cloister with their amazing variety of forms, all carved out of the same glowing golden stone.

The **chapter house,** just off the cloister, is a vast rectangular room daringly designed to avoid all central supports. So dangerous was its construction—the roof fell in twice—that only prisoners condemned to death were employed to build it. In an unceremonious changing of the guard every half-hour, two soldiers stand with stony expressions at the tomb of two unknown Portuguese soldiers. A small Aladdin's lamp with the "Flame of the Nation" burns patriotically on Portuguese olive oil. On the wall hangs a mutilated crucifix from a World War I battlefield in Flanders where Portuguese soldiers fought and died.

To the north of the royal cloister, past the barrel vaulted granary (now used as an exhibition hall), the **cloister of Dom Afonso V's** light decoration and heavy pillars make it more sober than its sibling. From here you can go outside to visit the chapels behind the chancel of the church. Begun in the early sixteenth century and known as the **Capelas Imperfeitas** (Unfinished Chapels), they surround a central octagon that has the beginnings of massive buttresses designed to support a large dome. The west portal (the door you come through) is an example of the Manueline style at its most effusive. Swirls and swirls of molding, like layers of icing on a wedding cake, canopy upward in a majestic series of sensuous curves. As you walk back to the bus stop, you'll pass old houses and the parish **Igreja de Santa Cruz,** which has a superb Manueline doorway.

Should you find yourself waylaid for the night, stop at **Pensão Vitória** (tel. 966 78), on Largo de Misericórdia in front of the bus stop. Be warned that the aesthetically unpleasing rooms are small, cramped, and untidy. (Singles and doubles 1500$ in summer, 900$ in winter.)

Turismo (tel. 961 80) is in the shopping mall complex at the freeway entrance. The helpful staff can offer great bus information. (Open Mon.-Fri. 10am-1pm and 3-7pm, Sat.-Sun. 10am-1pm and 3-6pm; Oct.-April Mon.-Fri. 10am-1pm and 3-6pm, Sat.-Sun. 10am-1pm and 3-5pm.) The **post office** (tel. 962 63) is just around the corner. (Open Mon.-Fri. 9am-12:30pm and 2:30-6pm.) The **postal code** is 2440. Batalha's central location makes for convenient **bus** connections to Leiria (8 per day, 95$), Alcobaça (6 per day, 205$), Nazaré (9 per day, 250$), Fátima (4 per day, 120$), Tomar (4 per day, 340$), and Lisbon (3 express per day, 600$).

Fátima

Portugal's answer to Santiago de Compostela, Fátima is likewise considered a holy site, drawing millions of faithful pilgrims each year. In this humble setting three children—Lucia, Francisco, and Jacinta—sat tending their sheep while most of the world was embroiled in war. On May 13, 1917, Mary allegedly appeared before the three little shepherds to issue a call for peace and to warn the world of the tragic events that would stem from Russia's godless communism. Not surprisingly, the incident aroused its share of heated controversy. The three peasant children remained steadfast in their belief despite attacks calling them mere sensationalists. Word of the vision spread throughout Portugal. Hundreds and then thousands flocked to the site as Our Lady of Fátima returned on the same day over the next five months. On her final appearance, Mary promised a miracle: The noonday sun spun around in a furious light spectacle and appeared to plunge into the earth. The townspeople were convinced by the divine, "fiery signature of God" and built a small chapel at the site to honor Mary. Fátima's exalted status was recognized by the Pope's visit in 1967 on the 50th anniversary of the first apparition. To this day, the eves of the 12th and 13th of each month witness torch-lit processions of believers.

No longer is Fátima the simple village of three little shepherds. Dominating the town is an astounding, ultra-modern religious complex. The sanctuary is set amidst vibrant parks enclosed by tall leafy trees, blocking out the surrounding commercial areas. At the end of the sunken plaza, rises the **Basílica do Rosário** (1928) whose very construction is intended to leave you in awe. Adorned by the stately statues of saints, the **colonnade** is supported by columns and decorated with tiles telling of the Via Sacra. The *azulejo*-covered walls embrace the plaza and focus attention on the tower. The white marble statue of Mary was sculpted by an American priest. A crystal cross that is lit during the candlelight procession sits atop a seven-ton brown crown. At the base of the tower, a sign proclaims "*Feliz Aquela que Acreditou*" (Happy are those who believed). Inside, the off-white stone hall with its tall cylindrical ceiling and twin rows of simple arches and columns leads to the blinding high altar. The centerpiece of the simple yet striking altar is a painting of Mary appearing before the three little sheperds. (You'll see *many* a variation on this theme before you leave Fátima.)

Sheltered beneath a modern metal and glass canopy, the original **Capelinha das Aparições** (Little Chapel of the Apparitions) was built in 1919. Considered to be the spiritual center of the entire sanctuary, the chapel is now surrounded by a pulpit where concelebrations are given all morning in six languages. The faithful crawl around the pulpit and pray before the serene statue of Our Lady of Fátima. Beside the chapel stands the **Azinheira Grande,** the large holm oak from which Mary appeared before the three children.

Outside the sanctuary, the **Museu de Cera de Fátima** (wax museum) is a definite must. Here, the incredible story of the town unfolds in a series of vivid scenes, like something out of a Fantasyland ride in Disney World. Whether or not you choose to believe in the apparitions, you'll still find the "fairytale" interesting, and absolutely indispensable for understanding the town. Something you wouldn't find at the Magic Kingdom, however, is the disturbing "Vision of Hell." Fiery, flourescent parts of contorted bodies rasp in agony from behind an iron screen. An art-nouveau fountain in the courtyard is perhaps the most original rendition of the appearance of Mary. Three crude faces carved in dark stone stare up at a pristine pair of outstretched hands. The museum is located near the bus station. Turn right as you exit and then take your first left uphill; make a right on Rua Jacinta Marto. (Open daily 9am-8pm; Nov.-March daily 9am-5pm. Admission 300$.)

If you have the time, you might want to hike 1km to **Aljustrel,** the small village where the three little shepherds lived. The entire town has been turned into a museum showpiece. Nevertheless, the sheer simplicity of the town gives you an idea of what Fátima was once like. To reach Aljustrel, walk past Turismo along Avda. D. José Alves Correia da Silva.

Having readjusted your senses to the surrounding glory, you're likely to be offended by the town's tasteless hubbub of religious commerce. Numerous shops stock religious paraphernalia ranging from simple color postcards to tacky glow-in-the-dark rosaries. Given its small size, Fátima certainly has a disproportionate share of *pensões* and *hoteles,*each with an uncanny religious name. You needn't worry about finding a place to stay except during the grand celebrations on the 13th of May and October, the first and last appearances of Mary, when reservations are strongly recommended. **Residencial Aleluia,** Avda. D. José Alves Correia da Silva, 120 (tel. 515 40), is a simple right turn from the bus station. Absolutely sparkling doubles, all with private bath, cost 2000$. A well-kept secret are the large, though stuffy, rooms at **Snack-Bar A Paragem** (tel. 515 58), just upstairs form the bus terminal. (Singles 1000$. Doubles 1500$.) You can bargain the price down to 750$ for a single when business is slow. This pension is a mixed blessing as the cold-water baths are in an ungodly state of disrepair. Don't expect to order anything on the menu; the place is a restaurant in name only. Fátima is in dire need of good restaurants at any price. Grab some sinful cakes and pastries at **Pastelaria Santo Agostinho,** Avda. de Santo Agostinho (tel. 518 42), the uphill street between the bus station and the wax museum. (Open daily 8:30am-midnight.)

The **tourist office,** Avda. D. José Alves Correia da Silva (tel. 511 39), is a 10-minute walk from the bus station. Simply turn right and walk down the tree-lined avenue. (Open Mon.-Fri. 9am-7pm, Sat.-Sun. 10am-1pm and 3-7pm; in winter Mon.-Fri. 9am-6pm, Sat.-Sun. 10am-1pm and 3-6pm.) The modern **post office,** Rua Conego Formigão (tel. 511 10), is on your left before Turismo. (Open Mon.-Fri. 8:30am-6pm; in summer Mon.-Fri. 8:30am-6pm, Sat. 3-8pm, Sun. 9am-noon.) Fátima's **bus station** is listed as "Cova da Iria" on all schedules, while the "Fátima (est.)" listing refers to the **train station** some 20km out of town. Given Fátima's national and international appeal, there are buses daily to nearly all major cities in Portugal, including Batalha (3 per day, 120$), Leiria (6 per day, 195$), and Tomar (3 per day, 260$).

Leiria

Capital of the surrounding district and an important transportation center, Leiria is a pleasant, if unspectacular, medium-sized town lying 22km from the coast in the fertile valley of the Rio Lena.

Leiria's oldest and most magnificent historic pile is the **castelo,** a granite fortification built by Dom Afonso Henriques in 1135 on the crest of a volcanic hill overlooking the northern edge of town. Dom Afonso constructed his castle in the severe Castilian style, but later proprietors, such as Dom Dinis, made the castle more livable by introducing Romanesque architectural elements. The **torre de menagem** (homage tower) displays Dom Dinis's coat of arms. The fortifications also shelter a roofless Manueline sacristy, an oasis of delicate and charming stonework in this military compound. Perhaps the most attractive aspect of the castle is the view from either the southern facade or the central tower—on clear days, the sea is plainly visible. At night, the castle is lit with a fantastic array of color lights and shines like a star atop a Christmas tree. (*Castelo* open daily 9am-7pm. Admission 40$.)

A more curious religious edifice lies at the southern end of town. The **Santuário de Nossa Senhora de Encarnação** (Sanctuary of Our Lady of the Incarnation) sits upon a wooded hill in full view of the rest of the town. From without, the sanctuary looks fairly ordinary, but if you can make your way in (try the unbolted door on the southern wall; the church is officially open only on Sun. and has no caretaker), its marvelously colorful decorations will astound you. Above, the vault is embellished with an astonishing variety of religious symbols and images of life, growth, and work: The murals painted just above the choir include two portrayals of local miracles attributed to Mary. Due in part to these fantastic scenes of salvation, life itself seems to be celebrated, and the interior lacks the gloom of other halls of worship where one ponders the mysteries of death and an uncertain afterlife.

Leiria's proximity to the seashore and the museum towns of Batalha and Alcobaça makes it an ideal base for culture vultures who also want a bit of sun on their beaks. The very clean and comfortable **Pousada de Juventude (IYHF),** on Largo Cândido dos Reis, 7D (tel. 318 68), offers members the cheapest beds in town and the company of two cats. Kitchen and laundry facilities are available, and the gracious warden will make your stay in this cozy hostel very pleasant. The feeble cold showers are the only drawback. (Reception open 9-10:30am and 6-10pm. 500$ per night.) **Pensão Leiriense,** Rua Afonso de Albuquerque, 6 (tel. 320 61), has pretty rooms with ornate ceilings and balconies with trellises. Be careful not to get stuck in a depressing windowless room (usually a single). (Singles 1700$, with bath 2000$. Doubles 1800$, with bath 3200$.) From Turismo, walk toward the castle and make a right under a blue-tiled overpass at Praça Rodrigues Lobo. Dull and uninspiring rooms with old beds can be found at **Pensão Alcoa,** Rua Rodrigues Cordeiro, 24 (tel. 326 90), 4 blocks to the right of the youth hostel. (Singles 1200$. Doubles 1700$.)

For munchies, **Café-Restaurante Casa Nova,** Rua Barão de Viamonte, 53 (tel. 252 63), serves up hearty eats in a pleasing cafe decor with green tablecloths and white chairs. Delicious *frango* (½-chicken, 400$) and *bacalhau* (cod, 650$) come with large servings of rice, salad, and fries. (Open Sun.-Fri. noon-3pm and 7-10pm.) The restaurant is on the narrow street that continues from Rua Cândido dos Reis at your far right. If your escudos are running low and you're not particularly choosy about what enters your stomach, visit **Casa das Febras,** Rua Mestre de Aviz, 27 (tel. 323 21). Welcome to a Portuguese cafeteria—service without a smile and the ultimate in blandness. If show up at dinner time, your meal (300-400$) has probably been soaking in grease all day. (Open Mon.-Sat. noon-8pm.)

You will probably arrive in Leiria at the **bus station,** just off Praça Paulo VI in the new part of town. Buses leave here for Lisbon (12 express per day, 650$), Coimbra (8 per day, 475$), Oporto (6 per day, 750$), Nazaré (4 per day, 350$), Fátima (6 per day, 300$), and Batalha (8 per day, 95$). To reach **Turismo** (tel. 327 48), walk right across the Jardim Camões to the modern building that looks out on the fountain. Pry maps and information about the buses going to the beaches of **São Pedro Moel, Vieira,** and **Pedrógão** from the unfriendly staff. In summer, there is a 400$ round-trip bus fare available to Pedrógão. (Office open Mon.-Fri. 9am-7pm, Sat.-Sun. 10am-1pm and 3-7pm; Oct.-April Mon.-Fri. 9am-6pm, Sat.-Sun. 10am-1pm and 3-6pm.)

The **post office** (tel. 241 66) is a five-minute walk past the bus station in the new town at Avda. Herbis de Angola, 101. (Open Mon.-Fri. 8:30am-6:30pm, Sat. 9am-12:30pm.) The **postal code** is 2400. For **medical assistance** call 321 33; for **police,** dial 320 22. Leiria has a **train station,** but it is located 3km outside of town and is accessible only by taxi.

Coimbra

An attractive university town surrounded by the rice fields and pinewood forests of the Beira Litoral province, Coimbra is sometimes described as the "Lusitanian Athens." While this district capital does not teem with wizened old sages quaffing hemlock in the shade of pagan temples, the presence of numerous bookstores, Old World print shops, and chain-smoking protestors provide the town with an unmistakable atmosphere of "old academia."

Built upon the steep banks of the Rio Mondego, the town is composed of a commercial section of Victorian shops and cobbled avenues by the river, and the university quarter on top of the hill, a mishmash of centuries-old buildings and monuments of fascist architecture erected by Salazar, who was an economics student here.

The university (1290) earned great fame throughout medieval Europe. Although later transfered to Lisbon, the university eventually was reestablished in Coimbra, where it became Portugal's most famous center of learning. Luís de Camões, Portugal's Shakespeare, studied here as did most of the major political figures in Portuguese history.

In addition to being home to many historical monuments and the burial place for Portugal's first two kings, Coimbra is the site of the famous "Miracle of the Roses": When the Sainted Queen Isabel was distributing food among the poor, the bread in her lap suddenly turned into flowers. A statue commemorates this religious event.

Orientation and Practical Information

Coimbra's center, a confusing maze of narrow streets, can be divided roughly into two areas. The lower town lies between the triangle formed by the river, **Largo da Portagem,** and **Praça 8 de Maio.** The upper town spreads on the adjoining hill, accessible through the **Arco de Almedina.** Coimbra has two train stations: Coimbra-A, near the town center by the bridge, and Coimbra-B, a half-hour hike outside the center of town to the northwest.

Tourist Office: Largo da Portagem (tel. 255 76 or 238 86), an olive-green building 2 blocks east of Coimbra-A station. With your back to the main entrance, walk straight along Avda. Emídio Navarro with the Mondego River on your right. The busy, understaffed office can provide you with a great map and helpful information for the surrounding region. Open Mon.-Sat. 9am-8pm, Sun. 9am-12:30pm and 2-6pm; mid-Sept. to mid-June Mon.-Fri. 9am-7pm, Sat.-Sun. 9am-12:30pm and 2-6pm.

After-Hours Currency Exchange: Hotel Astória, across the *largo* from Turismo, changes money after banking hours.

Post Office: Rua Olímpio Nicolau Rui Fernandes (tel. 281 81), just past the Manga rotunda. Central office is in the pink powder puff on Avda. Fernão de Magalhães. Open Mon.-Fri. 8:30am-6:30pm, Sat. 9am-12:30pm. Branch office at Praça da República is open Mon.-Fri. 9am-12:30pm and 2:30-6pm. **Postal Code:** 3000.

Telephone Code: 039.

Train Stations: Estação Coimbra-A (tel. 349 98 for information) and **Estação Coimbra-B** (tel. 256 32). Trains from cities outside the region stop only in Coimbra-B, while regional trains stop at both stations. Frequent shuttles connect the two stations. To Lisbon (14 per day, 740$; 8 express per day, 1380$), Oporto (24 per day, 500$), Viseu (7 per day, 440$), and Figueira da Foz (17 per day, 170$).

Bus Station: Avda. Fernão de Magalhães (tel. 270 81). To reach Turismo, turn right from the station and follow the avenue to the train station and then Largo da Portagem (15-min. walk). Turismo is the green building on the other side of the square. To Lisbon (14 per day, 775$), Oporto (9 per day, 600$), and Vila Real (2 per day, 850$).

Baggage Check: Available at the train stations. 30$ per item for 4 hr., 94$ per item for full day.

Swimming Pool: Piscina Municipal (tel. 71 29 95). Take bus #5 São José or Solum or #7T Tovim from Largo da Portagem outside the tourist office. The pool is near the stadium. Open Mon.-Fri. 10am-7:30pm, Sat.-Sun. 10am-7pm; in winter Mon.-Fri. 12:30-1:30pm.

Hospital: Hospital da Universidade de Coimbra, Cruz de Celas (tel. 72 21 15).

Police: Rua Olímpio Nicolau Rui Fernandes (tel. 220 22). **Emergency:** Tel. 115.

Accommodations and Camping

Coimbra is not known for pleasant budget accommodations. Notoriously cheap and seedy *penões* line **Rua da Sota** and the surrounding streets across from Coimbra-A station. Anything decent starts at 1800$ for doubles; pay less and pay the consequences. Fortunately for all, an excellent new IYHF youth hostel opened its doors this past year. It's a 45-minute walk from downtown, so consider investing in a 10-ride bus ticket booklet (240$). (One ride normally chomps 87.50$ from your pocket.) Booklets and tourist passes can be purchased at the counter in Bar Navarro, between Largo da Portagem and the river.

Pousada de Juventude (IYHF), Rua António Henriques Seco, 14 (tel. 229 55). From either Coimbra-A or Largo da Portagem, take bus #7, 8, 29, or 46. Sparkling new hostel with a running list of amenities—including a gorgeous patio, coin-op laundry machine, TV room with VCR, and travel counter that sells tickets and passes. Well-stocked kitchen. Curfew midnight. Reception open 9am-noon and 6pm-midnight. Members only, 550$. Breakfast included.

Residencial Internacional de Coimbra, Avda. Emídio Navarro, 4 (tel. 255 03), in front of the train station. You can't beat the location, but get ready for the noise. Renovated *pensão* with simple, comfortable rooms and fresh-smelling baths. Top-floor rooms with sloping ceilings are a terrific deal for groups of 3 or 4 at 2000$. Singles 1200$. Doubles 1800$.

Pensão Residencial Parque, Avda. Emídio Navarro, 42 (tel. 292 02), a couple of doors to the right of Turismo. Grand, spacious rooms in a pleasant *penão* overlooking the river. Less noisy than the above, but often full. Singles 1200$. Doubles 2000$, with bath 3000$.

Pensão Aviz, Avda. Fernão de Magalhães, 64 (tel. 237 18), a 10-min. walk from Coimbra-A station toward the post office. An oldish place with friendly proprietors. Streetside rooms are very noisy. Small, closet-like singles 600-700$, large singles with double beds 1450$, with bath 1820$. Doubles 2120$, with bath $2410.

Pensão Rivoli, Praça do Comércio, 27 (tel. 255 50), off busy Rua Ferreira Borges, which originates in Largo da Portagem. Well-furnished rooms with white walls. Lockout 1am (no ifs, ands, or buts). In theory, a night watchman will admit you after 3am, but if you can find him, you deserve a prize. Singles from 1000$. Doubles from 1500$.

One of the least attractive **campsites** in Portugal lies near Coimbra's municipal stadium close to a major road (tel. 71 29 97). Take bus #5 Estadio from the stop in front of the tourist office. (90$ per person, 70$ per tent, 120$ per car.)

Food

If you're looking for cheap eats, scout out **Rua Direita,** running west off Praça 8 de Maio; the side streets to the west of Praça 8 de Maio and Largo da Portagem; and the university district around **Praça da República.** When the university is in session (Oct.-June), you might try to eat at some of the student bars and cafeterias. One is located in the old college courtyard.

Churrasquéria do Mondego, Rua do Sargento Mór, 27 (tel. 233 55), off Rua da Sota, 1 block west of the Largo da Portagem. Serves possibly the tastiest meals for the money in Coimbra. Their *medio frango na churrasco* (½-chicken) leaves Colonel Sanders squawking in the dust (240$). Ask for a brushing of *piri-piri* sauce (it's hot!). Cheap seafood is also served at the counter, as well as scrumptious salads and pastry desserts. Open daily noon-3pm and 6-9:30pm.

Restaurante Adega Funchal, Rua das Azeiteiras, 18 (tel. 241 37), on a side street off Praça do Comércio. Elegantly rustic atmosphere. Generous helpings of A-1 Portuguese cuisine at affordable prices. Try *chanfana à chefe* (goat broiled in red wine, 560$) or *medalhões de vitela com champignons* (tenderloin of veal with mushrooms, 650$). ½-portions available. Open daily noon-3:30pm and 6-10:30pm.

Restaurante Democrática, Travessa da Rua Nova, 5-7 (tel. 237 84), on a tiny lane off Rua da Sofia (1st full left after city hall). A very popular place, with spontaneous mass uprisings. Most meals cost 500$ or less. Specialties change daily. You might even hear some impromptu *fado.* Open Mon.-Sat. noon-3pm and 7-10pm.

Combinado, Avda. Fernão de Magalhães, 34 (tel. 236 67). Another good restaurant with reasonable fixed prices. *Prata do dia* includes soup, entree, bread, and wine for 500$. Other entrees 250-300$. Open Sun.-Fri. 11:30am-9:30pm.

Café Moçambique, Praça da República 38. Student hangout. Indulge in sandwiches and combo plates for 250-450$. Open Mon.-Sat. 7am-midnight.

Sights and Entertainment

To reach the old center of town, pass through the **Arco de Almedina,** the remnant of a Moorish town wall, next to the Banco Pinto and Sotto Mayor on Rua Ferreira Borges. The gate leads to a stepped street where a left on Rua de Sub-Ripas brings you to a delightful enclave of small Renaissance buildings. The most prominent of these is the sixteenth-century **Paço de Sub-Ripas** (with the Alice-in-Wonderland doorway). Legend has it that Maria Teles was murdered here by her gullible husband, who was duped by his wife's envious sister, Queen Leonor. Just beyond, under the medieval Torre do Anto, lies the late-sixteenth-century **Colegio Novo.** An unusual Renaissance cloister where arches alternate with rectangular openings framed by columns supporting a Greek-style pediment is inside.

Through a narrow stone stairway looms the massive hulk of the twelfth-century **Sé Velha** (Old Cathedral), perhaps Portugal's finest Romanesque structure. Inside, a wide-springing arcade rests on huge square pillars that support a gallery. The heaviness of the interior is relieved by a splendid high altar. Particularly noteworthy are the highly expressive, contorted features of the two thieves hanging crucified next to Jesus. From the south aisle, a flight of steps leads up to the early Gothic **cloister** (admission 25$); here, rounded arches are set in pointed bays embossed with discs. (Open daily 9:30am-12:30pm and 2-5pm.)

From Praça da Sé Velha, walk uphill behind the old cathedral on Rua Borges Carneiro to reach the **Museu Machado de Castro,** justly famous for its superb Gothic sculptures and seventeenth-century polychrome figures. The first rooms hold fascinating medieval and Visigothic pieces as well as some excellent sixteenth-century wooden sculptures. From here, you will pass a stupendous view of the city and river off the courtyard. In the next section, look for the dramatic, seventeenth-century *Santas Mulheres,* made from terra-cotta, which depicts a serene Mary in the company of saints. The sixteenth-century *Martiro de São Bartolomeu* portrays the martyred saint in the act of losing his skin. Don't miss the Retablos room, with the larger-than-life terra-cotta *Last Supper* by Philipe Hodart (sixteenth century). You can tell Judas by his eyes. In the basement of the museum, you'll find catacomb-like Roman passageways exhibiting ancient sculpture. Upstairs, the museum has an interesting collection of thirteenth- to sixteenth-century paintings as well as porcelain and clay work. (Open Tues.-Sun. 10am-12:30pm and 2-5pm. Admission 150$, students with ISIC free.)

Across from the museum in Largo da Feira stands the **Sé Nova** (New Cathedral), originally built for the Jesuits in the late sixteenth century. The early baroque facade gets progressively more elaborate as it reaches skyward because it was built in two stages. The lower part was built in the sixteenth century, with Renaissance proportions according to a Jesuit model. The top third is seventeenth-century baroque, and the bell towers are an even later addition. In contrast, the interior is austere and self-consciously antique. The chancel contains paintings of the life of Jesus (left) and Mary (right). (Open daily 10am-12:30pm and 2-4:40pm.)

Rua Sáo Pedro, flanked by the grim facades of the new university buildings, leads to a seventeenth-century portal, the **Porta Férrea** (Iron Gate). Pass through into the old college courtyard and take the staircase at the right up to the **Senate House.** In its main hall, the Sala dos Capelos, portraits of the kings of Portugal hang on the walls below a beautifully painted seventeenth-century ceiling. An arcaded gallery (known as the Via Latina, since Latin was once the only language permitted here) heads to a terrace overlooking the city and the Mondego River. In the Sala dos Exames Privados, the smaller room off the corridor, curious portraits of former university rectors are displayed below a fine wooden ceiling. (Open daily 9am-noon and 2-5pm.) As you leave the Senate House and pass the baroque clock tower, you'll come to the **university chapel.** Its festive Manueline doorway opens into an interior remarkable for its seventeenth-century *azulejos* and enormous red and gold baroque organ. The jewel of the academic complex, the old **university library,** stands next door. Built by Dom João IV between 1717 and 1728, the library shelters 143,000 books in three lofty halls each painted with Chinese motifs. Press the buzzer to the left of the door to enter. (Open daily 9am-12:30pm and 2-5pm. A multi lingual guide gives a brief description. A 25-50$ tip is appropiate.)

From the university, it's a short walk downhill alongside the **Aqueduto de São Sebastião** to the lush **Jardim Botânico,** ornamented with sculpture and fountains. Laid out by Pombal in 1774, it is one of the most beautiful public parks in Europe and the site of many weddings. Other gardens for pleasant ambling include **Parque** de Santa Cruz, off Praça da República, and **Parque Dr. Manuel Braga,** with a lovely colonnade of trees. The branches form a canopied walkway alongside the river.

The main attraction in the lower part of the city is the **Mosteiro de Santa Cruz** (Monastery of the Holy Cross), founded in 1131 but greatly altered and enlarged in the sixteenth century. The baroque love of three-dimensionality is evident in the unusual entranceway, part of which forms a separate structure crowned by wind-swept angels triumphantly blowing brass trumpets. The interior is most notable for its Renaissance pulpit (1522), one of the great masterpieces of Portuguese sculpture. From the fantastic hydra-headed dragon at its base to the finely carved Manueline heraldry above the niches, this work displays an intricacy rarely attained in stone—it looks almost like ivory. Complementing the sculpture are the blue and white *azulejos* added to the wall behind it in the eighteenth century. The Founders' Tombs (1520), on either side of the high altar, show the first two kings of Portugal lying in Crusade armor among a great profusion of sacred elements, flowers, medal-lions, and figurines. In the splendid barrel-vaulted sacristy—it looks like a miniature Roman bath—hang a number of important paintings by Portuguese artists. Adjoin-ing the sacristy is the sixteenth-century **Claustro do Silêncio,** entered through the large, vaulted chapter house. Three exquisite bas-reliefs in the corners show scenes of the Passion modeled after Dürer engravings. Up the staircase in the cloister's corner is the *coro alto* where the choir stalls are decorated with gilded reliefs of epi-sodes from the voyages of Vasco da Gama (1505). (Open daily 9am-noon and 2-5pm. Admission to the cloister 50$.)

Rua da Sofia (Street of Learning) branches off the western corner of Praça 8 de Maio. Of the theological colleges that once lined this *rua,* the most interesting one still standing is the **Igreja do Carmo** (1597). Light from an antique chandelier casts an eerie glow over the timeless interior. Eighteenth-century paintings of clerics wearing enormous hats cover the walls, while in the right transept, a statue of São Bento dressed in a sinister black robe raises its hands as if to command an audience. The finely gilded high altar is separated into panels with a playful contrast between two-dimensional paintings and three-dimensional sculptures. Inside are eighteenth-century paintings of clerics wearing enormous hats and a particularly macabre St. Francis caressing a cross (left transept). The sacristy, which adjoins a Renaissance cloister, contains a stunning *Entombment of Christ* (similar to the one in the city's museum), in which two men dressed in Oriental garb hold the Winding Sheet at either end, while Mary and the Apostles quietly mourn from behind.

Across the bridge, the partially submerged mass of **Convento de Santa Clara-a-Velha** is not to be missed. The ruins are all that remain of the great convent erected by Isabel, who was canonized after her death as the Holy Queen. The devastating floods of the Mondego cause the foundation to sink deeper into the sand each year; today more than half the church lies underground. You can enter the church from the rear and walk along concrete platforms built above the level of the arches atop the columns. If you recall the height of most Portuguese churches and behold the huge void left by the rose window, you'll really appreciate this unearthly experience. (Open daily 10am-7pm.) To replace the vanishing convent, the **Convento de Santa Clara-a-Nova** was built on a nearby hill (1649-1677). These lovely white buildings, prominently visible from the other side of the river, are now used as army barracks. The convent's church, however, is open to the public and contains both the old fourteenth-century Gothic tombs of the queen—barely discernible through a wrought-iron grille in the back—and a new silver one perched on top of the high altar. Adjoining the church (access through the door near the chancel) is a monu-mental Renaissance cloister. (Open daily 10am-1pm and 3-5pm.)

The most popular late-night coffeehouse, the **Santa Cruz,** Praça 8 de Maio, occu-pies the building that was once a chapel for the church next door. Underneath its beautiful, vaulted ceiling, students occasionally sing *fados.* To hear the most unre-strained and heartfelt singers, go after dinner to the bar **Diligência,** down Travessa da Rua Nova off Rua da Sofia (open until midnight). **Pinto d'Ouro** is a popular pub located across the river on the main road to Tomar, not far from Santa Clara a Velha. The disco **Scotch** is nearby (cover 500$). The best disco in the area, however, is accessible only by car: **Lagar** is 5km to the east of town on the road to Guarda (cover 600$).

Coimbra opens its social season in May with the annual **student festivals.** The celebration features midnight *serenatas,* groups of black-clad serenading youth (a more mournful version of the Spanish *tunas*), and *gaiteiros,* wandering musical ensembles who play popular songs. There are scheduled concerts and folkdancing as well. Parades with floats sporting various school colors add to the activities. One of the best times to come to Coimbra is during the **Festas da Rainha Santa,** held in even-numbered years during the first week of July. Throughout this religious festival, the choral music of numerous groups echoes through the festooned streets.

Near Coimbra

Conimbriga

The largest Roman settlement yet to be excavated in Portugal, Conimbriga lies only 15km south of Coimbra. If you're expecting another Pompeii, forget it. Still, the ruins illustrate Roman genius in art and engineering. Most impressive is the so-called **House of Fountains,** where the layout of the rooms, atrium, and peristyle is easily discernible. Particularly beautiful, the mosaics on the house show a rich inventiveness in design. Another important structure, the **House of Cantaber,** contains small, private baths with the typical triads of pools: *frigidarium* (cold), *tepidarium* (warm), and *caldarium* (hot). The nearby **Museu Monográfico** displays artifacts unearthed in the area, including a colossal bust of Augustus that once stood in a temple dedicated to the emperor.

AVIC runs a direct bus to Conimbriga leaving from Hotel Astória (Mon.-Fri. at 9:05am, Sat.-Sun at 9:35am). It also stops near the Pinto d'Ouro on the far side of the bridge before continuing to the site. The return bus departs Conimbriga daily at 12:55pm.

Buçaco Forest

Rocky paths shaded by luxurious foliage have drawn solitary wanderers to the Buçaco Forest for centuries. More than 300 years ago, the Carmelite brothers selected the forest as the perfect site for *desertos,* isolated dwellings for penitence and absolute silence. They so jealously guarded their solitude that they obtained two papal bulls prohibiting the entrance of women into the enclosure and the defilement of the woods, both upon pain of excommunication. The decrees are still visible, carved in the Coimbra Gate, and silence still reigns over the 250 acres of woodland, though religious orders were abolished when the forest became national property in 1834. The park is famed for its extraordinary variety of trees and rich vegetation, crowning the northernmost peak of the Serra do Buçaco.

In the late nineteenth century, one of the last kings of Portugal chose to build a palace here, a neo-Manueline fantasy with an elaborate gallery of double arches modeled after the cloister of the Hieronymite Monastery in Lisbon. The palace's overwrought excess is the perfect stone counterpart to the forest's natural abundance. Buçaco's historical quiet was broken only briefly by a battle in 1810, when Wellington won a decisive victory over the French, prefiguring his success at Waterloo. A military museum contains relics of the battle where more than 4000 French troops were lost.

Wandering freely in the forest is a bit confusing, so pick up a map at the small refreshment stand near the palace. A typical walk passes through the **Fonte Fria** (Cold Fountain), whose waters cascade over a series of steps, **Fern Alley,** and the **Coimbra Gate.** Giant cedars line the path from the gate back to the palace. For the ambitious, a two-and-a-half-hour walk along the Via Sacra goes past little seventeenth-century chapels. Peek into them for a look at some terra-cotta figures. The hardy will be rewarded at the conclusion of their hike, when the view opens to a tremendous panorama of the surrounding countryside.

If you want to spend some money (about 1150$ per meal), dine at the **Palace,** now a luxury hotel. Otherwise, plan to bring food and picnic by Fonte Fria. A 40-minute walk downhill brings you to **Luso,** a pleasant old-fashioned spa town with a couple of inexpensive restaurants. The bus to Coimbra stops in Luso.

Five buses per day (Sat.-Sun. 2 per day) connect Coimbra to Buçaco (45 min., 205$) about every two hours beginning at 7:50am (Sat.-Sun. at 9am). Service continues to Viseu. Buses leave from the station on Avda. Fernão de Magalhães, a 15-minute walk from downtown. The last returning bus leaves Buçaco at 6:45pm.

Figueira da Foz

Blessed with a lush interior and a privileged position on the ocean, the sun-splashed resort town of Figueira da Foz is definitely not your average Portuguese town. Fancy homes and their well-kept gardens join modern seaside buildings to give this speck on the map a newly acquired air of importance. Fiqueira has little by way of tradition. Its single attraction is its huge beach, over 1km wide and 3km long, which attracts mobs of sun-worshipers. Many of the fun-seekers here are Portuguese; this seems to have kept prices down.

Orientation and Practical Information

Packed with hotels and "aparthotels," **Avda. 25 de Abril** is the busy lifeline that separates town from the beach. Four blocks inland and running parallel to the avenue, **Rua Bernardo Lopes** harbors many affordable *pensões* and restaurants. Much of the action in Figueira happens here in this casino-cinema-disco complex when the hordes withdraw from the beach.

Tourist Office: Avda. 25 de Abril (tel. 226 10), next to Aparthotel Atlântico at the very end of the airport terminal-like complex. Pleasant and helpful staff can give you a useful map as well as the lowdown on events. Open daily 9am-midnight; Oct.-May Mon.-Sat. 9am-12:30pm and 2-5:30pm, Sun. 10am-12:30pm and 2-5pm.

After-Hours Currency Exchange: Aparthotel Atlântico or Grande Hotel da Figueira, Avda. 25 de Abril near Turismo.

Post Office: Rua Miguel Bombarda, 76 (tel. 220 56). Open Mon.-Fri. 9:30-12:30pm and 2:30-6pm. **Postal Code:** 3080.

Train Station: Largo da Estação (tel. 243 56), near the bridge. Easy 20-min. walk to Turismo and the beach. Keeping the river to your left, walk down Avda. Saraiva de Carvalho, which becomes Rua 5 de Outubro at the fountain. Continuing straight, you'll curve into Avda. 25 de Abril. "Caminhos de Ferro-Buarcos" bus (25$) passes by the beachfront avenue. Frequent connections to Coimbra (17 per day, 170$); change there for other destinations.

Bus Station: Rua José da Silva Fonseca (tel. 230 95). Inconvenient and infrequent connections to Coimbra. **AFGA,** Rua Miguel Bombarde, 79 (tel. 277 77), near the post office, runs to the Algarve (1 per day, 1300$), Evora (1 per day, 875$), Lisbon (2 per day, 750$), and Oporto (2 per day, 650$).

Hospital: Gala (tel. 221 33 or 221 38).

Accommodations and Camping

Accommodations in Figueira are generally comfortable and modern. However, prices vary greatly depending on the time of year, peaking in July and August. Not only are *pensões* expensive, but they're also full. Arrive early in the day to check on vacancies, or better yet, make reservations.

Pensão Peninsular, Rua Bernardo Lopes, 35 (tel. 223 20), on the corner of Bernardo Lopes and Dr. António Dinis. Just about the only budget refuge during those awful summer months. Simple and comfortable rooms with tall ceilings and carpeting. Nice lobby with TV. Singles 1100$. Doubles 1850$. Breakfast included.

Pensão Residencial Bela Figueira, Rua Miguel Bombarda, 13 (tel. 227 28), 2 blocks from the beach. By far the most spectacular *pensão* for the money—if you arrive at the right time of the year. Gorgeous, comfortable rooms and spotless bathrooms. Cool outdoor terrace and kind English-speaking manager. July: Singles 1150$. Doubles 2150$. Aug.: Singles 2750$. Doubles 3250$. Sept.-June Singles 950$. Doubles 1500$. Rooms with bath available. Breakfast included.

Pensão Residencial Rio-Mar, Rua Dr. António Dinis, 90 (tel. 230 53), perpendicular to Rua Bernardo Lopes. Spacious and comfortable (albeit old) rooms. Singles 1860$, with shower 2360$. Doubles 2100$, with shower 2600$, with bath 3500$. Breakfast included. Prices 20-30% lower in winter.

About 2½ km inland, **Parque Municipal de Campismo** (tel. 231 16) has one of the best campsites in Portugal, complete with an Olympic-size swimming pool and tennis courts. (100$ per person, 100-115$ per tent, 125$ per car. Showers 60$.) From the beach, go all the way up Avda. 25 de Abril and turn right at the roundabout on Rua Alexandra Herculano. Make a left at Parque Santa Catarina going up Rua Joaquim Sotto-Mayor past the Palácio Sotto-Mayor. It's an enjoyable walk, past a lot of pretty homes and gardens.

Food

The restaurants in town are quite good, though slightly more expensive than the Portuguese norm. Budget eateries line **Rua Bernardo Lopes.** The local **market** is beside the municipal garden on Rua 5 de Outubro. (Open daily 8am-7pm; in winter Sun.-Fri. 8am-5pm, Sat. 8am-1pm.)

Restaurante Rancho, Rua Miguel Bombardo, 40-44 (tel. 220 19), 2 blocks up from Turismo. Packed with locals at lunchtime. Hefty, delicious meals 300-600$. For the adventurous, *coelho à caçador* (hunter's rabbit) is a good gamble at 450$. Open Mon.-Sat. 10:30am-9:30pm.

Restaurante O Escondidinho, Rua Dr. António Dinis, 62. An unusual alternative that offers close encounters with tourists from all over Europe. Serves Portuguese and Goanese Indian cuisine. Curry and *piri-piri* dishes 550-750$. Open daily noon-2:30pm and 7:30-11pm.

Snack Bar A Doca, Rua Bernardo Lopes, 57 (no phone). Limited menu, but cheap filling meals. Eat your *febras grelhadas* (380$) at the cozy bar. Open daily 9am-midnight.

Sights and Entertainment

Behind the glare of Figueira's amazing expanse of sand (gravelly, so wear slippers), there are a few cultural attractions to keep those sun-baked brain cells operating. One of Portugal's finest museums, the **Museu Municipal do Dr. Santos Rocha** houses exhibitions ranging from ancient coins to the decadent fashions of Portuguese nobility. The museum's pride and joy are its archeological exhibits, primarily the ceramic vases excavated in Figueira da Foz and Caldas da Rainha. Certain ethnographic artifacts from Angola and Mozambique will undoubtedly look somewhat familiar—impressive handwoven baskets with geometric patterns and an African band ensemble complete with Angolan ukeleles and *marimbas,* Mozambique's answer to the xylophone. Other items—notably an Angolan figurine with an unnerving, ghost-like expression and nails protruding from its body—leave more room to the imagination. The museum entrance faces Rua Calouste Gulbenkian, while the building itself lies in Parque Abadias, smack in the middle of the residential district. (Open Tues.-Sun. 9am-12:30pm and 2-6pm. Free.) Walk up through the large city park, veering left at the roundabout on Avda. Dr. Joaquim Carvalho. The first right, Rua Joaquim Sotto-Mayor, will lead you to the garden estate of **Palácio Sotto-Mayor.** The relatively modest exterior belies the almost shamelss extravagance inside. The ground floor, with the study and living room, is the most impressive. Lavish green marble columns line the main hallway, and the tall ceiling is plastered with paintings and decorative panels trimmed in gold-leaf. The bedrooms upstairs and the kitchen downstairs will awe you with their sheer size. (Open Tues.-Sun. 2-6pm.)

Back in the beach quarter, the triangular **Forte de Santa Catarina** fronts the junction of the Atlantic and the Rio Mondego. Inside the walls of the seventeenth-century fort sits a small chapel with a statue of the patron saint. As you head back toward the train station, glance at the **Casa do Paço** (Paço Manor House), decorated with 6888 Delft tiles that washed ashore after a shipwreck.

Figueira's party mode shifts from high gear to warp speed during the **Festa de São João** (June 23-24). People line the streets all hours of the night indulging in unofficial merrymaking; more organized activities occur at the fair. At 5am, a you've-got-to-see-it-to-believe-it ritual will make "rub a dub dub, three men in a tub" seem like child's play. A large procession heads for Buarcos, where all involved take a communal bath in the ocean. For tamer entertainment, the town hosts the **Gala Internacional dos Pequenos Cantores,** a singing competition for children's groups from many countries in mid-July. For ten days in September, the **Figueira da Foz Cinema Festival** features intellectual international flicks.

From the nearby village of **Buarcos,** which also has a large beach, you can watch fishers haul in the day's catch. The old, medieval-style houses overlook the shore from behind a thick wall built to protect the town from pirate attacks. The **tourist office** is at the town's entrance, Largo Tomás Aquino (tel. 250 19). (Open in summer daily 9am-9pm.) Frequent buses for Buarcos leave from the train station and stop along Avda. 25 de Abril.

The forested region north of Figueira is excellent for a nature getaway. The **Serra da Boa Viagem** (4km) have several vantage points that offer spectacular panoramas of the shoreline below. A short hike in this thickly wooded region is worthwhile. Farther north, the **Quiaios Lakes** offer limpid pools in a verdant countryside with countless idyllic spots to satisfy the throngs of naturalists and weekend picnickers. These jaunts can be made by bicycle. **AFGA** rents bikes for 200$ per hour, 500$ per half-day, and 550$ for a full day (plus 17% I.V.A.). Their office is open Monday through Friday from 9:30am to 1pm and 3 to 7pm, but there is almost always someone there.

Aveiro

Residents brag that Aveiro compares to Venice or Amsterdam. Not quite. Nonetheless, Aveiro is graced with a few charming (though at times smelly) canals. The town was an important port in the sixteenth century, but gradually declined as silt sealed off the estuary. Although silting proved initially disastrous to the community, the phenomena helped create the vast **ria** (lagoon) that extends 45km up the coast, protected by a long sand bar. Islands, salt marshes, sand dunes, and an occasional pine forest now dot the water. The region is mysteriously beautiful and unlike any other in Portugal.

Along these aged waterways, some remnants of the region's traditional livelihood remain: boats of every vivid color and form imaginable. Streamlined *barcos moliceiros* drift through the water laden with seaweed, their brightly painted bows rising high and curling into fearsome horns. Less impressive *barcos saleiros* whisk through the canals past the glistening white salt beds. *Marnotos* (people who work the salt pans) still gather salt into baskets and transport it to warehouses along the Canal de São Rogue.

Orientation and Practical Information

Aviero is split by Avda. Dr. Lourenço Peixinho and the Canal Central. North of this line lies the magnetic fishermen's quarter, **Beira Mar.** The southern port of town is the "new" residential district, which oddly enough contains all of the town's historical monuments. The narrow, winding streets, however, are living reminders of days gone by.

Tourist Office: Praça da República (tel. 236 80), above Banco Fonsecas & Burnay. In the *praça* just across the main bridge in the new district. Very helpful English-speaking staff has color brochures and bus schedules for the entire Rota da Luz region. Tickets for boat trips on the *ria* 900$. Open daily 9am-9pm; mid-Sept. to mid-June Mon.-Sat. 9am-8pm.

Post Office: Praça Marquês de Pombal (tel. 231 51). Follow either street past town hall from Turismo. Open Mon.-Fri. 8:30am-6:30pm, Sat. 9am-12:30pm. **Postal Code:** 3800.

Train Station: Largo da Estação, at the end of Avda. Dr. Laurenço Peixinho. Turismo is 1km away down the main avenue across the bridge. Buses from the train station bring you right to the bridge. (80$ or get a pre-purchased ticket at a kiosk for only 27$.) To Oporto (30 per day, 335$), Coimbra (23 per day, 295$), and Viseu (2 per day, 470$).

Bus Station: Nearest Rodoviária station is in Agueda, 19km away. Trains are most convenient for travel in and out of Aveiro and the Rota da Luz region. Buses to Forte da Barra (hourly 7:15am-6:40pm, 110$) leave from a stop by the canal down the street from Turismo.

Hospital: Avda. Artur Ravara (tel. 221 33).

Police: Praça Marquês de Pombal (tel. 220 22).

Accommodations and Camping

Budget *pensões* are conveniently clustered across the canal from Turismo.

Hospedagem Rossio, Rua Dr. Barbosa de Magalhães, 24 (tel. 298 57), near the *rossio*. Cross the bridge from Turismo and turn left on the street adjacent to the canal walking toward the palm trees. Plants line the entrance to this homey *pensão*. Spacious, beautiful rooms. Singles 1200$. Doubles 1800$.

Pensão Residencial Estrela, Rua José Estevão, 4 (tel. 238 18). Cross the bridge from Turismo; the *pensão* is on the corner of the street to your right. Grand stairway with oval skylight. Rooms are comfortable despite bare walls and floors. All top-floor rooms have low sloping ceilings; some are especially small and cramped. Singles 1300$. Doubles 2500$, with bath 3500$.

Residencial Palmeira, Rua da Palmeira, 7-11 (tel. 225 21). From Rua Morais (parallel to Rua José Estevão), turn left 1 block before the church. Cheerful rooms in a renovated establishment. Friendly management. Singles and doubles 2000$. Breakfast included.

Residencial Beira, Rua José Estevão, 18 (tel. 242 97), up the street from Estrela. Ugly color scheme on walls. Old-looking interior and unappealing bare wood floors. Darling of a hostess. Singles 2200$. Doubles 2600$, with shower 4000$. Breakfast included.

There aren't any camping sites in Aveiro itself, but several dot the coast. The Rota da Luz can be quite a haven for campers as campsites border both the *ria* and the beach. Closest to Aveiro is **Parque Municipal da Praia da Barra** (tel. 36 94 25), just across the *ria*. A very popular site, this isn't the place to come if you want to skip the crowds. **Orbitur** (tel. 79 16 18) has a superb campsite on the beach at Vagueira. (286$ per person, 220$ per tent, 260$ per car. Hot showers 90$.)

Food

Delicious, filling meals at low prices are easy to find. Seafood restaurants abound, but they can be expensive. For daytrips and campers, the **market** is off Avda. Dr. Laurenço Peixinho and open daily from 5am to 1pm. The "28th Boutique" is the big market day held on (you guessed it) the 28th of every month.

Restaurante Zico, Rua José Estêvão, 52 (tel. 296 49). The "in" place and cool by Aviero standards. Especially popular with young people. Fill up on *prego de porco* (pork steak with fries, 270$) or try the Portuguese shish kebab, *esfetada mista no churrasco* (490$). Save room for the tempting desserts: *tarte de cereja* (cherry tart, 100$) and *ananás ao vinho do Porto* (pineapple dipped in port, 250$). Open Mon.-Sat. noon-11pm.

Restaurante Marisqueira O Mercantel, Cais dos Mercanteis, 13 (tel. 280 57), near the fish market. One of the finest restaurants in town. Expensive, but worth it. The fish here were just pulled from the ocean. House specialty *arroz de gambas* (shrimp rice, 1000$) makes a delicious meal for two. Open daily noon-3pm and 7-10pm.

Restaurante Salimar, Rua de Luís Cipriano, 19 (tel. 251 08), 1 block up from Turismo. Cute nautical decor. Fragrant *bacalhau no churrasco* (barbecued cod, 500$). Bubbling orange-red broth swimming with seafood called *arroz de marisco*, 850$. Open daily 9am-midnight.

Restaurante Snack-Bar Amazonas, Rua Capitão Sousa Pizarro, 15 (tel. 276 60), on a street leading to the park. Glistening modern decor. The friendly manager serves a hamburger patty that tastes like sausage. Open Sun.-Fri. noon-midnight.

Sights

Across from Turismo in Praça da República, the regal **Paço do Concelho** (Town Hall) radiates a somber elegance with its eighteenth-century French window and bell tower. The **Igreja da Misericórdia** is certain to capture your attention with its simple yet striking, blue-tile facade. Seventeenth-century Lisbon tiles cover the walls and complement the white windows crowned with richly gilded placards.

The town's primary attraction is the **Museu de Aveiro.** Though its assorted religious pieces are not especially thrilling, the exuberant, gilded baroque woodwork that covers the church interior may be the most beautiful of its kind in Portugal. In 1472, a dramatic scene took place between King Afonso and his daughter the Infante Joana, who wished to enter a life of seclusion against the king's will. Sitting beneath *azulejo* panels depicting the princess' life, Santa Joana's Italian Renaissance tomb is one of the most famous works of art in Portugal. Sculpted in white marble in a checker pattern reminiscent of the Indo-Portuguese style, the tomb is supported by the heads of four angels. (Open Tues.-Sun. 10am-12:30pm and 2-5pm. Admission 150$, students with ISIC free.)

Stop at the nearby **Igreja das Carmelitas** for a look at a display of eighteenth-century *azulejos* and a stunningly symmetrical interior. The ceiling of the nave and the chancel is decorated with paintings depicting the life of Santa Teresa. If (and only if) you have time to kill, slip into the one-room **Museu de Caça e Pesca** (Museum of Hunting and Fishing), in the municipal park, and sneak a peak at stuffed animals and a rather tasteless presentation of guns and traps. (Open Mon.-Fri. 10am-noon and 2-5pm. Free.)

In late July, the entire *ria* rocks with the **Feira de Região de Aveiro** (FARAV), a mammoth region-wide fair featuring handicrafts and an awesome *moliceiro* (seaweed barge) regatta.

While in Aveiro, you should make at least a daytrip to the neighboring shore communities and visit the national park, **Dunas de São Jacinto,** which boasts one of Europe's finest expanses of sand dunes. Buses leave for São Jacinto and other beaches from a stop by the canal down the street from the tourist office. (Pick up schedules at Turismo.) The bus stops off at Forte da Barra (hourly, 110$), where you can catch a ferry to the town of **São Jacinto** (45$, no cars allowed). At the port, an unglamorous *trolley carro* (tram pulled by a tractor) will take you to the beach or the dunes (30$). Otherwise, with your back to the port, the beach lies a solid 20-minute walk, while the park is a 15-minute walk to your left. If you plan to spend the night in ths area, you can either camp on your own along the long, deserted shoreline (keep a low profile and don't prolong your stay) or stay at the **Orbitur Campsite.** (Tel. 482 84. 253$ per person, 190$ per tent. Hot showers 75$.) Another alternative is **Pensão Jardim** (tel. 367 45), in Forte da Barra across the square from the bus stop. Clean rooms, a restaurant, and friendly management make it an ideal base for travelers who prefer to be near the beaches rather than in the city of Aviero. (July-Sept.: Doubles 2000-2500$, with bath 2500-3000$. Discount for singles.) Ferries from Forte da Barra to the beach town of Barra cost 20$ and leave every hour and a half.

Costa Verde

Aptly named for its greenery, the Costa Verde occupies the northwestern corner of Portuagal and extends from the Douro River by Oporto up to the Minho River by the Spanish frontier. Though similar to Spanish Galicia in its fertile, rolling hills and Celtic influence, the Costa Verde is far less populated and developed. In 1143

Afonso Henriques defeated the Moors here and declared himself in Guimaraes ruler of the Kingdom of Portugal. Since then, the region has produced more than its share of the country's historic monuments and its most colorful *romarias* (pilgrimages) and folk festivals. Traveling through the lush countryside, you'll see hundreds of trellised vineyards where the famous *porto* and *vinho verde* wines are made. Houses with brilliantly colored tiles dot the landscape and line the town streets. The traditional feminine costume that includes layer upon layer of gold necklaces encrusted with charms attests to the region's mineral wealth.

Considering its natural beauty and rich folklore, the Costa Verde is strikingly untouristed, especially when compared with Lisbon and the Algarve. The mild, year-round climate of the north is not hot enough to attract the beach crowd until late July, while the beautiful towns of the interior—Ponte do Lima, Braga, and Guimarães—are only visited by a few far-reaching travelers.

Oporto (Porto)

As its name suggests (simply "The Port"), Oporto epitomizes the European port city, at once grimy and alluring, shabby and stately. A large percentage of Portugal's income is earned here, and the city's workaday mentality is illustrated by the old proverb: "Coimbra sings, Braga prays, Lisbon shows off, and Oporto works." According to an anecdote, when the Portuguese fleet needed provisions for the 1415 invasion of Ceuta, the populace of Oporto willingly slaughtered all their cattle, gave away all the meat, and kept only the entrails (tripe) for their own consumption. The dish *tripas à moda do Porto* stems from this incident of culinary self-sacrifice and to this day the people of Oporto are known as "*tripeiros*" (tripe-eaters).

On a dramatic gorge cut by the Douro River, Oporto lies only 6km from the sea. Orange-tiled houses packed closely together cascade down to the river, and Europe's most graceful arched bridges span the gorge above. Gerard Eiffel gave his soaring lines to the oldest one, the Dona Maria Pia Bridge, completed in 1877. The granite towers of the city's many churches pierce the skyline.

Oporto's fame, however, springs not from the beauty of its buildings but from the taste of its **Port wine.** First extensively developed by English merchants in the early eighteenth century, the Port industry still plays a major role in the city's economy. Now as before, only human feet can crush the grapes, and a lacing of brandy is added for an extra kick. The 80-odd Port warehouses lining the Nova de Gaia side of the river testify to this phenomenon. Many of them still offer free tours which include generous "tastes" of the sweet, sweet stuff.

Orientation and Practical Information

The heart of Oporto is **Avenida dos Aliados,** a wide thoroughfare that forms a long, rectangular square bordered on the north by **Praça General H. Delgado** and on the south by **Praça da Liberdade.** Statues in the center of mosaic walkways are surrounded by a constant bustle of traffic and a chaotic maze of one-way streets. The São Bento train station lies smack in the middle of town. The **Ribeira** district is a few blocks to the south, directly across the bridge from **Vila Nova de Gaia,** the *adega* (wine warehouse) area.

Tourist Office: Rua Clube dos Fenianos, 25 (tel. 31 27 40), west side of city hall. Extremely friendly and helpful staff provides maps, accommodations information, and advice on *adega* and *caves* tours to inspect Port wine production (see also Sights and Entertainment). Open Mon.-Fri. 9am-7pm, Sat. 9am-4pm, Sun. 10am-1pm.

Consulates: U.S., Rua Júlio Dinis, 826, 3rd floor (tel. 69 00 09). 24-hour service. Open Mon.-Fri. 8:30am-1pm and 2-5:30pm. **British,** Avda. da Buavista, 3072 (tel. 68 47 89). Open Mon.-Fri. 9:30am-12:30pm and 3-5pm.

Currency Exchange: Banco Pinto & Sotto Mayor, Praça da Liberdade. Open July-Sept. Mon.-Fri. 8:30am-7pm, Sat.-Sun. 9am-1pm.

American Express Representative: Star Travel Service, Avda. dos Aliados, 210 (tel. 236 37), near the post office. Not the most friendly staff. Mail, lost check, and personal check-cashing services for members. Open Mon.-Fri. 9am-12:30pm and 2-6pm.

Post Office: Praça General H. Delgado (tel. 38 02 51), across the avenue from Turismo. Poste Restante 27$ per item. Open for stamps Mon.-Fri. 8am-10pm. **Postal Code:** 4000.

Telephones: Praça da Liberdade, 62. Open daily 8am-11:30pm. **Telephone Code:** 02.

Train Stations: São Bento Station (tel. 227 22), 1 block from Pr. da Liberdade, for routes north and to the interior. **Campanhã Station** (tel. 56 41 41), to the west of the center, connected with São Bento by numerous trains, for southern and international routes. To Viana do Castelo (12 per day, 355$), Coimbra (15 per day, normal 500$; rapid 950$), Lisbon (8 per day, 1045-1900$), Vila Real (4 per day, 525$), and Aveiro (19 per day, 205$). The train line also runs buses to Viseu (3 per day, 615$) from São Bento.

Bus Station: To Lisbon and points south, **Garagem Atlântico,** Rua Alexandre Herculano, 366 (tel. 269 54). To Lisbon (2 per day, 1000$), Coimbra (6 per day, 600$), Viseu (1 per day Mon.-Fri. only, 700$). To Viana do Castelo and points north, **Estação de Camionagem,** Praça de D. Filipa de Lencastre (tel. 261 21), 1 block from Avda. dos Aliados. To Viana do Castelo (hourly 6:30am-7:30pm, 415$) and Braga (hourly 6:40pm-8pm, 360$). To Vila Real and the Montanhas, **Cabanelas,** Rua do Ateneu Comercial do Porto (old Travessa P. Manuel; tel. 243 98), 1 block form Rua de Sã da Bandeira. To Vial Real (5 per day, 540$).

Taxis: Tel. 48 80 61. 24-hour service. Taxi stand on Avda. dos Aliados.

English Bookstore: Livraría Diário de Notícias, Rua de Sá da Bandeira, 5, across from São Bento Station. Open Mon.-Fri. 9am-12:30pm and 2:30-7pm, Sat. 9am-1pm; in summer Mon.-Fri. 9am-12:30pm and 2:30-7pm.

Laundromat: Penguin, Shopping Center Brasilia, 3rd floor (tel. 69 50 32). Take bus #2 or 20 from Pr. da Liberdade. Self-service. 400$ per load for wash and dry. Open Mon.-Sat. 10am-midnight.

Swimming Pool: Piscina de Municipal, Rua Almirante Leute do Rêgo (tel. 49 33 27). Open daily 10am-12:30pm and 2-6:30pm. 50$ per person Mon.-Fri., 180$ Sat.-Sun.

Medical Services: Hospital de Santo António, Rua Prof. Vicente José de Carvalho (tel. 273 54). **Ambulance:** Tel. 115.

Police: Rua de Alexandre Herculano (tel. 268 21). **Emergency:** Tel. 115.

Accommodations and Camping

Accommodations in Oporto are some of the nicest in Portugal, but finding a vacancy in summer can prove hellish. Most of the city's *pensões* lie west of Avda. dos Aliados. Though plentiful, they tend to fill up by late evening in July or August. Rates for singles are absolutely criminal; solo travelers might want to team up and share a room. Recruit roomies from among the youth hostel's rejectees. Also try the tourist office. Unfortunately, the city's one and only IYHF youth hostel is pitifully small and obtaining a room there from July to September is possible only for superhumans. Even if you manage to save a room for yourself in the morning, the unsympathetic warden may bump you off the bed list to make room for large groups that arrive unheralded.

Pousada de Juventude do Porto (IYHF), Rua Rodrigues Lobo, 95 (tel. 655 35), about 2km from the center of town. Take bus #3, 19, 20, or 52 from the stop on the lower west end of Pr. da Liberdade and get off at Rua Júlio Dinis (the conductor knows the hostel stop). Small, cozy rooms with good kitchen facilities. If you arrive in town anytime after the morning reception hours, don't even think about this place. 3-night max. stay when the hostel is full (i.e. always). Curfew midnight. Reception open 9-10am and 6-11pm. July-Sept. 700$, Oct.-June 550$. Breakfast included.

Residencial Porto Chique, Rua Conde Vizela, 26 (tel. 38 00 69). From São Bento station, walk across Praça da Liberdade and up Rua Clérigos, taking your first right at the end of the street. Well-lighted *pensão* with big, comfy rooms. Some even have trellised balconies. No noise! Singles 1000$, with bath 1500$. Doubles 1500$, with bath 2500$.

Residencial Porto Rico, Rua do Almada, 237 (tel. 31 87 85). From Avda. dos Aliados, go up Rua Elísio de Melo after 2 left-hand blocks, and turn right on Rua do Almada. Very comfortable rooms make you feel right at home. The sweet landlady keeps the place spotless. Singles 1700$. Doubles 1800-2000$, with bath 2500$.

Pensão dos Aliados, Rua Elísio de Melo, 27 (tel. 248 53), on your left as you walk up Avda. dos Aliados. Gorgeous rooms with telephones and wall-to-wall carpeting. Living room with TV. Light sleepers take heed: Noise from the avenue filters in at all hours. Singles 1850$. Doubles 2000$, with bath 2800$. Breakfast included.

Residencial Vera Cruz, Rua de Ramalho Ortigão, 14 (tel. 32 33 96), on the side street before Turismo. The elevator creeps up to hallways covered with funky wallpaper. The rooms themselves are typical examples of Portuguese elegance. Singles 1400$. Doubles 1900$, with shower 2500$. Breakfast included.

You'll find a good **campsite, Prelada,** in Parque de Prelada (tel. 626 16), 5km from the beach. (220$ per person, 120$ per tent, 200$ per car.) Take bus #6 from Praça da Liberdade.

Food

The specialty of the city is *tripas à moda do Porto* (tripe served with beans and curry powder). If you're nonplussed by calf intestines, try the fresh and well-prepared fish dishes.

The most colorful and inexpensive restaurants are along the river in the Ribeira district, especially on **Cais de Ribeira, Rua Reboleira,** and **Rua de Cima do Muro.** You'll find budget fare in much rowdier and seedier surroundings near Praça da Batalha on **Rua do Cimo de Vila** and **Rua do Cativo.**

Churrasqueira Moura, Rua do Almada, 219-233 (tel. 256 36). Delicious, dirt-cheap meals (mostly 200$). Absolutely packed with locals at mealtimes. Hamburger with egg or *frango no churrasco* (barbecued chicken with fries) only 200$. Rice and fries also come as inexpensive side-orders. Open Mon.-Sat. 11:30am-10pm.

Taberna Típica, Rua Reboleira, 12 (tel. 32 03 73). Stone walls and cute nautical decor complement its riverside location. The seafood rice specialty *arroz de marisco* is a bargain at 650$, while solid *pratos do dia* cost 495$. Open Tues.-Sun. noon-2pm and 7-11pm.

Restaurante Boa Nova, Muro dos Bacalhoeiros, 115 (tel. 260 86), across the square from the above. Still pours wine from huge, wooden barrels. The dining room downstairs serves entrees for 400-500$. Open Mon.-Sat. noon-10:30pm.

Casa Filha da Mãe Preta, Cais da Ribeira, 40 (tel. 31 55 15), overlooking the river. Gorgeous dining room upstairs with stucco walls and beautiful *azulejo* tiles. Serves tasty entrees 350-850$. Open daily noon-3pm and 6-10pm.

Taberna do Bebobos, Cais da Ribeira, 21-25 (tel. 31 35 65). Steep prices, but come here for the atmosphere. Stone walls, candlelight, and handmade articles adorn round tables. Most meals 750-1000$. Open Mon.-Sat. noon-2:30pm and 7-9:30pm.

Brasa Churrasqueira, Praça da Batalha, 117, east of São Bento Station at the end of Rua 31 de Janeiro. You can find this place from its barbecue smoke. A whole barbecued chicken 320$, ½-chicken 200$. Open Wed.-Mon. 9am-10pm.

A Brasileira, Rua do Bonjardim, 18, 1 block from the train station. The interior is a mixture of art deco and turn-of-the-century Edwardian. A great place to enjoy morning coffee and pastries. The restaurant in back serves sandwich combos, hamburgers, and ice cream desserts. Open Mon.-Sat. 8am-9:30pm.

Sights

Busy Praça da Liberdade and adjoining Avenida dos Aliados make up the city's principal square and center of town. Lining this large open space are Oporto's most important commercial buildings. Their many domes, towers, and mansard roofs proclaim a late nineteenth-century exuberance, although the avenue was actually built up in the 1920s. Sitting behind a wide plaza, the neo-Renaissance **city hall** provides the perfect finish to this grand European time capsule.

Walking south past the alluring blue and yellow *azulejo* facade of the **Igreja dos Congregados,** you approach one of Oporto's oldest residencial districts. Here, ramshackle homes undulate in a sea of red tiles as Oporto's splendid landmarks stand to majestically against the skyline. Ponderous and fortified, the heavy Romanesque husk of Oporto's thirteenth-century **catedral** sits on a hill above the Ribeira. The Blessed Sacrament Chapel to the left of the high altar is made of solid silver. During the Napoleonic invasion the altar was whitewashed to protect it from vandalism. (Call the sacristan to turn on the light; otherwise its tarnished surface looks like coal.) Also note the extremely ornate choir stalls in the chancel, and the early eighteenth-century organ above. The late fourteenth-century cloister is wrapped in *azulejo* panels. Peek through the keyhole to see the remains of the Gothic cloister. (Open daily 9am-12:30pm and 3-6pm.)

Narrow Rua de Dom Hugo runs just behind the cathedral through the old city and past the **Casa-Museu de Guerra Junqueiro.** This comfortable home and its surrounding garden house a pleasant if unexceptional collection of seventeenth- to nineteenth-century furniture, pottery, and tapestries. (Open Tues.-Thurs. 10am-12:30pm and 2-5:30pm, Fri.-Sat. 10am-12:30pm and 2-6pm, Sun. 2-6pm. Admission 50$, students and Sat.-Sun free.)

Rua de Dom Hugo curls back around to the front of the cathedral. Take the staircase down to a terrace overlooking the city's many churches and old houses. The church immediately below, São Laurenço, better known as **Igreja dos Grilos,** dates from 1577. Its unusual facade is a masterful composition of overlaid planes designed to create a rich three-dimensional surface. Walk through the narrow, sloping streets past irresistably charming homes and amidst strange smells, screaming babies, sleeping dogs, parading chickens, and a colorful cascade of hanging laundry.

The narrow street in front of the church leads to Rua Mouzinho da Silveira. From here follow signs to the **Palácio da Bolsa** (Stock Exchange), built between 1834 and 1842 and still radiating a nineteenth-century elegance. Dominating the palace, the glass-covered Court of Nations is emblazoned with the coat-of-arms of every nation having commercial relations with Portugal at the turn of the century. The Goldsmith Association presents an exquisite exhibition of gold and silver tableware and jewelry. The Old Commercial Court houses a great deal of inlaid Brazilian wood and giant wall paintings depicting the role of Port in the region's economy. Almost elliptical in shape, the lavish Arab Hall sparkles in white and every imaginable shade of green. The design is modeled after the Alhambra in Granada and the walls are covered with the ironic inscription: "Allah protects Queen Maria II" in Arabic. (Open Mon.-Fri. 9am-6pm, Sat.-Sun. 10am-noon and 2-5pm; in off-season Mon.-Fri. 9am-5pm, Sat.-Sun. 10am-noon and 2-4pm. Admission 150$, students free.)

The much restored birthplace of Prince Henry the Navigator stands south of the Bolsa past Praça Infante Dom Henrique on Rua da Alfândega. It's now a museum and home of the municipal archives. A few feet away lies the **Ribeira** (Esplanade), skirted by a marvelous quay filled with shops and restaurants. The view encompasses the river and the Ponte de Dom Ruis I (1886). For further exploration of the Ribeira, take trolley #1 from the nearby São Francisco church. The cars run along the river on Rua do Ouro to the Foz do Douro, Oporto's beach community.

As you head back to the Bolsa you'll come to the **Igreja de São Francisco.** Originally Gothic, the church was remodeled in the seventeenth and eighteenth centuries with what is one of the most elaborate gilded wood interiors in Portugal—wear your sunglasses or run the risk of temporary blindness from all the glory. (Open Tues.-Sat. 9am-5pm. Admission 25$.)

Continuing west past the trolley stop, a right and a left will bring you to the **Igreja de São João Novo.** Its restrained, late seventeenth-century interior contains an exquisite organ. The **Museu de Etnografia e História** hosts a particularly interesting exhibit of models of the different boats used in the region in an incongruous rococo palace across from the church. (Open Tues.-Sat. 10am-noon and 2-5pm. Free.)

From Rua de Belomonte, east of the museum, a staircase leads to a terrace overlooking the city and then connects to a path that leads to Rua São Bento Davitaria. Midway up this street stands the imposing facade of the **Igreja de São Bento da Vitória** (1704), the most beautiful in the city. Two enormous, festive organs guard the entrance to the sanctuary, whose unusual galleries look like box seats in a grand opera house. Behind the deep chancel rises a soaring altar.

Just beyond the São Bento Church rises the 82-meter **Torre dos Clérigos** (Tower of Clerics). Built in the middle of the eighteenth century and long the city's most prominent landmark, its strong granite tower is decorated like some splendid processional candle. Climb the 240 steps for a panorama of the city and the Douro Tiver Valley. (Open Mon.-Fri. 7:30-9:30am, 10:30am-noon and 3:30-8pm, Sun. 10am-1:15pm and 8:30-10:30pm. Admission 25$.)

Past the base of the tower and beyond the university stand the twin eighteenth-century **Churches of the Carmelitas** and **Nossa Senhora do Carmo.** The exterior of the latter is decorated with enormous panels of *azulejos* framed in gray stone. Inside the Carmelitas you'll find a particularly gruesome collection of votive offerings: faded photographs and wax limbs and faces. (Carmelitas open daily 5-7:30pm; Carmo open daily 9am-noon and 2-5pm.)

On Rua D. Manuel II, past the churches and a forested park, the **Museu Nacional de Soares dos Reis** houses one of Portugal's most important art collections. Built in the eighteenth century as a royal residence, the present-day museum is dedicated to works by the noted nineteenth-century sculptor, Soares dos Reis, Portugal's Michelangelo. Study the solemn expresssions on his commissioned military busts and statues. His statue of Dom Afonso Henriques greets you at the entrance of both the museum here and the tenth-century castle in Guimarães. However, the sculptor's best works were in his free time. The most popular face in Portugal is that of *A Flor Agreste,* fair features of a young boy frozen in marble. If Soares dos Reis were Michelangelo, his *David* would be *O Desterrado.* As you behold the soothing marble statue of a young man sitting on a rock, you'll see that the comparision is not at all overblown. Note especially the life-like intricacy of the intertwined fingers. The museum also contains an excellent collection of impressionist paintings. Some of the best works in this collection are by a young genius named Henrique Pousão, whose creations are starkly realistic. His masterpiece is *Esperando o successo,* a playful painting of an Italian boy holding up a stickman sketch. These days, the painting is often presented in caricature of aspiring politician also "waiting for success." (Open Tues.-Sun. 10am-5pm. Admission 150$, students free.)

No visit to Oporto would be complete without a stop at one of the city's many *caves* or *adegas* (wine lodges), which produce the famous liquor. Most offer free tours of the wineries, where both red and white Port is aged and blended in huge oak barrels. After touring the processing and bottling factories, you can sample the various vintages in the tasting rooms. Most of the lodges are located across the river, in **Vila Nova de Gaia.** Walk across the lower level of the bridge and take a sharp right. The listing below only indicates a fraction of the *caves* that are open to the public. For more information, inquire at the tourist office or check listings in the yellow pages.

Cálem, Avda. Diogo Leite (tel. 39 40 41), the first warehouse on the street. Very friendly multilingual guides conduct tours daily 9:30am-5:45pm. Free.

Sandeman, Largo Miguel Bombarda (tel. 30 40 81), off Diogo Leite. Stocks the best Port and runs the best-organized (perhaps too organized) tours. Reservations necessary for large groups. Open daily 9:30am-5:30pm. Free.

Ferreira, Avda. Diogo Leite, 70 (tel. 308 66, ext. 315 *turismo*). The tourist crowds are smaller here than at Sandeman's and the Port is nearly as good. Open Mon.-Sat. 9am-noon and 2:30-5pm. Free.

Guimarães

An hour's bus ride south from Braga brings you to Guimarães, a mid-sized country town known throughout Portugal as the "cradle of the nation." Here, in 1110, Dom Afonso Henriques was born, and here, in 1143, he proclaimed himself the first King of Portugal. This event came after a Christian victory over the Moors and was widely perceived as a signal that the tide had turned against the Muslim invaders.

Guimarães is, however, older than the kingdom of Portugal itself. The Galician countess Mumadona founded a Benedictine monastery here in the tenth century and supervised the construction of the **castle,** the keep of which remains intact. The castle is regarded as Portugal's foremost historical monument, not only for its great age, but also because Dom Afonso Henriques was born behind its walls. (The castle is located in a park on the north edge of town. Open daily 9am-9pm. Free.)

While the sturdy stone and impressive fortifications of the castle may have kept its inhabitants reasonably safe from the onslaughts of the Normans and the Moors, its severe utilitarian construction offered few creature comforts. Consequently, the local noble family of a less bellicose age, the Dukes of Bragança, obtained the services of a French architect, Mestre Anton, who built for them in the fifteenth century a palacial manor house next to the castle which came to be known as **Paço dos Duques de Bragança.**

The elegant *paço,* modeled after the late Gothic palaces of Northern Europe, became celebrated as one of the finest noble houses in Portugal. In an act of regal justice, the crown confiscated the property following the death of the second Duke of Bragança in 1483. Perhaps out of spite, the kings of Portugal did not bother to keep up their new possession. By the seventeenth century, the abandoned *paço* had fallen into ruins and the local capuchin friars were granted permission to use its stones for the construction of their monastary. Further scavenging and vandalism continued until 1880 when the Portuguese government declared the *paço* a historic monument and began the process of restoration.

Today, the Paço dos Duques de Bragança stands as a museum of fifteenth-century Portugese aristocratic lifestyle and merits a visit. The Gothic courtyard overlooked by a gallery of Ionic pillars supporting a sloping, tiled roof is one of the largest to be found in a nobleman's manor. The rooms of the *paço* are also impressive and display an astonishing collection of centuries-old furniture, silverware, crockery, and weapons. Don't miss the several D'Aubisson tapestries (fifteenth century) that depict the Portuguese military expedition into North Africa. As you walk into the Banquet Hall, admire the wooden ceiling shaped like an inverted boat. The tables in this room date from the fifteenth century and have been the setting of lavish dinners not only for Portuguese nobles, but also for the presidents of Portugal who regularly attend conventions here. When the president is in residence, at least a quarter of the 39 fireplaces are kept burning in order to spread a cheery warmth throughout the building. (Open Mon.-Sat. 9am-6pm, Sun. 10am-5pm; mid-Sept. to May daily 10am-5pm. Admission 150$, tour in Portuguese included.)

From the *paço,* walk back into the center of town to visit the **Museu de Alberto Sampaio,** located in the Renaissance cloister of the **Igreja Colegiada de Nossa Senhora da Oliveira.** The church entrance fronts a medieval square where arches and an outdoor temple transport you to a different time. Like the castle, the church was commissioned by the Galician countess Mumadona in the tenth century. Although considerably remodeled since then, evidence of the original Latin-Byzantine architectural style remains in the church's interior. Next door, the museum houses a fascinating collection of late Gothic and Renaissance art, including silver processional crosses and gold-plated carvings of exquisite detail. The fifteenth-century Gothic chapel of São Braz houses the granite tomb of Dona Constança de Noronha, first dutchess of Bragrança. In the courtyard, an *oliveira* (olive tree) symbolizes the patron saint of Guimarães. (Open Tues.-Sun. 10am-1pm and 2-5:30pm; in winter Tues.-Sun. 10am-12:30pm and 2-5pm. Admission 150$. Tour in French or Portuguese included.) As you leave the museum, you'll catch a glimpse of what might make the perfect fairytale setting. An enchanting garden runs the street to the **Templo de Santos Passos** (a.k.a. Nossa Senhora de Consolação), where delicate Gothic towers soar from a cylindrical facade of *azulejos* and gray stone. Behind the "Bavarian castle," rolling green hills dotted with pastoral homes complete this scene fit for any *Princess Bride.*

Nearby on Alameda da Resistência al Facismo, the **Igreja de São Francisco** boasts an attractive interior of white stone arches and brilliant *azulejo* displays that cover the entire front wall. Archeology devotees should head for the **Museu da Sociedade de Martins Sarmento,** on Rua Paio Galvão. A private foundation and library, this small museum has an unexpectedly extensive collection of paleolithic tools and primitive pottery. In addition to the archeological display, one chamber is devoted to artwork ranging from Angolan wood sculpture to local paintings. (Open Tues.-Sun. 9:30am-noon and 2-5pm. Admission 80$.)

Guimarães offers few budget accommodations and restaurants. Try not to spend the night. If you must stay, by choice or by accident, try the **Pensão Imperial,** Avda. da Resistência al Fascismo (formerly Alameda Salazar, of course), 113 (tel. 41 51 63), above a restaurant. The spartan rooms have barewood floors and decrepit ceilings. The 1000$ rooms are actually better, if smaller, than 1500$ rooms. (Singles 1000-1500$. Doubles 1750$). The *pensão* has a decent restaurant with prices ranging from 350-550$ per entree.

More meals at a fair price can be enjoyed at **Café Mourão,** Praça Toural, 94 (tel. 41 50 60), where the well-priced *diárias* (daily specials) come with soup for 330$. (Open Sun.-Fri. noon-3pm and 7pm-1am.)

Turismo (tel. 41 24 50) is on Avda. da Resistência al Facismo, facing Praça Toural. Across the street, a makeshift castle declares "*Aqui nasceu Portugal*" (Portugal was born here). The staff here is pathetically uninformed and only offers outdated tourist brochures and a poorly drawn map. They do have a list of accommodations. (Open Mon.-Fri. 9am-12:30pm and 1-7pm; Oct.-June Mon.-Sat. 9:30am-12:30pm and 2-5pm.) To get here from the **bus station,** follow the long street on the bank in front of you, Rua Paio Galvão, to the end of Praça Toural. Eleven buses per day (last one at 8:25pm) leave for Braga (205$). The **train station** is a 10-minute walk south of Turismo down Avda. Afonso Henriques. The **post office** is at Rua de São António, 89 (tel. 41 50 32; open Mon.-Fri. 8:30am-6:30pm, Sat. 9am-12:30pm). The **postal code** is 4800. The **hospital** is on Rua Dr. Joaquim de Meira (tel. 41 26 12), and the **police** are on Rua Moleirinho (tel. 41 13 34; in an emergency 115).

Braga

Surrounded by rolling green hills and dotted with elegant parks, Braga is an important commercial and religious center. Known as Bracara Augusta in Roman times, the city was one of the three administrative capitals of the Roman province of Lusitania. After the town was sacked by the Arabs in 716, it remained a backwater for four centuries until it was designated the seat of a newly created archdiocese. The city's many splendid baroque churches owe their existence to Archbishop Diego de Sousa, who in the sixteenth century initiated a building program that turned the city into what *bacarenses* like to think of as Portugal's Rome. The influence of the church has not waned: Braga's people are considered by some the most pious, by others the most fanatic, and by all the most politically conservative in the country. Braga's Holy Week, at once solemn and festive, features a great religious procession similar to the more famous one in Sevilla.

Orientation and Practical Information

Praça de República lies in the heart of the city. The wide **Avda. da Liberdade** runs north to south from the *praça* to the hills of Pinheiro da Gregório. Perpendicular to Avda. da Liberdade, Avda. Central (formerly Avda. dos Combatentes) has a small park lining its length. Posh stores line **Rua do Souto,** a bustling pedestrian thoroughfare that runs from the Arco da Porta Nova (arch) near the train station to the *praça*.

Tourist Office: Avda. Central, 1 (tel. 225 50), at the corner of Avda. da Liberdade. Businessman-like staff hands out outdated maps with a dreadful coding system. Open daily 9am-7pm; in winter Mon.-Sat. 9am-7pm.

After-Hours Currency Exchange: Hotel Carandá, Avda. da Liberdade, 96 (tel. 770 27), a 10-min. walk from the *praça.* Open daily 8am-10pm.

Post Office: Avda. da Liberdade (tel. 241 31), 2 blocks south of Turismo. Open Mon.-Fri. 8:30am-6:30pm, Sat. 9am-12:30pm. **Postal Code:** 4700.

Telephones: In the post office building. **Telephone Code:** 053.

Train Station: Largo da Estaçao (tel. 221 66), a 15-min. walk to Turismo. Swing a right up Rua Andrade Corvo and continue under the arch. The *praça* is at the end of Rua do Souto and Turismo is just across the avenue. To Oporto (16 per day, 405$), Viana do Castelo (15 per day, 255$), Coimbra (12 per day, 620$), and Vigo in Galicia (3 per day, 692$).

Bus Station: Central de Camionagem (tel. 270 01), a few blocks north of the center. As you leave the station from the upper level, follow Avda. Gerneral Norton de Matos (on your left) up to a small square. Continue straight and Rua dos Chãos will take you to Praça da República. To Oporto (every ½-hr., 360$), Guimarães (11 per day, 205$), Coimbra (3 per day, 750$), and Lisbon (2 per day, 1185$). Reservation required for Lisbon.

Hospital: São Marcos Hospital, on Largo Carlos Amarante (tel. 240 42).

Police: Campo de Santiago (tel. 719 50). **Emergency:** Tel. 115.

Accommodations and Camping

Braga has many *pensões.* The cheapest are concentrated around the Hospital de São Marcos, the more expensive ones around Avda. Central. Unmarried couples and single (especially American) women may be looked upon with suspicion in this conservative town.

Pousada de Juventude (IYHF), Rua Santa Margarida, 6 (tel. 781 63). From Turismo walk down Avda. Central and turn left on Largo da Senhora-a-Branca. Popular with people traveling to or from Peneda-Gerês National Park. Relaxing, modern hostel with spotless kitchen and bath facilities. The friendly warden is a god among wardens, in fact. He's a fountain of information and will store your stuff if you go to Gerês. Reception open daily 9am-1pm and 6pm-midnight. Members only, 500$.

Residência Grande Avenida, Avda. da Liberdade, 738 (tel. 229 55), around the corner from Turismo. Reception on 3rd floor. A classy *pensão,* with elegant mirrors and furniture, run by very amiable folks. Singles 1250$, with bath 1500$. Doubles 2500$, with bath 3500$. Breakfast included.

Pensão Económica, Largo de João do Souto (tel. 231 60), behind the cathedral. Unpleasant management. Decent rooms. Singles 1400$. Doubles 2600$. Breakfast included.

Casa das Velinhas, Rua de São Bento, 23 (tel. 239 19), Largo Carlos Amarante. The cheapest rooms in town. The bare wood-floor rooms are simple and neat, though somewhat dark. You must know how to tread water to use the bathroom. Singles 840$. Doubles 1500$.

Hotel Carandá, Avda. da Liberdade, 96 (tel. 770 27). A good place to treat yourself: Melt in the comfort of these rooms with A/C, radios, telephones, sparkling baths, and terrific views of the city and Bom Jesús. Singles 2800-3000$. Doubles 3500-4000$. Enormous breakfast on the rooftop terrace included.

Camping is at **Parque da Ponte** (tel. 733 55), 2km down Avda. Liberdade from the center, next to the stadium and the municipal pool. (120$ per person, 100$ per tent. Showers 25$.)

Food

The budget restaurants in Braga are among the best in all of Iberia.

Restaurante Chinês, Rua do Raio, 279-301, in the Centro Comercial do Rechich, 71-72 (tel. 798 30). Run by a charming Shanghai couple. One of the best Chinese restaurants in Portugal. Hospitable service and well-priced entrees. Delicious vegetarian dishes. Open daily 11am-3:30pm and 6-11pm.

Restaurante A Marisqueira, Rua do Castelo, 3-15 (tel. 221 52), 1st right on Rua do Souto. *Prato do dia* (260$) is available only for lunch. Other entrees are significantly more expensive. Open daily noon-11pm.

A Brasileira, Largo Barão de São Martinho (no phone), in the square before Rua do Souto. Intellectual, romantic cafe. Great for coffee and people watching. Open Mon-Sat. 7am-midnight.

Sights and Entertainment

When Braga isn't ablaze with religious fervor, the city relaxes into an affluent lull. One of the wealthiest cities in Portugal, Braga's ultra-modern buildings rise by its many historical monuments. Considered Portugal's oldest cathedral, Braga's **sé** is a heavy granite structure that has undergone significant renovation since its construction in the eleventh and twelfth centuries. A two-towered facade opens to an elaborate Gothic portico decorated with delicate columns. The sanctuary, enclosed by thick walls and pierced by strikingly slender windows, leads to a chancel notable for its intricate ribbed vaulting and carved altar. To the right, the Chapel of the Holy Sacrament shelters a seventeenth-century polychrome altar lost among a riot of pink walls gilded with rococo decoration. The cathedral **treasury** houses the usual assortment of vestments and reliquaries crammed together in a series of stale-smelling rooms awash in harsh fluorescent light. Still, the tour of the treasury is worthwhile for the close-up view of the fabulously carved organ case in the *coro alto* (raised choir) and the fine fifteenth-century choir stalls supported by sensuous caryatids. In the adjacent room is the silver cross used in the first Mass celebrated in Brazil. Adjacent to the church, off a Renaissance cloister, are two beautiful chapels. The **Capela dos Reis** (Kings' Chapel) has an exquisite vaulted ceiling whose ribs spring from tiny human heads. At the far end of the right wall lie the mummified remains (note the protruding teeth and long fingernails) of Dom Lourenço Vicente, a fourteenth-century archbishop. The **Capela de Nossa Senhora da Gloria,** across the courtyard, is decorated with Moorish-style murals and contains the carved tomb of Archbishop Gonçalo Pereira (1336). (Treasury and chapels open daily 8:30am-6:30pm; Oct.-June daily 8:30am-12:30pm and 1:30-5:30pm. Admission 100$.)

The street behind the chapel leads to a lovely square flanked by the seventeenth-century **Capela de Nossa Senhora da Conceiçao** and the picturesque **Casa dos Coimbras.** The chapel has an interior faced with *azulejos* depicting the story of Adam and Eve and a finely carved *Entombment of Christ.* The Coimbra family mansion is noted for its Manueline windows. (Open Mon.-Fri. 9:30am-1pm and 2:30-7pm.)

The rococo facade of the **Igreja de Santa Cruz** stands across from the monumental **Hospital de São Marcos** on Largo dos Crivos. Statues of the 12 Apostles dramatically gesturing to an imaginary audience below crown the latter's facade, while the bald convex facade of the former demonstrates the baroque love for rich three-dimensional compositions. Farther along stands the city's most impressive palace, the **Casa do Raio** (House of Rays). Erected between 1754 and 1755, its large rococo windows are played against vibrant *azulejo* walls. The smiling figures on top of the balconies capture perfectly the festive spirit of the entire building. Of a completely different spirit is the **Casa das Gelosias** (House of Screens) on Rua São Marcos. Its Moorish system of latticed screen window coverings was once a common feature in the city, especially in homes occupied by merchants and other members of the upper middle class.

Elegantly sculpted in a rainbow of colors, the **Jardim de Santa Bárbara** fronts an archaic set of arches, creating a picture-perfect setting. Go behind the arches to sneak a peak at the **public library.** The stone-walled auditorium looks like something out of King Arthur's court. Heavy black iron chandeliers hang from decorative ceilings. Walk through the small library with your eyes fixed on the beautiful hardwood ceilings, but don't walk into a shelf of books—that can be embarrassing. (Open Mon.-Fri. 9am-noon and 2-8pm.)

Braga's most famous landmark is actually 5km out of town. Here, on a hillside carpeted in greenery, the **Igreja do Bom Jesús** overlooks the city. The eighteenth-century sanctuary itself can be taken in quickly: The main attraction here is the enormous set of double staircases leading up to it in a fascinating geometric zigzag adorned with symmetrical fountains and grim sculptures. Each terrace is lined with chapels dug out of rock depicting scenes from the Passion. Buses labeled "Bom Jesús" leave from the stop in front of the Hospital de São Marcos at 20 and 50 minutes past the hour (100$, if pre-purchased at kiosk 75$). The bus stops at the bottom of the lush hill. The best way to take in the beautiful wooded area is to take the elegant granite stairway up (or down, down is nice) the monument. A funicular whizzes up and down the hill (35$).

For those who enjoy out-of-the-way, unspoiled attractions, the **Mosteiro de Tibães** is a piece of the past lost in a wonderful wooded forest. Don't expect to see the sparkling monasteries of Alcobaça and Batalha; becoming of its isolation, this eleventh-century Bededictine monastery reflects centuries of neglect. Several treasures await beyond all the weathered, discolored plaster. Stone tombs rattle eerily underfoot as you walk through the weathered **cemetery cloister.** On the walls, eighteenth-century *azulejos* (many are missing) tell the story of São Bento. The restored wood panel ceilings give the place a "brand new" feel, and therefore seem awkward. Adjoining the cloister is a magnificently preserved **church,** built on the site of a sixth-century chapel. A high, narrow, cylindrical ceiling leads to a profusely ornate, rococo high altar. Walk through the kitchen and the back woods area to a small, tile-covered chapel. The chapel itself is not of any special interest, but the view of the church framed between the trees is spectacular. The long, stone stairway, interrupted every now and then by a small fountain, was the inspiration for Bom Jesús. The monastery is about 6km outside of Braga and accessible by city bus (every 2 hr., 100$). (Open Tues.-Sun. 9am-noon and 2-7pm. Guided tour free.)

Despite its conservative reputation, Braga's nightlife is happening. Discos, pubs, and cafes line **Avda. da Liberdade** and nearby streets. Try **Club '84,** a disco under Hotel Turismo on the main avenue.

Near Braga: Peneda-Gerês National Park

A splendidly unspoiled expanse of mountains, lakes, vegetation, and wildlife, **Peneda-Gerês National Park** occupies the Alto Minho Valley just south of the Spanish border at Portela do Homem, 43km north of Braga. You'll have to trust Turismo that deer, wild boars, and wild ponies make their home here—they are far too clever to come out for a snapshot. Hiking routes between the main village of Gerês and Pedra Bela (6.5km) will take you past glistening waterfalls and natural pools. On summer weekends, a bus connects several of the sparse villages that inhabit the huge park.

Turismo is in the village of **Gerês** (Tel. 651 33. Open daily 9am-noon and 2-6pm.) Several *pensões* are clustered in the area. The cheapest is **A Floresta** on Rua Boaudía (tel. 652 34), where singles and doubles start at 1200$. There are two **IYHF youth hostels** in the park itself. The first is near **Lindoso** (tel. (058) 473 05), a village of stone houses. From the village, it's a 3-kilometer hike up a mountain (follow the signs); expect it to take about an hour. The old ranger house, now the men's dormitory, is quite nice, but the women's barracks are stuffy and in disrepair. You can also camp around the hostel for a fraction of the 500$. The hostel has a kitchen, and nearby a small **store** sells basic food items. The Lindoso hostel is open from May to September. There are five direct buses daily from Braga to Lindoso (400$), and three return trips, the last one at 5pm. The second hostel, at **Vilarinho das Furnas,** is in the eastern section of the park; this area is simply amazing. On a clear day, you can see Braga and Bom Jesús from the mountaintop. The barracks (dorms) are not very nice, but reconstruction is in the works. (500$. Lunch or dinner 350$, but the food is horrible.) For more comfort, stay in the modern hotel rooms where doubles run 2000$.

If you don't have much time and want to see the park, there are excellent **minibus tours** that pass through key sites. They take an afternoon and cost about 550$. Inquire at Hotel do Parque, Rua dos Chãos, 38 (tel. 651 12), in Braga.

Viana do Castelo

Viana do Castelo has a river, mountains, and the best beaches north of Oporto. The town's tranquil streets, lined with granite houses, radiate from a lovely square. Once a Roman outpost and later the center of the British wine trade, Viana remains a small, pleasant base from which to explore the Upper Minho and the northern Costa Verde. Sixty kilometers north of Oporto on the coast, Viana do Castelo is the first major town south of the Spanish border.

Orientation and Practical Information

Avenida dos Combatentes da Grande Guerra is the main avenue, running from the train station south to Rio Lima. The beautiful old town lies east of the avenue, while most services and accommodations are on its side streets.

Tourist Office: Praça da Erva (tel. 226 20), 1 block east of the main avenue. Extremely kind and helpful staff. An excellent map of the town. Information on the region, Lisbon, and the Algarve. Open July-Aug. Mon.-Fri. 9am-8pm, Sat. 9:30am-12:30pm and 2:30-6pm, Sun. 9:30am-12:30pm; Sept.-June Mon.-Sat. 9:30am-12:30pm and 2:30-6pm, Sun. 9:30am-12:30pm.

Currency Exchange: Some hotels exchange money, but rates are better at travel agencies. **AVIC,** Avda. dos Combatentes, 206 (tel. 240 81). Open Mon.-Fri. 9am-12:30pm and 2:30-6:30pm, Sat. 9am-12:30pm.

Post Office: Avda. dos Combatentes (tel. 220 01), across from the train station. Open Mon.-Fri. 8:30am-6:30pm, Sat. 9am-12:30pm. **Postal Code:** 4900.

Telephones: In the post office. **Telephone code:** 058.

Train Station: At the northern end of Avda. dos Combatentes, directly under Santa Luzia hill. To get to Turismo, walk straight down the avenue, turn left after 4 blocks on Rua Picota, and take your first right. To Oporto (11 per day, 355$), Barcelos (15 per day, 160$), and Vigo, Spain (3 per day, 487$).

Bus Station: Central de Camionagem, on the eastern edge of the city. Catch a bus at any stop along Avda. dos Combatentes (50$). **Rodoviária** runs buses to Braga (8 per day, 360$). **Auto-Viação do Minho** runs buses to Oporto (12 per day, 415$).

Hospital: Avda. 25 Abril (tel. 24 911).

Police: Rua de Avelro (tel. 220 22). **Emergency:** Tel. 115.

Accommodations and Camping

Aside from the week of the Romaria de Nossa Senhora da Agonia (3rd weekend in Aug.), accommodations in Viana are easy to find and typically clean and charming, if not particularly cheap. Most young people, however, opt for the lodgings in private homes which charge reasonable rates, especially for longer stays. To get such a room, stand around the train station and look homeless (a woman should approach you within 5 min.) or walk a couple of blocks into town, turn right off the avenue, and repeat the homeless strategy. Expect to pay 800-1200$ for singles, 1000-1500$ for doubles. Always bargain.

Residência Laranjeira, Rua General Luís do Rego, 45 (tel. 222 61), 1 block down from the train station on your left. A bit expensive, but worth it. Sparkling *pensão* with large, comfortable rooms. Singles 2000$. Doubles 2250$, with bath 3600$. Breakfast included.

Pensão Residencial Magalhães, Rua Manuel Espregueira, 62 (tel. 232 93), 3 blocks from the train station on your left. Friendly, English-speaking owner runs a cozy *pensão* with spacious, airy rooms decorated with pretty wood furnishings and a carpet. Clean common bath. Singles 2300$. Doubles 2500$, with bath 3100$. Breakfast included.

Residência Viana Mar, Avda. dos Combatentes, 215 (tel. 230 54). Clean, modern, noisy rooms. Singles 2000$, with bath 2500$. Doubles 2500$, with bath 3000$.

Pensão Guerreiro, Rua Grande, 14 (tel. 220 99), 2 blocks up from the river. Restaurant downstairs in your right. Ugly wood floors in rooms with an authentic Portuguese apartment feel. Bathroom in a constant state of moisture. Singles 1000$. Doubles 2000$. Breakfast included. Down the street at #72 is a private home turned *pensão* with some of the cheapest rooms in town.

Pensão A Nova Floresta, Rua do Anjinho, 34 (tel. 224 92), 3 blocks up from the river on your left. Despite its name, anything but new. The lack of windows and *eau de toilette* (not the perfume) make being indoors quite unpleasant. Rough bar downstairs with gruff owner. Singles 800$. Doubles 1000$, with bath (a must if personal hygiene means anything at all to you) 2000$.

Orbitur (tel. 232 42) runs a campground on Praia do Cabedelo, the beach 3km from town. (253$ per person, 190$ per tent, 210$ per car. Showers 75$.) Take the bus ("Cabedelo," 50$) directly from the bus station or behind the train station near the funicular stop.

Food

One of the heftier local specialties is *arroz de sarabulha,* rice cooked in blood (it sounds terrible but just looks "seasoned") and served with sausages and potatoes.

Restaurante Diplomático, Avda. Rocha Páris, 202 (tel. 256 56), 3 blocks east of the main avenue. Filled with locals indulging in the excellent food and refreshing atmosphere. Entrees 600-800$, but the complete *prato do dia* runs only 350$. Open daily 8am-midnight.

Restaurante F. Meira, Praça 1° de Maio, 66-70 (tel. 294 61). Cafeteria atmosphere. *Prato do dia* 300$. Other dishes run 400-500$. Open Sun.-Fri. 9:30am-10pm.

Dolce Vita, Rua do Poça, 44 (tel. 248 60), across the *praça* from Turismo. Great place for pizza or spaghetti (400-500$). Portuguese dishes cost more (600-800$). Large selection of tempting ice cream desserts. Open daily noon-10:30pm; in off-season daily noon-3pm and 7:30-10:30pm.

Café Sport, Rua dos Manjovos (tel. 221 17), 2 blocks up from the river on your left. Cool cafe and restaurant adjacent to each other. *Arroz de lulas* (shrimp rice) 525$. The scrumptuous pastries won't leave you alone; buy one. Open Thurs.-Tues. 7am-2am.

Sights

Even in a country famous for charming squares, Viana's **Praça da República** is exceptional. In its center stands a sixteenth-century fountain encrusted with sculptural decoration and crowned by an sphere bearing a Cross of the Order of Christ. The small **Paço do Concelho** (1502), formerly the town hall, seals the square to the east, while diagonally across stands the **Igreja da Misericórdia** (1598). Its playful facade, enlivened by flowering geraniums, is supported by Assyrian-looking granite caryatids. Rebuilt in 1714, the church has a typical interior filled with *azulejos* and gilded altars covered by a ceiling sporting great swirls of color.

The **Museu Municipal,** west of Avda. dos Combatentes da G. Guerra on Largo São Domingos, is housed in an eighteenth-century palace and exhibits marvelous *azulejos* depicting the four continents. The collection includes a delicate fifteenth-century map of Africa, an eighteenth-century spinning wheel, and an eighteenth-century chapel, with a chestnut altar and walls covered with *azulejos.* The prize of the museum's collection of furniture, pottery, and sculpture is a beautiful wooden *oratorio,* with a middle panel that opens to reveal an exquisite terra-cotta crucifix. (Open Tues.-Sun. 9:30am-noon and 2-5pm. Admission 20$. Tour included.) Across from the museum stands the large, late sixteenth-century **Igreja de São Domingos.**

The cliff-like **hill of Santa Luzia** rises north of the city, crowned by a turn-of-the-century neo-Byzantine church. While the view of the town and Lima River is pleasant enough, the truly spectacular panorama lies to the north; look for a vantage point in the forested section away from the funicular. To reach the hilltop, you can either walk 4km of gently climbing, twisting road or take the funicular, which is 200m behind the train station. (Walk through the station, over the tracks, and up a set of stone steps.) Two cars inch their way up and down every half-hour from 9am to 8pm (30$). The basilica sheds the solemnity of most churches and the vibrant interior seems more regal than religious. The petals of the gigantic rose windows spring to colorful life indoors and surround the church on three sides.

The nearby **beach** on Rio Lima is gravelly and full of hungry insects. For more enjoyable sunbathing and swimming, take the **ferry** behind the parking lot at the end of Avda. dos Combatentes to the ocean beach. (Ferries every ½-hr. May-June 7:50am-8pm; July until 10:30pm; Aug. until midnight. 35$ per ride.)

Near Viana do Castelo: Barcelos

Sitting astride the Rio Cávado in the green heart of northern Portugal's wine country, Barcelos is a pretty and curious town, worthy of a daytrip from either Viana do Castelo (30km) or Braga (22km). Known throughout Portugal for the quality of its handicrafts, it is especially famous for its brightly colored earthenware cockerels. The cockerel became an unofficial national symbol as the result of a miracle said to have occurred in Barcelos during the Middle Ages. A Galician pilgrim on his way to Santiago de Compostela was mistakenly accused of theft; he received the death sentence from a judge who was deaf to his plea of innocence. The pilgrim then prayed to San Tiago (St. James), and, knowing that the judge's dinner was to be roast capon, asked the saint to affirm his innocence by making the cooked fowl stand on its legs before the judge. The judge missed out on his chicken dinner and freed the pilgrim. The Galician later returned and built a monument to San Tiago. The fourteenth-century *cruceiro* (cross) stands to this day on the grouds of the archeological museum.

Alighting from the bus in Barcelos, you step onto the **Campo da República,** one of the largest town squares in Portugal. A renowned, monstrous **fair** is held here every Thursday. The town springs to life with people wheeling and dealing in clothes, shoes, ceramics, rugs, and fresh fruit. Just around the corner from the fairground is the lovely **Jardim das Barrocas,** whose colorful plants complement the medieval stone buildings in the **Largo da Porta Nova.** Standing out amidst the shops and wonderful cafes, the **Igreja do Senhor da Cruz** hides an unusually round interior that's capped by an impressive dome. The five rows of medieval leather seats and the play of dancing candlelight accentuate the structure's curious feel; even the cross at the altar is bordered by a tacky set of Christmas lights.

Diagonally across the *praça* from the church, the fifteenth-century Torre de Menagem (Homage Tower) now houses the **tourist office** and the handicraft center (tel. 81 18 82). Actually, the office is nothing but a counter in the corner, and the staff here is more interested in selling than in telling. Nevertheless, flag down an employee and try to pry away a rare town map. (Open Mon.-Wed. 9am-12:30pm and 2-5:30pm, Thurs. 9am-5:30pm. Handicraft store open Fri.-Sat.)**Residencial Abrantes,** near Largo Bom Jesús de Cruz, offers spotless rooms with carpeting and comfortable beds. (Singles 1450$, with shower 1700$. Doubles 2000$, with shower 2400$. Breakfast included.) For more expensive meals and accommodations, visit **Pensão Bagoeira,** Avda. Dr. Sidónio Pais, 57 (tel. 822 36), just down the street from the bus station. The atmospheric, medieval restaurant serves up succulent portions of *cabrito assado* (roast kid) for 700$. Other entrees run 550-650$. Upstairs, the cheery rooms cost 2500$ each and fill quickly.

Buses are the quickest and most convenient way to get to Barcelos, but there is no bus service to Viana do Castelo. The bus stop is by the Rodoviária office, on Avda. Dr. Sidónio Pais, which faces the large fairground. To get to Turismo, turn right as you get off the bus and make a left at the square. Buses connect Barcelos to Braga (10 per day, 180$). The **train station** is located at the end of Avda. Alcaides de Faria, which changes to Avda. dos Combatentes da Grande Guerra as you approach downtown. It's a good half-hour walk, so you may want to take a bus or taxi. If you decide to walk, head left around the fairground onto Avda. da Liberdada to the square. Trains run to Viana do Castelo (15 per day, 160$).

The **post office** is on Rua Cândido dos Reis, 28 (tel. 81 24 44), off Avda. da Liberdade. (Open Mon.-Fri. 9am-12:30pm and 2-5:30pm.) The **postal code** is 4750. Call the **hospital** at 820 71, and the **police** at 832 00. Dial 115 in an **emergency.**

Also within easy reach of Viana is **Valença do Minho.** Dutifully guarding the entrance to northern Portugal, the town is primarily of interest for its seventeenth-century fortifications. These consist of three concentric ramparts intermittently pierced by stone arches and cannon portals. From Valença, a winding road rapidly rises to the summit of **Monte do Faro,** which offers a breathtaking panorama of the coastline, the Minho Valley, and the Galician mountains.

Pensão Rio Minho, near the train station, offers acceptable rooms. (Singles 1600$. Doubles 2000$.) Inquire at **Turismo,** Avda. de Espanha (tel. 233 74; open daily 9am-7pm, in off-season Mon.-Sat. 9:30am-12:30pm and 2:30-6pm) about somewhat less expensive rooms in *casas particulares.* Campers can pitch their tents for free in the nearby field with a fountain. Valença is a stop on the Oporto-Vigo train line. From Viana, 11 trains per day run to Valença (235$), three of which continue to Vigo.

For an unforgettable daytrip, hop a bus to **Ponte de Lima,** a beautiful town on the south bank of the Lima River. Nearly ½-kilometer-wide here, the river is spanned by a 16-arch stone bridge. Normally you can cross the river on foot in shorts, and it affords pleasant, warm water for swimming and wading compared to the coastal waters. The town's **Igreja de São Francisco,** now a museum for temporary exhibits, has stunning, carved wood altarpieces and two unusual wooden pulpits built into the wall. If you decide to stay overnight, inquire at **Restaurante Catrina** (tel. 94 12 67), near the bridge facing the river. The owner has lovely rooms in his hotel (doubles 1500$). **Turismo,** in Praça da República (tel. 94 23 35) provides information on accommodations and will arrange for a private home rental if you decide to spend more time here. (Open daily 9am-8pm; in off-season Mon.-Sat. 9:30am-12:30pm and 2:30-6pm.) For a meal, Restaurante Catrina, listed above, or **Restaurante Encanada** (tel. 94 11 89), near the park with a terrace overlooking the river, both serve delicious and enormous portions for about 500$. Try the *sarrabulha* (rice and sausage) or the *bacalhau* (cod). Ponte de Lima is in the middle of white *vinho verde* country—don't neglect to have a glass.

Montanhas

Trás-Os-Montes ("behind the mountains"), the **Beira Alta** ("high edge"), and Beira Baixa ("low edge") compose the only region of Portugal where snow falls. Geographically separated, these three mountainous provinces remain more tradition-bound than most of the surrounding country.

The transportation system is downright archaic. Train connections are few and far between, and much of the service off the main lines is provided by the wheezing ancestors of the modern diesel train; they pull along passenger cars that date from the '30s. This mode of travel is picturesque, but you should expect insufferably long journeys and crowded trains. Buses are quicker, more reliable, and more expensive. They're worth the extra cost, but those prone to carsickness should beware of the sharp curves and steep hills on the routes.

If the horrendous transportation system hasn't scared you off, you'll find in this region small hamlets, beautiful mountain scenery, and a refreshing absence of tourists. Those who want to forge eastward should aim for the fortress town of **Bragança,** which sits astride the Serra da Nogueira. The town is an eight-hour bus ride from Oporto, but its ancient walls and twelfth-century castle are worth a visit.

Vila Real

Overlooking the confluence of the Cabril and Corgo Rivers, Vila Real perches quietly atop rocky ravines. Not to be confused with Vila Real de Santo Antonio in the Algarve, this town serves as the principal commercial center for the southern farms of Trás-Os-Montes. The town is famous for its black pottery with a leaden sheen. Cement mixers have lately become as much a part of the local scenery as donkey carts, and the old town center is now ringed by new boroughs reaching into the hills. The older architecture stands out, constructed of the smoky grey granite that characterizes the region. But the most compelling reason to come here is the countryside; Vila Real makes a good base for excursions into the fertile fields and rocky slopes of the Serra do Marão.

Orientation and Practical Information

Vila Real lies north of Viseu and east of Oporto. It is somewhat difficult to reach by public transportation. Train service is slow and erratic, and the buses from Oporto, Viseu, and Bragança take their time winding along the mountain roads.

The old town center, along **Avenida Carvalho Araújo,** is a wide avenue lined with trees and mosaic sidewalks.

Tourist Office: Avda. Carvalho Araújo, 94 (tel. 228 19). Open Mon.-Fri. 9:30am-7pm, Sat.-Sun. 9:30am-12:30pm and 2-7pm; in off-season Mon.-Sat. 9:30am-12:30pm and 2-5pm.

Post Office: Avda. Carvalho Araújo (tel. 220 01), up the street from the tourist office. Open Mon.-Fri. 8:30am-6:30pm. **Postal Code:** 5000.

Telephone Code: 059.

Train Station: At the end of Rua Jeronimo Amaral (tel. 221 93). From here to the town center, cross the iron bridge onto Rua Miguel Bombarda, and turn left on Rua Roque da Silveira. Continue to bear left until you reach Avda. Primeiro de Maio. To Oporto (5 per day via Régua, 525$).

Buses: Cabanelas, Rua D. Pedro de Castro (tel. 221 93), on a square directly uphill from Turismo. To Oporto (2 per day, 540-595$), Bragança (1 per day, 615$), Guimarães (1 per day via Amarante, 465$), and Lisbon (1 per day, 1300$). **Rodoviária Nacional,** Rua Gonçalo Cristóvão, 16 (tel. 247 61), near Cabanelas. To Lisbon (1 per day, 1350$), Coimbra (850$), and Viseu (650$).

Hospital: District Hospital of Vila Real, on Rua das Viaturas (tel. 221 33), off the main avenue next to the town hall.

Police: Tel. 220 22. **Emergency:** Tel. 115.

Accommodations, Camping, and Food

Pensão Mondego, Travessa São Domingo, 11 (tel. 230 97), off Avda. Carvalho Araújo near the cathedral. Spacious rooms with old carpets. Spotless modern baths. Singles and doubles 1000$.

Residencial Restaurante, Avda. Carvalho Araújo, 78 (225 32), a couple doors down from Turismo. Spartan rooms with uneven barewood floors. All the furniture tilts to one side of the room. Comfortable, and the bath spews great hot showers. Singles 800$. Doubles 1000$, with bath 2500$. Hip outdoor cafe downstairs.

Pensão Coutinho, Travessa São Domingo, 33 (tel. 220 39). Look under the yellow restaurant canopy. A cut above the others. Spacious, carpeted rooms with stereo amp for soothing music. Singles 1500$. Doubles 2500$. Breakfast included.

Flor de Corco, Travessa São Domingo, 19 (tel. 231 34). The cramped, windowless rooms may be stifling, but you pay for what you get. Technically a private home, so bargain. Singles 1000$. Doubles 1500$.

Camping facilities lie just outside town at **Parque de Campismo** (tel. 247 24), near the Corgo River. Get on the Avda. Marginal and follow the signs to the site. (180$

per person, 150$ per tent, and per car.) The setting is idyllic. Go for a swim in the river.

For meals, try **Restaurante Churrasco,** Rua António de Azevedo, 24 (tel. 223 13), a relaxed bar with chummy locals in front and a blissfully cool restaurant in back. Meals run 450-500$. (Open daily noon-3pm and 6:45-11:30pm.) The **market** is just across the street from the bus station. (Open Tues.-Fri. 8am-1pm.)

Sights

At the lower end of Avda. Carvalho Araújo stands the fifteenth-century **sé** (cathedral), with its simple interior divided by thick, arched columns. The old town's narrow streets, lined with eighteenth-century buildings, squeeze between the main avenue and the gorge created by the Corgo River. Two blocks east of the cathedral stands the **Capela Nova** (New Chapel), with a bizarre floral facade. At the end of Rua Combatentes da Grande Guerra sits the **Igreja de São Pedro,** decorated with seventeenth-century *azulejos.* Three statues look down from its baroque facade.

Walking downhill from the main avenue past the town hall, you'll come to the site of the old town walls. Though there is virtually nothing left of the fortress, a very pleasant esplanade stretches down into the ravine. Beyond the town cemetery, the land narrows to a vantage point that overlooks the valley. The views from vertical outcroppings of rock scattered among the fields are breathtaking.

The village of **Mateus,** 3km east of Vila Real, is world-renowned for its rosé wine. Set against the mountains and surrounded by orchards and vineyards is the baroque **Mateus Manor,** where the various manor houses are reflected in a large pool with paths leading off to side gardens. French, Portuguese, and Chinese pieces from the seventeenth century furnish the rooms, each with a beautifully carved wood ceiling. A nearby room contains personal belongings of the Mateus family, as well as an original edition of the epic poem *Os Lusíadas* by Luis de Camões. (Open daily 9am-1pm and 2-6pm. Admission to gardens 200$, 100$ more to mansion.) Behind the manor house, well-maintained hedges weave geometric patterns on the ground. Gnarled and knotted branches create a cool passageway several meters high and equally wide. At the tunnel's end, trellised vines lead down to fields and vineyards.

Cabanelas operates nine buses per day along the loop from Vila Real to Mateus and back again (each way 80$). If it's a nice day, walk the 3km from town: Take the road going east toward Sabrosa, pass over a metal bridge, and continue beyond the train station.

Half the fun of being in the mountains involves escaping the population centers and roughing it. Vila Real makes an ideal base for those hardy souls who wish to explore the **Parque Natural do Alvão,** a protected area in the heights of the Serra do Marão. After making inquiries at the tourist office, you can walk or hitch northward to the hill town of **Lamas de Olo,** which lies some 1000m above sea level. A four-hour hike rewards you with a spectacular view of the Rio Olo gorge and a chance to examine some of the starkly beautiful granite dwellings of the inhabitants in this area. No buses serve this region nor are there any *pensões,* so pack at least a sleeping bag and be prepared to do a lot of walking.

Viseu

Amidst the wooded hills of some of Portugal's finest wine country, Viseu is a vibrant, vaguely sleazy city that has preserved a lovely old district of flowery balconies and narrow streets. In summer, music is piped out into the shady *rossio,* where the locals congregate in outdoor cafes. Although Viseu has few monuments, it makes a good stopover in transit to or from Spain. Relax here and treat yourself to a meal in one of the city's fine inexpensive restaurants.

Orientation and Practical Information

The pace of life here is as slow as the rickety train that crawls through the vineyards to reach the city. If you are coming from the south, it might be more convenient to take the express bus to Viseu from Coimbra. To get to the town center from the bus station, go right (uphill) along the wide avenue out front until you reach the *rossio,* the main boulevard, bordered by a wall that shimmers with nineteenth-century *azulejos.*

Tourist Office: Avda. de Calouste Gulbenkian (tel. 279 94), directly uphill along the avenue from the *rossio.* Friendly staff distributes a colorful English booklet about Viseu and a decent map. Open Mon.-Fri. 9am-7:30pm, Sat. 10am-12:30pm and 2-5:30pm, Sun. 10am-6pm; in off-season Mon.-Fri. 9am-6pm, Sat. 10am-12:30pm and 2-5:30pm.

Post Office: Rua dos Combatentes da Grande Guerra (tel. 241 68). Open Mon.-Fri. 8:30am-6:30pm. **Postal Code:** 5000.

Telephone Code: 032.

Train Station: Avda. Dr. António José de Almeida (tel. 220 11), at the end of the avenue. To Aveiro (2 per day, 470$), Coimbra (3 per day, 585$), Oporto (5 per day, 650$), and Lisbon (3 per day, 1510$).

Bus Station: Central de Camionagem, Avda. Dr. António José de Almeida (tel. 250 62). To Aveiro (1 per day, 510$), Coimbra (6 per day, 525$), Oporto (1 per day, 700$), and Lisbon (4 per day, 975$).

Baggage Check: At the bus station. 20$ per bag.

Hospital: Rua do Hospital (tel. 271 31). From the tourist office, go down short Rua João Barros.

Police: Tel. 220 41. **Emergency:** Tel. 115.

Accommodations, Camping, and Food

Residecial Viseense, Avda. Alberto Sampaio, 31 (tel. 279 00). Turn right at the end of the *rossio.* The only enjoyable *pensão* in town. Old, crumbling exterior belies large, luxurious rooms with new beds. Singles 1500$. Doubles 2500$, with bath 3000$. Breakfast 500$.

Pensão Europa, Rua Direita, 57 (tel. 253 94), the main street in the old town. Dark, mysterious hallways with neon pink and dull green walls. Likely to be full. Singles 500$. Doubles 1000$.

Pensão Bocage, Travessa São Domingos, 5 (tel. 223 75). From the *rossio,* walk down pedestrian Rua Formosa and turn left on Rua Direita, making another left at the fork. Scary *pensão* that belongs in an Alfred Hitchcock movie. Large rooms are poorly lit, but tolerable. The 700$ singles have no windows. Top floor rooms are the best of the lot. Singles 800$. Doubles 1250$.

The **Orbitur Campsite** (tel. 255 47), in **Fontelo** on the northeast edge of town (walk from the *rossio* to Largo de Sta. Cristina, and take a sharp left) offers excellent facilities for a price. (253$ per person, 190$ per tent, 210$ per car. Showers 75$.)

Food

Inexpensive restaurants concentrate around the *rossio.* On Avda. Alberto Sampaio, **Restaurante Moderno,** at #47, serves 450$ entrees. (Open Sun.-Fri.) In the old town, **Restaurante Cortiço,** Rua Augusto Hilário, 36-47 (formerly Rua Nova; tel. 238 53), is by far the best restaurant in town. The walls and ceilings are lined with fan mail and paper napkins scribbled with praise in many languages. Try the *polvo* (fried octopus, 900$) or the *cabrito* (roast kid, 950$). A full and memorable meal for two costs 1200-1400$. (Open daily noon-3pm and 7-11pm.) Downhill at #35, the Spanish shack called **O Hilário** (tel. 265 87) serves tasty meals from its wide menu at the lowest prices in town. Try *vitela con ervilhas à beirão* (veal with peas, 400$) and, for dessert, *morcela caseira frita* (fried homemade black pudding).

Sights

Viseu's old town is dominated by its stolid **sé,** built in the twelfth century and later extensively remodeled. Its interior is remarkable for its Manueline ceiling, where the ribbed vaulting is fashioned into knotted cables. The magnificent, gilded eighteenth-century altar crowned by a fourteenth-century statue of Mary rises from behind a deep chancel lined with finely crafted choir stalls. A staircase in the north transept ascends to the *coro alto* (upper choir), where you'll find a four-sided, sixteenth-century wooden lectern from Brazil. Adjacent to the church, the Renaissance cloister is surrounded by columns and lined with *azulejos.*

No tour of the sé is complete without a visit to the **treasury,** accessible through the stairs to the left of the altar. For an entrance fee of 50$, Portugal's only combination museum guide-magician-standup comic will whisk you through the cathedral's fascinating collection of religious art and pull escudos out of your ears. When you aren't busy laughing at the guide's antics, admire such priceless exhibits as a twelfth-century Bible, some remarkable medieval statuettes of saints, and a gold reliquary containing the dessicated forearm of Santo António, the first Portuguese saint. (Treasury open daily 9am-noon and 2-5pm. Cathedral open until 7pm.)

In the sixteenth century, Viseu was the center of one of the great Portuguese schools of painting. Fine canvases from this period are housed in the **Museu de Grão Vasco,** next to the cathedral. The collection boasts some excellent fourteenth- and fifteenth-century wood and terra-cotta sculpture, as well as a selection of nineteenth- and twentieth-century paintings, including works by the realist Alberto Sousa. (Open Tues.-Sun. 9:30am-12:30pm and 2-5pm. Admission 150$, students free.) The glorious white facade across from the cathedral belongs to the **Igreja da Misericórdia** (1775); its twin towers rise above elegant windows and a doorway enhanced by Corinthian columns.

Madeira (Ilha da Madeira)

Created 35 million years ago by a massive volcanic eruption, the autonomous archipelago of Madeira now forms the summit of an underwater mountain range rising 4 miles above the floor of the Atlantic. Closer to Africa than Portugal, Madeira is 450km north of the Canary Islands and 550km off the coast of Morocco. Madeira shares Morocco's temperate, sunny weather, but unlike her desert cousin, Madeira is an island paradise, dominated by stunning plantlife. Sheer cliffs plunge into turquoise water; terraced fields of fruit trees and innumerable varieties of exotic flowers form patches of vibrant color; and the jagged volcanic peaks—now enshrouded in lush greenery—brood in the mist.

Legend has it that the island was discovered by a pair of shipwrecked lovers fleeing from England in 1346. Robert Machim and Anne d'Arfet are said to have landed where the town of Machico (apparently named after him) now stands. History books report, however, report that Prince Henry the Navigator started Portugal's worldwide empire by commissioning the successful Madeira expedition. Portugese explorer João Gonçalves Zarco discovered the island of Porto Santo in 1418. One year later, he arrived on the uninhabited, thickly wooded island and formally claimed Ilha da Madeira (Island of Wood) for the king.

Madeira is usually associated with its deservedly world-famous wines. Prince Henry introduced to the island vines from Cyprus and Crete, as well as sugar cane from Sicily and spices from the East. The fine quality of the wine and sugar attracted merchants from all over Europe. Among them was Christopher Columbus himself, who married the daughter of Porto Santo's governor and set up house on that island. Some of the paintings found in local museums—particularly Flemish masterpieces—were acquired in exchange for wine, sugar, or fruit preserves. Madeira wine production was later undertaken and standardized by British traders, whose names still appear on the labels.

Because of the main island's relatively recent volcanic origins, sandy beaches are scarce; the only sizable one is on the nearby island of Porto Santo. Luxury hotels lining the coast west of Funchal have tried to compensate by building swimming pools on the cliffs overlooking the ocean, some of which are open to the tourists for a fee. Some natural seawater pools lie on the north side of Madeira at Porto Moniz and Ponta Delgada. Once you've experienced the island's tremendous natural beauty, however, you won't miss the feeling of sand between your toes.

Most tourists here are middle-aged Europeans who stay in the big hotels. Prices, therefore, tend to be high. Expect everything except the local wine to cost 10-15% more than on the mainland. Backpackers are—for better or worse—still a novelty. Tourism has not spoiled Madeira's incredible scenery, which alone makes a trip here worth the cost of the airfare.

Annual events of interest to the visitor include the Mardi Gras celebrations of **carnaval** in February, the exotic flower floats of the dazzling **Flower Festival** in May, the **Madeira Music Festival** in June, and the year-end **festas** of St. Sylvester, which culminate on New Year's Eve with a fireworks display over Funchal's harbor. Pick up a copy of the unwittingly hilarious *Madeira Island Bulletin,* an English-language monthly available free at tourist offices and filled with helpful information and a local calendar of events.

Getting There and Getting Around

The only practical way to get to Madeira is to fly. Although the city of Funchal is an important port-of-call on Atlantic sea routes, the only boats to Madeira are cruise ships, cargo ships, and military vessels. Still, you might luck out and be able to convince a cargo ship captain to take you on board for the four- to five-day trip. Ask around the Lisbon port. Most flights to Madeira go through Lisbon, but the number of European cities with direct service to Madeira is increasing. **TAP Air Portugal** connects Madeira to Lisbon with five or six flights per day. Madeira's little airstrip is actually a ridge carved out of the mountainside and running alongside the ocean. The approach and landing will make your adrenaline jump to unprecedented levels.

Regular round-trip fare between Lisbon and Funchal is 27600$ (one way 13800$), but round-trip excursion fares are available for 17900$, with the condition that you stay in Madeira no less than six and no more than 30 days. You can change your return date on the island after six days have passed. Excursion tickets be purchased only in Portugal. Regular round-trip airfare from London on TAP or **GB Airways** costs £508, but APEX fares bring the price down to £291. TAP runs one Sunday flight to and from Las Palmas for 31200$ round-trip. Madeira's Santa Catarina Airport is 21km north of Funchal, near Santa Cruz. A taxi into town costs 1800$, the bus runs 250$. Bus schedules are posted outside the exit of the baggage claim area. The airport Turismo office is rarely open.

Madeira is only 57km at its longest point and 22km at its widest. However, the extremely mountainous topography of the island coupled with its winding cliffside roads make distances much longer. The most comfortable (and most expensive) way to explore Madeira is to hire a **taxi.** A list of prices is available at the tourist office. Expect a taxi to cost you up to 8000$ per day; split four or five ways, it's manageable. Taxis are usually parked on Avda. Arriaga opposite the tourist office. If you prefer to drive, go to one of the dozen or so **car rental** agencies on the island. A Renault 5 costs 4000$ per day or 26000$ per week; a Ford Escort 5500$ per day or 36000$ per week. The twisting, narrow mountain roads require extra caution; honk and flicker your lights when you swing around blind curves to alert drivers coming from the other direction. Don't be spooked by the car remains at the bottom of the ravines; not *all* of them are from crashes—Madeirans use the precipices as junkyards. A far more interesting and economical way to see the island, local **buses,** parked along Avda. do Mar, will get you almost anywhere you want to go. Madeiran buses are comfortable, and many trips cost about 100$.

The simplest way to get to know Madeira is on **foot,** trudging through the terraced fields, *levadas,* and mountain paths. Hikers should pick up a copy of *Landscapes of Madeira: a Countryside Guide,* by John and Pat Underwood (1625$ at the Turismo and kiosks around the island). The book details long and short walks, as well as a number of car tours, and offers many helpful tips, including suggestions for picnic sites.

Funchal

The capital city of the now autonomous archipelago takes its name from *funcho,* or fennel, a wild herb with a strong licorice aroma that was abundant when the island was settled. On the southeastern tip of the island, Funchal is Madeira's largest city and home to half its inhabitants. The city's many gardens and parks nourish a seemingly infinite variety of plants, shrubs, flowers, and trees, many of them imported from all over the world. (Spring allergy sufferers should definitely bring their medicine.) A nighttime stroll down Avda. do Infante and Avda. Arriaga is a must. The fountains of the parks sparkle under an array of colorful lights. Still more spectacular, the city lights glow brightly, set against a jet black sky slipping into the ocean.

Host to a great many tourists, Funchal manages to nurture a cosmopolitan atmosphere without swallowing up the strong traditions of the local people. Sidewalk cafes are as much at home in Funchal as are the Spanish-tile roofs and the green shutters of traditional Madeiran homes. The black brick city streets and the patterned-tile sidewalks exemplify Funchal's successful mixture of sophistication and tradition. Since most of the island's services and accommodations are here, Funchal makes a good base from which to explore the rest of Madeira.

Orientation and Practical Information

Funchal lies draped over hills that slope south toward the bay. Running east-west along the waterfront is **Avenida do Mar,** a wide boulevard traveled by most city and intercity buses. Perpendicular to Avda. do Mar, **Avenida Zarco** runs north-south and connects the harbor area to the upper part of town. A block north and parallel to Avda. do Mar is **Avenida Arriaga,** Funchal's main thoroughfare, with the cathedral (*sé*) at its eastern end and **Praça do Infante** and its fountain at the western end. To the east, Avda. Arriaga becomes **Rua Aljube,** and to the west, it changes to **Avenida do Infante.**

Tourist Office: Turismo, Avda. Arriaga, 16-18 (tel. 256 58). Kind and helpful multilingual staff. Ask for maps and daytrip suggestions. Bus schedules for all routes 100$. Schedules posted for the ferry to Porto Santo. Ask for the *Tábela de preços máximos e mínimos,* a list of official rates that hotels, apartment-hotels, and pensões are allowed to charge. If you are overcharged, the Turismo will deal directly with the establishment. Pick up a copy of the *Madeira Island Bulletin.* Open Mon.-Sat. 9am-7pm, Sun. 9am-1pm.

Consulates: U.S., Avda. Luís de Camões, bloco B4, Apt. B (tel. 474 29), off Avda. do Infante. **U.K.:** Rua da Sé, 14, 1st floor (tel. 212 21), off Rua João Tavira beside the *sé.* The British consulate serves citizens of all Commonwealth nations.

Currency Exchange: Banks offer the best rates. They charge a flat commision of 545$ per transaction, so you may wish to change as much as you can at one time. Many banks line Avda. Arriaga.

American Express: Star Travel Office, Avda. Arriaga, 23 (tel. 320 01), next to the bank. Open Mon.-Fri. 9am-12:30pm and 2-6pm. In an emergency when the office is closed, call 303 54.

Post Office: Avda. Zarco (tel. 321 31). Poste Restante. You must ask for Madeira stamps specifically. Open Mon.-Fri. 8:30am-8pm, Sat. 9am-12:30pm. **Postal Code:** 9000.

Telephones: In the post office complex. International telephone and **telegram** services. Open daily 8:30am-midnight.

Airport: Santa Catarina Airport (tel. 522 73), near Santa Cruz. Buses to Funchal leave at 8:15am, 11:15am, 4:35pm, 8:15pm, and 11:15pm (also Fri. at 2pm, 45 min., 250$). You can also share a taxi into town (1800$). Buses to the airport leave from Avda. do Mar, straight down from Rua João Tavira, at 7:15am, 9:15am, 12:45pm, 7:15pm, and 9:15pm. **TAP Air Portugal:** Avda. Do Mar, 10 (tel. 301 51), at Rua João Tavira. Open Mon.-Fri. 9am-6pm.

Bus Station: Main bus park at the eastern end of Avda. do Mar. The bus schedule booklet lists the bus stops for popular destinations. Buses to Camacha, Santa da Serra, and Camico leave from a small *praça* at the eastern end of Rua da Alfândega (parallel to Avda. do Mar), near the market.

English Bookstore: Livraria Inglesa, Rua da Carreira, 43 (tel. 244 90), at the entrance to O Patio Restaurant. In a charming courtyard café setting; worth a visit just to see the delightful set-up. Open Mon.-Fri. 10am-7pm, Sat. 10am-1pm.

Laundromat: Lavandaria Açucena, Rua do Surdo, 5A (tel. 235 48), off Rua da Carreira at the end of Zarco. Wash-and-dry service 200$ per kg. 5-kilogram min. Open Mon.-Fri. 9am-7:30pm, Sat. 9am-1pm.

Weather: Tel. 331 61, 24 hours. Also at the tourist office. Important for hikers and sailing and fishing trips.

Pharmacy: English Chemist, on Avda. Zarco at Rua de Câmara Pestana. **Farmácia do Carmo,** Largo do Phelps, 8 (tel. 237 83). A list of on-duty pharmacies is posted on the door if these places are closed.

Medical Emergency: Hospital Tel. 421 11. **Red Cross,** Tel. 200 00.

Police: Tel. 220 22. **Emergency:** Tel. 115.

Accommodations

Luxury hotels line the shore west of the city, but there are a number of less expensive *pensões* and *residências* in the town center off Avda. Arriaga. Prices do not vary significantly from one season to the next, but lodgings are harder to come by in high season (May-Oct.), especially in late summer. Make sure you are charged according to the **Tabela de Preços,** or register your complaint at the Turismo before you pay.

Pensão Astória, Rua de João Gago, 10 (tel. 238 20), behind the cathedral. Reception on 4th floor. The best deal in town. Plain but big, well-lit rooms with pleasant furnishings. Rooms along Rua Aljube can be noisy, but the view complements. The jolly old man who runs the place would make a believable Santa Claus. Curfew midnight. Singles 1500$. Doubles 2500$. Add 250$ if staying for only one night. Hot showers and breakfast included.

Pensão Residência Colombo, Rua da Carreira, 182 (tel. 252 13). Walk up Avda. Zarco, and turn left at Rua da Carreira. Almost luxuriously, modern rooms. Elegant wood furnishings and immaculate bathrooms. Rooms facing the street have patios, but rooms in the back are quieter. June-Sept. singles 2600$, doubles 4000$; Oct.-Dec. prices slightly higher; Jan.-May lower prices. Hot bath and breakfast included.

Pensão Universal, Rua do João Tarira, 4 (tel. 206 18), on your left as you approach the cathedral from Avda. Arriaga. 2500$ rooms are airy with worn floors and private baths. 1000$ rooms are up the street in a dingy, rotting annex that looks like something out of a Hitchcock movie. Filthy walls and floors.

Pensão Greco, Rua do Carmo, 16 (tel. 300 81). From the cathedral, walk up Rua Aljube, cross the bridge over the *ribeira,* and continue left all the way to Rua do Carmo. Comfortable rooms with carpeting. Singles 3300$. Doubles facing the street 4500$, 5000$ rooms in back with a balcony and a delightful view of the hills.

Food

Fish and fruit in Funchal are always fresh. Grilled *bife de atum* (tuna steak) is delicious served with fried corn bread. Don't let the corn bread burn your tongue—the inside stays hot after the outside has cooled off. The flavor of Madeira's own black *espada* (scabbard fish) is also best appreciated *grelhado* (grilled). A popular local soup, *sopa típica,* is made from a tasty combination of tomato, egg, and onion. Other local delicacies are sure to satisfy your sweet tooth. *Bolo de mel* is a rich, dark molasses cake with nuts. You'll find it in all pastry shops. *Pudim caramelo,* a caramel pudding dessert (dipped in Madeira wine), is served in all the island's restaurants. The variety of fresh, exotic fruits make their way into the juices and ice cream. *Manga* (mango) and *maracujá* (passion fruit) are heavenly treats. Needless to say, you should not leave Madeira without sampling the island's world-famous wines—*Maluasia, Sercial, Verdelho,* and *Bual.*

A number of inexpensive restaurants frequented by locals lie along **Rua Queimada de Cima,** off Rua João Tavira. For a notch up in quality, check out the area around **Rua da Carreira** and **Rua Ivens,** north of Avda. Arriaga. The restaurants in the **Zona Velha** (old part of the city) will assault your senses and exact a high price for it.

Madeiran prices are likely to wreak havoc on your budget, but the **market** called **Mercado dos Lavradores** (see Sights) offers less expensive fruit and produce. Shops nearby sell bread, yogurt, and other dairy products. (Open Mon. 7am-2pm, Tues.-Thurs. 7am-4pm, Fri. 6am-8pm, and Sat. 6am-4pm.)

Restaurante Adega da Queimada, Rue da Queimada de Baixo, 46 (tel. 241 57), 1 block from the cathedral up Rua João Tavira. Cozy, small restaurant filled with lively locals. Tasty and filling food. *Bife de atum* and *espada* with rice and fries 400$. *Pudim de caramelo* for dessert 120$. Inexpensive steak dishes. Open Mon.-Sat. 7am-midnight.

Miraflores, Largo do Phelps, 24 (tel. 218 27), at Rua 31 de Janeiro. Follow Rua Aljube across the *ribeira.* Busy, but informal restaurant-bar atmosphere. Don't let the zombie-like waiters bother you. Various *espada* dishes with potatoes and salad 445$. Try the delicious *pudim caseiro* (homemade pudding, 135$). Open daily 8am-10pm.

Arco Velho, Rua Dom Carlos I, 42 (tel. 256 83), 2 blocks down from Supermercado dos Lauradores in Zona Velha. Touristy but elegant outdoor cafe. The exhaust coming from the busy road can be annoying; go at odd hours to avoid the traffic. If you're feeling exotic, try the octopus sandwich (160$). Wide variety of *sumos* (fruit juices) and *batidos* (fresh shakes) 120-150$. Open daily 10am-8pm.

A Indiana, Rua do Aljube, 1a3, across from the cathedral. A must. The pastries here are like cheap sex: inexpensive and absolutely orgasmic (45-70$). Ice cream served in crunchy, homemade cones (80$ per two scoops). Pay the cashier first. Open daily 8am-11pm.

O Fofinho, Rua Dr. Dernão Ornelas, 57. A stand-up sandwich bar great for a quick lunch or snack. Have one of the many interesting fruit drinks, ice cream, or coffee. You can't beat the name for entertainment value—listen to it being pronounced by those who can do so. Open Mon.-Fri. 8am-8pm, Sat. 8am-2pm.

Sights

Funchal's main street, Avenida Arriaga, is a favorite place to stroll in the evening. It's lined with mosaic sidewalks and trimmed with Jacaranda trees that bloom with fragrant purple flowers in spring. At the eastern end of Arriaga is Funchal's fifteenth-century **sé,** Portugal's first overseas cathedral. The *sé* is lit by columns of candles, and the narrow slits that serve as windows give the building an enigmatic feel. You can smell its antiquity in the musty wood odor that permeates the building's dark, spacious interior. The *sé* still holds services and is packed on religious holidays. If you follow Rua João Tavira uphill from the cathedral and turn right at the end, you will find the **Praça do Município,** covered with mosaic patterns that simulate the choppy currents around Madeira. On the eastern side of the square stands the eighteenth-century **Câmara Municipal,** a government building that doubles as a free museum. (Open Mon.-Fri. 9am-12:30pm and 2-5pm, Sat. 9am-1pm.) On the southern end of the *praça,* you will find the **Museu de Arte Sacra** (Sacred Art Museum), Rua do Bispo, 21. Madeira's particularly rich collection of religious art is displayed here, including items donated by *emigrantes* who made their fortunes elsewhere. (Open Tues.-Sat. 10am-12:30pm and 2:30-5:30pm, Sun. 10am-1pm. Admission 100$.)

Leaving Praça do Município, walk downhill on Rua dos Ferreiros (on the east side of the *praça*), and turn left on Rua Aljube onto the small footbridge that crosses the *ribeira.* At the end of Rua Dr. Fernão Ornelas, the busy commercial street on the other side of the bridge, stands the **Mercado dos Lavradores** (Laborers' Market), housed in a large, yellow building. The marketplace is most lively in the morning, when everyone vies for the best of the freshly arrived produce. At the entrance, women dressed in traditional red-and-yellow-striped Madeiran skirts sell flowers; inside is a cheerful, crowded courtyard with *azulejos* in blue and yellow, the island's colors. The stalls are filled with produce, wickerware, and leather goods. In the large warehouse room toward the back, fish for sale are spread out on large stone tables. Enormous tunas are expertly hacked into steak-size hunks with knives the width of the fish peddlers' arms. Look for the bulging eyes and sharp teeth of the eel-like **espada.** (The black *espada* are found at depths of 2400-4800 ft. only in the waters of Madeira and off the shores of Japan.) Huge octopuses are piled in enormous slippery heaps, while coils of silvery eels are carefully arranged in crates. Upstairs, fresh vegetables and fruits rest in shallow wicker baskets.

Bordering the market, down Rua Boa Viagem, spreads the **Zona Velha,** Funchal's old city. Here, narrow, winding cobbled streets are lined with whitewashed buildings. All the building's share Spanish tile roofs and traditional, dark green shutters. Ten minutes east along Rua de Santa Maria, past the tempting fragrances of meals-in-the-making, you'll arrive at the **Igreja de Santa Maria Maior.** The church's eighteenth-century facade was crafted out of black volcanic rock; black volcanic stones laced with white rock tile the small terrace. The interior is illuminated by crystal chandeliers, and the ceiling is painted in an illusory style. The tremendously ornate altar is filled with gold-leaf columns and fresh flowers—typically Madeiran. The church rests on a cliff, overlooking the reflective ocean below. The spectacular view alone is worth the trip. (Open daily 7:30am-8pm except Sun. afternoons. Free.)

West of the old city you will come to **Avenida do Mar,** the wide waterfront boulevard. Halfway down the avenue, a small pedestrian pier juts into the harbor. From the end of the platform, you can see the houses of Funchal spread before you, like the audience in an amphitheater, with the jagged peaks of the interior as a backdrop. This view is especially spectacular at night. If you're feeling touristy, have a drink at **The Beatles,** where you'll feel absolutely silly sitting in their little boats, fashioned as tables. At the west end of Avda. Arriaga (10 min. away), a stairway leads to the **Parque Santa Catarina.** Approach the statue, and step into the famous picture-postcard view. From here, paths lead to tropical gardens full of palm trees, flowering plants, and cacti. A small lagoon is surrounded by aviaries with exotic bird species; an outdoor cafe sells drinks nearby. Another garden worth a special trip is the **Jardim Botânico.** Cobblestoned paths, chirping birds, and a thousand varieties of flowers make this a marvelous spot for a stroll. Peacocks roam pleasant trellised areas. A magnificent view of Funchal and the harbor spreads below. Take bus #30, which leaves hourly from Avda. do Mar. (Open Mon.-Sat. 8am-6pm. Admission 80$.) In addition, you may catch word of an exquisitely beautiful park on a private estate. This is the **Quinto do Palheiro,** 5km from Funchal. Much of the commotion results from its supposed exclusiveness. The park is not shown on maps and tour buses aren't officially allowed to bring sightseers (they do). In reality, anyone willing to spend the time and the 300$ for admission is allowed in to view the dull fields with a few grazing bovines. The city gardens in Funchal require a fraction of the time and trouble to visit—and are many times more beautiful. If, however, you insist on the drudgery, take bus #29 at Avda. do Mar for Camacha at 10am (97.50$). (Park open—despite the warning signs—9:30am-12:30pm.)

No visit to Madeira is complete until you have seen the **Madeira Wine Company,** at Avda. Arriaga, 28 (next to Turismo), where you can watch the island's renowned *vinho* being processed and bottled. Upstairs is a small museum; downstairs is free wine tasting. Be sure to try the popular "Rainwater," a medium dry blend, and the rich, sweet, 10-year-old Malmsey. All bottles here are sold at bargain prices. (Open Mon.-Fri. 9am-1pm and 3-7pm, Sat. 9am-1pm.)

Entertainment

Funchal nights are full of life, but only near the big hotels on the west side (a 20-min., uphill walk along Avda. Arriaga and Avda. Infante). Elsewhere, cafes and restaurants are pretty much deserted by 11:30pm. Almost every luxury hotel has its own club. At the Madeira Sheraton's nightclub **O Farol**, the DJ plays many slow oldies to attract the older crowd. If you're into dancing, you'll enjoy the huge dance floor and big picture windows. Madeiran folk dancing and music is featured at different hotels every day of the week. (Check the *Island Bulletin* for details.) There are vast differences among the different dancing groups; some have forsaken all tradition to please the tourists. Ask the tourist office to recommend a troupe.

Near Funchal

The countryside around Funchal can be defined in one word: mountainous. Getting out of the city in any direction means climbing sometimes incredibly steep, narrow, winding roads. Pay no attention to the driver's maneuverings and enjoy the dazzling views.

Take an excursion to the little town of **Monte** for its gardens and its toboggans. Luxuriantly green, Monte's gardens creep up the hillside overlooking Funchal's harbor just north of the capital. In the middle of the carefully trimmed hedges and well-maintained paths, a steep hill with dozens of steps leads to the **Igreja de Nossa Senhora do Monte** (Church of Our Lady of the Mountain). Dedicated to the appropriately chosen patron of Madeira, this church is the site of an annual mid-August pilgrimage. To the left of the nave is the tomb of Emperor Karl I of Austria, who died in exile on the island in 1922. Below the church, the incredible Madeiran **carros de cesto** (wicker toboggans) begin their runs. You can climb into a wicker cart with wooden runners and slide all the way down to Funchal. A pair of white-clad men steer and control the speed by pulling thick ropes as you breeze along over the slippery cobbled pathway worn smooth by generations of tobogganers. The ride, which lasts an adventuresome 20 minutes, costs 1400$ per person. For a longer thrill, start from Terreiro da Luta, slightly higher up the mountainside (2300$).

Funchal buses #20 and 21 leave for Monte from Avda. do Mar, about 2 blocks east of Avda Zarco (every 15-30min., ½ hr., 97.50$). For a daytrip to Monte, take a late morning bus and toboggan back to Funchal after lunch (eat lightly).

When Madeira was settled, one town's beach was so filled with seals that Zarco named the village **Câmara de Lobos** (Chamber of Seals). Today, the only seals left in the archipelago are found in sparse colonies around the unpopulated Ilhas Desertas. Câmara de Lobos, a fishing town 8km west of Funchal, is famous for its *polvo* (octopus) and *lapas* (limpets), a mollusk notorious for sticking to rocks with steadfast zeal. The town showcases two "octopus" trees at the village's main entrance; their leaves supposedly resemble the slippery invertebrate.

Câmara de Lobos is an easy 20-minute bus ride from Funchal. Buses #1, 4, 6, 7, 27, 96, or 107 depart frequently from Avda. do Mar. The bus will drop you next to a band shelter in the town center. From the nearby trellised balcony, you can take in the view of the stone-covered beach below, where the townspeople dry their laundry using the stones to hold down the corners of the sheets and towels. Lizards darting among the rocks supervise the operation suspiciously. West along the shoreline, row after row of banana trees march up the hillside to the edge of the cliff. Looming in the distance beyond the fields is **Cabo Girão**, the second highest cliff in the world, rising almost 2000 feet from the pounding ocean below. Bus #154 (Mon.-Fri. at 9:15am, 1hr., 157.50$) will take you all the way to the lookout point on Cabo Girão. Once there, you'll share the spectacular view with the many local vendors selling their goods to the droves of tourists.

Curral das Freiras is a small, isolated village at the bottom of the crater of an extinct volcano in Madeira's deepest valley. In the sixteenth century, when the island was attacked by French pirates, the nuns of the Convent of Santa Clara took refuge here (*curral das freiras* means "nuns' corral"). The walls of jagged rock surrounding the town reach heights of 3200 feet. The sloping sides of the crater basin are covered with rows of terraced fields and peppered with small groups of houses. Come on Sunday, when women with delicate lace scarves over their heads mill about the village, while in nearby cafes the men consume cup after cup of wine. Blue and white *azulejos* line the inside of the church in front of which is the town's cemetery. A frighteningly realistic sculpture of Jesus' body after the crucifixion will startle you to the left of the entrance.

To get here from Funchal, take bus #81 at the western end of Avda. do Mar (3-4 per day, 1 1/3) hr., 200$). On the way, you'll climb through groves of tall eucalyptus trees and pass by cliffs over which narrow waterfalls plunge from tremendous heights. If you're driving or taking a taxi, stop at **Eira do Serrado,** a lookout point high on the top of the crater.

Santana

On the north side of Madeira lies Santana, famous for its brightly painted A-frame houses with thatched roofs. This small town is a good starting point for trips to nearby Queimadas Park and Pico Ruivo and a nice place to wander around in its own right. The road from Funchal presents some of the island's most spectacular scenery, cutting through elevated mountain passes that overlook verdant valleys. The whitewashed houses and terraced fields here cling to even the highest slopes. Occasionally, a house in the middle of a near-vertical incline will baffle you. The road itself climbs upward through forests of pine trees and then descends once more, snaking around hairpin turns within inches of sheer, hair-raising drops. Don't let this frighten you: The beauty of the trip alone merits a visit to Santana.

From Santana you can take a taxi (800$) or hike the 5km to **Parque das Queimadas.** (As the route from Santana to Queimadas is all uphill, you may wish to take a taxi there and walk back.) Queimadas is a lovely park of lush green paths, huge pine trees, and ivy-covered walls; water sprays over the rocks into a pool inhabited by a pair of black swans with bright red bills. (The few houses here are government property and accommodate employees on their holidays.)

Not far from Queimadas, **Pico Ruivo** rises 1936m above sea level, the highest point on the island. To get here, take a taxi from Santana to Achada do Teixeira, where the road ends (1000$). A 40-minute walk along a stone path leads to the peak. Before leaving the parking area, however, walk around to the northeast side (away from Pico Ruivo) and downhill a short distance to have a look at the unusual formation of vertical, black basaltic rocks known as *homem em pé* ("the standing man")—its odd shape resembles a large man standing on the slope. If the skies are clear as you walk to the peak, you'll have a tremendous view of the surrounding mountains and valley. On a misty day the walk has a different magic—the peaks appear and disappear, and the bleatings of sheep sound from the fog. The *casa de abrigo* (rest house) near the top sells drinks. It's also possible to spend the night here in one of the cozy bedrooms. (200$ per person. You must arrange this with Turismo in Funchal. The 3-night max. may be extended if you insist.) Simple kitchen facilities are available, so pack your own food. The summit is a 10-minute walk from the rest house. When the weather is clear, Curral das Freiras is visible to the south, and to the northeast you can see Santana, São Jorge, and the ocean beyond. To the southeast lies **Arieiro Peak,** which can be reached by foot if you don't mind the three-hour hike. This mountain path is not as well-maintained as the main one, and anyone with even a touch of vertigo may have some difficulty.

Bus #103 leaves Funchal from the eastern end of Avda. do Santana (see the map in the bus schedule booklet) for Samana (2½ hr.—be prepared for delays, 300$), continuing to the town of Bonaventura. You'll need to buy your ticket (at the kiosk under the palm tree) a few hours in advance for the 4 or 6pm buses and a day in advance for the 7:30am bus. For a lovely daytrip, take the early morning bus to Santana, hail a taxi to Achada do Teixeira, and hike from there to Pico Ruivo and back down to Santana via Queimadas. You'll get back to Santana in time to catch the 5:30pm bus to Funchal. (Get to the bus stop 30 min. early since the drivers come and go as they please.) No matter what the season, get the forecast before leaving Funchal (ask at Turismo or call 331 61 for a recording in both Portuguese and English), since wet weather can make the trip dangerous. Wear sturdy shoes, and be sure to pack lunch, water, and a sweater (even in summer the higher altitudes are chilly). In winter, the peak is snow-covered, and the hike can be treacherous.

Northern Coast

The northern coast of Madeira between Porto Moniz and Santana has some of the island's most spectacular scenery. Because there is greater rainfall here, the vegetation is even thicker and lusher on this side. The coast itself is lined with steep cliff faces and sprinkled with waterfalls that cascade down to the turquoise sea. The road between Ribeira Brava on the south coast and São Vicente on the north passes through the verdant **Serra de Aqua,** whose striking peaks form a deep valley fed by mountain streams. En route between north and south, be sure to stop at **Encumeada,** a breathtaking lookout point where you can see as far north as São Vicente and the ocean on one side, and deep into the valley made by the Serra de Aqua on the other. North of Encumeada, the road winds down through **Chao dos Louros,** where a large, fragrant grove of laurel trees makes an ideal spot for a picnic. **Quebra-Mar** in **São Vicente** is a good if somewhat expensive restaurant on the waterfront. All tables have a view of the coast through the big glass windows. Entrees start at 700$.

To the west along the coast, the road turns into a narrow ledge chiseled out of a cliff. Between **São Vicente** and **Seixal** the views are no less than stupendous—water pours from slender cascades near tunnels in the rock. The shoreline continues westward to **Porto Moniz,** where you can take a dip in the clear, blue seawater pools among the rocks. An artificial seawater pool at the edge of the ocean has been built at **Ponta Delgada,** east of São Vicente.

Getting here by public transportation is not exactly a snap. The trip from Funchal to Porto Moniz is long, and bus connections make it impossible to return to Funchal on the same day. Although there are no *pensões* or hotels in Porto Moniz, you can rent a room in a private house for around 700$. Ask around at the restaurants in town. From Funchal, take bus #6 to São Vicente, and transfer to bus #150 to Porto Moniz. If you don't have time to spend the night at Porto Moniz, your should hire a taxi or rent a car. It's a full day's drive from Funchal to Porto Moniz, down the southwestern coast, and back to Funchal.

Porto Santo

Forty kilometers northeast of Madeira, the tiny island of Porto Santo contrasts sharply with its neighbor: While Madeira is lush and green, Porto Santo is windswept and barren. The island's major attraction is its 7-kilometer beach of powdery, golden sand and crystalline waters. (Much of the sand arrives via the Gulf Stream all the way from the Gulf of Mexico.) Since Madeira has no beaches, the population of Porto Santo doubles to 10,000 in August and September. The catamaran departs at 8am Wednesday through Monday from the dock at the eastern end of Avda. do Mar, leaving Port Santo for Funchal at 6pm (90 min.; round-trip 3500$, same day round-trip 4000$). Buy your tickets at the marina. Even in the best weather, the crossing can be rough. Try to eat little or nothing beforehand and sit in the middle of the boat. You may even want to pop a few motion sickness pills (e.g., Dramamine). A friendly, uniformed woman hands out seasickness bags en route in case your precautions should prove futile. Alternately, TAP Air operates six or seven flights daily to Porto Santo (30 min., round-trip 4560$). The convenient schedule and the ever-increasing number of flights have made flying the preferred option.

Pensão Palmeira, Avda. Vieira de Castro (tel. 98 21 12), rents singles with bath for 2500$, doubles with bath for 3500$, breakfast included. **Residêncial Zarco,** Rua João Gonçalves Zarco, 66, is also clean and comfortable with doubles for 2200$, with kitchenette for 3500$, all rooms with bath. **Camping** is feasible in the sandy fields near the beach. Be aware that in late summer all accommodations are likely to be full. If you can't make reservations, you may have to settle for a daytrip from Funchal.

MOROCCO

US $1 = 8.29 dirhams (dh)
CDN $1 = 6.87dh
UK £1 = 14.01dh
AUS $1 = 6.64dh
NZ $1 = 5.49dh

1dh = US $0.12
100dh = CDN $0.15
100dh = UK £0.07
100dh = AUS $0.15
100dh = NZ $0.18

Once There

Plan to use the larger cities in Morocco as transportation hubs and civilization pit stops, places to catch up on current events and stock up on pharmaceutical goods and English books. There are laundromats in the large cities, but often the maid in your hotel will wash your clothes for a few dirhams. Agree on the price beforehand (20-30dh). It is usually safe to store your backpack at the CTM depot baggage check. If you do not have padlocks on the zippers, however, your bags may not be accepted. Private companies also check baggage. They are trustworthy and accept any kind of bag. Exchange money in banks, where rates are uniform and no commission is charged. Keep the receipts if you want to get rid of dirhams at the border—you won't be able to change them anywhere else. Black market transactions are illegal and potentially perilous; hustlers have a full bag of tricks for ripping you off, including forgery. Finally, practice your deep knee bends before trying your luck on a Moroccan toilet; if you are a real maestro, you can try it on a moving train. Have toilet paper with you at all times, since locals use methods that some Westerners consider unattractive.

Orientation

Most large Moroccan cities are divided into a New City (*ville nouvelle*), designed by the French during colonial rule, and a labyrinthine Old City, or medina ("town" in Arabic). The ratio of monuments, mosques, and markets between the two is roughly 100 to 1 in favor of the medina. The *Kasbah* refers to the old fortress and in many cities is now another quarter. The *mellah* is the old Jewish quarter and usually adjoins the medina; the *medersa* is the late medieval Koranic school and dormitory often adjoining a mosque. Because non-Muslims are not permitted to enter mosques, the *medersa* is often the major tourist attraction. In addition to craft *souks* (markets), nearly every city has a weekly *souk* where townspeople and peasants come together to transact business and to catch up on local gossip. The produce, handicrafts, and clothing seen and sold in these *souks* vary greatly from region to region. Go early in the day. As you look for addresses, keep in mind that many streets, especially those with foreign names, are currently being renamed and the houses renumbered. In some places, *zankat* or *derb* is taking the place of *rue* or *calle*.

Ramadan is a holy month during which Muslims fast from sun-up until sundown to cultivate spiritual and physical well-being and to foster compassion and charity: no eating, no drinking, no smoking, and no sex until the sun is low enough that a black thread and a white thread can no longer be distinguished from one another (in summer about 4:30am-8:30pm). Ramadan after dark is another story: A siren prompts every Moroccan to swill a bowl of *harira*, after which religious services and feasting are the two major activities. City streets explode with pedestrians, often to the accompaniment of music and festivities. The transmission of the Koran to Mohammed is celebrated on the 27th day of Ramadan, known as the Night of Destiny, when all mosques are illuminated and children are initiated into the fasting ritual. The appearance of the new moon, marking the end of the holy month, is

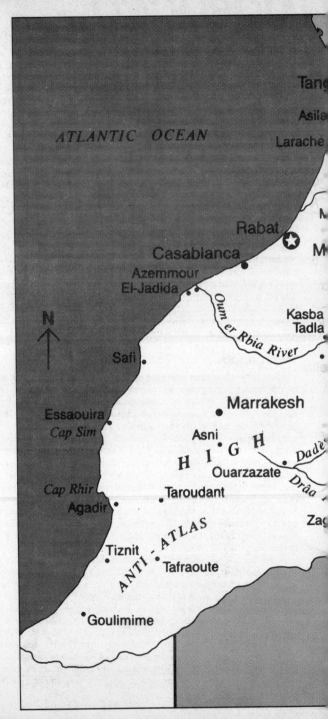

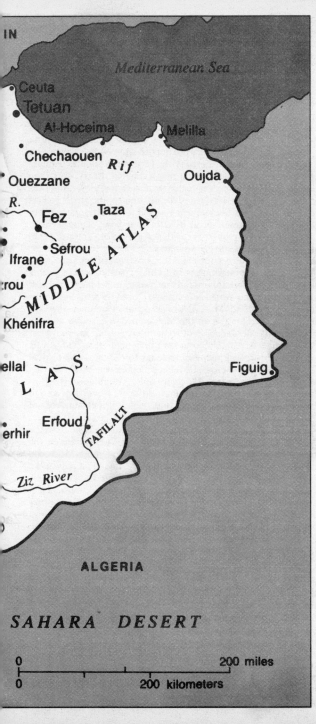

IN

Mediterranean Sea

Ceuta
Tetuan
Al-Hoceima   Melilla
Chechaouen   *Rif*
Ouezzane   Oujda
R.
Fez   Taza

MIDDLE ATLAS

Ifrane
Sefrou
rou
Khénifra

L   A   S
ellal
Figuig
Erfoud
erhir   TAFILALT

Ziz River

ALGERIA

SAHARA   DESERT

0 _____ 200 miles
0 _____ 200 kilometers

proclaimed by the king, and the daylight fast is broken with Aid Es-Saghir, a public holiday with big family breakfasts and gifts to the children.

Despite modernization, observance of Ramadan has by no means waned in Morocco. Though city services continue to operate for the most part, restaurants and cafes that cater to locals close down during the day, and all Muslims, including working people, observe the fast. Ramadan falls at a slightly different time each year so that over the course of three decades it will make a full cycle. In 1989, it will run approximately from April 6 to May 5 ("approximately" because Ramadan is on the Arab lunar calendar). If you're stuck on a crowded bus in 110° weather, sip from your canteen as unobtrusively as possible, since tempers flare along with the heat. During daylight hours, try to do your eating, drinking, and smoking in private, particularly in rural areas, where locals are not accustomed to tourists, and a lack of sensitivity can provoke outright hostility. In large cities such as Tangier and Rabat, many restaurants stay open all day during Ramadan. Elsewhere in the country, all but the fancier establishments that cater to tourists will close from sunrise to sunset. A good way to enter into the spirit of the fast and appreciate its powerful emotional hold over the country is to observe it yourself for an afternoon. Then, at sunset, seek out a popular restaurant, sit in front of your bowl of *harira,* wait for the cannon to sound, pause while prayers are said, and plunge in. You will probably savor this meal above all others during your stay.

Moussems are local Islamic holidays equivalent to Christian patron saint days. Most last several days and include pilgrimages to local shrines as well as events ranging from bustling bazaars and agricultural fairs to "fantasias" come to life with charging cavalcades of costumed and armed equestrians. Dozens of tents and traditional music and dancing are standard. Most *moussems* occur in summer; they fall at different days each year according to both the Mohammedan calendar and the discretion of local governments. Be warned that some *moussems* are more tourist traps than expressions of religious zeal. Use your own judgment; genuine festivals are wonderful. The grandest Moroccan *moussem* belongs to Meknes. The festival is actually held in Tissan, on the outskirts of Meknes, September 20-27. During Aid el K'bir (The Big Feast), around July 12, each family slaughters a sheep to commemorate Abraham's biblical sacrifice. Another festive event worth trying to catch is the Marrakech Folklore Festival in early June, which brings hundreds of performers in regional finery from all over Morocco for music, song, and dance.

Conversion calendars from Muslim to Gregorian and back are available from the Islamic Center of New York (see Practical Information and Publications in the General Introduction). The booklet *Leisure in Morocco,* free at most Moroccan tourist offices, contains helpful information on dates and places of annual *moussems,* as well as weekly *souks* (markets). Also check local, French-language newspapers.

Friday is the Muslim day of rest, and at least within the medina, most places will be closed. Since Morocco is adapting to western calendars, Sunday is an appropriate day of rest for non-Muslims. Office hours are usually from 8am to 2pm in summer and from 8am to noon and 4 to 6pm in off-season and during Ramadan.

Hustlers and Guides

"Welcome to Morocco! Hello friend, *bonjour!* American? Speak English?"—these words will greet you wherever you turn in Morocco. Especially in Tangier, Tetuan, Fes, and Marrakech, you will be continually approached by young men claiming to be the guide you need. Moroccan hustlers are famed for their ability to swindle Europeans and, especially, Americans. They will ask the time to find out what language you speak and examine your dress, guidebook, or T-shirt to determine your nationality. Don't fall for the old line "if you buy a *djellaba,* you will not be hassled as people will assume you are a Moroccan." Most hustlers speak flawless French, competent English, and a few words of German; some can rattle on in Danish, Spanish, or Italian. There is genuine need and poverty in Morocco, and you will see many outstretched palms. The trick is to distinguish the innocent, poverty-stricken beggar from the slick con-artist. Moroccans can be some of the most hospitable people in the world, however; don't let fear reduce you to paranoia and prevent the spontaneous friendships that make travel worthwhile.

When you do encounter hustlers, explain to them, amiably but firmly, that you know where you are going and don't need any help. Hustlers are persistent; dismissals or refusals to interact will occasionally meet with threatening retorts. Never be impolite or patronizing, and don't lose your temper: This will only infuriate them. Keep hustlers guessing about your next move; answer, for example, in a language that is sure to stump them. Don't be frightened or too adamant in your refusals unless it's called for. A simple question or compliment on the city may transform the person from a bird of prey into an impromptu protector. A visitor who is interested is far less likely to run into problems than one whose belligerence and suspicion are revealed in every action.

Above all, never permit these would-be guides to control your movements. One common trick is to tell tourists that the sight they are headed to is closed and then proceed on a circuitous tour leading nowhere to get the tourist lost and demand more money. Don't leave your car or valuables anywhere you can't find on your own, and don't trust anyone with anything of value. Even after traveling with Moroccans for days and gaining their friendship, you may be ripped off in the end. If someone offers you something you don't want, make your refusal absolutely clear from the start.

You will be invited home for "soup" several times each day. In the larger cities, be wary of all invitations and never accept any that is extended immediately. In smaller towns, though, sharing a meal with someone can become one of the most appealing parts of your trip. Remember that tipping is a way of life in Morocco, and Moroccans realize that there is a fine line between honest acquaintance and hustling; you will have to draw the line in your own mind.

In certain situations you may wish to have someone show you around: in the huge, labyrinthine medina of Fes, for example, or if you have only a day in town and want to get from sight to sight quickly, or sometimes just to keep hustlers away. The "guides" who approach you in the street are illegal, often incompetent, and sometimes dangerous. Beware of anyone who is too insistent or who tells you he's just a student (or a Club Med employee or an art teacher) wanting to practice his English—this is the oldest line in the book. Some escorts demand money for merely pointing you in the right direction, an innocuous form of begging. Others will tag along and attempt to extort money from you upon arrival at your destination. At the end of a tour, the guide may intentionally get his client lost in order to squeeze more dirhams from the confused foreigner. If you do hire a guide, agree on the price beforehand.

The safest option—though usually the most expensive—is to head for the local tourist office to procure an official guide. Always go to the tourist bureau; don't be taken in by official-looking badges and papers. Competent, knowledgeable, and moderately honest official guides can get you where you want to go efficiently and painlessly. As always, agree on the price before setting off—the rate is fixed by the tourist office at 30dh half-day, 50dh per day. No matter what they say, official guides do indeed skim off a commission on anything you buy, and often on whatever you eat as well. For the most part, you'll be better off with a good map and no guide. Despite what the hustlers tell you, guides are never "required by law."

Note that you don't owe the guardian of a monument anything unless he gives you a tour—unlike official guides, he's paid by the state. A small tip is always appreciated, though, and many times the only key required to open locked gates is the magical glitter of a few dirhams. Nuts, cigarettes, and aspirin (especially in rural areas) will often work wonders as well.

The other kind of "hustler" also abounds in Morocco. If you are a woman traveling alone, or with another woman, exercise extreme caution. Take both threats and offers seriously and refuse them firmly. Women should always wear a bra; bare knees and shoulders should be avoided by males and females alike, especially in the interior. By refusing to honor this Moroccan custom, travelers are only begging for trouble.

Getting Around

Trains are faster than buses, and if you travel third class, they're also cheaper. Train service is fairly reliable and surprisingly prompt throughout the country. Second-class rail fares are fairly inexpensive and infinitely more comfortable than buses. Couchettes are available for an extra 30dh over the price of the first- or second-class ticket. Fourth-class trains are the cheapest but have the creature comforts of a cattle car, plus a tin potty in the corner and a thick haze of hashish. Unfortunately, Morocco's national rail company, **Office National de Chemin de Fer (ONCF)**, has a somewhat limited network. The Eurailpass is not valid in Morocco, but InterRail is. (See General Introduction.) Rail fares here are cheap enough so that a pass won't be a bargain unless you do a fair amount of traveling outside the country.

Bus service in Morocco is more frequent than train service, and among the myriad companies you can get anywhere you want to go from anywhere you happen to be. You definitely trade comfort for convenience, however, so carefully consider the potential misery of long hauls. If you plan to see the country, you really won't have a choice; only buses run between the smaller towns.

The national busline, **Compagnie de Transports du Maroc (CTM)**, is the most luxurious and most expensive. Nonetheless, the average fare works out to only about 12dh per 100km. If you pay extra for reserved seats, you'll get your wad's worth in comfort. The largest of the country's many other companyies is SATAS, equally fast and reliable though somewhat less comfortable. The countless other private lines, sometimes referred to as *cars publiques,* run both long-distance city-to-city routes and local trips to smaller towns and the tiniest villages. These buses have no fixed schedules and depart only when very full.

Before you get on any bus, check on return service and connections from your destination. Many routes run only once or twice per day, and you can get stranded if you get off in a small town that sees buses only infrequently. Most buses make at least one half-hour stop. If you wish to explore or stretch your legs, let the driver know you're continuing on the bus so that it doesn't leave without you. If your bus originates in another city, it may arrive full, causing long delays. Try to board a bus that originates at your point of departure. Remember that wherever you inquire about bus information, you get only the schedule for that particular company. It takes some shopping around to get a comprehensive view of its bus connections.

The buses themselves aren't too appealing: There are five cramped seats per row, terrible ventilation, and the bus may stop at every little village along the way. But they're full of color with wailing horns, beggars, sermonizing mystics, water-carriers, and hard-boiled egg vendors passing through at every stop.

When exploring off the beaten track (especially south of Marrakech and inland from the Atlas Mountains), groups of four or more should consider renting a **car**. Major international companies such as Avis, Hertz, and Europcar operate in Morocco, as do a number of such national companies as Afric Car, Moroloc, and Locoto. Also explore the options at cut-rate rental agencies in Casablanca and Agadir. The average weekly rental will cost US$100-200 per week, excluding gas. The Renault 4 is the most common budget car. The least expensive deal will cost about 110dh per day plus 1.20dh per kilometer, or about 1500dh per week with unlimited mileage. In Agadir, a Renault 4 with unlimited mileage, 12% tax, and personal and automobile insurance (which you should never allow to lapse) costs 1060dh per week. Gas costs about 5.50dh per liter. Reserve a few days in advance. Because renting a car in Morocco is more expensive than in Europe, you'll save by procuring your rental car on the continent, especially if you wish to take an extended trip. The difficulty is finding a European company that will insure you for driving in Morocco. Try Europe-By-Car, which offers an arrangement whereby the leasee purchases the car from the company for a prearranged period, after which the company buys the vehicle back. The rates are low and the insurance terms good, but you must pay in the U.S. and pick the car up in Europe, rather than in Morocco. For more information, contact Europe-By-Car, 1 Rockefeller Pl., New York, NY 10020.

Principal roads (*routes goudronées*), designated with a "P," are paved and connect most cities. Secondary roads (*bonne pistes*), designated with an "S," are less smooth. You may have to contend with tortuous mountain roads made yet more hazardous by loose gravel. Buy several detailed maps, and ask locals if the routes you intend to take are passable. In regions such as the Sahara, spring thaws and showers on the mountains can turn into flash floods, destroying event the most carefully laid automobile itineraries. Roads indicated on maps have a way of turning into river-beds, stony mule tracks, and dune-swept obstacle courses. Conversely, some roads marked as impassable on maps may have been recently cleared and paved. Also be prepared for goats, cows, and sheep and their child-shepherds all nonchalantly crossing the road. If you drive in the desert, bring along at least 10 liters of bottled water per person and radiator, a spare tire, and an extra fuel tank (remember not to fill it to the brim to allow for the expansion of gasoline in the heat). Move rapidly over sand: If you start to bog down, put the car in low gear and rapidly swivel the steering wheel. If you come to a stop in soft sand, it's better to get out and push than to sink into tire trenches. Don't drive or park on beaches; it's very easy to strand your car in the deep, loose sand.

Don't be surprised if you're pulled over for security checks by the police—this is routine throughout Morocco, especially in and around major northern cities. All cops speak French. You may be queried about your driving or your travel plans, and your vehicle and passengers may even be searched. A good way to dissolve the tension is to ask directions to your destination immediately after you're stopped. Always drive with your passport and car papers. Seatbelts are required by law out-side major towns. If you are flagged for a traffic violation, the officer may ask you to pay the fine on the spot—make sure you get a receipt.

Petits taxis operate within cities and are very cheap—fares usually run 4-6dh and rarely exceed 8dh. Always ask the driver to turn on the meter; it's the law in Morocco. If a driver wants to fix a price, chances are he will overcharge you. Expect a 50% surcharge an night fares. **Grands taxis,** which run from city to city—and from anywhere to anywhere else for that matter—are about twice as expensive. Al-ways agree on a price before hopping in. Your best insurance against rip-offs is to know the standard charge for the trip you'll be making; ask a travel agency, a guest at a large hotel, or a local friend. Your other cab travel option in Morocco is the **collective taxi,** which may be your only alternative for long-distance trips. Collec-tive taxis have specific destinations and depart only when they're full—they may end up resembling a crowded bus, but the rates are reasonable (usually 10-20% more than the comparable bus fare), and it's a good way to meet other travelers or befriend a few Moroccans. Watch what the locals pay and insist on paying the same. Taxis are hailed either on the street or at marked taxi stands.

Hitchhiking in Morocco is generally undependable, even on well-traveled roads. It's best to wait for someone who can take you all the way to your destination rather than to accept short hops that may leave you stranded for another ride. The tradi-tional symbol for hitching here is not the outstretched thumb, but the forefinger pointed a little ahead and downward (though the thumb up has been gaining recog-nition in recent years). Hitching isn't necessarily a free ride here. Truck drivers may request payment in excess of bus fares. Campgrounds are an excellent place to hook up with drivers. Women should never thumb alone.

Picking up hitchhikers yourself is generally safe and a good way to meet locals, but don't expect payment; tourists are widely held to be rich, and you will not be offered a dirham. Beware that if you are pulled over by the police and a hitchhiker whom you have picked up or the driver from whom you've accepted a ride is carry-ing hashish, everyone in the car will go to jail together. Be particularly wary of this danger in the north around major cities, a favorite area for road checks.

Getting to Tunisia and Algeria

The easiest and probably the cheapest way to get from Morocco to Tunisia is to fly: **Air Tunis** and **Royal Air Maroc** both fly from Casablanca's Airport Mohammed V to Tunis for about 1400dh, ages under 26 1000dh. As the Saharan conflict reaches a resolution, train travel to **Algeria** has once again been restored. However, until recently, trains only went as far east as Oujda on the Moroccan side and as far west at Tlemcen on the Algerian side. Several buses per day ran from Oujda and Tlemcen to the border. You were forced to make your way across the border any way you could. Before attempting a crossing make sure that the on-again-off-again train service is working. If you try to cross the border on foot, you may be refused entry.

No matter how you enter, you'll be required to change 1000 Algerian dinars, about $260. (Students are exempt, but will need more evidence of their student status than just an ISIC.) Beware of the following scam: In Oujda and Figuig, Moroccans and Algerians will approach you and ask to change an Algerian 500-dinar note. The notes look genuine because they are genuine—and worthless; due to an excessive number of counterfeits the 500-dinar notes have been withdrawn from circulation.

To hitch a ride into Algeria, talk to the tourist office in Oujda (pl. du XVI d'Août, tel. 43 29; open daily 8am-2pm) or ask other travelers in town. Avoid traveling with employees of American oil companies; they are often the object of much hostility (which could make your crossing somewhat difficult) as well as terrorist attacks (which would make your crossing impossible). If you do hook up with a ride, empty the contents of your backpack into a suitcase, look respectable, and say you're with them. If the Algerian customs officer notices that your passport stamp date-of-entry into Morocco is different from theirs, however, you will be sent back. In either case, expect to have your bags ripped apart. If you are unable to enter by car, you will be refused entry at Oujda and will have to enter at Figuig. If you are traveling with strangers, remember that you will be jailed with them if they are found carrying any illicit substances.

The simplest way to get into Algeria for the car-less student is to pick up an Algerian visa (required of Americans, Canadians, and Australians, but not the British) at the United Arab Emirates Consulate for Algerian Affairs in Rabat, 12 rue d'Azrou (tel. 242 37; open Mon.-Fri. 9am-1pm). Bring four photographs, about US$15, and plenty of patience (about two days worth). Then take a bus south from Oujda for 369km to the border-oasis town of Figuig. The seven-hour, 30dh ride leaves daily at 6am, 10am, and 4pm from Pl. du Maroc. Most bus company offices are clustered on rue du Marrakech. The CTM office at rue Sidi Brahmin (tel. 20 47) is around the corner.

The Banque Populaire in Figuig does not take traveler's checks, and the Algerian border bank accepts only French currency in cash. It's a 4-kilometer walk or hitch to the border unless you find Figuig's only taxi. If you don't make it over the border, hitch back to town and relax on the terrace of the Hotel Sahara by the bus stop until the changing of the guard. Once in Algeria, it's a 1½-kilometer walk to Beni Ounif, where you can pick up a bus to Béchar (100km away). From here you can take a train back north to the Algerian-Mediterranean coast. Coming back to Morocco from Algeria is a breeze.

Accommodations

While finding a dirt-cheap place to sleep in Morocco isn't tough, avoiding the dirt is more of a challenge. The price of a room often includes armies of vermin. Enter dark rooms ahead of the proprietor, flick on the lights, and watch for scurrying creatures. Their size and quantity may inspire you to bargain despite the already-low rates; a hem and a haw will often get you an even better deal. Also take the room's ventilation into consideration. Often the proprietor will let you sleep on the roof for a fraction of the price of a room. In the Sahara, this can actually be the best room in the house. Don't expect spotless—or even sanitary—rooms and you won't be disappointed. And shop around: You'll be astonished at what you can find for a few dirhams more. If *Let's Go* lists one price for an establishment, its the high season price; the same room is often cheaper in off-season.

Youth hostels are run by the International Youth Hostel Federation affiliate, **Union Marocaine des Auberges de Jeunesse,** 6 pl. Amiral Phillibert, in Casablanca. Hostels vary in quality, but even those that lack amenities and a convenient location are worth considering since, at 10dh per night, they're usually the cheapest bed in town (though you get as little as you pay for). There are hostels in Casablanca, Fes, Marrakech, Meknes, Rabat, Tetuan, and in a number of smaller cities and towns.

There are two major categories of Moroccan **hotels:** *classé* and *non-classé. Classé* hotels are government regulated and rated by a system of stars. Within each rating there is a subdivision of A or B. For example, 1-star B is lower than 1-star A; 5-stars A is the best. All *classé* hotels are listed in the **Royaume du Maroc: Guide des Hotels,** free at any tourist office. Further, all *classé* hotels have been assigned maximum prices by the government. A list of these prices is also available at any tourist office.

Non-classé hotels do not have government-fixed prices, and do not meet government hotel standards. As a result, *non-classé* hotels are much cheaper. Many are clean and are run by friendly Moroccan families. With a bit of caution and some careful exploring, you may find the hotel of your dreams for a mere 30dh per night.

As a rule, the cheapest hotels are in the medina, where the action is. Hotelkeepers sometimes charge per room, not per person, making it economical to find roommates. An acceptable rate for a budget room is 20dh, but remember that while 20-30dh will get you a fleabag room in the medina, 40-60dh will land you a large, comfortable room in a one-star hotel. For 130-200dh, you can stay in a four-star luxury hotel complete with such amenities as poolside cafes, *kepi'*d and turbaned bellhops, red carpets, and possibly, the Atlantic Ocean at your doorstep. The opulence is ridiculously cheap and you might want to treat yourself at least once. Rooms can often be rented on a weekly basis at a rate equal to 50% of the nightly charge. Showers, when available, cost 2-4dh; in cheaper places hot water is generally available only during certain hours. *Hamam* (public Turkish baths) or *bains-douches* (individual public showers) run 2-3dh and are the best source of hot water.

Camping is by far the least expensive option at 3-5dh per person plus 3-5dh per tent. "Camping" often designates a place where you can rent a small hut or bungalow, or pitch a small tent for a fee. Some campgrounds are virtual citadels, with most necessary conveniences within arm's reach, including entertainment. Be ready to share your space, however, with lots of northern European teenagers. Avoid off-the-road camping: There are too many stories of tourists returning from a quick skinnydip to find themselves *sans* clothes, passport, or airplane ticket. If you do camp unofficially, always pick a spot where others are camping. It is unwise for women to do this, either alone or with other women.

Hashish

The most famous hashish fields in the world lie in the Rif (which rhymes with *kif,* the Arabic word for marijuana). Workers in the Rif painstakingly tap the upper leaves and distill branches of *Cannabis indica,* the female hemp plant, for the resin which is kneaded, rolled, and then dried into cakes.

Although *kif* and hash (sometimes called chocolate or, in Arabic, *shit*) are bountiful and often openly smoked, drugs are *not* legal for foreigners. Moroccan law forbids the transport of drugs, and foreigners, even if they're not actually in motion, are officially *always* in transport: That's the catch. As you walk down any street in Morocco, you'll be surrounded by hustlers murmuring the refrain of "hashish, hashish." If you answer at all, say you don't smoke, and never admit to having something on you: Many Moroccan dealers double as narcotics agents.

There are also frequent road checks throughout the country. Sometimes an entire bus will be stopped and searched. Though the degree to which the law is enforced varies from region to region (much more frequently along northern roads around the Rif and in major cities), caution is highly advisable. Police are always far more stringent with tourists than they are with locals; Moroccan authorities arrest about 100 Americans on drug charges per year—in most cases for possession of only a few grams. Choose your traveling companions carefully: Innocent passengers in a vehicle in which drugs are found receive the same penalties as the possessor.

For the sake of a little buzz, you can get up to six years in a dusty jail cell, the ultimate tourist trap. If you're arrested, you'll find American diplomatic officials remarkably unsympathetic. Another nasty catch-22 can compound your misery: The U.S. embassy refuses to contact a detainee's family unless he or she personally requests that they be informed, something Moroccan drug enforcement policies often make difficult. Never bring drugs from Morocco into Spain or Algeria. Fines and sentences are stiff—ranging in Algeria from 10 years to the death penalty.

Bargaining

Bargaining is the rule—not the exception—in all handicraft shops and anywhere else you suspect the price has been inflated just for tourists. This includes places that display a *prix fixe* sign. Don't rely on any formula (such as offering one-third of the merchant's starting price); you must know what the product is worth and how easily you can find it elsewhere. This is easier said than done since locals employ a nearly iron-clad dual price system against foreigners. Merchants often start with a price 40 times the object's real value. They then allow you the satisfaction of bargaining them down to one quarter of their original offer—still 10 times the item's actual worth. Don't buy anything your first day on the town, and avoid buying anything in big cities such as Tangier and Tetuan. Instead, find out what Moroccans pay for the article—goods are surprisingly cheap. Bartering is more effective than bargaining in small villages. American cigarettes (buy a duty-free carton at the airport before you leave the U.S.), T-shirts, jeans, or anything with English printing are good substitutes for currency. If you plan to do a lot of bartering, stock up on cheap (US$10 variety) digital watches, which can buy much more than their cash equivalent in rural areas. Keep in mind that bargaining can take a long time—it may take 45 minutes to bring a 400dh cloth *djellaba* down to 90dh. Wool *djellabas* will cost at least 250dh.

Once you know what you want and how much you want to pay for it, it's time to match wits with the merchant. Share a cup of tea, but remember that you're still not obligated to buy. If asked how much you paid for your Arabic threads, a noncommittal "I traded it for an old shirt" is the best reply. Don't wait until you've found just what you want to talk money. Merchants always try to postpone questions concerning price indefinitely. Insist on figures. Keep up a steady patter on the cost of this and that as you look things over. When you're ready to do real business, maintain a poker face, point to your desired object, but decline to open the bidding. Your opponent's first inflated price requires something to the effect of "I'll start doing business with you when you give me a reasonable price." If you're trying something on, take it off and hand it back, or meticulously search for imperfections and point them out. Offer a ridiculously low price (never let a figure pass your lips unless you're willing to pay). Stay amicable throughout the merchant's bitter laughter, hurt looks, and another cup of tea. Declare the article very beautiful, but add that as a poor student you can't afford it (more effective when your watch and camera are not in sight), and walk out. You can always come back. If you're followed out the door, you'll often get a price in your range. Close the deal with a *wachá* (OK) and a handshake. Never go shopping with a guide; official, preadolescent, or otherwise, he will collect at least a 30% commission on anything you buy. If you see something you like, return later on your own. If you decide to take your chances and later discover that you were grossly overcharged while shopping with an official guide, report him promptly to the tourist office and demand that your money be refunded. Never purchase anything if someone is loitering around who the merchant may be led to believe is your guide. Many local boys follow tourists unobtrusively, stand outside a shop as a transaction is being completed, and later claim a commission—without ever exchanging a word with the tourist.

Life and Times

History and Politics

Much as the desert sands blow across the Sahara in changing patterns and formations, the various cultures of modern Morocco have followed one another over the centuries, erasing, building, and combining to create something new. More than a dozen invasions and coups have swept over Morocco's deserts and mountains in its 3000 years of history, and much of its culture has been molded by the powers around it rather than from within.

Founded on the periphery of Mediterranean civilization in 1100 B.C.E., Morocco gradually became a commercial crossroads, linking Africa with Europe. The Berbers, whose original languages are unwritten and unintelligible even to Arabs, have lived in the mountains and plateaus since time immemorial. Phoenician colonists were the first to join these nomadic tribes on the coast of North Africa, and the Carthaginians followed. The Romans granted the North African province a long period of peace and prosperity during their rule. Jews have lived in Morocco since before the third century B.C.E.; historical records indicate that the first Jews in the region may have come from Jerusalem after the destruction of the temple by Titus. The many blacks in the country share a common history. Descended from individuals originally brought from Mali, Guinea, and Senegal, they are living testimony to a once-thriving slave trade.

The Vandal invasion broke off Roman influence in 429. Although tenuous ties to the West were revived in the sixth century under the Byzantine Empire, Morocco drifted into anarchy as the nomadic tribes began to war among themselves.

In 683, the first Islamic invasion burst across the African continent to alter forever the course of Moroccan history. A zealous Islamic army under Uqua Ibn Nabir converted the pagans, founded Koranic schools, and made Arabic the dominant language. By 711, after many decades of resistance, converted Berbers had extended Islam north to the Pyrenees.

Morocco first emerged as an independent state when Idris (I) Ibn Abdallah, a distant relation to Mohammed the Prophet, fled the Abbasid court in Baghdad and founded a kingdom near the old Roman settlement of Volubilis. (Volubilis is also the city in which U.S. General George Patton believed he was stationed as a Roman Centurion in a previous life. When visiting the ruin, he declined an offer for a guided tour—he knew his way around perfectly.) The eleventh century saw the beginning of a series of invasions from the south: First the Almoravids overthrew the decadent dynasty in the north, spreading their puritanical rule to Spain. In a new invasion, the Almohads established the greatest of the western Islam empires, ruling from Tripoli to Castille. The Koutoubia Mosque in Marrakech and the Hassan tower in Rabat were built in this period of flourishing cultural and intellectual activity.

Morocco declined in successive centuries under the Merinids and Wattasids. The Spanish and Portuguese reconquered the Iberian peninsula and by the fifteenth century occupied the major ports on the Moroccan coast. The second wave of Jewish immigrants, the Sephardim, came in 1492, when Spain's Jews and Moors were expelled during the Inquisition. The Saadis drove out foreign influence and reunited Morocco, but the Alawites staged a coup and founded what may prove to be the most stable of the dynasties; the present-day King Hassan II is the nineteenth in this line.

Morocco's strength waned during the age of imperialism as the European powers vied for colonial influence in Africa. Defeat by France in 1844 at Isly and by Spain in 1860 at Tetuan forced Morocco to become dependent on foreign aid and policy. By the end of the nineteenth century, both nations had secured protectorates in the country, and from 1912 to 1956 both Spanish and French Morocco were under foreign rule.

In 1924, a rebellion led by Abdel Krim in the Rif Country proved futile. In the Battle of Anoual, 18,000 Spaniards were killed or captured and 10,000 more were lost in the Spanish retreat from Chechaouèn to Tetuan in 1925. Eventually, Abdel Krim and his forces were forced to surrender. However, this uprising demonstrated the strength of the Moroccan people's commitment to independence from foriegn domination.

In 1944, the Independence Party was founded and the beginnings of a nationalist movement rallied around Sultan Mohammed V. With the creation of the state of Israel in 1948, most Jews left Morocco, and today, except for a few artisan villages, much of the remaining Jewish population lives in the large cities. The French deported nationalist leaders and deposed Sultan Mohammed V in 1952, but only provoked popular unrest to such an extent that the French were forced to reinstate him. In 1955, the French and Moroccans met to discuss independence, which was achieved for French Morocco in 1956, and in Spanish Morocco (Sidi Ifni) in 1969.

Mohammed V's successor, Hassan II, tried to introduce a democratic constitution in the '60s, but two abortive military coups and divisions within the government delayed parliamentary elections until 1977. The country is currently in the midst of a transition toward a more balanced constitutional monarchy. Although there is an elected parliament, the king continues to wield tremendous power. The fact that some citizens are not entirely comfortable criticizing the present regime suggests that civil liberties have not yet become fully established.

Morocco reinstituted diplomatic relations with Algeria in June, 1988. In the Western Sahara, the Algerians had backed the Polisario guerillas against whom the Moroccans had built a 1500-mile defensive wall. Diplomatic tensions still run high and the conflict over the Southern Sahara remains unpredictable. In August, 1988, soldiers were still being sent south despite an impending Algerian peace agreement.

Islam

Although science and technology have influenced and changed Moroccan culture, Islam remains very much a part of public and private life. Islam remains the state religion, and the king of Morocco retains the title "Commander of the Faith." The youngest of the major world religions, Islam is considered by believers to be the perfect and final faith of the world. Even a basic knowledge of Islam will help you avoid misunderstandings.

In 610, a vision revealed to the prophet Mohammed that he was a messenger of God. Opposition to his teachings arose among the threatened merchant class in his native city of Mecca (in modern Saudi Arabia) in 622. This persecution drove him and his adherents away from Mecca to Medina, a town north of Mecca. Mohammed rallied the tribes of the area and ultimately returned victoriously to Mecca. Following his death, the faith expanded under the Caliph 'Uman to encompass lands as far as Egypt, Syria, Iraq, and Iran.

The vision of this charismatic messenger of God was later recorded by his followers in the Koran, a work about equal in size to the Greek scriptures. Islam's conservative nature comes at least in part from the doctrinal absolutism attributed to this holy Arabic book. Because they consider the law divine (and therefore immutable), Muslims engage in a minimum of scriptural interpretation. Moreover, the Koran is also considered civil code and prescribes correct conduct and religious duty as well as the all-important theological doctrine of monotheism. *Allah* means only "god" and is not a proper name.

The five pillars of responsibility incumbent upon every Muslim are prayer at sunrise, noon, afternoon, sunset, and midnight (each time summoned by a caller from the mosque tower, or minaret); a one-time profession of faith testifying to belief in one God whose prophet is Mohammed; fasting during Ramadan; almsgiving; and, if at all possible, pilgrimage (*hajj*) to Mecca. However, Islam is far more than this. To many, the religion connotes a sense of inner peace; but more than anything else, it is a sense of community and identity based on the concept of a worldwide Muslim state. Even if they do not share a common language, Muslims from Morocco to Indonesia feel united by the threads of their religion.

Islam has also taken on a strong political dimension, rooted in its history, that non-Muslim travelers in this area cannot ignore. Many Muslims see the rapid influx of Western culture as a threat to their religious and cultural identity; caution should be taken not to offend their standards of behavior and morality. Political issues such as the existence of Israel and the state of Christian-Muslim relations have acquired a religious meaning to some Muslims—be careful when entering into political discussions with Moroccan acquaintances. This is particularly true if you are a North American, for many Muslims see the U.S. as an enemy of Islam and the Islamic "nation," especially because of the U.S.'s support of Israel.

The absence of any ordained clergy in Islam (the *Imam* is only leader of the Friday prayers) fosters a certain equality, although an unquestionable system of male authority prevails: While men relate directly to God, women relate to God only through men, and only since 1971 have women been permitted to enter mosques for Friday prayer. Rather than praying at the local mosque, most women still prefer to practice their faith at a nearby *koubba*, or saint's tomb. Muslim culture also emphasizes the family and community, prescribing fairly rigid duties for each member. In fact, there is essentially no concept of the Muslim as an individual; instead, one is defined by his or her part in an overall framework.

Separate from orthodox Islam is a body of diverse animistic and supernatural beliefs including saint worship; belief in the evil eye *el-Ain,* which is warded off by the downward-pointing Hand of Fatima, the door knocker that represents the hand of the prophet Mohammed's daughter; belief in genies (*djin*), enchanted springs and caves, and the magical powers of women; and such healing rituals as burning and ingesting verses of the Koran. Moroccan pharmacies and spice shops sell an array of potions and preparations, which include red ants, snakeskin shampoo, and magic beads.

Language

Avoid the temptation to deal only in broken French; learn to mispronounce at least a few words of Arabic, Morocco's official tongue. (The Moroccan dialect of Arabic is closer to the classical Arabic than it is to that spoken in Algeria, Tunisia, or Egypt, though the dialects are mutually intelligible and all alphabets are identical.) Even a simple *shokran* (thank you) or *la shokra' Allah wajib* (you're welcome) will be rewarded with an appreciative smile. *La bess* (the equivalent of "How're you doing?"), *na-am* or *aywa* (yes), *laa* (no), *wachá* (OK), *smáhli* (excuse me), *salám alékum* (hello), and *bisléhmah* (goodbye) can all be easily acquired. Other helpful phrases are *imshee* (go away), *safi* (enough!), *minfadlik* (please), *muezyen* (good), *l'hamdullah* (Thank Allah, I'm well; in response to *la bess* or *ça va*). Other commonly used words include *bzef* (a lot, too much, or big) and *schwia* (a little, small).

Berber, the native tongue of Morocco's earliest settlers, is widely heard in the mountain regions, though many Berbers also speak Arabic. Berber is a member of the Hamitic family of languages (a sub-group of the Afro-Asiatic languages) and is now unwritten, though at one time it was recorded in Arabic script and before that may have had its own characters. While the Braber dialect is intelligible to both the Rifian and the Chleuh, the latter two are quite different and mutually unintelligible.

Due to Morocco's brief term as a protectorate of France, French is considered the country's first foreign language and remains the most widely spoken commercial tongue. Streets are known by two names; bear this in mind when reading maps or following directions. In northern Morocco you're likely to hear Spanish, and in major cities you'll undoubtedly encounter English speakers—but beware that English is the specialty of hustlers. If you don't speak Arabic or Berber, it's best to have a French-English dictionary or phrasebook handy.

Architecture

The mosques, *medersas,* and medina walls you'll see in Morocco have their architectural roots in eighth-century Spain, where the Moorish style was influenced by the arts of the conquered lands. Just as the daily life of the devout Muslim has changed little over the centuries, and just as the sacred Koran has been subject to a minimal scriptural interpretation, so, too, have the features of Hispano-Moorish architecture remained fairly constant. The style is marked by its simplicity of line: Structure, which is horizontal, is always subordinated to decoration, which includes wood, stone, or plaster carving, and patterned tilework. Architectural embellishment must not, according to Koranic law, depict any of God's perfect works of nature. As a result, interior design is always highlighted by geometric or abstract motifs.

The sole purpose of the Islamic house of worship, the **mosque** (*djemma* in Arabic, which also means "assembly"), is to mark off a sacred space for the worshiper. The *mihrab,* a prayer niche carved out of the *kibla* (wall), points the supplicant toward Mecca, and the movable *minbar* (pulpit), from which Friday prayers are announced, need be no more than a set of steps but is often a lavish, inlaid work of art. The minarets, or towers from which Muslims are called to worship, are the only vertical lines in the style. The wide, spacious feel of the overall structure fosters the directness of the human-divine relationship in Islamic worship, where there is no mediating clergy.

The Mezquita mosque in Córdoba, Spain, best exemplifies the earliest Moorish architectural features, with its horseshoe arches (both round and pointed, smooth and cusped), arched *mihrab,* domed and decorated *minbar,* and square minarets. In the eleventh century, the Almoravids of Marrakech built with brick and cement and used floral motifs in their decorations, from which the word "arabesque" derives. In the following century, the Almohads employed geometric patterns ranging from the plain square or cross to the more intricate interlocking almond and hexagon. The last innovation in Hispano-Moorish style was introduced in the thirteenth century by the Merinids, who combined floral and geometric patterns and arranged in *zellij* (mosaic tiles) colorful patterns of both curved and straight-edged shapes.

The **medersa,** or theological school attached to mosques, were built in Morocco from the eighth century and became ubiquitous by the fourteenth. These tiny colleges consist of a courtyard with a fountain around which classrooms, libraries, and the prayer hall with its *mihrab* are situated. The students' sleeping quarters are usually on an upper level. The decoration on the *medersa* in Marrakech is a fine example of the range of wood and marble carving, mosaic work, and decorative inscriptions.

As fine as the minarets and *mihrabs* are the dwellings you'll pass on the residential streets inside the medina walls. Here, too, rooms wrap around a central courtyard with fountain and garden. Observe the silver doorknockers in the shape of the Hand of Fatima, the brightly colored tiles in blue and yellow or green and white, the wrought-iron railings, and floral cornices with their bits of colored glass. The rooftops often serve as gathering places for the townswomen who call to one another to speak of the day's affairs. If you are fortunate enough to be invited up, you will see that they afford views not only of the neighboring housetops but also of the gracious, green-tiled minarets and the mountain ranges beyond the city.

Literature

The first good guidebook to Morocco was written early in the twentieth century. Edith Wharton's *In Morocco* is a collection of wonderfully impressionistic descriptions of Rabat, Salé, Fes, and Meknes. Paul Bowles, a celebrated avant garde American author living in Tangier, has written a number of works about Morocco. His best is *Their Heads are Green and Their Hands are Blue.* For an autobiographical account of an American woman and her family living in the Marrakech medina, read Elizabeth Warnock Fernea's *A Street in Marrakech.* Paul Rabinow's *Reflec-*

tions on Fieldwork in Morocco is a delightful little book of anecdotes about an American anthropologist's experiences in a remote Middle Atlas village.

A number of British authors have also concerned themselves with Morocco. Walter Harris's *Morocco That Was* is an extremely readable journalist's diary about the country in the late nineteenth and early twentieth centuries. *A Year in Marrakech* by Peter Mayne is full of insightful observations about modern Moroccan society. For the experiences of a Bulgarian-born writer, read *The Voices of Marrakech* by Nobel Prize winner Elias Canetti; it's a beautiful, aphoristic record of a month-long visit to Marrakech.

Contemporary Moroccan writer **Mohammed Mrabet** has had most of his works translated by his friend Paul Bowles. Read *Love With a Few Hairs, M'hashish,* or *The Lemon.* He and Bowles have also published a joint collection of poems entitled *Scenes.* For a fascinating account of the traditional Islamic faith of the Atlas Mountain Berbers, read *Saints of the Atlas* by Ernst Gallner. For more information on the Riffian rebellion, read David Montgomery Hart's *The Aith Waryagher of the Moroccan Rif* or Vincint Sheean's *An American Among the Riffi.*

One of the best books on modern Moroccan history is Gavin Maxwell's *Lords of the Atlas.* It's a riveting account of the rise and fall of the colonial puppet leader from 1893 to 1956. (The book has been banned in Morocco and may be seized by local authorities if found.) Youssef Necrouf's *The Battle of Three Kings* is an interesting ancient history by a modern Moroccan author.

The best comprehensive guides to sights in Morocco are in French. Hachette's *Guide Bleu* is unbelievably thorough (an English edition was last printed in 1966) and available in all major Moroccan cities. Michelin's *Guide Vert* is also good and easy to find in Morocco. Christopher Kininmonth's *Morocco: The Traveller's Guide* is the best of the lot in English. Check out the *Shoestring Guide to Africa* and *The Rough Guide,* by Mark Ellingham, for tips on travel in Africa.

Food

Don't be deterred by the dingy surroundings in medina eateries; the chefs in such hole-in-the-wall restaurants often turn out to be culinary wizards. The Moroccan earth yields a fine supply of aromatic spices and excellent produce, meat, poultry, and game.

Couscous—named for the covered ceramic bowl in which it is cooked and served—is the national dish of semolina grain covered with saffron-flavored chicken, beef, lamb, or fish and cooked with onions, fruits, beans, and nuts. Local restaurants invariably serve chicken, lamb, beef, or fish either roasted or smothered in *tajine,* a scrumptious fruit and vegetable stew cooked with olives, prunes, or artichokes. You can always enjoy a steaming bowl of *harira,* a delicious soup of chicken, chickpeas, and assorted spices, for about 3dh. *Poulet roti* (chicken roasted on a spit with olives) or *poulet limon* (lemon chicken) are both good choices. Finely minced and heavily spiced Moroccan salad—predecessor of Andalusian gazpacho—or sweet natural yogurt accompanied by mounds of peaches, nectarines, or strawberries (about 1.50dh per glass and up) make light meals that won't weigh you down in the heat. You can always find *brochettes* (skewers of grilled lamb, beef, brains, or liver) and *kefta* (balls of delicately seasoned ground meat) for 1-2dh per skewer. Every medina features one-table brochette cubbyholes where you can fill up for a mere 15dh. Keep your eyes open for festive and regional treats: Try *mechoui,* a whole lamb spitted and roasted over an open fire, or *pastilla,* a culinary masterpiece concocted with squab, almonds, eggs, butter, cinnamon, and sugar in a wafer-thin pastry shell. Meat dishes are usually prepared with some combination of spices, oil, butter, pepper, ginger, cumin, saffron, honey, and sugar. Moroccans frequently munch on fresh fruit: Grapes, honeydew melon, watermelon, plums, apricots, figs, and dates are the most popular. Briny olives (at about 1dh per kg), roasted almonds, and cactus bud innards are great snacking foods. In areas of extreme heat, carry a basket of fruit covered with wet leaves—it's better to eat lightly throughout the day than to eat two or three heavy meals. Beans, carrots, tomatoes, beets, and artichokes are popular vegetables in Moroccan cuisine. A "complete" or "standard" restaurant meal will include a your of entree (*tajine, couscous,* or occasionally a 3rd choice), salad or *harira,* a side order of vegetables, and an orange or yogurt for dessert. If the tip is not automatically included, 10% is more than ample.

Although first introduced to the country only in the eighteenth century by the English, the ritual of preparing tea, made with sprigs of fresh mint (and great quantities of sugar), figures prominently in the daily routine of contemporary Moroccan life (1-1.50dh per glass and several dirhams per potful). You'll find that in hot weather, a glass of water will shake your thirst better than any cold drink. If you're lucky enough to be invited to a traditional rural feast or into a private home, don't expect silverware. Scoop up mouthfuls of your supper with pieces of bread or simply shovel with the middle three fingers of your right hand (never the left, which is saved a later stage of the digestive process). The third cup of mint tea signals the end of a visit. Freshly squeezed orange juice (2dh per glass, 6dh per liter) is also widely available. Although Muslims do not drink alcohol, both French and Spanish wines are sold and served along with a number of indigenous vintages (less common in southern regions).

For the sake of your health, drink *Sidi Ali* or *Sidi Harazem* (the former tends to be better), heavily chlorinated mineral water sold everywhere for 3-5dh per 1½-liter bottle. If the bottle isn't completely sealed, it's probably tap water, so be careful. Although the water is said to be safe in the north, unpurified water and uncooked vegetables are likely to wreak havoc on your bowels. In general, peel all fruit. A one-day fast and a strong dose of industrial strength medication is the best cure for diarrhea. Otherwise, stick to a small diet of bread, yogurt, boiled vegetables, and tea, and avoid sweet or greasy foods, milk, and non-citrus fruits.

Climate

Morocco has been described as "a cold country with a hot sun." Most visitors prepare for the blistering desert heat but are surprised by the chilly nights, ocean breezes, and snow-covered mountains. Pack some sweaters and a warm sleeping bag along with your sandals and shorts. Only in the Atlas Mountains are winters truly wintery, but the hot, dry days can be followed by cool and even cold desert nights throughout the country. Winters are warmer inland than on the coast, and accordingly, July and August are much hotter. Despite the lack of humidity, stifling is not an unfair description of summer in Morocco's interior cities. The north gets the best of Moroccan summer weather, the south is more pleasant in winter; despite the unpredictable rainstorms, autumn and spring are the optimal seasons for travel here.

Northwest

For centuries the primary gateway to the African continent, the northwestern corner of Morocco welcomes the traveler with a greeting that can be as exhilarating as it is harsh. As soon as you arrive in the port cities of Tangier and Tetuan, you'll be bombarded with hustlers. Once you've dispatched with them, you'll find that the labyrinthine medinas bubble with activity, as hooded men, veiled women, and singing street-peddlers joust with one another in chaotic open-air markets.

Visitors who restrict their tour of Morocco to Tangier or Tetuan often come away exhausted, dizzy, and pickpocketed. Even if you're visiting only for a few days, be sure to travel beyond these cities. Relax for a few days at one of the nearby tranquil resorts such as Asilah or Chechaouèn. For a quieter introduction to Morocco's cities, leave the lingering Mediterranean breeze behind and visit Meknes, the old capital of the Moorish Kingdom, or continue on to Rabat, where King Hassan II lives and hustlers and beggars are kept out of sight.

Tangier

While most people who visit believe it is a decent if rather uninteresting place, a vocal minority is devoted to giving Tangier a bad reputation. Take Mark Twain's epithet of "that African perdition called Tangier" with a grain of salt. Be prepared for a minor culture shock when you step off the ferry, since hustling wide-eyed, freshly arrived tourists has become a formidable industry here. (See Hustlers and Guides in the Morocco introduction.) The hustlers in Tangier are at the forefront of what may be called "the science of wrestling money from any foreigner." Foreigners are followed, sometimes discreetly, other times blatantly. The key is to firmly dispatch any hustler as soon and as politely as possible. Simply ignoring these persistent parasites doesn't always work. Be especially cautious in the medina, where hustlers and shop owners alike are especially hot tempered.

Nonethless, you will find Tangier not entirely unappealing. The city's peculair charm tends to grow on you: It is a bit of Europe on the African continent. You can hear throbbing drums in the Kasbah, as if you were in a remote oasis in the deep Sahara, yet you can sip espresso at a Parisian-style sidewalk cafe just around the corner. Tangier is just foreign enough to retain an exotic air, yet familiar enough for a Westerner to feel at ease (eventually).

Phoenecians and Romans built settlements here centuries before the Moors arrived. The first Europeans to capture Tangier were the Portuguese. With the marriage of England's King Charles II to Portugal's Princess of Braga, Tangier and Bombay were turned over to the British. Some Tangerines speculate that King Charles married the Portuguese princess in pursuit of Tangier. Though by 1912 the French and Spanish had established themselves in Morocco, Tangier preserved its unique neutral status, and a 1923 statute recognized the city as an international zone to be administered by a council of six Moroccan Jews, six Muslims, and representatives from seven European nations. A haven for smugglers in the '40s and '50s, Tangier maintained a certain intrigue as an international outpost of lawlessness. With Moroccan independence in 1956, the territory became part of the kingdom and the foreign community began gradually to dissolve. Nevertheless, the boulevards and cafes of the new city retain ample traces of the port's cosmopolitan heritage.

Orientation and Practical Information

An hour by hydrofoil and two and a half hours by ferry from Spain, Tangier's main virtue is its train and bus service to points south.

Allow enough time (1-1½ hr. in summer) to embark when leaving from Tangier. First, obtain a boarding pass from the ferry line representative at the port. Beware of hustlers trying to sell customs departure cards: You can get them for free from customs agents and ferry line representatives. Fill out the departure cards, and have your passport stamped before going through customs. There are long lines for all of these procedures. Try to get rid of your last dirhams before you come to the port since travel agents never adhere to the official rates. Once on board, prepare yourself for a delayed departure: Hundreds of fish and crabs gather around the docked boat.

Disembarking entails the same procedure in reverse, minus the boarding pass. Just as the fish and crustaceans surrounded the ship, you'll soon be surrounded by the Moroccan sharks. The port area is crawling with creepy, clinging hustlers, "guides," "students," and others who will insist that you need someone to show you around. You don't. As you walk from the port, firmly dispatch them. Explain politely but clearly that you know where you're going. The train station is the large, white building about 2 blocks to the left of the port; the bus station is in the square, directly across from the port. If you are taking a bus, ask information only of policemen or the blue-coated personnel. Give baggage directly to the ticket taker, and tip 1dh-3dh per bag, if anything.

Check immediately into a safe hotel where you can leave your telltale backpack. It's possible to walk to either the medina or to the *ville nouvelle* (new city), but if you are going to the new city, you might be better off hopping into one of the blue *petits taxis* in front of the port and leaving the pandemonium behind. Negotiate the fare in advance (about 3dh) and put your bags on top. If you let a "guide" show you to your hotel, don't let him stick around, no matter how nice he is. Say that you want to take a nap or are meeting a friend later, and give him 5dh, the "going rate." As you pay the hustler, show your gratitude by shaking hands and smiling profusely. Less money will make hustlers stick around for more, while significantly more will make them think they've found a sucker.

The port lies directly below the medina, which is small compared to the sprawling *ville nouvelle.* The new city has expanded from the port area in all directions, mainly to the east, along the beaches of the beautiful bay. Buses serve the entire city, but it is safer to use the abundant *petits taxis,* provided you have a general idea of where you're going and negotiate your fare in advance. All roads in Tangier have an old European name and a new Moroccan name. Almost all street signs give the old name, while most good maps record the new.

Tourist Office: 29 blvd. Pasteur (tel. 329 96), a 15-min. walk from the port. Cross ave. d'Espagne, turn left onto rue Salah Eddinel el-Ayoubi, and turn left again onto rue Anoual, which curves sharply uphill and to the right. At the end of the street (Grand Socco), make 2 left turns onto blvd. Pasteur. It's perhaps best to take a cab. Very sketchy maps. Train, bus, car, and ferry information. Open July-Aug. Mon.-Fri. 9am-3pm; Sept.-June Mon.-Fri. 8:30am-noon and 2:30-6:30pm; Ramadan Mon.-Fri. 9am-3 or 4pm.

Visa Extension Office: Hotel de Police, rue Ibn Toumert (tel. 404 27). Go to Control des Etrangers (the foreigner's desk). Not very hospitable. Your passport stamp is good for 3 months.

Consulates: U.S., rue El Achouak (tel. 359 04). Open Mon.-Fri. 7am-noon and 1:30-5:30pm. **U.K.,** 9 rue Amerique du Sud (tel. 358 95).

After-Hours Currency Exchange: Many hotels will change money, but some exact a hefty commission. Check the rate carefully. Travel agencies near the port are also required to change money at official rates, but they sometimes give you less, especially if you are exchanging pesetas for dirhams or are selling dirhams back to them. If you feel you are being taken for a ride, demand a receipt. Beware of hustlers asking you to change money: black market transactions are illegal and can be dangerous.

American Express: Voyages Schwartz, 54 blvd. Pasteur (tel. 334 59). Open for mail pick-up Mon.-Fri. 9am-12:30pm and 3-7pm, Sat. 9am-12:30pm; Ramadan Mon.-Fri. 9am-12:30pm and 3-6pm, Sat. 9am-12:30pm. Like all Moroccan AmEx offices, this is a branch office and cannot receive wired money, nor will it cash cardholders' personal checks.

Post Office: 33 blvd. Mohammed V (tel. 356 57), on the continuation of blvd. Pasteur. Open Mon.-Fri. 8:30am-12:15pm and 2:30-5:45pm.

Telephones: 33 blvd. Mohammed V., in the post office. Phones are along the right wall. Open 24 hours.

Train Station: ave. d'Espagne (tel. 312 01), to the left as you leave the port. Unless you're bound for the lovely Rif mountains or Tetuan (served only by bus), the train is the quickest and most comfortable way to plunge into the interior. 2nd-class tickets cost roughly as much as bus tickets; adventurous and unsavory 4th ("E") class costs about half. Express to Rabat (72dh) and Casablanca (93dh) at 4:22pm and 5:22pm. Non-express to Rabat (57dh) and Casablanca (74dh) at 8:50pm. To continue to Marrakech (135dh), change at Casablanca. Direct to Meknes (50dh) and Fes (61dh) at 8:12pm.

Bus Station: In the chaotic square to the left of the port. **CTM** (tel. 324 15), at the exit of the port area to the right. CTM runs 5 buses per day 11am-midnight to Rabat (6½ hr., 59dh), Casablanca (79dh), and points in between. To Fes (2 per day, 6 hr., 55dh). CTM doesn't serve Tetuan and Ceuta. Instead, hourly private buses provide service. They leave from Gare Provisoire Castilla, a dirt lot nowhere near the port. Take a *petit taxi* from anywhere in the city (5dh). Other companies around the square are slightly less expensive but have no fixed schedules—these clunkers leave if and when they are very, very full (watch your pack until departure time).

Ferries: Buy tickets at any travel agency. Try **Voyages Hispamaroc,** on blvd. Pasteur at rue el-Jabba el-Quatania (tel. 359 07, 327 18, or 331 13). Open Mon.-Thurs. 7am-7pm, Fri. 7am-noon, Sat. 7am-2pm. To Algeciras (3 per day at 7:30am, 12:30pm and 3:30pm; 2½ hr.; Class

A 3290ptas or 219dh, Class B 2550ptas or 170dh) and Tarifa (1 per at 2:30pm; 1½ hr., one way 160dh, return 340dh). Gibline catamaran to Gibraltar departs Mon. at 9am and 5:30pm; Wed. 2:30pm and Fri. 2:30pm and 6:30pm; Sun. 5:30pm (2½ hr.; one way 210dh, same-day return 310dh, open-ended return 340dh).

Taxis: A fast, comfortable way to points not served by rail. 2.50dh per km. On round-trips, the return fare is 1.50dh per km. If you're going to Tetuan, it's best to share a taxi (20dh per person). Pick-up points are along blvd. Pasteur and the Grand Socco.

Car Rental: Avis, 54 blvd. Pasteur (tel. 330 31), and **Hertz,** 36 ave. Mohammed V (tel. 333 22) offer cars at 177dh per day plus 1.95dh per km or 2464dh for 7 days with unlimited mileage.

Baggage Check: At the train station. *Consigne* checks locked bags (3.50dh).

Foreign Bookstore: Librairie des Colonnes, 54 blvd. Pasteur (tel. 369 55). An excellent collection of maps and guidebooks, mostly in French. Novels and books on Moroccan culture are also available. Open Mon.-Fri. 10am-1pm and 4-7pm, Sat. 10am-1pm.

24-hour Pharmacy: 22 rue de Fes (tel. 326 19).

First Aid: Hôpital Al-Kortobi, rue Garibaldi (tel. 310 73). **Red Cross Clinic:** Tel. 311 99. **Ambulance:** Tel. 15.

Police: Tel. 19.

Accommodations and Camping

In the Medina

Rooms in the medina are cheaper, a bit dirtier, and nearer to the port than the more comfortable options in the *ville nouvelle*. At night, the medina can be unsafe. The most easily accessible accommodations here cluster near **rue Mokhtar Ahardan,** formerly known as **rue des Postes,** off the Petit Socco. To enter the medina from the port area, make a U-turn around the CTM office and head west along rue de Cadiz until you come upon a set of stairs on your left, just before the lower gate entrance to the Kasbah. At the top of the steps is the bottom of rue des Postes. From the tourist office on blvd. Pasteur, head toward pl. de France and turn right on rue de la Liberté, which leads into the Grand Socco, a noisy square. Cross the square and take the first right down rue Semmarine (formerly Siaghines), which brings you to the Petit Socco. Rue Mokhtar Ahardan begins at the end of the Petit Socco closest to the port.

Pension Palace, 2 rue Mokhtar Ahardan (tel. 361 28). By far the best deal in the medina. Spacious, spotless, airy rooms, some overlooking the port and adjacent green-tiled buildings. Bathroom looks grungy but is clean. A beautiful courtyard and gracious management. Singles 25dh. Doubles 50dh. Hot showers 9am-noon included.

Hotel Mamora, 19 rue Mokhtar Ahardan (tel. 341 05). Unexpected elegance in the heart of the medina. Immaculate rooms, some with a view of the port. Attentive management. Singles 87dh, with bath 110dh. Doubles 104dh, with bath 129dh.

Pension Tan Tan, 33 rue Mokhtar Ahardan (tel. 326 41). The only virtue of these decrepit rooms is their proximity to the port side of the medina entrance. Rooms on the ground floor may be unsafe. Singles 20dh. Doubles 30dh.

Pension Fuentis, rue Arfaoui, 2nd floor (tel. 346 69), at the end of rue Mokhtar Ahardan at the Petit Socco. A last-resort dive: The only attraction here is the price. 15dh per person.

In the Ville Nouvelle

In the *ville nouvelle* a strip of inexpensive pensions runs along **rue Salah Eddine el-Ayoubi.** To reach this area from the train station, head east along ave. d'Espagne and take your first right. However, you'll get better values and better rooms farther up from the waterfront in the heart of the new city.

Hotel Valencia, 72 ave. d'Espagne, at the bottom corner of rue Salah Eddine el-Ayoubi. From the port, turn right onto ave d'Espagne. Excellent location near the port and the medina. Luxurious, carpeted hallways and richly decorated interior. First-rate rooms. Incredible lounge and TV room. Singles 63dh, with shower 85dh, with toilet 108dh. Doubles 83dh, with shower 100dh, with toilet 125dh.

Hotel de Paris, 42 blvd. Pasteur (tel. 381 26 or 318 77), across from the tourist office. Far and away the best deal in the new city. The rooms—some with balconies overlooking the boulevard—are spacious, sparkling clean, and comfortable, but can be noisy. Helpful management. Singles 49dh, with shower 62dh, with toilet 79dh. Doubles 57dh, with shower 79dh, with toilet 91dh.

Hotel Cecil, 112 ave. d'Espagne (tel. 310 87), a 10-min. walk from the port, along the waterfront. Ornate interior. Airy, spacious rooms with carpet and new furnishings. Bathrooms are clean, but a little old. A great deal. Singles 40dh. Doubles 60dh.

Pension Miami, 126 rue Salah Eddine el-Ayoubi (tel. 329 00). The most palatable of the many budget hotels on the block. Bright rooms, beautifully carved ceilings, and a balconied cloister on each floor. Singles 40dh. Doubles 40dh. Hot showers 5dh.

Pension Plaza, 53 rue Salah Eddine el-Ayoubi (tel. 353 69). Plain, but extremely clean. The bedding provides a touch of class to this drab pension. No showers and the bathrooms look old. Singles 25dh. Doubles 35dh.

However peaceful a Tangier campground might seem, you should be careful with your valuables. **Camping Tingis** (tel. 401 91), 2km from the beach on the Malabata road near Mar-Bel, has showers, a swimming pool, a grocery store, modern facilities, and tight security. Be careful walking to the beach—there have been muggings and rapes in the deserted woods. (10dh per person, 6dh per tent, 6dh per car.) **Camping Miramonte** (tel. 371 38), 1km from the town center (the route is well marked with signs), has a bar, grocery store, and restaurant. It's a beautiful, surprisingly green location, but not quite as posh as the above. (Open 8am-noon and 3-8pm. 10dh per person, 6dh per tent, 5dh per car.)

Food

In the Medina

You can put together the least expensive meal in town by hopping from one stall in the medina to the next. Sample the various specialties of those lining the **Grand Socco,** particularly in the evening. The medina also features standard Moroccan fare in adequate, budget restaurants along **rue Mokhtar Ahardan.**

Restaurant Ahlen, 8 rue Mokhtar Ahardan (tel. 219 54). A recently renovated establishment where the friendly owner serves generous salads (2.50dh), lamb *couscous* (15dh), or chicken (14dh). Open daily 10am-9pm.

Palace Marmounia, 6 rue Semmarine (tel. 350 99), near the exit to the Grand Socco. Rich Moroccan decor coupled with commendable Moroccan hospitality. Waiters are decked out in traditional garb, and during the meal you're serenaded by a folkloric band and entertained by male acrobats who balance trays of burning candles on their heads. Best time to go is 9pm, when the belly dancers strut their stuff. 3-course *menu touristique* 100dh. Service 15%. Open daily 11am-11pm.

Restaurant Aladin and **Restaurant Andalus,** both on rue du Commerce, an alley off rue Jamaa Kebir at the Petit Socco and rue Mokhtar Ahardan. Small dining grottos bustling with chaotic activity. If it's not the noise outside, it's the flies inside. The former serves *harira* and *tajine de kefta;* the latter specializes in thick, sizzling brochettes. Full meals 20dh. No fixed hours.

In the Ville Nouvelle

The vestiges of Tangier's status as an international zone are evident in *ville nouvelle* cuisine. Quality and price vary widely. For Moroccan fare, head for the restaurants lining **rue Salah Eddine el-Ayoubi,** across from the train station and leading up to the *ville nouvelle.* For hot sandwiches, try the storefronts off **boulevard Pasteur.**

Café Restaurant Hassi Baida, 81 rue Salah el-Ayoubi (tel. 367 26). Engaged in fierce competition with its slightly more expensive neighbors. Breakfast with cafe au lait, roll, butter, cheese, and jam 5dh. As you're enjoying *tajine* or *couscous* (12-13dh), contemplate the painting of

Mohammed V (the present king's father) giving an olive branch to a nuptially dressed, lion-escorted personification of Tangier. Open daily 9am-10pm.

El Dorado, 21 rue Allal ben Abdellah (tel. 433 53), near the Chella Hotel. Go up the street across from the post office. Unique Jewish-run establishment popular with locals and specializing in *kebab.* Belt-loosening meals 35dh. The *crevettes pil-pil* is superb. Open daily 11am-3pm and 6:30-11pm.

Restaurante Africa, 83 rue Salah Eddine el-Ayoubi (tel. 354 36). An airy place that serves excellent soups and scrumptious lamb *couscous.* 4-course *menu du jour* 30dh. Open daily 9am-1am.

Restaurant Chez Larbi (a.k.a. Dolce Vita), 18 rue Mohamed Abdou, near the Fes market and Cinema Mauretania. From pl. de France, walk down rue de Fes, turning left after 2 blocks. Small sandwich bar. *Tajine* 18-20dh, sandwiches 15dh, 3-course meals 35dh. Open daily 11am-4am.

Restaurant Hammadi, rue d'Italie (tel. 345 14). Follow the walls of the medina. Extravagant interior with wall-to-wall Moroccan carpeting and plush cushions. Elegant candlelight settings and musical entertainment. Specializing in *tajine* (25dh) and *couscous.* Service 19%. Open daily noon-3pm and 7:30pm-midnight.

La Grenouille, 3 rue el-Jabha el-Quatania, just off blvd. Pasteur. Popular with the expatriate community. Offers a melange of Moroccan, French, and English dishes. Fixed *menu* 36dh. Service 19%. Open Tues.-Sun. noon-2:30pm and 8pm-midnight.

Sights

As any hustler will tell you, the medina is the city's most interesting quarter. Although you do not need a guide to show you around, it is dangerous for tourists to wander through the medina or on the beaches at night (don't be surprised if the police and your consulate are bored by your crime report). Restrict your post-sunset sight-seeing to the *ville nouvelle.*

Start at the medina's commercial center, the **Grand Socco,** a bustling square and traffic circle cluttered with fruit vendors, parsley stands, and *kebab* and fish stalls. Bordering the square to the northeast is the **Main Market,** where the aroma of fresh spices wafts through narrow rows of orange, mint, fig, and melon stalls. The adjacent indoor **fish market** overflows with fresh crab, squid, eel, shark, and ray. To the northwest, where rue Bou Arrakia joins the Grand Socco (through the door marked #50) lie the shady **Jardins de la Mendoubia** (formerly Jardin du Tribunal du Sada), where a cache of seventeenth- and eighteenth-century bronze cannons stand amidst the greenery. **Rue Bou Arrakia,** the junk-dealer's alley, is lined with a motley collection ranging from used batteries to brass bedposts.

To reach the **Kasbah,** follow rue d'Italie north from the Grand Socco all the way through **Bab Fahs,** the Moorish gateway, and up to the steep, uphill incline of rue de la Kasbah, which terminates at the horseshoe-shaped **porte de la Kasbah,** guarded by particularly industrious hustlers. Rue Riad Sultan runs from this main portal alongside the Jardins du Sultan, where artisans weave carpets. (Open Mon.-Sat. 8am-2pm; in off-season 8:30am-noon and 2:30-6pm. Admission 5dh.) The approach culminates in **place de la Kasbah,** a sunny courtyard where an adjacent promontory offers a view of the Atlantic all the way to Spain. With your back to the vista, walk straight ahead and right toward the far corner of the plaza. The marble columns incorporated into the exterior walls of the adjacent buildings are Roman, plundered from the spoils of the earlier settlement. Just round the corner, the **Mosque of the Kasbah** sports an octagonal minaret that pokes above the surrounding rooftops.

Facing the mosque is the main entrance to **Dar-el-Makhzen,** a sumptuous palace where the ruling pasha of Tangier once resided. Begun during the reign of Moulay Ismail, the mansion was enlarged by subsequent rulers. A rich collection of handwoven tapestries, inlaid ceilings, and foliated archways grace the princely interior, along with two museums. The **Museum of Moroccan Art** features a first-rate collection of Fes ceramics, Berber and Arabic carpets, copper and silver jewelry from Marrakech, and an ensemble of Andalusian musical instruments. In the neighboring

Museum of Antiquities, the archeological history of Tangier is documented with a collection of ancient tools. Also noteworthy is the elegant Roman mosaic **Navigation of Venus,** excavated at Volubilis. (Complex open Sun.-Mon. and Wed.-Sat. 9am-noon and 3-6pm. Free.)

The **Old American Legation,** 8 rue America, stands south of pl. de la Kasbah in the far corner of the medina. (Enter the medina from rue du Portugal, and look for the yellow archway emblazoned with the U.S. seal.) The stone battlements you pass through were built in the 1600s by the Portuguese. Morocco was the site of the first American ambassadorial residence, established in 1777. This stately edifice combines the regality of the White House with a Moroccan splendor. Now a museum, it displays a wonderful collection of antique maps as well as works by twentieth-century American artists who have resided in Morocco. Downstairs you can view the correspondence between Sultan Moulay ben Abdellah and George Washington that led to Morocco's distinction as the first country to recognize the independence fo the United States. The curator, a knowledgeable Swiss woman, will lead you on a fact-filled tour in English. (Open daily 9am-1pm and 4-6:30pm. Free.)

In the new city, **St. Andrew's Church,** 1 block southwest of the Grand Socco on rue d'Angleterre, is an Anglican house of worship designed like a mosque. The Lord's Prayer is carved on the chancel arch in decorative Arabic. Constructed by British imperialists in 1894, the church is now used by Tangier's local British expatriates. A shady garden on its grounds contains the tombs of some of Tangier's most prominent British residents. The city's most recent monumental construction is the towering **New Mosque,** a tasteful ochre and white structure on **place el-Koweit,** southwest of the Grand Socco along rue Sidi Bouabib. It was a gift from the king of Kuwait and occupies the largest site of any house of worship in North Africa.

The **Fes Market** is a colorful shopping area where local merchants sell fresh fruits, vegetables, flowers, fish, and meat at reasonable prices. The relatively relaxed pace here appeals to Tangier's European community. To reach the market from the Grand Socco, head south on rue de la Liberté across pl. de France and onto rue de Fes—the market will appear 2 blocks down on your right. A more festive **country market** comes to town on Thursday and Sunday in the Dradeb district, when Rifian Berbers ride into town to sell their pottery, parsley, olives, mountain mint, and fresh fruit. To reach the Dradeb market, head west from the Grand Socco along rue Bou Arrakia and then northwest on rue de la Montagne.

The **Forbes Museum of Military Miniatures** (owned by American tycoon Malcolm Forbes) is home to the world's largest collection of toy soldiers. Various historic battles are meticulously recorded in graphic detail: Tiny figurines march through sand, snow, and rain and decapitate one another. Take rue de la Kasbah north from the Grand Socco, and turn left at the top onto rue de la Corse. Bear right at the fork onto H. Assad Ibn Farrat and continue straight ahead onto rue du Marshan until you reach an unmarked square. Rue Shakespeare, on which the museum is located, sprouts from the diagonal corner of the plaza. It's about a 15-minute walk from the Kasbah. (Open Mon.-Sat. 10am-5pm. Free.)

Entertainment

Ave. d'Espagne runs along Tangier's expansive **beach.** Stick to the main portions frequented by tourists—the deserted areas are prime locations for muggings. Watch all your belongings carefully.

The most popular evening activity in Tangier is to settle into one of the cafes along **boulevard Pasteur,** sip mint tea, and watch the crowds. The passing throng is particularly thick during Ramadan. If you don't mind paying twice as much for a pot of tea (5-6dh), you can enjoy the atmosphere at one of the two teahouses where Tangier's intelligentsia come to sip and quip: **Café de Paris,** 1 pl. de France, or **Madame Porte,** on ave. du Prince Moulay Abdellah at rue el-Mou Hanabi.

Treat yourself to an evening of folk music and dance in a more traditional setting at the **Morocco Palace,** ave. du Prince Moulay Abdellah, just off blvd. Pasteur. Chanting belly-dancers, beanie-twirling Ghaoua tribesmen, and wailing Berber women perform to the rhythms of lute, violin, tambourine, and bongo drums. Watch the way the drummer runs his fingers on a single drumskin to create virtually any tone. (Open nightly from 10pm. Best on Sat. Cover including 1 drink, 45dh.)

Near Tangier

A mountainous promontory covered with shady umbrella pines, **Cape Spartel** overlooks the Atlantic at the northwest corner of Africa. Only 14km from Tangier, it offers a pleasant if windy picnic spot and a fabulous panorama of the coast. Traces of prehistoric life have been discovered in the **Caves of Hercules,** 4km south of the wooded peninsula along the coast. Some caves here have been continuously inhabited since the Neolithic era. (Open 10am-sunset. Admission 1dh.) Just down the coast lie the ruins of the Phoenician city of **Cotta,** whose primary industry was the netting and salting of tuna. From this point, the Atlantic beach stretches south to Asilah. If you've just come from the Algarve, you'll wonder why you didn't come sooner—the expanse of sand is gloriously deserted. Do not, however, enter water above your waist—the current is strong, and several people drown here every year. (You can safely ride the gentle surf into shore, since the water depth drops off slowly.) Avoid driving on the beach (your car will sink), and although it seems inviting, don't camp here—there's a safe campground just up the road near the Caves of Hercules. **Robinson Plage Camping,** across from the Grottes d'Hercules Hotel, charges 5dh per person and 3dh per car. Halfway back toward Cape Spartel, overlooking a beautiful beach, the **Restaurant Sol** specializes in sardines (9-14dh) and *calamares* (18dh). Unfortunately, the only way to get to Cape Spartel is by *grand taxi* (round-trip, 200dh).

Cape Malabata, 12km east of Tangier along the Mediterranean coast, is crowned by a weather-beaten lighthouse and commands a beautiful view of Tangier and the coastline. **Ksar es Séghir,** a tiny fishing village 38km past the cape on the coastal road, harbors the ruins of a Portuguese citadel. Another 10km brings you to the foot of **Jbel Mousa,** the coastline's tallest mountain (842m). As there is no public transportation, take a *grand taxi* (not more than 160dh 5 passengers).

Asilah

Only 46km south of the tensions of Tangier, Asilah soothes the soul of the harried tourist with its quiet streets, golden beach, and glowing white medina. Inevitably, tour buses from Tangier attract a few of that city's handicraft shops and self-appointed guides. Fortunately, the guides here are easy to dismiss. Though Asilah is not quite the unspoiled resort it was only a few years ago, it remains tranquil and is an excellent base for exploring the beaches and ruins along Morocco's northwest Atlantic coast.

Asilah's most interesting inhabitant Raissouli built the Palais de Raissouli in the medina around the turn of the century. A bizarre figure in Moroccan history, Raissouli was an active criminal locally before he began his infamous international career kidnapping and ransoming Europeans. One of his victims was British novelist Walter Harris, who subsequently wrote about the event in one of his journals on Morocco.

Orientation and Practical Information

There is no tourist office in Asilah, despite promises from tourist authorities. The town is small enough that a map is not necessary. The main street into town is **boulevard Mohammed V,** which ends at the town's focal point, **place Mohammed V,** an unimpressive traffic circle. The road on your right leads to a fork in the stony confines of the medina. To your right is **rue Zallakah; avenue Hassan II** lies on your left, tracing the walls of the medina. The medina itself is relatively easy to navigate.

Post Office: Place des Nations Unis, on the right as you leave town. Street sign is hard to see. Open Mon.-Thurs. 8am-3pm, Fri. 8am-12:30pm.

Train Station: 2km from town on the Asilah-Tangier highway, near a strip of excellent campgrounds. To Tangier (6 per day, 1½ hr., 1st class 13.50dh, 2nd class 9dh) and Casablanca, with connections to Rabat and Marrakech (6 per day). A taxi from town costs about 10dh. A bus (1dh) takes you from the station to town, but it leaves *immediately* after your train arrives.

Bus Station: CTM, off pl. Mohammed V. CTM and private buses to Tangier leave hourly 7am-6:30pm in front of the office. Buses to Larache follow roughly the same schedule (40 min., 5dh). Buses depart frequently, but that's about the only thing you can be sure of; there's no fixed timetable.

Taxis: At pl. Mohammed V, across from the bus station. *Grand taxis* only. To Larache 100dh. To train station 10dh.

Pharmacy: Pharmacie Loukili, ave. Liberté (tel. 72 78), 1 block from pl. Mohammed V, across from the police station.

Police: Service de Police, on ave. Liberté at blvd. Mohammed V (tel. 19), 1 block from pl. Mohammed V. Helpful if you arrive at night.

Accommodations

You can rent rooms in a small pension or a private home for 15-20dh per person—ask around the waterfront or along rue Zallakah by the walls of the medina. Otherwise, a variety of pleasant and reasonably priced hotels lie within walking distance of the beach.

Hotel Marhaba, 9 rue Zallakah (tel. 71 44), on the right as you approach the medina from pl. Mohammed V. Excellent location, cheap rates, more than adequate rooms, and spotless bathroom. Run by 2 soft-spoken brothers who will let you climb on the terrace to hang your laundry or to enjoy the sunset over the Atlantic. Singles 28dh. Doubles 44dh. Hot showers 5dh.

Hotel Asilah, 79 ave. Hassan II (tel. 72 86). From rue Zallakah, turn left and follow the walls of the medina along ave. Hassan II. Enter on a side street. Small, clean, spartan rooms. Singles 42dh. Doubles 57dh.

Hotel Sahara, 9 rue Tarfaya (tel. 71 85). From pl. Mohammed V, walk along blvd. Mohammed V. Turn right at ave. Liberté and left at the next block. Small rooms. Clean showers and bath. Singles 42dh. Doubles 57dh. Hot showers 5dh.

Hotel Oued El Makhazine, ave. Melilla (tel. 70 90), facing the beach. Walk up blvd. Mohammed V until you hit rue Khalir Gailan. Follow this street for 3 blocks, and turn right. The hotel is behind a dirt lot. Don't come here unless you have money to burn; it's pricier than it's worth. Plain, modestly sized rooms boast nice private baths (hot shower included). The rooms look tidy, but difficult to enjoy through the small windows. Singles 110dh. Doubles 129dh.

Camping

Asilah is bursting with campgrounds, some of which offer small, inexpensive "bungalows" to those without tents or sleeping bags. Most campgrounds lie near or on the shore in a row toward the train station; others lie along the road to Cape Spartel.

Camping Echrigui, (tel. 71 82), 500m from the train station toward town. Along a beautiful beach and the walk to town isn't too bad. Kind, English-speaking manager. 6dh per person, 5dh per tent, 5dh per car. Bungalows with bath and hot shower 50dh.

Camping Sahara, 2km north of the train station. Quieter and less crowded. Campsites are covered with tough weeds. 5dh per person, 7dh per tent. New 1st-class bungalows are close to the shore (140dh); older 2nd-class bungalows are clean and quite bare (120dh).

Briech Camping, 12km north of Asilah, just before the Port de Mohammed V. Take a nonexpress bus from Asilah to Tangier and ask to be let off before the bridge. On a soft, sandy lagoon—great for a few days of sunny oblivion. Restaurant a bit expensive. Try Tahadart

Restaurant across the highway. 7dh per person, per tent, and per car. 2- or 3-person bungalow 50dh.

Food

Asilah's cheapest and most authentic restaurants are on **ave. Hassan II,** along the walls of the medina. You can eat your heart out in one of the tiny stalls with green doors for 10-20dh.

Restaurant Café Rabie, ave. Hassan II, across from the entrance to the medina. Many foreigners visit this small hideaway. Flies dance to the strains of Bob Marley and ABBA. The chicken, beef, and fish dinners are excellent deals (10-12dh). Open daily 11am-11pm.

Restaurant Lixus, pl. Mohammed V (tel. 73 79). Bland atmosphere, but generous portions for little money (20-30dh). Open daily 8am-10pm.

La Alcazaba Restaurant, end of rue Zallakah (tel. 70 12). Reputedly the best restaurant in town, but bus tours from Tangier have made it more expensive. Nonetheless, the food is good enough for a moderate splurge. Sit inside or across the street on a terrace overlooking the street. Wine served. Service 19%. Open Mon.-Sat. 11:30am-2:30pm and 6:30-10:30pm.

Sights

Asilah has two all-star attractions: the **beach** and the spotless **medina.** The beach is smooth, sandy, and sprawling, with bracing waves. The company is generally congenial, but don't bring your passport or valuables along. Hustlers have been known to liberate clothes and money during the briefest of dips. And don't settle right near the medina: The beaches north of Asilah are cleaner.

The medina, which lies within heavily fortified stone walls, is easy to navigate. Just enter—unescorted—through **Bab Hamar** at the intersection of ave. Hassan II and rue Zallakah. From here you can make your way to the Portuguese **Palais de Raissouli** (on the coastal side of the medina across from the *bab*), which features intricately painted Portuguese stalactite arches and brightly tiled burial markers. The palace is open to the public, but the caretaker opens only sporadically.

It's fun to explore the whitewashed residential district of the medina, with its freshly painted private entrances and ancient cobbled alleyways. Try to find the handicraft shops, but don't be deceived by their serene and secluded locations—the merchants will vastly overcharge if they can. Don't pay more than 90dh for a *djellaba* (Moroccan robe). European aristocrats own most of the homes just inside the Portuguese walls along the waterfront; the view of the glittering Atlantic and the washed medina side by side should not be missed. The lower portions of the opposite walls facing ave. Hassan II date back to Carthaginian and possibly Phoenician times. Though market day here is Thursday, there is also a colorful daily **fruit and vegetable market** on ave. Hassan II. For a secluded beach with cliffs (perfect for diving), walk all the way down ave. Hassan II and turn left at the waterfront. Walk along the coast for about 2km. Don't travel here alone, as assaults have been reported.

On Sunday mornings the place to be is the Berber market at **souk el-Had el-Gharbia,** 9km inland from Asilah. Berbers from as far away as the Rif Mountains converge on the enclosed area by the tiny village to peddle their wares. Tour buses from Tangier also regularly attend the market, and the locals have become accustomed to taking tourists for a handsome ride. Two kilometers farther inland, the scanty remains of the once sizable Roman metropolis of **Admercuri** line a dusty road. Ask local children to point the way.

In August, artists from all over the world flock to Asilah for the famous **cultural museum festival.** Painters adorn the white walls with murals, and musicians enliven the beach with their sounds.

Larache

Fifty kilometers south of Asilah, Larache is less attractive and correspondingly less touristed. A subtle Spanish flavor permeates the architecture, above all, and can be traced to the town's remaining a Spanish possession well into this century. Only recently have the street names been changed from Spanish to Arabic.

If you tell a Moroccan in Asilah that you're going to Larache, you'll recieve a puzzled expression followed by a short commentary on how there is nothing to see or do there. The Moroccans are right. Larache serves best as a sight-seeing break or as a base for exploring Lixus and Moulay Bousselham (see Near Larache).

Most accommodations and restaurants center around **place de la Libération,** a traffic circle with a beautiful fountain and palm trees. To get there from the bus station, turn right. When you reach ave. Moulay Mohammed Ben Abdellah, turn right again and continue for 10 minutes. As you approach pl. de la Libération, you'll come across several uninspiring pensions. **Pension Amal,** 8 rue Abdellah Ben Yassine (tel. 27 88), a side street off ave. Mouly Mohammed Ben Abdellah, offers immaculate rooms, but no showers. (Singles 15dh. Doubles 30dh.) There's a public bath on the same street, however. Farther down the street, **Pension Salama** (tel. 29 55) charges the same prices, but the facility is a step down in quality. There are common baths. **Pension Es Saada** (a.k.a. Hotel Saada), on the same street (tel. 36 41), lets small, white rooms and showers in a dingy closet on the ground floor. The Moroccan toilets look sanitarily imposing (Singles 25dh. Doubles 50dh.)

On pl. de la Libération are several decent restaurants, though you can find the cheapest food just inside the medina if you're not picky about sharing your meat with flies. For fresh seafood and healthy portions, try **Restaurant Lixus** (tel. 21 07). They serve a hearty meal of *omelette françáis,* marlin filets, and dessert for 35dh. **Restaurant Larache** on ave. Moulay Mohammed Ben Abdellah offers delicious seafood dishes for 20-23dh. (Open daily 9am-midnight.) The french fries come with a hot tomato sauce (6dh). The clean restaurant is a refreshing change.

The medina is bustling with the usuals, along with a smattering of fish vendors. The entrance is off pl. de la Libération, through the long, brown brick arch. The **post office** is 100m from pl. de la Libération on blvd. Mohammed V. The **telephone code** is 091. The **bus station** has buses leaving constantly for Tangier via Asilah (10.50dh) and several daily to Fes (30.50dh). A modern **pharmacy** (tel. 23 46 or 23 47) is near the plaza on ave. Moulay Mohammed Ben Abdellah. (Open daily 9am-1pm and 3-8pm.)

Near Larache: Lixus and Moulay Bousselham

Perched on a lofty hill overlooking the Loukos River, the ruins of ancient **Lixus** are both scenic and archeologically significant. The second most extensive Roman site in Morocco after Volubilis, Lixus in its heyday ranked as the largest city in West Africa. Founded by Phoenicians, the city thrived in part because of its strategic location. The town's economy was based on garum (a salted fish by-product) and sea salt; the latter is still gathered in the same riverside marshes. Near its modern counterpart, by the main highway, are the ruins of the **salt factory,** which once smoked fish and prepared salt for shipping. A dirt footpath leads up the hill from the highway to the Roman **amphitheater.** Circuses of wild animals once entertained local audiences here. Look for the faded but still imposing **Mosaic of Oceanus,** then scramble up to the summit for a panoramic view of the serpentine Loukos, terraced salt flats, and minarets of Larache. The **acropolis** sprawls downward, strewn with traces of a temple's oratory, altars, columns, and vaulted chamber.

To reach Lixus from Larache, head 4km north on the road to Tangier and stop on the left at the sign for Plage Ras Rimel, or take a *petit taxi* (20dh) at pl. de la Libération. A more time-consuming, expensive—and scenic—route is the shuttle rowboat along the meandering Loukos River; you can charter one of these, along with a rower (2 hr., 50-80dh). (Site open all day. Free.)

Some 50km south of Larache, the tiny coastal resort of **Moulay Bousselham** overlooks the Atlantic at the mouth of a spacious lagoon teeming with fish and pint-sized rowboats. Long revered as a holy place and famous for fishing, Moulay Bousselham has blossomed in recent years into a fashionable retreat, where shorts and bikinis are proudly sported by wealthy Moroccans on the main street of town. The community's remote location, 40km off the main north-south road, has kept it small and exclusive, and it remains worth visiting for its roomy beach, succulent and inexpensive seafood, and the glimpse it affords of success Moroccan-style.

The least expensive place to rest your body is **Camping/Caravaning Moulay Bousselham,** an ultra-modern, high-security operation on the shores of the lagoon. (6dh per person, 7dh per tent, 5dh per car, 4dh for electricity and shower.) The next cheapest arrangement—especially if you plan to stay for a week or more—is to rent a house. Ask at Restaurant Chez Cherif for details. In peak season, a three-bedroom, furnished villa with kitchen, bathroom, and refrigerator runs 1500dh per month. Weekly rates are negotiable. You'll pay dearly for overnight accommodations at **Hotel de Lagon.** (Luxurious singles 150dh. Doubles 200dh. Triples 280dh.) Several cafes and restaurants line the main street; the best is **Restaurant Chez Cherif.** The complete menu features what might be the best seafood dinner of your life, with mixed salad, mint tea, and gargantuan portions of fish, all for 20dh.

Dominating the town, the **Marabout of Moulay Bousselham** is dedicated to the tenth-century Egyptian saint who still commands a popular following here. Every year in late June or early July, pilgrims journey to the tomb to sacrifice bulls and sheep, and a lively festival is held in honor of the priest. Nearby, tucked away in a small cave, is the **Tomb of Joseph,** son of Aristotle. The cave is endowed with a sacred stalactite secreting tiny droplets of salt water that pilgrims like to suck on for good luck. You can also take a short boat excursion (30-40dh) to glimpse a neighboring colony of pink flamingos.

Moulay Bousselham is difficult to reach without a car. It is served by infrequent buses (35dh) and frequent taxis (50dh) from Souk el-Arba (Souk-Larba du Gharb), on the main inland highway between Larache and Rabat.

Tetuan

Crowded with Berbers from nearby fishing villages and farming communities, yet only 90 minutes by bus from Tangier and 20 minutes from Spanish Ceuta, Tetuan carries you into a world different from both. Despite its homely new town and its hustlers, Tetuan sustains a small-town authenticity that eludes more international cities. Its harsh, medium-sized medina can be one of the most engaging you will see.

Tetuan was founded in the fourteenth century as a guerilla base for attacks on Ceuta and flourished as a prosperous pirates' retreat before being razed by the Spaniards. Two centuries later, the city was resettled by Muslims and Jews fleeing persecution in Spain. In 1913, the Spanish made Tetuan the capital of their Moroccan protectorate, and *castellano* is still widely spoken. Tetuan wasn't returned to Morocco until 1958; the centuries of Spanish domination are evident in the neo-Andalusian architecture.

Orientation and Practical Information

In Djibliya, the language spoken by local Berbers, "Tetuan" means "Open your eyes." Be aware that Tetuan is second only to Tangier in its hustler-to-tourist ratio.

Leave your pack in a hotel as soon as you arrive. Hustlers will surround you at the bus station: Either dismiss them by explaining that you know where you are going, or offer about 5dh to lead you to the hotel you specify. Once there, tell them you want to rest, and don't let them wait. If you do decide later to engage an unofficial guide, be sure to check the Hustlers and Guides and Bargaining sections of our introduction to Morocco.

Tetuan's two main squares, **place Hassan II,** in front of the medina, and **place Moulay el-Mehdi,** with its handsome central fountain, are connected by the commercial artery, **avenue Mohammed V.** Most banks, offices, and safe accommodations can be found on or near these three locations. Running parallel to the above, **avenue Mohammed ben el-Arbi Torres** (or **avenue Mohammed Torres**) is lined with inexpensive restaurants and cafes.

Tourist Office: 30 ave. Mohammed V (tel. 70 09 or 44 07). From the upper floor of the bus station, turn left as you exit, then right onto blvd. Sidi Mandri. Walk right for 3 blocks, and turn left at ave. Mohammed V; the office is 2½ blocks down. Friendly advice. Ask to borrow the one and only map of the city underneath the glass counter, and have it photocopied across the street (1dh). Best to go in morning or late afternoon. Open July-Aug. Mon.-Fri. 8am-3pm; Sept.-June Mon.-Thurs. 8:30am-noon and 2:30-6:30pm, Fri. 8:30-11:30am and 3-6:30pm; Ramadan Mon.-Fri. 9am-3pm.

After Hours Exchange: Banque Marocaine (**B.M.C.E.**), pl. Moulay el-Mehdi. Open Mon.-Fri. 8am-9pm, Sat.-Sun. 9am-1pm and 3-8pm.

Post Office: pl. Moulay el-Mehdi (tel. 67 98). Best service available before 11am. Poste Restante 1.20 dh per item. Open July-Aug. Mon.-Sat. 8:30-3:30pm; Sept.-June Mon.-Sat. 8:30am-12:15pm and 2:30-6:45pm; Ramadan Mon.-Sat. 9am-4pm.

Telephones: In the post office along the far wall. Open daily 8:30am-9pm. Public phones right outside the entrance.

Bus Station: blvd. Ouad al-Makhazine, upper level, and blvd. Sidi Mandri, lower level. Buy your ticket early and ask for a numbered seat, or you may be bumped. **CTM** (tel. 62 63) operates service to Casablanca (2 per day, 75dh) and Rabat (1 per day, 60dh). Other companies serve many more destinations with greater frequency, including Oned Laou (3 per day, 5.10dh), Ceuta (hourly, 8dh), and Tangier (hourly, 9dh). There is **shuttle service** to the beaches of Cabo Negro, Mdiq, Restinga-Smir, and Martil (2dh), or you can take the bus for Centa and clap loudly several times when you want to get off. In summer, buses leave from the station and also from behind the green and white palace a few blocks down the road to Ceuta. Refuse to pay extra for baggage.

Taxis: Petits taxis, blvd. Ouad al-Makhazine, on your left as you exit the upper floor of the bus station. **Collective Grands taxis,** at a taxi stop on blvd. Maarakah Annoual. From the bus station (upper level), turn right along blvd. Ouad al-Makhazine and left at blvd. Med al-Khatib. To Ceuta (10-15dh per person). At ave. Moulay Abbas, at the gas station across from the lower level of the bus station. To Tangier (15-20dh per person). Taxis are the best way to get to Centa, Tangier, or Oued-Laou; the schedules are flexible, seats comfortable, and the pandemonium of riding Moroccan buses is left in the dust.

Hospital: blvd. Sidi Mandri and blvd. Generalíssimo Franco, 1 door above the police station.

Police: Tel. 19, on blvd. Sidi Mandri at blvd. Generalíssimo Franco, 1 block above ave. Mohammed V.

Accommodations

There are scads of cheap pensions in the medina, but most are hard to find and even harder to stomach. The following, in the new city, are all near the lively main squares, place Hassan II and place Moulay el-Mehdi.

Pension Iberia, 12 pl. Moulay el-Mehdi, 3rd floor (tel. 36 79), just above the B.M.C.E. bank at #5. From the bus station, turn right, go straight up blvd. Yacoub el-Mansour, and turn right again up toward pl. Moulay el-Mehdi with the fountain. Airy, spacious rooms and a clean common bath. Kind, Spanish-speaking manager. Safe and convenient. Singles 17dh. Doubles 28dh. Hot showers 3dh.

Hotel Regina, 8 blvd. Sidi Mandri (tel. 21 13). Turn left as you exit the bus station from the upper floor; it's the 1st right. A cut above the others. Spotless, comfortable rooms with stucco walls and a modern interior. Lively restaurant below. Singles with shower 46dh. Doubles with shower 82dh.

Hotel Nacional, 8 rue Mohammed Torres (tel. 32 90). From the bus station's upper level, turn left onto blvd. Sidi Mandri and right after 2 blocks. Posh rooms with ornate Moroccan lamp and ceiling. Come here for a break from the drab pension atmosphere. Singles 44dh, with shower 60dh, with toilet 77dh. Doubles 55dh, with shower 77dh, with toilet 89dh.

Hotel Trébol, 3 blvd. Yacoub el-Mansour al-Mouahidi (tel. 20 93). Exit the bus station from the lower level and walk a few steps uphill to the right; it's the 1st left. Convenient and clean. Calculate your bill carefully. Fills up quickly because of its location. Singles 41dh, with shower 60dh, with toilet 77dh. Doubles 55dh, with shower 77dh, with toilet 89dh.

Hotel Príncipe, 20 blvd. Youssef Ibn Tachfine (tel. 27 95). Go up blvd. Yacoub el-Mansour al-Mouahidi and turn right after 1 block. Manager is rather cold. The rooms are small, but clean. Singles 43dh, with shower 62dh. Doubles 59dh, with shower 82dh.

Food

There is not much to do in Tetuan except eat, but at least you can do that well. The cheapest food is in the medina. Pass through the entrance across from Pension Central on pl. Hassan II, and take your first left to find a host of small restaurants and stalls. Try **Restaurant Saffa** on rue Msallah for good *couscous* and brochettes (10dh each). In general, however, the most pleasant dining is in the new city, particularly along **Pasaje Achach.** Numerous pastry shops (cake 2.50dh per slice), ice cream shops (served in small scoops), and *bocadillo* (hero sandwich) bars line ave. Mohammed V.

Restaurante Moderno, 1 Pasaje Achach (no phone), between ave. Mohammed V and ave. Mohammed Torres. From pl. Hassan II, cross through the marble-tiled alley opposite the Cinema Español. A lively, local place featuring brochettes (16dh), *harira, couscous,* fish, and tender chicken with rice. Try the *tajine de kefta,* an aromatic meatball and egg concoction for 18dh. The nameless restaurant next door serves many of the same dishes during the same hours. Open daily 9am-9pm.

Bocadillos Alfath, 25 ave. Mohammed V, near pl. Monday el-Mehdi. Enjoy hefty sandwiches with everything on 'em (small 2.50dh, large 5dh, 1dh extra for an egg), while gaping at the unique seashell patterns on the ceiling. The small sandwiches are more than enough for a big snack. Icy cold drinks (get your Sidi Ali here). Open daily 8am-10pm.

Restaurant Zarhoun, 7 rue Mohammed Torres (tel. 30 64), 1½ blocks from Pasaje Achach. The fanciest restaurant in town and great for a modest splurge. Elegant *salon marocain* with sofas and engraved tabletop. Complete *menu* 35-45dh. Open daily noon-4pm and 6:30-10:30pm.

Café la Union, across from Restaurante Moderno on Pasaje Achach (no phone). A crowded place good for sipping tea, nibbling snacks, and meeting people. Buy a drink and ask for a set of parchesi, checkers, or dominos; it won't be long before a local pulls up a chair and teaches you the Moroccan rules. Open daily until midnight.

Bocadillos Chatt, rue Mohammed Torres at blvd. Mohammed Ibn Abderrahman (tel. 20 12), kitty corner to Restaurant Zarhoun. A fast-food place *à la marocaine.* Lean over the counter and select sandwich fillings from the sometimes mysterious but always fresh meats and vegetables. Large, well-stuffed sandwich 5dh, ½-sandwich 2.50dh. Open daily 5am-11pm.

Sights and Entertainment

Tetuan's **medina** climbs the side of a hill above the new city. If you enter through Bab an-Nawadir, near pl. Moulay el-Mehdi, you'll find yourself directly in the teeming **market area,** with frequent flea markets and *souks.* The old quarter is especially picturesque on Wednesdays and Saturdays, when Rif Mountain Berbers loaded down with fruits, vegetables, and handicrafts inundate the medina. Should you decide to accept a guide, agree on a price in advance (about 10-20dh for a few hours). It's a better idea to venture into the medina on your own and drift around at your own sweet pace. Remember not to shop if you are with a guide, since you'll be forced to pay him a commission.

A climb through the winding alleys to the top of the medina will reward you with a view of the whitewashed city and surrounding mountains. The outer walls were constructed in the sixteenth century to protect the city from the Portuguese. Before leaving, visit the ornate **Brisha Palace,** which houses an expensive tourist tea room, or the **Mellah el-Bali** (Jewish Quarter) and the "new" (300-year-old) Jewish section on **rue Msallah.** The palace lies just beyond pl. Hassan II.

Outside the walls, across from the old gate of Bab el-Okla, the **Escuela de Arte** shelters an interesting historical and folkloric museum. (Open Mon.-Fri. 8:30am-noon and 2:30-5:30pm, Sat. 8:30am-noon. Admission 3dh.) Potters, coppersmiths, tile-makers, and other artisans fashion their wares on the patio outside. Their handicrafts can be purchased at the **Exposition Artisanale**, 6 Derb Seffar (tel. 41 71). The **Ensemble Artisanale**, a few blocks down the road to Ceuta, runs a blanket and carpet workshop where you can watch the artists at work. (Open Mon.-Fri. 8am-1pm and 2:30-8pm, Sat. 8am-1pm.) The small, two-story **Museo Arqueológico** on blvd. Aljazaer, 1 block north of Mohammed V, features prehistoric, Phoenician, and Roman objects excavated from Lixus and Tamada. (Open Mon. and Wed.-Thurs. 8:30am-noon and 2:30-6:30pm, Fri. 8:30-11:30am and 3-6:30pm. Admission 3dh.)

Evenings underscore the soothingly slow pace of life in Tetuan. Strollers gravitate toward place Hussan II; ave. Mohammed V and ave. Mohammed Torres spring to life from their afternoon languor. Prices for goods are higher in Tetuan than in other Moroccan cities, and storeowners don't seem to appreciate the fine art of bargaining; do your buying elsewhere.

Near Tetuan

Croissant Rifain

The coastline from Ceuta almost to Tetuan is a sandy crescent of largely deserted beach. Across from the overpriced tourist village and the empty beach at **Restinga Smir,** you'll find spartan **Camping Fraja** (tel. 77 22; 5dh per person, 7dh per tent, 7dh per car). Farther south, the village of **Mdiq** has a popular, pebbly beach. The tiny harbor is filled with fishing boats and strewn with nets; the village bursts with tourist shops. Luckily the only hustlers in town are easy to dismiss. Clean, comfortable accommodations are available at the Hotel Playa (tel. 85 10; 15dh per person).

Closer to Tetuan and served by frequent buses are the resort beaches of **Martil** and **Cabo Negro.** Although both are somewhat overdeveloped, the 5-kilometer coastline between them is unspoiled and makes an ideal daytrip from Tetuan. Cabo Negro is dominated by the unsightly **Hotel Petit Merou,** but the resort complex houses a couple of comfortable cafes that offer relief from the sun. Martil is a mushrooming coastal town brimming with the seaside homes of Tetuan's well-to-do. Although crowded in summer, the beach is excellent and easily accessible from Tetuan. Just up from the waterfront, you can stay in adequate rooms at either **Hostal Nuzha** or **Pension Merhaba**—both charge about 20dh per person. **Camping Martil** (tel. 93 39) is by the beach at the southern end of town (3dh per person, 5dh per big tent, 3dh per small tent).

Oued-Laou

Basking in the Mediterranean sun, the coastal village of Oued-Laou, 42km south of Tetuan, lies on a curve of deserted beach at the foot of the Rif Mountains. It's a mellow seaside retreat which cultivates an appreciation for life's simpler things. The village is inhabited by a community of Berbers who fish and make and sell the terracotta pottery for which the town is famous. On Saturdays, the village comes alive with a **country market.** Berbers come down from the Rif to peddle their crafts and cannabis crop, while local potters display their wares. A bumpy but beautiful road leads inland from Oued-Laou toward Chechaouèn through the foothills of the Rif. Adjoining most of the roadside domiciles are the old-fashioned kilns in which the local ceramics are fired. Farther east along the coast are numerous deserted, dark, sandy beaches and scenic mountainous coastline.

From the sleepy main street, where the buses and taxis make their drop-offs, walk 1 block towards the ocean onto a gravel road. Everything you'll need here will be on your left. To the far left **Hotel Oued-Laou** offers immaculate, earthy rooms with mattresses on the floor and Moroccan decor (15dh per person). You can sip soft drinks in its pleasant, thatched-roof cafe overlooking the beach. **Hotel Laayoun** (nearby, with the yellow 2nd story) brings you back to the basics with their bare adobe rooms and new beds. The rooftop terrace commands a superb view of the beach and is an ideal place to catch some rays. (Singles 17dh. Doubles 25dh. Rooms for up to six available. Cold shower included.) If you're planning to stay for awhile, take a look at the many white houses that dot the beaches. With no electricity or any other creature comfort, these homes underscore the town's simplicity.

Next door to Hotel Laayoun, **Café Rosa Restaurant** is a colorful establishment serving 15dh meals outdoors, where you can bask in the sun and try to decipher the color scheme used in the wall mural. (Open daily 8am-midnight.)

Inconvenient and unreliable **buses** leave for Oued-Laou from Tetuan at 6:30am and 4pm, returning to Tetuan at 7:30am and 6pm (8dh). Save yourself many headaches by taking a **grand taxi** (15-20dh per person if you share a taxi). In Tetuan, a local taxi will bring you to the Oued-Laou taxi stop, 1km down the road to Ceuta (don't pay more than 7dh). There is no taxi service at the end of Ramadan.

From Oeud-Laou, your best bet is to get up early and try to find a taxi on the main street. You will face stiff competition, especially on a work day. If you hitchhike and a truck takes you back, you will probably have nightmares about the cliffs for the rest of your life.

Ceuta (Spain)

Lying on the African side of the Strait of Gibraltar, Ceuta (or Sebta in Arabic) is situated on a peninsula that juts out from the northern coast of Morocco. Despite its mismatched geography, Ceuta is thoroughly Spanish and is a more accessible and less harrowing introduction to Morocco than Tangier.

Unfortunately, Ceuta is known to Spaniards as the place to stock up on duty-free goods; this frequently makes it crowded. But this attractive city has a fascinating history. The small Spanish protectorate successfully combines the flavor of Andalucía with the comforts of a modern city. The result is an idyllic scene: Spanish plazas, cafes, and shops line ocean boulevards as palm leaves sway in the gentle breeze under the blue Mediterranean sky.

If you're coming from Morocco, you'll welcome the efficiency of this minimetropolis with open arms, especially after the hour-long nightmare at Moroccan customs. Get your yellow departure cards from customs agents and avoid hustlers selling white photocopies. At the Spanish border, **taxis** will take you into town or to the **port** (500 ptas). Pesetas, not dirhams, are the legal tender, and Ceuta is one hour ahead of Morocco (2 hr. ahead in summer). The **ferry to Algeciras** (late June-early Sept. Mon.-Fri. 12 per day 8:30am-10:30pm, Sun. 6 per day; mid-Sept. to mid-June Mon.-Sat. 6 per day 8am-9pm, Sun. 3 per day; 11/3 hr.; 1140 ptas) departs frequently.

If you're going to Morocco, enjoy your last minutes of peaceful bliss in one of the city's flowery, sun-soaked plazas. Then hop on bus #7, which leaves from **Plaza de la Constitución** for the *frontera* (45 ptas). After an hour wait at passport and baggage control, take a *grand taxi* to Tetuan (70dh, which can be split 5 ways). The bus to Tetuan leaves about 3km from the border. Don't let any guides tag along.

Traces of Ceuta's 2500-year history are present throughout the peninsula. During the time of the Greeks and Romans, **Monte Hacho** of Ceuta and the Rock of Gibraltar was thought to guard the passage to Hades as the pillars of Hercules. Today, Monte Hacho still dominates the skyline, watching over the mouth of the canal.

Atop Monte Hacho, the **Ermita de San Antonio** (Hermitage) offers an outstanding panorama of the city below. Traveling into the city from the port, you will see the stone battlements of the **Foso de la Muralla Real** (Moat of the Royal Wall), left behind by the Portuguese in the fifteenth century. Follow the curve along C. Edrissis onto the city's main oceanside promenade, **Paseo de las Palmeras.** Before walking down the Mediterranean *paseo,* turn into **Plaza de Africa.** In the middle of the plaza, amidst the greenery, rests the **Monumento a los Caídos en la Guerra de Africa** (Monument to the Fallen in the African War). Standing majestically behind the palm trees is the city's **cathedral,** with its characteristic two steeples and black marble portal. The facade of the fifteenth-century **Iglesia de Nuestra Señora** de Africa (Church of Our Lady of Africa) is only slightly less inspiring.

Paseo de las Palmeras leads directly to **Plaza da la Constitución,** the heart of the city. Near the plaza are several *pensións.* **Pensión Revellín,** Paseo del Revellín, 2 (tel. 51 67 62), is on your right at the fork. The hallways are dark, but the old rooms fill quickly. (Singles 900ptas. Doubles 1600ptas. Cold shower 100ptas, hot shower 200ptas.) **Pensión Oriente,** C. Teniente Arrabal, 3 (tel. 51 11 15), 100m ,from the plaza is a slightly better operation. (Singles 1000ptas. Doubles 1600ptas.) For a great meal and a spectacular view, walk 2 blocks perpendicular to the *paseo* to C. Independencia, on the other side of the peninsula. **Cafetería Regina,** C. Independencia, 5 (no phone), has a laid-back, small bar-restaurant atmosphere and is popular with locals. Have your pick of seafood dishes (500ptas) or *bocadillos* (200ptas), and enjoy the scenery. (Open daily noon-4pm and 7pm-midnight.)

The **tourist office** (tel. 51 13 79) is at the end of Muelle Cañonero Dato. From the port, turn left onto the main road, and walk all the way to the end. The office will provide you with a helpful map and high-quality brochures. (Open Mon.-Fri. 9am-2pm and 4-6pm, Sat. 9am-2pm.) The **post office,** C. Cervantes, 3 (tel. 51 24 09), is on the other side of town. (Open Mon.-Fri. 8am-2pm, Sat. 9am-2pm.) The **postal code** is 11017.

Meknes

Lazy, friendly, and sprawling, Meknes is an imperial city with a provincial warmth. The monumental mosques and *medersas* (Koranic schools) of the old city peer intently over the valley at the brutal concrete columns of the new; both are tempered by the medina, a smaller, tamer version of its eastern cousin at Fes. Even the hustlers are courteous here, although at night, when the sleepy streets come alive, the city assumes a slightly reckless—and all the more exhilirating—character.

Meknes was transformed from an unremarkable provincial capital into an emerald city by the dictator Moulay Ismail, who chose the city as his seat of power in 1672. The child of his scheme was the tragically ambitious **Dar el-Kebira,** the largest palace in the world, which now lies largely in shambles; it's a monument to a megalomaniac, built by armies of Christian and African slaves. Today, the city is capital to the Berbers and has the largest Berber population in Morocco.

Orientation and Practical Information

The old town, graced by the monuments of the *ville impériale* is separated from the modern **ville nouvelle** by the **Oued Boufrekane,** a long valley about ½km wide. You can either cross it on foot along ave. Moulay Ismail or catch one of the local buses (#5, 7, or 9) that shuttle between the CTM bus station in the *ville nouvelle* and **Bab Mansour,** the colossal entrance to the imperial complex that contains most of the medina's main attractions. All major services in the *ville nouvelle* center around **place Administrative** (also called **place de la Grande Poste**).

Tourist Office: pl. Administrative (tel. 244 26). From the small train station, turn left after 1 block onto ave. Gambetta, turn left onto an unmarked street, walk straight ahead 4 blocks, then head to the right of Hotel de Ville for pl. Administrative. The staff is friendly and the maps decent. Official guides 30dh per ½-day, 3 times the price of unofficial guides. Neither is necessary. Open July to mid-Sept. Mon.-Fri. 8:30am-2:30pm; mid-Sept. to late May Mon.-Fri. 8:30am-noon and 2:30-6:30pm; Ramadan Mon.-Fri. 9am-3pm.

Syndicat d'Initiative: Esplanade de la Foire (tel. 201 91), just inside the big yellow gate aves. Hassan II and Moulay Ismail. Open same hours as tourist office.

After-Hours Currency Exchange: Hotel Rif, Zankat Accra (tel. 225 91), around the corner from the tourist office. Gives regular bank currency rates. Open daily 7am-11pm.

Post Office: pl. Administrative. Open same hours as the tourist office. **Telephones** available daily 8am-9pm. Use the side entrance when the post office is closed. **Branch office:** rue Dar Smen, near the medina. Open same hours. **Telephone Code:** 05.

Train Stations: ave. de la Basse, more than 1km east of the center of the *ville nouvelle.* Get off instead at smaller, more centrally located **Meknes el-Amir Abdelkader station,** rue d'Alger, 2 blocks from blvd. Mohammed V. 8 trains per day to Rabat (43dh), Casablanca (63dh), Fes (14dh), and Oujda (99.50dh).

Bus Stations: CTM, 47 blvd. Mohammed V (tel. 225 83), near rue des Forces Armées Royales. To Rabat (7 per day) Casablanca (7 per day), Fes (6 per day), Tangier (1 per day), Ifrane (1 per day), Azrou (1 per day), and Ouezzane (2 per day). The bus to Fes often arrives full, so try to board early in the morning. **Private companies,** at the pink stone terminal at the foot of the hill just below Bab Mansour. Buses leave for most cities only when full, but service to the Middle Atlas is much more frequent here.

Laundromat: Inexplicably, Meknes is a lavophile's dream, with laundromats lining rue Dar Smen, ave. Rouzaine, and the new city. Most charge by the piece (about 7dh); ask for a per kilo price. **Pressing de la Poste,** 8 rue Dar Smen, in the old city across from the post office. Open Mon.-Sat. 8am-noon and 2-8pm.

Swimming Pools: Municipal pool, ave. Moulay Ismail at ave. des Forces Armées Royales, by Oued Boufrekane. Open May-Sept. daily 10am-4pm. Admission 2dh. A few steps farther down the driveway is a cleaner and less crowded **private pool** with a lawn. Admission 7.50dh.

After-Hours Pharmacy: Croissant Rouge Pharmacie d'Urgence, pl. Administrative. Side entrance to the Hotel de Ville (tel. 233 75, 24 hours). Open 8:30am-8:30pm.

Medical Emergencies: Hospital Moulay Ismail, rue des Forces Armées Royales (tel. 228 05 or 228 06), near ave. Moulay Youssef. **Hospital Mohammed V,** Tel. 211 34.

Accommodations and Camping

In the Medina

There is little point in staying in Meknes unless you stay near the medina, the soul of the city. Coming from the *ville nouvelle,* exuberant **avenue Roumazine** goes up toward **pl. el-Hedime.** Budget hotels line either side. From the bus terminal below Bab Mansour, climb the hill to the Bab and follow the street as it hooks left to become rue Dar Smen, which leads into pl. el-Hedime; from there, turn right onto avenue Roumazine.

Hotel Maroc, 103 ave. Benbrahim (tel. 307 05), just off ave. Roumazine. The best and one of the cheapest in town. Clean, safe rooms overlook a pleasant garden. Singles 20dh, doubles 35dh. Wash basins in every room.

Hotel Regina, 19 rue Dar Smen (tel. 302 80). Turn left at the end of ave. Roumazine, where rue Dar Smen runs to pl. el-Hedime. The rooms are hot and grimy, but still the cleanest this close to Bab Mansour. Hip hot pink lobby with black and white tile floor. Singles 25dh, doubles 30dh, triples 40dh. Several even greater dives next door or up the street, toward the Bab.

In the Ville Nouvelle

Staying in the ugly, sprawling *ville nouvelle* means additional comfort but also additional cost, and the inconvenience of shuttling across the Oued Boufrekane or just retiring early. (Nearly everything in the *ville nouvelle* closes after 11pm.) Some of the least expensive hotels are found along **avenue Allal ben Abdallah.**

Youth Hostel (IYHF), ave. Okba Ibn Nafi (tel. 246 98), near the Stade Municipal. Follow the arrows toward Hotel Trans Atlantique. Spartan rooms around a verdant garden. Outdoor café tables as well as indoor facilities. Clean toilets. Warden is helpful, informative, and dedicated. No curfew. Reception open May-late Sept. Mon.-Sat. 7-10am, noon-4pm, and 7pm-midnight, Sun. 7-10am and 6pm-midnight; Oct.-late Apr. Mon.-Sat. 8-10am, noon-3pm, and 6-10:30pm, Sun. 8-10am and 6-10:30pm. 10dh per person with card. Breakfast 3.50dh.

Hotel Moderne, 54 ave. Allal Ben Abdallah (tel. 217 43), 2 blocks straight out from the small train station. Clean rooms with small balconies. Singles 85dh, with shower 108dh. Doubles 100dh, with shower 125dh. No hot water.

Hotel Touring, 34 ave. Allal Ben Abdallah (tel. 223 51). Clean and spacious rooms. Singles 46dh, with shower 56dh. Doubles 68dh, with shower 79dh.

Hotel Excelsior, 57 ave. des Forces Armées Royales (tel. 219 00). Clean, recently renovated rooms on a big avenue that runs in front of CTM station. Singles 45dh, with shower 62dh. Doubles 64dh, with shower 81dh.

Hotel Continental, 92 ave. des Forces Armées Royales (tel. 202 00), hidden behind Restaurant Continental. Comfortable, clean, and airy. Singles 51dh, with shower 70dh. Doubles with shower 88dh.

Hotel Majestic, 19 ave. Mohammed V (tel. 220 35), closest to the small train station. Neat, spacious rooms; gracious management; spotless showers; and a rustic motif in the hallways. Engaging, if incongruous, bamboo walls and wooden doors. Singles 65dh, with shower 87dh. Doubles 87dh, with shower 104dh.

The municipal **Camping Agdal** (tel. 307 12)—the nicest place to stay in Meknes—lies on the side of the tomb of Moulay Ismail opposite the medina, just beyond the ramparts of the old city, next door to the Agricultural Park, and near the Heri. The complex is in a wooded park above a beautiful lake, originally part of the imperial palace gardens, and has excellent amenities, including hot showers, a grocery store, and cooking facilities. Crowds come here in the summer. (10dh per adult, 5dh per child, 5dh per tent, 5dh per car, and 6dh per shower. Rooms 50dh. Reception open daily 8am-1pm and 4-8pm.) The **restaurant** serves a three-course *menu* for 30dh. Hitchhikers can find rides here.

Food

The best belly-filling bargains come sizzling off the one-person stalls along **rue Dar Smen** in the medina, between ave. Roumazine and pl. el-Hedime. Here, whole lambs hang on hooks, and well-done brochettes cost 1dh each. On **place el-Hedime,** try a glass of fresh orange juice for 2dh and, in the evening, a bowl of piping hot *harira* for 2dh.

Rotisserie Oumnia, 8 Derb Ain el-Fouki, across ave. Roumazine from the Apollo Cinema. Too many tourists, but still a good deal. Order from the 30dh *menu.* Ask to sit in the plush *salon marocain,* behind the kitchen. The server will tell you that you are eating in his or her home, and it almost seems like it—genuine Moroccan hospitality and setting. Open daily 10am-10pm.

Rotisserie Karim, 2 ave. Ghannah (tel. 224 75), in the *ville nouvelle,* right off ave. Hassan II. Their 20dh *menu* features *salade marocaine,* a choice of hamburger or *poulet roti,* and dessert. The 24dh *menu* offers a *tajine* entree. Open daily 11am-11pm.

Restaurant la Coupole, rue Ghannah (tel. 224 83), across the street from Rotisserie Karim. More expensive, but excellent food. Try the delicate chicken *tajine* with lemon and olives (30dh). Service charge is not included. Open daily noon-3pm and 7-10pm.

Restaurant Novelty, 12 rue de Paris (tel. 221 56), at rue d'Annaba. Plastic setting. A complete dinner of salad, sausage, fried calves' brains, and dessert 35dh. Open daily 11am-11pm.

Sights and Entertainment

Emasculated by decades of war and weathering, the ramparts of the **Dar el-Kebira** (Imperial City) still testify to Meknes's former preeminence as a capital city. The ruthless Moulay Ismail spared no effort in the realization of his architectural ambitions. Strolling about the site with a pickax in hand, he personally supervised the city's construction, encouraging, criticizing, and flogging at will. Plundering priceless materials from other parts of the kingdom (notably from the Badi Palace in Marrakech and Roman marble from Volubilis), the sultan raised for himself a radiant city. But the fantasy was fleeting: The Lisbon earthquake of 1755 and several subsequent wars took their toll on the great palace, sparing only the heavy walls and several large monuments. The most tell-tale remnant is **Bab Mansour,** one of Morocco's most awesome gateways. Its splendid tilework is in Meknes's traditional green and black. The impressive main arch is flanked by marble Corinthian columns, while crenelated ramparts stretch away in either direction.

Passing through the Bab, shake off the amiable guides and hug the wall to your right; after the second gate, keep to the right and you'll see the emerald green roof of the little **Salle des Ambassadeurs.** Now rebuilt, this is where Moulay Ismail conducted diplomatic meetings. Ask the guard to unlock the door leading to the underground **Christian Dungeon,** where the sultans kept 60,000 Christian slaves. (Open Sat.-Thurs. 8:30am-noon and 2:30-6pm, Fri. 8am-noon and 3-6pm.)

As you leave the dungeon, walk through the arch marked by the blue arrow to the left; here stands the mosque that houses the **Tomb of Moulay Ismail.** The number 1082, posted on the front door, is the Islamic year in which Moulay Ismail began his 57-year reign. Not surprisingly, the "Roi Soleil" of Morocco built himself a resting place more like a palace than a mausoleum. It's the only mosque in Morocco open to non-Muslims, but you must dress modestly to gain entrance. Men should cover their legs and shoulders; women should hide everything but their heads. When you reach the tomb proper, remove your shoes and proceed into the prayer area, where crisp straw mats crunch softly under your feet. All the creamy, finely sculpted marble gracing the tomb was imported from Italy. (Open Mon.-Sat. 8am-noon and 2-6pm. Admission 3dh.)

As you exit Bab Mansour, walk straight across busy pl. el-Hedime to the huge polychrome mosaic on the outer wall of the nineteenth-century **Dar Jamai Palace.** This courtly mansion was raised by Moulay Hassan's powerful vizier Jamai, whose second residence in Fes bears the same name. Today the **Museum of Moroccan Art** (tel. 308 63), the palace houses the usual assortment of Koranic parchments, traditional garb, tools, and trinkets. More interesting is the stunning if somewhat bizarre interior, assembled from fragments of earlier seventeenth- and eighteenth-century mosques and *medersas.* Stroll through the shady courtyard garden and climb upstairs to view the luxurious master bedroom, strewn with dozens of embroidered divans and crowned with a magnificent cupola. (Open Sat.-Thurs. 8am-noon and 3-6pm. Admission 3dh.)

As you leave the palace, immediately turn left onto rue Sidi Amar to enter the medina. Follow the alley as it turns left and then forks right to the splendid green, glazed tile minaret of the **Mosquée Kebira** (Great Mosque). Directly across from the mosque is the breathtaking fourteenth-century **Medersa Bou Inania,** an outstanding example of Merinid architecture. Come here for relief from the heavy-handed opulence of Moulay Ismail's monuments. The roof (a terrace) affords a superb close-up view of the mosque. (Open 9am-noon and 4-7pm; in off-season 8am-noon and 2:30-6pm. Admission 3dh.)

Meknes's **medina** sways and hums with a rhythm all its own. Spacious, well-worn streets roofed with scalloped sheets of tin run down and across its length. In mornings and early evenings, the alleys teem with merchants and their stalls, juice bars, and barbershops. Start just west of the Dar Jamai; as you face the museum, take the alley to the left of the entrance. Plunge straight ahead, past drooping loops of braided silk rope, Berber carpets, and rows of embroidered *babouches* to reach **Souk en Nejjarin,** a major east-west thoroughfare lined with shops and stands of every imaginable variety. Bear east (right) past the Medersa of Bou Inania, then south onto the alleyway hugging the eastern wall of the Great Mosque. After passing a couple of lavish portals, watch for a tiny opening on the left, signaled by a set of crumbling, beautifully painted cedar doors. This is the crowded **Berber Market,** where you can watch metalworkers hammer silver into tiny chests, cups, and plates. Sporadic auctions—volatile affairs where local women occasionally come to blows over the merchandise—are held nearby following afternoon prayer. To cover the medina from bottom to top, return by **rue Karmouni.** This street rambles north through the **El-Mansour Palace,** a nineteenth-century residential area now transformed into a *souk.* Back at pl. el-Hedime, beside Bab Mansour, don't miss the **vegetable market.**

The **Agdal Basin** was originally intended for use as a private pool for Moulay Ismail's wives and a reservoir in case of siege. The lake now irrigates the numerous gardens and meadows that crowd the city environs. To reach the basin, head east from Bab Mansour, following the imperial walls halfway round. A wide staircase leads up the hill to a shady park overlooking the reservoir. Tiny **Café Agdal** serves cold drinks here for 3dh. Back beside the staircase, a doorway opens into the **Héri** (storehouse), a gargantuan granary with enormous cisterns and an endless succession of arcaded stables that once housed 12,000 horses. A long but invigorating hike from here northeast along the walls past the Agdal Basin will bring you to **Bab el-Khemis,** the magnificent western gateway to the city. Northeast of the Agdal reservoir, just beside the campground on the far side of the fortifications, stretch the **Agricultural Grounds,** the perfect spot for a shady picnic or evening promenade.

Just about the only live evening **entertainment** is in the *ville nouvelle* at the Hotel Rif, on rue Accra (tel. 225 91), near the post office on pl. Administrative. There is a belly dance floorshow nightly (8-10pm) followed by disco music. (Admission 80dh, including 1 drink.)

Near Meknes

Moulay-Idriss

The white burial place of Moulay Idriss I reminded Edith Wharton of cream cheese; bring your own bagel. Founder of the country's first dynasty, the Royal Kingdom of Morocco, and the city of Fes, Moulay Idriss I was the first to successfully unify the Berber tribes. Feared and respected for the force of his *baraka* (mystical powers), he was elected *imam* of the local tribespeople. During his active life, he acquired 500 wives, 1000 children, and 12,000 horses. After his death in 791, the city of Moulay-Idriss grew up around his tomb, which is still revered as the country's most sacred religious shrine. Within city limits, bars, cinemas, banks, swimming pools, and hotels are strictly forbidden. Non-Muslims are not permitted to spend the night. (Even the English and French instructors who teach in the local school are required to commute.) But if you conduct yourself with sensitivity and respect (don't wear shorts and don't enter places of worship), you'll find the locals perfectly hospitable. No matter what the fast-talking guides at the approach to the city may claim, you do not need their services.

Thirty kilometers directly north of Meknes, Moulay-Idriss climbs up and around the twin conical hills of **Tasga** and **Khiber.** In the hollow between the hills, you'll see the handsome minaret and emerald green roofing of the **Great Mosque,** the town's showpiece. Adjoining it is the sacred **Mausoleum of Moulay Idriss,** where the faithful whisper their prayers. The medina is a wonderful labyrinth of cobbled streets, commercial passageways, and cheerful *souks.* Come for the Saturday market. Climb down to the base of Tasga, and back up to the parking lot at the top of Khiber to view a lovely, green-striped cylindrical minaret.

The most important *moussem* in Morocco is celebrated at Moulay-Idriss. Starting on the last Thursday in August and lasting several weeks, celebrations alternate with sacrifices and prayers. Ask the tourist office in Meknes for details. Buses to Moulay-Idriss leave the Bab Mansour station approximately hourly (3.50dh); collective taxis cost 5dh.

Volubilis

Once a thriving metropolis of 20,000, Volubilis is the best-preserved Roman site in Morocco. Its premier attraction is an extensive collection of Roman mosaics that bask beneath the scalding North African sun. Founded in 25 B.C.E. by the Berber king of Mauritania, Juba II, the city flourished under Roman rule, reaching its zenith during the second century C.E. as capital of the province of Mauritania Tingitania. In the eighth century, Moulay-Idriss siphoned the population off into Fes and Meknes; Volubilis was left to an isolated colony of Jews and Christianized Berbers.

The **city walls** still stretch for over 2350m around the site. Pick your way through the paths to reach the **House of Orpheus,** so named for one of the fine mosaics that pave its floors. Just up the road, several Corinthian columns jut defiantly above the crumbled ruins at the **Capitole,** a former temple. The **Decumanus Maximus,** a wide boulevard surrounded by ruins, marches straight up the hill to the **Porte de Tanger,** a lone archway leading out of the crumbled city. From the top, there's a terrific view of Moulay-Idriss clinging to the sides of its two hills. Notice the stone-covered aqueduct running up the length of the Decumanus; it channeled water through the city and over the brilliant mosaics so that wealthy Romans could stroll about on cool stones all summer long. Return to the entrance via the Porte de Tanger for a sweeping view of the whole site. (Open 8am-6:30pm. Admission 8dh.) The **Café-Restaurant Corbeille Florie** offers a filling, five-course *menu* for 40dh and beverages for 3.50dh.

The only lodgings in the immediate vicinity are the monastic quarters of the **Refuge Zerhoun** (tel. 440 10 or 441 03), 1km north of Volubilis, off the road to Col du Zegotta (3dh per person; no women allowed).

Volubilis lies 3km from Moulay-Idriss; you can walk, hitch, take one of the occasional collective taxis, or hire a cab from Meknes to take you to both Moulay-Idriss and Volubilis (round-trip 60dh). The parking lot at Volubilis is a great place to hitch rides from other travelers.

Fes

Once the capital of Moroccan intellectual, political, and religious life, Fes survives as a crumbling monument to former glory. The foremost symbol of its decline is the Karaouiyne, reputed to be the oldest university in the world (founded in 859 C.E.). The Karaouiyne nurtured many great minds, including that of Pope Sylvester II, who introduced algebra and the number system to Europe. Today the university is solely a Koranic school, all other studies having moved to Rabat. As a religious center the city retains little of its past influence. To the outsider's eye, Fes's decline seems merely seems to have sharpened the exoticism of the city—all at the expense, however, of an impoverished populace.

Labyrinthine and fortified, Fes has never treated its invaders gently. Travelers who presume to penetrate the city today should be prepared for a devastating counterattack. Even before you stumble from the bus, the cacophony of multilingual greetings and the groping hands of hustlers besiege you through the windows. At its worst, a visit to Fes is enervating and infuriating. At its best, the siege of the senses can be exhilarating. Within the old walls are the smells and sounds of a cauldron of activity simmering since medieval times. The ringing of hammers on sheets of brass, the droning wail of the prayer-criers from countless minarets, children balancing trays of rolled dough on their heads, the thicket of bodies in the needle-narrow streets, the mouth-watering aroma of brochettes on open grills, the acrid whiffs of hash, the stench of tanning lye, donkey droppings, and the sweet scents of cedar shavings and freshly cut mint leaves—here is the medina of medinas, its delights and frustrations both larger than life.

Orientation and Practical Information

Fes is an extreme case of the modern Moroccan paradox: The broad, orderly boulevards of the French-built **ville nouvelle** seem far removed from the knotted tangle of the most labyrinthine of Morocco's medinas. The CTM station in the heart of the new city forms an equilateral triangle with the bus station at the **Bab Boujeloud** entrance to the medina and the train station at the outskirts of the *ville nouvelle.* The old city is divided into two fortified sections. **Fes el-Bali** (Old Fes) was founded in the ninth century by Moulay Idriss I. (His son, Idriss II, made the city his capital.) This section can be traversed along **rue Tala Kebira,** which runs southwest-northeast from Bab Boujeloud to the Karaouiyne Mosque. As you leave the medina through Bab Boujeloud, you'll meet **avenue des Français.** This leads to the entrance to the second part of the old city, **Fes el-Jdid** (New Fes), built under the Merinid

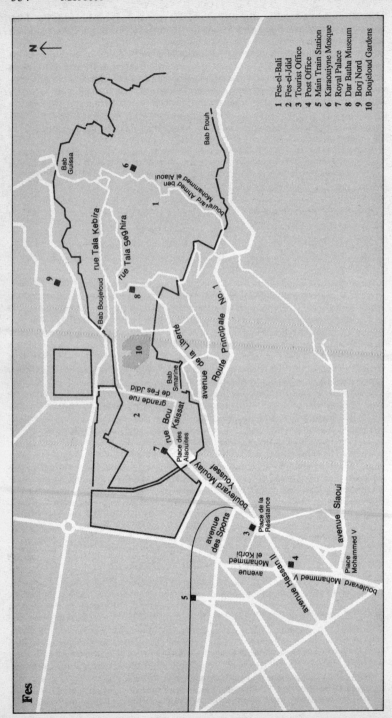

Fes

1 Fes-el-Bali
2 Fes-el-Jdid
3 Tourist Office
4 Post Office
5 Main Train Station
6 Karaouiyne Mosque
7 Royal Palace
8 Dar Batha Museum
9 Borj Nord
10 Boujeloud Gardens

Dynasty in the thirteenth century. South of this entrance is **grande rue de Fes Jdid,** a dead end. Here, **rue Bou Ksissat** leads (to the right) to the Royal Palace at Place des Alaouites.

You can reach Bab Boujeloud from the *ville nouvelle* either by *petit taxi* (8dh) or by bus #2 or 9 (1.10 dh) from the stop on **avenue Hassan II,** near **place de la Résistance,** the hub for most of the city's buses. Bus #18 runs from pl. de la Résistance to Bab Ftouh at the opposite end of the medina, near the Andalous Quarter. Bus #3 runs to Place des Alaouites, the entrance to Fes el-Jdid.

Office National Marocain du Tourisme (ONMT): pl. de la Résistance (tel. 23 46 0), at ave. Hassan II. From the CTM station, turn left onto blvd. Mohammed V and then right past the post office onto palm-lined ave. Hassan II; it's 5 blocks up on the left. From the train station, head straight along rue Chenguit, bear left at pl. Kennedy along ave. de France, and turn left on ave. Hassan II; also 5 blocks up on the left. From Bab Boujeloud Gare Routière, your best bet is a *petit taxi* (5dh). Friendly and helpful staff speaks English and dispenses sketchy maps. Open July to mid-Sept. Mon.-Fri. 8am-2pm; mid-Sept. to June Mon.-Fri. 8:30am-noon and 2:30-6:30pm; Ramadan Mon.-Fri. 9am-3pm.

Syndicat d'Initiative: pl. Mohammed V. (tel. 247 69), on blvd. Mohammed V. Also friendly, but not as well stocked as ONMT. Maps available. Official guides hang out here (30dh per ½-day). Open Mon.-Fri. 8:30-11:30am and 4:15-6pm, Sat. 8:30-11:30am; Ramadan Mon.-Fri. 10am-3pm.

After-Hours Currency Exchange: Les Merinides, in the Borj Nord (tel. 452 25). Open daily 6-10pm.

Post Office: At ave. Hassan II and blvd. Mohammed V in the *ville nouvelle.* Poste Restante. Open July-Sept. 15 Mon.-Fri. 8am-3pm; Sept. 16-June Mon.-Thurs. 8:30am-noon and 2:30-6:45pm, Fri. 8:30-11:30am and 3-6pm; Ramadan Mon.-Fri. 9am-2pm. Stamps also sold from the Hassan II entrance Sat. 8-11am. Branch offices at pl. d'Atlas and in the medina at pl. Batha. Open same hours Mon.-Fri.

Telephones: In the main post office. International calls and **telegrams.** Enter from blvd. Mohammed V. Open daily 8am-9pm. **Telephone Code: 06.**

Airport: Aèrodrome de Fes-Saiss, 12km out of town along the road to Immouzzér (tel. 247 12 or 247 99). To Casablanca (205dh), Marrakech (335dh), Agadir (510dh), Oujda, Rabat, and Tangier, as well as occasional flights to Paris. Catch bus #16 at pl. Mohammed V (2dh) or get a collective taxi (5dh if full). **Royal Air Maroc,** ave. Hassan II (tel. 255 16 or 255 17).

Train Station: ave. des Almohades (tel. 250 01), at rue Chenguit. 2nd-class prices are slightly higher than buses, but trains are more comfortable. To Casablanca (8 per day, 66dh, change for Marrakech), Rabat (8 per day, 47dh), Meknes (9 per day, 11.40dh), Oujda (4 per day, 60.50dh), Tangier (3 per day, only direct connection at 1:16pm, 64dh).

Bus Stations: CTM, blvd. Mohammed V (tel. 220 41 or 220 42), at rue Ksar el-Kebir. To Rabat (7 per day, 36.10dh), Casablanca (7 per day, 53dh), Marrakech (2 per day, 53.85dh), Meknes (4 per day, 9.65dh), Tangier (1 per day, 47.30dh), Tetuan (1 per day, 42.25dh), Ouezzane (1 per day, 30dh), Taza and Oujda (1 per day). The **SMTL station,** just behind the CTM, has more buses to the Middle Atlas from **Gare Routière,** Bab Boujeloud (tel 335 29). Buses leave when full.

Taxis: Major stands at the post office, the syndicat d'initiative, Bab Boujeloud, and (in case you emerge from the wrong end of the medina) Bab Guissa. Intra-city taxi and bus fares double July-Sept. 15 after 8:30pm, Sept. 16-June after 8pm.

Car Rental: Avis, 23 rue de la Liberté (tel. 217 76). **Hertz,** Hotel de Fes, ave. des Forces Armées Royales (tel. 228 12), at the southwestern end of ave. Hassan II. **Goldcar,** 2 blvd. Mohammed V (tel. 204 95).

English Bookstore: English Bookstore of Fes, 68 ave. Hassan II (tel. 208 42), near pl. de la Résistance. Large selection of novels and guide books as well as phrase books. Delightful English-speaking staff. Open Mon.-Fri. 8:30am-12:30pm and 3-7pm.

Maps: Librarie du Centre, blvd. Mohammed V (tel. 225 69), near the main post office. Also French-Arabic phrase books. Open Mon.-Fri. 9am-12:30pm and 3-8pm.

Swimming Pools: Municipal Pool, ave. des Sports, near the stadium in the *ville nouvelle.* Very crowded. Open July-Sept. 15. Admission 5dh. **Camping Moulay Slimane** (tel. 415 37). Call ahead to see if there's water. **Hotel de Fes,** ave. des Forces Armées Royales (tel. 230 06), at the opposite end of ave. Hassan II from the tourist office. A beautiful pool; call ahead to see if there's room for nonguests. If not, try **Hotel Zalaah**, ave. Mohammed Diouri.

After-Hours Pharmacy: In the Municipalité de Fes, blvd. Moulay Youssef (tel. 233 80). Open daily 8pm-8am.

Police: Tel. 19.

Accommodations and Camping

Ville Nouvelle

The new city is nondescript and far from the medina, but attractive in comparision to the old city, where hustlers are so aggressive that travelers staying in the medina often feel like prisoners in their rooms. All of the inexpensive lodgings in the *ville nouvelle* cluster conveniently on or just off the west side of **boulevard Mohammed V** between ave. Slaoui, near the train station, and ave. Hassan II, near the post office.

Auberge de Jeunesse (IYHF), rue Abdsalam-Sergeni (tel. 240 85). From the ONMT tourist office, cross the street, turn left onto blvd. Chechaouèn, walk 4 blocks, turn left to the street below, and look for the sign. Friendly, English-speaking proprietors. Reasonably clean rooms and showers with hot water in winter only. Open daily 8-9am, noon-3pm, 6-10pm. 10dh, nonmembers 12.50dh. IYHF card available 75dh and 2 photos.

Hotel Central, 50 rue Nador (tel. 223 33), 3 blocks from the CTM station, off blvd. Mohammed V. Often full in summer—come early. Fine management and tidy rooms. Singles 43dh, with bath 62dh. Doubles 69dh, with bath 81dh. Common hot shower around back.

Hotel Excelsior, 107 rue Larbi el Kaghat (tel. 256 02), 3 more blocks down blvd. Mohammed V. Clean rooms, some with carpets; sanitary toilets and showers. Hot water in winter only. Singles with shower 54dh. Doubles with shower 69dh.

Hotel Jeanne d'Arc, 36 ave. Slaoui (tel. 212 23), up the next street on the right from Excelsior. Plain but clean rooms. Adequate facilities. Singles 30dh. Doubles 40dh.

Hotel Renaissance, 47 rue Abdelkrim el-Khattabi (tel. 221 93), near pl. Mohammed V. Reasonably clean rooms; those with balconies overlooking the street are less musty. Singles 25dh. Doubles 40dh.

Fes el-Bali

The few budget accommodations here cluster just around **Bab Boujeloud** and charge as much as the market will bear. Come prepared to haggle. Cleanliness may prove a problem.

Hotel du Jardin Public, 153 Kasbah Boujeloud (tel. 330 86), a small alley, the first on your right as you approach Bab Boujeloud from outside the medina. Relatively sanitary rooms, some with good views. Winding hallways surround a small, airy lobby, where you can chat with the friendly staff. Singles 25dh. Doubles 35dh. Moroccan showers and toilets. Hot water 4dh (on tap in winter only).

Hotel Erraha (tel. 332 26), 1 block farther from the *bab,* also on the right as you approach. Helpful owner speaks only Arabic. Small rooms open onto an airy lobby. Singles 25dh. Doubles 35dh. Showers and clean tiled toilets included.

Hotel Cascade, just inside the Bab on the right (tel. 339 91). Adequate rooms. Rooftop terrace and large, yellow foyers. Passable pit toilets and cold showers. Singles 30dh. doubles 40dh.

Fes el-Jdid

Escape the new city prices and the Bab Boujeloud hustlers here. The lively main street, **grande rue de Fes Jhdid,** runs from Bab Smarine, near the Palais Royal, to Bab de Kakene, near the Boujeloud gardens.

Hotel le Croissant, 285 grande rue de Fes Jhdid (tel. 256 37). You guessed it: hot and flaky. Some rooms with balconies overlooking the street. Better rooms off a renovated court in back. Singles 20dh. Doubles 35dh.

Hotel du Parc, at the other end of grande rue Fes de Jhdid (no phone), near ave. des Français. Same recipe. Singles 20dh. Doubles 30dh.

Food

Ville Nouvelle

Inexpensive food awaits on the little streets to either side of **boulevard Mohammed V.** Beware that restaurants in the new city sometimes overcharge tourists by either adding the bill incorrectly or charging you for dishes you never ordered. **Rue Kaid Ahmed** has a number of good places. To get here, walk a few blocks down blvd. Mohammed V from the main post office. The street will be on your left.

For a great breakfast, pick up some pastries at the **Boulangerie Patisserie Epi D'or** at 81 blvd. Mohammed V, then continue along the street to **Café Zanzi Bar** at rue Abdelkrim el-Khattabi, where you can sip some of the best coffee and mint tea in Fes.

Casse-Croute Belkayat, 41 rue Kaid Ahmed (tel. 266 05). Six skewers of lamb, minced meat, or liver roasted over a smoky grill and served smothered in a spicy tomato sauce, all stuffed in a large pocket of bread (10dh). Open daily 8am-midnight.

Restaurant Chamonix, 5 rue Kaid Ahmed (tel. 266 38). Clean. A filling *couscous à la Fassi* (Fes-style) *menu* with *salade marocaine* and dessert 35dh. Open daily 10am-midnight.

Casse Croute, 45 rue Kaid Ahmed (tel 232 06). This family-run establishment offers steaks, liver, *tajines,* or six brochettes for only 15dh. Salad 6dh. Open daily noon-midnight.

Café-Sandwich Rialto, 23 rue Abdelkrim el-Khattabi, off blvd. Mohammed V. (Café Zanzi Bar is on the corner where the 2 streets meet.) Somewhat drab, but soup or salad, steak, vegetables, bread, and dessert cost 40dh. Take a look at the photo of the medina on the wall. Open daily noon-midnight.

Restaurant Es Saada, ave. Slaoui, a couple of blocks off Mohammed V on the right. The 35dh *menu* of delicious, generous portions attracts the locals. Service charge 12-20%. Open daily until 11pm.

Restaurant Roi de la Bière, 59 blvd. Mohammed V (tel. 253 24). One of the most elegant of the city's lower-priced restaurants. The dining room and its beautiful carved ceilings are illuminated by attractive brass lanterns. A/C. 3-course meals 55dh. Open daily noon-4pm and 6pm-midnight.

Restaurant des Voyageurs, 41 blvd. Mohammed V (tel. 255 37), near the CTM station. Try the *menu touristique* of lamb *tajine almondine* with *pastilla* and dessert, all delicious (45dh). Service included. Open daily noon-4pm and 6pm-midnight.

A la Tour d'Argent, 30 ave. Slaoui (tel. 226 89). One of the finest French restaurants in town—be kind to your stomach here. The finest 3-course *menu* costs 60dh. Service 15%.

L'Adour Restaurant, rue Abdelkrim el-Khattabi (tel. 221 48 or 267 70), in the Hotel Splendid. Tasty French cooking in the middle of the budget hotel district. Full meals 75dh.

Fes el-Bali and Fes el-Jdid

Food stalls line the beginning of **Tala Kebira** and **Tala Seghira,** the two streets that split off rue Serrajine as you enter through the *bab.* The food here may not be cheap, especially for foreigners, since no price list is posted, and checks are often "calculated" on an individual basis. Ask for prices before you order. The selection is limited to *couscous, harira,* brochettes, *kefta-burghers* (make sure they're cooked thoroughly), and a jumble of oily, diced tomatoes and cucumbers not really worthy of the name *salade.* The budget eateries here cluster just inside Bab Boujeloud.

Restaurant des Jeunes, 16 rue Serrajine (tel. 349 75), on the right as you enter the *bab.* Best budget restaurant in the medina. *Harira,* lamb *tajine,* veggies, and fresh fruit 25dh. Open daily 6am-midnight.

Restaurant Bouayad, 26 rue Serrajine, on the right and farther down from the above. Try gazelle horn pastry (3dh) for dessert. *Menu* 40dh, student *menu* 17dh. Open 24 hours to serve traveling merchants.

Dar Saada, 21 rue Attarine (tel. 333 43), deep in the heart of the medina. Worth visiting whether you eat here or not: housed in a former palace with cedarwood carvings and arched doorways. Half the palace now serves as an overpriced emporium. The other half serves excellent, expensive Moroccan entrees (36-45dh). Open Sat.-Thurs. 11am-11pm.

A few stands and nameless restaurants do business two-thirds of the way down **grande rue Fes Jdid** toward rue Bou Ksissat. These are somewhat cleaner and cheaper than their Fes el-Bali counterparts. They're not really worth a detour, however, so save these for your trek to the Royal Palace. **Place des Alaouites** has a number of pleasant cafes, where you can sip almond juice mixed with milk (2dh) and recover from sight-seeing.

Sights

The life-sized maze that is the **medina** (15km in circumference) is the largest and most difficult to navigate in Morocco. From your first moment, you will be asked "Do you want to see the medina?" by every man and child on the street. The greatest advantage of having a guide is the guarantee that the other guides and hustlers will stay away for the rest of the day. (See Hustlers and Guides in the Morocco introduction for general advice.) You can hire an **official guide** at either the ONMT tourist office or the syndicat d'initiative. A morning tour costs 30dh and ends at noon, so arrange to meet your guide at 8am to get the most for your money. Especially in summer, visit the medina in the morning, when it's at its liveliest. A "full day" tour costs 50dh, but unless you can make special arrangements, your guide will probably insist on taking two or three hours for lunch and then end the afternoon promptly at 6pm. It may be hard to find an official guide much later than 11am, since many go home if there are no morning takers. Tell the tourist office exactly what you have in mind—what language you want your guide to speak, for instance. When you meet your guide, invest five minutes in making sure he understands what you expect and vice-versa. If you don't like him, ask for another. Remember that the price of an official guide is *not* per person. At the end of the day, your guide may expect a tip; you are not obligated to pay it.

If you're alone and an official guide too expensive (don't forget to figure the costs and maddening frustration of being ripped off by a hustler), be patient and seek out an **unofficial guide** whom you like. Don't pay in advance, allow your camera to be carried, or tour after sunset. If you're with a group, don't be tricked into paying per person: A deluxe three- to four-hour tour should cost less than 25dh. You can always ask what a guide plans to show you and then compare the list with the sights *Let's Go* describes. Avoid all shops (if you buy in the presence of a guide, a hefty commission will be tagged on).

Beware that the oldest and most successful hustler's ploy in Fes is for your guide to blackmail you deep within the medina, usually toward evening, announcing that he will show you the way out only in return for a wad of dirhams. The second oldest trick is for your guide to have you park your car at an obscure side entrance, informing you about an hour later that if you ever want to see it again, it will cost you dearly.

If pride or a sense of adventure compels you to strike out on your own and if not knowing exactly—or even vaguely—where you are doesn't faze you, you should at least prepare yourself for constant harassment by hustlers. If you are armed with a decent map, consider saving Bab Boujeloud until the end of your visit. This will keep the hustlers who hang out there from descending upon you from the start. The best strategy is to enter the medina from a side entrance just before Bab Boujeloud. For example, take a *petit taxi* to Bab Guissa, and work your way down the main streets to Bab Boujeloud. From pl. de l'Istiqlal, just downhill from the Dar Batha Museum, head to the top of the square. Bear left, then immediately right down a long, skinny street. Cross the first busy thoroughfare you meet, passing the Mosque of Sidi Lezzaz. The next big street will be **Tala Kebira,** the main artery commencing at Bab Boujeloud and running the full length of the medina. Alternately, enter Bab Boujeloud on the heels of a tour group and try to blend in until you leave the hustlers behind. If you have a car, park just outside Bab Boujeloud at pl. Moulay Idriss—this way you'll be able to easily find your car later. If you have a map, park in the small lot near Bab Ftouh, and begin your tour from the rear of the medina. Better still, take a bus to the medina.

When you get lost in the medina, ask people to point you back to the *bab*. Choose your own sources of information—don't let them choose you. Shopkeepers are usually reliable, while would-be "guides" will misinform you about opening hours and street directions in order to shake your confidence.

Dar Batha and Bab Boujeloud

One of Morocco's most well-kept and beautiful museums, the **Dar Batha,** is housed in a lovely nineteenth-century palace. The spacious Moorish mansion was headquarters for Sultan Hassan I and his son Moulay Abd el-Aziz during the final years of Moroccan royal decadence before the French occupation. The extraordinary collection features Moroccan folk art, including intricately illuminated Koranic manuscripts penned in multicolored inks, a stamp collection, a number of musical instruments (including a Stradivarius violin), fine embroidery, Berber carpets, and excellent *mashrabiyya* and wood sculptures from the local *medersas* and mosques.

To reach the Dar Batha from the *ville nouvelle,* take bus #9 in front of the Grand Hotel or a *petit taxi* to pl. l'Istiqlal outside the medina near Bab Boujeloud, and look for the pyramidal, green tile roofs of the palace. Turn left at the corner from the bus stop to enter the square and head up the hill on your first left. The entrance is marked by red flags on your right. (Open Wed.-Thurs. and Sat.-Mon. 8am-noon and 3:30-6:30pm, Fri. 4-6:30pm. Admission 3dh.) During the *moussem* of Moulay Idriss in September, the museum is the scene of concerts of traditional Moroccan music.

Fes el-Bali

Plan on at least a full morning to make your tour of Fes el-Bali (Old Fes). From Tala Kebira, just inside Bab Boujeloud, keep your eyes peeled for a carved wooden contraption on the left that overlooks the street from the second story of an ancient shop (just after the Mosque of Sidi Lezzaz). This is the **medieval clock,** which dating from 1357, is Fes's oldest timepiece. The circular bronze hammers strapped to its ornate facade pounded the hour out in booming, musical notes. Across the street awaits the **Medersa of Bou Inania,** the best-preserved Koranic school in Morocco. Built under the Merinid Dynasty in the mid-fourteenth century, its beautifully carved white plastered walls and *mihrab* remain in remarkably good condition. The attached mosque, adorned by the original colorful glass windows, is separated from the school by a tiny canal. (Open daily 8:30am-1pm and 4-7pm. Admission 3dh.)

Back on rue Tala Kebira, head right, passing the **Tijania Zaouia** on your immediate left. Next door is the trim **Mosque of Sidi Ahmed Tijani,** graced by an elegant minaret. As you plunge ahead on Tala Kebira, watch carefully for side-street *fondouks,* two-story neighborhood **souks** set up in private courtyards. On your left, you'll come to a colorful fountain where cool water spouts into a rectangular basin. Pursue the main route a bit farther until a small, tiled minaret appears on your right; this is the **Mzara of Moulay Idriss,** an ancient house of worship. According to legend, Sultan Moulay Idriss I sat here when he announced that a city should be founded on the spot. Next door is the lively **drum makers' fondouk,** where traditional ceramic tamtams of all sizes and shapes are displayed. Just up and across the street, in the **sheepskin fondouk,** untanned woolly hides are bartered by the dozen. From here, rue Tala Kebira bows slightly to the right, changing its name to **rue ech Cherabliyyan.** Around the corner on the left is a traditional **hamman** (bath). Peek in the doorway to glimpse the interior. Up the road, at the crest of a hill, is a view of the **Cherabliyyan Mosque,** with one of the most picturesque minarets in Fes. Hack your way onward through the crowds entering the **leather souk,** where wallets, sandals, belts, bags, and bracelets cram the alley.

In the thick of this area, take a narrow right and then your first left to reach **place Nejarine,** a small, triangular plaza dominated by Fes's most beautiful tiled fountain, the **Fontaine Nejarine.** Women and small children gather here to socialize and collect their household water. Just below, an arched doorway leads into the **Nejarine Fondouk,** a fabulous eighteenth-century shopping area of delicate *mashrabiyya* and handsome balconies. If the door is locked, peer through the crack for a peek at the remarkable interior. Across the way is a lively **carpenters' fondouk,** where skilled artisans whittle, plane, sand, and hammer cedarwood chests and tables.

At the opposite end of the plaza from the fountain is one corner of the great **Zaouia of Moulay Idriss II,** honoring the saint, sultan, and son of the founder of Fes. The Zaouia includes the Mosque of Chorfa. Inside, an ornate shrine houses the saint's tomb. You can glimpse the intricate stalactite ceiling and the exquisite *mihrab* through the door. The wide doorway also affords a view of the faithful worshipers who arrive each morning to pray at the tomb. Around the side, counterclockwise from the main doorway, watch for a tiny brass star with a gold slot set in the wall of the shrine. From here, you can touch the back of the tomb—a practice believed to channel **baraka** (good luck) from the saint to his followers. Surrounding shops sell candles to burn as offerings. The **henna souk,** a steep side street up the western wall of the shrine, is a fragrant, spice-filled alley. Look for the bright orange diamond patterns tatooed on the hands of local women with this natural dye. Also notice the blue tatoos on the forehead and chin of many of the women. These tatoos specify individual Berber tribes.

Return to the Zaouia, passing its great doorway and skirting its southern wall counter-clockwise. Make a left turn at the corner of the building and then take an immediate right to reach the **Karaouiyne Mosque,** the largest in northern Africa. (If you're lost, just look for its 10th-century minaret, which rises majestically above the frenzied labyrinth.) Every Friday, 2000 faithful flock here to worship—though the mosque can hold up to 20,000 men and 2000 women, who worship on the sides and behind the men. The mosque is said to have been founded in 857 by Fatima, daughter of the founder of Karaouiyne (Kairouan in modern-day Tunisia). Today, the mosque houses Karaouiyne University, where a few hundred students study Koranic law. Although the most exquisite portions of the interior are off-limits, the view through the front portal is still a treat. Notice the tiled canal bordering the entrance: Worshipers can remove their shoes and simply walk through to clean their feet before praying. Walk clockwise around the mosque to view the shimmering interior from several different angles. On the way, you'll pass the **Medersa el-Attarine,** at the top of the first main intersection. It's the finest Merinid monument in Fes, and the prayer hall is now open to all. (Open 8am-noon and 4-7pm. Admission is a 3dh tip for the guard.)

Continuing clockwise around the Karaouiyne Mosque, after the next sharp right-hand corner, you'll see a beautiful *fondouk.* Farther on, hugging the walls of the great mosque, the **Palais de Fes** will appear on your left. Once a luxurious mansion, the palace now houses a grand carpet emporium. Continue south along the walls of the mosque until you reach **place Seffarine;** it's the noisiest spot in the medina. Smiths hammer out enormous metal cauldrons while artisans cut and chisel their sheets of copper into works of art. On the left stands the thirteenth-century **Medersa Seffarine.** Dating from 1280, this is the oldest Merinid Koranic school in Morocco. Its roof offers a fascinating view of the buzzing hive of the medina. From pl. Seffarine, complete your circle of the Karaouiyne Mosque, rounding the corner until the seventeenth-century **Medersa ech Cherratin** appears on your left.

Returning to pl. Seffarine, walk around the Medersa Seffarine and bear left, following the skinny, cobbled side street north until you notice an overpowering, pungent scent. A miniscule alley on your right leads from here straight down into the large, outdoor **leather tannery.** No guides are necessary since everything is in plain view in the courtyard, where you can wander freely. The skins are first soaked in a green liquid to remove all hair and rinsed in a cross between a washing machine and a cement mixer. Next, the sheepskins and goatskins are soaked in diluted pigeon excrement to make them more supple, while the cowhides and camelhides are immersed in a porridge of water-logged wheat husks to the same end. After another rinse, the goatskins are sunk in a vat of yellow dye (a saffron and grenadine mix), while the cowskins and camelskins are placed in a brown cedarwood dye, and the sheephides are lowered into a red dye extracted from poppies. All skins are then placed on the roof to dry. The process takes anywhere from a few months to a year.

Turn left as you exit the tanneries and take your first left where the route bends right; turn immediately left again to reach the **Pont Bein el-Moudoun** over the **Oued Fes,** a murky gray river even before it reaches the tanneries. To your right and slightly behind you up the hill sprouts the cheerful green minaret of the **Mosque el-Rsif.** From here, you can either cross the *oued* and head straight into the Andalous Quarter, or you can return to pl. Seffarine and head for the smoky **wool and silk dyers' row.** Take the road leading south from beside the Medersa Seffarine and away from the Karaouiyne Mosque; head left at the fork and make a sharp right when you reach the river. The dyes here are boiled over wood fires blazing in old garbage cans. The finished skeins of wool in brilliant crimson, green, and golden yellow are so shiny that they appear wet even when dry. From here, the covered Pont Sidi el-Aouad humps over the river, and leads into the Andalous Quarter.

Andalous Quarter

Across the Oued Fes from the heart of Fes el-Bali lies the Andalous Quarter. Though once a separate region, it has now been absorbed into the medina. During the Christian Reconquest of Spain in the late fifteenth century, Spanish Muslims fled the Iberian peninsula to Morocco. Many of these displaced Moors resettled around the great Almohad house of worship in Fes now known as the **Andalous Mosque.** The city's second largest religious monument, the mosque's main attraction to non-Muslims is its grandiose thirteenth-century doorway. To reach the mosque, head northwest from Bab Ftouh on the east end of the medina and take your first major left. If you're coming from Fes el-Bali, cross over the Oued Fes at Port Bein el-Moudoun near the tanneries, and head straight down rue Seffrah to the mosque; or cross at Pont Sidi el-Aouad near the dyers' *souk,* bear left at the fork, then left again at the end of the street.

A few doors southwest of the mosque stands the **Medersa es Sahrij,** an elegant Koranic school dating from 1321. Nearby is the smaller **Medersa es Sebbaiyin,** with an interesting facade and ornate interior. Farther down the same street from the Andalous Mosque, the nineteenth-century **Medersa el-Oued** sparkles even under a grimy layer of dust, with intricate, carving and a tiny courtyard.

Fes el-Jdid

Constructed by the Merinids in the thirteenth century on the edge of the old medina, Fes el-Jdid (New Fes) has hosted a series of communities distinct in various ways from the resident Muslim population. Inhabited for centuries by Christian families, the quarter later housed Fes's Jewish residents. Traces of an ancient synagogue still lie within the bowels of the district. Today, the 700-year-old neighborhood retains a medieval aura, with its narrow side streets, covered *souks,* and ornamental *mashrabiyya* balconies. A tour of Fes el-Jdid will take two to three hours and is far easier to negotiate than the labyrinthine medina. There's no need to hire a guide here.

Fes el-Jdid falls into two parts. On the north is the city itself, traversed by the arrow-straight **grande rue de Fes el-Jdid.** To the south is the adjacent *mellah,* cut by its main artery grande rue des Merinides. In the middle of the two areas sits **Bab Semmarin,** a chunky, twentieth-century, crenelated gate. To reach Bab Semmarin from the *ville nouvelle,* take either bus #4 or 9 from in front of the Grand Hotel and tell the driver where you want to go. From Fes el-Bali, bus #9 returns by way of Bab Semmarin. You can also walk from the *ville nouvelle* to the *mellah* (15 min.). Take ave. Hassan II north past the PTT, veer left at the fork 2 blocks later on blvd. Moulay Hassan, and head straight for the Grand Place des Alaouites, where the *mellah* and grand rue des Merinides begin.

Bordering Sultan Hassan II's sprawling modern palace, the **Dar el-Makhzen** is the sweeping patio of **place des Alouites.** The ostentatious brass doors of the king's palace open onto the top of the plaza. Running diagonally off the plaza, grande rue des Merinides runs up to Bab Semmarin on the other end of the *mellah.* Plunge onto this main route and drift past its shops. The meter-wide side streets open into miniature underground tailors' shops, half-timbered houses, and hidden alleyways. At the top of grande rue des Merinides, you'll come to the glittering **jewelers' souk,** with its innumerable bangles and baubles. From here run into **Bab Semmarin,** the entrance to Fes el-Jdid proper. Inside the gate, an animated covered market will be on the right. Cackling chickens, salty fish, dry okra, purple grapes, and shiny eggplants vie for attention. Toward the top of the avenue, the *souks* are covered, shading rainbows of *kaftans* and gold-stitched *babouches.* Bear left at the end into the **Petit Mechouar;** on your left is **Bab Dekaken,** the back entrance to the Dar el-Makhzen. Tunnel straight by and through the tiny archway for a look at the city walls and the Oued Fes. Then retrace your steps and head through **Bab es Seba,** an imperial gate opening onto the **Grand Méchouar,** a roomy plaza lined with streetlamps.

Circuit of the Medina

Fes is actually more enchanting when viewed from without. Borj Nord and Borj Sud can easily be reached by bus, or you can hire a *petit taxi* with a few other travelers and drive the whole circuit. If you're driving, bear east from blvd. Moulay Hassan in the *ville nouvelle* toward Taza and Oujda—the highway winds along the city fortifications. After 4km, take a right-hand turnoff toward **Borj Sud,** a sixteenth-century hilltop fortress guarding the southern end of Fes el-Bali. The castle, built by Christian slaves, is largely in ruins, but it still commands an excellent view of the city. The main highway continues east to **Bab Ftouh,** which sits in a medieval cemetery.

Bend around the eastern end of Fes, hugging the crenelated ramparts, to reach **Bab Khoukha.** From here, the walls curve wildly to **Bab Sidi Boujida.** A kink in the highway then brings you to the **Jamai Palace,** an exquisite nineteenth-century dream house raised by Sultan Moulay Hassan's powerful vizier, and now a luxury hotel. The palace is tucked inside **Bab Guissa,** where a pigeon and parakeet market is held every Friday morning. To continue the circuit, keep to the outer road and follow the signs for Hotel des Merinides, which overlooks the ruins of the **Merinid Tombs.** The tombs once formed the second-largest Merinid necropolis (after the Chellah in Rabat), but little remains of their former glory. At the base of the hill, numerous caves are burrowed out of the hillside. These troglodyte domiciles comprised the **lepers' quarters** in medieval times.

Borj Nord, a short walk down the road from Hotel des Merinides, looks like a crumbling hilltop fortress guarding the northern end of the city. The inside, however, has been renovated and houses the fascinating **Museum of Arms,** an extraordinary cache of weaponry bound to kindle the interest even of pacifists. The guided tour in French takes over an hour. (Open Wed.-Mon. 8:30am-noon and 3-5:30pm. Admission 3dh.)

Consider returning to either Borj Sud or Borj Nord just before sunset: The view of the medina and surrounding countryside is golden.

Ville Nouvelle

The main attraction of the *ville nouvelle* is the superb **Ensemble Artisanal** on blvd. Allah ben Abdallah at the southwestern end of ave. Hassan II. The display features exquisite Arab carpets, Berber blankets, and other examples of handiwork. In the garden of the courtyard you can watch the masterful artisans at work. Look into the weaving rooms where hundreds of young girls in perpetual motion and with hardly a glance at the blueprints, poke, thread, knot, snip, and pack spools of colored wool to create lavish masterpieces in a glorified sweatshop. (Open daily 8:30am-6:30pm.)

Follow local crowds into the busy, aromatic **municipal market,** where the households of Fes stock up on fresh fruit, vegetables, fish, meat, and spices. The market is across the street from Café Zanzi Bar, just off blvd. Mohammed V.

Entertainment

Catch the live Moroccan music, belly-dancing, and wailing in the *salon marocain* of palatial **Restaurant Firadous.** It's in the Palais Jamai complex in the medina, on the right, inside Bab Guissa. An entire evening, beginning with a sumptuous dinner at 8:30pm, costs a cool 140dh, including cover. For a chance to dance, **Night Club Oriental** features disco for a 40dh cover, including one drink. They're in the Grand Hotel on blvd. Chefchaouni (tel. 255 11), in the center of the *ville nouvelle.*

Atlantic Coast

An endless string of breathtaking beaches unfurls along Morocco's sandy Atlantic coastline, punctuated by a handful of major urban centers: Salé, with its ancient fortifications and lively *souk;* Rabat, the spacious capital; Casablanca, Morocco's largest metropolis; and Agadir, a bustling resort. South of Casablanca, the towns of Azemmour, El-Jadida, and Essaouira harbor labyrinthine medinas within their Portuguese walls. Between these cities lie only unspoiled beaches. As you travel south and the air grows hotter, the surf, which is swept by ocean currents, grows colder.

Rabat

Rabat is clean, orderly, and efficient in marked contrast to the rest of Morocco. The old twelfth-century city of the Almohads has been superseded by the new, French-flavored city with its European clothes, newspapers, and attitudes. But unlike the showpieces of other nations, Rabat has not become sterile, alienating, or vulgar: Big city cosmopolitanism meets small town warmth to create a graceful capital both intimate and spacious. Thanks to the King's unflagging interest in his own back yard, discreetly ubiquitous soldiers keep the city free of hustlers and hassles. Stop in for a day on your way south, and you may be lulled into staying a week. But resist the temptation: No matter how hard it tries, Rabat can never capture the soul of Morocco. For solo women, the city may be an acceptable compromise for safety reasons.

The Rabat of today was built around, rather than atop, the older structures. Its name comes from the tenth-century transformation of the town into a *ribat,* a religious and military stronghold. At the time, the city was threatened by heretical Barghawata Berber tribes to the south. In the twelfth century, Yacoub el-Mansour, credited with trying to make Rabat into an imperial capital, built the fortified walls and the grandiose Hassan mosque. However, his dream remained unfulfilled until 1912, when the French colonial administration chose the city as its capital. After Morocco became independent, Rabat retained its special status.

Orientation and Practical Information

Rabat could not be more conveniently organized. **Avenue Mohammed V** runs north-south from the Grande Essouna Mosque, past the train station and the post office, right through the medina. Perpendicular to Mohammed V is **avenue Hassan II,** which heads east along the medina's southern walls toward Rabat's sibling city **Salé,** and west into the **route de Casablanca,** where the "central" bus station is inconveniently located.

Office National Marocain du Tourisme (ONMT): 22 rue el-Jazair (tel. 212 52). Far away, but helpful. From the train station, walk up ave. Mohammed V to the Grande Essouna Mosque, turn left on ave. Moulay Hassan, and 7 blocks later (on the right-hand side of the street), bear right into rue el-Jazair. Knowledgeable, English-speaking staff. Sketchy maps of Rabat and other large cities available. Open Mon.-Fri. 8:30am-noon and 2:30-6:30pm; Ramadan Mon.-Fri. 9am-3pm.

Syndicat d'Initiative: rue Patrice Lumumba (tel. 232 72). More centrally located. From the post office, cross ave. Mohammed V and head to the right along rue el-Kahira, which intersects rue Patrice Lumumba a few blocks down. Well-informed staff. Open same hours as the ONMT.

Embassies: U.S., 2 ave. de Marrakech. Look for the Stars and Stripes fluttering over blvd. Tarik Ibn Ziyad, which runs beside the fortifications on the southeastern edge of town along the river. Consular section open Mon.-Fri. 8:30am-noon and 1-5:30pm. In an emergency, dial 622 65 24 hours. **Canadian,** 13 Joafar Essadik, Agday (tel. 713 76). Open Mon.-Fri. 8am-2pm. **British,** 17 blvd. de la Tour Hassan (tel. 209 05). Also takes care of citizens of **Australia** and **New Zealand. Tunisian,** 6 ave. de Fes (tel. 306 36), around the corner from the ONMT.

Algerian Visas: Algerian Consulate, 12 rue d'Azrou. Visas about US$15. Open Mon.-Fri. 9am-1pm.

After-Hours Currency Exchange: Hotel Tour Hassan, 34 ave. Abderrahman Annegai (tel. 214 01). From the train station, head across pl. des Alaouites onto el-Forat, cross pl. du Golan (pl. de la Cathédrale) onto Laghouat, walk to the next block, and turn left onto Abederrahman Annegai. Official bank rates. Open 8am-7pm.

Post Office: ave. Mohammed V (tel. 207 31), at rue Soekarno. From the train station, turn left and walk 2 blocks down Mohammed V. Open Mon.-Fri. 8:30am-noon and 2-6:45pm. **Telephones** and Poste Restante are located just on the other side of rue Soekarno. Open 8am-midnight; lines are shortest noon-3pm.

Airport: 6 buses per day (at 4.30am, 6am, 8am, 10am, 12:30pm, and 6pm) leave from in front of Hotel Terminus, ave. Mohammed V, across ave. Moulay Youssef from the train station, to Casablanca's international **Aeroport Mohammed V.** One-way tickets 45dh. **Royal Air Maroc,** ave. Mohammed V (tel. 322 96), across from the train station. Open Mon.-Fri. 8:30am-12:15pm and 2:30-6:15pm, Sat. 8:30am-noon and 2:30-6pm. **Air France,** 281 ave. Mohammed V. Open Mon.-Fri. 8:30am-noon and 2:30-6:15pm, Sat. 9am-noon.

Train Station: ave. Mohammed V (tel. 232 40), at ave. Moulay Youssef. Economy class to Tangier (5 per day, 35.50dh), Fes (8 per day, 28.50dh), Oujda (4 per day, 71dh), and Casablanca (15 per day, 11dh), where you can change trains for Marrakech (29.50dh).

Bus Station: route de Casablanca (tel. 751 24), at pl. Mohammed Zerktouni. Incredibly far from the town center. Pay 10dh for a *petit taxi* or take bus #30 from ave. Hassan near rue Mohammed V (2.70dh). All intercity bus companies operate from here. CTM tickets sold at windows #14 and 15; the other 13 windows belong to companies that post their schedules in Arabic only and depart only when the buses are really full. CTM buses to Tangier (4 per day, 59dh), Tetuan (2 per day, 60dh), Ouezzane (3 per day, 20.40dh), Marrakech (3 per day, 56dh), Meknes (5 per day, 31dh), Fes (4 per day, 44dh), Azrou (2 per day, 44.50dh), and Casablanca (12 per day, 16dh).

Taxis: Stands are located next to the train station, in front of the bus station along ave. Hassan II, and across from Bab Oudaias.

Car Rental: Avis, 7 Abou Faris el-Marini and at Rabat-Salé Airport (tel. 208 88). **Hertz,** 467 ave. Mohammed V and at the airport (tel. 344 75).

Baggage Check: In train station for 3dh.

English Bookstore: American Bookstore, 4 rue Tanja (tel. 610 16). From the train station, bear right along ave. Mohammed V, which veers to the left of the Grande Mosquée. Zankat Tanja is about 4 blocks farther, on the left; the bookstore is another 10 blocks or so up rue Tanja. An excellent shelf on Morocco and Islam, fine selection of classics, and an equally fine, friendly, and helpful staff. Open Mon.-Fri. 9:30am-12:30pm and 2:30-6:30pm, Sat. 10am-1pm.

English Libraries: George Washington Library, 35 ave. al Fahs (tel. 507 88), in Souissi near Hôpital Avicenne. Current newspapers, periodicals, and a library. Open 10am-noon and 4-6pm. The **British Council,** 24 ave. Moulay Youssef (tel. 693 53), has a similar set-up.

Arab Conversation Guides: Libraire Populaire, 16 rue de Ghazzah (tel. 388 67), off ave. Mohammed V, 2 blocks up from the medina. **Libraire Livre Service,** 38 ave. Allal ben Abdallah (tel. 244 95), right off rue de Ghazzah. French-Moroccan phrasebook 30dh.

American Language Center: 4 rue Tanja (tel. 612 69), in the same building as the American Bookstore. 2nd-run American films shown during the week.

English-Language Newspapers: Try the newsstand in the train station and the one on the right side of ave. Mohammed V, just before blvd. Hassan II. *USA Today* available.

Laundromat: Rabat Pressing, 67 ave. Hassan II (tel. 263 61), at Allal ben Abdallah. Pants 7.50dh, jackets 8-9dh. Open Mon.-Sat. 8am-12:30pm and 2-7pm.

After-Hours Pharmacy: Pharmacie de Préfecture, rue Moulay Sliman (no phone), across from Residence Moulay Ismail, signified by a hanging white crescent moon. Open Fri.-Mon. 8pm-8am.

Hospital: Hôpital Avicenne, at the southern end of blvd. d'Argonne (ave. Ibn Sina; tel. 728 71), in Souissi just south of Agdal. Morocco's best emergency medical care is available here free of charge to both locals and tourists. U.S. citizens can also go to the U.S. Embassy for medical care.

Ambulance: Tel. 15.

Police: rue Soekarno (tel. 19), 2 blocks down from the post office off ave. Mohammed V.

Accommodations and Camping

In the Medina

The cheapest rooms in town are in the medina. Most medina digs cost about 25dh, but most also feature roaches rather than showers. Since the heart of Rabat is more in the new city than the old, nothing but the low prices compels you to stay in the medina.

Hotel Marrakech, 10 rue Sebbahi (tel. 277 03), at ave. Mohammed V. Enter the medina from ave. Mohammed V and turn right 3 blocks later. The friendly management boasts that two women scrub down the whole place every day. One of the rare habitable establishments in the medina: Tiny rooms, clean toilets and showers, towels changed daily. Singles 25dh, doubles 40dh. An extra bed 5dh. Showers 2.50dh.

Hotel France, rue Souk Semara (tel. 234 57), at pl. du Marché. Turn left as you enter the medina on ave. Mohammed V. A banana tree in the courtyard and a rooftop terrace. Floor upon floor of dark, dingy rooms. Moroccan guests not permitted in rooms. Payment in advance. Large singles 24dh, doubles theoretically 38dh but can be as little as 29dh if traffic is slow. Rooms with showers 50dh.

Ville Nouvelle

You can find a host of comfortable hotels up from the medina, along and just off ave. Mohammed V and Allal ben Abdallah. From the train station's main entrance, turn left onto Mohammed V and walk toward the medina.

Auberge de Jeunesse (IYHF), 34 rue Marassa (tel. 257 69), just outside the medina walls several blocks north of Bab el Had. Recently moved to new premises, the hostel is now one of the best in Morocco. Still rather grungy. No curfew. Doors open 7-9:30am, noon-3pm, and 7pm-midnight. 10dh, nonmembers 12.50dh.

Hotel Central, 2 rue el-Basra (tel. 673 56). From the train station, cross Mohammed V and walk 2 blocks toward the medina; the hotel will be on your 2nd right immediately after Hotel Balima. Clean, decent rooms. Payment in advance. Singles 50dh, doubles 60dh. Hot water 7am-noon. Showers 8.50dh.

Hotel Splendide, 24 rue Ghazzah (tel. 232 83), just off ave. Mohammed V, the 2nd left from the medina or the 7th right from the train station. Spacious, almost spotless rooms, some overlooking a garden. Singles 65dh, with shower 87dh. Doubles 87dh, with shower 104dh. Hot water mornings and evenings.

Hotel de la Paix, 2 rue Ghazzah (tel. 229 26 or 320 31), just down the street from the Hotel Splendide. Immaculate singles, worn marble lobby. Singles 65dh, doubles 87dh. Hot water 9pm-noon.

Hotel Capitol, 34 ave. Allal ben Abdallah (tel. 312 36 or 312 37), in the arcade around the corner, to the left of Hotel de la Paix. Modern little lobby and creaky elevator. Well-scrubbed rooms. Singles 46dh, with shower 57dh. Doubles 66dh, with shower 91dh. Hot water at night.

Hotel Royal, 1 rue Amman (tel. 211 71), up the street from Hotel Capitol. A cut above the rest. Comfortable singles 87dh, with toilet 110dh. Doubles 104dh, with toilet 129dh.

Hotel Galois, 1 rue Hims (tel. 305 73), a block down Mohammed V from the post office and to the left. Interesting lobby with traditionally carved Moroccan furniture. Clean rooms and showers. Singles 51dh, with shower 80dh. Doubles 64dh, with shower 80dh.

Hotel Balima, rue Jakarta (tel. 216 71 or 677 55), facing ave. Mohammed V, 2 blocks toward the medina from the train station. The only centrally located splurge in Rabat. Fine rooms with full bathrooms. Day or night, the teeming outdoor cafe in front of the hotel is a fantastic place to meet locals and foreigners alike. Singles 161dh, doubles 217dh.

Camping de la Plage, on the beach across from the Bou Regreg River in Salé (tel. 823 68), has running water, toilets, and a provision shop/restaurant. Take bus #6 from ave. Hassan II near ave. Allal ben Abdallah to Salé's Bab Bou Haja (7dh), and follow the signs. The management is friendly and mellow, the facilities primitive, and the prices couldn't be better: 8dh per person, 3dh per tent, 5dh per car, slightly more for vans or larger vehicles. Cold showers and electricity are included. (Open daily 8am-8pm.)

Food

The chief virtue of Rabat's medina is its well-endowed food stalls. The tremendous covered market that sprawls from the entrance of the medina to pl. du Marché should keep you out of restaurants for a week. Try the delicious Andalouse meat pastries (tangy chicken cooked in a flaky pie) at one of the *patisseries*.

Inside the medina, several inexpensive places line ave. Mohammed V. Just through the walls is a square filled with food stalls, grills, and tables, where 15dh will bring you a plateful of tripe; a meal of veal cutlet, salad, and bread might run 17dh. There's plenty of local company here—both human and insect.

Some of the best budget eateries in the new city cluster around **ave. Mohammed V** and **ave. Allal ben Abdallah,** a block or two from the medina, and in the area around the train station, just off **ave. Moulay Youssef.**

Restaurant el-Bahia, ave. Hassan II (tel. 345 04), to your right as you approach the medina on ave. Mohammed V. Built into the walls of the medina with an interior court and fountain. Excellent food at budget prices. Upstairs is a lavish *salon marocain,* complete with embroidered sofas and puffy pillows. Try *tajine de kefta aux oeufs* or *tajine de poulet.* Fixed *menu* 25dh. Service charge 10%.

Restaurant Taghazout, 7 rue Sebbahi (tel. 256 47), in the medina, off Mohammed V to the right. Pull a chair up to one of the long tables and strike up a conversation with a local. If you peek through the service window, you can watch your lamb (17dh) or tripe (17dh) roasting over a glowing charcoal pit.

Café Restaurant La Clef, near the train station (tel. 619 71). As you leave the station, make a hairpin turn right onto ave. Moulay Youssef; enter the 1st alley on your left. Beautiful interior, superb food, and reasonable prices. The *salon marocain* has low-slung couches. Choose from a selection of *tajine pigeon* (tender pigeon stewed with prunes, almonds, and onions), *tajine kefta aux oeufs,* or *tajine poulet aux amandes* (34.50-38dh). Their best is the *pastilla aux poulets* (28.50dh). Service charge 19%. Open 11am-11pm.

Restaurant Ghazzah, rue Ghazza (no phone), across the street from Hotel Splendide. Fresh orange juice (6dh), *omelette aux crevettes* with vegetables (20dh), and *filet du Merlan* (21dh).

Café Restaurant Taghazout, 6 rue Jeddah (no phone), 1 block farther up Mohammed V than the above. The sign erroneously says "self-service." Looks like a misplaced sushi bar. An abundant *salade niçoise* with tuna and a lightly fried fillet of *merlan* with greenbeans and fries (30dh, including dessert). For dessert try the cool blend of milk and mashed banana (8dh). Open daily noon-midnight.

Restaurant Saadi, 87 ave. Allal ben Abdallah (tel. 699 03), a right turn off rue Jeddah coming from ave. Mohammed V in the arcade. A great place for a modest splurge. Lamb *couscous* you can really sink your teeth into (45dh). Open daily 10am-11pm.

Sights and Entertainment

Time your sightseeing so that you arrive at either the Chellah or Oudaias Kasbah at sunset, when the ancient fortifications are bathed in an orange glow, and the views over the **Bou Regreg River** are at their most impressive.

The eighteenth-century **Essouna Grand Mosque** at ave. Mohammed V and ave. Moulay Hassan is a good starting point. A sand-colored arch and gold-trimmed windows grace the renovated building's white plaster walls. Above, the tan and green minaret, pierced by arched windows on five levels, towers over the green shingle roof. Through the front door you can see the intricately carved walls and arches. (Entrance forbidden to non-Muslims.)

Ave. Moulay Hassan leads to the salmon-pink Almohad **Bab er Rouah** (Gate of the Winds). The Kufic inscriptions and arabesque flourishes of the relief work form concentric rippling arches. Inside the gate, to the right as you look in from outside, is a gallery of contemporary Moroccan paintings. Exhibits change every few weeks, and the artists occasionally sip mint tea in the corner. (Open daily 8:30am-noon and 2:30-8pm.)

Walk back through Bab er Rouah and turn right through the wall at the first gate onto the tree-lined promenade that leads to the **Dar el-Makhzen** (Royal Palace). Although it was begun in the eighteenth century, most of the present palace postdates the French occupation. The main entrance is through a beautiful, high arch supported by four white marble pillars. Farther along is another entrance lavishly decorated with turquoise ceramic tiles; four gray marble columns sustain a rich wooden mantle. Visitors are not permitted inside—if you come too close, you will be chased away by the unmistakable armed guards. They wear the traditional *serouel* (pleated, baggy white pants), a red sash, and a blue turban with a white diamond on the front. Don't make any sudden movements in front of the palace—the guards have strict orders and tend to be edgy. Next to the palace sprawl the **Royal Stables,** theoretically open to the public on Sunday at 3pm, but don't trot out of your way to visit. Directly across from the entrance to the royal estate lies the handsome, modern **Mosque of Ahl Fas** (Royal Mosque), where the sultan worships publicly on religious occasions. Stop by just after noontime prayers to glimpse the entourage of dignitaries emerging from the royal house of worship in traditional dress. The pageant reaches its zenith Fridays from 12:30 to 1pm.

Outside **Bab Zaers,** beyond the southern extremity of the palace grounds at the end of ave. Yacoub el-Mansour, loom the impressive remains of the **Chellah,** a fortified royal necropolis revered since the time of the Almohads. The ruins have been likened to the feverish hallucination of a weary desert rambler. Overgrown with trees, cacti, and exotic flowers, the interior of the ancient burial complex today forms a public park where narrow footpaths wind through well-tended gardens and picturesque ruins; it makes a splendid picnic spot. Enter through the majestic, crenelated **Chellah Gate,** a fortified archway flanked by twin hexagonal turrets. Abou Hassan erected the portal and the sturdy cemetery walls in the fourteenth century to protect the necropolis from robbers. Legend has it that a fabulous horde of treasure is buried beneath the great gate. Proceed down the path, past a pair of small white *marabouts,* to Hassan's **mausoleum;** his tombstone is the white prism in the back. The burial complex is comprised of several adjacent monuments. The most outstanding is the colorfully tiled minaret of the now-ruined mosque. The best-preserved chamber sits at the base of the minaret, arranged around a turquoise and emerald pool. The tower itself now serves as an apartment block for a community of storks. The mosque is no longer in use and is therefore open to the public. Up the path a few paces stand the ruins of **Sala Colonia,** once a Roman settlement. You can see the foundations of an avenue of boutiques. Also climb down to the sacred **absolution basin,** which is nourished by an underground spring. Since pre-Islamic times the waters of this tiny fountain have been revered for their healing powers, and worshipers still frequent the pool, burning candles and praying for health. (Chellah open 8:30am-6pm. Admission 3dh.)

Across town along ave. Abi Regreg (near the Pont Moulay Hassan to Salé), the **Mausoleum of Mohammed V** is a monumental and graceful example of Islamic architecture. A white cube crowned by a sea-green pyramidal roof serves as the final resting place of the popular monarch, who led the country from French and Spanish colonialism to independence. The marble exterior is topped by the traditional triplet of golden spheres set on a common vertical axis. The interior explodes in a rush of opulence; sapphire stained-glass windows bejewel the gold leaf dome, and the ivory-colored marble tomb lies in the center of an amazingly well-polished, black marble floor. Amid pomp and shaky trumpet calls, the costumed guards lower the flag daily at 5pm. (Open daily 8am-last prayer, around 10pm in summer, 8pm in winter. Free.)

In front of the mausoleum stands the imposing **Hassan Tower,** the unfinished minaret of the twelfth century's largest western mosque. Sultan Yacoub el-Mansour, intending to construct the three greatest towers in the world, raised the Giralda minaret of Sevilla and the Koutoubia of Marrakech before turning to this lofty spire. The project was never completed after his death in 1195, but at 55m, the unfinished turret towers above both its famous siblings. (Interior closed to the public.)

In the northern corner of the medina along Tarik el-Marsa are the walls of the famous **Kasbah des Oudaias,** the *ribat* where, in the tenth century, a garrison of the Oudaia tribe was stationed to protect the city. Andalusian refugees settled around the area in the seventeenth century. The most interesting of the gates is **Bab Oudaia,** at the top of the hill. The **Oudaias Gardens** inside are flower-strewn and peaceful. Also inside is the **Museum of Moroccan Arts,** housed in two separate parts of the seventeenth-century palace of Moulay Ismail. It contains a fascinating collection of traditional Moorish carpets, ceramics, and jewelry in one building and musical instruments, clothing, and Korans in the other. (Both open Wed.-Mon. 8:30am-noon and 3-6:30pm. Admission 3dh.)

Although less medieval than others, Rabat's **medina** is wonderful for a stroll, especially since you will be left in peace. Enter via ave. Mohammed V. To your left, you'll see the **fruit and vegetable market.** The first right off Mohammed V, **rue Souiqa,** is a lively street where merchants peddle everything from sheeps' heads and pigs' feet to running shoes. This eventually turns into **Souk es Sebat,** a narrow alley covered with straw mats for protection from the blazing sun. Adjoining the *souk,* the medina's **Grande Mosque** is built on Merinid foundations but was renovated in 1887 by Moulay Hassan. At the end of Souk es Sabat, branching off to the right, rue des Consuls becomes the **carpet souk.** It's lined with expensive tourist shops and ends at the Kasbah des Oudaia and **Souk el-Ghezal.** The large emporiums here are noticeably overpriced.

South of pl. de la Grande Mosquée, the **archeological museum** houses a brilliant collection of Volubilis bronze works, all dating from 25 B.C.E. and earlier. The museum also includes artifacts from the paleolithic and neolithic eras, and Phoenician and Carthaginian relics. To get there, walk down ave. Mohammed V, and take a left onto Abd Al Aziz at the Grand Mosque. The museum is on the next street, right off Abd Al Aziz. (Open Wed.-Mon. 8:30am-noon and 2-6:30pm. Admission 3dh.)

Nightlife in Rabat is limited to cinemas and expensive, pseudo-European discos. If you're itching for something interesting, call the palatial **Tour Hassan Hotel,** 34 ave. Abderrahman Anneigai (tel. 214 01), to find out if there will be a Moroccan music and dance performance that evening (70dh). Otherwise, you can sit at one of the outdoor tables of **Café Balima** (in front of Hotel Balima on ave. Mohammed V), sip mint tea, and watch—or even meet—the citizens of Rabat.

On March 3, the **Fête du Trone** is held to celebrate the anniversary of the king's accession; on July 9, there is the **Royal Birthday;** on November 6, the **Fête de la Marche Verte** celebrates the 1975 return of the southwestern Sahara; and on November 18, there are festivities in honor of independence.

Near Rabat

Salé

Less than a half-hour walk from Rabat, Salé has mellowed with age. Yet the medina of Rabat's riverside neighbor still offers what most visitors to Morocco are looking for: a well-preserved medieval city with enchanting *souks* free of tourist emporiums and hustlers.

Enter the medina through the towering horseshoe arch of **Bab Mrisa,** the most monumental of the city's ancient gates, constructed in the thirteenth century to control the flow of boats navigating the river. The **mellah** (old Jewish quarter) is on your left as you enter. Keep walking straight, and the mazelike alleyways of the *souk* will appear on your right. You don't need a guide; just plunge in and explore. Turn onto rue Bab el-Khebbaz, and your fourth right will be **Souk Sidi Merzuk,** the jewelers', embroiderers', and silkwinders' market. At the end, off to the left, branches the pretty **Souk Kissaria,** the basketmakers' quarter. Some of the alleys moving toward the heart of the medina sport handsome, wooden roof coverings and feature a separate cluster of shops for each specialty, including the carpet *souk,* footwear *souk,* and *djellaba* and kaftan *souk.* Also explore **rue Kechachine**—the stone-carvers' *souk*—and **rue Haddadine**—the blacksmiths' and brass-workers' *souk.* In the center of the medina, the **Grand Souk** is filled with wool-dyers who display their brightly-colored samples and weigh purchases on huge scales. From here, follow the crowds along **rue Bab Sebta,** an alley lined with an interminable row of squatting fruit and vegetable vendors.

To reach the twelfth-century **Grand Mosque,** retrace your steps and zero in on the towering minaret at the northern end of the medina, near Bab Malka. A tiny, ornate doorway adjoining the mosque leads to the **Medersa of Abou el-Hassan.** Its interior consists of geometric patterns and flourishes. Stairs lead to two tiers of students' seminary cells, each with a window overlooking the central courtyard. A final flight of stairs leads to a rooftop terrace with a spectacular view of Salé and Rabat. (Open 8am-noon and 2:30-6pm. Admission 5dh.)

Just behind the medersa and the Grand Mosque stands the blue and white-tiled **Marabout of Sidi Abdallah ben Hassoun,** who is revered as the spiritual guardian of boaters. (Seventeenth-century Salé was the home of the "Salé rovers," the notorious corsairs who pirated Europe's Atlantic coast.) Entrance to the shrine is forbidden to non-Muslims, but peek through the window to admire the lavish mausoleum. Straight ahead at the ocean's edge, and also worth a glimpse from the outside is the sumptuous **Marabout of Sidi ben Ashir.**

To reach Salé, cross the river on Pont Moulay Hassan, near the Mausoleum of Mohammed V, or, for more fun, take a rowboat (.50dh) from the Ramp Sidi Maklouf. Here you'll also find the popular and dirty **municipal beach.**

Temara and Sidi Bouknadel

The public beaches of Rabat and Salé are mobbed in the summer, while the sands of the coastline south of Rabat are almost always roomier. The most accessible spot for the car-free is the beach at **Temara.** Take bus #17 (2.20dh) from blvd. Hassan II near ave. Mohammed V, or take a collective taxi from blvd. Hassan II south to Temara and walk the 3km. Be prepared to meet up with half of Rabat. **Camping Palmeraie** charges 4dh per person, 3dh per tent, and 3dh per car. The fancy **Hotel La Felouque,** about 3km south on the beach (tel. (07) 442 37), offers the only accommodations. (Doubles with full board 210dh.) Farther south, on Skhirat Beach, **Hotel Amphitrite** (tel. 422 36) charges similar rates. Public showers at Temara and Skhirat beaches cost 1dh. If you tire of the ocean, visit the **Municipal Zoo** in Temara or the **Sunday market** in Skhirat.

South from Temara, you will reach Plage Bouznika, Plage Dahomey, Plage Assanoubar, and Plage Itilal—each more deserted and beautiful than the last. **Camping Dahomey** charges 6dh per person, per tent, and per car.

The most beautiful beach near Rabat is **Plage des Nations Unies,** just north of **Sidi Bouknadel,** 12km north of Rabat. Northbound buses leave from the Bab Mrisa in Salé. You can also take a collective taxi from Rabat (8dh). It's a 1-km walk from the Rabat-Khenitra highway. Sidi Bouknadel also boasts the appropriately named **Exotic Gardens,** with an array of bizarre botanical aberrations. The complex, laid out by an expatriate French ecologist, displays international plant life. The extensive grounds include Japanese bridges, bamboo pleasure huts, Amazon rope bridges, a cage of monkeys, and ponds brimming with water lilies and snapping turtles. (Open 9am-6:30pm. Admission 9dh.)

Mehdia and Khenitra

The monstrous beach at the tiny resort of **Mehdia** lies 39km north of Rabat and is thoroughly jammed on summer afternoons. In the off-season, however, this crescent of sand is one of the most breathtaking sights on the northern Atlantic coast. The local hotel is almost always booked solid, but you can stay at **Camping Mehdia** just south of the beach (tel. 48 49). Facilities are both crowded and minimal. (6dh per person, 5dh per tent, 3dh per car, and 4dh for electricity.)

The remarkable **Kasbah de Mehdia** dominates the length of a clifftop 2km north of the resort, looking down on the spectacular mouth of the Sebou River. The well-preserved walls date from the seventeenth century, while the stunning main gate was built during the reign of Moulay Ismail. Sequestered in the interior of the Kasbah, a decorated stone archway leads into the remains of the seventeenth-century governor's palace. (Open daily sunrise-sunset. Free, but tip the custodian.)

Comfortable accommodations are available 8km away at **Khenitra,** one of Morocco's largest and ugliest cities, but also a major transportation hub for travelers continuing north. Next door to each other, **Hotel d'Europe,** 63 ave. Mohammed Diouri (tel. 35 49), and **Hotel la Rotonde,** 50 ave. Mohammed Diouri (tel. 33 43), charge 50dh for singles and similar rates for doubles. **Camping La Chenaie** (tel. 33 73) charges 5dh per person, per car, and per tent. Mehdia is accessible only by collective taxi.

Casablanca

You must remember this: There is no Rick's Café Américain in the Kasbah; no getaway plane at the airport; and no one looking at you, kid, except the hustlers who prowl the port and the medina.

"Casa" has combined the charm of French heavy industry with the efficiency of Moroccan feudalism to create an ugly, smelly, noisy hybrid that only a resident could love. Even the most devoted Bogie-worshipers will be dismayed at Morocco's commercial capital and largest city. Nonetheless, there is something endearing about the city, though it may take careful searching to find it.

Orientation and Practical Information

Almost 100km directly south of Rabat, Casablanca is easily accessible by plane, bus, and train—provided you get off at the correct station. All international flights and most domestic ones fly into **Aeroport Mohammed V,** 30km south of Casablanca. From there, regular buses bring you into the centrally located CTM station.

Everyone ends up confused by Casa's two train stations. **Casa Port** is close to the CTM station and the youth hostel; **Casa Voyageurs** is close to nothing and about a 50-minute walk from Casa Port. If you have any choice, get off at Casa Port; if you don't, take a *petit taxi* to the city's center (about 7dh). To get from the port to the CTM station (which lets you check your locked bags for 3dh), cross the street, turn left, and after a few blocks, look for the tremendous Hotel Safir—the station is behind it to the right.

Tourist Office: 55 rue Omar Slaoui (tel. 27 11 77), off Rue Reitzer. Walk south along ave. Hassan II, turn left onto rue Reitzer, and then right onto rue Omar Slaoui. Open Mon.-Thurs. 8:30am-noon and 2:30-6:30pm, Fri. 8:30-11am and 3-6:30pm; Ramadan Mon.-Fri. 9am-4pm.

Syndicat d'Initiative: 98 blvd. Mohammed V (tel. 22 15 24), at rue Colbert. Facing the CTM station, walk 1 block right on ave. des Forces Armées Royales, then left up rue Colbert. Well-stocked with good maps and lists of Casa's movie theaters, health clubs, and swinging discos. Open Mon.-Sat. 9am-noon and 3-6:30pm, Sun. 9am-noon; Ramadan 9am-4pm; hours are always flexible in their favor.

Consulates: U.S., 8 blvd. Moulay Youssef (tel. 22 41 49). Open Mon.-Fri. 8am-4:30pm; in off-season Mon.-Fri. 8am-5:30pm. **British,** 60 blvd. d'Anfa (tel 26 14 41 or 26 14 40). Open Mon. 8:30am-12:30pm and 2-6pm, Tues.-Fri. 8:30am-12:30pm and 2-5:30pm.

Currency Exchange: Larger hotels will change money at official rates after banks have closed and on weekends. Try the new Hyatt Regency and Hotel Suisse.

American Express: Voyages Schwartz, 112 ave. du Prince Moulay Abdallah (tel. 22 29 47 or 27 80 54). All the services of a normal AmEx office and a helpful, cheerful staff. Open Mon.-Sat. 8:30am-noon and 2:30-6:30pm.

Post Office: ave. de Paris at ave. Hassan II, 1 block north of pl. des Nations Unies. Open Mon.-Thurs. 8:30am-12:15pm, Fri. 8:30-11:30am. **Branch office,** 116 ave. Mohammed V, conveniently located next to the *syndicat.* Open Mon.-Thurs. 8:30am-12:15pm and 2:30-6:45pm, Fri. 8:30-11:30am and 3-6:45pm. Poste Restante available only at main office.

Telephones: Collect calls can be made at the main post office. Open daily 8am-10pm. International pay phones are on blvd. d'Anfa, just south of blvd. de Paris. Open 24 hours. **Telephone Code:** 0.

Airports: Aeroport Mohammed V, Tel. 33 90 40. All international and most domestic flights. **Aeroport de Casablanca: ANFA,** Tel. 36 41 84. Other domestic flights. **Royal Air Maroc Ticket Office,** 44 ave. des Forces Armées Royales (tel. 31 41 41). Shuttle buses (20dh) run from the main bus station to the international airport. Domestic airport accessible by taxi only.

Train Station: Casa Port, Port de Casablanca (tel. 22 30 11), near the CTM station and the youth hostel. **Casa Voyageurs,** blvd. Ba Hammed (tel. 24 58 01), near nothing. The former offers better northbound service (21 trains per day to Rabat, 22dh); the latter better southbound service (4 trains per day to Marrakech).

Bus Stations: CTM, 23 rue Léon L'Africain (tel. 26 80 61), off rue Colbert. *Baggage consigne* 2dh. Service to Rabat (11 per day, 15dh). To Essaouira via El-Jadida (3 per day, 39dh) and Marrakech (3 per day, 35dh). Shuttle bus to international airport (5am-9pm 1 per hour., 45 min., 20dh). Other companies leave from pl. Benjdia to Marrakech and points south.

Car Rental: Avis, 19 ave. des Forces Armée Royales and at airport (tel. 31 24 24). **Hertz,** 30 ave. des Forces Armée Royales and at airport (tel. 31 22 33).

English Bookstore: American Bookstore, blvd. Moulay Youssef (tel. 27 95 59), 2 blocks west of the U.S. consulate. A warm, friendly staff and a wide selection of novels and reference books. Open Mon.-Fri. 9:30am-12:30pm and 3:30-7:30pm, Sat. 10am-noon.

After-Hours Pharmacy: Pharmacie de Nuit, pl. des Nations Unies (tel. 26 94 91). Open 24 hours.

Medical Services: Croissant Rouge Marocain, blvd. El Massira El Khadia (tel. 25 25 21). **Salle de Soins,** R1 Bloc 17, #6, Sidi Othman. Open daily 8pm-8am. **Ambulance,** Tel. 15.

Police: Tel. 19.

Accommodations

A group of fleabags lines **rue Colbert,** leading up to the *syndicat.* If none of these options appeals to you, ask the *syndicat* for its exhaustive, graded list.

Auberge de Jeunesse (IYHF), 6 pl. Amiral Philibert (tel. 22 05 51), 3 min. from the port train station. Cross the street in front of station, turn right, and walk along the walls until you can turn left up a small flight of stairs. A friendly, French-speaking staff will welcome you to their hole-in-the-wall. Space is always available in this dirty, barren hostel. No curfew. Open daily 8-10am, noon-2pm, and 6-11pm. 15dh, nonmembers 17.50dh. Bread and coffee at breakfast included.

Hotel Colbert, 30 rue Colbert (tel. 31 42 41). Dark, narrow hallways lead to small, decrepit rooms, some of which overlook a run-down garden. The night cashier speaks "petit" English. Singles 43dh, with shower 69dh. Doubles 59dh, with shower 93dh.

Hotel Guynemer, 2 rue Pegoud (tel. 27 76 19), near the pl. des Nations Unies. A comfortable, endearingly ramshackle place, with fake classical friezes outside and miniature reproductions of the Old Masters inside. Clean rooms. Singles 58dh, with shower 71dh. Doubles 68dh, with shower 87dh.

Hotel Windsor, 93 pl. Oued El Makhazine (tel. 27 88 74). Recently refurbished, the immaculate, spacious rooms are a refreshing change. A bit expensive, but worth it. Singles with shower 111dh, with bath 140dh. Doubles with shower 143dh, with bath 175dh.

Food

If there aren't cats inside, it isn't authentic.

Rotisserie Centrale, rue Colbert (no phone). From the *syndicat,* turn right onto rue Colbert. Greasy, spicy, and delicious ¼ chicken roasted on a spit with olives and served with a hunk of bread 10dh. Open daily 11am-11pm.

Café des Negociants, ave. Mohammed V (tel. 31 41 86), across from the *syndicat* on the corner. Sit back and watch the wheelings and dealings of Moroccan businessmen as you enjoy a filling meal of meat brochettes, fries, salad, and bread (8.50dh). Open daily 11am-11pm.

Restaurant Widad, 9 rue de Fes (no phone), off Mohammed V in the old medina by blvd. Mohammed el-Hansali. A local *couscous* hole. Meat or chicken *couscous,* salad, bread, and fruit 20dh. Open noon-10:30pm.

International Seamen's Center, 118 blvd. Moulay Abderhamane (tel. 30 99 50). Turn left off ave. des Forces Armées Royales onto rue du Azilal; it's 100 yds. up on the right. If you walk in without baggage but with a confident air, the "members only" requirement may be waived. Don't sign in; sit in the garden and touch base with the West. Cheeseburger 10dh, with fries 4dh. Open daily 10am-11pm.

Casa's French-style ice cream and pastry shops are excellent. **Glacier Gloria,** rue XI de Janvier, sells big sundaes and cafe drinks for around 7dh. Try *fraise melba,* a delicious concoction with tart strawberry sherbet and vanilla ice cream, fresh whipped cream, and big sweet strawberries (13dh). For staples, shop at the clean and sprawling **Central Market Halls,** 7 rue Colbert.

Sights and Entertainment

Casablanca remains the only place in Morocco devoid of sights. You can wander through the **old medina** or the **new medina** (the Habbous quarter) to reclaim any stolen goods, at reasonable prices of course, or to buy Moroccan goods. Get cheap *babouches* (slippers) for around 40dh and *djellabas* (robes) for about 90dh in either medina, but be prepared to bargain.

The **aquarium,** on rue Flaubert at Sidi Mohammed, has been closed indefinitely and will not reopen until funding difficulties are cleared up. The **place des Nations Unies** tries to pass for a nice area of the city. Here, the shiny, neo-Islamic facades of the city hall, post office, municipal theater, and Grand Mosque all face a glittery central fountain.

You should know from the movie not to come to Casa for the waters. The **municipal beach,** at the southwestern edge of town, is pretty but hopelessly crowded. Nearby is the **municipal pool.** (Open June-Sept. until 8pm. About 15dh per day.) You can also try **Ain Diab;** it hosts several private beaches and pools (22-35dh), as well as a number of western-style discos.

El-Jadida

Less wind blown than Essaouira, more authentic than Agadir, less crowded than the resort of Mohammedia, El Jadida is the prime Atlantic resort in Morocco. With a charming medina, crenelated Portuguese battlements, palm-studded boulevards, and a splendid beach, it is the ideal spot for recovering from Marrakech or Rabat. Though Phoenicians originally founded the area, the Portuguese fortified El-Jadida and named it Mazagan in the sixteenth century. In 1769, it became the last Portuguese citadel in Morocco to fall. After independence the name was changed to El-Jadida ("The New One"), and the town was launched on its career as a summer retreat for wealthy Marrakech families. By far one of the most tranquil cities on the Atlantic coast, El-Jadida also retains ample evidence of its heritage.

Orientation and Practical Information

Less than 100km south of Casablanca, El Jadida is close enough to the major population centers of the north to be constantly overcrowded with beachcombers. The bus station is at the southern end of town, about a 15-minute walk to most of the hotels and the Portugese Town or medina. From the bus station walk toward the beach and turn left on **avenue Mohammed V,** which leads to all the action.

Tourist Office: Delegation Provencale de Tourism d'El Jadida, rue Ibn Khaldoun, down the street from Hotel de Bruxelles. New office. Open Mon.-Fri. 8:30am-3pm; mid-Sept. to June Mon.-Fri. 8am-noon and 2-6pm.

After-Hours Currency Exchange: Hotel Dar es Salaam des Doukkala, ave. de la Ligue Arabe (tel. 35 75), facing the beach. They will change traveler's checks for a 5% commission.

Post Office: Pl. Mohammed V. Open Mon.-Fri. 8am-2:30pm, Sat. 8:30-11:30am.

Telephones: In the post office. **Telephone Code:** 034.

Buses: rue de Mohammed V, a 10-min. walk from the post office. To Casablanca (4 luxury per day, 18.50dh; others every ½-hr., 13.50dh), Essaouira (1 per day, 32.50dh), Safi (4 per day, 26.50dh), and Agadir (1 per day, 57.50dh).

After-Hours Pharmacy: Ave. de la Ligue Arabe, off pl. Mohammed V. Look for the plaque next door to the Croissant Rouge Marocain.

Hospital: Rue Sidi Bouzit, near rue Boucharette at the southern edge of town.

Police: Just around the corner from the Croissant Rouge Marocain, down from pl. Mohammed V. Tel. 19.

Accommodations and Camping

Amazingly, this quiet coastal town has many good-quality budget hotels. Most center around **place Mohammed V** and are only a few blocks from the sea. More than anywhere else in Morocco, it's worth calling for a room in advance as all hotels can be booked solid during the summer.

Hotel de Provence, 42 rue Fquih Mohammed Errafi (tel. 23 47), from the post office head away from the beach. It's on the right, several blocks inland. One of the best deals in Morocco: clean, classy, and friendly—an oasis of tranquility. Singles 53dh, with shower 61dh. Doubles 64dh, with shower 78dh. Showers 3dh. Continental breakfast 13dh.

Hotel de Bruxelles, 40 rue Ibn Khaldoun (tel. 20 72). Cozy, bright rooms with balconies. Singles 60dh. Doubles 80dh.

Hotel de la Plage, ave. de la Ligue Arabe (tel. 26 48). Moderately clean and near the beach. Singles 35dh. Doubles 50dh.

Hotel Royal, blvd. Mohammed V (tel. 28 39), past the post office on the right. Large, clean rooms close to both the beach and the center of town. Singles 49dh. Doubles 60dh.

Hotel Suisse, blvd. Zerktouni (tel. 28 16). Follow blvd. Mohammed V south from the post office, bear left at the fork, turn left at the dead end onto blvd. Zerktouni; its up the street on the left. A bit nicer than Hotel Royal, but rooms in the front can be noisy. Singles 51dh, with shower 79dh. Doubles 64dh, with shower 93dh.

Camping International (tel. 27 55) is a large campground with standard facilities on ave. des Nations Unies. (5dh per person, per tent, and per car.)

Food

El-Jadida does not excel in Moroccan *haute cuisine,* but a few good restaurants surrounding **pl. Mohammed V** offer tasty meals at cheap prices.

Restaurant La Broche, pl. el-Hansali (tel. 22 99 or 25 60), next to the Paris Cinema. The best deal in town. *Menu* 30dh. Try the *tajine de kefta aux oeufs.* Selection of juices 2-6dh. Great breakfasts 5-15dh. Open daily 7am-midnight.

Restaurant-Bar-Grill Royal, in the hotel of the same name. Great for quick lunches. Try *poulet roti* (12dh) or *tajine* (12dh).

Restaurant de l'Hotel de Provence, in the hotel of the same name. Prepares delicate, delicious meals served in a tranquil garden. The *menu complet* (45dh) changes daily.

Safari Grill Restaurant, rue Fquih M'hamid er Rafi (tel. 28 86), just off pl. Mohammed V. Expensive and delicious. Complete *menus* with soup or salad, entree, and dessert, 38dh and 62dh. Open daily noon-4pm and 6pm-midnight.

Sights

The highlight of El-Jadida is its Portuguese-built **medina,** fortified with stout bastions and ramparts. Raised in 1502, the citadel formed the first Portuguese stronghold in North Africa and was so well-designed that it was held longer than any other outpost on the Moroccan coast. Before retreating, the Portuguese dusted the entire city with gunpowder and detonated it just as the evacuation was completed. The medina remained abandoned until the early nineteenth century, when it was renovated by Sultan Moulay Abderrahman and became a *mellah,* or Jewish quarter. The nooks and crannies of the old section brim with iron balconies, garlanded cornices, and pillared doorways bearing witness to the Portuguese legacy.

Enter from rue de Carrcira through a sturdy, fortified gate opening off pl. Sidi Mohammed ben Abdallah, at the top of blvd. de Suez. A few yards up rue de Carreira on the left, a yellow plaque marks the entrance to the imposing **Portuguese Cisterns,** constructed in 1562. This underground complex supplied the city's water during the frequent sieges, survived the fireworks of the Portuguese retreat, and later housed a fencing school. The subterranean hallway resembles a miniature cathedral. The rainwater on the floor reflects the entire interior—Orson Welles couldn't resist the haunting scene as a backdrop for his movie, *Othello.* On display by the entrance, a tiny diorama depicts the original Portuguese city, complete with moats and drawbridges. Ask the custodian to unlock the access to the roof; at the top of the steps awaits a sixteenth-century fortress. (Cisterns open Mon.-Fri. 9am-noon and 2-7pm. Admission 3dh, plus tip for the custodian.)

Porta do Mar, the great archway at the end of rue de Carreira, leads to the harbor. Head right (north) onto the massive seaside ramparts to inspect the collection of rusty, bronze cannons. At the top of the incline, the **Bastion de l'Ange** commands a fine view of the harbor's fishing vessels and nets. From here, you can walk along the walls to the **Bastion of St. Sebastian,** flanked by a Portuguese chapel, or stroll along the jetty to see the entire town. In the center of the city at pl. Moussa stands the Gothic **Church of the Assumption,** now an assembly hall. Nearby is the old Portuguese **Tribunal,** converted into a synagogue after the resettlement of Jews here in 1815. It is now abandoned. The **souk,** held on Wednesday near the lighthouse, is a lively event. Aside from the usual vegetables and fruit, you'll find an extraordinary array of hanging meats here: Ram heads, cow lungs, and bull genitalia all bask in the heat.

Near El-Jadida

Azemmour

Isolated and amiable, the village of Azemmour sits at the juncture of the Oum er Rbia (Rbia River) and the Atlantic, 16km north of El-Jadida. The community is fortified by a series of sixteenth-century Portuguese ramparts that overlook the river and wrap around the whitewashed medina in a rectangle of mighty, crenelated wall. About 2km north of pl. du Souk past a small eucalyptus forest, you'll find the smooth beach of **Haouzia,** just south of the mouth of the river. A slew of beautiful beaches runs from here all the way to Casablanca.

The best view of Azemmour is from the **bridge** spanning the Oum er Rbia east of town, where you can soak in the scene of heavy medieval walls and tiny houses. Plunge into town for a closer look at the ramparts, punctuated by powerful bastions still equipped with Portuguese cannons. Within the medina, many houses retain Portuguese-style doorways with rounded arches and carved keystones.

Hotel de la Poste, in the main square outside the walls of the medina, offers basic rooms for around 25dh per person. For information on letting private rooms, inquire at the **Syndicat d'Initiative,** 1 block up from the hotel. (Open, sort of, Mon.-Sat.) Azemmour is accessible by several buses per day from Casablanca and by buses every half-hour from El-Jadida.

Boulaouane

The **Kasbah of Boulaouane** stands in solitary grandeur atop a hill overlooking rolling brown farmland dotted with straw-laden camels. The surrounding parched hills of Boulaouane were once noted for their succulent vineyards. Sultan Moulay Ismail established the Kasbah here in 1710 to levy a tax on these fertile fields. According to local lore, Moulay Ismail was so pleased with a woman named Halima that one afternoon in the Kasbah's minaret, he gave her all the lands in sight. From that day on, she lived in a palace within the Kasbah ramparts; when she died the sultan closed the castle and never returned to Boulaouane again. A ruined mosque inside the Kasbah is still paved with turquoise and green tiles.

Public transportation will take you only as far as the village of Boulaouane—take the bus for Settat from El-Jadida. You'll have to walk or hitch the final 8km. If you're coming from El-Jadida by car, take the inconspicuous right turn immediately before the village of Boulaouane—the route is marked by signs from there. Try to catch one of the markets on the way between Boulaouane and El-Jadida: The **souk** is on Sunday at Had Od Frej, Tuesday at Sidi Bennour, and Wednesday at Annout.

Oualidia

One of Morocco's loveliest ocean retreats has remained almost a complete secret to foreign visitors. Beside a lagoon with calm waters and a lonely beach, Oualidia is one of the favorite vacation spots of the Moroccan aristocracy. Restaurants and hotels are on the expensive side, but a pair of campgrounds and daily buses along the coastal road from El-Jadida (84km) and Safi (67km) make the resort accessible to budget travelers. On a hilltop overlooking the lagoon perch the partially inhabited remains of a twelfth-century **Kasbah,** while directly below stands a waterside summer pavilion erected by Sultan Mohammed V in 1947. Beware that the lagoon is linked to the ocean by two narrow channels cut into the natural rock barrier, and the current is dangerously strong.

In town by the highway, **Auberge de la Lagune** (tel. 105) charges 66dh per person for rooms with bath. The terrace restaurant overlooks the ocean and features a seafood feast for 50dh. More luxurious, and a better deal, **Hotel Hippocampe** (tel. 111), at the northern end of the beach, offers comfortable bungalows for 66dh for two, 84dh for three. **Camping International** (tel. 33 29 or 39 50) houses a tourist complex of tentsites, hotel rooms, bungalows, restaurant, and parking lot. Camping costs 5dh per person, per car, and per small tent; 7dh per large tent. Two-person hotel rooms cost 110dh. Six-person bungalows rent for 200dh and include hot showers. The restaurant here has a superb view of the lagoon and features a 39dh fixed seafood *menu.*

Running along rugged coastline, the raised highway from Oualidia to Safi skirts cliffs overlooking both beaches and barren land. **Playa Beddouza,** halfway between Oualidia and Safi near the village and cape of the same name, is a popular spot for unofficial camping, but watch your belongings with eagle eyes.

Safi

In a country where it sometimes seems that only the flies operate efficiently, Safi's industry is almost refreshing. Morocco's principal port for exporting phosphates (a major source of national income), Safi is also the kingdom's largest sardine canning center. Thor Heyerdahl set sail from here in *Ra* and *Ra II* in 1969 and in 1970 to prove that ancient Egyptians could have crossed the Atlantic in papyrus boats and reached the Americas before Columbus.

If you're traveling by bus between El-Jadida and Essaouira, you will most likely have to change buses at the centrally located station in Safi. During your layover, be sure to wander down to the medina, flanked by beautifully preserved Portuguese citadels and brimming with some of Morocco's finest ceramics.

Orientation and Practical Information

The post office, banks, travel agencies, and public offices are on or near **place de l'Indépendence.**

Tourist Office: Just off ave. Moulay Youssef (tel. 21 45), behind the post office. Open Mon.-Fri. 9am-2pm.

Post Office: Main office in pl. Administrative, up the hill from the old city. Open Mon.-Fri. 8am-noon and 3-6pm, Sat. 9am-1pm. Branch office at pl. de l'Independence. Open Mon.-Fri. 8am-noon and 3-6pm, Sat. 9am-1pm.

Telephones: In the main post office. Open daily 8am-9pm. **Telephone Code:** 046.

Train Station: At the southern end of town (tel. 24 08). Trains run to Benguérir on the Casablanca-Marrakech line, but they primarily move phosphates. Unless you're devoted to your train pass, travel by bus from Safi.

Bus Station: Gare Routière, rue de Président Kennedy. Frequent buses to Casablanca (31dh), Marrakech (22dh), and Essaouira (19dh).

Laundromat: Pressing Alafrah, 266 rue de R'bat.

Accommodations and Camping

Scads of cheap hotels jam the medina—each grungier than the next; most charge about 25dh.

Hotel Majestic, just within the walls of the medina, across from the entrance to the Dar el-Bahar (tel. 31 31). Comparatively clean, but noisy. Singles 25dh. Doubles 45dh.

Hotel Novelty, 6 rue Marrakech (tel. 29 29), just off rue de R'bat outside the medina. Big rooms but a bit stuffy. Definitely a bargain. 25dh per person.

Hotel L'Ocean, rue du R'bat (tel. 42 07), just up the hill from the post office at pl. d'Independence. More luxurious. Modern rooms and bathrooms. Singles 35dh. Doubles 45dh. Showers 5dh.

Hotel Les Mimosas, ave. Ibn Zaidoune (tel. 32 08). A very comfortable splurge. Singles with bath 137dh. Doubles with bath 169dh.

Safi has a wonderful municipal campground, **Camping de Sidi Bouzid.** It's 2km north of town in a lovely, wooded enclosure with a swimming pool and excellent facilities. (5dh per person, per tent, and per car.)

Food

The medina is full of inexpensive hole-in-the-wall joints that charge about 30dh for full meals. For a few more dirhams, you can get much better food.

Café-Restaurant Calypso, pl. de l'Indépendence. A pleasant, stylish place, with a tiled courtyard. Full meal about 40dh.

M'zoughen, pl. de l'Indépendance, across from the bus station. Comfortable cafe with excellent coffee and the usual assortment of pastries. A great spot to hang out.

Sights

Built by the Portuguese in the sixteenth century, the **Dar el-Bahar fortress** (Chateau de Mer), at the old port, commands a fine view of Safi's medina. (Open Mon.-Fri. 8am-noon and 2-6pm.) Enter the **medina** from here. Along **rue de Bab Chaaba,** Berber women sell rock shampoo, lipstick stones, green henna mud for hair-dying, and sticks of *swak* (a kind of toothpaste). The food stalls offer sweet and greasy pastries and strange, spongy pancakes—all hidden under swarms of bees and flies. Just off rue de Bab Chaaba is the sixteenth-century **Portuguese Chapel** (follow the signs past the Grand Mosque). The lively market street terminates at **Bab Chaaba,** a chunky twelfth-century arch marking the end of the medina. Outside this gate, story-tellers and musicians carry on their antics.

Just around the corner is the **Colline des Potiers** (Potters' Hill), Safi's claim to fame before sardine cans and phosphates took over. Fine ceramics are displayed in the outdoor *souk* where dozens of tiny shops line the street. It's a buyers' market, so let the merchants bargain each other down. To the left of the white-domed, turquoise-trimmed mosque you'll find Safi's fat, vase-shaped kilns puffing away. Climb up and examine the glazing pots, underground wheels, mounds of broken orange rock, and unglazed plates, roof tiles, and *tajine* vessels.

The **Borjel-Dar** (old Kechla) is a towering, walled Portuguese citadel up the hill from the potter's quarter. Constructed during the sixteenth century, the fortified quadrangle harbors the **Dar el-Makhzen** (royal palace), with a view of Safi's medina and environs.

Near Safi

The best beach near Safi is the stretch near the tiny resort of **Souira Kedima,** 30km to the south. Several buses per day run the route in the summer. The sand-covered fragments of a ruined Kasbah lie by the beach. The **municipal campground** consists of a large enclosed sand lot packed with tents and adjoined by showers and lavatories. (5dh per person, 5dh per tent, 3dh per car.) The beachside **Restaurant de Souira Kedima** is a wonderful surprise: Beneath bamboo covering is a plush *salon marocain* with cushioned divans and savory *tajine de boeuf.*

The eighteenth-century ruins of **Kasbah Hamidouch,** a hilltop fortress defended by towers and battlements, stand 76km south of Safi. Raised by the notorious Sultan Moulay Ismail, the Kasbah overlooks the Tensift River, still protected by a gaping ditch which once contained a moat. The castle houses the remains of a mosque and several domiciles. To reach Kasbah Hamidouch, take the coastal road to Souira Kedima, turn left by the turn-off for the beach, and head inland for 13km on a dirt track. Upon arrival in the tiny village of **Dar-Caï-Hadji** (roughly 7km), continue along the left bank of the river until you reach the Kasbah.

There are also a number of nice beaches near Safi. Thirty kilometers to the south lies the beach of **Souiria.** Bus #10 leaves from the municipal bus terminal next to the post office every hour (3dh). To the north lie the beaches of **Lalla Faina Mohamd** (15km from Safi) and **Cape Beddouza** (20km from Safi), accessible by bus #15 (same frequency, 3dh).

Essaouira

The powerful Sultan Mohammed ben Abdallah leveled the Portuguese city of Mogador and raised the ramparts and bastions of Essaouira (the name means "well-designed") to protect his band of pirates. The walls of the fortified town were ingeniously designed by Théodore Cornut, a French prisoner of the sultan who played the role of city architect during his captivity.

Many Moroccan cognoscenti agree that today Essaouira is the loveliest community in the country, but their reasons vary. Some stress Essaouira's architectural beauty: The medina is an artist's canvas of whitewashed walls and bright blue shutters enclosed in a frame of medieval bastions and ramparts. Others mention Essaouira's cool and persistent ocean breezes (which attract hordes of windsurfers), the town's courteous inhabitants, and its soft, sandy beach.

The town's virtues were also evident to Jimi Hendrix, who came here in 1968 and triggered a mass migration in his wake. Over the next five years Essaouira achieved international notoriety as a magnet for wandering hippies. Now that most of the hash smoke has cleared, the only legacy of the '60s is the cafe proprietors' propensity for hard rock. Often neglected by tourists, Essaouira is an ideal place to relax after a few nerve-taxing days in a Moroccan metropolis.

Orientation and Practical Information

Halfway down the coast between Safi and Agadir, Essaouira is neither as industrial nor as visited as either. The medina has two main entrances: **Bab Doukkala,** where the buses arrive, and **Porte Portugaise** (also called Porte de la Marine), facing the harbor. **Avenue de l'Isiqlal,** the main shopping street of the medina, runs from one gate to the other. The medina's other main artery, **rue Allal ben Abdallah,** runs parallel to l'Isiqlal.

Tourist Office: Across from Porte Portugaise in front of the harbor (no phone). Little help. Open Mon.-Sat. 8am-noon and 4-7pm.

After-Hours Currency Exchange: Hotel les Iles, ave. Mohammed V, just outside the medina facing the beach.

Post Office: ave. el-Moqaquamah, at Lalla Aicha, 1 block inland from the beginning of the beach at Hôtel les Iles. Open Mon.-Fri. 8am-2pm; Oct.-June 8am-noon.

Telephone Code: 047.

Buses: CTM, next to Bab Doukkala. To Casablanca (3 per day, 7 hr., 38dh), Agadir (2 per day, 3½ hr., 25dh), Taroudannt (1 per day, 5 hr., 35dh), and Marrakech (7 per day, 4 hr., 22dh; this is the famous "Marrakech Express" of CSNY). If you don't take one of these, you're at the mercy of the smaller private bus companies that operate from here too.

Foreign Newspapers and Magazines: 3 rue Allal ben Abdallah. Open daily 9am-11pm.

Hospital: Ave. el-Moqaquamah, next to the post office.

Police: Tel. 19.

Accommodations and Camping

Unfortunately, the medina is overflowing with the usual assortment of 20dh fleabags. At the city's **Bain-Douche,** next to the Hotel Tafraoute, 2.50dh entitles you to fulfill a fantasy shared by every budget traveler in Morocco: to stand under a private, hot shower for as long as one pleases.

Hotel du Tourisme, rue Mohammed ben Messaoud (tel. 20 75), along the medina walls. With your back to the tourist office, walk right along the outside of the walls until you see the sign. Remarkably inexpensive, moderately clean, and full of friendly cats. Singles 20dh. Doubles 28-35dh. Triples 40-45dh.

Hotel du Mechouar, ave. de l'Istiqual (tel. 20 18). A wonderful old hotel with spacious rooms. Singles 50dh. Doubles 70dh.

Hotel Sahara, ave. de l'Istiqual (tel. 23 79), next to the above. Spiffy, modern, Moroccan-decorated hotel. Singles 43dh. Doubles 59dh. Whether you stay or not, their traditional *salon marocain* with tiled walls and carved ceiling is a great place for coffee, mint tea, or a continental breakfast (8dh).

Hotel Tafraoute, 7 rue de Marrakech (tel. 21 20). Take your first left after entering the medina through Porte Portugaise and step beneath the clock tower; then immediately turn right and follow the inside of the ramparts—signs will point the way from here. The nicest of the hotels in the heart of the medina, though many of the rooms are windowless. Singles 42dh. Doubles 57dh. Triples 89dh.

The **municipal campground** (7dh per person) on ave. Mohammed V, at the far end of the beach, has only one virtue: It's near the ocean. But it is usually so windy that it's impossible to sleep (or sometimes even to set up your tent).

Food

The cheapest places to eat are the so-called **Berber cafes** at the end of rue Marrakech, just off ave. de l'Isiqlal. These places have low tables and straw floor mats and serve super fish *tajine* or *couscous* for around 15dh. If you take a right after the second archway beyond the Porte Portugaise, you'll reach a handful of Berber cafes that sell delicious *kefta* and meatballs for a dirham apiece. Just take a seat at the communal table and point to what you want, but establish prices before chowing down. During the day (and even for breakfast), you can get six or eight fried sardines at the port (enter the harbor behind the tourist office) for about 5dh, including bread, lemon, and tomatoes. If you've got the money, you can have fresh crab, mackerel, or lobster grilled to perfection over charcoal. Essaouira's restaurants are concentrated in the medina, in the port, and along the waterfront on ave. Mohammed V.

Café-Restaurant Essalem, pl. Moulay Hassan (no phone). The best budget restaurant in town. Scanty but delicious portions at comparatively low prices. *Menus* 20dh and 30dh. The *tajine boeuf,* stewed with prunes and onions, is scrumptious. Open Fri.-Wed. noon-11pm.

Restaurant la Petite Algue, ave. Mohammed V, just past Hotel Tafoukt on the waterfront. Fancy upstairs dining room filled with hammered brass and inlaid guns. *Very* formal service and excellent food. *Menus* 50dh and 60dh. Order the excellent *moules marinières* (marinated mussels).

Café-Restaurant Bab Lachour, pl. Moulay Hassan. Nice outdoor cafe for hanging out. Snack on their delicious *salade niçoise* or a bowl of *harira.* The restaurant inside is expensive but excellent; their specialty is lobster (90dh per ½ kg). Open 8am-midnight; restaurant opens at 6pm.

Sights

Essaouira is a bright beach town with a lively medina of arched *souk* stalls. Indigo-tiled fountains and carefully tended flowerbeds enhance the street, while Portuguese-style blue shutters and doors contrast with the whitewashed walls of the houses. Burly palm trees nod their fronds under a pale blue sky and ceremonious cannons squat between medina arches. Off pl. Moulay Hassan, rue Sidi Mohammed ben Abdallah plunges into the heart of the **medina.** Numerous alleyways branch off, some burrowing under the massive vaults of the city's fortifications. These arched subterranean passageways were originally used for escape and smuggling. The most dramatic portion of the medina is the sea-sprayed **Kasbah** (Village Sqala). Take the narrow alley across the street from the CTM station. A stone ramp leads up to a crenelated lookout post, where a battery of Catalan cannons, gun turrets, and fortress ramparts withstand the pounding surf. Below the Kasbah is the charming **carpenters' district.** In the tiny, vaulted caverns lining the inside of the ramparts, skilled woodworkers carry on a centuries-old tradition. Ebony, silver, and lemon-wood are inlaid onto the surfaces of fragrant thuya wood boxes in splendid floral and geometric patterns. You'll find that with only a little bargaining you can purchase woodcrafts much more inexpensively directly from the carpenters. However, the selection is wider and the finest pieces available at the more expensive woodwork emporiums along rue Abdul Aziz el-Fechtaly, off rue Sidi ben Abdallah in the medina. Just inside the medina is Essaouira's **museum,** located next to the Centre Artisanal, which houses a varied collection of traditional costumes, jewelry, musical instruments, pottery, and arms, but no legs. (Open daily 8am-3pm. Admission 3dh.)

Near Essaouira

Isle of Mogador

Like a mythological land sprung from the tales of Tolkien, Mogador, the largest of the Isles Purpuraires, has an ancient and tumultuous history. The Berber king of Mauritania, Juba II, established dye factories on the islands around 100 B.C.E. The red dye gave the islands their name (*purpureus* means "red" in Latin). In 1506, under King Manuel, the Portuguese contributed a fortress, and Moulay Hassan added a prison. The islands are now deserted, but you can arrange with a fisher to row out in a dinghy. There's a pleasant view of Essaouira and the coast from here.

Diabat

Jimi Hendrix attempted to purchase Diabat from the Moroccan government, but his offer was refused. In an unrelated fit of anger, some Moroccan junkies killed several tourists sleeping on the beach; as a consequence the police closed down all the accommodations in Diabat—at least officially. The situation has relaxed again, and a campground and one hotel have opened near the beach.

You can walk to Diabat on the rocky access road (off the coastal route to Agadir), which involves the perilous crossing of a dilapidated modern bridge, or simply walk along the beach. The latter approach sweeps along Essaouira's bay to a cape 2km away.

Diabat's only hotel, **Auberge Tangaro,** is a ramshackle but cheerful outfit run by a hospitable French proprietor. Next door, there are rooms without beds where you can spread your sleeping bag on a mattress. The tastefully decorated adjoining **restaurant** honors musical requests. The meager **Camping Tangaro,** in the adjacent enclosure, is the best ground for quite a ways. Both the hotel and the campground (5km from Essaouira) lie on the access road between the highway to Agadir and the Diabat beach—just follow the signs from the highway.

Cap Sim

Ten kilometers south of Essaouira along the road to Agadir, Rte. 6604 heads to Cap Sim, a long, empty beach marked by a lonely whitewashed *marabout*. There are no buses from Essaouira, but you can try hitching (though there's little traffic) or take a taxi. If you're driving to Cap Sim, follow the highway to Agadir south until you reach a paved turn-off on your right marked "Marabout of Sidi Kaouki"—that's your road. From here it's another 11km to the coast.

The incongruous sight of camels plodding along the seashore isn't a mirage. You can haggle with camel drivers who hang out under the shady trees 100m behind the *marabout* and ride a camel along the beach. Alternatively, consider embarking cum camel on a four-hour trek to the impressive **Dunes of Cap Sim.** Hide your camera and look less than eager to ride the ugly beasts. The camel is your friend, but don't become too attached to one. Camels, unlike toilet seats, do carry syphilis; most are muzzled. If you're not a camel enthusiast, consider a full day's excursion to the dunes on foot. Halfway between the cape and Diabat beach, a wash-out dirt road (virtually impassable by car) winds there from Diabat. It's impossible to drive to the dunes themselves.

Jbel Amsittene

The summit of Jbel Amsittene (58km) makes a lovely daytrip from Essaouria. The solitary ancient watchtower (recently renovated) at the summit shades you from the intense sun and provides an excellent view of the surrounding Haha region. A beekeeper lives next door to the tower. He will escort you up the tower and thank you graciously if you reward him with a small tip. The mountain is otherwise uninhabited, and there are no accommodations in the vicinity. Local buses from Essaouira will take you only as far as the turn-off from the highway. From here it is a lonely 9km trek to the summit. Be forewarned: In mid-summer the afternoon sun can make the trip grueling.

If you're driving from Essaouira, take the highway toward Agadir until the village of **Smimou.** Continue another 7km along the highway—on your left will be a dirt road that turns inland with a sign marked "Tnine Imin Tlet" (the name of a neighboring village). Stay on the main dirt road (bearing right at the first fork and left at the second fork), and it will take you right to the watchtower on the summit. The track is stony and crumbling, but passable.

Agadir

Agadir is definitely not Moroccan, but not quite European either. It's a pleasant shock to come here from somewhere else in Morocco—no hustlers (well, almost none), fine sandy beaches, and pizzerias. Completely the invention of tourist-minded Moroccans, today's Agadir was transplanted several kilometers from its original location after the earthquake of 1960. You'll find less artificiality a few kilometers north, where desolate stretches of pure sand are accessible by local bus.

Orientation and Practical Information

Buses arrive and depart around the corner from **place Lachen Tamri,** where all the best budget hotels are located. From here it is a five-minute walk directly east on rue Allal ben Abdullah to most of the city's services, located on and around **boulevard Hassan II.** From here its another five-minute walk directly east to the beach.

Tourist Offices: pl. du Prince Héretier Sidi Mohammed (tel. 228 94), in the shopping mall across from the PTT. Open July to mid-Sept. Mon.-Sat. 8:30am-3pm; mid Sept. to June Mon.-Sat. 8am-noon and 2:30-6:30pm; during Ramadan Mon.-Sat. 10am-4pm. **Syndicat d'Initiative:** ave. Mohammed V (tel. 226 95), at the intersection of ave. du General Ketani. A glorified brochure stand. Don't worry about the hours; all useful information is displayed in the window. Has a list of local *souks.* Same hours as tourist office.

Currency Exchange: Outside bank hours, **Hotel Sahara** runs an SGMB Bank window in its lobby. Open Sat. mornings, too. Most 4- and 5-star hotels will change traveler's checks if they like your looks. **Hotel Sindibad** and **Hotel Ayour** both exchange at bank rates for their guests.

American Express: Voyages Schwartz (tel. 228 94), Hassan II, by the tourist office. Up 1 flight of stairs in the Mopatours Building. Minimal services. No emergency cash refunds given on weekends or on Wed. Open Mon.-Fri. 9:30am-12:30pm.

Post Office: Across from pl. du Marché in the building without windows (the one that looks like it will be the last thing standing after the next earthquake). Open Mon.-Fri. 8am-2pm, Sat. 8am-noon; Sept.-June 8:30am-noon and 3-6:30pm, Sat. 8:30am-noon. Night service around the corner with **telephones** open Mon.-Sat. 8am-8pm. **Telephone Code:** 8.

Airport: Several kilometers south of town, accessible by taxi (10dh). **Royal Air Maroc,** ave. du General Ketani (tel. 220 06). Open Mon.-Fri. 8:30am-noon and 3-7pm, Sat. 9am-noon and 3-4pm.

Buses: CTM, Satas, and other lines are located on ave. Yacoub el Mansour, around the corner from pl. Lachen Tamri. CTM buses to Essaouira (1 per day, 30dh), Casablanca (3 per day, 100dh), Tiznit (1 per day, 15dh), and Marrakech (1 per day, 42dh). Satas buses to Essaouira (5 per day, 27dh), Casablanca (3 per day, 72.80dh), Marrakech (4 per day, 37dh), and Taroudannt (5 per day, 11dh). **Municipal buses,** including #12 to Taghazoute and #14 to Tamri, leave from pl. Salam (about 5dh).

Car Rental: Agadir is the cheapest and most convenient place to rent a car in Morocco. Agencies are on blvd. Mohammed V by the *Syndicat.* **Afric Cars** (tel. 237 50) usually has the best 3-day rates. There is also a handful of companies along ave. Hassan II. **Rent-A-Car/Location de Voitures** (tel. 259 45), has the cheapest rates for Renaults.

American Express: Voyages Schwartz (tel. 228 94), Hassan II, by the tourist office. Up 1 flight of stairs in the Mopatours Building. Minimal services. No emergency cash refunds given on weekends or on Wed. Open Mon.-Fri. 9:30am-12:30pm.

English Bookstore: Crown English Bookstore, by the tourist office. Good collection of novels and second-hand books. Stock up now—you won't be able to find any English books south of here. Open Mon.-Sat. 9:30am-12:30pm and 2:30-7pm.

Foreign Newspapers: Rialto Bureau de Tabac, ave. Hassan II. Large selection of newspapers and magazines.

Public Showers: Around the corner from Hotel de la Baie, ave. Allal ben Abdallah. Hot showers 1.80dh.

24-Hour Pharmacy: In the mall next to the municipal hall.

Hospital: Hospital Hassan II, route de Marrakech (tel. 224 77).

Medical Emergencies: Mon.-Fri. 8pm-8am and 24 hours Sat.-Sun. Tel. 226 85 for on-call French-speaking physician.

Police: Hotel de Police, rue du XVIII Novembre (tel. 19).

Accommodations and Camping

In July and August, finding a hotel room in Agadir is difficult. Start early, and look first in **pl. Lachen Tamri,** around the corner from the main bus station.

Hotel el Bahia, pl. Lachen Tamri (tel. 227 24), in the southwest corner of the square. This is the best hotel in the area, but not the cheapest. Friendly management and clean rooms. Singles 38dh, with shower 64dh. Doubles 52dh, with shower 78dh. Hot showers 4dh. Continental breakfast 8dh.

Hôtel Sindibad, pl. Lachen Tamri (tel. 234 77), closer to the buses than el Bahia. Sharp and spiffy—trying to imitate the luxury hotels by the beach. Small pool on the roof. Better buys can be found nearby. Singles with bath 110dh. Doubles with bath 129dh. Breakfast 14dh.

Hôtel Massa, pl. Lachen Tamri (no phone), next door to Sinibad. Much cheaper and dirtier, but friendly. Singles 40dh. Doubles 60dh.

Hôtel Ayour, rue de l'Entraide (tel. 249 76), off rue du XXIX Février, 1 block inland from ave. du Prince Moulay Abdallah. A shade more expensive but worth it: plush rooms and spotless showers. A great place to recuperate from the desert. They also cash traveler's checks for guests at bank rates. *Salon marocain* on the premises. Singles 110dh. Doubles 129dh. Triples 167dh.

Hôtel de la Baie, ave. Allal ben Abdallah (tel. 230 14), across from Café les Arcades. Clean rooms, some with balconies, and a lovely courtyard with absolutely repugnant murals. Singles 42dh. Doubles 57dh. Triples 89dh. Showers 5dh.

Hôtel la Tour Eiffel, 25 ave. du XXIX Février (tel. 237 12), 1 block south and around the corner to the left of the above. Small but clean rooms. Doubles 50dh. Triples 65dh. The cafe-restaurant downstairs makes a lot of noise but serves decent meals for 12-18dh.

The **campsite** (tel. 295 40) on ave. Mohammed V, a few blocks up from the northern end of the beach, is well-protected, well-equipped, safe, and crowded (5dh per person, everything else extra).

Food

Place Lachen Tamri has several cheap cafes and sandwich shops that offer filling meals for under 20dh. Down the street on rue Allal Ben Abdallah try **Café les Arcades.** A *menu* of salad or *harira, tajine* or *couscous,* and dessert costs 20dh. Closer to the beach and the resort life is **rue des Oranges,** a side street off blvd. Hassan II lined with fertile orange trees and opening onto a small plaza.

Restaurant L'Amirante, rue des Oranges (tel. 242 60). Smiling service, delectable food, and reasonable prices. Fish is the specialty: hot spiced shrimp *pil pil* 25dh, breaded *escalope* 19dh. A huge *menu* of *spécialités marocaines* 28dh. Open daily 10am-11:30pm.

Restaurant Tanalt, rue des Oranges (tel. 212 57), across the street from the above. Tuna salad 12dh, grilled sardines 14dh, *spaghetti bolognaise* 17dh. Moroccan *menu* 27dh, fish *menu* 33dh. Open daily 10am-11pm.

Restaurant Daffy (a.k.a. **Chez Houjayemi**), 2 rue des Oranges (tel. 200 68), around the corner from Tanalt. More expensive, slightly better quality, no duck. Moroccan *menu* 46dh. Open daily 10am-midnight.

Sights

The **Kasbah,** on a hilltop overlooking the port, occupies the original site of Agadir. In 1960, a 15-second earthquake leveled the entire city, leaving 15,000 dead and 20,000 homeless. The Portuguese fortress and old fortified medina were wiped out; the only relic, Kasbah ramparts perched above the ocean, command a spectacular view of Agadir and the surrounding coastline. Since the new city has been relocated to the south, the hilltop is wonderfully secluded and offers relief from the city's honking horns. Unfortunately, an entourage of rip-off camel-ride peddlers and self-proclaimed guides cluck and flutter about the main entrance. To reach the Kasbah, walk or take bus #12, 13, or 14 to the port and follow the signs from here.

On Saturday and Sunday, the surrounding countryside migrates to the outskirts of town for the crowded **souk** (follow the signs from the main highway just south of downtown off blvd. Mohammed V). You can procure everything from saffron to cellophane, but concentrate on the hammered brass and copperware—sold here at better prices than in the tourist bazaars in the center of town. Mounds of fragrant spices are arranged in pyramids across counters. Pick through mountains of surplus army uniforms and denim jackets, haggle over exquisite silver bracelets and earrings, or sample the tasty figs, dates, and nectarines.

The coolest place to sightsee is also the town's main attraction. The **municipal beach** is a glorious, fine-grained band of sand. The water is clean and, for these parts, extremely warm.

Near Agadir

Taghazoute

Just 15km north, the lovely (but no longer unspoiled) beach by the fishing village of Taghazoute is renowned as a vintage hippie hangout. The alkaloid and bean-sprout crowd is still thriving despite occasional visits from the Moroccan police. The best time to visit Taghazoute is between September and June, when only a few Europeans are around. In recent summers the beach has become popular with vacationing and weekending Moroccans, and the tents of unofficial campers extend for several miles.

To reach Taghazoute from Agadir, take a taxi or bus #12 from pl. Sallam—it leaves every 45 minutes from 5:15am to 8:15pm (about 3dh). The last bus back to Agadir leaves at 7:30pm.

If you don't care for the urban bustle of Agadir, the campground at Taghazoute is a good base for exploring the region to the north, since it is more conveniently located for both Immouzzèr and Imsoune. The coastline just north of Taghazoute features several less crowded and equally beautiful beaches. To reach them, take bus #14 from either Agadir or Taghazoute village. It leaves pl. Sallam in Agadir every two hours from 5am to 7pm. The fare to the most northern beaches is about 10dh. Tell the driver where you want to get off. The last bus back to Agadir and Taghazoute leaves Tamri at 5pm.

Imsoune

Surrounded by dramatic coastal scenery, the remote village of Imsoune sits next to a lovely patch of beach where in the summer a handful of Moroccan families pitch tents and enjoy the lively surf. On both sides, the precipitous coastline of **Igui n Tama Point** plunges down to the ocean. The road to Imsoune affords breathtaking panoramas of a tortuous shoreline. Between the highway and the coast, the road passes through a grove of peculiar trees: Unique to this part of Morocco, these argan trees are an ancient relative of the olive tree. Watch the goats climb them to graze on leaves and fruits; they balance on even the weakest of branches in order to reach the higher leaves. If you look carefully through the grove, you might find a large tree with as many as 15 goats strung out like surreal Christmas ornaments. The locals collect the excrement of the goats and extract argan oil from it—a coveted, traditional Moroccan seasoning. If you purchase some, eat it quickly—it doesn't keep.

The paved road to Imsoune branches off the Agadir-Essaouira highway toward the coast 91km north of Agadir, between the villages of Tamri and Tamanar. Local bus service will take you only as far as the turn-off. From there you'll either have to hoof or hitch the 14km, though it's only a couple of kilometers to the beginning of the argan grove.

Immouzzèr

The only paved road to the waterfalls of Immouzzèr Ida-Outanane is Rte. 7002, which begins 9km north of Agadir, just before the village of Tamrahrt. This spectacular road winds through the foliated canyons of the Ida-Outanane, a confederation of hospitable Berber tribes. Only two buses per day run to Immouzzèr, and the locals rely on tourists for transportation. You should rely on thumb, taxi, moped, or rented car from Agadir.

The road runs through the aptly named **Paradise Valley,** discovered in 1966 by two British backpackers. The road first cuts through the slabs of twisted, stratified stone of the **Tamrahrt Gorge.** Rock hounds will love the roadside shops selling crystals, fossil shells, and onyx calcite. Next comes a grove of shady palm and banana trees; wind your way past lily-padded pools and streams to a makeshift cafe in a stone cabin. You can also camp with the hippies who come up from Taghazoute when the police clamp down on the drug laws. Ask the locals to show you the *thin* plant (indigenous to the valley) from which Morocco's best honey is made.

From the oasis, the road plunges into the **Tarhat Gorge;** the sheer rock walls climb higher and higher as you move inland. Farther along toward Immouzzèr, the terrain becomes wilder and the villages more traditional. Grain is threshed by donkeys circling maypoles planted in the center of stone courts, and villagers dwarfed by weird rock formations stride with staffs in hand. If you reach Immouzzèr on a Thursday, you can explore the *souk,* a jumbled cluster of whitewashed stores bustling with activity. The rest of the week, however, the town is rather dull. Five kilometers down from the town along switchbacked roads you'll come to the **Cascades d'Immouzzèr des Ida Outanane.** From the bottom of the shady cleft, it is a short walk to the falls. During and just after the rainy season, water gushes forth and leaps over the brown rock, plummeting 45m into a pool. In the summer, on the other hand, the falls peter out to something far short of awe-inspiring, and by late August they have all the majesty and power of a leaky youth-hostel shower. Don't miss a dip in the cool, clean waters of the 25m-deep pool. The rock ledges above make perfect diving platforms. (Local hustlers will demonstrate and demand compensation for their performances.)

Auberge les Cascades (tel. 16), in town, charges an outrageous price per person with obligatory half-board. Not to fear: There's usually plenty of room, and with persistence they can be bargained down to a fraction of the quoted price. (Doubles 175dh.)

Marrakech

Marrakech is intense. From its mid-summer temperatures of over 90°F to the cacophonous circus of the Djemâa el-Fna with its snake charmers, musicians, singers, dancers, medicine men, acrobats, gamblers, beggars, peddlers, and the usual array of hustlers and hash vendors—this gateway to the desert is always intense. Through its salmon-colored streets and alleys streams an endless parade of *djellaba-*

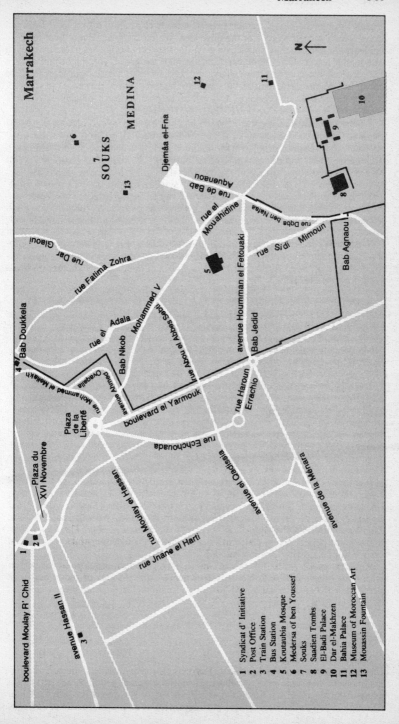

Marrakech

MEDINA

SOUKS

Djemāa el-Fna

rue de Bab Aguenaou

rue el Mouahidine

rue Dqba ben Nafaa

avenue Houmman el Fetouaki

rue Sidi Mimoun

Bab Jedid

Bab Agnaou

rue Fatima Zohra

rue Dar Gtaoui

Bab Doukkela

rue el Adala

Bab Nkob

Mohammed V

rue el Abbassett

rue Moh.ammed el Mellakt

avenue Ahmed Ouagfia

rue Haroun

Errachio

boulevard el Yarmouk

rue Echchouada

avenue el Qadissia

avenue de la Ménara

Plaza de la Liberté

Plaza du XVI Novembre

rue Moulay el Hassan

rue Jnane el Harti

avenue Hassan II

boulevard Moulay R' Chid

1   Syndicat d' Initiative
2   Post Office
3   Train Station
4   Bus Station
5   Koutoubia Mosque
6   Medersa of ben Youssef
7   Souks
8   Saadien Tombs
9   El-Badi Palace
10 Dar el-Makhzen
11 Bahia Palace
12 Museum of Moroccan Art
13 Mouassin Fountain

and *gandura*-clad Berber tribespeople, Arab artisans, French ex-colonists, Western tourists, Blue People from the desert, and troupes of merchants and performers from Mali, Niger, and Mauritania.

The mild winter is the best time to visit. Temperatures drop even more at night, as cool air wafts down from the High Atlas. If you do visit in hot weather, early morning and early evening are the most tolerable times to be active.

Orientation and Practical Information

All the life and excitement centers around the **Djemâa el Fna** and surrounding **medina.** The best budget food and accommodations are found here. Past the towering **Koutoubia minaret,** down ave. Mohammed V is the **Guéliz** or *ville nouvelle.* The bus station, train station, administration buildings, and luxury hotels are found here. Between the new town and the old are all the car rentals, newsstands, banks, and travel agencies. To travel from one to the other hop on bus #1, which runs between the minaret and the heart of the new city along the length of ave. Mohammed V (1.20dh). You can also take one of the many *petits taxis* (bargain down to 3-5dh per person) or the horse-drawn carriages (again bargain fiercely to 20dh per hr.).

If you don't sleep and eat near the Djemâa el-Fna, you'll spend all your time and energy commuting. As everywhere in Morocco, there are plenty of guides; as always you don't need them. (See Hustlers and Guides in the Introduction to Morocco for more specifics.)

Tourist Offices: Office National Marocain du Tourisme (ONMT), ave. Mohammed V at pl. Abdel Moumen ben Ali (tel. 302 58, but the phone is only ornamental). Bus #1 stops here. A laissez-faire attitude toward tourism, but English is spoken and the free brochures have good maps of the *souks* in the medina. Open July-Aug. daily 8am-2:30pm; Sept.-June daily 8am-noon and 2-6pm; Ramadan daily 9am-3pm. Official guides for hire: half-day 30dh, full day 50dh. **Syndicat d'Initiative,** 176 ave. Mohammed V (tel. 330 97), between the post office and ONMT. Binders full of useful information. Open Mon.-Fri. 9am-1:30pm and 4-7pm, Sat. 9am-1:30pm; Sept. 13-June Mon.-Fri. 8am-noon and 3-6pm, Sat. 8am-noon.

Currency Exchange: The quickest place to change money in the Djemâa el-Fna is the SGBM Bank on rue Bab Agnaou, 2 blocks from the post office. Open daily 8am-2pm and 4-8pm. Most of the luxury hotels in the *ville nouvelle* and Hotel Tazi, rue Bab Agnaou in the medina, will change money at late hours.

American Express: Voyages Schwartz, rue Mauritania, 2nd floor (tel. 328 31). Rue Mauritania meets ave. Mohammed V across from the *syndicat;* it's the last building on the left of the 1st block. Office open Mon.-Fri. 8:30am-12:30pm and 3-6:30pm; bank open Mon.-Fri. 8:30am-1:45pm.

Post Office: Pl. du XVI Novembre, off ave. Mohammed V. Very crowded. Open Mon.-Sat. 8am-9pm. Branch in the Djemâa (Marrakech-Medina). Open Mon.-Fri. 8am-2pm.

Telephones: Downstairs in the post office at Djemâa-el-Fna, around the corner on rue Bab Agnaou. Less crowded than the main post at pl. du XVI Novembre. Open Mon.-Fri. 8am-2:30pm. **Telephone Code:** 04.

Airport: Aeroport de Marrakech Menara, 5km south of town (tel. 303 38). Taxi service (5dh), but no bus. Domestic and international flights on Royal Air Maroc and Royal Air Inter. **Royal Air Maroc,** 197 ave. Mohammed V (tel. 319 38). To Casablanca (240dh), Paris (3065dh), London (3515dh), and New York via Casablanca (4960dh) among other destinations.

Train Station: Ave. Hassan II, a 5-min. walk from ave. Mohammed V and pl. du XVI Novembre. The best way to head north, with departures for Casablanca (7 per day, 97dh), Tangier (4 per day, 121dh), Meknes (5 per day, 97.50dh), and Fes (5 per day, 110dh).

Bus Station: All lines leave from the new main station just outside the walls of the medina by Bab Doukkala—not marked on any maps. There's 1 CTM window; the other windows represent private companies with lower prices, lower standards, and much more frequent service to specific destinations. To Agadir (CTM, 1 per day, 35dh), Casablanca (CTM, 3 per day, 38dh), Fes (CTM, 2 per day, 58dh), Ouarzazate (CTM, 4 per day, 40dh), Zagora (CTM, 4 per day, 69dh), Essaouira (6 per day, 24dh). SATAS buses run to Taroudannt at 5am and 4:30pm for 45dh. This bus doesn't go through the Tizi-n-Test pass—only the small private company with a bus at 3am goes this thrilling route, for which tickets must be purchased at least 24 hours in advance. Most private buses also stop outside the Bab er Rob, just south of Djemâa el-Fna—but seats are usually gone by then. Buses to Setti-Fatma in the High Atlas originate here (every ½ hr., 7dh).

Taxis: Collective taxis leave from Bab er Rob for nearby destinations, such as Asui and Setti-Fatma (10dh).

Car Rental: 213 ave. Mohammed V. 5 rental agencies all here claim the best deal. Price falls 75% per hour of arguing. You can bargain a Renault 4 down to 1000dh for 3 days, no restrictions, including tax and insurance. **Sud Car** (tel. 327 80) and **Europcar** (no phone) can get you started on the bargaining and even **Budget** (tel. 346 04) may jump into the act. Or go directly to shady **Haouz Car,** 1 ave. Mohammed V (tel. 482 35), and see what kind of deal they'll make.

Horse-and-Buggies: Across from Banque du Maroc on the edge of the Djemâa el-Fna, along ave. Mohammed V. Bargain to about 20-25dh per hr. for the whole carriage.

Municipal Swimming Pool: In the medina off ave. Mohammed V, the next left heading toward the new city from the Koutoubia (3.50dh, men only). Sneak into any of the luxury hotels in the *ville nouvelle* for a less chaotic dip.

Medical Emergency: Doctor on call at the pharmacy near Hotel Marrakech down the road from the post office (near the fire station at pl. de la Liberté). Open until 10pm. At all costs avoid the unsanitary government-run polyclinique. Instead, have a pharmacist recommend a private physician.

Private Doctors: Dr. Djoudi (tel. 224 01), rue Moulay Ismail, next to the Mamounia Hotel. Dr. Louraoui (tel. 30 04), blvd. Mohammed Zerktouni, Guéliz.

Accommodations and Camping

Apart from the youth hostel and the campgrounds, which are far from the medina but close to the train station, all cheap accommodations are within a stone's throw of the Djemâa el-Fna.

Djemâa el-Fna

The last three hotels listed will look after your bags for a few weeks if you want to take an extended trip to the mountains or the Sahara. These also have rooms with private showers and tubs—an important consideration during the summer.

Auberge de Jeuness (IYHF), rue el-Jahid (tel. 328 31), in the Quartier Industriel, 5 min. from the train station. Cross ave. Hassan II, walk to the right, and take your first left. Using your imagination, continue as straight as possible, passing, in turn, railroad tracks, rue Ibn el-Qadi, and a cluster of wandering streets. Take a right when you come to the vacant lot full of eucalyptus trees; the hostel is the only building on your left, at the end of the street. Exceptionally clean, with courtyard and terrace. Cold showers only. Open daily 8-9am, noon-2pm, and 6-10pm. Members only, 10dh.

Hôtel de la Jeunesse, 56 Derb Sidi Bouloukate (tel. 436 31). The cleanest and friendliest of the dozen or so budget hotels lining this street, a narrow alleyway to your right as you face the Hotel CTM on Djemâa el-Fna or down the alley to the right as you face the square from the Banque du Maroc. Singles 20dh. Doubles 30dh. Triples 40dh.

Hôtel Smarma, 77 Derb Sidi (tel. 255 68). A dusty little place with an unfinished courtyard. Singles 20dh. Doubles 25dh. Triples 29dh.

Hôtel des Amis, Riad Zitoune el-Kedim (tel. 425 15). Facing the Djemâa el-Fna CTM station, walk left and through an arch onto Riad el-Kedim; it's immediately to your right. A modest place. Singles 20dh. Doubles 30dh.

Hôtel de France, 197 Riad Zitoune el-Kedim (tel. 430 67), a bit farther along (not to be confused with the Hotel Café Restaurant de France overlooking the Djemâa el-Fna). Honorable proprietor will look after your bags if you wish to climb Mt. Toubkal. Large and friendly. Clean bathrooms. Singles 25dh. Doubles and triples 40dh. Cold showers 2dh, hot showers 3dh.

Hôtel Chella, on the 3rd street on the right after the above (tel. 419 77); follow the small signs on the left side of the street. Complete with charming courtyard, Saharan motif murals, and tea room. The calmest, coolest place around. Doubles 50dh.

Hôtel CTM, facing Djemâa el-Fna (tel. 223 25), next door to the defunct bus station. The least expensive of the comfortable hotels in the neighborhood and a great bargain. Friendly and family-run. The courtyard and large terrace overlook the Djemâa—a fabulous view. If you're a light sleeper, ask for one of the rooms in the back. Singles 60dh, with bath 77dh. Doubles 77dh, with bath 89dh.

Grand Hôtel Tazi, ave. el-Mouahidine at rue Bab Agnaou (tel. 221 52), 1 block from the Djemâa. Many rooms are beautifully painted and have plush furniture. Rooftop cafe open to guests all night. Sporadic hot water. Singles with bath 90dh. Doubles with bath 110dh. Triples with bath 126dh. Breakfast 10dh.

Hôtel Galia, rue de la Recette (tel. 459 13), parallel and to the left of Riad Zitoun el-Kedim coming from the Djemâa. Clean rooms in the heart of the medina. Singles with bath 86dh. Doubles with bath 106dh.

Ville Nouvelle

Hôtel Excelsior, rue Tarik Ibn Zaid and rue Ibn Aicha (tel. 317 33). The proprietor runs a tight ship, clean and efficient. Singles with bath 108dh. Doubles with bath 125dh.

Hôtel Koutoubia, 51 ave. Mansour Eddahbi (tel. 309 21), at the corner of rue de Yougoslavie. Dark rooms. Courtyard and swimming pool. Singles with shower 137dh. Doubles with shower 169dh.

Hôtel du Haouz, 66 ave. Hassan II (tel. 319 89), halfway between the train station and the PTT. Clean and convenient to the train station, but not the best deal for your money. All rooms 70dh. Bargain hard.

Marrakech has only one campground, **Camping-Caravaning Municipal,** in a partially wooded park. The good sites are usually full, leaving only rocky, shadeless terrain. The facilities are adequate, but the premises are crawling with hustlers and thieves—watch your belongings very carefully. From the train station, walk east (left as you exit) to pl. Haile Selassie, make a right onto rue de France, and take your second right. (8dh per person. 7dh per tent. 5.50dh per car.)

Food

Djemâa el-Fna

For cheap and often delicious food, chow down in the stalls of the Djemâa. Lots of restaurants are here, but the number of eating places increases three-fold in the evenings when food vendors set up their benches. Delicious *tajine, couscous,* and other main courses cost about 10dh. Settle prices before you eat. If you're unsure of the correct price for a dish, hang around and see how much the locals pay. Before your main course, stop off at a *harira*-stand and order a bowl (.80dh).

Try the succulent pulp of the prickly cactus buds, but first ask a local to pinch off the ends and peel back the skin (1dh per kg). Freshly squeezed orange juice costs about 1.50dh per glass or 7.50dh per 1½ liters, and the sweet natural yogurts (straight up or with fresh strawberries) are refreshing for 1.50dh. Prepare to bargain firmly.

Café-Restaurant-Hotel de France, pl. Djemâa el-Fna. The standard mediocre *menu,* but in pleasant surroundings—pillows, tiles, chandeliers, and pretty ceilings—for 35dh. The *salon marocain* is the coolest place to eat, though the rooftop offers the best view at night. Open daily 8am-midnight.

Café-Restaurant Marocain, pl. Djemâa el-Fna, farther along toward the *souks.* You'll recognize it by the yellow 4-leaf grille pattern. Simple fare at rock-bottom prices: soup, salad, brochettes, omelette, bread, and beverage, 12dh. Open daily 8am-11pm.

Café du Grand Balcon, pl. Djemâa el-Fna next to Hôtel CTM. Climb up to the terrace, order a soft drink (4dh) or mint tea (3dh) and enjoy a good view of the Djemâa. The best place for breakfast. Munch on the *patisseries* you buy at the bakery across the way and sip coffee as you listen to the drums and flutes of the snake charmers of pl. Djemâa el-Fna. Open daily 6am-midnight.

The Medina

Café-Restaurant Oriental, 33 rue Bab Agnaou, off the Djemâa. Facing CTM, it's 100m down the left side of the first major street on your right (with the Banque Marocaine on the corner). Very good food served more hygienically but at slightly higher prices than at vendors. Large selection of *menus. Tajine* or *couscous,* salad and dessert, 22dh. Open daily 11am-11pm.

Restaurant Etoile de Marrakech, rue Bab Agnaou, toward the Djemâa from the above. Comfortable upstairs dining, also a *terrasse panoramique.* The only place in the neighborhood where you can order a la carte without hassle. Daily *menu* 25dh. Open daily 11am-11pm.

Restaurant Tazi, in the Grand Hotel Tazi at ave. el-Mouahidine and rue Bab Agnaou. For a light meal, try the *hors d'oeuvres variées* (15dh): all you can eat, featuring salad ingredients, cold squash with tomato sauce, veggie stew, beets, rice, and fruit salad. Or have continental breakfast on top of the hotel for 10dh. Otherwise, meals are expensive. Open daily 7am-10pm.

Restaurant de Foucauld, rue del Mouahidine (tel. 254 99), across from small park, between the Koutoubia minaret and the Djemâa el-Fna, in the hotel of the same name. Acceptable splurge and the only place you can get an alcoholic beverage near the Djemâa. Tasty 4-course *menu* with a wide selection of entrees for 50dh or 60dh. Open daily 10am-midnight.

Ville Nouvelle

La Taverne, 23 blvd. Zerktouni. This garden restaurant has a fountain and pleasant shade. Excellent *tajine* or *couscous* 20dh. The 4-course French meal is also delicious and filling (50dh).

Sights

Djemâa el-Fna

A dusty and lively market square by day, the Djemâa el-Fna transmutes at night into a chaotic outdoor circus filled with an unbelievable array of characters. Djemâa el-Fna means "Assembly of the Dead"—this desert sideshow was once the spot where sultans had criminals decapitated. As a warning to would-be troublemakers, the dried heads were impaled on spikes for public viewing. The grisly task of preserving the heads by pickling them with salt was relegated to the Jews (hence the traditional name of Moroccan Jewish quarters, *mellah,* meaning "salt"). Today audiences, often numbering in the thousands, cluster in tight circles around frenzied performers: While in one corner impassioned storytellers recount religious lore and folktales, in another wild-eyed snake charmers hypnotize flat-headed cobras. Carnival acrobats tumble and leap, and fortune-tellers use Spanish cards to predict the future. Nearby, self-proclaimed dentists sell secondhand dentures and display gory arrays of brown molars extracted with a single blow of the hammer for a few dirhams. Patient scribes sit crosslegged on the ground, ready to pen a dictated letter in either French or Arabic for any illiterate customer. Flashy dancers in velvet trousers and tassled Fes hats twirl and twist in unison. Medicine men surrounded by colorful spices, gnarled roots, lizards, and toads chant as they concoct potions and powder treatments. Colorful clusters of balloons billow above the crowds, and the air resounds with the deafening pounding of drums, jangling of tambourines, and wailing of flutes. Horse-drawn carriages navigate through throngs of blind beggars, veiled women, timid tourists, wandering trinket bearers, juice vendors, and basket sellers. As always, hungry hustlers lurk in every crowd, ready to pounce on any unwary soul.

The Djemâa doesn't really get rolling until late afternoon, an hour or two before sunset, when the blistering heat has begun to subside. The snake charmers are notorious tourist extortionists. After enticing a hooded cobra from its lair and playing with a black scorpion, the tamer will carry several coral snakes and pit vipers toward the crowd. Draping one of his poisonous pets about the neck of an unsuspecting observer, he will demand 20dh as the price of liberation—and rarely get an argument. If you find yourself the unhappy recipient of a reptile necklace, remember that the creatures have all been defanged, so there's no danger. A 2dh tip for the privilege will suffice. Most of the other performers will pass the hat before starting their shows. Keep a pocketful of change handy for both observation and picture-taking privileges.

After sunset the odder sorts clear out and the food vendors take over. Beggars flit from stall to stall tugging on arms, and musicians and storytellers wind up for after-dinner clapping and rapping. By 10pm the square is carpeted with eager merchants plugging ceramics, weavings, carpets, clothing, and souvenirs; this is a great time for comparison shopping. The crowds jostle on until midnight. The tide begins to recede around 1am, until all that remains are comatose Moroccans sacked out in doorways and the one constant in this arena of insanity—rows of refreshing juice bars, piled high with oranges and blocks of ice.

Almost every tour of Marrakech begins at the twelfth-century **Koutoubia Mosque,** with its magnificent minaret presiding over Djemâa el-Fna. The minaret, crowned by a lantern of three golden spheres, is the oldest and best surviving example of the art of the Almohads, who made Marrakech their capital (1130-1213) and at one time ruled the region from Spain to present-day Tunisia.

The history of the Koutoubia parallels the early history of Marrakech. In the eleventh century, the Lemtouna, nomadic Berber tribes of the Sahara, crossed the High Atlas mountains and settled in the Haouz Valley. The Almoravid chieftain Abou Bekr, also known as Sanhadja, led the tribes to a spot much frequented by traders and travelers—today's Marrakech (from *marroukech,* Berber for "swift market"). His cousin Youssef ben Tachfin extended Almoravid possessions to northern Morocco, crossed the Straits of Gibraltar, and bloodied the Iberian Peninsula in a blaze of conquest. At Youssef's demise, the helm of the Almoravid Empire passed on to Ali ben Youssef, who built the first mosque within the walls of the Kasr el-Hajar, the Kasbah of his displaced uncle. Under Abd el-Mumin in 1147, the Almohads stormed Marrakech, razed the town, and built the first Koutoubia Mosque over the ruins of the Kasr el-Hajar. Ten years later, Sultan Abd el-Mumin acquired a holy copy of the Koran—probably stolen in Córdoba. This was one of the four authorized editions that had been sent to the far corners of the Muslim empire by Uthman Ibn Affanboth, relative of the Prophet, to spread Islam. Abd used it as a talisman in battle and it served as inspiration for the second Koutoubia. Built the following year in 1158, this is the mosque that stands today. Possession of the holy relic made Marrakech a seat of learning, and booksellers thrived around the mosque. The name Koutoubia can be traced to the Arabic *kutubiyyin,* which means "of the books" or "libraries." Entrance to the mosque is forbidden to non-Muslims, as is the case in all Moroccan mosques.

The Medina

The medina of Marrakech resonates with a chorus of shouting merchants, humming craftspeople, and laughing children. The proportions of this tangle of side streets are grander than those of most Moroccan medinas, with roomier streets and higher houses—all on a scale befitting an imperial city. This area is a centuries-old meeting place for desert nomads, Berber tribespeople, and wealthy Arabs. Here lies the largest *souk* in Morocco.

To begin your explorations enter the medina to the left of Café el Fati. This is the medina's main thoroughfare, **Souk Smarine,** which takes a turn at the **potters' souk.** Past the mounds of dates, nuts, sunflower seeds, mint, and chickpeas lies the **fabric souk.** Berber blankets are woven by families who spin fleece to wool in a tangle of dowels, string, and cards of yarn. Skeins of wool float by, draped across the bony backs of straining donkeys. After you pass through a large orange gateway, the first opening on your right leads to the **Zahba Kedima,** a small plaza surrounded by the **spice souk** on one side and the carpet souk on the other. Ask the friendly merchants to explain the appropriate uses of the most exotic goods: *sweck* (bark) is used for brushing teeth; dried twigs serve as natural toothpicks; dried sea urchins pin-pricked with pine needles are burned to calm down hyperactive children; and crushed herbs and insects are used as aphrodisiacs. There are also live chameleons for sale here. (Their precise use seems to be a Moroccan secret.)

The merchants in the **carpet souk** can make you a semi-expert on carpet-buying in no time. Backtrack and continue through the bolts of silks and satins on the Souk Smarine until the road forks. Take the left road, the **Souk Attarine,** past a few copper and silver merchants. A few hundred meters later the road forks again. The path to the left takes you into the center of the **woodworkers souk,** where skilled artisans carve tiny chess pieces with astonishing speed. Artisans use both hands and feet to power the lathe and to carve. The second street on your left passes through a section of basketweavers where you can purchase everything from a straw sun visor to huge baskets for your donkeys to carry. Past the baskets lies the **dyers souk,** with little stalls crammed full of bubbling cauldrons of material dyes. Loops of raw wool freshly tinted to shades of rich crimson, deep blue, and sunny gold line the walls. At the end of the street, northeast of the sixteenth-century Mosque of Mouassin, hides the **Mouassin Fountain.** Though clouded with dust and grime, the fountain sports gilded cedar corbels and decorative carving.

The residential area west of the fountain is worth exploring for a look at the medina's domestic side. Tiny doorways lead off the main street and open into two-story mini-*souks,* which center about rectangular courtyards. These offshoots are the **fondouks,** neighborhood markets once surrounded on three sides by arcades of shops.

For a retreat from the heat, visit the sixteenth-century **Medersa of ben Youssef.** The largest Koranic school in the Maghreb, this *medersa* was raised in 1565 by Sultan Moulay Abdallah and remained in use until 1956. The superb bas-relief carving inside brightens the shady courtyard, while brilliant tilework and the sturdy cedar corbels bake in the desert sun. The light from a single doorway splashes into the prayer room, and a marble ablution basin entwined with heraldic birds reclines in the entrance corridor. Poke around upstairs in the university dormitory, where over 900 students lived in medieval times. The *medersa* stands north of the *souks,* above the leather market; look for the ochre and green minaret of the neighboring Mosque of ben Youssef. (Open Tues.-Sun. 8am-noon and 3-7pm; in winter Tues.-Sun. 8am-noon and 2-6pm. Free, but tip the guard.) To the south, around the corner beside the neighboring mosque, juts the squat, unpainted cupola of the twelfth-century **Koubba el-Ba'adiyn,** the oldest monument in town. Peek at the underside of the fanciful tower, carved in a rich floral arabesque pattern. The guard will open an ancient, wooden door to reveal the subterranean cisterns. (Open daily 8am-noon and 3-7pm. Free, but tip the custodian.)

The path to the right off Souk Attarine is the **babouche souk,** where an endless selection of traditional Moroccan slippers is displayed. At the end of the street, turn right to the **cherratine souk,** which joins the *babouche souk* to the Souk el-Kbir, the right fork off rue Smarine as you enter the medina. This street is the **leather souk**—not as large, but just as colorful and smelly as the one in Fes. Hides are painstakingly prepared, cut into strips, punched with gold foil, and transformed into *babouches,* boots, bags, belts, and bookcovers. These butter-soft, handcrafted leather goods go for ridiculously low prices—if you're a skillful haggler. Around the corner Berber farmers barter raw hides.

Return to the Djemâa el-Fna by turning right on the **Souk el-Kbir.** As you descend toward the Djemâa, you'll see on your right the **Anciennes Kissarias,** rows of small parallel streets that connect the Souk Attarine and the *babouche souk* to the Souk el-Kmir. Here everything from *djellabas* to fur coats are sold. On the left of the Souk el-Kmir, you can glimpse at the gleaming merchandise in the **jewelers' souk.** Hammered copperware, lacy silver bracelets, pewter perfume bottles, and gem-studded scabbards are all laid out. If you have a strong stomach, visit the bubbling cauldrons of the **tannery,** just inside Bab ed Debbagh, in the northeast corner of the medina. Climb Bab ed Debbagh for an aerial view of the earthen vats of this foul factory, each brewing a different concoction. The vilest containers hold a chemical compound which softens the dried leather. Other vats are for dying, rinsing, or cleaning. Children dive in to recover the immersed skins and emerge covered with a muddy, olive-purple ooze. The treated leather is available for purchase; the oozing kids are not.

Encircling the city on all sides are more than 2km of pinkish **fortifications.** Renovated over the course of several centuries, most of these bulky battlements were assembled in the twelfth century by the Almoravid Sultan Ali ben Youssef. Thousands of Christian slaves lost their lives in the course of constructing the walls, and legend proclaims that as they died, their corpses were plastered into the mudbrick walls by their enslaved compatriots. Successive sultans have added to the ramparts with less bloodthirsty techniques. The most dazzling gate is the twelfth-century **Bab Agnaou** (3 blocks south of the Koutoubia minaret), former portal to the Kasbah of Yacoub el-Mansour. More decorative than defensive, this gate was the spot where the mutilated corpses and heads of slain enemies were often hung as trophies of war. The neighboring **Bab er Rob** formed the southern doorway to the city. North from here, above pl. Mourabite off ave. d'el-Jadida, the tiny **Marjorelle Gardens** shelter birds and spiny cacti. They're the brainchild of the French expatriate artist Louis Marjorelle. A long swing around town to the northeast corner of Marrakech will bring you to **Bab el-Khemis,** site of a lively Thursday market. The bastion was reputedly designed and built by Andalusian architects and artisans. Farther south, **Bab Aylen** marks the spot where the Almohads suffered a crushing defeat in 1130 in their first attack on the Almoravid city. A large **fruit and vegetable market** occurs daily just outside **Bab Aghmat,** the next gateway in line. Opening onto the grounds of the royal palace is **Bab Ahmar,** an Alouite gate. Visiting these and all the other city gates in a day is pretty ambitious, so try to incorporate them into other parts of your itinerary.

Palaces

The dazzling **Saadien Tombs,** modeled after the interior of the Alhambra in Granada, form Morocco's most lavish mausoleum. The tombs served as the royal Saadien necropolis during the sixteenth and seventeenth centuries and were walled off by Moulay Ismail, who wished to efface the memory of his predecessors. For two centuries the Saadien sultans rested in peace, but in 1912 the necropolis was rediscovered. The first of the two mausolea was constructed for Moulay Ahmed el-Mansour. The first of its three chambers brims with tiles, marble columns, and stucco carving that culminates in a gleaming *mihrab.* Originally intended as an antechamber rather than a burial site, the room houses the tombs of Saadien children and the Alouite sultan, Moulay el-Yazid. In the neighboring Hall of the Twelve Columns, the trapezoidal tombs appear to float on a pool of polished marble. The tiny doorway, originally constructed as a window, affords an enchanting glimpse of the tomb of Moulay Ahmed el-Mansour. The Saadien sultan made his fortune by trading, pound for pound, salt for Sudanese gold, and sugar for Italian marble. His four legitimate wives, 23 concubines, and the most favored of his hundreds of children are buried close by. The unmarked tombs are the women's. The less splendid second mausoleum is lathered in batches of brilliant green tile. To reach the Saadien Tombs, pass through Bab Agnaou into the Kasbah quarter a few blocks south of the Koutoubia minaret. The turquoise minaret of the **Mosque of the Kasbah,** private worshiping place of Sultan Yacoub el-Mansour, flags the way; veer right into the alley adjoining the mosque. (Open daily 8:30am-noon and 2:30-6pm. Admission 3dh plus tip for the tour.)

The sultan's grand viziers were sometimes more powerful than the king himself. This was certainly the case in the late nineteenth century, when the royal advisors wallowed in the wealth of the kingdom and masked the ugly truth of colonial domination and national impoverishment from the monarchs. Sidi Moussa, grand vizier to Sultan Sidi Mohammed ben Abd er Rahman, and Sidi Moussa's son Ba Ahmed, chief advisor and favorite of the sultans Moulay el-Hassan and Moulay Abd el-Aziz, fell into this category. On the eve of Morocco's fall from independence at the turn of the century, they constructed the magnificent **Bahia Palace.** The name means "The Riches," of which ample traces remain: Dazzling tilework, crimson curtains, and mahogany furniture fill a seemingly endless procession of reception halls, tea rooms, courtyards, and patios. The roomiest chamber is the **Court of Honor,** a 50m-long, marble-paved corridor. The **Moorish Garden** blooms with jasmine, mint, orange, grapefruit, and banana trees. The palace is currently owned by Sultan Hassan II, making it the only royal palace in Morocco open to the public. Facing the defunct CTM station in the Djemâa, head left through an archway onto rue Riad Zitoun el-Kedim; follow the main thoroughfare to the end, and bear left through pl. des Ferblantiers, curving around 180°. To your right, a reddish-brown archway will open into a long, tree-lined avenue leading up to the palace doorway. (Open daily 9:30am-1pm and 4-7pm; in winter daily 9:30am-11:45am and 2:30-6pm. Free, but tip the guide.)

The Dar Si Said, a nineteenth-century palace built by Si Said, brother of Grand Vizier Ba Ahmed and chamberlain of Sultan Moulay el-Hassan, now houses the **Museum of Moroccan Art.** The collection features splendid Berber carpets, pottery, jewelry, Essaouiran ebony, and Saadien woodcarving. The gleaming Dar Si Said lies in a tiny alley off rue Riad Zitoun el-Jadid, the second right as you head north toward the Djemâa el-Fna from the Bahia Palace. (Open Wed.-Mon. 9am-noon and 4-7pm. Admission 3dh.)

Only a great open square remains of the sixteenth-century **el-Badi Palace.** After a resounding victory over the Portuguese at the Battle of the Three Kings, Sultan Ahmed el-Mansour retired to Marrakech to construct the enormous festival palace in 1578. Architects and materials alike were imported from all over Morocco and Southern Europe to complete the task. A century later Moulay Ismail ordered its destruction. It took the sultan a dozen years to dismantle the arena and deposit the proceeds in his other palaces. All that remains today are some pools of water ringed by drooping orange trees, fragments of delicately carved stucco and sculpted cedar, and one solitary *minbar.* (Open only during the el-Badi Festival in June.)

When Sultan Hassan II visits Marrakech, he resides at **Dar el-Makhzen,** a sprawling ochre palace roofed with rounded grass-green tiles. Founded by the Almohads and enlarged by the Saadien Dynasty, the present royal residence was largely constructed by Alouite sultans. Although the interior is closed to the public, you can swing around through Bab Ahmar to ogle the **Grand Méchouar,** a walled court where European diplomats and heads of state were once received amid much pomp. Overlooking the plaza, a roofed portal opens onto the **Agdal Gardens,** a 3km enclosure filled with scrubby olive and fruit trees. Follow the central alley to the south where a great pond borders the former palace of **Dar el-Hana.** From here, a sunny terrace affords a panorama of the surrounding palm-studded plain.

The **Menara Gardens,** a vast enclave of olive groves around an enormous pond, appear most beautiful at sunset, when the mauve- and tangerine-tinted light dances unpredictably on the smooth surface of the artificial lake. The cold green reservoir, 800m by 1200m, dates from the Almohad era. A charming, nineteenth-century, balustraded pavilion stands on the southern brink silhouetted against the backdrop of the snowy peaks of the High Atlas. To reach the Menara, head west through Bab el-Jedid and straight down ave. de la Menara, the wide boulevard that resembles an airport landing strip. To the south (left) lies the expanse of the **Olive Grove of Bab Jedid,** a continuation of the Menara gardens.

Entertainment

If you're in town, don't miss the fantasia held outside Bab Jedid in the early evening. At the sound of a gunshot, former Berber soldiers, reliving the days when they swept down from the mountains to fight the French, emerge from pointy-topped tents and mount their proud Arabian stallions. With *koumiya* knives dangling at their sides and *moukkahla* muskets arched over their shoulders, the screaming equestrians gallop hell for leather down the field in a cloud of dust and, at a signal, turn back on their mounts at a precarious angle, swivel their guns, and fire.

The old el-Bedi Palace is now the site of the annual **Folklore Festival,** which begins the first Friday in June and continues for two or three weeks. The extravaganza involves hundreds of performers, mostly acrobats and saber, rifle, and Ghedra dancers (toned down for the tourist audiences). In the evenings, three-hour sound and light shows are held by the palace pools (9pm nightly, 40dh).

If you prefer the light shows and sounds of the West, you can opt for one of the several western-style discos attached to the luxury hotels in town. **Diamond Noir** is one of your best choices. Attached to Hotel Marrakech, pl. de la Liberté (tel. 343 51), the disco has no dress code and no cover charge, but nails you for 50dh per drink.

Atlas Mountains

The Atlas Mountains are divided into three geographically and culturally distinct ranges. Intermediate in size, the plateaus of the Middle Atlas are laced with verdant cedar forests, bubbling natural springs, and cascading waterfalls. They are rich areas that serve vacationers (mostly from Fes), including the King, who has a huge summer residence in Ifrane. Traditional Berber communities encircle the villages of Azrou, Sefrou, and Ifrane. The most dramatic Moroccan alpine scenery is offered by the High Atlas. The range is capped by Mount Toubkal, North Africa's highest summit. With its excellent hiking and scenery the High Atlas are the most interesting for tourists. The jagged and barren peaks of the Anti-Atlas conceal vast canyons of bizarre rock formations. All three are difficult to traverse, as bus routes are skeletal; the least interesting Middle Atlas are the best-connected thanks to their proximity to Fes. Access to much of the region is at least partially limited to those with their own vehicle.

Middle Atlas

Remarkably lush in spots (by Moroccan standards), the Middle Atlas range is blessed with an abundance of water: It irrigates the grain fields of Kasbah-Tadla, is dammed at Bin el-Ouidane for hydroelectric power, and is bottled into Sidi Harazem near Fes. It also gushes over the falls of Ouzoud and soaks the roots of the great Cedar Forest. Wintertime here is even blessed with snowfall. Best of all, in the calm mountain resorts of Immouzzèr du Kandar, Ifrane, and Azrou, you can roam freely without harassment by hustlers and self-appointed guides.

Transportation is limited in this area, and you may find yourself using Fes as a base. Sefrou can be reached only via Fes. Immouzzèr, Ifrane, and Azrou hinge upon the same route south from Fes. However, buses are infrequent; getting off at Immouzzèr or Ifrane may mean having to stay in their more expensive accommodations when it's best to rest in Azrou and venture on from there.

Sefrou

Only 28km south of Fes, sober Sefrou combines an enchanting medina with a dignified new town, both surrounded by rustic hills and waterfalls only minutes away. For centuries, the town has been a trading center at the foot of the Middle Atlas and, until Moulay Idriss I's conversion campaign, this was an ancient enclosure of Judaism. Today, the town celebrates its abundant cherry harvest with the June **Fête des Cerises.** Try to time daytrips to coincide with the colorful Thursday *souk.*

Enter Sefrou's **medina** through Bab Lamkam, which doubles as the bus station. From here, Sefrou's fascinating **souks** wind chaotically several blocks up to the left. The **mellah** (old Jewish quarter) lies across the Aggai River on the right, a solemn reminder of the pre-Idrissean era. Rugs, the fruit of Sefrou's looms, can be purchased year-round at the **Cooperative Artisanale.** This red-roofed building is across from the bus station; it's worthwhile just to watch the famous carpetmakers engaged in their intricate craft. The cooperative welcomes Berbers, buyers, and browsers alike. (Open Mon.-Sat. 8am-noon and 2-7pm. Free.)

From the entrance to Sefrou's medina, walk to the right and then across the concrete steps that span the valley to reach the new city and Sefrou's accommodations. To the right and up the hill is Sefrou's finest sleep spot, the **Hotel Sidi Lahcen Lyoussi** (tel. 604 97), featuring fading elegance in the form of studded lights around the reception desk, a terraced garden, spacious, comfortable rooms, and an outdoor pool (occasionally full). (Singles with bath 140dh. Doubles with bath 175dh.) The more budget-conscious should follow the signs to Sefrou's **campground,** a barren affair charging 3dh per person, per tent, and per car. If you're feeling adventurous, continue up the mountain, following the signs to **Les Cascades.** You may be accompanied on the 20-minute hike by swarms of village children. The 15-meter falls themselves are anticlimactic—more like a powerful spigot than a cascade—but you can strip down in the rock cavity and enjoy a mild scalp massage.

Sefrou's barren **Syndicat d'Initiative** is on ave. Moulay Hassan. (Open daily 8am-1pm and 3-6:30pm; in winter 8am-noon and 2:30-6pm, except when it isn't.) Sefrou is served by frequent private **buses** from Fes's Bab Boujeloud and by SMTL buses (5.50dh) that leave from behind Fes's CTM station. If you're driving from Immouzzèr du Kandar, don't take the direct dirt road via Jbel Abad—it's in miserable condition. Ignore the road signs and drive the northern route via Bhalil.

The hills surrounding Sefrou are sprinkled with traditional communities. The most accessible is the hilltown of **Bhalil,** which lies along the paved road to Immouzzèr du Kandar (10km northwest of Sefrou). An enormous canal, built to control rushing floods, bisects the town, but the old part of the community has no running water whatsoever. Cave dwellings are recessed into the mountainside, which affords splendid views of the surrounding plains.

Immouzzèr du Kandar

Crisp, peaceful, and halfway between Fes (37km) and Azrou (30km), little Immouzzèr du Kandar makes a good base for exploring the surrounding **Kandar Mountains** of the northern Middle Atlas and the archipelago of tiny mountain lakes that dot the region to the southeast. There's nothing much to do in the town itself, which hugs both sides of a single road, except visit the meager **Ensemble Artisanale** (follow the signs), breathe in the brisk mountain air, and gape at the greenery. Try to come during the Monday *souk* or the July **Fête des Pommes** (harvest festival). The friendly **Hotel du Centre,** next to the bus stop, offers acceptable rooms. (Singles 50dh. Doubles 75dh.) The best 25dh meal in town is available across the way at **Restaurant de la Place,** but you may do better at the outdoor brochette stands next door (2dh). Take a plunge at the municipal pool just south of town (2dh). (Open June-Sept. 8am-5pm.) Buses journey to Ifrane (4 per day) and Fes (4 per day, 5dh); collective taxis shuttle to Ifrane and Sefrou.

Jbel Abad offers a pleasant 10-kilometer walk or drive from Immouzzèr. Follow the dirt road (*not* the paved road) to Sefrou 6km out of town to an unmarked pebble track that branches off to the left and climbs up to the summit (1768m). Be careful if you're driving, since the road is lined with sharp stones that can puncture your tires. Proceed slowly and carry a spare. A stone tower that marks the top affords a magnificent panorama. If you are without a car and don't mind the additional expense, a *grande taxi* can take you on the same route. Hitching is not advisable in this area.

An alternative excursion is to **Dayet Aouwa,** a 7km lake with plenty of cushy grass and shady spots for comfortable, free camping. You can bed down at the graceful old **Chalet du Lac,** decorated with dazzling Berber rugs. (112dh per person includes both hygiene and half-board.) The four-course *menu* is a bit steep for nonguests at 80dh. Dayet Aouwa lies 20km north of Ifrane and 5km south of Immouzzèr on the main highway. Ask the bus driver to let you off at the turn-off. From Dayet Aouwa begins the **Circuit des Lacs,** a 70km loop that passes by numerous mountain lakes ending at Ifrane.

Ifrane

What's a modern Swiss skiing village doing smack in the middle of Morocco? This wealthy holiday village of stone houses and modern streetlamps, *sans* flies and hustlers, was built in the '20s by a French colonial governor who found the mountain air salubrious. A twilight-zone atmosphere pervades the place, exemplified by the cavernous, empty resort hotel that looms eerily above the town on a nearby mountain. A few years ago, the King ordered it evacuated and indefinitely locked when he caught one of the guests trying to peer with binoculars into the royal retreat across the valley.

The frigid waters of the **Cascades of Ifrane** tumble and splash 4km out of town along the old road to Meknes (ask for the road to Ozouyia). Nearby, a tiny source bubbles with mountain mineral water. From January through March, the **Mischliffen ski area** offers pleasant slopes for beginners. You can rent equipment and hitch out. In summer, there's no public transportation, but if you can get here, you'll find that the alpine meadows offer wonderful, secluded picnic spots and an opportunity for discreet camping.

Ever since the Auberge de Moyen Atlas was closed down for renting rooms by the hour, there have been no budget accommodations in Ifrane—just three large and exorbitantly priced resort hotels. The least expensive is **Hotel Perce-Neige,** rue des Asphodelles. (Tel. 62 10. Singles with bath 137dh. Doubles with bath 169dh.) Like its friends, the hotel is empty most of the year, except for a few weeks in the winter and summer (mid-July to Aug.), when it may be full. Only campers can avoid the extortionate hotel rates, but must make reservations at the overflowing **Camping Ifrane** (tel. 61 56), on ave. Mohammed V. (4dh per person and per large tent, 3dh per small tent, 3dh per car, and an obligatory jolting 6dh for electricity.) Ask here or around the Mobil station about renting a room in a private home (around 50dh). Ifrane's handful of cafes and restaurants line ave. Jramchek, which begins by the post office. At the simple **Restaurant de la Rose,** a tastebud treat of lamb *tajine,* salad, and dessert comes to only 35dh. On Sunday there is a large *souk.*

Ifrane is 17km north of Azrou and 67km south of Fes. In the center of town, around the corner and uphill from the Mobil station, the **Syndicat d'Initiative** (tel. 62 73) has a good map, brochures, and a friendly staff. (Open daily 8am-noon and 4-6pm; in winter daily 8am-noon and 2-6pm.) The **post office** (with **telephones**), just in front of the Mobil station, keeps identical hours. There is no bank in town, but you can try the **money exchange** at the luxury Hotel Mischliffen. The **municipal pool,** down the hill on the road to Fes, is open daily in the summer (3dh). Fes-bound **buses** leave for Ifrane seven times per day from Azrou; from Fes, take any bus headed for Azrou. In Ifrane, buses leave from beside the post office across from the Mobil station. There are direct buses to Fes (2 per day, 11dh), and one early-morning direct bus to Meknes; there are also frequent connections from Azrou to Meknes. Private buses leave from about 2km outside of town, along the road to Meknes.

Azrou

Surrounded by cedar forest and shaded by the craggy peaks of the Atlas Mountains, Azrou is seductive in spite of itself. The town center is a parking lot and a gas station, and the crowded Berber medina seems suspicious of intruders. But authenticity and earnestness, complemented by the raw beauty of the landscape, make Azrou the most appealing town in the Middle Atlas.

Azrou is the trading center for the Beni M'Guild tribe. The sheared sheep grazing on the hillsides are the source of Azrou's livelihood, rug-making. Shop here for rugs, blankets, and wood crafts. Compared to Fes and Meknes, prices here are lower and hassles fewer. At the **Ensemble Artisanal,** downhill from pl. Hassan II, you can watch women spin raw wool into yarn using ordinary wooden sticks, while carpenters transform blocks of wood into cranes, storks, and fish. The exhibition room displays handmade Berber carpets, embroidered bags, shawls, sculptures, and figurines. Familiarize yourself with quality and prices here, but do your shopping and haggling with private merchants elsewhere in town; you'll get a much better deal. (Open Mon.-Sat. 8:30am-7pm; in winter Mon.-Sat. 8:30am-noon and 2:30-6pm.) Fifty meters down the hill is the refreshing **municipal pool** (3dh), but for a wet dream, wander from pl. Mohammed V to the **town well,** a conglomeration of spigots, pools, and channels.

The bus stops at pl. Hassan II. The threadbare **IYHF youth hostel** (tel. 83 82), about 2km up the road to Midelt, offers nothing but serenity. The toilets are primitive, the sheets musty, and the curfew 11pm. (10dh.) For slightly more back in town, you can stay at the earthy **Hotel Ziz** on pl. Moulay Hachem ben Salah—turn right off the right side of pl. Mohammed V. (Singles 15-20dh. Doubles 20-30dh.) Across the square at #45 is the best deal in Azrou, the bright **Hotel Beausejour** (tel. 21 01), where the tiny, tidy rooms have balconies overlooking the lively square. (Singles 24dh. Doubles 36dh.) The outdoor stalls along and around **place Hassan II** have a frightening variety of delicious food. Brochettes cost 2dh apiece, cubes of spicy *kefta* 1dh, and blackened sheep stomachs—for those interested—run 7dh.

Azrou is 78km south of Fes and 67km south of Meknes. There are seven **buses** per day to Fes (15dh) and Ifrane, four to Meknes. Buses to Marrakech are few and usually arrive full, so it's a good idea to reserve a seat on a later Fes-Marrakech bus (preferably with CTM) before you get to Azrou. There is also one bus per day to Er-Rachidia (9 hr., 44dh).

Beni M'Guild Region

The land of the Beni M'Guild tribe, fanning out from Azrou in all directions, features beautiful cedar woods and quiet villages that specialize in rug-making and wood-carving. Even if you are on foot, there are a number of fine excursions to make from Azrou. Monkeys roam the dense **Gouraud Cedar Forest,** named for the one-armed French general. An eight-century-old cedar guards the forest entrance at the end of a dirt road that begins 6km from Azrou. Walk up the road to Midelt, and turn right at the sign that points toward Ain Leuh. You can return to Azrou down the steep, pebbly mountain—just follow the droppings or the bleating of the shepherded goats. Free, shady camping spots are easy to find, but there's no running water. If you have a car, continue along the Midelt road south through more lovely cedar forest. After 14km, a paved road leads to Mischliffen, then loops back toward Azrou via Ifrane.

If you continue south along the road to Midelt, you'll reach **Aguelmane de Sidi Ali** (55km from Azrou), an isolated mountain lake accessible by a small dirt-road turn-off. It's a great spot for trout and carp fishing. For an even more spectacular route, continue 17km along the road from Azrou toward Meknes (hop any Meknes-bound bus). The road climbs up to the **Tigrigra Balcony** (also called the **Belvedere of Ito**), an elevated plateau embracing a grand panorama. To reach the stone fountain at **Ain Leuh,** travel 17km south from Azrou toward Marrakech, then 13km east by secondary road, and 3km up the mountain. You can walk down the road to the town's main street and nose about the *souk* on Wednesdays.

The magnificent, cascading **sources of the Oum er Rbia** lie 25km farther south along the secondary road from Ain Leuh. The route is treacherous, crowded with crossing animals and the carcasses of automobiles that failed to avoid them. After passing a mountain lake, the road plunges into a valley cut by a cliff gorge, then crosses two bridges and turns onto a dirt track that leads to the tiny parking lot next to the springs. Forty-five ice-cold springwater sources converge into foamy rapids at the basin. A winding footpath follows the rapids up the falls (15 min.) where the current has sculpted a series of canyons and gorges. Take care when swimming in the basin; the current is deceptively strong and the rocks slippery. Ten kilometers farther along is **Lac Ouiouane,** whose fertile shores attract donkeys, camels, and horses. From the lake it's only 24km to Khénifra. Those on the main road between Azrou and Khénifra can stop at the Thursday **horse market** in the village of **Mrirt** (51km south of Azrou).

Kasbah-Tadla

Kasbah-Tadla, 70km southeast on P24 toward Beni-Mellal and Marrakech, is the site of a handsome seventeenth-century **Kasbah**—including two mosques and a paiace—overlooking the Oued Oum er Rbia. Today, the town is an important agricultural center. In the mountain town of **El Ksiba** (22km north of Kasbah-Tadla along the road to Khénifra), you can stay at the **Hostellerie Henri IV** (tel. 2; singles 54dh, doubles 64dh) or at **Camping Taghalout** (3dh per person, per tent, and per car). Come by on Sunday for the *souk*.

Twenty-two kilometers east of Kasbah-Tadla on P24, a very poor road turns off to the right and climbs high into the Ait Haddidou, reaching **Imilchil** after 100km. This village is famous for its three-day **marriage festival,** held the first week in September. Young men court young women by holding hands and sweet-talking, while fathers and brothers play escort. In this cross between a mass marriage and a Sadie Hawkins dance, women decide their futures on the basis of a handshake and a smile in a few short minutes.

High Atlas

The High Atlas Mountains and their showpiece Mount Toubkal (4167m, the highest in North Africa) rise out of the Sahara, providing dramatic and welcome contrasts to the dry, hot monotony of the surrounding plain. Cool air and spacious valleys supply the perfect antidote to the endless hassles, outstretched hands, and oppressive heat of Marrakech. Some of North Africa's tallest mountains lie only 50km south of the city. Frosted with snow year-round, the summit of Mount Toubkal features Morocco's most mind-boggling panorama, while the slopes of Mount Oukaimeden are the site of the country's most famous ski resort. On June 21, the vernal equinox, villagers climb the highest peaks in the region to honor an ancient pre-Islamic rite that calls for the sacrifice of an animal.

Transportation is very limited in this area. If you rent a car only once in Morocco, this is the place to do it. Otherwise, there are infrequent **buses** to Setti Fatma in the Ourika Valley, several buses per day to Ouarzazate through the Tizi-n-Tichka Pass, and only one other bus that goes the way of the Tizi-n-Test Pass leaving Marrakech for Taroudannt at 3am. You can catch **Berber trucks** in the High Atlas with good frequency. Before you leave Marrakech, be sure to change enough money to last you a while; there is no currency exhange in the mountains. (If you wish to climb Mount Toubkal, read through the Mount Toubkal section *before* leaving Marrakech.)

Asni

At the beginning of the dramatic rise up to the Tizi-n-Test Pass, the tiny roadside village of Asni (elev. 1150m) serves as the primary gateway to Imlil and Mount Toubkal National Park and offers a fantastic opportunity to get away from the hustle and bustle (mostly hustle) of Marrakech. The dusty road to Asni winds through outcroppings of red rock and adobe villages. Boys ride tail-swishing donkeys sidesaddle and trudge by rows of sunflowers and cacti. The bus chugs up the winding road—at points only three donkeys wide—and coughs black smoke at the peasants washing clothes by the streams. Clumps of grass yield to patches of corn and wheat as the bus rises into the foothills of the High Atlas. The only life that comes to Asni is the delightful Saturday *souk,* which is liveliest in the morning. But tourists will be swamped with jewelry sellers all the time. Attractive, thinly plated copper and silver Berber bracelets and snuff boxes can be traded for T-shirts and cigarettes.

Facing the market's side entrance, just uphill from the bus stop, is Asni's modest **IYHF youth hostel,** about 100m to the right as you face the market's facade. Inhabited by families of ducks and cats, a dog, a few donkeys, cows, and two delightful wardens, the hostel comes complete with a dry toilet, a well, and shady trees. It is also possible to camp in the hostel's yard. The relaxing atmosphere of the shady lawn and sound of nearby stream are reason alone to visit the hostel (members and nonmembers 10dh). The other accommodations in town are highly overpriced. When buying food in Asni, don't pay more than 1.10dh for bread, and beware that the local merchants often save their rotten produce to pawn off on tourists.

Buses leave for Asni on the hour from the main bus station in Marrakech by the Bab er Rob. The two-and-a-half-hour bus ride (45 min. by car) costs about 8dh and 3dh per backpack. Much quicker and more comfortable is the collective **taxi** (12dh); taxis also leave from the Bab er Rob. For Mount Toubkal, continue directly to Imlil, either by the blue truck (20-30 passengers with luggage) that leaves every couple of hours (12dh), or by the town's only taxi, if you can round up five passengers (12dh each). If you're driving, continue past Asni in the opposite direction from Marrakech, and the turn-off for Imlil will be on your left.

Imlil

Most visitors to this tiny mountain village whiz through it on their way up the trail to Mount Toubkal. But the surrounding valleys are breathtaking, with cascades, scenic hikes, and some of the lushest vegetation you're likely to see in Morocco. The beautiful costumes worn by the workers in the fields are not for the tourists' benefit—in fact, they prefer not to be photographed. You can arrange to rent cramped private rooms in Imlil or one of the neighboring villages for around 12dh per person, but more comfortable lodgings are available at the stone **Refuge d'Imlil,** run—like all the refuges in the High Atlas—by Club Alpin Français. The refuge has decent cooking facilities (4dh for use of gas burners) and bunk beds (18dh, nonmembers 20dh; 2dh for the guardian). At nightfall ask the custodian to light a gas lamp for you. The best place to eat is **Café Resta,** across from the refuge. The proprietor will fix a salad and an omelette for only 8dh and throw in a pot of mint tea for 2dh.

Directly below in the **shopping center,** the most experienced (and English-speaking) guide of Mount Toubkal has a large selection of second-hand hiking boots for sale or rent. He also has the most exhaustive guide to the mountain, Robin Collomb's *Atlas Mountain Guide.* Since there is no electricity in Imlil, or anywhere else higher in the mountains, bring a flashlight.

The area around Imlil offers a host of pleasant hikes. If you arrive late in the day, two short **excursions** are possible. A trail leads across the river (branching to the left off the direct trail to Toubkal) and winds through verdant, terraced fields, meandering past several itsy-bitsy villages, before ending finally in the large central village of **Aremd.** The more spectacular unpaved road starts at the edge of town (branching to the right off the direct trail to Toubkal) and winds straight up, affording a terrific panorama of the Imlil Valley and ending in Aremd. Since the village lies at the foot of the main trail to Mount Toubkal, either one of these trails makes a nice alternative route to or from Toubkal. You can also shave roughly an hour off your hike to Toubkal by staying the night at Aremd (8dh). For the way down, you can arrange for a *couscous* meal (15dh) or a pot of tea here. This is also an opportunity to take a sobering closer look at the austerity and poverty of Moroccan mountain village life.

Besides the trail to Neltner, two other ambitious hikes begin from Imlil. The more difficult one leads to **Refuge Lepiney** (3000m) by the village of **Tazaghart,** a 5km climb from Imlil (get a very early start). To reach Lepiney, take the unpaved road to Aremd until just before it switches back, then follow the footpath. (If you have trouble, ask local villagers to point out the way.) The key for the refuge is kept in the village of **Tizi Oussem** (halfway along the trail). The other trail leads to the village of **Tachdirt** (2300m), where you can stay at the **Refuge de Tachdirt** and hike down to **Setti-Fatma** in the Ourika Valley the following day. For the hike to either Lepiney or Tachdirt, consider hiring a guide (about 150dh per day), since the trails become a bit hazy in places. The refuges at Lepiney and Tachdirt both cost 16dh with ISIC or IYHF cards, 30dh without, plus 2dh per person for the custodian and

5dh for cooking facilities. (Before taking these hikes, read the section on Mount Toubkal.)

Mount Toubkal

Starting from Marrakech, climbing Mount Toubkal (Jbel Toubkal) at a leisurely pace will take four days: one day to reach Imlil, one day to reach Neltner, one day to ascend to the summit, and one day to return.

Leave most of your luggage at the refuge in Imlil or the hostel in Asni, but don't forget to load up your day pack with a sweater, a waterproof windbreaker, an army knife, a canteen, and a warm sleeping bag for Neltner. **Topographic maps** of Mount Toubkal are available at the Imlil refuge for 50dh. Before you begin the trek to the summit, make sure you are adequately clothed. Wear **sturdy shoes** or lighter canvas-gortex boots, particularly for ankle support on the loose shale rocks of the more slippery trails. Thin cotton socks inside thick wool ones will keep your feet dry and help you avoid blisters. Bring a pair of **shorts** for afternoon hiking. For the final ascent, wear a pair of **long pants** for protection against thorns, jagged rocks, and cooler mountain temperatures, and don a pair of sunglasses to shield the glare. Bring **water purification tablets** as all the streams have the parasite *jardia* in them. Don't be fooled by locals drinking out of the stream water—they already host the parasite. Also bring plenty of **bottled water** and **suntan lotion.** Lastly, bring enough **food** (canned goods, bread, chocolate, oranges) to last through several days of exploring. Imlil is a good place to stock up; the last shop on the right bakes bread for the whole region. Food prices will rise with the altitude, as you will see in Neltner.

In Imlil many of the locals will offer their services as guides. The official guide rate fixed by Club Alpin Français is around 60dh per day. However, if you're careful and inquire of passing shepherds whether you're on track, hiring a guide is unnecessary.

The hike is usually made in two stages: first to Neltner Alpine Refuge (3207m), then to the peak itself (4167m). You do not need a guide to reach Neltner. Hiring a burro to carry your packs makes the going much easier. The hike can take as long as six hours from Imlil, an hour less from Aremd. Follow the stone road beginning past the village to the fork by the river. To the left across the river is a pleasant alternative route that winds past hamlets to culminate at the larger village of Aremd. For Mount Toubkal, continue right to the fork less than 100m away. To the right of here is a broad stone road that climbs above the irrigated valley in switchbacks; this cars-and-carts road leads indirectly to Aremd and is now being carved out of the mountains. To the left, marked by a long, horizontal tree branch, the steep trail to the peak of Mount Toubkal begins. This trail runs south toward Toubkal along the western side of the river gorge (Aremd is on the eastern side) and then descends into the valley.

Continuing toward Toubkal, the trail passes a clump of trees and crosses the valley floor's stony riverbed onto the eastern side of the long river valley (not the smaller terraced valley that begins at the base of Aremd over your left shoulder). You can pick up the trail to Sidi-Chamharouch 500m farther along the valley on the left. From here over the tree-line to Neltner, the trail is well-marked with burro blots and red rectangles painted on large rocks. About halfway to Neltner, the trail crosses the river again, so you can escape the midday heat by dipping into its refreshing pools. A few steps past the river is the tiny community of **Sidi-Chamharouch**—your last chance to buy food, at even more inflated prices. You can also arrange for meals or lodgings at Aremd here. Buying provisions at Sidi-Chamharouch calls for furious bargaining. Soft drinks are chilled in the river by the village, but beware of the local scam: They quickly dip the warm bottle into the river when you're not looking so that it feels cold to a quick touch. Check all food before paying; flat Cokes and stale chocolate are common, though the hollowed-out French bread does not seem to be a problem in this region.

All water upstream from here and even upstream from Neltner is *undrinkable*. It may look pure and fresh, but it's not. Drink only water that comes from a well or from a mountain that clearly has no villages on it. Even then, it's a good idea to boil it or use the foul-tasting but effective Halazone water purification tablets (paradichlorosulfamoyl benzoic acid).

Snakes, salamanders, and herds of bawling goats cross this path to Neltner, which first curves west from Sidi-Chamharouch and then gradually heads back south-southwest, parallel to the trail from Aremd to Sidi-Chamharouch. Well below the footpath, but above the valley gorges, hawks pirouette over their prey. **Refuge Louis Neltner** has water, cooking facilities, rows of beds in the attic, beautiful views, and fantastic trails heading off in every direction (14dh, nonmembers 19dh; 5dh for cooking facilities). The refuge is not a bad place to shop. The scrupulously honest warden has a small collection of handicrafts on hand to swap or sell to tourists. Bring enough food to last several days of exploring.

The final ascent to the summit is a bit perplexing. Start early. Your options include hiring a guide (almost 50dh per day), following discreetly behind someone who knows the way, or just going it alone. In any case be cautious: Don't hesitate to return to the refuge to ask directions from the innkeeper. Any attempts to find shortcuts out of the valley will require serious rock climbing. Unless you want to end up dangling on a ledge, caught in some remote and inaccessible cleft, don't trail-blaze. The trail to the peak cuts east across the valley, perpendicular to the essentially north-south trail to Neltner. With the refuge's toilet to your back, the Toubkal trail goes over the V-shaped crest. After crossing the river, climb the loose, pebbly wall for about 200m (the ascent from the left-hand side of this stony field is more direct, the ascent from the right-hand side easier) until you reach a skewed outcropping of layered rock. The trail up to the top of the crest begins behind this stratified rock sandwich. At the crest, Toubkal looms ahead, its broad peak resembling a camel's hump. To reach the crest at the base of Toubkal, take the trail farthest to the left. Before the actual ascent to the summit, the trail swerves right to avoid a steep cliff, then hooks left at the base. Don't despair: The trail becomes progressively clearer as you make the climb. It can take four to seven hours depending on how the altitude and heat affect you. A tripod marks the summit.

The view from North Africa's highest point defies description. A trickling stream should still be active toward the top of the trail, so stop here if you exhaust your water supply. If the stream is dry (most likely in Aug.), refill your canteen with snow and drink it as it melts.

Above 3500m you may suffer dizziness or headaches. Proceed slowly. Yawn or swallow to pop your ears in order to adjust to the low pressure. If you still feel sick, descend. The best way to avoid altitude-sickness is simply not to rush. Start early, schedule your climb at a leisurely pace, plan on walking from sunrise to sunset, and take lots of short rests to regain your breath and your equilibrium and to soothe any throbbing in your head.

Besides Toubkal, a number of other peaks, either just under or just over 4000m, are accessible from Neltner. If you wish to spend several days climbing, consider hiring a mule at Imlil or Aremd to bring up all your provisions (officially 40dh one way, 70dh round-trip—but can be bargained down).

The well-marked continuation of the trail to Neltner is not to Toubkal—it leads to the idyllic **Lake Ifni** and makes a pleasant two-day excursion. If you follow the valley trail, stay to the right of the river for the first 1½ km from the refuge. Cross the river following the trail for 6km until you reach the lake. The hike takes approximately six hours, and the final portion involves a dramatic descent. To visit the lake, you must be equipped for cold-weather camping and have sufficient supplies for a few days. You can hire a mule to carry your provisions between Neltner and Lake Ifni for 50dh each way. Due to the steep uphill return, it is impossible to return to Neltner on the same day. To avoid the grueling ascent back to Neltner, most visitors continue on from Ifni to the Ourika Valley. If you attempt this without a guide, bring along a regional map of the High Atlas; *Guide Alpin* to the High Atlas is available at the refuge in either Imlil or Neltner.

Tizi-n-Test

Beyond Asni begins the most dramatic stretch of road in Morocco. The engine whines as the chassis scrapes against stones, dust, and flies, and horns honk unseen around the bend—the adventure has begun. You're on your way to the Tizi-n-Test Pass. The steep, rugged road winds up through the High Atlas mountains from Marrakech in the direction of Taroudannt, 175km away. As you leave Asni and its pushy jewelry peddlers, tall pine trees appear along the route, and the air becomes lighter and purer. The hills light up with intense reds, greens, and browns, a spectacular background for the tiny Berber villages that dot the landscape.

The major attraction along the Tizi-n-Test route, the handsome crenelated turrets of the **Mosque of Tin Mal,** nestle in a lonely mountain valley. Its soaring minaret recalls the carriage of its sibling tower, the Koutoubia in Marrakech, constructed by the same ruler just a few years later. By the time of the mosque's construction, Tin Mal had already passed from the limelight, eclipsed by Marrakech.

Enter through the wooden door to explore the crumbling interior where cracking columns retain their foliated capitals. Facing southeast (not quite toward Mecca) the lovely *mihrab* survives intact. The mosque is also graced with a colony of brilliant, turquoise birds who nest in the clefts in the walls. Admission is free, but tip the guide. If the mosque is closed, try to unearth the custodian who lives in the nearby village.

Across the Oued Nfiss from the mosque stands the **Kasbah of Tagoundaft,** built at the beginning of this century. Below, in the village of **Souk Larba,** you can eat inexpensively at the **Restaurant Tin Mal** and poke around at the Thursday *souk.* Halfway between Asni and Tin Mal, in the village of **Ouirgane,** the **Auberge au Sanglier Qui Fume** has an efficient French proprietor who offers very tidy lodgings, including hot showers, at reasonable rates. (Singles 55dh. Doubles 68dh.) The *auberge* restaurant is expensive (55dh for a 4-course *menu*), but the food is fantastic (try the frogs' legs) and offers reason enough to stop off at Ouirgane. **Restaurant Tighardine,** just down the highway toward Tin Mal, has a 25dh *menu.*

Perhaps the best town in which to spend the night is **Idni.** This quiet five-house, five-cafe village is a popular pit stop for truck drivers. You can sleep either on a rooftop or one of the cafes' few beds for 5dh. Idni is about 40km short of the actual pass.

The route climaxes at **Tizi-n-Test** (2092m), the pinnacle of the pass, with its fantastic panorama of the Sous Valley. Overlooking the pass, **Cassecroute Restaurant** sells lukewarm soft drinks (3dh) and a large collection of quartz, pyrite, topaz, agate, and other rocks. Past Tizi-n-Test, the landscape and flora change from rock to pine, to palms, to arable land, and finally to the blistering desert foothills of the Anti-Atlas, guarded by the walled city of Taroudannt.

Public transportation to this region is a bit sparse. There are a few **buses** per day between Marrakech and Tin Mal, but to reach destinations farther than this is difficult. There is only service between Taroudannt and Marrakech on a bus that usually doesn't stop. (1 per day, leaves Taroudannt 5am, leaves Marrakech 3am; 8 hr., 45dh.)

Ourika Valley

The narrow, verdant Ourika Valley (33km from Bab er Rob in Marrakech) forks off from the road to Oukaimeden just before the village of Arbalou and stretches southeast to the tiny village of Setti-Fatma. Dotted with picturesque adobe villages and lined with lush, terraced fields, the valley is divided by the bubbling Ourika River and surrounded by the vaulting peaks of the High Atlas. In summer, the entire length of the valley is filled with campers and vacationing Moroccans. To reach the Ourika Valley by public transportation, take either a **bus** (8dh) or a collective **taxi** (12dh per person) from Bab er Rob in Marrakech. To get here by car, take S513 toward Oukaimeden and turn left where the road forks with signs for Oukaimeden (up to the right) and Setti-Fatma (down and to the left).

At the far end of the valley, the village of **Setti-Fatma** overlooks the mouth of the river, ensconced by tiny waterfalls. Sit at one of the outdoor tables of **Café Setti-Fatma** and watch the crystal-clear water flow past. **Café de la Cascade** features rock music, outdoor tables, and little else besides an adjacent pool in the river. Next to the cafe begins the delightful trail, winding past stunning mountain scenery, up to the **Cascades of Setti-Fatma.** A half-hour hike from the cafe, the first cascade (most dramatic in spring) presents an imposing column of falling water. The fourth and highest of the cascades is also the most impressive: The water drops from a height of 140m. Unfortunately these waterfalls are virtually dry in July and August, but the trip to the area is still rewarding and peaceful.

The entire Ourika Valley is strewn with restaurants interrupted by an occasional hotel. **Hotel-Restaurant la Chaumiere,** 1km before Setti-Fatma on the main highway, is the best place to stay at the far end of the valley (39dh). Their four-course *menu* costs 34dh. At the opposite end of the valley, by the village of **Arbalou** (just beyond the turn-off for Oukaimeden), the pleasant, rustic **Auberge Ramuntcho** (tel. 118), run by a French expatriate, serves a tasty 72dh *menu.* Five kilometers into the valley from Arbalou, the cheap and grimy **Hotel Nadia,** in the little town of **Oulmess,** charges only 20dh per person.

Oukaimeden

For a breathtaking and refreshing excursion, take a trip up the sinuous, steeply ascending road to Oukaimeden. From Bab Aganaou in Marrakech, it's a 75km climb up to this mountain resort, which boasts the highest ski-lift in Africa (3200m). The road winds through a dark green valley up to the bare, rocky peaks of the High Atlas. You'll pass numerous fruit stands before you leave the terraced hillsides and make the final ascent to the tourist village on the slopes of Mount Oukaimeden.

During the ski season (Dec.-Feb.), Oukaimeden is hopping with activity. In summer the tourist village is almost completely sealed up and provides a peaceful base for exploring the High Atlas. Oukaimeden features a tiny artificial lake and a host of hiking trails branching in every direction. Directly above the village, **Point Tizerag** (2740m) has a collection of Morocco's most galactic-looking telecommunications antennas and a terrific panorama of the High Atlas, complete with a plaque identifying individual peaks. Beyond the summit, a sandstone cliff drops almost 35m straight down.

In winter, both Chez Juju and the Hotel Imlil rent **ski** equipment. The ski lift operates from December 15 until the snow melts (Feb. or March). In the beautiful valleys near Oukaimeden, terraced fields and mud-brick villages paint a picture of rustic beauty. One particularly breathtaking excursion leads to the lush agricultural fields of the stunning Oussertik Valley (8-12 hr. round-trip hike).

There's no public transportation up to Oukaimeden, but you can take a shared **taxi** or **bus** (11dh for either one) to the village of Ourika from Bab Aganaou in Marrakech. Ask the driver to let you off at the crossroads (43km from Marrakech) to Oukaimeden; from here it is a 32km hitch (be prepared to pay for the ride). Club Alpin Français runs a **refuge** at the bottom of the road to Oukaimeden (12dh, nonmembers 18dh). The caretaker of the refuge can be found in the adjoining village. If you have dirhams to spare and an aversion to hitching, collect a group of five people and hire a *grand taxi* to take you all the way from Marrakech to Oukaimeden for a whopping 285dh (bargaining necessary).

Only a handful of accommodations remain open year-round. The best option is Hotel de l'Angour (tel. 05), known more affectionately as **Chez Juju.** Rates are a bit steep, but they include bath and half-board. (96dh per person, 130dh with full board.) However, there's a very comfortable six-bed dormitory room in back, where you can stay for only 18dh, including showers. The restaurant serves large portions of delectable French cuisine—*plat du jour* 40dh, complete four-course *menu* 60dh. **Club Alpin,** just down the road, also rents dormitory rooms. (12dh, nonmembers 18dh.) To call from Marrakech, dial 045 90 before the number.

Between Asni and Oukaimeden, a scenic but rather difficult dirt road runs from the village of **Tahanoute** (10km along the Tizi-n-Test from Asni toward Marrakech) to the base of Oukaimeden, winding past the pretty village of **Tadmamt** and the panoramic pass of **Tizi-n-Taslitane** (2200m). The route stretches only about 40km but still ends up taking more time than driving via Marrakech due to the poor conditions. Start with a full tank of gas. If your car breaks down in Oukaimeden, dial 310 40 in Marrakech for assistance.

Tizi-n-Tichka

A spectacular 200-kilometer mountain road leads from Marrakech through the High Atlas via the scenic Tizi-n-Tichka Pass (2260m—the highest in Morocco), culminating finally in the desert plains of Ouarzazate. The pass is sometimes closed in the winter; the CTM window at Marrakech's Gare Routiere will know the prevailing road conditions. Along the way, half-crazed chickens scramble about in front of red and brown mud houses, and teams of horses circle platformed courts threshing golden wheat under the keen eye of whip-cracking farmers.

Several **buses** per day traverse the Tizi-n-Tichka, most of them stopping at all major villages along the route. All along the highway, on either side of Tizi-n-Tichka, in the villages and on the roadside, aggressive vendors sell samples of rare rocks and precious minerals. Supply far exceeds demand here, so ignore the starting offers (often around 120dh); simply walk away and let the merchants bargain themselves down. Before you're out of earshot they'll probably agree to your original price. A small piece of manganese should cost 4dh to 5dh.

The road begins by the bus station at Bab Doukkala and winds its way through the vast palm groves of Marrakech, arriving 36km later at the bridge over the Oued Zat. As you cross the parched river bed, the scenery suddenly becomes dramatic. From the bed of the Zat River the road ascends continuously, arriving eventually at the picturesque village of **Toufliht**. You'll find a refreshing natural spring 1km farther down the road, where the villagers come for water.

Perhaps the most pleasant spot to stay overnight is the mountain village of **Taddart** (1650m), 86km from Marrakech and only 14km before the pass. The **Auberge Le Noyer** (no sign), facing the highway, is run by a gracious French expatriate and has spartan but adequate accommodations. (Singles 30dh. Doubles 37dh.) If you have a car, ask to shelter it in the garage here. A smoky **restaurant** across the street serves *harira,* tasty brochettes, and *tajine.* After browsing through Taddart's ramshackle tourist shops, climb down into the adjoining valley and follow the footpaths across the corn fields and up to the top of the butte on the opposite side. Electricity and gas are turned off in town at 11:30pm, so have a flashlight ready. Just down the road, the **Tizi-n-Tichka Pass** marks the precise halfway point (100km) of the route. The summit of the pass, which divides the provinces of Ouarzazate and Marrakech, is not as spectacular as the landscape that precedes it, and the summit is windy and barren. A few kilometers before the pass, you'll find the **Refuge de Tizi-n-Tichka,** run by the Club Alpin Français. (16dh, nonmembers 20dh.)

A few kilometers down the road from the Tizi-n-Tichka Pass, an acute left turn snakes steeply into the heart of a secluded valley. The 21-kilometer pitted asphalt road passes several stone hamlets and leads to the village of **Telouet,** where the weathered **Kasbah of the Glaoui,** a haunting pile of turrets and tile roofs, roasts silently beside the parched Oued Imarene. Home of the Glaoui, a native Berber clan who ruled the rebellious south at the turn of the century, this was the fortress into which sultan Moulay Hassan was taken after his fateful campaign of 1893. Enter through a gargantuan cedar doorway studded with brass nails and opened by the guard with an enormous pewter key. Lofty ceilings and lovely wooden doorways highlight the now-bare apartments leading into the heart of the Kasbah. The lavish dining room, paved with bright tiles, frames a majestic view of the valley with a delicate horseshoe arch window. (Free, but tip the guardian and the guide.)

If you haven't got your own wheels, the way to Telouet can be painful. Your best bet is to take a **bus** through the Tizi-n-Tichka Pass to the turn-off for Telouet and hitch the last 21km from here. Be forewarned: The road is sparsely traveled, and you may have a long wait. Arrive early and bring plenty of water.

The hospitable little hamlet of **Irherm-n-Ougdal,** dominated by a squat box-shaped Kasbah, lies 12km beyond the Telouet turn-off. Beyond this town, the road descends rapidly as the mountain air gives way to dusty winds and the foothills of the High Atlas yield to the sunbaked desert cliffs of the Sahara. Along the way you'll pass a number of Kasbahs, some enchanting, others dilapidated.

Anti-Atlas

Stretching from just northeast of Taroudannt to beyond Irherm and Tafraoute in the south, the Anti-Atlas forms a mountainous barrier protecting the Sous River Valley from the Sahara's brutal winds. Because of a great lack of transportation, the Anti-Atlas mountains are the least tourist-oriented and the least visited of the Atlas Mountains. The rock formations border on the bizarre and make for excellent photographic subjects. The sedentary Berber who populate the region have preserved many of their ancestral customs even though the government of King Hassan II has tried repeatedly to outlaw and destroy their ways and language.

Removed from the sea and enclosed in an oven of radiating, sun-baked rock, the canyons here cook to temperatures regularly exceeding 100°F in summer. Take the same precautions here as you would in the Sahara: Wear a hat (or turban), and drink fluids constantly.

Tafraoute

Tafraoute is a must for any visitor who is serious about seeing southern Morocco. The jewel of the region, this town is surrounded by naturally sculpted rock gardens. Located in the heart of the Anti-Atlas, the range is best visited by driving along one of the two routes that connect Tafraoute with the rest of Morocco.

Perhaps the most visually stimulating route is the drive from Agadir, which winds through the most dramatic scenery in the Anti-Atlas. South of Ait-Batha (where you'll find the last gas station before Tafraoute, 85km to the south), the precipitously rising terrain is punctuated by villages pasted against the bases of mountains and heaped together in hilltop clumps. Toward Tafraoute, the road is lined with stratified rocks of splotchy tones, and scrawny argan trees begin to appear.

Those traveling by bus have to transfer in Tiznit. Rte. #7074 climbs up through the desert past Assaka, a modest oasis, into the ochre-purple windy hills of the range. Here, rocky plateaus protrude from valleys and the softer rock has eroded away at the peaks, leaving only the jagged pieces of more durable rocks. The scenery is best at the **Kardouss Pass** (1100m), where the panorama embraces rows of peaks in every direction.

According to popular myth and certain Moroccan cartographers, there is a third road to Tafraoute, from Taroudannt via Irherm. Although the stretch from Taroudannt to Irherm is paved—except for a brief tract across a stony river bed near Freija—the last 100km along Rte. 7038 to Tafraoute is unpaved and thus best negotiated by donkey or a high-clearance, four-wheel-drive vehicle. A normal car couldn't possibly make it. Four-wheel-drive collective taxis, originating in Tiznit and Irherm, sometimes negotiate the road between Irherm and Tafraoute.

Deep within the mountains, Tafraoute is set in a dramatic slice of landscape where mammoth rose-tinged granite boulders and pillars are piled together in improbable rock formations. Pink Kasbahs are offset by a brilliant green oasis of palm, olive, fruit, and almond trees. Providentially, except for a brief invasion of four buses per day from Agadir, the spectacle remains unpolluted by tourists—and hustlers—throughout the year. The only exception is Wednesday (market day), when the four buses from Agadir come to town and many local cafes and shops temporarily double their prices. For several days every February when the trees blossom, all the town's hotels are booked and all of Tafraoute comes alive for the **Almond**

Festival (inquire at tourist offices in Agadir for precise dates). You can buy a bag of the nuts, Tafraoute's delicacy, at any time of year.

Tafraoute's budget hotels are clustered around the main square. The cheapest one is **Hotel Tangier** (singles 15dh, doubles 25dh—negotiable), but it's not a very cool place. You may want to try **Hotel Redouane** (tel. 66), which has pool and foosball tables downstairs and a **cafe-restaurant** that serves decent meals. (All rooms 35dh—negotiable. Hot showers 5dh.) The best food in town—and the only daytime meals during Ramadan—can be enjoyed at the splashy **Restaurant Etoile du Sud,** where you can dine in a large desert tent made of velvet. The proprietor will sprinkle you with rosewater and show you pictures of some of the restaurant's many guests. A complete meal here costs 46dh, a steep price for the standard *tajine, couscous,* and brochettes that they offer.

On pl. Hassan II, you'll find the **PTT** (open 8:30am-noon and 2-6pm), **Banque Populaire,** and **Banque MCE.** (Both banks open Mon.-Fri. 9-11:30am.) After-hours **phone** calls can be made from the hilltop Hotel des Amandiers for a 30% service fee; you may also be able to change money here after hours (though their official policy is to change only for guests). Signs point the way from pl. Hassan II to the **douches** (showers, 5dh).

The area around Tafraoute is graced with some of the most charming villages in Morocco. Walk or drive 3km out of town along the road to Tiznit to reach the village of **Adai,** at the center of an unforgettable landscape. The boulders threaten to tumble down and crush the tiny homes below at any moment. The most feasible and rewarding on-foot excursion is to the village of **Agard-Oudad,** 4km south of town on Rte. 7075. The village sits at the base of a legendary rock formation christened **Le Chapeau de Napoleon,** but a more discerning eye will notice that the rock's profile looks like a gorilla sucking its thumb. The gorilla, like most, is best appreciated from afar. At sunset, admire it silhouetted against the horizon—to attain the proper perspective, walk ½km down the road past the turn-off for the village. In Agard-Oudad, you'll find Morocco's only drive-in mosque and a series of steps leading to the trail up to the summit of Napoleon's Hat.

The most spectacular landscape is found to the north, along the Vallée des Ameln (Valley of the Almond Trees). This daytrip can be accomplished only on foot, with considerable exertion and a very early start. About 10km north of town on the road to Agadir (Rte. 7147) is the jumbled village of **Oumesnat** (look for the marked turn-off on your left) carved in pink stone. Drivers should park here. Proceed by foot to view the mud-brick homes. Several kilometers before the turn-off for Oumesnat, a road branches off the highway to Agadir into the heart of the almond valley generously sprinkled with Kasbahs. (There are over 20 within a 10km radius of Tafraoute.) The most challenging road leads to the spectacularly situated village of Tagudicht, clinging to the upper shoulders of the massive **Jbel Lekst** (2374m). To reach the village, look for a turn-off from the Vallée des Ameln marked "Ecole Tamaloukt." Drive by the school building, and turn off the road from Tamaloukt upward, following the endless switchbacks straight up the mountainside.

Taroudannt

The long, winding descent to the Tizi-n-Test Pass through the High Atlas comes to a halt at the tall, sandy ramparts of Taroudannt. The northern gateway to the Anti-Atlas, its bastions have controlled traffic between the mountain ranges for centuries. Encased in an enormous rectangle of crenelated fortifications, Taroudannt is one of Morocco's best preserved walled cities, with enchanting *souks* and remarkably few tourists. A road leads all the way around the ramparts and is best taken at sunset when the temperature is tolerable and the walls are bathed in a mauve-orange glow. The oldest battlements date from the early sixteenth century, when Taroudannt thrived as one of the cultural and military centers of the Saadian Dynasty. However, the remains are mostly eighteenth-century work. In town, all revolves around **place Assarag,** the central square at the entrance to the **souks.** Along with Tiznit, Taroudannt is Morocco's center for silverwork, and the jewelry *souk* sells intricate brooches and lavishly adorned daggers. The town is also famous for its peculiar gray and red rocks, which local artisans carve into wonderful stone figures.

A host of mediocre hotels cluster in and around pl. Assarag. Most charge 20-25dh per person (like **Hotel de la Place**), but around the corner to the right facing the above is **Hotel Restaurant,** where you can bargain a room down to 12dh per person. For the best ambience, go to the antique **Hotel Taroudannt** (tel. 24 16) on pl. Assarag. Rooms are clean and comfortable, and there's an inviting central courtyard that looks like a small tropical rain forest. Singles are 60dh, doubles 77dh. Their filling four-course *menú* (55dh) is one of the best European meals you'll find in the south. Off the other square, place Talmoclat, **Hotel Mentaga** (tel. 23 83) has modern, cheery, slightly overpriced singles (40dh) and doubles (50dh). The best budget eatery is **Restaurant de la Place** (in the hotel of the same name), pl. Assarag, with *tajines* for 12.50dh and tasty brochettes for 2dh apiece.

The places for **after-hours currency exchange** are Hotels Salam and Gazelle d'Or, both just outside the town walls (follow the signs). Near the hotels is the **post office.** Poste Restante and **telephones** are in this office. (Open Mon.-Fri. 8am-11pm and 3-7pm, Sat. 8-11am.) The town's **telephone code** is 085.

The **bus station** in Taroudannt is on pl. Assarag. There is only one CTM bus to Agadir and Casablanca at 5pm, so getting here from Marrakech is an ordeal. Buses leave the main station in Marrakech for Taroudannt each day at 3am; buses headed the other way leave at 5am (45dh). Connections from Agadir to Taroudannt are more convenient (4 per day, 12dh). If you're coming from the south, get off at the town of **Inezgane,** 12km from Agadir. A big public transportation center, the city has much more frequent service to neighboring towns such as Taroudannt (every 2 hr.). Be advised: This is local service that stops everywhere, but since the trip is only two hours long it's worth bypassing Agadir and catching a connection here. You can also reach here by *grande taxi* from Inzegane to Houara (6dh), and then from Houara to Taroudannt (6dh). The entire trip takes just over one hour.

Tioute

The lush palm grove and ruined Kasbah by the tiny village of Tioute, at the northern edge of the Anti-Atlas Range, offers a pleasant daytrip (37km) from Taroudannt. There's no bus service, so if you don't have a car, you'll have to hitch, hire a taxi, or haggle with Hotel Salam (tel. 130) for their expensive guided tour. If you're driving, continue 8km south along the road to Ourazazate, and turn onto the road to Irherm. Shortly after the turn-off you'll cross the broad, dusty bottom of the Sous River (bone dry almost year-round), overlooked by the hilltop ruins of the **Kasbah of Freija.** After continuing along the road to Irherm for rougly 24km, you'll reach (on your right) the dirt road for Tioute (5km).

The **Kasbah of Tioute** affords a terrific view of the surrounding oasis. On clear days you can see all the way to Taroudannt. Wiped out by the 1960 earthquake of Agadir, the Kasbah now houses only a few well-preserved chambers. Above, on a neighboring hill, are the remains of a Portuguese fortress, while directly below lies the tomb of an anonymous rabbi. Local Berbers will point out the **Palace of Tiouti Mohammed,** once the official seat of the regional pasha. Next door, a **hotel** should now be open. Follow the road past the village to the **Source de Tioute,** a natural spring bubbling up from the ground and channeled into a rectangular reservoir. Adjoining the spring, at the edge of the palm grove, sprawl the ruins of the *mellah,* where a community of Jewish silversmiths once dwelt.

Sahara

The Sahara is best approached with caution and respect. The world's largest desert spans an area as big as the continental United States. The war in the south appears near resolution. By press time, the Algerians had agreed to reopen diplomatic relations with Morocco, though this does not necessarily mean a ceasefire will occur. But even without war, the region is dangerous to travel. While it is impossible (and undesirable) for tourists to get anywhere near the war zone, traveling to the Kasbah- and palm grove-strewn Ziz and Drâa River valleys affords the rare opportunity to see one of the last camel caravans crossing the oasis. Even in the pre-Sahara you will be amazed by the imposing military presence in every town and on every road. Don't let this, or the searing heat, deter you from climbing the orange, mountain-like sand dunes of Merzouga and enjoying the mirage of your choice.

Practical Information

Wear lip balm, strong sunblock, head covering, and light, loose-fitting clothes to protect your skin. If you venture into any dune areas, a bandana is indispensable for preventing sand inhalation. Always carry plenty of bottled water—*at least two gallons of water per day*. Drink regularly, even when you're not thirsty. Thirst is the first sign of dehydration, which strikes quickly. You can't merely drink huge quantities of water after the fact—indeed, it's dangerous. "Moroccan Whiskey," mint tea, is not only cultural but practical—it is the best thing around for supplying liquids while decreasing thirst (due to salts in the mint). Bring food with you if you like, but you will probably find that the heat takes your appetite away. Yogurt, fresh vegetables, melons, dried fruit, and nuts are good hot-weather sustenance, though it's best to eat large quantities only after sundown. Restrict activity to the morning and the evening after sundown; spend the afternoons sleeping or relaxing in the shade. Moroccan life is generally built around these hours. Most places can be reached by bus.

If you're **driving** in the desert, appropriate preparation and extreme caution are essential. Every year several foolhardy tourists hop into their car, head thoughtlessly off into the Sahara, strand themselves on a sandswept road, and die of sunstroke or thirst. Before you leave any main road—even for a short excursion—fill your gas tank, and ask locals or roadside police about road conditions. Before embarking on an isolated track far from villages, pack up large supplies of reserve water and a reserve can of gas. If you'll be traveling along remote routes, inform local authorities of your precise travel plans. For such ventures, also be sure to bring materials to construct a shady refuge (or brick house) from the sun. Take all warnings concerning poor road conditions seriously. The ideal arrangement is to travel with two four-wheel-drive vehicles, so if one of breaks down you can still return to civilization. Cars can be rented in Ouarzazate for the Drâa and Ziz Valleys or in Agadir for Goulimime.

Inhabitants of the Sahara have virtually no source of income. There is neither agriculture nor industry. Many people have nothing, so they will persist even when it is clear that they have nothing to gain. As a result, they must be handled much more delicately than the streetwise youths of the cities. In general, people are very friendly and will eagerly tell you about the desert or give you a quick lesson in Arabic.

Goulimime

Due to its proximity to the beach resort of Agadir, the desert outpost of Goulimime has the honor of being both the most popular and the least attractive portal to the Sahara. Goulimime's attraction is its status as the meeting ground of two very different worlds: the sedentary Berber merchants of the town and the nomadic Blue People of the open Sahara. Although of radically divergent cultures, they share a common language, allowing the trading vital to Goulimime's mercantile economy.

Blue People, so named because they have blue skin colored by the dye of their clothing, are extremely rare today. Most of them are hustlers dressed up as nomads attempting to make a quick rip-off. But occasionally you will see a real Touareg (tribal name for Blue People). The same events that have attracted the Blues for centuries lure Western travelers here today: the weekly camel market held every Saturday morning and the spectacular seven-day festival, or moussem, held annually only Allah knows when. Unbelievable though it may seem, this grand event is somewhat impromptu.

Be prepared for the desert heat here: Summer temperatures soar to 120°F. Fortunately, proximity to the coast sometimes brings cool ocean breezes through the valley and a bearable climate all year-round. *Water is scarce here;* treat it with respect at all times.

Orientation and Practical Information

The only place well-connected to Goulimime by bus is Tiznit. Very infrequent buses hook Goulimime to Agadir (or Inezgane), and it is often necessary to change at Tiznit. The easiest way to go from Goulimime to Sidi Ifni is via collective taxi.

From the **bus station** ask directions for **pl. Hassan II,** which is a sort of commerce/*souk* center as well as the only place to find good food. To reach pl. Bar Nzarine, home to the **post office** and the only bank, **Banque Populaire,** walk uphill along rue Mohammed V. (Both open Mon.-Fri. 8:30am-noon and 2-4pm; July-Aug. Mon.-Fri. 8am-2pm.)

Accommodations and Camping

The accommodations scene here is bad. Only three budget places and several cafes let you sleep on the terrace, but the latter don't have running water.

Hotel Salam, route de Tan Tan (tel. 20 57). The only sanitary establishment in town and by far the most expensive. Its extra comfort (and the luxury of baths in each room) is worth the money. Singles with bath 84dh. Doubles with bath 102dh.

Hotel l'Ère Nouvelle, 113 rue Mohammed V (tel. 122). Much less than the above in all respects. Cold showers available. Singles 32dh. Doubles 40dh. Cold showers available.

Hotel la Jeunesse, rue Mohammed V (no telephone), diagonally across from the above. Slightly less still than the above. Singles and doubles 30dh—negotiable.

Cafe Alag, pl. Hassan II (no phone). No running water. Roof space 7dh.

Camping facilities are minimal but peaceful and outside of the city. Follow the signs from pl. Hassan II—it's about 1½ km out located in a safe and fairly well-guarded wooded area. Water is available. (5dh per person, 2dh per tent and per car.)

Sights

Visit Goulimime on market day—otherwise it's a waste of time. Every Saturday morning, a fascinating **camel market** is held in the enclosure 1km south of town on the road to Tan Tan. At 10am busloads of camera-toting rubbernecks arrive from Agadir, so if you want to see more dromedaries than Europeans, go early (the market begins at 5am and lasts until 11am), or consider arriving in town Friday night. Poke around the camel and check its teeth to determine its age. The camels come with standard equipment (1 hump, not 2) and list for about 900dh. Shopping at the camel market requires vigorous bargaining, since the locals have become accustomed to an extraordinarily naive breed of tourists.

Goulimime, a caravan port for centuries, was the end of the road for traders in gold, salt, and slaves from Niger, Mauritania, and Senegal. Today, trade goods from central Africa occasionally find their way this far north. With a little shopping around in the bazaars, you can find bracelets from the Ivory Coast, beadwork from Senegal, and beautifully decorated saddlebags from Mali.

A spectacular sight is the annual religious festival or **moussem,** where Saouhari tribes (Blue People) traditionally come from as far away as Mauritania and Timbuctu in Mali to attend the festivities. Recently, the conflict in the Sahara has somewhat dampened the migration of nomads. During the *moussem* all of Goulimime is given a face lift: While people strut about in their folkloric finery, streets are refurbished and houses repainted. The event usually takes place at the outskirts of town on the road to Agadir. Two rows of camel-skin tents are set up along either side of a cleared, wide thoroughfare, at the end of which three huge chieftain tents are staked. Inside these tents at night, you can see the *guedra,* an exotic desert dance of unmistakeably erotic origin, often performed by courtesans. The kneeling women harmonize expressive gesticulations with the pulsating drumbeats and syncopated clapping of musicians. If you miss the *moussem,* you can still glimpse the regional *guedra* dance: Every Saturday at noon and 9pm a performance for tourists is given at **Hotels Mauritania** and **l'Ère Nouvelle** (20dh), or every Friday night at the **Rendez-Vous des Hommes Bleus Restaurant,** on the road to Agadir.

Near Goulimime

Ait-Boukha and Plage Blanche

If you're in Goulimime on any day other than a Saturday, there are just two worthwhile places to go—both involve leaving town. The **Ait-Boukha Oasis,** a cluster of small Berber villages in a grove of palm and olive trees, lies 17km southeast of town. You can take a taxi (team up with other tourists if possible), but bargain furiously. The road is only paved as far as Asrir (10km), where it turns off onto a dirt road (4-wheel-drive is unnecessary) and heads off to the northeast. You'll be able to make out the palm grove 7km in the distance. A guide is not necessary—definitely ignore the hustlers' prattle about caravans and tents with Blue People on the way to the oasis—they're setting you up for the local scam that involves extorting a fortune in exchange for meeting phony nomads.

The other worthwhile venture from Goulimime is only safe in a four-wheel-drive vehicle: **Plage Blanche** (65km southwest) offers miles of pure, isolated, sandy beach. The road to Plage Blanche branches off the highway to Agadir just as you leave town.

The only other possibility, if you don't come to Goulimime on market day, is to visit a *souk* at one of the neighboring desert villages: **Tighmert** has a Thursday *souk,* **Ait Ourir** a Tuesday *souk,* and **Tamslout** a Friday *souk.*

Sidi Ifni

Since the Spanish colonial masters withdrew in 1969 and the territory was incorporated into the Kingdom of Morocco, this tiny art deco port resort has undergone dramatic decline. The faded white, pink, and light blue Spanish colonial mansions and official buildings stand in a state of disrepair. With the handful of remaining hotels desperate for business, Sidi Ifni seems on the verge of becoming a ghost town. Nonetheless, the coastal road from Ifni to Tiznit offers a scenic alternative route to or from Goulimime, and the cool coastal breezes afford relief from the ruthless desert sun. Sidi Ifni's white, sandy beach lies directly below the town, at the foot of a cove of rising cliffs. Bring warm clothes—even in mid-summer it can become remarkably chilly here. Clouds are often generated when the hot desert air meets the cool Atlantic winds, completely eclipsing the sun.

The clean, quiet **Hotel Belle Vue** (tel. 50 72) is above the beach on pl. Hassan II. (Singles with shower 77dh. Doubles with shower 89dh.) Their restaurant serves a *menu complet* with a fish or *couscous* entree (49dh). **Hotel Ait Ba-Amran,** ave. de la Plage (tel. 51 73), has comfortable rooms right on the beach for similar prices.

Sidi Ifni is served by collective taxi from either Goulimime (10dh) or Tiznit (13dh), as well as occasional direct buses from Tiznit (10dh). The paved road from Tiznit meets the coast at the tiny village of **Gourizim** (52km from Ifni), which has a ruined hilltop Kasbah and a wonderful little beach (2km south of town). In the summer a small enclave of campers sets up here. If you join them, guard your goods, especially from the local children.

Tiznit

Romantically ensconced within a crenelated wall, Tiznit bakes upon an arid plain at the foothills of the Anti-Atlas Range. Most of the fortifications still standing at this pre-Saharan outpost, famous for its silversmiths and warrior sons, were constructed after 1882 during the reign of Sultan Moulay Hassan. In the last century, Tiznit has become the primary administrative center and transportation hub for the western Sahara. Tourists traveling by bus to Goulimime, Sidi Ifni, or Tafraoute will inevitably find themselves stranded at Tiznit for several hours, if not overnight. Try to come here at the end of August, when Tiznit celebrates the **Moussem of Sidi Ali ou Moussa.**

The nineteenth-century **city walls** extend around the outskirts of town. Ramble about the dusty alley of the medina for a taste of the town's marketing district. At the eastern edge, the minaret of the **Grand Mosque** rears its crusty turret. A hundred meters north of the mosque, the sparkling waters of a tiny source bubble. Lalla Tiznit, a pious fisher who dwelled here, is said to have prayed that any community founded on the spot would carry her name. Follow the walls north to **Bab Tarqua,** where you can mount the ramparts for a panorama of the town and desert. Later, head for the *souk,* with its **jewelers quarter** (with your back to the Hotel Atlas, walk to the right and enter the gateway at the left end of the square) to take in the silver crafts for which Tiznit is known. Fine jewelry and handmade *djellabas* and *kaftans* can be purchased here at reasonable prices with relatively little bargaining. Thursday is market day.

Buses stop in the main square called the **Méchouar.** Here there are plentiful sleazy and cheap accommodations. However, your best choice is **Hotel CTM** (tel. 22 11), which has clean, spacious rooms (25dh per person) as well as a good, cheap restaurant (a full meal for around 20dh). It is located across from the **post office.** (Open Mon.-Fri. 8am-3:30pm; Sept.-June Mon.-Fri. 8am-12:15pm and 6-7:30pm.) Closer to the Méchouar, **Hôtel-Restaurant au Bon Accueil** offers spartan rooms (20dh per person) and has a pleasant restaurant downstairs. Travelers with a larger budget may want to try **Hotel Mauritania,** rue de Goulimime (tel. 20 72), boasting small and spotless carpeted rooms, all with full bath. (Singles 77dh. Doubles 89dh.) Turn left when exiting Méchouar via the main gate, walk about ¾ km to the large intersection with rue Goulimime; it's on the right just past the gas station. The **police station** is nearby on blvd. Mohammed V. In the square between the Hotel CTM and the post office are collective taxis that regurlarly head for Agadir (20dh), Goulimime (15dh), and Sidi Ifni (13dh). The **Syndicat d'Initiative** is inconveniently located outside the medina walls on the Agadir-Goulimime highway. Across from it is the **Tiznit Hotel,** which has the only swimming pool in town. (Admission 20dh for nonresidents.)

Sidi Moussa d'Aglou Beach, 17km northwest of town along an infrequently trafficked route, is quite inviting: On weekends and in the summer, Moroccan families pitch tents above the beach. **Motel Aglou** is a lonely, run-down establishment on the beach. The equally dilapidated **Camping Aglou** sits 1km up the hill toward Tiznit off the main road.

Bou Izakarn to Zagora

A fascinating route begins at **Bou Izakarn** (41km north of Goulimime) and slices east across the heart of the Moroccan Sahara to Zagora via the large oasis of Tata. Much of the road is hazardous sand track best crossed by four-wheel-drives, though parts of it are more easily accessible. Bou Izakarn offers a shadier and more hassle-free overnight stop on the Tiznit-Goulimime highway than Goulimime. **Hotel Anti-Atlas,** on the main highway (tel. 34), has comparatively clean, toasty rooms with creaky beds and cold showers. The summer sun will heat the shower water to lukewarm. Their *menu touristique* is the only solid meal available in town. The **PTT** (open 8am-noon and 4-7pm) is just down the road toward Tiznit from the hotels.

Tuesday is market day in town. **Ifrane de l'Anti-Atlas,** 14km away, along a more difficult road to Tafraoute, consists of a lovely cluster of 30 *ksours* (southern-style settlements) scattered about an inviting oasis.

The road from Bou Izakarn is paved for the first 114km to the east, but thereafter it degenerates rapidly. Gas, food, and some form of accommodations are available at Foum Zguid, Tissint, Tata, Akka, and Foum el-Hassan—the five regional administrative centers along the way. The two most beautiful of the oases are Tissint and Tata: Tiny **Tissint** consists of five *ksours* cut by a trickling *oued* (stream) and affords a fine view of Jbel Bani, but the route's main attraction is the large, enchanting oasis of **Tata** at the convergence of three streams flowing down from the Anti-Atlas. With a sturdy vehicle, Tata is accessible from Tafraoute via a poor road that starts at Irherm.

Ouarzazate

It's almost impossible to travel in the Moroccan Sahara without spending at least one night in Ouarzazate. The center of the town stands at the crossroads of four of southern Morocco's major arteries: the Tizi-n-Tichka Pass, the Dadès Valley, the Drâa Valley, and the desert road to Agadir. Ouarzazate is where the desert plains meet the foothills of the High Atlas. It is a big center for artisanry produced by the nomadic and sedentary tribes to the east, as well as the administrative seat of the Moroccan Sahara.

Orientation and Practical Information

Most administrative buildings, cafes, and restaurants are located along **ave. Mohammed V.** Inexpensive lodgings can be found either here or on the streets parallel and to the north of it.

Tourist Offices: Ave. Mohammed V (tel. 24 85), where the road forks to follow both the Oued Draâ and the Oued Dadès. Helpful, friendly staff. Thorough bus information and a list of local *souks* and *moussems*. Open Mon.-Fri. 8am-2pm; Sept. 14-June Mon.-Fri. 7:30am-noon and 2-6pm. **Syndicat d'Initiative,** 2km east from the center of town, along the road to Oued Dadès, next to the Kasbah. Cheerful, knowledgeable staff. Same hours as tourist office.

After-Hours Currency Exchange: Hotels at the eastern edge of town (Hotel Azghor, Hotel Tichka, and Hotel Le Zat).

Post Office: Ave. Mohammed V, next to the tourist office. In the same building are **international telephones.** Both open Mon.-Sat. 7am-2:30pm; Sept. 14-June Mon.-Sat. 8:30am-noon and 2:30-6pm. **Telephone Code:** 088.

Bus Stations: CTM, ave. Mohammed V, next to the post office. To Marrakech (5 per day, 5½ hr., 45dh), Tinghir via the Oued Dadès and Boumalne (2 per day, 4 hr., 26.40dh), and M'hamid via Oned Drâa and Zagora (1 per day, 8 hr., 44.20dh). **Private buses** travel the area around Ouarzazate more frequently. They leave from a station 100m west of CTM in pl. Mouhadine.

Collective Taxis: Pl. Mouhadine. They have slightly higher prices but can leave at any time and are much faster. To Marrakech (4 hr., 50dh per person) and Zagora (3 hr., 35dh per person).

Car Rental: Hertz, Mohammed V. **Budget,** 1km past town near Hotel la Gazelle.

After-Hours Pharmacy: Pharmacie de Nuit, ave. Mohammed V (tel. 27 08), across from the post office. Open daily 8am-7:30pm.

Private Doctor: Georges P. Apostolakis, ave. Mohammed V, across from Cafe Dimitri.

Police: Ave. Mohammed V. Tel. 19

Accommodations and Camping

The Ouarzazate accommodations scene is a budget traveler's dream. There are several clean, cheap hotels in town, convenient to the bus stations, and medium-priced hotel nearby. Unless you're willing to spend a fortune, you'll probably end up spending almost nothing at all.

Hotel Royal, 24 ave. Mohammed V (tel. 22 58), next to Cafe Dimitri. The town's best budget hotel. Rooms with big windows and a courtyard. Fun and friendly staff. Singles 20-30dh. Doubles 40-50dh. Triples 45-70dh.

Hotel Atlas, 13 rue du Marché (tel. 23 07), parallel to ave. Mohammed V, by the market. Moderately clean. Singles 26dh, with shower 32dh. Doubles 32dh, with shower 42dh.

Hotel El Salam, ave. Mohammed V (no phone), across from Hotel Royal. Clean, but nothing fancy. Large rooms. Singles 35dh. Doubles 45dh.

Hotel la Gazelle, ave. Mohammed V (tel. 21 51). The elusive gazelle has at last been found—outside of town (1km) toward Marrakech, on the right. Sparkling clean rooms surrounding a gorgeous garden. Pool. Ouarzazate's only medium-priced hotel. Worth the walk. Singles 84dh. Doubles 102dh.

Camping Ouarzazate (tel. 25 78) is 2km east of town. Facilities are adequate and safe, including toilets and cold showers. (5dh per person, 3.50dh per tent and per car.) The **restaurant** offers breakfast, a three-course lunch or dinner, and cold drinks.

Food

Restaurant du Sud, ave. Mohammed V (no phone), next to the CTM station. The place to eat while you wait for your bus. The manager loves American music and is constantly playing selections from his cassette collection. *Harira* 1.50dh, *tajine* 16dh. Open daily 6am-1am.

Restaurant es Salam, ave. Prince Héretier Sidi Mohammed (tel. 27 63), around the corner from Hotel Atlas. Noon-time watering hole for Moroccan soldiers. Decent meals at decent prices. *Couscous* 25dh, omelette 6dh. Open daily 8am-11pm.

Restaurant-Cafe Royal, ave. Mohammed V (tel. 24 75), under the signs for the hotel. Best budget restaurant in town. Salad 3.50dh, lamb *tajine* 16dh. Open daily 7am-11pm.

Restaurant el-Helal, 6 rue de Marché (no phone), up the street form Hotel Atlas. *Harira* 1.80dh, *couscous* or *tajine* with lamb 18dh. Open daily 9am-10pm.

Sights

The **Kasbah of Taourirt,** 1½km east of town, rises from a sandy riverbed and cradles a neighboring *ksour* within its impervious ramparts. Constructed at the turn of the century, the fortress is under restoration, but a small portion of the palace interior is open to the public. Enter through the doorway just south of the Syndicat d'Initiative and avoid the crush of self-proclaimed guides pressing about the entrance. (Open daily 8am-7pm; in winter 8am-6pm. Admission to palace 5dh.) The most authentic parts of the fortress are its imposing ramparts and the village they circumscribe, all of which you can tour for free. Head down the alley just to your left as you face the palace entrance. Within you'll find a fabulously preserved medieval labyrinth. The village is crowded with shuffling grannies, toothless shopkeepers, and screaming adolescent soccer enthusiasts. Across the highway, a tiny **Centre Artisanale** displays local crafts (same hours as the palace). From the southern end of Taourirt you can make out the handsome profile of the **Kasbah de la Cigogne,** a 2-kilometer walk through the desert from Taourirt.

Near Ouarzazate

Ait Benhaddou

The descent to Ouarzazate is periodically interrupted by small Berber Kasbahs, all quadruply turreted gingerbread hovels. This side of the Atlas is hot and dry, a painted desert of vast stony fields and distant buttes. The colors, miraculously buttressed by the blistering African sun, come alive as the sun begins to set and then fade softly into pastels. Two kilometers past the Kasbah of El Mdint, the turn-off for Tamdaght leads 9km to the ancient *ksour* of Ait Benhaddou. Reddish-brown sun-baked fortresses with massive walls and crenelated brick towers rise proudly from the southern face of a khaki butte; houses are piled side by side in an extraordinary ensemble that no urban planner could ever have devised. Though seemingly abandoned, the fortified *ksour* is inhabited by a handful of Berber families. The forest of tapered turrets, sculpted with checkerboard arches, climbs steeply to the crest of the mount, culminating in the ruined Kasbah that commands the desert hilltop.

Although there are no hotels in Ait Benhaddou, the village does offer the possibility of a decent meal. **Restaurant La Kasbah** features a fine view of the *ksour,* a pleasant *salon marocain* dining room, and a fixed *menu* for 35dh. To reach Ait Benhaddou without private automobile, you can hire a taxi in Ouarzazate (about 150dh round-trip). This taxi option is best combined with a stop-off at Tiffletout on the way back for the same fare.

Tiffletout

The baked, burgeoning battlements of the **Kasbah of Tiffletout** stand guard from a lofty riverside hilltop. Once the haunt of the caliph of the Glaoui, who housed a standing army within its walls, the Kasbah was temporarily converted into a swanky four-star hotel before lapsing into its present state of relative neglect. Inhabited by a colony of pigeons and the usual crew of friendly storks, the castle maintains an imposing fortified facade. Inside, the central courtyard is strewn with the modern vestiges of the former hotel, and the terrace offers a fabulous view of the surrounding desertscape. The fortress is occasionally the site of traditional festive bellydancing. Inquire at the Ouarzazate Club Med for times and prices.

To reach Tiffletout by public transport from Ouarzazate, hire a **taxi** with others if possible (60dh round-trip).

Jbel Siroua

A massive volcano that emptied in the prehistoric period depositing volcanic rock throughout southern Morocco, Jbel Siroua (3304m) lies 95km west of Ouarzazate. The most direct road to Jbel Siroua starts from the tiny village of Anezaal, 56km away. However, the route is virtually impassable with a regular vehicle. It is therefore necessary to go via the town of Aoulouz, on the desert route between Agadir and Ouarzazate, serviced by four buses per day. Along the way the bus stops at **Taznakht,** an interesting *ksour* with a lively Saturday *souk,* and **Taliouine,** a mudbrick community seated amid a lush orchard of almond trees. A good unpaved road leads south from Taznakht to the oasis of **Foum-Zguid. Hotel Ibn Toumert** (tel. 29) in Taliouine wins the prize as the country's most luxurious hotel in the middle of nowhere. It comes complete with swimming pool and cushy rooms with telephones and private baths. (Singles 213dh. Doubles 265dh.)

The dirt track that leads up to the northern slopes of the volcano is in fairly poor condition and should be attempted only by a sturdy vehicle. The first portion of the route passes through the land of the Ouzguita tribe of Berbers, famous for their fabrics and weavings. Their most superb handicrafts are the shimmering black *khenifs* decorated with reddish medallions and the stark black-and-white knotted carpets. Snow covers the summit of the volcano year-round. Guides can be hired to lead the way to the top at any of the tiny villages situated along the foot of its naked, rocky slopes. From Aoulouz you can easily continue on by bus or collective taxi to Taroudannt (83km), near the foothills of the Anti-Atlas. Due to the difficulty of obtaining transportation from Aoulouz into the Jbel Siroua region, however, the excursion is best undertaken in a rented vehicle.

Drâa Valley

The lush but narrow oasis-strewn Drâa Valley is flanked by the bone-dry pre-Saharan steppes where the *cherugi* (desert wind) slaps you in the face. Images are so distorted by the heat here that squinting eyes see cars as bright glints and Berber villages as smudges. From Agdz to M'hamid, the caravan port where the Drâa sinks into the sands of the vast Sahara, the river valley is a continuous grove of palm trees dotted with Kasbahs. The Drâa Valley is the place to come if you want to visit unspoiled southern Morocco.

Buses leave Marrakech for Zagora via Ouarzazate (2 per day, 7-8 hr., 61.85dh), but the route is best toured by car so that you can get out and walk through the ancient villages. Both hard liquor and audio cassettes can be traded in the Drâa for wonderful native handicrafts.

Northern Drâa

As you leave Ouarzazate southbound on P31, you'll find the scene almost instantly transformed. A lunar landscape strewn with volcanic rock stretches in all directions. Farther south, the scenery assumes more fanciful proportions as magnificent cusps of black cliff loom eerily on the horizon. The roadside terrain is sprinkled with ancient lookout towers, each one within sight of the next. The first *ksour* you'll meet is **Ait Saoun.** From here the road winds over the **Tizi-n-Tinifift** pass to Ourika, passing a sinister black gorge.

Toward Zagora, the tourist center of the valley, the road passes **Agdz** in a beautiful setting below Jbel Kissane. The CTM bus stops here for about a half-hour. Agdz is a good place to shop for Berber carpets and rock sculptures. **Café Communal,** in the center of the village, has genuinely cold soft drinks for 5dh per bottle.

Directly south of Agdz the highway intersects the Drâa River and the long string of lush oases begins. Women in brightly decorated capes wear black kaftans to cover their heads. The architecture of the villages is remarkable: Each community is divided into several clusters that are scattered about the oasis with smaller domiciles adjoining central fortified Kasbahs. The first truly breathtaking *ksour* along the route, **Igdâoun** is identifiable by its oddly shaped towers. Many of the smaller villages are also worth exploring: **Tansihkt** offers an explosion of palm trees, **Ouaouzgour** boasts a fine valley view, **Tamezmoute** has an impressive Kasbah, and **El Had** hosts a Sunday *souk*. **Oulad Slimane** is a particularly imposing fortified village, and **Tinezouline,** a large central village with a pretty Kasbah, is well-known for its lively Monday market. Just before Zagora, after cutting through the tiny narrow gorge of the **Azlag Pass,** the valley opens up into a magnificent ocean of palms.

Zagora

The stifling hot town of Zagora is the tourist center of the region and a good base for exploring the Drâa Valley. Almost everything there can be found along **avenue Mohammed V,** the main artery of this desert outpost. Bordering the avenue on the northern edge of Zagora is the biweekly *souk,* primarily a livestock affair, laced with an occasional jewelry vendor. At the opposite side of town, the avenue ends at the **Cercle de Zagora,** the administrative bureau where you should ask about travel to M'hamid and other points in the extreme south. In between, along the avenue, lie the town's PTT, banks, restaurants, and hotels.

The best place to stay is **Hotel La Palmerie** (tel. 8), just across from the Cercle de Zagora on ave. Mohammed V. They'll let you sleep on their concrete terrace for only 5dh per person. (Clean doubles 59-68dh. Triples 72-83dh.) If that's too hot, in summer you can sack out in their huge tent for 10dh. For Morocco's southernmost luxury accommodations, head for **Hotel Tinsouline** (tel. 22), encased in a modern imitation Kasbah, complete with swimming pool and air-conditioned bar. (Singles with shower 125-159dh. Doubles with shower 158-193dh.) You can just pay 30dh for a dip in the pool. Down the road (west of the highway) lies the primitive, palm-studded **Camping D'Amezrou** (5dh per car and per person, 3dh per tent). One kilometer in the opposite direction at the foot of Jbel Zagora is **Camping de la Montagne de Zagora,** with better facilities but slightly less picturesque premises. (5dh per car, 4dh per person, 3dh per tent.)

Budget meals in town are available at the friendly **Restaurant des Amis** (in the hotel of the same name), where you can buy a satisfying menu for 28dh. The **Restaurant Tinsouline,** also in the hotel of the same name, has a wider selection of entrees but places a bigger strain on the budget (*menu touristique* 75dh). The best place to fill your stomach, however, lies about 3km outside town, just across the Oued Drâa, along the road to M'hamid. **Restaurant La Fibule du Drâa** is a wonderful establishment with an ornate, traditional dining room, a lovely central garden, generous portions of excellent food, and startlingly reasonable prices—39dh for a three-course *menu* including straw fans, incense, and slow but gracious service.

You can arrange a **camel excursion** through either the Hotel La Palmerie or the Cercle de Zagora. The official rates for camel and guide are 70dh per four hours (tea included), 150dh per day, and 150dh per day for two or three days including evenings and homecooked dinner. Prices are negotiable if the manager is in a good mood. Try to spend at least one night in the desert; it's an experience. **La Palmerie's** guides are excellent cooks and can be very entertaining. The standard overnight trip takes you up the palm groves of the Drâa Valley (camping in the open with the guide preparing the *tajine*) and returns via the desert. Longer excursions can also be arranged. (There is a half-serious sign at the Cercle de Zagora for a 52-day journey to Timbuktu.)

Two buses per day travel from Zagora to Ouarzazate (4 hr., 29dh; connect for Marrakech). Collective taxis leave whenever you want from the station (2½ hr., 35dh per person).

Southern Drâa

To cross the Drâa at the southern edge of Zagora, push on 3km into the desert and watch for a dirt road scouting off to the left (at the sign for Camping de la Montagne de Zagora). This rough track trundles its way to **Jbel Zagora,** a lone volcanic outcropping overlooking the fertile Drâa. The mountain is best visited at sunset, when the simmering mauve sunlight daubs the peaks with a surreal glow. At **Amazraou,** ½km south of the turn-off for Jbel Zagora along the main road, an ancient Jewish Kasbah contemplates the encroaching desert.

In **Tamegroute,** a lively oasis where turreted *ksours* alternate with shady date palms, a tiny nut of scholarship is tucked away: This otherwise ordinary village is renowned for its **Koranic library,** which houses a collection of thirteenth-century hand-illuminated manuscripts etched on gazelle hides. Ask the caretaker to show you the Berber poetry (penned in a phoneticized Arabic script no longer in use), the Turkish-Arabic dictionary, the astronomy lists, astrology charts, algebra tables, and Koranic commentaries. The Saturday **market** attracts valley neighbors and features local pottery. Arrive early, it's over by noon. You can eat in town at either **Restaurant L'Oasis** or **Restaurant du Drâa.**

Whisked into swollen, ethereal shapes by fierce desert gusts, the **Dunes of Tinfou** rise from the valley floor in smooth golden mounds of ultra-fine sand. These natural sculptures, flowing in gentle waves, are buffeted into remarkably beautiful forms of exquisite delicacy. Cusped on top with a razor-fine edge, the transient mountains evolve and dissolve in ever-changing configurations. To reach the dunes of Tinfou, follow the main highway south from Tamegroute and watch for the well-marked dirt turn-off on the left—the yellow humps are visible from the road. From Zagora the taxi fare anywhere in this area is steep (at least 300dh).

M'hamid

Ninety kilometers south of Zagora on P31, M'hamid sits at the end of the Drâa Valley. Here, the Drâa disappears into the sands of the desert. Transportation in the area is so inconvenient that you are wiser to do your dune-climbing in Merzouga.

Due to a peace agreement with Algeria, it is no longer necessary to obtain permission from the authorities in the Cercle de Zagora before traveling to M'hamid. However, given the volatility of the situation in this region, the Moroccan government may decide to reinstate this procedure at any time. Check at the Cerde de Zagora or a local hotel for information. It is also advisable to hire a guide (50dh per day), as the trail to M'hamid is sometimes unclear.

Renting a taxi and a guide/driver for a day usually costs 300dh, which can be split among six people in the car. Be sure to bargain. You can't stay in the secure zone overnight, so get an early start if you wish to see any of the local *souks.* The first military checkpoint is 34km south of Zagora, just beyond the Dunes of Tinfoud. The sprawling oasis of **Tagounite,** 33km beyond the checkpoint, hosts an interesting Sunday *souk.* The road farther south climbs up to give a splendid view of the palm groves of Tagounite, then passes through the black rock landscape of the **Tizi-Ben-Selmane Pass.** The vast palm groves of M'hamid begin 15km before the village. The community itself is the least interesting part of the route unless you arrive in time for the Monday morning **camel souk,** a weekly rendezvous between the sedentary and nomadic peoples of the Sahara. Beyond M'hamid, the Drâa fades into the **Debaia,** a vast ocean of sand that eventually merges with the **Hammada**—the inhospitable desert plateau dividing Algeria and Morocco, where not a bird or a blade of grass is to be found.

Dadès Valley

To the east of Ouarzazate begins the scenic Dadès Valley, known as the "Valley of a Thousand Kasbahs." Indeed, the roadside is littered with Kasbahs of every imaginable shape, size, and construction. Buses leave daily from Ouarzazate bound eastward for Tinerhir. Here you can get bus connections to er-Rachidia and Rissani, but you may have to wait an entire day for them.

The luxurious oasis village of **Skoura,** famous for its rosewater, is surrounded by fields of grain and—as you might expect—roses. Among the numerous, magnificent Kasbahs in town, those of **Amerhidil** and **Dar Ait Sidi el-Mati** are the most impressive. Rooms in private homes go for about 20dh per person. The best place to eat between Ouarzazate and Skoura is **Restaurant du Lac,** which overlooks a large artificial lake. (Take the turn-off south, 19km east of Ouarzazate.) The first 40km east of Skoura are a flat expanse of rock and dust. Then a 10km explosion of green plantations and palm groves runs parallel to the highway, crowned on either side by scores of imposing Kasbahs overlooking the river valley.

Dadès Gorge

Comparable to the Todra Gorge in size and natural beauty, the Dadès Gorge is much more difficult to navigate and hence thankfully less visited. **Boumalne** is the uninteresting town marking the entrance to the gorge. It is not worth lingering here, so grab a taxi or hitch a ride out as quickly as possible.

Across from **Café Bougafr** (doubles 40dh), local **trucks** leave from the taxi island to carry passengers up to the gorge for 10-15dh, depending on how far you wish to go. A **bus** also leaves from the Boumalne bus station at about 2pm daily and goes into the Dadès Gorge River Valley as far as Msemir (16dh per person).

As you enter the river valley you'll be dazzled by the fruit trees and red rocks as well as the picturesque Kasbahs framed by some of the strangest rock formations you'll see in Morocco. The village of **Tamlalt** (15km from Boumalne) is a good spot to spend the night; if possible, continue 9km more until the road ends in the village of Ait Oudinar. In Tamlalt, the **Hotel-Restaurant Kasbah de la Vieille Tradition** offers simple, spotless doubles for about 12dh per person. Their reasonably priced restaurant has a comfortable *salon marocain* dining room and outdoor Berber tents.

The **Hotel-Restaurant Tamlalt,** 100m up the road, has basic rooms. (Singles 17dh. Doubles 28dh.) The **campsite** 3km up the road charges only 3dh per person. The village has no electricity, so have a candle or flashlight handy.

The most dramatic portion of the excursion begins right after the paved road ends, about 2km after the untouched, quiet village of **Ait Oudinar** (24km from Boumalne). On the fringe of the village you can sleep under the camel hair tents of **Auberge du Gorges** for 10dh or camp next door for less. Past the village and closer to the beginning of the gorge are two tourist traps: **Auberge des Gorges Dadès** (22dh per room, 4dh per person to camp, 20dh for *tajine* or *couscous*) and **Restaurant-Camping Aux Col du Gorge de Dadès,** which has a fabulously scenic location and a variety of lodgings. (You can sleep in the cafe, on the roof, or in your own tent for 3dh per person.) The restaurant serves a three-course *menu* featuring *tajine* for 18dh. From the green river basin by the restaurant, the road goes up the gorge, affording tremendous views. Farther on, the cliff walls create a shady tunnel filled with crystal-clear water perfect for swimming. With a high clearance four-wheel-drive vehicle you can drive from here all the way to the Todra Gorges, but even the locals say this is more than an ambitious enterprise.

Todra

Morocco's most famous natural wonder, the Todra Gorges rank among the most impressive geological formations in all of Africa. In Tinerhir you can rent donkeys or take a taxi and then continue on foot to explore the riverside trail through the gorges. This is a wonderful place to hike and camp, but beware of large felines and wild sheep, both rumored to roam the area. Plan on at least a full day to view the gorges.

Tinerhir

The town of Tinerhir is divided into a modern quarter with the bus station, hotels, restaurants, and a splendid castle, and the much more fascinating old quarter, which lies to the east across the riverbed. It is a village of mud-brick homes nestled in an oasis of pomegranate, olive, and date palm trees.

Hotel Todgha, located in the main square (tel. 09), offers clean, spacious rooms with showers and a friendly staff. (Singles 84dh. Doubles 102dh.) For 20dh, you can swim in the luxurious **pool** at Hotel Sargho (top of the hill). Right on the main plaza are a slew of restaurants and cafes that will satisfy your appetite for a reasonable price. Try **Cafe-Restaurant Gazelle d'Or,** where a complete *menu* of *tajine* or *couscous* costs 30dh.

Buses and collective taxis connect Tinerhir with Er-Rachidia and Boumalne. Two CTM buses connect Tinerhir to Ouarzazate (5 hr., 32dh), while one bus goes to Er-Rachidia (3 hr., 17.50dh). If you're traveling between Tinerhir and Tafilalt, you'll have to change at Er-Rachidia. Summer hitchhikers should expect a lot of competition. Those driving to Tafilalt will be glad to find that the road from Tinejdad to Erfoud is paved.

Todra River Valley and Todra Gorges

The **Todra River Valley** winds through the desert heat toward the gorges. The shady oasis forest, paved with farmland, emits a cool, damp breath of fresh air. Though less dramatic than the gorges themselves, the valley is easily accessible. Coming along the highway from Tinerhir, you'll encounter a trio of beautiful campsites, all charging 5dh per person, per tent, and per car. **Camping Source des Poissons Sacrés** is the friendliest, while **Camping Atlas** has slightly better facilities.

The towering **Todra Gorges** are paved with a rocky riverbed. From the bottom, the desert sky appears to be a clear blue racing stripe framed by golden cliffs. During the spring, the mountains shed their icy winter caps and the river comes rolling down the gorge, sometimes flooding the floor and the road. By summer, however, the waters subside, preparing for next year's cycle of droughts and floods.

Collective taxis leave the main plaza in Tinerhir to traverse the 14km between the city and the gorges several times per day (about 7dh per person). Several hotels are conveniently located in the most beautiful portion of Todra. At the mouth of the gorge stands **Café-Restaurant Hotel el Mansour,** just after the pavement ends (no phone). (Doubles 35dh. Sleep in your sleeping bag on a couch or on the terrace for 10dh.) Their 40dh *menu* is the cheapest around. Another ½ km into the gorge, under towering walls of orange rock, the more comfortable **Hotel les Roches** rents rooms with two double beds for 40dh and will let you sleep on the terrace for 10dh. Next door, the **Hotel-Restaurant Yasmina** rents singles for 35dh and doubles for 40dh, but you can sleep in the cushioned *salon marocain* for 12dh, or on the roof for 10dh.

The proprietor of the El Mansour Hotel will help you arrange **donkey rentals** for a two- or three-hour excursion (20dh) or a full day's ride (100dh). A complete circuit of the Dadès and Todra Gorges is possible by car, but it's very difficult even during the dry season. You can start from Tinerhir and cross over to Msemir in the Dadès from Tamtattouche in the Todra along Rte. 3444. From Msemir you can descend to Boumalne (along 100km of nasty tracks and only 40km of paved road). Starting from the Dadès Valley, the road is reportedly passable as far north as Msemir, but the abandoned, rusting cars suggest otherwise. You can, however, travel about 20km up the gorge, which is far enough to view the terrain and see some of the most handsome fortresses in the canyon. Starting from the Todra Valley, the drive to the cloistered, traditional community of **Tamtattouche** is easy and worthwhile.

Tafilalt

A fertile finger of palm groves reaching deep into the Sahara, the Tafilalt is irrigated by the Ziz and Ghéris, rivers that originate in the High Atlas. The cluster of oases known as the Tafilalt is a region of fortified villages with crumbling minarets. In October, after harvesting the fruit from the region's palms, the annual **Date Festival** is celebrated in Erfoud. The triweekly *souk* in Rissani and the rolling sand dunes of Merzouga are the major tourist attractions of the area. Unfortunately, the recent tourist boom has dragged the usual army of con artists along in its wake. Unless you are driving to Merzouga in your own car, it is unnecessary to hire a guide.

The bus ride south to the Tafilalt region and the deep Sahara beyond is a pines-to-palms roller coaster ride you won't soon forget (12 hr., 60dh from Fes to Er Rachidia; plus 2 hr., 12dh from Er Rachidia to Rissani). If you're not in a hurry, break up the haul by stopping off in one of the towns of the Middle Atlas: Azrou and Midelt have inexpensive hotels. If you are touring the Tafilalt by car, watch out for the following scam: A soldier waves your car to a halt, demands your passport, briefly searches your vehicle, and extracts a fine on some pretense. Never hand your passport to anyone other than an authorized official (in uniform, with a badge and a pistol holster). If you're stopped by an ordinary foot soldier dressed in khaki, demand to see his official police identification.

Erfoud and Rissani

The biggest attraction of **Erfoud** is that it is only one hour away from Rissani. As the gateway to the Tafilalt, Erfoud has the last **post office** and **telephones** (at the intersection of Mohammed V and Moulay Ismail). **Banque Populaire** has branches here and in Rissani (next to the bus station).

If you can't get all the way to Rissani or back to Er-Rachidia, there are three places to stay here. **Hotel Restaurant La Gazelle** (tel. 116), on Moulay Ismail, will rent spacious but dirty rooms for around 40dh after bargaining. **Hotel-Restaurant**

Tafilalet, ave. Moulay Ismail (tel. 60 36), sports a new pool and large, comfortable rooms. (Singles with bath 137dh. Doubles with bath 169dh.) The expensive **Hotel Sijilmassa** has a great swimming pool (admission 15dh for nonguests) and will change money after hours. The **municipal campground**, off ave. Moulay Ismail, has depressing bungalow rooms (8dh) and camping (5dh per person, per tent, and per car). Erfoud's sole tourist attraction, **Borj-Est** (3km from town), is a fortress-capped hilltop with a superb panorama.

The town of **Rissani** (accessible by bus or collective taxi from Erfoud) comes alive on market days (Sun., Tues., and Thurs.; the best and biggest on Sun.) when Berbers of the Ait Hasilbiyod tribe come in from the desert to trade. Go to the **donkey market** (the large area next to the market enclosure is the "donkey parking lot," where the locals moor these furry tug-boats of the Sahara), and visit the medicine vendors who dispense gazelle horns, live lizards, dried storks, and a hundred kinds of herbs. Despite its small size, Rissani has an incongruous bunch of hustlers. Insist firmly that you don't need a guide, that you don't want to go to Merzouga (even though you probably do), and that you're leaving the area today. If you do want a guide for the drive to Merzouga, wait to declare your intentions until you find someone you like.

There is one **hotel** and several rooftops to sleep on in town. **Hotel El Filalia** (tel. 51) is 50m from the bus station—to the right on the main street. Despite what hustlers may say, there is running water here. Rooms are 55dh or 70dh. If you don't mind the sandstorms, they will let you sleep on the terrace. If you can stand the heat, march 2½km east to the crumbling **Tomb of Moulay-Ali-Chérif**, the seventeenth-century chieftain who was a direct descendant of the prophet Mohammed. Next door is the ruined nineteenth-century **Ksar d'Abbar**, and 1km southeast stands the **Ksar of Oulad Abdelhalim**, the most glorious of the Tafilalt's fortresses. Just to the west of Rissani you'll find the ancient Moroccan capital of **Sijilmassa**.

If Allah has blessed you with a car, you can tour the whole **Circuit Touristique**, a 21km loop south of Rissani that winds by date palms and tiny fortified villages. (The middle 7km involve a somewhat dilapidated dirt road.) A turn-off leads southwest to the elevated **Ksar of Tinerheras**, where there is a fine view of the Tafilalt and, on clear days, the High Atlas in the distance.

Merzouga

For the archetypal Saharan fantasy, descend from Erfoud or Rissani to Merzouga. The creamy sand rises in sharp peaks and soft, sculpted dales. Both *Marco Polo* and St. Exupéry's *The Little Prince* were filmed in Merzouga (look for the miniature Aéroplane de Poste Française by the local restaurant). There's a spree at predawn to catch the glorious sunrise over the dunes.

Getting to Merzouga has become fairly easy and cheap. Remember to take plenty of bottled water; "this is the desert" is how locals will answer your requests for water. From Rissani you can ride in a **Landrover** for 10-15dh per person or climb into the back of a **Berber truck** for 8-10dh. Most leave after 4pm to avoid the scalding desert heat; the bumpy, 25-kilometer ride takes about one-and-a-half hours.

Driving in your own **car** is quite difficult. You'll find hundreds of dirt tracks crisscross in all directions with neither signpost nor landmark for miles. Don't drive to Merzouga alone. Though an ordinary car can negotiate the road, it can also easily sink into the sand, requiring a hefty push from more than one person. It's best to follow a tourist vehicle that has taken on a private guide. Start down the road toward Merzouga from Rissani around 4:30pm, when the desert cools, and flag down the next passing car. If their destination is Merzouga, tag along. A 12dh tip is in order for the guide upon arrival. (Let the guide conduct his own business with the group who has hired him. He may well be charging them a fortune, but as long as you keep quiet he won't mind your presence.) Fill up the gas tank before setting out—you must be prepared for the possibility of spending the night in the desert. The route is fairly well-traveled in early morning by tourists seeking the sunrise, and you will be able to get help then as long as you stay within sight of the main route. You can also set out for Merzouga an hour or two before dawn and hope to latch onto another vehicle, but be aware that if there's any trouble, you'll spend the day—not the night—in the desert. From Rissani, the dirt road to Merzouga heads southeast off the main highway. As the paved main road curves to the right, the Merzouga track continues straight. Ask directions frequently to confirm that you're on the correct route, and don't go so far that you can't return if you fail to hook up with another group. From Erfoud, the road to Merzouga heads off beside the mountain road. The return trip is much easier. Shortly after sunrise tourists beat a hasty retreat to avoid confronting the brutal Saharan sun. Simply wait for a group to leave and follow them discreetly.

If you're car-free, grab a ride to Merzouga from people at the campsites in Erfoud or Meski and have them let you off in Rissani on the way back. Hitching back from Merzouga in the morning is a breeze. There are also Landrover excursions leaving Erfoud in late afternoon or early evening (35-50dh per person, or 400dh for a 9-person vehicle; inquire at the Hotel Tafilalet in Erfoud).

On the side of the dunes nearest Rissani, you can scarf down a meal of *tajine* or *couscous* for 25dh at **Restaurant Merzouga;** sleep on their terrace for 10dh. Most visitors, however, prefer to doze near the restaurant in the cool desert beneath a sparkling night sky (watch your valuables). Down the road, **Café Simm** offers the same for slightly higher prices. Your car will be safest if you park it with other vehicles next to one of these establishments.

The small *ksar* and oasis of Merzouga lie 15km beyond the dunes. The equally tiny and even more remote **Ksar of Taouz** marks Morocco's southeastern corner. On the way back, stop at one of the Berber tents to haggle for some fruit of the loom (blankets that is). Look for the black band of rock before a low hill (about 10km along the road); it's littered with marine fossils and is a not-so-subtle reminder that the Sahara was once a vast ocean.

Ziz Valley

A bucolic strip of well-irrigated and cultivated land, the Ziz Valley introduces many visitors to Southern Morocco. The stunning Ziz Gorges and the cozy natural springs at Meski are two reasons to linger here. Daily buses run from Fes and Ouarzazate to Er-Rachidia (formerly Ksar es-Souk), the commercial capital and administrative center of the valley. The landscape becomes increasingly arid and the climate hotter as you approach this important transportation hub where you can catch buses for Tinerhrir and Ouarzazate (the transfer point to Marrakech), or journey east to Figuig on the Algerian border (200km away). Travelers en route to either the Tafilalt or Todra will change buses here and probably have to spend the night as well. From the bridge over the Ziz River there is a great view of the valley with its fortresses and palm trees. *Souks* are held in town, just off ave. Moulay Ali Cherif, on Saturday, Tuesday, and Thursday.

The easiest hotel to find (just follow the signs) is **Hotel Oasis,** 4 rue Abou Abdallah (tel. 26 19). It offers spacious, traditionally-decorated rooms with showers. (Singles 110dh. Doubles 129dh.) **Hotel Meski,** ave. Moulay Ali Cherif (tel. 20 65), has similar accommodations and a pool. (Singles 86dh. Doubles 106dh.) Both hotels have restaurants; many cafes surround the town square. For travel information, visit the **National Tourist Delegation,** 16 blvd. Moulay Ali Cherif (tel. 27 33), next to Hotel Meski.

The highway north from Er-Rachidia passes right through the stunning **Ziz Gorges.** You can hire donkeys to explore the region (ask at Hotels Oasis and Meski) or just hop any northbound bus. The floor of the gorges is carpeted with palms, fruit trees, and corn fields and dotted with splendid fortified villages. The route sidles alongside a large, crystalline artificial lake created by the massive **Hassan Addakhil Dam** (turn-off 16km north of Er-Rachidia). Farther north, the cliff walls form a dramatic 10-kilometer canyon and broaden again after the **Legionnaire's Tunnel.** The roadside is lined with children hawking grapes and figs. If you're traveling through the gorges between the Ziz Valley and the north, consider breaking your trip halfway at the quiet plateau town of **Midelt.** The **Cirque de Jaffar** makes a 79km loop along dirt roads to the foot of **Jbel Agachi,** passing small villages and stone Kasbahs.

The greatest concentration of tourists in southern Morocco is at the **Source Bleu de Meski,** 18km north of Er-Rachidia. This mountain-fed swimming pool is set in a palm grove. However tempting, don't swim anywhere but in the pool—the standing water in the neighboring streams carries infectious diseases. On the road to Erfoud and near the track to Bourfar and Figuig, Meski makes for a great hitching center, particularly for travelers headed to Todra or Merzouga; hang out in the parking lot. Entrance to the Meski complex (whether you want to swim, camp, or just park) costs per car and 5dh per person. The restaurant serves a 27dh *menu* and 10dh omelettes. (Open noon-2pm and 8-10pm.)

To reach Meski by public transportation from Er-Rachidia, take the Erfoud bus and ask the driver to let you off at the turn-off for Meski; from there it's about a ½-kilometer walk.

Northeast

Although easily accessible from Tetuan and Tangier, northeastern Morocco remains the least explored region of the kingdom. It is also one of the most beautiful. While the modernization Morocco has undergone in the past 25 years is evident in this region, tradition survives. People still identify with their ethnic origins, which are associated with certain trades: Berbers are weavers, Jews work with leather, Andalusians craft and sell copper and brass items, and Arabs make shoes. Travelers usually come either to sample the flourishing marijuana of the Rif Mountains or to cross the Algerian border at Oujda. Whatever your motivations, linger awhile at the lovely Andalusian medina of Chechaouèn, on the deserted beaches along the eastern Mediterranean coast, or in the unspoiled mountains around Taza. Since Morocco's big-name cities are located elsewhere, this region maintains an appealing tranquility.

Chechaouèn (Chaouen)

The surest remedy for the hustlers and headaches of Tetuan and Tangier is the next bus to Chechaouèn. The ride provides dazzling vistas of the Rif Mountains, and the town presents a steeply climbing medina laced with terraces that overlook the sparkling streams and craggy hills of the valley below, frequently bathed in the mellow gold of the northeastern sun.

Chechaouèn literally means "look at the horns," and the townspeople will tell you that the two peaks rising above the village resemble bovine horns. Note the distinctive costume of the local Berber women, as well as their chin and forehead tattoos, which establish their tribal identity.

Orientation and Practical Information

From the bus stop, shake off the hustlers (a gentler strain than in Tetuan, although they are catching on fast), and exit around the corner to your left. As you walk away from the station, the marketplace will be on your left. Climb the broad stairs to the right, near the Hotel Magou. As you emerge from the market, you will be on **avenue Hassan II,** which leads on the left to **place Mohammed V** and on the right to **rue Tarik Ibn Ziad.** Walk to the right to find **Bab en Sou,** the entrance to the **medina.** The medina is arranged around **place Uta el-Hammam** at its top. The *ville nouvelle* is essentially a cluster of buildings built around the base of the medina. To get to Uta el-Hammam, just climb up the steep, winding main street, **Calle Horra.**

Syndicat d'Initiative: Off pl. Mohammed V. No maps, little information. Open July to mid-Sept. Mon.-Sat. 9am-3pm; mid-Sept to June Mon.-Fri. 9am-noon and 2:30-6:30pm, Sat. 9am-noon; Ramadan Mon.-Fri. 8:30am-3pm. Hours may vary at whim.

Student Travel Office: Agence des Voyages, 65 ave. Tarik Ibn Ziad (tel. 60 09). 25% discounts on all tickets—land, sea, and air—for those under 26 with student ID. Energetic, amusing young couple run the agency with a smile. Open Mon.-Sat. 8am-noon and 2:30-7pm.

Currency Exchange: ave. Hassan II, across from Bab en Sour. Also between pl. Mohammed V and the post office on ave. Hassan II. Both open Mon.-Fri. 9am-noon and 4:15-6pm. For **after-hours exchange,** go to Hotel Asmaa.

Post Office: Ave. Hassan II, by the steps that lead down into the marketplace. 1-eyed clerk speaks excellent English and can help place long-distance calls. Open July-Sept. 15 Mon.-Sat. 8:30am-3:30pm; Sept. 16-June Mon.-Fri. 9am-1pm and 2:30-5:30pm, Sat. 9am-1pm.

Telephone Code: 098.

Swimming Pool: Hotel Asmaa. Follow the signs and enjoy the hike up the mountain. Non-guests 15dh.

Pharmacy: A block south of ave. Hassan II, next to Hotel Magou (follow the signs for the hotel). Open Mon.-Tues. 9am-1pm and 3:30-9pm, Wed.-Sat. 9am-1pm and 4-9pm.

Accommodations and Camping

Unlike most, the pensions in Chechaouèn's medina are perfectly safe and engagingly funky—colorful Moroccan decor and terraces recall the days when hippies flocked here in search of cheap highs and cheaper beds. Although the medina is not very big, it can be disorienting. Consider investing 5dh to let a local kid guide you to the hotel of your choice. For relatively more comfort, stay in the *ville nouvelle,* on the road that surrounds the base of the medina.

Auberge de Jeunesse (IYHF) (no phone), Inconveniently located at the top of the town, next to the campsite. Follow signs to Hotel Asmaa (25 min.). Open daily 8am-noon and 4-10pm. Spartan dorm rooms 5dh.

Hotel Salam, 39 rue Tarik Ibn Ziad (tel. 62 39). Follow the street to the right of the medina entrance up the hill. A magic place, perhaps the best deal in town. Authentic Moroccan decor, stunning views, and meals on the patio terrace. Rooms overlooking the terrace are noisy. Single bed 20dh. Double bed 40dh.

Pension Mauritania, 20 rue Kadi Alami (tel. 61 84). Follow the signs from Uta el-Hammam or get a guide. Adequate rooms, dorm-style beds, beautiful courtyard, and plenty of rock music. 12.50dh per person. Showers 4dh.

Hotel Andaluz, 1 rue Sidi Salem (tel. 60 34). Enter the medina at Bab en Sou and follow C. Horra until a small plaza with a little cafe. Turn right; the hotel will be right on the corner of the first street you hit. Moroccan decor and clean, comfortable rooms. 7-14dh per person. Roof 5dh. Hot showers 4dh, cold showers 2dh.

Pension La Castillana, 4 rue Sidi Ahmed Bouhali (tel. 62 95), just off pl. Uta el-Hammam in a good location. Follow the signs. Good location. Some dark and musty rooms, so be choosy. They may let you sleep on the roof if full. 10dh per person.

Hotel Rif, 29 rue Tarik Ibn Ziad (tel. 62 07), just down the street from the Salam. Clean, modern rooms. Singles 77dh. Doubles 89dh.

Chechaouèn's only **campground** (no phone) has a remarkably scenic but inconvenient location at the very top of town. Follow the signs for Hotel Asmaa. You can pitch your tent in a small forest, but it's crowded in summer. 2dh per person, 3dh per tent and per car. It's a good place to hitch rides.

Food

Cafe Restaurant Cafeteria Restaurant, pl. Uta el-Hammam in the medina. This isn't the real name of the place, but it's what Westerners unfamiliar with Arabic can read. Cheap, satisfying fare. In the afternoon, you may have to eat amidst tenacious flies. Brochettes 1dh, salads 2dh, and *harira* 2.50dh. Open daily 11am-2pm and 4-10pm.

Snack Mounir, pl. Uta el-Hammam, across from the above. Great location, good selection of omelettes, *tajine de kefta*, or *tajine de poulet* 5-10dh. Fresh orange juice 2dh. Open daily 9am-midnight.

Restaurant Azhar, off ave. Hassan II by the steps at the post office. Complete with flies and reggae music. Their sign says it all: "Good Food and Yummy OJ." Delicious lamb stew, *couscous*, and *tajine* 10dh. Open daily 11am-9pm.

Restaurant Bar Omo Rabi (tel. 61 80), next to the travel agency on rue Tarik Ibn Ziad. Incomprehensible sign. Complete Moroccan or French meals 25-30dh. "French" means you can get wine or beer, and if you've been in Morocco long enough, you'll appreciate that. Open Mon.-Sat. 11:30am-2:30pm and 6-10pm.

Sights

Chechaouèn's steep medina is perhaps Morocco's friendliest and brightest. Merchants will nod their heads as you pass by, asking "*la bess?*" ("*ça va?*") from their shops. Enter from ave. Hassan II through the medieval **Bab en Sour**. Narrow, cobbled passageways wind steeply up the mountain, converging on the hilltop at place Uta el-Hammam. The Kasbah across the square houses pleasant gardens and the remains of a palace built by Moulay Ismail. (Open Mon.-Sat. 8am-2pm and 4-8pm; Ramadan Mon.-Sat. 8am-3pm. Admission 1dh.)

Northeast of the square, up the side street across from the Kasbah entrance, sits a tiny **caravansary**, which is especially active on market days. To enter the *souks*, cross Uta el-Hammam and head down the alley that begins beside the mosque. An array of brightly dyed handwoven wool and cotton will greet you. As you move farther from the main square, the shops become increasingly less expensive. Before leaving the medina, head past pl. Uta el-Hammam to **place el-Makhzen** to see the underside view of the soaring twin cow horn peaks.

Chechaouèn's **souk** is held Mondays and Thursdays in the new city in the square beside Hotel Magou (just down the stairs from ave. Hassan II). Berbers descend from all parts of the Rif to trade with one another. Notice how the women greet each other: a quick handshake followed by a kiss on their own hands. Also in the new city, place Mohammed V sports a delightful garden with a fountain. The nameless **cafe** on the western side offers cold drinks, chess, and parchesi in the early evenings.

Rif

Laced with pink oleander, green cedar forests, and rippling streams, the Rif Mountains offer some of the most extraordinary scenery in Morocco. During the '60s and early '70s, backpackers stormed this region to stock up on *kif*. Almost two decades later, security measures have tightened and tourism has dropped considerably. Expect police roadblocks along every major route in or out of the Rif. Buses and cars are subject to thorough searches on a random basis. Picking up hitchhikers in the region is a bad idea because if anything illegal is found in your passengers' possession, you will accompany them to prison.

The native Berbers jealously guard their traditional culture. During the colonial period, the Spanish authorities met with fierce, fiery, and sometimes bloody opposition to their attempts to remold the indigenous society. Local peasant women still wear the pink striped skirt, green facial tattoos, and blue hat pom-pom of their particular tribes. The most fascinating day to visit the backwoods of the area is June 21, the summer solstice, when everyday rules are suspended and otherwise forbidden pagan rites are enacted. Visitors need to be aware of their privileged situation when allowed to witness these ceremonies. Insensitive intruders have been chased away by angry locals.

Ouezzane

At the western foothills of the Rif, Ouezzane (Wazzan) is a traditional town with a cluster of *souks* tucked into the rambling alleyways of its tiny medina. Logistically, it's the perfect stopover between Chechaouèn and Fes or Meknes. Despite Ouezzane's colorful history, most travelers find themselves leaving town very quickly, using it only as a transportation hub. The road from Chechaouèn offers a pleasant glimpse of the Rif as it sidles along the waters of the Oued Loukkos. Ouezzane, reknowned as the most lawless town in nineteenth-century Morocco, preserves a distinctly Andalusian flavor. At the turn of the century, the last of the great sharifs (descendants of the prophet Mohammed through his daughter Fatima) married an English woman of high society. After his death, the feared Berbers of the western Rif worshiped this foreign woman as a saint whom they believed had inherited the *baraka* (mystical powers) of her husband. Today, the small community is peaceful, though it remains devoted to its sacred shrines.

The **Mosque S'Ma des Zaouia** (also known as the Green Mosque), headquarters of the Zouaia sect, is situated inside the medina just above pl. du Marché. Look for the enchanting minaret plastered with green tiles. Follow the main thoroughfare east under an archway to reach the nearby **Mosque of Moulay Abdallah Sharif.** From here, bear right 180° and loop back to pl. du Marché, drifting through the covered alleyways of the colorful **souks,** which burst with the usual assortment of spices, fruits, and *djellabas.* A colorful regional **market** occurs on Wednesdays and Thursdays in the new city at pl. de l'Indépendence. A 3-kilometer excursion from here will bring you to **Jbel Bou Hellal,** a wooded mountain towering above Ouezzane. It affords a sweeping panorama of the town and the Rif Mountains.

Everything in Ouezzane revolves around **place de l'Indépendence.** Here, all in a row, you'll find the town's three hotels. The cheapest is **Hotel L'Horloge** (singles 30dh, doubles 46dh); the most comfortable is **Grand Hotel d'Ouezzane** (singles 40dh, doubles 50dh); and the friendliest is **Hotel El Alem** (singles 40dh, doubles 50dh, triples 60dh). All have mediocre, inexpensive **restaurants.** Avenue Mohammed V, the main commercial drag, connects place de l'Indépendence with **place du Marché,** where outdoor vendors peddle their wares. From here, signs point to the adjoining **Cooperative Artisanal.** (Open daily 8am-7pm; in winter daily 8am-noon and 2:30-6pm.)

Ketama

Throughout Morocco the name Ketama is synonymous with hashish. If you're driving, as soon as you turn onto the road to Ketama you'll be approached by the first of a horde of roadside hash sellers, often standing only a few meters apart. You may also encounter groups of young boys forming human roadblocks to help along business transactions. Just keep driving—at the last minute they'll jump out of the way. More difficult to manage are situations in which dealers in cars attempt to run your vehicle off the road. Don't try to outrun the hasslers, and don't stop your car or get out. If you're cool-headed and insistent in your refusals to do business, you should be able to travel here without too much trouble.

Just before Ketama the road sinks into a cool cedar forest boasting some of the largest trees in North Africa. The town is a large clearinghouse, crawling with pushy dealers. As soon as you step off the bus, expect to be mobbed. If you find yourself in serious trouble, head for the **police station,** just northeast of town along the road to Tetuan. Avoid traveling through Ketama alone (especially if you're a woman) and, unless you have to, avoid traveling through Ketama at all.

Unity Road

The Unity Road, which runs through the most spectacular portion of the Rif, was built by thousands of young Moroccan volunteers shortly after independence in order to link the formerly French and Spanish zones. The road winds its way from Ketama through rich forests of cedar wood and past the highest peaks of the range, finally descending to Fes (164km). If you have a car, the route is well-worth going out of your way to tour—especially if you have the time for a half-day side excursion to the breathtaking summit of **Jbel Lalla-Outka.**

Halfway between Ketama and Fes, the village of **Taounate** hosts an interesting Friday *souk* and a traditional **moussem** in September. Roughly 8km south of the village, a paved road branches west to **Ourtzahr** (28km), where you can enjoy the splendid vista of **Mount Lalla-Outka.** To reach the mountain, take the paved road north to Rhafsi—from here the route changes to a bearable dirt road until Tamesnite. At Tamesnite the road to the summit begins and rapidly degenerates into a treacherous but still passable route. The commanding view from the summit, overlooking the Rif, is awe-inspiring.

The village of **Tissa,** (114km south of Ketama), situated beside the road to Fes, celebrates a magnificent **moussem** annually from the end of August to the beginning of September, attracting tribespeople from the entire region and featuring raucous festivities.

Al-Hoceima

Popular with vacationing Moroccans, the resort of Al-Hoceima lies beside towering gray cliffs and the teeming blue Mediterranean. In May, June, and September it's a warm and wonderful place to sun and surf, but in July and August it's crammed with tourists. Year-round it's expensive and devoid of traditional Moroccan culture.

Orientation and Practical Information

Most everything in Al-Hoceima lies between the bus stop at one end of avenue Mohammed V in place du Rif and Hotel Mohammed V toward the beach on Plage Quernado at the end of ave. Mohammed V.

Tourist Office: Delegation Regionale du Ministre du Tourisme, C. Tario Ibn Zeyyad (tel. 28 30), 8 blocks down from ave. Mohammed V. Open July-Sept. Mon.-Fri. 8am-3pm; Sept.-June Mon.-Fri. 8:30am-noon and 2:30-6:30pm; Ramadan Mon.-Fri. 9am-3pm.

After Hours Currency Exchange: Hotel Mohammed V, on Plage Quemado (tel. 22 33). Hotel National cannot exchange traveler's checks.

Telephone Code: 093.

Bus Stop: At pl. du Rif. To Tetuan (2 per day, 10 hr., 36.85dh), Chaouen (2 per day, 8 hr., 29.25dh), and Nador (1 per day, 5 hr., 18.50dh).

Taxis: At pl. du Rif or tel. 22 91.

Accommodations and Food

There are many grungy little places between pl. du Rif and Hotel Mohammed V, but few are palatable.

Hotel Bilbao, 28 ave. Mohammed V (no phone). The only decent and inexpensive hotel in town. Friendly manager, grungy rooms. 11dh per person. Cold showers only.

Annexe de l'Hotel Al Maghreb El-Jadid, passage Soussan El Yakoubi (tel. 25 11), across ave. Mohammed V from the luxury hotel of the same name. Friendly, easy-going management. Singles with shower 56dh. Doubles with shower 70dh.

Hotel Marrakech, 114 rue Abdellah Hamou (tel. 30 25). A sign on ave. Mohammed V marks the corner. The newest kid on the block boasts spotless, modestly elegant rooms with full bathrooms. Well worth the price. Singles 77dh. Doubles 89dh.

There are two **campsites** 2km east or more out of town toward the beach. **Camping Plage El Jamil** (tel. 20 09) and **Camping Cala Tris** (no phone) are both crowded in summer and within earshot of soothing waves.

All the fancy hotels in town offer appropriately fancy restaurants with menus for 45-60dh. Inexpensive fare can be found around pl. du Rif or around the upper part of Mohammed V.

Restaurant Marhaba, pl. du Rif (no phone), next to Hotel Mahati. Excellent *viande hachée* (grilled ground meat) 6dh. Friendly, swift service and a tiny ceiling fan that works.

Restaurant Familial, 19 ave. Mohammed V, across from Hotel Bilbao. Remarkably distasteful decor, but cheap food. *Tajine* 15dh. Open Mon.-Fri. 11am-3pm and 7-11pm.

Café-Restaurant Tamsamon, C. Al Amir Moulay Abdallah (tel. 28 30), 1 street over from Hotel National. Cheerful staff and tasty fare. Surprisingly filling *oeuf et pomme de terre* (egg and potatoes, 5dh). Brochettes 2dh each. Open daily 10am-midnight.

Sights

The newest attraction in town is the **Ensemble Artisanal,** a year-round exhibition of local crafts. It was due to open in the fall of 1988. Ask the tourist office for its location. Most travelers, however, come to enjoy Al-Hoceima's sun and surf. **Plage Quemado,** the town beach, is crowded beyond belief in summer. (Admission 1.5dh.) For a little more leg and elbow room, drive or hitch the 5½km to **Plage Espalmerado,** a rockier beach just off the road to Nador. For the beach of your dreams, continue 9km east until you reach the turn-off for **Plage Al-Mouyahidine.** Surrounded on three sides by dramatic coastal cliffs, the tranquil bay is one of Morocco's most breathtaking Mediterranean haunts. The shoreline consists of a sweeping, fine-grained gray beach, where you can camp for 5dh per night. Even in July and August, this spacious crescent remains quiet and uncrowded. Facing the beach is the tiny **Peñón de Alhucemas.** The history of this lovely promontory is particularly fascinating. Due to its strategic position on the lower lip of the Mediterranean's mouth, the *peñón* was long coveted by European powers. Beginning in the seventeenth century, England, France, and Spain each dispatched admirals to the island to install an outpost on its rocky summit. Each installation was eventually squelched by the Moroccan king until finally, in 1673, the Spanish raised a fortress, village, and tiny church atop the rock. Due to the islet's offshore location, periodic raids from the neighboring Rif mountains were all too easily mounted. The outpost, lost to Morocco in the Rifian War, never gained a commanding position in the southern Mediterranean. But the sheer walls of the castle still jut proudly from the bay, a fantasy-white fortified island swimming in an ocean of aquamarine blue.

For a similar sandy beach, overlooking a fortified Spanish island, head for the more remote cove near **Torres de Alcalá** (110km from Al-Hoceima), facing the islet of **Peñón de Vélez de la Gomera.** The idyllic fishing spot of **Kalad Iris** lies 4km to the west.

If taking the bus or driving east to Nador, you'll pass through the lovely **Nekor River Valley.** Just before the road crosses a bridge (42km from Al-Hoceima), a turn-off leads to the **Kasbah of El Arba de Taourirt,** which commands a splendid view of the valley. The road to Taza via Aknoul, which branches south just beyond here, offers a wonderful glimpse of the unspoiled eastern foothills of the Rif.

Mediterranean Coast

Morocco's eastern Mediterranean coast offers miles of windswept beaches; they are overwhelmingly crowded in July and August, but prove to be idyllic retreats the rest of the year. The area is also a transportation hub, linking Morocco to Spain and France. Thus, travelers come here to get away from it all, or just to get away from Morocco.

Melilla (Spain)

Melilla is a pleasant respite from the rigors and hassles of Moroccan travel. The town also makes for a gentler approach to Morocco than frenzied Tangier. Founded by the Spanish as a colony in 1479, this territory remains an Andalusian outpost on the African continent. If you've been in Morocco long, come to enjoy the Spanish food and tax-free liquor. If you've been in Morocco too long, come to take one of the regular ferries to Spain.

The two main tourist attractions are the **municipal museum** (open Tues.-Sun. 10am-1pm and 4-8pm) and the picturesque **Medina Sidouia Quarter** (also called the **Pueblo**), the old town enclosed by sixteenth-century ramparts. Otherwise, the main sources of entertainment here are shopping, eating, and drinking. English-speaking technicians on weekend leave from their posts in Morocco gather at the **Café Metropole** on pl. de España to debate the merits of Melilla's restaurants. **Restaurantes Duala, Victoria,** and **Napoli** are good, but **Granada** and **Salazones** serve the freshest seafood at moderate prices. Cheap hotels are tough to come by, but many dives line the streets off **Avenida del General Macías** at the port. Try the **Hostal de París,** with rooms for 600ptas. Rooms start at 1500ptas at **Hotel Nacional,** C. Primo de Riviera, 10 (tel. 68 45 40), near Pl. España.

The **tourist office** at C. del General Aizpura, 20 (tel. 68 42 04), is helpful and can provide information on travel options. (Open Mon.-Fri. 9am-2pm, Sat. 10am-noon.) The **post office** is on C. de Pablo Vallesca. (Open Mon.-Fri. 9am-noon and 4-8pm.) **Compañía Transmediterránea,** pl. de España, operates ferries from Melilla to Málaga (July 13-Sept. 11 Mon. at 1am, Wed. 8:30am, Thurs. 11:30pm, and Sun. 8:30am; Sept. 12-July 12 Tues., Thurs., and Sat. at 11:30pm; 8hrs; deck fare 2040ptas). If you have a car, you can save tons of money by driving to Ceuta and crossing there. Also check out the new ferry service from Nador to Sete, France. (See Nador below.) The ferries to Málaga and Almería leave from **Estación Marítima,** on a dock jutting out from the base of the old city. **Iberia** flights to Málaga depart from Melilla's airstrip, which can be reached by taxi.

Nador

Tourists come to this failed experiment in modernization to cross the border near Melilla, to plunge into the Mediterranean waters of the **Sebkha bou Areg Lagune,** or to catch the **Rif ferry** to Sete, France (mid-June to late Sept. 7-8 per month, 37hrs., from 850dh).

The bus for Melilla leaves from the **main bus station** (every 45min., 2dh); you can also take a *grand taxi* (about 10dh). Buses leave for Al-Hoceima (4 per day, 8 hr., 18.50dh), Casablanca (2 per day), Fes (4 per day), Taza (2 per day), Oujda (10 per day), and Tetuan (4 per day). The **consigne** will accept any baggage (2dh per item).

The accommodations scene here remains bleak. The town's handful of fleabag hotels are full in summer, and the only alternative is the exorbitant **Hotel Rif,** ave. Youssef Ibn Tachfine (tel. 23 37; singles 174dh, doubles 214dh). You're better off heading for the less crowded beach at **Kariet Arkmane** (23km). You can stay at **Camping Karia Plage** right on the beach for 3dh per person, per tent, and per car. Kariet Arkmane has no bus service, but collective taxis run from Nador in summer. You can exchange dirhams and pesetas at **Banque Populaire,** rue de la Ligue Arabe, or the **BMCF,** ave. Ibn Rochd at ave. Youssef ben Tachfine. You must have bank receipts proving you've exchanged twice the amount in dirhams you wish to cash back.

Saidia

If you're exploring the Beni-Snassen Mountains or waiting for a visa at Oujda, this is the place to cool off. Timid Mediterranean swells bathe 14km of sandy coastline that begin at the Algerian border. Pleasant woods seal the beach to the south. An interesting Sunday **souk** takes place at the edge of town, and an ancient **Kasbah** is now inhabited by local villagers. The **buses** from Oujda (60km, 7.60dh) arrive and depart at the Kasbah. It's a five-minute walk directly north to the beach and another 10 minutes to accommodations. The cheapest is **Hotel Select** on blvd. de la Moulouya (tel. 51 10), which is closed in off-season. (Singles with shower are 60dh, doubles with shower 77dh.) Another block west is the **Hotel Al Kalaa,** slightly nicer and more expensive. (Singles with bath 84dh. Doubles with bath 102dh.) In front is **Camping Tennis** (tel. 52 52; 3dh per person, 10dh per car).

Taza

Gateway between the eastern and western Maghreb, the **Taza Gap** forms a natural corridor through which marching Romans, galloping Arabs, and renegade sultans have passed on their way into Morocco. Today, Taza remains the administrative seat of its own province, with a European *ville nouvelle* crouching below the hilltop fortifications of its medina. The city also forms a pleasant base for excursions into neighboring Jbel Tazzeka National Park.

Orientation and Practical Information

All public offices and facilities and almost the accommodations are found in the *ville nouvelle,* clustered around the **place de l'Indépendence.** From this square there is frequent service by *petit taxi* to the medina on the top of the hill.

Syndicat d'Initiative: 56 ave. Mohammed V. Inquire about excursions to Jbel Tazzeka National Park. Open mid-June to Aug. Mon.-Fri. 8am-2pm; Sept. to mid-June Mon.-Fri. 8:30am-noon and 2-6:30pm.

Post Office: Rue Moussa Ibn Noussair at rue Allal ben Abdallah, next to pl. de l'Indépendence. Open mid-June to Aug. Mon.-Fri. 8am-3pm; Sept. to mid-June Mon.-Thurs. 8am-noon and 4-7pm, Fri. 9am-noon. Open Sat. 4-6pm for Poste Restante and telephone calls only.

Telephones: In the same building. Open in summer until 6pm. Can be uncooperative about placing international calls. **Telephone Code:** 067.

Train Station: On the northern edge of the *ville nouvelle,* a 30- to 40-min. walk from pl. de l'Indépendence. Buses go to the station from pl. Moulay in the medina. A *petit taxi* from pl. de l'Indépendence should cost 5-7dh. Daily connections to Casablanca, Rabat, Oujda, and Fes. Change at Sidi Kacem or Sidi Slimane for Tangier.

Bus Station: CTM, just off pl. de l'Indépendence. More reliable is the **bus terminal** next to the train station, a 30- to 40-min. walk from pl. de l'Indépendence (or a *petit taxi* for 5-7dh). To Oujda (1 per day), Fes (2 per day, 16.50dh), and Nador (1 per day).

Police: Hotel de Police (not a place to spend the night), on pl. de l'Indépendence (tel. 19), facing the more pleasant Grand Hotel du Dauphiné. Tel. 19.

Accommodations and Food

The cheaper hotels are centrally located **Hotel-Restaurant Brasserie,** pl. de l'Indépendence (tel. 23 47; singles 25dh, doubles 40dh), and **Hôtel de la Gare,** by the train and bus station (same prices). Much nicer is the **Grand Hotel du Dauphiné,** pl. de l'Indépendence (tel. 35 67). Vintage art deco adorns the airy rooms and fine balconies. (Singles 63dh, with shower 85dh. Doubles 83dh, with shower 100dh, with complete bath 125dh. Hot water 7pm-10am.) Finally there is the barren wasteland named **Camping Oliveraie;** follow the signs to Hotel Friouato-Salam.

The most inexpensive meals are available in the evening from the tiny cafes and outdoor stalls adjoining place Moulay Hassan in the medina. Restaurants in the *ville nouvelle* are expensive and scarce. The best budget restaurant is **Restaurant Majestic,** 26 ave. Mohammed V. A complete *menu* with generous portions costs 28dh. The **Restaurant Dauphiné,** pl. de l'Indépendence, next to the hotel of the same name, offers a 40dh *menu.* (Both open daily 11am-11pm.)

Sights

Take a *petit taxi* (3-5dh) or a **bus** (0.90dh) from pl. de l'Indépendence up to the **medina,** overlooking the valleys and ridges of the Taza Gap. Its most formidable battlement, the sixteenth-century **bastion,** rears its 3-meter-thick walls at the southeast corner of the old city. From here, follow the ramparts south to the main intersection at **Bab el-Guebar.** Head up rue Bab el-Guebar until you see the yellow archway to your left—the entrance to the medina. If you go straight on through the underpasses, passageways, and narrow walls, you'll reach the **Mosquée des Andalous,** topped by a twelfth-century minaret. Head right and then immediately left to reach **rue Sidi Ali Derrar** (which eventually changes to rue Kettanine), the main east-west thoroughfare of the medina. Here, the route widens into the **Méchouar,** a small plaza filled with soccer and volleyball enthusiasts and lined with mansions.

Pass straight on through the Méchouar beside the charming **Mosquée du Marché** to reach the **souks.** Fresh vegetables, glittering *kaftans,* dried spices, and shiny silk thread hang there. Continue straight along the main thoroughfare, veering left and then right around the **Great Mosque** to reach **Bab er Rih,** a crumbling bastion guarding the western extremity of the town. From here, you can gaze across the swells of the dissipating Middle Atlas mountains. Try to arrive at sunset, when the endless panorama glows with a glorious orange.

Near Taza: Jbel Tazzeka National Park

The mountainous forest of the Jbel Tazzeka, which forms the southern pincer of the Taza Gap, has been set aside as one of Morocco's two major national parks (the other is Jbel Toubkal). The 123-kilometer circuit through the park can be a daytrip from Taza, but due to the scarcity of traffic, it's not so easy without a car. Your best bet is to hook up with other tourists in Taza (if there are any) and hitch a ride for the day. There are no accommodations in the area. Although they are not official agents, the staff at Hotel Dauphiné will provide information on tours of the park.

From Taza, take highway 5311 up the hill and east from Bab el-Guebar, climbing into the mountains above Taza. Eight kilometers from town watch for the turn-off for Ras el-Ma, where water gushes from under boulders. The run-off stream is shaded by a tiny grove of olive and cherry trees. Don't drink from or swim in the algae-choked catchment basin below the source. From here the road winds upward, and the views are spectacular. About 10km farther, you'll reach a plateau, surrounded by peaks and paved for several miles with wheatfields. You may see a donkey napping in the sun, or even a family of storks. This bucolic pasture borders the entrance to the mysterious and totally amazing **Gouffre du Friouato,** a grotto tunneling 750m into the earth. Watch for the right-hand turn-off leading up to the cave; it's guarded by a shack. From here, stone steps descend into the abyss. At the bottom, the staircase continues for several hundred meters into a natural museum of stalactite-filled recesses. Bring a powerful flashlight and come prepared to squirm between narrow wedges of slippery rock if you wish to spelunk down this final portion of the stairway. Follow the stairs at all times and proceed with caution. (Admission 5dh.) There are equally dramatic caves off the main road toward Taza, just 3km before the turn-off for the Gouffre du Friouato by the tiny lake. The **Grottoes of Chiker,** which sink nearly 5km into the earth, are open to tourists only with a professional escort; the Speleology Club of Taza organizes visits. For more information, write to either **The Alpine Club,** 13 blvd. de la Résistance, Rabat, or the **Mountain and Ski Federation,** 53 rue Allal ben Abdallah, Casablanca.

The breathtaking view from the top of **Jbel Tazzeka** (1980m) extends across the Taza Gap, encompassing both the Middle Atlas and Rif Mountains. Fields of ferns and stripped cork trees line the 15-kilometer route between the Gouffre du Friouato and the right-hand dirt turn-off up the mountain. Plan on a difficult, stony climb to the top, and don't attempt to drive up the track in the rainy season. The descent from Jbel Tazzeka back to Taza passes through the lonely cliffs of the **Gorges of** the **Oued Zireg** before rejoining the main road 30km west of Taza. If you're traveling the circuit beginning with the gorges, take the turn-off toward Bab Azhar off the main Fes-Taza highway that twists under the train tracks.

East

The eastern end of the country is visited almost exclusively by travelers between Morocco and Algeria. Tourists waiting for visas to be processed at the Algerian consulate in Oujda often find themselves spending a great deal more time in the area than they had planned. Many take the bus up to Saidia and cool off in the Mediterranean, or rent a car in Oujda and explore the nearby Beni-Snassen Mountains.

Oujda

Morocco's gateway to Algeria is a clean, modern, and unremarkable city that seems somewhat bewildered by the annual summer migration of backpackers. Its most interesting feature is a small **medina** surrounded by crenelated walls and containing a compact cluster of *souks.* **Bab Sidi Abed el-Ouahab,** at the end of ave. des Marchés, is the medina's most imposing entrance. **Place el-Attarine** hosts portions of the city's Wednesday and Sunday markets. Local handicrafts are displayed at the **Ensemble Artisanal** on pl. Dar el-Makhzen or at the **Maison de l'Artisanat** on blvd. Allal ben Abdallah.

Some of the cheapest beds in town are available at musty **Café-Hotel Hassania,** on rue de Casablanca. (Singles 20dh. Doubles 30dh.) Much more comfortable lodgings are available at either **Hotel Ziri,** on blvd. Mohammed V (tel. 43 05; singles 61dh, doubles 78dh), or **Hotel Lutetia,** 44 blvd. Hassan Loukili (tel. 33 65; singles 68dh, doubles 84dh).

The **tourist office** is on pl. du XVI Août (tel. 43 29; open daily 8am-noon and 2:30-6:30pm, Ramadan 9am-3pm). If you've just arrived from Algeria, you have four ways besides hitching to put Oujda behind you. The **CTM bus station** is on rue Sidi Brahim (tel. 20 47), providing buses to Casablanca and the border. The **private bus companies** as well as other CTM lines are at Oned Nachef, also called the **Gare Routière.** Buses run to Saidia (6 per day, 7.60dh), Rabat and Casablanca (3 per day, 125dh), Fes (2 per day, 47dh), and Nador (4 per day, 18dh). A 10-minute walk away the train station, pl. de l'Unité Africaine (tel. 27 01), offers 3 connections per day to Taza (37.50dh), Fes, and Tangier. The **airport,** is 15km out of town (tel. 47 11), with flights to Casablanca. Finally, you can rent a car from either **Avis,** through Maroc Voyages, 110 ave. Allal ben Abdallah (tel. 39 93), or from **Hertz,** 20 blvd. Fetouaki (tel. 28 38). You can cash traveler's checks after hours at any of the town's three luxury hotels.

Most travelers in Oujda focus on a single point: the **Algerian consulate,** 11 blvd. de Taza (tel. 36 76). Remember that visas are issued only at the consulate in Rabat and that the mandatory currency exchange in Algeria is 1000dh. (See Morocco Introduction.) The handsome walled city of **Tlemcen,** only 85km from Oujda, boasts an impressive collection of mosques and minarets, including the excellent **antiquities museum,** on pl. Abdelkeder (open 8am-noon and 2-6pm), and the **Almoravid Grand Mosque.** The town of **Mansourah,** 11km south of Tlemcen, contains the ruins of two wonderful Merinid mosques, as well as the remains of a Roman city. All three of these Algerian mosques are open to non-Muslims, unlike their Moroccan counterparts.

Beni-Snassen

The calcite massif of the Beni-Snassen Mountains (named for the Berber tribe who inhabit the region) bulges from the fertile flatland northwest of Oujda. The dusty range cuts east-west through one of Morocco's most populous areas, dividing the well-irrigated Triffa Plains to the north from the Angad Plains in the south.

The mountains are best toured by car from Oujda (170km round-trip) via a paved *circuit touristique* that winds over the jagged peaks and crests of the range before circling back to Oujda by way of the regional center of Berkane. You can take a bus from Oujda to Berkane and proceed from there by collective taxi, private trucks, or thumb. If you are driving, bring a picnic, plenty to drink, and a good road map. Don't attempt to negotiate the route in the wet season—passing rainstorms cause flash floods and the road can become completely washed out.

From Oujda, take highway P27 northwest for 24km and then turn left onto route 5319 toward the village of Aines Sfa. The route borders the plains of Angad for 12km before meeting highway 5308. From here, take the right-hand turn onto the winding route to ascend directly into the mountains. When you reach the first major fork, 10km after turning onto highway 5308, bear left and cruise up to **Oulad Jabeur Fouaga**, a charming hamlet skirted by almond groves and forests. A left-hand dirt turn-off departs from the main route just outside town for **Ras Fourhal**, the highest point in the Beni-Snassen massif (1532m). The scramble to the summit must be undertaken on foot. The highway descends tortuously from here. To complete the circuit, take the right fork 17km beyond Oulad Jabeur Fouaga and then turn right again 4km later at the ruined pile of a stone cottage. Finally, a third right, 5km farther, passes through calcite boulders. With a little luck you should be able to admire the dramatic landscape without one of these squashing you. Take your next left onto route 5306 toward Taforalt to embark on the enjoyable detour into the **Zegzel Valley.** Soon after the turn, a small left-hand turn leads south to the calcite-filled **Grotto of Chameau.** Regain route 5306 and continue on to the well-marked turn-off toward the **Zegzel Gorges,** a precipitous mountain pass bounded by olive groves, orange orchards, and wheat-dusted terraces. Retrace your tracks onto 5306, bearing left at the main crossroads for the town of **Berkane.** Buses leave from here for Saidia, Nador, and Oujda. Besides being the only place in the area where you can cash traveler's checks, Berkane makes a pleasant base for exploring the area at a leisurely pace. To high-tail it back to Oujda, highway 5306 (60km) returns through the fertile expanse of the Triffa Plains.

Figuig

Unless you're an impassioned desert enthusiast, the only reason to come to Figuig is to cross the border into southern Algeria. (See Morocco Introduction.) Buses leave from the Oued Nachet station in Oujda for Figuig at 6am, 10am, and 4pm (369km, 7 hr., 33dh). The road from Rissani to Figuig is treacherous in places, so bring plenty of water and extra gas. Most reputable guidebooks describe Figuig in glowing terms, but don't hold your breath. Recent years have taken their toll. Figuig's role as a strategic military outpost, a major border crossing, and a regional administrative headquarters have all played a part in eroding the oasis. Mud brick homes yield to tasteless concrete cubes, and military personnel are gradually outnumbering the Saharan Berbers.

The only accommodations in the center, **Hotel Sahara,** by the bus stop, will let you sleep on their terrace for 12dh. For a more Saharan setting, the **Auberge de la Palmerie** (tel. 62), in Kasr Zanega, offers rooms for 28dh per person. The **administrative center** is modern and ugly, but if you have the time, explore some of the fortified villages on the periphery of the oasis. **Zanega** is the largest, **El-Hammam el-Foukani** has a hot spring and the ancient mausoleum of a saint. The two most picturesque *ksars* are **El-Oudarhir** and **El-Maiz;** the most dramatic palm groves are found on the eastern edge of Figuig in the **Zousfana River Valley.**

INDEX

About Let's Go

In 1960, Harvard Student Agencies, a three-year-old nonprofit corporation established to provide employment opportunities to Harvard and Radcliffe students, was doing a booming business selling charter flights to Europe. One of the extras HSA offered passengers on these flights was a 20-page mimeographed pamphlet entitled *1960 European Guide,* a collection of tips on continental travel compiled by the staff at HSA. The following year, Harvard and Radcliffe students traveling to Europe made notes and researched the first full-fledged edition of *Let's Go: Europe,* a pocket-sized book with a smattering of tips on budget accommodations, irreverent write-ups of sights, and a decidedly youthful slant. The first editions proclaimed themselves to be helpmates to the "adventurous and often pecunious student." Throughout the sixties, the series reflected its era: A section of the 1968 *Let's Go: Europe* was entitled "Street Singing in Europe on No Dollars a Day"; the 1969 guide to America led off with a feature on drug-ridden Haight Ashbury.

During the seventies, *Let's Go* gradually became a large-scale operation, adding regional guides to parts of Europe and slowly expanding into North Africa and nearby Asia. In 1981, *Let's Go: USA* returned after an eight-year hiatus, and in the next year HSA joined forces with its current publisher, St. Martin's Press. Since then, the series has continually blossomed; the additions of *Let's Go: Pacific Northwest, Western Canada, and Alaska* and *Let's Go: California and Hawaii* in 1988 brought the the total numbers of titles to eleven.

Each spring, over 150 Harvard students compete for some 70 positions as *Let's Go* researcher/writers. An editorial staff of 14 carefully reads stacks of 10-page applications and conducts thorough interviews. Those hired possess a rare combination of budget travel sense, writing ability, stamina, and courage. Each researcher/writer travels on a shoestring budget for seven weeks, researching and writing seven days per week, and mailing back their copy to Cambridge—about 500 pages in six installments. Train strikes, grumpy proprietors, noisy hostels, irate tourist officials are all in a day's work, but sometimes things become more serious. The afflictions of the summer of 1988 included one tear gassing, two totaled cars, one concussion, one near-drowning, and, in the most bizarre tale to date, one researcher/writer was chased up a tree by a pack of reindeer.

Back in a cluttered basement in Harvard Yard, an editorial staff of 25 and countless typists and proofreaders spend four months poring over more than 50,000 pages of manuscript as they push the copy through 12 comprehensive stages of intensive editing. In September the collected efforts of the summer are converted from computer diskette to nine-track tapes and delivered to Com Com in Allentown, Pennsylvania, where their computerized typesetting equipment turns them into books in record time. And even before the books hit the stands, the next year's editions are well underway.